W9-DDY-666

Warman's ANTIQUES AND COLLECTIBLES
PRICE GUIDE
—— 34TH EDITION ——

EDITED BY ELLEN T. SCHROY

© 2000 by
Ellen T. Schroy

All rights reserved.
No part of this publication may be reproduced or transmitted in any form or by any means,
electronic or mechanical, including photocopy, recording or any information storage and retrieval system, without
permission in writing from the author, except by a reviewer who may quote brief passages in a critical article or
review to be printed in a magazine or newspaper
or electronically transmitted on radio or television.

Published by

krause
publications

700 East State St., Iola, WI 54990-0001
715-445-2214
www.krause.com

Please, call or write us for our free catalog of antiques and collectibles publications.
To place an order or receive our free catalog, call 800-258-0929. For editorial comment and further information,
use our regular business telephone at (715) 445-2214

Library of Congress Catalog Number: 82-643543
ISBN: 0-87341-700-3

Printed in the United States of America

INTRODUCTION

Warman's: Serving the trade for more than 50 years

In 1994, *Warman's Antiques and Their Prices* became *Warman's Antiques and Collectibles Price Guide*. The last edition is bigger than ever—physically, that is. Longtime *Warman's* users may find it difficult to imagine that the amount of information in this larger-size book is identical to that found in the earlier smaller-size editions. Yet, it is true. While the page, text, and photograph sizes are larger, the content is the same. You can always expect more, never less, from *Warman's*.

Individuals in the trade refer to this book simply as *Warman's*, a fitting tribute to E. G. Warman and the product he created. *Warman's* has been around for 51 years, 26 years longer than its closest rival. We are proud as peacocks that *Warman's* continues to establish the standards for general antiques and collectibles price guides in 2000, just as it did in 1972 when its first rival appeared on the scene.

Warman's, the antiques and collectibles "bible," covers objects made between 1700 and the present. It always has. Because it reflects market trends, *Warman's* has added more and more 20th-century material to each edition. Remember, 1900 was 100 years ago—the distant past to the new generation of twenty-something and thirty-something collectors.

The general "antiques" market consists of antiques (for the purposes of this book, objects made before 1945), collectibles (objects of the post-World War II era that enjoy an established secondary market), and desirables (contemporary objects that are collected, but speculative in price). Although *Warman's* contains information on all three market segments, its greatest emphasis is on antiques and collectibles. In fact, this book is the essential field guide to the antiques and collectibles marketplace, which indicates that *Warman's* is much more than a list of object descriptions and prices. It is a basic guide to the field as a whole, providing you with the key information you need every time you encounter a new object or collecting category.

'*Warman's* is the Key'

Warman's provides the keys needed by auctioneers, collectors, dealers, and others to understand and deal with the complexities of the antiques and collectibles market. A price list is only one of many keys needed today. *Warman's 34th Edition* contains many additional keys including: histories, marks, reference books, periodicals, collectors' clubs, museums, reproductions, videotapes, and special auctions. Useful buying and collecting hints also are provided. Used properly, there are few doors these keys will not open.

Warman's is designed to be your first key to the exciting world of antiques and collectibles. As you use the keys this book provides to advance further in your specialized collecting areas, *Warman's* hopes you will remember with fondness where you received your start. When you encounter items outside your area of specialty, remember *Warman's* remains your key to unlocking the information you need, just as it has for more than 40 years.

Organization

Listings: Objects are listed alphabetically by category, beginning with ABC Plates and ending with Zsolnay Pottery. If you have trouble identifying the category to which your object belongs, use the extensive index in the back of the book. It will guide you to the proper category.

We have made the listings descriptive enough so that specific objects can be identified. We also emphasize items that are actively being sold in the marketplace. Some harder-to-find objects are included to demonstrate market spread—useful information worth considering when you have not traded actively in a category recently.

Each year as the market changes, we carefully review our categories—adding, dropping, and combining to provide the most comprehensive coverage possible. *Warman's* quick response to developing trends in the marketplace is one of the prime reasons for its continued leadership in the field.

Krause Publications also publishes other *Warman's* titles. Each utilizes the *Warman's* format and concentrates on a specific collecting group, e.g., American pottery and porcelain; Americana and collectibles; coins and currency; country, English and continental pottery and porcelain; glass; and jewelry Several are second or subsequent editions. Their expanded coverage compliments the information found in *Warman's Antiques and Collectibles Price Guide*.

History: Collectors and dealers enhance their appreciation of objects by knowing something about their history. We present a capsule history for each category. In many cases, this history contains collecting hints or other useful information.

References: Books are listed in most categories to help you learn more about the objects. Included are author, title, publisher, and date of publication or most recent edition. If a book has been published by a small firm or individual, we have indicated (published by author). To assist in finding these sometimes hard-to-locate authors, we have included the address.

Many of the books included in the lists are hard to find. The antiques and collectibles field is blessed with a dedicated core of book dealers who stock these specialized publications. You will find them at flea markets and antiques shows and through their advertisements in trade publications. Books go out of print quickly, yet many books printed more than 25 years ago remain the standard work in a category. Used book dealers often can locate many of these valuable reference sources. Many dealers publish annual or semi-annual catalogs. Ask to be put on their mailing lists.

Periodicals: The newsletter or bulletin of a collectors' club usually provides the concentrated focus sought by specialty collectors and dealers. However, there are publications, not associated with collectors' clubs, about which collectors and dealers should be aware. These are listed in their appropriate category introductions.

In addition, there are several general interest newspapers and magazines which deserve to be brought to our users' attention. These are:

Antique & The Arts Weekly, Bee Publishing Company, 5 Church Hill Road, Newton, CT 06470; http://www.the-bee.com/aweb

Antique Review, P.O. Box 538, Worthington, OH 43085

Antique Trader Weekly, P.O. Box 1050, Dubuque, IA 52001; http://www.csmonline.com

AntiqueWeek, P.O. Box 90, Knightstown, IN 46148; http://www.antiqueweek.com

Antiques (The Magazine Antiques), 551 Fifth Avenue, New York, NY 10017

Antiques & Collecting, 1006 South Michigan Avenue, Chicago, IL 60605

Inside Collector, 225 Main St., Suite 300, Northport, NY 11768

Maine Antique Digest, P.O. Box 358, Waldoboro, ME 04572; http://www.maineantiquedigest.com

MidAtlantic Monthly Antiques Magazine, P.O. Box 908, Henderson, NC 27536

New England Antiques Journal, 4 Church St., Ware, MA 01082

New York-Pennsylvania Collector, Drawer C, Fishers, NY 14453

Space does not permit listing all the national and regional publications in the antiques and collectibles field. The above is a sampling. For more publications, see David J. Maloney Jr.'s *Maloney's Antiques & Collectibles Resource Directory*, 4th edition (Antique Trader Books, 1997).

Collectors' Clubs: Collectors' clubs add vitality to the antiques and collectibles field. Their publications and conventions produce knowledge which often cannot be found elsewhere. Many of these clubs are short-lived; others are so strong that they have regional and local chapters.

Museums: The best way to study a specific field is to see as many documented examples as possible. For this reason, we have listed museums where significant collections in that category are on display. Special attention must be directed to the complex of museums which make up the Smithsonian Institution in Washington, D.C.

Reproductions: Reproductions are a major concern to all collectors and dealers. Throughout this edition, boxes will alert you to known reproductions and keys to recognizing them. Most reproductions are unmarked; the newness of their appearance is often the best clue to uncovering them. Specific objects known to be reproduced are marked within the listings with an asterisk (*). The information is designed to serve as a reminder of past reproductions and prevent you from buying them, believing them to be period.

We strongly recommend subscribing to *Antique & Collectors Reproduction News*, a monthly newsletter that reports on past and present reproductions, copycats, fantasies, and fakes. Send $32 for twelve issues to: ACRN, Box 12130, Des Moines, IA 50312-9403. This newsletter has been published for several years. Consider buying all

available back issues. The information they contain will be of service long into the future.

Special Auctions: In the 34th edition, we have chosen to again feature boxes highlighting auction houses. To qualify for placement in one of these boxes, auction houses have to meet several specific requirements. First, they must actively hold auctions solely devoted to that specialty. Second, they must provide a catalog and prices realized. Often the catalogs become an important part of a collection, serving as reference and identification guides. Many of the auction companies featured hold more than one auction annually; some work with a particular collectors' club or society. It is our hope that these boxes will give collectors and those searching for specific objects a better idea of who to contact. *Warman's* is designed to give collectors and dealers a lot of clues to find out what they have, what it is worth, and where to sell it!

These special auction boxes are not intended, however, to diminish the outstanding work done by the generalists, those auctioneers who handle all types of material. The fine auctions like Garth's, Skinner's, and Sloan's, provide us with excellent catalogs all through the year covering many aspects of the antiques and collectibles marketplace. Several categories had too many auction houses to list. For example, most auctioneers sell furniture, clocks, and fine arts. We just couldn't list them all. In addition to these auction-house boxes, we hope you will consult the master list of auction houses included in this edition. We are sure that any one of them will be eager to assist in consigning or selling antiques and collectibles.

Index: A great deal of effort has been expended to make our index useful. Always begin by looking for the most specific reference. For example, if you have a piece of china, look first for the maker's name and second for the type. Remember, many objects can be classified in three or more categories. If at first you don't succeed, try, try again.

Black-and-white photographs: You may encounter a piece you cannot identify well enough to use the index. Consult the photographs and marks. If you own several editions of Warman's, you have available a valuable photographic reference to the antiques and collectibles field. Learn to use it.

Price notes

In assigning prices, we assume the object is in very good condition. If otherwise, we note this in our description. It would be ideal to suggest that mint, or unused, examples of all objects exist. The reality is that objects from the past were used, whether they be glass, china, dolls, or toys. Because of this, some normal wear must be expected. In fact, if an object such as a piece of furniture does not show wear, its origins may be more suspect than if it does show wear.

Whenever possible, we have tried to provide a broad listing of prices within a category so you have a "feel" for the market. We emphasize the middle range of prices within a category, while also listing some objects of high and low value to show market spread.

We do not use ranges because they tend to confuse, rather than help the collector and dealer. How do you determine if your object is at the high or low end of the range? There is a high degree of flexibility in pricing in the antiques field. If you want to set ranges, add or subtract 10 percent from our prices.

One of the hardest variants with which to deal is the regional fluctuations of prices. Victorian furniture brings widely differing prices in New York, Chicago, New Orleans, or San Francisco. We have tried to strike a balance. Know your region and subject before investing heavily. If the best buys for cameo glass are in Montreal or Toronto, then be prepared to go there if you want to save money or add choice pieces to your collection. Research and patience are key factors to building a collection of merit.

Another factor that affects prices is a sale by a leading dealer or private collector. We temper both dealer and auction house figures.

Price research

Everyone asks, "Where do you get your prices?"

They come from many sources.

First, we rely on auctions. Auction houses and auctioneers do not always command the highest prices. If they did, why do so many dealers buy from them? The key to understanding auction prices is to know when a price is high or low in the range. We think we do this and do it well. The 34th edition represents a concentrated effort to contact more regional auction houses, both large and small. The cooperation has been outstanding and has resulted in an ever-growing pool of auction prices and trends to help us determine the most up-to-date auction prices.

Second, we work closely with dealers. We screen our contacts to make certain they have full knowledge of the market. Dealers make their living from selling antiques; they cannot afford to have a price guide which is not in touch with the market.

More than 50 antiques and collectibles magazines, newspapers, and journals come into our office regularly. They are excellent barometers of what is moving and what is not. We don't hesitate to call an advertiser and ask if his listed merchandise sold.

When the editorial staff is doing field work, we identify ourselves. Our conversations with dealers and collectors around the country have enhanced this book. Teams from *Warman's* are in the field at antiques shows, malls, flea markets, and auctions recording prices and taking photographs.

Collectors work closely with us. They are specialists whose devotion to research and accurate information is inspiring. Generally, they are not dealers. Whenever we have asked them for help, they have responded willingly and admirably.

Board of advisors

Our Board of Advisors is made up of specialists, both dealers and collectors, who feel a commitment to accurate information. You'll find their names listed in the front of the book. Several have authored a major reference work on their subject.

Our esteemed Board of Advisors has increased in number and scope. Participants have all provided detailed information regarding the history and reference section of their particular area of expertise, as well as preparing price listings. Many furnished excellent photographs and even shared with us their thoughts on the state of the market.

We are delighted to include those who are valuable members, officers, and founders of collectors' clubs. They are authors of books and articles, and many frequently lecture to groups about their specialties. Most of our advisors have been involved with antiques and collectibles for more than 20 years. Several are retired, and the antiques and collectibles business is a hobby which encompasses most of their free time. Others are a bit younger and either work full time or part time in the antiques and collectibles profession. We asked them about their favorite publications, and most responded with the names of specialized trade papers. Many told us they are regular readers of *AntiqueWeek* and the *Maine Antique Digest*.

One thing they all have in common is their enthusiasm for the antiques and collectibles marketplace. They are eager to share their knowledge with collectors. Many have developed wonderful friendships through their efforts and are enriched by them. If you wish to buy or sell an object in the field of expertise of any of our advisors, drop them a note along with an SASE. If time permits, they will respond.

Buyer's guide, not seller's guide

Warman's is designed to be a buyer's guide, suggesting what you would have to pay to purchase an object on the open market from a dealer or collector. It is not a seller's guide to prices. People frequently make this mistake. In doing so, they deceive themselves. If you have an object listed in this book and wish to sell it to a dealer, you should expect to receive approximately 50 percent of the listed value. If the object will not resell quickly, expect to receive even less.

Private collectors may pay more, perhaps 70 to 80 percent of our listed price, if your object is something needed for their collection. If you have an extremely rare object or an object of exceptionally high value, these guidelines do not apply.

Examine your piece as objectively as possible. As an antiques and collectibles appraiser, I spend a great deal of time telling people their treasures are not "rare" at all, but items readily available in the marketplace.

In respect to buying and selling, a simple philosophy is that a good purchase occurs when the buyer and seller are happy with the price. Don't look back. Hindsight has little value in the antiques and collectibles field. Given time, things tend to balance out.

Always improving

Warman's is always trying to improve. Space is freely given to long price descriptions, to help you understand that the piece looks like, perhaps what's special about it. With this edition, we've arranged some old formats, using more bold words to help you find what you're looking for. Some categories have been arranged so that if the only thing you know is how high, you can start there. Many times, identifying what you've got is the hardest part. Well, the first place to start is how big—grab that ruler and see what you can find that's a comparable size. You are still going to have to make a determination about what the object is made of, be it china, glass, porcelain, wood, or other materials. Use all your senses to discover what you've got. Ask questions about your object, who made it, and why, how was it used, where, and when. As you find answers to these questions, you'll be helping yourself figure out just what the treasure is all about. Now take that information and you'll be able to look it up and discover the value.

Eager to hear from readers

At *Warman's* and Krause Publications, we're always eager to hear what you think about *Warman's* and how we can improve it. Write to either Ellen Schroy, *Warman's* Editor, P.O. Box 392, Quakertown, PA 18951-0392 or e-mail at schroy@voicenet.com. The fine staff at Krause Publications can be reached at 700 E. State St., Iola, WI 54990. It's our goal to continue in the *Warman's* tradition and make it the best price guide available.

STATE of the MARKET

Every edition of *Warman's Antiques and Collectibles Price Guide* contains a few paragraphs about the current state of the antiques and collectibles marketplace. To make this a timely report, I find myself doing a lot of reading, reflecting, and interviewing those in different aspects of the antiques and collectibles field. This year was a particularly good one to reflect on what has been in the past and what the future may bring to those who enjoy participating in this wonderful marketplace.

The good news is that the antiques and collectibles marketplace seems alive and well. Perhaps it's changing a bit to respond to changes in the world-wide marketplace, and let's assume that change is a good thing, even in antiques. As for the past few years, the high end of the market is secure and prices seem to be soaring to even greater heights. The middle market is somewhat more conservative, perhaps a little soft, with some collecting areas seeing stable or slightly declining prices. The lower end of the marketplace, the under $100 per item collectors, seem to be doing better in 1999 than they did in the late 1990s. Folks are happily buying back their childhood memories, adding to collections, and even starting new collections.

Something that has helped to spur interest in high-end antiques is the popular PBS television program, "Antiques Roadshow." More and more folks are enjoying that show and go on to discover that they, too, have a treasure in their possession. I've been asked many times about the impact this television show is having on collectors and it's got to be positive for all concerned. People are thinking about what they have, re-discovering some family heirlooms and trying to learn how to recognize what they own. I'd be remiss if I didn't mention that I don't always agree with the values presented and perhaps some of these high values are giving people false expectations, but in general, it's been very positive. Other television shows are helping folks to identify what they own and determine values and every one is a winner.

One of the most encouraging side effects is the number of appraisal clinics that are popping up all across the country, some to benefit a local charity or event, which are allowing appraisers and collectors to meet on an informal basis. Every time I'm involved in one of these fun days, I come away with a new appreciation for what "savers" we all are and what kinds of things folks hold dear. I love to meet the owners, hear the stories, and often learn how they don't want to sell their treasure, but want to keep it in the family for future generations. It's been a year full of radio interviews for me, many with call-ins, again allowing me to hear what's important to folks all across the country. From Maine to Texas to Portland, OR, I've talked about toys, glass, all kinds of advertising, and political memorabilia, while discussing what folks collect. And no one should ignore that sweet little old lady who may appear at a yard sale—they are turning out to be the most savvy of shoppers. One called into a Canadian show I was doing one morning and carefully described a Rolling Stones' concert program she had purchased quite reasonably. She told me she figured it was worth the small amount she had paid for it and was now going to look for a rock 'n' roll memorabilia collector who might really enjoy it.

Following a summer where many dealers added Beanie Babies to their inventories, it's nice to see the autumn antique shows where the same dealers didn't bring them to shows. The impact of Beanie-Baby collectors will be felt for some time to come. It's taught folks of all ages about the fun of collecting, organizing their treasures, seeking out rare examples, learning how to store and properly maintain their collection. For some dealers, the income from selling these charming toys has helped them through slow periods, keeping their spirits somewhat elated.

From what I experienced in the autumn antique show circuit, dealers were happy and selling their wares, and the shows were well attended by folks of all ages. At any given antique and collectible show, I could find a range of ages, from young couples who may have been looking for a wonderful accent piece for their new home, to middle-aged couples who may have been looking for a special piece to add a growing collection, to senior citizens who sometimes were looking for a replacement piece or simply adding to their collections. Through the past several months, I've spoken with a number of senior citizens who wanted to find a replacement or additional serving piece to the china, glassware, or silver they started housekeeping with, as they wanted to give a complete set to a beloved grand child. The other good news in this story is that the lucky grand children are usually very appreciative of the gift—treasuring that bit of family history.

Summer flea markets were delights in that they, too, were hubs of activities, with collectors eager to examine the wares. Many times I heard conversations of how items were used, why a collector was interested in a certain item, discussions of company histories, etc. This exchange of information helps keep the antiques and collectibles field interesting for all. Probably the funniest experience all summer was a poor gentleman who had taken to a sneezing fit, to which he promptly declared, "Guess I'm allergic to all these antiques" and his wife chuckled, simply grabbed his arm and told him bluntly, "Too bad, let's go." The same husband was later seen to be carrying several bags, and didn't look too worse for the wear.

The one underlying fear that crept into conversations all year long was, What will the Internet do to the antiques world? So far it looks like it's having a rather positive effect. Now I bet some of you readers are wondering, how can that be? Well, if you consider the Internet to be nothing more than that of a giant antiques mall filled with booth after booth and at the end of the mall is a big auction center, with many auctioneers offering all kinds of goods for sale, aren't you just about in antiques heaven? The interesting part is that if you're computer savvy, you can let your fingers to the walking, using search engines, favorite websites, etc. to help find the items you're interested in. Sure, sure, many times the descriptions used by the Internet dealers are a bit confusing, sometimes almost comical. However, if you're an educated consumer, you might be able to find some interesting bargains. And, how do you get this education? By reading the myriad sources available on the Internet, and also the print world of excellent trade publications, reference books, and, of course, price guides like *Warman's*.

I have heard grumblings all year long about "all the good stuff going on the 'Net"—it just isn't so; many "good things" are still available. Perhaps you need to drive a little further or look a little harder to find them, but they are still there. Some things just don't do well on the Internet and dealers are finding that out. If I had a working crystal ball, I might see that the treasures dealers are not selling on the Internet will be finding their way back to traditional venues, like antique shows, shops, malls, and flea markets. Why? Because, the bottom line to any dealer is that he's got to resell his merchandise. Keeping it for months or years is not going to help his profit statement. And like any other commercial enterprise, antiques and collectibles dealers are hoping to be prosperous.

One area that seems to be strong to me as we begin 2000 is auctions. Again, you get some grumbling that live auctions are not getting as good a supply of merchandise because the Internet is taking the best examples out of the arena. Personally, I don't see that happening. Yes, some exciting examples are offered on the Internet, perhaps allowing collectors in remote areas to sell or buy items that would not be readily available without the Internet. However, considering the antiques and collectibles field is one fed by consumer supply and demand, aren't auctions still a great source for dealers?

I recently read a wonderful column in *AntiqueWeek* (a great weekly publication by Mayhill Publications, Inc.) that supports my theory. John Steve Proffitt III (Steve to his readers) always writes a well-researched column, but I found his "Top Ten Predictions for the Year 2000" to be really quite thought probing and right on the money in several areas. One of Steve's predictions is that "non-auctioneer auctions" (you know, those online, radio, television, newspaper, etc. "auctions") will continue to grow, both in number and value of assets sold. This is a result of the enormous increase in the popularity of auction marketing, and it will result in an even greater increase in the popularity of auction marketing. Steve goes on to explain why he believes this and challenges the old-time auctioneers to remember that the horse and buggy days are over and they should get with the program and learn about on-line and other types of computer-related auctions. I think he correctly states, "The Internet is not our enemy, but our newest and best tool for dynamic auction marketing in the 21st century."

The next prediction offered by Steve is that, "Live, auctioneer-conducted auctions will continue to grow in number and value of assets sold." I'm afraid Steve's comment about the graying of the Baby Boomers is perhaps a little too close to home for me. But, I must also acknowledge that he's probably 100% correct that this graying will "trigger the greatest transfer of wealth in the history of the world, and auctioneers will be riding the crest of it."

Many of us graying Baby Boomers are finding ourselves trying to deal with elderly parents and disposing of their households, while watching our own children grow and create their first nests. The phone calls and letters I get asking where to dispose of antiques and collectibles because a fellow Baby Boomer's parents are going to an elderly care facility are becoming more frequent. And, to be perfectly honest, I refer many of them to local auctioneers. In most cases, time is of an essence, learning how to operate a new computer, investigate on-line auctions, and learning how to ship things is pretty difficult when you're dealing with the every-day problems of dealing with those aging parents and youngsters at home, too.

Steve's article goes on to encourage auctioneers to get as much education as possible, a good idea for collectors and dealers too. His predictions are well thought out and it will be interesting to see how many will become truthful. Since he is an auctioneer and lawyer, I trust that Steve will inform readers at a later date as to how well his thoughts did in 2000 and beyond.

As I end this traditional "State of the Market Report," my thoughts drift to some wonderful items I have added to personal collections this past year. Of course, I feel all were purchased at a fair price: some were great yard-sale bargains, some were found during hot summer trips to flea markets, another pretty plate came home with me during a very early morning trip to a foggy flea market and represents a good buy and a happy memory of a couple of hours spent with good friends, and a few great auction buys round out the warm feeling. And, add to that many hours spent talking with dealers, collectors, auctioneers, show promoters, friends, and fellow writers about their views, all of which help me learn more, reflect on a positive market.

RECORD PRICES

Every year, new price levels are attained in the antiques and collectibles market—and 1999 was no exception. With increased interest in this marketplace, more record prices are being reported on the evening news, leading us all to want to know more about the pieces, why did it sell for so much, and the "oh, won't it be wonderful if I owned one, too" optimism.

Skinner Inc., auctioneers and appraisers of antiques and fine arts (The Heritage on the Garden, Boston, and Bolton, MA) had a wonderful year. Its October Americana auction was the third consecutive record-breaking Americana auction, topping expectations by nearly $1 million. Its June Americana auction grossed more than $2 million, and its August Americana auction was the most successful summer auction of the season. Skinner reports international interest in its auctions, as well as a record number of telephone bidders.

Classy furniture finds

Some highlights from the October Americana sale include an inlaid cherry chest of drawers made by cabinetmaker Nathan Lombard, in western Massachusetts. This Federal chest is lavishly inlaid and had descended through a Connecticut family. The chest sold for $365,500, setting a new record for the maker. The Charleston Museum, Charleston, SC, benefited from the sale of a Philadelphia Chippendale mahogany carved tea table. The table, which also descended through a New England family, sold for $343,500. Extraordinary furniture crossed the auctioneers block all through this auction, bringing exciting prices. One set of nine Classical bird's eye maple chairs brought $23,000, quite an value appreciation since the chairs were documented as selling new in 1826 for $82.50. Eben White, the Boston chairmaker who made these chairs, might have been pretty surprised at this significant increase.

Another museum, the High Museum of Art in Atlanta, secured a great example of Aesthetic Movement/Renaissance Revival furniture when it purchased a cabinet created by Pottier & Stymus at the July auction of the New Orleans Auction Gallery. The hammer price was $104,500. Many fine examples of documented furniture is also going into private collections.

If bidding on all this classy furniture made the bidders thirsty, a fine tumbler made by John Frederick Amelung sold for $51,750. It is delicately etched and blown early glass. Additional lots sold in many areas, such as painted boxes, and glazed chintz bed textiles, which far exceeded their pre-sale expectations. Will Skinner's next Americana auction, scheduled for February 2000, bring such prices? Only the bidders will answer that.

Toy treaures

Bidding was brisk for the horse-drawn omnibus toy that sold for $48,300 at Skinner's July auction. The toy, attributed to Francis, Field and Francis of Philadelphia, was made in the 1850s from tinplate. A mechanical bank, known as "New Bank" to collectors, and made by J. & E. Stevens, far exceeded it's pre-sale estimate of $2,200,

when the hammer struck for more than $10,000. This toy auction also included a number of high-priced dolls and their accessories. Teddy bears were also strong in July, as a Steiff cream mohair brought $9,775 and an early Bing ginger mohair bear brought $2,300.

Native American items

Another area that is gaining strong collector attention is Native American artifacts. Many auction houses report strong results in this area. Again, Skinner's delighted collectors with a CA Cahuilla coiled basketry bowl that sold for an impressive $23,000, far above it's pre-sale estimates. Also at the same June auction, a Northern Plains beaded hide war shirt sold for $21,850. Many other items brought outstanding prices.

Period jewelry

Perhaps your tastes run to smaller objects, like jewelry. Again, several record prices were achieved during the past year. If the Edwardian style of jewelry catches your eye, you may wish to know that a brooch made with a Kashmir sapphire of 6.50 cts and surrounded by diamonds brought a price of $55,200. Prefer something from the Art Deco period? Perhaps the Tiffany & Co. brooch of platinum and diamonds would be more appealing, as it sold for $18,400. Jewelry from all periods did well this year, especially well marked and documented pieces.

Silvery finery

English silver did well in June, with an exquisite George II basket selling for $54,050. The basket was made by Phillips Garden, date marked 1751, and was a fine example of a Rococo piece. It has boldly scrolled feet topped by the head of the goddess Ceres, shells on the rim and busts of summer and autumn goddesses, and the cast handle displays herm uprights, topped by a wind god. A Swedish covered serving dish sold for $16,100, well beyond Skinner's original expectations. American silver was well represented and a set of Tiffany silver gilt side plates, with engraved centers of fruit sprigs, brought more than $14,000.

A Meissen porcelain tea caddy with it's original cover, in the manner of C. F. Höroldt, sold for $10,000 at Lawson's in Sydney, Australia. The sale auction featured a Japanese silver openwork cloisonné teapot that sold for $12,000. Other international success stories include a Louis XV "Commedia dell'Arte" clock which brought $1,251,500 at the auction house of Galerie Killer, in Zurich, Switzerland.

Musical instruments

Would you like a little music to entertain you? How about a few tunes from the fabulous Art Deco piano sold by Christie's New York in November for more than $600,000. The stunning piano is made of ebony and amboyna, has convex-sides and was made by Jacques-Emile Rhulmann with works by Gaveau. The piano was made for a 1925 exhibition in Paris. You'll be delighted to know the purchase price included a chair. Other types of musical instruments also set record prices at other auctions. Like furniture and other antiques, pristine condition is paramount in achieving high prices.

Swann successes

Swann Galleries, New York City, also experienced a great year, with a copy of *Williamson's Catalogue of the Collection of Jewels and Precious Works of Arts, The Property of J. Pierpoint Morgan,* selling for $19,550. This 1910 catalog is believed to be one of only 40 numbered copies on Japanese vellum and had an additional suite of 46 hand-colored plates. Its October Photograph Auction saw a group of six cartes-de-visite of the James Younger Gang of Outlaws sell for $39,100. The price of $19,550 was realized for an oversized outdoor daguerreotype of a mid-1850s California frontier scene. The high price was paid for a circa 1868 albumen print of Carleton Watkin's view of *The Golden Gate from Telegraph Hill, San Francisco.* A 1623 copy of *Burton's Anatomy of Melancholy,* printed in Oxford, England, realized $17,250. Well known for its high-quality book, autograph, photograph and print-oriented auctions, Swann's pulled a real magic trick when selling a circa-1890 automation of a Negro conjurer by Lambert of Paris, in working order of course, for $32,200 at its annual Magic auction.

Reeling them in

Time for the outdoors—Lang's again set some records with its successful auctions of fishing collectibles. A Perfection trout reel brought $8,525, a Hardy Cascapedia model salmon reel realized $7,920, and an empty lure box brought $2,860 for a Michigan Life-Like Minnow box.

These prices are a mere sampling of some of the record prices realized this past year. Visit the auction houses or their websites for more information about these prices and details of these spectacular antiques.

Live auctions all around the world experienced similar success. On-line auctions also claimed some victories. With the current favorable economic climate, the expectations for 2000 are even better. Auction houses will continue to bring exciting examples of all types of antiques and collectibles to delight bidders, collectors, and even spectators. As the live auctions learn to combine with on-line bidding, the whole world of auctioning will continue to reach more and more bidders. Will they be willing to pay such high prices? Let's wait and see.

BOARD of ADVISORS

Dale Abrams
Tea Leaf Antiques
960 Bryden Rd
Columbus, OH 43205
(614) 258-5258
e-mail: 70003.2061@com-
puserve.com
Tea Leaf Ironstone

John and Alice Ahlfeld
2634 Royal Rd
Lancaster, PA 17603
(717) 397-7313
Pattern Glass

Bob Armstrong
15 Monadnock Road
Worcester, MA 01609
(508) 799-0644
Puzzles

Susan and Al Bagdade
The Country Peasants
1325 N. State Parkway, Apt. 15A
Chicago IL 60610
(312) 397-1321
Quimper

Johanna S. Billings
P.O. Box 244
Danielsville, PA 18038-0244
e-mail: bankie@concentric.net
Rose Bowls

Wendy Hamilton Blue
FANA
Suite 128, 1409 N. Cedar Crest Blvd.
Allentown PA 18104
Whitehall, PA 18052
Fans

Bill Boyd
1034 Sherwood Ave.
Marysville, OH 43040
Shaving Mugs

Tina M. Carter
882 S. Mollison Ave.
El Cajon, CA 92020
(619) 440-5043
e-mail: premos2@aol.com
Teapots

Loretta DeLozier
1101 Polk St.
Bedford, IA 50833
(712) 523-2289
e-mail: LeftonLady@aol.com
website: http://members.aol.com/
leftonlady/
Lefton China

Craig Dinner
P.O. Box 4399
Sunnyside, NY 11104
(718) 729-3850
Doorstops

Roselyn Gerson
12 Alnwick Road
Malverne, NY 11565
(516) 593-8746
Compacts

Ted Hake
Hake's Americana & Collectibles
P.O. Box 1444
York, PA 17405
(717) 848-1333; fax 717-852-0344
Disneyana; Political Items

Mary D. Harris
2205 Berkshire Rd
Lancaster PA 17603
(717) 872-8288

Majolica

Tom Hoepf
P.O. Box 90
27 Jefferson St.
Knightstown, IN 46148
(800) 876-5135
e-mail: antiqueth@aol.com
Cameras

Joan Hull
1376 Nevada
Huron, SD 57350
(605) 352-1685
Hull Pottery

David Irons
Irons Antiques
223 Covered Bridge Rd
Northampton, PA 18067
(610) 262-9335
Irons

Michael Ivankovich
P.O. Box 2458
Doylestown, PA 18901
(215) 345-6094
e-mail: Wnutting@comcat.com
*Wallace Nutting; Wallace Nutting-
Like Photographers*

Dorothy Kamm
P.O. Box 7460
Port St. Lucie, FL 34985-7460
(561) 465-4008
e-mail: dorothy.kamm@usa.net
American Painted Porcelain

James D. Kaufman
248 Highland St.
Dedham, MA 02026
(800) 283-8070
Dedham Pottery

W. D. and M. J. Keagy
P.O. Box 106
Bloomfield, IN 47424
(812) 384-3471
Yard-Long Prints

Ellen G. King
King's Antiques
102 North Main St.
Butler, PA 16001
(724) 894-2596
e-mail: eking@attglobal.net
Flow Blue; Mulberry China

Michael Krumme
P.O. Box 48225
Los Angeles, CA 90048-0225
email: mkrumme@pacbell.net
Paden City

Elizabeth M. Kurella
The Lace Merchant
P.O. Box 222
Plainfield, MI 49080
(616) 685-9792
e-mail: ekurella@accn.org
Lace and Linens

Robert Levy
The Unique One
2802 Centre St.
Pennsauken, NJ 08109
(609) 663-2554
Coin-Operated Items

Clarence and Betty Maier
The Burmese Cruet
P.O. Box 432
Montgomeryville, PA 18936
(215) 855-5388
*Burmese Glass; Crown Milano;
Royal Flemish*

James S. Maxwell, Jr.
P.O. Box 367
Lampeter, PA 17537
(717) 464-5573
Banks, Mechanical

Jocelyn C. Mousley
137 Main St.
Quakertown, PA 18951
(215) 536-9211
Animal Collectibles

Bob Perzel
4 Mine St., P.O. Box 1057
Flemington, NJ 08822
(908) 782-9631
  Stangl Birds

Richard Porter
P.O. Box 944
Onset, MA 02558
  Thermometers

Evalene Pulati
National Valentine Collectors Association
P.O. Box 1404
Santa Ana, CA 92702
  Valentines

John D. Querry
RD 2, Box 137B
Martinsburg, PA 16662
(814) 793-3185
  Gaudy Dutch

David Rago
333 North Main St.
Lambertville, NJ 08530
(609) 397-9374
website: http://www.ragoarts.com
  *Art Pottery, General; Arts and
    Crafts Movement, Fulper Pottery,
    Grueby Pottery, Newcomb Col-
    lege Pottery*

Charles and Joan Rhoden
8693 N. 1950 East Road
Georgetown, IL 61846-6264
(217) 662-8046
e-mail: rhoden@soltec.net
  Yard-Long Prints

Ferill J. Rice
302 Pheasant Run
Kaukauna, WI 54130
  Fenton

Julie P. Robinson
P.O. Box 117
Upper Jay, NY 12987
(518) 946-7753
  Celluloid

Jim and Nancy Schaut
7147 W. Angela Drive
Glendale, AZ 85308
(602) 878-4293
e-mail: Jnschaut@aol.com
  Automobiles, Automobilia

Kenneth E. Schneringer
271 Sabrina Ct.
Woodstock, GA 30188
(707) 926-9383
e-mail: trademan68@aol.com
  Catalogs

Susan Scott
882 Queen Street West
Toronto Ontario M6J 1G3
Canada
(416) 538-8691 fax
e-mail:
Susan@collecting20thcentury.com
  Chintz Patterned China, Clarice Cliff

Lissa Bryan-Smith and Richard M.
Smith
17 Market St.
Lewisburg PA 17837
e-mail: lbs8253@ptdprolog.net
  Christmas Items

George Sparacio
P.O. Box 791
Malaga, NJ 08328-0791
(856) 694-4167
(856) 694-4536 fax
e-mail: mrvesta1@aol.com
  Match Safes

Louis O. St. Aubin, Jr.
44 North Water St.
New Bedford, MA 02740
(508) 993-4944
  Mount Washington

George Theofiles
Miscellaneous Man
Box 1776
New Freedom, PA 17349
(717) 235-4766
  Posters

Clifford Wallach
277 West 10th Street, Ph-H
New York, NY 10014
(212) 243-1007
  Tramp Art

Lewis S. Walters
143 Lincoln Lane
Berlin, NJ 08008
(856) 719-1513
e-mail: lew6@erols.com
  Phonographs; Radios

Web Wilson
P.O. Box 506
Portsmouth, RI 02871
(800) 508-0022
  Door Knobs & Builders Hardware

AUCTION HOUSES

The following auction houses cooperate with Warman's by providing catalogs of their auctions and price lists. This information is used to prepare *Warman's Antiques and Collectibles Price Guide*, volumes in the Warman's Encyclopedia of Antiques and Collectibles. This support is truly appreciated.

Albrecht & Cooper Auction Services
3884 Saginaw Rd
Vassar, MI 48768
(517) 823-8835

Sanford Alderfer Auction Company
501 Fairgrounds Rd
Hatfield, PA 19440
(215) 393-3000
web site: http://www.alderfer
company.com

American Social History and Social
Movements
4025 Saline St.
Pittsburgh, PA 15217
(412) 421-5230

Andre Ammelounx
The Stein Auction Company
P.O. Box 136
Palantine, IL 60078
(847) 991-5927

Apple Tree Auction Center
1616 W. Church St.
Newark, OH 43055
(614) 344-4282

Arthur Auctioneering
RD 2, P.O. Box 155
Hughesville, PA 17737
(717) 584-3697

Auction Team Köln
Jane Herz
6731 Ashley Court
Sarasota, FL 34241
(941) 925-0385
Fax: (941) 925-0487

Auction Team Köln
Postfach 50 11 19
D-50971 Köln, Germany
Tel: 0221-38-70-49
Fax: 02-21-37-48-78
email: auction@breker.com

Noel Barrett Antiques & Auctions, Ltd.
P.O. Box 1001
Carversville, PA 18913
(610) 297-5109

Robert F. Batchelder
1 W Butler Ave.
Ambler, PA 19002
(610) 643-1430

Bear Pen Antiques
2318 Bear Pen Hollow Road
Lock Haven, PA 17745
(717) 769-6655

Beverly Hills Auctioneers
9454 Wilshire Blvd., Suite 202
Beverly Hills, CA 90212
(310) 278-8115

Bill Bertoia Auctions
1881 Spring Rd
Vineland, NJ 08360
(609) 692-1881

Biders Antiques Inc.
241 S. Union St.
Lawrence, MA 01843
(508) 688-4347

Brown Auction & Real Estate
900 East Kansas
Greensburg, KS 67054
(316) 723-2111

Buttefields
755 Church Rd
Elgin, IL 60123
(847) 741-3483
web site: http:.//www:butterfields.com

Butterfields
7601 Sunset Blvd.
Los Angeles, CA 90046
(213) 850-7500
web site: http:.//www:butterfields.com

Butterfields
220 San Bruno Ave.
San Francisco, CA 94103
(415) 861-7500
web site: http:.//www:butterfields.com

C. C. Auction Gallery
416 Court
Clay Center, KS 67432
(913) 632-6021

W. E. Channing & Co., Inc.
53 Old Santa Fe Trail
Santa Fe, NM 87501
(505) 988-1078

Chicago Art Galleries
5039 Oakton St.
Skokie, IL 60077
(847) 677-6080

Childers & Smith
1415 Horseshoe Pike
Glenmoore, PA 19343
(610) 269-1036
e-mail: harold@smithauctionco.com

Christie's
502 Park Ave.
New York, NY 10022
(212) 546-1000
web site: http://www.christies.com

Christie's East
219 E. 67th St.
New York, NY 10021
(212) 606-0400
web site: http://www.christies.com

Cincinnati Art Galleries
635 Main St.
Cincinnati, OH 45202
(513) 381-2128

Mike Clum, Inc.
P.O. Box 2
Rushville, OH 43150
(614) 536-9220

Cobb's Doll Auctions
1909 Harrison Road
Johnstown OH 43031-9539
(740) 964-0444

Cohasco Inc.
Postal 821
Yonkers, NY 10702
(914) 476-8500

Collection Liquidators Auction Service
341 Lafayette St.
New York, NY 10012
(212) 505-2455
website: http://www.rtam.com/coliq/
bid.html
e-mail: coliq@erols.com

Collector's Sales and Service
P.O. Box 4037
Middletown RI02842
(401) 849-5012
website: http://www.anti-
quechina.com

Coole Park Books and Autographs
P.O. Box 199049
Indianapolis, IN 46219
(317) 351-8495
e-mail: cooleprk@indy.net

Copeke Auction
226 Route 7A
Cokepe, NY 12516
(518) 329-1142

Samuel J. Cottonne
15 Genesee St.
Mt. Morris, NY 14510
(716) 583-3119

Craftsman Auctions
1485 W. Housatoric
Pittsfield MA 01202
(413) 442-7003
web site: http://www.artsncrafts.com

Dargate Auction Galleries
5607 Baum Blvd.
Pittsburgh, PA 15206
(412) 362-3558
web site: http://www.dargate.com

Dawson's
128 American Road
Morris Plains, NJ 07950
(973) 984-6900
web site: http://www.idt.net/-dawson1

DeWolfe & Wood
P.O. Box 425
Alfred, ME 04002
(207) 490-5572

Marlin G. Denlinger
RR3, Box 3775
Morrisville, VT 05661
(802) 888-2775

Dixie Sporting Collectibles
1206 Rama Rd.
Charlotte, NC 28211
(704) 364-2900
web site: http://www.sportauction.com

William Doyle Galleries, Inc.
175 E. 87th St.
New York, NY 10128
(212) 427-2730
web site: http://www.doylegalleries.com

Dunbar Gallery
76 Haven St.
Milford, MA 01757
(508) 634-8697

Early Auction Co.
123 Main St.
Milford, OH 45150
(513) 831-4833

Fain & Co.
P.O. Box 1330
Grants Pass, OR 97526
(888) 324-6726

Ken Farmer Realty & Auction Co.
105A Harrison St.
Radford, VA 24141
(703) 639-0939
web site: http://kenfarmer.com

Fine Tool Journal
27 Fickett Rd
Pownal, ME 04069
(207) 688-4962
web site: http://www.wowpages.com/
FTJ/

Steve Finer Rare Books
P.O. Box 758
Greenfield, MA 01302
(413) 773-5811

Flomaton Antique Auction
207 Palafox St.
Flomaton, AL 36441
(334) 296-3059

Fontaine's Auction Gallery
1485 W. Housatonic St.
Pittsbfield, MA 01201
(413) 488-8922

William A. Fox Auctions Inc.
676 Morris Ave.
Springfield, NJ 07081
(201) 467-2366

Freeman\Fine Arts Co. of Philadelphia, Inc.
1808 Chestnut St.
Philadelphia, PA 19103
(215) 563-9275

Garth's Auction, Inc.
2690 Stratford Rd
P.O. Box 369
Delaware, OH 43015
(740) 362-4771

Greenberg Auctions
7566 Main St.
Skysville, MD 21784
(410) 795-7447

Green Valley Auction Inc.
Route 2, Box 434
Mt. Crawford, VA 22841
(540) 434-4260

Guerney's
136 E. 73rd St.
New York, NY 10021
(212) 794-2280

Hake's Americana & Collectibles
P.O. Box 1444
York, PA 17405
(717) 848-1333

Gene Harris Antique Auction Center,
Inc.
203 South 18th Ave.
P.O. Box 476
Marshalltown, IA 50158
(515) 752-0600

Norman C. Heckler & Company
Bradford Corner Rd
Woodstock Valley, CT 06282
(203) 974-1634

High Noon
9929 Venice Blvd.
Los Angeles CA 90034
(310) 202-9010

Michael Ivankovich Auction Co.
P.O. Box 2458
Doylestown, PA 18901
(215) 345-6094
web site: http://www.nutting.com

Jackson's Auctioneers & Appraisers
2229 Lincoln St.
Cedar Falls, IA 50613
(319) 277-2256
web site: http://www.jacksonauction.com

James D. Julia Inc.
Rt. 201 Skowhegan Rd
P.O. Box 830
Fairfield, ME 04937
(207) 453-7125

J. W. Auction Co.
54 Rochester Hill Rd
Rochester, NH 03867
(603) 332-0192

Lang's Sporting Collectables, Inc.
31 R Turthle Cove
Raymond, ME 04071
(207) 655-4265

La Rue Auction Service
201 S. Miller St.
Sweet Springs, MO 65351
(816) 335-4538

Leonard's Auction Company
1631 State Rd
Duncannon, PA 17020
(717) 957-3324

Howard Lowery
3818 W. Magnolia Blvd.
Burbank, CA 91505
(818) 972-9080

Joy Luke
The Gallery
300 E. Grove St.
Bloomington, IL 61701
(309) 828-5533

Mapes Auctioneers & Appraisers
1729 Vestal Pkwy
Vestal, NY 13850
(607) 754-9193

Martin Auctioneers Inc.
P.O. Box 477
Intercourse, PA 17534
(717) 768-8108

McMasters Doll Auctions
P.O. Box 1755
Cambridge, OH 43725
(614) 432-4419

Metropolitan Book Auction
123 W. 18th St., 4th Floor
New York, NY 10011
(212) 929-7099

Wm. Frost Mobley
P.O. Box 10
Schoharie, NY 12157
(518) 295-7978

Wm. Morford
RD #2
Cazenovia, NY 13035
(315) 662-7625

Neal Auction Company
4038 Magazine St.
New Orleans, LA 7015
(504) 899-5329
web site: http://www.nealauction.com

New England Auction Gallery
P.O. Box 2273
W Peabody, MA 01960
(508) 535-3140

New Orleans Auction St. Charles
Auction Gallery, Inc.
1330 St. Charles Avenue
New Orleans, LA 70130
(504) 586-8733
web site: http://www.neworleansauc-
tion.com

New Hampshire Book Auctions
P.O. Box 460
92 Woodbury Rd
Weare, NH 03281
(603) 529-7432

Norton Auctioneers of Michigan Inc.
50 West Pearl at Monroe
Coldwater MI 49036
(517) 279-9063

Old Barn Auction
10040 St. Rt. 224 West
Findlay, OH 45840
(419) 422-8531
web site: http://www.oldbarn.com

Ohio Cola Traders
4411 Bazetta Rd
Cortland, OH 44410

Richard Opfer Auctioneering Inc.
1919 Greenspring Dr.
Timonium, MD 21093
(410) 252-5035

Pacific Book Auction Galleries
133 Kerney St., 4th Floor
San Francisco, CA 94108
(415) 989-2665
web site: http://www.nbn.com/~pba/

Pettigrew Auction Company
1645 S Tejon St.
Colorado Springs, CO 80906
(719) 633-7963

Phillips Ltd.
406 E. 79th St.
New York, NY 10021
(212) 570-4830
web site: http://www.phillips-auc-
tion.com

Postcards International
2321 Whitney Ave., Suite 102
P.O. Box 5398
Hamden, CT 06518
(203) 248-6621
web site: http://www.csmonline.com/
postcardsint/

Poster Auctions International
601 W. 26th St.
New York, NY 10001
(212) 787-4000

Profitt Auction Company
P.O. Box 796
Columbia, VA 23038
(804) 747-6353

Provenance
P.O. Box 3487
Wallington, NJ 07057
(201) 779-8725

David Rago Auctions, Inc.
333 S. Main St.
Lambertville, NJ 08530
(609) 397-9374
web site: http://www.ragoarts.com

Lloyd Ralston Toys
173 Post Rd
Fairfield, CT 06432
(203) 255-1233

James J. Reeves
P.O. Box 219
Huntingdon, PA 16652-0219
(814) 643-5497
website: www.JamesJReeves.com

Mickey Reichel Auctioneer
1440 Ashley Rd
Boonville MO 65233
(816) 882-5292

Sandy Rosnick Auctions
15 Front St.
Salem MA 01970
(508) 741-1130

Thomas Schmidt
7099 McKean Rd
Ypsilanti, MI 48197
(313) 485-8606

Seeck Auctions
P.O. Box 377
Mason City, IA 50402
(515) 424-1116
website: www.willowtree.com/
~seeckauctions

L. H. Selman Ltd.
761 Chestnut St.
Santa Cruz, CA 95060
(408) 427-1177
web site: http://www.selman.com

Sentry Auction
113 School St.
Apollo, PA 15613
(412) 478-1989

Skinner Inc.
Bolton Gallery
357 Main St.
Bolton, MA 01740
(978) 779-6241
web site: http://www.skinnerinc.com

Skinner, Inc.
The Heritage on the Garden
63 Park Plaza
Boston MA 02116
(978) 350-5429
web site: http://www.skinnerinc.com

C. G. Sloan & Company Inc.
4920 Wyaconda Rd
North Bethesda, MD 20852
(301) 468-4911
web site: http://www.cgsloan.com

Smith & Jones, Inc., Auctions
12 Clark Lane
Sudbury MA 01776
(508) 443-5517

Smith House Toy Sales
26 Adlington Rd
Eliot, ME 03903
(207) 439-4614

R. M. Smythe & Co.
26 Broadway
New York, NY 10004-1710
(212) 943-1880
web site: http://www.rm-smythe.com

Sotheby's
1334 York Ave.
New York, NY 10021
(212) 606-7000
web site: http://www.sothebys.com

Southern Folk Pottery Collectors
Society
1828 N. Howard Mill Rd.
Robbins, NC 27325
(910) 464-3961

Stanton's Auctioneers
P.O. Box 146
144 South Main St.
Vermontville, MI 49096
(517) 726-0181

Stout Auctions
11 W. Third St.
Williamsport, IN 47993-1119
(765) 764-6901

Michael Strawser
200 N. Main St.
P.O. Box 332
Wolcottville, IN 46795
(219) 854-2859

Swann Galleries Inc.
104 E. 25th St.
New York, NY 10010
(212) 254-4710

Swartz Auction Services
2404 N. Mattis Ave.
Champaign, IL 61826-7166
(217) 357-0197
web site: http://www/SwartzAuc-
tion.com

The House In The Woods
S91 W37851 Antique Lane
Eagle, WI 53119
(414) 594-2334

Theriault's
P.O. Box 151
Annapolis, MD 21401
(301) 224-3655
web site: http://www.theriaults.com

Toy Scouts
137 Casterton Ave.
Akron, OH 44303
(216) 836-0668
e-mail: toyscout@salamander.net

Treadway Gallery, Inc.
2029 Madison Rd
Cincinnati, OH 45208
(513) 321-6742
web site: http://www.a3c2net.com/
treadwaygallery

Unique Antiques & Auction Gallery
449 Highway 72 West
Collierville, TN 38017
(901) 854-1141

Venable Estate Auction
423 W. Fayette St.
Pittsfield, IL 62363
(217) 285-2560
e-mail: sandiv@msn.com

Victorian Images
P.O. Box 284
Marlton, NJ 08053
(609) 985-7711

Victorian Lady
P.O. Box 424
Waxhaw, NC 28173
(704) 843-4467

Vintage Cover Story
P.O. Box 975
Burlington, NC 27215
(919) 584-6900

Bruce and Vicki Waasdorp
P.O. Box 434
10931 Main St.
Clarence, NY 14031
(716) 759-2361

Web Wilson Antiques
P.O. Box 506
Portsmouth, RI 02871
1-800-508-0022

Winter Associates
21 Cooke St. Box 823
Plainville, CT 06062
(203) 793-0288

Wolf's Auctioneers
1239 W. 6th St.
Cleveland, OH 44113
(614) 362-4711

Woody Auction
Douglass, KS 67039
(316) 746-2694

York Town Auction, Inc.
1625 Haviland Rd
York, PA 17404
(717) 751-0211
e-mail: yorktownauction@cyberia.com

ABBREVIATIONS

The following are standard abbreviations which we have used throughout this edition of *Warman's*.

4to = 8" x 10"
8vo = 5" x 7"
12mo = 3" x 5"
ABP = American Brilliant Period
ADS = Autograph Document Signed
adv = advertising
ah = applied handle
ALS = Autograph Letter Signed
AQS = Autograph Quotation Signed
C = century
c = circa
Cal. = caliber
circ = circular
cyl. = cylinder
cov = cover
CS = Card Signed
d = diameter or depth
dec = decorated
dj = dust jacket
DQ = Diamond Quilted
DS = Document Signed
ed = edition
emb = embossed
ext. = exterior
eyep. = eyepiece
Folio = 12" x 16"
ftd = footed
ga = gauge
gal = gallon
ground = background
h = height
horiz. = horizontal
hp = hand painted
hs = high standard
HT = hard top
illus = illustrated, illustration
imp = impressed
int. = interior
irid = iridescent
IVT = inverted thumbprint
j = jewels
K = karat
l = length
lb = pound

litho = lithograph
ll = lower left
lr = lower right
ls = low standard
LS = Letter Signed
mfg = manufactured
MIB = mint in box
MOP = mother-of-pearl
n/c = no closure
ND = no date
NE = New England
No. = number
ns = no stopper
r/c = reproduction closure
o/c = original closure
opal = opalescent
orig = original
os = orig stopper
oz = ounce
pat = patent
pcs = pieces
pgs = pages
PUG = printed under the glaze
pr = pair
PS = Photograph Signed
pt = pint
qt = quart
rds = roadster
RM = red mark
rect = rectangular
sgd = signed
S. N. = Serial Number
sngl = single
SP = silver plated
SS = Sterling silver
sq = square
TLS = Typed Letter Signed
unp = unpaged
vert. = vertical
vol = volume
w = width
yg = yellow gold
# = numbered

ABC PLATES

History: The majority of early ABC plates were manufactured in England and imported into the United States. They achieved their greatest popularity from 1780 to 1860. Since a formal education was uncommon in the early 19th century, the ABC plate was a method of educating the poor for a few pennies.

ABC plates were made of glass, pewter, porcelain, pottery, or tin. Porcelain plates range in diameter from 4-3/8 to slightly over 9-1/2 inches. The rim usually contains the alphabet and/or numbers; the center features animals, great men, maxims, or nursery rhymes.

References: Susan and Al Bagdade, Warman's English & Continental Pottery & Porcelain, 3rd Edition, Krause Publications, 1998; Mildred L. and Joseph P. Chalala, A Collector's Guide to ABC Plates, Mugs and Things, Pridemark Press, 1980; Irene and Ralph Lindsey, ABC Plates & Mugs, Collector Books, 1997; Noel Riley, Gifts for Good Children, Richard Dennis Publications, 1991.

Collectors' Club: ABC Plate/Mug Collector's Circle, 67 Stevens Ave., Old Bridge, NJ 08857.

Glass

Christmas Eve, Santa on chimney, clear, 6" d 75.00
Clock face center, Arabic and Roman numerals, alphabet
   center, frosted and clear, 7" d 75.00
Duck, amber, 6" d 45.00
Elephant with howdah, three waving Brownies, Ripley & Co., clear,
   6" d 135.00
Frosted Stork, flake 125.00
Little Bo Peep, center scene, raised alphabet border,
   6" d 50.00
Plain center, clear, white scalloped edge, 6" d 65.00
Young Girl, portrait, clear, 6" d 65.00

Pottery or Porcelain

Boy, stringed instrument, bird on fence, brown transfer, emb alphabet
   border, mkd "Adams," 7-1/4" d 80.00
Child reading, black transfer, polychrome enamel, Staffordshire, 5" d,
   short hairline, small back edge flakes 35.00

Pearlware, alphabets emb around rim, center transfer prints, clockwise: bird in nest, $350; England's Home, Prince of Wales, $550; Victoria Regina, $450.

Crusoe Finding the Footprints, 7 1/2" d 80.00
Fox Hunt, brown transfer, 7" d 125.00
Gathering Cotton, 6" d 425.00
Horses for Hire or Sale, brown transfer and polychrome dec,
   6-3/4" d 145.00
Keep Within Compass, soft paste, enamel, minor
   damage 85.00
Little Boy Blue 80.00
Make Hay, soft paste, enamel, minor damage 55.00
Old Mother Hubbard, brown transfer, polychrome enamel trim, alphabet border, mkd "Tunstall," 7-1/2" d 200.00
Swing Swong 115.00
Take Your Time Miss Lucy, black transfer of money and cat, polychrome enamel, titled, molded hops rim, red trim, ironstone, imp
   "Meakin," 6" d 125.00
Wandering Pie, birds, Staffordshire, 1890s 125.00

Tin

Girl on swing, lithographed center, printed alphabet border,
   3-1/2" d 60.00
Mary Had A Little Lamb, light rust, 9" d 115.00
Two kittens playing with basket of wood, 4-1/2" d q80.00
Who Killed Cock Robin, 7-3/4" d 120.00

ADVERTISING

History: Before the days of mass media, advertisers relied on colorful product labels and advertising giveaways to promote their products. Containers were made to appeal to the buyer through the use of stylish lithographs and bright colors. Many of the illustrations used the product in the advertisement so that even an illiterate buyer could identify a product.

Advertisements were put on almost every household object imaginable and were constant reminders to use the product or visit a certain establishment.

References: *Advertising & Figural Tape Measures*, L-W Book Sales, 1995; A. Walker Bingham, *Snake-Oil Syndrome*, Christopher Publishing House, 1994; Lagretta Metzger Bajorek, *American's Early Advertising Paper Dolls*, Schiffer Publishing, 1999; Michael Bruner, *Advertising Clocks*, Schiffer Publishing, 1995; ——, *Encyclopedia of Porcelain Enamel Advertising*, 2nd ed., Schiffer Publishing, 1999; ——, *More Porcelain Enamel Advertising*, Schiffer Publishing, 1997; *Collector's Digest Letter Openers: Advertising & Figural*, L-W Book Sales, 1996; Doug Collins, *America's Favorite Food: The Story of Campbell Soup Company*, Harry N Abrams, 1994; Fred Dodge, *Antique Tins*, 1995, 1999 value update, Collector Books; ——, *Antique Tins*, Book II, (1998), Book III (1999), Collector Books; Warren Dotz, *Advertising Character Collectibles*, Collector Books, 1993, 1997 values updated; ——, *What a Character! 20th Century American Advertising Icons*, Chronicle Books, 1996; Bill and Pauline Hogan, *Charlton Standard Catalogue of Canadian Country Store Collectables*, Charlton Press, 1996; Bob and Sharon Huxford, *Huxford's Collectible Advertising*, 4th ed., Collector Books, 1998; Ray Klug, *Antique Advertising Encyclopedia*, Vol. 1 (1978, 1993 value update) and Vol. 2 (1985), L-W Promotions; Mary Jane Lamphier, *Zany Characters of the Ad World*, Collector Books, 1995; Rex Miller, *The Investor's Guide to Vintage Character Collectibles*, Krause Publications, 1999; Tom Morrison, *More Root Beer Advertising &*

Collectibles, Schiffer Publishing, 1997; Richard A. Penn, *Mom and Pop Stores*, Schiffer Publishing, 1998; Gerald S. Petrone, *Tobacco Advertising*, Schiffer Publishing, 1996; Don and Carol Raycraft, *Wallace-Homestead Price Guide to American Country Antiques*, 16th ed., Krause Publications, 1999; Robert Reed, *Bears and Dolls in Advertising*, Antique Trader Books, 1998; ——, *Paper Advertising Collectibles: Treasures from Almanacs to Window Signs*, Antique Trader Books, 1998; Bob Sloan and Steve Guarnaccia, *A Stiff Drink and a Close Shave*, Chronicle Books, 1995; Louis Storino, *Chewing Tobacco Tin Tags*, Schiffer Publishing, 1995; B. J. Summers, *Value Guide to Advertising Memorabilia*, 2nd ed., Collector Books, 1999; Richard White, *Advertising Cutlery*, Schiffer Publishing, 1999; Neil Wood, *Smoking Collectibles*, L-W Book Sales, 1994; David and Micki Young, *Campbell's Soup Collectibles from A to Z*, Krause Publications, 1998; David Zimmerman, *The Encyclopedia of Advertising Tins*, Vol. 1 (1994) and Vol. II (1998), Collector Books.

Periodicals: *Advertising Collectors Express*, P.O. Box 221, Mayview, MO 64071; *Creamers*, P.O. Box 11, Lake Villa, IL 60046; *Paper Collectors' Marketplace*, P.O. Box 128, Scandinavia, WI 54917; *Paper & Advertising Collector* (PAC), P.O. Box 500, Mount Joy, PA 17552.

Collectors' Clubs: Advertising Cup and Mug Collectors of America, P.O. Box 680, Solon, IL 52333; Antique Advertising Association of America, P.O. Box 1121, Morton Grove, IL 60053; Ephemera Society of America, P.O. Box 95, Cazenovia, NY 13035; Inner Seal Collectors Club, 4585 Saron Drive, Lexington, KY 40515; National Association of Paper and Advertising Collectibles, P.O. Box 500, Mount Joy, PA 17552; Porcelain Advertising Collectors Club, P.O. Box 381, Marshfield Hills, MA 02051; Tin Container Collectors Association, P. O. Box 440101, Aurora, CO 80044.

Museums: American Advertising Museum, Portland, OR; Museum of Transportation, Brookline, MA; National Museum of American History, Archives Center, Smithsonian Institution, Washington, DC.

Additional Listings: See Warman's Americana & Collectibles for more examples.

Ashtray, tin
    Green River Whiskey, match holder, c1900 .... 25.00
      Kellogg Telephone Co., emb telephone, 50th anniversary 38.00
Bean Pot, Heinz 57, brown glazed ceramic, emb letters 115.00
Bill Hook, "Don't Forget to Order J. G. Davis Co.'s Granite Flour," gray and dark blue, 5-1/2" x 3-5/8" 210.00
Biscuit Box, Columbia, Missouri Can Co., red, white, and blue, Miss Columbia, pre-1900 .... 115.00
Biscuit Jar, 10-1/2" h, glass jar, glass lid, "Sunshine Biscuits" emb on front "Loose-Wiles Biscuit Company" on back 350.00
Blotter, unused
    Culliman Shoe Hospital, J. L. Vick, Prop., 1930s, 3" x 6" 4.00
    Gordon Keith Studio, Oakland, CA, elegant couple dancing, "For a rhythmic thrill learn the new Latin American Dances! Conga! Tango! Rhumba! And the season's newest - Samba," black and white, 4" x 9" 10.00
    I. Tucker Show Repair, Moultrie, GA, 1930s, 3" x 5" 3.50
    Miller's Leather Store, Waverly, IA, 1930s, 3-1/8" x 6" 4.00
    Reichert Miling Co., girl wearing wooden shoes, boy playing accordion, multicolored, c1910, 3-1/4" x 6" 7.50
Booklet, Knott's Berry Farm and Ghost Town, Buena Park, 1950s, 8" x 11" 25.00
Bookmark, Geneva National Mineral Water, celluloid, diecut water fountain, adv on back, c1905 .... 35.00

Apple Butter Crock, Heinz, paper label, $350.

SPECIAL AUCTIONS

Bear Pen Antiques
2318 Bear Pen Hollow Road
Lock Haven, PA 17745
(717) 769-6655

Bill Bertoia Auctions
1881 Spring Rd
Vineland, NJ 08360
(609) 692-1881

Hake's Americana & Collectibles
P.O. Box 1444, Dept. 344
York, PA 17405
(717) 848-1333

James D. Julia, Inc.
P.O. Box 830
Fairfield, ME 04937
(207) 453-7125

Richard Opfer Auctioneering
1919 Greenspring Dr.
Timonium, MD 21093

William Morford Auctions
Rd#2
Cazenovia, NY 13035

Sandy Rosnick Auctions
15 Front St.
Salem, MA 01970

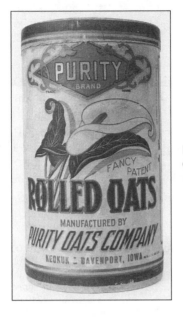

Box, Purity Brand Rolled Oats, $75.

Box, cardboard
    Adams Sappota Chewing Gum, 7-1/2" x 8-1/2", two Victorian
        ladies, graphic labels 90.00
    Andy Gump Sunshine Biscuits, cardboard, 5" x 3" x 2".........425.00
    Fairbank's Gold Dust Washing Powder, tri-panel, 3 printed panels
        on front and back, 19" x 9-1/4"_____1,000.00
    Williams Brothers Valvriggans, men's long underwear............15.00

Calendar, A. J. Russlow, Livery & Feed Stable, Randolph, VT, 1908, 14-1/4" x 10", $18.

Cake tin, Purity Highest Quality Fruit Cake, Chicago's Best Cake, $30.

Calendar
    1885, L. L. Ferriss, boots, shoes, and rubbers, framed,
        6" x 8-1/2" 70.00
    1894, Nestle's Food, "Give the Babies Nestle's Food," ©1894, starts
        with May, 1894, ends April, 1895, framed to show both sides,
        5-1/2" x 11-3/4" x 35-1/2" 50.00
    1909, DeLaval Cream Separator, full pad, 19-1/2" x
        12-1/2" 475.00
    1911, M. A. Theoford's Black Draught Liver Medicine and McElree's
        Wine of Cardui Woman's Relief Medicine, 1911, metal edge....40.00
    1913, Swift's Premium, 4 pages, each with different scene,
        17" x 9" 20.00
    1921, McCormick-Deering, young girl sitting on fence at edge of
        wheat field, 24" x 12" 30.00
Candy Pail
    Lovell & Covel, Queen of Hearts design, 3" x 2-7/8", 3 oz, slot
        added later to lid 110.00

Cigar box, College Maid, $60.

Riley's Rum & Butter Toffee, Halifax, England, 7-1/4" x 7", emb name, silhouettes of children playing with kite, slip lid..........50.00

Sharps' Toffee, 10" x 3-1/4", colorful parrot 55.00

Canister, North Pole Cut Plug, Hasker & Marcuse, Richmond, VA, pre-1901, 1#, horizontal, oval top, two polar bears playing 1,400.00

Chair, wooden, folding, adv on both sides of backrest

Cross-Cut Cigarettes, Victorian Lady, slogan, and illus of package, 30-1/2" h 200.00

Duke's Cigarettes, Victorian Lady and slogan, 32" h.............150.00

Cigar Box, Kin-To, full 40.00

Cigar Lighter, hotel lobby type

Midland Spark, wood base, Model L, c1920, 15" x 7-1/4" x 7" ...400.00

Rising Sun Stove Polish, oak, lighter and cigar cutter, 23" x 9"...1,600.00

Clip, Spencerian Pens 20.00

Coffee Tin

Battleship, warship illus, 1 pound, keywind 90.00

Bestaste, 1 pound, keywind...295.00

Chateau Frontenac Brand Coffee, Kearney Bros., Canada, bright graphics 165.00

Dillworth's Golden Urn, 1 pound, keywind...............................225.00

Don-De, Weppner-Weil Co., Cleveland, OH, 1 pound, keywind.150.00

Donald Duck Coffee, Free Sample, orig bank style lid, 3" x 2-1/4" 570.00

First Pick, 1 pound, keywind..220.00

Garden of Allah, Delano, Potter & Co., Boston, 1 pound, keywind 95.00

High Park, 1 pound, keywind, plantation scenes...................125.00

McFadden's Electric Brand, 1 pound......................................75.00

Millard's May-Day, 1 pound, top circular label 65.00

Monticello, view of mansion, 1 pound, keywind....................200.00

Old Boston, horse-drawn stage coach, ©1941, 1 pound, keywind...250.00

Old Master, Blodgett-Beckley Co., Toledo, OH, 3 pound, snap top..140.00

Page's Devotion, 1 pound, snap top.......................................290.00

Parke's Newport, sprawling factory scene, 1 pound, snap top ...180.00

Princess Patt, 1 pound, keywind 240.00

Red Rooster, 1 pound, keywind...75.00

Cocoa tin, Baby Stuart, 1 lb, $70.

Star Cup, Mogar Coffee Co., king drinking coffee, 1 pound, keywind...225.00

Sunny Sky, image of sun's rays over coffee plantation, 1 pound, keywind...355.00

White Swan, swan in circle on front, red ground, 1 pound, keywind...50.00

White Villa, touring car and villa, 1 pound, snap top, some surface rust..45.00

Counter Display

Beech-Nut Gum, back of tin display shows little girl with package of gum, mounted on metal pedestal, 14-3/4" h 1,450.00

Bicycle Playing Cards, tin display, front shows royal flush, sides simulated wood grain, 12-1/2" x 4-1/2" x 8" 100.00

Dana's Sarsaparilla, metal rim and glass, fancy Art Nouveau filigree on all corners, glass etched "Dana's Sarsaparilla," 5-1/2" x 10" x 10" 50.00

Ever-ready Shaving Brushes, tin, oversized shaving brush on left side, right side with bald man shaves "trademark" face, shaving brushes displayed behind window, 12" h, 15" w 450.00

Horseshow Tobacco, wood, hinged display box, decal on glass lid, orig tax stamp, 13" x 13" x 4"...200.00

Regal Elastic Web, slanted oak case, int. compartmentalized for corset supplies, 7" x 6" x 18" 400.00

Sir Walter Raleigh Tin, 6 orig pocket tins...............................130.00

Cup and Saucer, Hills Bros. Tea and Coffee, china, Hills Man on front, 2-3/8" h, 5" d 150.00

Dispenser, Karo Tape, porcelain..25.00

Display Cabinet

Arrow Collar, vertical, adv on front glass door, brass trim, 7" x 7" x 47" 750.00

JP Clarks, spool

2 drawer, "Best Six Cord Thread," and "J&P Coats" on drawers, decals on other 3 sides adv "J. & P. Coats Cottons," 6-1/2" x 14" x 20" 100.00

4 drawer, lift lid top, orig knobs, 29-1/2" x 20" 410.00

Slant front, oak, partial orig decal on front, roll top front, 24" x 32" x 9" 525.00

Diamond Dyes, wooden case, emb tin panel

Lady drying clothes, Kellogg &Bulkeley Co., Hartford, Conn. Lithographer, orig paper label inside, 29-1/2" h, 22-1/4" w, 9-3/4" l 650.00

Mrs. Knight Bought a Remnant, 5 children in vintage clothing playing with balloon in front of mansion, cardboard adv on back, inner compartments, plus approx. 50 packs of orig Diamond Dye, ©1908, Meek Co. Lithographer, 24-1/4" h, 15-1/4" w, 8" l..800.00

The Governess, children playing in park, ©1906, slight surface rust, 29-3/4" h, 22-1/4" w, 9-3/4" l...................................500.00

Dr. Scholl's, metal, wood grain emb 240.00

Ferry's 5¢ Seeds, cabinet with rack, 27" x 12" x 5-1/2" 200.00

Humphrey's Remedies, wooden cabinet, tin front lists remedies, approx. 60 unopened packages inside, 27-1/2" h, 21" w, 10" d...1,250.00

Lorillard & Co., P., countertop type, front doors stenciled, 4 etched panes of glass, 17-1/2" x 33" x 32-1/2" 900.00

Putnam Dyes, wood, countertop type, trademark scene, British Red Coats chasing George Washington, 10" x 21" x 8-1/4".......115.00

Rubberite Varnish, tiger decal, 15" x 26" x 12-1/2"..................40.00

Star Braid, thread, wood..650.00

Display Case

Ever Ready Daylo, glass, 20" x 14" x 12".............................250.00

Primley's, J. P., Gum, small countertop curved glass display case, etched "J. P. Primley's California Fruit and Pepsin Chewing Gum," orig silver, gold and copper paint on etching, 9-1/2" x 18-1/2" x 12-1/4" 900.00

Display Rack

Samoset Chocolate, circular metal stand, metal marquee sign "Samoset Chocolate Pocket Packets 10 Cents," 6" x 22" 25.00

Yello-Bole Pipe, revolving...95.00

Mirror, Beau-tyskin, Chichester Chemical Co., Phila., girl in pink dress, yellow flowers, green ground, 2-1/2" x 1-1/2", $40.

Figure
   Dr. Scholl's Foot Comfort, meal, blue 160.00
   Nathan's Ankle Support, display foot, orig box 90.00
   Old Crow, ceramic 35.00
   William Atkinson's Bear's Grease, 15-1/4" l, earthenware bear, hand modeled, ribbon extending over back with adv, England, c1860, firing lines, chips to ears, glaze loss to feet 1,265.00
Jar, Squirrel Brand Nuts, bulbous glass jar, emb "Squirrel Brand Salted Nut" trademark, glass lid 130.00
Ledger Marker, Bagley's May-Flower Chewing Tobacco, tin, ship scene on left, fan with little girls picture on right, 3" x 12" 100.00
Lunch Box, litho tin
   Blue and Scarlet Plug Cut, Booker Tobacco Co., Richmond, clasp missing, some fading 100.00
   Fashion Cut Plug Tobacco, couple strolling 360.00
   Great West Tobacco, Canadian, red and black, wear 60.00
Magazine Tear Sheet, back cover of Youth's Companion, Proctor & Gamble, 14" h, 11-1/4" w
   Ivory Flakes, hand washing stockings, June 11, 1925 .... 10.00
   Naptha Soap, Sept. 13, 1923 .... 8.00
Mirror, beveled, countertop type
   Duke's Tobacco, brass base, stenciled "Smoke and Chew Duke's Special Long Cut," W. Dukesons & Co., 17-1/2" x 10" x 6" 700.00
   Y&N Corsets, lady in her "Diagonal Seam Corset," wood frame, 25-3/4" x 16-1/2" 300.00
Mirror, Pocket, Tydol Veedol Petroleum Products, celluloid, birthstones, 2" d 80.00
Mug
   Dove Brand Ginger Ale, Penn's Bottling & Supple Co., 3 coves on branch, two hairline cracks, 5" h 55.00
   Good Cheer Cigar 55.00
Paint Set
   American Crayon, Pied Piper Set, 1930s 40.00
   DeVoe Water Colors with Indian Pictures 45.00
Paperweight, Socony Motor Oils, palm type mirror back, 3-1/2" d ... 160.00
Peanut Butter Tin, litho tin
   Harvard, Millard Supply Co., Chicago, 10" x 8", 10#, peanut dressed as graduating student, "Educate the Taste" 140.00
   Squirrel, Canada Nut Company Limited, Vancouver, BC, snap-top tin
      3-3/4" x 3", 13 oz 165.00
      4-1/4" x 4", 27 oz 160.00
      4-3/4" x 5-1/4", 48 oz 90.00

   5-1/2" x 5", 57 oz 95.00
   6-1/2" x 5-1/4", #5, horizontal scratch on front 120.00
Pinback Button, multicolored
   American Express, red, white, and blue corporate flag centered on "World Service" globe image, c1920 .... 15.00
   Forest City Paint, fleshtone arm holding black, white, and gray paint can, ivory white ground, black letters 25.00
   Hamilton Brown Shoe Co., red, white, blue, and gray, "Keep the Quality Up," 1920s 20.00
   Pontiac Strain Furs, black and white image of seated fox over gold profile of Indian head, red, blue, and gold accents 70.00
   Quaker Oats, package on white ground, red lettering 45.00
   South Bend Watch Co., image of pocket watch encased in block of ice, blue ground, white letters, c1920 .... 20.00
   Stephenson Underwear, red underwear shirt held by gentleman in blue and white striped dress shirt, white ground, black letters, 1920s 75.00
   Waterloo Boy Tractor, farm boy in broad brimmed straw hat, image of early 1900s steam farm tractor 100.00
   White Rose Butter, white rose, green petals, dark blue ground, white letters 25.00
   Wilbur's Cocoa, cupid stirring cup of steaming cocoa 65.00
Pot Scraper
   Delco-Light Brand, Farm Electric Generators, never used, 3-1/4" x 2-1/2" 725.00
   Penn Furnaces/Stoves 100.00
Ruler, Toldedo Metal Co., litho tin, diecut, children playing at well, 5-1/4" 500.00
Saleman's Sample
   Calendar, titled "Advertising That Advertises," F. J. Offreman Art Works, Inc., Buffalo, IN, green Art Nouveau border, two colorful tigers in center, 1934 calendar pad, 30" x 41" 125.00
   Display Showcase, German silver steeple case curved glass, 9" x 6" x 5-1/2" 7,500.00
   Furnace, Holland Furnace, orig carrying case, cast iron and sheet metal, 12" x 13" x 10" 100.00
   Stove, cast iron, mkd "Little Eva N. S. Cate Boston," 19th C, 11-1/4" w, 13-1/2" d, minor rust 345.00
Shipping Crate
   Castile Soap, Chicago, 1900, wooden, paper label 10.00
   Warner's Safe Yeast, wooden, printed 20.00
Soap, Goblin Soap, wrapped bar, orig box, graphics both sides .. 30.00
Store Canister/Bin
   A & P Coffee, metal 200.00
   Alburn Eskimo Cigar, early 1900s, 5" x 5" 25.00
   Gloor, R. G. & Co. Coffee, stenciled front, pre-1900, 8-1/2" sq .. 120.00
   Horlick's Malt Milk, raised blue enameled lettering, 4-5/8" h .. 475.00
   Nestle's Hot Chocolate, large 100.00
   Roundy's Mustard, stenciling, pre-1900, 7" x 5-1/2" x 9-1/2" .. 70.00
   Sweet Cuba Fine Cut, large, yellow and orange 325.00
   Sweet Mist, sq, cardboard lift top 150.00
   Thompson's Malted Milk 70.00
Signs
   Anheuser-Busch, Budweiser, King of Bottled Beer, tin, 49" x 14-1/2" 250.00
   Barrett, Lawrence, Mild Havana Cigar, 10 and 15 cents, portrait of Barrett, porcelain, 20" x 34" 125.00
   Brubaker & Bros., W. L., paper, roll-down type, tin strips on top and bottom, portrait of woman on green foliage background, professional restoration to one side, framed, 24" x 17" 450.00
   Bulldog Seats, oval, emb tin, arrogant looking black and white bulldog standing on toilet seat, "Joints Won't Let Go," 9-3/4" x 6-1/2", 880.00
   Canada Dry, diecut tin, bottle shape, 40" h 750.00
   Cetacolor, "Not a Soap, Prevents Wash Good from Fading, 10 cents Package," graphic of Gibson style girl, linen, framed, 36" x 12" 125.00
   Chew Corn Bread Tobacco, heavy paper, Compton & Sons litho, yellow ground, red and black lettering, 30" x 18" 530.00
   Columbia Records, cardboard, Columbia Phonograph cylinder packages on either side of highly emb American eagle standing stop stars and stripes shield, 11 x 14-1/2" 200.00

Columbian Rope, linen, seaman carrying coil of rope, 49" x 29-1/2"..325.00

Cremo Cigar, litho tin, round, 17" d.........................225.00

Crown Prince Coffees, paper, lady in vintage clothing standing in garden, holding roses, matted and framed, 27-1/2" x 13-1/2".......400.00

Dr. Coc's Barbed Wire Liniment, Carlisle, Indiana, cardboard....150.00

Eagle Rock Wine, emb diecut cardboard, western scene, riding roping cowgirl, framed, 15-3/4" x 19" 900.00

Edgemont Tobacco, linen, shows two colorful packages, framed, 36" x 12"...70.00

Elgin National Watch Works, paper, black and white, factory scene, various horse drawn carriages and early automobiles along streets, orig wood frame mkd "Elgin," 15-1/4" x 33-1/4" 125.00

Fiske, J., Boston, figural pocket watch, wood, gold, white, and black paint, 24" h...440.00

Fritz Bros. Best 5¢ Cigars, reverse foil under glass, framed, some professional repairs, 17-1/4" l 250.00

Grants Hygienic Crackers for Constipation, cardboard, 11" x 14"...30.00

Helmar Turkish Cigarettes, porcelain, 24" x 12" 80.00

Hickman-Ebbert Co., self framed tin, couple picking apples, loading them into Ebbert wagon, "In the Shade of the Old Apple Tree," ©1906, Chas. W. Shonk Co., Litho, 25-1/2" x 37-1/2" 700.00

Hires Root Beer, diecut cardboard, 33-1/2" x 14-1/2"............200.00

Hood Dairy

    Guernsey Cow and milk maid 125.00

    Jersey cow 225.00

Independence Indemnity Insurance, tin litho, 15" x 18"...........55.00

Illinois Springfield Watches, tin, view of Observatory of Illinois Watch Co., Springfield, orig wood frame, some surface rust to upper portion, overall fading, 17-1/2" x 23-1/2"....................200.00

Kawannee, elevators, wagons, tin, 20" x 11"..........................55.00

Keene, Tom, Cigars 5 Cents, yellow, blue, and white, porcelain, 40" x 18"...300.00

Lipschultz 44 Cigar, two sided diecut tin litho oval, flange, 18" x 13"...250.00

London Life Cigarettes, two sided, porcelain, diecut flange, 16" 500.00

Masury's House Paints, reverse glass, corner sign, "Masury's Pure Linseed Oil House Paints," wood frame, 21" x 16-1/2" 275.00

Mellin's Food, diecut, stand-up, baby sitting in highchair, adv on back "Why Your Baby Should Have Mellin's Food," framed to show both sides, 12 x 10-1/4" 150.00

Moxie

    Diecut, tin, two sided, Moxie Car, blue, man in Moxie coat riding white horse in blue car, patented Feb 27, 1917, lithographer H. D. Beach Co., 6-1/2" h, 8-1/2" l...............................1,700.00

    Self framed tin, oval, "Yes, We Sell Moxie, Very Healthy, Feeds the Nerves," Kaufmann & Strass Co., NY litho, 27" x 19-1/2" ..500.00

Navy Cut Plug, emb tin, self framed, emb battleships and horse shoe designs on sides, horse shoe flags hanging in air, 35" x 23" 3,750.00

Nesbitt's Soda Pop, tin, showing bottle, 24" sq 275.00

Nu-Wood Insulating Wall Board and Lath, porcelain, house among trees, mfg. by Veribrite Signs, 22-1/2" x 35" 100.00

Old Boone Distillery, Tixton, Millett & Co. Distillers, old time distillery in backwoods of KY, ©1904, Haeusermann M. M. Co. Litho, crease in lift side, 18" x 26"...500.00

Old Reliable Coffee, tin, H. D. Beach Co., Coshocton, Ohio, orig nail holes around edges, 9-1/4" x 6-1/2" 135.00

Owl Cigar, two sided diecut cardboard, owl in cage sitting atop Owl Cigar, ©1902, framed to show both sides..........................300.00

Pickwick Ale, self framed tin, jovial old men toasting beer at table in front of fireplace, Charles W. Shank, Chicago, Lithographer, 22" x 28-1/2"...300.00

Piedmont, the Virginia Cigarettes, porcelain, shows package

    14" x 16", curved 450.00

    30" x 46"...200.00

Red Coon, Sun Cured Chewing Tobacco, heavy paper, red and black raccoon, yellow ground, black lettering, 18" x 22".......60.00

San Antonia Brewery, cardboard, western scene of "The Jersey Lilly," home of Judge Roy Bean, wood frame, 26" x 36".....550.00

Segal Key, double sided, diecut tin litho, key shape, 31" l.....170.00

Shepherd, W., serpentine frame painted yellow, red scroll border, center panel painted with stars and rays above eagle and shield flanked by flag, banner, and arrows, MA, early 19th C, 59-1/4" w, 49-1/2" h 3,740.00

Sickle Cut Plug, linen, framed with plastic-pac, 36" x 12" 65.00

Smoke Moonstruck Cigars, reverse painted under glass, early, some restoration, 16" x 9"...450.00

St Louis Shot Tower Co., paper, factory scene, vintage horse drawer vehicles on upper portion, lower section with successful duck hunter, A. Lambrecht & Co. Lithographer, St. Louis Mo., wooden frame holds vials of company's different shot sizes, 16-1/2" x 25-1/2" 3,900.00

Sullivan, R. G., Manchester, NH, two sided tin, "7-20-4 10¢ Cigars," 5-1/2" x 4-1/2"...50.00

Sunlight Soap, Cincinnati, tin...300.00

Tatem-Wright Dry Goods Co., diecut cardboard, 4 little ladies dressed in Sunday best, riding in rose dec vehicle, matted and framed, 7-1/2" x 11-1/4"..100.00

Union Leader, cardboard, Uncle Sam reading the Naval Review, images of named U. S. Fleet, c1909, framed, 17-1/2" x 26"....700.00

U. S. Marine Cut Plug, sailor leaning out of porthole with package, double matted and framed, 19-1/2" x 25" 1,050.00

Velvet Tobacco, porcelain, 42" x 11".................................225.00

Vienna Pudding, paper, comical dinner guests looking as family dog runs between butler's legs, spilling the Vienna Pudding, border trimmed, 12-1/4" x 9" 80.00

Warren, E. K. Grocery Store, pine, worn and weather black and yellow paint, blue and yellow on crown molded frame, 20-1/2" h, 48-3/4" w 800.00

Weller, J. H., dealer in ready made clothing and sewing machines, imperfections, 21-1/4" x 74-1/4"..1,380.00

Wrigley's Spearmint Chewing Gum, countertop type, two sided, cardboard, orig metal frame, "Wrigley's" engraved on both sides, 14" x 18" 100.00

Thermometer

    American Seal Paints, Uncle Sam carrying paint bucket, wood, 21" h, 9" w 210.00

    Ex Lax, porcelain, 36" h, 8-1/4" w.....................................140.00

    Mail Pouch Chewing Tobacco Co., blue, red, and white, 39" h, 8" w, minor paint chips...400.00

    Moxie, tin, Moxie Man image, 9-1/2" x 25" 425.00

Tins

    Baking Powder

        Clabber Girl...10.00

        Rabbit's Foot Baking Powder, 5-1/2" x 3-1/4" 775.00

        Royal Powder...10.00

    Bacon, Stickney 1834 Coffee House, Bacon, Stickney Co., Albany, NY, 3-7/8" x 5"..400.00

        Wigwam Coffee, 1 lb, prytop, lid missing 40.00

    Gum, Adams California Fruit Gum, illus of packs of Adams California Fruit Gum on all 4 sides, 6" x 6-3/4" x 4-3/4" 550.00

    Marshmallow

        Bunte Brothers, Chicago, #5, slip top, factory view on one side, dapper child on other, 12-3/4" x 5" 230.00

        Circus Club Mallows, Harry Horne Co., Toronto, hat shape, 6-1/2" 150.00

    Peanut Tin, Cream Dove, 1 pound, 9-1/2" x 8-1/4", orig top . 165.00

    Razor, Yankee Brand Safety Razor, hinged lid, father faced man, eagles, 1-1/2" x 2-1/2" x 1-3/4" 825.00

Tip Tray

    Climax Plug, colorful..115.00

    DeLaval Cream Separators, lady separating cream in family kitchen, little boy, ©1906, 4-1/4" d....................................140.00

    Globe-Wernicke Sectional Bookcases, couple sorting books in stacking bookcases, 4-1/4" d...95.00

    Junket, little girl eating bowl, "Have Some Junket," mfg. By Chr. Hansens Laboratory, Little Falls, NY, 4-1/4' d 200.00

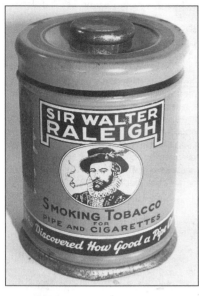

Tobacco tin, Sir Walter Raleigh, $40.

Kenney, C. D., Co., America's Pride, patriotic stars and stripes border, sailor and solider in vintage uniforms, background shows Gatlin guns, airplanes, and battleship, 4-1/4" d 275.00

King's Pure Malt, nurse in vintage garb carrying tray of "King's Pure Malt," 6" x 4-1/4" 75.00

Krebs, E. K., adv President Suspenders, glass applied over base of tray protecting image of Grecian looking woman, wear to rim, 4-1/4" d 125.00

Lehnert's Beer, beautiful woman head, 4-1/4" d.................... 100.00

Red Raven Splits, Red Raven logo next to vintage bottle, "For High Livers' Livers," Chas. W. Shonk Co. Litho Chicago, 4-1/4" d...50.00

Rockford Watches, lady in waiting, sitting on water's edge, scalloped edge rim, 5" x 3-1/4" 300.00

Welsbach Mantle 85.00

Tobacco Tin, vertical pocket type
Abbey, 10¢, 4" h, full.. 370.00
Bagdad, tall version, litho top, 4-1/4" h 440.00
Bambino, silhouette of the Babe, red ground 2,930.00
Big Ben 35.00
Bon Air 500.00
Briggs, "Complimentary tin, not for sale," full........................ 165.00
Bulldog, blue, full, 4-1/2" h 600.00
Central Union.. 340.00
Checkers, red and black, gold letters, short version............. 340.00
Coach & Four 245.00
Dial, "for pipe and cigarettes" 140.00
Dill's, concave, girl in red dress 135.00
Edgeworth Junior.. 95.00
Ensign, Washington and Lee, Perfection Cut..................... 1,210.00
Fairmount, white lid, 10¢ 310.00
Forest & Stream, fisherman, creel top 125.00
Four Roses, flat top, 4-1/4" h.. 545.00
Full Dress
   Flip top, overall wear 200.00
   Sears Roebuck & Co. 1,335.00
Gold Bond, 4-1/2" h, 3" w 235.00
Guide, full 335.00
Handmade, woman's hand illus... 500.00
Hi-Plane, red ground, white plane and lettering 60.00
Honeymoon 600.00
John Middleton Club Mixture 1,350.00
King Edward 515.00
Kingsbury, Christian Paper Tob. Co., St. Louis, MO, 4-1/2" h 755.00
Life... 825.00
London Sherbet Mixture, block letters, green
   ground 260.00

Look Out, scratch on front 1,215.00
Lucky Strike, 4-1/2" h 100.00
Manhattan Cocktail, rooster and cocktail glass 1,115.00
Maryland Club, flip top, rust to lid and top left 250.00
Master Mason.. 330.00
Matoaka, some overall wear and rust spots 1,650.00
Moonshine, dents 1,180.00
Old Colony, silver, 4-3/8" h 215.00
Peachy... 225.00
Pipe Major, dark variation 200.00
Plug Crumb Cut 445.00
Q-Boid
   Flat, granulated plug 100.00
   Oval.. 80.00
Rex 265.00
Shot, shows rifle and long peace pipe................................... 275.00
Sun Cured, slight fading to one side................................... 1,835.00
Stag, tall... 115.00
Three Squares, 2-3/4" x 2", complimentary sample, full.......... 75.00
Times Square, some rust on lid.. 335.00
Torpedo, Canadian
   Destroyer... 1,455.00
   Submarine, concave 7,720.00
Union Leader, five color 110.00
US Marine, 4-1/4" h, full 360.00
Wagon Wheel, yellow ground, red and black trim 1,025.00
Wellington, full 1,055.00
Yacht Club, red ground, some dents to base, worn............ 1,100.00
Tray, Hall Ice Cream, Binghamton, NY, 13" x 10-1/2" 1,650.00
Watch Fob, Green River, silvered brass, horseshoe shape, center trademark image of caretaker and horse, "Green River" jug suspended from saddle, slogan "She Was Bred In Old Kentucky," reverse inscription "Official Whiskey of the U. S. Marine Hospital Service," lists six international awards from 1900-1907 .... 40.00

ADVERTISING TRADE CARDS

History: Advertising trade cards are small, thin cardboard cards made to advertise the merits of a product. They usually bear the name and address of a merchant.

With the invention of lithography, colorful trade cards became a popular way to advertise in the late 19th and early 20th centuries. They were made to appeal especially to children. Young and old alike collected and treasured them in albums and scrapbooks. Very few are dated; the prime years for trade card production were 1880 to 1893; cards made between 1810 and 1850 can be found, but rarely. By 1900 trade cards were rapidly losing their popularity, and by 1910 they had all but vanished.

References: Kit Barry, *Advertising Trade Card*, Book 1, published by author, 1981; Dave Cheadle, *Victorian Trade Cards*, Collector Books, 1996; Robert Jay, *Trade Card in Nineteenth-Century America*, University of Missouri Press, 1987; Murray Cards (International) Ltd. (comp.), *Cigarette Card Values*, Murray Cards (International) Ltd., 1994.

Periodicals: *Card Times*, 70 Winified Lane, Aughton, Ormskirk, Lancashire L38 5DL England; *Trade Card Journal*, 109 Main St., Brattleboro, VT 05301.

Collectors' Club: Trade Card Collector's Association, P.O. Box 284, Marlton, NJ 08053.

Additional Listings: See *Warman's Americana & Collectibles* for more examples.

Beverages

Arbuckle Brothers Coffee

    Eskimos, seals, Alaska scenery, adv and Alaska history on back, 3" x 5".. 10.00

    Indians, miners, Montana scenery, 1892, 3" x 5"..................... 15.00

Ayer's Sarsaparilla

    "Ayer's Sarsaparilla Makes the Weak Strong," two gentlemen..... 18.00

    "The Old Folks at Home," 8" x 12", bottle of tonic 325.00

Duff's Malt Whiskey, man in red jacket working on formula 30.00

Hermitage Sour Mash Whiskey, two rats and bottle 30.00

Lion Coffee, canaries and parakeets 12.00

Gibson's Pure Rye Whiskey 35.00

Mayer Brewing, Palest Brewery, New York, diecut 65.00

Union Pacific Tea, young lad sailors with American flag, includes Easter greeting 8.00

Clothing

A. S. Shaw Footwear, floral chromo, c1885, 4-1/2" x 7" 12.00

Ball's Corsets, center corset illus, child and mother holding baby 25.00

Child's & Staples, Gilbertsville, ME, young girl chasing butterfly, 2-3/4" x 4-1/2" 12.00

Hapke Knit Goods, 1876 Centennial, light green knitting machine vignette.. 45.00

Mattmueller, C., Boots, Shoes and Rubbers, Cleveland, floral designs, 1880s, 4-1/2" x 2-1/2" 9.00

Solar Tip Shoes, Girard College, Philadelphia, Where Boys Wear our Solar Tip Shoes.. 20.00

Strauss, Levi & Co., multi-fold, multiple images of children and adults wearing jeans, when folded it's shape of pair of Levi Strauss jeans showing both front and back pockets.................................... 275.00

Thompson's Glove Fitting Corsets, lady and cupids 35.00

Farm Machinery & Supplies

Gale Mfg. Co., Daisy Sulky Hay Rake, folder type, 4 panels, field scene... 75.00

Keystone Agricultural Implements, Uncle Sam talking to world representatives, metamorphic 75.00

Mast & Foos Columbia Steel Wind Mill, folder type, child with pump. 45.00

New Essay Lawn Mower, scene of Statue of Liberty, New York harbor... 35.00

Reid's Flower Seeds, two high wheeled bicyclers admiring flowers held by three ladies 15.00

McCormick Harvesting Machine Co., To Our Friends at the Annual Fairs, 1885, 6-1/4" x 4-1/16", $15.

Pillsbury Best XXXX is the Best, This Flour Always On Top, 5-1/2" x 3-1/2", $6.50.

Sheridan's, To Make Hens Lay, Use Sheridan's Condition Powder, before and after views of farmer in chicken house 25.00

Food

Bardenwerper, C. E., Dealer in Choice Meats & Poultry, NY, front adv, floral dec, c1880, 2" x 3-1/2" 7.50

Batsford, W. A., Dealer in Milk in Orange Co., NY, floral motif, c1880, 2" x 3-1/2' 6.00

Czar Baking Powder, black woman and boy with giant biscuit 25.00

Enterprise Meat and Food Chopper.. 45.00

Heinz Apple Butter, diecut, pickle shape...................................... 45.00

Hornby's Oats, diecut of girl peeking out of box 35.00

Pearl Baking Powder, light blue and sepia, reverse with order blank, c1890 .... 35.00

Royal Hams, Chief Joseph & His Tribe examining barrel of hams 48.00

Thurber Connoisseur Ketchup, product label illus 70.00

E. Tunison Grocer, elf standing next to pansies 15.00

Woolson Spice, Lion Coffee, young children portraying Cinderella ... 25.00

Health and Beauty

Ayer's Hair Vigor, four mermaids, ship in background 7.00

Golf Queen Perfume, Ricksecker Co., c1895, blotter type 12.00

Hill's Hair and Whisker Dye, New York proprietor........................ 40.00

Hoyt's German Cologne, E. M. Hoyt & Co., mother cat and kittens... 25.00

Laundry and Soaps

Empire Wringer Co., Auburn, NY, child helping "I Can Help Mama" .. 35.00

Higgin's Soap, comical black scene showing various uses for soap, set of 7 cards, framed, 29-1/2" x 8"... 150.00

Ivorine Cleanser, lettering on side of elephant, other animals 15.00

Mrs. Potts' Sad Irons, sign painters 35.00

Sapolio Soap, young black face peering out of watermelon center ... 18.00

Soapine, Kendall Mfg. Co., Providence, RI

    Carriage... 15.00

    Soapine on mantle, product box plus name spelled out over mantle.. 15.00

    Steam Engine 10.00

    Street Scene.. 10.00

    Wizard, lady talking to wizard.. 10.00

The Fort Wayne Improved Western Washer, Horton Manufacturing Co., Fort Wayne, Ind, one lady watching as other works new machine . 35.00

Medicine

Dr. Kilmer & Co., Binghamton, NY, 36" x 60", Standard Herbal Remedies, detailed graphics 395.00
King of the Blood Medicine, Automation Musical Band, Barnum's Traveling Museum 45.00
Perry Davis, Pain Killer for Wounds, armored man of war ships battle scene 25.00
Quaker Bitters, Standard Family Medicine, child in barrel 17.50
Scott's Emulsion of Cod Liver Oil, man with large fish over back, vertical format 20.00
Shaker Family Pills, little girl in white bonnet 38.00

Miscellaneous

Archer's Champion Refrigerators, Fulton St, Brooklyn, front adv with floral design, back listing products, 1880s, 2-1/2" x 4-1/2" 7.50
Bear Hunt Bank, J. & E. Stevens Co. 60.00
Drew's Good Singing Canaries Only, NY, fox and hounds racing on front, 2" x 3-1/2" 7.50
Emerson Piano Co., black and white illus 40.00
Forbes, C. P., Jewelry, Greenfield, MA, Santa in front of fireplace, toys on table 15.00
Granite Iron Ware, 3 ladies gossiping over tea 25.00
Middleton, Walter, Photographer, floral insert, baby face, gold trim, c1880, NH, 2-3/4" x 4" 6.00
Read McCraney, Sonora, Tuolumne Co., CA, Diamonds and Watches, Jewelry & Optical Goods, 1890s, 2-1/2" x 4" 10.00
The American Machine Co., Manufacturers of Hardware Specialties, three women ironing, vertical format 40.00
Two Headed Lady, 8th Wonder of the World 150.00
Wells Portrait & Landscape Photographer, Sonora, CA, adv on front, ship motif, gold and silver trim, 4-1/4" x 6" 35.00

Stoves and Ranges

Andes Stove, black children.. 15.00
Dixon's Stove Polish, Brownies illus 20.00
Florence Oil Stove, colorful illus of 2 women and 2 children 40.00
Rising Sun Stove Polish, folder type, "The Modern Cinderella".... 50.00
Rutland Stove Lining, child talking to parrot............................. 115.00

Thread and Sewing

Brooks' Spool Cotton, 3 kittens playing instruments made from spools... 25.00
Clark's Thread, Mile End Spool Cotton
    Two children riding high wheeled bike made from spools, others falling 12.00
    Two circus clowns... 15.00
Corticelli Spool Silks, Nonotuck Silk Co., diecut leaf shape with silkworm, green and white, c1888, 2" 10.00
Singer Manufacturing Co., choir of children singing as bird's listen....20.00
White Sewing Machine Co., elves working at sewing machine 15.00

Tobacco

Capadura Cigar, two baseball players, "Judgment, Judgment is always decided in favor of the Capadura Cigar" 30.00
Horsehead Tobacco, Dansman Tobacco Co., horse head illus 15.00

AGATA GLASS

History: Agata glass was invented in 1887 by Joseph Locke of the New England Glass Company, Cambridge, Massachusetts.

Agata glass was produced by coating a piece of peachblow glass with metallic stain, spattering the surface with alcohol, and firing. The resulting high-gloss, mottled finish looked like oil droplets floating on a watery surface. Shading usually ranged from opaque pink to dark rose, although pieces in a pastel opaque green also exist. A few pieces have been found in a satin finish.

Whiskey taster, 2-5/8" h, $550.

Bowl, 8" d, 4" h, green opaque body, staining and gold trim.... 1,150.00
Celery Vase, 7" h, sq, fluted top.................................... 625.00
Creamer 1,200.00
Finger Bowl
    5-1/4" d, 2-1/2" h, shiny, ruffled, peachblow opaque body, large areas of black mottling, lace-like gold tracery 685.00
    5-1/4" d, 2-5/8" h, crushed raspberry shading to creamy pink, all over gold mottling, blue accents 995.00
    5-1/4" d, 3" h, ruffled, peachblow opaque body, allover bright blue staining spots.. 750.00
    Pitcher, 6-3/8" h, crimped rim 1,750.00
Spooner, 4-1/2" h, 2-1/2" w, sq top, wild rose peachblow ground, small areas of wear 400.00
Toothpick Holder, 2-1/4" h, flared, green opaque, orig blue oil spots, green trim... 795.00
Tumbler, 3-7/8" h, peachblow ground, gold tracery, bold black splotches 785.00
Vase
    6" h, lily, crimson peachblow ground, large black splotches.. 885.00
    8" h, lily, shiny surface, crimson peachblow ground, large black splotches... 1,085.00

AMBERINA GLASS

History: Joseph Locke developed Amberina glass in 1883 for the New England Glass Works. "Amberina," a trade name, describes a transparent glass which shades from deep ruby to amber. It was made by adding powdered gold to the ingredients for an amber-glass batch. A portion of the glass was reheated later to produce the shading effect. Usually it was the bottom which was reheated to form the deep red; however, reverse examples have been found.

Most early Amberina is flint-quality glass, blown or pattern molded. Patterns include Diamond Quilted, Daisy and Button, Venetian Diamond, Diamond and Star, and Thumbprint.

In addition to the New England Glass Works, the Mount. Washington Glass Company of New Bedford, Massachusetts, copied the glass in the 1880s and sold it at first under the Amberina trade name and later as "Rose Amber." It is difficult to distinguish pieces from these two New England factories. Boston and Sandwich Glass Works never produced the glass.

Amberina glass also was made in the 1890s by several Midwest factories, among which was Hobbs, Brockunier &

Co. Trade names included "Ruby Amber Ware" and "Watermelon." The Midwest glass shaded from cranberry to amber, and the color resulted from the application of a thin flashing of cranberry to the reheated portion. This created a sharp demarcation between the two colors. This less-expensive version was the death knell for the New England variety.

In 1884, Edward D. Libbey was given the use of the trade name "Amberina" by the New England Glass Works. Production took place during 1900, but ceased shortly thereafter. In the 1920s, Edward Libbey renewed production at his Toledo, Ohio, plant for a short period. The glass was of high quality.

Marks: Amberina made by Edward Libbey in the 1920s is marked "Libbey" in script on the pontil.

References: Gary Baker et al., Wheeling Glass 1829-1939, Oglebay Institute, 1994 (distributed by Antique Publications); Neila and Tom Bredehoft, Hobbs, Brockunier & Co. Glass, Collector Books, 1997; Kenneth Wilson, American Glass 1760-1930, 2 vols., Hudson Hill Press and The Toledo Museum of Art, 1994.

Reproduction Alert: Reproductions abound.

Additional Listings: Mount Washington.

Beverage Set, Optic Diamond Quilted pattern, 7" h pitcher, 3 punch cups, 2 tumblers, New England, 6 pcs 825.00
Bonbon, 7" d, 1-1/2" h, wavy six pointed 1-1/2" w rim, fuchsia shading to pale amber, sgd "Libbey" 625.00
Bowl
    4-1/2" d, 2-1/4" h, tricorn, fuchsia shading to amber, Venetian Diamond design 325.00
    4-1/2" d, 2-1/2" h, Optic Diamond Quilted pattern 125.00
Butter Pat, 2-3/4 d, Daisy and Button pattern, sq, notched corners, pr 250.00
Celery Boat, 14" l, 5" w, 2-1/2" h, Daisy and Button pattern, Hobbs, Brockunier, minute roughness on bow 750.00
Celery Vase
    Diamond Quilted pattern, sq scalloped rim. 6-1/8" h 275.00
    Inverted Thumbprint pattern 145.00
    Optic Expanded Diamond pattern, New England Glass Works, 6-1/2" h 345.00
Centerpiece, 14" l, canoe, Daisy and Button pattern, Hobbs Brockunier 950.00
Cordial, 4-1/2" h, trumpet shape 225.00
Cracker Jar, cov, 8" h, 5-3/4" d, Inverted Thumbprint pattern, barrel shape, rare glass cov, applied amber knob finial, attributed to Hobbs, c1885 .... 785.00
Cream Pitcher and Sugar, 2-3/4" h, Optic Thumbprint pattern, blood red neck and shoulder, honey colored lower half, shape #77, Mt. Washington, damage to handle of sugar 485.00
Cruet, 5-1/2" h, Inverted Thumbprint pattern, fuchsia trefoil spout, neck, and shoulder, Mt. Washington 435.00
Decanter
    Optic Diamond Quilted pattern, solid amber faceted stopper, 12" h 485.00
    Reverse Inverted Thumbprint pattern, ground and polished pontil 125.00
Ice Cream Plate, 5-1/2" sq, Daisy and Button pattern, Hobbs Brockunier 95.00
Juice Tumbler, 3-1/2" h, tapered cylindrical, applied reeded handle 150.00
Lemonade Glass, 4-7/8" h, 16 optic ribs, upper 2" blushed with color 215.00
Pickle Castor Insert, 4-1/4" h, 4" d, Inverted Thumbprint pattern, Mt. Washington 425.00
Pitcher
    4-1/2" h, sq top, Inverted Thumbprint pattern, applied amber reeded handle 325.00

Tumbler, Baby Inverted Thumbprint pattern, 4-1/8" h, $48.

    5" h, Daisy and Button pattern, Hobbs Brockunier 425.00
    8" h, 5" d, amberina-opalescent, clear reeded handle, ruffled top, wide flange petticoat shape 650.00
    10" h, 4-3/4" d, Optic Diamond Quilted pattern, applied amber handle, ground pontil 235.00
Punch Cup, 2-1/2" h, applied reeded amber handle, slight ribbing, tapered body, attributed to Mt. Washington 245.00
Sauce Dish, Daisy and Button, scalloped, set of 6 .... 450.00
Spooner, 4-1/2" h, Inverted Thumbprint pattern, New England Glass Works 100.00
Syrup Pitcher, Hobnail pattern, orig pewter top std "Pat. Jan 29 84," Hobbs, Brockunier & Co., 3 hobs chipped 300.00
Tankard
    6-5/8" h, ten paneled cylinder, applied reeded handle 395.00
    7" h, flared cylinder, Diamond Quilted pattern, applied handle 450.00
Toothpick Holder
    2-1/4" h, 1-1/2" w, Inverted Thumbprint pattern, sq top 295.00
    2-1/2" h, Optic Diamond Quilted pattern, sq, shape #8, Mt. Washington 285.00
Tumbler, fuchsia shading to rich honey-amber, slight rim flake 50.00
Vase
    6-3/4" h, roll down lip, optic diamond body 300.00
    9-1/2" h, lily, ribbed trumpet form, tricorn rim, disk base 400.00
    10-1/4" h, lily, ribbed trumpet form, tricorn rim, round disk base. 350.00
    10-1/2" h, swagged and ruffled lip, snake form entwined around neck, heavy enameled goldfinches perched on thistle blossoms, attributed to Le Gras, c1890 .... 595.00
    12-1/4" h, 3-1/4" d, swirled calla lily shape, cranberry shading to golden amber foot, amber applied spiral trim 165.00
    11-1/4" h, shape #3004, sgd "Libbey" 1,200.00
    15" h, lily shape, deep red shading to amber, large lily top, flint, c1880 .... 825.00

AMBERINA GLASS, PLATED

History: The New England Glass Company, Cambridge, Massachusetts, first made Plated Amberina in 1886; Edward Libbey patented the process for the company in 1889.

Plated Amberina was made by taking a gather of chartreuse or cream opalescent glass, dipping it in Amberina, and working the two, often utilizing a mold. The finished

Cruet, applied amber handle, amber faceted stopper, 6-3/4" h, $3,200.

product had a deep amber to deep ruby red shading, a fiery opalescent lining, and often vertical ribbing for enhancement. Designs ranged from simple forms to complex pieces with collars, feet, gilding, and etching.

A cased Wheeling glass of similar appearance had an opaque white lining but is not opalescent and does not have a ribbed body.

Bowl, 8" w, 3-1/2" h, border of deep dark mahogany, 12 vertical stripes alternating with 12 vertical opalescent fuchsia stripes, off-white casing 7,500.00
Celery Vase... 2,750.00
Cruet, 6-3/4" h, faceted amber stopper.................................... 3,200.00
Lamp Shade, 14" d, hanging, swirled, ribbed 4,750.00
Milk Pitcher, applied amber handle, orig "Aurora" label 7,500.00
Punch Cup, vertical ribs, applied handle................................ 1,500.00
Salt Shaker, vertical ribs, orig top 1,200.00
Tumbler, 2-1/2" d, 3-3/4" h, vertical ribbed cylinder, deep fuchsia-red at top shading to golden yellow base, creamy opal lining 1,750.00
Vase, 7-1/4" h, lily shape, raspberry red shading to bright amber, opal white casing 2,750.00

AMERICAN PAINTED PORCELAIN

History: The American china painting movement began in 1876 and remained popular over the next 50 years. Thousands of artisans-professional and amateur-decorated tableware, desk accessories, dresser sets, and many other items with florals, fruits, and geometric designs and occasionally with portraits, birds and landscapes. Some American firms, such as Lenox and Willetts Manufacturing Co. of Trenton, New Jersey, produced Belleek, a special type of porcelain, that china painters decorated, but a majority of porcelain was imported from France, Germany, Austria, Czechoslovakia, and Japan.

Marks: American painted porcelains bear foreign factory marks. However, the American style was distinctive, whether naturalistic or conventional (geometric). Some pieces were sgd and dated by the artist.

References: Dorothy Kamm, *American Painted Porcelain: Collector's Identification & Value Guide*, Collector Books, 1999; — *Comprehensive Guide to American Painted Porcelain*, Antique Trader Books, 1999.

Periodical: Dorothy Kamm's *Porcelain Collector's Companion Newsletter*, P.O. Box 7460, Port St. Lucie, FL 34985-7460.

Museums: Museum of Porcelain Art, International Porcelain Artists & Teachers, Inc., Grapevine, Texas; World Organization of China Painters Foundation Center & Museum, Oklahoma City, Oklahoma.

Advisor: Dorothy Kamm.

Notes: The quality of the artwork, the amount of detail, and technical excellence—not the amount of the gilding or the design or manufacturer of the porcelain itself-are key pricing factors. Unusual subjects and uncommon forms also influence value.

Berry Set, three-piece, 10-7/8" w, 9-1/4"d handled tray, sugar and creamer, blackberry decorations, burnished gold scrolls and rims, sgd "Slocum," mkd "Gurud, Limoges, France," c1920 .... 125.00
Berry Spoon Holder, 9-3/4" w, strawberry dec, burnished gold rim and handles, sgd "A.E.Pierce," mkd with crossed lines, "KPM," Germany, c1910-18 .... 25.00
Bread and Butter Plate, 6-1/8" d coupe, border design of Queen Anne's lace in palladium, sgd "M/Wagner," c1950 .... 18.00
Bon Bon Bowl, 5-1/2" d, ftd, double handled, pink and yellow rose dec, burnished gold rim, handles and feet, c1900-25 .... 50.00
Butter Dish, domed cover and plate, 7-1/2" d, dec with branches of pink wild roses, yellow enamel centers, burnished gold handle, mkd "Haviland, France," c1894-1931 .... 60.00
Cake Plate, 9-1/2" d, double handled, border design of pink wild roses on pale blue band, ivory center, burnished gold rim and handles, c1900-20 .... 50.00
Celery Dish, 12" l, 5" w, red poppy dec, burnished gold rim, sgd "E. ZOOST," c1900-20 .... 45.00
Compote, 8-1/2"w, border design of conventional-style grapes, burnished gold outlines, border and rim, sgd "McCarthy, Schulz, Stuhl," mkd "UNO-IT, Favorite, Bavaria," c1908-18 .... 45.00
Comport, single handle, 10-3/4"l, pink wild rose dec, burnished gold rim and handle; sgd "Milne," mkd "W. G. & Co., Limoges, France," c1901 .... 55.00

Butter dish, domed cover, branches of pink wild roses, yellow enamel centers, burnished gold handle, mkd "Haviland, France," c1894-1931, 7-1/2" d, $60. Photo courtesy of Dorothy Kamm.

Condiment Set, four pieces, 7-3/8" l, 4-1/2" w tray, salt and pepper shakers; toothpick holder, poppy border dec, burnished gold rims and tops, mkd "Germany," c1891-1914 .... 50.00

Cracker Jar, 9" d, white wild rose border dec, burnished gold handles, sgd "A.S.S.," mkd "Royal wreath, O. & E. G.," 1898-1918 .... 65.00

Cup and Saucer, ruby rose and white wild rose border design on burnished gold ground, burnished gold handle, sgd "M.N. Stenger," mkd "Germany," c1891-1914 .... 30.00

Dresser set, four pieces, 5" h candlesticks, 4-7/8" h hat pin holder, puff box, hair receiver; conventional-style chicory design, silver borders and tops, various French manufacturers, c1900-15................. 190.00

Fern Pot, hanging, 6-1/4" l, pink wild rose dec, burnished gold rim and handles, sgd "M. ARIZER," c1900-20 .... 55.00

Hand Mirror, 10-1/4" l, 6-1/8" w, pink rose decoration, brass frame, c1890-1915 .... 125.00

Incense Jar, 4-1/2" d, 3-1/8" h, conventional-style clover border design in burnished gold, pale green ground, burnished gold lid, sgd ""Xmas 1926, From Emma," mkd "Prov. Sxe. E. S. Germany" 45.00

Jardiniere, 5-1/2" h, colored enamel floral dec, burnished gold rim, border, and feet , sgd "Clara M. Smith, January 1928," mkd with Belleek palette, Lenox... 90.00

Mustard Pot, 3-1/2" h, matching spoon and plate, conventional-style decoration in light green and burnished gold on various yellow brown grounds with burnished gold rims and handles, sgd "E.L.H.," mkd with wreath and scepter, "R.S. Germany," c1904-38................... 55.00

Nut Bowl, 7" d, chestnut decoration, opal luster int., burnished gold rim, mkd "Royal wreath, O. & E. G.," Austria, c1898-1918................ 60.00

Olive or Bon Bon Dish, 6-1/2" d, with two open handles, decorated with an inner border design in palladium of conventional florals and striped, 1940s-50s... 35.00

Pancake Server, 7-3/16" d plate, 4-3/4" d, 3-1/4" h open handled lid, Art Nouveau-style border decoration of columbine in pale yellow brown and blood red, with burnished gold bands and panels, light pompadour ground, blood red handle, sgd "MBCAMERON," mkd "GDA France," c1900-15 .... 75.00

Plate and Bowl, 9"d coupe plate, 10" l, 7-1/4" w, 2-3/8" h oval bowl, both decorated with etched leaf borders covered with palladium, sgd "MWAGNER," c1950 .... 80.00

Plate, 8-3/8" d, peacocks in forest, border of peacock feathers and butterflies, burnished gold trim, mkd "Leonard, Vienna," c1890 ...... 45.00

Pin Tray, 3-1/2" l, violet dec, burnished gold border, sgd "M. Burnet," mkd "Royal wreath, O. & E. G.," c1898-1918 .... 22.00

Punch Cup, 3" h, decorated with conventional-style grape design, mkd "Royal wreath, O. & E. G.," c1898-1918, pr..................................... 60.00

Salt and Pepper Shakers, pr, 3" h, decorated with garlands of pink roses and forget-me-nots on an ivory ground, pale blue bands, burnished gold tops, c1900-20 .... 25.00

Relish Dish, 9" l, 3-3/4" w, clematis dec, burnished gold rim and handles, sgd "M. GATE(S?)," mkd with crown, crossed scepters, "Rosenthal," c1891-1907.. 35.00

Sugar and Creamer, decorated with a stylized pink rose design, with opal luster bands, knob and handles, mkd "KPM, Silesia Germany," c1914-27 .... 35.00

Tea Set, three pieces, sugar, creamer and tea pot, burnished gold chrysanthemum medallions in burnished gold, burnished gold rims, handles, and spout, sgd "MSF," mkd "Willets Belleek," mid-1880s-1909..... 325.00

Vase, 10-3/4" h, wild carrot decoration with burnished gold rim, sgd "M.J. Leber, 1915," mkd with crown, "H & Co., Selb, Bavaria". 165.00

AMPHORA

History: The Amphora Porcelain Works was one of several pottery companies located in the Teplitz-Turn region of Bohemia in the late 19th and early 20th centuries. It is best known for art pottery, especially Art Nouveau and Art Deco pieces.

Marks: Several markings were used, including the name and location of the pottery and the Imperial mark, which included a crown. Prior to World War I, Bohemia was part of the Austro-Hungarian Empire, so the word "Austria" may appear as part of the mark. After World War I the word "Czechoslovakia" may be part of the mark.

Additional Listings: Teplitz.

Center Bowl, 2-1/8" h, incised dec outlined in black, enameled blue-green and pink cabochons, mottled tan matte ground, 4 legs, circular base 200.00

Creamer, 5-1/4" h, gold trim, raised flowers, sgd "Turin, Teplitz, Amphora" 215.00

Ewer, 14-1/2" h, pink, gold, and green floral dec, gold accents, salamander entwined handle, c1900 .... 575.00

Figure

16-1/4" h, peasant woman carries basket on back, reaching for another basket at feet, tan clothes, gold highlights, crown mark and "Austria" 550.00

Pancake server, Art Nouveau-style border decoration of columbine in pale yellow brown and blood red, with burnished gold bands and panels, light pompadour ground, blood red handle, sgd "MBCAMERON," mkd "GDA France," c1900-15, 7-3/16" d plate, 4-3/4" d, 3-1/4" h open handled lid, $75. Photo courtesy of Dorothy Kamm.

Vase, pink roses, green shaded ground, imp crown and Amphora marks, minor chips on roses, 11" h, $320.

18-1/2" h, peasant woman empties apron of greens into basket, tan, gold highlights, crown mark and "Austria" 550.00

Pitcher, 11" h, emb owl sitting on branch 165.00

Vase

5-1/4" h, 3 buttressed handles dec with naturalistic leafy rose vines, rose hip clusters, matte green rose on mottled brown round, gilt highlights, imp mark and stamp on base 250.00

5-1/2" h, 3-3/4" d, bottle shape, portrait of Art Nouveau style woman, enameled flowers in her hair, imp "Amphora/492" 400.00

6" h, flattened spherical form, shoulder dec with alternating large and small moths in shades of blue, pink, and yellow, raised gilt outline, relief spider webs and enameled disk centers, gilt highlights on green and blue ground, imp "Amphora" in oval, printed "R. S. & K. Turn-Teplitz Bohemia" with maker's device on base 900.00

8-1/2" h, 5" d, bulbous, 4 sided, Art Nouveau profile of woman against blooming forest glaze, umber, gilded details, stamp mark "Teplitz" 1,200.00

10" h, shouldered form, textured green and blue glaze, gilt accents 650.00

11-1/8" h, pear shape, extended neck, 2 tri-part handles, mottled matte green and brown glaze, inscribed cipher, R. S. & K, Teplitz, Bohemia, c1900, crazing, base chip 1,035.00

ANIMAL COLLECTIBLES

History: The representation of animals in fine arts, decorative arts, and on utilitarian products dates back to antiquity. Some religions endowed certain animals with mystical properties. Authors throughout written history used human characteristics when portraying animals.

Glass has been a popular material in making animal-related collectibles. Dishes with an animal-theme cover were fashionable in the early 19th century. In the years between World Wars I and II, glass manufacturers such as Fostoria Glass Company and A. H. Heisey & Company created a number of glass animal figures for the novelty and decorative-accessory markets. In the 1950s and early 1960s, a second glass-animal craze swept America led by companies such as Duncan & Miller and New Martinsville-Viking Glass Company. A third craze struck in the early 1980s when companies such as Boyd Crystal Art Glass, Guernsey Glass, Pisello Art Glass, and Summit Art Glass began offering the same animal figure in a wide variety of collectible glass colors, with some colors in limited production.

The formation of collectors' clubs and marketing crazes, e.g., flamingo, pig, and penguin, during the 1970s increased the popularity of this collecting field.

References: Felicia Browell, *Breyer Animal Collector's Guide*, 2nd ed., Collector Books, 1999; Elaine Butler, *Poodle Collectibles of the 50's & 60's*, L-W Book Sales, 1995; Diana Callow et al., *Charlton Price Guide to Beswick Animals*, The Charlton Press, 1994; Dana Cain, *Film & TV Animal Star Collectibles*, Antique Trader Books, 1998; Jean Dale, *Charlton Standard Catalogue of Royal Doulton Animals*, 2nd Edition, The Charlton Press, 1998; ——, *Charlton Standard Catalogue of Royal Doulton Beswick Storybook Figurines*, The Charlton Press, 1994; Candace Sten Davis and Patricia Baugh, *A Treasury of Scottie Dog Collectibles*, Collector Books, Volume I (1998), Volume II (1999); Marbena Jean Fyke, *Collectible Cats*, Book I (1993, 1995 value update), Book II (1996), Collector Books; Lee Garmon and Dick Spencer, *Glass Animals of the Depression Era*, Col-

lector Books, 1993; Everett Grist, *Covered Animal Dishes*, Collector Books, 1988, 1993 value update; Christopher Payne, *Animals in Bronze*, *Reference and Price Guide*, Antique Collectors' Club, 1999.

Periodicals: *Boyd Crystal Art Glass Newsletter*, P.O. Box 127, 1203 Morton Ave., Cambridge, OH 43725; *Canine Collector's Companion*, P.O. Box 2948, Portland, OR 97208; *Collectively Speaking*, 428 Philadelphia Rd., Joppa, MD 21085; *Collie Courier*, 428 Philadelphia Rd., Joppa, MD 21085; *Hobby Horse News*, 5492 Tallapoosa Rd., Tallahassee, FL 32303; *Jumbo Jargon*, 1002 West 25th St., Erie, PA 16502; *MOOsletter*, 240 Wahl Ave., Evans City, PA 16033; *TRR Pony Express*, 71 Aloha Circle, Little Rock, AR 72120.

Collectors' Clubs: Boyd Art Glass Collectors Guild, P.O. Box 52, Hatboro, PA 19040; Canine Collectibles Club of America, Suite 314, 736 N. Western Ave., Lake Forest, IL 60045; Cat Collectors, 33161 Wendy Dr., Sterling Heights, MI 48310; Folk Art Society of America, P.O. Box 17041, Richmond, VA 23226; Frog Pond, P.O. Box 193, Beech Grove, IN 46107; National Elephant Collector's Society, 380 Medford St., Somerville, MA 02145; Squirrel Lovers Club, 318 W. Fremont Ave., Elmhurst, IL 60126; Wee Scots, Inc., P.O. Box 1597, Winchester, VA 22604-1597.

Museums: American Kennel Club, New York, NY; American Saddle Horse Museum Association, Lexington, KY; Dog Museum, St. Louis, MO; Frog Fantasies Museum, Eureka Springs, AR; International Museum of the Horse, Lexington, KY; Stradling Museum of the Horse, Patagonia, AZ.

Additional Listings: See specific animal collectible categories in Warman's Americana & Collectibles.

Advisor: Jocelyn C. Mousley.

Cookie jar, Eeyore, blue, gray, and black, white lid int., mkd "Walt Disney," $600. Photo courtesy of Green Valley Auctions, Inc.

Barnyard

Bank, mechanical, cast iron

Tricky Pig Bank, old repaint, 7-1/2" l, teller replaced 420.00

Trick Pony, worn polychrome.................................. 1,210.00

Bank, still, 5" l, pig, white ironstone, black spatter spots, one ear replaced 110.00

Bottle, 7-1/2" h, pig, dark brown Albany slip, incised "Good Old Rye in Hogs" and "Our oil diggins, pure lard in a flowing well," Anna Pottery, IL 880.00

Cookie Jar, hen on nest, Brush.................................. 125.00

Creamer

8-1/4" l, cow, Rockingham glaze, gilt dec 220.00

10-1/2" l, 6-7/8" h, Continental silver, mid 18th C, realistically modeled as standing heifer, upturned tail as handle, oval hinged lip on back, 21 troy oz 2,760.00

Figure

4-1/2" h, cow and calf, white clay, dark brown glaze 580.00

4-3/4" h, rooster, bronze, cold painted in naturalistic tones, stamped "Austria," c1920 .... 1,035.00

6-1/2" h, pig, porcelain, realistic brown and beige enamel 110.00

6-1/2" l, ram, carved green stone, on stand, orig box.............. 66.00

7" h, Donkey in Love, Llardo.................................... 70.00

9" l, sheep, sewer pipe, rough textured coat, chips............... 165.00

Painting, 18" x 24", oil on canvas, "Cows at Rest, Twilight," sgd and dated "...Thorpe 1878," mounted to masonite, scattered retouch, prevalent craquelure, framed 300.00

Pip-Squeak, 6-1/4" w, 7-1/4" h, felt and feather rooster, wooden cage with red and black litho paper covering, orig drawer, working bellows, mkd "Made in Germany," minor edge damage.......................... 275.00

Platter, 9-3/4" l, 7" w, blue transfer, romantic scene with castle and cows, minor staining.. 300.00

Range Shakers, pr, Twin Winton.................................. 250.00

Rug, hooked. 25" x 38", cow in landscape with foliage in spandrels, edge stripes, rows of scalloped gray felt, red, brown, blue, gray, olive, and white, some fading 615.00

Weathervane, 20-3/4" h, pig, zinc, cast iron directional arrow 415.00

Birds

Andirons, pr, 15-1/2" h, owls, cast iron, yellow and black glass eyes. 85.00

Ashtray, Rook, Rookwood, #1139 .... 325.00

Bank, still, 5-1/4" h, duck in top hat, "Save For A Rainy Day," polychrome dec 215.00

Candy Container, figural, baby chick 195.00

Child's Riding Toy, 39-1/2" l, wood, cutout silhouettes of roosters, orig dark red, green, and yellow paint, adjustable seat, rockers and folding wheels, wear and edge damage, partial paper label on bottom 715.00

Dish, 14-1/4" l, swan, sterling silver, Mexican 140.00

Doorstop, parrot, cast iron 140.00

Figure

6" h, rooster, carved wood, worn polychrome, edge damage.. 770.00

8-1/4" h, owl, sewer pipe, solid, incised "Tim Gibson" 140.00

11" l, mother bird facing baby bird, black, red, yellow, and white, metal feet, wooden base.................................... 1,100.00

12-1/2" h, owl, matte finish, polychrome enamel, mkd "Great Horned Owl by Andrea," 60.00

22" l, pheasants, bronze, worn polychrome dec, pr.............. 770.00

24-1/2" h, owl, earthenware, redware body, naturalistic colored enamels, inset glass eyes, German, 19th C, repair to branch 2,415.00

Game Plate, 11-5/8" d, pair of quail, sgd "A. Broussilion," gilt rim, mkd "Coronet, Limoges, France," 140.00

Hen on Nest, Staffordshire, porcelain, polychrome dec

7-1/2" l, egg cup insert, one cup damaged and glued 635.00

10-1/2" l, good color, minor edge wear, chips on inner flange 715.00

Painting, 18" x 12", oil on canvas, Parrot Perched in a Sunset Landscape, sgd and dated "J. O'B Inman April 8 '90," (John Edward O'Brien Inman, 1890,) framed 1,150.00

Plate, 9-1/2" d, peacock, blue Royal Bayreuth mark.................. 600.00

Prints, 12-1/2 x 10-1/2", hand-colored engravings, sgd "George Edwards," book pages with English and French text on reverse side, old gilt frames vary, set of 6 .... 885.50

Shooting Gallery Target, 3" h, cast iron, set of 2.................... 100.00

Stuffed Toy, 6" h, Peggy Penguin, Steiff 60.00

Tape Dispenser, pelican, cast metal 130.00

Toy, tin wind-up

4" l, pecking chickens, finger activated, good polychrome dec .. 360.00

7-1/2" l, duck pulls cart with three small ducks, Lehmann 315.00

Weathervane, rooster

21-1/4" x 25", sheet metal, traces of old paint, 20th C, modern base.. 360.00

25-1/4" h, tin silhouette, double cone base 470.00

31" x 31-1/2", sheet metal, cast iron, and zinc, red tin tail, Rochester Ironwork.. 1,500.00

32" x 34", cast and sheet iron, American, c1850............... 4,890.00

Cats

Children's Book

Millions of Cats, Wanda Gag, NY, 1928, plates and text illus by Gag, orig board slipcase, 1 of 250 numbered copies sgd by Gang, orig sgd and numbered wood engraving 1,725.00

The Tale of Tom Kitten, Beatrix Potter, Warne, London, 1907, first edition, 27 color plates and other illus, 12mo, gray-green paper boards, spine bit faded, ends slightly bumped................... 400.00

Figure

3-1/4" h, white Persian, green eyes, sitting 30.00

7" h, sewer pipe, solid, seated................................ 165.00

10-7/8" h, seated, redware, black glaze, yellow glass eyes, imp "Zanesware, Made in U.S.A." 105.00

13" h, Galle Faience, yellow enamel ground, black trimmed blue dec, glass eyes, imp mark, early 20th C, restored.. 230.00

Model, 13" h, yellow ground, blue and white designs, glass eyes, artist sgd, attributed to Emile Galle, French Faience, late 19th/early 20th C .. 750.00

Painting, 21" x 25-3/4", oil on canvas, sgd "Brunel Neuville," French, 1879-1907, framed.. 3,100.00

Pip-Squeak, 7-1/4" h, wood and composition, worn white flannel and painted brown and gray cat, white button eyes, worn painted pupils, neck and voice box damaged 110.00

Print, 11-7/8" x 9-1/4", lithograph on paper, numbered "49/90", sgd "T. L. Foujita," Japanese, 1886-1968, matted 1,610.00

Quilt, 84-1/2" x 63", pierced and appliquéd, repeating design of seated cats, America, c1930.. 1,265.00

Shooting Gallery Target, 14-3/4" h, stuffed canvas, painted features, leather strap added to weighted base 110.00

Dogs

Advertising Sign, 20" w, 31" h, self framed tin, "To school well fed on Grape-Nuts, There's a Reason," little girl walking beside St. Bernard, dog carrying bag in mouth.................................... 1,600.00

Bank, still, cast iron, St. Bernard, black with gold, minor wear ... 130.00

Book

Hertig, Maddelena, Mix with Love, Cookbook for Dogs, Dorrance & Co., 1978, 1st ed., autographed 20.00

Twain, Mark, A Dog's Tale, London, 1903, 4 illus, 8vo, orig buff paper wrappers, printed for National Anti-Vivisection Society.......... 290.00

Weatherwax, Rudd, The Lassie Method, Raising & Training Your Dog with Patience, Firmness & Love, 1971 .... 10.00

Bookends, pr, 7-3/4" l, bronze, modeled as two hunting dogs on point, artist sgd "Jules Moignieze," dark brown patina, mounted on golden ebony brass base.. 2,300.00

Boot Scraper, 18-3/4" w, 11-1/2" d, 15-1/2" h, cast zinc full bodied pointing Spaniel, cast iron base, black and white repaint 275.00

Box, 2" d, leaded glass, paperweight top, French Bulldog in domed top, French 1,955.00

Calendar, beautiful cowgirl twirls lariat around herself and sitting dog, Rolf Armstrong 65.00

Child's Book, ABC Dogs, Clara Tice, NY, 1940, color plates after etchings

Painting, one of pair of hunt scene, oil on canvas by Russian/ German artist Vyasheslav G. Shvarts, (price for pair) $17,360. Photo courtesy of Jackson's Auctioneers & Appraisers.

by Tice featuring different breeds of dogs for each letter, 4to, cloth backed pictorial boards, first edition 135.00
Dish, covered
    Champ Terrier, caramel slag 170.00
    Scottie, Akro Agate, blue and white swirls 165.00
Figure
    1-1/2" x 3", Scottie, bronze, mkd "J. B." 80.00
    5-5/8" h, seated, free standing front legs, oval base, traces of red paint cast iron 110.00
    6-3/4" h, 5-1/2" d, Poodle, white, tan base, brown collar, blue bow, gold trim padlock 155.00
    9-1/2" h, Ohio buff clay, black painted finish, glitter trim 412.50
    9-1/2" l, Harlequin Great Dane, laying down, gray and white .. 65.00
    10" h, seated, Ohio pottery, unglazed buff clay, reddish paint stain, black painted details, attributed to Newcomerstown 550.00
    10" h, 7" w, 3" d, Staffordshire, copper spots, gold and black eyes, emb numbers 225.00
    12-1/2" h, sewer pipe, seated, imp label "Superior Clay Corp, Uhrichsville, OH," incised "Samantha," uneven glaze 335.00
    13-1/2" h, Staffordshire, seated, red and white, gold, black, and ochre trim, mkd "Staffordshire, Kent, Made in England," pr ... 385.00
    20" h, bulldogs, bemused look, sitting on hind legs, terra cotta, Continental, pr 3,250.00
    27" h, Foo Dog, cast stone, 20th C 115.00
    Cocker Spaniel, standing, Royal Doulton 75.00
    Dachshund, Beswick, begging 55.00
Game Plate, 10" d, dog with deer, gold trim, mkd "Limoges" 135.00
Glasses, RCA Nipper giveaway, pr 30.00
Lamp Base, 15" h, Bulldogs, cold painted white metal, dogs standing by tree, electrified, 20th C 1,265.00
Painting, 22" x 33-3/4", watercolor on board, "The Day's Catch/Huntsmen and Dogs with Game," sgd "J. Hardy J." in pencil lower right, three men, 2 dogs, pack horse, c1860, framed 575.00
Pin
    German Shepherd, white gold collar, chased 14K yellow gold mount, dated "April 19th, '29," 4.5 dwt 200.00
    Poodle Head, 18K yellow gold, gold twisted wire, cabochon sapphire eyes, sgd "Tiffany & Co., France," French maker's mark, 12.4 dwt 820.00
Plate, 11" d, majolica, dog center, American 175.00
Stuffed Toy, Tige, Buster Brown, Steiff, all jointed 550.00
Teapot, Dachshund, Erphila 110.00

Tobacco Tin, Flick and Flock, 6" x 4" x 5", images of two dogs, some surface rust 660.00

Horses

Bank, 5-3/8" h, Circus Horse, tub, black, brown, silver, and red . 140.00
Book, Mark Twain, *A Horse's Tale*, illus by Lucius Hitchcock, 8vo, pictorial red cloth cover, first edition 60.00
Candy Container, papier-mâché, prancing, orig saddle and reins ... 250.00
Figure
    5" x 4", papier-mâché and wood, on platform, wheels, Germany 125.00
    28-1/2" x 24-3/4" h, full figured head, carved walnut, mounted in molded frame, late 19th C, minor losses 690.00
    Dappled Grey Foal, Cybis 325.00
    Draft Horse, large, Melbaware 100.00
    Palomino, large, Goebel 125.00
Plate, Plough Horses, Royal Doulton 85.00
Pull Toy
    12-1/4" l, wood and composition, brown hair cloth covering, tack eyes, old colorful harness, steel wheels, old replaced mane and tail 220.00
    30" l, wool fabric body, mohair mane and tail, glass eyes, leatherette harness, wood base, wheels missing, fiber loss 175.00
Rug, hooked yarn
    23" x 35", braided yarn border, horse head, brown, beige, black, and white, light green ground 200.00
    30-1/2" x 51", pictorial ground, saddled horse on variegated ground, New England, 19th C, mounted 2,185.00
Tray, 14" x 23-3/4", multicolored wood veneer, image of running horse, mahogany gallery edge , corners missing 330.00
Weather Vane
    15" x 17-1/2", zinc and copper, trotting, applied mane and tail, C. J. Howard, Bridgewater, MA, late 19th C 2,300.00
    15-1/2" x 25", copper, running, fine verdigris surface, one bullet hole, America, late 19th C 1,380.00
    25-1/2" x 34", gilt copper, WA Snow, Boston, late 19th C ... 2,415.00
Windmill Weight, 17" l, 16-1/2" h, cast iron, Dempster Mill Manufacturing Co., Beatrice, NE, old black paint 385.00

Automata, Monkey Band, c1930, $2,100. Photo courtesy of Auction Team Breker.

Wild Life

Bank, still, cast iron
  Begging Bear, gold paint, some wear.......................................90.00
  Polar Bear, white, some wear, 5-1/4" h..................................385.00
Bread Plate, two handles, lion in center....................................65.00
Candy Container, 7" h, rabbit, papier-mâché, orig white paint, pink and red trim, glass eyes, wooden legs, mkd "Germany"................110.00
Dish, covered, lion, lacy base, purple slag..................................245.00
Display Jar, 14-1/2" h, "Squirrel Brand Salted Nuts," name and squirrel emb on front...395.00
Doorstop, 9" l, lion, cast iron, full bodied, old gold and silver repaint 110.00
Figure
  3" h, elephant, carved wood, orig gray paint, black, red, white, and yellow, mkd "Joe" on blanket...27.50
  3-1/2" h, walrus, carved ivory...85.00
  5-1/2" l, bear, bronze, cold painted in browns and white, Austrian, c1920...980.00
  5-7/8" h, 5-1/2" d, frog, blue overlay diamond quilted glass, crystal legs, climbing glass tree stump, fancy scalloped base, applied crystal eyes and legs, mouth open, white lining................275.00
  6" l, frog, sewer pipe, hollow int. incised "Al Frail March 5, 1908" and "Alfred Frail March 5, 1908," chips and short hairline..175.00
  6-3/4" h, squirrel, sewer pipe, yellow slip eye, solid, imp "cm1980"...27.50
  7" l, frog, sewer pipe, solid...105.00
  7-1/4" l, lions, recumbent, pressed colorless glass, oval base, imp anchor symbol of Davidson, English registry mark for July 4, 1874, very minor chips, pr...115.00
  8-1/2" h, lion, sewer pipe, unglazed red clay, molded detail, rect base, incised "Wadsworth, Ohio, 7-16-52"..........................220.00
  10" h, 9" l, lion, pottery, cream colored clay, tan highlights, unglazed, some incised detail..110.00
  15-1/4" l, raccoon, sewer pipe, white slip detail, green painted eyes, incised "J. C."...165.00
Hunting Set, fox with hounds, lead, orig box, Germany.............125.00
Perfume Bottle, monkey, brown, Schuco....................................385.00
Pip-Squeak, 7" w, 7-3/4" h, furry rabbit in cage, wooden cage with red and black litho paper covering, edge damage, drawer missing, bellows squeak, string attachment broken.....................................110.00
Sugar Tongs, pr, 5-1/2" l, silver, Victorian, English, London, 1884, Leuchars & Son makers, outstretched money, front paws as nips, back feet on crabstock handles, 2 troy oz....................................920.00
Teapot, rabbit, Erphila..150.00
Tobacco Tin, Stag, red ground, oval vignette of standing stag...100.00

ARCHITECTURAL ELEMENTS

History: Architectural elements, many of which are hand-crafted, are those items which have been removed or salvaged from buildings, ships, or gardens. Part of their desirability is due to the fact that it would be extremely costly to duplicate the items today.

Beginning about 1840 decorative building styles began to feature carved wood and stone, stained glass, and ornate ironwork. At the same time, builders and manufacturers also began to use fancy doorknobs, doorplates, hinges, bells, window locks, shutter pulls, and other decorative hardware as finishing touches to elaborate new homes and commercial buildings.

Hardware was primarily produced from bronze, brass, and iron, and doorknobs also were made from clear, colored, and cut glass. Highly ornate hardware began appearing in the late 1860s and remained popular through the early 1900s. Figural pieces that featured animals, birds, and heroic and mythological images were very popular, as were ornate and very graphic designs that complimented the many architectural styles that emerged in the late 19th century.

Fraternal groups, government and educational institutions, and individual businesses all ordered special hardware for their buildings. Catalogs from the era show hundreds of patterns, often with a dozen different pieces available in each design.

The current trends of preservation and recycling of architectural elements has led to the establishment and growth of organized salvage operations that specialize in removal and resale of elements. Special auctions are now held to sell architectural elements from churches, mansions, office buildings, etc. Today's decorators often design an entire room around one architectural element, such as a Victorian marble bar or mural, or use several as key accent pieces.

References: Bakewell & Mullins, *Victorian Architectural Sheet-Metal Ornaments*, Dover Publications, 1999; Ronald S. Barlow (comp.), Victorian Houseware, Hardware and Kitchenware, Windmill Publishing, 1991; Margarete Baur-Heinhold, *Decorative Ironwork*, Schiffer Publishing, 1996; Louis Blanc, *Decorative French Ironwork Designs*, Dover, 1999; Len Blumin, *Victorian Decorative Art*, available from ADCA (P.O. Box 126, Eola, IL 60519), n.d.; Michael Breza and Craig R. Olson (eds.), *Identification and Dating of Round Oak Heating Stoves*, Southwestern Michigan College Museum (58900 Cherry Grove Rd, Dowagiac, MI 49047), 1995; Henri Clouzet, *Art Deco Decorative Ironwork*, Dover Publications, 1997; A. Dureanne, *Ornamental Ironwork*, Dover Publications, 1998; Maude Eastwood wrote several books about doorknobs which are available from P.O. Box 126, Eola, IL 60519; David A. Hanks, *The Decorative Designs of Frank Lloyd Wright*, Dover Publications, 1999; Barbara Israel, *Antique Graden Ornaments: Two Centuries of American Taste*, Harry N. Abrams, 1999; Alistair Morris, *Antiques from the Garden*, Antique Collectors' Club, 1999; Ernest Rettelbusch, *Handbook of Historic Ornament from Ancient Times to Biedermeier*, Dover Publications, 1996; Edward Shaw, *Modern Architect* (reprint), Dover Publications, 1996; Turn of the Century Doors, Windows and Decorative Millwork, Dover Publications, 1995 reprint; Stanley Shuler, *Architectal Details from Old New England Homes*, Schiffer Publishing, 1997; Web Wilson, *Great Glass in American Architecture*, E. P. Dutton, New York, 1986; — Antique Hardware Price Guide, Krause Publications, 1999.

Periodical: *American Bungalow*, P.O. Box 756, Sierra Madre, CA 91204.

Collectors' Club: *Antique Doorknob Collectors of America*, Inc., P.O. Box 126, Eola, IL 60519.

Museum: American Sanitary Plumbing Museum, Worcester, MA.

SPECIAL AUCTIONS

Web Wilson Antique Hardware Auction
P.O. Box 506
Portsmouth, RI 02871
(800) 508-0022

Additional Listings: Doorknobs & Builders' Hardware, Stained Glass.

Bird Bath, 19" d, 33-1/2" h, cast iron, shallow basin, gadrooned rim mounted by 2 doves, fluted baluster form standard on circular base cast with pierced rose design 300.00
Bird Cage, 21" x 19-1/2" x 18", house form, grand entrance, front porch, bay windows, dormers, cupola, painted green, trimmed with red painted wooden buttons, knobs, and perches, some paint loss .230.00
Catalog
   Arkansas Soft Pine Bureau, Little Rock, AR, 36 pgs, 8-1/4" x 11", 1918, loose sheets in company folder 32.00
   Burhans & Black, Inc., Syracuse, NY, 42 pgs, c1923, spring and summer hardware 32.00
   Janusch Manuf Co., NY, 152 pgs, 9" x 12", 1922, Cat. No. 33, fireplace implements, bathroom cabinets, electrical grates, screens, hoods, etc. 55.00
   National Trade Journals, NY, 368 pgs, 8-1/2" x 11-1/4", 1931, Home Builders Catalog, 5th ed., contractor's reference work 36.00
   Sears, Roebuck & Co., Chicago, IL, 78 pgs, 8-1/2" x 11-1/2", 1930, "Honor Bilt," building materials, doors, moldings, cabinets, etc..50.00
   Webber Lumber & Supply Co., Fitchburg, MA, 48 pgs, 7" x 10", c1930, Cat. No. 95, "The Home from Cellar to Shingles" 35.00
Column
   25-1/2" h, green marble, black marble base, Italian, pr 1,500.00
   86" h, Baroque-style giltwood, spiraled form, trailing vines, grape clusters, and putti, Spanish, 19th C, minor losses, flaking .5,750.00
Eagle, 5-3/4" h, cast iron, gilt, stepped rect base, minor gilt wear, America, 19th C, pr 175.00
Fern Stand, 25" d, 57-1/2" h, wire-work, three graduated scrollwork baskets with everted rims, tripod base with scroll feet, 19th C. 375.00
Fountain
   32" h, cast iron, boy holding goose...550.00
   61-7/8" h, frieze of Neptune holding dolphin, one basin with screen insert 1,200.00
Fountain, patinated bronze
   36" h, swan form, outstretched neck, pr 1,800.00
   46-3/4" h, figural young boy astride large fish mounted, rocky outcrop base 2,100.00
   55" h, figural young boy with crane, rocky outcrop base with turtle and large fish 2,900.00
   77-1/2" h, 41" d, shallow shell cast basin, swan with outstretched wings carrying winged putto on back, leaf capped base mounted by mer-children with linked hands 8,000.00
Fountain Group, 24-1/2" h, marble, figural boy and dolphin, entwined figures, rockwork base 1,495.00
Garden Furniture
   Settee, Rococo Revival, painted cast iron, attributed to New York City or Boston, late 19th C, curving crests, arms, legs and feet, scrolls and leafage, Gothic revival elements, old white repaint, minor paint loss, pr 3,200.00
Garden Post, 41" h, 3-1/2" d top, 7" d base, painted cast iron, two part casting, tree trunk form, brown bark and limb scars, entwined with red grapes, green foliage and vines, cutouts and holes for cross pieces, minor wear, repainted, pr 900.00
Garden Statue, 27-1/2" h, cast iron, 4 putto musicians............1,300.00
Garden Urn, cast iron
   54-1/2" h, campana form, everted rim, body flanked by 2 looped handles and frieze, pedestal base, pr..............................1,900.00
   31" d, 62-1/2" h, loped campana form, sides cast with classical figures, applied lion mask handles, sq tapering pedestal base with paneled sides, each centered by winged putti, pr............1,100.00
Jardiniere
   25-1/4" d, 44" h, patinated bronze and porcelain, scroll cast circlet supporting Oriental porcelain fish bowl dec in underglaze blue, 3 chimera-headed monopodi surrounded by scalloped shells, joined by X-form stretchers, pr..4,000.00
   31" w, 30" h, cast iron, urn form, ribbed body with everted undulating rim, ribbed base flanked by pierced foliate scrolls, pr ...550.00
Lectern, 27" h, figural eagle, pine, old mellow finishing.................3,100.00

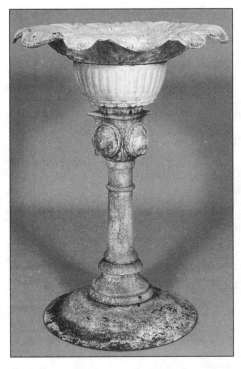

Planter, cast iron, acanthus leaf dec, turned pedestal base, sq top with cherub's head on each of 4 sides, Victorian, 48" h, 36" d, $1,568. Photo courtesy of Jackson's Auctioneers & Appraisers.

Mantle
   Carved Carerra marble, Empire, stepped molded rect top, over carved pilasters with acanthus leaf carved molding, paw feet, molded block plinth base, 55" w, 16" d, 40" h 2,000.00
   Poplar, old worn finish, applied moldings, face turned circular medallions, 33" h x 35" w opening, 63" h shelf, 52-1/4" w, 52" h waist, found in OH 110.00
Obelisk, 31-1/2" h, faux grained wood and composition, raised on four gold painted supports, plinth base, 20th C, pr................................460.00
Planter, 12" x 19" x 11-1/4", cast iron, shaped rect body, cast scrolls, athemia, ivy wreaths, rose garlands, scalloped handles, scrolled feet, pr 275.00
Sundial, 17" d, 34" h, lead, circular, alpha numerics, terra cotta base shaped like 3 gargoyles, shaped plinth 850.00
Terrace Urn
   22-1/2" d, 29-1/4" h, cast iron, lobed campana form body, everted gadrooned rim, sides case with rinceaux, applied handles, fluted socle raised on rect plinth, pr..1,200.00
   24-1/2" d, 27" h, patinated bronze, campana shaped body, beaded rim, sides with applied Herculean heads mounted on lion skins, socle raised on sq plinth 950.00
Urn with Column, pr, 68-1/4" h, Regency style, cov red marble urns, 4 sided solid peach marble column tapering to red marble base, 15,000.00
Wall Fountain, 30" w, 14" h, Baroque taste, bronze, winged putto head 500.00

ART DECO

History: The Art Deco period was named after an exhibition, "l'Exposition Internationale des Arts Déecorative et Industriels Modernes," held in Paris in 1927. Its beginnings succeed those of the Art Nouveau period, but the two overlap in time as well as in style.

   Art Deco designs are angular with simple lines. This was the period of skyscrapers, movie idols, and the Cubist works of Picasso and Legras. Art Deco motifs were used for every conceivable object being produced in the 1920s and 1930s (ceramics, furniture, glass, and metals) not only in Europe but in America as well.

References: Victor Arwas, *Glass: Art Nouveau to Art Deco*, Rizzoli, 1977; Bryan Catley, *Art Deco and Other Figures*, Antique Collectors' Club, 1999; Henri Clouzet, *Art Deco Decorative Ironwork*, Dover Publications, 1997; Jean L. Druesedow (ed.), *Authentic Art Deco Interiors and Furniture in Full Color*, Dover Pub., 1997; Alfred W. Edward, *Art Deco Sculpture and Metalware*, Schiffer Publishing, 1996; Mary Gaston, *Collector's Guide to Art Deco*, 2nd ed., Collector Books, 1997; Ken Hutchinson and Greg Johnson, *Affordable Art Deco*, Collector Books, 1999; Jim Linz, *Art Deco Chrome*, Schiffer Publishing, 1999; Henrie Martinie, *Art Deco Ornamental Ironwork*, Dover Publications, 1996; Theodore Menten, *Art Deco Style*, Dover Publications, n.d.; Paula Ockner and Leslie Piña, *Art Deco Aluminum: Kensington*, Schiffer Publishing, 1997; Leslie Piña and Paula Ockner, *Depression Era Art Deco Glass*, Schiffer Publishing, 1999; Tina Skinner, *Art Deco Era Textile Designs*, Schiffer Publishing, 1998; Wolf Uecker, *Art Nouveau and Art Deco Lamps and Candlesticks*, Abbeville Press, 1986; Howard and Pat Watson, *Collecting Art Deco Ceramics*, Kevin Francis, 1993.

Periodical: Echoes Report, P.O. Box 2321, Mashpee, MA 02649.

Collectors' Clubs: Canadian Art Deco Society, #302-884 Bute St., Vancouver, British Columbia V6E 1YA Canada; Carlton Ware International, P.O. Box 161, Sevenoaks, Kent TN15 6GA England; Chase Collectors Society, 2149 W. Jibsail Loop, Mesa, AZ 85202; International Coalition of Art Deco Societies, One Murdock Terrace, Brighton, MA 02135; Miami Design Preservation League, P.O. Box Bin L, Miami Beach, FL 33119; Twentieth Century Society, 70 Cowcross St., London EC1M 6DR England.

Museums: Art Institute of Chicago, Chicago, IL; Copper-Hewitt Museum, National Museum of Design, Smithsonian Institution, New York, NY; Corning Museum of Glass, Corning, NY; Jones Museum of Glass and Ceramics, Sebago, ME; Virginia Museum of Fine Arts, Richmond, VA.

Additional Listings: Furniture; Jewelry. Also check glass, pottery, and metal categories.

Andirons, pr, 15-7/8" h, figural owls, angled geometric features, "P" at lower center, c1930 .... 115.00
Architectural Panels, pr, 29" x 98", plaster, frieze of reclining woman surrounded by flower and fruit motifs 1,000.00
Bookends, pr
    4-4/8" h, cast bronze, stepped base supports 2 columns joined by pediment, green patina, center medallion of Katarina Elizabeth Geothe, brown patina, sgd "E. Stelzer, Frankfurt" 400.00
    6-1/2" h, patinated metal figures, nude dancing maidens, felted half-oval base, imp "203" near base 230.00
Books, *Arts et Metiers Graphiques*, Volumes 1 to 68, Paris, 1927-39, 4to, orig wrappers, some spines worn, very good condition covers and spines, each volume with color and black and white tipped in plates 1,955.00
Box, 2-7/8" d, mother-of-pearl and brass inlaid Bakelite, circular, grasshopper with ong antennae inlaid in lid, French 175.00
Bust, 8-3/4" h, woman, wearing turban, white marble, gray-veined marble bodice, Continental 500.00
Centerpiece Bowl, 5-1/2" h, gray glass bowl cut with foliage and geometric details, stepped chrome foot 100.00
Chandelier
    15" w, 34" l, press-molded yellow frosted glass plaffonier light bowl, 5 matching shades mounted on cast iron frame, chain and ceiling

Cigarette box, 2 compartments, painted brass, red ground, black highlights, 7-1/4" l, 3-1/2" w, 3" h, $80.

    mount with floral and geometric dec, America, c1930, corrosion to metal 350.00
    17-1/2" w, 21" h, 5 press-molded frosted amber shades with floral dec, suspended from gilt and enameled metal mount with linear and floral dec, imp and raised marks "Halcolite Co. P750 Pat Pend" on ceiling mount, wear to gilt, minor chips 520.00
    23-1/2" d, 28-1/2" h, gilt metal and frosted glass, 7-light, triangular, rope-twist basket supporting conforming glass inverted shade, 6 foliate candle branches 600.00
Compact and Cigarette Case, 5" x 2-3/4", sterling silver, top enameled in green over scalloped ground, opening off-center to reveal cigarette compartment and mirrored compact, engine turning on underside, Birmingham, England, c1913 .... 650.00
Console Set, 12" d bowl, four 3-3/4" h candleholders, shallow center bowl, crystal, cut sq foot, bases stamped "Libby," 1939-42...... 290.00
Desk Set, comb, mirror, cov etched glass jar, two brushes, enamel dec with fan motif in black and creamy white, lavender engine-turned ground, sterling silver mounts, imp "F & B sterling," attributed to Theodore W. Foster and Bros. Co., Providence, RI, c1930, 5 pcs, some enamel loss 800.00
Dish, 6" l, silver, ovoid, swirled pattern, extending to curved tripartite handle accented with row of graduated beading, 3 ball feet, monogrammed, Tiffany & Co., pr, 10 troy oz.................................... 520.00
Furniture
    Bed, brass, stylized sunburst design on headboard and footboard, side rails, c1930, 48-3/4" w, 42-1/2" h 300.00
    Bureau Plat, French, attributed to Ruhlmann, burl inlaid, ebonized and Palisander, rect top, rounded corners, gold-tooled saddle leather writing surface, fluted structure with side slides, central long drawer flanked by two pairs of short drawers, structure inlaid with stylized cascading flora, brass-capped ebonized tapering sq legs, 75" w, 36" d, 30-1/4" h... 20,000.00
    Cabinet, step-back, veneered wood, chrome pulls, rect single door compartment on setback conforming top, 2 long drawers over two cabinet doors in base, c1935, 29-3/8" w, 60" h, nicks, wear to veneer... 800.00
    Canapé, c1920, carved walnut, slightly arched padded back, leaf-carved frame surmounted by leaf-carved crest, continuing into similarly padded curved arms, loose cushion seat raised on carved block feet, 77-1/2" l 700.00
    Chair, rattan, Heywood Wakefield, c1935, curvilinear arms, gold Naugahyde seats, one with arm for newspaper, one 40" d, 30" h, other 31" d, 30-1/2" h, pr... 800.00
    Desk, lady's, French, c1920, molded rect top, leather-lined writing slide opening, lidded compartments, superstructure with 2 hinged banks of drawers opening to int. with 2 open shelves flanked by tambour-fronted end sections, turned, tapered and reeded legs, 24-3/4" w, 16-3/4" d, 38-1/4" h... 550.00
    Dining Table, walnut, rect expanded top, plain frieze, rhomboidal support, plinth base, stepped feet, 58-1/2" l, 36-1/2" d, 29-3/4" h . 700.00

Hall Rack, 42-3/4" w, 6-3/4" d, 72" h, chromed metal framework, long hat shelf over center mirror and shelf, flanked by disk shaped coat hooks over side storage racks, some wear, mirror replaced. 3,750.00

Sideboard, Chinoiserie eglomise, shaped mirrored top, 2 doors with polychromed and gilt dec exotic birds and flowering trees flanking 4 drawers, peach and white flora with gilt highlights, plinth base, 72" l, 15" d, 34" h 1,200.00

Vanity and Mirror, gallery top, mirror-faced rect top, backsplash over center drawer flanked by 4 half drawers, chrome and glass pulls, rect mirror with center attached disk shaped mirror, mirror loss to one leg 490.00

Vitrine, ebonized and teak, breakfront form top, ebonized trim over 3 doors, trapezoidal glazed panels above 3 drawers, reeded and ebonized bun feet, 67" w, 19-3/4" d, 79" h 800.00

Lamp

Boudoir, 10-1/4" h, chrome, cylindrical base, shaped shade depicting woman's head, imp linear facial features, America, c1930 ...... 230.00

Desk, 11-1/4" l, 7-5/8" h, figural, airplane, frosted colorless glass body, silver paint accents, nickel plated wings, tail, and base, looped metal support on flat rect base with rolled ends, c1935 .... 375.00

Floor, 69-1/4" h, wrought iron, crimped and angular geometric shaft, tripod base, striated bronze finish, later frosted and colorless green glass shade with geometric design, John Sartori 800.00

Floor, 71" h, 22" w, torcheres, bronze, alabaster bowl, reeded and pierced shaft, gilt-toned arrow motifs, pierced and shaped round base, pr 275.00

Floor, 74" h, wrought iron, shaft with applied scrolls, trifid S-scroll legs, fitted with later glass dome 225.00

Table, 16-1/2" h, metal figure of woman in architectural setting, green patina, backlit by frosted glass panel, black marble base, emb "Fayral" at side, "Made in France, Ovington New York" at back, wear to patina 2,300.00

Table, 20" h, opalescent glass and copper, shade and base with 4 cornucopia form appliqués 425.00

Mantel Garniture, pink and Verte Antico marble, 14-1/2" shaped angular clock case, inlaid marble forming "X" across front, pair of tapered vases, French, c1930 .... 400.00

Pedestal, 18-3/4" w, 14" d, 31" h, rect marble top inset within carved frieze, tapering sq supports resting on plinth base 200.00

Perfume Atomizer, 6" h, shaped sq with pulls at shoulders, blue glass body with uniform bubbles, remnants of orig paper label 45.00

Perfume Bottle

4-7/8" h, tapered sq form, molded geometric pattern, transparent smoky amethyst glass, gilt-metal screw cap 190.00

6" h, sq prismatic shape, teardrop shaped stopper, cut colorless to ruby, stylized flowers 225.00

Sauce Boat, 8-7/8" l, English silver, Birmingham, 1934, Wilson & Gill makers, paneled boat shape, stepped foot, 2 cylindrical ivory handles, one side engraved and dated 1936, 8 troy oz 750.00

Snuff Box, 3" x 2" x 1/2", .935 fine silver and enamel, rect, black enamel sides within chased silver borders, hinged lid with central red enamel, bordered by black, engine turned bottom and gilt int. 410.00

Tea Cart, 31-1/2" l, 18-1/2" w, 25-3/4" h, oval chromed metal curvilinear framework, oblong smoky glass top and shelf 800.00

Tea Set, 5-1/2" h teapot, 3-1/4" h creamer, 3-1/4" h sugar, chrome over cream glazed ceramic body, Bakelite finial, mkd "Ellgrave...Co. Ltd., Burslem England," matching tea cozy, c1930 .... 250.00

Vase

8-3/4" h, foil under opalescent white, copper, gold, yellow, and black, gilt sgd "C. Faure Limoges" 3,450.00

11-1/2" h, tapered oval, flared rim, geometric shapes in foil under shades of blue, black, and opalescent white enamel, gilt "C. Faure Limoges" signature near base, some corrosion to metal on base, minor stress crack below surface 3,565.00

11-1/2" h, 8-1/2" d, pottery, ftd pillow, molded musicians, instruments, and notes under mottled semi-matte bottle-green glaze, imp artist's mark, attributed to Cleveland School 200.00

ART NOUVEAU

History: Art Nouveau is the French term for the "new art" which had its beginning in the early 1890s and continued for the next 40 years. The flowing and sensuous female forms used in this period were popular in Europe and America. Among the most recognized artists of this period were Gallé, Lalique, and Tiffany.

The Art Nouveau style can be identified by flowing, sensuous lines, florals, insects, and the feminine form. These designs were incorporated into almost everything produced during the period, from art glass to furniture, silver, and personal objects. Later wares demonstrate some of the characteristics of the evolving Art Deco style.

References: Victor Arwas, *Glass: Art Nouveau to Art Deco*, Rizzoli, 1977; Graham Dry, *Art Nouveau Domestic Metalwork*, Antique Collectors' Club, 1999; Alastair Duncan, The Paris Salons 1895-1914, Vol. IV, *Ceramics and Glass*, Antique Collectors' Club, 1998; Albert Christian Revi, *American Art Nouveau Glass*, reprint, Schiffer Publishing, 1981; Wolf Uecker, *Art Nouveau and Art Deco Lamps and Candlesticks*, Abbeville Press, 1986; Kenneth Wilson, *American Glass 1760–1930*, 2 vols., Hudson Hill Press and The Toledo Museum of Art, 1994.

Museum: Virginia Museum of Fine Arts, Richmond, VA.

Additional Listings: Furniture; Jewelry. Also check glass, pottery, and metal categories.

Basket, 11-1/2" w, 9" h, pewter, floral relief dec, Kayserzinn 260.00

Blotter Corners, 2-1/2" l, gilt bronze, cast relief of woman's head, c1900, worn patina, set of 4 .... 250.00

Box, cov, 14-1/2" w, 8" d, 5-1/2" h, brass covered, two-drawer wooden box, emb flower and vine motif, inset with colored glass flower centers, sgd "Daguet" 350.00

Bowl, 13" d, 6-1/2" h, broad oval, 4 peaked handles, relief dec as stylized basket, opal blue over came-colored glazed ground, matte black drip glaze at top rim, imp European maker's mark 200.00

Brush, sterling silver, wear 45.00

Candlesticks, pr

8" h, gilt metal, foliate and floral dec, c1900, minor scratches 345.00

10-1/2" h, gilt metal, partially clad maidens carrying vessels on heads, oval base, imp "MP," and "D. P. Muller" around base, patina and gilt loss 375.00

Chandelier, 30" w, 44" h, bronze, pierced dish with foliage motifs, 5 scrolling candle arms, hung by rod and twisted chains 850.00

Charger, 14-3/4" d, porcelain, circular, molded open handles, central painting of black, blue, and red parrot on perch, yellow ground, Limoges 225.00

Cigarette Case, 2-1/4" x 3", silver, rect, repousse of maiden, hair issuing flowers and scrolls, Mauser, 3.64 troy oz 375.00

Clock

Desk, 3-3/4" w, 4-3/8" h, bronze, Chelsea Clock movement, gilt-metal and glass mount, red enamel dec devices, ftd base, circular face with Arabic chapters, imp "Chelsea Clock Co., Boston, USA, 155252" on inside clock works, worn patina 460.00

Figural, 12-1/2" h, enameled cast white metal, relief of woman's head, flowing hair, leaves, thistles, Seth Thomas movement, circular dial with Roman numerals, c1900, minor wear 300.00

Mantel, 10" h, pottery, bronze glaze surmounted by foliage head, flowing hair, center circular clock face, recessed panels depicting hp songbird and flowers, gray ground, enameled cabochons, mkd "Bretby, England" on base, c1900 .... 1,495.00

Tall Case, 17-1/2" w, 9-3/4" d, 84" h, oak case with molded cornice above block, trunk with beveled glazed panels, carved central medallion, plinth base, clock with brass chapter ring, painted Arabic numerals, German, c1910-20 .... 900.00

Desk Set, enameled pewter, 4-3/4" h cov biscuit box designed by

Figure, Walrath Pottery, nude lying on stomach, face supported by hands, mustard glaze, green base, imp "Walrath/1912," 4-3/4" l, $465.

Archibald Knox, pr of candlesticks, pen tray, blue-green enameled foil disks and hearts, raised leaf and vine dec, imp "English Pewter Made by Liberty & Co." 1,725.00

Dresser Set, sterling silver, hand mirror, hair brush, clothes brush, nail file, each with repousse of woman's face, swirling florals, hairbrush monogrammed, Wm B. Kerr & Co., early 20th C 520.00

Ewer, 12-1/2" h, art pottery, tapered oviform, exotic bird perched on branch, gray-blue shaded cream ground, sgd on base "Royal Jubilee," and "hand painted Holland" 175.00

Figure
6" h, 4-1/2" l, nude, white porcelain, Germany 75.00
21-1/2" h, Renaissance Woman, reading, silvered bronze, ivory features, circular red marble base, after Albert Carrier-Belleuse 5,750.00
48-1/4" h, patinated bronze chalkware, standing female, holding jug 200.00

Fire Fender, 52-1/2" l, brass, sq section rail raised at each end by architectural plinth, stylized plant motif, molded base with rounded corners, c1900 ....225.00

Floor Vase, cov, 38" h, Serves-style, figural panels with cherubs framed within stylized floral designs, France, c1900 ....6,900.00

Garniture, centerpiece with bronze patina, female spelter figure of "L. Historie," flanked by spelter plinth with clock, enameled dial with painted Arabic numbers, sgd "L. Satre-A Pont. Aven," rect molded marble base with center bronze gilt neoclassical mounting, bronze gilded bun feet, pr of bronze patina spelter Louis XVI style urns, ribbons and swags centering figural medallion, sq marble base, bronze gilded feet.......................950.00

High Chair, 15" w, 13-1/2" d, 38" h, walnut, straight backrest with shaped and floral carved top rail, spindle-turned gallery, emb leather panel, flanked by downswept armrests, emb leather seat, sq legs joined by turned stretchers, c1900 ....200.00

Inkwell, 14" l, 5" h, brass, double, pen tray, gargoyle handles, imp flowers, bronze patina, incised "O. Hoffmann," repatination to ink well.......850.00

Jardiniere and Pedestal, 27-1/2" h, 9-1/2" d, Langley Ware, underglaze blue irises on green ground, pate-sur-pate stenciling of stylized pattern in white and green on celadon, stamped "Lovatt/Langley Ware/England," short line to rim of both pcs.......................1,400.00

Lantern Holders, pr, wrought iron, painted black, round twisted plated centered by four cast leaves issuing S-scroll arm with cast leaves and tulip-like flowers.......................750.00

Mirror, 12" h, hammered brass, curved, stepped, rect frame, attached hinged stand, imp Rorag Wien maker's mark, Vienna, early 20th C, minor discoloration.......................260.00

Nested Tables, 18" w x 28-3/4" h, 20-1/2" w x 29-1/2" h, 23-3/4" w x 30" h, rect table tops inlaid with various fruitwood marquetry of flowers and leafy vines, branded "C. G. Pa...r Nancy," set of 3 ....2,750.00

Photo Frame, 6" x 7-1/2", bronze, scrolling floral border, applied details on corners, stamped "K. & Co.," American.......................150.00

Plant Stand, 67-1/2" h, wrought iron, each foot of trifid base rising to scrolling vine topped by leaf-form surface at stepped intervals, central stem continuing to vine-form book.......................400.00

Plate, 7-1/4" d, silver, chased and emb with profile of woman with flowing tresses, background of reeded formed as stylized sun's rays, shaped edge, Gorham, 1883, 6 troy oz.................................1,150.00

Stove, coal, 28-1/2" w, 22" d, 36" h, bronze and iron, shaped structure, pierced bronze plaque with "S" scroll motifs centering pineapple, applied bronze medallions with female profiles, stamped "Deville Pailliette Forest, No. 17, Charlesville, Ardennes," c1900.........375.00

Table Lamp
21-1/2" h, Steuben catalog #964 calcite shades, pulled gold aurene leaf dec, gold int., bronze rope arms with dolphin finials, bronze bell shaped bases with ropetwist dec, green and brown patina, shades mkd with silver Steuben stamp, pr 4,025.00
22-1/2" h, 17" d domed leaded shade, radiating caramel slag glass segments, 3 socket patinated metal base, stylized floral and lineal dec, wear to patina, 2 cracked segments 635.00
29" h, figural, metal, stylized woman in diaphanous dress, arms outstretched, holding two Steuben gold aurene ribbed bell shaped shades, floral mounts, dark bronze and green patina, silver Steuben stamp.......................1,100.00

Teapot and Plate, 5" h teapot, 10-1/2" d plate, repeating rose and leaf dec, pink and green on creamy white ground, black Royal Doulton stamp on base, repairs to teapot.......................90.00

Tile, 6" w, 6" h
Six tile frieze, repeating stylized lotus blossoms in relief, rose and tan glossy glazed flowers on dark green ground, raised "England" mark, scratches, some chipped edges 325.00
Stylized floral pattern, raised "Made in Belgium" mark.......................65.00

Torah Breast Plate, 9-1/2" h, Russian silver, cartouche form, surmounted by crown, above candelabra and decalogue among bold foliate designs of tulips, grape clusters, cattails, bells and suspension chain, mkd "84," marker's mark, early 20th C, three bells missing 2,530.00

Tray
Hammered copper, 24" x 11", rect, emb handles, heavily rolled rim, orig dark patina, unmarked, attributed to Benedict.............600.00
Porcelain inset of yellow water iris and lily pads, green, blue, and white ground, pierced mixed metal surround.....................575.00

Umbrella Stand, 23" h, pottery, tapering cylinder, spray of yellow and red tulips against glossy shaded green and brown ground, imp "Ruko" on base, A. Radford Pottery, Clarksburg, WV 525.00

Vase
4-1/2" h, tapered oviform, lightly irid dark blue enameled metal, dragonfly motif 275.00
5-3/4" h, ovoid, ruffled edge, colorless rising to yellow, raised enameled flower 145.00
8-1/2" h, 6" d, pewter, Tudric pattern, Liberty & Co., England, some dents 175.00
8-7/8" h, porcelain, quatrefoil rim flaring to bulbous base, high relief pendulous molded bell flowers, stems, and leaves, soft green and yellow, gilt rim and highlights, small chips and repair to one leaf 175.00
10-1/4" h, irid cylindrical vase, naturalistic conforming iris bronze mount with gilt bronze bloom, Austria.......................525.00
11-1/4" h, porcelain, elongated oviform, gilt finished ext. linear and floral motifs in black, artist Sidney T. Callowhill signature on base, Boston.......................200.00
12-3/4" h, ceramic, bulbed ovoid, tapered to diamond-shaped base, blossom cluster near rim, 2 side handles, central modeled woman's head, matte tan, rust, and green-blue glaze, sgd "Grumbach" on side, imp marks on base 230.00

Vitrine, 41" w, 15-1/2" d, 73" h, oak, molded rect cornice over plain frieze, pr of cupboard doors with glazed panels, stylized floral motifs, shelved fitted int., long drawer, c1910-20.......................750.00

ART POTTERY (GENERAL)

History: America's interest in art pottery can be traced to the Centennial Exposition in Philadelphia, Pennsylvania, in 1877, where Europe's finest producers of decorative art displayed an impressive selection of their wares. Our young artists rose to the challenge immediately, and by 1900, native artisans were winning gold medals for decorative ceramics here and abroad.

The Art Pottery "Movement" in America lasted from about 1880 until the first World War. During this time, more than 200 companies, in most states, produced decorative ceramics ranging from borderline production ware to intricately decorated, labor intensive artware establishing America as a decorative art powerhouse.

Below is a listing of the work by various factories and studios, with pricing, from a number of these companies. The location of these outlets are included to give the reader a sense of how nationally-based the industry was.

References: Susan and Al Bagdade, *Warman's Americana Pottery and Porcelain*, Wallace-Homestead, 1994; Carol and Jim Carlton, *Colorado Pottery*, Collector Books, 1994; Paul Evans, *Art Pottery of the United States*, 2nd ed., Feingold & Lewis Publishing, 1987; Lucile Henzke, *Art Pottery of America*, revised ed., Schiffer Publishing, 1996; Norman Karlson, *American Art Tile*, 1876-1941, Rizzoli Publications, 1998; Ralph and Terry Kovel, *Kovels' American Art Pottery*, Crown Publishers, 1993; Richard and Hilary Myers, *William Morris Tiles*, Richard Dennis (distributed by Antique Collectors' Club), 1996; David Rago, *American Art Pottery*, Knickerbocker Press, 1997; Jim Riebel, *Sanfords Guide to Nicodemus*, Adelmore Press, 1998.

Periodicals: Style 1900, 17 S. Main St., Lambertville, NJ 08530.

Collectors' Clubs: American Art Pottery Association, P.O. Box 834, Westport, MA 02790-0697, http://www.amartpot.org; Pottery Lovers Reunion, 4969 Hudson Dr., Stow, OH 44224.

SPECIAL AUCTIONS

Cincinnati Art Galleries
635 Main St
Cincinnati, OH 45202
(513) 381-2128

Jackson's Auctioneers & Appraisers
2220 Lincoln St.
Cedar Falls, IA 50613
(319) 277-2256

David Rago Auctions, Inc.
333 North Main St.
Lambertville, NJ 08530
(609) 397-9374

Treadway Gallery, Inc.
2029 Madison Rd.
Cincinnati, OH 45208
(513) 321-6742

Museums: Cincinnati Art Museum, Cincinnati, OH; Everson Museum of Art of Syracuse and Onondaga County, Syracuse, NY; Los Angeles County Museum of Art, Los Angeles, CA; Metropolitan Museum of Art, New York, NY; Newcomb College Art Gallery, New Orleans, LA; Zanesville Art Center, Zanesville, OH.

Additional Listings: See Clewell; Clifton; Cowan; Dedham; Fulper; Grueby; Jugtown; Marblehead; Moorcroft; Newcomb; North Dakota School of Mines; Ohr; Paul Revere; Peters and Reed; Rookwood; Roseville; Van Briggle; Weller; Zanesville.

Notes: Condition, design, size, execution, and glaze quality are the key considerations when buying art pottery. This category includes only companies not found elsewhere in this book.

Advisor: David Rago.

Arequipa
Bowl, 6-1/2" d, 2-1/4" h, closed-in, emb eucalyptus branches, matte green and dark blue glaze, stamped mark, incised "KH/11"..... 800.00
Vase
    4-1/4" h, 7" d, squat, closed handles, plant with white berries, semi-matte blue-gray glaze, incised "AP/1911" 600.00
    7" h, 4" d, bulbous, squeezebag wreath of heart-shaped leaves, frothy matte green glaze, Rhead period blue and white enamel mark.. 4,250.00
Bachelder, O. L., vase, 5" h, 3-3/4" d, bulbous, cobalt blue and teal sheer glossy glaze, incised "OLB/R," ink cipher....................... 500.00
Brouwer, vase
    5-1/2" h, 5-1/4" w, bulbous, lustered purple and black glaze, incised flame.. 800.00
    8-1/2" h, 5-1/4" h, straight rim, green and purple flame-painted glaze, incised flame 1,600.00
Cole, A. R., urn, 18-1/2" h, 9-1/2" d, hand-thrown, 3 fanciful twisted handles, mirror black glaze, unmarked, shallow scratches...... 400.00
Crook, Russel, urn, 16-1/2" h, 10" d, wax-resist, cowboys on horseback, brown clay under glossy, mottled dark blue glaze, incised "John Lampus/potter/RCrook/92", 1892, restored small rim chip, larger chip at base.. 3,750.00
Denaura, Denver
Vase
    6-3/4" h, 3-1/4"d , ovoid, emb mistletoe, semi-matte Robin's egg blue glaze, stamped "Denver," stilt pull........................... 1,200.00
    9" h, 5" d, ovoid, emb tulips and leaves, matte green glaze, "Denaura U.S.A 1903," written on base, stamped "Denver," and ink stamp 2,600.00
Jervis, 5-1/2" h, 6-1/2" d, hand carved, enamel glazed blue flowers, green foliage, teal-green ground, fine glaze nicks at edge, incised "Jervis" 950.00
Merrimac
    Jar, cov, 5-1/4" h, 3-1/4" d, glossy speckled brown glaze, paper label, stilt-pulls to int. rim of lid... 450.00
    Umbrella Stand, 22-3/4" h, 8-1/2"d , tooled and applied leaves, leathery matte green glaze, paper label, base crack, few small chips to dec, some glaze pooling..................................... 3,750.00
    Vase, 10" h, 5" d, bulbous, cylindrical neck, green and mirrored black mottled glaze, unmarked....................................... 1,500.00
    Vessel, 4" h, 9" l, broad squat, matte green glaze, imp mark, minute fleck to rim 1,200.00
Pewabic
Cabinet Vase
    2-1/4" h, 2-1/4" d, Persian blue crackled glaze, circular stamp and "40B" 225.00
    2-1/2" h, 2" d, fine celadon and oxblood lustered glaze, stamped mark 350.00
    2-1/2" h, 2-3/4" d, fine and thick pink, gold, and blue lustered dripping glaze, circular stamp "Pewabic/Detroit/PP"............. 1,200.00

Plate, 10-3/4" d, blue slip dragonflies, white crackled ground, stamped "PEWABIC," several glaze flakes and chips to foot ring 1,000.00
Vase
  3-3/4" h, 3-3/4" d, bulbous, fine dripping turquoise and purple lustered glaze, stamped circular mark.................................... 400.00
  4-3/4" h, 3-1/2" d, ovoid, gold and mauve lustered glaze, circular stamp 650.00
  4-3/4" h, 4" d, bulbous, lustered celadon and purple glaze, stamped cylindrical mark, remnant of paper label 500.00
  4-3/4" h, 4" d, bulbous, vibrant mirrored gold glaze dripping over glossy blue ground, circular stamp, small firing base chip 1,100.00

Pisgah Forest
Tea Set, Cameo Ware, wagon and landscape dec, dark matte green ground, raised mark and date 1943, 5-1/4" h teapot with fleck to rim and spout, creamer, rim chip on sugar................................... 700.00
Vase
  5" h, 4-3/4" d, bulbous, white and amber glaze, blue crystals, raised potter's mark and date 1940 .... 325.00
  5-1/2" h, 3-1/2" d, bulbous, amber glaze, white and blue crystals, raised potter's mark and illegible date 275.00
  6-1/2" h, 4" d, classical shape, fine amber glaze, tightly packed white and blue crystals, raised potter's mark and date 1940............. 600.00
  6-1/2" h, 4-1/2" d, corseted, amber glaze, gray crystals, raised potter's mark, illegible date 375.00
  7" h, 4" d, bulbous, brown and amber flambé glaze, clusters of large blue crystals, emb mark, grinding chip to base.......... 550.00
  7-3/4" h, 4-3/4" d, classical shape, amber glaze, white and blue crystals, raised potter's mark and date 1949 .... 700.00
  8" h, 5-1/4" d, bottle shape, white glaze with white crystals, raised potter's mark and date 1941 .... 650.00

Vessel
  3-3/4" h, 4-1/2" d, spherical, amber flambé glaze, celadon crystals, raised Stephen mark and illegible date.............................. 275.00
  3-3/4" h, 5-3/4" d, spherical, white glaze, white crystals, raised "Cameo/Stephen" mark and date 1951 .... 275.00
  5" h, 5-3/4" d, spherical, amber glaze, white and blue crystals, raised potter's mark and date 1947 .... 350.00
  7-1/2" h, 4-3/4" d, baluster, amber flambé glaze, few blue crystals, raised "Pisgah Forest" and illegible date 475.00

Teco
Vase
  5-1/2" h, 3-1/2"d, ovoid, 4 lobes, matte green glaze,stamped "Teco" 950.00

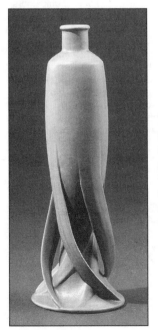

Teco, vase, reticulated blade-shaped leaves around foot, smooth matte green with charcoal glaze, stamped "Teco," 18" h, 6" d, minor chip to edge of one blade, $60,000. Photo courtesy of David Rago Auctions, Inc.

  10-1/2" h, 3-3/4" d, bottle shape, Aventurine, mirrored black, gold, and amber microcrystalline flambé glaze, stamped "Teco".......... 2,700.00
  12" h, 5" d, buttressed, tulip shape, smooth matte green glaze, stamped "Teco/463," designed by F. Moreau, small nick to one corner.. 3,750.00
  16-1/2" h, 8" d, organically shaped, sq base, tall neck, green and charcoal matte glaze, stamped "Teco," few restored chips to rim and lobe on body 1,200.00
Wall Pocket, 16-3/4" h, 6-1/2" d, emb stylized leaves, smooth matte green glaze, stamped "Teco/156A" 1,900.00

Volkmar
Vase, 12-1/4" h, 7-3/4" w, 3-3/4" d, pillow shape, painted barotine, sepia scenes of horses pulling carts, sgd "Chas. Volkmar," pr 5,000.00
Vessel, 5-1/2" h, 5-3/4" d, spherical, mottled Robin's egg blue vellum glaze, incised "Volkmar" and dated 650.00

Walrath
Sculpture, 4" h, 6" l, kneeling nude picking rose, sheer matte green glaze, yellow details, incised "Walrath"....................................... 300.00
Vase
  5-1/4" h, 3-3/4" d, bell shape, ochre and red painted landscape of cypress trees, blue-gray ground, incised "Walrath Pottery" ..5,000.00
  6-1/4" h, 4" d, painted stylized purple and dark green flowers, light gray-green ground, incised "Walrath Pottery" 4,000.00

Wheatley
Bust, 11-1/2" h, 15" w, Dante, frothy matte green glaze, unmarked, base chip 900.00
Garden Fountain, 7-3/4" h, 11-1/2" w, 8-1/4" d, large frog, matte green glaze, restoration to mouth and corner of base 850.00
Jardiniere, 6" h, 8-1/2" d, tapering rim, frothy matte green glaze, unmarked, bruise to rim 750.00
Lamp, 22" h, 18" d, matte green glaze, green leaded slag glass shade with row of white flowers, remnants of paper label on base, some breaks to glass panes, small chips to rim of vase................. 5,500.00
Pitcher, 8" h, 7-3/4" d, corseted, emb grape clusters and vines, frothy matte green glaze, imp "WI".. 700.00
Urn, 11" h, 11" d, bulbous, collar rim, frothy matte green glaze, unmarked, glaze flake to handle, possibly in the making, hairline to rim 450.00
Vase
  5-3/4" h, 7-3/4" d, organic, 2 handles, frothy matte green glaze, unmarked... 2,000.00
  9-3/4" h, 6" d, tapering ribbed rim, frothy matte green glaze, unmarked... 450.00

ARTS and CRAFTS MOVEMENT

History: The Arts and Crafts Movement in American decorative arts took place between 1895 and 1920. Leading proponents of the movement were Elbert Hubbard and his Roycrofters, the brothers Stickley, Frank Lloyd Wright, Charles and Henry Greene, George Niedecken, and Lucia and Arthur Mathews.

The movement was marked by individualistic design (although the movement was national in scope) and re-emphasis on handcraftsmanship and appearance. A reform of industrial Society was part of the long-range goal. Most pieces of furniture favored a rectilinear approach and were made of oak.

The Arts and Crafts Movement embraced all aspects of the decorative arts, including metalwork, ceramics, embroidery, woodblock printing, and the crafting of jewelry.

References: Steven Adams, *Arts & Crafts Movement*, Chartwell Books, 1987; *Arts and Crafts Furniture: The Complete Brooks Catalog of 1912*, Dover Publications, 1996;

Annette Carruthers and Mary Greensted, eds., *Simplicity of Splendour Arts and Crafts Living*, Lund Humphries, distributed by Antique Collectors' Club, 1999; Michael E. Clark and Jill Thomas-Clark (eds.), *J. M. Young Arts and Crafts Furniture*, Dover Publications, 1994; Paul Evans, *Art Pottery of the United States*, 2nd ed., Feingold & Lewis Publishing, 1987; *Furniture of the Arts & Crafts Period With Prices*, L-W Book Sales, 1992, 1995 value update; Charlotte Gere and Geoffrey Munn, *Pre-Raphaelite to Arts & Crafts Jewelry*, Antique Collectors' Club, 1999; Bruce Johnson, *Pegged Joint*, Knock on Wood Publications, 1995; Elyse Zorn Karlin, *Jewelry and Metalwork in the Arts and Crafts Tradition*, Schiffer Publishing, 1993; *Limbert Arts and Crafts Furniture: The Complete 1903 Catalog*, Dover Publications, n.d.; Thomas K. Maher, *The Jarvie Shop: The Candlesticks and Metalwork of Robert R. Jarvie*, Turn of the Century Editions, 1997; James Massey and Shirley Maxwell, Arts & Crafts, Abbeville Press, 1995; ——, *Arts & Crafts Design in America: A State-By-State Guide*, Chronicle Books, 1998; Kevin McConnell, *More Roycroft Art Metal*, Schiffer Publishing, 1995; Richard and Hilary Myers, *William Morris Tiles*, Richard Dennis (distributed by Antique Collectors' Club), 1996; David Rago, *American Art Pottery*, Knickerbocker Press, 1997; Roycrofters, *Roycroft Furniture Catalog*, 1906, Dover Publications, 1994; Paul Royka, *Mission Furniture, from the American Arts & Crafts Movement*, Schiffer Publishing, 1997; Joanna Wissinger, *Arts and Crafts: Metalwork and Silver and Pottery and Ceramics*, Chronicle Books, 1994.

Periodicals: American Bungalow, P.O. Box 756, Sierra Madre, CA 91204; Style 1900, 333 N. Main St., Lambertville, NJ 08530. American Bungalow focuses on the contemporary owner of Period homes and the refurbishing of same. Style 1900 has a more historically oriented approach to the turn of the century artisans.

Collectors' Clubs: Foundation for the Study of the Arts & Crafts Movement, Roycroft Campus, 31 S. Grove St., East Aurora, NY 14052; Roycrofters-At-Large Association, P.O. Box 417, East Aurora, NY 14052; William Morris Society of Canada, 1942 Delaney Dr., Mississaugua, Ontario, L5J 3L1, Canada. Students of the Arts and Crafts Movement are encouraged to participate in the two major conferences now

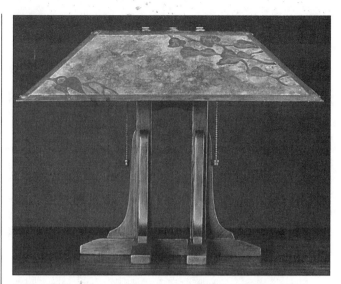

Lamp, table, Limbert, 4 panel mica shade set in copper frame, leaf-shaped cut-outs, base with 2 columns of long corbels resting on shoe feet, mint orig mica, orig patina, some refinishing to base, carved Limbert mark, 19" h, 24-1/2" w, 17" d, $19,000. Photo courtesy of David Rago Auctions, Inc.

available. The Grove Park Inn Conference is held annually in Ashville, NC, in February, by Bruce Johnson.

Museums: Cooper Hewitt Museum, Manhattan, NY; Elbert Hubbard Library-Museum, East Aurora, NY; Los Angeles County Museum of Art, Los Angeles, CA; Metropolitan Museum of Art, Manhattan, NY; Museum of Modern Art, New York, NY; Richmond Museum of Art, Richmond, VA.

Advisor: David Rago.

Additional Listings: Roycroft; Stickleys; art pottery categories.

Book, All Year Round, James Whitcomb Riley, 1912, 12-color wood-
    block illus by Gustav Baumann 125.00
Bookcase, 42" w, 17-3/4" d, 54-3/4" h, chestnut and oak, double doors,
    small glass panes around larger one, Gustav Stickley copper V-pulls,
    rough orig finish, small chips 2,100.00
Bowl, 13-1/2" d, 4" h, hammered copper, flaring, petal feet, floriform rim,
    cleaned patina, imp "BT" or "TB," in the style of M. Zimmerman... 125.00
China Cabinet, 55" w, 16" d, 54" h, double door, through tenon top and
    gallery, paneled back, orig hardware and finish, Limbert 4,000.00
Console Table, 96" l, 24" d, 29-1/2" h, trestle, long narrow top and
    lower shelf, new finish, replaced toe to one side 2,300.00
Dining Chair, 17" w, 17" d, 49-1/2" h, attributed to Majestic Chair Co.,
    tall back, 3 long vertical back slats, orig worn inset rush seat, new fin-
    ish, unmarked 1,900.00
Dining Table, 48" d, 31" h, No. 419, circular top, 4 leaves, 5 legs, over-
    coat to orig finish, branded Limbert mark 2,600.00
Lamp, table
    19" h, 21" d Dirk Van Erp hammered copper and mica 4 panel shade,
        4 socket fitting, bulbous base, orig patina and mica, closed box
        mark, inner cap missing from top of bulb stem 55,000.00
    19" h, 24-1/2" x 17", Limbert, 4 panel mica shade, set on copper
        frame, leaf shaped cut-outs, base with 2 columns of long corbels
        resting on shoe feet, mint orig mica, orig patina, some refinishing
        to base, carved Limbert mark 19,000.00
    25" h, 16" d six-sided shade with green slag glass panels, fluted
        bronze base, dark patina 600.00
Lamp Table, 29-1/4" d, 29" h, circular top, lower shelf over cross-
    stretchers, new dark finish 1,700.00

BOX SPECIAL AUCTIONS

Craftsman Auctions
1485 West Housatonic
Pittsfield, MA 01201
(413) 448-8922

David Rago Auctions, Inc.
333 North Main St.
Lambertville, NJ 08530
(609) 397-9374

Treadway Gallery, Inc.
2029 Madison Rd.
Cincinnati, OH 45208
(513) 321-6742

Library Table, 48" l, 34" d, 29" h, two drawer, overhanging top, long corbels, overcoat to dark finish, branded Limbert mark 1,300.00

Pedestal, 15-1/4" sq, 37-3/4" h, circular top, 4 sided cut-out column, flaring base, unmarked, style of Greene and Greene, refinished top, alligatored finish on base 1,200.00

Plate, copper, Art Crafts Shop

5-1/2" d, enameled stylized blue flowers, grin foliage, stamp mark and "401," minor wear to light brown patina 300.00

5-1/2" x 7-1/2", rect, two blue enameled poppies, bright green leaves, dark green stems, orig medium brown patina, stamp mark and "406A," minor losses to enamel 550.00

6" sq, enameled stylized blue flowers, green foliage, light brown patina, die-stamped mark and "410" 550.00

6-1/2" sq, enameled stylized blue, green and black border, orig dark patina, stamp mark and "2-134" 700.00

7" sq, enameled red flowers, green foliage, orig dark patina, stamp mark and "407," minor flecks to enamel............................ 750.00

7-1/4" sq, enameled stylized blue and black flowers, green foliage, light brown patina, die-stamped mark and "404," minute loss of enamel 450.00

7-1/2" x 5-1/4", rect, enameled red poppies, green leaves, orig medium brown patina, stamp mark and "406," minor enamel loss 350.00

8" d, enameled blue flowers, green stems, orig dark patina, stamp mark and "408," minor flecks to enamel.............................. 750.00

Print, woodblock, matted and framed

5-1/2" h, 4-1/2" w, William S. Rice, The Buoy, orange, blue, and green, pencil sgd and titled, c1936 .... 700.00

7" h, 9" w, William S. Rice, Eucalypti Sunset, silhouetted trees in front of cloudy sky, sgd and titled.................................... 2,000.00

12" h, 7" w, Waldo Chase, Nomad, silhouetted ship at sunset, blue, sgd and dated "1932" lower right 750.00

14-1/4" h, 8-1/2" w, Bertha Lum, courtyard view from doorway, blue, orange, and chartreuse, on rice paper, pencil sgd, matted and mounted in Arts & Crafts frame, small tear and stain on margin 1,500.00

Rocker, 27-1/4" w, 29-3/4" d, 35-1/2" h, tapering vertical slats on back and under curved arms, drop-in spring seat cov in brown leather, Harden, new dark finish 475.00

Screen, 58-1/2" w, 68" h, 3 sections, wooden, horizontal and vertical panels, pyrography band of red poppies, green ground, orig finish, few minor blind cracks.. 900.00

Server, 36" w, 16-1/2" d, 38-1/2" h, Ebon-Oak, backsplash, 2 shelves, orig finish, branded Limbert mark, minor split to post............ 2,000.00

Silent Butler, 11" h, 7-1/2" d, silver plated hammered copper, monogrammed "AAG," stamped open box Dirk Van Erp mark 450.00

Smoking Set, hammered copper, 8" h x 7" d humidor with riveted lid, curled handle; bulbous cigarette and match holders, rect tray, incised Jarvie Shop mark, cleaned patina, soldered lid handle............ 125.00

Smoking Stand, hammered copper, 4 rods riveted to hemispherical top and base, orig finish, Dirk Van Erp closed box mark............. 2,300.00

Taboret, 18" d, 22" h, mahogany, circular top, lower shelf, varnished, stains to top 350.00

Trestle Table, 95-1/2" l, 29" d, 31" h, plank top, lower shelf mortised with through-tenons, orig reddish-brown finish, some alligatoring to top 3,750.00

Vase, 5-3/4" h, 3-1/2" d, bottle shape, sunstone glaze, Pilkington die-stamped animal logo and "England" 750.00

AUSTRIAN WARE

History: More than 100 potteries were located in the Austro-Hungarian Empire in the late 19th and early 20th centuries. Although Carlsbad was the center of the industry, the factories spread as far as the modern-day Czech Republic.

Many of the factories were either owned or supported by Americans; hence, their wares were produced mainly for export to the United States.

Marks: Many wares do not have a factory mark but only the

Bowl, scalloped edge, swirl and shell relief, white ground, 2 rose floral motifs, gilded, 11" d, 2-7/8" h, $70.

word "Austrian" in response to the 1891 law specifying that the country of origin had to be marked on imported products.

Additional Listings: Amphora; Carlsbad; Royal Dux; Royal Vienna.

Bowl, 7-7/8" d, 2-3/4" h, pottery, circular form tapering to base, radiating streaked turquoise and blue glossy glaze, imp "Made in Austria, WW.IV," on base, glass bubbles in center int. 175.00

Bulb Vase, 11-3/4" h, mold-blown triple bulbed form, striated textured irid surface, flanking festoons, amber shading to ruby, early 20th C... 350.00

Cabinet Plate, 9-5/8" d, enamel dec center with nymph by stream, gilt dec pink and burgundy ground border, 19th C............................ 520.00

Cup and Saucer, 4" h, 6" d, hp, ornate classical scenes of figures and putti, blue field, gilt accents, cup with gilt int., cup mkd "Apollo und de Musen," saucer with shield mark and "F/Vienna/D, Austria," both also artist sgd.. 420.00

Ewer, 11-3/4" h, 6" d, rococo gold scroll, hp pink and yellow wild roses, gold outlines, 4 ftd 125.00

Figure

3-3/4" h, bronze, huntsman, cold painted, c1920 .... 350.00

4-1/4" h, bronze, courting couple, cold painted 750.00

8" h, porcelain, five children in various poses, mounted on circular base, printed beehive mark, late 19th C, restoration 175.00

Lamp, 15-1/2" h, 9" d, metal shade dec with 3 red glass inserts, 3 foliate stem arms, reticulated bronzed Secessionist-inspired base 850.00

Rose Bowl, 3-1/2" d, spherical, tricorn rim, colorless, lightly irid yellow and green spot and pulled swirls, polished pontil, dark inclusions, burst bubble 275.00

Salt, 3" h, figural, donkey, 2 dish shaped baskets on back, c1915... 265.00

Tray, 7" l, 2 bronze dancers, round green and white marble base, imp mark, c1925, abrasions 175.00

Vase

4-1/4" h, eight-rib form, raised ruffled rim, olive green, overall irid panels, loose grid of threaded lines, c1900, two pinpoint bubble bursts 200.00

5" h, baluster, pinched and ruffled rim, purple and yellow swirled body, pulled irid ext. dec, polished pontil, c1900................. 165.00

6" h, pinched ovoid, elongated neck of colorless glass, ext. dec with highly textured irid gold dimpled glass, polished pontil....... 690.00

6-3/4" h, double bulbed translucent opal green, amber spotted dec on lower portion, overall dark red threading, 2 applied opal blue-green handles 750.00

AUTOGRAPHS

History: Autographs appear on a wide variety of formats—letters, documents, photographs, books, cards, etc. Most collectors focus on a particular person, country, or category, e.g., signers of the Declaration of Independence.

References: Mark Allen Baker, *All-Sport Autographs*, Krause Publications, 1995; ——, *Collector's Guide to Celebrity Autographs*, Krause Publications, 1996; *Standard Guide to Collecting Autographs*, Krause Publications, 1999; Kevin Martin, *Signatures of the Stars*, Antique Trader Books, 1998; Kenneth W. Rendell, *Forging History: The Detection of Fake Letters & Documents*, University of Oklahoma Press, 1994; ——, *History Comes to Life*, University of Oklahoma Press, 1996; George Sanders, Helen Sanders and Ralph Roberts, *Sanders Price Guide to Sports Autographs*, 2nd ed., Alexander Books, 1997; ——, *Sanders Price Guide to Autographs*, 4th ed., Alexander Books, 1997.

Periodicals: *Autograph Collector*, 510-A S. Corona Mall, Corona, CA 91720-1420, http://www.autographcollector.com/acm.htm; *Autograph Review*, 305 Carlton Rd., Syracuse, NY 13207; *Autograph Times*, 1125 W. Baseline Rd., #2-153-M, Mesa, AZ 85210-9501, http://celebrityconnection.com/at.htm; *Autographs & Memorabilia*, P.O. Box 224, Coffeyville, KS 67337; *The Collector*, P.O. Box 255, Hunter, NY 12442; *Celebrity Access*, 20 Sunnyside Ave., Sutie A241, Mill Valley, CA 94941-1928; V.I.P. *Autogramm-Magazine*, 3000 W. Olympic Blvd, Blvd. 3, Suite 2415, Santa Monica, CA 90404, http://www.vip-entertainment.com.

Collectors' Clubs: International Autograph Collectors Club & Dealers Alliance, 4575 Sheriden St., Suite 111, Hollywood, FL 33021-3575, http://www.iacc-da.com; Manuscript Society, 350 N Niagara Street, Burbank, CA 95105-3648, http://www.manuscript.org; Universal Autograph Collectors Club, P.O. Box 6181, Washington, DC 20044; Washington Historical Autograph & Certificate Organization, P.O. Box 2428, Springfield, VA 22152-2428, http://www.whaco.com.

Additional Listings: See *Warman's Americana & Collectibles* for more examples.

Notes: The condition and content of letters and documents bear significantly on value. Collectors should know their source since forgeries abound and copy machines compound the problem. Further, some signatures of recent presidents and movie stars were done by machine rather than by the persons themselves. A good dealer or advanced collector can help spot the differences.

Abbreviations: The following are used to describe autograph materials and their sizes.

Materials:

ADS	Autograph Document Signed
ALS	Autograph Letter Signed
AQS	Autograph Quotation Signed
CS	Card Signed
DS	Document Signed
FDC	First Day Cover
LS	Letter Signed
PS	Photograph Signed
TLS	Typed Letter Signed

Sizes (approximate):

Folio	12 x 16 inches
4to	8 x 10 inches
8vo	7 x 7 inches
12mo	3 x 5 inches

Colonial America

Chittenden, Thomas, first Governor of Vermont, DS, 1 page small oblong folio, May 8, 1781, headed "His Excellency Thomas Chittenden, Esquire, Captain-General, Governor, and Commander of Chief in and over the State of Vermont," electing Thomas Whipple a Lieutenant in the Militia of Vermont, countersigned by Joseph Thay as State Secretary, paper seal, wear to folds, few small holes, silked on reverse 950.00

Hancock, John, partially printed DS, sgd as Governor and Commander in Chief of Massachusetts, 1 page small folio, Boston, Nov 23, 1787, appointing Aaron Mighill of Brimfield as Coroner of Hampshire County, Massachusetts, countersigned by John Avery as Secretary, paper seal, very dark signature 4,500.00

Henry, Patrick, DS, partially printed, 1 page small 4to, April 1, 1785, as Governor of VA, officer's commission, heading "The Commonwealth of Virginia," ornate borders, paper seal, dark signature 3,975.00

Penn, William, DS, 1 page 4to on vellum, April 13, 1684, land grant to Griffith Jones for property near the Delaware River running along Walnut Street from Front to Second Streets in Philadelphia, wax and paper pendant seal present 3,900.00

Trumbull, Jonathan, Governor of Colony and later State of Connecticut, partially printed document, sgd "Jonth. Trumble Asnt," 1 page oblong 8vo, Lebanon, Connecticut, May 10, 1758, certifying Ezekiel Kellogg is voluntarily enlisting as "...a Soldier to serve his Majesty King George the Second...to be commanded by Col. Nathan Whitiny for invading Canada..." 375.00

Walton, George, signed of Declaration of Independence, free franked address leaf panel, address to "His Excellency, the Governor of the State of George," free franked "Public Service, George Walton," stamped "FREE" below signature 1,500.00

Washington, George, DS, partially printed military document, 1 page oblong small 4to, "Headquarters, August 14, 1778, warrant to William Palfrey, Paymaster General of the Forces of the United States," ordering money to be paid for recruiting, sgd "By his Excellency's Command G. Washington," countersigned by Robert Hanson Harrison, aide-de-camp, also sgd by John Clark as auditor 15,000.00

Foreign

Catherine II (the Great), ALS, sgd as Empress, in Russina, 1 page 4to, Saint Petersburg, Aug. 12, 1788, to Ivan Ivanovich, ordering repairs to be made at horse stables of Cavalary Regiment Guards at Imperial Winter Palace, framed in gold wood and matted in red velvet with portrait engraving of Catherine... 1,150.00

George II, ALS, sgd as Prince of Wales, in French, 2 pages 4to, Leicester House, Jan 11/22, 1723, to Madame Marygrove, sending sympathies on loss of her close relation, written completely in the hand of George II 1,000.00

Lafayette, Marie Joseph, Marquis De, ALS, 1 page, 5-5/8" x 6", Paris, Jan. 8, (c1811-17) in English, to James Monroe, asking about progress in helping with Lafayette's financial complications, double matted and framed in silver antiqued wood frame with engraved portrait of Lafayette 2,800.00

Napoleon, ALS, signed as "Napol," while emperor of France, 1 page 4to, Rambouillet, August 13, 1811, to Count Nicholas-Francois Mollien, sending his minister to public treasury "...sending rather surprising records concerning the finances of the Army of the North," noting "it would be necessary to have the same kind of records concerning the armies of Spain." 1,450.00

SPECIAL AUCTIONS

Swann Galleries, Inc.
104 E. 25th St.
New York, NY 10010
(212) 254-4710

General

Barton, Clara, ALS, 4 pgs 8vo, Oxford (Mass), Dec. 22, 1905, to Miss Mary Kensel, National First Aid Association, conforming items to be printed in pamphlet...395.00

Dali, Salvador, DS, loan agreement, typed, 1 page 4to on Museum of Modern Art letterhead, Jan. 4, 1965, bold blue ink full signature, arranging for loan of 3 pieces to museum 285.00

Dalton, Emmett, sgd and inscribed 8vo page from his personal copy of his book, The Daltons Rode, 1931, inscribed "Private Property of Emmett Dalton" 1,100.00

Edison, Thomas, stock certificate, Edison Phonograph Works for 41 and 116/1000 shares, New Jersey, June 26, 1888, issued to Thomas A. Edison, signed by Edison as President, 10-1/4" x 5-3/4", sgd second time on verso as endorsement........................2,800.00

Lindbergh, Charles A., sgd photograph, 8" x 10", oblong, sepia, Lindbergh wearing duster over civilian attire, standing between friend Carl Squier and unidentified man, both in uniform, airfield background, sgd in full with "May 1933" over light portion of his coat................1,650.00

Morse, Samuel F. B., ALS, 2 full pages 4to with integral leaf, Poughkeepsie, NY, Nov. 1, 1854, to S. M. Door of Chatham 4 Corners, length letter in which he expresses his views on Kansas-Nebraska Act 7,000.00

Remington, Frederic, orig sketch of artist's palette, penned by Remington , sgd below and dated "New Rochelle, NY, 1901," 1-1/2" x 2-1/4" sketch, signature 4" l, on 7-1/2 x 4-3/4" album page, verso with signature of Theodore Roosevelt as President, dated Nov. 28, 1902, and Charles W. Fairbanks, dated April 17, 1907....................4,500.00

Literature

Dalziel, George and Edward, child's book sgd, The Brothers Dalziel: A Record of Fifty Years' Work in Conjunction with Many of the Most Distinguished Artists of the Period 1840-1890, London, 1901, first edition, sgd by both, inscribed, 4to, publisher's blue cloth gilt covers 320.00

Doyle, Arthur Conan, Sir, book sgd, Through the Magic Door, dated "November 21, 1907," 8vo, gilt pictorial red cloth.....................920.00

Irving, Washington, manuscript sgd, 1 pg small 8vo, undated, page from Mahomet and His Successors, words in Irving's hand, including revisions and cross-outs, mounted to matching paper.............700.00

Rackam, Arthur, child's book sgd, Fairy Tales, London, 1932, 12 mounted color plates with lettered tissue guards, 4to, vellum gilt, moderately soiled and rubbed, 1 of 525 numbered signed copies..1,100.00

Sinclair, Upton, book sgd with TLS, The Jungle, 8vo, pictorial green cloth, rubbed, rear hinged cracked, TLS dated July 1, 1909, Cutchogue, Long Island, NY...145.00

Tarrington, Booth, book sgd, The Gentleman from Indiana, (NY, 1899), 8vo, publisher's cloth, first edition, inscribed and sgd, 1941, Kennebunkport 435.00

Twain, Mark, book, To the Person Sitting in Darkness, Anti-Imperialist League, NY, 1901, with cut signature, sgd "Mark Twain" in pen, 60 x 10 mm on torn sq of laid paper, laid in 550.00

Wyeth, N. C., child's book, The Little Shepherd of Kingdom Come, John Fox Jr., NY, 1931, 14 color plates by Wyeth, tissue guards, 4to, 1/4 vellum, discoloring to spine, custom cloth slipcase, 1 of 512 copies sgd by Wyeth...750.00

Military

Bormann, Martin, TLS, in Germany, 1 page large 4to, stationery printed with "Administration Obersalzberg Reichsleiter Martin Bormann, Main Quarters of the Fuhrer," June 20, 1944, to Prof. Heinrich Michaels at Chieming on Chiemsee, instructing Professor to buy works of art for a government sponsored exhibition 900.00

Heath, William, Revoluntary War General, DS, 2 pages folio, Boston, June 1, 1777, court martial proceedings involving desertion and theft of two soldiers, marginal chipping slightly affecting few words of text, writing bold and dark 1,400.00

MacArthur, Douglas, two line autographed note, sgd "D. Mack," 1 pg, 4 to, ALS, Oct 21, 1959..375.00

Ward, Artemus, Continental Major General, Commander in Chief of Massachusetts troops, second in command to Washington, directed

Battle of Bunker Hill, DS, 1-1/2 pgs 4to, Headquarters, Boston, Aug. 26, 1776, ordering Army Paymaster General Ebene, second in command to Washington, directed Battle of Bunker Hill, DS, 1-1/2 pgs 4to, Headquarters, Boston, Aug. 26, 1776, ordering Army Paymaster General Ebenezer Hancock to pay artillery Capt. Edward Burbeck…to pay his company of artillery in the service of the United American States for the month of July last…"......................1,200.00

Muhlenberg, Henry, ALS, 1 page 4to, Aug. 23, 1830, to War Dept. in Washington, regarding officers and soldiers eligible for Revolutionary War soldier pension, postmarked integral address leaf 125.00

Wheeler, Joseph, Confederate major general, cavalry officer, ALS, 2 pgs 8vo, Mexico City, Dec. 14, 1904, discussing daughter's trip to Ashville and his social plans 185.00

Music

Ellington, Edward Kennedy (Duke), FDC, honoring American composer Edward MacDowell, postmarked May 13, 1940, with small printed photograph of Ellington 225.00

Handy, W. C., FDC, honoring American composer John Philip Sousa, Handy sgd twice, once as "William C. Handy," other as "W. C. Handy," dated 4-24-43, postmarked May 3, 1940..300.00

Ravel, Maurice, autographed note signed on picture postcard, June 10, (1905) to Maurice Delage, sending greetings, image of 1905 International Exposition at Liege 650.00

Strauss, Richad, ALS on postcard, in German, Berlin, Nov 14, 1901, to Ernst von Schuch, Dresden conductor, writing about rehearsals..850.00

Tchaikovsky, Peterilich, signed sepia cabinet photo, 4-1/4" x 6-1/2", head and shoulders pose, facing to left, sgd and dated, inscribed to French poet Paul Colin, inscription in French, 1888 ....6,500.00

Wagner, Richard, ALS, written in French, 2 pgs 8vo, Zürich, Dec. 12, 1857, to Mr. Anderson concerning score for performance at Royal Court in London..3,500.00

Presidents

Ford, Gerald R., typed DS, typescript of the Presidential Oath of Office, August 9, 1974, 1 page 4to, large penned signature under typed oath 900.00

Jackson, Andrew, DS, patent for an improvement in horse power, 1 page large folio on vellum, March 30, 1835, countersigned by John Forsyth as Secretary of State and Benjamin F. Butler as Attorney General 1,600.00

Jefferson, Thomas, free franked address panel, addressed to firm of Matthew Cary & Son of Philadelphia, franked by him "free Th. Jefferson," at

Dwight D. Eisenhower, matted and framed photograph, autograph on card, $90.

upper left, manuscript "Free" at upper right and dark circular black "Charlot May 12" postmark........................3,900.00

Johnson, Andrew, DS, 1 page small 4to, Executive Office, June 18, 1865, giving approval for certain officers to be mustered out of service, some fold wear, dark signature..................................1,750.00

Kennedy, John F., photograph signed and inscribed, 8" x 10", black and white, oblong, matte surface, showing Kennedy in left profile in conversation with Congressman King, wide lower margin inscribed "For Cecil King - With the esteem and best wishes of his friend - John Kennedy" in bold black felt-tip marker, photograph taken in 1962 at Biltmore Hotel in Los Angeles................................4,800.00

Lincoln, Abraham, autographed note signed as President, 1 page, 2-3/4" x 4" sheet, May 9, 1861, to Secretary of War Simon Cameron, requesting Secretary of War Simon Cameron accept a volunteer regiment from Illinois, matted in blue, engraving of Lincoln, framed in antique gold wood frame..10,800.00

Nixon, Richard M., PS, full color page of booklet from Dedication of New Wing of Eisenhower Museum, Oct. 14, 1971, 14 pgs 4to, also sgd on page with full color photo by Mamie Eisenhower, other pgs sgd by General Launis Norstad and Kansas Senator Harry Darby........185.00

Roosevelt, Franklin D., TLS, as Governor of NY and Democratic Presidential candidate, 1 page 4to on official letterhead, Albany, July 9, 1932 to Aymar Johnson, Esq. In London, thanking old friend for political contribution 650.00

Truman, Harry S., DS, 1 page folio, Feb 6, 1948, appointing Howard L. Doyle as U. S. Attorney for southern district of Illinois, sgd by Tom Clark as Attorney General, bright gold seal 775.00

Show Business

Bogart, Humphrey, DS, 1 page 4to, Aug. 29, 1955, letter from Robert Hunter, an employee of Bogart, dealing with purchase of automobile for Hunter 1,400.00

Clark Gable, DS, Gone with the Wind contract, MGM stationery, Culver City, Aug. 3, 1939 ....6,500.00

Reagan, Ronald, ALS, 1 page 4to, Los Angeles, Dec. 9, 1949, to Leonard B. Elliott, mentioning Amos and Andy, mentions just returning from location..............................1,250.00

Swanson, Gloria, CS, printed instructions for Security First National Bank, sgd by her, but not filled in with info 150.00

Statesmen

Bancroft, George, ALS, 1 page 8vo, Newport, RI, July 1, 1884, to (John Jay) Knox, thanking him for a copy of his book, United States Notes… 125.00

Benjamin, Judah P., Confederate, free franked envelope, "J. P. Benjamin, U.S.S.," addressed to Lt. M. P. Small at Fort Monroe, Old Point Comfort, VA, circular black Washington City postmark, small tear 400.00

Clay, Henry, ALS, 1 page 4to, Washington, March 18, 1828, to John Scott in Missouri, re proposition before Congress....................450.00

Harrison, William Henry, manuscript document sgd, "Approved, 19th Decemr 1811, Willm Henry Harrison," 1 page 4to, sgd as Territorial Governor of Indiana and Superintendent of Indian Affairs 1,600.00

Kennedy, Edward M., US Senator, note sgd, in pencil, 1 page small 8vo, request for 7 theater tickets for Camelot movie................150.00

Rockefeller, John D., DS, 4 pgs folio, Dec. 18, 1896, title deed buying 17-1/2 acres of land in North Tarrytown, NY, bold signature .2,200.00

Vanderbilt, Cornelius, manuscript document sgd, 7 pgs, 4 legal folio sheets, orig fasteners, June 12, 1865, declaration of trust between Vanderbilt and John M. Tobin, of one part, and the Hudson River Rail Road Co. of the other part, establishing boundaries, etc., sgd by Vanderbilt, Tobin, and Edwin Quackenbush, some fold repairs 1,650.00

Western

Chaffee, Jerome, US Senator, ALS, dated 1880, Little Pittsburg Mining Co. letterhead..325.00

Diamond City, Montana Territory, ALS, 1866, describing killing and mining activity..300.00

Fort Halleck, Idaho Territory, ALS, Civil War era soldier 175.00

Leadville, CO, 1880, ALS, describing mining activity, hand-drawn illus of mine in mountains 190.00

New Mexico Fort, 1880, ALS 180.00

Parker, Issac, "Hanging Judge," book, from personal library, name stamped on cov with gold lettering, sgd on frontispiece...........300.00

AUTOMOBILES

History: Automobiles are generally classified into two categories, vehicles manufactured before World War II, and those manufactured after the conflict. The Antique Automobile Club of America, the world's oldest and largest automobile historical society, considers motor vehicles manufactured before 1930 officially "antique." The Contemporary Historical Vehicle Society, however, accepts cars and trucks that are twenty-five years old. There are scores of clubs dedicated to specific marques, like the Willys/Kaiser/AMC Jeep Club, and the Edsel Owners Club. Some states, such as Pennsylvania, have devised a dual registration system for older cars—antique and classic. Models from the 1960s and 1970s, especially convertibles and limited-production vehicles (under 10,000 produced), fall into their "classic" designation if they are not used as daily transportation. Many states have also allowed collectible vehicles to sport "year of issue" license plates, thus allowing the owner of a 1964 1/2 Mustang to legally use a 1964 license plate from his or her home state. Many older cars, especially original and unrestored models, are worth well more than $20,000. Restoration costs have skyrocketed, making it advisable to purchase a complete, running and original vehicle or one that has been completely restored rather than a car or truck needing thousands of dollars invested for mechanical, body and paint work.

Prices of high-powered 1964-1972 "muscle cars" will continue to escalate, while the value of pre-war cars will remain steady for all but unique custom-built roadsters and limousines. There is renewed interest in the original Volkswagen Beetle since the introduction of the updated '90s' version. Look for prices of these economical little cars to climb as well. The prices of old pickup trucks will continue to climb as vintage trucks remain popular with consumers for their style and usefulness. Auctions, more than any other source, determine the value of antique and classic automobiles. Values have remained steady for some years, but the combination of increased demand and fewer available vehicles is sure to drive prices up.

References: Dennis A. Adler, *Corvettes*, Krause Publications, 1996; John Chevedden & Ron Kowalke, *Standard Catalog of Oldsmobile, 1897-1997*, Krause Publications, 1997; James M. Flammang, *Standard Catalog of American Cars, 1976-1999*, 3rd ed., Krause Publications, 1999; ——, *Standard Catalog of Imported Cars, 1946-1990*, Krause Publications, 1992; ——, *Volkswagen Beetles, Buses and Beyond*, Krause Publications, 1996; Patrick R. Foster, *American Motors, The Last Independent*, Krause Publications, 1993; *The Metropolitan Story*, Krause Publications, 1996; Gordon Gardner and Alistair Morris, *Automobilia, 20th Century International Reference with Price Guide*, 3rd ed., Antique Collectors' Club, 1999; Robert Genat, *The American Car Dealership*, MBI Publishing, 1999; John Gunnell, *American Work Trucks*, Krause Publications, 1994; ——, *Marques of America*, Krause Publications, 1994; —— (ed.), *100 Years of American Cars*, Krause

Publications, 1993; ——, Standard Catalog of American Light Duty Trucks, 1896-1986, 2nd ed., Krause Publications, 1993; ——, *Standard Catalog of Chevrolet Trucks, Pickups & Other Light Duty Trucks, 1918-1995*, Krause Publications, 1995; Beverly Kimes and Henry Austin Clark, Jr., *Standard Catalog of American Cars, 1805–1942*, 3rd ed., Krause Publications, 1996; Ron Kowalke, *Old Car Wrecks*, Krause Publications, 1997; ——, *Standard Guide to American Cars, 1946-1975*, 3rd ed., Krause Publications, 1997; ——, *Standard Guide to American Muscle Cars, 1949-1995*, 2nd ed., Krause Publications, 1996; Jim Lenzke and Ken Buttolph, *Standard Guide to Cars & Prices*, 12th ed., Krause Publications, 1999; Albert Mroz, *The Illustrated Encyclopedia of American Trucks & Commercial Vehicles*, Krause Publications, 1996; Robert Murfin (ed.), *Miller's Collectors Cars Price Guide*, Reed International Books (distributed by Antique Collectors' Club), 1996; Gerald Perschbacher, *Wheels in Motion*, Krause Publications, 1996; Edwin J. Sanow, *Chevrolet Police Cars*, Krause Publications, 1997; Ed Lindley Peterson, *First to the Flames*, Krause Publications, 1999; Donald F. Wood and Wayne Sorensen, *Big City Fire Trucks, 1951-1997*, Krause Publications, Volume I, 1996, Volume II, 1997; Peter Winnewisser, *The Legendary Model A Ford*, Krause Publications, 1999. Krause Publications' Standard Catalog series includes special marque volumes, including *Standard Catalog of Cadillac, 1903-1990; Standard Catalog of Chrysler, 1925-1990; Standard Catalog of Pontiac, 1926-1995; Standard Catalog of Ford, 1903-1990; Standard Catalog of Chevrolet, 1912-1990; Standard Catalog of American Motors, 1902-1987; Standard Catalog of Oldsmobile, 1897-1997; Standard Catalog of Buick, 1903-1990*.

Periodicals: *Automobile Quarterly*, 15040 Kutztown Rd., P.O. Box 348, Kutztown, PA 19530; *Cars & Parts*, P.O. Box 482, Sydney, OH 45365; *Classic Car Source*, http://www.classicar.com; *Hemmings Motor News*, P.O. Box 256, Bennington, VT 05201; *Old Cars Price Guide*, 700 E. State St., Iola, WI 54990; *Old Cars Weekly, News & Marketplace*, 700 E. State St., Iola, WI 54990.

Collectors' Clubs: Antique Automobile Club of America, 501 West Governor Rd., P.O. Box 417, Hershey, PA 17033, http://www.aaca.org; Contemporary Historical Vehicle Association, P.O. Box 98, Tecumseh, KS 66542; Horseless Carriage Club of America, 128 S. Cypress St., Orange, CA 92866, http://www.horseless.com; Milestone Car Society, P.O. Box 24612, Indianapolis, IN 46224; Veteran Motor Car Club of America, P.O. Box 360788, Strongsville, OH 44136; Willys/Kaiser/AMC Jeep Club, 1511 19th Ave. W., Bradenton, FL 34205.

Museum: AACA Library and Research Center, Hershey PA.

Advisors: Jim and Nancy Schaut.

Notes: The prices indicated are for cars in running condition, with either a high proportion of original parts or somewhere between 60 and 80 percent restoration. Prices can vary by as much as 50 percent in either direction for lesser vehicles.

AMC
   1960 Rambler Station Wagon 5,500.00
   1968 AMX Fastback coupe 8,500.00
Amphicar, 1962 conv 19,500.00
Auburn
   1929 Auburn boattail speedster 58,000.00

Chevrolet Cameo Pickup Trick, 1957, $18,000. Photo courtesy of Jim and Nancy Schaut.

   1935, Model 6-653, 4d sedan, 6cyl 23,000.00
Bricklin, 1975, Model SV-1, gullwing coupe 12,500.00
Buick
   1911 Model 38 Roadster, conv, 4cyl 26,500.00
   1941 Roadmaster, 4dr sedan, 8cyl 17,500.00
   1986 Regal, Grand National 10,500.00
Cadillac
   1931 Model 370, Cabriolet, V-12 .... 147,000.00
   1957 Eldorado Barritz Conv, V8 .... 28,000.00
Checker, 1963, Aerobus 6,500.00
Chevrolet
   1932 Model AE, 2dr sedan, 6cyl 12,000.00
   1953 Bel Air Conv 25,000.00
   1955 Cameo Pickup Truck 19,500.00
   1964 Chevelle Super Sport, coupe 15,000.00
   1967 Corvette Stingray Coupe 32,000.00
   1969 Camaro Convertible 18,000.00
Chrysler
   1932 Imperial Sedan, 6cyl 18,000.00
   1956 New Yorker, Hemi engine, 2dr hardtop 15,000.00
   1970 300, 2dr. "Hurst" edition 9,500.00
Cord, 1931 4dr. convertible sedan, celebrity owned 225,000.00
Crosley, 1950 "Hot Shot" Roadster 8,900.00
Dodge
   1915, 2dr roadster 14,500.00
   1932 2dr Rally Sport conv 25,000.00
   1948 Power Wagon 9500.00
   1957 "Sweptline" Pickup, 101 made 14,000.00
   1970 Challenger T/A 25,000.00
Essex, 1929 Challenger Series, 4dr Town Sedan 9,500.00
Edsel, 1958 Ranger 2dr HT 12,000.00
Ferrari Testarosa coupe, 1985 .... 52,000.00
Ford
   1924 Model T coupe 8,500.00
   1931 Model A rds 18,500.00
   1934 5W coupe 22,000.00
   1956 F-100 pickup 7,500.00
   1959 Thunderbird 2dr HT 19,500.00
   1970 Mustang Boss 302 .... 30,000.00
Henry J, 1953, Allstate 8,500.00
Hudson
   1937 Terraplane pickup, 1 of 5 known 49,000.00
   1951 Hudson Hornet 18,000.00
Hummer, 1985, government sale, served in Desert Storm 21,500.00
International Scout, 4x4, 1966 .... 6,500.00
Jaguar, 1964 XKE, roadster 52,000.00
Jeep, 1966 Wagoneer, 4dr, 4x4 .... 8,500.00
Julian, 1922 Model 60 coupe, 6cyl 9,500.00
Kaiser
   1953 Manhattan, 4dr sedan 12,000.00

1954 Kaiser Darrin, 2dr, 1 of 435	50,000.00
Lambert, 1909, roadster, 6cyl	12,500.00
Lamborghini, 1975, P200	90,000.00
La Salle, 1928 2dr business coupe	32,000.00
Lincoln	
1935 Dietrich conv. Coupe, V-12	38,000.00
1957 Continental Mark II, 2dr HT	32,000.00
1973 Lincoln Cont. Mark IV, 10,000 miles	6,000.00
Mercedes-Benz, 1964 300Se Coupe	25,000.00
Mercury	
1940 convertible, 8 cyl	25,000.00
1966 Comet Cyclone GT	12,000.00
1969 Cougar XR-7 HT	7,500.00
Nash	
Ambassador, 1954, 2dr HT	4,500.00
Metropolitan, 1956, conv	8,500.00
Oakland, 1930 sedan	7,500.00
Oldsmobile	
1901 curved dash, 1cyl	34,000.00
1934 Business coupe	11,000.00
1967 Toronado	9,500.00
1970 Vista Cruiser Station Wagon	6,500.00
Packard	
1930 Model 745 Deluxe Eight, limo	72,000.00
1946 Clipper, sedan	12,000.00
Plymouth	
1942 Model P14S, 2dr. sedan, 6cyl	6,500.00
1959 Sport Fury convertible	24,000.00
1970 Barracuda, 1 of 1,554	11,000.00
Pontiac	
1934 2dr sedan	9,500.00
1955 Star Chief custom Safari	19,500.00
1966 2+2 convertible	13,500.00
1970 GTO 2dr HT	15,000.00
Porsche, 1961, 356B, Rds	35,000.00
Rolls Royce, 1951 Silver Wraith	49,000.00
Studebaker	
1932 Rockne, 2 passenger coupe	12,500.00
1962 Gran Turismo Hawk	12,750.00
1962 Lark	4,500.00
1963 Avanti coupe	17,000.00
Toyota, 1967 2000GT	75,000.00
Triumph, 1956 TR-3, rds	11,000.00
Volkswagen	
1949 sedan	10,500.00
1974 Super Beetle	6,500.00
Willys-Knight, 1928 Model 70, roadster	22,000.00
Willys, 1954, Eagle	8,500.00

AUTOMOBILIA

History: Automobilia is a wide-ranging category that covers just about anything concerning automobiles and trucks from fine art costing thousands of dollars to new diecast toys costing less than a dollar. Car parts are not usually considered automobilia, although there are a few exceptions like a beautiful glass radiator ornaments by Lalique or an upholstered sofa made from the tail fins of a 1959 Cadillac.

Advertising from dealers and manufacturers comprise a major part of most automobilia collections. Signs, salesman's jewelry and desk ornaments, and metal or plastic promotional model cars are hot sellers. Collectible memorabilia is not restricted to antique automobiles and it is not necessary to actually own an antique car to enjoy automobile, bus, truck and motorcycle advertising. Modern automobilists often collect advertising brochures or diecast models of their daily driver, be it Jeep Grand Cherokee or Toyota truck.

The most popular automobilia reflects the most popular collector cars. Right now, muscle cars from the late 1960s are hot and the market for Mustang, Pontiac GTO, Oldsmobile 4-4-2 and Chevrolet Corvette and Super Sport memorabilia remains strong. Most material changes hands at automobile swap meets, specialty auctions like Krause and Internet auction venues held throughout the year.

References: Mark Anderton, *Encyclopedia of Petroliana, Identification and Price Guide*, Krause Publications, 1999; Mark Allen Baker, *Auto Racing Memorabilia and Price Guide*, Krause Publications, 1996; Scott Benjamin and Wayne Henderson, *Gas Pump Globes*, Motorbooks International, 1993; Mike Bruner, *Gasoline Treasures*, Schiffer Publishing, 1996; Bob and Chuck Crisler, *License Plates of the United States*, Interstate Directory Publishing Co. (420 Jericho Tpk., Jericho, NY 11753), 1997; Leila Dunbar, *Automobilia*, Schiffer Publishing, 1998;—, *Motorcycle Collectibles*, Schiffer Publishing, 1996; James K. Fox, *License Plates of the United States*, A Pictorial History 1903 to the Present, Interstate Directory Publishing Co., 1996; John A. Gunnel, *Car Memorabilia Price Guide*, Krause Publications, 1995; Ron Kowalke and Ken Buttolph, *Car Memorabilia Price Guide*, 2nd ed., Krause Publications, 1997; Rick Pease, *A Tour With Texaco*, Schiffer Publishing, 1997; Jim and Nancy Schaut, *American Automobilia*, Wallace-Homestead, 1994.

Periodicals: *Check the Oil*, 30 W. Olentangy St., Powell, OH 43065-9764; *Hemmings Motor News*, P.O. Box 256, Bennington, VT 05201; *Mobilia*, P.O. Box 575, Middlebury, VT 05753; *Old Cars Weekly*, Krause Publications, 700 E. State, Iola WI 54990; *Toy Cars & Vehicles*, Krause Publications, 700 E. State, Iola WI 54990; WOCCO, 36100 Chardon Rd., Willoughby, OH 44094.

Collectors' Clubs: Automobile License Plates Collectors Association, 226 Ridgeway Drive, Bridgeport, WV 26330; Automobile Objects D'Art Club, 252 N. 7th St., Allentown, PA 18102; Classic Gauge & Oiler Hounds, Rte 1, Box 9, Farview, SD 57027; Hubcap Collectors Club, P.O. Box 54, Buckley, MI 49620; International Petroliana Collectors Association, P.O. Box 937, Powell, OH 43065-9764;

Ashtray, '49 Nash, Hotter than a Depot Stove, ceramic, $75. Photo courtesy of Jim and Nancy Schaut.

National Indy 500 Collectors Club, 10505 N. Delaware, Indianapolis IN 46280; Spark Plug Collectors of America, 14018 NE 85th St., Elk River, MN 55330.

Advisors: Jim and Nancy Schaut.

Ashtray
    Figural pot bellied stove, orange and black ceramic, decal says "49 Nash, hotter than a depot stove" 75.00
    Tire, green depression glass insert, 1936 Texas exposition .. 125.00
Badge, attendant's hat,
    Sinclair Grease, celluloid, 3" d 350.00
    Texaco, 1930s era, with Scottie dogs 750.00
Badge, driver's hat, Trailways Bus Lines, enamel 225.00
Bank, shaggy dog, "Ford" on collar, marked "Florence Ceramics" .. 65.00
Blotter, Sunoco advertising, Disney's Goofy character, near mint 60.00
Box, Mobil oil "Gargoyle" logo, designed to hold lubrication charts 45.00
Bud Vase, Fostoria glass, hard-to-find mounting bracket, unusual
    pattern 150.00
Calendar, 1966 Texaco station, "girlie" type, unsigned 15.00
Can, motor oil
    D-A Speed Sport, racing oil, yellow tin with black & white checkered
    flags, near mint, full quart 50.00
    Duplex, 8oz. Tin, Outboard Motor Oil, Quaker State, near mint ... 60.00
    Ronson, Wayne Oil Company, Philadelphia, racing streamlined car,
    airplane and car, full quart 900.00
Clock
    Atlas Tires and Batteries, wall clock, 1950s 175.00
    Pontiac Service, glass front, dark blue painted rim 300.00
    Studebaker, 15" h, gold metal rim, red/blue emblem, electric .. 400.00
Compression Tester, Hasting's Piston Ring advertising on dial, orig
    metal storage box 45.00
Credit Card, Husky, 1961, fair to good condition 25.00
Decanter, figural race car, Lionstone, Al Unser's Johnny Lightning Special,
    1970 and 1972 Indianapolis 500 Winner 75.00
Display
    Champion Spark Plugs, 12" h, 19" w, 5 1/2" d, tin, yellow with black
    lettering 200.00
    Exide battery, 40" high, tin and metal, black with orange
    lettering 150.00
Display Cabinet
    Gates fan belts, hangers inside for various sizes, painted tin front,
    15" l, 30" w, 24"h 75.00
    Auto Lite Spark Plug, 18 1/2"h, 13" w, painted metal cabinet, glass
    front 125.00
    Schrader tire gauge cabinet, figural tire gauge, opens to reveal
    parts 350.00
Emblem, Wolverine, model made only a few years by Reo 50.00
Gas Pump Globe
    Mobilgas Special, red Pegasus logo 275.00
    Shell, figural white Shell 450.00
    Thorobred, horse head 2,800.00
Gas Pump Salt & Pepper set, plastic, decals crazed, Phillips 66 . 45.00
Grill Badge, Sports Car Club of America, black and red wire wheel
    logo, cloisonné, early 1960s era 50.00
Hood Ornament, 1955 Chevrolet, mint, unused 275.00
Key Fob
    1960 Oldsmobile, color print in clear Lucite............................ 10.00
    Esso Tiger logo, 1960s, engraved serial number for lost key
    return 10.00
Knife, Cadillac Crest, 958 Certified Mechanic, orig box 80.00
Light, red bubble light for roof, 6 volts, early 1950s emergency
    vehicle 225.00
Lighter, Zippo, 1953 Buick Suggestion Winner, Buick Crest engraved,

Pin, Certified Craftsman, 1947, Cadillac, 10K gold, $85. Photo courtesy of Jim and Nancy Schaut.

    mint and unused in orig box 125.00
Map
    1938 Standard Oil Map of Idaho 25.00
    1967 Texaco, map of Texas 5.00
Map Rack, gas station display, Conoco, "branding iron" logo 95.00
Motometer, Boyce, unpitted chrome, working condition 135.00
Nodder, Chrysler advertising, "Little Profit" 60.00
Paperweight
    1938 Pontiac, cast pot metal car on base, probably by Banthrico. 95.00
    Laughing Bear cast metal on base, advertising Bear Wheel Align-
    ment, 4" h 200.00
Pencil, mechanical, "floating" 1953 Cadillac in clear top, dealer adver-
    tising on side 45.00
Pin, "Chevrolet Corvette Owner," 10K, makers' mark on reverse . 300.00
Plate, Ford Rotunda logo, 10" d 125.00
Playing cards, AMC Pacer Wagon, still sealed, dealer
    giveaway 25.00
Service Pin
    Buick, 25 years, screwback,10K gold, 1930s logo 50.00
    Lincoln-Mercury Registered Mechanic, 10K gold filled 25.00
    Shell Oil 15 year tiebar, 10K gold, dated 1944 .... 75.00
Sign
    Oilzum, 10" by 15 1/2", double sided, few chips 450.00
    Reo Sales & Service, 18" by 24" 1,000.00
    Triple X Trucking, Phoenix, Arizona, porcelain over steel 250.00
Thermometer
    Buick Motor Cars, 27" h, porcelain, blue, c1918 .... 300.00
    Texaco, Plastic Pole Thermometer, 6" h 75.00
Tin
    American Motors, 1 quart all season coolant, no rust 20.00
    Cadillac, Blue Coral Wax, no rust, light scratches 25.00
    Mopar, polishing cloth, red, yellow, blue tin, 1950s Chrysler Corp.
    logo, excellent condition 35.00
Tie Bar, replica of 1950s Ford truck grill 60.00
Tire Patch Repair Kit, Belnord/Cornell Tires, (Pep Boys), tin, orig
    contents 25.00
Tissue Dispenser, chrome, Buick logo affixed, mounts under dash and
    swivels out for access, mint, orig box 40.00
Watch Fob
    "Good Roads," celluloid logo affixed to metal fob 75.00
    Thomas Flyer, cloisonné, reverse unmarked 250.00
Weathervane, 27" by 32", Mobil service station, double sided, porce-
    lain, flying red horse, ... 1,500.00

BACCARAT GLASS

History: The Sainte-Anne glassworks at Baccarat in Voges, France, was founded in 1764 and produced utilitarian soda glass. In 1816, Aime-Gabriel d'Artiques purchased the glassworks, and a Royal Warrant was issued in 1817 for the opening of Verrerie de Vonâoche éa Baccarat. The firm concentrated on lead-crystal glass products. In 1824, a limited company was created.

From 1823 to 1857, Baccarat and Saint-Louis glassworks had a commercial agreement and used the same outlets. No merger occurred. Baccarat began the production of paperweights in 1846. In the late 19th century, the firm achieved an international reputation for cut glass table services, chandeliers, display vases, centerpieces, and sculptures. Products eventually included all forms of glassware. The firm still is active today.

Reference: Jean-Louis Curtis, Baccarat, Harry N. Abrams, 1992; Paul Jokelson and Dena Tarshis, Baccarat Paperweights and Related Glass, Paperweight Press, 1990.

Additional Listings: Paperweights.

Box, cov, 2-3/4" d, 2-1/4" h, white airplane design on sides, etched mark 125.00
Candelabrum, 24-1/2" h, Alfante, colorless and frosted, two candle branches issuing from removable standard, figure of cherub supporting knopped stem, circular foot with frosted glass lobed details, was pans suspending beads and prismatic drops, conforming lobed candlecups 475.00
Centerpiece, 20-1/4" h, crystal bowl with shaped rim, cut details, ormolu stand cast with berried laurel, feet cast to simulate branches, open handles, ormolu stamped, late 19th/early 20th C 400.00
Chandelier, 42" h, 29" w, 12 scrolling candle arm, foliate crown surmounting figures, prisms 12,500.00
Cologne Bottle, 7" h, colorless, frosted rosette ground, gold floral swags and bows, cut faceted stopper, pr 345.00
Decanter, 11-1/4" h, matching stopper 150.00
Ice Bucket, 6-1/2" h, multi-sectioned body, two reeded bands, swing handle, silvered metal mounts, ball finial 200.00
Jar, cov, 7" d, cameo cut, gilt metal mounts, imp mark 350.00

Fairy lamp, maroon shading to clear, sgd, 3-5/8" h, $225.

Pitcher, 9-1/4" h, Rose Tiente, Helical Twist pattern 300.00
Sculpture, 14-1/4" l, 5" h, trout, naturalistic form, colorless glass, frosted and polished details, conforming base, chips 525.00
Toothpick Holder, 2-1/2" h, Rose Tiente 115.00
Vase
    6" h, colorless, swollen rectilinear vessel, dec with band of engraved water birds in stream, flowers on shore, pattern of raised curvilinear stripes 290.00
    12" h, flared cylinder, enameled lavender, rust, and white iris, gilded foliage, frosted and textured surface, base mkd "Les Vaporisateurs Paris Baccarat," wear to gilding at rim 350.00
Wine Decanter, 10" h, 5" d, Rose Tiente, Zipper pattern, matching stopper 225.00

BANKS, MECHANICAL

History: Banks which display some form of action while accepting a coin are considered mechanical banks. Mechanical banks date back to ancient Greece and Rome, but the majority of collectors are interested in those made between 1867 and 1928 in Germany, England, and the United States. Recently, there has been an upsurge of interest in later types, some of which date into the 1970s.

Initial research suggested that approximately 250 to 300 different or variant designs of banks were made in the early period. Today that number has been revised to 2,000-3,000 types and varieties. The field remains ripe for discovery and research.

More than 80 percent of all cast-iron mechanical banks produced between 1869 and 1928 were made by J. E. Stevens Co., Cromwell, Connecticut. Tin banks are usually of German origin.

References: Collectors Encyclopedia of Toys and Banks, L-W Book Sales, 1986, 1993 value update; Al Davidson, Penny Lane, A History of Antique Mechanical Toy Banks, Long's Americana, 1987; Don Duer, A Penny Saved: Still and Mechanical Banks, Schiffer Publishing, 1993; Bill Norman, The Bank Book: The Encyclopedia of Mechanical Bank Collecting, Collectors' Showcase, 1984.

Collectors' Club: Mechanical Bank Collectors of America, P.O. Box 128, Allegan, MI 49010.

Reproduction Alert: Reproductions, fakes, and forgeries exist for many banks. Forgeries of some mechanical banks were made as early as 1937, so age alone is not a guarantee of authenticity. In the following price listing, two asterisks indicate banks for which serious forgeries exist, and one asterisk indicates banks for which casual reproductions have been made.

Notes: While rarity is a factor in value, appeal of design, action, quality of manufacture, country of origin, and history of collector interest also are important. Radical price fluctuations may occur when there is an imbalance in these factors. Rare banks may sell for a few hundred dollars while one of more common design with greater appeal will sell in the thousands.

The values in the list below accurately represent the selling prices of mechanical banks in the specialized collectors' market. As some banks are hard to find, and the market is quite volatile both up and down in price structure, consultation of a competent specialist in mechanical banks, with up to the moment information, is advised prior to selling any mechanical bank.

The prices listed are for original old mechanical banks with no repairs, in sound operating condition, and with a majority of the original paint intact.

Advisor: James S. Maxwell, Jr.

Note: Prices quoted are for 100 percent original examples, no repairs, no repaint, and have at least 90 percent bright original paint. An * indicates casual reproductions; † denotes examples where casual reproductions and serious fakes exist.

†Acrobat...1,500.00
†Afghanistan...775.00
African Bank, black bust, back emb "African Bank"....................750.00
American Bank, sewing machine..850.00
*Artillery...1,800.00
Atlas, iron, steel, wood, paper.....................................750.00
Automatic Chocolate Vending, tin....................................750.00
Automatic Coin Savings, predicts future, tin.......................250.00
Automatic Fortune Bank, tin..3,700.00
Automatic Savings Bank, tin, soldier................................450.00
Automatic Savings Bank, tin, sailor.................................200.00
Automatic Surprise Money Box, wood.................................6,500.00
†Baby Elephant X-O'clock, lead and wood..........................1,700.00
*Bad Accident...3,200.00
Bambovila, black bust, back emb "Bambula".........................4,700.00
Bank Teller, man behind 3-sided fancy grillwork...................5,500.00
Bank of Education and Economy, must have orig paper reel.....2,800.00
Barking Dog, wood...500.00
Bear, tin...450.00
†Bear and Tree Stump...3,500.00
†Bear, slot in chest..400.00
†Bill E. Grin...500.00
†Billy Goat Bank..350.00
Bird In Cage, tin...250.00
†Bird on Roof...1,245.00
†Bismark Bank..18,500.00
Bonzo, tin..350.00
Book-Keepers Magic Bank, tin......................................22,000.00

Bow-ery Bank, iron, paper, wood...................................2,500.00
Bowing Man in Cupola..3,200.00
†Bowling Alley..5,500.00
†Boy Robbing Birds Nest...1,750.00
*Boy Scout Camp...2,500.00
†Boy and bull dog...8,500.00
†Boy on trapeze...6,000.00
†Boys stealing watermelons..1,350.00
Bread Winners...2,700.00
British Clown, tin...12,000.00
†Bucking Mule...4,500.00
*Bull Dog, place coin on nose.....................................3,700.00
†Bull and Bear...75,000.00
Bull Dog Savings, clockwork.......................................1,100.00
†Bull Dog, standing...1,500.00
Bureau, wood, Serrill patent......................................5,500.00
Bureau, Lewando's, wood..22,000.00
Bureau, wood, John R. Jennings Patent.............................7,500.00
Burnett Postman, tin man with tray................................3,500.00
†Butting Buffalo..850.00
†Butting Goat...2,700.00
†Butting Ram..375.00
*Cabin, black man flips...1,200.00
Caller Vending, tin...3,500.00
†Calamity...4,500.00
†Called Out...2,800.00
Calumet, tin and cardboard, with Calumet kid........................200.00
Calumet, tin and cardboard, with sailor..........................14,000.00
Calumet, tin and Cardboard, with soldier.........................18,000.00
†Camera...1,100.00
*Cat and Mouse..1,200.00
†Cat and Mouse, giant cat standing on top........................40,000.00
Chandlers...2,000.00
Chandlers with clock..350.00
*Chief Big Moon...1,800.00
Child's Bank, wood..850.00
Chinaman in Boat, lead..3,500.00
Chinaman with queue, tin..400.00
Chocolate Menier, tin...1,750.00
†Chrysler Pig...800.00
Cigarette Vending, tin..700.00
Cigarette Vending, lead...2,000.00
Circus, clown on cart in circular ring............................2,000.00
†Circus, ticket collector...350.00
Clever Dick, tin..200.00
Clown Bust, iron..2,500.00
Clown, Chein, tin..65.00
†Clown on Bar, tin and iron.......................................2,200.00
*Clown on Globe...5,500.00
Clown and Dog, tin..250.00
Clown with arched top, tin..250.00
Clown with black face, tin..2,000.00
Clown with white face, tin..125.00
Clown with white face, round, tin.................................3,700.00
Cockatoo Pelican, tin...200.00
Coin Registering, many variants...................................1,000.00
Columbian Magic Savings, iron.......................................200.00
Columbian magic Savings, wood and Paper..........................15,000.00
Confectionery...2,200.00
Coolie Bust, lead...400.00
Cowboy with tray, tin...350.00
†Creedmoor..1,275.00
Crescent Cash Register..4,200.00
Cross Legged Minstrel, tin..350.00
Crowing Rooster, circular base, tin...............................6,500.00
Cupid at Piano, pot metal, musical..................................750.00
†Cupola...1,050.00
Dapper Dan, tin...2,500.00
*Darktown Battery...3,500.00
Darky Bust, tin, tiny size..200.00

Banks, mechanical Chief Big Moon, 1899, $1,475. Photo courtesy of Auction Team Breker.

Baby elephant, x' o' clock, unlocks at x' o' clock, lead and wood, side with elephant feeding monkey to alligator, emb, "If I Had Only Some Money in the Bank," patented Nov. 16, 1880, Manuf by Charles A. Bailey, Cobalt, CT, $1,700.

†Darky Fisherman, lead..8,500.00
†Darky Watermelon, man kicks football at watermelon 7,500.00
†Dentist...3,700.00
Dinah, iron..500.00
Dinah, aluminum...250.00
Ding Dong Bell, tin, windup...3,500.00
Dog on turntable..950.00
†Dog with tray..650.00
Domed vending, tin..4,000.00
Driver's Service Vending, tin.......................................2,800.00
Droste Chocolate..1,500.00
*Eagle and Eaglettes..1,200.00
Electric Safe, steel..2,200.00
*Elephant and Three Clowns..1,850.00
*Elephant, locked howdah...450.00
Elephant, made in Canada...10,500.00
Elephant, man pops out, wood, cloth, iron............................550.00
†Elephant, no stars...3,700.00
*Elephant, pull tail..1,050.00
Elephant, three stars...1,200.00
*Elephant, trunk swings, large.......................................350.00
*Elephant, trunk swings, small.......................................250.00
Elephant, trunk swings, raised coin slot............................1,500.00
†Elephant with tusks, on wheels......................................500.00
Empire Cinema, tin...775.00
English Bulldog, tin...450.00
Feed the Goose, pot metal..800.00
5 cents Adding...250.00
Flip the Frog, tin...450.00
Football, English football..1,800.00
Fortune Savings, tin, horse race....................................1,050.00
Fortune Teller, Savings, safe,......................................2,200.00
†Fowler...2,200.00
†Freedman's Bank, wood, lead, brass, tin, paper, etc............75,000.00
Frog on arched track, tin...1,200.00
Frog on rock..1,400.00
*Frog on round base..950.00
†Frogs, two frogs...1,200.00
Fun Producing Savings, tin..3,200.00
*Gem, dog with blgd...2,800.00
German Sportsman, lead and iron.....................................1,500.00
German Vending, tin...1,500.00
†Germania Exchange, iron, lead, tin.................................2,000.00

†Giant in Tower...1,200.00
†Giant, standing by rock..2,200.00
Girl Feeding Geese, tin, paper, lead...............................22,000.00
†Girl Skipping Rope,...16,000.00
†Girl in Victorian chair..2,000.00
Give Me A Penny, wood...8,000.00
Grenadier...1,875.00
Guessing, man's figure, lead, steel, iron...........................8,800.00
Guessing, woman's figure, iron......................................2,200.00
Guessing, woman's figure, lead......................................1,400.00
Gwenda Money Box, tin...3,500.00
Hall's Excelsior, iron, wood...750.00
Hall's Liliput, no tray..400.00
Hall's Liliput, with tray..250.00
†Harlequin..7,500.00
Harold Lloyd, tin..450.00
Hartwig and Vogel, vending, tin.....................................1,500.00
Hen and Chick...1,650.00
Highwayman, tin..650.00
Hillman Coin Target...1,500.00
*Hindu, bust...750.00
†Hold the Fort, 2 varieties, each...................................1,050.00
Home, tin building...950.00
*Home, iron..400.00
Hoop-La...5,500.00
*Horse Race, 2 varieties, each......................................2,000.00
†Humpty Dumpty, bust of clown with name on back, iron 2,800.00
Humpty Dumpty, aluminum, English.....................................350.00
Huntley and Palmers, tin, vending...................................1,800.00
*I Always Did 'spise a Mule, black man on bench.....................1,050.00
*I Always Did 'spise a Mule, black man on mule......................1,550.00
Ideal Bureau, tin...3,700.00
*Indian and Bear..1,250.00
†Indian Chief, black man bust with Indian feathered headdress,
   aluminum..750.00
Indiana Paddlewheel Boat..1,050.00
†Initiating Bank, first degree......................................1,000.00
Initiating Bank, second degree......................................1,200.00
Japanese Ball Tosser, tin, wood, paper..............................1,500.00
Joe Socko Novelty Bank, tin..450.00
John Bull's Money Box...2,000.00
John R. Jennings Trick Drawer Money Box, wood.....................15,000.00
Jolly Joe Clown, tin..3,200.00
*Jolly Nigger, American..650.00
*Jolly Nigger, English...350.00
Jolly Nigger, lettering in Greek.....................................375.00
Jolly Nigger, lettering in Arabic...................................1,800.00
*Jolly Nigger, raises hat, lead.....................................1,500.00
*Jolly Nigger, raises hat, iron.....................................2,200.00
*Jolly Nigger, stationary ears.......................................250.00
*Jolly Nigger, stationary eyes.......................................450.00
*Jolly Nigger, with fez, aluminum....................................750.00
Jolly Sambo Bank..2,800.00
*Jonah and The Whale Bank, large rectangular base...................2,000.00
†Jonah and The Whale Bank, stands on 2 ornate legs with rectangular
   coin box at center..8,500.00
†Jumbo, elephant on wheels...500.00
Kick Inn Bank, wood...2,500.00
Kiltie...650.00
Lawrence Steinberg's Bureau Bank, wood.............................12,000.00
†Leap Frog..2,200.00
Lehmann Berlin Tower, tin..350.00
Lehmann, London Tower, tin...400.00
†Light of Asia...450.00
†Lighthouse Bank...500.00
Lion, tin..575.00
Lion Hunter...1,650.00
†Lion and Two Monkeys...1,850.00
*Little High Hat...1,500.00
Little Jocko, tin..650.00

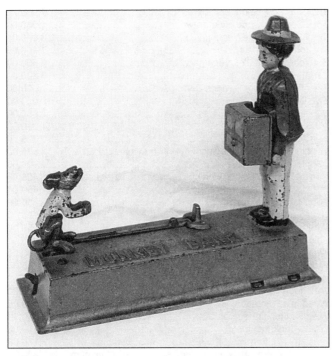

Monkey and Organ Grinder bank, (trick monkey bank), iron, made by Hubley Toy Co., Lancester, PA, c1906-30, $1,450.

*Little Joe Bank	950.00
Little Moe Bank	350.00
Lucky wheel Money Box, tin	4,200.00
*Magic Bank, iron house	650.00
Magic Bank, tin	300.00
Magic, safe, tin	450.00
†Magician	1,800.00
†Mama Katzenjammer	2,650.00
†Mammy and Child	2,000.00
*Mason	2,800.00
Memorial Money Box	400.00
*Merry-Go-Round, mechanical, coin activates	2,800.00
†Merry-Go-Round, semi-mechanical, spin by hand	850.00
Mickey Mouse, tin	2,350.00
Mikado Bank	7,500.00
†Milking Cow	3,600.00
Minstrel, tin	2,8800.00
Model Railroad Drink Dispenser, tin	15,000.00
Model Savings Bank, tin, cash register	4,200.00
*Monkey and Coconut	1,600.00
Monkey and Parrot, tin	1,400.00
†Monkey Bank	1,450.00
Monkey, chimpanzee in ornate circular bldg, iron	1,050.00
Monkey Face, tin with arched top	3,200.00
Monkey, pot metal, nods head	750.00
†Monkey, slot in stomach	375.00
Monkey, tin, tips hat	450.00
Monkey with Tray, tin	950.00
Mosque	450.00
Motor Bank, coin activates trolley	2,000.00
Mule Entering Barn	1,875.00
Music Bank, tin	375.00
Musical Church, wood	575.00
Musical Savings Bank, Regina	2,800.00
Musical Savings, tin	325.00
Musical Savings, velvet covered easel	450.00
Musical Savings, velvet covered frame	500.00
Musical Savings, wood house	950.00

National Bank	950.00
National, Your Savings, cash register	2,800.00
Nestle's Automatic Chocolate, cardboard, vending	2,800.00
*New Bank, lever at center	400.00
*New Bank, lever at left	300.00
†New Creedmoor Bank	320.00
Nodding Clown, pewter and brass	750.00
Nodding Dog, painted tin	375.00
†North Pole Bank	1,875.00
*Novelty Bank	1,450.00
Octagonal Fort Bank	1,600.00
Old Mother Hubbard, tin	750.00
*Organ Bank, boy and girl	950.00
*Organ Bank, cat and dog	750.00
*Organ Bank, medium, only monkey figure	450.00
*Organ Bank, tiny, only monkey figure	350.00
Organ Grinder and Dancing Bear	1,275.00
Owl, slot in book	275.00
Owl, slot in head	325.00
*Owl, turns head	400.00
*Paddy and the Pig	1,850.00
Panorama Bank	1,675.00
Pascal Chocolate Cigarettes, vending, tin	1,800.00
Patronize the Blind Man	1,200.00
Pay Phone Bank, iron	2,800.00
Pay Phone Bank, tin	850.00
†Peg-Leg Beggar	675.00
*Pelican, Arab head pops out	575.00
*Pelican, Mammy head pops out	525.00
*Pelican, man thumbs nose	500.00
*Pelican, rabbit pops out	450.00
†Perfection Registering, girl and dog at blackboard	1,850.00
Piano, musical	450.00
*Picture Gallery	2,650.00
Pig in High Chair	450.00
Pinball Vending, tin	2,200.00
Pistol Bank, iron	575.00
Pistol Bank, iron, Uncle Sam figure pops out	2,200.00
Pistol Bank, litho, tin	3,700.00
Pistol Bank, sheet steel	1,200.00
Policeman, tin	500.00
Popeye Knockout, tin	1,650.00
Post Office Savings, steel	2,000.00
†Preacher in the Pulpit	9,500.00
†Presto, iron building	950.00
Presto, mouse on roof, wood and paper	950.00
*Presto, penny changes optically to quarter	1,275.00
*Professor Pug Frog	4,200.00
Pump and Bucket	4,700.00
*Punch and Judy, iron	2,450.00
Punch and Judy, iron front, tin back	750.00
Punch and Judy, litho tin, circa 1910	475.00
Punch and Judy, litho tin, circa 1930	275.00
†Queen Victoria. bust, brass	2,800.00
†Queen Victoria, bust, iron	4,200.00
Rabbit in Cabbage	350.00
†Rabbit Standing, large	675.00
†Rabbit Standing, small	375.00
Reclining Chinaman with cards	2,100.00
Record Money Box, tin scales	6,700.00
†Red Riding Hood, iron	3,300.00
Red Riding Hood, tin, vending	1,500.00
†Rival Bank	2,650.00
Robot Bank, aluminum	650.00
Robot Bank, iron	1,050.00
Roller-Skating Bank	2,850.00
Rooster	2,000.00
Royal Trick Elephant, tin	5,500.00
Safe Deposit Bank, tin, elephant	1,650.00
Safety Locomotive, semi	1,850.00

Sailor Face, tin, pointed top 3,200.00
Sailor Money Box, wood 450.00
Saluting Sailor, tin 850.00
Sam Segal's Aim to Save, brass and wood 1,300.00
Sam Segal's Aim to Save, iron 1,800.00
*Santa Claus 1,650.00
Savo, circular, tin 650.00
Savo, rectangular, tin 575.00
†Schley Bottling Up Cevera 975.00
Schokolade Automat, tin, vending 1,700.00
School Teacher, tin and wood, American 1,200.00
School Teacher, tin, German 675.00
Scotchman, tin 1,875.00
Seek Him Frisk 3,200.00
Sentry Bank, tin 375.00
Sentry Bugler, tin 275.00
†Shoot That Hat Bank 2,700.00
†Shoot the Chute Bank 2,300.00
Signal Cabin, tin 1,875.00
†Smith X-ray Bank 1,275.00
Snake and Frog in Pond, tin 12,000.00
*Snap-It Bank 1,400.00
Snow White, tin and lead 875.00
*Speaking Dog 1,875.00
Spring Jawed Alligator, pot metal 250.00
Spring Jawed Bonzo, pot metal 250.00
Spring Jawed Bulldog, pot metal 225.00
Spring Jawed Cat, pot metal 275.00
Spring Jawed Chinaman, pot metal 1,400.00
Spring Jawed Donkey, pot metal 225.00
Spring Jawed Felix the Cat, pot metal 3,700.00
Spring Jawed Mickey Mouse, pot metal 12,500.00
Spring Jawed Monkey, pot metal 225.00
Spring Jawed Parrot, pot metal 250.00
Spring Jawed Penguin, pot metal 275.00
Springing Cat 4,200.00
†Squirrel and Tree Stump 675.00
Starkies Aeroplane, aluminum, cardboard 12,000.00
Starkies Aeroplane, aluminum, steel 16,000.00
Stollwerk Bros., vending, tin 1,050.00
Stollwerk Bros., 2 penny, vending, tin 1,400.00
Stollwerk Bros., Progressive Sampler, tin 550.00
Stollwerk Bros., Victoria, spar-automat, tin 950.00
Stollwerk Bros., large vending, tin 1,600.00
*Stump Speaker Bank 2,800.00
Sweet Thrift, tin, vending 575.00
Symphonium Musical Savings, wood 2,400.00
†Tabby 375.00
*Tammany Bank 375.00
Tank and Cannon, aluminum 2,000.00
Tank and Cannon, iron 2,800.00
†Target Bank 875.00
†Target In Vestibule 950.00
*Teddy and The Bear 1,650.00
Ten Cent Adding Bank 3,800.00
Thrifty Animal Bank, tin 850.00
Thrift Scotchman, wood, paper 4,500.00
Thrifty Tom's Jigger, tin 2,500.00
Tid-Bits Money Box, tin 350.00
Tiger, tin 450.00
Time Is Money 1,050.00
Time Lock Savings 575.00
Time Registering Bank 750.00
*Toad on Stump 750.00
Toilet Bank, tin 650.00
Tommy Bank 950.00
Treasure Chest Music Bank 250.00
*Trick Dog, 6 part base 2,300.00
*Trick Dog, solid base 850.00
*Trick Pony Bank 1,200.00

Trick Savings, wood, end drawer 1,050.00
Trick Savings, wood, side drawer 1,050.00
Tropical Chocolate Vending, tin 3,000.00
Try your Weight, tin, semi 950.00
Try Your Weight, tin, mechanical 2,600.00
†Turtle Bank 3,200.00
Twentieth Century Savings Bank 500.00
Two Ducks Bank, lead 9,000.00
U.S. Bank, Building 850.00
†U.S. and Spain 1,200.00
†Uncle Remus Bank 1,275.00
†Uncle Sam Bank, standing figure with satchel 1,875.00
†Uncle Sam, bust 400.00
†Uncle Tom, no lapels, with star 425.00
†Uncle Tom, lapels, with star 400.00
†Uncle Tom, no star 350.00
United States Bank, safe 550.00
Viennese soldier 1,050.00
Volunteer bank 950.00
Watch Bank, blank face, tin 200.00
Watch Bank, dime disappears, tin 275.00
Watch Bank, stamped face, tin 140.00
Watchdog Safe 650.00
Weeden's Plantation, tin, wood 850.00
Weight Lifter, tin 650.00
Whale Bank, pot metal 850.00
*William Tell, iron 2,175.00
William Tell, crossbow, Australian, sheet steel, aluminum 3,200.00
Wimbledon Bank 1,500.00
Winner Savings Bank, tin 1,050.00
Wireless Bank, tin, wood, iron 875.00
Woodpecker Bank, tin 875.00
World's Banker, tin 750.00
*World's Fair Bank 1,200.00
Zentral Sparkasse, steel 1,350.00
Zig Zag Bank, iron, tin, papier-mâché 4,200.00
*Zoo 1,500.00

BANKS, STILL

History: Banks with no mechanical action are known as still banks. The first still banks were made of wood or pottery or from gourds. Redware and stoneware banks, made by America's early potters, are prized possessions of today's collectors.

Still banks reached a golden age with the arrival of the cast-iron bank. Leading manufacturing companies include Arcade Mfg. Co., J. Chein & Co., Hubley, J. & E. Stevens, and A. C. Williams. The banks often were ornately painted to enhance their appeal. During the cast-iron era, banks and other businesses used the still bank as a form of advertising.

The tin lithograph bank, again frequently a tool for advertising, reach its zenith during the years 1930 to 1955. The tin bank was an important premium, whether a Pabst Blue Ribbon beer can bank or a Gerber's Orange Juice bank. Most tin advertising banks resembled the packaging of the product.

Almost every substance has been used to make a still bank—die-cast white metal, aluminum, brass, plastic, glass, etc. Many of the early glass candy containers also converted to a bank after the candy was eaten. Thousands of varieties of still banks were made, and hundreds of new varieties appear on the market each year.

References: *Collector's Encyclopedia of Toys and Banks*, L-W Book Sales, 1986, 1993 value update; Don Duer, *Penny*

Banks Around the World, Schiffer Publishing, 1997; Earnest Ida and Jane Pitman, *Dictionary of Still Banks*, Long's Americana, 1980; Beverly and Jim Mangus, *Collector's Guide to Banks*, Collector Books, 1998; Andy and Susan Moore, *Penny Bank Book, Collecting Still Banks*, Schiffer Publishing, 1984, 1997 value update; Tom and Loretta Stoddard, *Ceramic Coin Banks*, Collector Books, 1997.

Periodicals: *Glass Bank Collector*, P.O. Box 155, Poland, NY 13431; *Heuser's Quarterly Collectible Diecast Newsletter*, P.O. Box 300, West Winfield, NY 13491.

Collectors' Club: Still Bank Collectors Club of America, 4175 Millersville Rd., Indianapolis, IN 46205.

Museum: Margaret Woodbury Strong Museum, Rochester, NY.

Aluminum, Lindy, 6-1/2" h, aluminum and painted gold metal, Grannis & Tolton, US, bust type, wearing hat and goggles, c1928........ 125.00
Brass, beehive, 4" h, 4-1/2" d, EOS, well detailed, base mkd "A. B. Dalames Bank"... 385.00
Cast Iron
Auto, 3-1/2 x 6-3/4" l, A. C. Williams, painted green, slot on door, gold painted spoked wheels, three passengers 1,430.00
Bird, 4-7/8" h, old gold repaint, tip of tail broken, M664 .... 55.00
Boston Bull Terrier, 5-1/4 x 5-3/4", Vindex, painted brown and white 415.00
Bugs Bunny at Barrel, Metal Moss Mfg Co., 5-3/4" w 150.00
Buffalo, 3" h, old gold repaint, M560 .... 75.00
Building
   2-1/2" h, 2" w, John Brown's Fort, slotted sides.................. 1,100.00
   2-3/4 to 4-3/4" h, Kyser & Rex, Town Hall and Log Cabin, chimney on left side, "Town Hall Bank" painted yellow, c1882 .... 260.00
   3-1/4" h, Kenton, State, japanned, gold and bronze highlights ... 180.00
   3-3/4" h, Grey Iron Ceiling Co., bungalow, porch, painted..... 470.00
Cab, Arcade
   7-3/4" l, Yellow Cab, painted orange and black, stenciling on doors, seated driver, rubber tires, painted metal wheels, coin slot in roof... 935.00
   8" l, Yellow Cab, painted orange and black, iron wheels, rubber tires, stenciled "Yellow Cab Main 4321" on door, spare tire missing... 3,575.00
   8-1/4" l, Green Cab, painted green, white, and black, coin slot in front hood, head lamps, seated figure, disc wheels, new license plate, spare tire attached to rear 1,870.00
Cat, 4-1/4" h, traces of dark paint, M366 .... 125.00
Circus Dog, old repaint, M359 .... 75.00
Coronation, 6-5/8" h, Syndeham & McOustra, England, ornately detained, emb busts in center, England, c1911........................ 200.00
Dresser, 6-3/4" h, very detailed casting, columned panel, simulated wood carving, key lock opens center drawer, painted brown and black .990.00
Duck, 4-3/4" h, Hubley, colorfully painted, outstretched wings, slot on back... 165.00
Dutch Boy and Girl, 5-1/4" and 5-1/8" h, Hubley, colorfully painted, boy on barrel, girl holding flowers, c1930, price for pr 260.00
Egyptian Tomb, 6-1/4" x 5-1/4", green finish, pharaoh's tomb entrance, hieroglyphics on front panel 275.00
Elk, 9-1/2" h, painted gold, full antlers.................................... 154.00
Globe Savings Fund, 7-1/4" h, worn polychrome, incomplete, gilt cover on window missing, M1199 .... 690.00
Hall Clock, 5-3/4" h, swinging pendulum visible through panel... 110.00
Horse, horseshoe, 3-1/4" h, wire grill, old gold paint.................... 85.00
Husky, 5" h, Grey Iron Casting Co., painted brown, black eyes, yellow box, repaired 365.00
Jewel Chest, 6-1/8 x 4-5/8", ornate casting, ftd bank, brass combination lock on front, top lifts for coin retrieval, crack at corner 90.00
Kodak, 4-1/4 x 5" w, J & E Stevens, nickeled, highly detailed casting, intricate pattern, emb "Kodak Bank" on front opening panel, c1905...225.00
Lion, 5-1/4" h, traces of gold paint, screw replaced, M762 .... 95.00

Mailbox, 5-1/2" h, Hubley, painted green, emb "Air Mail," with eagle, standing type... 220.00
Maine, 4-1/2" l, worn silver paint, some rust, replaced screw, M1440 .... 200.00
Mammy, 5-1/4" h, Hubley, hands on hips, colorfully painted....... 300.00
Merry-Go-Round, 4-5/8 x 4-3/8", nickeled, Grey Iron Casting Co., ornate, round merry-go-round mounted on pedestal for spinning, replaced shaft... 105.00
North Pole, 4-1/4" h, nickeled, Grey Iron Casting Co., depicts wooden pole with handle, emb lettering 415.00
Owl, 4-1/4" h, polychrome, minor wear, M597 .... 200.00
People Savings Bank,10-3/4" h, brown gabled roof, cream walls, caption "Property of…Grand Rapids, Mich." 1,100.00
Pig, 2-1/2" h, 5-1/4" l, Hubley, laughing, painted brown, trap on bottom 120.00
Professor Pug Frog, 3-1/4" h, A.C. Williams, painted gold, blue jacket, new twist pin.. 195.00
Radio, Kenton
   2-7/8" h, 4-1/2" w, painted red, nickeled combination on front panel, three dial style, orig Kenton tag 440.00
   4-1/2" h, metal sides and back, painted green, nickeled front panel in Art Deco style.. 435.00
Rearing Horse, 7-1/2" h, worn black and silver paint, M520 .... 95.00
Reindeer, 9-1/8" h, 5-1/4" l, A. C. Williams, painted gold, full rack of antlers, replaced screw 55.00
Rumplestiltskin, 6" h, painted gold, long red hat, base and feet, mkd "Do You Know Me," c1910 .... 210.00
Safe
   Egyptian, gilt motifs on black ground, 4-1/2" h 520.00
   Floral, J. & E. Stevens, colored floral dec, gold ground, 4-3/4" h345.00
   Key lock, J. & E. Stevens 85.00
Saint Bernard
   3-3/4" h, with pack, old black and gold paint, M439 .... 80.00
   8" l, worn black, gold, and silver paint, M437 .... 55.00
Seal 3-1/2 x 4-1/4", Arcade, painted japanned, basking on rock platform 75.00
Sharecropper, 5-1/2" h, A. C. Williams, painted black, gold, and red, toes visible on one foot 240.00
Skyscraper, A. C. Williams, 4 corner towers, gilt finish, 5-3/4" h .. 90.00
Stag, 9" h, gold repaint, M737 .... 65.00
State Bank
   6-3/4" h, Kenton Grey Iron Casting Co., cupola and dormer windows 575.00
   8-3/4" h, japanning, gold and bronze paint, M1078............... 300.00
Steamboat, 7-1/2" l, Arcade, painted gold 190.00
Stove
   3-3/4 x 3-3/4", Roper, arcade, cast iron and sheet metal, painted white, burner cover lifts open... 1,045.00
   4-3/4" h, Gem, Abendroth Bros., traces of bronzing, back mkd "Gem Heaters Save Money"... 275.00
   5-1/2 x 4", gas, Berstein Co., NY, cast iron and sheet metal, metallic scale version of early stove, railed handle on top 150.00
   5-3/4" h, upright, enameled violet color, mkd "Tiger" on back, removable base plate 360.00
   6-7/8" h, parlor, nickeled finial and center bands, ornately cast, free standing 360.00
Tank, 9-1/2" l, 4" w, Ferrosteel, side mounted guns, rear spoke wheels, emb on sides, c1919... 385.00
US Mail
   4-3/4" h, Kenton, painted silver, red highlights on lettering, small combo trap on back panel 195.00
   5-1/8" h, Kenton, painted silver, gold painted emb eagle, red lettering large trap on back panel 180.00
   6-7/8" h, 4-3/8" w, D.B. Fish, painted silver, red emb lettering, nickeled combination lock on front panel, c1903 .... 130.00
World Time, 4-1/8 x 2-5/8", Arcade, paper time-tables of various cities around the world 315.00
Yellow Cab, 7-3/4" l, Arcade, painted yellow and black, slot on door, stenciled on doors 2,970.00

Shawnee Pottery, Winnie, combination bank and cookie jar, $325. Photo courtesy of Green Valley Auctions, Inc.

Chalk, Winston Churchill, 5-1/4" h, bust, painted green, back etched "Save for Victory," wood base 55.00

Glass, Charles Chaplin, 3-3/4" h, Geo Borgfeldt & Co., painted figure standing next to barrel slotted on lid, name emb on base 220.00

Lead

Boxer, 2-5/8" h, Germany, head, painted brown, black facial details, lock on collar, bent in back 130.00

Burro, 3-1/2" x 3-1/2", Japan, lock on saddle mkd "Plymouth, VT" .. 125.00

Ocean Liner, 2-3/4" x 7-5/8" l, bronze electroplated, three smoking stacks, hinged trap on deck, small hole 180.00

Pug, 2-3/4" h, Germany, painted, stenciled "Hershey Park" on side, lock on collar 300.00

Pottery

Cat, 3" h, head, white clay, green glaze 275.00

Dog, 2-1/2" h, head, white clay, dark green glaze, flake at coin slot. 110.00

Pig, Germany, two pigs on see-saw on top of money bag 120.00

Steel

Life Boat, 14" l, pressed, painted yellow and blue, boat length decal mkd "Contributions for Royal National Life Boat Institution," deck lifts for coin removal, over painted 360.00

Piano, 5-1/8" x 5-7/8", Lyon & Healy's, free standing, etched wording on cabinet panel 380.00

Postal Savings, 4-5/8" h, 5-3/8" w, copper finish, glass view front panel, paper registering strips, emb "U.S.Mail" on sides, top lifts to reveal four coin slots, patent 1902 .... 95.00

Tin Lithograph, Panama-Pacific Expo, Bliss Can Manuf Co., talc can shape, 4" h, 2-1/2"w, 1-1/4" d 150.00

White Metal

Amish Boy, seated on bale of straw, 4-3/4" x 3-3/8", US, painted in bright colors, key lock trap on bottom 55.00

Cat with Bow, 4-1/8" h, painted white, blue bow 155.00

Gorilla, colorfully painted in brown hues, seated position, trap on bottom 165.00

Pig, 4-3/8" h, painted white, decal mkd "West Point, N.Y." on belly 30.00

Rabbit, 4-1/2" h, seated, painted brown, painted eyes, trap on bottom, crack in ear 30.00

Santa, 5-7/8" l, colorfully painted, full figure of standing Santa, holding toy bag, book and box mkd "York National Trust Co." 165.00

BARBER BOTTLES

History: Barber bottles, colorful glass bottles found on shelves and counters in barber shops, held the liquids bar-

bers used daily. A specific liquid was kept in a specific bottle, which the barber knew by color, design, or lettering. The bulk liquids were kept in utilitarian containers under the counter or in a storage room.

Barber bottles are found in many types of glass—art glass with various decorations, pattern glass, and commercially prepared and labeled bottles.

References: *Barbershop Collectibles*, L-W Book Sales, 1996; Keith E. Estep, *Shaving Mug & Barber Bottle Book*, Schiffer Publishing, 1995; Richard Holiner, *Collecting Barber Bottles*, Collector Books, 1986; Ralph & Terry Kovel, *Kovels' Bottles Price List*, 11th ed., Three Rivers Press, 1999.

Museums: Atwater Kent History Museum, Philadelphia, PA; Barber Museum, Canal Winchester, OH; Lightner Museum, Saint Augustine, FL.

Note: Prices are for bottles without original stoppers unless otherwise noted.

Amber, Hobb's Hobnail 250.00

Amethyst, Mary Gregory type dec, white enameled child and flowers, 8" h 250.00

Cobalt Blue, cylindrical, bulbous body, long neck, white enamel, traces of gold dec, tooled mouth, pontil scar, 7-1/4" h 100.00

Emerald Green, cylindrical bell form, long neck, orange and white enameled floral dec, sheared mouth, pontil scar, some int. haze, 8-1/2" h 210.00

Latticino, cylindrical, bulbous, long neck, clear frosted glass, white, red, and pale green vertical stripes, tooled mouth, pontil scar, 8-1/4" h 200.00

Lime Green, satin glass, classical bird claw grasping ball, ground mouth, smooth base, 7" h, pr 100.00

Milk Glass, Witch Hazel, painted letters and flowers, 9" h 115.00

Opalescent

Coin Spot, blue 300.00

Seaweed, cranberry, bulbous 465.00

Spanish Lace, electric blue ground, sq, long neck, tooled mouth, smooth base, 7-7/8" h, pr 250.00

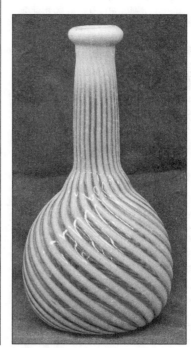

Blue, opalescent swirl, 6-7/8" h, $125.

Stars and Stripes, cranberry, pale blue, tooled mouth, smooth base, 7-1/4" h, pr 600.00
Sapphire Blue, enameled white and yellow daisies, green leaves, 8-5/8" h 125.00

BAROMETERS

History: A barometer is an instrument which measures atmospheric pressure, which, in turn, aids weather forecasting. Low pressure indicates the coming of rain, snow, or storm; high pressure signifies fair weather.

Most barometers use an evacuated and graduated glass tube, which contains a column of mercury. These are classified by the shape of the case. An aneroid barometer has no liquid and works by a needle connected to the top of a metal box in which a partial vacuum is maintained. The movement of the top moves the needle.

Reference: Nicholas Goodison, English Barometers, 1680-1860, Antique Collectors' Club, 1999.

Aneriode, circular, floral wreath dec, enamel dial mkd "I. Cassio & Co.," dore bronze, French 1,100.00
32" h, wall, giltwood and gilt composition, foliate cresting, octagonal barometer face, mounted with pair of associated two-light sconces, French, 19th C 2,760.00
33" d, wheel, carved oak, foliage and C-scrolls, English, late 19th C 230.00
34" l, stick, sgd E. Kendall, N. Lebanon, mahogany, etched steel face, mirrored well cov 550.00

Banjo, English, mahogany case, hygrometer, thermometer, barometer, balancing level, A & V Cattania of York, 38-1/2" l, $395.

37" l, lyre form, giltwood, crest with thermometer, painted dial in lower hexagonal section, borders modeled with foliage, French, mid 19th C 690.00
37-1/2" h, C. J. Verga, Bath, mahogany wheel, 19th C 300.00
38" h, wheel, giltwood, ribbon-tied cresting, bellflower frame, painted dial, French, 19th C, lacking hand and thermometer 690.00
38-1/4" h, banjo, mahogany inlaid, T. and H. Doublet, Moorgate St. Bank, early 19th C, shaped case with engraved thermometer and barometer dials, convex mirror, restoration 750.00
38-3/4" h, banjo, mahogany, dial engraved "P. Nossi & Co. Boston," broken pediment cresting above shaped case with thermometer, circular barometer dial flanked by inlaid paterae 690.00
39" h, wall, pierced crest above paper dial in rect frame, scrolling brackets continuing to shaped base with applied boss, painted black, Thomas Shaw, England, early 19th C, minor imperfections 690.00
39-1/2" h, stick, Georgian style, mahogany, swan's neck cresting, carved well cov, engraved steel face, 20th C 290.00
39-3/4" h, banjo, shell inlaid, painted black, Kirner Bros., Oxford, Victorian, mid 19th C 460.00
40" h, mahogany veneer, brass trim, dials inscribed "P. F. Ballenbach, Chicago, Illinois," 20th C, wear and some veneer damage 175.00
41" h, stick, retailer plaque Williams, Page & Co., Boston, paper labels, two thermometers, Victorian, c1850, losses 290.00
41-1/2" h, cased, Storm King, E. C. Spooner, Boston, late 19th C .. 445.00
42" h, wheel, L. Solomons, Bath Warantes, Regency period, early 19th C, shaped case 850.00

BASKETS

History: Baskets were invented when man first required containers to gather, store, and transport goods. Today's collectors, influenced by the country look, focus on baskets made of splint, rye straw, or willow. Emphasis is placed on handmade examples. Nails or staples, wide splints which are thin and evenly cut, or a wire bail handle denote factory construction which can date back to the mid-19th century. Decorated painted or woven baskets rarely are handmade, unless they are American Indian in origin.

Baskets are collected by (a) type—berry, egg, or field, (b) region—Nantucket or Shaker, and (c) composition—splint, rye, or willow.

Reference: Don and Carol Raycraft, *Collector's Guide to Country Baskets*, Collector Books, 1985, 1994 value update.

Museums: Heard Museum, Phoenix, AZ; Old Salem, Inc., Winston-Salem, NC.

Reproduction Alert: Modern reproductions abound, made by diverse groups ranging from craft revivalists to foreign manufacturers.

Note: Limit purchases to baskets in very good condition; damaged ones are a poor investment even at a low price.

Cheese, 21" d, woven splint, old patina, some damage, string wrapped repair at rims 115.00
Gathering
11" d, 7" h plus bentwood handle, woven splint, round, old green paint 385.00
11" w, 14-1/2" l, 6-1/2" h, woven splint, oblong, bottom ends of bentwood end handles form feet, minor damage 360.00
13" x 21-1/2", woven splint, Woodland Indian, faded colored stripes and old brown stain 275.00
14" x 16-1/2", 7-3/4" h, woven splint, buttocks, 30 ribs, old worn patina, bentwood handle, minor damage 220.00
15" x 21" x 5-1/2" h, rye straw, oval, wear and damage 85.00
15-1/2" d, 9-1/2" h, woven splint, round 300.00
16" d, 8" h plus bentwood handle, woven splint, round, old patina 165.00

Oval, attributed to W. D. Appleton, c1900, finely woven, brass ears, medium brown color, finely carved handle, 6" x 9-1/2", $2,000.

16" x 17", 8" h plus bentwood handle, woven splint, red repaint 275.00
20" d, 11" h, woven splint, round, bentwood handles, old patina, minor damage 200.00
Key, 8-3/4" l, 4-1/2" h, black leather, tooled leaves, vines, and floral dec, overall wear, replaced lining, replaced end tabs below heart cutouts, stitching added around rim, with five old keys, VA or TN provenance 4,400.00
Laundry, 35" l, 21-1/2" d, 2, 14" h, splint, rect, two handles, America, 19th C 350.00
Loom, 9-1/2" w, 8-3/4" h, woven splint, hanging type, natural, pink, and green, varnished 95.00
Miniature, 4-3/4" x 5" x 2-1/2" h, woven splint, buttocks, 24 ribs, bentwood handle, good patina, minor edge damage 385.00
Nantucket
   5-1/4" h, 6" d, minor imperfections, 19th C 1,100.00
   5-7/8" d, 4-1/2" h, turned wooden bottom, splint and cane, bentwood swivel handle, traces of paper label, two small holes in one side 525.00
   6" h, pocketbook style, whalebone plaque on lid, imperfections.175.00
   7-3/4" d, 4-7/8" h, paper label on base "Lightship Basket made by Fred S. Chadwick Nantucket Mass. 4 Pine St.," early 20th C 920.00
   10" d, 7-1/4" h, 20th C, minor imperfections....................... 1,100.00
   11" d, 7" h, early 20th C, scattered minor breaks and losses 575.00
Oak, 11-1/2" h, 14" d top, peach, initials "CMT".......................... 235.00
Rye Straw
   23" d, dough rising, shallow, hickory splint binding, PA, late 19th C 125.00
   24" d, domed lid, wear, edge damage, one bentwood rim handle missing... 300.00
Storage, cov, 28" h, woven splint, shaped cylindrical form, fancy porcupine and plain weaving, 2 ring shaped handles to side, 2 looped handles on cover, America, 19th C 460.00
Woven Splint, bentwood handle
   7" x 7-1/2" x 4" h, buttocks, 38 ribs, natural patina 140.00
   7-1/4" x 7-1/4" x 4-1/4" h, buttocks, 26 ribs, natural patina, faded red and green 220.00
   10-1/2" d, 5-1/2" h, round, good patina.................................. 275.00
   10-1/2 x 13" x 5-3/4", rect, courses of splint have unfaded dyed color, red, blue, yellow, and brown...................................... 385.00

11" x 13" x 6-1/2" h, buttocks, old dark green paint, some wear, 28 ribs, wear and holes in bottom... 275.00
12-1/2" x 12-1/2" x 6-1/2" h, buttocks, 58 ribs, old orange-tan pigmented varnish, twisted detail at handle........................... 550.00
13" x 16-1/2" x 9" h, buttocks, 44 ribs, scrubbed finish, some exposure damage 110.00
13-1/4" d, 7" h, old green paint.. 440.00
13-1/2" x 14" x 7" h, buttocks, 40 ribs, old gray paint 60.00
13-1/2" x 16-1/2" x 8-1/2" h, buttocks, 22 ribs, blue and black stripes 140.00
14" d, buttocks, single handle... 160.00
15" d, melon shaped, single handle, minor loss 85.00
15-1/2" x 23" x 10-3/4" h, yellow bands, blue potato print designs, bentwood swivel handle, minor damage 275.00
16" d, market type, single handle 90.00

BATTERSEA ENAMELS

History: Battersea enamel is a generic term for English enamel-on-copper objects of the 18th century.

In 1753, Stephen Theodore Janssen established a factory to produce "Trinkets and Curiosities Enamelled on Copper" at York House, Battersea, London. Here the new invention of transfer printing developed to a high degree of excellence, and the resulting trifles delighted fashionable Georgian society.

Recent research has shown that enamels actually were being produced in London and the Midlands several years before York House was established. However, most enamel trinkets still are referred to as "Battersea Enamels," even though they were probably made in other workshops in London, Birmingham, Bilston, Wednesbury, or Liverpool.

All manner of charming items were made, including snuff and patch boxes bearing mottos and memory gems. (By adding a mirror inside the lid, a snuff box became a patch box). Many figural whimsies, called "toys," were created to amuse a gay and fashionable world. Many other elaborate articles, e.g., candlesticks, salts, tea caddies, and bonbonnières, were made for the tables of the newly rich middle classes.

Reference: Susan Benjamin, *English Enamel Boxes*, Merrimack Publishers Circle, 1978.

Box, St. Ann's Well, Buxton, scenic, black letters and scene, gold trim, white, blue base, 1-3/4" x 1-1/2" x 1", $395.

Bonbonniere, reclining cow, natural colors, grassy mound, floral lid, Bilston, c1770...3,750.00

Box, 1-3/4" l, With Greatful Heart this Trifle I Present as such accept it & I'm Content, enamel on copper, blue inscription, white lid, polychrome lovebirds, professional repair 240.00

Candlesticks, pr, 6" h, pink ground, allover nosegays, pastels, Bilston, 1770..3,500.00

Etui, white tapered column, pastoral scenes within reserves, gilt scrolling and diaper work, int. fitted with perfume bottle, writing slide, pencil, and bodkin, Bilston, c1770...3,400.00

Mirror Knobs, 2-7/8" d, rural genre scenes, woman on shore, two restored, 3 pc set 350.00

Patch Box, oval
   1-1/2" l, pastoral riverside scene, full color, pale green top and base, Bilston, c1780 ....650.00
   2-1/2" x 1-3/4" x 1-1/2", black and white King Charles Spaniel, pink ground, floral dec, around sides 2,750.00

Portrait Medallion, 4" l, oval, enameled portrait of George II, third quarter 18th C, painted en grisaille 1,465.00

Snuff Box, 3" l, molded spaniel cover, landscape painted base, lines 1,465.00

Tiebacks, 2-1/2" d, enamel and brass, Cupid dec, pr 150.00

BAVARIAN CHINA

History: Bavaria, Germany, was an important porcelain production center, similar to the Staffordshire district in England. The phrase "Bavarian China" refers to the products of companies operating in Bavaria, among which were Hutschenreuther, Thomas, and Zeh, Scherzer & Co. (Z. S. & Co.). Very little of the production from this area was imported into the United States prior to 1870.

Cake Plate, 7-1/2" d, whimsical pattern, mkd "Winterling Marktleuthen Bavaria"...65.00

Celery Tray, 11" l, center with basket of fruit, luster edge, c1900 ....45.00

Charger, scalloped rim, game bird in woodland scene, bunches of pink and yellow roses, connecting garlands 95.00

Chocolate Set, cov chocolate pot, 6 cups and saucers, shaded blue and white, large white leaves, pink, red, and white roses, crown mark 295.00

Creamer and Sugar, purple and white pansy dec, mkd "Meschendorf, Bavaria" 65.00

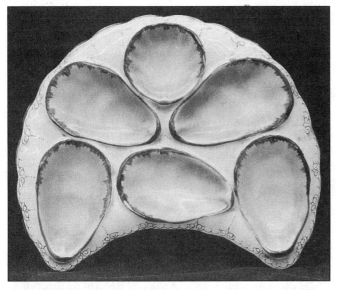

Oyster plate, half-moon shape, six oyster wells, shaded blue, gold border, 9" d, $75.

Cup and Saucer, roses and foliage, gold handle 25.00

Dinner Plate, 10-1/4" d, Black Knight, floral and foliate design, cream and mint green ground, mkd "Hohenberg, Bavaria," set of six ... 150.00

Figure, 10-1/2" h, dark blue and pale orange marabou standing beside tan and navy cactus, mkd "Hutschenreuther Selb-Bavaria, K. Tutter" 285.00

Fish Set, 13 plates, matching sauce boat, artist sgd 295.00

Hair Receiver, 3-1/2" x 2-1/2", apple blossom dec, mkd "T. S. & Co." 60.00

Pipe, 4" l, molded as man holding keg, wear...............................50.00

Pitcher, 9" h, bulbous, blackberry dec, shaded ground, burnished gold lizard handle, sgd "D. Churchill" 125.00

Portrait Plate, 16" l, side view of lady, sgd "L. B. Chaffee, R. C. Bavaria"..95.00

Ramekin, underplate, ruffled, small red roses with green foliage, gold rim 45.00

Salt and Pepper Shakers, pr, pink apple blossom sprays, white ground, reticulated gold tops...35.00

Shaving Mug, pink carnations, mkd "Royal Bavarian" 65.00

Sugar Shaker, hp, pastel pansies 60.00

Vase, 6" h, pink and yellow roses, green leaves, white ground, sgd.. 40.00

BELLEEK

History: Belleek, a thin, ivory-colored, almost-iridescent porcelain, was first made in 1857 in county Fermanagh, Ireland. Production continued until World War I, was discontinued for a period of time, and then resumed. The Shamrock pattern is most familiar, but many patterns were made, including Limpet, Tridacna, and Grasses.

There is an Irish saying: If a newly married couple receives a gift of Belleek, their marriage will be blessed with lasting happiness.

Several American firms made a Belleek-type porcelain. The first was Ott and Brewer Co. of Trenton, New Jersey, in 1884, followed by Willets. Other firms producing this ware included The Ceramic Art Co. (1889), American Art China Works (1892), Columbian Art Co. (1893), and Lenox, Inc. (1904).

Marks: The European Belleek company used specific marks during given time periods, which makes it relatively easy to date a piece of Irish Belleek. Variations in mark color are important, as well as the symbols and words.

First mark............................. BlackHarp, Hound, and Castle1863-1890

Second mark...................................BlackHarp, Hound, and Castle and the words "Co. Fermanagh,
....Ireland"1891-1926

Third mark...........................Black"Deanta in Eirinn" added1926-1946

Fourth mark.......................................Greensame as third mark except
....for color1946-1955

Fifth mark............................Green"R" inside a circle added1955-1965

Sixth mark...............Green"Co. Fermanagh" omitted1965-March 1980

Seventh markGold .... "Deanta in Eirinn" omitted .... April 1980-Dec. 1992

Eighth markBlue..Blue version of the second mark with "R" inside a
circle added..Jan. 1993-present

References: Susan and Al Bagdade, *Warman's English & Continental Pottery & Porcelain*, 3rd Edition, Krause Publications, 1998; Richard K. Degenhardt, *Belleek*, 2nd ed., Wallace-Homestead, 1993.

Collectors' Club: The Belleek Collectors' Society, 144 W. Britannia St., Taunton, MA 02780.

Museum: Museum of Ceramics at East Liverpool, East Liverpool, OH.

Cup and saucer, white, gold trim, Willetts, $95.

Additional Listings: Lenox.

American

Bowl
  5" w, 2" h, Art Nouveau enameled dec, gold feet, Lenox palette mark, c1906-24 .... 125.00
  9" d, green, heavy gold trim, white curled handle, Lenox green wreath mark 95.00
Christmas Plate, 1972 .... 75.00
Cup and Saucer, 6" h, sq pedestal base, undecorated, Willets brown mark 45.00
Dresser Set, cov powder box, pink tray, buffer and container, nail brush, pin cushion, hp violets, artist sgd "M. R.," Willets brown mark 600.00
Figure, 4" h, Lenox green wreath mark
  Elephant, white 325.00
  Swan, green 75.00
Floor Vase, 18-1/2" h, 9" d, ovoid, china painted with gilded details, ink stamped "Willets Belleek," short hairline to base 700.00
Loving Cup, 3 handles, wine keeper in wine cellar dec, artist sgd, SS repousse collar, CAC mark 195.00
Mustache Cup, gold leaves, butterflies 100.00
Perfume Bottle, figural, rabbit, white, Lenox green wreath mark 550.00
Powder Box, 4" x 6", pink, gold wheat on lid, Lenox green wreath mark 60.00
Salt, 2" d, gold ftd, green ground, pink roses, Lenox green palette mark 40.00
Vase, 5" h, 5" d, tree trunk shape, transfer printed flowers, polychrome dec, red Ott & Brewer stamp 450.00

Irish

Basket, 8" d, Melvin, sq, decorative border, twig handles, turquoise-blue, 4 applied violet floral sprays, green leaves 625.00
Box, cov, 3" h, Forget-Me-Not, globular, ftd, applied flowerheads, conical knob, pearl luster glaze, 3BM 395.00
Butter Dish, cov, figural, cottage, 6th mark 160.00
Cake Plate, Limpet pattern, 2BM 195.00
Creamer, Lotus pattern, green handle, 2BM 95.00
Cup and Saucer, Shamrock pattern, 2BM 200.00
Demitasse Cup and Saucer, Shamrock pattern, 6th mark 55.00
Dish, coral and shell, 6th mark 35.00
Figure
  3-1/2" h, terrier, 4GM 45.00
  5-1/2" h, fish on rocky pedestal, 7th mark 75.00
Flower Holder, 3-1/2" h, Seahorse, one with one head, other with brown, 1BM, pr 1,400.00
Mustache Cup, Tridacna pattern, first black mark 125.00
Plate, 9" d, Harp and Shamrock pattern, 5th mark 60.00
Sandwich Tray, Mask pattern, 2BM 285.00

Spill Jug, 7" h, Limerick pattern, 5th mark 70.00
Tea and Toast Set, Tridacna pattern, 6th mark 90.00
Vase, 6-1/2" h, Harp and Shamrock pattern, 5GM 70.00

BELLS

History: Bells have been used for centuries for many different purposes. They have been traced as far back as 2697 b.c., though at that time they did not have any true tone. One of the oldest bells is the "crotal," a tiny sphere with small holes, a ball, and a stone or metal interior. This type now appears as sleigh bells.

True bell making began when bronze, a mixture of tin and copper, was invented. Bells are now made out of many types of materials—almost as many materials as there are uses for them.

Bells of the late 19th century show a high degree of workmanship and artistic style. Glass bells from this period are examples of the glassblower's talent and the glass manufacturer's product.

Collectors' Clubs: American Bell Association, Alter Rd., Box 386, Natrona Heights, PA 15065; American Bell Association International, Inc., 7210 Bellbrook Dr., San Antonio, TX 78227.

Museum: Bell Haven, Tarentum, PA.

Bicycle, cast brass, nickel plated, eagle 90.00
Brass, 4" h, 3-1/4" d, Jacobean head finial, emb figures around sides 120.00
Church, cast brass
  20" h, wrought-iron ringer, suspended from chain, Reading, PA, late 18th C 980.00
  24" h, mounted on wrought iron frame, c1772, from Manheim, Lancaster County, PA church 8,000.00
Desk, bronze, white marble base, side tap, c1875 .... 65.00
Glass
  Amethyst, flint, metal lace trim, painted crowing rooster on top of handle 375.00
  Custard, souvenir, "Alamo-Built 1718, San Antonio, Texas," gilt band 120.00
  Vaseline, flint, ornate metal lace trim, elephant with green eyes and red mouth on top of handle 350.00

Cigar counter type, brass, cast iron base, mkd "Russell & Erwin Mfg. Co., New Britain, CT, USA, Pat'd Aug. 1, 96, Rd. No. 269895," 8" x 7", $250.

Hemony, 6-3/4" h, 3-3/8" d, brass, figural knight handle, figures emb around sides, name "Hemony".. 120.00
Locomotive, 17" x 17", brass, cradle and yoke 850.00
School, 10-1/4" h, turned curly maple handle 385.00
Sleigh, leather strap, 24 bells... 110.00
Table, 4-5/8" h, sterling silver, cupid blowing horn, figural handle, foliate strap work border, frosted finish, Gorham, c1870 .... 750.00

BENNINGTON and BENNINGTON-TYPE POTTERY

History: In 1845, Christopher Webber Fenton joined Julius Norton, his brother-in-law, in the manufacturing of stoneware pottery in Bennington, Vermont. Fenton sought to expand the company's products and glazes; Norton wanted to concentrate solely on stoneware. In 1847, Fenton broke away and established his own factory.

Fenton introduced to America the famous Rockingham glaze, developed in England and named after the Marquis of Rockingham. In 1849, he patented a flint enamel glaze, "Fenton's Enamel," which added flecks, spots, or streaks of color (usually blues, greens, yellows, and oranges) to the brown Rockingham glaze. Forms included candlesticks, coachman bottles, cow creamers, poodles, sugar bowls, and toby pitchers.

Fenton produced the little-known scroddled ware, commonly called lava or agate ware. Scroddled ware is composed of differently colored clays, which are mixed with cream-colored clay, molded, turned on a potter's wheel, coated with feldspar and flint, and fired. It was not produced in quantity, as there was little demand for it.

Fenton also introduced Parian ware to America. Parian was developed in England in 1842 and known as "Statuary ware." Parian is a translucent porcelain which has no glaze and resembles marble. Bennington made the blue and white variety in the form of vases, cologne bottles, and trinkets.

The hound-handled pitcher is probably the best-known Bennington piece. Hound-handled pitchers were made by about 30 different potteries in more than 55 variations. Rockingham glaze was used by more than 150 potteries in 11 states, mainly in the Midwest, between 1830 and 1900.

Marks: Five different marks were used, with many variations. Only about twenty percent of the pieces carried any mark; some forms were almost always marked, others never. Marks include:

1849 mark (4 variations) for flint enamel and Rockingham

E. Fenton's Works, 1845-1847, on Parian and occasionally on scroddled ware

U. S. Pottery Co., ribbon mark, 1852-1858, on Parian and blue and white porcelain

U. S. Pottery Co., lozenge mark, 1852-1858, on Parian

U. S. Pottery, oval mark, 1853-1858, mainly on scroddled ware

References: Richard Carter Barret, *How to Identify Bennington Pottery*, Stephen Greene Press, 1964; William C. Ketchum Jr., *American Pottery and Porcelain*, Avon Books, 1994.

Museums: Bennington Museum, Bennington, VT; East Liverpool Museum of Ceramics, East Liverpool, OH.

Additional Listings: Stoneware.

Candlesticks, pr, flint enamel, brown and olive, trumpet stand, 8-1/4" h, $1,200.

Bank, 6-1/2" h, flint enamel, c1850-60 .... 865.00
Bowl, 7-1/8" d, shallow, brown and yellow Rockingham glaze, Fenton's 1849 mark 775.00
Candlestick, 8-1/4" h, flint enamel glaze 875.00
Churn, stoneware, 6 gallon, cobalt blue cornucopia of flowers, orig dasher, mkd "A. J. Norton & Co." 8,800.00
Curtain Tiebacks, 4-1/2" l, 1849-58, Barrett plate 200, one chipped, pr 175.00
Cuspidor, 6-3/4" h, flint enamel, imp 1849 mark on base, mold cracks, chips to base 250.00
Figure
   7-1/2" h, 10" l, lion, facing left, coleslaw mane, tongue up, flint enamel, Barrett plate 377, minor repair to tail, repaired chip on paw .4,315.00
   8-1/2" h, 9" l, poodle, standing, basket in mouth, Barrett plate 367, repairs to tail and hind quarters 2,500.00
Flask, book, flint enamel, title imp on spine, 1849-58, Barrett plate 411
   5-3/4" h, titled "Bennington Battle".. 750.00
   5-3/4" h, untitled 460.00
   6" h, titled "Hermit's Life & Suffering"................................... 980.00
   7" h, titled "Ladies Companion" 690.00
   8" h, titled "Bennington Companion G" 750.00
Jar, 4-3/8" h, 4-1/4" d, Parian, blue and white, Acanthus Leaf pattern, lid missing 85.00
Jug, 10-3/4" h, stoneware, strap handle, imp label "F. B. Norton & Co., Worcester, Mass," cobalt blue slip floral design 220.00
Nameplate, 8" l, Rockingham glaze... 135.00
Paperweight, 3" h, 4-1/2" w, spaniel, 1849-58, Barrett plate 407 .. 815.00
Picture Frame, 9-1/2" h, oval, 1948-58, Barrett plate VIII, chips and repairs, pr 230.00
Pie Plate, 9" d, brown and yellow Rockingham glaze, Fenton's 1949 mark, minor wear 925.00
Pitcher
   8" h, hunting scene, Barrett pate 26, chips........................... 175.00
   9-1/2" h, hound handle, 1852-67, Barrett plate 32, crack and repair to spout 345.00
Planter, 11" h, stump form, stoneware, base mkd "F. B. Norton & Co., Worcester," minor chips 320.00
Spittoon, 9-1/2" d, flint enamel glaze, rare 1849 mark 450.00

Jug, J. Norton & Co., 1859-61, 4 gallon, cobalt blue double bird on flower, 17-1/2" h, $750.

Sugar Bowl, cov, 3-3/4" h, Parian, blue and white, Repeated Oak Leaves pattern, raised grapevine dec on lid 150.00
Teapot, cov, flint enamel, Alternate Rib pattern, pierced pouring spout 425.00
Toby Bottle, 10-1/2" h, Barrett plate 421, marked on base, mold cracks, top of foot repaired, other foot chipped 550.00
Wash Bowl
    13-1/2" d, flint enamel, twelve-sided, hairline, chip 250.00
    14-3/4" d, flint enamel, relief border dec, hairline, chip 265.00

Bennington-Type
Bank, 3-1/4" h, 3-3/4" w, chest of drawers shape, Rockingham glaze, Barrett plate 428, small chip to front top edge 150.00
Creamer, 5-1/2" h, 6-3/4" l, figural, cow, Rockingham glaze, Barrett plate 378, chipped cov, repairs 115.00
Figure, 4-3/4" l, brown glazed earthenware, 19th C, chips to base ..345.00
Flask, book
    5-1/2" h, untitled, Rockingham glaze, 19th C, small chips to edge 175.00
    7" h, titled "Spiritual Manifestations By" imp on spine, Rockingham glaze, mid 19th C, crack 260.00
Foot Warmer, 11-1/4" l, Rockingham glaze, 19th C 190.00
Spittoon, 8-1/2" d, scallop shell form, Rockingham glaze, 19th C 175.00
Toby Bottle, 9" h, barrel, Rockingham glaze, mid 19thC, rim and base chips 175.00

BISCUIT JARS

History: The biscuit or cracker jar was the forerunner of the cookie jar. Biscuit jars were made of various materials by leading glassworks and potteries of the late 19th and early 20th centuries.

Note: All items listed have silver-plated mountings unless otherwise noted.

5" h, Wedgwood, 3 color jasper, central dark blue ground, light blue borders, applied white classical relief, silver plated rim, handle, and cov, imp mark, 19th C 300.00

6-1/4" h, cased, blue, enameled pink roses and green leaves, SP top, rim and handle 145.00
6-1/2" h
    Bristol glass, allover enameled pink, blue, white and yellow floral dec, green leaves, SP top, rim, and handle 125.00
    Loetz-type, translucent white mother-of-pearl irid green raindrop spatter, melon swirls, SP lid, rim, and handle 225.00
6-3/4" h, Mount Washington, Crown Milano, hp floral and gold enamel dec, sgd "CM," crown mark, silver plated rim, bail and cov, mkd "MW 4404" 750.00
7" h, 6-1/2" d, Peleton, white, yellow, blue, and pink strands, molded vertical ribs, SP fittings 785.00
7-1/4" h, pink satin, molded shell base, enameled floral dec, SP lid and handle 315.00
7-1/2" h, 4-1/2" w, Nippon china, sq, white, multicolored floral bands, gold outlines and trim 110.00
9" h, Wave Crest, yellow roses, molded multicolored swirl ground, incised floral and leaf dec on lid, mkd "Quadruple Plate" 400.00
9" h, 6-1/4" d, cranberry, two applied clear ring handles, applied clear feet and flower prunt pontil, ribbed finial knob 195.00
9-1/2" h, burnt orange, floral dec, blown-out floral base, sgd "Pairpoint" 350.00

BISQUE

History: Bisque or biscuit china is the name given to wares that have been fired once and have not been glazed.

Bisque figurines and busts, which were popular during the Victorian era, were used on fireplace mantels, dining room buffets, and end tables. Manufacturing was centered

Nodder, seated child with basket, white dress, yellow basket, unmarked, 4-1/2" h, $125.

in the United States and Europe. By the mid-20th century, Japan was the principal source of bisque items, especially character-related items.

References: Susan and Al Bagdade, *Warman's English & Continental Pottery & Porcelain*, 3rd Edition, Krause Publications, 1998; Elyse Karlin, *Children Figurines of Bisque and Chinawares*, Schiffer Publishing, 1990; Sharon Weintraub, *Naughties, Nudies and Bathing Beauties*, Hobby House Press, 1993.

Center Bowl, 8-3/4" h, figural, pierced bowl supported by tripod feet modeled as cherubs, white, France, 19th C 575.00
Dish, cov, 9" x 6-1/2" x 5-1/2", dog, brown, and white, green blanket, white and gilt basketweave base 500.00
Figure
    4-3/4" h, Three Bears, painted outfits, orig 5-8/8" w x 6-1/4" box, c1910 .... 230.00
    28" h, man holding fishing net, woman holding small keg, gilt and yellow enamel dec, German, 19th C, pr 920.00
Funerary Jar, 14" h, nude male figure weeping to forefront of a bust head statue, Berlin scepter mark, 19th C 345.00
Match Holder, figural, Dutch girl, copper and gold trim 45.00
Nodder, 2-1/2" x 3-1/2", jester, seated holding pipe, pastel peach and white, gold trim 85.00
Piano Baby
    Crawling, crying, mkd "Made in Japan" 20.00
    Lying on stomach, wearing bib, dog, and cat, 6-3/4" l, German . 100.00
Planter, carriage, four wheels, pale blue and pink, white ground, gold dots, royal markings 165.00
Salt, 3" d, figural, walnut, cream, branch base, matching spoon .. 75.00
Wall Plaque, 10-1/4" d, light green, scrolled and pierced scallop, white relief figures in center, man playing mandolin, lady wearing hat, c1900, pr 275.00

BITTERS BOTTLES

History: Bitters, a "remedy" made from natural herbs and other mixtures with an alcohol base, often was viewed as the universal cure-all. The names given to various bitter mixtures were imaginative, though the bitters seldom cured what their makers claimed.

The manufacturers of bitters needed a way to sell and advertise their products. They designed bottles in many shapes, sizes, and colors to attract the buyer. Many forms of advertising, including trade cards, billboards, signs, almanacs, and novelties, proclaimed the virtues of a specific bitter.

During the Civil War, a tax was levied on alcoholic beverages. Since bitters were identified as medicines, they were exempt from this tax. The alcoholic content was never mentioned. In 1907, when the Pure Foods Regulations went into effect, "an honest statement of content on every label" put most of the manufacturers out of business.

References: Ralph and Terry Kovel, *Kovels' Bottles Price List*, 11th ed., Three Rivers Press, 1999; John Odell, *Digger Odell's Official Antique Bottle and Glass Collector Magazine Price Guide Series*, Vol. 2, published by author (1910 Shawhan Rd., Morrow, OH 45152), 1995; Carlyn Ring, For Bitters Only, published by author 203 Kensington Rd., Hampton Falls, NH 03844), 1980; J. H. Thompson, *Bitters Bottles*, Century House, 1947; Richard Watson, *Bitters Bottles*, Thomas Nelson and Sons, 1965; Jeff Wichmann, *Antique Western Bitter Bottles*, Pacific Glass Books, 1999;

—, *The Best of the West Antique Western Bitters Bottles*, Pacific Glass Books, 1999.

Periodicals: *Antique Bottle and Glass Collector*, P.O. Box 187, East Greenville, PA 18041; *Bitters Report*, P.O. Box 1253, Bunnell, FL 32110.

Alpine Herb Bitters, amber, sq, smooth base, tooled lip, 9-5/8" h 175.00
Baker's Orange Grove Bitters, yellowish-amber, smooth base, applied mouth, 9-1/2" h 185.00
Bell's Cocktail Bitters, Jas. M. Bell & Co., New York, amber, applied ring, smooth base, 10-1/2" h 450.00
Browns Celebrated Indian Herb Bitters/Patented Feb. 11, 1868, figural, emb, golden amber, ground lip, smooth base, 12-1/4" h 350.00
Bourbon Whiskey Bitters, barrel shape, cherry puce, applied sq collar, smooth base, 9-3/4" h 500.00
Caldwell's Herb Bitters/The Great Tonic, triangular, beveled and lattice work panels, yellowish-amber, applied tapered lip, iron pontil . 395.00
Clarke's Vegetable Sherry Wine Bitters, aqua, smooth base, applied mouth, 14" h 575.00
Dr. Loew's Celebrated Stomach Bitters & Nerve Tonic, green, smooth base, tooled lip, 9-1/4" h 150.00
Drake's Plantation Bitters, puce, Arabaseque design, tapered lip, smooth base, 9-3/4" h 295.00
Godfrey's Celebrated Cordial Bitters, NY, aqua, pontil, applied mouth, 10" h 1,225.00
Greeley's Bourbon Bitters, barrel shape, smokey gray-brown, sq collared lip, smooth base, 9-1/4" h 225.00
Hibernia Bitters, amber, sq, smooth base, tooled lip, 9-1/4" h 125.00
Hops & Malt Bitters, golden amber, tapered collar lip, smooth base, 9-1/8" h 250.00
J. C.& Co., molded pineapple form, deep golden amber, blown molded, 19th C, 8-1/2" h 460.00
Kelly's Old Cabin Bitters, cabin shape, amber, sloping collar lip, smooth base, 9" h 725.00
Keystone Bitters, barrel shape, golden amber, applied tapered collar, sq lip, smooth base, 9-3/4" h 175.00
Mist of the Morning Sole Agents Barnett & Lumley, golden amber, sloping collar lip, smooth base, 9-3/4" h 300.00

Augauer Bitters, green, orig label front and back, $75.

National Bitters, corn cob shape, puce amber, applied ring lip, smooth
  base, 12-5/8" h 350.00
Red Jacket Bitters, Monheimer & Co., sq, amber, tooled lip, smooth
  base, 9-1/2" h 100.00
Simon's Centennial Bitters, George Washington bust shape, aqua,
  applied mouth, smooth base, 9-1/8" h 650.00
Suffolk Bitters, Philbrook & Tucker, Boston, pig shape, amber, applied
  mouth, smooth base, 10-1/8" l 600.00
Sunny Castle Stomach Bitters, Jos. Dudenhoefer, Milwaukee, sq,
  amber, tooled lip, smooth base, 9" h 125.00
Tippecanoe, Warner & Co., amber, applied mushroom lip, 9" h ... 95.00
Warner's Safe Bitters, amber, applied mouth, smooth base,
  8-1/2" h 265.00

BLACK MEMORABILIA

History: The term "Black memorabilia" refers to a broad range of collectibles that often overlap other collecting fields, e.g., toys and postcards. It also encompasses African artifacts, items created by slaves or related to the slavery era, modern Black cultural contributions to literature, art, etc., and material associated with the Civil Rights Movement and the Black experience throughout history.

The earliest known examples of Black memorabilia include primitive African designs and tribal artifacts. Black Americana dates back to the arrival of African natives upon American shores.

The advent of the 1900s saw an incredible amount and variety of material depicting Blacks, most often·in a derogatory and dehumanizing manner that clearly reflected the stereotypical attitude held toward the Black race during this period. The popularity of Black portrayals in this unflattering fashion flourished as the century wore on.

As the growth of the Civil Rights Movement escalated and aroused public awareness to the Black plight, attitudes changed. Public outrage and pressure during the early 1950s eventually put a halt to these offensive stereotypes.

Black representations are still being produced in many forms, but no longer in the demoralizing designs of the past. These modern objects, while not as historically significant as earlier examples, will become the Black memorabilia of tomorrow.

References: Douglas Congdon-Martin, *Images in Black: 150 Years of Black Collectibles*, 2nd ed., Schiffer, 1999; Dee Hockenberry, E*nchanting Friends: Collectible Poohs, Raggedies, Golliwoggs & Roosevelt Bears*, Schiffer Publishing, 1995; Kyle Husfloen (ed.), *Black Americana Price Guide*, Antique Trader Books, 1997; Jan Lindenberger, B*lack Memorabilia for the Kitchen: A Handbook and Price Guide*, 2nd ed., Schiffer, 1999; —, *More Black Memorabilia*, 2nd ed., Schiffer Publishing, 1999; J. L. Mashburn, *Black Postcard Price Guide*, 2nd ed., Colonial House, 1999; Dawn Reno,

Encyclopedia of Black Collectibles, Wallace-Homestead/ Krause, 1996; J. P. Thompson, *Collecting Black Memorabilia*, L-W Book Sales, 1996; Jean Williams Turner, *Collectible Aunt Jemima*, Schiffer Publishing, 1994.

Periodical: *Blackin*, 559 22nd Ave., Rock Island, IL 61201; *Doll-E-Gram*, P.O. Box 1212, Bellevue, WA 98009-1212; *International Golliwogg Collectors Club*, P.O. Box 612, Woodstock, NY 12498, http://www.teddybears.com/golliwog; *Lookin Back at Black*, 6087 Glen Harbor Dr., San Jose CA 95123.

Collectors' Club: Black Memorabilia Collector's Association, 2482 Devoe Ter, Bronx, NY 10468.

Museums: Great Plains Black Museum, Omaha, NE 68110; Museum of African American History, Detroit, MI.

Reproduction Alert: Reproductions are becoming an increasing problem, from advertising signs (Bull Durham tobacco) to mechanical banks (Jolly Nigger). If the object looks new to you, chances are that it is new.

Advertising Broadside, 14" w, cardboard, adv "Coloreds Only Dance,
  Rendville, OH, Armistice Day" 200.00
Advertising Sign, heavy cardboard, multicolored
  14" w, Picanniny Freeze 5¢, 1922 .... 100.00
  19" w, "Paul Jones Whiskey the Temptation of St. Anthony," some
    surface discoloration 725.00
Book
  Harris, Joel Chandler, *Uncle Remus: His Songs and Sayings,* NY,
    1881, illus by Frederick S. Church and James H. Moser, 8vo, publisher's gilt-pictorial green cloth, first edition 1,610.00
  Stowe, Harriet Beecher, *Uncle Tom's Cabin: or, Life among the
    Lowly,* J. P. Jewett and Co., Boston, 1852, 2 volumes, 8vo, illus,
    publisher's gilt pictorial plum cloth cover, first edition, bookplates,
    some wear 12,650.00
Bust, 3-5/8" h, woman, carved ivory, large facial features, elaborate
  hairstyle, African 100.00

Advertising tin, Durham's Cocoanut, $175.

SPECIAL AUCTIONS

Collection Liquidators
341 Lafayette Street
New York, NY 10012
(212) 505-2455
http://www.rtam.com/coliq/bid.html

Doll, Golliwogg, black face, jacket, shorts, white shirt, gloves, red tie, pants, mkd "Made in England," $185.

Candle Holder, 6" d, ceramic, seated black with melon on head, ring handle 700.00
Children's Book, Ten Little Negros Boys, Nora Case, England, blue hardcover, 5-1/2" h, black, red, and white dust jacket 195.00
Cigarette Holder, ceramic, multicolored lusterware
    3" h, boy sitting, hollowed out hat holds cigarettes 200.00
    3-1/2" h, dog barking at scared black couple 140.00
    4" h, multicolored black man playing banjo, ashtray base, mkd "St. Petersburg," pre-war Japan 95.00
Coat Rack, 13" w, bronze, 4 hooks, classic Johnny Griffin head, mkd "1592 Austria," c1880 .... 225.00
Dexterity Game, 2-1/4" sq, 5 black boys on fence covet little black boy's melon slice, mkd "Souvenir Indian Lakes, Ohio" 200.00
Doorstop, 8" w, green, red, and brown, 3 black boys eating melon behind fence, 60% paint loss 300.00
Egg, 6" h ostrich egg, detailed engraving of slave in chains, "Abolish Slavery," verso 1860 American eagle "We Are One" 865.00
Face Jug, grotesque, ceramic, hand fired
    6-1/2" h, dark brown, pink, and white, exaggerated expression .225.00
    8-1/2" h, dark brown, blue, and white, "XX Slave Jo Flowers" 200.00
Floor Polish Tin, 4" d, Piccanniny, smiling black boy, "Twice the Shine, Half the Time," directions on verse, England, ... 200.00
Food Tin
    3" h, Negro Head Oysters, litho label, 1930s, sealed 175.00
    9" w, Huntley's Biscuits, England, black and white minstrels, litho label 160.00
Game, Ten Little Niggers, Parker Bros., 6" w multicolored box, 1890s, orig instructions 800.00
Golliwog, hand made cloth doll, black and white eyes, played with condition
    18" h, red shirt, green pants 185.00
    20" h, white shirt, black jacket with long tails, striped pants 195.00
    26" h, green, black, and tan 125.00
Lunch Box, Dixie Kid Cut Plug, black boy illus, litho tin 290.00
Epherma, printed document, 1 pg, 7-1/2" x 7-7/8", c1826, used for sale of slaves from estate of Thomas Jefferson by Thomas Jefferson Randolph, grandson and executor, blank spaces for name of buyer, amount to be paid, "...negro slave named___late the property of

Thomas Jefferson deceased," document concludes with statement that title to the slave/s is warranted forever........................... 2,800.00
Figure
    11" h, wax, hand painted, multicolored whistling black man.. 100.00
    16" w, chalk, 3 boys sitting behind fence eating melon 335.00
Hand Towel, 17" l, heavy paper, red, and white, exaggerated expressions and dialect, black man "Yas Suh/dis am a towel," 1930s.. 85.00
License Plate Holder, 11-1/2" w, painted cast iron, multicolored, Negro Ocean Playground 110.00
Match Holder
    4" h, chalk, hand painted, brown ground, white bust, Johnny Griffin style head 230.00
    11" h, ceramic, red, yellow, green, and blue, Mammy with platter, matchbox held on base, wall mounted 200.00
Nutcracker, 8" h, painted wood, red, black, and white, big toothed Mammy, mkd "Ahab," c1900 .... 850.00
Painting, 21" h, 17" w, oil on canvas, smiling boy with tattered hat and red shirt, unsgd, gold gesso frame 550.00
Pin Cushion, 5-1/2" h, stuffed cloth, multicolored smiling Mammy, metal earrings, holding large melon 200.00
Pipe Rack, 13" w, bronze, copper wash, holds 6 pipes, classic Johnny Griffin head, mkd "1502," Austria, 1880s 200.00
Plate, 10" d, Nigger Head, white, gold trim, adv, minor back chips.. 125.00
Portrait, oil on board, 6-1/2" x 5", inscribed and dated "...1893" in pencil on reverse, one of man, other woman, identified as "from Louisiana," framed, price for pr,.. 4,600.00
Print, 24" w, chromolithograph, blacks eating melon, hand carved melon frame, 1880s 800.00
Puzzle, 3-3/4" d, round, Lil Niggers, black and gold, orig instructions260.00
Shaving Mug, 4" h, ceramic, multicolored, blacks in razor fight, "A Close Shave," mkd "KPM," Germany, 1880s 400.00
Slave Tax Badge, Charleston, SC, copper
    1-1/2" x 1-1/2", stamped "Charleston 998 Servant 1857," wear, patination 1,495.00
    1-1/2" x 1-1/2", stamped "Charleston 1851 Servant 2376," wear, patination 1,840.00
    2" x 2", stamped "Charleston 2083 Servant 1835," wear, cleaned, lacquered 1,840.00
    2-1/8" x 2", stamped "Charleston 1828 Porter No. 254," reverse stamped "LA FAR" in rect, wear, cleaned, lacquered 3,220.00
Smoking Stand, 6-4/5" w, majolica, multicolored minstrel playing banjo, holds cigars, matches, ashtray, back strike, c1880 .... 450.00
Souvenir Spoon, sterling silver, 3-3/4" l
    Pinehurst, NJ, torso of black boy surrounded by corn as double sided handle, "Sunny South" engraved in gold washed bowl........... 125.00
    Savannah, GA, "Georgia" along stem, detailed eagle over black boys head, enameled collar, "Savannah" in bowl 150.00
    Mobile, Alabama, detailed bowl with black playing banjo, seated on cotton bale, second black works at tree 125.00
    Summerville, SC, detailed double-sided full-figured black holding melon as handle, engraved bowl 110.00
Stein, 8" h, minstrel, playing banjo, Austria, 1880s..................... 800.00
Tobacco Jar, cov, ceramic, multicolored
    5-3/4" h, black woman, teeth missing, Austrian, 1880s......... 925.00
    6-3/4" h, black boy holding pipe, sitting on pineapple, 1880s.. 450.00
    7" h, hand painted bisque, smiling black man, peaked cap, Austrian, 1800s 800.00
    8" h, screaming black man, Germany, 1880s..................... 1,500.00
Tobacco Tin
    Bigger Hair, Fiji Islander, black woman with large rings through ears and nose, full 115.00
    Burley Boy Tobacco, "The white man's hope," white ground, red and black dec.. 1,000.00
Toy
    Dice, 2" d, multicolored, spring activated, mkd "Alco Britain HK" . 90.00
    Ramp Walker, 4-1/2" h, multicolored, cloth, USA, c1920s....... 65.00

BLOWN THREE MOLD

History: The Jamestown colony in Virginia introduced

glassmaking into America. The artisans used a "free-blown" method.

Blowing molten glass into molds was not introduced into America until the early 1800s. Blown three-mold glass used a predesigned mold that consisted of two, three, or more hinged parts. The glassmaker placed a quantity of molten glass on the tip of a rod or tube, inserted it into the mold, blew air into the tube, waited until the glass cooled, and removed the finished product. The three-part mold is the most common and lends its name to this entire category.

The impressed decorations on blown-mold glass usually are reversed, i.e., what is raised or convex on the outside will be concave on the inside. This is useful in identifying the blown form.

By 1850, American-made glassware was relatively common. Increased demand led to large factories and the creation of a technology, which eliminated the smaller companies.

Reference: George S. and Helen McKearin, *American Glass*, reprint, Crown Publishers, 1941, 1948.

Collectors' Club: Early American Pattern Glass Society, P.O. Box 266, Colesburg, IA 52035; National Early American Glass Club, P.O. Box 8489, Silver Spring, MD 20907.

Museum: Sandwich Glass Museum, Sandwich, MA.

Bottle, 7-1/4" h, olive green, McKearin GIII-16............................330.00
Bowl, 5-3/8" d, colorless, folded rim, pontil, 12 diamond base, McKearin GII-6 ....125.00
Celery Vase, colorless, Pittsburgh, McKearin GV-21 ....650.00
Cordial, 2-7/8" h, colorless, ringed base, pontil, heavy circular foot, freehand formed, McKearinGII-18..550.00
Creamer, 3-1/2" h, colorless, applied handle 125.00
Cruet, 7-3/4" h, cobalt blue, scroll scale pattern, ribbed base, pontil, applied handle, French..265.00
Decanter
    6-3/4" h, olive-amber, pint, attributed to Marlboro Street Glass Works, Keene, NH, some abrasions...................................460.00
    8" h, colorless, 3 applied rings, McKearin GII-18, replaced wheel stopper 110.00
    8-1/4" h, colorless, McKearin GII-19, replaced wheel stopper....115.00
    9-1/2" h, colorless, 3 applied rings and vintage band in white and blue enamel, orig stopper 420.00
    10" h, colorless, arch and fern design, snake medallion, McKearin GIV-7, minor chips, mold imperfections 165.00
    11" h, colorless, sunburst in square, minor chips, mold imperfections 150.00
    Dish, colorless
        5-1/4" d, McKearin GII-16...65.00
        5-1/2" d, McKearin GII-18...50.00
Flask, 5-1/4" h, colorless, arch and diamond pattern, sheared mouth, pontil, Continental 300.00
Flip Glass, colorless
    5-1/2" h, McKearin GII-18...165.00
    6" h, McKearin GII-18...125.00
Ink Bottle, 2-1/4" d, deep olive green, McKearin GII-2...............195.00
Miniature, 2-5/8" h decanter, colorless, McKearin GIII-12 ....165.00
Mustard, 4-1/4" h, colorless, pontil, cork stopper, orig paper label, McKearin GI-15 ....85.00
Pitcher, 7" h, colorless, base of handle reglued, McKearin GIII-5 ....145.00
Salt, basket shape, colorless 120.00
Toilet Water Bottle, 5-3/4" h, cobalt blue, tam-o-shanter cap......300.00
Tumbler, 6-1/4" h, colorless, McKearin GII-19 ....155.00

Vase, 9" h, colorless, engraved flowers, leaves, and berries, McKearin GV-21 ....7,500.00
Vinegar Bottle, cobalt blue, ribbed, orig stopper, McKearin GI-7 ....285.00
Whiskey Glass, 2-3/8" h, colorless, applied handle, McKearin GII-18 ....285.00

BOEHM PORCELAINS

History: Edward Marshall Boehm was born on Aug. 21, 1913. Boehm's childhood was spent at the McConogh School, a rural Baltimore County, Maryland, school. He studied animal husbandry at the University of Maryland, serving as manager of Longacre Farms on the Eastern Shore of Maryland upon graduation. After serving in the air force during World War II, Boehm moved to Great Neck, Long Island, and worked as an assistant veterinarian.

In 1949, Boehm opened a pottery studio in Trenton, New Jersey. His initial hard-paste porcelain sculptures consisted of Herefords, Percherons, and dogs. The first five to six years were a struggle, with several partnerships beginning and ending during the period. In the early 1950s, Boehm's art porcelain sculptures began appearing in major department stores. When Eisenhower presented a Boehm sculpture to Queen Elizabeth and Prince Philip during their visit to the United States in 1957, Boehm's career accelerated.

Boehm contributed the ideas for the images and the techniques used to produce the sculptures. Thousands of prototype sculptures were made, with more than 400 put into production. The actual work was done by skilled artisans. Boehm died on Jan. 29, 1969.

In the early 1970s, a second production site, called Boehm Studios, was opened in Malvern, England. The tradition begun by Boehm continues today.

Many collectors specialize in Boehm porcelain birds or flowers. Like all of Boehm's sculptures, pieces in these series are highly detailed, signed, and numbered.

Reference: Reese Palley, *Porcelain Art of Edward Marshall Boehm*, Harrison House, 1988.

Collectors' Club: Boehm Porcelain Society, P.O. Box 5051, Trenton, NJ 08638.

Birds

American Avocet, #40134...1,250.00
American Eagle, #498...1,000.00
Blue Jay, #436, 4-1/2" h 130.00
Bob White Quail, #407 ....1,400.00
California Quail, #433, pr 1,800.00
Cape May Warbler, 9-1/4" h, one leaf loose 270.00
Cardinal, female, #415, 15" h 700.00
Crested Flycatcher, baby, #458C..250.00
Fledgling Eastern Bluebird, #442...175.00
Hummingbird, 8-1/4" h 220.00
Kingfisher, #449 ....175.00
Northern Oriole, 12" h, limited edition #83 ....100.00
Oven Bird, 10" h 800.00
Pelican, #40161 ....1,000.00
Ruby Crowned Kinglets, #434 ....900.00
Tumbler Pigeons, #416...850.00

Flowers

Blue Nile Rose, #300-80...1,300.00
Crocus, 5" h 200.00

Daisies, #3002 .... 800.00
Magnolia Grandiflora, #300-12 .... 1,500.00
Pussy Willows, #200-28, pr 300.00
Queen Elizabeth Rose, #30091 .... 1,450.00
Other, Madonna La Pieta, 4-1/2" h, c1958 .... 115.00

BOHEMIAN GLASS

History: The once independent country of Bohemia, now a part of the Czech Republic, produced a variety of fine glassware: etched, cut, overlay, and colored. Their glassware, which first appeared in America in the early 1820s, continues to be exported to the U.S. today.

Bohemia is known for its "flashed" glass that was produced in the familiar ruby color, as well as in amber, green, blue, and black. Common patterns include Deer and Castle, Deer and Pine Tree, and Vintage.

Most of the Bohemian glass encountered in today's market is from 1875 to 1900. Bohemian-type glass also was made in England, Switzerland, and Germany.

References: Dr. James D. Henderson, *Bohemian Decorated Porcelain*, Schiffer Publishing, 1999; Sylvia Petrova and Jean-Luc Olivie (eds.), *Bohemian Glass*, Abrams, 1990; Robert and Deborah Truitt, *Collectible Bohemian Glass*, R & D Glass, 1995.

Reproduction Alert.

Bowl, 12-1/2" d, double cut overlay, cobalt blue cut to clear 265.00
Box, domed lid, ruby flashed, Vintage, engraved clear and frosted grape clusters and vines, gilt brass fittings 165.00
Centerpiece Bowl, 8" l, 5" h, broad dimpled form, ruffled rim, irid amber glass 300.00
Centerpiece, 14-1/8" h, bowl with shaped rim, floral panels, flanked by diamond cut panels, large base with enameled female portrait medallion, verso with floral bouquet, flanked by diamond cut panels, bordered by dec gilding 650.00
Chandelier, 21-1/2" h, cut glass, baluster form column surmounted by domed canopy, 5 scrolled candle branches, all suspending prismatic drops 200.00
Cologne Bottle, 5" h, cobalt blue, tiered body dec, white and gold flowers and scrolls 175.00
Compote, 7" d, amber flashed, cut leaf and floral dec, green band at top, pedestal base 125.00
Console Set, 12" d x 12" h ftd center bowl, pr candlesticks, amber, etched foliate and landscape designs, late 19th/early 20th C .. 250.00
Decanter, 18-3/4" h, blue cut to clear, cut gilt dec scallops above and below rect panels, gilt bands around neck, rim, and base, tall sphere shaped faceted stopper, alternating squiggle line dec to facets .. 490.00
Glassware, amber, 14" h decanter, fifteen 5-1/4" h water glasses, eleven 4" h stemmed glasses, fourteen 4-1/2" stemmed glasses, nine 6" h stemmed glasses, twelve 3-5/8" h stemmed sherbets, late 19th/early 20th C 460.00
Goblet
    5-3/4" h, double overlay, pink cut to clear, white int., 19th C . 115.00
    5-7/8" h, overlay, blue cut to clear, etched titled scenes, dated 1857, flower-form foot, third quarter 19th C 300.00
    6" h, eight panels, flared ftd oviform, central alternating enameled flower medallions on fine diamond cut ground, amber colored gilt rim, gilt outlines, 19th C, set of 8 .... 300.00
Jack-In-The-Pulpit-Vase, 6-3/4" h, bulbous translucent lightly irid light blue body, amber spotting and light blue threading, flared top, early 20th C 375.00
Jar, 6" h, quatraform, green, maroon-red threading, metal rim, swing bail handle and cover 250.00
Jug, 8-1/4" h, dark olive green spherical body, irid pulled feather silvery

luster, applied offset twisted basket handle, raised pedestal foot, berry prunt at pontil 1,265.00
Lemonade Set, 10-1/2" h slightly ribbed tankard pitcher, four 4-3/4" h tumblers, amber glass, light blue handles, gilded and enameled Oriental floral motif, polished pontil, c1880, wear to gilding 750.00
Spill Vase, 6-3/8" h, overlay, cut white to cranberry, 19th C, very minor chips, pr 420.00
Rose Bowl, vaseline, enameled white flowers, gilt trim 90.00
Tumbler, 5-1/2" h, wheel cut stag and architectural scene flanked by dec cartouche, ruby cut to clear, late 19th C, set of six 120.00
Vase
    4-1/4" h, tapered cylinder, ruffled rim, teal, five pulled arches of white and magenta, overall irid luster, polished pontil 275.00
    5" h, double bulbed body, irid green, vertical stripes interspersed with round spots, molded base, top rim smoothed 250.00
    5-1/4" h, bulbous body, flared rim, lightly irid colorless body, 2 applied elephant head handles, applied fish dec, blue, green, and white enamel, polished pontil, attributed to Harrach, c1890350.00
    6-3/4" h, mold-blown pinched ovoid body, vine-like ribs, ruffled rim, light blue luster, polished pontil, bubbled irid 175.00
    7-3/4" h, ovoid, trumpet form neck, central dec of bird on branch, ruby cut to clear, late 19th C, pr 90.00
    8-1/2" d, green jade, molded as 3 women dancing in vineyard, deep green to creamy green, faceted rim and base, Schlevogt Ingrid series, c1935 .... 350.00
    8-3/4" h, cut glass, trumpet form, circular foot, cut amber to clear, cut facets, wide central grapevine motif 300.00
    8-3/4" h, tapered oviform, green glass body with int. texture, etched and enameled mauve and yellow iris, gilt accents 520.00
    9-1/2" h, bulbous form, spiral ribbed neck, 2 applied handles, slightly irid surface, dark blue and gold enamel foliate design, sgd "F. H. 5547 182" in gold enamel (Fritz Heckert), c1890, gilt wear 115.00
    9-1/2" h, urn form, amber ground, 2 applied fish, overall multicolored enamel dec of dragonfly, pond lilies, and flowers, 2 handles, Harrach, c1890, wear to enamel 200.00
    9-3/4" h, pale amber tapered cylinder with dark metal mount with Art Nouveau stylized flowers 250.00
    11" h, tapered oval, lightly crackled and irid colorless body, applied handle, wrap at neck, Art Nouveau foliate style gold, white, green, blue, and red enameling, large polished pontil, late 19th C, chips to applied neck wrap 275.00
    12" h, tapered cylindrical, cameo etched berries, hawthorn branches surrounded by ice-chip finish, enameled orange berries, green leaves, maroon ground, polished pontil 350.00
    12-1/4" h, amber glass blown into ormolu-style support, highlighted by heraldic shield, double chamfered rim 300.00

BOOKS, ARCHITECTURE

History: Books relating to architecture, building, and landscape gardening are popular with both book collectors and those who study and appreciate old houses, buildings, and gardens.

Architecture books are very much like the "style" books associated with some of the great furniture makers. These books were eagerly read by early builders to learn what was the most popular styles, how to build some of the newest designs, etc. Some architects, including Frank Lloyd Wright, also designed furniture and accessories to complement his building design. Mr. Wright was not only a well-known architect, but also a frequent author.

To the collector restoring an old house, an architectural book containing drawings of the "correct" period might just have the keys to understanding their unique structure.

References: Allen Ahearn, *Book Collecting: A Comprehensive Guide*, G. P. Putnam's Sons, 1995; Allen and Patricia Ahearn, *Collected Books: The Guide to Values*, F. P. Putnam's Sons, 1997; *American Book Prices Current*, Bancroft Parkman, published annually; Geoffrey Ashall Glaister, *Encyclopedia of the Book*, 2nd ed., available from Spoon River Press, 1996; John R. Gretton, *Baedeker's Guidebooks: A Checklist of English-Language Editions 1861-1939*, available from Spoon River Press, 1994; Sharon and Bob Huxford, *Huxford's Old Book Value Guide*, 11th ed., Collector Books, 1999; Ian C. Ellis, Book Finds, Berkley Publishing, 1996; Norma Levarie, *Art & History of Books*, available from Spoon River Press, 1995; Catherine Porter, *Collecting Books*, available from Spoon River Press, 1995; Caroline Seebohm, Estelle Ellis, and Christopher Simon Sykes, *At Home with Books: How Book Lovers Live with and Care for Their Libraries*, available from Spoon River Press, 1996; Henry Toledano, *The Modern Library Price Guide 1917-1995*, available from Spoon River Press, 1995; *John Wade, Tomart's Price Guide to 20th Century Books*, Tomart Publications, 1994; Edward N. Zempel and Linda A. Verkler (eds.), *Book Prices: Used and Rare 1996*, Spoon River Press, 1996; —, *First Editions: A Guide to Identification*, 3rd ed., Spoon River Press, (2319C W. Rohmann, Peoria, IL 61604) 1995.

Periodicals: *AB Bookman's Weekly*, P.O. Box AB, Clifton, NJ 07015; *Biblio Magazine*, 845 Wilamette St., P.O. Box 10603, Eugene, OR 97401; *Book Source Monthly*, 2007 Syosett Dr., P.O. Box 567, Cazenovia, NY 13035; *Rare Book Bulletin*, P.O. Box 201, Peoria, IL 61650; *The Book Collector's Magazine*, P.O. Box 65166, Tucson, AZ 85728.

Collectors' Club: Antiquarian Booksellers Association of America, 20 West 44th St., 4th Floor, New York, NY 10036.
Benjamin, Asher

>   *Practice of Architecture*, 2nd ed., Boston, 1835, 60 plates, 4to, contemporary calf, moderately rubbed, some plates foxed or browned, few marginal repairs 300.00
>   *The Architect, or, Practical House Carpenter*, L. Coffin, Boston, 1844, 64 engraved plates, 4to, contemporary calf, heavily scuffed, scattered light soiling..460.00

Brandon, Raphael and J. Arthur Brandon, *The Old Timber Roofs of the Middle Ages*, London, 1860, 43 plates, some in color, 4to, publisher's green cloth, splitting along spine, rubbed, rear hinge cracked.175.00
Bridaham, Lester Burbank, *Gargoyles, Chimeres, and the Grotesque in French Gothic Sculpture*, Architectural Book Publishing, NY, 1930,

---

SPECIAL AUCTIONS

New Hampshire Book Auctions
P.O. Box 460
Weare, NH 03281
(603) 529-7432

Pacific Book Auction Galleries
133 Kerney St., 4th Fl
San Francisco, CA 94108
(415) 896-2665

Swann Galleries, Inc.
104 E. 25th St.
New York, NY 10010
(212) 254-4710

---

intro by Ralph Adams Cram, photographic plates, 4to, gilt pictorial cloth, scattered light foxing, dust jacket, moderate wear 230.00
Britton, John, *The History and Antiquities of the Metropolitical Church of York*, London, 1819, 36 engraves plates of views, elevations, plans, and details, 4to, 1/2 evergreen morocco, extremities rubbed, scattered light foxing 175.00
Chicago Tribune Tower Competition, *The International Competition for a New Administration Building for the Chicago Tribune MCMMMXII Containing All the Designs Submitted in Response to the Chicago Tribune's $100,000 Offer*, Chicago, 1923, 282 plates, small folio, coarse cloth, joints cracked and frayed.................................230.00
Corner, James M. and E. E. Soderholtz, *Examples of Domestic Colonial Architecture: In New England, in Maryland and Virginia*, 3rd ed., Boston, 1892, 50 heliogravure plates of ext. and int., small folio, contents loose as issued, gilt lettered cloth portfolios...................375.00
Creswell, K. A. C., *Early Muslim Architecture*, 2nd ed., Oxford, 1969, Vol. 1, 140 plates, folio, green cloth gilt, dust jacket, tears 635.00
Downing, Andrew Jackson, T*he Architecture of Country Houses*, New York, 1852, 320 plates and illus, 4to, publisher's gilt pictorial green cloth, some portions faded...320.00
Elmes, James, *Memoirs of the Life and Works, Sir Christopher Wren*, London, 1823, 12 engraved plates, thick 4to, red morocco gilt extra, extremities moderately rubbed, scattered foxing 1,495.00
Emerson, William and Georges Gromore, *Old Bridges of France*, American Institute of Architects, NY, 1925, 24 mounted color reproductions after watercolors by Pierre Vignal, 35 black and white illus, 44 measured dwgs, photographic plates, diagrams, and maps, folio, contents loose as issued, publisher's cloth portfolio, 1 of 1,000 numbered copies...460.00
Gotch, J. Alfred, *Architecture of the Renaissance in England*, London, 1894, 145 plates, diagrams, and plans, 180 text illus, 2 volumes, folio, publisher's 1/2 morocco gilt, rubbed 100.00
Hegemann, Werner and Elbet Peets, *The American Vitruvius: An Architect's Handbook of Civic Art*, New York, 1922, 1,203 photographic plates and illus, folio, gilt lettered sky blue cloth, dust jacket, head of spine panel chipped 400.00
Hills, Chester, *The Builder's Guide*, D. W. Kellogg & Co., Hartford, 1834, first edition, 70 litho plates, 2 volumes in one, folio, 19th C calf, worn, foxing, scattered dampstaining......................................320.00
Jekyll, Gertrude, *Home and Garden*, London, 1900, 53 photographic plates, large 8vo, orig gilt pictorial cloth, extremely faded, moderately soiled and rubbed, owner's inscriptions 95.00
Kern, G. M., *Practical Landscape Gardening*, Cincinnati, 1855, wood engraved plates and garden plans, 8vo, orig pictorial cloth gilt, spine slightly darkened and worn 115.00
Lacey, Adin Benedict, *American Competitions Published by the T Square Club*, Philadelphia, 1907, 160 plates of plans and elevations from entries to 7 architectural competitions, 4to, publisher's green cloth, leather spine label, 1 of 750 numbered copies...............115.00
McKim, Mead, and White, *A Monograph of the Work...1879-1915*, New York, 1915-18, hundreds of photographic plates, plans, and elevations, 4 volumes, folio, publisher's orig brown cloth bindings, worn.....2,990.00
Moholy-Nagy, Sibyl, *Native Genius in Anonymous Architecture*, New York, 1957, 126 photographic plates and illus, sq 4to, 1/2 cloth, dust jacket...140.00
Platt, Charles A., *Monograph of the Work of Charles A. Platt*, New York, 1925, 183 plates, folio, cloth 490.00
Reynolds, Helen Wilkinson, *Dutchess County Doorways and Other Examples of Period-Work in Wood*, 1730-1830, New York, 1931, 240 photographic plates, 4to, cloth gilt, slipcase...........................165.00
Richardson, A. E. and H. Donaldson Eberlein, *The Smaller English House of the Later Renaissance*, 1660-1830, New York, 1925, illus, 4to, cloth...115.00
Semsch, O. E., *A History of the Singer Building Construction*, New York, 1908, detailed photographic plates, plans, and elevations, 4to, publisher's gilt lettered cloth, spine ends and tips rubbed........150.00
Shaw, Edward

>   *Civil Architecture: or, A Complete Theoretical and Practical System of Building*, Third Edition, Revised and Enlarged, Boston, 1834,

100 engraved plates, 4to, contemporary calf, heavily scuffed, scattered foxing, becoming loose 375.00

Practical Masonry; or, A Theoretical and Operative Treatise of Building, Boston, 1846, 44 engraved plates, 4to, publisher's sheep, quite worn, covers detached, foxing 175.00

Thornton, William, *The Octagon*, American Institute of Architects, Washington, c1925, 30 plates and elevations of Colonel John Tayloe 1798 home, folio, text and plates loose as issued in cloth portfolio, worn 100.00

Tipping, Henry Avray, *English Homes*, London, 1920-28, photographic plates and illus, 8 volumes, folio, 1/2 cloth, moderately worn 1,610.00

Triggs, H. Inigo, *Formal Gardens in England and Scotland*, London, 1902, 122 plates, folio, contemporary 1/2 olive morocco gilt, scuffed, spine faded.. 230.00

Walcot, William, *Architectural Water-Colours and Etchings*, New York and London, 1919, color and black and white plates of European architecture, folio, gilt lettered brown cloth 300.00

Wright, Frank Lloyd

An Autobiography, London and New York, 1932, plates, small sq 4to, pictorial cloth, lightly rubbed, bookplates, first edition.. 260.00

Buildings, Plans, and Designs, Horizon Press, NY, 1963, 100 plates, folio, 640 x 400 mm, text, bookplate, and unbound plates laid-in, paper sleeve, 1/2 cloth portfolio as issued 900.00

Schumacher's Taliesin Line of Decorative Wallpaper, Bredemeier, Chicago, c1855, salesman's copy, 26 wallpaper samples, 6 pgs of photographic plates, folio, orig dec boards 1,265.00

The Future of Architecture, Horizon Press, NY, 1953, photographic plates, 4to, cloth, dust jacket, first edition, sgd by Wright on front free endpaper 1,840.00

Young, John, *A Series of Designs for Shop Fronts, Porticoes, and Entrances to Buildings, Public and Private*, London, 1835, 30 plates by Young, engraved by Adlard, 4to, rebound 525.00

BOOTJACKS

History: Bootjacks are metal or wooden devices that facilitate the removal of boots. Bootjacks are used by placing the heel of the boot in the U-shaped opening, putting the other foot on the back of the bootjack, and pulling the boot off the front foot.

Cast Iron

9-1/2" h, adv, emb "Use Musselmans - Bootjack - Plug Tobacco," orig gold paint, geometric scroll design.. 170.00

10" h, Naughty Nellie, head turned to left, orig red paint 300.00

10-1/4" h, lyre shape... 85.00

10-1/2" h, cricket, bulging black eyes, painted green and black, c1920 .... 125.00

11" h, stag head, scroll dec, c1880 .... 650.00

11-1/4" h, double ended, half circles in middle, quarter moon each end, early 20th C 175.00

11-1/2" h, intertwined scrolls form letter "M" 75.00

11-3/4" h, Tree of Life, vulture heads, cutout heart base, c1890. 220.00

12" h, forked end, central open diamond design, ring at opposite end 150.00

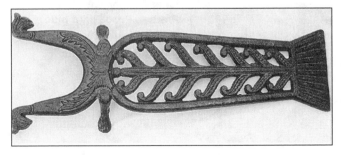

Beetle, cast iron, $60.

13" h, dress boots, two scrolls, c1870 .... 450.00

13" h, emb "Whittier's, American Centennial Book Jack, 1876," around cutout star, "Hyde Park" circles 2nd star, also "Mass – 1776".. 450.00

13-1/4", woman in bloomers, made in Czechoslovakia, early 20th C 750.00

13-1/2" h, cutout scroll design, cutout lettering "Downs & Co." with reversed "N" and "S" 200.00

14" h, raised stylized floral design, heart base 300.00

15-5/8" h, tapering flat wedge, 3 cutout hearts, 5 cutout circles... 450.00

Wood

10" h, folding, hand carved pistol, brass hinges and pins, c1865 350.00

10" h, folding, walnut, lady's legs, pointed toes, brass hinges and pins, c1865 .... 350.00

12" h, lady's leg, hinged brass fittings, boot strap pulls inset inside, early 20th C 900.00

13" h, maple hand hewn.. 65.00

24" h, pine, rose head nails, pierced for hanging 70.00

25-1/2" h, heart shaped loop at top, fork at other end............. 135.00

BOTTLES, GENERAL

History: Cosmetic bottles held special creams, oils, and cosmetics designed to enhance the beauty of the user. Some also claimed, especially on their colorful labels, to cure or provide relief from common ailments.

A number of household items, e.g., cleaning fluids and polishes, required glass storage containers. Many are collected for their fine lithographed labels.

Mineral water bottles contained water from a natural spring. Spring water was favored by health-conscious people between the 1850s and 1900s.

Nursing bottles, used to feed the young and sickly, were a great help to the housewife because of their graduated measure markings, replaceable nipples, and the ease with which they could be cleaned, sterilized, and reused.

References: Ralph & Terry Kovel, *Kovels' Bottles Price List*, 11th ed., Three Rivers Press, 1999; Peck and Audie Markota, *Western Blob Top Soda and Mineral Bottles*, 2nd ed., published by authors, 1994; John Odell, *Digger Odell's Official Antique Bottle and Glass Collector Magazine Price Guide Series*, Vols. 1 through 8, published by author (1910 Shawhan Rd., Morrow, OH 45152), 1995; Diane Ostrander, *Guide to American Nursing Bottles*, 1984, revised ed. by American Collectors of Infant Feeders, 1992; Michael Polak, *Bottles*, 2nd ed., Avon Books, 1997; Dick Roller (comp.), *Indiana Glass Factories Notes*, Acorn Press, 1994; Jeff Wichmann, *Antique Western Bitter Bottles*, Pacific Glass Books, 1999; —, *The Best of the West Antique Western Bitters Bottles*, Pacific Glass Books, 1999.

Periodicals: *Antique Bottle and Glass Collector*, P.O. Box 187, East Greenville, PA 18041; *Canadian Bottle and Stoneware Collector*, 179D Woodridge Crescent, Nepean, Ontario K2B 7T2 Canada.

Collectors' Clubs: American Collectors of Infant Feeders, 5161 W. 59th St., Indianapolis, IN 46254; Antique Bottle Club of Northern Illinois, P.O. Box 571, Lake Geneva, WI 53147; Baltimore Antique Bottle Club, P.O. Box 36031, Townson, MD 21296-6061; Empire State Bottle Collectors Association, 22 Paris Rd., New Hartford, NY 13413; Feder-

SPECIAL AUCTIONS

Norman C. Heckler & Company
Bradford Corner Rd
Woodstock Valley, CT 02682

ation of Historical Bottle Collectors, Inc.; 88 Sweetbriar Branch, Longwood, FL 32750; First Chicago Bottle Club, P.O. Box A3382, Chicago, IL 60690; Forks of the Delaware Bottle Collectors Association, P.O. Box 693, Easton, PA 18042; Historical Bottle Diggers of Virginia, 1176 S Dogwood Dr., Harrisonburg, VA 22801; Las Vegas Antique Bottle & Collectibles Club, 3901 E Stewart #16, Las Vegas, NV 89110-3152; Midwest Antique Fruit Jar & Bottle Club, P.O. Box 38, Flat Rock, IN 47234; New England Antique Bottle Club, 120 Commonwealth Rd, Lynn, MA 01904; North Jersey Antique Bottle Collectors Association, 117 Lincoln Place, Waldwick, NJ 07463-2114; Pennsylvania Bottle Collector's Association, 251 Eastland Ave., York, PA 17402-1105; San Bernardino County Historical Bottle and Collectible Club, P.O. Box 6759, San Bernardino, CA 92412; Southeastern Antique Bottle Club, 143 Scatterfoot Dr., Peachtree City, GA 30269-1853.

Museums: Hawaii Bottle Museum, Honolulu, HI; National Bottle Museum, Ballston Spa, NY, http://www.crisny.org/not-for-profit/nbm; Old Bottle Museum, Salem, NJ.

Additional Listings: Barber Bottles; Bitter Bottles; Figural Bottles; Food Bottles; Ink Bottles; Medicine Bottles; Poison Bottles; Sarsaparilla Bottles; Snuff Bottles. Also see the bottle categories in Warman's Americana & Collectibles for more examples.

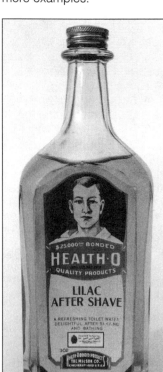

Health-O Lilac After Shave, $30.

Beverage

Arny & Shinn, Georgetown, D. C., "This Bottle Is Never Sold," soda water, squat cylindrical, yellow ground, applied heavy collared mouth, smooth base, half pink, professionally cleaned 150.00
Cole & Southey Washington DC, soda water, squat cylindrical, aquamarine, applied sloping collared mouth with ring, smooth base, half pint, professionally cleaned 110.00
M. Flanagan Petersburg Va, Philadelphia XXX Porter & Ale, squat cylindrical, green with olive tone, heavy applied collared mouth, iron pontil mark, half pint, overall ext. wear 230.00
Stromeyer's Grape Punch, syrup bottle, reverse with glass label, orig cup lid, 12-1/2" h 200.00
Vanderbergh & Co., olive green, Netherlands, early 19th C, seal with emb lettering, bell and star, sq tapering sides, applied flat lip, pontil scar, 9" h, minor wear, set of six 750.00
W. H. Buck Norfolk VA, soda water, squat cylindrical, deep green, applied heavy collard mouth, iron pontil mark, half pint, some ext. wear and scratches 240.00

Cosmetic

De Vry's Dandero-Off Hair Tonic, clear, paper label, 6-1/2" h 15.00
For the Hair, Lyon's Hair Tonic, Kathairon, New York, emb, aqua, rolled lip, 6" h 85.00
Kickapoo Sage Hair Tonic, cylindrical, cobalt blue, tooled mouth, matching stopper, smooth base, 5" h 160.00
Pompeian Massage Cream, amethyst, 2-3/4" h 9.00
Tricopherous for the Skin and Hair, Barry's, New York, emb, pale aqua, 6-3/8" h 40.00
Violet Dulce Vanishing Cream, eight panels, 2-1/2" h 7.50

Household

Glue, Bull Dog Brand Liquid Glue, aqua, ring collar, 3-1/2" 6.50
Ink, Waterman's, paper label with bottle of ink, wooden bullet shaped case, orig paper label, 4-1/4" h 10.00
Sewing Machine Oil, Sperm Brand, clear, 5-1/2" h 5.00
Shoe Polish, Everett & Barron Co., oval, clear, 4-3/4" 5.00
Vanilla, Sauer's Vanilla Extract, wood box, graphic label 25.00

Mineral or Spring Water

Alburgh A. Spring, VT, cylindrical, golden yellow, applied sloping collared mouth with ring, smooth base, quart 800.00

Adams Spring Mineral Water, Lake County, CA, Dr. W. R. Prather, Prop., light blue, c1895, 11-1/2" h, $15.

Chalybeate Water of the American Spa Spring Co., N. J., cylindrical, light to medium blue green, olive green slag striation I neck, applied heavy collared mouth, smooth base, pint.................................. 400.00

Champlain Spring, Alkaline Chalybeate, Highgate, VT, cylindrical, emerald green, applied sloping collared mouth with ring, smooth base, quart 200.00

Gettysburgh Katalysine Water, yellow olive, applied sloping collared mouth with ring, smooth base, quart 200.00

Guilford Mineral Sprig Water, Guilford VT, cylindrical, yellow-olive, applied sloping collard mouth with ring, smooth base, quart.... 475.00

Hopkins Chalybeate Baltimore, cylindrical, dense amber, applied double collared mouth, iron pontil mark, pint 130.00

Middletown Healing Springs, Grays & Clark, Middletown, VT, cylindrical, yellow apricot amber, applied sloping collared mouth with ring, smooth base, quart 1,200.00

Missiquoi, A. Springs, cylindrical, apricot amber, applied sloping collared mouth with ring, smooth base, quart 150.00

Saratoga (star) Springs, cylindrical, dark olive green, applied sloping collared mouth, smooth base, quart 300.00

Vermont Spring, Saxe & Co., Sheldon, VT, cylindrical, citron, applied sloping collared mouth with ring, smooth base, quart 600.00

Nursing

Acme, clear, lay-down, emb.. 65.00
Cala Nurser, oval, clear, emb, ring on neck, 7-1/8" h...................... 8.00
Empire Nursing Bottle, bent neck, 6-1/2" h.................................. 50.00
Mother's Comfort, clear, turtle type.. 25.00
Nonpareil Nurser, aqua, 5-1/2" h.. 20.00

BRASS

History: Brass is a durable, malleable, and ductile metal alloy consisting mainly of copper and zinc. The height of its popularity for utilitarian and decorative art items occurred in the 18th and 19th centuries.

References: Mary Frank Gaston, *Antique Brass & Copper*, Collector Books, 1992, 1994 value update; Rupert Gentle and Rachael Feild, *Domestic Metalwork 1640-1820*, Revised, *Antique Collectors' Club*, 1994; Henry J. Kaufmann, *Early American Copper, Tin & Brass*, Astragal Press, 1995.

Reproduction Alert: Many modern reproductions are being made of earlier brass forms, especially such items as buckets, fireplace equipment, and kettles.

Additional Listings: Bells; Candlesticks; Fireplace Equipment; Scientific Instruments.

Bedwarmer
41-1/2" l, highly tooled lid with starflower and cross, cast and turned brass handle, European.. 525.00
43" l, engraved lid with floral design, refinished turned maple handle 470.00
43-1/4" l, engraved floral design, worn iron handle, old repairs in pan and hinge 275.00
Bookends, pr, 7" w, 4" d, 4-3/4" h, rect, etched and emb flower stalks outlined in green, imp "Carence Craft" mark, some discoloration.......290.00
Box
3" h, dome top, eight sided, double hinged, minor pitting, Netherlands, 18th C..200.00
4" l, dome top, cast, relief eagle and crowns, England, 19th C 175.00
Bucket, spun, 9-1/2" d, 13" d, wrought iron bale handles, "W. A. Hayden's Patent" labels, dents, damage, and old repair, price for pair..........330.00
Candle Sconce, 11-3/8" l, cast brass fixture, scrolled arm, cup, and drip dish fitted into stepped circular bracket, 19th C 375.00
Candlestick, single
4-3/4" h, capstan base.. 600.00

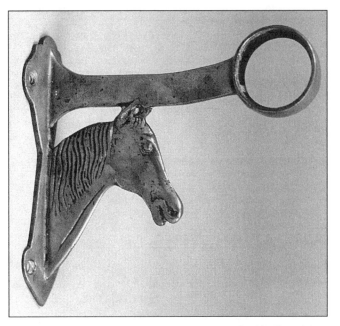

Bar Rail Hardware, figural horse head, 6-1/2" h, 7" w, $35.

5-1/4" h, capstan base, repair to top flange........................... 495.00
5-3/4" h, drum base, bulbous stem, old soldered repairs 440.00
7-3/8" h, Queen Anne, scalloped base and lip, soldered repairs 360.00
7-1/2" h, Queen Anne, scalloped base and well shaped stem, socket flange restored 550.00
7-1/2" h, Queen Anne, scalloped base, baluster, and lip, repairs to socket, added push-up 330.00
7-3/4" h, Queen Anne, scalloped base................................. 495.00
8-5/8" h, round domed base with scalloped edge, somewhat battered, old soldered repairs 110.00
9-1/8" h, Neo-classical, sq base with push-up, casting hole in stem 275.00
11-3/4" h, quatrefoil base with feet, stem screws into base... 155.00
Chamberstick
3-1/2" h, push-up, dent and old repair 110.00
4-1/4" h, old replaced iron thumb piece on push-up 140.00
4-3/4" h, rect base with push-up, conical snuffer and scissors wick trimmers.. 660.00
7" h, scrolled edge pan, side knob push-up, conical snuffer and wick trimming scissors, splits in pan 385.00
Chandelier, 10-1/2" h, three scrolling candle arms, orig hanging chain, early 20th C.. 250.00
Chestnut Roaster, 26-1/2" l, wooden handle, 20th C................. 150.00
Clock Jack, 17" h, mkd "Geo. Salter & Co. Improved, Warranted" ..200.00
Desk Set, 7-1/2" l, oval base with 4 feet, 2 candle sockets, sander and 2 compartments with domed lids, late 18th or early 19th C, minor seam separation at gallery edge 990.00
Footman, shaped brass top with central piercing, front with stylized piercing, two straight rear and two ogee front feet joined by straight and shaped stretchers... 230.00
Glove Warmer, 10" l, brass pan with emb lid, turned wooden handle430.00
Honor Box
4-1/2" x 9" x 8-3/4" h, rect, turned ball beet, T-shaped coin slot, spring latch lid, repairs.. 550.00
5-3/4" l, rect, turned feet and T-shaped coin slot, top with engraved designs and inscription "A sixpence put into the till, when the lid opens you may fill, when you have fill'd with out delay, shut down the lid or a shilling pay," also inscribed "William Shankle," orig key, English 4,620.00
Kettle Shelf, 7-1/2" d, round sliding shelf with simple scroll detail, wrought iron hook for attachment to fender, repairs.................. 90.00

Knife Box, 10-3/4" x 15", paw feet, reticulated sides, divided, and bottom, soldered repair to one end 770.00
Scissor Wick Trimmers, 9-1/" l, scrolled edge pan, battered 200.00
Stamp Box, 3-1/8" l, 1-3/4" w, 1-1/4" h, floral, fleur-de-lis, and putti motifs in relief, imp "T" on base 290.00
Teapot, 8-3/8" h, engraved floral design, hand made, 20th C 165.00
Tobacco Box
    3-1/2" l, oval, couple on each side, plain int., Dutch, 18th C . 175.00
    5-1/4" l, oval, incised figures and verses, Holland, 18th C 230.00
    6-7/8" l, two sections, lids, stepped feet, engraved "E. Ingham 1860," one foot bent 200.00
Trivet
    6-3/8" l, reticulated scrolled top, turned feet 190.00
    14" l, reticulated, gallery, turned handle 275.00
Wall Sconce, 17" h, cast, figural, pierced and foliate Rococo style back plate, scrolled and pierced foliate candle branch with drop pan, surmounted by putto bearing swag of berried laurel, pr 450.00

BREAD PLATES

History: Beginning in the mid-1880s special trays or platters were made for serving bread and rolls. Designated "bread plates" by collectors, these small trays or platters can be found in porcelain, glass (especially pattern glass), and metals.

Bread plates often were part of a china or glass set. However, many glass companies made special plates, which honored national heroes, commemorated historical or special events, offered a moral maxim, or supported a religious attitude. The subject matter appears either horizontally or vertically. Most of these plates are oval and ten inches in length.

Reference: Anna Maude Stuart, *Bread Plates and Platters*, published by author, 1965.

Additional Listings: Pattern Glass.

Majolica
    Apple and Pear, brown ground, minor wear rim 385.00
    Bamboo and Fern, cobalt blue, Wardles 395.00
    Corn, yellow center, minor rim chip on back 440.00
    Give Us This Day Our Daily Bread, cobalt border and basket center, wheat handles 360.00
    Picket Fence and Floral, cobalt blue 385.00
    Pineapple, cobalt blue center 440.00
    Pond Lily, very minor rim repair 440.00
    Water Lily, 12" l, surface wear 110.00
Milk Glass, Wheat & Barley 65.00
Mottos, pressed glass, clear
    Be Industrious, handles, oval 50.00
    Give Us this Day, round, rosette center and border 65.00
    Rock of Ages, 12-7/8" l 175.00
    Waste Not Want Not 35.00
Pattern Glass, clear unless otherwise noted
    Actress, Miss Nielson 80.00
    Beaded Grape, sq 35.00
    Butterfly & Fan 40.00
    Canadian, 10" d 45.00
    Cleopatra, wear 55.00
    Cupid and Venus, amber 85.00
    Deer and Pine Tree, amber 110.00
    Egyptian, Cleopatra center 60.00
    Frosted Lion, rope edge, closed handles, 10-1/4" d 55.00
    Garden of Eden, wear 35.00
    Good Luck 45.00
    Iowa, motto 80.00
    Lion, amber, lion handles, motto 135.00

    Scroll and Flowers, 12" d 40.00
    Tennessee, colored jewels 75.00
    Train 75.00
Silver, sterling, American
    6" d, plain circular form, reeded rim, 19 oz, 2 dwt, price for 8 pc set 300.00
    11" l, oval, fluted sides, Poole, 10 oz, 4 dwt 100.00
    11-3/4" l, Francis I, oval, chased and emb edge, shaped rim, Reed & Barton, 1953, 14 troy oz 400.00
Souvenir and Commemorative
    Old State House, sapphire blue 185.00
    Three Presidents, frosted center 95.00
    Virginia Dare 135.00
    William J. Bryan, milk glass 45.00

BRIDE'S BASKETS

History: A ruffled-edge glass bowl in a metal holder was a popular wedding gift between 1880 and 1910, hence the name "bride's basket." These bowls can be found in most glass types of the period. The metal holder was generally silver plated with a bail handle, thus enhancing the basket image.

Over the years, bowls and bases became separated and married pieces resulted. If the base has been lost, the bowl should be sold separately.

Reference: John Mebane, *Collecting Bride's Baskets and Other Glass Fancies*, Wallace-Homestead, 1976.

Reproduction Alert: The glass bowls have been reproduced.

Note: Items listed below have a silver-plated holder unless otherwise noted.

8" d pink cased bowl with hp florals, crimped edge, 9" w x 14" h ornate brass frame with small porcelain flowers, beveled mirrors between brass leaves, center mirror on high back with hand panted flowers 650.00
8" d, 2-1/8" h, bowl only, satin overlay, shaded pink, clear edging on base, gold and silver sanded flowers and leaves dec, ruffled, off-white lining, ground pontil 155.00
8-1/4" w, sq, cased, deep rose and white ext., whit int., dragon, floral, and leaf dec, ruffled edge, Mt Washington 675.00
9-3/8" d, cased, shaded pink int. with gold floral dec, clear ruffled rim, whit ext. 110.00
9-3/4" d, 2-3/4" h, 3" d, base, bowl only, shaded pink overlay, ruffled edge, white underside, colored enameled flowers and foliage dec, clear and opaque ribbon applied edge 220.00
9-3/4" h, 10" d, deep blue shading to lighter blue, enameled pink and tan flowers, clear edging, resilvered stand 395.00
9-7/8" d, 3" h, 3-3/4" base, bowl only, peachblow, glossy finish, deep pink shading to pale 250.00
10" d, 11" h, Vasa Murrhina, outer amber layer, center layer with hundreds of cream colored spots, random toffee colored spots, dark veins, gold mica flakes, mulberry pink lining, crossed rod thorn handles 635.00
10" w, sq, custard, melon ribbed, enameled daisies, applied rubena crystal rim, twisted and beaded handle, ftd, emb SP frame, mkd "Wilcox" 450.00
10-1/2" d, Hobnail, pink, enameled flowers, ruffled rim, reticulated SP frame 250.00
10-3/4" d, 3-1/2" h, bowl only
    Overlay, heavenly blue, enameled white flowers, green leaves, white underside, ruffled 215.00
    Satin, shaded purple, white underside, dainty purple and white flowers, lacy foliage dec 225.00
11" x 15-1/2", satin, deep rose, enamel swan and floral dec, heavy bronze holder with birds perched on top 425.00

11-1/8" d, 3-3/4" h, bowl only, satin, brown shaded to cream overlay, raised dots, dainty gold and silver flowers and leaves dec, ruffled 250.00

11-3/8" d, 3-1/4" h, 2-7/8" d base, bowl only, maroon shaded to cream overlay, fancy leaf edges with circle and slot emb designs, dainty enameled pink flowers, gold leaves, white underside 215.00

11-1/2" d, 3-5/8" h, bowl only, shaded green overlay satin, ruffled emb lattice edge, white underside.. 210.00

14" d, satin, rose pink, scalloped, rippled, ribbed, and swirled, lacy all-over enamel and gold flower pattern, figural SP base with hummingbird, sgd "Eagle & Co." 1,200.00

BRISTOL GLASS

History: Bristol glass is a designation given to a semi-opaque glass, usually decorated with enamel and cased with another color.

Initially, the term referred only to glass made in Bristol, England, in the 17th and 18th centuries. By the Victorian era, firms on the Continent and in America were copying the glass and its forms.

Biscuit Jar, 6-1/2" h, white, brown leaves and white flowers....... 165.00

Bowl, light blue, Cupid playing mandolin, gold trim...................... 40.00

Box, cov, 2-1/2" d, round, hinged, Cupid on lid, purple floral dec 150.00

Cake Stand, celadon green, enameled herons in flight, gold trim 135.00

Candlesticks, pr, 7" h, soft green, gold band................................ 75.00

Decanter, 11-1/2" h, ruffled stopper, enameled flowers and butterfly 75.00

Dresser Set, two cologne bottles, cov powder jar, white, gilt butterflies dec, clear stoppers 75.00

Ewer, 6-3/8" h, 2-5/8" d, pink ground, fancy gold designs, bands, and leaves, applied handle with gold trim 135.00

Finger Bowl, 4-3/8" d, blue, faceted sides, early 20th C, 8 pc set 500.00

Hatpin Holder, 6-1/8" h, ftd, blue, enameled jewels, gold dec..... 100.00

Lamp, table, 21-1/2" h, 8-1/2" d, turquoise blue stem, font and shade, gold bands, heavy black glass base, orig chimney 395.00

Mug, 5" h, white, eagle and "Liberty" 375.00

Perfume Bottle, 3-1/4" h, squatty, blue, gold band, white enameled flowers and leaves, matching stopper 100.00

Pitcher, smoky gray, blue handle, gold dec, 5-1/2" h, $45.

Puff Box, cov, round, blue, gold dec 35.00

Rose bowl, 3-1/2" d, shaded blue, crimped edge 65.00

Sugar Shaker, 4-3/4" h, white, hp flowers.................................... 60.00

Sweetmeat Jar, 3" x 5-1/2", deep pink, enameled flying duck, leaves, blue flower dec, white lining, SP rim, lid, and bail handle 110.00

Urn, 18" h, pink, boy and girl with lamp 550.00

Vase

12" h, blue, enamel dec... 90.00

16" h, blue, roses dec.. 200.00

Wine Glass, 5" h, green, England, 19th C, price for set of 6 ...... 260.00

BRITISH ROYALTY COMMEMORATIVES

History: British commemorative china, souvenirs to commemorate coronations and other royal events, dates from the 1600s, with the early pieces being rather crude in design and form. With the development of transfer printing, c1780, the images on the wares more closely resembled the monarchs.

Few commemorative pieces predating Queen Victoria's reign are found today at popular prices. Items associated with Queen Elizabeth II and her children, e.g., the wedding of HRH Prince Andrew and Miss Sarah Ferguson and the subsequent birth of their daughter HRH Princess Beatrice, are very common.

Some British Royalty commemoratives are easily recognized by their portraits of past or present monarchs. Some may be in silhouette profile. Royal symbols include crowns, dragons, royal coats of arms, national flowers, swords, scepters, dates, messages, and monograms.

References: Susan and Al Bagdade, *Warman's English & Continental Pottery & Porcelain*, 3rd Edition, Krause Publications, 1998; Douglas H. Flynn and Alan H. Bolton, *British Royalty Commemoratives*, Schiffer Publishing, 1994; Lincoln Hallinan, *British Commemoratives*, Antique Collectors' Club, 1999; Eric Knowles, *Miller's Royal Memorabilia*, Reed Consumer Books, 1994.

Collectors' Club: Commemorative Collector's Society, The Gardens, Gainsborough Rd, Winthrope, New Newark, Nottingham NG24 2NR England.

Periodical: The Commemorative Collector Newsletter, P.O. Box 294, Lititz, PA 17543-0294.

Additional Listings: See Warman's Americana & Collectibles for more examples.

Autograph

King George II, LS, sgd "George R," 1 page folio, St. James, 12/13 Jan. 1741 to the Margrave Carl Wilhelm Friedrich of Brandenburg, in German, New Year's greetings, addressed to "Sereniest Prince, dear cousin," large paper and wax seal.................. 600.00

King William III, LS, sgd "Guilielmus R." as king, 2 pages folio, Sept. 1, 1699, written in Latin, to Duke Bernhard of Saxony, formal letter of condolence on death of Bernard's brother, Duke Albrecht of Saxony... 1,850.00

King William IV, LS, sgd "William Henry," 2 pages large 8vo, Nov 18 1787, from naval vessel off cost of New Jersey, writing to request drawing supplies from London, contains comments about life aboard ship, etc. 575.00

Queen Mary II, LS, 1 page, Türnhout, April 26, 1687, written in German, to Frederick Wilhelm, The Great Elector of Brandenburg, heartfelt letter of condolence on death of Elector's son... 2,200.00

Tumbler, Coronation of George VI, 1937, 4-3/8" h, $40.

Beaker, George IV and Elizabeth, 1937 Coronation, Grindley, 4" h ...48.00
Book, Mark Twain, Queen Victorian Jubilee, The Great Procession of June 22, 1897, in the Queen's Honor, 4to, orig maroon cloth backed white boards, moderately soiled, 1 of 195 numbered copies ... 375.00
Bowl
 Charles, 1969 Investiture, Aynsley, 5-1/2" d 55.00
 Edward VII, 1937 Coronation, profile in well, pressed glass, 10 d 70.00
 Elizabeth II, 1953 Coronation, pressed glass, 4-3/4" h 60.00
 George VI and Elizabeth, 1937 Coronation, coat of arms, Paragon, 5-1/2" d 55.00
Box, cov, Elizabeth the Queen Mother, 1980, 80th Birthday, color portrait, Crown Staffordshire, 4" d 75.00
Brochure, Canadian Visit, 1959, Queen Elizabeth II and Prince Philip, opening of St. Lawrence Seaway, 8-1/2" x 11" 15.00
Cup and Saucer
 Andrew and Sarah, 1986 Wedding, Colclough 30.00
 Edward VII and Alexandra, 1888 Silver Wedding Anniversary, coat of arms 185.00
 Elizabeth II, portrait flanked by flags, coronation, pairs of flags inside cup and on saucer, mkd "Alfred Meakin England," 3" h x 3-1/4" d cup, 6" d saucer, ... 45.00
 George V and Mary, 1911 Coronation, color portraits 60.00
Figure, 5-1/4" h, Elizabeth I, carved ivory, lower section of skirt hinged to reveal triptych of Queen and Sir Walter Raleigh, Continental, 19th C, hairlines 550.00
Handkerchief, white fabric, small red, white, and blue stitched British flag above printed full color view across Thames towards Buckingham Palace, Westminster Abbey, rural countryside scenes on border, May, 1937, orig small cardboard price tag, 10-1/2" x 11" 20.00
Jug
 Elizabeth II, 1953 Coronation, emb crowning scene, Burleigh Ware, 8-1/4" h 250.00
 Victoria, 1887 Gold Jubilee, black and white portraits, 5" h ... 145.00
Lithophane, cup, crown, and cypher, 2-3/4" h
 Alexandra, 1902 .... 195.00
 George V, 1911 .... 165.00
Loving Cup
 Elizabeth II and Philip, 1972 Silver Wedding Anniversary, Paragon, 3" h 175.00
 George VI and Elizabeth, 1937 Coronation, brown Marcus Adams portraits, 3-1/4" h 145.00
Magic Lantern Slide, Victoria and Albert 15.00
Medallion, Anne and Mark, 1973 Wedding, molded pale pink portraits, pink frame, Hutchenreuther 3-1/4" d 60.00

Mug
 Edward VIII, Coronation, 1937, sepia portrait of king flanked by multicolored flags, reverse with Union Jack and Flag of commonwealth, flanking names of some of the nations, topped by crown, gold trim, 2-1/2" h, 2-1/2" d, crest mark and "Empire England" 50.00
 Elizabeth II, Coronation, portrait of Queen facing left, "Coronation of Her Majesty Queen Elizabeth" on reverse, gold trim, 3" h, 3" d, crown and "Radfords Bone China Made in England" mark .. 45.00
Paperweight, Charles and Diana, 1981 Wedding, white sulphide portraits, cobalt blue ground, CR Albret, France, 2-3/4" d 225.00
Pinback Button
 Edward VIII, multicolored, for 1937 coronation, 7/8" d 15.00
 George V and Queen Mary Silver Jubilee, black and white oval portraits, pale turquoise ground, full color British flags, 1" d 20.00
 George VI and Elizabeth, black and white, May 2, 1937, coronation, 1-1/4" 20.00
 Prince of Wales, c1910 portrait, 7/8" d 30.00
 Victoria, Queen of England, multicolored, from 1900 series, 1-1/4" d 35.00
Pin Tray, Elizabeth II, 1977 Silver Jubilee, black silhouette, Coalport, 3-3/4" d 35.00
Pitcher, 8-3/4" h, marriage of Princess Charlotte and Prince Leopold, c1816, relief dec, double scroll handle, Pratt ware, minor enamel loss 1,265.00
Plate
 Edward VII and Alexandra, 1902 Coronation, blue and white, Royal Copenhagen, 7" d 200.00
 George VI and Elizabeth, Canadian visit, 1939, word "Canada" in relief under portraits in center, "King George IV, Queen Elizabeth, 1939" in relief on rim 65.00
Program
 Prince of Wales Royal Investiture, July 1, 1969, glossy paper, 6-1/2" x 9" 12.00
 Queen Elizabeth II, Silver Jubilee, 1977, 42 pgs, glossy paper, 8-1/4" x 11-3/4" 10.00
Snuff Box, 3" d, round, bronze, round, dark patina, angel riding lion with "Regent," reverse emb inscription "In record of the reign of George III" covered by sunburst and cross, visible on int., engraved paper bust and "H.R.H. George Augustus Frederick Prince Regent...Feb 1811" 2,100.00
Teapot
 Charlotte, 1817 In Memoriam, black and white dec, 6" h 275.00
 Victoria, 1897 Diamond Jubilee, color coat of arms, Aynsley .. 225.00
Tin
 Queen Elizabeth II, coronation, sq, Queen Elizabeth II on horseback, full view, mkd "Sharp Assorted Toffee," stamped "Made In England by Edward Sharp & Sons Ltd. Of Maidstone Kent," 7" x 6" x 2", minor scratches and edge rubbing 40.00
 Queen Elizabeth II and Prince Philip, round, coats of arms of the commonwealth nations on sides alternating with pictures of Buckingham Palace, Westminster Abbey, Windsor Castle, and Palace of Holyrood, mkd "Huntley & Palmer Biscuits Reading & London, England," 7-1/2" d 30.00

BRONZE

History: Bronze is an alloy of copper, tin, and traces of other metals. It has been used since Biblical times not only for art objects, but also for utilitarian wares. After a slump in the Middle Ages, the use of bronze was revived in the 17th century and continued to be popular until the early 20th century.

References: Harold Berman, *Bronzes: Sculptors & Founders 1800-1930*, Vols. 1-4 and Index, distributed by Schiffer Publishing, 1996; James Mackay, *The Dictionary of Sculptors in Bronze*, Antique Collectors' Club, 1999; Christopher Payne, *Animals in Bronze*, Reference and

Price Guide, Antique Collectors' Club, 1999; Stuart Pivar, *The Bayre Bronzes, A Catalogue Raisonné*, Antique Collectors' Club, 1999.

Notes: Do not confuse a "bronzed" object with a true bronze. A bronzed item usually is made of white metal and then coated with a reddish-brown material to give it a bronze appearance. A magnet will stick to it but not to anything made of true bronze.

A signed bronze commands a higher market price than an unsigned one. There also are "signed" reproductions on the market. It is very important to know the history of the mold and the background of the foundry.

Andirons, pr, 18-1/2" h, 30" l, Rococo-style, openwork rocaille form, elongated cabochons, joined by trelliswork fender 460.00
Box, cov, French, gilt bronze, enamel dec, retailed in US, late 19th C
    4" x 3-1/2" x 1-3/4", rect, canted corners, sides with berried laurel swags suspended from stylized arches, lid with central relief medallion of children at play 225.00
    5-3/8" l, oval, sides cast with continuous band of scrolling foliage, lid with relief medallion of courting couple, gentleman teaches lady to play pipe, fountain and landscape in background ... 300.00
Bust, 8" h, Seneca, fitted to waisted circular socle, mounted to dark green marble plinth, Continental, 19th C................................... 230.00
Candelabra, pr
    25" h, Renaissance Revival, seven-light, gilt bronze, urn shouldered by winged animals, central shaft, 6 C-scroll branches cast with acanthus and lyres, bobeche and candle cups, architectural form base, winged term capped paw feet centered by grotesque mask, applied dec and borders, 19th C, electrified.......... 1,100.00
    36" h, nine-light, gilt bronze, elaborately modeled with foliage, masks, and scrolls, stamped "F. Barbedienne," late 19th/early 20th C 6,325.00
Candelabrum, 21" h, two-light, Louis XV style, gilt bronze, acanthus cast shaft with conforming cast scroll branches, bobeche and cup, circular foot, later central mount with shaft and adjustable shade, late 19th C, electrified 800.00
Candlesticks, pr
    2-3/4" h, hammered, short baluster form, stepped circular base, unmarked 230.00
    6-1/4" h, Louis XV style, bronze dore, tapering, cartouche and scrolls on body, acanthus cast candlecups, foliate cast feet, late 19th C 120.00
    10-1/4" h, cast, baluster shape, hammered bronze textured center section, spotting... 145.00
Chandelier, 21-1/2" drop, 21-1/2" w wingspan, figural bat, 3 full bodied flying bats in triangular formation, each facing outward, wings touching side to side, suspended from bronze chains, metal ceiling mount, suspending 3 brass foliate light figures, brown patina, 20th C.......7,200.00
Chenets, pr, Louis XVI style, shaped base cast with openwork foliate and garland sides supporting figure of cherub draped in ribbon, late 19th C.. 950.00
Figure
    5-3/8" h, 6-3/4" l, Standing Horse, greenish-brown patinated bronze, sgd "Alfred Barye" on base, French, 19th C 1,955.00
    8" h, Diana the Huntress, mounted on rect base, dark green patina, illegible signature, 20th C 865.00
    8-1/2" h, 9-1/2" l, Braying Stag, brown patinated bronze, sgd "Isadore Bonheur," c1880 .... 1,150.00
    16" l, Charioteer, light brown patination, marble base, paw feet, Continental, one foot missing 575.00
    20-3/4" h, 27" l, standing bull, patinated 600.00
    24-1/2" h, Marly Horse, rearing horse restrained by figure, light to medium brown patination, after Coustou 1,380.00
    30" h, two birds in bulrushes, imp signature, also imp "L. Martin, Foundeur," bronze socle base, 19th C............................1,840.00
    39-1/2" h, young girl, hip-shot pose, classical drapery, long hair, holding arms aloft, patinated..1,100.00

Statue, Reronsseur de la Reanissance, Ernest Rancoulet, sgd and titled on base, 26-3/8" h, $2,000. Photo courtesy of Freeman\FineArts.

Lamp Base, 17" h, fox below fruiting tree with bird, pierced base, Japanese, early 20th C, pr... 2,760.00
Paperweight, figural
    5-1/2" l, frog 275.00
    8" l, dead Sparrow, sgd "H. Parris," 19th C 375.00
Plaque, 38" l, 29" w, George Washington, brown and reddish-brown patina, by Anthony W. Jones, sgd and located "A. J. Jones, Sculp. N.Y." 950.00
Sconces, pr
    11-3/4" h, Louis XVI style, bronze dore, rect back plate, central sunflower and cornered foliate swags, suspending figure of putti alighting on shield holding torch, campana form candlecup475.00
    21" h, 16-1/2" w, 9-1/2" d, Rococo style, bronze dore, 2-light, coiled dragon had back plate, elaborately curving arms 3,000.00
    21-1/2" h, figural flying bat, brass foliate light fixture suspended from rings at mouth, dark brown patina, 20th C, pr 5,175.00
Sculpture, 25-7/8" h, Flower Fairies, golden-brown patina, sgd "Moreau," also inscribed "S. Marchi Eder" 2,200.00
Standish, 17" l, modeled with lions, masks, cabochons, and foliage, ball feet, gilt, Renaissance Revival, c1870................................ 345.00
Table Pedestal, 30-3/4" h, patinated, baluster shape standard, elaborately case with floral swags, gadrooning and scrollwork, beaded capital applied with 4 melusines with entwined arms, foliate tails forming support brackets, stepped circular base, lion paw feet550.00
Tray, 14-1/4" d, circular, variegated patina, gilt berry and foliate handles, Carl Sorensen... 50.00
Vase, 12-1/2" h, 5" d, classic shape, overlaid with sterling silver dancing maidens, Heintz, stamped "Hams/R. H. Macy & Co." and "Patent"700.00

BUFFALO POTTERY

History: Buffalo Pottery Co., Buffalo, New York, was chartered in 1901. The first kiln was fired in October 1903. Larkin Soap Company established Buffalo Pottery to produce premiums for its extensive mail-order business. Wares also were sold to the public by better department and jewelry stores. Elbert Hubbard and Frank Lloyd Wright, who designed the Larkin Administration Building in Buffalo in 1904, were two prominent names associated with the Larkin Company.

Early Buffalo Pottery production consisted mainly of semi-vitreous china dinner sets. Buffalo was the first pottery in the United States to produce successfully the Blue Willow pattern. Buffalo also made a line of hand-decorated, multicolored willow ware, called Gaudy Willow. Other early items include a series of game, fowl, and fish sets, pitchers, jugs, and a line of commemorative, historical, and advertising plates and mugs.

From 1908-1909 and again from 1921-1923, Buffalo Pottery produced the line for which it is most famous—Deldare Ware. The earliest of this olive green, semi-vitreous china displays hand-decorated scenes from English artist Cecil Aldin's Fallowfield Hunt. Hunt scenes were done only from 1908 to 1909. English village scenes also were characteristic of the ware and were used during both periods. Most pieces are artist signed.

In 1911, Buffalo Pottery produced Emerald Deldare, which used scenes from Goldsmith's The Three Tours of Dr. Syntax and an Art Nouveau-type border. Completely decorated Art Nouveau pieces also were made.

Abino, which was introduced in 1912, had a Deldare body and displayed scenes of sailboats, windmills, or the sea. Rust was the main color used, and all pieces were signed by the artist and numbered.

In 1915, the manufacturing process was modernized, giving the company the ability to produce vitrified china. Consequently, hotel and institutional ware became the main production items, with hand-decorated ware de-emphasized. The Buffalo firm became a leader in producing and designing the most-famous railroad, hotel, and restaurant patterns. These wares, especially railroad items, are eagerly sought by collectors.

In the early 1920s, fine china was made for home use. Bluebird is one of the patterns from this era. In 1950 Buffalo made their first Christmas plate. These were given away to customers and employees primarily from 1950 to 1960. However, it is known that Hample Equipment Co. ordered some as late as 1962. The Christmas plates are very scarce in today's resale market.

The Buffalo China Company made "Buffalo Pottery" and "Buffalo China"—the difference being that one is semi-vitreous ware and the other vitrified. In 1956, the company was reorganized, and Buffalo China became the corporate name. Today Buffalo China is owned by Oneida Silver Company. The Larkin family no longer is involved.

Marks: Blue Willow pattern is marked "First Old Willow Ware Mfg. in America."

Reference: Seymour and Violet Altman, *Book of Buffalo Pottery*, reprinted by Schiffer Publishing, 1987.

Abino Ware

Candlestick, 9" h, sailing ships, 1913...475.00
Pitcher, 7" h, Portland Head Light...700.00
Tankard, 10-1/2" h, sailing scene...900.00

Deldare

Bowl, 9" d, Fallowfield Hunt, the Death, sgd "W. Foster," 1908 ....450.00
Calendar Plate, 1910, 9-1/4" d, sgd "W. Foster" 575.00
Calling Card Tray
    Street scene 395.00

Three Pigeons 450.00
Candlesticks, pr, street scene 895.00
Cereal Bowl, 6" d, Fallowfield Hunt...250.00
Chop Plate, 14" d
    Fallowfield Hunt 795.00
    Street scene 695.00
Creamer and Sugar, Scenes of Village Life in Ye Olden Days, creamer sgd "F. Mae," sugar sgd "O Sauter," 1909 ....500.00
Cup and Saucer, street scene 225.00
Fruit Bowl, street scene 575.00
Hair Receiver, street scene, 1909...450.00
Jardiniere, street scene...995.00
Mug
    Fallowfield Hunt
        3-1/2" h...395.00
        4-1/2" h...475.00
    Street scene
        3-1/2" h...350.00
        4-1/2" h...395.00
Pin Tray, street scene...325.00
Pitcher
    Street scene
        6" h...495.00
        9" h...750.00
    The Great Controversy, 7" w, 12" h, sgd "W. Fozter," stamped mark 290.00
Plaque, 12-1/2" l, Fallowfield Hunt, Breakfast at the Three Pigeons, c1910 ....295.00
Plate, 8-1/4" d, Fallowfield Hunt, The Death, artist sgd "Egowlman," 1909 ....225.00
Powder Jar, street scene 395.00
Punch Cup, Fallowfield Hunt...375.00
Soup Plate, 9" d, street scene 425.00
Tankard, Three Pigeons...1,175.00
Teapot, cov, large, street scene 395.00
Tea Tile
    Fallowfield Hunt 395.00
    Street scene 395.00
Tea Tray, street scene...650.00
Vase
    7" h, street scene...450.00
    7-3/4" h, 6-1/2" d, King Fisher, green and white dec, olive ground, stamped mark, artist signature 1,380.00

Emerald Deldare

Creamer..450.00
Fruit Bowl...1,450.00
Mug, 4-1/2" h..475.00
Vase, 8-1/2" h, 6-1/2" h, stylized foliate motif, shades of green and white, olive ground, stamp mark 810.00

Roycroft China, all ivory with green and red border, stamped "Buffalo Pottery" and orb and cross mark, left: four 9" d luncheon plates, $850; two rect serving dishes and teapot (with hairline, small chips) $550; 10" d serving plate with 2 handles, $425; three soup bowls, bread plate, and saucer, $275. Photo courtesy of David Rago Auctions, Inc.

Roycroft, Dard Hunter geometric design

Compote, 9" d, 3-3/4" h, orb and cross mark 1,300.00
Luncheon Plate, 9" d, green and red border, ivory ground, stamped
   "Buffalo Pottery,"" orb and cross mark, set
   of 4 .... 850.00
Salt and Pepper Shakers, pr, 3" h, 2" d, stylized green and brown geo-
   metric dec, white ground 375.00
Serving Plate, 10" d, green and red border, ivory ground, stamped
   "Buffalo Pottery," orb and cross mark 425.00

BURMESE GLASS

History: Burmese glass is a translucent art glass originated by Frederick Shirley and manufactured by the Mt.
Washington Glass Co., New Bedford, Massachusetts, from
1885 to c1891.

Burmese glass colors shade from a soft lemon to a
salmon pink. Uranium was used to attain the yellow color,
and gold was added to the batch so that on reheating, one
end turned pink. Upon reheating again, the edges would
revert to the yellow coloring. The blending of the colors
was so gradual that it is difficult to determine where one
color ends and the other begins.

Although some of the glass has a glossy surface, most
pieces were acid finished. The majority of the items were
free blown, but some were blown molded in a ribbed, hobnail, or diamond-quilted design.

American-made Burmese is quite thin and, therefore, is
fragile, and brittle. English Burmese was made by Thos.
Webb & Sons. Out of deference to Queen Victoria, they
called their wares "Queen's Burmese Ware."

Collectors Club: Mount Washington Art Glass Society,
P.O. Box 24094, Fort Worth, TX 76124-1094.

Reproduction Alert: Reproductions abound in almost
every form. Since uranium can no longer be used, some of
the reproductions are easy to spot. In the 1950s, Gundersen produced many pieces in imitation of Burmese.

Advisors: Clarence and Betty Maier.

Bonbon, 6-1/2" l, 4-3/4" w, 2-3/8" to top of handle, Mt. Washington,
   shiny, lemon-yellow, 3 applied prunts, applied handle, re-fired heart
   shaped rim 950.00
Charger, 10" d, shallow, disk shape 285.00
Cream Pitcher and Sugar, 4-1/8" h pitcher, 2-5/8" h sugar, Mt. Washington, shape #99, diamond quilt design, heat check on creamer 465.00
Cruet
   6-1/2" h, satin finish, delicate blush on shoulders, melon ribbed
     body, soft lemon-yellow handle and faceted stopper 1,0855.00
   7" h, shiny finish, mushroom stopper, each rib (of 30) has hint of
     pink, refired buttery yellow tip of spout 1,250.00
Demitasse Cup and Saucer, 2-3/8" h, 3-1/8" d cup, 4-5/8" d saucer, Mt.
   Washington, undecorated, orig paper label on saucer 585.00
Fairy Lamp
   3-3/4" h, Webb, pyramid, Burmese shade, unsigned clear glass
     base 145.00
   4" h, pyramid, pressed glass base has molded-in "S. Clarke Fairy
     Pyramid" and dancing fairy logo signature 335.00
   4-3/4" h, pyramid, Burmese shade, clear base sgd "S. Clarke's Pyr-
     amid Fairy" 335.00
   5-1/2" h, 5-3/4" w, Webb, Cricklite, short crimped skirt flares out
     from the top of the bowl-shaped base, impressed signature
     "Thos. Webb & Sons Queens Burmeseware Patented," clear
     glass candle cup is signed, "S Clarke Fairy Trade Mark Patent,"
     unused wax candle 950.00

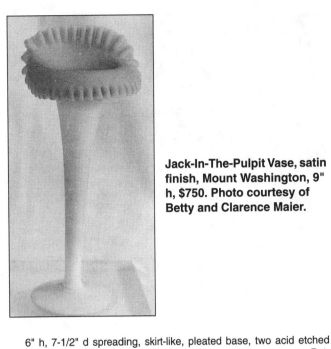

Jack-In-The-Pulpit Vase, satin finish, Mount Washington, 9" h, $750. Photo courtesy of Betty and Clarence Maier.

   6" h, 7-1/2" d spreading, skirt-like, pleated base, two acid etched
     signatures, "Thos Webb & Sons Queen's Burmeseware Pat-
     ented" and "S. Clarke's Fairy Patent Trade Mark,", clear glass
     candle cup signed, "Clarke's Criklite Trade Mark" 950.00
Jack-In-The-Pulpit Vase, 9" h, refired yellow margin of pie-crimped
   edge, subtle blush of color at mouth and throat, soft yellow standard
   and base, Mt. Washington 750.00
Rose Bowl
   2-1/2" h, 2-1/2" d, Mt. Washington 285.00
   3-1/4" h, Webb, prunus blossom dec, sq top 285.00
Salt Shaker, 4-1/4" h, Mt. Washington, blushed upper half, lemon-yel-
   low lower half, 2 part metal top 265.00
Toothpick Holder
   2-1/2" h, Mt Washington, optic diamond quilt design,
     pinched tricorn top 535.00
   2-1/2" h, Webb, sq top, bulbous body 285.00
Tumbler, Mt. Washington
   Pastel salmon shading to a creamy-yellow 285.00
   Shiny finish, egg-shell thin satin body 375.00
Vase
   7" h, Mt. Washington, lily, delicate blush to the mouth of the "lily,"
     refired yellow rim 650.00
   8" h, gourd shape, roses and forget-me-nots, three lovely peach-col-
     ored rose blossoms cling to leafed branch which swirl down rim,
     around body and down to the base, entwining strands of turquoise-
     colored forget-me-not blossoms, double gourd shaped..... 1,050.00
   9-1/2" d, h, encrusted gold, Crown Milano, thorny rose branches
     laden with single petaled blossoms, buds and leaves, 9-1/2" tall,
     original paper label 1,450.00
   11" h, 6" d base, white daisies with distinctive yellow-dot
     centers 1,750.00
   11-1/2" h, acid finished, ovoid, hp Egyptian desert scene, pyramids
     and ibis in flight, gilt highlights 4,500.00
   12" h, Mt. Washington, #146 .... 385.00
Whiskey Taster, 2-3/4" tall, molded-in elongated diamond quilted
   design.. 285.00

BUSTS

History: The portrait bust has its origins in pagan and
Christian traditions. Greek and Roman heroes dominate the earliest examples. Later, images of Christian

Cavalier, sepia colors, mkd "Teplitz,"" c1910, 8-1/2" h, $185.

saints were used. Busts of the "ordinary man" first appeared during the Renaissance.

During the 18th and 19th centuries, nobility, poets, and other notable persons were the most frequent subjects, especially on those busts designed for use in a home library. Because of the large number of these library busts, excellent examples can be found at reasonable prices, depending on artist, subject, and material.

Additional Listings: Ivory; Parian Ware; Soapstone; Wedgwood.

10" h, Cicero, black basalt, waisted circular socle, imp title and Wedgwood & Bentley mark, c1775, chips to socle rim 2,300.00
12" h, young boy, patinated bronze, illegibly sgd, shaped marble base, Continental, early 20th C 435.00
14-3/4" h, Woman in Hat, inscribed title, Victorian, spelter 375.00
15" h, Athena, bronze, wearing full regalia, tapered socle, Continental, 19th C...800.00
18" h, elegant woman, brown patinated bronze, sgd "Caesar Ceribelli," late 19th C 750.00
20" h, lady with rose, marble, incised "A. Testi," associated partial alabaster pedestal with spiral fluted stem 2,645.00
21" h
   Caesar, Augustus, Roman-style Carrara and Verte Antico marble, 20th C, cracks to tunic, losses 3,100.00
   Child, after Shiela Estelle Russell-Taylor, carved sandstone, Arthur Bryan 385.00
   Christ, carved wood and plaster, naturalistic features and paint, Continental, 19th C, some worming..................................635.00
   Goethe, locking dexter, sgd "Ga. Aix," Italian carved Carrara marble, late 19th C...................................1,150.00
21-1/4" h, Smiling Gypsy Girl, plaster, Continental 450.00
21-3/4" h, young woman, Italian faience, polychromed Renaissance style attire, initialed...350.00
23" h, man in Roman dress, Carrara marble, incised on back as being modeled and carved by N. N. Burnard, late 19th C 1,380.00
25" h, young beauty, sgd "J. Arduino," dated 1900, marble, rusticated red marble fluted socle...2,645.00
26" h, young pious woman, lace and flower bodice, hair in long braid, marble, matching 6" h marble socle, Italian, late 19th C 7,475.00
35" h, George Washington, cast plaster, orig bronze finish 195.00

BUTTER PRINTS

History: There are two types of butter prints: butter molds and butter stamps. Butter molds are generally of three-piece construction—the design, the screw-in handle, and the case. Molds both shape and stamp the butter at the same time. Butter stamps are generally of one-piece construction but can be of two-piece construction if the handle is from a separate piece of wood. Stamps decorate the top of butter after it is molded.

The earliest prints are one piece and were hand carved, often heavily and deeply. Later prints were factory made with the design forced into the wood by a metal die.

Some of the most common designs are sheaves of wheat, leaves, flowers, and pineapples. Animal designs and Germanic tulips are difficult to find. Prints with designs on both sides are rare, as are those in unusual shapes, such as half-rounded or lollipop.

Reference: Paul E. Kindig, *Butter Prints and Molds*, Schiffer Publishing, 1986.

Reproduction Alert: Reproductions of butter prints were made as early as the 1940s.

Mold
2" d, pineapple, round, cased 125.00
2-3/4" d, anchor, carved wood 185.00
2-7/8" d, pineapple, round, cased 150.00
3-1/2" d, sunflower, carved wood...................................85.00
4-3/8" d, pineapple, carved wood 325.00
4-3/4" d, deer, round, repairs to case.............................200.00
5" x 8", roses, carved maple, serrated edges 165.00

Stamp
2-1/2" d, round, turned handle, thistle...50.00
2-7/8" d, 4-1/2" l, carved fruitwood, strawberry 50.00
3-1/4" l, turned inserted handle, leaf, refinished 50.00
3-3/8" d, round, eagle 90.00
3-3/8" x 6-1/8", deeply cut stylized floral and double heart design, pine, soft worn patina..525.00
3-5/8" d, 2-1/4" l, fruitwood, leaf and branch................................65.00
3-3/4" d
   Pinwheel, 4 teardrop and triangular arms form design, old dark finish 115.00

Floral and relief carved crosshatch dec, chip carved, double sided, lollipop handle, $200.

Round, pinwheel, hole for inserted handle, poplar, old worn patina,
   some edge damage 200.00
4" d, round, one pc turned handle, poplar, old scrubbed patina
   Beehive, age cracks 195.00
   Eagle, edge wear and cracks 275.00
4-1/8" d x 4-1/2", star design, similar carving on handle 145.00
4-1/4" d, round, turned handle
   Cow, poplar, old scrubbed patina, age cracks, edge damage 200.00
   Leaf design, dark waxy finish 200.00
   Sunflower, feather leaves, old dark finish 435.00
   Swan 125.00
4-1/2" d, round, sturdy handle, stylized tulip 125.00
4-5/8" d, round, turned handle, pineapple 95.00
4-3/4" d, round, handle, geometric design 95.00
4-3/4" d, 5-1/2" l, walnut, foliage and flowers, elaborate carving .. 85.00

4-7/8" d, round
   Pinwheel, one pc handle 225.00
   Stylized tulip and stars, deep cut, one pc turned handle,
      poplar, old patina 425.00
5-7/8" l, carved hardwood, lollipop style, rosette 110.00
6-3/4" l, sheaf of wheat, stylized design, notched rim band 200.00
7" l
   Lollipop style, star, zig-zag band rim, flared end handle, old
      patina 300.00
   Semi-circular, flower with foliage, insert turned handle, poplar, old
      soft patina 300.00
   Semi-circular, heart with foliage, insert turned handle 385.00
   Semi-circular, pineapple, insert turned handle 350.00
   Semi-circular, sheaf, insert turned handles, poplar, old soft
      patina 300.00

CALENDAR PLATES

History: Calendar plates were first made in England in the late 1880s. They became popular in the United States after 1900, the peak years being 1909 to 1915. The majority of the advertising plates were made of porcelain or pottery and the design included a calendar, the name of a store or business, and either a scene, portrait, animal, or flowers. Some also were made of glass or tin.

Periodical: *The Calendar*, 710 N. Lake Shore Dr., Barrington, IL 60010.

Additional Listings: See *Warman's Americana & Collectibles* for more examples.

1906, holly and roses, 9" d 40.00
1907, Santa and holly, 9-1/2" d 80.00
1908, hunting dog, Pittstown, PA 40.00
1908, roses center 55.00
1909, woman and man in patio garden, 9" d 35.00
1910, Betsy Ross, Dresden 35.00
1910, ships and windmills 30.00
1911, Souvenir of Detroit, MI, months in center, hen and yellow chicks, gold edge 28.00
1912, Martha Washington 40.00
1912, Milford Square, PA, floral center 35.00
1913, roses and holly 30.00
1914, Point Arena, CA, 6-3/4" d 30.00
1915, black boy eating watermelon, 9" d 60.00
1916, man in canoe, IA, 7-1/2" d 35.00
1916, eagle with shield, American flag, 8-1/4" d 40.00
1917, cat center 35.00
1919, ship center 30.00
1920, The Great War, MO 30.00
1921, bluebirds and fruit, 9" d 35.00
1922, dog watching rabbit 35.00

1912, airplane motif, green border, H. A. Boyer Furniture, West Hanover, PA, color transfer, sterling highlights, $75.

CALLING CARD CASES and RECEIVERS

History: Calling cards, usually carried in specially designed cases, played an important social role in the United States from the Civil War until the end of World War I. When making formal visits, callers left their card in a receiver (card dish) in the front hall. Strict rules of etiquette developed. For example, the lady in a family was expected to make calls of congratulations and condolence and visits to the ill.

The cards themselves were small, embossed or engraved with the caller's name and often decorated with a floral design. Many handmade examples, especially in Spencerian script, can be found. The cards themselves are considered collectible and range in price from a few cents to several dollars.

Note: Don't confuse a calling card case with a match safe.

Case

2-1/2" x 3-3/4", sterling silver, Whiting, c1900, central monogrammed medallion bordered by entwined foliage, decorative borders, orig fitted box, 2.89 troy ozs... 425.00
3" x 4-3/8", Mauchline Ware, White Fern pattern...................... 225.00
3-3/8" x 2", mother-of-pearl inlaid tortoiseshell, rect, veneered case inlaid on front and back with large floral sprays, side thumb piece opens hinged lid, Continental, late 19th C 360.00

Silver, shaped edges, engine turning dec, worn center monogram, hinged top, 3-1/2" x 1-1/2", $90.

3-3/4" l, rect, tortoiseshell, ivory inlay, nacre and colored metal ...95.00
3-3/4" x 2-1/2", red wool, moose hair dec of flowers, Native American, late 18th or 19th C 660.00
3-7/8" x 2-3/4", sterling silver, plaid and ribbon type pattern, monogrammed, ES hallmark, Birmingham, c1857 .... 375.00
4" l, rect, ivory, wood inlay, block rows, center framed with diamond design rim band 175.00
4" l, 2-7/8" w, silver, Victorian, Birmingham, 1868, maker's mark rubbed, shaped rect, engraved overall with floral scrolls, central navette, fitted velvet lined case 400.00
4" x 3"
  Mother-of-pearl, rect, veneered with allover diamond pattern, central diamond of silver chased with circular monogrammed medallion, Continental, c1800 .... 550.00
  Tortoiseshell, flat rect form, fitted with small Swiss watch, appointment pad with pencil, Victorian, late 19th C 460.00
  White metal, bird and floral motif, green and black enamel highlights, Victorian 230.00
4-1/8" x 2-1/2", Shakudo, silver, yellow, white, and rose gold, applied dec of cranes in bamboo, reverse with vase with flowers, Victorian..... 635.00

Receiver

Bronze, 7" l, monkey, Victorian 135.00
Cast Metal, figural Art Deco lady, painted green 90.00
Crystal, blown out flowers, pedestal base 45.00
Hand Painted China, 10" l, roses, foliage, gold handles 45.00
Majolica, 5" l, duck and bird, Continental, minor rim nicks 90.00
Stone and Glass, polished onyx-type oval dish, fitted at each end by ribbed gold Favrile glass handles, inscribed "Schlumberger/Made in France/Tiffany" 865.00

CAMBRIDGE GLASS

History: Cambridge Glass Company, Cambridge, Ohio, was incorporated in 1901. Initially, the company made clear tableware, later expanding into colored, etched, and engraved glass. More than 40 different hues were produced in blown and pressed glass.

The plant closed in 1954. Some of the molds were later sold to the Imperial Glass Company, Bellaire, Ohio.

Marks: Five different marks were employed during the production years, but not every piece was marked.

References: Gene Florence, *Elegant Glassware of the Depression Era*, 8th ed., Collector Books, 1998; National Cambridge Collectors, Inc., *Cambridge Glass Co., Cambridge, Ohio* (reprint of 1930 catalog and supplements through 1934), Collector Books, 1976, 1998 value update; ——, *Cambridge Glass Co., Cambridge, Ohio*, 1949 thru 1953 (catalog reprint), Collector Books, 1976, 1996 value update; ——, *Colors in Cambridge Glass*, Collector Books, 1984, 1993 value update; ——, *"Nearcut"* (reprint of 1910 catalog), 1997; Naomi L. Over, *Ruby Glass of the 20th Century*, Antique Publications, 1990, 1993-94 value update; Miami Valley (Ohio) Study Group, *Etchings by Cambridge*, Volume 1, Brookville Publishing, 1997; Bill and Phyllis Smith, *Cambridge Glass 1927-1929* (1986) and *Identification Guide to Cambridge Glass 1927-1929* (updated prices 1996), published by authors (4003 Old Columbus Rd., Springfield, OH 45502).

Periodical: *The Daze*, P.O. Box 57, Otisville, MI 48463.

Collectors' Club: National Cambridge Collectors, Inc., P.O. Box 416, Cambridge, OH 43725.

Museums: Cambridge Glass Museum, Cambridge, OH; Museum of the National Cambridge Collectors, Inc., Cambridge, OH.

Ashtray, Stack Away, 4 ashtrays, blue, green, pink, and yellow, wood base 55.00
Banana Bowl, Inverted Thistle, 7" l, radium green, mkd "Near-cut" ... 95.00
Basket
  Apple Blossom, crystal, 7" 475.00
  Hunts Scene, pink, 11" h 215.00
Bell, Blossom Time, crystal 90.00
Bonbon, Diane, crystal, 8-1/2" 25.00
Bookends, pr, eagle, crystal 55.00
Bowl
  10" d, Wildflower, crystal, gold krystol, matching 12-1/2" d plate, sgd 375.00
  15" d, Rose Point, crystal 100.00
Butter Dish, cov
  Gadroon, crystal 45.00
  Rose Point, crystal, quarter pound 750.00
Candlestick
  Caprice, blue, 3-lite, #1338 .... 75.00
  Cascade, crystal, 1-lite, pr 47.50
  Diane, crystal, 5" 20.00
  Doric, black, 9-1/2" h, pr 160.00
  Rose Point, crystal, 2 lite, keyhole, pr 95.00
Candy Dish, cov, 3 ftd
  Caprice, Alpine Blue 130.00
  Wildflower, crystal, 8" d, 3 part 75.00
Champagne, Wildflower, crystal, 6 oz 20.00
Cigarette Box, Caprice, blue, 3-1/2" x 4-1/2" 70.00
Claret, Wildflower, crystal, 4-1/2 oz 42.00
Cocktail
  Caprice, blue 47.50
  Diane, crystal, 3 oz 14.00
  Rose Point, crystal, 3 oz 35.00
  Stradivary 50.00
Comport
  Caprice, crystal, low, ftd, 7" 19.00
  Honeycomb, Rubena, 9" d, 4-3/4" h, ftd 150.00
  Krome Kraft, 7 1/2" h, cutout grape motif, amethyst 55.00
  Rose Point, crystal, 5-1/2" 50.00
Condiment Set, Pristine, crystal, 5 pc 98.50
Cordial
  Caprice, blue 120.00
  Chantilly, crystal 58.00
  Stradivary 65.00
  Wildflower, crystal, 1oz 60.00
Corn Dish, Portia, crystal 50.00
Creamer
  Inverted Thistle, dark marigold, mkd "Near-cut," slight rim damage 65.00
  Martha Washington, amber, clear stick handle 15.00
Creamer and Sugar
  Cascade, emerald green 35.00
  Decagon, blue, flat bottom 18.00
Creamer and Sugar, tray, Caprice, crystal 40.00
Cream Soup, orig liner
  Decagon, green 35.00
  Willow Blue, #3400/55 .... 25.00
Cup and Saucer
  Caprice, crystal 14.00
  Decagon, pink 7.00
  Martha Washington, amber 12.00
Decanter, Nautilus, #84482, crystal 45.00
Decanter Set, decanter, stopper, 6 handled 2-1/2 oz tumblers, Tally Ho, amethyst 185.00
Dressing Bottle, Chantilly, crystal, silver base 150.00
Finger Bowl, Adam, yellow 25.00

Flower Frog
   Draped Lady, 8-1/2" h
      Amber 190.00
      Crown Tuscan 1,850.00
      Crystal, frosted, ribbed base 75.00
      Dark pink 150.00
      Frosted green 150.00
      Green 160.00
      Light pink 160.00
   Eagle, pink 365.00
   Jay, green 365.00
   Nude, 6-1/2" h, 3-1/4" d, clear 95.00
   Rose Lady
      Amber 260.00
      Green 250.00
      Mocha, tall base 275.00
      Pink 250.00
   Seagull 65.00
   Two Kids, clear 155.00
Fruit Bowl, Decagon, pink, 5-1/2" 5.50
Goblet
   Caprice, blue 40.00
   Cascade, crystal 13.00
   Diane, crystal 25.00
   Heirloom, crystal, 9 oz 17.50
   Rose Point, crystal, 10 oz 30.00
Ice Bucket
   Blossom Time, crystal 125.00
   Chrysanthemum, pink, silver handle 85.00
   Tally Ho, cobalt blue 175.00
Iced Tea Tumbler, ftd
   Lexington, #7966, trumpet, 12 oz 17.50
   Wildflower, crystal, 12 oz 28.00
Jam Jar, Krome Kraft base and lid, amber 35.00
Juice Tumbler, ftd
   Candlelight etch, 5 oz, #3114 .... 38.50
   Diane, crystal, ftd 15.00
Lamp, Martha Washington, crystal, 9", electric, portable 95.00
Lemon Plate, Caprice, blue, 5" d 15.00
Martini Pitcher, Rose Point, crystal 700.00
Mustard, cov, Farber Brothers, cobalt blue 50.00

Lemonade Set, Christmas, amberina with Rockwell silver overlay, 10" h pitcher, five 5-3/8" h cups with "C" in triangle marks, wear to silver gilt rims, $1,430. Photo courtesy of Garth's Auctions.

Oil Cruet, Chantilly etch, 4 oz 95.00
Oyster Cocktail, Portia, crystal 40.00
Pitcher
   Mt. Vernon, forest green 300.00
   Tally Ho, crystal, metal spout and lid 105.00
Plate
   Apple Blossom, pink, 8-1/2" d 20.00
   Caprice, crystal, 9-1/2" d 38.00
   Crown Tuscan, 7" d 45.00
   Decagon, pink, 8" 5.00
   Martha Washington, amber, lunch 12.00
   Rose Point, crystal, 8" d, ftd 70.00
Platter, Caprice, crystal, 14" l, ftd 30.00
Relish
   Mt. Vernon, crystal, 5 part 35.00
   Rose Point, crystal, 12" l, 5 part 100.00
   Tally Ho, blue, 8-1/4" l, 3 part, handle 25.00
Salad Bowl, Caprice, blue, 10" d 250.00
Salt Shaker
   Decagon, cobalt blue 40.00
   Farber Brothers, amethyst, pr 40.00
Sauce Dish, Inverted Strawberry, 5" d, marigold ... 25.00
Seafood Cocktail, Seashell, #110, Crown Tuscan, 4-1/2" oz 95.00
Server, center handle
   Apple Blossom, amber 30.00
   Decagon, blue 16.00
Sherbet
   Caprice, blue 325.00
   Carmine, crystal 17.00
   Diane, crystal, low 14.00
   Regency, low 12.00
   Rose Point, crystal, 7 oz 24.00
Sherry, Portia, gold encrusted 60.00
Sugar, Martha Washington, crystal 17.50
Torte Plate, Rose Point, crystal, 13" d, 3 ftd 95.00
Tray, #3500/112, 3 part, 15" 38.50
Tumbler
   Adam, yellow, ftd 25.00
   Caprice
      Blue, 12 oz, ftd 40.00
      Crystal, 5 oz, ftd 14.00
   Carmine, crystal, 12 oz 25.00
   Decagon, blue, ftd
      5 oz 10.00
      8 oz 12.00
      12 oz 20.00
Vase
   Crown Tuscan
      Flying nude, hp roses and violets dec, creamy pink molded shell
        bowl held by nude woman, 9" h, 12" l 175.00
      Nautilus, ftd, 7" h 67.50
      Rose Point, #278, gold encrusted, 11" h 475.00
   Diane, crystal, keyhole, 12" h 110.00
   Songbird and Butterfly, #402, 12" h, blue 375.00
   Tall Flat Panel, swung, 19-1/4" h, sgd 105.00
   Wildflower, 12" h, flip 800.00
Whiskey, Caprice, blue, 2-1/2 oz 225.00
Wine
   Caprice, crystal 24.00
   Diane, crystal, 2-1/2 oz 30.00
   Rose Point, crystal, 2-1/2 oz 57.50

CAMEO GLASS

History: Cameo glass is a form of cased glass. A shell of glass was prepared; then one or more layers of glass of a different color(s) was faced to the first. A design was then cut through the outer layer(s) leaving the inner layer(s) exposed.

This type of art glass originated in Alexandria, Egypt between 100 and 200 a.d. The oldest and most famous example of cameo glass is the Barberini or Portland vase which was found near Rome in 1582. It contained the ashes of Emperor Alexander Serverus, who was assassinated in 235 a.d.

Emile Gallé is probably one of the best-known cameo glass artists. He established a factory at Nancy, France, in 1884. Although much of the glass bears his signature, he was primarily the designer. Assistants did the actual work on many pieces, even signing Gallé's name. Other makers of French cameo glass include D'Argental, Daum Nancy, LeGras, and Delatte.

English cameo pieces do not have as many layers of glass (colors) and cuttings as do French pieces. The outer layer is usually white, and cuttings are very fine and delicate. Most pieces are not signed. The best-known makers are Thomas Webb & Sons and Stevens and Williams.

Marks: A star before the name Gallé on a piece by that company indicates that it was made after Gallé's death in 1904.

References: Victor Arwas, *Glass Art Nouveau to Art Deco*, Rizzoli International Publications, 1977; Alastair Duncan and George DeBartha, *Glass by Gallé*, Harry N. Abrams, 1984; Ray and Lee Grover, English Cameo Glass, Crown Publishers, 1980; Albert C. Revi, *Nineteenth Century Glass*, reprint, Schiffer Publishing, 1981; John A. Shuman, III, *Collector's Encyclopedia of American Art Glass*, Collector Books, 1988, 1994 value update.

American

Gillander American Glass Co., attributed to, 4" h, overlaid in white, cameo etched morning glory blossoms, buds, and leafy vines, shaded blue cased to white oval body 825.00
Harrach, vase, 8" h, 4" d, bright white carved daffodils, leaves, and stems, frosted and green ground 950.00
Honesdale Glass, vase, 12" h, green etched to clear, gold dec trim 1,295.00
Mount Washington
  Bowl, 8" d, 4" h, sq, ruffled edge, two winged Griffins holding up scroll and spray of flowers design, blue over white ground 1,475.00
  Lamp, 17" h, 10" d shade, fluid font and shade composed of opal white opaque glass overlaid in bright rose pink, acid etched butterflies, ribbons, and bouquets centering cameo portrait medallions in classical manner, mounted on silverplated metal fittings, imp "Pairpoint Mfg. Co. 3013," electrified.......................... 3,105.00
  Lamp, 21" h, 10" d shade, brilliant deep yellow over white, base figural woman with basket of flowers, matching floral design on shade, fancy brass base and font, orig chimney 8,500.00

English

Florentine Art, cruet, 6-1/2" h, ruby-red body, textured white enamel meadowland scene, Meadowlark on tall plant stalk, smaller scene on reverse, white rim, trefoil spout, clear frosted handle, teardrop shaped stopper, pontil mark sgd "59".. 750.00
Stevens and Williams
  Vase, 4-1/2" h, broad bright blue oval, overlaid in opaque white glass, cameo etched and cut clusters of cherries on leafy boughs, circular mark on base "Stevens & Williams Art Glass Stourbridge"...1,265.00
  Vase, 6-1/4" h, Rose du Barry, lush pink rose oval body, etched with white six-petaled blossoms and buds, intricate leaves, butterfly at reverse, linear border......................... 1,610.00
Unknown Maker
  Plaque, 5-1/2" l, 3-1/2" w, citron yellow, five white carved carnation flowers, leaf... 1,275.00

Vase, 7" h, 5" w, corset shape, cranberry, white overlay, carved sprays of sweet peas, leaves, branches, butterfly in flight 1,750.00
Webb
  Bonbon, 7-1/2" h, 5" d, morning glory blossoms, white on red on citron, deep yellow base layer, creamy white lining, hammered sterling silver standard and lid, lid stamped "800," silversmith's mark obscured by finial, attributed to Webb 1,950.00
  Cup and Saucer, handleless, 2-3/4" h, 5" d, cranberry over crystal, prunous blossom carving, leaves, and branches, 10 blossoms on cup with large butterfly and 25 buds 550.00
  Perfume Bottle, 3-3/4" l, flattened teardrop shape, bright blue, etched forget-me-nots all around, two butterflies on shoulder, one chip on surface flower, wear to gilt metal screw cap........... 435.00
  Perfume Bottle, 5-1/2" l, 2-3/4" w, sq, citron yellow, white overlay, allover carved wild roses, leaves, and buds, orig silver spring-hinge cov 2,750.00
  Scent Bottle, 4" l, flattened teardrop shape, sapphire blue, white ferns and grasses dec, butterfly at side, gilt metal hinged cover 920.00
  Vase, 7-1/2" h, bulbous baluster, gold ground, carved white geraniums, carved white coral bells on reverse, sgd "Webb" 1,750.00
  Vase, 10-1/4" h, pink single petal roses, white DQ MOP, attributed to Webb 1,750.00

French

Arsall, vase, 5" h, flared, pink mottled yellow overlaid ground, green layer etched as decumbent blossoms, buds, and leafy stems, sgd "Arsall" in design 325.00
Burgen, Schverer and Cie, Alsace-Lorraine, vase, ftd broad ovoid, frosted colorless glass, amethyst overlay etched and engraved trailing nasturtium blossom, gilt highlights, elaborate gold enamel trademark on base, c1900, enamel wear 2,760.00
D'Argental
  Atomizer, 4" h, cylindrical amber perfume bottle, green and brown overlay, etched landscape of leafy trees, wild geese in flight, sgd "D'Argental" on side, gilt metal fittings mkd "Le Parisien Made in France," "BTE, S.G.D.G." 825.00
  Vase, 10-1/2" h, 4-1/2" d, 3 acid cuttings, brown cut to tan to gold, forest scene, mountains, castle on hill, sgd 1,300.00
Daum Nancy
  Bowl, 7-3/4" d, 3" h, pinched rim, mottled white, pink, purple, and yellow, etched and intricately enameled Coreopsis daisies in shaded yellows, green foliage, sgd in enamel "Daum Nancy France" on side, c1910, burst int. bubble 2,100.00
  Candy Dish, 5-1/4" d, heavy walled sq dish, mottled yellow and red, layered in dark green, etched trees by lake, cameo sgd "Daum Nancy," nick to rim, center burst bubble.............................. 635.00
  Lamp Base, 10-1/4" h, broad ovoid body, mottled gold, yellows, and cream overlaid in deep orange and brown, intricately etched flowering magnolia branches, gilded floral lamp fixtures, inscribed "Daum (cross) Nancy France" near base 3,450.00
  Lamp Base, 23-1/4" h, elongated body, mottled orange overlaid in dark orange and brown, cameo etched trumpet flowers rising from broad leaves, engraved "Daum (cross) Nancy" at side, metal lamp fittings.. 1,380.00
  Night Light, 8-3/4" h, slender tapered form, frosted pale pink and green, cameo etched and enameled black trees in rain, illuminated patinated metal stand 3,450.00
  Perfume Bottle, 5" h, ovoid red body, acid etched and enameled spray of daisies, gold enamel highlights, chased silver base and stopper, sgd "Daum (cross) Nancy" in gold enamel........ 1,035.00
  Salt, 1-3/8" h, bucket form, two upright handles, frosted colorless ground, cameo etched and enameled black tree lined shore, distant ruins, gilt rim, sgd "Daum (cross) Nancy" in gilt on base, small rim chips 575.00
  Vase, 4-1/4" h, two handles, light green and pale red, etched Japanese-style scene of herons and water plants, gilded trailing vines, mounted in finely cast and chased silver mounts with roses and foliage on rim and base, French hallmarks 925 fine, etched and gilt signature "Daum Nancy" on base 3,100.00

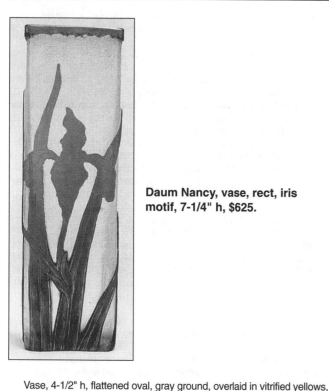

Daum Nancy, vase, rect, iris motif, 7-1/4" h, $625.

Vase, 4-1/2" h, flattened oval, gray ground, overlaid in vitrified yellows, light greens, and rose pink, etched rose hips among leaves, polished to enhance design, sgd "Daum Nancy (cross)," c1910 ....1,150.00

Vase, 8-1/2" h, trumpet form, light green and pink rising to colorless, etched and intricately enameled purple and red cyclamen among green leaves, gilded highlights, sgd "Daum Nancy" at side ..2,450.00

Vase, 9" h, elongated bell form, slender bulbed neck, pink ground, overlaid in grass green, carved and etched flowering thistle, Martele ground, base inscribed "(cross) Daum Nancy".......... 1,610.00

Vase, 15-1/4" h, elongated and swollen body, mottled yellow rising to white, etched and intricately enameled iris in naturalistic greens and yellows, sgd "Daum Nancy (cross)" among leaves, c1900 ...3,750.00

Vase, 15-1/2" h, oval body with raised rim, shaded gray to sky yellow to gray, vitrified autumn colors on falling leaves above and below landscape scene, medial cameo mark "Daum Nancy (cross)"...... 3750.00

Wine Glass, 7-3/4" h, slender, opalescent and frosted sea green, etched and enameled violets in pale rose and green, gilded rims, base inscribed and enameled "Daum Nancy Rube 62 B2 Haussmann Paris," light wear to gilding and enameling, pr.......2,185.00

Degue, vase, 5-1/2" h, cylindrical, tapered raised rim, mottled shades of frosted orange, layered in dark brown, etched desert oasis scene, camels and palm trees, side cameo sgd, small inside rim chip 750.00

Delatte, vase, 6-1/8" h, flared cylindrical form, frosted colorless ground, brown enamel and etched tree lined shore and rocky outcropping, distant hills, gilt metal pedestal, raised leaf pattern, sgd "A. Delatte Nancy" on lower side...520.00

De Vez

Rose Bowl, 3-1/2" d, cobalt blue foliated trees and mountains, pink to yellow sky and water, scalloped rim, sgd 500.00

Vase, 6" h, maroon and fiery amber oval body, etched cottages, mother, child, under tall trees, sgd "de Vez" at side, polished rim...900.00

Vase, 8" h, tubular, three color scenic brown castle and trees, blue mountains, frosted ground, sgd 1,400.00

Vase, 10" h, elongated oviform, frosted colorless body cased in amber, olive, and deep blue, cameo etched silhouetted trees overlooking water, distant villages and mountains, sgd "de Vez" in cameo lower side...1,150.00

Galle

Bowl, 6" d, tricorn, frosted colorless and pale yellow pinched bowl,

lavender and blue layers, etched flowering myrtle vines, sgd "Galle" on side, nick at base 800.00

Bowl, 7-3/4" d, 4-1/4" h, ftd, 4 pulled points, pale pink ground, light yellow-green and amber overlay, etched clusters of blossoms on leafy branches, sgd "H Galle" among leaves, several bubble bursts and int. wear 690.00

Decanter, 10-1/4" h, flattened oval body, upturned rim, conical stopper, frosted colorless and purple ground, overlaid in deep purple, etched iris, engraved "Cristallerie de Galle Nancy modele et decor deposes" on base 2,530.00

Tazza, 10-3/4" d, amber-yellow ground, maroon layer etched as flowering clematis vines, short maroon foot, sgd "Galle" on underside, light wear, matte surface to rim, two bubble bursts on top....1,150.00

Vase, 3-1/2" h, bulbous, raised neck, opaque pink cased to colorless ext., olive green layer etched as round berries among leaves, sgd "Galle" on side, black inclusion 460.00

Vase, 4-3/4" h, broad ovoid body, raised rim, frosted colorless ground, yellow, orange, and green layers, etched daffodils in meadow, flowers polished, sgd "Galle" near base, nick near base...............980.00

Vase, 5" h, flattened ovoid, wide flaring neck, frosted yellow ground, layered with aubergine, cameo etched clusters of wildflowers, inscribed "Galle" near base, nick on base 575.00

Vase, 5" h, ovoid, flared rim, pale frosted blue ground cased in purple and olive green, etched primrose among leaves, sgd "Galle" on side, dark inclusion on top rim 400.00

Vase, 6-1/4" h, oval, flared mouth, frosted colorless and yellow-green ground, purple overlay, etched blueberry branches, sgd "Galle" in cameo at side..350.00

Vase, 6-1/2" h, elongated ovoid, bulbed and flared neck, amber glass overlaid in leafy green, etched ferns, sgd "H Galle" among ferns..550.00

Vase, 6-1/2" h, flattened ovoid, shell pink layered in white, periwinkle, and green, etched flowering hydrangea branch, sgd "Galle" in cameo on side, nick to signature, bubble burst below neck 980.00

Vase, 6-3/4" h, flattened spherical form, elongated neck, pale yellow cased to colorless, brown layer, etched woodland orchids, sgd "Galle" among leaves...525.00

Vase, 7-7/8" h, ovoid, elongated neck, frosted colorless and pink ground, periwinkle and green layer, etched flowering hydrangea branches, sgd "H Galle" near base...................................750.00

Vase, 8" h, bulbous, elongated neck, gray with pink streaked ground, periwinkle and green layers, acid etched stalk of stylized flowers, sgd "Galle" near base...875.00

Vase, 8" h, bulbous, flared neck, pink layered with olive green, etched spray of berries among leaves, sgd "Galle" on side, bubble bursts 400.00

Vase, 8" h, stepped cylindrical, colorless ground, overlaid in pink and purple etched crocus in field, sgd "Galle" near base 1,265.00

Vase, 8-1/2" h, barrel form, transparent topaz colored ground, etched and naturalistic colored enameled grains of barley, sgd "Galle" near base, some wear to enamel..........................865.00

Vase, 11" h, brown berry and vine dec, clambroth ground, fire polished, mounted as lamp..400.00

Vase, 13" h, ovoid, amber and frosted colorless ground, light green and olive layers etched as leafy maple branch, sgd "Galle" near base 920.00

Vase, 13-1/4" h, cylindrical, frosted colorless ground, yellow, pink, and mauve overlay cut as columbine flowers, faint Galle cameo signature near base 1,150.00

Legras

Bowl, 4-3/4" l, 1-3/4" h, frosted colorless shaped oval, scenic dec of shepherd and flock of sheep among mountainous landscape, enameled natural colors, sgd "Legras" at end, rim roughness..........175.00

Bowl, 10" d, 3-3/4" h, olive green body, heavily etched and engraved Art Deco swag and drapery design, fire polished, acid etched "Legras"" near base 825.00

Vase, 4-3/4" h, spherical body, quatreform rim, colorless ground, enameled bare trees in snow at sunset, yellow, orange, brown, black, and white, sgd "Legras" near base..........................410.00

Vase, 5-5/8" h, pinched rim, swollen and waisted vessel, colorless body, etched and enameled dark fuchsia ivy on textured and frosted surface, sgd "Legras" on side, light scratches to enameled surface 350.00

Vase, 8-3/4" h, scalloped oval shape, landscape scene, green, brown, peach, and frosty white 50.00

Michel

Vase, 7-1/2" h, 4-3/4" d, maroon overlay, yellow opaque satin ground, sailboats, branches, and leaves frame border, sgd "Michel, Paris" 725.00

Vase, 14-1/8" h, baluster, frosted cream overlaid yellow, orange, brown, and dark blue, cameo etched bayou scene at sunset, "Michel" at lower side, burst bubbles 990.00

Richard

Bowl, 6" l, 2-3/4" h, brilliant cased poppy red, brown overlay, acid-etched stylized foliate motif, sgd "Richard" at side.............. 460.00

Vase, 7-1/4" h, yellow cased oval, layered in brown, cameo etched mountainous village waterfront scene, applied brown-black handles at each side, sgd "Richard" at side............................ 825.00

Wine, 7-3/4" h, cobalt blue scenic water and sailboats, frosted ground, notched stem 400.00

Velez, vase, 8-1/2" h, ftd, tapered, deep cranberry shaded sky silhouettes autumn green trees and woodland grasses, pale green hills and trees along river bank, sgd "Velez" 1,100.00

CAMERAS

History: Photography became a viable enterprise in the 1840s, but few early cameras have survived. Cameras made before the 1880s are seldom available on the market, and when found, their prices are prohibitive for most collectors.

George Eastman's introduction of the Kodak camera in 1888, the first commercially marketed roll film camera, put photography in the hands of the public.

Most collectors start with a general interest that becomes more defined. After collecting a broad range of Kodak cameras, a collector may decide to specialize in Retina models. Camera collectors tend to prefer unusual and scarce cameras to the most common models, which were mass-produced by the millions.

Because a surplus exists for many common cameras, such as most Kodak box and folding models, collectors are wise to acquire only examples in excellent condition. Shutters should function properly. Minimal wear is generally acceptable. Avoid cameras that have missing parts, damaged bellows, and major cosmetic problems.

References: Brian Coe and Paul Gates, *The Snapshot Photograph*, Ash and Grant Ltd., 1977; John F. Maloney, *Vintage Cameras and Images*, Books Americana, 1981; James and Joan McKeown, *McKeown's Price Guide to Antique & Classic Cameras*, 1997-1998, Centennial Photo Service, 1996; Beaumont Newhall, *The History of Photography*, The Museum of Modern Art, 1982.

Periodicals: *Camera Shopper*, P.O. Box 1086, New Cannan, CT 06840; *Classic Camera*, P.O. Box 1270, New York, NY 10157-2078; *Shutterbug*, 5211 S. Washington Ave., Titusville, FL 32780.

Collectors' Clubs: American Photographic Historical Society, Inc., 1150 Avenue of the Americas, New York, NY 10036; American Society of Camera Collectors, 4918 Alcove Ave., North Hollywood, CA 91607; International Kodak Historical Society, P.O. Box 21, Flourtown, PA 19301; Leica Historical Society of America, 7611 Dornoch Lane, Dallas, TX 75248; National Stereoscopic Association, P.O. Box 14801, Columbus, OH 43214; Nikon Historical Society, P.O. Box 3213, Munster, IN 46321; Photographic Historical Society, P.O. Box 39563, Rochester, NY 14604; The Movie Machine Society, 50 Old Country Rd., Hudson, MA 01749; Zeiss Historical Society, 300 Waxwing Drive, Cranbury, NJ 08512.

Museums: Cameras & Images International, Boston, MA; Fleetwood Museum, North Plainfield, NJ; George Eastman Museum, Rochester, NY; International Cinema Museum, Chicago, IL; Smithsonian Institution, Washington, DC.

Additional Listings: See *Warman's Americana & Collectibles* for more examples.

Advisor: Tom Hoepf.

Bell & Howell, Dial 35, half-frame 35 mm, c1963-67, spring-powered auto wind, unique styling, molded plastic case, also found with Canon nameplate 60.00

Eastman Kodak

Retina IIIC, c 1958, f2/50 mm Xenon lens, built-in exposure meter, similar to earlier IIIc except viewfinder windows are same size and bigger, near mint, everready case 750.00

Kodak Signet 35, 1951-58, f3.5/44mm lens, Kodak Synchro 300 shutter 25.00

Kodak Town & Country Outfit featuring Bantam RF Camera, case, flash, cord, hang tag, mint in original box, 1953-57 .... 45.00

Franke & Heidecke, Germany

Heidoscop, three-lens stereo camera, 1925-41, Carl Zeiss Jena Tessar f4.5 55 mm lenses, 45" x 107" mm exposure size .. 600.00

Rolleiflex Gray Baby, twin lens reflex, c1958, f3.5 Xenar, with flash, filters, lens hoods 275.00

Gundlach, Korona 4" x 5" view camera, c 1900-1950, polished cherrywood, antique lens 175.00

Ihagee, Germany, Kine Exakta I, 35mm single lens reflex, rect focusing magnifier, 1937-49, with Tessar or Exaktar f3.5/50mm lens 175.00

Kamera Werkstatten, Germany, Patent Etui, 9x12cm folding camera,

Zeiss Ikon Contessa, Tessar f2.8/45mm lens, lens cover folds down, $115.

c1937, f6.3 Tessar lens, Compur shutter, black leather covering body and bellow, with sheet film holder 100.00
Kemper, Kombi, miniature box camera, 1890s, metal body doubles as a transparency viewer, engraved decorated front 300.00
Konica, Japan
  Baby Pearl, c 1940 folding camera, f4.5/50mm Hexar lens, 127 film 125.00
    Konica, 35 mm rangefinder, original model, c1948, f2.8 Hexar lens, marked "Made in Occupied Japan" 75.00
Nikon, Japan, Nikon S2, 35mm rangefinder, f1.4/50mm lens, c1955, chrome finish with black leather, case, near mint 700.00
Paillard (Switzerland), Bolex-H-16 movie camera, 3-lens turret 225.00
Stirn, Concealed Vest Camera No. 2, c1890, round metal "detective" camera, 7" diameter, takes 4 pictures on round glass negatives, original neck string 2,500.00
Thornton-Pickard, England, Folding Ruby, c1920, 3-1/4" x 4-1/4" folding plate camera, polished wood interior, Cooke Anastigmat lens 250.00
Voigtlander , Germany, Sterophotoskop, 45 x 107 mm stereo camera, c1907, with magazine back for 12 plates, f4.5 Herliers lens 400.00
Whittaker, Micro 16, 16mm subminiature, c1950, Achromatic doublet lens, single shutter speed, with slide-on metal viewfinder and film cartridge, chrome body 65.00
Ziess, Germany
  Box Tengor 54/2, c1935, box camera, 6 x 9 cm image on 120 film 30.00
    Ikoflex lc, twin lens reflex, c1956, f3.5/75mm Tessar, working meter, near mint 300.00

CAMPHOR GLASS

History: Camphor glass derives its name from its color. Most pieces have a cloudy white appearance, similar to gum camphor; others have a pale tint. Camphor glass is made by treating the glass with hydrofluoric acid vapors.

Bowl, 10" d, fluted rim, polished pontil 125.00
Box, cov, 5" d, hinged, enameled holly spray 75.00
Candlesticks, pr, 7" h, hp roses 75.00
Creamer, 3-1/4" h 25.00
Cruet, hp enameled roses, orig stopper 45.00
Perfume Bottle, 8-1/2" h, pinch type, mushroom cap 50.00
Place Card Holder, 3-3/4" h, ftd 35.00
Plate, 7-1/4" d, hp owl 40.00
Rose Bowl, hp violets, green leaves 50.00
Salt and Pepper Shakers, pr, Swirl pattern, blue, orig tops 45.00
Toothpick Holder, bucket shape 30.00
Vase, 8" h, fan shape, clear leaf design and trim 85.00

CANDLESTICKS

History: The domestic use of candlesticks is traced to the 14th century. The earliest was a picket type, named for the sharp point used to hold the candle. The socket type was established by the mid-1660s.

From 1700 to the present, candlestick design mirrored furniture design. By the late 17th century, a baluster stem was introduced, replacing the earlier Doric or clustered column stem. After 1730 candlesticks reflected rococo ornateness. Neoclassic styles followed in the 1760s. Each new era produced a new style of candlesticks; however, some styles became universal and remained in production for centuries. Therefore, when attempting to date a candlestick, it is important to try to determine the techniques used to manufacture the piece.

References: Margaret and Douglas Archer, *Collector's Encyclopedia of Glass Candlesticks*, Collector Books, 1983; Veronika Baur, *Metal Candlesticks*, Schiffer Publishing, 1996; Gene Florence, *Glass Candlesticks of the Depression Era*, Collector Books, 1999; Ronald F. Michaels, *Old Domestic Base-Metal Candlesticks*, Antique Collectors' Club, 1999; Kenneth Wilson, *American Glass 1760-1930*, 2 Vols., Hudson Hills Press and The Toledo Museum of Art, 1994.

Art Glass, 8-3/4" h, hollow baluster stem, applied flared circular base, irid amethyst glass bobeche, pr 260.00
Brass
  4-1/2" h, Queen Anne style, scalloped bases, pr 600.00
  5-3/8" h, rounded scalloped bases, tulip-like sockets, pr 385.00
  6-1/4" h, square base with feet, scalloped apron, baluster stem, minor splits in base, pr 635.00
  7-7/8" h, Queen Anne style, scalloped base, well shaped stem with scalloped edge socket rim, minor casting flaws, single 660.00
  8-1/4" h, sheet brass, trumpet base, mid drip pan, single .. 1,045.00
  8-1/2" h, domed base, bulbous stem, battered and repaired base, single 440.00
  8-3/4" h, octagonal, good detail, traces of silver plate on underside, early, repairs, pr 365.00
  11-1/2" h, The Queen of Diamonds, push-ups, Victorian, pr . 300.00
  11-7/8" h, The Diamond Prince, push-ups, Victorian, pr 300.00
  12-1/2" h, King of Diamonds, push-ups, Victorian, pr 440.00
  12-3/8" h, The Coronation 1902, push-ups missing, Victorian, pr 525.00
  15" h, picket, bulbous stem, ball feet, ecclesiastical markings, wide drip pans, pr 3,300.00
Bronze, 11-1/2" h, 5" d, circular base, ovoid bobeche, orig patina, mkd "Jarvie," pr 1,100.00
Hogscraper
  6-3/8" h, push-up knob replaced, lip hanger, single 115.00
  8-1/4" h, push-up mkd "Shaw's Brim," lip repair, hanger missing, single 90.00
Pewter, 8-3/4" h, English, push-up, 1800-25, pr 395.00
Sheet Iron, 7-1/4" h, Wedding Band, hog scraper, brass ring around shaft, one thumbpiece broken off, pr 520.00

Porcelain, Dresden, cupid holding torch, multicolored flowers, gilt dec, blue crossed swords mark, 10" h, $350.

Silver
    6" h, weighted stem topped by beading and flowerheads, beaded removable bobeche, domed foot with 3 bands of beading, two centered with flowerheads, Goodnow & Jenks, late 19th/early 20th C, set of 4 .... 990.00
    13-1/2" h, English, Mappin and Webb, Birmingham, 1807, Corinthian column wrapped with trailing vines, spread foot, acanthus and urn dec, weighted 2,000.00
Tin, 7-1/4" h, round weighted base, single 460.00
Wrought Iron, 11-1/2" h, scrolled handle and feet, lip handle, notched push-up, pr 550.00

CANDY CONTAINERS

History: In 1876, Croft, Wilbur and Co. filled small glass Liberty Bells with candy and sold them at the Centennial Exposition in Philadelphia. From that date until the 1960s, glass candy containers remained popular. They reflect historical changes, particularly in transportation.

Jeannette, Pennsylvania, a center for the packaging of candy in containers, was home for J. C. Crosetti, J. H. Millstein, T. H. Stough, and Victory Glass. Other early manufacturers included: George Borgfeldt, New York, New York; Cambridge Glass, Cambridge, Ohio; Eagle Glass, Wheeling, West Virginia; L. E. Smith, Mt. Pleasant, Pennsylvania; and West Brothers, Grapeville, Pennsylvania.

References: *Candy Containers*, L-W Book Sales, 1996; Douglas M. Dezso, J. Lion Poirier & Rose D. Poirier, *Collector's Guide to Candy Containers*, Collector Books, 1998; George Eikelberner and Serge Agadjanian, *Complete American Glass Candy Containers Handbook*, revised and published by Adele L. Bowden, 1986; Jennie Long, *Album of Candy Containers*, published by author, Vol. I (1978), Vol. II (1983).

Collectors' Club: Candy Container Collectors of America, P.O. Box 352, Chelmsford, MA 01824-0352.

Museums: Cambridge Glass Museum, Cambridge, OH; L. E. Smith Glass, Mt. Pleasant, PA.

Additional Listings: See *Warman's Americana & Collectibles* for more examples.

Notes: Candy containers with original paint, candy, and closures command a high premium, but beware of reproduced parts and repainting. The closure is a critical part of each container; if it is missing, the value of the container drops considerably. Small figural perfumes and other miniatures often are sold as candy containers.

Airplane
    P-38 Lightning, orig wire clip, motors, and ground, no closure ...200.00
    Spirit of Goodwill, 98% paint, orig propeller, orig closure 180.00
    Spirit of St Louis, amber glass, all orig tin, orig closure 525.00

SPECIAL AUCTIONS

Old Barn Auction
10040 St. Rt. 244 West
Findlay, OH 45840
(419) 422-8531
www.oldbarn.com

Amos & Andy, glass, car, 2-3/4" x 4-1/2" x 1-1/2" 525.00
Auto, couple, long hood, orig tan snap-on strip, orig gold stamped tin wheels, orig closure 120.00
Barney Google and Bank
    Orig paint, orig closure 700.00
    Repainted, orig closure 550.00
Barney Google and Bell, 70% orig paint, orig closure 350.00
Baseball Player with Bat, 50% orig paint, orig closure 500.00
Bear on Circus Tub, orig tin, orig closure 500.00
Begging Dog, 3-1/2" h, pressed glass, clear, no closure 150.00
Black Cat for Luck, repainted, replaced closure 2,000.00
Bird on Mount, orig whistle, 80% orig paint, orig closure, some chips 550.00
Boat, USN Dreadnaught, orig closure 350.00
Boot, 3" h, clear glass, etched "Rick I Love You Penny" 35.00
Bulldog, 4-1/4" h, screw closure 60.00
Bus
    Chicago, replaced closure 270.00
    Jitney, orig tin, imperfect paint on top, crack to one wheel, orig closure 220.00
    New York-San Francisco, orig closure 375.00
    Victory Glass Co., replaced closure 300.00
Camera on tripod, 80% paint, all paints replaced 200.00
Cannon
    Cannon #1, orig carriage, orig closure 375.00
    Rapid Fire Gun, orig closure 425.00
    U. S. Defense Field Gun #17, orig closure 380.00
    Two Wheel Mount #1, orig carriage, orig closure 220.00
    Two Wheel Mount #2, orig carriage, orig closure, one replaced wheel 260.00
Cash Register, orig paint, orig closure 600.00
Cat, papier-mâché
    3-3/4" h, seated, gray and white paint, pink ribbon, glass eyes, touch up and repairs 375.00
    5" h, polychrome paint, glass eyes, boy's outfit 275.00
Chick, composition
    3" h, painted, orange, yellow, and white, lead legs 65.00
    5" h, cardboard, base, Germany 20.00
Clarinet, musical, tin whistle, cardboard tube 35.00
Coach, Esther Overland Limited, chipped glass coupler projections, replaced wheels 175.00
Delivery Truck, cream colored tin canopy, red lettering
    Bakery Truck, small chip 1,100.00
    Express Truck 2,100.00
    Grocery Truck, small chip 2,100.00

Frog and chickens, oval box, yellow crepe paper dec, 5-1/8" d, $45.

Ice Truck 690.00
Laundry Truck, small chip, crack on wheel
    flank 2,100.00
Dog by Barrel, 90% paint, chip on base, orig closure 220.00
Elf on Rocking Horse, 3-1/2" h, pressed glass, no closure 160.00
Felix the Cat, repainted, replaced closure 550.00
Fire Truck, with ladders 25.00
Flossie Fisher's Bed, yellow tin bed, dec with black silhouettes of chil-
    dren and animals 3,600.00
Flossie Fisher's Chair, Borgfeldt & Co. Ink stamp on back 715.00
Football, tin, Germany 20.00
Gentleman, 6" h, papier-mâché head and hollow body, large pink
    nose, closed smiling mouth, painted brown eyes, molded and
    painted yellow vest, black jacket, gray pants with black stripe, black
    shoes, green bow tie, brown cane in left hand 210.00
George Washington, 3" h, papier-mâché, with tricorn hat, white pony-
    tail and blue coat, standing beside cardboard cabin with deep roof
    and chimney, unmarked 165.00
Ghost Head, 3-1/2" h, papier-mâché, flannel shroud 150.00
Girl, celluloid, crepe paper dress 30.00
Goblin Head, 60% orig paint, orig closure 625.00
Green Taxi, orig wheels, orig closure, small chip 600.00
Gun, 5-3/4" l, West Specialty Co. 20.00
Hanging Basket, flashed ruby glass, orig chain, no closure 70.00
Hearse #2, replaced closure 80.00
Horse and Wagon, pressed glass 35.00
Hot Doggie, traces of paint, orig closure 525.00
House, all glass, 95% paint, orig closure 250.00
Independence Hall, corner steeple chip, orig closure 250.00
Indian, 5" l, pressed glass, riding motorcycle with sidecar, no
    closure 350.00
Jack-o-lantern
    Open top, 95% orig paint, no closure 350.00
    Pop eyed, 75% orig paint, orig closure, orig bail 475.00
    Screw on lid, 95% orig paint 360.00
Kettle, 2" h, 2-1/4" d, pressed glass, clear, T. H. Stough,
    cardboard closure 50.00
Kewpie on radio, orig paint, orig closure 650.00
Lantern, 3-3/4" h, mkd "Pat. Dec. 20, '04" 35.00
Lawn Swing, orig red and white tin canopy, orig closure 650.00
Learned Fox Bottle, large chips on closure threads, orig closure . 35.00
Limousine, orig wheels, orig closure, small chip 600.00
Little Boy, 6" h, papier-mâché head and hollow body, large pink nose,
    closed smiling mouth, painted brown eyes, molded and painted red
    vest, green jacket, yellow short pants, purple socks, black shoes,
    brown tie 210.00
Locomotive
    Jeant. Glass Co. #889, orig wheels, several small chips 160.00
    Mapother's 1892, orig closure 125.00
Lynne Clock Bank 750.00
Man on Motorcycle, side car, repainted, replaced closure 525.00
Mule, pulling two wheeled barrel with driver, 95% paint, orig
    closure 80.00
Nursing Bottle, pressed glass, clear, natural wood nipple closure, T. H.
    Stough, 1940-50 .... 20.00
Powder Horn, orig closure 30.00
Pumper, 5" l, pressed glass, tin wheels and bottom 110.00
Pump for Candy, yellow, both labels complete 235.00
Pumpkin Head Witch, 50% orig paint, orig closure 650.00
Puppy, 2-1/2" h, papier-mâché, painted, white, black muzzle, glass
    eyes 35.00
Rabbit, glass
    Rabbit Family, 95% orig paint, no closure 650.00
    Rabbit Mother and Daughter, orig closure, chipped tail 675.00
    Rabbit Pushing Chick in Shell Cart, orig closure 500.00
    Rabbit Wearing Hat, 90% orig paint above waist, repainted below
      waist, orig closure 900.00
    Rabbit With Basket on Arm, no paint, orig closure 120.00
Rabbit, papier-mâché, 10" l, glass eyes, removable head, hollow body,

4 wood legs, stamped "Germany" on base of body, pulling wooden
    cart with wood and cardboard wheels, tin egg in cart, some orig dec,
    light wear 225.00
Record Player with Horn 200.00
Rocking Horse, small chips on rockers, no closure 180.00
Rolling Pin, orig handles, orig closure 250.00
Rooster, 6-1/2" h, papier-mâché, pewter feet, orig polychrome paint,
    mkd "Germany" 225.00
Sailor, 6" h, papier-mâché head and hollow body, large pink nose,
    closed smiling mouth, protruding lower lip, molded and painted side-
    burns and hair, molded gray fez, painted blue eyes, molded and
    painted blue sailor uniform, black belt with knife case and sword,
    black shoes, unmarked 265.00
Santa Claus
    By sq chimney, 60% paint, replaced closure 180.00
    Double cuff, repainted, orig closure 75.00
    Paneled coat, orig closure 140.00
Soldier by the Tent, 95% orig paint, orig closure 2,700.00
Spark Plug, no paint, roughness in front, replaced closure 45.00
Statue of Liberty, 5-3/4" h, pressed glass, clear, lead top 1,200.00
Stop and Go, replaced switch handle, orig closure 440.00
Submarine F6, no periscope or flag, orig super structure, orig
    closure 250.00
Suitcase, milk glass, orig handle, traces of bear decal, orig
    closure 30.00
Swan Boat with Rabbit and Chick, repainted, replaced closure . 650.00
Tank, World War I, traces of orig paint, no closure 90.00
Telephone, small glass receiver 55.00
Toonerville Depot Line, orig paint, orig closure 575.00
Turkey, Gobbler, small chip under orig closure 100.00
Village Bank, with insert, log cabin roof 110.00
Wagon, orig closure 90.00
Wheelbarrow, orig wheel, no closure 35.00
Windmill
    Dutch Wind Mill, orig blades, chip on back, no closure 220.00
    Five Windows, ruby flashed orig blades, orig closure 475.00
    Teddy Wind Mill, all tin orig, orig closure 1,160.00

CANES

History: Canes and walking sticks were important accessories in a gentleman's wardrobe in the 18th and 19th centuries. They often served both a decorative and utilitarian
function. Glass canes and walking sticks were glassmakers' whimsies, ornamental rather than practical.

References: Linda L. Beeman, *Cane Collector's Directory*,
published by author, 1993; Joyce E. Blake, *Glasshouse
Whimsies*, published by author, 1984; *Catherine Dike*,
Cane Curiosa, Cane Curiosa Press (250 Dielman Rd.,
Ladue, MO 63124), 1983; ——, *Canes in the United States*,
Cane Curiosa Press (250 Dielman Rd., Ladue, MO 63124),
1994; ——, *La Cane Object díArt*; Cane Curiosa Press (250
Dielman Rd., Ladue, MO 63124), 1988; Ulrich Klever,
Walkingsticks, Schiffer Publishing, 1996; George H. Meyer,
American Folk Art Canes, Sandringham Press, 1992.

Periodical: *Cane Collector's Chronicle*, 99 Ludlum Crescent, Lower Hutt Welling, New Zealand.

Collectors' Club: International Cane Collectors, 24 Mag-
nolia Ave., Manchester-by-the-Sea, MA 01944; The Cane
Collector's Chronicle, 99 Ludlum Crescent, Lower Hutt,
Weelington, New Zealand.

Museums: Essex Institute, Salem, MA; Remington Gun
Museum, Ilion, NY; Valley Forge Historical Society, Valley
Forge, PA.

Handle, ivory, Liberty figure, 5-1/2" h, $170.

Notes: Carved wood and ivory canes are frequently considered folk art and collectors pay higher prices for them.

Cane

24-3/4" l, sword, 2-1/4" h elephant ivory handle, fluted ivory and snakewood, Continental, c1860 .... 1,600.00

33-1/4" l, folk art, carved wood, handle carved as pirate, painted eyes, American 250.00

35-1/4" l, folk aft, carved hickory, carved black male head wearing hat, glass eyes, dec metal ferrule, American, late 19th/early 20th C 175.00

35-1/2" l
Jugendstil, silver overlay, crook handle, ferrule creased by stylized intertwining sterling vine, brass finial, late 19th C 100.00
Vienna Secession, crook handle, stylized sterling overlay depicting cleaved hoof at termination of handle, brass finial 200.00

36" l, folk art, carved birch, imago head of pensive boxer dog, glass eyes, birch shaft, bone finial, American 200.00

38-5/8" l, folk art, carved and painted wood, "The House that Jack Built," various carved animal, figural, and human motifs, American, 19th C, minor cracks very minor paint loss 3,600.00

39" l, folk art, sampling, crook handle with carved eagle's head 185.00

43" l, gun, Remington, 3-1/2" l dog head molded gutta percha handle, nickel silver collar, gutta percha cov shaft, Remington mark and "Pat 1872" above separation, 22-caliber concealed gun 6,000.00

Walking Stick

25-1/2" l, worn red finish, brass ferrule horn handle, ivory leg and boot, crack in ivory, piece missing from horn 85.00

29" l, carved horn imago handle, diminutive boxer dog head, glass eyes, beaded metal collar ferrule, Continental, 19th C 150.00

31-1/4", Greunderzeit vermeil, opera handle, evening stick, floral and foliate repousse handle, central cartouche, ebony shaft, late 19th C 300.00

32-1/2" l, folk art, knob handle incised with inked diamond pattern extending 3" down shaft into radial wood ferrule, tri-color woven bamboo shaft, 4-1/2" wood finial, American 100.00

33" l, Malacca sterling knob handle, Art Nouveau motif scrolling flora and fauna, brass finial, Continental 150.00

33-1/4" l, birch imago, highly detailed carving, monkey head, beaded glass eyes, braided metal collar, ferrule with metal stud stamped "London," brass finial 200.00

33-1/2" l, Continental
Bamboo, brass roundel top, incised ruler numbers, shaft calibrated in inches and hands, 19th C 85.00
Carved ivory roundel top, inset with jade, 2-1/4" ogee turned ivory ferrule with mother-of-pearl circular eyelets, 1-1/2" ivory finial, late 18th/early 19th C 275.00
Malacca carved ivory, "L" shaped hairy hoof handle, gilt-metal buckle ferrule, attributed to Germany 200.00

34" l
American, spiral twist, snake on end, plain handle, worn dark paint 145.00
Continental, horn crook handle, pewter ferrule, shaft of horn discs, metal finial, 19th C 200.00

34-1/4", carved ivory, "L" shaped 4" h ivory handle, diamond-shaped cartouche on ferrule overhanging cabochon cartouche below, metal finial, German, 19th C 100.00

34-1/2" l
American, Bakelite knob, caramel colored knob with flash light, brass ferrule stamped "Neusilber," Bakelite finial, 20th C ... 150.00
Continental, porcelain roundel, embracing putti in celestial setting, gold dec cobalt blue ground, gilt-metal repousse dec ferrule, brass finial, 19th C 400.00
English, carved hickory, imago handle, Queen Victoria with nightcap, 19th C 200.00

34-3/4" l, birch, sterling knob, stalactites, mkd "RFS & Co. Sterling," brass finial, American, late 19th C 100.00

35" l
American, Tiffany, "L" shaped handle, crossed tennis rackets with overlapping branches and streamers, engraved "M. F. M. 1894" 400.00
Continental, carved "L" shaped handle, open mouth bridled horse head, obverse side of shaft carved male figure with walrus mustache, sgd "Kephvpa," brass finial, 19th C 300.00
Continental, ebony, opera handle, shaft with Chinoiserie floral silver metal inlay, late 19th C 175.00
Viennese, carved deer antler crook handle, Malacca, mournful greyhound, beaded glass eyes, late 19th C 350.00

35-1/4" l
American, raided root, late l9th/early 20th C 95.00
Continental, lady's, "L" shaped carved ivory handle, gadroon motif, gilt-metal ferrule with floral guillouche design, metal finial .. 275.00
Continental Malacca silver plate, imago knob handle, full bust of Bismarck, 19th C 200.00

35-1/2" l
American, diamond quilted shaft, two tone finish, bone handle 165.00
Continental, carved bone "L" shaped horse handle, glass beaded eyes, chased brass ferrule 325.00
Continental, silver and bone inlay, knob handle, silver stud engraved "Alfred," radials of silver and bone 2-1/4" down shaft, bone finial 175.00
English, marquetry pistol grip, inlaid handle with Edwardian floral and fauna motif, eyelets terminating in wood finial, late 19th C 125.00
Japanese, pearl, bamboo, carved shaft with climbing monkey, crook handle, brass finial, sgd with Japanese characters, c1890-1900 .... 75.00

35-3/4" l
Continental, carved hardstone knob with cross axis design, gold ferrule mkd "14K," bone finial 150.00
English, civilian, swagger stick, elongated pistol grip top highlighted with grained ivory, 2" burl neck, circular ivory ferrule, Malacca shaft ending in ivory finial, c1912 .... 150.00

36" l
Continental, Congo, pewter finish metal "L" shaped handle crafted in organic form to emulate shaft, brass finial, 19th C 100.00
Continental Malacca, silver plate, handle dec in Adams style, garlands on reeded background, metal finial, 19th C 175.00

Continental, sterling, "L" shaped handle, stylized arabesque design with cartouche, brass finial, late 19th/early 20th C 250.00
French, ebonized, carved ivory figural image of Jean Paul Marat, sterling ferrule, stamped "A. Taylor" 550.00
German, Blackthorn, carved deer antler, "L" shape, "Muenchner Bilderbogen," aggressive short man with long nose, gilt metal ferrule, c1850 ....300.00
Greunderzeit Malacca, opera, silver, floral and fauna repousse motif with cartouche on handle mkd "German 800 Fine," brass finial 275.00
Viennese, Tula, silver knob, profusely dec in geometric and champleve motif extending from handle down shaft for 10-1/2" to Tula ferrule, brass finial 275.00
36-1/4" l
Continental, silver plate, crook handle, finely detailed greyhound with collar, glass eyes, brass finial....................................225.00
German, carved ivory "L" 5" h handle intricately carved in "C" scroll motif, surmounting oblong cartouche with brass ferrule, wavy incised dotted lines, 1-3/4" ivory finial, late 18th/19th C 100.00
36-1/2" l, carved imago handle, ebony stained banded shaft, finely carved male head, fur hat, beaded glass eyes, 4-1/2" chased and banded ferrule, brass finial, Continental, early 19th C 250.00
36-3/4" l, carved wood, folk art, carved leaves, lizard and snake, green, rust, and yellow polychrome dec, black ground, America, 19th C, wear 920.00
37" l, French Malacca, crutch handle, carved ivory boxer dog with glass eyes knob 350.00
37-1/4" l, birch, sterling whistle handle, opera style handle, English sterling London hallmarks, stamped "Brigg London," brass finial, c1923 ....475.00
37-1/2" l, red shank, ivory knob, hairline in ivory.........................125.00
39" l, folk art, sapling, relief carved turtle, snake, and alligator...200.00

CANTON CHINA

History: Canton china is a type of Oriental porcelain made in the Canton region of China from the late 18th century to the present. It was produced largely for export. Canton china has a hand-decorated light- to dark-blue underglaze on white ground. Design motifs include houses, mountains, trees, boats, and bridges. A design similar to willow pattern is the most common.

Borders on early Canton feature a rain and cloud motif (a thick band of diagonal lines with a scalloped bottom). Later pieces usually have a straight-line border.

Early, c1790-1840, plates are very heavy and often have an unfinished bottom, while serving pieces have an overall "orange peel" bottom. Early covered pieces, such as tureens, vegetable dishes, and sugars, have strawberry finials and twisted handles. Later ones have round finials and a straight, single handle.

Marks: The markings "Made in China" and "China" indicate wares which date after 1891.

Reproduction Alert: Several museum gift shops and private manufacturers are issuing reproductions of Canton china.

Bowl, 9-1/2" d, cut corner, minor int. glaze imperfections, 19th C 920.00
Box, cov, sq, domed top, cloud and rain border on lids, early 19th C, pr 6,270.00
Cider Pitcher, cov, 8-1/4" h, double-woven strap handle with flower impressed ends, cover with fu dog finial, chips on base, 19th C 1,955.00
Coffeepot, 7-1/4" h, mismatched cover.......................................750.00
Cup and Underplates, handleless, 1-3/4" h, 5-1/2" d, Chinese Imperial, set of 8 ....300.00

Plate, water's edge scene, 10-1/8" d, $125.

Dish, 8-7/8" d, scalloped rim, blue and white, 1/4" glued rim chip....300.00
Egg Cup, 2-1/4" h, chips, cracked, 9 pc set................................345.00
Fish Platter, 13-1/2" l, glaze roughness 1,265.00
Fruit Basket
  9-1/4" d, minor chips...690.00
  10-1/2" l, reticulated, undertray 1,100.00
  11" l, reticulated, mismatched undertray, star crack, minor chips 345.00
Ginger Jar, cov...230.00
Milk Pitcher, 6-1/8" h, very minor chips......................................575.00
Pitcher, 3" to 6-1/2" h, chips, 4 pc set 2,760.00
Plate, early, c1820-30
  6" d, bread and butter...65.00
  7-1/2" d, salad..85.00
  8" d, dessert...95.00
  9" d, lunch...115.00
  10" d, dinner..150.00
Platter
  13-3/4" l, deep, minor glaze chips 375.00
  17" l, oval, butterflies, insects, and chrysanthemum blossoms, central gilt monogram, c1850-70....................................1,100.00
  18-3/8" l, rim chips, knife marks, pr 1,265.00
Pot de Creme, 4" h, 3 pc set...325.00
Salad Bowl, 9-3/4" d, rim roughness..815.00
Salt, 3-3/4" l, trench, chips, 3 pc set 550.00
Sauce Tureen
  6" l, minor chips..245.00
  8-1/2" l, mismatched cover...865.00
Serving Plate, 12" d, minor chips..435.00
Shrimp Dish, 10-1/4" d, minor edge roughness, pr..................690.00
Soup Tureen, 9" h, 11-3/4" d, mismatched cover......................635.00
Syllabub, 3" h, imperfections, 16 pc set...................................850.00
Tea Caddy, cov, 5-1/2" h, octagonal, 19th C 2,645.00
Tea Canister, cov, 11-1/2" h, restoration to lids, damage to one base, pr..3,336.00
Tureen, cov, undertray, 12-1/2" l, mismatched, cracks, chips.....815.00
Vegetable Dish, cov
  9-1/2" l, chips...250.00
  9-3/4" l, minute chips..400.00
  10-1/4" l, chips..265.00

Warming Dish, cov

    9" d, 3 pc set..500.00
    10-1/2" d, circular, pr..525.00

CAPO-DI-MONTE

History: In 1743, King Charles of Naples established a soft-paste porcelain factory near Naples. The firm made figurines and dinnerware. In 1760, many of the workmen and most of the molds were moved to Buen Retiro, near Madrid, Spain. A new factory, which also made hard-paste porcelains, opened in Naples in 1771. In 1834, the Doccia factory in Florence purchased the molds and continued production with them in Italy.

Capo-di-Monte was copied heavily by other factories in Hungary, Germany, France, and Italy.

Museums: Metropolitan Museum of Art, New York, NY; Museo of Capodimonte, Naples, Italy; Woodmere Art Museum, Philadelphia, PA.

Reproduction Alert: Many of the pieces in today's market are of recent vintage. Do not be fooled by the crown over the "N" mark; it also was copied.

Box, cov, gilt mounting

    6-1/8" l, hinged, rect, relief molded, 3 maidens and young, sides molded with baby Bacchantes tending to grapevine, overglaze blue crowned "N" mark 1,200.00
    11-1/2" l, oval, Greek gods molded on lid, ribbon tied floral garland, gilt ground, side frieze of mask flanked by 2 sphinxes between scrolling acanthus above gilt guilouche band enclosing flowerheads, underglaze blue crowned "N" mark......................1,350.00
Candleholder, 3" h, raised flowers and nude figures...................120.00
Compote, cov, 9" h, oval, relief molded cherubs on sides, cherub finial and handles..250.00
Cup and Saucer, molded cup ext. with sea nymphs swimming in the ocean, gilt int. with painted floral sprigs, molded putti on saucers, underglaze blue crowned "N" mark, set of 12 ....2,500.00
Demitasse Set, covered coffeepot, creamer, sugar, six ftd cups and saucers, large round ftd tray, artist sgd, 17 pc set...................275.00
Ferner, 11" l, oval, relief molded and enameled allegorical figures, full relief female mask at each end 110.00
Figural Group, 12-1/2" l, grazing gazelles, artist sgd, 20th C......175.00

Figurine, fighting leopards, G. Qurius, 17-1/2" l, $180.

Plaque, 6-1/2" x 8-1/2", cut corner rect, classical subject, set in brass mounted ebonized wood frame inset with colored porcelain medallions, 19th C 690.00
Plate, 9" d, raised classical figure in border surrounding central armorial crests, sgd on reverse "Palazzo Reale Napoli," 19th C, slight surface wear, 12 pc set 1,495.00
Snuff Box, 3-1/4" d, hinged lid, cartouche shape, molded basketweave and flowerhead ext., painted int. with court lady and page examining portrait of gentlemen, gold mountings, c1740, minor restoration1,650.00
Urn, cov, 21-1/8" h, ovoid, central molded frieze of Nerieds and putti, molded floral garlands, gadroon upper section, acanthus molded lower section, socle foot with putti, sq plinth base, applied ram's head handles, domed cov, acorn finial, underglaze crowned "N" mark, minor chips and losses, pr 1,650.00

CARLSBAD CHINA

History: Because of changing European boundaries during the last 100 years, German-speaking Carlsbad has found itself located first in the Austro-Hungarian Empire, then in Germany, and currently in the Czech Republic. Carlsbad was one of the leading pottery manufacturing centers in Bohemia.

Wares from the numerous Carlsbad potteries are lumped together under the term "Carlsbad China." Most pieces on the market are post-1891, although several potteries date to the early 19th century.

Ashtray, 5-1/4" d, multicolored Dutch men and women strolling waterfront 18.00
Bowl, 8-1/4" l, 7-1/4" w, 5" h, oval, ftd, Art Nouveau stylized foliate sides, green, blue and purple irid glaze, gold highlights, red stamp mark "Carlsbad Made in Austria" and crown on base 225.00
Butter Dish, cov, 7-1/4" d, pink flowers, green leaves, wavy gold lines, white ground...65.00
Chocolate Pot, cov, 10" h, blue, scenic portrait, mkd "Carlsbad Victoria" 115.00
Creamer and Sugar, Bluebird pattern, mkd "Victoria Carlsbad"....70.00
Ewer, 14" h, handles, light green, floral dec, gold trim, mkd "Carlsbad Victoria" 85.00

Vase, portrait center, deep pink ground, gold trim, mkd "Victoria, Carlsbad, Austria," artist sgd "Fr. Stahl," 9-1/2" h, $125.

Hair Receiver, 4" d, cobalt blue flowers, emb basketweave at top, gold trim, white ground..45.00
Oyster Plate
   8-1/4" d, 5 wells plus center well, stylized pink and blue peonies, green leaves, gold accents, mkd "Marx & Gutherz"...........120.00
   9-3/4" d, lavender flowers, gold outlining, white ground........125.00
Pin Tray, 8-1/2" l, irregular scalloped shape, roses, green leaves, white ground, mkd "Victoria Carlsbad Austria"...................................40.00
Pitcher, 8" h, gold floral dec, cream ground, ornate handle..........65.00
Plate, 9" d, hp cherries, artist sgd..35.00
Sugar Shaker, 5-1/2" h, egg shape, floral dec..............................70.00
Urn, 14-1/2" h, rose bouquet, shaded ivory ground, mkd "Carlsbad Austria"...155.00

CARNIVAL GLASS

History: Carnival glass, an American invention, is colored pressed glass with a fired-on iridescent finish. It was first manufactured about 1905 and was immensely popular both in America and abroad. More than 1,000 different patterns have been identified. Production of old carnival glass patterns ended in 1930.

Most of the popular patterns of carnival glass were produced by five companies—Dugan, Fenton, Imperial, Millersburg, and Northwood.

Marks: Northwood patterns frequently are found with the "N" trademark. Dugan used a diamond trademark on several patterns.

References: Gary E. Baker et al., *Wheeling Glass*, Oglebay Institute, 1994 (distributed by Antique Publications); Elaine and Fred Blair, *Carnival Hunter's Companion: A Guide to Pattern Recognition*, published by authors (P.O. Box 116335, Carrolton, TX 75011), 1995; Carl O. Burns, *Collector's Guide to Northwood Carnival Glass*, L-W Book Sales, 1994; ——, *Dugan and Diamond Carnival Glass*, 1909-1931; Collector Books, 1998; ——, *Imperial Carnival Glass*, Collector Books, 1996, 1998 value update; Dave Doty, *A Field Guide to Carnival Glass*, Antique Trader Publications, 1998; Bill Edwards and Mike Carwile, *Standard Encyclopedia of Carnival Glass*, 6th ed., Collector Books, 1998; Marion T. Hartung, *First Book of Carnival Glass to Tenth Book of Carnival Glass* (series of 10 books), published by author, 1968 to 1982; published by authors (36 N. Mernitz, Freeport, IL 61032), 1996; Glen and Steven Thistlewood, *Carnival Glass, The Magic & The Mystery*, Schiffer Publishing, 1998; Margaret and Ken Whitmyer, *Fenton Art Glass*: 1907-1939, Collector Books, 1996, 1999 value update.

Collectors' Clubs: American Carnival Glass Association, 9621 Springwater Ln, Miamisburg, OH 45342; Canadian Carnival Glass Association, 107 Montcalm Dr., Kitchner, Ontario N2B 2R4 Canada; Collectible Carnival Glass Association, 3103 Brentwood Circle, Grand Island, NE 68801; Heart of America Carnival Glass Association, 4305 W. 78th St., Prairie Village, KS 66208; International Carnival Glass Association, P.O. Box 306, Mentone, IN 46539; Lincoln-Land Carnival Glass Club, N951, Hwy 27, Conrath, WI 54731; National Duncan Glass Society, P.O. Box 965, Washington, PA 15301; New England Carnival Glass Club, 27 Wells Rd., Broad Brooks, CT 06016; Tampa Bay Carnival Glass Club, 101st Ave. N., Pinellas Park, FL 34666; WWW.CGA at http://www.woodsland.com.

SPECIAL AUCTIONS

Albrecht Auction Service, Inc.
3884 Saginaw Rd.
Vassar, MI 48768
(517) 823-8835

Ayers Auction Service
P.O. Box 320
Tremont, IL 61568

Mickey Reichel Auctioneer
1440 Ashley Rd.
Boonville, MO 65233
(816) 882-5292

Seeck Auction
P.O. Box 377
Mason City, IA 50402
(515) 424-1116

Woody Auction
Douglass, KS 67039
(316) 746-2694

Museums: National Duncan Glass Society, Washington, PA; Fenton Art Glass Co., Williamstown, WV.

Notes: Color is the most important factor in pricing carnival glass. The color of a piece is determined by holding it to the light and looking through it.

Acorn Burrs, Northwood
   Bowl, 4-3/4" d, marigold...30.00
   Tumbler, marigold...60.00
Acorns, Millersburg, compote, 6 ruffles, marigold and vaseline...3,750.00
Apple Blossom Twigs, Dugan
   Bowl, 9-1/2" d, low, ruffled, white, irid pink and green..........130.00
   Plate, low, ruffled, purple, electric purple and blue highlights..225.00
Basket of Roses, Northwood, bonbon, stippled, amethyst.........475.00
Beaded Cable, Northwood
   Candy Dish, ftd, amethyst..70.00
   Rose Bowl
      Aqua Opalescent, light butterscotch overlay, air bubbles, stress line in foot..135.00
      Ice Blue...425.00
Big Fish, Millersburg, bowl, 8-1/4" d, 6 ruffles, marigold, radium finish..550.00
Blackberry, Fenton, miniature compote
   Green...65.00
   Marigold...40.00
Blackberry Block, Fenton, tumbler, blue.....................................45.00
Blackberry Spray, Fenton, hat, 6-1/2" h
   Green, 2 sides up...95.00
   Red, small flake...365.00
   Vaseline, sq, 4 sides up..40.00
Blackberry Wreath, Millersburg
   Bowl, 7-1/2" d, six ruffles, green..65.00
   Bowl, 10-1/4" d, 6 ruffles, amethyst.....................................250.00
   Bowl, 10-1/2" d, 3 in 1 edge, green......................................155.00
   Ice Cream Bowl, 8" d, green, some wear to berries.................85.00
   Ice Cream Sauce, 5-1/2" d, dark marigold.............................110.00
   Sauce, 6" d, 6 ruffles, marigold..60.00

Sauce, 6-1/4" d, 6 ruffles, green, satiny finish 65.00
Blossomtime, Northwood, compote, marigold 200.00
Boggy Bayou, Fenton, vase, 9" h, black amethyst....................... 75.00
Border Plants, Dugan, bowl, 7" d, 10 ruffles edge, peach
    opalescent.. 225.00
Bouquet, Fenton
    Tumbler, blue.. 55.00
    Tumbler, marigold... 15.00
    Water Pitcher, marigold... 150.00
Bull's Eye & Beads, Imperial, vase, 7" h, flared, dark marigold 40.00
Bushel Basket, Northwood, aqua opalescent , light
    opalescence 195.00
Butterfly & Fern, Fenton
    Tumbler, blue.. 115.00
    Tumbler, green.. 55.00
    Water Pitcher, blue, radium finish................................. 800.00
Butterfly & Tulip, Dugan, bowl, sq, purple, satin irid................. 1,400.00
Captive Rose, Fenton, marigold, compote, marigold, crimped
    edge 42.00
Cherries, Dugan
    Banana Boat, electric blue, purple highlights, 3 ftd 275.00
    Sauce, low, ruffled, 6" d, purple 120.00
Cherries, Fenton, banana boat, blue, satin irid, cracked 250.00
Concave Diamond, Northwood
    Tumbler, celeste blue... 30.00
    Tumbler, vaseline.. 95.00
    Tumble-Up, russet green 900.00
    Vase, 6" h, celeste blue 175.00
Concord, Fenton, bowl, three-in-one edge, green 245.00
Cosmos, Millersburg, ice cream bowl, green, radium irid 115.00
Courthouse, Millersburg, ice cream bowl, 7-1/2" d, amethyst, lettered
    example 900.00
Daisy Wreath, Westmoreland, 8-1/2" d, ice cream bowl,
    moonstone 110.00
Dandelion, Northwood, tumbler, purple.............................. 55.00
Diamond Points, Northwood, vase, 10-1/4" h, aqua opalescent , irides-
    cent and opalescent from top to base 1,650.00
Diamond Rib, Fenton, vase, 9" h, purple 40.00
Diving Dolphins, Millersburg, compote, Rosiland int., green.... 1,700.00

**Dragon and Lotus, Fenton, bowl, collared base, marigold,
9" d, $160.**

Drapery, Northwood
    Rose Bowl
        Aqua opalescent, light butterscotch overlay.................... 250.00
        Frosty White 265.00
    Vase, 8-3/4" h, aqua opalescent 575.00
Drapery Variant, Northwood, dark marigold, radium
    finish.. 375.00
Embossed Scroll
    Bowl, 7" d, Hobstar & Tassel exterior, electric purple 400.00
    Sauce, 5" d, purple... 45.00
Embroidered Mums, Northwood
    Bowl, 9" d, ruffled, electric blue border, bronze highlighted
        center... 475.00
    Plate, 9" d, ice green 1,100.00
Enameled Grape, Northwood, water set, 6 pcs, blue, enamel dec.. 800.00
Fanciful, Dugan
    Bowl, low, ruffled, frosty white, pink, blue, and green
        highlights 115.00
    Plate, 9" d, blue, basketweave back, multicolored highlights 350.00
Fashion, Imperial
    Punch Cup, marigold.. 24.00
    Tumbler, marigold.. 90.00
    Water Set, marigold, 7 pc matched set 150.00
Fentonia, Fenton, tumbler, marigold...................................... 45.00
Fine Cut & Roses, Northwood, rose bowl
    Dark Ice Blue, fancy feet, slight damage to feet.................. 265.00
    Purple.. 135.00
Fine Rib, Fenton, vase
    10" h, powder blue... 60.00
    10-1/2" h, blue.. 85.00
    10-1/2" h, cherry red... 225.00
    10-1/2" h, marigold.. 40.00
    11-3/4" h, vaseline, marigold overlay................................. 70.00
Fishscale & Beads, Dugan
    Plate, 7" d, electric purple... 575.00
    Plate, 7" d, marigold, satin irid... 45.00
    Plate, 7-1/2" d, low, ruffled, purple................................... 325.00
Fleur-De-Lis, Millersburg, bowl, 10" d, six ruffle crimped edge, collar
    base, amethyst, radium finish 525.00
Floral & Optic, Imperial, bowl, 9" d, electric purple, electric blue
    irid 775.00
Flowers, Fenton, rose bowl
    Blue, multicolored irid... 110.00
    Blue, flake on foot... 45.00
Frosted Block, Imperial, rose bowl, deep marigold 30.00
Fruits & Flowers, Northwood
    Bonbon, handled
        Amethyst, light, electric highlights................................ 225.00
        Aqua opalescent , electric yellow iridescence, heavy opales-
            cence.. 600.00
        Dark ice blue 450.00
        Dark ice green, chip on base 245.00
        Frosty white 210.00
        Lavender 200.00
        Purple.. 85.00
    Sauce, 5-1/2" d, ruffled, purple... 55.00
Good Luck, Northwood
    Bowl, 9" d, ruffled, ribbed ext., marigold............................ 175.00
    Bowl, pie crust edge, blue 350.00
    Bowl, ruffled, electric blue.. 435.00
    Bowl, ruffled, purple... 300.00
Grape, Imperial
    Bowl, ruffled, 8-1/2" d, electric purple 135.00
    Decanter, electric purple, stopper missing........................... 85.00
    Water Carafe, electric purple, blue/purple irid 300.00
    Water Pitcher, electric purple... 600.00
Grape & Cable, Fenton
    Bowl, 6-1/2" d, smoky blue 40.00
    Bowl, 7-3/4" d, eight ruffles, brick red, satiny iridescence 300.00

Grape and Cable, Northwood
Banana Boat, purple 185.00
Berry Bowl, master, emerald green 145.00
Bonbon, 2 handles
Electric blue 155.00
Green, stippled 105.00
Marigold 55.00
Bowl, 8-1/2" d, ruffled, stippled, ribbed back, pumpkin
marigold 255.00
Butter Dish, cov
Green 175.00
Purple, small nick on lid 175.00
Cologne Bottle, marigold, no stopper 90.00
Cracker jar, cov., marigold 500.00
Hatpin Holder, purple 175.00
Sweetmeat Compote, cov, purple 170.00
Water Pitcher, dark ice green 8,000.00
Grape & Gothic Arches, Northwood, tumbler, electric blue 45.00
Grape Arbor, Northwood
Tankard Pitcher, dark marigold, radium finish 575.00
Tankard Pitcher, purple, blue irid highlights, bronze highlights at
base 400.00
Grapevine & Lattice, Dugan, tumbler, white 225.00
Grape Wreath, Millersburg
Bowl, 8-1/2" d, three-in-one-edge, green, radium finish 135.00
Bowl, 9" d, six ruffles, marigold, blue radium finish 65.00
Ice Cream Bowl, 8" d, amethyst, radium finish 155.00
Grape Wreath Variant, Millersburg, bowl, 7" d, three-in-one edge,
Feather center, purple, radium finish 115.00
Greek Key, Northwood, tumbler, purple 150.00
Hanging Cherries, Millersburg, compote, stemmed, round
Amethyst 2,100.00
Green 1,600.00
Marigold 700.00
Hearts & Flowers, Northwood
Bowl, ruffled, frosty white, multicolored pastel highlights 165.00
Compote
Aqua opalescent , pastel, small flake on base 800.00
Blue, electric blue highlights 450.00
Marigold, multicolored iridescence 170.00
Heavy Grape, Imperial
Chop Plate, 11" d, electric purple 400.00
Chop Plate, 11" d, helios green, flat, wear on high points 135.00
Nappy, 5" d, electric purple 110.00
Plate, 8" d, electric purple 165.00
Plate, 8" d, violet, minor wear on grapes 85.00
Heavy Iris, Dugan, tumbler, amethyst 75.00
Heavy Pineapple, Fenton, bowl, ftd, 10" d, amber, satiny
iridescence 500.00
Hobnail, Millersburg
Rose Bowl, purple 220.00
Spittoon, marigold 700.00
Hobnail Swirl, Millersburg, vase, 11" h, amethyst, radium
iridescence 250.00
Hobstar & Feather, Millersburg
Compote, round, clear 75.00
Compote, round, frosted 135.00
Punch Cup, crystal 25.00
Tumbler, crystal, clear 65.00
Tumbler, crystal, frosted 125.00
Holly, Fenton
Bowl, 9" d, ruffled, light amethyst 130.00
Compote, ruffled, lime green, marigold overlay 100.00
Jack-in-the-Pulpit Hat, crimped edge, marigold 50.00
Plate, 9" d, marigold 155.00
Holly Sprig, Millersburg
Bowl, 6-1/2" d, deep, tight crimped edge, amethyst 120.00
Bowl, 8-1/2" d, 6 ruffles, amethyst 150.00
Nappy, tri-corn, handle, green 160.00

Holly Sprig Variant, Millersburg, bowl, 8-1/2" d, Star center, ruffled and
crimped edge, amethyst, blue radium finish 465.00
Holly Whirl, Millersburg
Bonbon, Issac Benesch 54th Anniversary adv, marigold 150.00
Bowl, 9-1/2" d, ruffled, marigold, radium finish 85.00
Nappy, 2 handles, deep, flared, amethyst, radium
finish 100.00
Nappy, 2 handles, deep, flared, green, satin finish 110.00
Horse Head Medallion, Fenton
Jack-in-the-Pulpit Bowl, ftd, marigold 75.00
Plate, 7-1/2" d, crystal 105.00
Plate, 7-1/2" d, marigold 175.00
Inverted Strawberry, Cambridge, sauce dish, 5" d,
marigold 25.00
Inverted Thistle, Cambridge
Banana Bowl, 7" l, radium green, mkd "Near-Cut" 95.00
Creamer, dark marigold, mkd "Near-Cut," slight rim damage 65.00
Kittens, Fenton
Bowl, six ruffles, marigold 135.00
Cup and Saucer, marigold 245.00
Toothpick Holder, ruffled, marigold, radium finish 115.00
Lattice Hearts, Dugan, plate, 8-1/2" d, electric purple 115.00
Leaf & Beads, Northwood
Nut Bowl, ftd, aqua opalescent , butterscotch irid 1,525.00
Rose Bowl
Aqua opalescent 300.00
Blue, electric blue highlights 135.00
Ice blue 1,100.00
Marigold 55.00
Purple, floral int., ftd 75.00
Leaf and Little Flowers, Millersburg
Compote, flared, deep, green, radium finish with bright blue high-
lights 500.00
Compote, flared, deep, marigold, radium finish 225.00
Compote, 6 ruffles, amethyst 475.00
Compote, 6 ruffles, dark marigold 300.00
Compote, 6 ruffles, purple, radium finish 325.00
Leaf Columns, Northwood, vase, 10-1/2" h
Radium green, multicolored irid, slightly flared top 135.00
Sapphire blue, small flake on base 135.00
Leaf Swirl, Westmoreland, compote
Purple 65.00
Yellow 30.00
Leaf Tiers, Fenton, tumbler, ftd, marigold 80.00
Lotus & Poinsettia, Fenton, bowl, 10" d, ruffled, ftd, dark
marigold 75.00
Many Stars, Millersburg
Bowl, 10" d, 6 ruffles, green, five pointed star 650.00
Bowl, 10" d, three-in-one edge, amethyst, five point star and Trefoil
Fine Cut exterior 775.00
Bowl, 10-1/2" d, 6 ruffles, amethyst, five pointed star 525.00

Louisa, West-moreland, rose bowl, purple, $95.

Mayan, Millersburg, ice cream bowl, green, radium irid.............. 120.00
Memphis, Northwood
    Punch Bowl and Base, adv for Shannon's Furniture-Carpets, crystal, one small flake 125.00
    Punch Bowl Base, purple 45.00
Milady, Fenton, tumbler, blue 75.00
Morning Glory, Imperial
    Funeral Vase, 16-1/2" h, 4-3/4" d base, purple 250.00
    Vase, 6-1/2" h
        Marigold 20.00
        Olive Green 60.00
        Smoke, 4" flared top 50.00
Nesting Swan, Millersburg
    Bowl, 8-3/4" sq, crimped edge, green, radium finish 1,800.00
    Bowl, 9-3/4" d, 6 ruffles, amethyst, satiny finish 250.00
    Bowl, 10" d, 6 ruffles, amethyst, radium finish 375.00
    Bowl, 10" d, 6 ruffles, green, satiny finish 375.00
Night Stars, Millersburg, bonbon, 2 handles, 2 sides, olive green, blue radium finish 800.00
Ohio Star, Millersburg
    Cider Pitcher, 11" h tankard, crystal.................................... 250.00
    Cider Set, 6 pcs, 10" h tankard, crystal, chip on one tumbler 625.00
    Compote, 4-1/2" d, crystal 35.00
    Creamer and Sugar, open, crystal 45.00
    Punch Set, 10 pcs, crystal 1,550.00
    Toothpick Holder, crystal.. 115.00
    Water Carafe, crystal 255.00
Open Rose, Imperial
    Bowl, 8-1/2" d, electric purple 85.00
    Plate, 9" d, marigold 45.00
    Rose Bowl, electric purple int. and ext. 625.00
    Sauce, 5" d, electric purple 105.00
Optic & Buttons, Imperial, rose bowl, marigold 30.00
Orange Tree, Fenton
    Bowl, 9" d, ruffled, Tree Trunk center, white, blue irid 90.00
    Mug, standard size, amber, weak impression 55.00
    Plate, 9" d, frosty white, blue and pink highlights 155.00
    Plate, 9" d, marigold, radium finish 255.00
    Plate, 9-1/2" d, Tree Trunk center, white, frosty irid 185.00
    Powder Box, cov, blue 115.00
    Punch Set, punch bowl, stand, 12 cups, marigold 395.00
    Tumbler, blue 60.00
    Wine, blue 60.00
Oriental Poppy, Northwood, tumbler
    Light Marigold 25.00
    Purple 40.00
Peacock, Millersburg
    Berry Bowl, individual, 5" d, purple, radium finish 115.00
    Berry Bowl, master, 9" d, purple, radium finish, small nick 225.00
    Bowl, 9" d, ruffled, with bee and beads, amethyst, radium finish 650.00
    Bowl, 10" d, three-in-one edge, green, radium finish, blue highlights 425.00
    Ice Cream Bowl, 5" d, marigold, satiny irid 200.00
Peacock at Fountain, Dugan, tumbler, blue 35.00
Peacock at Fountain, Northwood
    Berry Bowl, 5" d, purple 35.00
    Punch Cup, white 20.00
    Tumbler, amethyst 25.00
    Water Pitcher, amethyst.. 250.00
Peacock at Urn, Fenton
    Compote, stemmed, celeste blue, marigold overlay 150.00
    Plate, 9" d, blue, bright red, blue, and green highlights 500.00
Peacock at Urn, Millersburg
    Berry Bowl, individual, 5" d, flared, marigold, radium irid with blue highlights 225.00
    Berry Bowl, master, 9" d, flared, marigold, radium irid with blue highlights 275.00
    Bowl, 9" d, green, satin irid... 700.00

Bowl, 10-1/2" d, 6 ruffles, green, satin finish, bee, no beading 250.00
Compote, stemmed, ruffled, large, amethyst.................... 1,600.00
Compote, stemmed, ruffled, large, green 1,500.00
Compote, stemmed, ruffled, large, marigold 2,300.00
Ice Cream Bowl, 9-3/4" d, amethyst, radium finish, bee, no beading 225.00
Plate, 6" d, amethyst, satin finish, no bee, no beading 1,200.00
Sauce, 6" d, ruffled, blue, no bee, no beading.................. 1,050.00
Peacock Tail Variant, Millersburg, compote, stemmed, ruffled
    Green... 55.00
    Marigold 85.00
    Purple 115.00
Peacocks, Northwood
    Bowl, pie crust edge, clambroth, multicolored irid 325.00
    Bowl, ruffled, aqua opalescent 1,650.00
    Plate, 9" d, electric blue, satin irid 1,025.00
Perfection, Millersburg, water pitcher, handle, ruffled top, purple 4,650.00
Persian Garden, Dugan, plate, 6-1/2" d, marigold 40.00
Persian Medallion, Fenton
    Bonbon, 2 handles, vaseline, marigold overlay 140.00
    Hair Receiver, frosty white... 130.00
    Plate, 6" d, marigold 25.00
    Rose Bowl, deep marigold.. 120.00
Petals, Northwood, compote, 7", marigold.................................. 30.00
Pinecone, Fenton, plate, 6" d, marigold...................................... 40.00
Plume Panels, Fenton, vase, 11" h, green.................................. 95.00
Poinsettia & Lattice, Northwood, bowl, 8-1/2" d, ruffled, rib ext.
    Blue 600.00
    Lavender.. 925.00
Pond Lily, Fenton, calling card tray, 2 handles, white, weak irid 25.00
Poppy, Millersburg, compote, flared, dark marigold................... 475.00
Poppy, Northwood, pickle dish, blue... 55.00
Poppy Show, Northwood, bowl, ruffled, marigold 400.00
Primrose, Millersburg, bowl, 9-1/2" d, ruffled, Fine Cut Heart exterior, marigold, radium finish with blue highlights................................ 95.00
Rays & Ribbons, Millersburg
    Bowl, 9-1/2" d, crimped edge, Cactus exterior, purple, blue radium irid 175.00
    Bowl, 9-3/4" d, 3-in-1 edge, marigold 140.00

Singing Bird, Northwood, mug, marigold, $275.

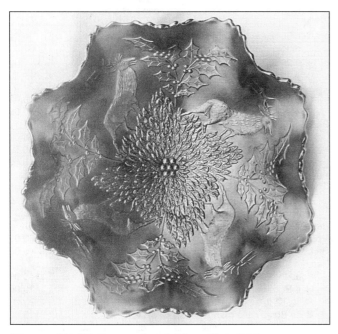

Stag and Holly, Fenton, bowl, blue, 8" d, $500.

Ribbon Tie, Fenton, bowl, three-in-one edge, low, blue 160.00
Ripple, Imperial, funeral vase, 17" h, marigold 115.00
Rosalind, Millersburg
    Bowl, 10-1/2" d, 6 ruffles, amethyst 225.00
    Bowl, 10-1/2" d, marigold satin 125.00
    Jelly, stemmed, flared, deep, 8-1/2" h, amethyst 3,500.00
Rose Columns, Millersburg, vase, green 3,000.00
Roses and Fruit, Millersburg, bonbon
    Green, 2 handles, ... 600.00
    Marigold, stemmed, handles 550.00
Rose Show, Northwood, bowl, ruffled, aqua opalescent , light butter-
    scotch overlay, opalescent highlights 775.00
Rose Spray, Fenton
    Goblet, marigold 30.00
    Jack In The Pulpit, celeste blue 65.00
Round-Up, Dugan
    Bowl, low, ruffled, peach opalescent 250.00
    Plate, 9" d, blue, basketweave back, blue and pink
        highlights 275.00
Rustic, Fenton
    Funeral Vase, 18-1/2" h, blue, electric blue highlights 675.00
    Swung Vase, 15" h, 4-1/4" d base, green, radium multicolored
        irid 110.00
Seacoast, Millersburg, pin tray, marigold 1,000.00
Seaweed, Millersburg
    Bowl, 10-1/4" d, 3-in-1 edge, green 400.00
    Bowl, 10-1/4" d, 3-in-1 edge, marigold, satiny irid 350.00
    Plate, 9" d, flared, green, satiny irid 1,900.00
    Plate, 9" d, flared, marigold 1,600.00
    Sauce, 5-1/2" d, ice cream shape, dark marigold 850.00
Ski Star, Dugan, plate, 6-1/2" d, tightly crimped edge, Compass ext.,
    peach opalescent 135.00
Smooth Rays, Dugan, berry, ruffled, Jeweled Heart ext.,
    amethyst 35.00
Squatty Thin Rib, Northwood, vase, 7" h, purple 60.00
Stag & Holly, Fenton
    Bowl, 10" d, ruffled, ftd, powder blue, marigold overlay 200.00
    Bowl, 10-1/2" d, crimped edge, ftd, marigold 125.00
    Bowl, 11-1/4" d, ruffled, ftd, light blue aqua base, marigold
        overlay 200.00
Stippled Petals, Dugan, plate, purple, dome ftd, tight crimped
    edge 750.00

Stippled Rays, Fenton
    Ice Cream Bowl, 6" d, cherry red 450.00
    Plate, 7" d, Scale Band back, marigold 25.00
Strawberry, Northwood
    Bowl, 8" d, pie crust edge
        Horehound, stippled, basketweave ext. 485.00
        Purple 100.00
    Plate, 9" d, basketweave back, dark marigold, etched "St. Joe,
        Mich" 155.00
    Plate, 9-1/4" d, basketweave back, green 235.00
Strawberry Wreath, Millersburg
    Bowl, 9" d, low crimped ruffled, purple 185.00
    Compote, 6 ruffles, amethyst 375.00
    Compote, 6 ruffles, dark marigold 175.00
    Compote, 6 ruffles, green 400.00
    Sauce, 5" sq, crimped edge, green 650.00
Swirl Hobnail, Millersburg, rose bowl, purple 275.00
Ten Mums, Fenton
    Bowl, 9" d, three-in-one edge, green 100.00
    Bowl, 10" d, six ruffles edge, emerald green base, multicolored
        irid 350.00
Thin Rib, Fenton, vase, 10" h, blue 60.00
Thin Rib, Northwood, vase, 10" h, blue, multicolored irid 55.00
Three Fruits, Northwood
    Bowl, 8 ruffles, stippled
        Green 315.00
        Pumpkin marigold 185.00
    Bowl, ruffles, stippled, ftd, Meander ext.
        Aqua opalescent 675.00
        Marigold 115.00
    Plate, 9" d, basketweave back, dark marigold 225.00
    Plate, 9" d, stippled, amethyst 300.00
Tiger Lily, Imperial, tumbler, marigold 75.00
Tree Trunk, Northwood
    Funeral Vase
        10-1/2" h, aqua opalescent, butterscotch overlay, opalescence
            extending to base 950.00
        11-1/2" h, dark marigold, radium finish with multicolored
            irid 175.00
        12-1/2" h at back, 10-1/2" h at front, green, radium
            finish 425.00

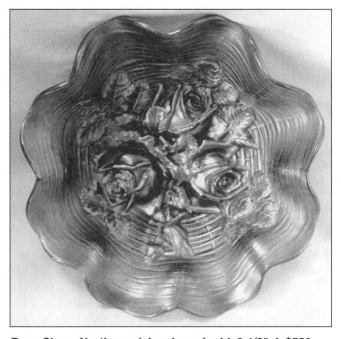

Rose Show, Northwood, bowl, marigold, 8-1/2" d, $550.

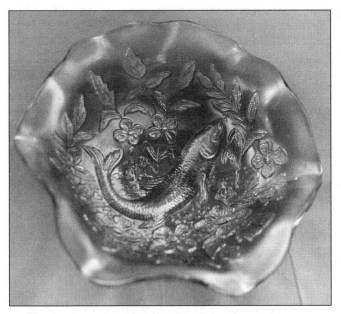

Trout and Fly, Millersburg, ice cream bowl, marigold, satiny finish, 8-1/4" d, $525.

18-1/2" h, electric blue, plunger base	3,500.00
Swung Vase, 11" h, blue, radium electric blue highlights	225.00

Trout and Fly, Millersburg

Bowl, 9" d, 3-in-1 edge, light amethyst	700.00
Ice Cream Bowl, 8-1/4" l, marigold, satiny finish	525.00
Ice Cream Bowl, 8-1/2" l, green, satiny finish, bruise on base	625.00

Two Flowers, Fenton

Bowl, 9" d, ftd, emerald green	275.00
Bowl, 11" d, ruffled, ftd, blue, small flake on foot	95.00
Vintage, Fenton, jack-in-the-pulpit vase, marigold	1,400.00

Whirling Leaves, Millersburg

Bowl, 9-1/2" d, 6 ruffles, amethyst	215.00
Bowl, tri-corn, crimped edge, amethyst	475.00
Wide Panel, Northwood, sherbet, russet green	20.00
Wild Berry, Westmoreland, powder jar, cov, marigold	210.00
Wild Flower, Northwood, compote, stemmed, light marigold	65.00
Wild Rose, Northwood, rose bowl, ftd, stippled rays int., electric purple	650.00
Wild Strawberry, Northwood, plate, 8" d, hand grip, basketweave back, electric purple	325.00

Windmill, Imperial

Pitcher, marigold	65.00
Sauce, 5" d, purple	55.00
Tumbler, purple	75.00
Wishbone & Spades, Dugan, chop plate, 10-3/4" d, plain back, purple, with electric purple and blue highlights	900.00

Wreath of Roses, Fenton, punch cups, Vintage interior

Blue	40.00
Green	40.00

Zig-Zag, Millersburg

Bowl, 10" d, 3 in 1 edge, amethyst	400.00
Bowl, tri-corn, crimped edge, amethyst	1,050.00

CAROUSEL FIGURES

History: By the late 17th century, carousels were found in most capital cities of Europe. In 1867, Gustav Dentzel carved America's first carousel. Other leading American firms include Charles I. D. Looff, Allan Herschell, Charles Parker, and William F. Mangels.

References: Charlotte Dinger, *Art of the Carousel*, Carousel Art, 1983; Tobin Fraley, *The Carousel Animal*, Tobin Fraley Studios, 1983; Frederick Fried, *Pictorial History of the Carrousel*, Vestal Press, 1964; William Manns, Peggy Shank, and Marianne Stevens, *Painted Ponies*, Zon International Publishing, 1986.

Periodicals: *Carousel Collecting & Crafting*, 3755 Avocado Blvd., Suite 164, La Mesa, CA 91941; *Carousel News & Trader*, Suite 206, 87 Park Avenue West, Mansfield, OH 44902; *Carousel Shopper*, Zon International Publishing, P.O. Box 6459, Santa Fe, NM 87502.

Collectors' Clubs: American Carousel Society, 3845 Telegraph Rd., Elkton, MD 21921; National Amusement Park Historical Association, P.O. Box 83, Mount Prospect, IL 60056; National Carousel Association, P. O. Box 4333, Evansville, IN 47724.

Museums: Carousel Museum of America, San Francisco, CA; Heritage Plantation of Sandwich, Sandwich, MA; Herschell Carousel Factory Museum, North Tonawanda, NY; International Museum of Carousel Art, Portland, OR; Merry-Go-Round Museum, Sandusky, OH; New England Carousel Museum, Inc., Bristol, CT.

Notes: Since carousel figures were repainted annually, original paint is not a critical factor to collectors. "Park paint" indicates layers of accumulated paint; "stripped" means paint has been removed to show carving; "restored" involves stripping and repainting in the original colors.

Camel

European, 1890	2,400.00
Loeff	7,000.00
Morris, E. Joy	8,000.00

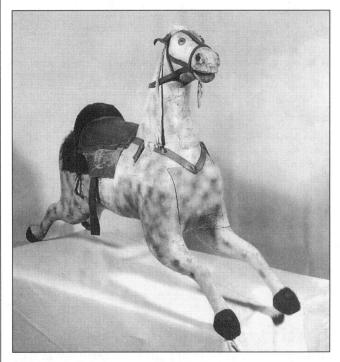

Horse, painted wood, orig halter, leather saddle, and corduroy blanket, eastern origin, c1840, $650.

Chariot Bench
  Loeff, gilded 625.00
  Parker, C. W. 12,500.00
  Spillman, with flowers 300.00
  Unknown maker, one panel having applied carved flowers, other side with applied carved eagle and horse,52" x 29" 800.00
Cow, Bayol, France 5,000.00
Elephant, fiberglass 600.00
Deer, P.T.C., orig paint 20,000.00
Donkey, Illions, from Willow Grove Amusement Park, Willow Grove, PA 17,000.00
Giraffe, Loeff 13,000.00
Goat, Loeff 7,500.00
Horse
  Anderson, J. R., jumper 5,000.00
  Bayol, France, jumper 3,000.00
  Carmel, jumper 3,700.00
  Dare, Charles W. F., New York Carousel Manufacturing Company, Brooklyn, NY, jumper
    56" l, 39" h, orig paint, old repair, minor imperfections .. 9,775.00
    60" l, 39" h, orig paint, very minor losses, paint wear and loss 8,625.00
  Dentzel
    Escape Jumper, restored in fiber glass 7,750.00
    Jumper, top knot 5,000.00
    Prancer, orig paint 8,000.00
  Herschell, Allen
    Combination wood and fiber glass 650.00
    Jumper, all wood, 1920 .... 2,000.00
    Metal, restored 800.00
    Trojan, restored 3,750.00
  Herschell-Spillman, North Tonawanda, NY, jumper, orange, green, and blue, 60" x 56" x 12" cast iron stand 2,750.00
  Heyn, Frederick 4,100.00
  Hubner, prancer, fully restored 4,250.00
  Illions, from Willow Grove Amusement Park, Willow Grove, PA
    Jumper 5,000.00
    Stander, armored 75,000.00
    Stander 13,000.00
  Loeff, stander, closed mouth 14,200.00
  Morris, E. J., stander 10,500.00
  Norman & Evans 1,500.00
  Ortega, jumper 300.00
  Parker, C. W. Abilene, KA, c1905, carved mane, saddle, American flag, glass eyes, old polychrome repaint, 56" h, added base and brass post, replaced tail and stirrups, old sheet metal repairs over seams and breaks in legs 1,760.00
  P.T.C., jumper 3,250.00
  Spillman
    Jumper, restored 3,300.00
    Stander, animal pelt 4,600.00
  Stein & Goldstein
    Jumper 2,750.00
    Stander 11,000.00
Indian Pony
  Parker, C. W., pelt saddle 9,000.00
  Spillman 4,500.00
Panel, carved wood
  37-1/2" x 45", cowboy on bucking bronco in panoramic view 200.00
  63" x 13", cherub at top, carved leaves overall 450.00
Pig
  Dentzel, restored 12,000.00
  Spillman, with pear 5,000.00

CASTLEFORD

History: Castleford is a soft-paste porcelain made in Yorkshire, England, in the 1800s for the American trade. The wares have a warm, white ground, scalloped rims (resembling castle tops), and are trimmed in deep blue. Occasionally pieces are decorated further with a coat of arms, eagles, or Lady Liberty.

Creamer, 4-1/4" h, Parian, white, deep blue striping, emb classical scenes of cherubs 100.00
Milk Jug, 4-3/4" h, oval, relief of American eagle on one side, Liberty and cap on reverse, acanthus leaf border 165.00
Sugar, cov, relief of classical figure leaning on urn, acanthus leaf panel, blue enamel border, scalloped edge, 3 enameled bands on cov 250.00
Teapot, cov, 6" h, molded eagle dec, early 1ith C, minor imperfections 245.00

CASTOR SETS

History: A castor set consists of matched condiment bottles held within a frame or holder. The bottles are for condiments such as salt, pepper, oil, vinegar, and mustard. The most commonly found castor sets consist of three, four, or five glass bottles in a silver-plated frame.

Although castor sets were made as early as the 1700s, most of the sets encountered today date from 1870-1915, the period when they enjoyed their greatest popularity.

3 Bottle, clear, Daisy and Button pattern, toothpick holder center, matching glass holder 125.00
3 Bottle, clear, Ribbed Palm pattern, pewter tops and frame 185.00
4 Bottle, clear, mold blown, pewter lids and frame, domed based, loop handle, mkd "I. Trask," early 19th C, 8" h 320.00
4 Bottle, cranberry bottles and jars, clear pressed glass frame, silver plated look handle, two brass caps, one pewter, 9-1/2" h 275.00
4 Bottle, green cut to clear, sq bottles, SP frame 340.00
4 Bottle, rubena, Venecia pattern, glass frame 200.00
4 Bottle, ruby stained, Ruby Thumbprint pattern, glass frame 360.00
5 Bottle, clear, Bellflower pattern, pressed stoppers, pewter frame with pedestal 295.00

3 bottle, pink milk glass, hand painted floral dec, pewter tops, fan shaped base, $95.

5 Bottle, clear, allover cut linear and geometric design, SS mounts and frame, shell shaped foot, English hallmarks, c1750, 8-1-2/" h . 625.00
5 Bottle, clear, Honeycomb pattern, ornate Wilcox frame 265.00
5 Bottle, cut glass, ornate Rogers & Bros. frame 295.00
5 Bottle, etched, wreath and polka dots pattern, rib trimmed frame 195.00
6 Bottle, china, Willow ware, matching frame 150.00
6 Bottle, clear, pressed bottles, SP Simpson Hall & Miller frame 150.00
6 Bottle, cut, diamond point panels, rotating sterling silver frame, all over flowers, paw feet, loop handle, Gorham Mfg. Co., c1880, 11-1/2" h 2,500.00
6 Bottle, cut, pewter frame with mechanical door housing, Gleason 1,500.00

CATALOGS

History: The first American mail-order catalog was issued by Benjamin Franklin in 1744. This popular advertising tool helped to spread inventions, innovations, fashions, and necessities of life to rural America. Catalogs were profusely illustrated and are studied today to date an object, identify its manufacturer, study its distribution, and determine its historical importance.

References: Ron Barlow and Ray Reynolds, *Insider's Guide to Old Books, Magazines, Newspapers, Trade Catalogs*, Windmill Publishing (2147 Windmill View Rd., Cajon, CA 92020), 1995; Lawrence B. Romaine, *Guide to American Trade Catalogs 1744-1900*, Dover Publications, n.d.

Museums: Grand Rapids Public Museum, Grand Rapids, MI; National Museum of Health and Medicine, Walter Reed Medical Center, Washington, DC.

Additional Listings: See Warman's Americana & Collectibles for more examples.

Advisor: Kenneth Schneringer.

A .G. Spalding & Bros., St. . Louis, MO, 1939, 32 pgs, 6-3/4" x 10", Fall & Winter Catalog of Sport Goods 47.00

Bellas Hess & Co., Catalogue No. 59, 1913, illus by Wanley J. Johnson, pink hair bow, holding pink roses, $24. Photo courtesy of Kenneth E. Schneringer.

American Colortype Co. New York, NY, ND, c1915, 49 pgs, 7-1/2" x 11-1/2", color illus, adv with cuts like P. Boileau cover of National Cloak & Suit, Swift & Co., label of Little Cook, individual packages, Anheuser-Busch post card 127.00
Animal Trap Co. of America, Lititz, PA, 1945, 48 pgs, 8-1/2" x 11", "How To Catch More Fur With Oneida Victor Traps" 41.00
Art Metal Construction Co., Jamestown, NY, c1919, 48 pgs, 7-1/2" x 10-1/2" Cat. No. 753, office furniture 36.00
Barclay Co., Narberth, PA, ND, c1929, 24 pgs, 4" x 9", 18" x 24" sheet folded as issued, Barclay Garden Ware 24.00
C. L. Berger & Sons, Boston, MA, 1910, 226 pgs, 6" x 9", Handbook & Illustrated Catalogue of Engineers' & Surveyors' Instruments, heavy wraps, used 128.00
Bird Food Co., Philadelphia, PA, 1912, 122 pgs, 4-1/2" x 5-3/4", No. 1 Fanciers' Hand Book 24.00
Bravman Furniture Co., Wilkes Barre, PA,1927, 24 pgs, 6" x 9", Kold King & Superior Refrigerators 32.00
Brooks Manufacturing Co., Saginaw?. MI, 1917, 64 pgs, 6-3/4" x 10", Cat. #32, Bookrs, Boats-raking Transom Stern Design, wraps, fade, loose 93.00
Buick Motor Co., Detroit, MI, ND, c1917?, 22 pgs, 5-3/4"x 9-3/4", "The Buick Value-In-Head," illus, some sheetslooseoning 67.00
Carbone Co., Boston, MA, 1932, 48 pgs, 7-1/4" x 10-1/2", "The Chard," pages loosening from rusted staples, good condition 23.00
Cash Buyer's Union, Chicago, IL,1910, 32 pgs, 6" x 9", Mfgr's & Wholesale Dealers Special Catalog A. No. 375, wraps, lay-ins, good illus 29.00
Central Oilgas Stove Co., Boston, MA, 1892, 42 pgs, 6" x 9", Fall Catalogue of Oilgas & Vaporizing Heating Stoves for Kerosene 31.00
Cessna Aircraft Co., Wichita, KS, 1965, 12 pgs, 8-1/4" x 11", laid-in price list, letter, chart, etc., The 411 by Cessna, 5 pictures of aircraft, plane interior, color 47.00
Claflin, Thayer & Co., New York, NY, 1899, 56 pgs, Fall, Vol. 14, Book of Shoes for Men, Women & Children 24.00
Henry N Clark Co., Boston, MA, ND, c1929, 24 pgs, 6" x 9", Cat. No. 929, Knickerbocker Refrigerators, oak exterior cases 62.00
Comm, Paolo Soprani /Figli, IT, ND, c1926, 40 pgs, 7-1/2" x 11-1/4", in Italian, music boxes, etc., some pages loosening, light stains... 38.00
Czechoslovak Music Co., New York, NY, ND, 1930s, 165 pgs, 8-1/2" x 11-3/4", musical instruments 128.00
Dominion Organ & Piano Co., Bowmanville, ON, ND, c1900, 40 pgs, 7" x 8 3/4", revised descriptive price list of pianos, bad gnaw rear wrap . 53.00
E. & T. Fairbanks & Co., St. Johnsbury, VT, ND, 1880s, 32 pgs, 4" x 6", Fairbanks' Standard Railroad, Hay, Coal, Platform & Counter Scales 44.00
Fairbanks, Morse & Co., Chicago IL, ND, early 1900, 28 pgs, 6" x 9-1/4", Simplex Gasoline Marine Engine 99.00
Folbot Corporation, Long Island City, NY, 1939, 40 pgs, 6" x 8-1/2", "The Greater Outdoors," well illus 33.00
Julien P. Friez & Son, Baltimore, MD, 1939, 32 pgs, 8-1/2" x 11", 17" x 40" sheet folded as issued, division of Bendix Aviation Corp., aviation instruments, weather instruments, etc., dusted 77.00
Galloway Terra-Cotta Co., Philadelphia PA, ND, 1924?, 24 pgs, 9-1/4" x 12", Pottery Catalog No. 24 for Garden and Interior, price list laid in, many illus 63.00
Richard Garrett & Son. Leiston, Great Britain, ND, early, 32 pgs, 9" x 11", Illustrated List of Parts for Garrett and other portable and semi-portable steam engines 122.00
Gimbel Brothers, New York, 1915, 226 pgs, 8" x 10-3/4", Fall & Winter, Paris, London & American styles for women and children 58.00
Haug Dept., Store, Spillville, IA, ND, 8 pgs, 11" x 16", Christmas Store, folded in half 24.00
Hawkins Co., S. Britain, CT, 1926, 14 pgs, 6" x 9", descriptive price list and catalog of Blake, Lamb & Co. Game Traps 44.00
Herring-Hall-Marvin Safe, New York, NY, 1924, 72 pgs, 8" x 10-1/2", Cat. No. 115, Fireproof Steel Safes, etc. 47.00
Holgate Brothers Co., Kane, PA, 1941, 28 pgs, 8-1/2" x 11", Cat. No. 18., Holgate Toys, sturdy wooden wagons and toys 38.00
Kelly Press Division, US, 1927, 30 pgs, 8-1/2" x 11", hard cover, "The Kelly Press" division of American Type Founders Co. 47.00

Kochs' Beauty Parlor Fixtures and Accessories, T. Noonan & Sons, Boston, Mass, tan cover with purple and pink, $100. Photo courtesy of Kenneth E. Schneringer.

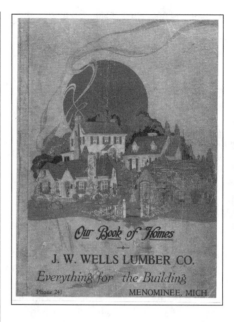

Our Book of Homes, J. W. Wells Lumber Co., Menominee, MI. $34. Photo courtesy of Kenneth E. Schneringer.

Keuffel & Esser Co., New York, NY, 1891, 36 pgs, 5-1/2" x 8-3/4", Manheim Slide Rule, complete manual, tables, dusted..38.00

Kimberly-Clark Co., Neenah, WI, 1924, 64 pgs, 8-1/2" x 11-1/2", advertising literature, cups, large number of ads, wraps roughed 26.00

King Sewing Machine Co., Buffalo, NY, 1909, 56 pgs, 6" x 9", The King, Direct From Factory to Home, dusted 24.00

Larkin Co., Buffalo, NY, 1907, 80 pgs, 8-1/4" x 10-1/4", premium list, some tape at spine 36.00

Leach Co., Oshkosh, WI, ND, c1940, 24 pgs, 7-3/4" x 10-1/4", Cat. No. 49, Oshkosh Pole Line Construction Eqpt, staples rust, wraps loose, intact..22.00

Long Beach Reed & Willow, New York, NY, ND, c1922, 45 pgs, 6" x 9-1/4", furniture......................................68.00

Macbeth-Evens Glass Co., Pittsburgh, PA, ND, c1915, 52 pgs, 6" x 9", Cat. #77, Ajax Lighting Equipment for Nitrogen Lamps, Type C, halftones of ceiling fixtures, other lightning 68.00

Manufacturers' Price List, US, 1907, 298 pgs, 7-3/4" x 10-1/4", No. 80, Jewelry Items, ... 110.00

Max Geisler Bird Co., Omaha, NE, 1929, 64 pgs, 6" x 8-3/4", Illustrated Catalogue of Animals, aquariums, cages, accessories..............46.00

Mid-Western Sport Togs, Berlin, WI, 1942, 24 pgs, 7-1/4" x 10-1/4", buckskin coats, etc. 30.00

Millers Harness Co., Inc., New York, NY, 1974, 112 pgs, 8-1/4" x 11", Miller's Catalog No. 106, Equestrian equipment, clothing, accessories 33.00

Monarch Telephone Mfg. Co., Chicago IL, ND, c1910, 48., 8" x 10-1/4", magneto switchboards, equipment 79.00

National Cash Register Co., Dayton, OH, 1928, 16 pgs, 5-1/2" x 8-1/2", Products of NCR Co., business machines 39.00

National Cash Register Co., Dayton, OH, ND, c1921, 88 pgs, 6" x 9", "How to Use Your National Cash Register," Class 900 Receipt . 27.00

Noonan & Sons Co., Chicago, IL, c1920, 160 pgs, 7-3/4" x 10-3/4", Kochs' Beauty Parlor Fixtures & Accessories, halftone illus 100.00

James Ohlen & Sons Saw Co., Columbus, OH, 1918, 116 pgs, 5-3/4"x 8-3/4", Cat. No. 56-8 of Saws..............................38.00

Oneida Community Limited, Niagara Falls, NY, 1895, 36 pgs, 7-1/2" x 10-1/2", Illustrated Catalog & Price List of Silver Plated Ware, roughed at binding, contents good.............................80.00

Parks Woodworking Machine, Cincinnati, OH, 1927, 48 pgs, 6" x 9", Catalog A, wood working machines, illus booklet laid in 46.00

Premier Cycle Works, Chicago, IL,1916, 64 pgs, 8-3/4" x 11-3/4", No. 66, Premier Bicycles, cuts of 13 models, accessories 139.00

Richard's New York, NY, ND, c1900, 26 pgs, 8" x 11-1/4", Richard's Fashion Album of Tailor Made Costumes for Women, colorful wraps, torn at binding, dusted.....................................43.00

J. U. Rutishauser Co., Inc., Chicago, IL, 1900, 224 pgs, 7-3/4" x 10", wholesale jewelry catalog, rear wrap missing 39.00

Samuel Kirk & Son, Inc., Baltimore, MD, 1940, 48 pgs, 6-1/4" x 9", silver flatware patterns, accessories.........................36.00

The Scout Executive, New York, NY, 1928, 42 pgs, 8" x 11", Equipment Vol. 9, No. 10, equipment, insignias, uniforms, etc. 32.00

Schwinn Bicycle Co., Chicago, IL,1980, 64 pgs, 5-1/2" x 8-1/2", bicycles and accessories, cuts of many models..........................29.00

Sears, Roebuck & Co., Chicago, IL, 1902, 62 pgs, 8-1/2" x 11", Cat. #112, vehicles, harness, saddles, etc. 72.00

Sears, Roebuck & Co., Chicago, IL, 1908, 66 pgs, 6-3/4" x 13-1/4", The Economy Chief Cream Separator 52.00

Sears, Roebuck & Co., Chicago, IL, 1911, 72 pgs, 8-1/2" x 10-3/4", Conley Cameras & Photographic Supplies................73.00

Smith & Barnes Piano Co., Chicago, IL, c1927, 19 pgs, 6" x 8-1/2", showing piano styles.......................................26.00

Sports, Inc., Chicago, IL, 1956, 40 pgs, 8-1/4" x 11", 1956 Catalog of Guns & Shooting Supplies 29.00

Star Shoe Co., Portsmouth, OH, 1896, 15 pgs, 5-3/4"x 8-3/4", Misses & Children's Fine Shoes for the Fall........................18.00

J. Stevens Arms Co., Chicopee Falls, MA, ND, 1934, 24 pgs, 7-1/4" x 9", Catalog of Rifles, Shotguns, Pistols & Accessories.............62.00

Studebacker Motors, Detroit, MI, 1930, 16 pgs, 8-3/4" x 11", World Famous Studebaker Commander Eight, colored cuts of 5 models, colorful wraps, light dampening.................................48.00

Sunray Stove Co., Delaware, OH, ND, c1926, 48 pgs, 7" x 10-1/4", Cat. E, Sunray Gas Heaters & Gas Ranges.................34.00

Taylor Fireworks Co., Kansas City, MO, 1966, 8 pgs, 8-1/2" x 11", Taylor's Fireworks- Zebra & Cat Brand Firecrackers, (Woody's Hardware, Golden City, MO), mail-out brochure with 2 order sheets, 33.00

Vischer & Co., Alfred, New York, NY, 1906, 12 pgs, 3-3/4" x 6-1/2", Minerva dolls, orig mail-out, illus envelope 122.00

Weber Lifelike Fly Co., Stevens Point, WI, 1937, 80 pgs, 6-1/4" x 9-1/4", Cat. No. 18, Flies & Fly Tackle, List of Fly Patterns........69.00

Josiah Wedgwood & Sons, New York NY, ND, 16 pgs, 4-1/2" x 6", Wedgwood Pottery with the Story of Wedgwood and the Making of His Pottery, illus...39.00

Willmarth Tackle Co., Roosevelt, NY, 1934, 60 pgs, 6" x 9", Fishing Tackle Catalog & Tackle Tinker's Guide 48.00

Wilson Dearborn & Co., Boston MA, 189_, 58 pgs, 9-1/2" x 12-1/4", Hair-dressers Purchasing Guide, color sheets, illus, wraps roughed 950.00

CELADON

History: The term "celadon," meaning a pale grayish green color, is derived from the theatrical character Celadon, who wore costumes of varying shades of grayish green, in Honore d'Urfe's 17th-century pastoral romance, L'Astree. French Jesuits living in China used the name to refer to a specific type of Chinese porcelain.

Celadon divides into two types. Northern celadon, made during the Sung Dynasty up to the 1120s, has a gray to brownish body, relief decoration, and monochromatic olive green glaze. Southern (Lung-ch'uan) celadon, made during the Sung Dynasty and much later, is paint-decorated with floral and other scenic designs and is found in forms which would appeal to the European and American export market. Many of the southern pieces date from 1825 to 1885. A blue square with Chinese or pseudo-Chinese characters appears on pieces after 1850. Later pieces also have a larger and sparser decorative patterning.

Reproduction Alert.

Bowl, 14-3/4" d, deep rounded sides, waisted rim,, everted lip, ext. with interwoven bands of flowering magnolias, 3 cylindrical applied monster head feet, pale gray-green glaze, unglazed base, Chinese...........975.00
Censor, 10-3/4" d, compressed globular form, 3 monster head supports, carved with Eight Trigrams, thick gray-green crackle glaze, int. central portion and glaze unglazed, kiln flaws, Lonquan, Ming Dynasty 675.00
Libation Cup, 3-3/4" h, steep tapering sides, foliate rim, dragon and clouds, blue-green glaze, 19th C 250.00
Plate, 7-3/8" d, polychrome flowers, birds, and butterflies, pr, one with chip on table ring...200.00
Umbrella Stand, 24-3/4" h, blue glazed dec, Chinese 275.00
Vase
    10-1/2" h, swelling block cylindrical form, mask and ring handles, Chinese, fitted as lamp 100.00
    16" h, club form, Chinese, fitted as lamp 120.00
    16-1/2" h, Rouleau form, front with blue and white scene of dancing figures, crackled, Chinese, Ming style, second half 19th C, sgd .. 700.00

CELLULOID ITEMS

History: In 1869, an Albany, NY printer named John W. Hyatt developed and patented the world's first commer-cially successful semi-synthetic thermoplastic. The moldable material was made from a combination of camphor—the crystalline resin from the heart of a particular evergreen tree, and collodion—a type of nitrated cellulose substance (also called Pyroxylin) which was extremely flammable. Hyatt and his brother Isaiah called their invention Celluloid, a name which they made up, by combining the words cellulose and colloid.

By 1873, the Hyatts were successfully producing raw pyroxylin plastic material at the Celluloid Manufacturing Company of Newark, NJ. In the early days of its commercial development, Celluloid was produced exclusively in two colors; flesh tone—for the manufacture of denture base material;and off white—which was primarily used for utilitarian applications like harness trimmings and knife handles.

However, during the late 1870s, advances in plastics technology brought about a shift in the ways that Celluloid could be used. Beautiful imitations of amber, ivory, tortoise shell, jet and coral were being produced and used in the fabrication of jewelry, fashion accessories and hair ornaments. Because the faux luxury materials were so realistic and affordable, Celluloid quickly advanced to the forefront of consumerism by the working and middle classes.

Throughout the 1880s and 1890s, competition in the infant plastics industry was rampant and a number of newly organized fabricating companies were aggressively molding their brands of pyroxylin plastic into a variety of consumer products. However, since there was such limited knowledge about the nature of the material, many companies failed due to inferior products or devastating fires.

By the early 20th century, there were four major American manufacturers firmly established as producers of quality pyroxylin plastics. In addition to the Celluloid Company of Newark, NJ, there was the Arlington Manufacturing Company of Arlington, NJ, which produced Pyralin; Fiberloid Corporation of Indian Orchard, MA makers of Fiberloid and the Viscoloid Company of Leominster, MA. Even though these companies branded their plastic products with their registered trade names, today the word "celluloid" is used in a general sense for all forms of this early plastic.

Celluloid-type plastic became increasingly popular as an alternative for costly and elusive natural substances. Within the fashion industry alone, it gained acceptance as a beautiful and affordable substitute for increasingly dwindling supplies of ivory and tortoise shell. However, it should be noted that celluloid's most successful application during the late 19th century was realized in the clothing industry; sheet stock in imitation of fine grade linen was fashioned into stylish waterproof cuffs and collars.

In sheet form, Celluloid found other successful applications as well. Printed political and advertising premiums, pin-back buttons, pocket mirrors and keepsakes items from 1890-1920 were turned out by the thousands. In addition, transparent sheet celluloid was ornately decorated by embossing, reverse painting and lamination, then used in the production of decorative boxes, booklets and albums. The toy industry also capitalized on the use of thin celluloid sheets for the production of blow-molded dolls, animal toys and figural novelties.

Brush Washer, 2-1/4" d, 2" h, $95.

The development of the motion picture industry helped celluloid fulfill a unique identity all its own; it was used for reels of camera film as well as in sheet form by animation artists who drew cartoons. Known as animation cels, these are still readily available to the collector for a costly sum, but because of the depredation of old celluloid, many early movies and cels have been lost forever.

By 1930, and the advent of the modern plastics age, the use of celluloid began to decline dramatically. The introduction of cellulose acetate plastic replaced the flammable pyroxylin plastic in jewelry and toys and the development of non-flammable safety film eventually put an end to its use in the movies. By 1950, the major manufacturers of celluloid in the United States had ceased production; however, many foreign companies continued manufacture. Today Japan, France, Italy and Korea continue to manufacture cellulose nitrate plastics in small amounts for specialty items such as musical instrument inlay, ping pong balls and designer fountain pens.

Beware of celluloid items that show signs of deterioration: oily residue, cracking, discoloration, and crystallization. Take care when cleaning celluloid items; it is best to use mild soap and water, avoiding alcohol- or acetone-based cleansers. Keep celluloid from excessive heat or flame and avoid direct sunlight.

References: Keith Lauer and Julie Robinson, Celluloid, *A Collector's Reference and Value Guide*, Collector Books, 1999; Karima Parry, *Bakelite Bangles, Price & Identification Guide,* Krause Publications, 1999; Joan Van Patten and Elmer and Peggy Williams, *Celluloid Treasures of the Victorian Era*, Collector Books, 1999.

Collectors' Club: American Plastics History Association, 534 Stublyn Rd., Granville, OH 43023-9554.

Museum: National Plastics Center & Museum, Leominster, MA 01453.

Marks: Viscoloid Co. manufactured a large variety of small hollow animals that ranged in size from 2 to 8 inches. Most of these toys are embossed with one of three trademarks: ""Made in USA," an intertwined "VCO," or an eagle with a shield.

Advisor: Julie P. Robinson.

Advertising & Souvenir Keepsake Items

Badge, 2" d
  Cream colored rect celluloid sheet with "Official" in black block letters, set in a gold tone filigree framework with pinback 12.00
  Printed with "P H" and two intertwined American flags, fraternal organization for Patrons of Husbandry - The Grange, Whitehead & Hoag Co., early 1900s, shaped metal pin back frame....... 20.00
Booklet, 4-3/4" x 3", memo, celluloid cover printed with lovely lady by Whitehead & Hoag, ad for Alphonse Judas Co. Season's Greetings 1906 .... 45.00
Bookmark
  3 1/4" l, 1/4" w, folded top for slipping over a page, violets dec, "Greetings" on the long flat surface 20.00
  4-1/2" l, diecut, emb rose motif, pierced and embroidered name "Amitie" in pink silk thread, silk tassel 20.00
  4 3/4" l, diecut ivory grained celluloid, poinsettia motif with "Footpath to Peace" by Henry Van Dyke.................................... 25.00

Card
  3-1/16" x 2", engraved "Baldwin & Gleason With Best Wishes," ivory grained sheet cream colored celluloid, deep blue floral motif.... 30.00
  4" x 3" folding paper card, emb celluloid front showing gold cornucopia with flowers and "Remembrance," unused.................. 12.00
Clothing Brush, 3-1/2" d, celluloid laminated printed paper showing Parisian Novelty Company of Chicago, USA - "Supplies for making Fiberloid Novelties and Advertising Specialties," rare 175.00
Comb, case, 4-1/2" x 7/8" ivory grained comb, case with blue and black graphics "New England Made Cigars" 35.00
Compact, 1-3/4" d, imitation ivory grained celluloid with gold Elk motif and "Third Annual Ball, BPOE, Leominster Lodge no. 1237, Jan. 26, 1917," produced by the Viscoloid Co. Of Leominster, MA.......... 55.00
Fan, 4" tall when closed, mottled turquoise and cream celluloid Brise fan, light blue ribbon, shows the Washington Monument and words "Washington D.C." in gold tone paint 15.00
Game Counter, 2-3/4" x 1" ivory grained celluloid, disks turn to keep baseball score, "Peter Doelger Bottled Beer - Expressly for the Home" 55.00
Ink Blotter
  2-1/2" x 6" rect booklet of blotters with holiday lantern motif, "May this be your Merriest Christmas and 1929 your Happiest Year," The Charis Corp of Allentown, PA 45.00
  4-1/8" x 2-7/8" ivory grained celluloid, front and back covers w/ blotters inside, engraved scene of Black Diamond File Works, Philadelphia, PA, 1890 calendar, Baldwin & Gleason Co. 45.00
Letter Opener
  6 3/4" l, multi purpose bookmark/opener connected by string; round medallion features Indian profile, "Souvenir of Quebec"....... 15.00
  8" l, ivory grained, tapered point, Smith and Nichols Wax Co. Of Boston.. 35.00
Match Safe, 2-1/2" x 1-1/2"
  Ivory grained safety match holder, red outline, blue lettering, "Joseph's Economy Store, 406 Penn St. Reading,PA" 18.00
  Sepia celluloid photo dec of historical scenes from Gettysburg, PA 20.00
Pencil Clip
  5/8" d, celluloid disc, red, white, and yellow graphics, image of pretty maiden in center diamond, "Diamond Crystal Shaker Salt"....... 20.00
  3/4" d, celluloid disc, red, white, and blue graphics and star, "Star Brand Shoes Are Better".. 15.00
Pin Back Button
  3/4" d, red celluloid. white lettering "I'm the Guy that put the oysters in Oyster Bay" 18.00
  1-1/4" d, bird series, cardinal, blue jay, robin, goldfinch, Whitehead & Hoag Co., Newark, NJ, each.. 7.50
  1-1/2" d, "Erin Go Braugh," crossed American and Irish flags, center shamrock and lyre motif 25.00
  1-1/2" x 1/2", oval, turquoise blue with black trim, "Johnstown," c1920 .... 10.00
Pin Holder, 1-3/4" d, celluloid disc, metal framework, "F Krupps Steel Works, Thomas Prosser & Son, NY," front shows advertising, back shows small child, engraved ivory grained celluloid.................. 40.00
Pocket Mirror
  1-3/4" d, topsy-turvy image of a smiling man, "This man trades at Hager's Store, Frostburg, MD," turned upside down the man is frowning and caption reads "This man does not. For a satisfied customer see other side" 110.00
  2-1/4" d, beautiful woman with long red hair, wearing teal blue dress and cloche, holding a bouquet of roses 45.00
  2-3/4" x 1-3/4," oval, pink rose motif, "Use Mennen's Flesh Tint Talcum Powder," info on curl Duplicate mirror 5 cents postage, Gerhard Mennen Co., Newark... 550.00
Postcard, 5-1/2" x 3-1/2", emb fan motif with applied fabric and metal script words "Many Happy Returns" applied over fabric, circa 1908.......... 10.00
Tape Measure
  1-1/4" d, pull out tape; colorful pretty girl with flowers, adv for "The First National Bank of Boswell, The Same Old Bank in its New Home," printed by P.N. Co. (Parisian Novelty Co. Of Chicago), Patent 7-10-17, emb in the side... 65.00

1-1/2" d, printed image of Indian in full head dress, scenic mountain and water background, "Johnstown, PA" 25.00

3" d, center winding key, cream colored celluloid, blue printing, "The GM Parks Co. Fitchburg, Mass, The Measure of Good Piping is Results," printed by Whitehead & Hoag 45.00

Template, 3-7/16" x 1-13/16", Remtico Typewriter Supplies, Remington Typewriter Co., printed by Whitehead & Hoag 25.00

Animals

Viscoloid Co. of Leominster, MA manufactured a variety of small hollow toy animals, birds and marine creatures. Most of which are emb with one of these three trade marks; "Made In USA," an intertwined "VCO" or an eagle with shield. A host of foreign countries also mass produced celluloid toys for export into the United States. Among the most prolific manufacturers were Ando Togoro of Japan whose toys bear the crossed circle trademark and Sekiguchi Co., which used a three petal flower motif as their logo. Paul Haneaus of Germany used an intertwined PH trademark and Petticolin of France branded their toys with an eagle head. Japanese and American made toys are plentiful, while those manufactured in Germany, England and France are more difficult to find.

Alligator

3", green, white tail tip, VCO/USA 18.00

5-3/4", tan, brown highlights, VCO/USA trademark 25.00

Animal Set, 6 circus animals, garish bright colors, mkd "Made In Occupied Japan," elephant, gorilla, giraffe, tiger, lion and hippo, set . 85.00

Bear

4" l, peach bear, purple highlights, poor details, Japan 15.00

5" w, cream bear, pink and gray highlights, VCO/USA 20.00

Bison, 3-1/4" l, dark brown, eagle and shield trademark 18.00

Boar, 3-1/4" l, brown, Paul Haneaus of Germany/ PH trademark . 75.00

Camel

2-1/4" l, cream, light brown highlights, Made in USA trademark ... 15.00

3-1/2" x 2-1/2", peach celluloid, pink and black highlights, mkd with crossed circle and Made in Japan 15.00

Cat

3" l, 2-1/4" h, cream or peach celluloid, black spots, pink bows, ears and mouth; floral trademark, JAPAN, and Made in Occupied Japan 25.00

5-1/4", cream, pink and black highlights, molded collar and bell, Made in USA trademark 60.00

Chick, 7/8", yellow, black eyes and beak, no trademark 8.00

Chicken (hen)

2-3/4" h, metal feet; Double Diamond, Made In Japan 18.00

3" h, standing in grass, cream, gray, yellow feet, VCO/USA trademark 22.00

Cow

4-1/2", cream and orange cow; intertwined VCO/USA 18.00

5-1/2", purple and cream, red rhinestone eyes; crossed circle, Made In Japan 25.00

7-1/2", cream, orange and black highlights, hand painted facial features; eagle mark 45.00

Dog

Airedale, 3" w, 2-1/2" h, white with pink and dark purple highlights, hand painted collar, plaster filled, nice detailing; Made In Japan trademark 18.00

Bulldog, 4-3/4" l, 2-1/2" h, spiked neck collar, translucent green color, rhinestone eyes, intertwined VCO/USA 30.00

Hound, 5", long tail, peach celluloid, gray highlights, crossed circle Japan 18.00

Scottie, 3-1/4" l, plaster filled cream colored celluloid, no detailing, mkd JAPAN 15.00

St. Bernard, 3-1/4" , tan, black highlights, intertwined VCO/USA . 18.00

Donkey

2-1/4", dark gray, Made in USA 18.00

4" l, 3-3/4" h, molded harnesses, saddles and blankets; grayish brown, red and orange highlights, intertwined VCO/USA 35.00

Duck

2-1/4", standing, cream colored celluloid, hand painted eyes and bills; original paper label, Made In Japan 18.00

3-1/2", yellow, green highlights, VCO/USA, circle 12.00

4", glossy surface, red and green, VCO/USA 15.00

4", yellow, applied green and orange, PH (Paul Hunaeus), "25 cents" on bottom 25.00

Elephant

2-3/8" x 1-1/2", white, gray highlights, VCO/USA 8.00

3", white and gray, purple ears, Made in Occupied Japan 20.00

3-1/2" x 2", peach, gray highlights, poor detailing, no trademark 5.00

6-3/4" x 4-3/4", gray elephant, tusks; Made In USA 35.00

Fish

2-1/2", medium reddish pink, molded scales and fins, nicely detailed, Japan 12.00

2-7/8", yellow, brown highlights, molded scales, intertwined VCO, circle 10.00

4-1/2", yellow and red, molded scales, Made in USA 12.00

6", red, rattle, sharp fin, molded scales, gold eyes, intertwined YM trademark and Japan 22.00

6-3/4", white and red, smooth shiny surface, molded fin, VCO/USA 15.00

Frog

1-1/4", green or yellow, stripe on back, intertwined VCO/USA 12.00

2-3/8", painted green, molded from white or yellow celluloid, spotted back; Made in USA inside circle or VCO in Circle over USA 15.00

2-3/4", white, painted green and black striped back, Made in Japan 15.00

Giraffe, 10" h, cream, beaded neck alternating brown and cream, brown and yellow painted highlights, detailed face, crossed circle mark of Ando Togoro, Made In Japan 110.00

Goat

2-1/8", white, hand painted facial features, poor detail, no trademark 15.00

3", white, curled horns, flower, "N" in circle, Japan 18.00

3-1/2", white, gray, beard & horns, VCO/USA 22.00

Hippopotamus, 3-3/4", pink, closed mouth, crossed circle, Japan 15.00

Horse

2-1/4" x 2", cream, brown highlights, Made in USA 10.00

4", yellow, rattle, orange highlights, painted reins and saddle, Made in USA 22.00

5-1/4", pink, black highlights, crossed circle, Japan 20.00

7", cream, purple and pink highlights, Made in USA 22.00

9-1/4" x 7-3/4", cream, grayish brown highlights, Made In USA ... 45.00

Leopard, 4-1/2", white, orange highlights, black spots, Made in Occupied Japan 25.00

Lion

3", orange, black highlights, Made in USA 15.00

3-3/4", tan, brown highlights, TS Made in Japan 20.00

4", rattle, tan, brown, black, VCO/USA trademark on belly 20.00

Lobster

1-3/4", bright red, detailed shell, no trademark 55.00

3-1/4", shiny red lobster, smooth surface, intertwined VCO/USA . 85.00

Parakeet, 6-3/8" l, cream colored, yellow and black highlights, mkd "Germany" 40.00

Parrot, 4", white, bright pink, green and yellow highlights, fine detailing; CT - Made In JAPAN 20.00

Pig

1-1/8", cream, pink highlights, VCO 30.00

4-1/2", pink, painted eyes, Made in USA 35.00

Polar Bear, 2-1/4" l, white, USA 10.00

Ram

2-1/2", cream, poor detailing, Japan 10.00

4-1/2", cream, gray highlights, Made in USA 18.00

Autograph Album, emb reverse painted lettering and floral motif, maroon velour back, 4" x 6", $75. Photo courtesy of Julie P. Robinson.

Rhino
    4", white, gray, smiling, double horn, Made in Occupied
        Japan 22.00
    5", gray, fine detail, PH trademark, Paul Haneaus 55.00
Seal, 4-1/2", gray, balancing red ball, VCO/USA 70.00
Sparrow
    3-1/4", balancing, yellow teal, tail weighted, oval Made in USA trademark near talon 18.00
    4-1/2", yellow, red highlights, Made in Japan 20.00
Squirrel, 2-7/8", brown celluloid, holding a nut, Made in USA.......40.00
Stork, 6-3/4", standing, white, pink legs, flower mark and Japan..22.00
Swan, 3-3/8", multicolored purple, pink yellow, crossed circle......15.00
Turtle
    1-3/8", two tone, brown top, yellow bottom, USA on foot 15.00
    3", cream, brown highlights, VCO/USA with circle 18.00
    4", cream, brownish gray highlights, CC in diamond and Made in Japan 20.00
Whale, 4-1/2", curled tail, smooth molded tails, cream, green, red, and yellow highlights 45.00

Decorative Albums & Boxes
Autograph Album
    4" x 5-1/2", printed pastoral scene of a couple giving thanks in a garden, celluloid front, paper covered back 75.00
    6" x 4", silver and violet clear celluloid coated paper, central emb oval with beautiful lady in wide brimmed hat, white dress and fur, maroon velvet back and binding 85.00
Collar Box, 6" h, 6" d, covered in gold paper with pink, green, and yellow flowers, clear celluloid overlay, central image of a pretty woman wearing ruffled dress with corsage..........................175.00
Dresser Set Box, 8" x 6-1/4" x 3-1/2" d, emb white celluloid, cornflower motif in two strips across top, blue satin lined, fitted with brush, mirror, salve box, file and nail cleaner, all original, pieces individually marked "Celluloid" 250.00
Hankie Box, 7" sq, 3" h, center vignette of pretty girl in hat and gown picking pink flowers, emb Greek key design on sides, overall pale yellow, green, and blue grapevine with leaf design..................165.00
Manicure Box, 5" x 7" x 2" h, cream colored emb celluloid, snowy house scene, puffed satin lining, manicure implements...........125.00
Necktie Box, 12-1/2" x 4", emb script "Neckties," cream-colored celluloid, emb circular design on sides 145.00
Photograph Album
    8" x 11", celluloid covered photo album, Gibson girl, lavender dress, hat with lavender plumes, emb corners, applied gilt paint ..195.00
    18" l, 6" w, standing lady in flowing red draped dress 275.00

Dolls and Toys
Baby Rattle
    2-1/4", peach horse on cream colored 4-1/2" d ring, two pink and white balls attached to ring, "Japan" on horse 45.00
    4-1/2", bright red celluloid, clown playing lute, intertwined "VCO/ USA" trademark on back, unusual color 55.00
    4-3/4", cream, bell shaped, bell, blue triangular painted dec, no trademark..35.00
    6-1/4", yellow pear, orange-red highlights, brown twig handle, finely detailed and realistic, no trademark..................................75.00
    6-1/2" l, ivory grained dumbbell, bell inside 45.00
Doll
    3-1/4" black baby, strung arms and legs, unidentified lantern trademark, Made in Japan 50.00
    3-3/4", toddler, pink snowsuit, yellow and red trim, F in diamond, Made In JAPAN 22.00
    5-3/4" Dutch girl, green, pink, yellow, and black details, butterfly trademark- Made In JAPAN, mfg. by Yoshino Sangyo Co....35.00
    6" girl and boy dressed in ethnic costumes, turtle in diamond trademark, Rheinische Gummiund Celluloid Fabrik Co. of Germany, pr...125.00
    7" all celluloid ,molded, moving arms, molded bracelet on right wrist, mermaid in shield trademark on back, DRP Germany, mfg. by Cellba, Celluloidwarenfabrik Co. 95.00
    8-1/2" side glancing googlie eyed, blue and white printed dress and kerchief trimmed in ric-rac, trademarked with unidentified lantern trademark, "Made in Japan"..55.00
    16-1/2" realistic baby, movable arms and legs, bright blue eyes, red hair, smiling face, made in USA by Viscoloid....................175.00
    18" realistic baby doll, stuffed textile body, beautifully molded celluloid head, blond, blue eyes, mfg. by Minerva, Buschow & Beck, helmet trademark, No.7-42, German 250.00
Roly Poly
    2-1/2", Buster Brown winking, cream, brown and black highlights, PH, Paul Hunaeus, Germany 225.00
    2-1/2", duckling, peach hat trimmed in flowers, jacket, necktie, green trim, cream celluloid, VCO trademark..................75.00
    3-1/2", gray man, spectacles; black and white highlights on pink base, emb "Palitoy, Made in England" 85.00
    4-1/2", baby face, green and white base, orange bow tie; sticker on bottom, lacking detail, Made In China................................40.00
    4-1/2", realistic child-like clown standing on hands, balancing on ball, cream, teal blue and pink highlights, Viscoloid intertwined VCO/USA trademark 75.00
Toy
    4", Bathing Beauty, double figural showing two little girls, pink and green bathing suit, umbrella, floral trademark, Made In Japan, mfg. by Sekiguchi Co...75.00
    5", steamer, gray and red, flag, intertwined PH 55.00
Whistle
    3-1/4" l, 2-1/4" h, Nightingale bird, yellow celluloid, green and red highlights; VCO/USA 22.00
    4-1/2" l, 1-1/2" w, 3-1/4" w at ends, black and cream graduated pipe, "Baby Grand" 28.00
    9-1/2" x 3/4" recorder, transparent teal celluloid, molded mouthpiece and 6 holes for playing notes, no trademark..25.00

Fashion Accessories
Bar Pin
    2-1/2" l, ivory grained rect shape, orange brown swirled pearlescent laminate, center hp florals.....................................18.00
    2-3/4" l, elongated oval, black imitation jet, molded cameo motif, C-clasp, on orig card that states "Persian Ivory collar or jabot pin" 85.00
Belt, 22" l, 3/4" x 1-1/2" rect mottled green celluloid slabs linked by chain, applied silver tone filigree dec 35.00
Bracelet, bangle
    Ivory colored, embedded with center row of red rhinestones and flanked by outside rows of clear rhinestones.....................75.00

Brooch, black cameo profile of woman, Victorian imitation of jet, c1880, 1-1/4" x 1-1/2", $55. Photo courtesy of Julie P. Robinson.

Molded imitation coral, imitation ivory, or imitation jade, allover floral dec, blue ink stamp "Made in Japan," 3" d, each 40.00

Translucent amber, single row of alternating red and amber rhinestones, further decorated with scored white painted scallop edging around stones 95.00

Translucent green, 1/2" wide, studded with 3 rows of aqua blue rhinestones 85.00

Bracelet, link, 3" d, 4 oblong two-tone cream and ivory links, attached by smaller round cream links 50.00

Brooch

1-1/4" d thin gold tint metal frame, blue and white enamel floral embellishment, clear celluloid, designed to hold photo, safety clasp 25.00

1-3/4" x 3/4", rect pearlized cream celluloid, black stencil silhouette of man and woman conversing over picket fence 30.00

1-3/4" x 2-1/8" oval, celluloid laminated paper with red roses on yellow and green ground, applied over dome shaped metal disk, C-clasp 35.00

Comb and Case

2-1/4" l, folding molded case, emb rose motif, imitation ivory 25.00

3" l cream colored celluloid comb, 3-1/4" x 1" pearlized amber and gray rhinestone studded case 15.00

Cuff Links, pr

Separable "Kum-a-part" Baer & Wilde Co., 1/4" sq shape divided by purple and black triangular shapes of celluloid, center diamond shape, Art Deco, mid 1920s. orig card 55.00

Toggle back, realistic molded celluloid lion heads, c1896 .... 95.00

Cuff links, pr, matching stickpin, lever back links of silver tone metal, octagonal framework with circular imitation ivory set with rhinestone 75.00

Dress Clips, pr, molded floral motif, semi-translucent cream celluloid, mkd "Japan" 35.00

Eyeglasses, Harold Lloyd type, black frames 15.00

Fan

Brise style, diecut and emb imitation ivory, silk ribbon, mirrored heart on end stick, pink floral motif, tassel 45.00

Cockade style, cream celluloid handles, bottom link clasp, pleated linen body, opens to full circle 55.00

Hair Comb, 4" x 5-1/4", imitation tortoiseshell, 24 teeth; applied metal trim studded with rhinestones and brad fastened Egyptian Revival pink and gold metal floral and beetle dec 145.00

Hair Pin Container; 2-1/2" holder, ivory, bird motif; dark gray lid 35.00

Hat Pin

4" l elephant head, tusks, black glass eyes, imitation ivory 95.00

10" l, diecut 1" filigree hollow egg, pale green paint applied over grained celluloid 45.00

12" l, conical, imitation tortoiseshell 20.00

Hat Ornament

3-1/2" h, Art Deco, pearlized red and cream half circles, rhinestone trim 45.00

4" l, amber feather, red rhinestones 18.00

4-1/2" h, calla lily, cream pearlized celluloid. white rhinestones, 1-1/2" l threaded pin with screw on celluloid point 25.00

Necklace, 2" elegant Art Nouveau filigree pendant, cream celluloid, oval cameo, profile of a beautiful woman, suspended from 20" cream celluloid beaded necklace 110.00

Purse Frame

4" l, black pointed horseshoe shape, rhinestones, white molded cameo clasp 95.00

6" l, imitation tortoiseshell, crescent shape, molded filigree and center cameo, celluloid push button latch and linked chain 110.00

Purse

4" d clasp, red rose, dangling leaves, green velvet bag, velvet handle, mkd "#35" on fame 1,250.00

4" d, round clam shell; imitation tortoiseshell and ivory; leather strap, celluloid findings and finger ring; applied celluloid leaf decoration 125.00

4-1/2" x 4-1/2", basketweave, link celluloid chain; mottled grain ivory and green 185.00

Holiday Items

Angels, 1-1/2" h, set of 3, one holding cross, star or lantern, Japan, Mt. Fuji trademark 25.00

Christmas Decoration, roly poly type house, opening in back for a small bulb, shows Santa approaching door, red and white, intertwined VCO/USA trademark 125.00

Christmas Ornament

3-3/4" little boy on swing, all celluloid, dark green highlights, holding onto string "ropes" for hanging on tree 145.00

3-3/4", Santa, horn and sack, hole in back for light bulb, trademarked "S" in circle, Japan 100.00

4" l, stripped green and white Christmas stocking filled with gifts including duck and kitten, crossed circle trademark, Ando Togoro ... 145.00

6-1/2", horn, red, pink and yellow 80.00

7-1/2", Santa holding gift box in arm, cream, red painted detailing, marked with oval Made in USA 125.00

Figure

3" x 3-1/2", bunny, dressed in top hat and tails, in teal shoe, crossed circle mark, Japan 85.00

3-3/4", Swan Boat, Easter rabbit and chick in eggshell, intertwined VCO/USA 145.00

4" h, Vegetable Person, orange carrot legs, sad face on one side, happy on other, applied black bat and owl shaped dec, VCO . 250.00

5-1/4", Uncle Sam, white celluloid, painted red, white, and blue patriotic clothing 175.00

7-3/4" h, Easter Rabbit, dressed in tails and top hat, holding chicken under arm, cream, pink and blue highlights, VCO 125.00

Halloween Favor, 4" l, orange horn, black witch and trim, intertwined VCO/USA 110.00

Rattle, 3-3/4" l, standing black cat, orange bow, intertwined VCO/USA 175.00

Reindeer, 3-1/2", white deer, gold glitter, red eyes and mouth, molded ears and antlers; USA 18.00

Roly Poly

3-1/2", black cat on orange pumpkin, intertwined VCO/USA 200.00

4", yellow owl, orange and black highlights, intertwined VCO/USA 185.00

Santa

4", yellow or mint green translucent celluloid, holding lantern and sack, Japanese, Mt. in circle trademark 40.00

5" h, basket of flowers, fur trimmed suit, nice detail, VCO/USA trademark 75.00

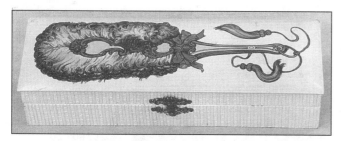

Fan Box, emb cream colored celluloid sides, reverse painted clear celluloid top, blue satin lining, 12" x 4" x 2", $225. Photo courtesy of Julie P. Robinson.

Toy

2-7/8" l, Easter rabbit in harness, attached to cart full of eggs, "Made in Japan" on cart, "Pat.15735" on rabbit 85.00

3-3/8" x 2", Santa driving house shaped automobile, white, applied red, yellow & green painted highlights, VCO/USA trademark 125.00

3-1/2", black Halloween cat pushing a witch in a pumpkin carriage, intertwined VCO/USA 245.00

4" x 2-1/8", reindeer pulling sleigh, Santa, sack and packages, red and white, VCO/USA trademark 125.00

4-3/4" h, Paddy, riding pig, movable legs, little boy with dunce cap riding on back, Japan 185.00

5-3/8" x 2", Santa riding on a train laden with holiday decorations and gifts including doll, puppy and rocking horse, cream, red and green highlights, VCO/USA on Santa 165.00

Novelty Items

Letter Opener

7" l, celluloid paper knife, bronze Art Nouveau cupid handle .. 95.00

7 3/8" l, ivory grained, magnifying glass in top, coiled metal snake, red glass eyes around the handle 85.00

8" l, solid celluloid, blade top by intricately detailed full figure lady holding a flask 80.00

9 5/8" l, solid celluloid, handle molded with lighthouse and filigree 95.00

Pin Cushion

2" h, rabbit with pin cushion baskets, mkd "Germany" 130.00

2-1/4" h, straight pin holder, brown hen on base 65.00

Tape Measure

1" h, strawberry with pull tap tape measure 200.00

1-1/4" d, basket of fruit, mkd "Made in Germany" 145.00

1-3/4" h, chariot, horse, and driver, imitation bronze 225.00

2" h, handled basket, flowers, mkd "Made in Japan" 125.00

2" h, Swashbuckler, ivory, ivory and tan highlights 250.00

2-1/2" h, Billiken, cream celluloid, applied brown highlights, mkd "Japan" 185.00

Utilitarian & Household Items

Bookends, pr, 4-1/4" h, 3-1/4" w, 2-1/4" d, mottled pink celluloid, emb ornamental gold neoclassic drape, plaster weighted, no trademark, c1930 .... 35.00

Candle Holders, pr, 5-1/4" h, cylindrical, round flared weighted bases, unmarked 60.00

Clock

3" sq, New Haven Clock Co., alarm, folding travel case, pearlescent pink laminated over amber celluloid 30.00

5-1/2" x 3", classical Gothic cathedral design, round face, dark yellow ivory grained celluloid, Germany 45.00

9" x 6-1/2", mantle clock, neoclassical design, front molded pearlized gray columns, imitation ivory weighted base and top, mkd "Made in USA," patented clockworks, Apr. 27, 1920 .... 65.00

Crumb Tray Set, two dust pan shaped trays

Ivory celluloid, one large and one small, unadorned, Fuller trademark 22.00

Ivory celluloid, dark blue dec border, monogrammed "T" in center of each tray 55.00

Game Keeper, grained celluloid, hand painted pansy dec, rotating disks, $30. Photo courtesy of Julie P. Robinson.

Cutlery, solid imitation ivory grained handle utensils, 8 forks, 8 knives in orig box, Standard Mfg. Co. 30.00

Frame

4" d, round, ivory grained, easel back 18.00

5-1/2" x 7", pearlized amber celluloid, diecut floral motif, attached over wood frame, celluloid butterflies in each corner 35.00

6" x 8", plain oval frame, imitation ivory grained celluloid, glass, easel back 30.00

Napkin Ring

1" w, basketweave strips of celluloid 12.00

1" w, ivory grained, monogram name "Agnes" 6.00

1-1/2" w, plain pale green celluloid 4.00

Pen Holder, 3" sq, black base, laminated pearlized top, conical holder attached in center 20.00

Stamp Box, 2-1/2" x 1-1/2", ivory grained box, hinged lid, two int. stamp sized compartments separated by a center divider 20.00

String Holder, round sphere on a weighted base, twist apart, center hole in top for string, imitation ivory grain, no trademark 65.00

Vase

6" h, imitation ivory, conical, fluted weighted base, flange around top 15.00

7" h, yellow, bulbous bottom, narrow opening, fluted top, painted pink and blue floral motif, no trademark 25.00

8" h, imitation tortoiseshell, weighted scalloped base 45.00

Watch Holder, 6-1/2" l, pearlescent blue green and amber, wall hanging banjo clock style, Wilcox trademark, late 1920s 22.00

Vanity Items

Dresser Boxes, pr, oval shaped pearlized peach boxes, dec shaped lids, mkd "Amerith," Lotus Pattern, c1929 .... 25.00

Dresser Set

3 piece, mirror, brush and comb, green pearlized celluloid, emb gold flower motif in center of each item, plaster filled mirror, orig cardboard box, poor quality unmarked set 15.00

8 piece, pearlized yellow laminated amber celluloid, black trim, mirror, brush, shoe horn, button hook, soap box, nail buffer, toothbrush holder, hair pin holder, mkd "Arch Amereth, Windsor," c1928, orig box 65.00

17 piece, Fairfax pattern, Fiberloid Company, mottled brown and gold, carved floral trim, comb, brush, mirror, powder box, hair receiver, nail file, scissors, button hook, and clothing brush, c1924 .... 125.00

Dresser Tray, 7-1/2" l, 5" w, oval, pearlized cream colored and amber

Toy, girl with Halloween jack-o-lantern in hand, green dress, red apron and hair bow, mkd "Made in Japan," 3-3/4" h, $65. Photo courtesy of Julie P. Robinson.

Cat, sleeping tabby, blue collar with red dots, 6" l, $125.

framework, Normandy lace inserted between double glass bottom, c1925 .... 30.00
Hair Receiver/Powder Box Set
    3-1/2" d, pearlized gray containers, octagonal lids, no
      trademark... 25.00
    4" d, ivory grained set, scalloped lids laminated in Goldaleur, mkd
      "The Celluloid Co.".. 45.00
Hat Pin Holder, weighted base
    5" h center post, round circular disc on top, circular base, cream
      celluloid, cranberry colored velvet cushion 90.00
    5" h, pale green celluloid, triangular shape, painted flower 20.00
Manicure Set, rolled up leather pouch fitted with 6 imitation tortoiseshell
    celluloid manicure tools, gold trim, pink velvet lining 30.00
Powder Box, 4" d, flared round box, fitted lid, imitation ivory grained
    celluloid, hand applied floral swag and ribbon dec in pink, white, and
    blue, includes down puff with blue satin and celluloid handle 65.00
Straight Razor
    Imitation wood grained celluloid, Germany.............................. 28.00
    Plain black or imitation ivory handle, Durham Duplex 6.00
Trinket Box, 5" l, 2" h, oval, amber, butterfly, grass and milkweed silk
    under clear celluloid lid, 1925.. 35.00
Vanity Set, amber, teal-green pearlescent laminate surface, dresser tray,
    octagonal amber hair receiver box with pearlized lid, nail buffer, scissors,
    and button hook, hp rose motif on all pcs, unmarked, c1930 .... 45.00

CHALKWARE

History: William Hutchinson, an Englishman, invented chalkware in 1848. It was a substance used by sculptors to imitate marble and also was used to harden plaster of paris, creating confusion between the two products.

Chalkware pieces, which often copied many of the popular Staffordshire items made between 1820 and 1870, was cheap, gaily decorated, and sold by vendors. The Pennsylvania German folk art pieces are from this period.

Carnivals, circuses, fairs, and amusement parks gave away chalkware prizes during the late 19th and the 20th centuries. These pieces often were poorly made and gaudy.

Additional Listings: See Carnival Chalkware in Warman's Americana & Collectibles.

Notes: Don't confuse the chalkware carnival giveaways with the earlier pieces.

Bank, 11" h, dove, worn orig polychrome paint........................... 350.00
Bust, Sheherazade, painted to resemble bronze....................... 250.00
Figure
    5" h, squirrel, worn red and green, base flakes 250.00
    5-1/4" h, cat, red and black details, PA, 19th C 200.00
    5-1/2" h, deer, red, black, and yellow, old worn paint, pr 935.00
    5-1/2" h, dog, molded detail, painted brown, black spots, red collar,
      PA, 19th C, pr 375.00
    6-3/8" h, reclining eye and lamb, grassy base, yellow border, PA,
      19th C, one ear repaired... 325.00
    9-7/8" h, seated cat, red, black, and yellow, old worn paint 1,430.00
    12" l, sleeping cat, old polychrome paint, wear, some edge rough-
      age... 425.00
    15" h hen, 20" h rooster, full bodied, comb, wattle, and feather
      detail, inset glass eyes, quatrefoil base, scrolled acanthus sup-
      port, repairs, pr 1,495.00
Mantel Ornament
    12-1/2" h, fruit and foliage design, American, 19th C, restoration,
      paint wear, pr 460.00
    16" l, 15-1/2" h, reclining stag, polychrome dec, minor paint
      loss 300.00
Match Holder, 6" h, figural, man with long nose and beard, Northwest-
    ern National Insurance Co. adv, c1890 .... 110.00
Nodder, 8-1/2" l, cat, white, black spots, late 19th C 1,495.00
Plaque, 9" h, horse head, orig polychrome paint 100.00
Wall Pocket, basket shape.. 35.00

CHARACTER and PERSONALITY ITEMS

History: In many cases, toys and other products using the images of fictional comic, movie, and radio characters occur simultaneously with the origin of the character. The first Dick Tracy toy was manufactured within less than a year after the strip first appeared.

The golden age of character material is the TV era of the mid-1950s through the late 1960s. Some radio premium collectors might argue this point. Today, television and movie producers often have their product licensing arranged well in advance of the initial release.

Do not overlook the characters created by advertising agencies, e.g., Tony the Tiger. They represent a major collecting subcategory.

References: Bill Blackbeard (ed.), *R. F. Outcault's The Yellow Kid,* Kitchen Sink Press, 1995; Bill Bruegman, *Cartoon Friends of the Baby Boom Era,* Cap'n Penny Productions, 1993; ——, *Superhero Collectibles,* Toy Scouts, 1996; *Cartoon & Character Toys of the 50s, 60s, & 70s,* L-W Book Sales, 1995; James D. Davis, *Collectible Novelty Phones,* Schiffer, 1998; Warren Dotz, *Advertising Character Collectibles,* Collector Books, 1993; ——, *What a Character!* 20th *Century American Advertising Icons,* Chronicle Books, 1996; Michael Friedman, *Cowboy Culture: The Last Frontier of American Antiques,* 2nd ed., Schiffer Publishing, 1999; Ted Hake, *Hake's Guide to Cowboy Character Collectibles,* Wallace-Homestead, 1994; ——, *Hake's Price Guide to Character Toys,* Gemstone Publishing, 1998; Jim Harmon, *Radio & TV Premiums,* Krause Publications, 1997; Clark Kidder, *Marilyn Monroe: Cover to Cover,* Krause Publications, 1999; Jack Koch, *Howdy Doody,* Collector Books, 1996; Mary Jane Lamphier, *Zany Characters of the Ad World,* Collector Books, 1995; Cynthia Boris Liljeblad, *TV Toys and the Shows That Inspired Them,* Krause Publications, 1996; Jan Lindenberger with Cher Porges, *Peanuts Gang Collectibles; An Unauthorized Handbook and Price Guide,* Schiffer, 1998; David Longest, *Character Toys and Collectibles* (1984, 1992 value update), 2nd Series (1987, 1990 value update), Collector Books; Rex Miller, *The Investor's Guide To Vintage Collectibles,* Krause Publications, 1999; Andrea Podley with Derrick Bang, *Peanuts Collectibles, Identification and Value Guide,* Collector Books, 1999; Jon R. Warren, *Collecting Hollywood: The Movie Poster Price Guide,* 3rd ed., American Collectors Exchange, 1994; David and Micki Young, *Campbell's Soup Collectibles from A to Z,* Krause Publications, 1998.

Periodicals: *Autograph Times,* 2303 N. 44th St., #225, Phoenix, AZ 85008; *Baby Boomer,* P.O. Box 1050, Dubuque, IA 52004; *Big Reel,* P.O. Box 1050, Dubuque, IA 52004; *Button Pusher,* P.O. Box 4, Coopersburg, PA 18036; *Celebrity Collector,* P.O. Box 1115, Boston, MA 02117; *Classic Images,* P.O. Box 809, Muscatine, IA 52761; *Collecting Hollywood,* American Collectors Exchange, 2401 Broad St., Chattanooga, TN 37408; *Cowboy Collector Newsletter,* P.O. Box 7486, Long Beach, CA 90807; *Frostbite Falls Far-Flung Flier,* P.O. Box 39, Macedonia, OH 44056; *Hollywood & Vine,* Box 717, Madison, NC 27025; *Hollywood Collectibles,* 4099 McEwen Dr., Suite 350, Dallas, TX 75224; *Movie Advertising Collector,* P.O. Box 28587, Philadelphia, PA 19149; *Movie Collector's World,* 17230 13 Mile Rd., Roseville, MI 48066; Television History Magazine, 700 E. Macoupin St., Staunton, IL 62088; *TV Collector Magazine,* P.O. Box 1088, Easton, MA 02334.

Collectors' Clubs: All About Marilyn, P.O. Box 291176, Hollywood, CA 90029; Beatles Fan Club, 397 Edgewood Ave., New Haven, CT 06511; Betty Boop Fan Club, P.O. Box 42, Moorhead, MN 56561; C.A.L./N-X-211 Collectors Society, 2820 Echo Way, Sacramento, CA 95821; Camel Joe & Friends, 2205 Hess Dr., Cresthill, IL 60435; Charlie Tuna Collectors Club, 7812 NW Hampton Rd, Kansas City, MO 64152; Dagwood-Blondie Fan Club, 541 El Paso, Jacksonville, TX 75766; Dick Tracy Fan Club, P.O. Box 632, Manitou Springs, CO 80829; Dionne Quint Collectors, P.O. Box 2527,

SPECIAL AUCTIONS

Hake's Americana & Collectibles
P.O. Box 1444, Dept. 344
York, PA 17405
(717) 848-1333

Toy Scouts
137 Casterton Ave.
Akron, OH 44303
(216) 836-0668

Woburn, MA 01888; Howdy Doody Memorabilia Collectors Club, 8 Hunt Ct., Flemington, NJ 08822; Official Popeye Fan Club, 1001 State St., Chester, IL 62233; R. F. Outcault Society, 103 Doubloon Dr., Slidell, LA 70461; Three Stooges Fan Club, P.O. Box 747, Gwynedd Valley, PA 19437.

Additional Listings: See *Warman's Americana & Collectibles* for expanded listings in Cartoon Characters, Cowboy Collectibles, Movie Personalities and Memorabilia, Shirley Temple, Space Adventurers, and TV Personalities and Memorabilia.

Character

Andy Gump, pinback button
   7/8" d, Andy Gump/The Gumps by Syndey Smith, black, white, and red, issued by Western Theatre Premium Co., 1930s 24.00
   1-1/4" d, "Andy Gump For President/I Endorse The Atwater Kent Receiving Set,"" red, white, blue, and fleshtone 40.00
Betty Boop
   Bank 20.00
   Decal Sheet, c1920, set of 12 .... 15.00
   Perfume Bottle, 3-1/2" h, figural, glass, c1930 .... 46.00
   Wall Pocket, Betty and Bimbo, luster glaze, ©Fleischer Studios 110.00

Buster Brown Roly Poly, celluloid, intertwined "PH," Paul Hunaeus, Germany, 2-1/2" h, $225. Photo courtesy of Julie P. Robinson.

Brownies, Palmer Cox
  Book, The Brownies, Their Book, Palmer Cox, NY, 1887, first edition, second issue, illus by Cox, 4to, pictorial glazed boards 230.00
  Doll, set of 8" dolls, stuffed cloth, Uncle Sam, Indian, Highlander, Chinaman, German, Sailor, Soldier, Canadian, Irishman, Policeman, John-Bull, and Dude, each has name stitched on back, colorful printed outfits, mkd "Copyright 1892 by Palmer Cox" on back of each, "Brownie's" on right foot of each, set of 12............760.00
  Pinback Button, 1-1/4" d, blue on white, 8 Brownies around board fence imprinted with calendar page for January, 1897, Whitehead & Hoag 20.00
  Plate, 7" d, octagonal, china, full color illus of 3 Brownies, dressed as Uncle Sam, Scotsman, and golfer, soft blue ground, gold trim, sgd "La Francaise Porcelain" 95.00

Buster Brown
  Bank, cast iron, Buster and Tige, c1910................................. 165.00
  Drawing Book, 8 pgs, thin film tracing sheets between each page, Emerson Piano Co., unused..70.00
  Mask, diecut, stiff paper, Froggy the Gremlin, 1946 ....45.00
  Paddle Board, 5" x 10", cardboard, rubber ball attached by string, 1946..65.00
  Pinback Button
    Buster Brown Bread, multicolored, yellow rim, red letters..20.00
    New York Herald Young Folks, Buster with dripping paint brush, c1905, 1-1/4" d 85.00
  Sign, 39" x 55", diecut, tin, Buster Brown in shoe being pulled by diecut Tige, ... 1,900.00
  Whistle, Buster Brown Shoes, litho tin, image of Buster, black inscriptions, ivory ground, bright gold underside, 1930s.......65.00

Campbell Kid
  Children's Dishes, "Campbell's Lunch Time," 4" x 14" x 17-1/2" unopened display carton, service for 6, child's hard plastic soup bowls and coaster plates, cups, saucers, spoons, and forks, prominent Campbell's marking, sealed in orig clear shrink wrap, six miniature placements on back, ©1984 ....45.00
  Menu Book, 5-1/2" x 7-1/2", softcover, ©1910, 48 pgs, menus for 30 days of the month, full color Campbell Kid art on cov......20.00
  Salt and Pepper Shakers, pr, 4-1/2" h, painted hard plastic, red and white outfits, yellow molded hair, ©Campbell Soup 40.00
  Sign, 11-1/2" x 17-1/2", tin, Kid holding spoon, red, white, and yellow...250.00

Charlie the Tuna
  Animation cel, 10-1/2" x 12" clear acetate sheet, centered smiling full figured 4" image of Charlie gesturing toward 4" image of goldfish holding scissors, 10-1/2" x 12-1/2" white paper sheet with matching blue/lead pencil 4" tall image of Charlie, c1960 ..150.00
  Figure, 7-1/2" h, soft vinyl, blue, dark pink opened mouth, black rimmed eyeglasses, orange cap inscribed "Charlie," ©1973 30.00
  Wristwatch, 1-1/2" d bright gold luster bezel, full color image of Charlie on silver background, ©1971 Star-Kist Foods, grained purple leather band 60.00

Dutch Boy, string holder, 14-1/2" x 30", diecut tin, Dutch Boy sitting on swing painting the sign for this product, White Lead Paint Bucket houses ball of string 300.00

Elsie The Cow, Borden
  Display, mechanical milk carton, cardboard and papier-mâché, figural milk carton rocks back and forth, eyes and mouth move from side to side, made for MN state fair circuit, 1940s 500.00
  Lamp, 4" x 4" x 10", Elsie and Baby, hollow ceramic figure base, Elsie reading to baby nestled on her lap, brass socket, c1950........125.00
  Mug, 3-1/4" h, white china, full color image of Elmer, gold accent line, orig sq box with image of child's alphabet block including panels "E for Elsie" and "B for Borden," Elmer pictured on one side panel, ©1950..95.00

Felix the Cat
  Figure, 1" h, dark copper colored plastic, loop at top, 1950s...10.00
  Pinback Button, 1" d, Herald and Examiner, c1930s...............45.00
  Place Card Holder, 1-3/4" h celluloid Felix, arched back black cat, base, glossy black holder, Japanese, 1930s 85.00

Howdy Doody mug, red plastic, orig decal, $55.

  Valentine, diecut, jointed cardboard, full color, "Purr Around If You Want To Be My Valentine" inscription, ©Pat Sullivan, c1920 ..20.00
  Vending Label, 3" x 3", red, white, blue, black, and fleshtone, Little King and Felix the Cat illus, for Popeye "Kid Kartoon Komics" button, ©King Features, mid 1940s 15.00
  Yarn Holder, 6-1/2", diecut wood, black images, inscription "Felix Keeps On Knitting," "Pathe Presents" symbol in center, c1930. 38.00

Happy Hooligan
  Figure, 8-1/4" h, bisque, worried expression, tin can hat, orange, black, blue, and yellow...75.00
  Pinback Button, 11-16" d, brown and cream, profile, inscribed "Son Of Rest," initials below "G.T.A.T.," c1910 ....30.00
  Stickpin, 2-1/4" l, brass..25.00

Howdy Doody
  Bank, 6-1/2" x 5", ceramic, riding pig 65.00
  Belt, suede, emb face 35.00
  Cake Decorating Set, unused..40.00
  Handkerchief, 8" x 8-1/4", cotton 20.00
  Pencil Case, vinyl, red 25.00

Jiggs and Maggie
  Paperweight glass 40.00
  Pinback Button
    3/4" d, The Knoxville Sentinel, black white image of Jiggs, red bow tie, c1920 ....15.00
    1" d, Herald And Examiner, black image, bright yellow ground, 1930s..30.00
  Salt and Pepper Shakers, pr, ceramic....................................48.00

Krazy Kat, pinback button
  7/8" d, full color, cigarette premium, c1912, Tokio back paper 20.00
  1-3/8" d, "Cash Prices See Comic Pages Daily," Los Angeles Evening Herald & Express, black on green litho, 1930s.......30.00

Little Annie Rooney, pinback button, 1-1/4" d, comic strip contest button, serial number type, c1930...25.00

Little Orphan Annie
  Clicker, red, white, and black, Mysto members, 1941 ....40.00
  Doll, ABC Toys, c1940...50.00
  Mug, Ovaltine 70.00
  Whistle, tin, signal type, 3 tones...40.00

Little Oscar, Oscar Mayer
  Doll, 30" inflatable soft vinyl, chef hat, white chef outfit, red inscriptions, 1970s 25.00
  Post Card, 3-1/2" x 5-1/2", traveling Wienermobile, sgd "Jerry Maren," portrayed Little Oscar in 1950s 10.00
  Ring, red plastic top, c1970...18.00
  Toy, 3" w, 10" l, 4-1/2" h, Wienermobile, pull toy, wheels turn and diecut Little Oscar moves up and down, c1950s 150.00

Mr. Peanut
  Ashtray, Golden Jubilee, 50th Anniversary, gold plated metal, figural, orig attached booklet, orig box, 5" h, 5-3/4" h............130.00

Bank, 8-1/2" x 4", full figure, orange plastic 725.00

Booklet, *Mr. Peanuts Guide to Tennis,* 6" x 9", ©1960, 24 illus pgs 20.00

Box, Planters Chocolate Covered Nut Assortment, silver alligator texture, 2 early Mr. Peanut figures, 8-1/4" sq.....................350.00

Case, salesman's sample, attaché, 9 different unopened vacuum pack display cans, orig promotional divider 475.00

Paint Book, *Planter's Paint Book No. 2,* 7-1/4" x 10-1/2", ©1929, 32 pgs, ... 35.00

Salad Set, ceramic tops, wooden fork and spoon, rhinestone monocle, 10" h 170.00

Shipping Box, corrugated cardboard, adv for Planters Salted Peanut 5¢ cellophane bags, 1950s, 17" x 14" x 11" 140.00

Toy, trailer truck, red cab, yellow and blue plastic trailer, 5-1/2" l. 275.00

Mr. Zip

Bank, 2-1/4" x 4" x 5-3/4", tin litho, mail box, red, white, and blue, photos of coins, chart on back, trap missing........................ 15.00

Decal, 6" d, red, white, and blue glossy paper, May, 1963, unused 5.00

First Day Cover, 3-1/2" x 6-1/2", with Zip Code commemorative stamp, "Saluting the U.S. Postal Service Zip Code System 1974" 10.00

Popeye

Charm, 1" h, bright copper luster plastic figure of Olive Oyl, 1930s 10.00

Children's Book, *Popeye Borrows A Baby Nurse,* Whitman, #712 .... 45.00

Figure, 14" h, chalkware 140.00

Mug, 4" h, Olive Oyl, figural 20.00

Pencil Sharpener, figural, Catalin plastic, dark yellow, multicolored decal, 1930s 60.00

Sticker Book, Lowe #2631 .... 40.00

Tie Bar, 2-1/2" l, 3/4" h enameled figure of Popeye, 1930s..... 45.00

Reddy Kilowatt

Bib, 10" x 10" fabric, printed nursery rhyme and Reddy, c1950....65.00

Employee Cap, white canvas fabric, 2" bright red, white, blue, and

Figure, gentleman and lady, colorful garb, detailed features, 6-1/2" h, $625.

yellow fabric patch for PA Power and Light Co., 1920-1996 commemorative date 10.00

Hot Pad, 6" d, laminated heat resistant cardboard, textured top surface with art and verse inscription "My name is Reddy Kilowatt-I keep things cold. I make things hot. I'm your cheap electric servant. Always ready on the spot," c1940 .... 40.00

Pinback Button

Inspectors Club, multicolored, silver rim, for nuclear plant of Consumers Power Co., c1960 .... 45.00

Please Don't Litter, blue and white, 1950s 15.00

Pocket Knife, metal cast, red figure image and title on one side, single knife blade, Zippo, c1950.. 60.00

Statuette, 5" h, 1-1/2" x 3" black plastic base, ivory white glow plastic head, gloves, and boots, translucent red body, c1950 ... 195.00

Stickpin, red enamel and silvered metal miniature diecut figure, c1950 .... 30.00

Rocky Jones, Space Ranger

Coloring Book, Whitman, cockpit cov, 1951 .... 40.00

Pinback Button, membership type... 45.00

Wings, pin... 40.00

Sambo

Doll, 4" x 6-1/2" x 9", tiger, plush stuffed, ear tag and name tags, 1977©, R. Dakin Co., orange striped, black and white muzzle, inset glass eyes, Sambo's name stamped in red on chest... 40.00

Pinback Button, Sambo's Pancakes, brown, orange, and white, c1960 .... 15.00

Token, wooden disk, printed in red on both sides, Sambo and tiger image on one side, other side with coffee cup "What This Country Needs Is A Good Cup of Coffee-Sambo's Has It," c1960....... 8.00

Yellow Kid

Cigar Box, 3-1/2" x 4-1/4" x 9", wood, illus and name inscription in bright gold, brass hinges, label inside "Smoke Yellow Kid Cigars/ Manuf'd by B. R. Fleming, Curwesville, Pa," tax label strips on back, c1896 .... 225.00

Fireworks, 5" l, 5/8" d, "Yellow Kid Salute," orig cartoon illus of Kid holding lit firecracker under his arm, "Don't touch me when I'se Lit," fuse missing... 850.00

Pinback Button

"There is Only One Yellow Kid/Big Bubble Chewing Gum," bright yellow and black, fleshtone details on Kid's head, c1910, 7/8" d 40.00

"Yellow Kid No. 1," Kid with huge beer mug, no back paper, blue number and copyright... 75.00

"Yellow Kid No. 13," Kid with wooden horse, Napoleon-style hat, text reference to Napoleon 20.00

"Yellow Kid No. 15," Kid with money and can of red paint, ready to "Paint new York Red," High Admiral Cigarettes on black tin reverse 20.00

"Yellow Kid No. 16," Kid hanging stocking for "Santie Klaws," orig back paper... 20.00

"Yellow Kid No. 72," Kid with Vassar pennant 25.00

"Yellow Kid No. 146," Kid with earrings, hair in pigtails, holds rifle and Madagascar flag 60.00

Personality

Amos and Andy

Ashtray and match holder, plaster 30.00

Diecut, 3" x 5", cardboard, Amos, Andy, and Kingfish, 1931 .... 22.00

Poster, 13" x 29", multicolored, Campbell's Soup ad, radio show listings, framed.. 145.00

Toy, Fresh Air Taxi, litho tin wind-up, Marx, 1929 .... 425.00

Ball, Lucille

Magazine, *Life,* April 6, 1953, 5 pg article, full color cover of Lucy, Desi Arnaz, Desi IV, and Lucy Desiree 30.00

Movie Lobby Card, 11" x 14", full color, 1949 Columbia Picture "Miss Grant Takes Richmond" 40.00

Captain Kangaroo

Badge, 2-1/4" h, emb tin shield, came on 1960s doll 15.00

Puzzle, 10" x 14", frame tray, Captain and nursery rhyme characters, 1956, Milton Bradley 20.00

Whisk Broom, 7" h, wood handle, blue and fleshtones, black, white, red, and yellow accents, ©R.K.A., 1960 ....40.00

Cassidy, Hopalong

Badge, silvered metal, star shape, raised center portrait, c1950 ....25.00

Coloring Book, 1950, large size..............................30.00

Rug, chenille 100.00

Tablet, 8" x 10", color photo cov, facsimile signature, unused.......24.00

Dionne Quintuplets

Advertisement, 5" x 7", Quintuplet Bread, Schultz Baking Co., diecut cardboard, loaf of bread, brown crust, bright red and blue letters, named silhouette portraits, text on reverse 70.00

Book, *Now We Are Five*, Jas Brough, 256 pgs, dj.....................7.50

Dolls in Ferris wheel, 18-5/8" h, five 6-1/2" h composition Madame Alexander dolls with brown painted eyes, closed mouth, orig white organdy dresses, lawn bibs, blue accented yellow and green wooden Ferris wheel, some paint loss, c1936....... 1,035.00

Fan, 8-1/4" x 8-3/4", diecut cardboard, titled "Sweethearts Of The World," full-color tinted portraits, light blue ground, ©1936, funeral director name on reverse 35.00

Garland, Judy

Pinback Button

1" h, "Judy Garland Doll," black and white photo, used on c1930 Ideal doll, name appears on curl, also "Metro-Goldwyn-Mayer Star" in tiny letters 125.00

1-1/4" d, "Oz/Your Dollars Will Work Magic in Hecht Month," Baltimore department store, multicolored.....................275.00

Sheet Music, *On The Atchison, Topeka, and the Sante Fe,* 1945 MGM movie "The Harvey Girls," sepia photo, purple, light pink, and brown cov 35.00

Gleason, Jackie

Coloring Book, "Jackie Gleason's Dan Dan Dandy Color Book," Abbott, ©1956, unused 25.00

Magazine, *TV Guide,* May 21, 1955, Philadelphia edition, 3 pg article on the Honeymooners..............................18.00

Pinback Button, 1-5/8" d, "Jackie Gleason Fan Club/And Awa-a-ay We Go!," blue on cream litho, checkered suit, 1950s 65.00

Houdini, Harry, big little book, *Houdini's Big Little Book of Magic,* Whitman, 1927, premium or American Oil and Amoco Gas, 192 pgs 35.00

Henie, Sonja

Pinback Button, 1-3/4" d, "Sonja Henie Ice Review," orange on blue, illus of skater, c1940s..............................20.00

Portrait Art, 15-1/2" x 19-1/2", rigid white art board, 12-1/2" x 16-1/2" paint and ink portrait by John Cullen Murphy, figure skater wearing cap with Olympic rings symbols, bottom margin with title in red pencil, "Once In A Lifetime," for nostalgia feature in Jan 1948 Sports Magazine 300.00

Laurel & Hardy

Bank, plastic, 14" h 45.00

Movie Poster, Laurel and Hardy in the Big Noise, Fox, 1944, Tooker Litho 300.00

Salt and Pepper Shakers, pr 230.00

Lone Ranger

Badge, 1" d, Safety Scout 20.00

Better Little Book, *The Lone Ranger and Dead Men's Mine,* Whitman, 1939..............................50.00

Cereal Box, Cheerios, Frontiertown 75.00

Coloring Book, Lone Ranger Ranch, Fun Book, Whitman, Cheerios premium, 1956..............................75.00

Gun and Holster Set, MIB..............................135.00

Hartland Figure, orig box 250.00

Pencil Case, 1" x 4" x 8-1/4", textured stiff cardboard, gold cov design, dark blue ground, American Lead Pencil Co., 1930s................45.00

Premium Ring, Six Shooter, metal, c1947..............................145.00

Print Set, orig box, unused, 1940s 45.00

Toothbrush Holder, plaster, painted, 1938, 4" h.....................75.00

Marx Brothers

Book, Beds, hardbound..............................45.00

Sheet Music, 9-1/2" x 12-1/4", *Alone* from MGM musical "A Night At The Opera," 1935, orange, blue, and white cov, blue tone photos of Groucho, Chico, Harpo, Allan Jones, and Kitty Carlisle ...30.00

Rogers, Roy

Bank, Roy on Trigger, porcelain, sgd "Roy Rogers" and "Trigger" 200.00

Bedspread 115.00

Camera..............................110.00

Comic Book, April, 1958..............................60.00

Guitar, orig box, 1950s 140.00

Ring, litho tin, Post's Raisin Bran premium, Dale Evans, ©1942 ....45.00

Toy, Roy Fit It Stagecoach, figure, Bullet, 2 horses, complete accessories 95.00

Yo-Yo, orig display box with 12 yo-yos 250.00

Watch, Roy and Dale..............................120.00

Temple, Shirley

Children's Book, *Shirley Temple's Birthday Book,* Dell Publishing Co., c1934, soft cover, 24 pgs 100.00

Figure, 6-1/2" h, salt-glazed 85.00

Handkerchief, Little Colonel, boxed set of 3 ....200.00

Magazine Advertisement, Lane Hope Chests, 1945 ....8.00

Magazine

Life, July 11, 1938, cover with young Shirley in field, article..............................28.00

Parade, Oct 20, 1957, Shirley and her children on cov......22.00

Three Stooges

Autograph, letter, 4-1/2" x 5-1/2" mailing envelope, two folded 6" x 8" sheets of "Three Stooges" letterhead, personally inked response to fan, sgd "Moe Howard," March 10, 1964 Los Angeles postmark 200.00

Badge, 4" d, cello, black and white upper face image of Curly-Joe on purple background, Clark Oil employee type..................20.00

Movie Poster

14" x 36", "The Three Stooges Meet Hercules," paper insert for 1961 Columbia Pictures movie, folded 60.00

27" x 41", "Snow White and The Three Stooges," 1961 20th Century Fox film, folded 60.00

Photo, 4" x 5" glossy black and white, facsimile signatures of Curly-Joe, Larry, and Moe, plus personal inscription in blue ink by Moe......95.00

Pinback Button, 7/8" d, black and white photo of Moe, series issued by "Button-Up Co." on the curl 8.00

CHILDREN'S BOOKS

History: Because there is a bit of the child in all of us, collectors always have been attracted to children's books. In the 19th century, books were popular gifts for children, with many of the children's classics written and published during this time. These books were treasured and often kept throughout a lifetime.

Developments in printing made it possible to include more attractive black and white illustrations and color plates. The work of artists and illustrators has added value beyond the text itself.

References: E. Lee Baumgarten, *Price Guide for Children's & Illustrated Books for the Years 1880-1960 Sorted by Artist and Sorted by Author,* published by author, 1996; David & Virginia Brown, *Whitman Juvenile Books,* Collector Books, 1997; Richard E. Dickerson, *Brownie Bibliography,* 2nd ed., Golden Pippin Press, 1995; Virginia Haviland, *Children's Literature, a Guide to Reference Sources (1966),* first supplement (1972), second supplement (1977), third supplement (1982), Library of Congress; John Henty, *The*

Collectable World of Mabel Lucie Attwell, Richard Dennis Publications, distributed by Antique Collectors' Club, 1999; Alan Horne, *Dictionary of 20th Century British Book Illustrators, available from* Spoon River Press, 1994; Simon Houfe, *Dictionary of 19th Century British Book Illustrators,* revised ed., available from Spoon River Press, 1996; E. Christian Mattson and Thomas B. Davis, *A Collector's Guide to Hardcover Boys' Series Books,* published by authors, 1996; Diane McClure Jones and Rosemary Jones, *Collector's Guide to Children's Books,* 1850 to 1950, Collector Books, 1997; Jack Matthews, *Toys Go to War,* Pictorial Histories Publishing, 1994; Edward S. Postal, *Price Guide & Bibliography to Children's & Illustrated Books,* M & P Press (available from Spoon River Press, 2319C W. Rohmann, Peoria, IL 61604), 1995; *Price Guide to Big Little Books & Better Little, Jumbo Tiny Tales, A Fast Action Story, etc.,* L-W Book Sales, 1995; Steve Santi, Collecting Little Golden Books, 3rd ed., Krause Publications, 1998; Albert Tillman, *Pop-Up! Pop-Up,* Whalesworth Farm Publishing, 1997.

Periodicals: *Book Source Monthly,* 2007 Syosett Dr., P.O. Box 567, Cazenovia, NY 13035; *Martha's KidLit Newsletter,* P.O. Box 1488, Ames, IA 50010; *Mystery & Adventure Series Review,* P.O. Box 3488, Tucson, AZ 85722; *The Authorized Edition Newsletter,* RR1, Box 73, Machias, ME 04654; *Yellowback Library,* P.O. Box 36172, Des Moines, IA 50315.

Collectors' Clubs: Horatio Alger Society, 4907 Allison Dr., Lansing, MI 48910; Movable Book Society, P.O. Box 11645, New Brunswick, NJ 08906; Society of Phantom Friends, P.O. Box 1437 North Highlands, CA 95660.

Libraries: American Antiquarian Society, Worcester, MA; Free Library of Philadelphia, Philadelphia, PA; Library of Congress, Washington, DC; Lucile Clark Memorial Children's Library, Central Michigan University, Mount Pleasant, MI; Pierpont Morgan Library, New York, NY; Toronto Public Library, Toronto, Ontario, Canada.

Additional Listings: See *Warman's Americana & Collectibles* for more examples and an extensive listing of collectors' clubs.

Abbreviations:

dj	dust jacket	n.d.	no date
4to	8" x 10"	pgs	pages
8vo	5" x 7"		

ABC Book, Charles Buckles Falls, Garden City, 1927, 26 color woodblock designs by Falls, 4to, cloth backed pictorial boards........ 100.00
Abe Lincoln Kentucky Boy, Raymond Warren, Reilly & Lee Publ, 1931 .... 10.00
A Child's Garden of Verses, color illus by Jessie Wilcox Smith, Schribner, 1905, 1st ed., one illus missing 17.50
Alice In Wonderland, MacMillan, 1877, red cloth cover with gold Alice, some wear.. 12.50
Alice's Adventures in Wonderland & Through the Looking-Glass, Lewis Carroll, color illus by John Tanniel, Macmillian, 1966, orig dg.... 12.00
An Alphabet of Animals, Carton Moore Park, Blackie and Son, London, 1899, black and white plates by Park, 4to, pictorial green boards, spine ends, bottom edge, and tips rubbed 100.00
Anything Can Happen, Alice and Jerry reader, 1940.................... 15.00
Around the Rocking Chair, Kate Tannatt Woods, 1870................. 30.00
Aunt Jaunty's Tales: Dame Brown's Visit to London, Marks & Son publisher, London, 6 hand colored plates, 8vo, pictorial wrappers, list of books on rear cover 80.00
Babar and His Children, Jean De Brunhoff, first edition, illus, 4to, pictorial boards 150.00
Billy Whiskers in An Aeroplane, Frances Trego Montgomery, Saalfield Publishing, color and black and white illus, 1912, orig dj 45.00
Black Beauty, Anna Sewell, color plates by Fritz Eichenberg, 1945 .... 7.50
Boy Scouts in the Canal Zone, Ralphson, some pgs missing 9.00
Chaucer for Children: A Golden Key, Mrs. H. R. Hawies, London, 1877, first edition, 8 color plates, numerous woodcut illus, 4to, gilt pictorial cloth 130.00
Cherry Ames, Dude Ranch Nurse, 1953, some light coloring 10.00
Cinderella, C. S. Evans, London, 1919, first trade edition, Arthur Rackham color illus and silhouettes, 4to, orig cloth backed pictorial boards, front joint cracked at bottom, dj 350.00
East of the Sun and West of the Moon, Kay Nielsen, London, 1914, first trade edition, 24 mounted color plates, lettered tissue guards, 4to, gilt pictorial cloth, spine ends and tips frayed................. 2,185.00
Giovani & the Other, Frances Hodgson Burnett, NY, Schribner, 1892, 1st ed., cover wear, gilt trim 40.00
Green Forest Series, Buster Bear's Twins, Thornton Burgess, illus by Harrison Cady, 1923 .... 28.00
Grimm's Goblins: German Popular Stories Translated From the Kinder und Haus Marchen, E. Taylor, R. Meek & Co., London, 1876, 24 steel engraved illus after George Cruikshank, 8vo, cloth backed pictoral boards, scuffed and rubbed, advertisements on end papers 75.00
Honey Bunch, Her First Little Treasure Hunt, Helen Thorndyke, 1937, wear to cover.. 7.00
Honey Bunch, Her First Twin Playmates, Helen Thorndyke, 1941, paper browned, slight tears to dg 7.00
In Fairyland. A Series of Pictures from the Elf-World by Richard Doyle, poem by Wm Allingham, London, 1870, first edition, 16 color printed wood engraved plates by Edmund Evans after Doyle, folio, rebound 920.00
Insects and Reptiles With Their Uses to Man, Darton & Clark, London, 1844, 10 hand colored litho plates, 4to, publisher's gilt pictorial cloth, wear along spine 100.00
Kidnapped, Robert Louis Stevenson, Milo Winter color illus, Rand McNally & Co., 1938 .... 35.00
Lincoln's Youth, Indiana Years, Seven to Twenty-One, Louis A. Warren, orig dj 10.00
Little Brown Koko, Blanche Seale Hunt, color illus by Dorothy Wagstaff, American Colortype Co., 1952 .... 50.00
Little Lord Fauntleroy, Frances Hodgson Burnett, NY, 1886, illus by Reginalrd Birch, first edition, 4to, publisher's red and gilt stamped pictorial cloth covers.. 165.00
Little Songs of Long Ago, H. Willebeek, Augener, London, 1912, illus by Le Mair, oblong 4to, tan cloth gilt with pictorial onlay, some scuffs and rubs, some repairs 140.00
Mother West Wind's Children, Thornton Burgess, illus by George Kerr, 1911 .... 22.00
Mother West Wind's Neighbors, Thornton Burgess, illus by George Kerr, 1941 .... 18.00
Now We Are Six, A. A. Milne, Dutton, London, 1927, first edition, illus by Ernest H. Shepard, 8vo, gilt pictorial red cloth, worn, hinges starting, owner's signature on half title 120.00
Nursery Rhymes, Claud Lovat Fraser, London, 1919, first edition, color illus, 4to, cloth backed pictorial boards 165.00
Old Woman and Her Silver Penny, Dean and Son, London, c1865, 8 hand colored plates with tab controlled movable pieces, 8vo, cloth backed pictorial boards, scuffed, scattered foxing, most plates and tabs repaired 260.00
Ragged Dick; or, Street Life in New York with the Boot-Blacks, Horatio Alger, Boston, c1868, illus, 8vo, publisher's green gilt cloth cover, first edition, owner's gift inscription 3,680.00
Raggedy Ann in the Garden, Johnny Gruelle, Perks Pub Co., 1934 .... 16.00
Raggedy Ann's Lucky Pennies, Johnny Gruelle, Mary & Wallace Stover color illus, Perks Pub Co., 1946 .... 16.00

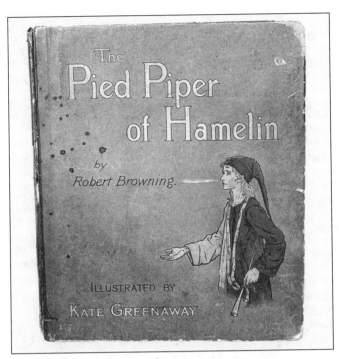

Pied Piper of Hamelin, Robert Browning, George Rut-
tledge & Sons, Kate Greenaway illus, $135.

Rudolph the Red-Nosed Reindeer, Robert L. May, illus by Denver
  Gillen, first edition for Montgomery Ward, c1939, 4to, pictorial stapled
  wrappers, spine worn, some tears near staples, child's name in pen-
  cil on front cover 400.00
Ten Ever Loving Blue-Eyed Years with Pogo, 1949-1959, Walt Kelly,
  Simon & Schuster, 1959 .... 15.00
The Affectionate Parent's Gift and the Good Child's Reward, Henry
  Sharpe Horsley, printed for T. Kelly, London, 1828, first edition, 100+
  engraved illus, 8vo, 19th C burgundy morocco gilt cover, rubbed,
  owner's inscriptions 375.00
The Book of Birds and Beasts, Mary Elliott, Wm Darton & Son, Lon-
  don, c1840, 48 hand colored plates, 12mo, orig patterned cloth with
  paper cover label, soiled 150.00
The Cat in the Hat Comes Back, Dr. Seuss, New York, 1958, first edition, illus by Seuss, 8vo, pictorial boards, light wear, dj 550.00
The Cat in the Hat in English & French, Dr. Seuss, Random House,
  1967, orig dj 25.00
The Children's Shakespeare, E. Nesbitt, Alltemus, c1900, slight edge
  wear 20.00
The Devil and Aunt Serena, Esther Kellner, Bobbs-Merrill, 1968, autographed by author 15.00
The Fables of Aesop and Others, Charles Bennett, London, 1858, first
  edition, 23 hand colored plates engraved by Swain, 4to, 1/2 morocco
  gilt cov, rubbed and scuffed, scattered light soiling 200.00
The Illustrated Family Bunyan, John Bunyan, Sangster, London,
  c1880, introductory essay by Rev'd W. Landels, 23 chromolitho-
  graphs after Edward Deanes, woodcuts by Dalziel Brothers ... 115.00
The King and the Goat, A. Jataka Tale, Dharma Publ, 1986, gilt dec,
  illus by Deborah Black 10.00
The Life and Adventures of Robinson Crusoe, William Lee, London &
  New York, c1870, 100 illus by Ernest Griset, Popular Edition, 8vo,
  black, silver, and gilt stamped pictorial cloth 140.00
The Lost Zoo, Countee Cullen and Christopher Cat, NY, 1940, first edi-
  tion, illus by Charles Sebree, 8vo, yellow cloth covers, edges rubbed,
  worn dj, publisher's review laid in 100.00
The Magical Land of Noom, Johnny Gruelle, P. F. Volland, NY, 1922,
  first edition, Gruelle illus, 4to, cloth backed pictorial boards 200.00
The Magic Flutes, Josef Kozisek, translated by Clara Winlow, New

York, 1929, Rudolf Mates color illus, oblong 4to, cloth backed pictorial boards 230.00
The New England Primer, J. Thomas & Co., Walpole, NH, 1814, woodcut illus, 16mo, paper covered wooden boards 260.00
*The Parlour Book, or, Favorite Conversations on Science and the Arts
  for the Use of Schools and Families,* William Martin, William Darton,
  London, c1837, color litho frontispiece, 15 black and white litho
  plates, vignettes, 8vo, later 19th C black calf, rubbed 225.00
The Pied Piper of Hamelin, Robert Browning, London, 1934, first trade
  edition, Arthur Rackum illus, 4 color plates, 8vo, orig pictorial stiff wrappers, bookplate, dj, spine panel darkened, repair on verse 375.00
The Slant Book, Peter Newell, NY, 1910, first edition, 22 color plates by
  Newell, slanted 4to, cloth backed pictorial boards, edges rubbed,
  custom cloth folding box with gilt lettered morocco labels 2,530.00
The Square Book of Animals, William Nicholson, Arthur Waugh
  rhymes, London, 1899, first edition, 12 plates by Nicholson, sq 4to,
  cloth backed pictorial boards, upper tips bumped 750.00
The Story of a Bad Boy, Thomas Bailey Aldrich, Boston, 1870, 8vo,
  illus, publisher's burgundy cloth, gilt pictorial spine, slightly faded,
  first edition 230.00
The Story of a Puppet, or, The Adventures of Pinocchio, Carlo Collodi,
  T. Fisher Unwin, London, 1892, first English edition, illus by C. Maz-
  zanti, 8vo, orig blue floral patterned cloth covers, spine darkened,
  ends frayed, tips rubbed, hinges cracked 2,990.00
The Tailor of Gloucester, Beatrix Potter, privately printed by Strange-
  ways and Sons, London, December 1902, frontispiece and 15 color
  plates, 12mo, orig pictorial pink boards, custom felt lined cloth folding
  box 4,140.00
The Tale of Jemima Puddle-Duck, Beatrix Potter, Frederick Warne &
  Co., London, 1908, first edition, color plates and illus, 12mo, green
  paper board with inset color pictorial label 700.00
The Tale of the Flopsy Bunnies, Beatrix Potter, Warne, London, 1909,
  first edition, 27 color plates and other illus, 12mo, dark green paper
  boards, color pictorial label on front cover, spine evenly faded,
  owner's inscription on half-title 635.00
The Tale of Timmy Tiptoes, Beatrix Potter, Warne, London, 1911, first
  edition, 27 color plates, other illus, 12mo, brown paper boards with
  color pictorial label on front cover, joints starting to loosen 400.00
The Tales of Peter Parley about America, Samuel Griswold Goodrich,
  Philadelphia, 1845, wood engraved illus 95.00
The True Story of a Little Boy who Cheated Himself, Tabart & Co., Lon-
  don, 1811, 12 hand colored engraved plates, sq 12mo, lettered stiff
  wrappers 1,035.00
The Witches, Ronald Dahl, NY, 1983, illus by Quentin Blake, 8vo, blue
  cloth covers, slipcase, 1 of 300 numbered copies sgd by Dahl and
  Blake 320.00
The Wonderful Wizard of Oz, L. Frank Baum, George M. Hill, Chicago
  & NY, 1900, color plates, text illus by W. W. Denslow, 4to, orig picto-
  rial cloth cover, first edition, 2nd issue, lightly soiled, spine slightly
  darkened 3,220.00
Tom Turner's Adventures with Radio, Whitman, 1924, first edition.... 27.50
Uncle Wiggily's Auto Sled, Howard Garis, color illus by Lang Campbell,
  Whitman Pub Co., 1936, some wear 35.00
When We Were Very Young, A. A. Milne, 1926, red cover, gold trim 12.50

CHILDREN'S FEEDING DISHES

History: Unlike toy dishes meant for play, children's feeding dishes are the items actually used in the feeding of a
child. Their colorful designs of animals, nursery rhymes,
and children's activities are meant to appeal to the child
and make mealtimes fun. Many plates have a unit to hold
hot water, thus keeping the food warm.

Although glass and porcelain examples from the late 19th
and early 20th centuries are most popular, collectors are
beginning to seek some of the plastic examples from the
1920s to 1940s, especially those with Disney designs on them.

Creamer, cream ground, brown rabbit, green branch, blue bird, Weller, 4-1/8" h, $55.

References: Maureen Batkin, *Gifts for Good Children, Part II, 1890-1990,* Antique Collectors' Club, 1996; Doris Lechler, *Children's Glass Dishes, China and Furniture,* Vol. I (1983), Vol. II (1986, 1993 value update), Collector Books; Noel Riley, *Gifts for Good Children: The History of Children's China, Part I, 1790-1890,* Richard Dennis Publications, 1991; Margaret and Kenn Whitmyer, *Collector's Encyclopedia of Children's Dishes: An Illustrated Value Guide,* Collector Books, 1993.

Bowl, Little Red Riding Hood 95.00
Butter Pat, 3-1/4" d, A Present For Ann, Blue transfer medallion 125.00
Cereal Set, Nursery Rhyme, amber, divided plate, Humpty Dumpty on mug and bowl, Tiara 125.00
Cup, Raggedy Ann, Johnny Gruelle, 1941, Crooksville China 65.00
Cup Plate, 4-5/8" d, "Constant dropping wears away stones and little strokes fell great oaks," green transfer, polychrome enamel dec 90.00
Feeding Dish
    Bunnies, puppies, Nippon 45.00
    Kiddieware, pink, Stangl 75.00
    Little Bo Peep, glass, divided, white, red trim 45.00
    Nursery Rhyme, green enamelware, mkd "Made in Germany" 40.00
    Raggedy Ann, Johnny Gruelle, 1941, Crooksville China, 8-3/4" d 85.00
    Sunbonnet Babies, sweeping, 7-1/4" d 400.00
Mug, yellow glazed, transfer print, England, c1850, glaze and transfer wear
    1-3/4" h, "A rabbit for William" 225.00
    2-1/8" h, "Keep thy shop and thy shop will keep thee," luster rim, minor chip 195.00
    2-1/8" h, two sheep reserve, luster rim 220.00
    2-1/4" h, red and green flower, leaf handle 200.00
    2-3/8" h, "A new doll for Margaret," very minor chips 490.00
    2-3/8" h, reddish brown transfer "My Son, if sinners entice thee, consent thou not lest disgrace come upon thee," leaf handle, small lip flakes 420.00
    2-1/2" h, "A rocking horse for John," minor chips 460.00
    2-1/2" h, reserve of townscape with bridge, luster rim 200.00

Plate
    6" d, Buster Brown, 1910, mint center image 135.00
    8" d, Nursery Rhymes, glass, green 30.00
    8" d, Where Are You Going My Pretty Maid, See Saw Margery Daw, 3 part, transparent green Depression-era glass 35.00
Sherbet, white Depression-era glass, red dec of Three Little Pigs 12.00

CHILDREN'S NURSERY ITEMS

History: The nursery is a place where children live in a miniature world. Things come in two sizes. Child scale designates items actually used for the care, housing, and feeding of the child. Toy or doll scale denotes items used by the child in play and for creating a fantasy environment which copies that of an adult or his own.

Cheap labor and building costs during the Victorian era encouraged the popularity of the nursery. Most collectors focus on items from the years 1880 to 1930.

References: Marguerite Fawdry, *International Survey of Rocking Horse Manufacture,* New Cavendish Books, 1992; Marcia Hersey, *Collecting Baby Rattles and Teethers: Identification and Value Guide,* Krause Publications, 1998; Sally Kevill-Davies, *Yesterday's Children, The Antiques and History of Childcare,* Antique Collectors' Club, 1999; Elizabeth Kurella, *The Complete Guide to Vintage Textiles,* Krause Publications, 1999; Doris Lechler, *Children's Glass Dishes, China and Furniture,* Vol. I (1983), Vol. II (1986, 1993 value update), Collector Books; Patricia Mullins, *Rocking Horse: A History of Moving Toy Horses,* New Cavendish Books, 1992; Lorraine May Punchard, *Playtime Kitchen Items and Table Accessories,* published by author, 1993; Herbert F. Schiffer and Peter B. Schiffer, *Miniature Antique Furniture: Doll House and Children's Furniture from the United States & Europe,* Schiffer Publishing, 1995; Tony Stevenson and Eva Marsden, *Rocking Horses: The Collector's Guide to Selecting, Restoring, and Enjoying New and Vintage Rocking Horses,* Courage Books, 1993.

Museum: The Victorian Perambulator Museum of Jefferson, Jefferson, OH.

Additional Listings: Children's Books; Children's Feeding Dishes; Children's Toy Dishes; Dolls; Games; Miniatures; Toys.

Baby Buggy, wicker, adjustable back, cast iron parasol holder, 1890s 375.00
Bib Clips, sterling silver, clothespin type 75.00
Blanket Chest, New England, late 18th C, grain painted, molded hinged top, dovetail constructed box, slightly flaring bracket feet, orig mustard and brown paint resembles exotic wood, repair, 20-1/2" l, 12" d, 14" h 1,840.00
Blocks
    Boxed set, ABC's, animals, litho of Noah and ark on cov, Victorian 185.00
    23 wooden blocks, colored litho dec of sailors, letters, etc.... 250.00
Boat, play, ice, 24" l, wood with iron runners, c1900 .... 460.00
Bureau, Empire, America, 19th C, grained and painted, rect top and backsplash, 2 glove drawers, case with single overhanging drawer above 3 full drawers flanked by serpentine columns, shaped skirt, wooden pulls, 3 drawers lined with compartments, pair of lovebirds painted on glove box top, yellow and pink roses on drawer fronts and case sides, blue paint on sides and bands on drawer fronts, one pull missing, minor wear and paint loss, 12-1/2" x 13-1/4" x 8" 690.00

Baby Carriage, molded composition horse covered with horse hide, horse hair mane and tail, carriage with orig paint, metal rails, buggy wheels, Victorian, English, 58" l, $2,300.

Chair, 28" h, 9" h seat, New England, 18th C, arm, slat back, old splint seat, needlepoint cushion, old refinish, minor height loss........490.00

Chamber Pot, 8" d, 4-3/4" h, blue and white Oriental scene.......165.00

Cradle Quilt, pieced cotton calico
  36" x 35", Delectable Mountain, blue, gray, red, and yellow patches, printed baby-blocks fabric back, diagonal line quilting, Mennonite, PA, late 19th C 3,165.00
  41" x 40", Sunburst, pink, red, green, navy blue, and orange patches, reverse with paisley fabric, field outline and diagonal line quilting, PA, early 20th C....865.00

Dog Cart, 60" l, two wooden wheels, painted dec of two birds and nest on sides, worn, incomplete......495.00

Doll Carriage, 36" l, 26-1/2" h, wood, black body, stenciled dec and striping, 8-spoked wood wheels, handle, convertible leatherette sun shade, attributed to Joel Ellis, c1869, fringe damaged 320.00

Doll's Cradle, 10-1/2" l, 5-1/4" w, 9" h, grain painted pine, dovetailed construction, carved and shaped hood and rockers, molded base, small age splint, minor paint loss 150.00

Highchair, New England, early 19th C
  32-1/2" h, 17-3/4" seat, old red paint, "TH" carved on underside of seat, minor surface imperfections....1,150.00
  35" h, 22" h seat, old black paint, mustard highlights, rush seat, imperfections 345.00

Jack in the Box, 6-1/2" l, pine box, paper covering, wooden figure with cloth costume, lace, and printed round cardboard head 470.00

Pram Coverlet, quilted silk, satin rosebud dec...........60.00

Print, Awake & Asleep, Bessie Gutman, double matted, orig frame 150.00

Rattle, 3-3/4" l, bone, whistle 95.00

Record Book, 8-1/4" x 10-1/2", Baby Days, Sunbonnet Babies, Bertha Corbett illus, 1910, unused....295.00

Rocker, child size, rustic, New York state, c1900, bent elements intertwined above solid splat, plant seat, sq stretchers and rockers, dark natural surface, 9-3/4" h seat 230.00

Rocking Horse, 40" l, platform type, painted, dapple-gray, hair mane and tail, leather saddle, red platform with painted and incised dec, one eye missing 800.00

Rocking Toy, 30" l, two duck silhouettes, platform base with turned spindle sides, orig ivory paint, black, gold and red trim, some paint missing, upholstered seat missing 165.00

Scooter, 43" l, 30-3/4" h, steel frame and wheels, wooden platform and handle, worn orig red paint, black and yellow striping, partial label "...Arrow Deluxe"....140.00

Sewing Machine, child's, Singer, 6-3/4" h, table model, cast iron and nickeled steel 150.00

Sled, wooden
  Iron rod tipped runners, scrolled finials, worn black paint, polychrome striping, flowers, small landscape, and "Black Bird" 395.00
  Peaked runners, red painted and polychrome dec, poplar and oak, shaped deck, turned frontal stretcher on rect legs with chamfered corners, seat dec with galloping horse in red, black, and white with yellow highlights, PA, 19th C, metal braces added, some loss to paint 990.00
  Steel runners, old green paint, yellow striping on runners, polychrome foliage in a circle on top, touch-up repaint, 35-1/2" l 235.00

Wagon
  15" l, 25" tongue, wood, orig dark blue and yellow paint, orange and black striping, gold stenciled "Express," stenciled label "Pat. Jan. 12, 1869"....1,185.00
  40" l, wood, metal fittings, Roller Bearing Coaster, black stenciled label, old red and brown paint, some orig paint, old repaint touchup repair 385.00

CHILDREN'S TOY DISHES

History: Dishes made for children often served a dual purpose—playthings and a means of learning social graces. Dish sets came in two sizes. The first was for actual use by the child when entertaining friends. The second, a smaller size than the first, was for use with dolls.

Children's dish sets often were made as a sideline to a major manufacturing line, either as a complement to the family service or as a way to use up the last of the day's batch of materials. The artwork of famous illustrators, such as Palmer Cox, Kate Greenaway, and Rose O'Neill, can be found on porcelain children's sets.

References: Doris Lechler, *Children's Glass Dishes, China and Furniture,* Vol. I (1983), Vol. II (1986, 1993 value update), Collector Books; Lorraine May Punchard, *Playtime Kitchen Items and Table Accessories,* published by author, 1993; ——, *Playtime Pottery & Porcelain from Europe and Asia,* Schiffer Publishing, 1996; ——, *Playtime Pottery and Porcelain from the United Kingdom and the United States,* Schiffer Publishing, 1996; Margaret and Kenn Whitmyer, *Collector's Encyclopedia of Children's Dishes,* Collector Books, 1993.

Collectors' Club: Toy Dish Collectors, P.O. Box 159, Bethlehem, CT 06751.

Butter Dish, Tappan pattern, clear, 3-3/4" d, $48.

Akro Agate
    Tea Set, Octagonal, large, green and white, Little American Maid, orig box, 17 pcs 225.00
    Water Set, Play Time, pink and blue, orig box, 7 pcs 125.00
Bohemian glass, decanter set, ruby flashed, Vintage dec, 5 pcs 135.00
China
    Cheese Dish, cov, hunting scene, Royal Bayreuth 65.00
    Chocolate Pot, Model T car with passengers 90.00
    Creamer, Phoenix Bird 20.00
    Cup and Saucer
        Phoenix Bird 15.00
        Willow Ware 10.00
    Dinner Set, Willow Ware, blue and white, Japanese 200.00
    Tea Set
        Children playing, cov teapot, creamer, cov sugar, 6 cups, saucers, and tea plates, German, Victorian 285.00
        Willow Ware, cov teapot, creamer, cov sugar, 4 cups, saucers and plates, Japan, orig box 250.00
Depression Glass, 14 pc set
    Cherry Blossom, pink 390.00
    Laurel, McKee, red trim 355.00
    Moderntone, turquoise, gold 210.00
Milk Glass
    Cheese Dish, blue opaque, McKee 65.00
    Creamer, Wild Rose 65.00
    Cup, Nursery Rhyme 24.00
    Ice Cream Platter, Wild Rose 60.00
Pattern Glass
    Berry Set, Wheat Sheaf, 7 pcs 85.00
    Butter, cov, Hobnail with Thumbprint base, blue 95.00
    Cake Stand
        Beautiful Lady, 4" h, 5" d, c1905 .... 25.00
        Palm Leaf Fan 35.00
    Creamer
        Buzz Saw 15.00
        Drum 70.00
        Lamb 75.00
    Cup and Saucer, Lion 50.00
    Pitcher, Oval Star, clear 20.00
    Punch Set, Wheat Sheaf, 7 pcs 75.00
    Spooner
        Mardi Gras 45.00
        Tulip and Honeycomb 20.00
    Sugar, cov
        Beaded Swirl 40.00
        Mardi Gras 65.00
    Water Set, Nursery Rhyme, pitcher, 6 tumblers 225.00

CHINESE CERAMICS

History: The Chinese pottery tradition has existed for thousands of years. By the 16th century, Chinese ceramic wares were being exported to India, Persia, and Egypt. During the Ming dynasty (1368-1643), earthenwares became more highly developed. The Ch'ien Lung period (1736-1795) of the Ch'ing dynasty marked the golden age of interchange with the West.

Trade between China and the West began in the 16th century when the Portuguese established Macao. The Dutch entered the trade early in the 17th century. With the establishment of the English East India Company, all of Europe sought Chinese-made pottery and porcelain. Styles, shapes, and colors were developed to suit Western tastes, a tradition which continued until the late 19th century.

Fine Oriental ceramics continued to be made into the 20th century, and modern artists enjoy equal fame with older counterparts.

References: Carl L. Crossman, *The Decorative Arts of the China Trade,* Antique Collectors' Club, 1999; Gloria and Robert Mascarelli, *Warman's Oriental Antiques,* Wallace-Homestead, 1992; Nancy N. Schiffer, *Imari, Satsuma, and Other Japanese Export Ceramics,* Schiffer Publishing, 1997.

Periodical: *Orientalia Journal,* P.O. Box 94, Flushing, NY 11363-0094, http://members.aol.com/Orientalia/index.html.

Collectors' Club: China Student's Club, 59 Standish Rd., Wellesley, MA 02181.

Museums: Art Institute of Chicago, Chicago, IL; Asian Art Museum of San Francisco, San Francisco, CA; George Walter Vincent Smith Art Museum, Springfield, MA; Morikami Museum & Japanese Gardens, Delray Beach, FL; Pacific Asia Museum, Pasadena, CA.

Additional Listings: Canton; Fitzhugh; Imari; Kutani; Nanking; Rose Medallion; Satsuma.

Bottle, 16" h, painted reserves of floral and bird scenes, light blue ground, Chinese Export, 19th C, wear 230.00
Bough Pot, 8-1/2" h, 8-1/4" w, 5-1/4" w base, 7-7/8" d, octagonal, applied dec of squirrels among grapes on canted corners which flank shaped lanes, central floral sprays, gilt dec base, famille rose palette, gilt rope twist handles, inserts with 5 circular apertures, gilt edges, Chinese Export for European market, c1775-85, gilt wear, 3 insert handles missing, pr 13,800.00

Bowl, Kakiemon style, white ground, blue, red, yellow, and aqua enamel asymmetrical scrolling floral dec, six radial ribs create notches at rim, Japanese, Edo period, 1695-1700, 5-9/16" d, foot ring chip, $1,150. Photo courtesy of Freeman\Fine Arts.

Bowl
  9-1/2" d, blue and white landscape dec, hairline, small rim restoration, 19th C 175.00
  10-1/2" d, 4-1/2" h, underglaze blue, polychrome enameled scenes with gilt, orange peel glaze, wear and hairline 1,540.00
Bowl, cov, 11" d, iron red and white, fish dec, Qing dynasty, 19th C 200.00
Brush Washer, 4-3/4" d, compressed circular form, splayed base, incurved rim, thick bluish-gray crackle glaze 175.00
Candlesticks, pr, 8" h, blue and white, dragons and precious object dec, Chinese 120.00
Censer, 3-1/2" h, compressed globular form, splayed raised foot, everted rim, countersunk band dec, 2 scroll handles, white glaze, 19th C.......................... 395.00
Charger, 18" d, iron red, fish dec, Qing dynasty, 19th C 175.00
Coffeepot, Chinese Export
  9" h, fruit final, intertwined handle with flowers and foliage, sepia colored and gilt dec landscape in almond-shaped reserve 550.00
  9-1/8" h, berry lid finial, intertwined handle with flower and leaf detail, round medallions with geese, red, blue, and gilt, minor wear and roughness at spout 1,100.00
Cup, 2-1/4" h, Blanc-De-Chine, molded animal and foliate dec, Qing dynasty, 18th C.......................... 100.00
Figure, 5-1/2" h, seated dog, Chinese characters on collar, Blanc de Chine 250.00
Fruit Basket and Undertray, 11" l, blue and white, reticulated, floral dec, Chinese 350.00
Garden Set, blue and white, 18-1/2" h 635.00
Garniture Set, two 14-1/2" h vases, three 13-1/2" h covered urns, Cabbage pattern, foo dog finials, 19th C, minor imperfections 3,335.00
Ginger Jar, cov, 3-1/2" h, blue and white porcelain, figural procession dec, wood cover.......................... 300.00
Jar, cov, blue and white porcelain
  3-3/4" h, petal shaped panels, figures and flower-filled jardinieres, Kangxi.......................... 225.00
  8" h, shaped panels with kylins on blue ground, floral dec, carved wood lid, Kangxi.......................... 425.00
  11" h, flowering prunus branch dec, crackled ice ground, fu dog finials, Qing dynasty, 19th C, price for pr 275.00
Plate, 9" d, scalloped edge, polychrome and gilt armorial dec, minor edge chips, late 18th C 635.00
Platter, 17-3/4" l, pierced insert, painted armorial of New York State, extensive restoration.......................... 375.00
Punch Bowl, sepia landscape medallion, white gilt and blue enamel border, Chinese Export, late 18th C, hairline firing blemishes..........1,265.00
Salad Bowl, 9-1/2" d, blue and white, floral dec, Chinese...........200.00
Sauceboat, 3" h, polychrome and gilt dec, gold edge band, int. scallop border, floral garland dec, chip, hairline, mid 18th C 250.00
Soup Plate, 9-5/8" d, Cabbage Leaf and Butterfly, 19th C, minor chips, gilt and enamel wear, 4 pc set.......................... 175.00
Teapot, 5-3/4" h, hp polychrome and gilt eagle with wings, down, and shield dec, entwined strap handle, chips, hairline, scratches, 19th C.......................... 690.00
Tea Set, partial, American Eagle, sepia and gilt dec, 5-1/4" h tea caddy, five 2-3/4" h mugs, three 2" h tea cups, plate, some damage 1,265.00
Umbrella Stand, 24" h, blue and white, Canton-style dec, Chinese 250.00
Urn, ovoid pottery body tapering to flat base, pair of small loop handles, high rounded shoulder painted red and black, 4 circles within sweeping concentric bands, Chinese, Neolithic, Yangshao period.................650.00
Vase
  9-1/8" h, baluster, Tobacco Leaf pattern, iron-red pheasants perched on flowering branch, enameled yellow, turquoise, green, and blue leaves, rose and yellow tobacco blossom, insects and floral springs on reverse, gilt ruyi lappet border with floral springs dec on iron-red hatchwork ground, gilt husk and dot band, ormolu pierced foliate scroll base, c1785.......................... 1,750.00
  12" h, blue and white, Chinese, Qing dynasty, 19th C, pr 300.00
  14-1/4" h, Sang de Boeuf, mounted as lamps, pr.................. 200.00

  17" h, polychrome dec court scenes, surrounded by pink and green foliate devices, blue ground, mask handles, pr, one with damage and repair.......................... 460.00
  19" h, two panels with court scenes surrounded by floral devices and medallions with figures, orange dec, gilt fruit-form handles, mounted as lamp, minor glaze loss 575.00
  27" h, blue and white, foliage, geometric band at mid-section, Chinese, 19th C.......................... 350.00
Vegetable Dish, cov, 12" l, 9-1/2" d, 5-1/2" h, One Thousand Butterflies pattern, diamond shaped, 19th C, crack 175.00

CHINTZ CHINA

History: Chintz china has been produced since the 17th century. The brightly colored exotic patterns produced on fabric imported from India to England during this century was then recreated on ceramics. Early chintz patterns were hand painted and featured large flowers, fantastical birds and widely spaced patterns. The advent of transfer printing resulted in the development of chintz dishes which could be produced cheaply enough to sell to the masses. By the 1830s, a number of Staffordshire potteries were producing chintzware for everyday use. These early patterns have not yet attracted the interest of most chintz collectors.

Collectors typically want the patterns dating from roughly 1920 until the 1950s. In 1920, A.G. Richardson "Crown Ducal" produced a range of all-over-transfer chintz patterns which were very popular in North America, particularly the East Coast. Patterns such as Florida, Festival, and Blue Chintz were originally introduced as tea sets and then expanded to full dinner services. Florida is the most popular of the Crown Ducal patterns in North America but Peony has become increasingly popular in the past year or two.

What most collectors consider the first modern chintz was designed by Leonard Grimwade in 1928 and named Marguerite. This pattern was very successful for many years but has never been highly regarded by collectors. Every year at the British Industries Fair factories vied with each other to introduce new patterns which would catch the buyers' eye. From the late 1920s until the mid-1950s, Royal Winton produced more than 80 chintz patterns. In some cases, the background color was varied and the name changed: Hazel, Spring and Welbeck is the same pattern in different colorways. After the second world war, Royal Winton created more than fifteen new patterns, many of which were more modern looking with large flowers and rich dark burgundy, blue or black backgrounds—patterns such as May Festival, Spring Glory and Peony. These patterns have not been very popular with collectors although other 1950s patterns such as Florence and Stratford have become almost as popular as Julia and Welbeck in the past year.

The 1930s were hard times in the potteries and factories struggled to survive. They copied any successful patterns from any other factories. James Kent Ltd. produced chintzes such as DuBarry, Apple Blossom and Rosalynde. These patterns were sold widely in North America and complete dinner sets still occasionally turn up. The most popular pattern for collectors is the white Hydrangea although Apple Blossom seems to be more and more sought after. Elijah Cotton "Lord Nelson" was another factory which produced large amounts of chintz. Cotton had always been known for the hundreds of utilitarian jugs they produced and they continued to be great producers of institutional ware. The workers at Elijah Cotton were never as skilled as the Grimwades' workers and usually the handles and the spouts of teapots and coffeepots were left undecorated. The shapes are chunky and the pottery thicker than the other factories. Collectors, however, love the Nelson Ware jugs and stacking teapots especially in Black Beauty and Green Tulip.

Although a number of factories produced bone china after World War II, only Shelley Pottery seems to be highly desired by today's collector.

By the late 1950s, young brides didn't want the dishes of their mothers and grandmothers but preferred the clean lines of modern Scandinavian furniture and dishes. Chintz gradually died out by the early 1960s and it was not until the 1990s that collectors began to search for the dishes their mothers had scorned.

References: Eileen Busby, *Royal Winton Porcelain,* The Glass Press Inc.1998; Susan Scott, *Charlton Standard Catalogue of Chintz,* Charlton Press, *3rd Edition;* 1999; Heller/Feljoy, *Chintz by Design,* Chintz International, 1997; Muriel Miller, *Collecting Royal Winton Chintz,* Francis Joseph Publications, 1996, Jo Anne Welch, *Chintz Ceramics,* 2nd Edition, Schiffer Publishing 1998.

Collectors' Clubs: Royal Winton International Collectors' Club, Dancer's End, Northall, Bedfordshire, England LU6 2EU; Royal Winton Collectors' Club, 2 Kareela Road, Baulkham Hills, Australia 2153.

Website: www.chintz.net/mail_list.

Reproduction Alert: In the last couple of years, with the rising prices of chintz, both Royal Winton and James Kent have started to reproduce some of their more popular patterns. Royal Winton is reproducing Welbeck, Florence, Summertime and Julia. In 1999, it added Marion, Majestic, Royalty, and Richmond and plan to add Stratford. James Kent reproduced Du Barry, Hydrangea, and Rosalynde, as well as creating several new colorways of old patterns. Contact the factories for current production lists to avoid confusing old and new chintz.

Advisor: Susan Scott.

Elijah Cotton "Lord Nelson"

Cake Plate, tab handles, Black Beauty pattern 245.00
Demitasse Cup and Saucer, Heather pattern 65.00
Jug, 5", Rosetime pattern 550.00
Muffineer, covered, Rosetime pattern 295.00
Plate, 8-1/2" sq, Rosetime pattern 175.00
Salt and Pepper on Tray, Marina pattern 250.00
Stacking Teapot, totally patterned, Skylark pattern 1,795.00

Grimwades Royal Winton

Basket, Rowsley, Shrewsbury pattern 500.00
Breakfast Set, Floral Feast pattern 1,450.00
Butter Pat, Somerset 95.00
Cheese Keep, Rex shape, Spring pattern 695.00
Coffeepot, Albans shape, Balmoral pattern 1,000.00
Cream and Sugar, Balmoral pattern 225.00
Cream and Sugar, on tray, Majestic pattern 495.00
Cup and Saucer, Marion pattern 115.00
Cup and Saucer, Julia pattern 245.00

Candy box, English Rose, Royal Winton, $395. Photo courtesy Susan Scott.

Jam Pot, Rheims, silver lid, Royalty pattern 395.00
Jug, Albans shape 4-1/2", Cotswold pattern 475.00
Nut Dish, large, Evesham 425.00
Plate, 10" round, Sweet Pea pattern 275.00
Salt and Pepper, on tray, Mayfair pattern 245.00
Teapot, Two cup, Albans shape, Sunshine pattern 750.00
Teapot, One cup Countess shape, Majestic pattern 795.00
Tennis Set, cup and undertray, Stratford pattern 425.00
Toast Rack, five bar, Eleanor pattern 375.00
Vase, bud , Welbeck pattern 425.00

James Kent Ltd.

Breakfast Set, Apple Blossom pattern 1,200.00
Cake Plate, Tab Handles, 10" x 9-1/2" Du Barry 175.00
Celery Dish, 13" x 6-1/2", Apple Blossom 325.00
Cream and Sugar, Du Barry pattern 150.00
Cup and saucer, Crazy Paving shape 95.00
Egg Cup Set, four egg cups on tray, Marigold pattern 395.00
Jug, Dutch shape 4", Silverdale pattern 195.00

Kinver bud vase, Royal Winton, $225. Photo courtesy Susan Scott.

Rheims jampots, Royal Winton, Hazel; small, $195; large, $225. Photo courtesy Susan Scott.

Nut Dish, 3" sq, Apple Blossom pattern 85.00
Plate, 7" round, Rosalynde pattern 135.00
Tray, 10" x 5", Hydrangea pattern 150.00

Midwinter Ltd.
Biscuit Barrel, chrome lid, Brama pattern 550.00
Bowl, salad, silver rim, Brama pattern 395.00

A.G. Richardson "Crown Ducal"
Bowl, 9-1/2" octagonal, Florida pattern.......................................650.00
Cake Plate, 8", metal handle, Primula pattern 125.00
Breakfast Set, Pink Chintz pattern 3,200.00
Comport, 8", Purple Chintz pattern 525.00
Cup and Saucer, Ivory Chintz pattern...125.00
Plate, 8" d, Ivory Chintz pattern 95.00
Teapot, four cup, Priscilla pattern..495.00
Vase
   6-1/4", Purple Chintz pattern 375.00
   9-1/4", Pink Chintz pattern...725.00

Shelley Potteries Ltd.
Cup and Saucer
   Melody pattern..125.00
   Oleander shape, Rock Garden pattern..................................165.00
Pin Dish, 4-1/2", Maytime pattern 70.00
Plate, 6", Summer Glory pattern 95.00
Teapot, six cup, Rock Garden pattern..775.00
Muffin Server, 8", covered, Primrose pattern 350.00

CHRISTMAS ITEMS

History: The celebration of Christmas dates back to Roman times. Several customs associated with modern Christmas celebrations are traced back to early pagan rituals.

Father Christmas, believed to have evolved in Europe in the 7th century, was a combination of the pagan god Thor, who judged and punished the good and bad, and St. Nicholas, the generous Bishop of Myra. Kris Kringle originated in Germany and was brought to America by the Germans and Swiss who settled in Pennsylvania in the late 18th century.

In 1822, Clement C. Moore wrote "A Visit From St. Nicholas" and developed the character of Santa Claus into the one we know today. Thomas Nast did a series of drawings for Harper's Weekly from 1863 until 1886 and further solidified the character and appearance of Santa Claus.

References: Robert Brenner, *Christmas Past*, 3rd ed., Schiffer Publishing, 1996; ——, *Christmas through the Decades*, Schiffer Publishing, 1993; Barbara Fahs Charles and J. R. Taylor, *Dream of Santa*, Gramercy Books, 1992; Beth Dees, *Santa's Guide to Contemporary Christmas Collectibles*, Krause Publications, 1997; Jill Gallina, *Christmas Pins Past and Present*, Collector Books, 1996; George Johnson, *Christmas Ornaments, Lights & Decorations* (1987, 1998 value update), Vol. II (1996), Vol. III (1996), Collector Books; Constance King, *Christmas Customs, Antiques, Decorations & Traditions*, Antique Collectors' Club, 1999; Chris Kirk, *Joy of Christmas Collecting*, L-W Book Sales, 1994; James S. Morrison, *Vintage View of Christmas Past*, Shuman Heritage Press, 1995; Mary Morrison, *Snow Babies, Santas and Elves: Collecting Christmas Bisque Figures,* Schiffer Publishing, 1993; Margaret Schiffer, *Christmas Ornaments: A Festive Study,* Schiffer Publisher, 1984, 1995 value update; Clara Johnson Scroggins, *Silver Christmas Ornaments,* Krause Publications, 1997; Lissa Bryan-Smith and Richard Smith, *Holiday Collectibles, Vintage Flea Market Treasures Price Guide,* Krause Publications, 1998; Margaret and Kenn Whitmyer, *Christmas Collectibles,* 2nd ed., 1994, 1996 value update, Collector Books.

Collectors' Club: Golden Glow of Christmas Past, 6401 Winsdale St, Golden Valley, MN 55427.

Additional Listings: See *Warman's Americana & Collectibles* for more examples.

Advisors: Lissa Bryan-Smith and Richard M. Smith.

Advertising
Bank, molded rubber, Santa Clause holding a coin, toys in pack, mkd "Christmas Club A. Corp, N.Y. 1972"...6.00
Booklet, "When All The World Is Kin," 5" x 4", collection of Christmas stories, Christmas giveaway, Fowler, Dick, and Walker, The Boston Store, Wilkes-Barre, PA" 7.00
Calendar, 3" h, 7" l, celluloid, Christmas scene with holly border and 1929 calendar, giveaway from the Penny Specialty Shop, Selinsgrove, PA...15.00

Bank, Santa Claus, chalkware, USA, 1950s, 14" h, $45. Photo courtesy of Lissa Bryan-Smith and Richard Smith.

Candy Tin, 9" l, rect, red and green holly on white ground, mkd "Satin Finish, hard candies, div. of Luden's Inc., Reading, PA" 18.00

Catalog, Boston Store, Milwaukee, WI, 1945, 48 pgs, 8-1/2" x 11", "For An American Christmas" 20.00

Cracker Tin, 2-1/2" h, 11" l, 8" w, Christmas scene on hinged lid, red and gold trim on sides, mkd "NBC" on base 25.00

Matches, 4" x 2", "Season's Greetings," winter scene on cover, intact matches create Christmas scene, Boehmer's Garage, Milton, MA.15.00

Trade Card, child holding snowballs, "The White is King of all Sewing Machines, 80,000 now in use," reverse reads "J. Saltzer, Pianos, Organs, and Sewing Machines, Bloomsburg, Pa." 10.00

Candy Box
cardboard

4-1/2" l, 3" h, Christmas Greetings, three carolers, USA 4.00

6" x 5", pocketbook style, tuck-in flap, Merry Christmas, Santa in store window with children outside, mkd "USA" 15.00

8" h, four sided cornucopia, Merry Christmas, Santa, sleigh, and reindeer over village rooftops, string bail, USA 35.00

Children's Book
The Night Before Christmas, Clement C. Moore, Corrine Malvern illustrator, A Golden Book, Golden Press, 1975 .... 8.00

Rudolph The Red-Nosed Reindeer, Robert I. May, Maxton Publishers, Inc., 1939 .... 12.00

The Littlest Snowman, Charles Tazewell, Grosset Dunlap, NY, 1958 .... 18.00

Feather Tree
4' h, green goose feather wrapped branches with metal candleholders, painted white with green trim round wooden base, mkd "Germany" 400.00

Figure
Father Christmas

7" h, composition, pink face, red cloth coat, painted blue pants, black boots, mounted on mica-covered cardboard base, mkd "Japan" 90.00

8" h, papier-mâché, hollow molded, plaster covered, white coat, black boots, sprinkled with mica 300.00

Nativity, 7" h, composition, shepherd holding lamb, mkd "Germany" 12.00

Reindeer

1" h, pot metal, mkd "Germany" 18.00

4" h, celluloid, white 7.00

Santa Claus

3" h, bisque, long red coat, mkd "Japan" 25.00

Fairy Christmas Box, Fairbank's Fairy Soap, cloth covered, latch, 16" x 16", $170. Photo courtesy of Lissa Bryan-Smith and Richard Smith.

3" h, cotton batting, red, attached to cardboard house, mkd "Japan" 48.00

3" l, celluloid, molded, one-piece Santa, sleigh, and reindeer. 35.00

5" h, hard plastic, Santa on green plastic skis, USA 120.00

10" h, pressed cardboard, red hat and jacket, black boots 90.00

14" h, pressed cardboard, head, store display 95.00

Sheep, 3" h, composition body, carved wooden legs, covered with cloth or wool, glass eyes 40.00

Greeting Card
"Christmas Greetings," booklet style, emb diecut cov, color litho pictures on int. pgs, The Art Lithographic Publishing Co. 18.00

"Loving Greetings," flat card, two girls pictured hanging garland, c1910, mkd "Germany" 8.00

"Merry Christmas," series of 6 envelopes, decreasing in size, small card in last envelope, American Greeting Publishers, Cleveland, USA, 1933 .... 12.00

"Sincere Good Wishes," purple pansy with green leaves, greeting inside, Raphael Tuck & Sons, 1892 .... 7.00

House
cardboard

2" x 2", mica covered, wire loop on top, mkd "Czechoslovakia" 7.00

4" x 5", house and fence, sponge trees, mkd "USA" 10.00

Lantern
8" h, four sided, peaked top, wire bail, metal candleholder in base, black cardboard, colored tissue paper scenes, 1940s 25.00

Ornament
Angel

4" h, wax over composition, human hair wig, spun glass wings, cloth dress, Germany 55.00

8" h, chromolithograph, tinsel and lametta trim, pr 15.00

Ball, 2" d, silvered glass, any color 3.00

Beads, 72" l, glass, half inch multicolored beads, paper label mkd "Japan" 8.00

Bulldog, 3" h, Dresden, three-dimensional, mkd "Germany" 250.00

Camel,. 4" h, cotton batting, Germany 160.00

Cross, 4" h, beaded, 2-sided, silvered, wire hanger, paper label mkd "Czechoslovakia" 18.00

Drummer Boy, 3" h, wax, hollow, metal ring hanger, USA 5.00

Father Christmas on Donkey, 10" h, chromolithograph, blue robe, tinsel trim 25.00

Mandolin, 5" h, unsilvered glass, wrapped in lametta and tinsel .. 45.00

Parakeet, 5" h, multicolored glass, spun glass tail, mounted on metal clip 23.00

Pear, 3" h, cotton batting, mica highlights, paper leaf, wire hanger, Japan 12.00

Santa Claus in Chimney, 4" h, glass, Germany 75.00

Swan, 5" x 6", Dresden, flat, gold with silver, green, and red highlights 150.00

Tree Top, 11" h, 3 spheres stacked with small clear glass balls, silvered, lametta and tinsel trim, attached to blown glass hooks 90.00

Postcard
Germany

"Happy Christmas Wishes," Santa steering ship 10.00

"May Your Christmas Be Merry and Gay," photo card, sepia tones, Father Christmas peeking between 2 large wooden doors, wearing fur cap 18.00

Putz
Brush Tree, 6" h, green, mica-covered branches, wooden base 8.00

Christmas Tree Fence

Cast iron, silver, ornate gold trim, fifteen 10" l segments with posts, Germany 600.00

Wood, folding red and green sections, 48" l, USA 35.00

Choir Boy, 3" h, hard plastic, red and white 4.00

Penny Wooden, two children on seesaw, hand carved wood, multicolored, Nurenberg or Erzgebrige 32.00

Toy

Jack-in-the-Box, 9-1/2" h, "Santa Pops," hard plastic, red felt hat, orig box, Tigrette Industries, 1956 .... 30.00

Merry-Go-Round, wind-up, celluloid, green and red base, 4 white reindeer heads, Santa sitting under umbrella, Santa spins around, stars hanging from umbrella bounce of bobbing deer heads, orig box, Japan 65.00

Santa, 10" h, battery operated, metal covered with red and white plush suit and hat, soft plastic face, holding metal want with white star light, wand moves up and down and lights up while Santa turns head....90.00

CIGAR CUTTERS

History: Counter and pocket cigar cutters were used at the end of the 19th and the beginning of the 20th centuries. They were a popular form of advertising. Pocket-type cigar cutters often were a fine piece of jewelry that attached to a watch chain.

Reference: Jerry Terranova and Douglas Congdon-Martin, *Antique Cigar Cutters and Lighters,* Schiffer Publishing, 1996; —, *Great Cigar Stuff for Collectors,* Schiffer Publishing, 1997.

Advertising

Betsy Ross 5¢ Cigars, nickel plated placard with paper image of Betsy surrounded by emb wording, cast iron base, lever on base pushed to expose cigar cutter, damage to adv 310.00

Brunhoff Manufacturing Co., framed Havana Cigar adv on top, 1906, cast iron, counter type 400.00

Country Gentleman 5c, chrome plated, ornate counter top plate 110.00

Fifth Avenue Cigar, keywind pocket type................................. 45.00

Home Run Cigars, reverse painted on glass, key wind mechanism, H. F. Kohler Cigar Manufacturer, Nashville, Pa., late 19th/early 20th C baseball game vignette on front, similar scenes on side, 8-1/4" w, 6-1/2" d, 4-1/2" h, some paint chipped off 1,600.00

Hotel Sherman, figural street light, red globe, ornate base, mkd "Reed & Barton"... 250.00

Lillian Russell Cigar Five Cents, cast metal, countertop, emb red letters, 8-1/2" l, 6-3/4" h 275.00

Scissors type, Castenada Perfecto, back emb with factory scene and "Castaneda Cigar Factories, Virtudes 129 Habana/Pat. March 20, '10, I.H.A. Struck, New York, USA, German Silver, $70.

Louis Bergdull Brewing Co., Philadelphia, china, patent 1904, cigar cutter and ashtray, wording around match holder on top, 5" w, 4" h.. 165.00

Master Workman, decal, long handle 85.00

Tutt's Liver Pills, captain's wheel, cast metal, adv on reverse, wheel spins to expose cigar cutters, 6" w, 6" h, some surface rust....550.00

Brass, cast, rect, keywind, cast inside "Erie Specialty Co. Erie Pa Pat. Feb 19 1888," 6-1/2" w, 5" d, 3-1/2" h 100.00

Figural

Arrowhead, SP, enamel dec, pocket knife type 125.00

Boy sitting on ornate rock, metal, 7" h.................................. 400.00

Burro, heavy cast iron, base lever pushed to operate cigar cutter, ears and tail move, cigar snuffer on saddle with emb pots and pans, minor paint loss 525.00

Crying Child, cast iron, painted black, gray base, cigar in mouth, 4-3/4" h, 4-1/2" l 415.00

Man wearing fez, cast metal, right hand lowered to activate cutter, shield dated "1881," wood base, 7" h 250.00

Ship's Wheel, brass plated tin, handle revolves to expose cigar cutter, 5" h, minor surface rust.. 65.00

Trumpet, brass, pocket knife type 50.00

Silver, sterling, pocket type

Fob 25.00

Scissors, repousse dec 45.00

CIGAR STORE FIGURES

History: Cigar store figures were familiar sights in front of cigar stores and tobacco shops starting about 1840. Figural themes included Sir Walter Raleigh, sailors, Punch figures, and ladies, with Indians being the most popular.

Most figures were carved in wood, although some also were made in metal and papier-mâché for a short time. Most carvings were life size or slightly smaller and were brightly painted. A coating of tar acted as a preservative against the weather. Of the few surviving figures, only a small number have their original bases. Most replacements were necessary because of years of wear and usage by dogs.

Use of figures declined when local ordinances were passed requiring shopkeepers to move the figures inside at night. This soon became too much trouble, and other forms of advertising developed.

References: Edwin O. Christensen, *Early American Wood Carvings,* Dover Publications, out of print; A.W. Pendergast and W. Porter Ware, *Cigar Store Figures,* The Lightner Publishing Corp., out of print.

Blackamore, 27" h, carved wood, old polychrome dec, 19th C, minor damage to right hand 4,750.00

Indian Brave, 17-1/2" h, carved wood, orig polychrome over green, 19th C, damage to right shoulder and chip from base 2,000.00

Indian Chief

27-1/2" h, counter type, pine, holding bunch of cigars in raised right hand, feathered headdress, orange costume, green cloak, leather fringed leggings, mounted on sq painted base, 19th C ... 8,250.00

88" h, pine, arm raised shielding eyes, bunch of cigars in other hand, one foot resting on rock, wearing feathered headdress, feather trimmed costume with leggings, painted green, red, and yellow, orig base inscribed "Ed A Feltham, Cigars and Tobacco," orig bars surround top of base, c1880 .... 36,500.00

Indian Princess, 61" h, carved wood, gold over polychrome, weathered, age cracks, loose three feather headdress................. 1,575.00

Indian Squaw, 45-1/2" h, carrying box quiver, applied carved and polychromed arrows, circular bosses and tomahawk, painted, mounted on metal base, left arm missing, American, c1870 .... 26,000.00

Punch, 50" h, pine, carved and painted, holding bunch of cigars in one

Indian, one outstretched, holding tomahawk, other holding long spear, worn base reads "Pipes and Tobacco," 9' h, $9,900.

hand, other hand raised, circular base, early 20th C 3,000.00
Scotsman, 38-1/2" h, carved and painted, orig polychrome over gesso, base carved "tobacco, snuff and cigars" 3,600.00
Turk
   19" h, carved wood, orig polychrome, smoking pipe, 19th C 2,000.00
   27" h, carved wood, orig polychrome over gesso, 19th c, 2 chips off base, missing chip from turban 2,800.00

CINNABAR

History: Cinnabar, a ware made of numerous layers of a heavy mercuric sulfide, often is referred to as vermilion because of the red hue of most pieces. It was carved into boxes, buttons, snuff bottles, and vases. The best examples were made in China.

Box, cov, Chinese figures in garden, 3-3/4" x 5-3/8", $95.

Bowl, 8" d, garden scene, blue enamel int................................. 225.00
Box, 3-3/4" x 5-3/8", Chinese figures in garden setting 95.00
Cup, 4-1/2" d, dragon handles, c1900 .... 225.00
Dish, 10-3/4" d, deeply carved, leafy melon vines, black lacquer base 900.00
Ginger Jar, 12" h, figural landscape dec, Chinese, mounted as lamp 425.00
Incense Burner, pagoda type, Taoist mask design, c1900 .... 1,300.00
Jar, 4" h, flowering plants, carved floral scrolls, diaper ground, domed cov, gilt metal rim and finial, price for pr 150.00
Plate, 12-3/4" d, double dragon design 375.00
Tray, 15" l, bird and flower scene, reddish brown 625.00
Vase, 10" h, carved continuous scenic dec, Chinese, pr 120.00

CIVIL WAR MEMORABILIA

History: America's heritage is rich in memories of the greatness of this nation, but it is also perhaps slightly blemished over the civil war that divided the country during the years of 1861 to 1865. This period of turmoil has been well documented so that we might learn from what our ancestors sacrificed; their diaries show us how hard life was during those times, just as the artifacts we have from this period reinforce what they valued, how fiercely they defended their principals.

Today collectors are still finding this historic period fascinating. And because of the numerous historical battlefield sites, museums, and other places of interest, many more are able to experience this exciting time. Some collectors specialize in the North or South, others find the photography or journals of the era more interesting. Because the impact of the war was so far reaching and so important to people's lives, many treasures await the collector.

References: Ron Manion, *American Military Collectibles Price Guide,* Antique Trader Books, 1995; Marc Newman, *Civil War Knives,* Paladin Press, 1998; H. A. Ogden, *Uniforms of the United States Army,* 1774-1889, Dover Publications, 1998; Sydney B. Vernon, *Vernon's Collectors' Guide to Orders, Medals, and Decorations,* published by author, 1986.

Periodicals: *Men at Arms,* 222 W. Exchange St., Providence, RI 02903; *Militaria Magazine,* P.O. Box 995, Southbury, CT 06488; *Military Collector Magazine,* P.O. Box 245, Lyon Station, PA 19536; *Military Collector News,* P.O. Box 702073, Tulsa, OK 74170; *Military Images,* RD1 Box 99A, Henryville, PA 18332; *Military Trader,* P.O. Box 1050, Dubuque, IA 52004; *North South Trader's Civil War,* P.O. Box Drawer 631, Orange, VA 22960.

Collectors' Clubs: American Society of Military Insignia Collectors, 526 Lafayette Ave., Palmerton, PA 18071; Association of American Military Uniform Collectors, P.O. Box 1876, Elyria, OH 44036; Company of Military Historians, North Main Street, Westbrook, CT, 06498; Imperial German Military Collectors Association, 82 Atlantic St., Keyport, NJ 07735; Karabiner Collector's Network, P.O. Box 5773, High Point, NC 27262; Militaria Collectors Society, 137 S. Almar Dr., Ft Lauderdale, FL 33334; Orders and Medals Society of America, P.O. Box 484, Glassboro, NJ 08028.

Museums: There are excellent Civil War-era museums located all through the country. Many are associated with a specific military unit or battle field.

Reproduction Alert: Civil War items have been reproduced for many years. Know your source and consider condition, provenance, and other standard measures of determining whether an item has been reproduced.

Autograph, carte-de-visite photograph
Grant, Ulysses S., half figure seated portrait, sgd "U. S. Grant/Lt. Gen. U.S.A." on lower mount, reverse printed "Published by E. & H. T. Anthony 501 Broadway, New York," dark image and dark signature 4,500.00
Lee, Robert E., sgd "R. E. Lee" on lower portion of front, sgd, inscribed, and dated Aug. 25th, 1868, on back by his wife, Mary Curtis Lee, back mkd "M. B. Brady & Co.'s National Photographic Portrait Gallery, 352 Pennsylvania Avenue, Washington," dark signature 7,000.00
Stuart, James Ewell Brown, Confederate general, killed at Chancellorsville, sgd "J. E. B. Stuart, Major General, C. S. A." 4,800.00
Autograph, letter signed, William Wirt Allen, sgd as Brig Gen. Commanding, 1 pg 8vo, Headquarters of Allen's Cavalry Div. (S Carolina), Feb 9, 1865, to Lt. Hudson, A.A.A. Genl, regarding safety of wagon train during Carolina Campaign 695.00
Badge
Eighth Corp., 1" six-pointed star, soldered button type shank . 30.00
Sixth Corp., 7/8" cross, soldered brass pins, two missing 30.00
Sixth Corp., 1-1/8", engraved cross, "Co. M. 9th N.Y. H.A.," traces of blue filler in center, spring pin back 95.00
Book
Hardee's Tactics, 1861, soft cover, identified in pencil "James C. Cole from his brother Dr. Whalin Cole C.S.A.," cover wear and stains 550.00
McElroy, John, *This Was Andersonville,* 16th Illinois Calvary, ©1966, dj 35.00
Randolph, J. W., *Regulation's of the Army of Confederate States,* Richmond, 1863, hard cover, penciled inscription "Arthur Huger, Dec 1863, Savannah," minor stains 550.00
Ropes, John Codman, *The Army Under Pope (Battle of Cedar Mountain thru the Battle of Chantilly)* 1881, illus and maps .. 35.00
Canteen, 7" d, 2-3/4" h, red painted wood, cheese box construction, yellow lettering, initialed "S. D." obverse, "14" on reverse, minor paint loss, hangers missing 980.00
Chevron, Sergeant's, yellow 70.00
Drum, worn eagle dec, wings and head remaining in flaking paint, red hoops, early repair, label inside "Edward Baack, N.Y.," head stenciled "D. C. Connelly Stewarts Run, PA," sold with copies of war record 800.00
Epaulets, pr, cased, 7-1/2" x 9-1/4" x 6-1/4", by Schuyler, Hartley & Graham, gilded finish, buttons marked "G. & Cie. Paris," tin box with worn japanning 165.00
Ephemera
Diary, Union Soldier's, Spencer Hall of Guersney Co., Ohio, served in 30th and 185th Companies of Ohio Infantry Volunteers, from July 1861 to Sept 1865, 12 mo pocket diary contains 37 pages of writing, orig leather-covered boards, begins just before enlistment, giving details of battles, marches, described Second Battle of Bull Run, other interesting content 1,900.00
Harpers Weekly Page, "A Rebel Guerilla in a Western Town," colored, gilt frame, 20" x 26-1/2" 85.00
Print, Battle of Malvern Hill, Currier & Ives, lithograph, stains and small tear, 11-3/8" x 13-7/8" 50.00
Rebellion Memorial, for Co. A. 9th N. H. Vol. Infantry, detailed print, some damage, shadow box frame, 19-1/4" x 23-1/2" 55.00
Regimental Roster, Co. B., 160th Regt. NY Vols, bright colors, short tear and stains at top, shadow box frame, 21-1/2" x 26-1/2" ... 140.00
Union Muster Roll, 54th Regiment, New York State Volunteers, partially printed document, 1-1/2" pgs large oblong folio, Arlington Heights, VA, Aug. 31, 1862, first page lists 11 officers and 59 privates of Company C, under command of Col. Eugene A. Kozlay, columns of information, many noted as being wounded at Battle of Bull Run on Aug. 29 .... 350.00
Flask, 4-7/8" l, Colt type revolver, eagle, stars, shield and "E. Pluribis Unum," good patina, minor dents 200.00

Hat
Artillery Kepi, mkd "Manufactured by Bent & Bush-Boston," red wool, white piping, black band around base, eagle "A" buttons, moth damage, lining separating 650.00
Hardee, sgd "U. S. Army extra manufacture," bugle, "I" and "Z" insignias, brass eagle and shield plate, 6" x 13-1/2", several repairs 1,550.00
Insignia
Artillery, brass, crossed cannons, one back loop missing, 1-3/4" x 3-1/4" 85.00
Artillery, embroidered, crossed cannons, work red velvet center, black velvet ground 140.00
Bugle, embroidered, small breaks in threads, 2-3/8" l 85.00
Corps of Engineers, brass, 1-1/2" x 1-3/4" 220.00
Crossed sabre, embroidered, very work, 2-7/8" l 55.00
Infantry Bugle, brass, 2" x 3-1/2" 75.00
Infantry Officer, heavy gold thread with sequins around bell and mouthpiece, backing cup in oval, moth holes 110.00
Infantry Officer, hat, gold embroidery, tufted area in crook of horn with silver, 2" x 3-3/8" 145.00
Infantry Officer, kepi, embroidered wreath, gold thread, applied brass "3," 2" x 3" 90.00
Officer's, emb brass, crossed cannon, 95% gilding remaining, 2-1/2" l 55.00
Ordinance, brass, good patina, one pin missing, 1-5/8" h 50.00
Photograph
2-3/8" x 2-5/8", eighth plate ambrotype, Infantryman, seated, wearing kepi with bugle insignia, cased 200.00
2-3/8" x 2-7/8", Brittian Brothers, Hamptons Legion, S.C., one ambrotype, other tin, cased as pair 550.00
2-3/8" x 2-7/8", eighth plate tintype, Infantryman and his wife, good image, tinting on faces, worn case 275.00
2-3/8" x 2-7/8", eighth plate tintype, Infantryman, waist-up image, wearing kepi with bugle insignia, patriotic case with restored hinge 145.00
2-3/8" x 2-7/8", eighth plate tintype, soldier, wearing kepi, crossed cannons, identified as "Elijah E. Clapp" inside case, PVT. Colvin's battery B., ILL, first Lt. Artillery, cased 220.00

Daugerreotype, soldier wearing full uniform, holding sword, gold dec liner, gutta percha case, 2-1/2" x 2", $125.

2-3/8" x 2-7/8", ninth plate ambrotype, Confederate, seated, wearing battle shirt with red trim, cased, small spots in background 385.00

2-3/8" x 2-7/8", ninth plate ambrotype, Confederate, seated, wearing slouch hat, cased, halo effect in emulsion 220.00

2-3/8" x 3", ninth plate ambrotype, first Lieutenant wearing double breasted Confederate regulation jacket, cased, minor scratches and discoloration along liner 150.00

2-1/2" x 3", eighth plate ambrotype, Confederate soldier, seated, holding Remington type revolver, minor background spots, thermoplastic case with edge chips 660.00

2-1/2" x 3", eighth plate tintype, seated Infantryman, holding sword, thermoplastic case with leaves and strawberries, small chips on edges 315.00

2-1/2" x 3", ninth plate ambrotype, Confederate holding musket, light image, damage to thermoplastic case 275.00

2-1/2" x 3", ninth plate ambrotype, Confederate Lieutenant, shoulder strap insignias and buttons with gilding, ornate thermoplastic case by Peck 550.00

2-1/2" x 3-3/4", ninth plate tintype, enlisted man wearing forage cap, coat, holding musket with bayonet, half case 250.00

2-5/8" x 3", ambrotype, two Confederate soldiers, brothers wearing battle shirts, 3 stars on front, faces tinted, scrollwork thermoplastic case, minor wear to case 550.00

3" x 3-5/8", sixth plate tintype, Union Infantryman, slouch hat, gilt insignia and epaulets, pants tinted blue, cased, small rust spots 175.00

3-1/8" x 3-5/8", eighth plate ambrotype, Confederate private, sixth plate, seated, double breasted coat with gilt buttons, mat sgd "Lanneau, Artist," replaced hinge on case 275.00

3-1/8" x 3-5/8", eighth plate ambrotype, Infantryman, blue tint on coat, holding hat, cased, minor scratches along edge of liner 200.00

3-1/8" x 3-5/8", quarter plate tintype, young Infantryman, full view, musket and cartridge box, cased 440.00

3-1/8" x 3-5/8", sixth plate ambrotype, seated Infantryman, wearing forage cap, bowie knife and revolver in belt, revolvers in each hand, patriotic case with gilding 450.00

3-1/8" x 3-5/8", sixth plate ambrotype, three Infantryman, 40th N. Y., all seated, kepis on table, cased...................450.00

3-1/8" x 3-5/8", sixth plate tintype, Infantryman, seated, holding small frame revolver across his chest, wearing kepi and U. S. oval belt plate, identified as "Geo. S. Marsh, Ohio Vol. Inf.," cased........475.00

3-1/8" x 3-5/8", sixth plate tintype, Infantryman, standing in uniform, musket and bayonet in belt, cased 315.00

3-1/8" x 3-5/8", sixth plate tintype, young Infantryman, kepi, musket, cartridge box, and cap box, gilt buttons and plate, patriotic case, minor emulsion spots 315.00

3-1/8" x 5-1/8", sixth plate tintype, Infantry second Lt., wearing kepi with gilded bugle and "8" insignia, shoulder insignia, cased, minor bends and spotting 165.00

3-1/8" x 5-1/8", sixth plate tintype, standing Infantryman, standing against backdrop, holding musket with bayonet, wearing kepi, bowtie, and colt revolver in belt, identified as Perry Haywood, Iowa, cased.................................385.00

3-1/4" x 3-5/8", tintype, seated officer, revolver in belt, cased, light studio backdrop, image clear................135.00

3-1/4" x 3-5/8", tintype, Union soldier in rain gear, standing before backdrop, cased 175.00

3-1/4" x 3-3/4", sixth plate tintype, Union sergeant, bold stripes, "I & 12" on collar, Littfield, Parsons & Co. thermoplastic case, two corner chips 250.00

3-1/4" x 3-3/4", tintype, Union officer, wearing Hardee hat, holder, and sword drawn from scabbard, gilding, thermoplastic case shows man and woman with palm trees, edge chips..........525.00

3-1/4" x 4-3/4", quarter plate ambrotype, Confederate soldier wearing belt with bayonet scabbard, holding musket, some spots in background, area of emulsion wear, cased 550.00

3-1/2" x 3-1/4", carte de visite, identified on reverse as Nathaniel Pottle, age 22, 8th Reg Maine Vol., killed at Petersburg, VA, July 4, 1864, leatherette case 195.00

3-5/8" x 3-1/4", tintype, Confederate wearing double breasted shell jacket, gilded buttons, cased 110.00

.3-5/8" x 4-5/8", quarter plate ambrotype, Union infantryman, wearing military coat and kepi, resting elbow on tinted red and white flag, cased, hinged damage................315.00

3-5/8" x 4-5/8", quarter plate tintype, cavalryman, standing against camp backdrop, wearing gauntlets, cased, minor bend in plate 380.00

3-5/8" x 4-5/8", quarter plate tintype, sergeant seated against backdrop holding sword, kepi, tinted red sash, cased...............385.00

3-3/4" x 3-1/4", sixth plate ambrotype, seated young man in uniform, holding rifle with fixed bayonet, thermoplastic union case with eagle, shield and flags.................................175.00

4-3/4" x 6-1/2", carte-de-visite, Infantryman in front of tents, haversack reads "71-N.Y.," glued to later mat, period frame with gold repaint 200.00

5" x 7", albumen photo, Capt. Daniel Nichols, 51st PA Vols., chest-up image, framed................145.00

5-1/4" x 7-3/8", albumen photo, Major Wm. W. Anderson, 20th PA Cavalry, 181st Regt., accidentally killed at Harper's Ferry, framed................475.00

Print, Currier & Ives, hand colored lithograph, 14-3/8" x 18-1/4" frame
   Battle of Chancellorsville, VA, margin stains, 10" x 14" 55.00
   Bombardment of Ft. Sumter, 12" x 15-1/8" 55.00

Snare Drum, 13 gold painted stars in an arch above name "Hubert O. Moore 36th RegT. Mass. Vols.," also lists 14 battles and engagements of the regiment, paper label on int. "Massachusetts Drum Manufactory John C. Haynes & Co. 38 Court St. Boston Wholesale & Retail Dealers in Sheet Music, Musical Instruments & Musical Merchandise," woven carrying strap, replaced rope, head missing 4,370.00

Shoulder Strap
   Captain of Sharp Shooters, gold thread on green ground, edge wear 75.00
   Colonel's, eagle, blue ground, wear 185.00
   Infantry Captain, medium blue ground, gold border, wear 80.00
   Major of Staff, with leaves, blue ground, wear......................195.00
   Second Lt. of Artillery, faded red backing 50.00
   Second Lt. of Cavalry, Smith Pat., yellow backing 65.00

Stereoview, E. & H. T. Anthony's War View Series
   Burial of Dead at Fredericksburg, VA 75.00
   Ft. Concoran, VA 100.00
   Lt. Gen. Grant at his headquarters, Brady standing at corner.................................120.00

Token, Dix, copper colored, picture of flag on reverse, 3/4" d, $65.

Signal Corp., Cobbs Hill 100.00
Stencil Kit, 8-3/4" h x 5-1/2" w tin case, brass alphabet stencils, pan, brush, nameplate "N. G. Batchelder" 110.00
Sword, Ames 1850 Infantry Officer, 30-1/4" etched and engraved blade "Chicopee, Mass" address, cast hilt with open work, 36-1/4" l leather scabbard and brass bands and drag, engraved "Lt. Geo. Trembley, 174th N.Y.S.I." 1,980.00
Tin Container, 3" h, 4-1/4" d, bale handle 85.00
Tobacco Box, 4-1/2" x 8-1/2" x 6-1/2", twist of Yankee Nests, machine dovetailing, good patina 145.00

CLEWELL POTTERY

History: Charles Walter Clewell was first a metal worker and secondarily a potter. In the early 1900s, he opened a small shop in Canton, Ohio, to produce metal overlay pottery.

Metal on pottery was not a new idea, but Clewell was perhaps the first to completely mask the ceramic body with copper, brass or "silvered" or "bronzed" metals. One result was a product whose patina added to the character of the piece over time.

Since Clewell operated on a small scale with little outside assistance, only a limited quantity of his artwork exists. He retired at the age of 79 in 1955, choosing not to reveal his technique to anyone else.

Marks: Most of the wares are marked with a simple incised "Clewell" along with a code number. Because Clewell used pottery blanks from other firms, the names "Owens" or "Weller" are sometimes found.

References: Paul Evans, *Art Pottery of the United States,* 2nd ed., Feingold & Lewis Publishing Corp., 1987; Ralph and Terry Kovel, *Kovels' American Art Pottery,* Crown Publishers, 1993.

Museum: John Besser Museum, Alpena, MI.

Candlesticks, pr, 7" h, 3-1/2" d, copper clad, 4 sided, dark bronzed patina, unmarked 1,300.00
Jardiniere, 14" h, ovoid, matte finish 130.00

Vase, relief flower design, twisted flask body, mkd "Z/ Owens/120," 4-3/4" h, $425.

Mug, 4-1/2" h, copper clad, riveted design, applied monogram, relief signature 65.00
Vase
  5" h, 4-1/2" d, spherical, copper clad, verdigris patina, partly varnished, incised "Clewell/382" 650.00
  7-1/2" h, 4" d, ovoid, copper clad, verdigris to bronze patina, incised "Clewell/351-25" 1,000.00
  11" h, 5" d, bulbous, copper clad, bronzed finish, incised "Clewell/ 357-5," cleaned some time ago 500.00
Vessel, 10-1/2" h, 8-1/4" d, milk can shape, copper clad, emb Oriental design, bronzed finish, illegible mark 800.00

CLARICE CLIFF

History: Clarice Cliff, born on Jan. 20, 1899, in Tunstall, Staffordshire, England, was one of the major pottery designers of the 20th century. At the age of 13, she left school and went to Lingard, Webster & Company where she learned freehand painting. In 1916, Cliff was employed at A. J. Wilkinson's Royal Staffordshire Pottery, Burslem. She supplemented her in-house training by attending a local school of art in the evening.

In 1927, her employer sent her to study sculpture for a few months at the Royal College of Art in London. Upon returning, she was placed in charge of a small team of female painters at the Newport Pottery, taken over by Wilkinson in 1920. Cliff designed a series of decorative motifs which were marketed as "Bizarre Ware" at the 1928 British Industries Fair.

Throughout the 1930s, Cliff added new shapes and designs to the line. Her inspiration came from art magazines, books on gardening, and plants and flowers. Cliff and her Bizarre Girls gave painting demonstrations in the stores of leading English retailers. The popularity of the line increased.

World War II halted production. When the war ended, the hand painting of china was not resumed. In 1964, Midwinter bought the Wilkinson and Newport firms.

The original names for some patterns have not survived. It is safe to rely on the handwritten or transfer-printed name on the base. The Newport pattern books in the Wilkinson's archives at the Hanley Library also are helpful.

Clarice Cliff's birth centenary was marked in 1999, with several major exhibitions in England. Christie's South Kensington, in London, held three Clarice Cliff auctions and plan three more for the year 2000. Clarice attracts more collectors every year and every auction breaks another price record.

Marks: In the summer of 1985, Midwinters produced a series of limited-edition reproductions to honor Clarice Cliff. They are clearly marked "1985" and contain a special amalgamated backstamp.

References: Susan and Al Bagdade, *Warman's English & Continental Pottery & Porcelain,* 3rd Edition, Krause Publications, 1998; Richard Green and Des Jones, *Rich Designs of Clarice Cliff,* published by authors, 1995 (available from Carole A. Berk, Ltd., 8020 Norfolk Ave., Bethesda, MD 20814); Leonard R. Griffin, *Clarice Cliff: The Art of Bizarre,* Pavilion Books, 1999; Leonard R. Griffin and Susan Pear Meisel, *Clarice Cliff,* Harry N. Abrams, 1994; Howard and Pat Watson, *Clarice Cliff Price Guide,* Francis-

Joseph Books, 1995.

Collectors' Club: Clarice Cliff Collector's Club, Fantasque House, Tennis Drive, The Park, Nottingham, NG7 1AE, England.

Website: http://www.claricecliff.com/

Advisor: Susan Scott.

Reproduction Alert: In 1986, fake *Lotus* vases appeared in London and quickly spread worldwide. Very poor painting and patchy, uneven toffee-colored honey glaze are the clues to spotting them. Collectors also must be alert to marked pieces on which patterns were added to originally plain ground.

Notes: Bizarre and Fantasque are not patterns. Rather they indicate the time frame of production—Bizarre being used from 1928-1937 and Fantasque from 1929-1934.

Candlesticks, pr, 3-1/4" h, Melon pattern, band of overlapping fruit, orange glaze, yellow, blue-green, and brown outline, stamped on base in black ink "Hand Painted Fantasque by Clarice Cliff Wilkinson Ltd. England," c1930, minor glaze nicks, 2 small firing cracks to inside of rim of one candlestick 1,380.00
Cup, 3-5/8" h, Chintz pattern, predominately orange, brown, and black glaze, stamped "Hand Painted Bizarre by Clarice Cliff, Newport Pottery, England," gilt Lawley's stamp 460.00
Cup and Saucer
    Bizarre, conical shape, Orange Autumn, printed factory marks 425.00
    Fantasque Bizarre, Pastel Melon, printed factory marks 550.00
Honey Pot
    3-3/4" h, Bizarre, Orange Roof Cottage, printed factory marks 1,565.00
    4" h, Beehive, Crocus, printed factory marks 585.00
Jam Pot, 4" h, Melon pattern, band of overlapping fruit, orange, yellow, blue, and green, brown outline, stamped on base in black ink, c1930, restoration to rim and side.. 690.00
Lotus Jug
    11-1/2" h, Fantasque Bizarre, twin handles, Autumn between orange bands 3,125.00
    12" h, Bizarre, single-handle, Viscaria, printed factory marks.. 1,475.00
Pitcher
    5-1/8" h, squared base, flattened spherical sides, Autumn (Balloon Trees) pattern, blue, yellow, green, orange, black, and purple, stamped on base "Registration Applied for Fantasque Hand Painted Bizarre by Clarice Cliff Newport Pottery England," minor glaze bubbles and nicks 920.00
    6-3/8" h, octagonal, Alpine pattern, trees and house dec, orange and black borders, stamped in black on base "Hand Painted Fantasque by Clarice Cliff Wilkinson, England," minor glaze flakes........ 1,725.00
Plate, Fantasque Bizarre
    7" d, Red Gardenia inside orange and yellow bands, printed factory marks 625.00
    9" d, House & Bridge inside orange, yellow, and black bands, printed factory marks 1,465.00
    10" d, Autumn (Balloon Trees), blue, yellow, green, and purple trees, orange striped border bands, base stamped "Fantasque Hand Painted Bizarre by Clarice Cliff Newport Pottery England," scratches 1,725.00
Preserve, 4-1/4" h, Bon Jour shape, Rhodanthe, printed factory marks 395.00
Sugar Shifter
    5" h, Bizarre, Bon Jour shape, Blue Firs, printed factory marks 3,125.00
    5" h, Bizarre, Lynton shape, Newlyn, printed factory marks .. 785.00
    5" h, Bon Jour Shape, Coral First, printed factory marks ... 1,750.00
    5-1/2" h, Bizarre, Conical, Mountain, printed factory marks 3,715.00
    5-3/4" h, Bizarre, Conical, Trees and House (Alpine) pattern, orange and black borders and trees, green rooftop and grass, base stamped

"Hand Painted Bizarre by Clarice Cliff Newport Pottery England," minor nicks to glaze, hairline to base 1,380.00
Teapot, 4-1/2" h, Bizarre, inverted conical form, angled handle and spout, orange, yellow, and black, lid stamped "Hand Painted Bizarre

Vases, from top left: Red Gardenia, Gibraltar and Red House & Tree. Photo courtesy Christie's South Kensington.

Charger, Coral Firs. Photo courtesy Christie's South Kensington.

by Clarice Cliff Newport Pottery, England," small glaze flakes, small chip to spout 2,185.00

Vase

2" h, miniature, ovoid, Sliced Fruit, between yellow and orange bands, printed factory marks 585.00

6" h, Original Bizarre, shape 186, band of triangles in red, blue, and yellow between red and blue bands, printed factory marks 780.00

8" h, Bizarre, shape 358, Appliqué Avignon between orange and black bands, printed and painted marks 3,500.00

8" h, Fantasque Bizarre, shape 360, Floreat between yellow and orange bands, printed factory marks 1,175.00

Zodiac Sign, 6-3/4" d, star shape, modeled in low relief, "Pisces"....875.00

CLIFTON POTTERY

History: The Clifton Art Pottery, Newark, New Jersey, was established by William A. Long, once associated with Lonhuda Pottery, and Fred Tschirner, a chemist.

Production consisted of two major lines: Crystal Patina, which resembled true porcelain with a subdued crystal-like glaze, and Indian Ware or Western Influence, an adaptation of the American Indians' unglazed and decorated pottery with a high-glazed black interior. Other lines included Robin's-Egg Blue and Tirrube. Robin's-Egg Blue is a variation of the crystal patina line but in blue-green instead of straw-colored hues and with a less-prominent crushed-crystal effect in the glaze. Tirrube, which is often artist signed, features brightly colored, slip-decorated flowers on a terra-cotta ground.

Marks: Marks are incised or impressed. Early pieces may be dated and impressed with a shape number. Indian wares are identified by tribes.

References: Paul Evans, *Art Pottery of the United States,* 2nd ed., Feingold & Lewis Publishing Corp., 1987; Ralph and Terry Kovel, *Kovels' American Art Pottery,* Crown Publishers, 1993.

Biscuit Jar, cov, 7" h, 4-1/4" d, gray-brown ground, enameled running ostrich and stork, florals, bail handle 300.00

Creamer, Crystal Patina, incised "Clifton," dated 225.00

Bowl, Indian Ware, red clay body, feather design, glazed black int., c1906, 3-1/2" d, 2-1/2" deep, $200.

Decanter, 11-1/2" h, rose shading to deep rose, purple flowers, gilt butterfly on neck, applied handle, marbleized rose and white stopper... 150.00

Jardiniere, 8-1/2" h, 11" d, Four Mile Ruin, Arizona, incised and painted motif, buff and black on brown ground, imp mark and incised inscription, hairline to rim 400.00

Sweetmeat Jar, 4" h, hp ducks and cranes, robin's egg blue ground, cow finial 375.00

Teapot, 6" h, brown and black geometric design 200.00

Vase

6-1/2" h, bulbous, Crystal Patina, incised "Clifton," dated 250.00

9-1/2" h, 4-1/2" d, bottle shape, Crystal Patina, incised "Clifton/158" 350.00

10" h, 7" d, angular handles, Crystal Patina, incised "Clifton"450.00

Vessel

4-1/2" h, ovoid, two handles, Crystal Patina, incised "Clifton," dated, firing line to base 65.00

8" h, 11" d, squat, Homolobi, bands of geometric umber designs, terra cotta ground, incised "Clifton/233," titled, flaking of glaze 450.00

CLOCKS

History: The sundial was the first man-made device for measuring time. Its basic disadvantage is well expressed by the saying: "Do like the sundial, count only the sunny days."

Needing greater dependability, man developed the water clock, oil clock, and the sand clock, respectively. All these clocks worked on the same principle—time was measured by the amount of material passing from one container to another.

The wheel clock was the next major step. These clocks can be traced back to the 13th century. Many improvements on the basic wheel clock were made and continue to be made. In 1934 the quartz crystal movement was introduced.

The recently invented atomic clock, which measures time by radiation frequency, only varies one second in a thousand years.

References: Robert W. D. Ball, *American Shelf and Wall Clocks,* Schiffer Publishing, 1992; F. J. Britten, *Old Clocks and Watches & Their Makers,* Antique Collectors' Club, 1999; Cesinsky & Webster, *English Domestic Clocks,* Antique Collectors' Club, 1999; J. E. Connell, *The Charlton Standard Catalogue of Canadian Clocks,* 2nd ed., Charlton Press, 1999; Brian Loomes, *Brass Dial Clocks,* Antique Collectors' Club, 1999; —, *Painted Dial Clocks,* Antique Collector's Club, 1994; Tran Duy Ly, *Seth Thomas Clocks & Movements,* Arlington Book Co., 1996; Derek Roberts, *Skeleton Clocks,* Antique Collectors' Club, 1999; Tom Robinson, *The Longcase Clock,* Antique Collectors' Club, 1999; Ronald Rose, *English Dial Clocks,* Antique Collectors' Club, 1999; Robert and Harriet Swedberg, *Price Guide to Antique Clocks,* Krause Publications, 1998; John Ware Willard, *Simon Willard and His Clocks,* Dover Publications, n.d.

Periodicals: *Clocks,* 4314 W. 238th St., Torrance, CA 90505.

Collectors' Club: National Association of Watch and Clock Collectors, Inc., 514 Poplar St., Columbia, PA 17512.

Museums: American Clock & Watch Museum, Bristol, CT; Greensboro Clock Museum, Greensboro, NC; National Association of Watch and Clock Collectors Museum, Columbia, PA; National Museum of American History, Washington, DC; Old Clock Museum, Pharr, TX; The Time Museum, Rockford, IL; Willard House & Clock Museum, Grafton, MA.

World Time Clock, technically sophisticated pendulum clock by Aug. Anderson, Lund, Sweden, c1900, $2,815. Photo courtesy of Auction Team Breker.

Notes: Identifying the proper model name for a clock is critical in establishing price. Condition of the works also is a critical factor. Examine the works to see how many original parts remain. If repairs are needed, try to include this in your estimate of purchase price. Few clocks are purchased purely for decorative value.

Advertising

Chew Friendship Cub Plug, face of man with moving mouth chewing Friendship Tobacco to the tic of the clock, pat'd Mar 2, 1886, 4" h...900.00

Electric Ad Clock Co., Chicago, cathedral shaped clock, drum in lower window rotates to promote advertising, wood front, rest sheet metal, c1933, 21-1/2" x 13", some chipping to veneer........................200.00

Gruen Watch, Williams Jewelry Co. on marquee at bottom, blue neon around perimeter, 15" x 15"......................................600.00

Hire's Root Beer, "Drink Hires Root Beer with Root Barks, Herbs," 15" d...250.00

Longine's Watches, "The World's Most Honored Watch," brass, 18-1/2" d..300.00

None Such Mincemeat, pumpkin face, 8-1/2" w, some wear......300.00

Reddy Kilowatt, compliments of Philadelphia Light and Electric, West-clox alarm clock, 5" h 350.00

Victrola Records, orig pendulum...2,100.00

Alarm

Attleboro, 36 hour, nickel plated case, owl dec, 9" h....................75.00

Bradley, brass, double bells, Germany 40.00

Champion, 30 hour, American movement, metal frame, ornamental feet, 9" h 75.00

New Haven, c1900, 30 hour, SP case, perfume bottle shape, beveled glass mirror, removable cut glass scent bottle, beaded handle 185.00

Thomas, Seth, 1919, one day time and alarm movement, second bit, metal case, 10 1/4" h...50.00

Banjo, Federal

Unidentified Maker

Massachusetts, c1820, mahogany and gilt gesso, mahogany case with molded brass bezel enclosing white painted metal dial, 8-day weight driven movement, eglomise tablets framed by gilt sepia moldings, flanked by brass side brackets, old refinish, restorations, 22-1/2" h...1,495.00

New England, c1825, mahogany, brass bezel enclosing white painted metal dial, 8-day weight-driven movement, eglomise table with house in landscape, half-round moldings, some imperfections, 32-1/2" h..1,265.00

Rhode Island, c1820, mahogany and gilt gesso, mahogany case with molded brass bezel enclosing white painted iron dial, A-frame type weight-driven movement, eglomise tablets showing Helios framed by spiral moldings, flanked by pierced brass slide brackets, restoration, 34" h...............................4,315.00

Willard, Simon, Roxbury, MA, c1815, mahogany inlaid, circular molded brass bezel enclosing white painted iron dial, 8-day weight driven brass movement, mahogany string inlaid and crossbanded framed throat and pendulum, box with white and green eglomise tablets, lower with fan design, oak leaves, and acorns, inscribed "S. Willard's Patent," flanking brass vine and brackets, restoration, 29-1/4" h.........................17,250.00

Bracket

Parke, Solomon, Federal case, mahogany veneer, old finish, brass feet, brass hands, brass fusee works, painted steel face with "Strike" and "Silent," labeled "Solomon Parke, Philadelphia," some veneer damage, old veneer repair, pendulum and keys, 17-3/4" h plus top handle 9,350.00

Regency, Bennett & Co., Norwich, c1810, brass inlaid and gilt bronze mounted mahogany, dial and backplate sgd, oak leaf spandrels, case inlaid with scrolls, gadrooned bun feet, 17" h, chips 4,325.00

Tiffany & Co., bronze, stepped rect shaped top, four acorn finials, cast foliate frieze, four capitals with reeded columns, shaped and foliate cast base, beveled glass door and panels, circular face dial with Roman numerals, mkd "Famiel Marti Medaille...Paris 1900, Tiffany & Co.," 13" h 600.00

Carriage

French, oval, brass, four beveled glass panels, fine cut flowers in border to sides, top oval glass panels initialed "M.E.H.," dial painted with woman and cupid, decorative D-shaped handle on top, 5-1/2" h...........1,150.00

New Haven Clock Co., gilded brass case, beveled glass, gold repaint to case, orig pendulum and key, 11-1/2" h 315.00

Cartel, Continental, late 19th/early 20th C, gilt brass, two train-chiming movement, metal face with enamel Roman numerals, topped by urn flanked by lion's heads suspending loops, round face flanked by scrolls and foliate finials, body ending in dolphin flanked urn suspending stylized fleur-de-lis, 34" h, 17" w 2,530.00

Desk, American, shaped rect, brass case, white enamel bordering cobalt blue, stylized applied monogram, decorative brass corners, central dial with Arabic numerals, 4-3/4" h 150.00

Dwarf, attributed to Noah Ranlet, Gilmanton, NH, early 19th C, pine, cased, scrolled cresting joining 3 finials on sq plinths, flat cornice molding, sq door with glazed dial opening, attached wooden bezel framing painted dial, 8-day weight driven movement, waist with thumb-molded door, small glazed aperture, flanked by quarter columns, cove molded base and cut-out feet, old refinished, replaced dial, 48" h 6,325.00

Garniture, Napoleon III, black marble, clock with central dial, painted Roman numerals, flanked by marble scrolls, supported on rect base with motifs, short round feet, pr black marble tazza on plinth base, gilded floral highlights...500.00

Half, Aaron Willard Jr., Hepplewhite case, figured mahogany with inlay, old finish, French feet, shaped apron, molding at base of hood with

French, gilded, cast brass, cherubs and cat faces, foliage, etc., 4 painted scenic porcelain panels, one side panel repaired, 16" h, $550. Photo courtesy of Garth's Auctions.

molded and fretwork cornice, brass finials, brass banjo works with hourly strike, weight, and pendulum, painted face labeled "Aaron Willard Junior, Washington Street Boston," orig paper label on back of case "directions for putting up the time piece," repairs to case, some old veneer repair, minor touch-up to face, 35-1/2" h 27,500.00

Mantel

Birge and Fuller, 1844-48, Gothic, double steeple, mahogany, peaked case, 2 glazed doors, painted zinc dial, 8-day wagon spring driven movement, tablets of fruit motifs flanked by gothic spires, turned feet, minor imperfections, 13-1/8" w, 4" d, 27" h 3,105.00

Deniere a Paris, Napoleon III, c1880, bronze and black marble, scholarly classical figure atop case fitted with frieze of processing putti, works sgd "Deniere a Paris," no pendulum, 20" w, 23" h 475.00

Empire Style, gilt bronze mounted Sienna marble, temple form, eagle finial and column form supports on shaped base, 14" w, 25-1/2" h 1,725.00

French Empire, attributed to Jean-Francoise Deniere, c1805-11, bronze dore, patinated bronze, standing Orpheus figure with lyre, resting arm on bronze-dore plinth surmounted by urn with garland of flowers, gilt-bronze dial with enamel Roman numerals over bronze-dore mountings in Neoclassical taste, rect molded base with ornate cast frieze representing Orpheus in underworld playing lyre for Pluto and Proserpine, other mythological figures, paw feet, movement with silk suspension and outside count week, 24" w, 8-3/4" d, 35-1/4" h 8,500.00

French Empire Revival, gilt bronze and ebonized, lyre form, foliate cornucopia modeled mounts, plinth with glass dome, c1850-75, 19-1/2" h, glass dome cracked 800.00

French, gilt bronze, cloisonné, and porcelain, frame with foliate scrolled cloisonné, porcelain plaques depicting Neoclassical maidens, dial with faux jeweled bezel, 16" h 3,105.00

French, Second Empire, gilt bronze and mahogany, Portico, single architectural structure, bronze dore mounting highlights, stamped "France," 9-1/2" w, 5-3/4" d, 18-1/2" h 900.00

J. and J. G. Low, tile body designed by Arthur Osborne, emb putti around hourglass, set in brass housing emb with swirls, reconditioned New Haven Clock Co. works, emb mark on tile, 12-1/4" h, 9" w, 6" d, hairline to front tile, several hairlines on porcelain dial 5,500.00

Louis Philippe, inlaid and ebonized, enameled dial with Roman numerals, gilt metal bezel, surmounted by scroll crest raised on 4 twist-turned columns, molded plinth, inlaid with scrolling foliage, 21-1/4" h 550.00

Louis XVI-style, gilt bronze, figural, enameled dial with Roman numerals within gilt bronze case gadrooned rim, trailing swags with fruit, flanked by allegorical gilt metal figures, gilt bronze base dec with paterae and vitruvian scroll flanking malachite insert, 25-3/4" w, 15" h 700.00

Mirror, attributed to Benjamin Morrill, Boscawen, NH, c1830, rect case with hinged split baluster framed gilt and black painted door, enclosing stenciled tablet framing white painted iron dial and brass wheelbarrow weight driven movement above mirror plate, minor imperfections, 15" w, 4" d, 30" h 5,175.00

Novelty, figural

American, c1880, three stacked rifles supporting drum form pendant housing movement, brass and copper, 10-3/4" h 345.00

French, 19th C, sedan shape, bronze dore, body with low relief depicting cherubs within low relief within scrolling foliate borders, central enamel dial with Arabic numerals over applied ivory panel depicting cherub, each side with miniature portrait of elegant lady, one sgd "r. peter," other "Renner," 11-1/4" h 1,500.00

Pillar and Scroll

Downes, Ephraim, Bristol, CT, 1825, mahogany, 30 hr wooden weight movement, old finish, imperfections, 31" h 950.00

Leavenworth and Son, Mark, Waterbury, CT, c1825, mahogany, 30 hr wooden movement, imperfections, 16-1/2" w, 4-1/2" d, 29-3/4" h. 950.00

Thomas, Seth, , c1825, Federal, mahogany, scrolled cresting joining 3 brass urn finials above glazed door, 30-hour wooden weight-driven movement, polychrome and gilt dec dial, landscape tablet, flanked by freestanding columns on cut bracket feet, old refinish, minor imperfections, 17-1/4" w, 4-1/2" d, 32" h 2,185.00

Shelf

Ansonia, gingerbread, carved and pressed walnut case, paper on zinc dial, silver dec glass, 8 day time and strike movement with pendulum, 22" h 185.00

Atkins and Downs, eight day triple, reverse painted glass with buildings, pendulum window and split columns, middle section with mirror and full columns, top section with dec dial, split columns, top crest with spread eagle, most of orig label remains, 38" h, 17" w, 6" d 450.00

Botsford's Improved Patent Timepiece, Coe & Co. 52 Dey St., New York, papier-mâché, scrolled front, gilt, polychrome embellishments, mother of pearl floral designs, circular enamel dial inscribed "Saml. S. Spencer," lever spring-driven movement, mounted on dec oval base, brass ball feet, glass dome, 11" h 1,265.00

Brown, J. C. and Forestville Mfg Co., laminated rosewood veneered case, painted tablet with floral dec and geometric designs, painted zinc dial, 8 day time and strike double fusee movement with pendulum, 19" h 5,000.00

Classical, Norris North, Torrington, CT, c1825, mahogany, flat cornice above glazed door, eglomise tablet of young woman flanked by engaged black paint stenciled columns, polychrome and gilt white painted dial, thirty-hour wooden weight driven movement, 23-3/4" h, 13-1/2" w, 5-1/4" d 4,900.00

Empire, mahogany veneer, ebonized and stencil gilded pilasters and crest, wooden works with weights, key, and pendulum, very worn paper label "William Orion & Co.," door with mirror in base, replaced reverse painted glass in middle section, finials missing, some veneer damage and repair 350.00

Federal, New England, early 19th C, mahogany and mahogany veneer, shaped fretwork joining three plinths and brass urn finials, flat cornice, glazed veneer door, white painted wood dial with red painted drapery, lower projecting base with crossbanded frame and flame mahogany panel pierced for viewing pendulum, slightly flaring French feet, 39" h, 13-3/4" w, 5-1/2" d, imperfections, replaced old movement 1,500.00

Tiffany & Company, walnut case, worn finish, traces of gilding in incised carved detail, brass works, blue and white enameled face, mkd "Tiffany & Comp. New York," orig pendulum and key, 20" h 935.00

Willard, Aaron, Boston, c1825, Federal, mahogany, molded plinth above glazed door, eglomise tablet of lyre spandrels and foliate designs, oval inscribed "Aaron Willard Boston," wooden framed white painted concave iron dial, eight-day weight-drive brass movement, lower section with mirror, framed by rounded moldings, ball feet, refinished, imperfections, 31" h 7,500.00

Tall

Brown, Tho., Birmingham, English, early 19th C, mahogany and inlay,

William Cann, mahogany, sgd, $5,600.

two train chiming movement sgd "Wilson" to mechanism, painted face with phases of moon, allegorical depictions of continents in each corner, subsidiary seconds dial, face sgd "Tho. Brown, Birmingham," hood with swan's neck cresting, gilt metal roundels, glass door flanked by fluted columns mounted to top with gilt metal Corinthian capitals, body with fluted columns flanking central door, plain plinth base, 90-3/4" h 4,600.00

Claggett, William, Newport, RI, 18th C, cherry, flat top above arched cornice molding and glazed tombstone door, engraved columns enclosing 8 day weight driven movement, brass engraved dial with strike-silent indicator in arch flanked by cast dolphin spandrels, engraved chapter ring seconds hand, calendar aperture below and engraved panel "Wm. Claggett Newport" with cast spandrels, arch molded rect waist door, glazed bull's eye panel on molded base, ball feet, old refinish, restored, 100" h 9,200.00

Coxall, Samuel, George II, mid 18th C, quartered oak, arched hood with caddy top surmounted by 3 spire finials, outset arched cavetto cornice raised on parcel-gilt Doric columns flanking conforming door, trunk with molded and arched door, cavetto-molded base raised on plinth, silvered chapter ring with Roman numerals, subsidiary seconds dial, date aperture, and strike/silent in arch, lower gilt-metal foliate spandrels, dial sgd "Saml. Coxall/Royston," 91" h 2,700.00

Cummens, William, Roxbury, Massachusetts, c1790-1800, Federal, mahogany inlaid, hood with scrolled cresting above arched molded cornice, glazed inlaid tombstone door, white painted iron dial with polychrome farm scene in oval reserve above floral spandrels, second hands and calendar aperture, inscribed "Warrented by William Cummens," dial flanked by freestanding reeded columns, molded rect waist door with inlaid crossbanding and stringing, flanked by brass stop fluted quarter Columbus, conforming inlaid base, refinished, alternations, 88" h..10,235.00

Grotz, Issac, Easton, PA, 1810-35, Chippendale case, curly maple, mellow old refinishing, bonnet with freestanding columns, fluted and dentilated moldings, broken arch pediment with inlaid rosettes and turned finials, molded edge waist door with carved fan, fluted quarter columns, molded edge panel in base, moldings between sections, ogee feet, brass works with second hand and calendar movement, painted sheet face with phases of the moon dial, cornucopias in the spandrels and labeled "Issac Grotz, Easton," weights, pendulum, and key, finials and plinths replaced, minor repairs to case, calendar dial repainted or replaced, 103" h 28,600.00

Hostetter, Jacob, York County, PA, Chippendale case, cherry, old finish, bonnet with 4 fluted freestanding columns with brass fittings and Corinthian capitals on front columns, broken arch pediment with Greek key molding, carved floral rosettes and flame carved finials on reeded and fluted plinths, molded edge door with double arch top, molding between sections with fluted quarter columns in waist, fluted quarter columns and molded panel in base, ogee feet, brass works with second hand and calendar movement, pained steel face with spandrels, labeled "Jacob Hostetter," weights, pendulum, and key, touch-up and repair to face, feet replaced, minor repairs, 99-3/4" h............14,300.00

Park, Solomon, c1876, mahogany, shell and fan carving fluted quarter columns and well developed bonnet, brass works with engraved brass face with silvered dial, polychrome phases of the moon dial, second hand and calendar movement, labeled "Solomon Park, Philadelphia," weights, pendulum, and key, 101" h 5,500.00

Read, A., country Hepplewhite case, cherry with old mellow refinishing, bonnet with turned front columns and reeded pilasters in back, broken arch pediment and chip carving on arch, waist with chamfered corners, lamb's tongues and molded edge door, molding between sections, cutout feet and apron, painted wood face labeled "A. Read & Co. Xenia, Ohio," polychrome flowers and vintage dec, wooden works replaced with electric movement, age crack in base, minor pierced repairs, 94-1/2" h 4,400.00

Ringe, J. Woodward, New England, 1790, cherry, hood with pierced fretwork joining 3 reeded plinths above arched cornice molding, glazed tombstone door flanked by reeded free standing columns, painted iron dial with floral designs, inscribed "J. Woodward Ringe," 8-day brass weight driven movement, molded tombstone waist door flanked by reeded quarter columns on base, ogee bracket feet, refinished, repainted dial, 89-1/8" h...4,600.00

Smith, Elisha, Sanbornton, NH, early 19th C, Federal, birch inlaid, hood with flat cornice molding door above 2 quarter fan inlays, glazed tombstone door enclosing pained iron moon phase dial with seconds hand, calendar aperture, inscribed "Elisha Smith Sanbornton," flanked by freestanding columns, rect molded waist door with bird's eye maple veneer and mahogany crossbanded border flanked by reeded quarter columns on base with cut-out fee over which cast brass hairy paw feet have been added, old finish, dial repainted, lacks fretwork, 83" h..2,990.00

Willard, Aaron, Boston, MA, c1790, cherry, hood with arched cornice molding, pierced fretwork centering reeded plinth joining 3 brass ball finials, glazed tombstone door, flanking freestanding columns, white painted iron dial with floral designs, second hand and calendar aperture inscribed "Aaron Willard," 8-day brass weight driven movement, waist with thumb-molded arched door, base with applied molding, c1790, imperfections, 87" h...8,100.00

Willard, Benjamin, Chippendale case, cherry, old mellow refinishing

Arched top, bonnet with freestanding fluted columns with brass trim and stop fluting, molded curved cornice with fretwork and brass finials on plinths, overlapping door, moldings between sections, scrolled apron, bracket feet with replaced foot pads, brass works, brass face with engraved eagle and cast floral scroll work detail, engraved "Benja. Willard, Grafton" and "Tempus Fugit" under eagle and "No. 114" on second hand dial, calendar movement with weights, key, and cast lead pendulum with "Willard" label, 89" h..38,500.00

Bonnet with freestanding front columns and quarter pilaster back columns with arch and pagoda like hood with pierced starflower design, turned finials, overlapping waist door with scrolled top edge, molding between sections, bracket feet with scrolled apron, brass works with second hand and calendar movement, engraved brass face with cast foliage scroll designs, engraved label "Benja'n

Willard," Grafton fecit, weights, pendulum, and key, very minor repairs to case, 87-1/2" h 33,000.00

Willard, Ephraim, Hepplewhite case, mahogany with inlay, bonnet with freestanding front columns with brass stop fluting, molded curved cornice with fretwork and brass finials on fluted plinths, fluted quarter columns with brass fittings and brass stop fluting and molded edge door in base, molding between sections, base molding, ogee feet, stringing inlay with invected corners, brass works with second hand and calendar movements, painted steel face with polychrome flowers and birds, labeled "Warranted by Em. Willard," weights, pendulum, and key, repairs to feet, pierced repair where lock was removed on waist door, minor repairs to bonnet, 93-3/4" h.....................33,000.00

Willard, Simon

Hepplewhite case, mahogany with stringing and fans inlay, old finish, bonnet with fluted quarter columns, molded arch cornice and fretwork with fluted plinths, brass trim and stop fluting, eagle finials, molded edge door and fluted quarter columns, base moldings and moldings between sections, ogee feet, brass works with calendar movement, second hand and painted steel face with rocking ship with American flag, face labeled "S. Willard," weights, pendulum, and key, center plinth and fretwork restored, minor repairs to feet and age cracks in base, 94" h.................55,000.00

Hepplewhite Roxbury case, mahogany with inlay, varnish finish, bonnet with freestanding fluted columns, molded arch pediment with fretwork, gilded wooden finials on fluted plinths, stringing inlay with corner fans, brass trim, brass stop fluting on columns, brass works with phases of the moon dial, calendar movement and second hand, fluted quarter columns and molded edge door, molding between sections, bracket feet, painted steel face labeled "Simon Willard," Roman numerals have been repainted, wear to face, weights, pendulum, and key, 97" h..77,000.00

Wall

Ingraham, E. & Co., Bristol, CT, c1870, gilt gesso, molded circular glazed frame, white painted metal dial, 8 day spring driven movement, minor imperfections, 20" d...1,955.00

Ansonia, oak case, time and strike movements, 37" h, $400.

Little, W. Torrey, New England, early 19th C, gilt gesso, molded circular frame, convex painted wooden gilt dial inscribed "W. Torrey Little, Inc., Boston-Marshfield," 8 day weight driven movement, repainted dial, restoration, 29" h 1,495.00

Morrison, W., London, mahogany regulator, 19th C, 66-1/2" h 1,955.00

Victorian, American, inlaid walnut, serpentine molded top crest centered by urn finial, white dial with Roman numerals (replaced), surrounded by inlaid frame, 15" w, 5-1/4" d, 35" h 225.00

CLOISONNÉ

History: Cloisonné is the art of enameling on metal. The design is drawn on the metal body, then wires, which follow the design, are glued or soldered on. The cells thus created are packed with enamel and fired; this step is repeated several times until the level of enamel is higher than the wires. A buffing and polishing process brings the level of enamels flush to the surface of the wires.

This art form has been practiced in various countries since 1300 b.c. and in the Orient since the early 15th century. Most cloisonné found today is from the late Victorian era, 1870-1900, and was made in China or Japan.

Reference: Lawrence A. Cohen and Dorothy C. Ferster, *Japanese Cloisonné,* Charles E. Tuttle Co., 1990.

Collectors' Club: Cloisonne Collectors Club, P.O. Box 96, Rockport, MA 01966.

Periodical: *Orientalia Journal,* P.O. Box 94, Flushing, NY 11363-0094, http://members.aol.com/Orientalia/index.html

Museum: George Walter Vincent Smith Art Museum, Springfield, MA.

Box, cov

4-3/4" d, 2-3/4" h, rounded form, butterflies among flowering branches, turquoise ground, Chinese, 19th C 345.00

6" l, rect, rounded corners, wisteria, pines, scrolls, and birds of paradise, Japanese, inner flange separated, slight fracture to lid...325.00

Charger, 14-1/4" d, central phoenix, red ground, lotus and dragon panels on cream ground, late 19th or early 20th C 150.00

Animal, turtle like creature, green shell back, brown body, $220. Photo courtesy of Garth's Auctions.

Cup, 4" h, ftd, butterflies and flowers, lappet borders, Chinese, 19th C 100.00

Desk Set, brush pot, pen, pen tray, blotter, and paper holder, Japanese, price for set 130.00

Figure
    7-1/4" h, prancing horse, left front leg raised, neck curved, mouth open, allover tightly scrolled lotus, Chinese, 18th/19th C, damage 320.00
    9" h, bird chariot, bronze base, Chinese 100.00
    12" h, horse head, Chinese, Qing dynasty 250.00
    21" h, prancing deer carrying two handled vase on its back, two dragons chasing flaming pearl on rect base, Chinese, 19th/20th, losses 575.00

Garniture, 9" h, gilt bronze urn, multicolored cloisonné foliage design, two bronze putti, onyx base, French, early 20th C 865.00

Incense Burner, 19-3/4" h, globular, three dragon head feet, high curving handles, scrolling lotus and ancient bronzes motif, openwork lid, dragon finial, raised Quinlong six character mark, damage 815.00

Jar, cov, 6" h, ovoid, even green over central band of scrolling flowers, dome lid, ovoid finial, marked "Ando Jubei," 20th C 230.00

Planter, 11" l, quatralobe, classical symbol and scroll dec, blue ground, Chinese, pr 200.00

Tea Kettle, 10-1/2" h, multicolored scrolling lotus, medium blue ground, lappets border, waisted neck with band of raised auspicious symbols between keyfret borders, floral form finial, double handles, Chinese, 19th C 690.00

Teapot, 4-3/4" d, 3-1/4" h, central band of flowering chrysanthemums on pink ground, shoulder with shaped cartouches of phoenix and dragon on floral and patterned ground, lower border with chrysanthemum blossom on swirling ground, flat base with three small raised feet, single chrysanthemum design, spout and handle with floral design, lid with two writhing dragons on peach colored ground, Japanese, late 19th/early 20th C 4,025.00

Urn, 23-3/4" h, ovoid, slightly waisted neck, peony dec, black ground, base plaque marked "Takeuchi Chubei," Japanese, late 19th C, Shichi Ho Company, Owari 690.00

Vase
    3 5/8" h, shouldered form, long slender neck flaring at rim, colored enamels, spider chrysanthemums and songbirds, midnight blue ground, Japanese, Meiji period, pr 550.00
    4-3/4" h, ovoid, continual scene of geese on riverbank, flowering bushes and mountains in distance, Japanese 2,875.00
    6" h, six sided, each side with shield below floral band, alternating dragon and phoenix motif, flecked blue ground, Japanese, early 20th C 460.00
    7-1/4" h, blood red ground, pink and white apple blossoms .. 145.00
    7-1/4" h, partially wireless, crane looking at reflection, mountain in background, celadon ground, Japanese 225.00
    8-1/2" h, 3-1/8" d, dark colors, wide rust band, small colored flowers, bird in flight, goldstone in band, other bands of dainty flowers, pr 425.00
    8 7/8" h, flattened ovoid, large cartouches of dragon with serpent and phoenix flying among vines, surrounded by flowering vines, black ground, Japanese, Meiji period 8,350.00
    9 1/8" h, angled shoulder, ovoid, waisted neck, multicolored flowering chrysanthemum, bright blue ground, Meiji period, Ota, minor crazing 1,380.00
    9 5/8" h
        Angular baluster, single naturalistic scene of songbirds among flowering trees and bushes, midnight blue ground, lappet foot and rim borders, Japanese, early 20th C 1,725.00
        High angled shoulder, straight sides, short waisted neck, eagle perched on flowering cherry tree, wisteria and bamboo below, dark blue ground, lappet borders above and below, late 19th C, pr 2,300.00
    10" h, silver wire dec, slender iris, deep blue ground, Japanese, base sgd "Obei Tsukuru," scratches, fracture 375.00
    12" h, slender ovoid, waisted neck and foot, beetle and cricket resting on flowering branches, midnight blue ground, Japanese, early 20th C 1,955.00

12-1/4" h, ovoid, waisted neck, inverted rim, two songbirds among prunus and bamboo, colored enamels with silver wire, dark blue ground, stamped silver rim, wire Ando Jubei mark on base, Meiji period, orig fitted box 4,975.00

12-1/2" h, pigeon blood glaze, cranes in flight over sea, Japanese, Meiji Period, sgd "Matsuno," one with crazing, pr 1,000.00

12 7/8" h, pear form, single yellow rose, green ground, Ando Jubei, 20th C 1,100.00

14-3/4" h, Iron Age form, classical symbol and scroll dec, blue ground, Chinese, pr 300.00

CLOTHING and CLOTHING ACCESSORIES

History: While museums and a few private individuals have collected clothing for decades, it is only recently that collecting clothing has achieved a widespread popularity. Clothing reflects the social attitudes of a historical period.

Christening and wedding gowns abound and, hence, are not in large demand. Among the hardest items to find are men's clothing from the 19th and early 20th centuries. The most sought after clothing is by designers, such as Fortuny, Poirret, and Vionnet.

References: Blanche Cirker (ed.), *1920s Fashions From B. Altman & Company,* Dover, 1999; Roselyn Gerson, *Vintage & Contemporary Purse Accessories,* Collector Books, 1997; —, *Vintage Ladies Compacts,* Collector Books, 1996; —, *Vintage Vanity Bags and Purses,* Collector Books, 1994, 1997 value update; Michael Jay Goldberg, *The Ties That Blind,* Schiffer Publishing, 1997; Carol Belanger Grafton, Fashions of the Thirties, Dover Publications, 1993; —, *Shoes, Hats and Fashion Accessories,* Dover Publications, 1998; ——, *Victorian Fashion: A Pictorial Archive,* Dover Publications, 1999; Kristina Harris, *Authentic Victorian Dressmaking Techniques,* Dover Publications, 1999; ——, *Victorian & Edwardian Fashions for Women,* Schiffer Publishing, 1995; ——, *Vintage Fashions for Women,* Schiffer Publishing, 1996; Richard Holiner, *Antique Purses,* Collector Books, 1996 value update; Erhard Klepper, *Costume Through The Ages,* Dover Publications, 1999; Elizabeth Kurella, *The Complete Guide to Vintage Textiles,* Krause Publications, 1999; Susan Langley, *Vintage Hats & Bonnets, 1770-1970,* Collector Books, 1997; Ellie Laubner, *Fashions of the Roaring '20s,* Schiffer Publishing, 1996; Jan Lindenberger, *Clothing & Accessories from the '40s, '50s, & '60s,* Schiffer Publishing, 1996; Sally C. Luscomb, *The Collector's Encyclopedia of Buttons,* Schiffer Publishing, 1997; Herbert Norris, *Ancient European Costume and Fashion,* Dover Publications, 1999; Mary Brooks Picken, *A Dictionary of Costume and Fashion: Historic and Modern,* Dover, 1999; Leslie Piña, Lorita Winfield, and Constance Korosec, *Beads in Fashion, 1900-2000,* Schiffer Publishing, 1999; Maureen Reilly, *Hot Shoes, 100 Years,* Schiffer Publishing, 1998; Desire Smith, *Hats,* Schiffer Publishing, 1996; --, *Vintage Styles: 1920-1960,* Schiffer Publishing, 1997; Pamela Smith, *Vintage Fashion & Fabrics,* Alliance Publishers, 1995; Jeffrey B. Snyder, *Stetson Hats & The John B. Stetson Company 1865-1970,* Schiffer Publishing, 1997; Diane Snyder-Haug, *Antique & Vintage Clothing,* Collector Books, 1996; Geoffrey Warren, *Fashion & Accessories, 1840-1980,* Schiffer Publishing, 1997; Debra Wisniewski, *Antique and Collectible Buttons,* Collector Books, 1997.

Periodicals: *Glass Slipper,* 653 S. Orange Ave., Sarasota, FL 34236; *Lady's Gallery,* P.O. Box 1761, Independence, MO 64055; *Lill's Vintage Clothing Newsletter,* 19 Jamestown Dr., Cincinnati, OH 45241; *Vintage Clothing Newsletter,* P.O. Box 88892, Seattle, WA 98138; *Vintage Connection,* 904 N. 65th St., Springfield, OR 97478; *Vintage Gazette,* 194 Amity St., Amherst, MA 01002.

Collectors' Clubs: Textile Group of Los Angeles, Inc., 894 S. Bronson Ave., Los Angeles CA 9005-3605; The Costume Society of America, P.O. Box 73, Earleville, MD 21919, http://www.costumesocietyamerica.com; Vintage Fashion and Costume Jewelry Club, P.O. Box 265, Glen Oaks, NY 11004.

Museums: Bata Shoe Museum, Toronto, Canada; Fashion Institute of Technology, New York, NY; Los Angeles County Museum (Costume and Textile Dept.), Los Angeles, CA; Metropolitan Museum of Art, New York, NY; Museum of Costume, Bath, England; Philadelphia Museum of Art, Philadelphia, PA; Smithsonian Institution (Inaugural Gown Collection), Washington, DC; Wadsworth Athenaeum, Hartford, CT; Whiting and Davis Handbag Museum, Attleboro Falls, MA.

Additional Listings: See *Warman's Americana & Collectibles* for more examples.

Note: Condition, size, age, and completeness are critical factors in purchasing clothing. Collectors divide into two groups: those collecting for aesthetic and historic value and those desiring to wear the garment. Prices are higher on the West coast; major auction houses focus on designer clothes and high-fashion items.

Cape
    Beaded felt, large collar with bone button closure, multicolored bead swags, Inuit, Greenland, 20th C, 17" l 250.00
    Blue, black velvet collar, Edwardian 300.00
Collar, velvet, black, rhinestones, beads, and pearls, 1930s 35.00
Coat
    Raccoon, brown cloth lining, c1920 .... 275.00
    Wool, black, Edwardian, large fur collar 250.00
Corset
    Lady Marlene, strapless, padded cups, boned ribs, spandex and nylon, beige 15.00
    Saks Fifth Avenue Waist Finder, elastic, bone in sides, defined lace cups, adjustable straps 22.00
Dress
    Cotton, embroidered bodice, back, sleeves, and hemline, flowered, Victorian, somewhat fragile 135.00
    Cotton, flowered, large organdy collar, waist tie, Edwardian ... 85.00
    Cotton, polka dots, navy and white, c1930 .... 80.00
    Cotton, striped, black and white, Edwardian 70.00
    Lace, coral, flower trim, c1920, some repairs 55.00
    Lawn, child's, lace at neckline, around sleeves and down front panels, back button, c1900 .... 45.00
    Net, white, embroidered bodice and skirt 340.00
    Net, white, embroidered, pink satin ribbon trim, 4 rows of ruffles on skirt, attached satin underslip 235.00
    Satin, black, c1930 .... 85.00
    Satin and Lace, black, Victorian 295.00
    Silk, 2 pc, blue, lace trim, Victorian, lace replaced 375.00
    Tulle, white, satin ribbon trimmed bodice, 3/4 sleeves, ribbon circling skirt, waist cummerbund 225.00

Velvet and crepe, purple, matching jacket, c1920 .... 110.00
Wool bodice, cotton skirt, Gibson Girl style, ribbon trim 395.00
Gloves, pr
    Black, flared at wrist, embroidered design, 10" l, 1940s 20.00
    Black, satin, 11" l 18.00
    Orange, wrist length, 8" l, 1940s 18.00
    Silver lame, stretch, 13" l 20.00
Hat, lady's
    Doeskin Felt, purple, net, bow, 2-1/2" brim 35.00
    Evening, black sequin, net 30.00
    Feathers, spray of long black and beige feathers in front, Woodward & Lothrop, Washington, DC label 40.00
    Felt, red, black ostrich feather, netting, small turned up brim, 20" d 45.00
    Fur, lamb, dark brown, 22" 65.00
    Gold Lamé, 4" w brim in front, 3" w in back, bow in back, 1950s 35.00
    Navy, sgd "Skol Nips," woven nylon and netted material, side combs 25.00
    Straw, beige, rolled brim, small silk flowers and feather, Adoria 22.00
    Straw, black, Mr. John, tailored 35.00
    Straw, black, Victorian 95.00
    Straw, brown, Madras plaid band, Keens Colonials, 1950s 28.00
    Straw, navy blue, netting, small bow in front, 1930s 22.00
    Straw, turquoise and black, netting, large trim, "Sylvia New York & St Louis" on orig label 35.00
    Velvet, navy blue, large bow, Norman Paulvin, NY, label 28.00
    Wool Felt, black, small bows in back, netting in brim, "Genuine Fur Felt" label, 1930s 35.00
Hat, man's
    Suede, beige, Knox, size 7-1/4 .... 22.50
    Wool Felt, Stetson Ivy League, dark charcoal gray, size 7-1/8", 1950s 38.00
Headache Band, Flapper, white marabou feathers, amethyst stone center with tiny faux seed pearls (2 missing), black sequin stretch band 25.00
Muff, child's, fur, black, satin lining 70.00
Purse
    Appliqué, evening, Josef, white, faux pearls and white sequins,

Night Gown, white cotton, c1870, $45.

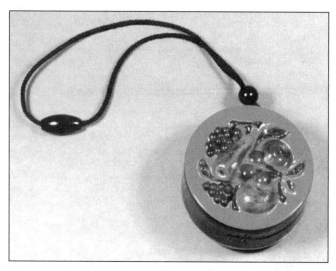

Purse, red celluloid top and bottom, blue celluloid sides, molded and painted fruit motif, cord handle with sliding bead, 3-1/2" d, $125. Photo courtesy of Julie P. Robinson.

goldtone frame, snap closure trimmed with pearl roping, thin gold link chain handle, ivory satin lining, matching wallet, tag "Bags by Josef Hand Beaded in France" 110.00

Bakelite, beaded, jet black beads, butterscotch Bakelite top, double twisted rope handle, black silk lining, glued in mirror, 5-1/2" x 9" x 1-1/2" 225.00

Beaded, Art Nouveau, sterling silver, allover black beaded design, beaded fringe, sterling silver frame with whiplash motif, link chain, sgd "Tiffany & Co.," repair to fabric near hinge 500.00

Beaded, Marshall Fields, tiny white seed beads, hand embroidered lowers and leaves, divided satin int., beaded handle, mkd "Made in Belgium for Marshall Fields," 8" w, 6" h.......................... 115.00

Beaded, midnight blue, beaded handle, c1950, 8-1/2" w, 3-1/2" d, 7-1/2" h 95.00

Beaded, white, orig label "Made by Dormer, Paris-Belgium-New York," 7-1/2" x 5-1/2" 75.00

Beaded, white, orig label "Made by Hebe Sanders," 8-1/2" x 4-3/4" 100.00

Lucite, clutch, blue, silver embedded sparkles, gold-plated clasp, 9-1/4" w, 1-3/8" h, 4-1/2" d 75.00

Lucite, ivory, trapezoid, heavy goldtone frame, goldtone rigid handle and snap closure, navy lining, 12" l, 8" w, c1950 .... 185.00

Lucite, pearly white and clear, single handle, gold colored tinsel type embedded dec, 6" w, 7-1/2" h, 3-1/4" d...................... 155.00

Mesh, Art Nouveau, German silver, sgd "HHC Co. German Silver," 5-1/2" x 6" 185.00

Mesh, sterling, ornate frame, layer of woven sterling lace along bottom, initials "ECG" and "800," 8" w, 8-3/4" l 425.00

Native American, cranberry ground, red, cream, black, and turquoise motif, plastic tortoise handles, white lining, tag "100% wool exclusive of ornamentation, Mfg. 4063, Sold and distributed by David S. Shehady, El Paso, Texas," 14" x 15" 110.00

Needlepoint, floral, pink, lavender, and green, chartreuse leather trim, swing handle, gold metal snap clasp and feet, lime green moiré int., zipped int. compartment and matching change purse, c1960, 10-1/2" x 9-1/2" 50.00

Snakeskin, clutch, charcoal, bright goldtone frame, gold front snap closure, 12-1/2" x 8", black leather int., orig tag "Genuine Snakeskin" 45.00

Tapestry, man and woman in outdoor setting, pink, green, and blue on ivory ground, gold filigree frame, swing handle, black leather snap closure, silk moiré lining, 13" w, 9" h.......................... 165.00

Riding Habit, side saddle, skirt buttons to create back bustle, black, Victorian 450.00

Robe, silk, embroidered, orange lining, c1920........................... 140.00

Shirt, man's, Hawaiian, blues, greens, turquoise, pinks, yellows, and red, bright, upper left pocket

Breakers label with man surfing, 1950s, 100% cotton, palm trees and tropical birds, plus writing, tropical drink, sea, wind, Aloha... 65.00

Pennys of Hawaii, 1960s, 100% rayon................................. 45.00

Network label, 1960s, 100% rayon.................................... 45.00

Shore Things label, orchids print. 50% rayon, 50% cotton...... 45.00

Slip

Barbizon, nylon/orlon, zipper at side, lace trim, adjustable straps 18.00

Pauline Gordon, taffeta, elastic bodice, fitted, lace trim, adjustable straps, navy 18.00

Saks Fifth Avenue, black, short elastic bodice, adjustable straps, back, and cups, polyester/nylon skirt, lace trim 20.00

Skirt

Cotton, aqua and orange, Victorian, fragile condition............. 25.00

Lawn, white, drawstring waist, train, Victorian...................... 150.00

Sport Coat, man's, wool, red, navy blue, and dark green plaid, 2 button front, 2 pockets with flaps, 4 buttons on sleeve, split tail, size 38/40, "Saks Fifth Avenue, 100% wool" label 48.00

Suit, black, 3 pcs, tatted lace on jacket, Victorian, needs repairs 175.00

Tie, man's

49" l, 4-1/2" h, hand painted, mallards and pheasants, rust shading to peach crepe-type fabric, pr................................... 45.00

54" l, 4" w, brown, rust, cream tan, and light blue, "Par Excellence" written on lining... 15.00

56" l, 4-1/4" w, orange-brown, gold, gray, cream, and blue, Cravateur.. 15.00

57" l, 3-1/2" w, black, rose, silver and light lavender, mkd "Ketch" 15.00

Walking Suit, navy blue, Edwardian, wear to jacket lining 250.00

Wallet, evening, embroidered satin, two chickadees nestled in ivy, tiny red glass seed beads, bifold, mkd "Made in France," 3-1/4" x 3-3/4" 45.00

Wedding Gown

Brocade, ecru, long train, side snaps, button front, pointed sleeves, c1930... 210.00

Chantilly Lace, fitted bodice, spaghetti straps, jacket with high neck and short puffed sleeves, ruffled skirt with narrow ruffles at waist and hips, deeper ruffles at hem and end of long train, c1939, clipping from Washington DC newspaper of orig owner 375.00

Flocked, c1940 .... 220.00

Jeweled bodice, white satin skirt, c1950 .... 110.00

Satin, candlelight, long train, c1940................................. 275.00

Satin, ivory, long train, c1940 .... 350.00

Satin, white, V-neck, c1940 .... 375.00

Silk, cream, lace trim, 2 pc, Edwardian 275.00

Silk, pink and black, pleating under skirt and train, lace trim collar and bodice, black velvet ribbon trim, 2 pc, c1890.............. 650.00

Silk, some lace and beading, c1920................................. 300.00

COALPORT

History: In the mid-1750s, Ambrose Gallimore established a pottery at Caughley in the Severn Gorge, Shropshire, England. Several other potteries, including Jackfield, developed in the area.

About 1795, John Rose and Edward Blakeway built a pottery at Coalport, a new town founded along the right-of-way of the Shropshire Canal. Other potteries located adjacent to the canal were those of Walter Bradley and Anstice, Horton, and Rose. In 1799, Rose and Blakeway bought the Royal Salopian China Manufactory at Caughley. In 1814, this operation was moved to Coalport.

A bankruptcy in 1803 led to refinancing and a new name—John Rose and Company. In 1814, Anstice, Horton, and Rose was acquired. The South Wales potteries at Swansea and Nantgarw were added. The expanded firm made fine-quality, highly decorated ware. The plant enjoyed a renaissance from 1888-1900.

World War I, decline in trade, and shift of the pottery industry away from the Severn Gorge brought hard times to Coalport. In 1926, the firm, now owned by Cauldon Potteries, moved from Coalport to Shelton. Later owners included Crescent Potteries, Brain & Co., Ltd., and finally, in 1967, Wedgwood.

References: Susan and Al Bagdade, *Warman's English & Continental Pottery & Porcelain,* 3rd Edition, Krause Publications, 1998; Michael Messenger, *Coalport 1795-1926,* Antique Collectors' Club, 1995; Tom Power, *The Charlton Standard Catalogue of Coalport Figures,* Charlton Press, 1997.

Collectors' Club: Coalport Collector Society, P.O. Box 99, Sudbury, CO10 6SN England.

Museums: Cincinnati Museum of Art, Cincinnati, OH; Coalport China works Museum, Ironbridge Gorge Museum Trust, Shropshire, England; Victoria & Albert Museum, London, England.

Additional Listings: Indian Tree

Box, cov, 6" l, porcelain, fan shape, lake scene 350.00
Compote, 12" d, round, pedestal on sq foot, gilt scroll molded rim, flower sprays within gilt and foliage surrounds, red ground, c1830 .... 475.00
Cup and Saucer, Harebell pattern 45.00
Dinner Service, gilt monogram and polychromed florets on white ground framed in cobalt blue, twelve bouillon cups and saucers, twelve breakfast cups and saucers, twelve butter pats, three compotes, two cream jugs, ten demitasse cups and twelve saucers, twelve 10-1/4" d dinner plates, twelve 5-3/8" d plates, twelve 6" plates, twenty-four 9" d plates, two 12-1/2" l oval platters with handles, four 13", 15", 16-3/4" platters, twelve ramekins, two cov sardine

Plate, crimped edging, gilt trim, Indian tobacco leaf design, 10" d, $150.

boxes, twelve 5" d sauce dishes, two 8-1/4" l serving bowls, two 11-3/4" l q serving dishes, twelve 9" d soup plates, two sugar bowls, twelve teacups and saucers, two cov vegetable dishes 12,650.00
Dish, leaf shape, apple green, garden flower bouquet, gilt foliate, c1820 .... 100.00
Figure
   6-3/4" h, Lady Bountiful, pink overshirt, green collar, blue bows, pink bonnet with blue ribbon, c1949 .... 445.00
   7-3/4" h, The Fire Fighter, black and orange,1985 .... 275.00
   9-1/2" h, Harlequin, multicolored, 1983 .... 750.00
Spill Vase, 5" h, pink, garden flowers and gilt scroll bands, bird's head handles with gilt rings, flared rim, sq base, 3 pc set 950.00

COCA-COLA ITEMS

History: The originator of Coca-Cola was John Pemberton, a pharmacist from Atlanta, Georgia. In 1886, Dr. Pemberton introduced a patent medicine to relieve headaches, stomach disorders, and other minor maladies. Unfortunately, his failing health and meager finances forced him to sell his interest.

In 1888, Asa G. Candler became the sole owner of Coca-Cola. Candler improved the formula, increased the advertising budget, and widened the distribution. A "patient" was accidentally given a dose of the syrup mixed with carbonated water instead of still water. The result was a tastier, more refreshing drink.

As sales increased in the 1890s, Candler recognized that the product was more suitable for the soft-drink market and began advertising it as such. From these beginnings, a myriad of advertising items have been issued to invite all to "Drink Coca-Cola."

References: Gael de Courtivron, Collectible *Coca-Cola Toy Trucks,* Collector Books, 1995; Steve Ebner, *Vintage Coca-Cola Machines,* Vol. II, published by author (available from FunTronics, Inc., P.O. Box 448, Middletown, MD 21769; Deborah Goldstein Hill, *Price Guide to Vintage Coca-Cola® Collectibles: 1896-1965,* Krause Publications, 1999; Allan Petretti, *Classic Coca-Cola Calendars,* Antique Trader Books, 1999; —, *Petretti's Coca-Cola Collectibles Price Guide,* 10th ed., Antique Trader Books, 1997;—, *Petretti's Soda Pop Collectibles Price Guide,* 2nd ed., Antique Trader Books, 1998; Allan Petretti and Chris Beyer, *Classic Coca-Cola Serving Trays,* Antique Trader Books, 1998; B. J. Summers, B. J. Summers' *Guide to Coca-Cola,* 2nd ed., Collector Books, 1999; Jeff Walters, *Complete Guide to Collectible Picnic Coolers & Ice Chests,* Memory Lane Publishing, 1994.

Collectors' Club: Cavanagh's Coca-Cola Christmas Collector's Society, 1000 Holcomb Woods Parkway, Suite 440B, Roswell, GA 30076; Coca-Cola Collectors Club, 400 Monemar Ave., Baltimore, MD 21228-5213; Coca-Cola Collectors Club International, P.O. Box 49166, Atlanta, GA 30359-1166; The Coca-Cola Club, P.O. Box 158715, Nashville, TN 32715.

Museums: Coca-Cola Memorabilia Museum of Elizabethtown, Inc., Elizabethtown, KY; World of Coca-Cola Pavilion, Atlanta, GA.

Additional Listings: See *Warman's Americana & Collectibles* for more examples.

Serving Tray, 1910, 10-1/2" x 13-1/4", $750.

Notes: Dates of interest: "Coke" was first used in advertising in 1941. The distinctively shaped bottle was registered as a trademark on April 12, 1960.

Badge, Bottlers Convention, 1930 .... 65.00
Bingo Card, c1940 .... 25.00
Bookmark, Romance of Coca-Cola, 1916 .... 30.00
Bottle
    Amber, mkd "Lewisburg" 30.00
    Christmas, Williamstown, WV 15.00
    Commemorative, Nascar Series, Bill Elliott, Dale Earnhardt, or Bobby Labonte 5.00
Bottle Opener, bottle shape, Glascock Mfg Co., Muncie, IN c1930 ...48.00
Calendar, 1913, 13-1/2" x 22-1/2", Hamilton King illus 900.00
Change Tray
    1914, Betty 150.00
    1941, girl with skates 45.00
    1970, Santa Claus 85.00
Cigarette Bow, cov, frosted glass, 50th Anniversary, 1936 .... 70.00
Clock, 9" x 19-1/2" d, light-up, "Drink Coca-Cola" some oxidation and pitting to gold plating 500.00
Door Push Bar, porcelain, 1960 .... 85.00
Hair Receiver, celluloid, incised red lettering "Drink Coca Cola". 250.00
Magazine Advertisement Tear Sheet
    National Geographic, Santa, c1942 .... 25.00
    Success Magazine, lady driving carriage, being served Coca-Cola in glass, 1906 .... 65.00
Paperweight, girl in white swimsuit 80.00
Pocket Mirror, 1-3/4 x 2-1/4", celluloid, aqua blue ground, black letters, red "Icy-O" logo, black soda dispenser, red and white Coca-Cola bottle, made by Parisian Novelty, Chicago 600.00
Sign
    4-1/2" x 12-1/2", emb tin, features 1923 Christmas bottle, c1931 .... 695.00

    16" x 43", tin, wrap-around type, fishtail, slight paint chips.... 375.00
    26" d, round, porcelain, red and white 95.00
    36" x 19-1/2", cardboard, c1944, framed 495.00
Thermometer, 16", "Trade Mark Registered, Bottle Pat Dec 25, 1923" 120.00
Tray
    1909, World's Fair, young lady 3,000.00
    1917, Elaine 200.00
    1925, girl with fur 185.00
    1930, bathing beauty 195.00
    1935, Madge Evans 165.00
    1938, girl in large brimmed hat 125.00

COFFEE MILLS

History: Coffee mills or grinders are utilitarian objects designed to grind fresh coffee beans. Before the advent of stay-fresh packaging, coffee mills were a necessity.

The first home-size coffee grinders were introduced about 1890. The large commercial grinders designed for use in stores, restaurants, and hotels often bear an earlier patent date.

Reference: Joseph Edward MacMillan, *MacMillan Index of Antique Coffee Mills,* Cherokee Publishing (657 Old Mountain Rd., Marietta, GA 30064), 1995; Michael L. White and Derek S. White, *Early American Coffee Mills,* published by authors (P.O. Box 483, Fraser, CO 80442).

Collectors' Club: Association of Coffee Mill Enthusiasts, 5941 Wilkerson Rd, Rex, GA 30273.

7-1/2" h, cast iron, brass trim, lion and unicorn label, English 175.00
8-1/2" h, refinished poplar, pewter hopper, bottom renailed 145.00
11" h, Arcade Imperial, wood, cast iron fittings 115.00
12" h, Landers, Frary & Clark, New Britain, CT, No. 2, two wheels cast iron 475.00
14-1/2" h, ceramic, blue and white Delft design, cast iron fittings, German, wall mounted 175.00

Wilmot Castle Co., $300.

22-1/2" h, cast iron, two wheels, wooden drawer, worn orig black paint with gold, yellow, and red, transfer design, "Enterprise Mfg. Co., Philadelphia, U.S.A.," hopper lid missing 315.00
27" h, Coles Mfg. No. 7, patented 1887, cast iron 525.00
60" h, Elgin National, red, store type, cast iron 395.00

COIN-OPERATED ITEMS

History: Coin-operated items include amusement games, pinball machines, jukeboxes, slot machines, vending machines, cash registers, and other items operated by coins.

The first jukebox was developed about 1934 and played 78-RPM records. Jukeboxes were important to teenagers before the advent of portable radios and television.

The first pinball machine was introduced in 1931 by Gottlieb. Pinball machines continued to be popular until the advent of solid-state games in 1977 and advanced electronic video games after that.

The first three-reel slot machine, the Liberty Bell, was invented in 1905 by Charles Fey in San Francisco. In 1910, Mills Novelty Company copyrighted the classic fruit symbols. Improvements and advancements have led to the sophisticated machines of today.

Vending machines for candy, gum, and peanuts were popular from 1910 until 1940 and can be found in a wide range of sizes and shapes.

References: Michael Adams, Jurgen Lukas, and Thomas Maschke, *Jukeboxes,* Schiffer Publishing, 1995; Michael F. Baute, *Always Jukin' Official Guide to Collectible Jukeboxes,* published by author (221 Yesler Way, Seattle, WA 98104), 1996; Richard M. Bueschel, *Collector's Guide to Vintage Coin Machines,* Schiffer Publishing, 1995; ——, *Guide to Vintage Trade Stimulators & Counter Games,* Schiffer Publishing, 1997; ——, *Lemons, Cherries and Bell-Fruit-Gum,* Royal Bell Books, 1995; ——, *Pinball 1,* Hoflin Publishing, 1988; ——, *Slots 1,* Hoflin Publishing, 1989; Richard Bueschel and Steve Gronowski, *Arcade 1,* Hoflin Publishing, 1993; Herbert Eiden and Jurgen Lukas, *Pinball Machines,* Schiffer Publishing, 1992, values updated 1997; Bill Enes, *Silent Salesmen Too, The Encyclopedia of Collectible Vending Machines,* published by author (8520 Lewis Dr., Lenexa, KS 66227), 1995; Eric Hatchell and Dick Bueschel, *Coin-Ops on Location,* published by authors, 1993; Bill Kurtz, *Arcade Treasures,* Schiffer Publishing, 1994; Joseph E. Meyer, *Protection: The Sealed Book,* 10th ed., Mead Publishing Co., 1999.

Periodicals: *Always Jukin',* 221 Yesler Way, Seattle, WA 98104; *Antique Amusements Slot Machines & Jukebox Gazette,* 909 26th St. NW, Washington, DC 20037; *Around the Vending Wheel,* 5417 Castana Ave., Lakewood, CA 90712; *Coin Drop International,* 5815 W. 52nd Ave., Denver, CO 80212; *Coin Machine Trader,* 569 Kansas SE, P.O. Box 602, Huron, SD 57350; *Gameroom Magazine,* 1014 Mt. Tabor Rd., New Albany, IN 47150; *Jukebox Collector,* 2545 SE 60th St., Des Moines, IA 50317; *Pin Game Journal,* 31937 Olde Franklin Dr., Farmington, MI, 48334; *Scopitone Newsletter,* 810 Courtland Dr., Ballwin, MO 63021.

Collectors' Club: Bubble-Gum Charm Collectors, 24 Seafoam St., Staten Island, NY 10306

Museum: Liberty Belle Saloon and Slot Machine Collection, Reno, NV.

Additional Listings: See *Warman's Americana & Collectibles* for separate categories for Jukeboxes, Pinball Machines, Slot Machines, and Vending Machines.

Advisor: Bob Levy.

Notes: Because of the heavy usage these coin-operated items received, many are restored or, at the very least, have been repainted by either the operator or manufacturer. Using reproduced mechanisms to restore pieces is acceptable in many cases, especially when the restored piece will then perform as originally intended.

Arcade
Fortune Teller, Princess Doraldina, Rochester, NY, c1928, 5 cent, life like, gives fortune 13,000.00
Grip Tester, Shake with Your Uncle Sam, Howard, c1904, 1 cent, 66" h 17,250.00
Photo Viewing Machine, American Mutoscope, NY, c1920, 1 cent, metal, orig photos and paper marquee 1,100.00
Gum Machines
Adams, c1934, four column, tab gum vendor, chrome, decal, 22" h 100.00
Ford, c1950, round globe, gum balls, large, organizational use, 12" h 75.00
Master, c1923, 1 cent, confection, 16" h 200.00
Penny King, c1935, four in one, rotates, Art Deco style, four glass compartments 500.00
Pulver, c1930, 1 cent, two column, porcelain, stick dispenser, policeman figure rotates, 21" h 600.00
Juke Boxes
Seeburg, Model 100R, c1954, high fidelity, classic style, plays 45s 2,000.00
Wurlitzer, Model 1015, c1946, The Bubbler 7,500.00

Little Duke, c1931, $1,900. Photo courtesy of Auction Team Breker.

Miscellaneous

Cash Register, National Brass, Model 317, c1910, barber shop size, orig marquee 800.00

Pinball, Jolly Roger, c196, four player 200.00

Scale, American Scale, Fortune Model, c1937, 1 cent, health chart 200.00

Slot Machines

Caille, Superior, c1929, three reel, fancy design, 5 cent 1,400.00

Groetchen, Columbia, c1936, three reel, high maintenance, 25 cent 500.00

Jennings, Standard Chief, c1947, three reel, classic design, 10 cent 1,400.00

Mills

    Jewel Hightop, c1948, three reels, rugged and popular style, 5 cent 1,400.00

    Puritan Bell, c1925, cash register design, 5 cent, 8" h, 8" w 700.00

Pace, All Star Comet, c1936, three reel, side mint vendor, 5 cent . 1,400.00

Watling, Rolatop, c1935, three reel, gold coins on front, 25 cent 3,200.00

Vending Machines

Card, slot dispenser, various subjects, exhibit supply, c1930, table top, 12" h, 10" w 225.00

Cigarettes, Advance, c1930, 15 cent, 30" h, 14" w 100.00

Coke, Vendo V81, c1955, 6-1/2, 8, or 10 oz bottles, orig condition 1,200.00

Food, Horn and Hardart Automat Dispenser, c1902, four item unit 1,200.00

Matches, Edwards Mfg Co., c1930, Diamond, one to four books, 13-1/2" h 225.00

Nut, Ajax, Newark, NH, c1947, three unit vendor, serves hot nuts, 21-1/2" h 300.00

Pen, Vendorama, Victor Corp., c1962, oak case, 20" h, 14" w ... 100.00

Perfume, Perfumatic, c1950, four fragrances, 10 cent spray, pink, 16" h, 18" w 325.00

Stamp, Dillion Mfg, c1930, two selections, 12" x 12" 75.00

COMPACTS

History: In the first quarter of the 20th century, attitudes regarding cosmetics changed drastically. The use of make-up during the day was no longer looked upon with disdain. As women became "liberated," and as more and more of them entered the business world, the use of cosmetics became a routine and necessary part of a woman's grooming. Portable containers for cosmetics became a necessity.

Compacts were made in myriad shapes, styles, combinations and motifs, all reflecting the mood of the times. Every conceivable natural or man-made material was used in the manufacture of compacts. Commemorative, premium, souvenir, patriotic, figural, Art Deco, and enamel compacts are a few examples of the types of compacts that were made in the United States and abroad. Compacts combined with other forms, such as cigarette cases, music boxes, watches, hatpins, canes, and lighters, also were very popular.

Compacts were made and used until the late 1950s when women opted for the "Au Naturel" look. The term "vintage" is used to describe the compacts from the first half of the 20th century as distinguished from contemporary examples.

References: Juliette Edwards, *Compacts,* published by author, 1994; Roselyn Gerson, *Ladies Compacts,* Wallace-Homestead, 1996; ——, *Vintage and Contemporary Purse Accessories, Solid Perfumes, Lipsticks, & Mirrors,* Collector Books, 1997; ——, *Vintage Ladies Compacts,* Collector Books, 1996; ——, *Vintage Vanity Bags and Purses: An Identification and Value Guide,* 1994, 1997 value update, Collector Books; Frances Johnson, *Compacts, Powder and Paint,* Schiffer Publishing, 1996; Laura M. Mueller, *Collector's Encyclopedia of Compacts, Carryalls & Face Powder Boxes* (1994, 1999 value update), Vol. II (1997), Collector Books.

Collectors' Club: Compact Collectors Club, P.O. Box 40, Lynbrook, NY 11563.

Additional Listings: See *Warman's Americana & Collectibles* for more examples.

Advisor: Roselyn Gerson.

Austrian, vanity bag, 3-3/4" x 2", silver and enamel, sectioned rect, ext. with cobalt blue enamel on sunburst ground flanked by enameled on engine-turning, central medallion of bird in star and swag circle, amethyst colored cabochon thumbpiece, int. with 2 small sections, larger mirrored section, Austrian 650.00

BOAC, British Overseas Airways Corp., 3" d, gold, black leatherette, gold metal logo, framed mirror, BOAC puff, royal blue felt cover 65.00

Celluloid, unknown maker

    1-1/2" d, 1-1/2" h, powder box, ornate wreath & fleur dis lis motif, pink & white cameo lid 40.00

    2" sq, metal compact, celluloid top showing pastoral scene with lovers, c1940 .... 45.00

    3" d, orange compact studded with floral rhinestone motif 45.00

    5" celluloid diamond shaped purse, 2" tassel and silk cord, mottled cream, green and brown with oval cameo attached to center top, mirror, powder puff and chrome scent vial 275.00

Coty, #405, envelope box 65.00

Daniel, black leather, portrait of lady encased in plastic dome, Paris 90.00

Djer Kiss, with fairy 95.00

Estee Lauder, compact necklace, oval silvertone engraved pendant suspended from ornate silvertone ball and tube chain, orig solid fragrance 45.00

Evans, goldtone, heart shape, black twisted carrying cord, lipstick concealed in black tassel suspended from bottom 250.00

Fifth Avenue, vanity case "Cosmetist," aquamarine enamel, powder, rouge, lipstick, cleansing cream, and mascara, England 175.00

Flato, 2-1/2" x 2-1/4" x 1/2", goldtone, faux emerald fir tree bijoux, framed mirror, mkd "Flato" inside 95.00

Foster & Bailey, Providence, vanity case

    Blue cloisonné suspended from enameled perfume container, powder and rouge compartments, lipstick attached at base, tassel and black enameled finger carrying ring 950.00

    Sterling silver and enamel, 3-1/2" x 2", rect, canted corners, lid enameled in center over diamond shaped starburst ground, vase of roses on white ground, bordered by turquoise enamel cornered by roses, green cabochon thumbpiece open to hinged mirror, off-center hinged double compartment each with cabochon thumbpiece, braided wrist chain, c1880 .... 800.00

Gray, Dorothy, engine turned goldtone, hat shape, ribbon and fruit dec 80.00

Halston, SP, name on puff, used 150.00

Italian, hand mirror shape, SS, stylized floral engraving, lipstick concealed in handle, coral cabochon thumb piece 325.00

Kigu, compact and cigarette case, silvered and goldtone, tandem lipstick and carrying chain, England 80.00

Lampi, light blue enamel, five colorful three dimensional scenes from Alice in Wonderland enclosed in plastic domes on lid 180.00

Max Factor, 2-1/4" d, solid perfume, round faux jade pendant, goldtone twisted braided wire disk, orig Khara fragrance 35.00

Norida, emb lady, silver tone 75.00

Rex Fifth Avenue, vanity-pochette, navy blue, gold polka dots, taffeta drawstring, mirror on outside base 90.00

R. G. & Co., vanity case, SS, yellow cloisonné enamel, finger chain, painted flowers on lid, chain, perfume tube suspended from enameled and silver finger ring chain 290.00

Schuco, teddy bear, apricot mohair, fully jointed, black steel eyes, embroidered nose and mouth, c1920, spotty fur loss 575.00

Tiffany & Co.
14K yellow gold, mirrored compartment, engraved case, engine turned design, sgd "Tiffany & Co.," minor dents 320.00
Sterling silver and 14K yellow gold, Art Deco, reeded silver sunburst, ruby and gold accents, brushed gold int. 345.00
Toilet Box, 3-3/8" x 2-1/2", sterling silver, rounded rect, lid cornered by pierced circles, Tiffany & Co., c1910, 3.9 oz 175.00

Unknown Maker, compact
Castanets shape, ebony wood, metal Paris insignia centered on lid, orange tasseled carrying cord 220.00
Flamingo motif 90.00
Sterling Silver, chain handle 90.00
Sterling Silver and Enamel, English, Birmingham, 2-1/8" x 3", rect, enameled pale green over scalloped sunburst ground stemming from thumbpiece 250.00
Sterling Silver and Enamel, English, Birmingham, 2-1/2" sq, canted corners, green enamel over "L" shaped engine-turning, scalloped sunray issuing from scrolls, c1940 .... 225.00
Sterling Silver and Enamel, English, Birmingham, 2-3/4" sq, canted corners, white enamel over sunburst bordered by engine-turning, int. with metal fitting and inscription, c1937 .... 300.00
Sterling Silver and Enamel, English, Birmingham, 2-7/8" sq, canted corners, blue enamel over spiraling engine-turning, central nautical flag with crown 250.00
Telephone dial shape, red, white, and blue, slogan "I Like Ike" imprinted on lid, red map of USA on lid center 225.00
Wagon Wheel, 4-1/2" d, goldtone, framed mirror, powder screen, orig puff, felt cover 55.00

Unknown Maker, compact and matching cigarette case, SS and 14K gold, reeded silver case with applied gold bow plaque, red stone accents, sgd "WAB" 490.00

Unknown Maker, powder tier, silvertone triple tier vanity case, swivel compartments for powder, rouge, and lipstick 195.00

Unknown Maker, vanity bag, SS mesh, hallmarked, octagonal, goldtone int. and finger ring carrying chain 500.00

Unknown maker, engine turned, gold toned, orig contents, puff, and felt pouch, $40.

Unknown Maker, vanity case, antique goldtone, two sided filigree, red stones set in lids, powder and rouge compartments, lipstick concealed in tassel, carrying chain 245.00

Volupte
2-7/8" sq, gold metal, top black, beaded bold edge, gold center medallion with shell-like raised edge, inlaid on gold leaves and rhinestone flowers, flannel case, orig Franklin Simon box.... 75.00
3" x 3", affixed silver bijou, 3 sapphire cabochons surrounded by rhinestones, black enameled top and bottom with silver trim, glued in mirror, powder screen, orig puff 95.00

Whiting & Davis Co., vanity bag, purple, black, and silver mesh, purple enameled vanity case on outside corner of frame, lined int., powder sifter, metal mirror, and rouge compartment on lid, carrying chain 500.00

CONSOLIDATED GLASS COMPANY

History: The Consolidated Lamp and Glass Company was formed as a result of the 1893 merger of the Wallace and McAfee Company, glass and lamp jobbers of Pittsburgh, and the Fostoria Shade & Lamp Company of Fostoria, Ohio. When the Fostoria, Ohio, plant burned down in 1895, Corapolis, Pennsylvania, donated a seven-acre tract of land near the center of town for a new factory. In 1911, the company was the largest lamp, globe, and shade works in the United States, employing more than 400 workers.

In 1925, Reuben Haley, owner of an independent design firm, convinced John Lewis, president of Consolidated, to enter the giftware field utilizing a series of designs inspired by the 1925 Paris Exposition (l'Exposition Internationale des Arts Décorative et Industriels Modernes) and the work of René Lalique. Initially, the glass was marketed by Howard Selden through his showroom at 225 Fifth Ave. in New York City. The first two lines were Catalonian and Martele.

Additional patterns were added in the late 1920s: Florentine (January 1927), Chintz (January 1927), Ruba Rombic (January 1928), and Line 700 (January 1929). On April 2, 1932, Consolidated closed it doors. Kenneth Harley moved about 40 molds to Phoenix. In March 1936, Consolidated reopened under new management, and the "Harley" molds were returned. During this period, the famous Dancing Nymph line, based on an eight-inch salad plate in the 1926 Martele series, was introduced.

In August 1962, Consolidated was sold to Dietz Brothers. A major fire damaged the plant during a 1963 labor dispute and in 1964 the company permanently closed its doors.

References: Ann Gilbert McDonald, *Evolution of the Night Lamp,* Wallace-Homestead, 1979; Jack D. Wilson, *Phoenix & Consolidated Art Glass,* 1926-1980, Antique Publications, 1989.

Collectors' Club: Phoenix and Consolidated Glass Collectors, 41 River View Dr., Essex Junction, VT 05452, http://www.collectoronline.com/club-PCGCC-wp.html.

Berry Bowl, master, Criss-Cross, cranberry opalescent, 8" d 175.00

Bon Bon, cov, 8" d, Ruba Rhombic, faceted, smoky topaz, catalog #832, c1931 .... 325.00

Bowl
5-1/2" d, Coronation, Martelé, flared, blue 75.00
8" d, Dancing Nymph, dark blue wash 365.00

Box, cov, 7" l, 5" w, Martelé line, Fruit and Leaf pattern, scalloped edge 85.00

Butter Dish, cov, Cosmos, pink band 200.00
Candlesticks, pr
  Hummingbird, Martelé line, oval body, jade green,
    6-3/4" h 245.00
  Ruba Rhombic, smoky topaz...215.00
Cocktail, Dancing Nymph, French Crystal 90.00
Cologne Bottle, orig stopper, 4-1/2" h, Cosmos 120.00
Cookie Jar, 6-1/2" h, Regent Line, #3758, Florette, rose pink over white
  opal casing 370.00
Creamer and Sugar, Ruba Rhombic, smoky topaz, angular
  handles 1,265.00
Cruet, orig stopper, Florette, pink satin 225.00
Cup and Saucer, Dancing Nymph, ruby flashed 265.00
Dinner Service, Five Fruits, service for six, goblet, plate, sherbet, one
  large serving plate, purple wash, mold imperfections, wear.....375.00
Goblet, Dancing Nymph, French Crystal 90.00
Humidor, Florette, pink satin 225.00
Jar, cov, Con-Cora, #3758-9, pine cone dec, irid 165.00
Jug, Spanish Knobs, 5-1/2" h, handle, pink 125.00
Lamp
  Cockatoo, 13" h, figural, orange and blue, black beak, brown stump,
    black base 450.00
  Elk, 13" h, chocolate brown, blue clock mounted between horns,
    black bass base, shallow annealing mark 1,000.00
  Flower Basket, 8" h, bouquet of roses and poppies, yellows, pinks,
    green leaves, brown basketweave, black glass base.........300.00
Mayonnaise Comport, Martelé Iris, green wash 55.00
Miniature Lamp, Cosmos, 7" h, fish net ground.....................350.00
Night Light, Santa Maria, block base 450.00
Old Fashioned Tumbler, 3-7/8" h, Catalonian, yellow 20.00
Pitcher, water, Florette, pink satin 200.00
Plate
  7" d, Catalonian, green 25.00
  8-1/4" d, Bird of Paradise, amber wash 40.00
  8-1/4" d, Dancing Nymph, French Crystal 85.00
  8-1/2" d, Five Fruits, green 40.00
  10-1/4" d, Catalonian, yellow 40.00
  12" d, Five Fruits, white 65.00
  12" d, Martelé, Orchid, pink, birds and flowers....................115.00
Platter, Dancing Nymph, Palace, dark blue wash 1,000.00
Puff Box, cov
  Hummingbirds, milk glass..75.00
  Lovebirds, blue 95.00
Salt and Pepper Shakers, pr
  Cone, pink 75.00
  Cosmos 185.00
  Guttate, green 85.00
Sauce Dish, Criss-Cross, cranberry opalescent 55.00
Sherbet, ftd
  Catalonian, green 20.00
  Dancing Nymph, French Crystal..80.00
Snack Set, Martelé Fruits, pink 45.00
Spooner, Criss-Cross, cranberry opalescent 75.00
Sugar Bowl, cov
  Catalonian, green 30.00
  Guttate, cased pink..120.00
Sugar Shaker, orig top
  Cone, green..95.00
  Guttate, cased pink, pewter top...200.00
Sundae, Martelé Russet Yellow Fruits 35.00
Syrup
  Cone, squatty, pink 295.00
  Cosmos, SP top..275.00
Toilet Bottle, Ruba Rhombic, cased jade green 650.00
Toothpick Holder
  Florette, cased pink 75.00
  Guttate, cranberry..185.00
Tumbler
  Catalonian, ftd, green, 5-1/4" h..30.00

Tumbler, Cosmos pattern, white ground, pink, blue, and yellow flowers, pink border, 3-3/4" h, $85.

Cosmos 85.00
Dancing Nymph, frosted pink, 6" h 175.00
Guttate, pink satin...60.00
Katydid, clambroth...165.00
Martelé Russet Yellow Fruits, ftd, 5-3/4" h...............................5.00
Ruba Rhombic, faceted, ftd, silver gray, 6" h.........................200.00
Umbrella Vase, Blackberry...550.00
Vase
  Catalonian, #1183, three tiers, honey, 6" h 165.00
  Con-Cora, milk glass, hp flowers, 12" h, 8-1/2" d 95.00
  Dancing Nymph, crimped, ruby stain, reverse French Crystal high-
    lights, 5" h 135.00
  Dancing Nymph, crimped, rust stain, reverse highlights,
    5" h 140.00
  Florentine, collared, flat, green, 12" h..................................275.00
  Freesia, white ceramic wash, fan 225.00
  Hummingbird, #2588, turquoise on satin custard,
    5-1/2" h 90.00
  Katydid, blue wash, fan shaped top, 8-1/2" h 300.00
  Lovebirds, custard yellow ground, pale green birds, coral colored
    flowers, 11-1/4" h, 10" w 600.00
  Poppy, green cased...550.00
  Purple leaf and berry design, opalescent, 9-3/4" h...............225.00
  Regent Line, #3758, cased blue stretch over white opal, pinched,
    6" h...175.00
  Ruba Rhombic, silver gray, c1931, 6-1/2" h 635.00
Whiskey Glass, 2-5/8" h, Ruba Rhombic, faceted, transparent jungle
  green, catalog #823 ....250.00

CONTINENTAL CHINA and PORCELAIN (GENERAL)

History: By 1700, porcelain factories existed in large numbers throughout Europe. In the mid-18th century, the German factories at Meissen and Nymphenburg were dominant. As the century ended, French potteries assumed the leadership role. The 1740s to the 1840s were the golden age of Continental china and porcelains.

Americans living in the last half of the 19th century eagerly sought the masterpieces of the European porcelain factories. In the early 20th century, this style of china and porcelain was considered "blue chip" by antiques collectors.

References: Susan and Al Bagdade, *Warman's English & Continental Pottery & Porcelain,* 3rd Edition, Krause Publications, 1998; Rachael Feild, *Macdonald Guide to Buying Antique Pottery & Porcelain,* Wallace-Homestead, 1987; Geoffrey Godden, *Godden's Guide to European Porcelain,* Random House, 1993.

Additional Listings: French—Haviland, Limoges, Old Paris, Sarreguemines, and Sevres; German—Austrian Ware, Bavarian China, Carlsbad China, Dresden/Meissen, Rosenthal, Royal Bayreuth, Royal Bonn, Royal Rudolstadt, Royal Vienna, Schlegelmilch, and Villeroy and Boch; Italian—Capo-di-Monte.

Berlin, urn, cov
    10-1/4" h, floral cartouche and molded foliage swags, mated pair 650.00
    17-1/2" h, ribbed body, figural cartouches enclosed by molded laurel wreath, ground floral spray and banded dec, lids surmounted by fully molded figure of bird, ormolu mounts with cast foliate dec, pr 4,250.00

French Faience
    Bulb Pot, 3-1/8" d, sq, molded acanthus-capped scroll feet, conforming handles, front with scene of courting couple, verso landscape, each side with floral sprays, sq form insert, gilt highlights, attributed to Marseilles, last quarter 18th C, pr 900.00
    Inkstand, 13-1/2" l, figural, cartouche shaped base molded with scrolls, front painted with harbor scene flanked by tower and knight shaped inkpots, back sections support large figure of lion with raised paw resting on shield with armorial 650.00
    Plate, 9" d, blue and white floral dec, foliate border 115.00
    Plate, 9" d, central vase and large floral blossoms, stylized garland border, yellow rim 150.00
    Sugar Caster, 8-1/2" h, brightly polychrome scene of courting couple in landscape, floral sprays borders, dec band of fleur-de-lis border, pierced cov with conforming dec, early 19th C 450.00

French, plate, multicolored hunting reserves, floral and trellis border, mid 19th C, "Gien Porcelaine Opaque" mark, $85. Photo courtesy Susan and Al Bagdade.

Hochst, figural group, 11" h, lovers, rococo arbor entwined with grapes, underglaze wheel mark, incised triangle, c1765, minor restoration 9,500.00
Hutschenreuther
    Plaque, 5-1/8" x 6-7/8", oval, Madonna and Child, giltwood frame, late 19ty C 600.00
    Service Plate, 10-7/8" d, central dec, summer flowers within heavily gilt cavetto, rim worked with scrolling acanthus, textured ground, underglaze green factory marks, minor rubbing, 12 pc set 1,600.00
Ludwigsburg, bowl, cov, underplate, 6-1/4" h, molded vine handles, applied pink flowers, scenes of putti at play, cobalt blue and gilt reserves, underplate with scalloped rim, conforming reserves, large floral sprays, c1800 .... 1,000.00
Naples, ewer, 20" h, relief dec, Bacchian orchard scene, female rising from leaf ornaments handle, late 19th C 395.00
Niderviller, charger, scalloped, Bleuett dec, cobalt blue rim, Count Philbert De Custine mark, c1780 .... 450.00
Paris
    Tea Set, partial, enamel dec floral design between wide gilt bands, teapot (cover missing), 7-1/2" h creamer, 7" h sugar, waste bowl, six cups and saucers, 19th C 635.00
    Vase, 9-1/2" h, oval form, red ground borders, paneled landscapes with children, 19th C, pr 320.00
    Vase, 14-1/2" h, blue ground with gilt foliate framed figural and floral cartouches, 19th C, pr 2,645.00
Petit, Jacob, clock case, 15-3/4" h, portrait of French courtesan, sgd, c1840, chips 1,200.00
Portuguese, shaving bowl, 3-5/8" h, molded indention in rim, central dec, blue, yellow, and green floral border 100.00
Potschappel, urn, cov, 19" h, cartouche with 3 women and musical instruments, enclosed by applied fruit and floral dec, sq plinth base with applied floral enclosed neoclassical style and floral cartouches ... 450.00
Rex, Augustus, urn, 14-1/2" h, molded with gilt and white ram's head form handles, supporting foliage garland in mask, body with figures of harbor side, pink diaper neck and foot, underglaze blue "Augustus Rex" mark, pr 2,900.00
Rue Thiroux, plate, 9-1/4" d, painted floral sprays, gilt scalloped rim, French, 18th C, pr 250.00
Saint Cloud
    Bonbonniere, cov, cat form, SS mountings, late 19th C 295.00
    Cup and Saucer, pr, tremleuse, c1750 .... 650.00
Samson
    Figural Group, 10-1/2" h, maiden in flowering robes, seated on shell, naturalistically molded rocky base, polychromed details, late 19th C 1,200.00
    Figural Group, 13-3/4" h, maiden with draping garment, one arm over face, other holding vessel, polychromed details, gilt highlights, late 19th C 750.00
    Figural Group, 19" h, Aurora seated in chariot, surrounded by cherubs on naturalistically molded cloud, 2 maidens attend to swans pulling chariot, floral garlands, polychromed details, highlights, late 19th C 2,600.00
    Standish, 5" l, oval form, 4 paw feet, plinth with ball feet, Chinese export style floral dec 300.00
Schumann, partial dinner service, alternating panels of floral sprays and courting couples, 36 pcs 450.00
Schwartzburg, Thuringia, figure, 11-1/4" h, Chinoiserie-style, man and woman reclining against pillows, polychrome and gilt highlights, sgd "H. Meisel," dated 1922, pr 3,850.00
Sitzendorf, mirror, 18-1/2" w, 33-1/2" h, Meissen style, rect plate, conforming frame profusely dec with applied flowers and putti, white ground, surmounted by mirrored cartouche flanked by 2 putti, rococo inspired cartouche with 3 short S-scroll arms ending in candlecups 800.00
Unknown Continental Maker
    Cup and Saucer, 4-1/2" h, panel depicting "Ludwigskirche," blue ground, gilt rim 350.00
    Portrait Plaque, 11-1/8" d, young boy, hexagonal plaque, gilt wood frame with oval opening 1,600.00

Unknown German Maker

Bowl, 12-1/4" h, oval, reticulated sides, molded open-work handles with center shells, floral and ribboned garland painted center, gilt highlights 100.00

Urn, cov, 14" h, figural and floral cartouches, gilt foliate dec, two caryatid form handles, one damaged, pr 600.00

Volkestadt

Figure, 12-3/4" h, Cupid and Psyche, rock molded circular base, white biscuit, printed mark, late 19th C, restorations 250.00

Teapot, swelled circular, faint ridging, dome top, applied purple berry finial, purple floral sprigs, applied scroll handles, underglaze blue crossed pitchforks mark, handle restored 400.00

COOKIE JARS

History: Cookie jars, colorful and often whimsical, are now an established collecting category. Do not be misled by the high prices realized at the 1988 Andy Warhol auction. Many of the same cookie jars that sold for more than $1,000 each can be found in the field for less than $100.

Cookie jars often were redesigned to reflect newer tastes. Hence, the same jar may be found in several different variations.

Marks: Many cookie jar shapes were manufactured by more than one company and, as a result, can be found with different marks. This often happened because of mergers or separations, e.g., Brush-McCoy which became Nelson McCoy. Molds also were traded and sold among companies.

References: Fred and Joyce Roerig, *Collector's Encyclopedia of Cookie Jars,* Book I (1991, 1997 value update), Book II (1994, 1999 value update), Book III (1998), Collector Books; Mike Schneider, *The Complete Cookie Jar Book,* 2nd ed., Schiffer, 1999; Mark and Ellen Supnick, *Wonderful World of Cookie Jars,* L-W Book Sales, 1995, 1998 value update; Ermagene Westfall, *Illustrated Value Guide to Cookie Jars,* Book I (1983, 1997 value update), Book II (1993, 1997 value update), Collector Books.

Periodical: *Cookie Jarrin',* RR 2, Box 504, Walterboro, SC 29488-9278.

Collectors' Club: American Cookie Jar Association, 1600 Navajo Rd., Norman, OK 73026, http://cookiejarclub.com.

Museum: The Cookie Jar Museum, Lemont, IL.

American Bisque

After School, school house shape, bell in lid, lid chipped 65.00

Coffeepot, yellow coffee cup, 9-1/2" h, 7-1/2" d, c1959 .... 75.00

Cow Jumped Over the Moon, flasher 900.00

Lamb, 11-1/2" h, design patent 137120, minor wear to paint 75.00

Liberty Bell 195.00

Spaceship with Astronaut 1,250.00

Brush

Donkey with cart 225.00

Hillbilly Frog 3,500.00

Lantern 100.00

Teddy Bear 225.00

California Originals

Tigger 200.00

Wonder Woman Cookie Bank, 1970s 900.00

Maddux of California, Queen of Tarts 525.00

McCoy

Asparagus 70.00

Dutch Treat Barn 65.00

Left: Dog in Basket, American Bisque, partial paint, flake under lid, $40; center: Milk Wagon, American Bisque, dark horse, $50; right: Peter Pan, large, Brush-McCoy, small area of darkened crazing inside base, $700; Photo courtesy of Green Valley Auctions, Inc.

Engine, #207, 8-1/2" h, mkd "McCoy USA" 295.00

Granny, #159, 11" h, mkd "USA" 125.00

Have A Happy Day, mkd "McCoy 235 USA," glaze skip, small factory blemish 50.00

Pineapple 75.00

Popeye and Whimpy, cylindrical 95.00

Touring Car 120.00

Mosaic Tile, Mammy, yellow 375.00

Nestle's, Toll House Cookie House 95.00

Regal

Alice in Wonderland, Walt Disney Productions copyright, 1950s, several small paint flakes 3,200.00

Quaker Oats 195.00

Robinson Ransbottom

Dutch Boy 85.00

Jock the Monkey 90.00

Shawnee

Dutch Boy 175.00

Winnie Pig 320.00

Treasure Craft

Cactus, bandanna and cowboy hat 50.00

Dinosaur, gray, large purple spots, blue spines, 11-1/2" h 65.00

Mickey Mouse, Disney copyright, 12" h 75.00

Nanna (Mammy) 95.00

Twin Winton

Cow Spots 75.00

Happy Bull 75.00

Jack in Box 70.00

Walt Disney, Dumbo, double sided, touch-up to paint, 14" h 195.00

COPELAND and SPODE

History: In 1749, Josiah Spode was apprenticed to Thomas Whieldon and in 1754 worked for William Banks in Stoke-on-Trent. In the early 1760s, Spode started his own pottery, making cream-colored earthenware and blue-printed whiteware. In 1770, he returned to Banks' factory as master, purchasing it in 1776.

Spode pioneered the use of steam-powered pottery-making machinery and mastered the art of transfer printing from copper plates. Spode opened a London shop in 1778 and sent William Copeland there about 1784. A number of larger London locations followed. At the turn of the century, Spode introduced bone china. In 1805, Josiah Spode II and William Copeland entered into a partnership for the London business. A series of partnerships between Josiah Spode II, Josiah Spode III, and William Taylor Copeland resulted.

In 1833, Copeland acquired Spode's London operations and seven years later the Stoke plants. William Taylor Copeland managed the business until his death in 1868. The firm remained in the hands of Copeland heirs. In 1923, the plant was electrified; other modernization followed.

In 1976, Spode merged with Worcester Royal Porcelain to become Royal Worcester Spode, Ltd.

References: Susan and Al Bagdade, *Warman's English & Continental Pottery & Porcelain,* 3rd Edition, Krause Publications, 1998; Robert Copeland, *Spode & Copeland Marks,* Cassell Academic, 1993; —, *Spode's Willow Pattern & Other Designs After The Chinese,* Blanford Press, 1990; D. Drakard & P. Holdway, *Spode Printed Wares,* Longmans, 1983; L. Whiter, *Spode: A History of the Family, Factory, and Wares,* 1733-1833, Random Century, 1989; Sydney B. Williams, *Antique Blue & White Spode,* David & Charles, 1988.

Museums: Cincinnati Art Museum, Cincinnati, OH; City of Stoke-On-Trent Museum, Hanley, England; Jones Museum of Glass & Ceramics, Sebago, ME; Spode Museum, Stoke-on-Trent, UK; Victoria & Albert Museum, London, England.

Cabinet Plate
    8-1/4" d, jeweled border, with coral and pearls, dark green ground, c1883 .... 600.00
    9-1/2" d, artist sgd "Samuel Alcock," 1-3/4" jeweled border, intricate gold, beading, pearl and turquoise jeweling, c1889 .... 750.00
Demitasse Cup and Saucer, Heather Rose, mkd "Spode's Jewel, Copeland Spode, England," registration, patent numbers, pattern name 20.00
Dish, 11-1/2" w, 2 handles, mushroom ground, gilt foliage, gilt scroll molded handles, puce Spode Feldspar mark, c1800 .... 150.00
Fish Plate, 9-3/4" d, artist sgd "H. C. Lea," four part gold swirled design, hp fly in each section, c1891 .... 175.00
Jar, cov, 10" h, globular, handles, Oriental style, apple green, birds on flowering peony branches, iron-red, pink, and gilt dec, gilt knob finial, Spode mark, Pat. #3086, c1820 .... 725.00
Pitcher, 7-1/2" h, deep blue glaze, raised white figures, tavern scenes and berries 225.00
Plate
    9-1/4" d, scalloped edge, hp pink border with gilding, blue, yellow, and green floral dec 80.00
    9-1/2" d, bird perched on snowy branch, holly leaves and berries 115.00
Platter, 15" l, blue transfer, mkd "Copeland, Spode's Tower," wear and scratches, minor edge chips 165.00
Potpourri Jar, 10" h, pierced cov, flared rim and foot, Imari style, flowering plants, gilt knob finial, Spode mark, Pat. #967, c1810 .... 625.00

Game Plates, each with different enameled reserves of birds among tall grasses, colored grounds, including pink, blue, white, and yellow, profuse gilding, c1875, 4 shown from set of 15, 8-1/4" d, $3,750. Photo courtesy of Freeman\Fine Arts.

Punch Set, 13" d punch bowl, 12 cups and ladle, c1920 .... 550.00
Soup Bowl, brown Rhine pattern, brown mark 30.00
Spill Vase, 4-3/4" h, flared rim, pale lilac, gilt octagonal panels with portrait of bearded man, band of pearls on rims and bases, Spode, c1920 .... 425.00
Urn, cov, 15" h, Louis XVI style, cobalt blue ground, medallions on each side with bouquet of roses, majolica, repair to one handle, nick to one lid, pr 900.00
Water Pitcher, 8-1/4" h, bulbous, tan acanthus leaf handle and spout, green field dec with white relief classical figures of dancing women, white relief banded floral garland dec at neck, mkd "Rd. No. 180288" 250.00

COPPER

History: Copper objects, such as kettles, teakettles, warming pans, and measures, played an important part in the 19th-century household. Outdoors, the apple-butter kettle and still were the two principal copper items. Copper culinary objects were lined with a thin protective coating of tin to prevent poisoning. They were relined as needed.

References: Mary Frank Gaston, *Antique Brass & Copper,* Collector Books, 1992, 1994 value update; Henry J. Kauffman, *Early American Copper, Tin, and Brass: Handcrafted Metalware from Colonial Times,* Astragal Press, 1995.

Reproduction Alert: Many modern reproductions exist.

Additional Listings: Arts and Crafts Movement; Roycroft.

Notes: Collectors place great emphasis on signed pieces, especially those by American craftsmen. Since copper objects were made abroad as well, it is hard to identify unsigned examples.

Bed Warmer, 38-1/2" l, engraved lid, wood handle, wrought iron ferule, European 90.00
Bowl, 9-3/4" d, 7-1/2" h, hammered, flaring ribbed form, scalloped rim, circular flared base, imp "Mark Zimmerman Maker" on base, 1912, polished 1,495.00
Candelabra, 24" h, long central stem flanked and joined by U-shaped stem, crimped edge candle cups, joined by scroll openwork dec, raised on domed and crimped circular base, dark patina, c1915 .... 690.00
Cigarette Box, 4-1/2" l, 1-1/2" h, oval, enameled medallion of tall ship on crashing waves, cedar lined, fine orig patina, attributed to Society of Arts & Crafts Boston 400.00

Pub Measure, Georgian, 1 quart, mid "1826 N P" on spout, 6-1/8" h, $250.

Coal Scuttle, 18" x 22" x 15", Art Nouveau, brass shovel, stylized flowers, English, break to 2 hinges..250.00
Colander, 12" d 75.00
Desk Set, hammered blotter, letter holder, bookends, stamp box, each with bone carved cabochon, branch and berry motif, Potter Studio, fine orig patina, die-stamp mark 750.00
Fish Poacher, cov, 20-1/2" l, oval, rolled rim, iron swing ball handle, 19th C...350.00
Haystack Measure, 12" h, stamped "Gallon," dovetailed, English....220.00
Lantern, 15" h, hexagonal beveled glass panels, circular handle, 19th C...275.00
Letter Holder, 5-1/2" w, 4-1/4" h, hammered, deep orig patina, enameled medallion of sailing ship, inscribed "Twichell," Getrude Twichell, Boston Society of Arts of Crafts, c1917 ....375.00
Milk Pail, 12" h, swing handle, stamped "1870," Dutch................500.00
Mirror, 35" w, 18-3/4" h, rect form, hammered copper, green and blue enameled circular ornament, beveled glass insert, c1916, minor crack to enamel...1,955.00
Pitcher, 17-1/2" h, 9" w, raised foliate design, brass handle and mount, imp diamond with bird mark for W. M. F., polished...................230.00
Sauce Pan, 7" d, dovetailed construction, cast iron handle..........70.00
Tea Kettle
    11-1/2" h, curved spout, upright swing handle, brass lid knob, imp "G. Tyron" on handle, dents, wear, PA, 19th C 690.00
    12-1/2" h, curved spout, upright swing handle, brass lid knob, imp "H. Dehuff" on handle, dents, wear, PA, 19th C 800.00
Tray, 16-1/2" l, 11-3/4", rect, wrought handles, Arts & Crafts, enameled peacocks, medium brown ground, some wear to orig patina.....95.00
Umbrella Stand, 25" h, hand hammered, flared rim, cylindrical body, 2 strap work loop handles, repousse medallion, riveted flared foot, c1910 ....650.00
Vase, 11-1/2" w, 6-7/8" h, patinated, ribbed flaring oval, scalloped rim, raised on oblong ftd base, dark brown and green patina, inscribed "M. Zimmerman maker 1463-1915 B," artist's cipher on base, scratches..4,325.00
Wall Plaque, 17" d, raised foliate design around woman's portrait, imp diamond with bird mark for W. M. F., polished........................175.00

CORALENE

History: Coralene refers to glass or china objects which have the design painted on the surface of the piece along with tiny colorless glass beads which were applied with a fixative. The piece was placed in a muffle to fix the enamel and set the beads.

Several American and English companies made glass coralene in the 1880s. Seaweed or coral were the most common design. Other motifs were Wheat Sheaf and Fleur-de-Lis. Most of the base glass was satin finished.

China and pottery coralene, made from the late 1890s until after World War II, is referred to as Japanese coralene. The beading is opaque and inserted into the soft clay. Hence, it is only one-half to three-quarters visible.

Reproduction Alert: Reproductions are on the market, some using an old glass base. The beaded decoration on new coralene has been glued and can be scraped off.

China
Condiment Set, open salt, cov mustard, pepper shaker, white opaque ground, floral coralene dec, SP stand 250.00
Pitcher, 4-1/2" h, 1909 pattern, red and brown ground, beaded yellow daffodil dec...950.00
Vase, 8" h, 6-3/4"w, melon ribbed, sq top, yellow drape coralene, rose shaded to pink ground, white int. 850.00
Glass
Cruet, pink satin, yellow coralene, orig stopper 420.00

Tumbler, seaweed coralene dec, pink diamond quilted satin glass body, mkd "0700," 2-3/4" d, 4" h, $225.

Fairy Lamp, 7" h, 6 rows of yellow coralene, white opaque shade with yellow tinting, brass colored metal holder 375.00
Lamp Shade, 4-1/2" h, egg shape, scalloped tops, coral pink with yellow beaded wheat design, pr 350.00
Lamp, table, 16-1/2" h, 5-1/2" d, green glass, pink, white, and yellow coralene flowers and leaves, coralene branch at top, white enameled dot dec, frosted shade with birds and bows 325.00
Vase
    5-1/2" h, 4" d, butterscotch MOP, Coinspot pattern, heavy coralene beading, pink and white flowers, yellow centers, green leaves525.00
    7" h, pink shaded and cased to white, DQ pattern, gold beading within design, pr..450.00
Cowan
Bookends, pr
    6-1/4" h, 4" d, Boy and Girl, Special Ivory glaze, stamped " Cowan" 350.00
    7-1/2" h, 5" w, Elephant, semi-matte green glaze, stamped "Cowan," minor nick to base of one 700.00
    8-1/2" h, 6" d, Flying Fish, Antique Green glaze, stamped "Cowan," restored point on each 600.00

COWAN POTTERY

History: R. Guy Cowan founded the Cowan Pottery in 1913 in Cleveland, Ohio. The establishment remained in almost continuous operation until 1931, when financial difficulties forced closure.

Early production was redware pottery. Later a porcelain-like finish was perfected with special emphasis placed on glazes, with lustreware being one of the most common types. Commercial wares marked "Lakeware" were produced from 1927 to 1931.

Marks: Early marks include an incised "Cowan Pottery" on the redware (1913-1917), an impressed "Cowan," and an impressed "Lakewood." The imprinted stylized semicircle, with or without the initials "R. G.," came later.

References: Mark Bassett and Victorian Naumann, *Cowan Pottery and the Cleveland School,* Schiffer Publishing, 1997; Leslie Piña, *Pottery, Modern Wares 1920-1960,* Schiffer Publishing, 1994; Tim and Jamie Saloff, *Collector's Encyclopedia of Cowan Pottery: Identification and Values,* Collector Books, 1994.

Candleholders, triple, ivory, 8-1/2" w, 4-7/8" h, mkd, $45.

Museums: Cowan Pottery Museum, Rocky River Public Library, Rocky River, OH; Everson Museum of Art, Syracuse, NY.

Bowl, 5-1/4" h, 5-1/2" d, ftd, cinnabar glaze, some glaze cracking at foot joint, imp mark 160.00
Charger, 11-1/4" d, emb undersea motif, light green fish and plants, blue-green ground, imp "Cowan" 500.00
Figure
   8" h, Pierrette, Old Ivory glaze, stamped "Cowan" 250.00
   9-1/2" x 9", horse, mahogany and gold flambé glaze, imp mark 1,500.00
Flower Frog
   7" h, figural nude, #698, Original Ivory glaze 250.00
   7-3/4" h, 4-1/4" d, Heavenward, Original Ivory glaze, stamped "Cowan" 175.00
   7-3/4" h, 6-1/4" d, Duet, Original Ivory glaze, stamped "Cowan," small shallow chip to base 450.00
   . 10" h, 5-1/4" d, Pan, Special Ivory glaze, stamped "Cowan," minor base nick 250.00
   10-1/4" h, Debutante, Special Ivory glaze, stamped "Cowan/S" 850.00
   10-3/4" h, 4" d, Swirl Dancer, Original Ivory glaze, stamped "Cowan" 850.00
   11-3/4" h, Loveliness, Original Ivory glaze, incised "B," crack to wrist 400.00
Lamp Base, 11-1/2" h, 9-1/2" d, bulbous, Oriental Red glaze, stamp mark, drilled at side and bottom 300.00
Paperweight, 4-1/2" h, 3-1/4" l, Elephant, Special Ivory glaze, stamped "Cowan" 300.00
Trivet, 6-1/2" d, woman's head and flowers, blue, cream, yellow, and pink, die-stamped mark, minor scratches 450.00
Vase
   7-1/4" h, 5" d, classical shape, dripping brown crystalline glaze, mirrored orange glaze, ink mark 300.00
   10" h, 10'"d, spherical, ribbed, leathery vermillion glaze, stamped "Cowan," two hairlines to rim 125.00

CRANBERRY GLASS

History: Cranberry glass is transparent and named for its color, achieved by adding powdered gold to a molten batch of amber glass and reheating at a low temperature to develop the cranberry or ruby color. The glass color first appeared in the last half of the 17th century but was not made in American glass factories until the last half of the 19th century.

Cranberry glass was blown, mold blown, or pressed. Examples often are decorated with gold or enamel. Less-expensive cranberry glass, made by substituting copper for gold, can be identified by its bluish purple tint.

Reference: William Heacock and William Gamble, *Encyclopedia of Victorian Colored Pattern Glass: Book 9, Cranberry Opalescent from A to Z,* Antique Publications, 1987.

Reproduction Alert: Reproductions abound. These pieces are heavier, off-color, and lack the quality of older examples.

Additional Listings: See specific categories, such as Bride's Baskets; Cruets; Jack-in-the-Pulpit Vases; etc.

Basket
   5" h, 3-1/2" d bowl, German silver filigree frame, plain cranberry bowl 115.00
   7" h, 5" w, ruffled edge, petticoat shape, crystal loop handle, c1890 .... 250.00
Bottle
   8" h, 3" d, gold mid-band, white enameled trim, clear faceted stopper 150.00
   8-1/2" h, 3-1/4" d, Inverted Thumbprint pattern, white enameled dot flowers and bands, gold trim, clear cut faceted stopper 165.00
Centerpiece, 19-1/2" h, central trumpet form vase, shallow dish, pedestal foot, gilt Greek key dec, Victorian 300.00
Condiment Dish and Underplate, 6-1/2" h, cranberry, scrolling vines and grapes dec, Continental 175.00
Creamer, 5" h, 2-3/4" d, Optic pattern, fluted to, applied clear handle 95.00
Cruet, 6-3/4" h, 4" d, white enameled flowers and leaves, applied clear handle, cut clear stopper 225.00
Epergne, 19" h, 11" d, 5 pcs, large ruffled bowl, tall center lily 3 jack-in-the-pulpit vases 1,200.00
Finger Bowl, Inverted Thumbprint pattern, deep color 200.00
Garniture, 14" d bowl, pr 11" h candlesticks, cranberry overlay cut to clear, faceted cut dec, Continental 450.00
Lamp, 10" h, 5" d, peg, silverplated base, ruffled rubena shade, emb daisies, chimney 265.00

Vase, applied yellow band and feet, English, 9-1/4" h, pr, $180.

Pipe, 18" l, hand blown, tapering bent neck, bulbous bowl, 3 bulbs at base, white enamel dec at outer rim of bowl 250.00

Pitcher

6-1/2" h, 4-1/8" d, Ripple and Thumbprint pattern, bulbous, round mouth, applied clear handle 175.00

10" h, 5" d, bulbous, ice bladder int., applied clear handle 250.00

11-3/8" h, 9" w, bulbous, internal vertical ribs, white and blue enameled floral dec, applied clear loop handle, c1895 .... 300.00

Rose Bowl, 5" h, heart shaped, Raindrop pattern, mkd "Rd 81051," attributed to Stevens & Williams 300.00

Salt, master, ftd, enameled floral dec 200.00

Tumble-Up, Inverted Thumbprint pattern 195.00

Tumbler, Inverted Thumbprint pattern 65.00

Vase

7-1/2" h, emb ribs, applied clear feet, 3 swirled applied clear leaves around base 120.00

8-7/8" h, bulbous, white enameled lilies of the valley dec, cylindrical neck 150.00

12" h, cylindrical, flared top and base, vaseline trim, enameled butterflies and flowers 395.00

Wine Decanter, 11" h, 5" d, heavy cut clear base, gold trim, clear cut faceted stopper, wear to gold trim 195.00

CROWN MILANO

History: Crown Milano is an American art glass produced by the Mt. Washington Glass Works, New Bedford, Massachusetts. The original patent was issued in 1886 to Frederick Shirley and Albert Steffin.

Normally, it is an opaque-white satin glass finished with light-beige or ivory-colored ground embellished with fancy florals, decorations, and elaborate and thick raised gold.

Through continuing research into the Mount Washington Glass Company, experts have now determined that shiny Crown Milano was originally named "Colonial Ware." Documentation of this includes the name used in an 1894 issue of the *Jewelers Circular and Horological Review,* which featured both Colonial Ware glass and Crown Milano.

Collectors Club: Mount Washington Art Glass Society, P.O. Box 24094, Fort Worth, TX 76124.-1094

Marks: Marked pieces have a purple enamel entwined "CM" with a crown on the base. Sometimes paper labels were used. Since both Mount Washington and Pairpoint supplied mountings, the silver-plated mounts often have "MW" impressed or a Pairpoint mark.

Advisors: Clarence and Betty Maier.

Biscuit Jar, cov

7-1/2" d, 9" h to top of raised bail, stark white background, scene of couple in Colonial garb, young lass, wearing fancy yellow and blue skirt, as tries to catch the bubbles blown by youthful lad, wearing a blue doublet over pink knickerbockers, framed by bold raised gold scrolls, reverse side with small white reserve, raised gold outline, gold line drawn florals. base is signed "3912/80," lid is signed "M.W.4419/c"" 785.00

5-1/2" d, 4" h, muted shades of gold, sepia and brown single-petaled rose blossoms with jewel centers, buds, and leaves, raised gold branches, alternating melon and cream colored jagged swirls, turtle plodding across floral emb lid, bail handle, sgd "M.W.4416/a" 1,385.00

Demitasse and Saucer, 2" h cup, raised golden vine laden with single petaled blossoms, buds and tiny leaves meanders around satin-white ext., each bordered by raised gold, coral center dots in 3 blos-

Biscuit Jar, melon shape, beige shading to coral ground, raised gold blossoms and foliage, silver plated cover, sgd "CM/crown/521," 6-1/4" d, 5-1/2" h, $990.

soms, other 3 blossoms with ring of black dots, sepia colored rococo scrolls entwined with floral dec, pale pink tint ext. and int. rim, curlicue handle, conforming dec on 5" saucer, sgd with logo 1,750.00

Ewer, 6-1/2" h, 7-1/2" d, Colonial Ware, 2 reserves of colorful flowers, framed by rococo borders of raised gold scrolls, fancy scroll borders, gold crosshatching across cream ground, rope handle, sgd "0100" 975.00

Muffineer, 4" d, 3" h, melon ribbed, butter yellow tint on body, powder blue and cream colored daisy blossoms encircle perimeter, metal collar and lid emb with butterfly, dragonfly, and blossoms 535.00

Vase

6" h, 5-3/4" d, butter-yellow neck and mouth with four-fold-down sides, 24 swirling molded-in ribs, cream colored body, heavily applied enamel blue and white forget-me-nots, delicate leaves and foliage 1,485.00

8-1/2" h, melon ribbed, cream ground, 3 long-stemmed thistles, each crowned with blossom of individual raised gold petals, pastel pink, aqua, and green leaves with off-white highlights, raised leaves and veins 1,450.00

9" h, Colonial Ware, white opaque, sprays of colorful blossoms, pink and yellow roses, blue cornflowers, daisies, shadow foliated branches of single petaled roses and buds, gold embellishments on neck, crown-like mouth, sgd with logo and "0615" 1,000.00

9" h, white, pearlescent pink-white Lotus Blossoms, purple and green pads, trailing stems, background gray shadow dec 1,500.00

10-1/2" h, petticoat shape, white body, pastel pansies, free-form gold accents 850.00

18" h, Colonial Ware, shiny, scene of youthful couple dancing, lady in formal yellow and pink gown, elegant hat, pink bows on shoes, male partner with baby blue satin waistcoat, fancy pantaloons, tricorner hat, walking stick, ruby colored garter, elaborate rococo scrollwork of raised gold, some loss to gold embellishments on applied wafer base, crown in wreath mark and "1029" 1,750.00

CRUETS

History: Cruets are small glass bottles used on the table and holding condiments such as oil, vinegar, and wine. The pinnacle of cruet use occurred during the Victorian era when a myriad of glass manufacturers made cruets in a wide assortment of patterns, colors, and sizes. All cruets had stoppers; most had handles.

References: Elaine Ezell and George Newhouse, *Cruets, Cruets, Cruets,* Vol. I, Antique Publications, 1991; William Heacock, *Encyclopedia of Victorian Colored Pattern Glass: Book 6, Oil Cruets from A to Z,* Antique Publications, 1981.

Additional Listings: Pattern Glass and specific glass categories such as Amberina, Cranberry, and Satin.

Amberina, 5-1/2" h, Inverted Thumbprint, trefoil spout, attributed to Mt. Washington Glass 385.00
Bluerina, 7-1/4" h, deep royal blue neck fades to clear at shoulder, optic inverted thumbprint design in body, applied clear glass handle, teardrop shaped airtrap stopper, in-the-making thin elongated bubble in neck 500.00
Bohemian, amber cut to clear, floral arrangement intaglio carved on ruby flashed ground of 3 oval panels with carved frames of floral swags, 5 cut-to-clear panels at neck, 3 embellished with gold scrolls, all edged in brilliant gold, 16 decorative panels edged in gold, base and stopper both sgd "4" 750.00
Burmese, 6-1/2" h, three striking chrysanthemum blossoms, two white and one yellow, coral colored detail stripes mushroom stopper, signed "88" in enamel 2,950.00
Custard Glass, Wild Bouquet pattern, fired-on dec.....................500.00
Frosted Blue, 12" h, 3" d, enameled large pink and white flower, green leaves, applied blue handle, matching blue frosted bubble stopper, gold trim 165.00
Green, 9-1/4" h, 3-1/8" d, white enameled dec, applied green handle, green bubble stopper 165.00
Greentown
    Cactus, chocolate, ns 125.00
    Leaf Bracket, chocolate, os 265.00
Opalescent Glass
    Daisy Fern, blue ground, Parian mold, orig stopper............225.00
    Stripes, pale blue ground, orig hollow stopper, solid amber handle, polished pontil mark 485.00
    Wild Bouquet, blue, orig stopper 495.00
Pattern Glass
    Beveled Star, green, os 225.00
    Big Button, ruby stained, os..250.00

Spatter Glass, red and white, applied clear handle, stopper missing, 4-1/2" h, $175.

    Croesus, large, green, gold trim, os 395.00
    Cut Log, os 60.00
    Daisy and Button with Crossbars, os...................................75.00
    Dakota, etched, ns 55.00
    Delaware, cranberry, gold trim, os 295.00
    Esther, green, gold trim, os 465.00
    Fandago, ns 85.00
    Fluted Scrolls, blue dec, os 265.00
    Louise, os 70.00
    Mardi Gras, ns 35.00
    Millard, amber stain, os 345.00
    Riverside's Ransom, vaseline, os.......................................225.00
    Tiny Optic, green, dec, os 150.00
Peachblow, 6-1/2" h, petticoat sape, orig cut amber stopper, Wheeling 1,750.00
Sapphire Blue
    7-1/4" h, Hobnail, faceted stopper, applied blue handle, damage to 3 hobs 385.00
    7-1/2" h, hp bridal white leafed branches, orig stopper with teardrop shaped airtrap 185.00
    7-1/2" h, 3-1/4" d, enameled pink, yellow, and blue flowers, green leaves, applied clear handle and foot, cut clear stopper.....165.00
Satin, 8-1/4" h, DQ, white shaded to gold, clear frosted handle, orig frosted clear knobby stopper...595.00

CUP PLATES

History: Many early cups were handleless and came with deep saucers. The hot liquid was poured into the saucer and sipped from it. This necessitated another plate for the cup, hence the "cup plate."

The first cup plates made of pottery were of the Staffordshire variety. From the mid-1830s to 1840s, glass cup plates were favored. The Boston and Sandwich Glass Company was one of the main manufacturers of the lacy glass type.

References: Ruth Webb Lee and James H. Rose, *American Glass Cup Plates,* published by author, 1948, Charles E. Tuttle Co. reprint, 1985; Kenneth Wilson, *American Glass 1760-1930,* 2 vols., Hudson Hills Press and The Toledo Museum of Art, 1994.

Collectors' Club: Pairpoint Cup Plate Collectors of America, P.O. Box 52D, East Weymouth, MA 02189.

Notes: It is extremely difficult to find glass cup plates in outstanding (mint) condition. Collectors expect some signs of use, such as slight rim roughness, minor chipping (best if under the rim), and, in rarer patterns, portions of scallops missing.

The numbers used are from the Lee-Rose book in which all plates are illustrated.

Prices are based on plates in average condition.

Glass
LR 26, 3-9/16" d, colorless, attributed to Sandwich or New England Glass Co. 160.00
LR 37, 3-1/4" d, opalescent, attributed to Sandwich or New England Glass Co. 200.00
LR 45, 3-9/16" d, pale opalescent, attributed to Sandwich or New England Glass Co. 200.00
LR 58, 3-3/8" d, clambroth, unlisted, Eastern origin 275.00
LR 61, 3-3/8" d, opalescent, attributed to Sandwich or New England Glass Co. 250.00
LR 75-A, 3-13/16" c, colorless, attributed to New England Glass Co..120.00
LR 81, 3-3/4" d, fiery red opalescent, New England origin 350.00

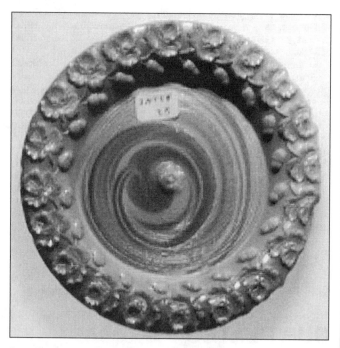

Lee-Rose #82, opaque blue, $2,900. Photo courtesy of Green Valley Auction, Inc.

LR 88, 3-11/16" d, deep opalescent opaque, attributed to Sandwich or New England Glass Co. 300.00
LR 100, 3-1/4" d, colorless, attributed to Philadelphia area, normal mold roughness.. 115.00
LR 121, colorless, lacy, Midwestern...150.00
LR 242-A, 3-1/2" d, black amethyst, lacy, Eastern origin, mold underfill and overfill 600.00
LR 247, 3-7/16" d, emerald green, lacy, attributed to Sandwich or New England Glass Co. 775.00
LR 253, 3-9/16" d, blue-green, Roman Rosette, Midwestern origin 350.00
LR 276, 3-7/16" d, blue, lacy, Boston and Sandwich Glass Co., slight opalescence bloom 350.00
LR 319, 3-5/16" d, colorless..120.00
LR 433, 4-1/8" d, colorless, mold roughness 95.00
LR 459-E, 3-7/16" d, colorless, hearts, 43 even scallops, attributed to Sandwich 75.00
LR 476, 3-5/16" d, colorless, hearts, 12 plain sides, attributed to Sandwich 75.00

Glass, Historical

LR 568, 3-7/16" d, colorless, attributed to Sandwich 165.00
LR 586-B, colorless, Ringgold, Palo Alto, stippled ground, small letters, attributed to Philadelphia area, 1847-48 ....665.00
LR695, 3" d, colorless, Midwestern origin, normal mold roughness 145.00

Pottery or Porcelain

Gaudy Dutch, Butterfly pattern..750.00
Leeds, 3-3/4" d, soft paste, gaudy blue and white floral dec, very minor pinpoint edge flakes 250.00
Majolica, leaf motif 250.00
Mulberry, cabbage roses, wheat border......................................175.00
Staffordshire, Historical
   3-1/4" d, Woodlands Estate near Philadelphia, dark blue 475.00
   3-1/2" d, Franklin Tomb, dark blue, Wood 650.00
   4" d, The Tyrants Foe, light blue, unknown maker 295.00
   4-5/8" d, Landing of Lafayette, dark blue, Clews, full border.......400.00

CUSTARD GLASS

History: Custard glass was developed in England in the early 1880s. Harry Northwood made the first American custard glass at his Indiana, Pennsylvania, factory in 1898.

From 1898 until 1915, many manufacturers produced custard glass patterns, e.g., Dugan Glass, Fenton, A. H. Heisey Glass Co., Jefferson Glass, Northwood, Tarentum Glass, and U.S. Glass. Cambridge and McKee continued the production of custard glass into the Depression.

The ivory or creamy yellow custard color is achieved by adding uranium salts to the molten hot glass. The chemical content makes the glass glow when held under a black light. The more uranium, the more luminous the color. Northwood's custard glass has the smallest amount of uranium, creating an ivory color; Heisey used more, creating a deep yellow color.

Custard glass was made in patterned tableware pieces. It also was made as souvenir items and novelty pieces. Souvenir pieces are include a place name or hand-painted decorations, e.g., flowers. Patterns of custard glass often were highlighted in gold, enameled colors, and stains.

References: Gary E. Baker et al., *Wheeling Glass 1829-1939,* Oglebay Institute, 1994, distributed by Antique Publications; William Heacock, *Encyclopedia of Victorian Colored Pattern Glass, Book IV: Custard Glass from A to Z,* Peacock Publications, 1980; William Heacock, James Measell and Berry Wiggins, *Harry Northwood: The Early Years 1881-1900,* Antique Publications, 1990.

Reproduction Alert: L. G. Wright Glass Co. has reproduced pieces in the Argonaut Shell and Grape and Cable patterns. It also introduced new patterns, such as Floral and Grape and Vintage Band. Mosser reproduced tooth-

Lee-Rose #68, colorless, one of 5 known, $4,500. Photo courtesy of Green Valley Auction, Inc.

picks in Argonaut Shell, Chrysanthemum Sprig, and Inverted Fan & Feather.

Additional Listings: Pattern Glass.

Banana Stand, Grape and Cable, Northwood, nutmeg stain...... 325.00
Berry Bowl, individual size
    Fan 45.00
    Ring Band, gold and rose dec 48.00
Berry Set, master
    Diamond with Peg 225.00
    Louis XV, gold trim 165.00
Berry Set, Intaglio, 7" master berry, six sauces 395.00
Bonbon, Fruits and Flowers, Northwood, nutmeg stain 225.00
Bowl, Grape and Cable, Northwood, 7-1/2" d, basketweave ext., nut-
    meg stain.. 65.00
Butter Dish, cov
    Everglades.. 375.00
    Grape and Cable, Northwood, nutmeg stain 450.00
    Tiny Thumbprint, Tarentum, dec.. 300.00
    Victoria... 300.00
Celery, Ring Band 300.00
Compote
    Argonaut Shell 85.00
    Geneva 65.00
Creamer
    Fluted Scrolls... 90.00
    Heart with Thumbprint 80.00
Cruet, Chrysanthemum Sprig, 7" h, gold dec............................. 485.00
Goblet, Grape and Gothic Arches, nutmeg stain 80.00
Hair Receiver, Winged Scroll 125.00
Nappy
    Northwood Grape 60.00
    Prayer Rug 65.00
Pitcher, Argonaut Shell 325.00
Plate, Grape and Cable, Northwood 55.00
Punch Cup
    Diamond with Peg 70.00
    Louis XV 65.00
Salt and Pepper Shakers, pr, Chrysanthemum Sprig 175.00
Sauce
    Cane Insert.. 35.00
    Intaglio 35.00
    Louis XV, gold trim... 40.00
    Peacock and Urn 40.00
Spooner
    Grape and Gothic Arches... 95.00
    Intaglio 115.00

Sugar, cov
    Georgia Gem, pink floral dec.. 185.00
    Tiny Thumbprint, rose dec 185.00
Table Set, cov butter, creamer, spooner, cov sugar
    Argonaut Shell 450.00
    Intaglio 500.00
Tankard Pitcher, Diamond with Peg 275.00
Toothpick Holder, Louis XV 200.00
Tumbler
    Cherry Scale... 50.00
    Geneva, green and red enamel dec...................................... 60.00
    Inverted Fan and Feather 90.00
    Vermont 110.00
    Wild Bouquet 45.00
Water Set, Ring Band, Heisey, blue floral dec, pitcher, 6
    tumblers 695.00

CUT GLASS, AMERICAN

History: Glass is cut by grinding decorations into the glass by means of abrasive-carrying metal or stone wheels. A very ancient craft, it was revived in 1600 by Bohemians and spread through Europe to Great Britain and America.

American cut glass came of age at the Centennial Exposition in 1876 and the World Columbian Exposition in 1893. The American public recognized American cut glass to be exceptional in quality and workmanship. America's most significant output of this high-quality glass occurred from 1880 to 1917, a period now known as the Brilliant Period.

Marks: Around 1890, some companies began adding an acid-etched "signature" to their glass. This signature may be the actual company name, its logo, or a chosen symbol. Today, signed pieces command a premium over unsigned pieces since the signature clearly establishes the origin. However, signatures should be carefully verified for authenticity since objects with forged signatures have been in existence for some time. One way to check is to run a finger tip or fingernail lightly over the signature area. As a general rule, a genuine signature cannot be felt; a forged signature has a raised surface.

Many companies never used the acid-etched signature on their glass and may or may not have affixed paper labels to the items originally. Dorflinger Glass and the Meriden Glass Co. made cut glass of the highest quality, yet never used an acid-etched signature. Furthermore, cut glass made before the 1890s was not signed. Many of these wood-polished items, cut on blown blanks, were of excellent quality and often won awards at exhibitions.

References: Bill and Louis Boggess, *Identifying American Brilliant Cut Glass,* 3rd ed., Schiffer Publishing, 1996; ——, *Reflections on American Brilliant Cut Glass,* Schiffer Publishing, 1995; Jo Evers, *Evers' Standard Cut Glass Value Guide,* Collector Books, 1975, 1995 value update; Bob Page and Dale Fredericksen, *A Collection of American Crystal,* Page-Fredericksen Publishing, 1995; ——, *Seneca Glass Company 1891-1983,* Page-Fredericksen Publishing, 1995; J. Michael Pearson, *Encyclopedia of American Cut & Engraved Glass,* Vols. I to III, published by author, 1975; Albert C. Revi, *American Cut & Engraved Glass,* Schiffer Publishing, 1965; Jane Shadel Spillman, *American Cut Glass, T. G. Hawkes and His Competitors,* Antique Collectors' Club, 1999; Martha Louise Swan, *American Cut

Creamer, Chrysanthemum Sprig, gold drape dec, 4-1/2" h, worn dec, $120.

and Engraved Glass, Krause Publications, 1998; Kenneth Wilson, *American Glass 1760-1930,* 2 vols., Hudson Hills Press and The Toledo Museum of Art, 1994.

Collectors' Club: American Cut Glass Association, P.O. Box 482, Ramona, CA 92065.

Museums: Corning Museum of Glass, Corning, NY; High Museum of Art, Atlanta, GA; Huntington Galleries, Huntington, WV; Lightner Museum, St. Augustine, FL; Toledo Museum Of Art, Toledo, OH.

Atomizer, 8" h, 2-1/2" h sq, Harvard pattern, gold washed atomizer, ABP 125.00
Banana Bowl, 11" d, 6-1/2" d, Harvard pattern, hobstar bottom, ABP 210.00
Basket
    6" l, 5-1/2" w, rect, applied clear glass handle, Visica miter cuts, hobstars, diamonds, and sunbursts 190.00
    6" h, 7" d, four cut hobstars, strawberry, diamond, and fan cutting, triple notched square cut handle, brilliant blank, ABP 350.00
    7-1/2" h, 8-1/2" d, four large hobstars, two fans applied crystal rope twisted handle, ABP 350.00
    8-1/2" h, 6-1/2" w, square-shaped, three large cut hobstars with panels of floral cut leaf design, double notched handle, ABP 500.00
    9" h, 10-1/2" d, low flaring basket, bands of twelve hobstars around side with fan cutting and panels of cross hatching, cut with huge hobstar in base, flat arched handle with notched edges and leaf cutting in center, clearly sgd "Hoare" on int. 3,500.00
    9-1/2" h, 11-1/2" d, five large hobstars, fancy emb floral silver handle and rim, ABP 225.00
Bon Bon, 8" d, 2" h, Broadway pattern, Huntly, minor flakes 135.00
Bowl
    8" d, Checker Board pattern 250.00
    8" d, Heart pattern 250.00
    9" d, deep cut, medallions, large pointed ovals, arches, and base, ABP 110.00
    10" d, deep cut buttons, stars, and fans, ABP 220.00
    11" l, oval, scalloped rim, ABP 85.00
    12" d, Holland pattern, rolled rim, sgd "Hawkes" 700.00
    12" d, 4-1/2" h, rolled down edge, cut and engraved flowers, leaves, and center thistle, notched serrated edge 275.00

Canoe, Plaza, Pitkin and Brooks, Chicago, IL, American Brilliant Period, 11-1/4" l, 4-3/4" w, $325.

Box, cov
    5" d, 2-3/4" h, cut paneled base, cover cut with large eight-pointed star with hobstar center surrounded by fans, C. F. Monroe 275.00
    6-1/2" d, hinged, hobstars, cross hatching, fan, Hawkes, ABP ..400.00
Bread Tray, 8" x 12", Anita, Libbey in circle mark, ABP 535.00
Butter Dish, cov, Hobstar, ABP 250.00
Candlesticks, pr
    9-1/2" h, hobstars, teardrop stem, hobstar base 250.00
    10" h, faceted cut knobs, large teardrop stems, ray base 425.00
    12" h, Adelaide pattern, amber, Pairpoint 250.00
Celery Vase, 9-3/4" h, fan and linear cuts, ABP 95.00
Centerpiece, 10-3/4" d, wheel cut and etched, molded, fruiting foliage, chips 490.00
Champagne
    Kalana Lily, pattern, Dorflinger 75.00
    Stone engraved rock crystal, Dorflinger, c1890 .... 85.00
Champagne Bucket, 7" h, 7" d, sgd "Hoare," ABP 400.00
Champagne Pitcher
    10" h, hobstars and cane, double thumbprint handle 210.00
    11" h, Prism pattern, triple notch handle, monogram sterling silver top 425.00
Cheese Dish, cov
    6" h dome, 9" d, plate, cobalt blue cut to clear, bull's eye and panel, large miter splints on bottom of plate, ABP 250.00
    8" h, 10-1/2" d plate, swirling pattern serving plate, matching high dome cov, faceted knob top, ABP, flat edge chip, minor wear. 550.00
Cider Pitcher, 7" h, hobstars, zippers, fine diamonds, honeycomb cut handle, 7" h, ABP 175.00
Cocktail Shaker, 12-1/2" h, 5-1/2" w, mallard duck in flight over marsh, fancy sterling silver rim and cover, both glass and sterling rim sgd "Hawkes" 210.00
Cologne Bottle
    6" h, Hob and Lace pattern, green cased to clear, pattern cut stopper, Dorflinger 625.00
    7-1/2" h, Holland pattern, faceted cut stopper 275.00
    7-1/2" h, 2-3/4" d, Parisian pattern, sq shape, Dorflinger, ABP, pr 700.00
Compote
    6" h, hobstar and arches, flared pedestal, ABP 150.00
    9" h, Pairpoint, intaglio cut fruit 445.00
    9" h, deep cut sunburst, arches and buttons, zippered stem, starcut petal base, ABP 150.00
Console Set, 12" d ftd bowl with wide flat rim, p 9-1/8" h baluster form candlesticks, cross-hatched diamond and flute cutting, ABP... 750.00
Creamer and Sugar, pr
    4-1/2" h, pedestal, geometric cuttings, zippered handles, teardrop full length of handle, sgd "Hawkes," ABP 750.00
    5-1/2" h, pedestal, Carolyn variation, notched handles, ABP 895.00
Decanter, orig stopper
    11-1/2" h, stars, arches, fans, cut neck, star cut mushroom stopper 95.00
    12-3/4" h, hobstar and fan pattern, large notched handle, sgd "Hoare," firing check at handle 75.00

Bowl, octagonal crimped edges, hobstar and cane, sgd "Niagara," American Brilliant Period, 8-1/4" d, $300.

13" h, cranberry cut to clear, bulbous body, fan and diamond cutting, notched panel neck, applied cut handle, faceted stopper, star-cut base, ABP 3,450.00

14" d, eight panels, hollow pointed stopper, sgd "Hawkes" ... 220.00

Dish
5" d, hobstar, pineapple, palm leaf, ABP 45.00
8" d, scalloped edge, all over hobstar medallions and hobs, ABP 175.00

Dresser Box, cov, 7" h, 7" w, Harvard pattern variation, three-ftd, silver plated fittings, orig beveled mirror on swivel hinge under lid, cut by Bergen Glass Co., couple of minute flakes 750.00

Fern Dish, 3-3/4" h, 8" w, round, silver-plate rim, C. F. Monroe, minor roughness to cut pattern, normal wear on base, no liner 200.00

Flower Center
5" h, 6" d, hobstars, flashed fans, hobstar chain and base, ABP 325.00
7-3/4" h, 12" d, etched and wheel cut motif, honeycomb flared neck, some wear 500.00
8" d, large hobstar base, step cut neck, ABP 325.00

Goblet
7" h, Buzzstar, pineapple, marked "B & B," ABP 40.00
8-1/2" h, intaglio vintage cut, 8-1/2" h, sgd "Sinclaire" 80.00

Hair Receiver, 4-1/4" d, deep cut arches, diamonds, engraved florals 60.00

Humidor, cov
7-1/2" d, Middlesex, hollow stopper, sponge holder in lid, Dorflinger, ABP 490.00
9" h, hobstars, beaded split vesicas, hobstar base, matching cut glass lid with hollow for sponge, ABP 575.00

Ice Bucket
6-1/2" h, 7" w, Harvard pattern, floral cutting, eight sided form, ABP, minor edge flaking on handles 100.00
7" h, hobstars and notched prisms, 8" d underplate, double handles, ABP 940.00

Ice Cream Set, Russian pattern, eight 7" d dishes, 8-1/2" d serving bowl, 11" d cake plate, some chips to edges, ABP, price for 10 pc set 500.00

Knife Rest, 4" l, ABP 90.00

Lamp
14" h, teardrop shade with engraved tulip blossoms, star-cut closed top, columnar shaft with sq silver plated platform base, dec with cherubs in vineyard scene, attributed to Pairpoint 550.00
15" h, 5" h x 10" d mushroom shade done cut with gravic cut style daisies and leaves, matching base, orig prisms, Pairpoint style ... 500.00
16-1/2" h, Regency-style, ormolu mounts, spherical glass body topped by ormolu mount issuing rosette capped S-scrolls, slender shaft ending in campana-form candle-cup, circular base with cast acanthus feet, pr 800.00

Loving Cup, 3 handles, sterling top, ABP 350.00

Nappy, two handles
6" d, hobstar center, intaglio floral, strawberry diamond button border, 6" d 45.00
9" d, deep cut arches, pointed sunbursts and medallions, ABP 135.00

Orange Bowl, 9-3/4" x 6-3/4" x 3-3/4" h, hobstars and strawberry diamond, ABP 200.00

Perfume Bottle
3-1/2" l, cranberry overlay, shaped sides, notched cuts, S. Mordan & Co., silver mounted cap 325.00
5-1/2" h, 3" d, six-sided, alternating panels of Harvard pattern and engraved florals, rayed base, matching faceted stopper, ABP 175.00
6-1/2" h, bulbous, all over cutting, orig stopper, ABP 220.00

Pickle Tray, 7" x 3", checkerboard, hobstar 45.00

Pitcher, 8-7/8" h, baluster form body, upper section vertically ribbed and cut, lower section with stylized flowerheads, facet cut handle, silverplated rim mount with beaded edging, monogrammed, mkd "Wilcox Silver Plate Co." 750.00

Powder Jar, cov, 2-1/2" h, circular, body wheel cut with ribboned garland, pink enamel over sunbursts ground on cov, unmarked, attributed to Hawkes 275.00

Plate
10" d, Carolyn pattern, J. Hoare 525.00
12" d, alternating hobstar and pinwheel 100.00

Punch Bowl
11" h, 10" w, 2 pc, Elgin pattern, Quaker City 600.00
14", 7" h, five large hobstars, central large hobstar, ABP ... 550.00

Punch Ladle, 11-1/2" l, silver plated emb shell bowl, cut and notched prism handle 165.00

Relish
8" l, two handles, divided, Jupiter pattern, Meriden 120.00
13" l, leaf shape, Clear Button Russian pattern, ABP 375.00

Salad Serving Fork and Spoon, silver plated, cross-cut diamond glass handles 300.00

Salt, open
Feather 20.00
Sawtooth, ftd, individual size 30.00

Salt Shaker, Notched prism columns 30.00

Spooner, 5" h, hobstar and arches, ABP 90.00

Tankard Pitcher
10-1/4" h, Harvard cut sides, pinwheel top, mini hobnails, thumbprint notched handle, ABP 200.00
11" h, hobstar, strawberry diamond, notched prism and fan, flared base with bull's eye, double thumbprint handle 275.00

Tray
12" d, round, Monarch, sgd "Hoare," ABP 975.00
12" d, round, Wilhelm, Fry, ABP 850.00
14" x 7-1/2", Sillsbee pattern, Pairpoint 335.00

Tumbler
Clear Button Russian pattern 95.00
Harvard, rayed base 45.00
Hobstars 40.00

Vase
8" h, 11" d, squatty body, short flaring neck, scalloped rim, ABP 550.00
11" h, fan, amber, engraved grape leaves and vines, round disk base, acid etched Hawkes mark, small chip on base 300.00
12" h, three cartouches of roses, star and hobstar cut ground 225.00
12" h, 5-1/2" w, triangular, three large and three small hobstars, double notched pedestal and flaring base, ABP 150.00
12-1/4" h, corset shape, cone and file band, deep cut leaves and flowers 85.00
12-1/2" h, 6-1/2" d, floral and diamond point engraving, sgd "Hawkes" 250.00
14" h, bowling pin shape, three 24 point hobstars on sides surrounded by notched prisms, strawberry diamond, hobstars, star, and checkered diamond fields 700.00
14" h, club form, ABP 300.00
14" h, pedestal, Florentine pattern, Higgins & Seiter, ABP 775.00
16" h, corset shape, well cut hobstar, strawberry diamond, prism, flashed star and fan 300.00

Water Carafe
Harvard pattern, ABP 185.00
Hobstars and notched prisms, ABP 125.00
Pinwheel and Fan cutting, notched neck, 8" h, 4" w 125.00

Water Pitcher
9-1/2" h, Harvard pattern panels and intaglio cut sprays of flowers and foliage, ABP 300.00
10" h, Keystone Rose pattern 190.00

Whiskey Jug, 6-1/4" h, bulbous, thistle and grape cutting, orig stopper, sgd "Sinclaire" 295.00

Wine
4" h, flint, cut panels, strawberry diamonds, and fans, Pittsburgh 60.00
4-1/8" h, flint, Gothic Arch, sheaf like ferns, Pittsburgh 75.00

CUT VELVET

History: Several glass manufacturers made cut velvet dur-

Vase, bottle shape, blue, white int., 6" h, $245.

Vase, red ground, black and brown desert oasis and pyramid scene, 10-3/4"h, $115.

ing the late Victorian era, c1870-1900. An outer layer of pastel color was applied over a white casing. The piece then was molded or cut in a high-relief ribbed or diamond shape, exposing portions of the casing. The finish had a satin velvety feel, hence the name "cut velvet."

Bowl, 5-1/4" h, 5-1/2" d, ftd, cinnabar glaze, some glaze cracking at foot joint, imp mark 160.00
Charger, 11-1/4" d, emb undersea motif, light green fish and plants, blue-green ground, imp "Cowan" 500.00
Figure
    8" h, Pierrette, Old Ivory glaze, stamped "Cowan" 250.00
    9-1/2" x 9", horse, mahogany and gold flambé glaze, imp mark 1,500.00
Flower Frog
    7" h, figural nude, #698, Original Ivory glaze 250.00
    7-3/4" h, 4-1/4" d, Heavenward, Original Ivory glaze, stamped "Cowan" 175.00
    7-3/4" h, 6-1/4" d, Duet, Original Ivory glaze, stamped "Cowan," small shallow chip to base 450.00
    10" h, 5-1/4" d, Pan, Special Ivory glaze, stamped "Cowan," minor base nick 250.00
    10-1/4" h, Debutante, Special Ivory glaze, stamped "Cowan/S" 850.00
    10-3/4" h, 4" d, Swirl Dancer, Original Ivory glaze, stamped "Cowan" 850.00
    11-3/4" h, Loveliness, Original Ivory glaze, incised "B," crack to wrist 400.00
Lamp Base, 11-1/2" h, 9-1/2" d, bulbous, Oriental Red glaze, stamp mark, drilled at side and bottom 300.00
Paperweight, 4-1/2" h, 3-1/4" l, Elephant, Special Ivory glaze, stamped "Cowan" 300.00
Trivet, 6-1/2" d, woman's head and flowers, blue, cream, yellow, and pink, die-stamped mark, minor scratches 450.00
Vase
    7-1/4" h, 5" d, classical shape, dripping brown crystalline glaze, mirrored orange glaze, ink mark 300.00
    10" h, 10'"d, spherical, ribbed, leathery vermillion glaze, stamped "Cowan," two hairlines to rim 125.00

CZECHOSLOVAKIAN ITEMS

History: Objects marked "Made in Czechoslovakia" were produced after 1918 when the country claimed its independence from the Austro-Hungarian Empire. The people became more cosmopolitan and liberated and expanded the scope of their lives. Their porcelains, pottery, and glassware reflect many influences.

Marks: A specific manufacturer's mark may include a date which precedes 1918, but this only indicates the factory existed during the years of the Bohemian or Austro-Hungarian Empire.

References: Dale and Diane Barta and Helen M. Rose, *Czechoslovakian Glass & Collectibles* (1992, 1995 values), Book II (1997) Collector Books; *Bohemian Glass*, n.d., distributed by Antique Publications; Ruth A. Forsythe, *Made in Czechoslovakia,* Antique Publications, 1995 value update; Jacquelyne Y. Jones-North, et. al., *Czechoslovakian Perfume Bottles and Boudoir Accessories,* Revised Ed., Antique Publications, 1999.

Periodical: *New Glass Review,* Bardounova 2140 149 00 Praha 4, Prague, Czech Republic.

Collectors' Club: Czechoslovakian Collectors Guild International, P.O. Box 901395, Kansas City, MO 64190.

Museum: Friends of the Glass Museum of Novy Bor, Kensington, MD.

Cologne Bottle, 4" h, porcelain, glossy blue, bow front 40.00
Decanter Set, 7-3/4" h decanter, seven 6" h wine glasses, Moorish style, heavily dec gold borders, red enamel, multicolored glass jewels .. 800.00
Demitasse Service, partial, hp, red Geisha tea house scene, 5 cups and saucers, cov sugar, 19-1/2" x 9-1/2" oval tray 120.00
Figure
    6" h, white horse 28.00
    8-1/2" h, doctor, orig label, set of 3 .... 450.00
Flower Frog, bird on stump, pottery 35.00
Goblet, 6-1/2" h, mold blown, cobalt blue, strong oil spot irid ext., acid-etched stamp "Czechoslovakia" 375.00
Lamp
    Boudoir, 13" h, enamel dec shade with raised enamel castle, mountainous landscape, sunset orange ground, baluster form glass

base with similar dec, base stamped "Made in Czechoslovakia" 400.00

Table, 14-1/2" h, 13-1/4" d conical shade, spherical base, frosted dark amber glass, acid etched and enameled Art Deco-style geometric diamond and triangle patterns in orange and green, silver stamp "Bulova Czechoslovakia" on base, c1930 .... 2,645.00

Perfume Bottle

8-1/4" h, colorless, wide stepped design, elaborate oval stopper engraved and etched as kneeling woman gathering flowers ...350.00

9-3/4" h, mold blown red glass, figural woman with butterfly wings, some frosting, colorless glass lily stopper frosted and polished 750.00

Pitcher, 6" h crackled, irid marigold flashing, hp underwater scene of fish and coral, polished pontil 150.00

Powder Box, cov, glass, round, yellow, black knob top 75.00

Stemware

Goblet, red bowls with silver overlay, vignettes of deer surrounded by floral ground, black stems, 10 pcs 325.00

............Sherbet, red bowl, silver trim, black stem, acid stamp mark, 12 pcs 350.00

Vase

6-1/4" h, cylindrical, mottled white and purple, cased to colorless, enameled stylized vignette of woman fishing, silver mounted rim with English hallmarks, c1930 .... 275.00

7-1/2" h, mold-blown ovoid, tapered neck, flared mouth, black glass, furnace dec winding ribbons of yellow-green to dark green, acid mark, c1930 .... 320.00

Beaded parrot on perch, multicolored beads, electric bulb inside, minor bead loss, 14-1/2" h, $1,210. Photo courtesy of Garth's Auctions.

DAVENPORT

History: John Davenport opened a pottery in Longport, Staffordshire, England, in 1793. His high-quality light-weight wares are cream colored with a beautiful velvety texture.

The firm's output included soft-paste (Old Blue) products, luster-trimmed pieces, and pink luster wares with black transfer. Pieces of Gaudy Dutch and Spatterware also have been found with the Davenport mark. Later Davenport became a leading maker of ironstone and early flow blue. His famous Cyprus pattern in mulberry became very popular. His heirs continued the business until the factory closed in 1886.

Reference: T. A. Lockett and Geoffrey A. Godden, China, *Earthenware & Glass*, 1794-1884, Random Century, 1990.

Museums: British Museum, London, England; Cincinnati Art Museum, Cincinnati, OH; Hanley Museum, Stoke-on-Trent, England; Liverpool Museum, Liverpool, England; Victoria & Albert Museum, London, England.

Charger, 17-1/2" l, oval, Venetian harbor scene, light blue
  transfer 80.00
Compote, 2-1/2" h, 8-1/2" d, turquoise and gold band, tiny raised flowers,
  hp scene with man fishing, cows at edge of lake, c1860, pr 225.00
Creamer, tan, jasperware, basketweave, incised anchor
  mark 60.00
Cup Plate, Teaberry pattern, pink luster 40.00
Dish, ftd, tricorn, Belvoir Castle dec 90.00
Ewer, 9" h, floral dec, multicolored, c1930 .... 190.00
Plate, 9-1/8" d, Legend of Montrose, transfer, c1850 .... 65.00
Platter
  18-1/4", stone china, polychrome dec blue transfer print bird and
    floral pattern, printed mark, c1810, glaze wear 230.00
  19-1/8" l, purple transfer, idyllic scene, boat and church, mkd "Dav-
    enport" 440.00
Sauce Tureen, cov, ladle, creamware, molded leaves, lime green vein-
  ing, early 450.00

Plate, Chantilly pattern, white ground, blue and orange floral dec, imp mark and red anchor, 8-3/4" d, $65.

Soup Tureen, matching stand, 13-1/4" l, stone china, polychrome dec
  blue transfer printed bird and floral patter, gilded lion mask handles,
  printed marks, c1810, large hairline on stand, glaze wear 1,610.00
Tea Service, Imari pattern, 18" l tray, teapot, creamer, cov sugar, four
  cups and saucers 850.00

DECOYS

History: During the past several years, carved wooden decoys, used to lure ducks and geese to the hunter, have become widely recognized as an indigenous American folk art form. Many decoys are from 1880-1930, when commercial gunners commonly hunted using rigs of several hundred decoys. Many fine carvers also worked through the 1930s and 1940s. Fish decoys were also carved by individuals and commercial decoy makers.

Because decoys were both hand made and machine made, and many examples exist, firm pricing is difficult to establish. The skill of the carver, rarity, type of bird, and age all effect the value.

References: Joel Barber, *Wild Fowl Decoys*, Dover Publications, n.d.; Russell J. Goldberger and Alan G. Haid, *Mason Decoys – A Complete Pictorial Guide*, Decoy Magazine, 1993; Bob and Sharon Huxford, *Collector's Guide to Decoys*, Vol. II, Collector Books, 1992; Carl F. Luckey, *Collecting Antique Bird Decoys and Duck Calls*: An Identification & Value Guide, 2nd ed., Books Americana, 1992; Donald J. Peterson, *Folk Art Fish Decoys*, Schiffer Publishing, 1996.

Periodicals: *Decoy Magazine*, P.O. Box 787, Lewes, DE, 19558; *North America Decoys*, P.O. Box 246, Spanish Fork, UT 84660; Sporting Collector's Monthly, RW Publishing, P.O. Box 305, Camden, DE 19934; *Wildfowl Art*, Ward Foundation, 909 South Schumaker Dr., Salisbury, MD 21801; *Wildfowl Carving & Collecting*, 500 Vaughn St., Harrisburg, PA 17110.

Collectors' Clubs: Midwest Collectors Association, 1100 Bayview Dr., Fox River Grove, IL 60021; Minnesota Decoy Collectors Association, P.O. Box 130084, St. Paul, MN 55113; Ohio Decoy Collectors & Carvers Association, P.O. Box 499, Richfield, OH 44286.

Museums: Chesapeake Bay Maritime Museum; Saint Michaels, MD; Havre de Grace Decoy Museum, Havre de Grace, MD; Museum at Stony Brook, Stony Brook, NY; Noyes Museum of Art, Oceanville, NJ; Peabody Museum of Salem, Salem, MA; Refuge Waterfowl Museum, Chincoteague, VA; Shelburne Museum, Inc., Shelburne, VT; Ward Museum of Wildfowl Art, Salisbury, MD.

Reproduction Alert.

Notes: A decoy's value is based on several factors: (1) fame of the carver, (2) quality of the carving, (3) species of wild fowl—the most desirable are herons, swans, mergansers, and shorebirds—and (4) condition of the original paint.

The inexperienced collector should be aware of several facts. The age of a decoy, per se, is usually of no importance in determining value. However, age does have some influence when it comes to a rare or important example. Since very few decoys were ever signed, it is quite difficult to attribute most decoys to known carvers. Anyone who

SPECIAL AUCTIONS

Gary Guyette & Frank Schmidt Inc.
P.O. Box 522
West Farmington, ME 04992
(207) 778-6256

has not examined a known carver's work will be hard pressed to determine if the paint on one of his decoys is indeed original. Repainting severely decreases a decoy's value. In addition, there are many fakes and reproductions on the market and even experienced collectors are occasionally fooled. Decoys represent a subject where dealing with a reputable dealer or auction house is important, especially those who offer a guarantee as to authenticity.

Decoys listed below are of average wear unless otherwise noted.

American Bittern Drake, miniature, H. Gibbs, sgd and identified in ink on base, 2-3/4" x 2-1/2" 375.00

Baldgate Wigeon Drake, miniature
A. Elmer, Crowell, East Harwich, MA, identified in ink, rect stamp on base, 2-1/2" x 4" 635.00
James Lapham, Dennisport, MA, sgd in ink, oval stamp, natural wood base, 3-3/4" x 5-3/4" 230.00

Black Bellied Bustard, miniature, H. Gills, initialed "H. G. 1957," identified in pencil, natural wood base, 3-1/2" x 4" 230.00

Black Bellied Plover, unknown American 20th C maker, orig paint, glass eyes, mounted on stick on lead base
12-1/2" h, minor paint loss, small chips to beak 2,530.00
13-1/2" h, minor paint loss, beak repair 1,725.00

Black Breasted Plover
A. E. Crowell, oval brand on bottom 2,750.00
Harry C. Shourds, orig paint 2,650.00

Black Duck
A. Elmer Crowell, East Harwich, MA, orig paint, glass eyes, stamped mark in oval on base, sleeping, wear, crack, 5-1/4" h 520.00
A. Elmer Crowell, East Harwich, MA, orig paint, glass eyes, stamped mark in oval on base, minor paint wear and wear to tip of beak, 7" h 460.00
Ira Hudson, preening, raised wings, outstretched neck, scratch feather paint 8,500.00
Mason Factory, challenge grade, snakey head, orig grade stamp on bottom 1,700.00
Charles Thomas, MA, glass eyes, orig paint 365.00
Unknown Maker, carved balsa body, wood head, glass eyes, orig pant, 15-1/2" l 150.00
Wildfowler, CT, inlet head, glass eyes, worn orig paint, green overpaint on bottom on sides, 13" l, c1900 .... 220.00

Black Drake, miniature
A. Elmer Crowell, East Harwich, MA, identified in ink, rect stamp on base, break at neck, reglued, minor paint loss, 3-1/2" x 4-3/4". 635.00
James Lapham, Dennisport, MA, identified in black ink, oval stamp, minor imperfections, 2-1/2" x 4" 290.00

Bluebill Drake
Jim Kelson, Mt. Clemens, MI, carved wing detail, feather stamping, glass eyes, orig paint, orig keep and weight, 13-1/2" l, c1930 .295.00
Sandusky, well shaped head, tack eyes, orig paint traces, 19th C 350.00

Bluebill Hen
Irving Miller, Monroe, MI, carved wood, glass eyes, orig paint, 11-1/2" l 165.00
Thomas Chambers, Canada Club, hollow body, glass eyes, old repaint, 15-3/4" l, c1900 .... 550.00

Bluebill, mated pair, Maryland, worn orig paint, 14" l, price for pair ..225.00

Blue-Wing Teal Drake, Mason Factory, premier grade, replaced eyes 850.00

Brant, Ward Brothers, MD, carved, hollow body, head turned left, sgd "Lem and Steve," dated 1917 .... 1,650.00

Bufflehead Drake
Bob Kerr, carved detail, glass eyes, orig paint, scratch carved signature, 10-1/2" l, c1980 .... 250.00
James Lagham, Dennisport, MA, identified in ink, oval stamp on base, 3" x 4-1/2" 345.00
Harry M. Shrouds, carved, hollow body, painted eyes 1,800.00

Canada Goose
A. Elmer Crowell, East Harwich, MA, rect stamp on base, 4" x 6" 750.00
Bill Eminght, Toledo, OH, cork body, wood head and keep, orig paint shot scars, sgd and dated 1968, 24-1/2" l 650.00
Hurley Conklin, carved, hollow body, swimming position, branded "H. Conklin" on bottom 600.00
H. Gibbs, identified and initialed "HG 1957" on natural wood base, 2-1/2" x 4-1/2" 290.00

Canvasback Drake
Thomas Chambers, Canada Club, Ontario, Canada, hollow body, glass eyes, worn orig paint, 14-1/2" l 600.00
Maryland, orig paint worn, 16" l, price for pair 250.00
Wisconsin, old working repaint, glass eyes, 15" l 200.00

Canvasback Drake, miniature
Cleon, identified and sgd "Cleon" in ink on base, minor paint loss, 3" x 5" 500.00
A. Elmer Crowell, East Harwich, MA, in feeding position, identified in ink, rect stamp on base, minor paint imperfections, 2-1/2" x 5" 865.00

Canvasback Hen
Charles Bean, carved wood, glass eyes, orig paint, 14-3/4" l 250.00
Frank Schmidt, orig paint, glass eyes, relief carved wing tips, 16-1/4" l 165.00

Common Golden Eye Drake, miniature, A. Elmer Crowell, East Harwich, MA, identified in ink, rect stamp on base, minor paint imperfections, 2-1/2" x 4" 825.00

Curlew
A. E. Crowell, hollow carved, orig paint 850.00
Harry V. Shrouds, orig paint 2,000.00
William Bowman, Long Island, NY, 1870-90 .... 57,500.00
William Gibian, carved wings and feathers, head turned back carved neck muscle, sgd on bottom 600.00

Elder Drake, unknown Maine maker, carved bill, inlet neck, chip carved body, turned-up tail, orig paint 700.00

Golden Eye Drake
A. Elmer Crowell, East Harwich, MA, minor paint wear, miniature, rect stamp, 3" h 630.00

Clockwise, from top: Canadian Goose by Madison Mitchell, $450; Canvasback, $225; Goldeneye, attributed to Joe Lincoln, $475.

Stevens Factory, repainted, branded on bottom.................... 460.00
Golden Eye Whistler Drake, miniature, J. Lapham, Dennisport, MA, identified, sgd in ink, oval stamp, natural wood base, 3" x 4-1/2"..........290.00
Green Wing Teal Duck, miniature, A. Elmer Crowell, East Harwich, MA, identified in ink, rect stamp on base, 2-1/2" x 4"............... 865.00
Heron, unknown maker, carved wing and tail, wrought iron legs.. 900.00
Herring Gull, Charles Wiber, Highland Heights, NJ, Barnegat Bay style, hollow body, carved splint wing tip, glass eyes, orig paint, 19" l....350.00
Hooded Merganser Drake, miniature, H. Gibbs, 1965, sgd in pencil on base, 2-1/2" x 2-3/4".. 290.00
Mallard Drake
  Ben Schmidt, Detroit, relief carved, feather stamping, glass eyes, orig paint, orig keep, mkd "Mallard drake Benj Schmidt, Detroit 1960," 15-1/4" l.. 450.00
  Bert Graves, carved, hollow body, orig weighted bottom, branded "E. I. Rogers" and "Cleary" 900.00
  James Lapham, Dennisport, MA, sgd and identified in ink on bottom, 4" x 5".. 435.00
  Mason Factory, standard grand, carved wood, glass eyes, orig paint, 15-3/4" l.. 225.00
Mallard Hen
  Ralph Johnston, Detroit, MI, high head, glass eyes, orig paint mkd "R. D. Johnston orig keel 1948" in pencil, 17-1/2" l............. 250.00
  Robert Elliston, carved, hollow body, orig paint................... 1,800.00
Merganser Drake
  A. Elmer Crowell, East Harwich, MA, miniature, rect stamp, 2-7/8" h 690.00
  Mason Factory, challenge grade, orig paint........................... 700.00
Merganser Hen
  George Boyd, head turned slightly, feathered paint 7,000.00
  Hurley Conklin, hollow body, carved wing tips, branded "H. Conklin" on bottom 375.00
Pigeon, carved and painted wood, America, late 19th/early 20th C, 12-1/4" l.. 575.00
Pintail Drake
  Mason Factory, premier grade, sloping breast, orig paint 750.00
  Zeke McDonald, MI, high head, hollow body, glass eyes, orig paint, c1910 .... 550.00
Pintail Hen, Mason Factory, premier grade, sloping breast, orig paint, mkd "Big Point Co. Pathcourt, Ont. James S. Meredith, member 1900-1920" 2,400.00
Pintail Hen, miniature, sgd "Cleon" in ink on bottom, 2-3/4" x 3-1/2" 250.00
Plover, Joe Lincoln, winter plumage, feather painting, orig paint 800.00
Red Breasted Merganser Drake
  George Boyd, NH, carved, orig paint.................................... 8,000.00
  Amos Wallace, ME, inlet neck, carved crest, detailed feathered paint 2,000.00
Red Breasted Merganser Drake, miniature, A. Elmer Crowell, East Harwich, MA, identified in ink, rect stamp on base, minor paint imperfections, 2-1/2" x 6" 980.00
Redhead Drake
  R Madison Mitchell, carved wood, orig paint, unused, 13" l .. 300.00
  Frank Schmidt, Detroit, MI, orig paint, glass eyes, relief carved wing tips, 15-1/2" l 250.00
Redhead Drake, miniature
  Crowell, A. Elmer, East Harwich, MA, identified in ink, rect stamp on base, minor paint imperfections, 2-1/2" x 4" 550.00
  Gibbs, H., sgd in pencil on natural wood base, 2-1/4" x 3-1/4" ...230.00
Robin Snipe, Obediah Verity, carved wings and eyes, orig paint 4,400.00
Ruddy Duck Drake, Len Carmeghi, Mt. Clemens, MI, hollow body, glass eyes, orig paint, sgd and dated, 10-3/4" l 250.00
Ruddy Duck, miniature, maker unknown, identified in ink on base, paint loss to bill, 2" x 2-3/4" 690.00
Ruffled Grouse, miniature, A. Elmer Crowell, East Harwich, MA, rect stamp, mounted on natural wood base, 3-1/2" x 4-1/2" 865.00

Sickle Bill Curlew, unknown maker, carved wood, glass eyes, pitchfork tine beak, orig paint, 22" l.. 150.00
Swan, unknown Chesapeake Bay, MD, maker, carved wood, braced neck, white paint, 30" l; 900.00
Widgeon, matted pair, Charlie Joiner, MD, sgd on bottom.......... 800.00
Wood Duck Drake, miniature, A. Elmer Crowell, East Harwich, MA, identified in ink, rect stamp on base, 3" x 4-1/2" 1,150.00
Yellowlegs, Joe Lincoln, carved wings, split tail, stippled paint, branded "S" on bottom 1,750.00

DEDHAM POTTERY

History: Alexander W. Robertson established a pottery in Chelsea, Massachusetts, about 1866. After his brother, Hugh Cornwall Robertson, joined him in 1868, the firm was called A. W. & H. C. Robertson. Their father, James Robertson, joined his sons in 1872, and the name Chelsea Keramic Art Works Robertson and Sons was used.

Their initial products were simple flower and bean pots, but the firm quickly expanded its output to include a wide variety of artistic pottery. The firm produced a very fine redware body used in classical forms, some with black backgrounds imitating ancient Greek and Apulian works. It experimented with underglaze slip decoration on vases. The Chelsea Keramic Art Works Pottery also produced high-glazed vases, pitchers, and plaques with a buff clay body with either sculpted or molded applied decoration.

James Robertson died in 1880 and Alexander moved to California in 1884, leaving Hugh C. Robertson alone in Chelsea where his tireless experiments eventually yielded a stunning imitation of the prized Chinese Ming-era blood-red glaze. Hugh's vases with that glaze were marked with an impressed "CKAW." Creating these red-glazed vases was very expensive, and even though they received great critical acclaim, the company declared bankruptcy in 1889.

Recapitalized by a circle of Boston art patrons in 1891, Hugh started the Chelsea Pottery U.S., which produced gray crackle-glazed dinnerware with cobalt blue decorations, the rabbit pattern being the most popular.

The business moved to new facilities in Dedham, Massachusetts, and began production in 1896 under the name Dedham Pottery. Hugh's son and grandson operated the business until it closed in 1943, by which time between 50 and 80 patterns had been produced, some very briefly.

Marks: The following marks help determine the approximate age of items:

"Chelsea Keramic Art Works Robertson and Sons," impressed, 1874-1880
"CKAW," impressed, 1875-1889
"CPUS," impressed in a cloverleaf, 1891-1895
Foreshortened rabbit only, impressed, 1894-1896
Conventional rabbit with "Dedham Pottery" in square blue stamped mark along with one impressed foreshortened rabbit, 1896-1928
Blue rabbit stamped mark with "registered" beneath along with two impressed foreshortened rabbit marks, 1929-1943

References: Lloyd E. Hawes, *Dedham Pottery and the Earlier Robertson's Chelsea Potteries*, Dedham Historical Society, 1968; Paul Evans, *Art Pottery of the United States*, Feingold & Lewis, 1974; Ralph and Terry Kovel, *Kovels' American Art Pottery*, Crown Publishers, 1993.

Collectors' Club: Dedham Pottery Collectors Society, 248 Highland St., Dedham, MA 02026.

Museum: Dedham Historical Society, Dedham, MA.

Reproduction Alert: Two companies make Dedham-like reproductions primarily utilizing the rabbit pattern, but always mark their work very differently from the original.

Advisor: James D. Kaufman.

Bowl, 8-1/2" sq
 Rabbit pattern, reg. stamp 600.00
 Rabbit pattern, reg. stamp, hairline crack..............275.00
 Swan pattern, reg. stamp 725.00
Candlesticks, pr
 Elephant pattern, reg. blue stamp 525.00
 Rabbit pattern, reg. blue stamp 325.00
Creamer and Sugar, type #1, 3-1/4" h, Duck pattern, blue stamp....650.00
Demitasse Cup and Saucer, Rabbit pattern, blue stamp 320.00
Knife Rest, Rabbit form, blue reg. stamp 575.00
Paperweight, Rabbit form, blue reg. stamp 495.00
Pickle Dish, 10-1/2" l, Elephant pattern, blue reg. stamp............750.00
Pitcher
 5" h, Rabbit pattern, blue stamp 325.00
 5-1/8" h, Chickens pattern, blue stamp................2,300.00
 7" h, Turkey pattern, blue stamp..........................585.00
 9" h, Rabbit pattern, blue stamp 700.00
 Style of 1850, blue reg. stamp...........................975.00
Plate
6" d
 Clover pattern, reg. stamp....................................625.00
 Dolphin pattern, blue reg. stamp, chip 225.00
 Iris pattern, blue stamp, Maude Davenport's "O" rebus ...280.00
 Rabbit pattern, blue stamp 145.00
8" d, Iris pattern, reg. stamp......................................230.00
8-1/2" d
 Chicken pattern, reg. blue stamp 1,450.00
 Crab central design, blue stamp 550.00
 Duck pattern, blue stamp, Maude Davenport's "O" rebus.....375.00
 Elephant pattern, blue reg. stamp 650.00

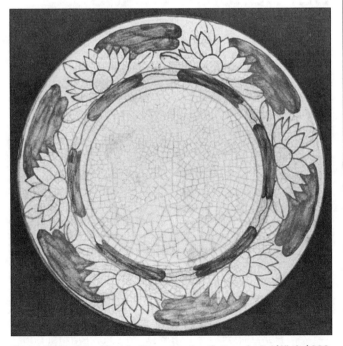

Plate, Water Lily, Maude Davenport artist mark, 6-1/4" d, $300.

 French Mushroom pattern, blue stamp 1,100.00
 Lobster central design, blue stamp 575.00
 Magnolia pattern, blue stamp..165.00
 Rabbit pattern, blue stamp...170.00
 Rabbit pattern, blue stamp, Maude Davenport's "O" rebus ..235.00
 Snow Tree pattern, blue stamp...210.00
 Upside down dolphin, CPUS...900.00
10" d
 Clover pattern, blue stamp..825.00
 Dolphin pattern, blue reg. stamp 875.00
 Elephant pattern, blue reg. stamp.....................................900.00
 Elephant pattern, blue reg. stamp, three small rim nicks ... 450.00
 Pine Apple pattern, CPUS...775.00
 Turkey pattern, blue stamp, Maude Davenport's "O" rebus..475.00
 Turtle pattern, reg. blue stamp 1,125.00
Platter, 14" x 8", oval, steak platter, Rabbit pattern, blue reg. stamp 825.00
Sherbet, two handles, Rabbit pattern, blue stamp......................350.00
Tea Cup and Saucer
 Azalea pattern, reg. stamp 130.00
 Butterfly pattern, blue stamp..345.00
 Duck pattern, reg. stamp 190.00
 Iris pattern, reg. stamp...155.00
 Rabbit pattern, reg. stamp...155.00
 Turtle pattern, reg. stamp 680.00
 Water Lily pattern, reg. stamp 130.00
Teapot, 6-1/8" h, Rabbit pattern, blue stamp 875.00
Vase, 9-1/2" d, 8-1/2" h, spherical, extended raised rim, tapered base, glossy mottled sea green glaze, incised "Dedham Pottery 10.11.96 H.C.R. 3016B" on base, modeled by Hugh Robertson, in-the-making glaze chips near base 2,100.00

DELFTWARE

History: Delftware is pottery with a soft, red-clay body and tin-enamel glaze. The white, dense, opaque color came from adding tin ash to lead glaze. The first examples had blue designs on a white ground. Polychrome examples followed.

The name originally applied to pottery made in the region around Delft, Holland, beginning in the 16th century and ending in the late 18th century. The tin used came from the Cornish mines in England. By the 17th and 18th centuries English potters in London, Bristol, and Liverpool were copying the glaze and designs. Some designs unique to English potters also developed.

In Germany and France the ware is known as Faience, and in Italy as Majolica.

Reproduction Alert: Since the late 19th century much Delft-type souvenir material has been produced to appeal to the foreign traveler. Don't confuse these modern pieces with the older examples.

Bowl
 7-1/2" d, blue and white, Chinese pavilion in landscape, England, 18th C 325.00
 8-3/4" d, shallow, blue and white, figure of young woman with bough..475.00
 12" d, shallow, blue and white, landscape with figure, edge chips 550.00
 12-1/2" d, 6-1/2" h, blue and white, broken, poorly repaired....1,155.00
 13" d, shallow, polychrome dec, minor edge wear, English 715.00
Bowl, attached strainer, 8-3/4" d, 3-1/2" h, blue and white floral dec, hairlines and deteriorating old repair 470.00
Charger
 12" d, blue and white, floral rim, landscape, edge chips 200.00

Charger, yellow, manganese, green, orange, and blue gallant on horseback, sword raised above his head, 3 manganese concentric rings on ext., English, 17th/18th C, 12-1/2" d, general wear, $560. Photo courtesy of Freeman\Fine Arts.

13" d, floral design, building scene, manganese and blue, edge chips 615.00
13-1/8" d, blue and white, foliate devices, Dutch, 19th C, chips, glaze wear 410.00
13-1/4" d, polychrome floral design, blue, red, yellow, green, and black, edge chips 880.00
13-5/8" d, blue and white, foliate devices, 19th C, chips, glass wear, restoration 320.00
14" d, polychrome floral dec, tree, edge chips 550.00
16 1/2" d, center branch with fruiting blossoms, two birds, conforming florals on wide rim, sgd "G. A. Kleynoven," c1655 ..... 2,250.00

Dish
8-1/4" d, molded rim, blue and white, stylized landscape and floral design, edge chips 315.00
12-3/8" l, fluted oval, blue and white floral design, attributed to Lambeth, chips 440.00

Flower Brick, 4-5/8" l, 2-1/2" h, blue and white, Chinese figures in landscape, Dutch, 18th C, chips, cracks 375.00
Garniture, 3 bulbous 17-1/4" h cov urns, 2 octagonal tapered 12-3/4" h vases, polychrome dec foliage surrounding central blue figural panels, Dutch, late 18th/early 19th C 8,625.00
Inkwell, 4-1/2" h, heart shape, blue and white floral dec, wear and edge chips 495.00
Jar, 5" h, blue and white, chips, pr 715.00
Model, 17-1/2" h, tall case clock, blue dec white ground, panels of figural and architectural landscapes between scrolled foliate borders, 19th C, slight glaze wear 320.00
Mug, 6-3/8" h, blue and white, armorial surrounded by exotic landscape, palm trees, mkd on base, Dutch, 19th C, minor chips, glaze wear 490.00

Plate
8-1/2" d, blue and white, floral, pots of flowers and insects, small edge chips, 5 pc set 825.00
8-5/8" d, blue and white, central reserves of foliate devices, neoclassical urn, Continental, 18th C 175.00
8-3/4" d, manganese, iron red, yellow, and underglaze blue floral design, chips 200.00
9" d, blue and white floral dec, Dutch inscription on front, another on back, edge chips 200.00
9" d, blue scene, bianco-sopra-bianco border, attributed to Bristol, hairline and chips 200.00
9" d, polychrome central reserve of basket of flowers, surrounded by foliate border, Dutch, early 19th C, minor chips and cracks, glaze wear, pr 635.00
9" d, polychrome iron red, yellow, and manganese, underglaze blue, Fazackerly design, chips, some touch-up repair to red and yellow 165.00
9" d, polychrome Oriental bridge scene, blue acanthus leaf border, chips 275.00
10-1/4" d, blue and white Bible illustration, small over reserve with bible reference and date "MAT 2:IV.00, 1752," small edge chips 770.00

Posset Pot
4-3/4" h, blue and white, birds among foliage, England, 19th C, minor chips and cracks 920.00
7-1/4" h, blue and white floral dec with bird, attributed to Lambeth, mismatched lid, base hairlines, minor edge chips 1,650.00

Sauce Boat, 8-1/4" l, applied scrolled handles, fluted flaring lip, blue and white Oriental design, edge chips and hairline, later added yellow enamel rim 440.00
Saucer, 8-3/4" d, table ring, blue, iron-red, yellow, and manganese bowl of flowers dec.. 825.00
Strainer Bowl, 9-1/8" d, blue and white floral design, three short feet, chips 520.00
Tea Caddy, 5-7/8" h, blue and white floral dec, scalloped bottom edge, mkd "MVS 1750," cork closure, wear, edge flakes, old filled in chip on lid 550.00
Tobacco Jar, 10" h, blue and white, Indians and "Siville," older brass stepped lid, chips 1,870.00
Vase, 19" h, tapering octagonal, molded lobes, blue, green, and red polychromed continuous band of birds of paradise within foliage, mkd "J.V.D.H.," late 19th C, pr 1,200.00
Vase, cov, 18-3/4" h, baluster, body with 3 cartouches depicting courting couple, sailing ships bordered by molded diaper work, foliate cast ormolu base with conforming dec cov, Holland, late 19th C, pr..3,000.00
Wall Pocket, 7-3/4" h, blue and white, cornucopia with cherub's head, attributed to Liverpool, small edge chips.............................. 1,100.00

DEPRESSION GLASS

History: Depression glass was made from 1920 to 1940. It was an inexpensive machine-made glass and was produced by several companies in various patterns and colors. The number of forms made in different patterns also varied.

Depression glass was sold through variety stores, given away as premiums, or packaged with certain products. Movie houses gave it away from 1935 until well into the 1940s.

Like pattern glass, knowing the proper name of a pattern is the key to collecting. Collectors should be prepared to do research.

References: Gene Florence, *Collectible Glassware from the 40's, 50's, 60's*, 5th ed., Collector Books, 1999; ——, *Collector's Encyclopedia of Depression Glass*, 14th ed., Collector Books, 1999; ——, *Elegant Glassware of the Depression Era*, 8th ed., Collector Books, 1998; ——, *Florence's Glassware Pattern Identification Guide*, Collector Books, 1998; ——, *Glass Candlesticks of the Depression Era*, Collector Books, 1999; ——, *Pocket Guide to Depression Glass & More, 1920-1960s*, 11th ed., Collector Books, 1999; ——, *Stemware Identification Featuring Cordials with Values*, 1920s-1960s, Collector Books, 1997; ———, *Very Rare Glassware of the Depression Era*, 1st Series (1988, 1991 value update), 2nd Series (1991), 3rd Series

(1993), 4th Series (1996), 5th Series (1996), Collector Books; Ralph and Terry Kovel, Kovels' *Depression Glass & American Dinnerware Price List*, 5th ed., Crown, 1995; Carl F. Luckey and Mary Burris, *Identification & Value Guide to Depression Era Glassware*, 3rd ed., Books Americana, 1994; Jim and Barbara Mauzy, *Mauzy's Comprehensive Handbook of Depression Glass Prices*, Schiffer, 1999, —, *Mauzy's Depression Glass*, Schiffer Publishing, 1999; Leslie Piña and Paula Ockner, *Depression Era Art Deco Glass*, Schiffer Publishing, 1999; Ellen T. Schroy, *Warman's Depression Glass*, Krause Publications, 1997; Kent G. Washburn, *Price Survey*, 4th ed., published by author, 1994; Hazel Marie Weatherman, *Colored Glassware of the Depression Era*, Book 2, published by author 1974, available in reprint; ——, *1984 Supplement & Price Trends for Colored Glassware of the Depression Era*, Book 1, published by author, 1984.

Periodical: *The Daze*, P.O. Box 57, Otisville, MI 48463.

Collectors' Clubs: Canadian Depression Glass Club, 1026 Forestwood Drive, Mississauga, Ontario L5C 1G8, Canada; National Depression Glass Association, Inc., P.O. Box 8264, Wichita, KS 67209; 20-30-40 Society, Inc., P.O. Box 856, LaGrange, IL 60525, plus many local and regional clubs.

Websites: DG Shopper Online, http://www.dgshopper.com; Facets Antiques & Collectibles Mall, http://www.Facets.net; Mega Show, http://www.glassshow.com.

Additional Listings: *See Warman's Americana & Collectibles* for more examples.

Reproduction Alert

The following is a partial listing of Depression Glass patterns that have been reproduced.

Adam (produced in the Far East and distributed through AA Importing of St. Louis) butter dish, pink.

Avocado (Indiana Glass Company) pitcher and tumbler, in amethyst, blue, green, pink, frosted pink, red, and yellow.

Cherry Blossom (large number of manufacturers and importers) numerous forms including two-handled tray, cup and saucer, and children's set, in blue, cobalt blue, Delphite, green, iridized colors, pink, and red.

Iris, plate and tumbler, in crystal.

Madrid (Indiana Glass Company) goblet, grill plate, shakers, vase, and more, in crystal (clear), blue, pink, and teal.

Mayfair, cookie jars, juice pitchers, shakers, shot glasses, and more, in amethyst, blue, cobalt blue, green, pink, and red.

Miss America, covered butter dish, pitcher, shakers, and tumbler, in cobalt blue, crystal (clear), green, ice blue, pink, and red amberina.

Sharon (privately produced) covered butter in blue, cobalt blue, green (light and dark), opalescent blue, red, and umber (burnt).

AMERICAN SWEETHEART

American Sweetheart, soup plate, flat, pink, $75.

Manufactured by MacBeth-Evans Glass Company, Charleroi, PA, from 1930 to 1936. Made in blue, Monax, pink, and red. Limited production in Cremax and color-trimmed Monax.

	Blue	Cremax	Monax	Monax with color-trim	Pink	Red
Berry Bowl, 9" d	-	36.00	60.00	150.00	50.00	-
Cereal Bowl, 6" d	-	11.00	14.00	37.50	16.00	-
Chop Plate, 11" d	-	-	15.00	-	-	-
Console Bowl, 18" d	1,000.00	-	375.00	-	-	850.00
Cream Soup, 4-1/2" d	-	-	120.00	-	75.00	-
Creamer, ftd	115.00	-	9.00	85.00	12.00	110.00
Cup	100.00	75.00	8.00	70.00	15.00	75.00
Lamp Shade	-	450.00	400.00		-	-
Pitcher, 60 oz, 7-1/2" h	-	-	-	-	675.00	-
Pitcher, 80 oz, 8" h	-	-	-	-	575.00	-
Plate, 6" d, bread & butter	-	-	4.50	13.00	5.50	-
Plate, 8" d, salad	75.00	25.00	7.50	-	11.00	75.00
Plate, 9" d, luncheon	-	-	10.00	35.00	-	-
Plate, 9-3/4" d, dinner	-	-	14.00	70.00	38.00	-
Plate, 10-1/4" d, dinner	-	-	24.00	-	38.00	-
Platter, 13" l, oval	-	-	75.00	-	55.00	-
Salt and Pepper Shakers, pr, ftd	-	-	325.00	-	425.00	-
Salver Plate, 12" d	180.00	-	18.00	-	22.00	125.00

Saucer	25.00	-	3.00	15.00	5.75	20.00
Serving Plate, 15-1/2" d	375.00	-	200.00	-	-	300.00
Sherbet, 3-3/4" h, ftd	-	-	10.50	-	22.00	-
Sherbet, 4-1/4" h, ftd	-	-	20.00	70.00	17.00	-
Soup Bowl, flat, 9-1/2" d	-	-	65.00	90.00	75.00	-
Sugar Lid	-	-	300.00	-	-	-
Sugar, open, ftd	115.00	-	7.50	85.00	11.00	100.00
Tidbit, 2 tier	250.00	-	95.00	-		200.00
Tumbler, 5 oz, 3-1/2" h	-	-	-	-	100.00	-
Tumbler, 9 oz, 4-1/4" h	-	-	-	-	85.00	-
Tumbler, 10 oz, 4-3/4" h	-	-	-	-	115.00	-
Vegetable Bowl, 11"	-	-	90.00	-	65.00	-

ANNIVERSARY

Manufactured by Jeannette Glass Company, Jeannette, PA, from 1947 to 1949, late 1960s to mid 1970s. Made in crystal, iridescent, and pink.

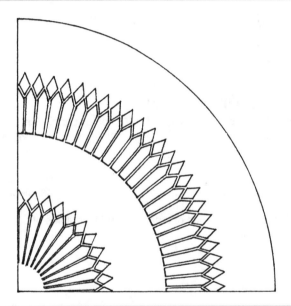

	Crystal	Iridescent	Pink
Berry Bowl, 4-7/8" d	3.50	4.50	11.00
Butter Dish, cov	30.00	-	57.00
Cake Plate, 12-3/8" w, square	7.00	-	16.50
Cake Plate, 12-1/2" d, round	7.50	-	17.50
Cake Plate, metal cover	15.00	-	-
Candlesticks, pr, 4-7/8" h	16.00	24.00	-
Candy Jar, cov	24.00	-	45.00
Comport, open, 3 legs	5.00	5.00	16.00
Comport, ruffled, 3 legs	6.50	-	-
Creamer, ftd	5.00	6.50	14.00

Cup	5.00	4.00	9.00
Fruit Bowl, 9" d	10.00	14.00	24.00
Pickle Dish 9" d	5.50	7.50	12.00
Plate, 6-1/4" d, sherbet	2.00	3.50	4.00
Plate, 9" d, dinner	5.00	8.00	17.00
Relish Dish, 8" d	5.60	7.50	14.00
Sandwich Server, 12-1/2" d	6.50	10.00	20.00
Saucer	1.00	1.50	6.00
Sherbet, ftd	4.00	-	10.00
Soup Bowl, 7-3/8" d	7.00	7.50	17.00
Sugar, cov	10.00	8.00	18.50
Tidbit, metal handle	14.00	-	-
Vase, 6-1/2" h	14.00	-	28.00
Wall Pocket	15.00	-	30.00
Wine, 2-1/2 oz	8.00	-	18.00

BLOCK OPTIC, Block

Manufactured by Hocking Glass Company, Lancaster, OH, from 1929- to 1933. Made in amber, crystal, green, pink, and yellow.

Production in amber was very limited. A 11-3/4" d console bowl is valued at $50, while a pair of matching 1-3/4" h candlesticks are valued at $110.00.

* There are five styles of creamers and four styles of cups, each have a relative value.

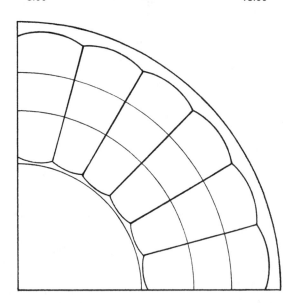

	Crystal	Green	Pink	Yellow
Berry Bowl, 8-1/2" d	20.00	35.00	40.00	-
Bowl, 4-1/4" d, 1-3/8" h	4.00	8.00	10.00	-
Bowl, 4-1/2" d, 1-1/2" h	-	28.00	-	-
Butter Dish, cov	-	50.00	-	-
Cake Plate, 10" d, ftd	18.00	-	-	-
Candlesticks, pr, 1-3/4" h	-	100.00	80.00	-
Candy Jar, cov, 2-1/4" h	30.00	60.00	55.00	65.00

Candy Jar, cov, 6-1/4" h	40.00	80.00	60.00	-
Cereal Bowl, 5-1/2" d	-	16.00	27.50	-
Champagne, 4-3/4" h	10.00	27.50	16.50	15.00
Cocktail, 4" h	-	35.00	35.00	-
Comport, 4" wide	-	36.00	70.00	-
Console Bowl, 11-3/4" d, rolled edge	-	70.00	95.00	-
Creamer*	10.00	12.50	18.00	15.00
Cup*	6.00	7.00	6.50	6.50
Goblet, 9 oz, 5-3/4" h	10.00	24.00	30.00	
Goblet, 9 oz, 7-1/2" h, thin	15.00	-	-	22.00
Ice Bucket	-	40.00	48.00	-
Ice Tub, open	-	48.00		-
Mug	-	35.00		-
Pitcher, 54 oz, 7-5/8" h, bulbous	-	70.00	70.00	-
Pitcher, 54 oz, 8-1/2" h	-	42.00	40.00	-
Pitcher, 80 oz, 8" h	-	88.50	80.00	-
Plate, 6" d, sherbet	1.50	3.50	3.25	3.50
Plate, 8" d, luncheon	3.50	5.50	7.00	8.50
Plate, 9" d, dinner	11.00	27.50	35.00	42.00
Plate, 9" d, dinner, snowflake center	-	16.50	-	-
Plate, 9" d, grill	15.00	27.50	30.00	42.00
Salad Bowl, 7-1/4" d	-	155.00	-	-
Salt and Pepper Shakers, pr, ftd	-	37.50	80.00	80.00
Salt and Pepper Shakers, pr, squatty	-	90.00	-	-
Sandwich Plate, 10-1/4" d	-	27.50	30.00	-
Sandwich Server, center handle	-	65.00	50.00	-
Saucer, 5-3/4" d	-	12.00	10.00	-
Saucer, 6-1/8" d	2.00	8.00	10.00	3.50
Sherbet, cone	-	6.00	5.50	-
Sherbet, 5-1/2 oz, 3-1/4" h	-	6.50	9.50	7.50
Sherbet, 6 oz, 4-3/4" h	7.00	15.50	15.00	16.00
Sugar, cone	-	12.00	9.50	12.00
Sugar, flat	-	10.00	10.00	-
Sugar, round, ftd	10.00	12.00	18.00	-
Tumbler, 3 oz, 2-5/8" h	-	27.50	25.00	-
Tumbler, 3 oz, 3-1/4" h, ftd	-	27.50	25.00	-

Tumbler, 5 oz, 3-1/2" h, flat	-	20.00	17.50	-
Tumbler, 5-3/8" h, ftd	-	-	19.50	18.00
Tumbler, 9" h, ftd	-	-	17.50	22.00
Tumbler, 9-1/2 oz, 3-13/16" h, flat	-	17.50	14.00	-
Tumbler, 10 or 11 oz, 5" h, flat	-	24.00	22.00	-
Tumbler, 12 oz, 4-7/8" h, flat	-	27.50	24.00	-
Tumbler, 15 oz, 5-1/4" h, flat	-	27.50	24.00	-
Tumble-Up, 3" h tumbler and bottle	-	87.50	75.00	-
Whiskey, 1 oz, 1-5/8" h	20.00	40.00	45.00	-
Whiskey, 2 oz, 2-1/4" h	15.00	35.00	30.00	-
Wine, 3-1/2" h	-	415.00	415.00	-
Wine, 4-1/2" h	15.00	35.00	32.00	-

BUBBLE, Bullseye, Provincial

Manufactured originally by Hocking Glass Company, and followed by Anchor Hocking Glass Corporation, Lancaster, OH, from 1937 to 1965. Made in crystal (1937), forest green (1937), pink, Royal Ruby (1963), and sapphire blue (1937).

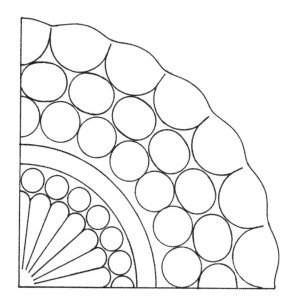

	Crystal	Forest Green	Royal Ruby	Sapphire Blue
Berry Bowl, 4" d	4.25	-	6.00	17.50
Berry Bowl, 8-3/4" d	12.00	15.00	18.00	17.50
Bowl, 9" d, fanged	8.00	-	-	335.00
Candlesticks, pr	24.00	40.00	-	-
Cereal Bowl, 5-1/4" d	7.00	16.50	-	15.00
Cocktail, 3-1/2 oz	4.50	10.00	10.00	-
Cocktail, 4-1/2 oz	4.50	12.50	12.50	-
Creamer	4.00	13.50	17.00	40.00
Cup	4.00	8.75	12.50	14.00
Fruit Bowl, 4-1/2" d	5.00	11.00	9.00	16.00

Goblet, 9 oz or 9-1/2 oz stem, 5-1/2" h	7.50	15.00	15.00	-
Iced Tea Goblet, 14 oz	8.00	17.50	-	-
Iced Tea Tumbler, 12 oz, 4-1/2" h	12.50	-	19.50	-
Juice Goblet, 4 oz	3.00	8.00	-	-
Juice Goblet, 5-1/2 oz	5.00	12.50	12.50	-
Juice Tumbler, 6 oz, ftd	4.00	11.50	10.00	-
Lamp 3 styles	42.00	-	-	-
Lemonade Tumbler, 16 oz, 5-7/8" h	16.00	-	16.00	-
Old Fashioned Tumbler, 8 oz, 3-1/4" h	6.50	16.00	16.00	-
Pitcher, 64 oz, ice lip	60.00	-	60.00	-
Plate, 6-3/4" d, bread and butter	3.50	4.50	-	3.75
Plate, 9-3/8" d, dinner	7.50	25.00	22.00	8.00
Plate, 9-3/8" d, grill	-	20.00	-	21.50
Platter, 12" l, oval	10.00	-	-	18.00
Sandwich Plate, 9-1/2" d	7.50	25.00	22.00	8.00
Saucer	1.50	5.00	5.00	1.50
Sherbet, 6 oz	3.50	6.50	12.00	-
Soup Bowl, flat, 7-3/4" d	8.50	-	-	16.00
Sugar	6.00	12.00	-	20.00
Tumbler, 9 oz, water	5.00	-	10.00	-

CAMEO, Ballerina, Dancing Girl

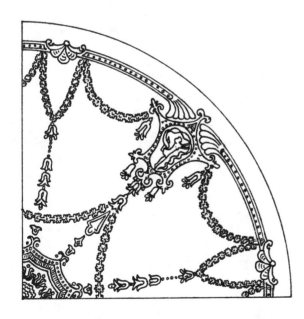

Cameo, plate, yellow, 10" d, $10.

Manufactured by Hocking Glass Company, Lancaster, OH, from 1930 to 1934. Made in crystal, green, pink, and yellow. Only crystal has a platinum rim.

Reproductions: † Salt shakers made in blue, green, and pink. Recently children's dishes have been made in green and pink, but were never part of the original pattern.

	Crystal	Green	Pink	Yellow
Butter Dish, cov	-	220.00	-	1,400.00
Cake Plate, 10" d, 3 legs	-	22.00	-	-
Cake Plate, 10-1/2" d, flat	-	95.00	150.00	-
Candlesticks, pr, 4" h	-	85.00	-	-
Candy Jar, cov, 4" h	-	75.00	495.00	80.00
Candy Jar, cov, 6-1/2" h	-	150.00	-	-
Cereal Bowl, 5-1/2" d	7.50	30.00	150.00	30.00
Cocktail Shaker	500.00	-	-	-
Comport, 5" w	-	32.00	200.00	-
Console Bowl, 3 legs, 11" d	-	75.00	45.00	95.00
Cookie Jar, cov	-	60.00	-	-
Cream Soup, 4-3/4" d	-	175.00	-	-
Creamer, 3-1/4" h	-	25.00	110.00	23.00
Creamer, 4-1/4" h	-	29.00	85.00	-
Cup	10.00	15.00	-	8.00
Decanter, 10" h	200.00	175.00	-	-
Domino Tray, 7" l	125.00	135.00	250.00	-
Goblet, 6" h, water	-	52.00	165.00	-
Ice Bowl, 3" h, 5-1/2" d	265.00	150.00	600.00	-
Jam Jar, cov, 2" h	175.00	165.00	-	-
Juice Pitcher, 6" h, 36 oz	-	60.00	-	-
Juice Tumbler, 3 oz, ftd	-	55.00	90.00	-
Pitcher, 8-1/2" h, 56 oz	550.00	50.00	1,200.00	-
Plate, 6" d, sherbet	4.00	6.00	85.00	2.50
Plate, 7" d, salad	12.00	-	-	-
Plate, 8" d, luncheon	14.00	12.00	36.00	10.00
Plate, 8-1/2", luncheon, sq	-	40.00	-	225.00
Plate, 9-1/2" d, dinner	-	18.00	75.00	9.00
Plate, 10-1/2" d, dinner, rimmed	-	90.00	145.00	-
Plate, 10-1/2" d, grill	-	10.00	55.00	6.00
Platter, 12" l	-	20.00	-	40.00
Relish, 7-1/2" l, ftd, 3 part	175.00	30.00	775.00	-
Salad Bowl, 7-1/4" d		60.00	-	-

Salt and Pepper Shakers, pr, ftd †	-	70.00	-	-
Sandwich Plate, 10" d	-	15.00	45.00	37.00
Saucer	4.00	3.00	90.00	4.50
Sherbet, 3-1/8" h, blown	-	15.00	75.00	-
Sherbet, 3-1/8" h, molded	-	16.00	75.00	40.00
Sherbet, 4-7/8" h	-	30.00	95.00	-
Soup Bowl, rimmed, 9" d	-	62.00	100.00	-
Sugar, 3-1/4" h	-	21.00	-	12.00
Sugar, 4-1/4" h	-	29.00	115.00	
Syrup Pitcher, 20 oz, 5-3/4" h	-	225.00	-	1,850.00
Tumbler, 9 oz, 4" h, 9 oz	16.00	30.00	80.00	-
Tumbler, 9 oz, 5"h, ftd	-	29.00	115.00	14.00
Tumbler, 10 oz, 4-3/4" h, flat	-	30.00	95.00	-
Tumbler, 11 oz, 5" h, flat	-	29.00	90.00	48.00
Tumbler, 11 oz, 5-3/4" h, ftd	-	60.00	125.00	-
Tumbler, 15 oz, 5-1/4" h	-	65.00	125.00	-
Vase, 8" h	-	40.00	-	-
Vegetable, oval, 10" l	-	30.00	-	45.00
Wine, 4" h	-	65.00	250.00	-

COLONIAL, Knife and Fork

Manufactured by Hocking Glass Company, Lancaster, OH, from 1934 to 1938. Made in crystal, green, and pink.

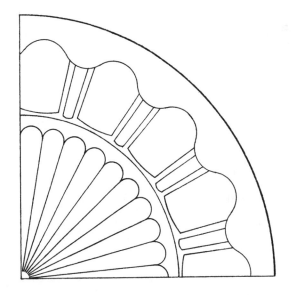

	Crystal	Green	Pink
Berry Bowl, 4-1/2"	10.00	17.00	15.00
Berry Bowl, 9" d	24.00	55.00	35.00
Butter Dish, cov	37.00	60.00	625.00

Cereal Bowl, 5-1/2" d	32.00	85.00	60.00
Claret, 4 oz, 5-1/4" h,	20.00	25.00	-
Cocktail, 3 oz, 4" h	15.00	25.00	-
Cordial, 1 oz, 3-3/4" h	20.00	30.00	-
Cream Soup Bowl, 4-1/2" d	70.00	70.00	70.00
Creamer, 8 oz, 5" h	17.00	25.00	60.00
Cup	8.00	12.00	12.00
Goblet, 8-1/2 oz, 5-3/4" h	24.00	35.00	40.00
Ice Tea Tumbler, 12 oz.,	28.00	55.00	45.00
Juice Tumbler, 5 oz, 3" h	17.50	27.50	20.00
Lemonade Tumbler, 15 oz	47.50	75.00	65.00
Milk Pitcher, 8 oz, 5" h	17.00	25.00	60.00
Mug, 12 oz, 5-1/2" h	-	825.00	500.00
Pitcher, 54 oz, 7" h, ice lip	40.00	45.00	48.00
Pitcher, 54 oz, 7" h, no lip	40.00	45.00	48.00
Pitcher, 68 oz, 7-3/4" h, ice lip	35.00	72.00	65.00
Pitcher, 68 oz, 7-3/4" h, no lip	35.00	72.00	65.00
Plate, 6" d, sherbet	4.50	7.50	6.50
Plate, 8-1/2" d, luncheon	8.00	9.00	11.00
Plate, 10" d, dinner	32.00	45.00	46.00
Plate, 10"d, grill	17.50	27.00	27.00
Plate, 12" d, oval	17.50	25.00	30.00
Platter, 12" l, oval	17.50	25.00	30.00
Salt and Pepper Shakers, pr.	65.00	140.00	145.00
Saucer	4.50	7.50	6.50
Sherbet, 3" h	-	-	24.00
Sherbet, 3-3/8" h	10.00	15.00	10.00
Soup Bowl, 7" d	30.00	95.00	85.00
Spoon Holder or Celery Vase	80.00	125.00	135.00
Sugar, cov	35.00	38.00	42.00
Sugar, 5", open	10.00	12.00	15.00
Tumbler, 3 oz, 3-1/4" h, ftd	11.00	15.00	14.00
Tumbler, 5 oz, 4" h, ftd	15.00	35.00	30.00
Tumbler, 9 oz, 4" h	15.00	20.00	25.00
Tumbler, 10 oz, 5-1/4" h, ftd	30.00	46.50	50.00
Tumbler, 11 oz, 5-1/8" h	25.00	37.00	40.00

Vegetable Bowl, 10" l, oval	18.00	25.00	30.00
Whiskey, 2-1/2" h, 1-1/2 oz.	9.00	20.00	15.00
Wine, 4-1/2" h, 2-1/2 oz	16.00	28.00	11.00

DIAMOND QUILTED, Flat Diamond

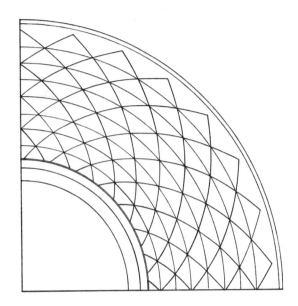

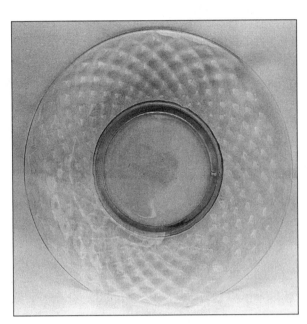

Diamond Quilted, luncheon plate, 8" d, pink, $8.50.

Manufactured by Imperial Glass Company, Bellaire, OH, from late 1920 to early 1930s. Made in amber, black, blue, crystal, green, pink, and red.

Amber and red prices would be valued slightly higher than black.

	Black	Blue	Crystal	Green	Pink
Bowl, 5-1/2" d, one handle	18.50	-	-	12.00	15.00
Bowl, 7" d, crimped edge	18.50	-	-	10.00	10.00
Cake Salver, 10" d, tall	-	-	-	60.00	65.00
Candlesticks, pr	60.00		50.00	32.00	28.00
Candy Jar, cov, ftd	-	-	25.00	65.00	65.00
Cereal Bowl, 5" d	15.00		6.00	8.50	8.00
Compote, cov, 11-1/2" d	-	-	-	80.00	75.00
Console Bowl, 10-1/2" d, rolled edge	65.00	60.00	15.00	20.00	24.00
Cream Soup Bowl, 4-3/4" d	22.00	20.00	20.00	12.00	14.00
Creamer	18.50	20.00	15.00	9.00	10.00
Cup	18.00	18.50	7.00	10.00	12.00
Ice Bucket	90.00	90.00	-	50.00	50.00
Mayonnaise Set, comport, plate, ladle	60.00	65.00	25.00	37.50	40.00
Pitcher, 64 oz	-	-	-	50.00	55.00

Plate, 6" d, sherbet	10.00	8.50	7.50	7.00	7.50
Plate, 7" d, salad	10.00	10.00	8.00	8.50	8.50
Plate, 8" d, luncheon	12.00	12.00	9.00	6.50	8.50
Punch Bowl and Stand	-	-	-	450.00	450.00
Sandwich Plate, 14" d	-	-	-	15.00	15.00
Sandwich Server, center handle	50.00	50.00	20.00	25.00	25.00
Saucer	5.00	5.00	2.00	4.00	4.00
Sherbet	16.00	16.00	14.00	6.00	5.00
Sugar	20.00	25.00	12.00	15.00	13.50
Tumbler, 6 oz, ftd	-	-	-	9.00	10.00
Tumbler, 9 oz	-	-	-	14.00	16.00
Tumbler, 9 oz, ftd	-	-	-	14.00	16.00
Tumbler, 12 oz, ftd	-	-	-	15.00	15.00
Vase, fan	80.00	75.00	-	50.00	50.00
Whiskey, 1-1/2" oz	-	-	-	10.00	12.00
Wine, 2 oz	-	-	-	12.50	12.50
Wine, 3 oz	-	-	-	15.00	15.00

LACED EDGE, Katy Blue

Manufactured by Imperial Glass Company, Bellaire, OH, early 1930s. Made in blue and green with opalescent edges.

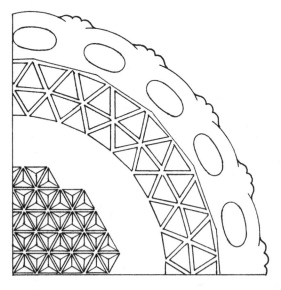

	Blue	Green
Bowl, 5" d	40.00	40.00
Bowl, 5-1/2" d	37.50	37.50
Bowl, 5-7/8" d	40.00	40.00
Bowl, 11" l, oval	285.00	285.00
Bowl, 11" l, oval, divided	130.00	130.00
Candlesticks, pr, double lite	165.00	180.00
Creamer	45.00	40.00
Cup	35.00	35.00
Fruit Bowl, 4-1/2" d	32.00	30.00
Mayonnaise, 3 piece	100.00	125.00
Plate, 6-1/2" d, bread and butter	20.00	20.00
Plate, 8" d, salad	32.00	32.00
Plate, 10" d, dinner	90.00	85.00
Plate, 12" d, luncheon	85.00	80.00
Platter, 13" l	165.00	150.00
Saucer	18.00	15.00
Soup Bowl, 7" d	85.00	80.00
Sugar	45.00	40.00
Tidbit, 2 tiers, 8 and 10" plates	110.00	100.00
Tumbler, 9 oz	60.00	60.00
Vegetable Bowl, 9" d	95.00	95.00

MAYFAIR

Manufactured by Federal Glass Company, Columbus, OH, 1934.
  Made in amber, crystal, and green.

	Amber	Crystal	Green
Cereal Bowl, 6" d	16.50	9.50	19.50
Cream Soup, 5" d	18.00	11.00	18.00
Creamer, ftd	13.50	11.00	16.00
Cup	8.50	5.00	8.50
Plate, 6-3/4" d, salad	7.00	4.50	8.50
Plate, 9-1/2" d, dinner	14.00	10.00	14.50
Plate, 9-1/2" d, grill	13.50	8.50	13.50
Platter, 12" l, oval	27.50	20.00	30.00
Sauce Bowl, 5" d	8.50	7.00	12.00
Saucer	4.50	2.50	4.50
Sugar, ftd	14.00	12.00	14.00
Tumbler, 9 oz, 4-1/2" h	27.50	15.00	32.00
Vegetable, 10" l, oval	30.00	30.00	30.00

MOROCCAN AMETHYST

Manufactured by Hazel Ware, division of Continental Can,
  1960s. Made in amethyst.

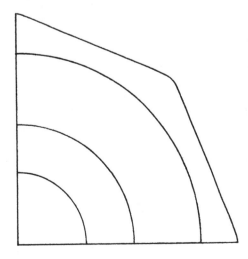

	Amethyst
Ashtray, 3-1/4" d, round	5.75
Ashtray, 3-1/4" w, triangular	5.75
Ashtray, 6-7/8" w, triangular	10.00
Ashtray, 8" w, square	14.00
Bowl, 5-3/4" w, deep, square	10.00
Bowl, 6" d, round	8.50
Bowl, 7-3/4" l, oval	17.50
Bowl, 7-3/4" l, rectangular	14.00
Bowl, 7-3/4" l, rectangular, metal handle	17.50
Bowls, 10-3/4" d	30.00
Candy, cov, short	35.00
Candy, cov, tall	32.00
Chip and Dip, 10-3/4" and 5-3/4" bowls in metal frame	40.00
Cocktail Shaker, chrome lid	30.00
Cocktail, stirrer, 16 oz, 6-1/4" h, lip	30.00
Cup	5.00
Fruit Bowl, 4-3/4" d, octagonal	9.00
Goblet, 9 oz, 5-1/2" h	10.00
Ice Bucket, 6" h	35.00
Iced Tea Tumbler, 16 oz, 6-1/2" h	16.00
Juice Goblet, 5-1/2 oz, 4-3/8" h	9.00
Juice Tumbler, 4 oz, 2-1/2" h	10.00
Old Fashioned Tumbler, 8 oz, 3-1/4" h	14.00
Plate, 5-3/4" d, sherbet	4.50
Plate, 7-1/4" d, salad	4.75
Plate, 9-3/4" d, dinner	7.00
Punch Bowl	85.00
Relish, 7-3/4" l	14.00
Salad Fork and Spoon	12.00
Sandwich Plate, 12" d, metal handle	15.00
Saucer	1.00
Sherbet, 7-1/2 oz, 4-1/4" h	8.00
Snack Plate, 10" l, fan shaped, cup rest	8.00
Snack Set, square plate, cup	12.00
Tumbler, 9 oz	10.00

Tumbler, 11 oz, 4-1/4" h, crinkled bottom	12.00
Tumbler, 11 oz, 4-5/8" h	12.00
Vase, 8-1/2" h, ruffled	40.00
Wine, 4-1/2 oz, 4" h	10.00

NEWPORT, Hairpin

Manufactured by Hazel Atlas Glass Company, Clarksburg, WV, and Zanesville, OH, from 1936 to the early 1950s. Made in amethyst, cobalt blue, pink (from 1936 to 1940), Platonite white and fired-on colors, from the 1940s to early 1950s.

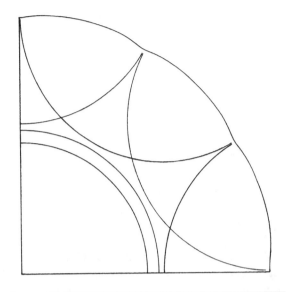

	Amethyst	Cobalt Blue	Fired-On Color	Platonite
Berry Bowl, 4-3/4" d	14.00	19.00	4.00	5.00
Berry Bowl, 8-1/4" d	35.00	22.50	14.00	10.00
Cereal Bowl, 5-1/4" d	30.00	34.00	-	-
Cream Soup, 4-3/4" d	20.00	22.50	6.00	8.50
Creamer	14.00	20.00	8.50	3.00
Cup	12.00	15.00	4.00	2.00
Plate, 6" d, sherbet	7.50	8.00	1.50	1.00
Plate, 8-1/2" d, luncheon	12.00	16.50	5.00	2.50
Plate, 8-13/16" d, dinner	30.00	30.00	15.00	12.00
Platter, 11-3/4" l, oval	35.00	45.00	18.00	12.00
Salt and Pepper Shakers, pr	42.00	45.00	24.00	18.00
Sandwich Plate, 11-1/2" d	48.00	50.00	12.00	10.00
Saucer	5.25	6.00	3.00	2.00
Sherbet	15.00	18.50	7.00	4.00
Sugar	14.00	20.00	9.50	5.00
Tumbler, 9 oz, 4-1/2" h	32.00	38.00	15.00	-

OVIDE

Manufactured by Hazel Atlas Glass Company, Clarksburg, WV,
and Zanesville, OH, 1930-35, 1950s. Made in black, green,
white Platonite with fired-on colors in the 1950s.

	Black	Green	Platonite
Berry Bowl, 4-3/4" d	-	-	7.50
Berry Bowl, 8" d	-	-	20.00
Candy Dish, cov	45.00	24.00	35.00
Cereal Bowl, 5-1/2" d	10.00	-	12.00
Creamer	7.00	4.50	18.00
Cup	6.50	3.50	14.00
Egg Cup	-	-	22.00
Fruit Cocktail, ftd	5.00	4.50	-
Plate, 6" d, sherbet	-	2.50	6.00
Plate, 8" d, luncheon	-	3.50	15.00
Plate, 9" d, dinner	-	-	25.00
Platter, 11" d	-	-	24.00
Salt and Pepper Shakers, pr	28.00	28.00	25.00
Saucer	3.50	3.50	6.00
Sherbet	6.50	3.50	15.00
Sugar, open	7.00	5.00	18.00
Tumbler	15.00	-	18.00

PARROT, Sylvan

Manufactured by Federal Glass Company, Columbus, OH, from 1931 to 1932.

Made in amber and green with limited production in blue and crystal.

	Amber	Green
Berry Bowl, 5" d	22.00	24.00
Berry Bowl, 8" d	75.00	80.00
Butter Dish, cov	1,150.00	375.00
Creamer, ftd	65.00	55.00
Cup	35.00	35.00
Plate, 5-3/4" d, sherbet	24.00	35.00
Plate, 7-1/2" d, salad	-	40.00
Plate, 9" d, dinner	49.00	38.00
Plate, 10-1/2" d, grill, square	-	27.00
Platter, 11-1/4" l, oblong	50.00	55.00
Salt and Pepper Shakers, pr	-	270.00
Saucer	18.00	18.00
Sherbet, ftd, cone	27.00	24.00
Soup Bowl, 7" d	32.00	42.00
Sugar, cov	450.00	175.00
Tumbler, 10 oz, 4-1/4" h	100.00	130.00
Tumbler, 12 oz, 5-1/2" h	115.00	160.00
Tumbler, 5-3/4" h, ftd, heavy	100.00	120.00
Vegetable Bowl, 10" l, oval	65.00	57.00

ROXANA

Manufactured by Hazel Atlas Glass Company, Clarksburg, WV, and Zanesville, OH, in 1932. Made in crystal, golden topaz, and white.

Production in white was limited to a 4-1/2" bowl, valued at $15.

	Crystal	Golden Topaz
Berry Bowl, 5" d	6.00	12.00
Bowl, 4-1/2 x 2-3/8"	6.00	12.00
Cereal Bowl, 6" d	7.50	15.00
Plate, 5-1/2" d	4.50	9.00
Plate, 6" d, sherbet	4.00	8.00
Sherbet, ftd	6.00	12.00
Tumbler, 9 oz, 4-1/4" h	8.50	17.00

ROYAL LACE

Royal Lace, tumbler, 5 oz, 3-1/2" h, cobalt blue, $65.

Manufactured by Hazel Atlas Glass Company, Clarksburg, WV, and Zanesville, OH, from 1934 to 1941. Made in cobalt blue, crystal, green, pink, and some amethyst.

Reproductions: † Reproductions include an 5 oz, 3-1/2" h tumbler, found in a darker cobalt blue.

	Cobalt Blue	Crystal	Green	Pink
Berry Bowl, 5" d	32.00	15.00	30.00	27.00
Berry Bowl, 10" d	66.00	20.00	32.00	28.00
Bowl, 10" d, 3 legs, rolled edge	-	190.00	75.00	50.00
Bowl, 10" d, 3 legs, ruffled edge	-	42.00	65.00	100.00
Bowl, 10" d, 3 legs, straight edge	-	24.00	45.00	40.00
Butter Dish, cov	-	65.00	250.00	150.00
Candlesticks, pr, rolled edge	-	45.00	85.00	60.00
Candlesticks, pr, ruffled edge	-	28.00	70.00	60.00
Candlesticks, pr, straight edge	-	30.00	75.00	55.00
Cookie Jar, cov	520.00	45.00	75.00	55.00
Cream Soup, 4-3/4" d	35.00	14.00	35.00	24.00
Creamer, ftd	60.00	15.00	25.00	20.00
Cup and Saucer	45.00	16.00	25.00	18.00
Nut Bowl	990.00	190.00	375.00	375.00
Pitcher, 48 oz, straight sides	150.00	40.00	110.00	85.00
Pitcher, 64 oz, 8" h	225.00	45.00	110.00	120.00
Pitcher, 68 oz, 8" h. ice lip	240.00	50.00	-	95.00
Pitcher, 86 oz, 8" h	-	50.00	135.00	95.00
Pitcher, 96 oz, 9-1/2" h, ice lip	265.00	69.00	140.00	100.00
Plate, 6" d, sherbet	14.00	5.00	10.00	15.00
Plate, 8-1/2" d, luncheon	30.00	7.50	15.00	20.00
Plate, 9-7/8" d, dinner	40.00	18.00	25.00	20.00
Plate, 9-7/8" d, grill	35.00	15.00	23.00	20.00
Platter, 13" l, oval	50.00	27.00	40.00	39.00
Salt and Pepper Shakers, pr	250.00	45.00	128.00	65.00
Sherbet, ftd	42.00	17.00	25.00	18.00
Sherbet, metal holder	28.00	4.00	-	-
Sugar, cov	42.00	32.00	30.00	50.00
Tumbler, 5 oz, 3-1/2" h †	65.00	15.00	30.00	35.00
Tumbler, 9 oz, 4-1/8" h	45.00	16.00	30.00	20.00
Tumbler, 10 oz, 4-7/8" h	100.00	25.00	60.00	60.00
Tumbler, 12 oz, 5-3/8" h	125.00	25.00	50.00	55.00
Vegetable Bowl, 11" l, oval	65.00	25.00	35.00	35.00

SUNFLOWER

Manufactured by Jeannette Glass Company, Jeannette, PA, 1930s.
Made in Delphite, green, pink, and some opaque colors.

	Delphite	Green	Pink	Opaque
Ashtray, 5" d	-	14.00	10.00	-
Cake Plate, 10" d, 3 legs	-	16.00	16.00	-
Creamer	85.00	20.00	20.00	85.00
Cup	-	14.50	12.50	75.00
Plate, 9" d, dinner	-	20.00	16.00	-
Saucer	-	13.50	10.00	85.00
Sugar	-	23.00	20.00	-
Trivet, 7" d, 3 legs, turned up edge	-	315.00	300.00	-
Tumbler, 8 oz, 4-3/8" h, ftd	-	35.00	30.00	-

THUMBPRINT

Manufactured by Federal Glass Company, Columbus, OH, from
1927-1930. Made in green.

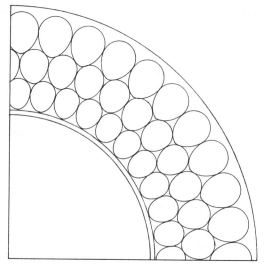

	Green
Berry Bowl, 4-3/4" d	7.00
Berry Bowl, 8" d	10.00

Cereal Bowl, 5" d	9.00
Creamer, ftd	8.00
Cup	6.00
Juice Tumbler, 4" h	6.00
Plate, 6" d, sherbet	3.00
Plate, 8" d, luncheon	5.00
Plate, 9-1/4" d, dinner	7.00
Salt and Pepper Shakers, pr.	25.00
Saucer	2.00
Sherbet	7.00
Sugar, ftd	8.00
Tumbler, 5" h	8.00
Tumbler, 5-1/2" h	10.00
Whiskey, 2-1/4" h	6.50

WINDSOR, Windsor Diamond

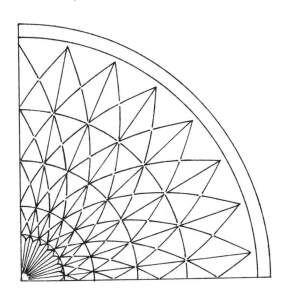

Windsor, pitcher, pink, 52 oz, 6-3/4" h, $33.

Manufactured by Jeannette Glass Company, Jeannette, PA, from 1936 to 1946. Made in crystal, green, and pink with limited production in amberina red, Delphite and ice blue.

	Crystal	Green	Pink
Ashtray, 5-3/4" d	13.50	45.00	35.00
Berry Bowl, 4-3/4" d	4.00	11.00	9.00
Berry Bowl, 8-1/2" d	6.50	17.50	18.50
Bowl, 5" l, pointed edge	5.00	-	17.50
Bowl, 7 x 11-3/4", boat shape	18.00	35.00	32.00
Bowl, 7-1/2" d, 3 legs	8.00	-	24.00

Bowl, 8" d, 2 handles	9.00	24.00	20.00
Bowl, 8" l, pointed edge	10.00	-	48.00
Bowl, 10-1/2" l, pointed edge	25.00	-	32.00
Butter Dish, cov	27.50	94.00	60.00
Cake Plate, 10-3/4" d, ftd	9.00	22.00	20.00
Candlesticks, pr, 3" h	20.00	-	85.00
Cereal Bowl, 5-3/8" d	9.00	22.00	25.00
Chop Plate, 13-5/8" d	19.00	40.00	42.00
Coaster, 3-1/4" d	8.50	18.00	25.00
Comport	9.00	-	-
Cream Soup, 5" d	6.00	30.00	25.00
Creamer	5.00	15.00	19.00
Cup and Saucer	9.00	24.00	15.00
Fruit Console, 12-1/2" d	25.00	-	95.00
Pitcher, 16 oz, 4-1/2" h	24.00	-	115.00
Pitcher, 52 oz, 6-3/4" h	15.00	55.00	33.00
Plate, 6" d, sherbet	3.75	8.00	5.00
Plate, 7" d, salad	4.50	20.00	18.00
Plate, 9" d, dinner	9.00	25.00	25.00
Platter, 11-1/2" l, oval	7.00	25.00	22.00
Powder Jar	15.00	-	55.00
Relish Platter, 11-1/2" l, divided	10.00	-	200.00
Salad Bowl, 10-1/2" d	12.00	-	-
Salt and Pepper Shakers, pr	16.00	48.00	39.00
Sandwich Plate, 10" d, open handles	7.50	17.00	17.00
Sherbet, ftd	3.50	15.00	13.00
Sugar, cov	9.00	39.00	19.00
Sugar, cov, Holiday shape	12.00	-	100.00
Tray, 4" sq	5.00	12.00	10.00
Tray, 4" sq, handles	6.00	-	40.00
Tray, 4-1/8 x 9"	5.00	16.00	10.00
Tray, 4-1/8 x 9", handles	9.00	-	50.00
Tray, 8-1/2 x 9-3/4"	7.00	35.00	25.00
Tray, 8-1/2 x 9-3/4", handles	14.00	45.00	85.00
Tumbler, 5 oz, 3-1/4" h	9.00	42.00	25.00
Tumbler, 9 oz, 4" h	7.50	38.00	22.00
Tumbler, 12 oz, 5" h	11.00	55.00	30.00
Vegetable Bowl, 9-1/2" l, oval	7.50	29.00	25.00

DISNEYANA

History: Walt Disney and the creations of the famous Disney Studios hold a place of fondness and enchantment in the hearts of people throughout the world. The 1928 release of "Steamboat Willie," featuring Mickey Mouse, heralded an entertainment empire.

Walt and his brother, Roy, were shrewd businessmen. From the beginning they licensed the reproduction of Disney characters on products ranging from wristwatches to clothing.

In 1984, Donald Duck celebrated his 50th birthday, and collectors took a renewed interest in material related to him.

References: Ted Hake, *Hake's Guide to Character Toys*, Gemstone Publishing (1966 Greenspring, Ste. 405, Timonium, MD 21093), 1998; Robert Heide and John Gilman, *Disneyana*, Hyperion, 1994; Maxine A. Pinsky, *Marx Toys: Robots, Space, Comic, Disney & TV Characters*, Schiffer Publishing, 1996; Rex Miller, *The Investor's Guide to Vintage Character Collectibles*, Krause Publications, 1999; Carol J. Smith, *Identification & Price Guide to Winnie the Pooh Collectibles*, Hobby House Press, 1994; Tom Tumbusch, *Tomart's Illustrated Disneyana Catalog and Price Guide*, Vols. 1, 2, 3, and 4, Tomart Publications, 1985; —, *Tomart's Illustrated Disneyana Catalog and Price Guide, Condensed Edition*, Wallace-Homestead, 1989.

Periodicals: *Mouse Rap Monthly*, P.O. Box 1064, Ojai, CA 93024; *Tomart's Disneyana Digest*, 3300 Encrete Ln, Dayton, OH 45439; *Tomart's Disneyana Update*, 3300 Encrete Ln, Dayton, OH 45439.

Collectors' Clubs: Imagination Guild, P.O. Box 907, Boulder Creek, CA 95006; Mouse Club East, P.O. Box 3195, Wakefield, MA 01880; National Fantasy Fan Club for Disneyana Collectors and Enthusiasts, P.O. Box 19212, Irvine, CA 92713.

Archives/Museum: Walt Disney Archives, Burbank, CA 91521.

Additional Listings: *See Warman's Americana & Collectibles* for more examples.

Advisor: Theodore L. Hake.

Davy Crockett

Chow Set, 4-1/4" x 7" colorful store card, browntone image of Davy at left holding long rifle, clear plastic covered diecut windows with 5-3/4" stainless steel spoon, 5-1/2" l fork, each with full figure image etched on blade, ©Walt Disney Productions, c1955 .... 60.00
Gum Card Set, 80 cards, full color photo front, Topps, 1958 ...... 265.00
Plate, 7" d, white, dark brown Davy staring down bear, facsimile signature below image, c1955 .... 45.00
Pocket Knife, 2-1/4" l, cream colored celluloid grip, black, white, and red image on one side, small inset circular photo of Davy against long rifle and tomahawk, black text "Walt Disney's Davy Crockett

SPECIAL AUCTIONS

Hake's Americana & Collectibles
P.O. Box 1444, Dept. 344
York, PA 17405
(717) 848-1333

Fess Parker as Davy Crockett," ©Walt Disney Productions, c1955 .... 45.00
Wallet, 3-1/4" x 4-1/2", brown vinyl, Davy Crockett Indian Fighter, c1955 .... 40.00

Disneyland

Ashtray, 5" d, glazed ceramic, white, 3 gold cigarette rests, colorful scene of castle and Tinker Bell, c1960 .... 25.00
Card Game, deck of 44 2-1/2" x 3-1/4" cards, clear plastic case, Whitman, copyright 1964, 11 different characters 30.00
Park Folder, Disneyland USA Tom Sawyer Island, 4" x 9", brown, white, green accent opens to 9" x 12" map, ©Walt Disney Productions, 1967 .... 60.00
Salt and Pepper Shakers, pr, 2-1/2" h, glazed ceramic, bell shape, one shows castle, other carousel, one with ©Walt Disney Productions, other has "Japan" sticker, c1960 .... 28.00
Souvenir Booklet, Disneyland Hi-Lites, 3" x 4-1/4", spiral bound, 12 stiff thin cardboard pages, 1960s 18.00
Tea Cup and Saucer, china, 2" h cup, 6" d, saucer, white, ridged design, gold rim and "Disneyland," Tinker Bell inside cup, castle with flags on saucer 35.00

Donald Duck

Bank, 4" x 4" x 8" h, painted composition, Uncle Scrooge, holding large money sack, green jacket, red spats, black hat, blue hand, c1960. 75.00
Blotter
   3-1/2" x 5-1/4", blue and white, color scene of Donald ice skating with 3 nephews playing ice hockey, imprint for insurance agent in San Jose, CA, text "1601 Ice Follies," c1940, unused 48.00
   4" x 7-1/2", Blue Sunoco, color scene of startled Donald in car being pushed down snowy road by ramming goat, ©Walt Disney Enterprises, 1938, unused 85.00
Cereal Bowl, 5-1/2" d, deep blue Beetleware, yellow and black accent art of Donald in center, alphabet letters at top rim, relief numbers 0 to 9, ©Walt Disney Enterprises, c1935, Post's 40% Bran Flakes, Grape-Nuts Flakes premium 48.00
Figure, 3-1/4" h, bisque, white, smiling smugly, hands up next to chest, blue outfit, red bow tie, Japan, ©Walt Disney, c1940 .... 85.00
Handkerchief, 8-1/2" sq, white cloth, color image of Donald in sailboat, nephews helping from dock, trimmed blue and white ocean design border, yellow rope around scene, c1950 .... 18.00
Magazine, Liberty, Oct. 19, 1940, 8-1/2" x 11-3/8", 68 black and white pages, patriotic Donald cover 38.00
Puppet Punch-Out Sheet, 7-1/2" x 9-3/4", Donald Duck Bread premium, white stiff paper, 1950s, unpunched 38.00

Dumbo

Figure, 2-3/8" h, ceramic, Thumper, brown and white, orange accents, seated, Goebel, tiny bee within "V" mark, mkd "W. Germany" ... 38.00
Picture Set, 11" x 11" paper sheet with circus tent train, animal cages, white silhouettes designated areas for placement of character cutouts from Donald Duck bread labels, 4 uncut 2-3/4" x 8-1/4" strips, 1950s, full set 85.00
Record Album, 10-1/2" x 12", Victor K-1, c1942, blue and white cardboard sleeve, orange accents, smiling baby Dumbo on front, 3 brown sleeves, records missing 14.00
Lady and the Tramp, Big Golden Book, 9-1/4" x 12-1/2", cover of Tramp giving Lady flower on house step, Jock and Trusty grin on back cover, wrap-around scene, 32 full color pgs, art by Claude Coach, Golden Press 1955 copyright, #10427 .... 45.00

Mickey Mouse

Bank, 6-3/4" h, composition, figural, powder blue suit, black bow tie and belt, red shirt, yellow shoes, ©Walt Disney Productions, Korea, early 1970s 45.00
Better Little Book, *Mickey Mouse and the Lazy Daisy Mystery*, Whitman #1439, ©1947, very fine condition 50.00
Bubble Gum Wrapper, 5" x 7" waxed paper wrapped, Mickey, Minnie, Pluto, Horace, and Clara Bell, ad for picture card album, 1930s, Gum Inc. 145.00

Mickey Mouse Hurdy Gurdy, litho tin wind-up, 6" l, 3" w, 8" h, $18,700. Photo courtesy of James D. Julia.

Cereal Bowl, 5" d, red Beetleware, black and yellow accent on inside of smiling Mickey, ©Walt Disney Enterprises, Post's 40% Bran Flakes/Grape Nuts 28.00

Christmas Card Giveaway, mechanical, 5" x 8" stiff paper, c1935, front and back image of Mickey holding paint brush, large gray painter's palette, small diecut window at top against blue ground, multicolored lettering, attached disk turned to produce movie, one side with Mickey skating, other with Minnie walking in snow, card opens to show other illus, front mkd "A Xmas Gift From Mickey Mouse," back with reversed image 225.00

Easter Egg Transfers, "Mickey Mouse Transfer-o-s For Easter Eggs," 5-1/2" x 5-1/2" sealed paper envelope, full color graphics, Mickey and bunny spinning yellow egg, also Mickey pulling off transfer image of Donald Duck, Paas Dye Co., ©Walt Disney Enterprises, c1936 .. .. 115.00

Figure, 2-3/4" w, 2-1/4" h, bisque, Mickey riding Pluto, using his ears as reins, c1935, "Japan" stamp 135.00

Pencil Sharpener, 1-1/2" x 1-1/4" x 4-3/4", figural, black Mickey, flesh-tone face, red shorts, brown shoes, red base, c1960, ©Walt Disney Productions, Hong Kong 45.00

Push Button Puppet, 1-1/8" d, 2-1/2" h, smiling Mickey, hands out to sides, red shorts, yellow shoes, blue base, black and silver foil label on front, Kohner, ©Walt Disney Productions, c1970 .... 25.00

Sheet Music, *The Wedding Party of Mickey Mouse*, 9" x 12", 8 pgs, ©1931, black, white, and red cover of Mickey and Minnie, laughing animals wedding party, bright red background, Stasny Music Corp., NY 125.00

Store Sign, 5-1/2" x 7", "Have You Seen the New Mickey Mouse Pencil Box," thin cardboard, red and black art and text, smiling Mickey at left, large red text title "School Sale," advertised Dixon pencil boxes, ©Walt Disney, c1933 .... 85.00

Ticket, 2-1/4" x 3-1/4", Southern California vs California at Los Angeles, Sat, Dec 9, 1939, white ticket, brown image of Mickey as Roman soldier holding SC shield, growling bear with UCLA on chest, Mickey ©WDP by special permission of Walt Disney Enterprises, Jefferies Bank Not. Co., blue art of football stadium layout on back 95.00

Wind-Up, 3-1/4" h Mickey, fleshtone face, white gloves, red shoes, 2-3/4" h Pluto, orange, red accent mouth and collar, black ears and tail, applied sticker eyes, Mickey walks, Pluto sits up, ©1977 Tomy, Korea, pr 35.00

Wrist Watch, 1" x 1-/8" chrome cased watch, color image of Mickey in center, red shorts, yellow hands and shoes, orig ed. vinyl band, Ingersoll, 1948, over-wound 115.00

Peter Pan

Little Golden Book, 6-3/4" x 8"
    Peter Pan and the Indians, cover with Peter meeting Indian chief, 28 full color pgs, art by Brice Mack and Dick Kinney, ©1952 Walt Disney Prod., 1st edition 18.00
    Peter Pan and Wendy, 6-5/8" x 8", cover with Peter and Wendy about to fly off, 28 full color pgs, art by Eyvind Earle, 1st edition 22.00

Pinocchio

Drinking Glass, design of full figure on one side, poem on reverse, c1940
    4-1/4" h, J. Worthington Foulfellow, red design 38.00
    4-3/4" h, Cleo, swimming orange figure, c1940 .... 28.00
Figure
    2-1/2" h, bisque, Figaro, black, white, and orange, gold nose tip, pink mouth, c1940 .... 60.00
    3-1/2" h, glazed china, Jiminy Cricket, smiling full figure, holding umbrella in right hand, National Porcelain Co., NJ, c1940 ... 45.00
    5-1/4" h, Syroco, Geppetto, dark brown, blue apron, repainted white hair, c1940 .... 45.00
Mask, 10" x 12", orig brown paper bag, printing in black, 2 different 9" x 10" diecut stiff paper full color masks, one of Pinocchio, other of Cleo, (from set of 6), 1939, Gillette razor blade premium 28.00

Snow White

Figure
    1-1/4" h, glazed ceramic, Dopey, Hagen, fleshtone, purple cap, green gown, black accent buttons and shoes, silver foil sticker, ©Walt Disney Prod., glued repair.. 28.00
    1-3/4" h, hollow metal, Britains, Dopey, red hat, dark green gown, yellow accent, some paint loss, c1930 .... 45.00
    4-3/4" h, bisque, Sleepy, green cap, gray jacket with brown patch, black pants, brown shoes, ©Walt Disney, 1930s, some paint missing.. 60.00
    4-3/4" h, bisque, Sneezy, brown cap, purple jacket, red pants, gray shoes, holding left hand to nose, ©Walt Disney, late 1930s. 75.00
Medal, 1-1/2" d, Snow White 50th Anniversary Grumpy, limited edition, .999 fine silver, circular clear plastic case, velvet box with hinged lid, from set of 11 different coins, each limited to 20,000, 1987, Rarities Mint 58.00
Picture, 11" x 11-1/2", Skylark Bread premium, full color, cottage in background, forest scene, wood grain design margins, white silhouettes for application of cut-out bread label characters, red, white, and blue design on reverse with directions, c1950 .... 80.00
Uncle Remus, Little Golden Book, 6-3/4" x 8", Uncle Remus, cover of Brer Fox and Brer Bear about to snare Brer Rabbit, 42 pgs, art by Bob Grant, ©1947 Walt Disney Prod, 4th printing...................... 18.00

Zorro

Action Figure, 6" x 9" blister card, 3-3/4" poseable figure, accessories, Gabriel #32710, copyright 1981 .... 65.00
Bowl, 5-1/2' d, white hard plastic, color image of Zorro, raised sword, riding horse, Sun-Valley, Chicago, late 1950s.......................... 35.00
Sun Picture, 2-1/2" x 3-3/4", black, white, red, yellow, silver foil envelope, complete contents, late 1950s, unused.......................... 22.00

DOLLHOUSES

History: Dollhouses date from the 18th century to modern times. Early dollhouses often were handmade, sometimes with only one room. The most common type was made for a young girl to fill with replicas of furniture scaled especially to fit into a dollhouse. Specially sized dolls also were made for dollhouses. All types of accessories in all types of styles were available, and dollhouses could portray any historical period.

References: Evelyn Ackerman, *Genius of Moritz Gottschalk*, Gold House Publishing, 1994; Mary Brett, *Tomart's Price Guide to Tin Litho Doll Houses and Plastic Doll House Furnishings*, Tomart Publications, 1997; Nora Earnshaw, *Collecting Dolls' Houses and Miniatures*, Pincushion Press, 1993; Flora Bill Jacobs, *Dolls' Houses in America: Historic Preservation in Miniature*, Charles Scribner's Sons, 1974; Margaret Towner, *Dollhouse Furniture, Courage Books*, 1993; Dian Zillner, *American Dollhouses and Furniture from the 20th Century*, Schiffer Publishing, 1995.

Periodicals: Doll Castle News, P.O. Box 247, Washington, NJ 07882; International Dolls' House News, P.O. Box 79, Southampton S09 7EZ England; Miniature Collector, 30595 Eight Mill, Livonia, MI 48152; Miniatures Showcase, P.O. Box 1612, Waukesha, WI 53187; Nutshell News, 21027 Crossroads Circle, P.O. Box 1612, Waukesha, WI 53187.

Collectors' Clubs: Dollhouse & Miniature Collectors, 9451 Lee Hwy #515, Fairfax, VA 22302; National Association of Miniature Enthusiasts, P.O. Box 69, Carmel, IN 46032; National Organization of Miniaturists and Dollers, 1300 Schroder, Normal, IL 61761.

Museums: Art Institute of Chicago, Chicago, IL; Margaret Woodbury Strong Museum, Rochester, NY; Museums at Stony Brook, Stony Brook, NY; Toy and Miniature Museum of Kansas City, Kansas City, MO; Washington Dolls' House and Toy Museum, Washington, DC.

American
    12-1/4" w, 13" d, 11" h, painted wood and board, bungalow style, blue building, cream and orange trim, red roof, one room with orig wall covering, 1920s, some paint wear, side door warped..300.00
    21-1/4" l, 28-3/4" h, Victorian, last quarter 19th C, two story house, modified Federal style, mansard roof with widow's walk, fenced in front garden, simulated grass and fountains, polychrome details 400.00
Bliss, chromolithograph paper on wood
    13" h, 2 story, litho blue roof, red wood base, 2 opening windows, working front door, orig litho walls and floors, mkd "R. Bliss" on front door, some wear, stains, and discoloration 900.00
    14" h, 2 story, house, blue litho paper on roof, blue wood on back, red wood chimney and base, two open lower windows and 2 upper windows, house opens in front, litho wall and floor coverings inside, mkd "R. Bliss" on door, some wear, one wall slightly warped 575.00
    14" h, 2 story, stable, red shingle roof, painted green roof and red spire on cupola, painted red base and side poles of stable, single opening door on second floor, brown papier-mâché horse, mkd "R. Bliss" 900.00
    16-1/2" h, 2 story, front porch with turned columns, working front door, overhanging roof with lattice-work balcony, blue-gray roof with dormer windows, hinged front, int. with two rooms, printed carpeting and wallpaper, celluloid windows with later lace curtains, electric lights, two scratch-built chairs 1,725.00
    19" h, 2 story, front porch with balcony, 2 real windows, working front door, litho windows on 2nd floor and sides, red litho shingles on roof, blue litho shingles on porch roof, litho wall and floor cov-

Two Story, working front door, porch with columns and porch swing, bay window on 2nd floor, orig yellow, green, and red paint, int. carpets, wallpaper, remnants of curtains, c1900, 27" w, 20" d, 35" h, $750. Photo courtesy of Alderfer Auction Co.

erings inside, wood chimney, mkd "R. Bliss" on porch balcony, some general soil and discoloration 1,200.00
Elastolin, Germany, 29" w, farmyard, house, barn, fencing, trees, and various figures 1,150.00
German, 35" w, 11-1/4" d, 17" h, Nuremberg Kitchen, dark yellow walls with deep red trim, red and black checkerboard floor, cream stove hood, green furniture, tin stove, tin and copper pots, set of scales, wash boiler, baking pans, utensils, pottery, porcelain, and pewter tableware, late 19th C, some paint wear and imperfections . 2,300.00
McLoughlin, 12" x 17" x 16", folding, house, 2 rooms, dec int., orig box 950.00
Schoenhut, 20" x 26" x 30", mansion, 2 story, 8 rooms, attic, tan brick design, red roof, large dormer, 20 glass windows, orig decal, 1923 .... 1,750.00
Tootsietoy, 21" w, 10-1/8" d, 16" h, house, furniture, and accessories, printed Masonite, half-timbered style, 2 rooms down, 2 up, removable roof, open back, orchid and pink bedroom sets, orchid bathroom, brown dining room set, flocked sofa and chairs, green and white kitchen pcs, piano, bench, lamps, telephone, cane-back sofa, rocker, some damage and wear to 3/4 scale furniture 525.00
Unmarked, 15" h, 11-1/2" w x 8" deep, log cabin, lithographed paper over wood, 2 story, two working windows on front, working door, two lithographed windows on each side, balcony across entire front, green painted roof 900.00

DOLLS

History: Dolls have been children's play toys for centuries. Dolls also have served other functions. From the 14th through 18th centuries, doll making was centered in Europe, mainly in Germany and France. The French dolls produced in this era were representations of adults and were dressed in the latest couturier designs. They were not children's toys.

During the mid-19th century, child and baby dolls, made in wax, cloth, bisque, and porcelain, were introduced. Facial features were hand painted; wigs were made of mohair and human hair; and the dolls were dressed in the current fashions for babies or children.

Doll making in the United States began to flourish in the 1900s with companies such as Effanbee, Madame Alexander, and Ideal.

Marks: Marks of the various manufacturers are found on the back of the head or neck or on the doll's back. These marks are very important in identifying a doll and its date of manufacture.

References: Johana Gast Anderton, *More Twentieth Century Dolls from Bisque to Vinyl*, vols. A–H, I–Z, revised eds., Wallace-Homestead, 1974; J. Michael Augustyniak, *Thirty Years of Mattel Fashion Dolls, 1967 Through 1997: Identification and Value Guide, Collector Books,* 1998; Kim Avery, *The World of Raggedy Ann Collectibles*, Collector Books, 1997; John Axe, Encyclopedia of Celebrity Dolls, Hobby House Press, 1983; Carol Corson, *Schoenhut Dolls*, Hobby House Press, 1993; Carla Marie Cross, *Modern Doll Rarities*, Antique Trader Books, 1997; Linda Crowsey, *Madame Alexander Collector's Dolls Price Guide #24*, Collector Books, 1999; Maryanne Dolan, *The World of Dolls, A Collector's Identification and Value Guide, Krause Publications, 1998*; Jan Foulke, *Doll Classics*, Hobby House Press, 1997; --, *Insider's Guide to China Doll Collecting*, Hobby House Press, 1995;——, *Insider's Guide to Doll Buying and Selling*, Hobby House Press, 1995; ——, *Insider's Guide to Germany "Dolly" Collecting*, Hobby House Press, 1995; ——, *13th Blue Book Dolls and Values*, Hobby House Press, 1997; Sandra Ann Garrison, *The Raggedy Ann and Andy Family Album,*2nd ed., Schiffer Publishing, 1999; Cynthia Gaskill, *Legendary Dolls of Madame Alexander*, Theriault's, 1995; Patricia Hall, *Johnny Gruelle: Creator of Raggedy Ann and Andy*, Pelican Publishing (1101 Monroe St., Gretna, LA 70053), 1993; Dawn Herlocher, *Antique Trader's Doll Makers & Marks*, Antique Trader Books, 1999; —, 200 Years of Dolls, Antique Trader Books, 1996; R. Lane Herron, *Warman's Dolls*, Krause Publications, 1998; Judity Izen, *Collector's Guide to Ideal Dolls*, 2nd ed., Collector Books, 1998; Judith Izen and Carol Sover, *Collector's Guide to Vogue Dolls*, Collector Books, 1998; Polly Judd, *African and Asian Costumed Dolls*, Hobby House Press, 1995: —, *Cloth Dolls*, Hobby House Press, 1990; Polly and Pam Judd, *Composition Dolls*, Vol. I (1991), Vol. II (1994), Hobby House Press; —, *European Costume Dolls*, Hobby House Press, 1994; —, *Glamour Dolls of the 1950s & 1960s*, revised ed., Hobby House Press, 1993; —, *Hard Plastic Dolls*, 3rd ed. (1993), Book II (1994), Hobby House Press; Michele Karl, *Composition & Wood Dolls and Toys: A Collector's Reference Guide*, Antique Trader Books, 1998; Constance King, *Collecting Dolls Reference and Price Guide*, Antique Collectors' Club, 1999; Kathy and Don Lewis, *Talking Toys of the 20th Century*, Collector Books, 1999; A. Glenn Mandeville, *Alexander Dolls*, 2nd ed., Hobby House Press, 1995; ——, *Ginny*, 3rd ed., Hobby House Press, 1998; Marcie Melilo, *The Ultimate Barbie Doll Book*, Krause Publications, 1997; Ursula R. Mertz, *Collector's Encyclopedia of American Composition Dolls*, 1900 to 1950, Collector Books, 1999; Patsy Moyer, *Doll Values, Antique to Modern*, 3rd ed., Collector Books, 1999; —, *Modern Collectible Dolls*, Collector Books, 1997, Vol II. (1997), Vol. III (1999) ; Myra Yellin Outwater, *Advertising Dolls*, Schiffer Publishing, 1997; Edward R. Pardella, *Shirley Temple Dolls and Fashion,* Schiffer Publishing, 1992; Sabine Reinelt, **Magic of Character Dolls**, Hobby House Press, 1993.

Lydia Richter, *China, Parian, and Bisque German Dolls*, Hobby House Press, 1993; Lydia and Joachim F. Richter, Bru Dolls, Hobby House Press, 1989; Lydia Richter and Karin Schmelcher, *Heubach Character Dolls and Figurines*, Hobby House Press, 1992; Joyce Rinehart, *Wonderful Raggedy Anns*, Schiffer Publishing, 1997; Jane Sarasohn-Kahn, *Contemporary Barbie*, Antique Trader Books, 1997; Patricia N. Schoonmaker, *Patsy Doll Family Encyclopedia*, Vol. II, Hobby House Press, 1998; Patricia R. Smith, *Antique Collector's Dolls*, vol. I (1975, 1991 value update), vol. II (1976, 1991 Value update), Collector Books;--, *Effanbee Dolls*, Collector Books, 1998 values update; ——, *Madame Alexander Collector's Dolls Price Guide #20*, Collector Books, 1995; ——, *Madame Alexander Dolls 1965-1990*, 1991, 1997 values update, Collector Books; ——, *Modern Collector's Dolls*, Series I through VIII (1973–1996 value updates), Collector Books; ——, *Patricia Smith's Doll Values Antique to Modern*, Eleventh Series, Collector Books, 1995; ——, *Shirley Temple Dolls and Collectibles*, Vol. I (1977, 1992 value update), Vol. II (1979, 1992 value update), Collector Books; Evelyn Robson Stahlendorf, *Charlton Standard Catalogue of Canadian Dolls*, 3rd ed., Charlton Press, 1997; Carl P. Stirn, *Turn-of-the-Century Dolls*, Toys and Games (1893 catalog reprint), Dover Publications, 1990; Florence Theriault, *The Beautiful Jumeau*, Gold Horse Publishing, 1997.

Periodicals: *Antique & Collectables*, P.O. Box 12589, El Cajon, CA 92002, http://www.collect.com/antiquesandcollectables; *Antique & Collectible Dolls*, 218 W. Woodin Blvd., Dallas, TX 75224; *Antique Doll Collector*, 6 Woodside Ave., Suite 300, Northport, NY 11768, http://www.antiqueDollCollector.com; *Cloth Doll Magazine*, P.O. Box 2167 Lake Oswego, OR 97035-0051, http://www.theclothdoll/com; *Costume Quarterly for Doll Collectors*, 118-01 Sutter Ave., Jamaica, NY 11420; *Doll Castle News*, P.O. Box 247, Washington, NJ 07882-0247, http://www.dollcastlenews.com; *Doll Collector's Price Guide*, 306 East Parr Rd, Berne, IN 46711; *Doll-E-Gram*, P.O. Box 1212, Bellevue, WA 98009-1212; *Doll Life*, 243 Newton-Sparta Rd, Newton, NJ 07860; *Doll Magazine*, Avalon Court, Star Rd, Patridge Green, West Sussex RH13 BRY +44(0) 1403 711511, http://www.dollmagazine.com; *Doll Reader*, 741 Miller Drive, SE, Harrisburg, PA 20175, http://www.cowles.com/maglist.html; *Doll Times*, 218 W Woodin Blvd., Dallas, TX 75224; *Doll World*, 306 East Parr Rd, Berne, IN 46711; *Dollmasters*, P.O. Box 151, Annapolis, MD 21404; *Dolls—The Collector's Magazine*, 170 Fifth Ave., 12th Floor, New York, NY 10010; *Patsy & Friends*, P.O. Box 311, Deming, NM 88031, http://www.zianet.com/patsyandfirends; *Rags*, P.O. Box 823, Atlanta, GA 30301.

SPECIAL AUCTIONS

McMasters Doll Auctions
P.O. Box 1755
Cambridge, OH 43725
(614) 432-4419

Skinner Inc.
Bolton Gallery
357 Main St.
Bolton, MA 01740
(508) 779-6241

Theriault's Auction
P.O. Box 151
Annapolis, MD 21404-0151

Collectors' Clubs: Annalee Doll Society, P.O. Box 708, Meredith, NH 03253, http://www.annalee.com; Doll Collector International, P.O. Box 2761, Oshkosh, WI 54903; Doll Costumers Guild, 7112 W Grovers Ave., Glendale, AZ 85308; Doll Doctor's Association, 6204 Ocean Front Ave., Virginia Beach, VA 23451; Ginny Doll Club, P.O. Box 338, Oakdale, CA 95361; International Golliwogg Collectors Club, P.O. Box 612, Woodstock, NY 12498, http://www.teddybears.com/golliwog; Ideal Toy Co. Collector's Club, P.O. Box 623, Lexington, MA 02173; Madame Alexander Doll Fan Club, P.O. Box 330, Mundeline, IL 60060; United Federation of Doll Clubs, 10920 N. Ambassador Drive, Suite 130, Kansas City, MO 64153, http://www.ufdc.org.

Museums: Aunt Len's Doll House, Inc., New York, NY; Children's Museum, Detroit, MI; Doll Castle Doll Museum, Washington, NJ; Doll Museum, Newport, RI; Toy and Miniature Museum of Kansas City, Kansas City, MO; Gay Nineties Button & Doll Museum, Eureka Springs, AR; Margaret Woodbury Strong Museum, Rochester, NY; Mary Merritt Doll Museum, Douglassville, PA; Mary Miller Doll Museum, Brunswick, GA; Prairie Museum of Art & History, Colby, KS; Washington Dolls' House & Toy Museum, Washington, DC; Yesteryears Museum, Sandwich, MA.

Additional Listings: *See Warman's Americana & Collectibles for more examples.*

Alt, Beck & Gottschalck, 23" h, 1361 baby, bisque socket head, blue sleep eyes, feathered brows, painted upper and lower lashes, open mouth with accented lips and 2 upper teeth, retracting tongue that falls back when eyes close, human hair wig, bent-limb composition baby body, new white baby dress and bonnet, mkd "ABG, 1361, 55," Made in Germany, 16" on back of head, light nose and cheek rubs, real lashes missing, normal wear 300.00
Amberg, L., newborn baby, solid dome bisque flange head, brown sleep eyes, softly blushed brows, painted upper and lower lashes, closed mouth, painted hair, cloth body with non-working crier, celluloid hands, white baby dress, mkd "©L. Amberg & Son, Germany, 8863" on back of head, faint stamp on body 300.00
American Character, 17" h, Annie Oakley, hard plastic head, blue sleep eyes with real lashes, single stroke brows, painted lower lashes, closed mouth, orig saran wig in braids, hard plastic body jointed at shoulders and hips, orig gold satin western-style blouse with green cuffs, matching vest and culottes skirt with gold fringe and embroidered name, gold satin scarf, black and gold felt western hat,

black boots, holster with one metal gun, mkd "Original American Character Annie Oakley" paper wrist tag 425.00
Belton
10-1/2" h, bisque socket head with flat top and 3 holes, set blue eyes, single stroke brows, painted upper and lower lashes, open-closed mouth with white space between lips, pierced-in ears, orig mohair wig, jointed wood and composition body with straight wrists, orig baby-type clothes, mkd "L 2/0" of head, some wear to body finish 500.00
11" h, bisque socket head with flat top, 2 small hand one larger hole on top, set blue eyes, single stroke brows, painted upper and lower lashes, open-closed mouth with accented lips, pierced-in ears, replaced mohair wig, jointed wood and composition body with shapely torso, 1-pc arms with straight wrists, wooden upper legs, antique white dress, mkd "L, 9/0" on back of head, pale coloring 425.00
Bergmann, C. M.
22" h, bisque head, brown sleep eyes, open mouth, fully jointed composition body, imp "C. M. Bergmann," wig missing, some paint wear to body 325.00
28-1/2" h, bisque socket head, set blue eyes, molded and feathered brows, painted lower lashes, open mouth with accented lips and 4 upper teeth, pierced ears, antique human hair wig, jointed wood and composition body, antique child's dress, mkd "S. M. Bergmann, Simon & Halbig, 13" on back of head, eyes set, real lashes missing, light wear to body 450.00
Bisque, unknown maker
8" h, all bisque, brown sleep glass eyes, close mouth, blond mohair wig, one piece head and body, jointed at shoulders and hips, molded pink socks and black shoes, imp "30 10" mark, Germany, late 19th C. 575.00
8-1/2" h, Shebee, all bisque, jointed at shoulders and imps, molded and painted features, white undershirt and pink booties, orig paper bib, imp "Germany" on back lower edge of undershirt, paper label on chest, Charles Twelve Trees character, 1923, top of left leg repaired 435.00

French, 19" Henri Alexandre Phoenix #90, bisque socket head, closed mouth, blue paperweight set eyes, pierced ears, original mohair wig and pate, original clothes including shoes and bebe phoenix waist ribbon, french ball jointed composition body, $4,250.

13" h, character boy, shoulder head, molded blond hair, blue painted intaglio eyes, open/closed mouth, kid body, bisque hands, imp "2 Germany" on back, c1900, damage to hands 750.00

17" h, man, bisque shoulder head, painted eyes, single stroke brows, closed mouth, molded and painted blond hair, cloth body, bisque lower arms, antique black wool suit with vest, unmarked......... 240.00

Bye-Lo Baby

16" h, 13-1/2" d, bisque flange head, brown sleep eyes, softly brushed brows, painted upper and lower lashes, closed mouth with accent line between lips, lightly molded and painted hair, cloth body with frog legs, celluloid hands, orig short white Bye-Low dress and slip, mkd "Copr. by Grace S. Putnam, Made in Germany" on back of head, "Bye-Lo Baby, Pat. Appl'd for Cop. Grace Storey Putnam" on front of body, turtle mark on hands, light aging to body, cracks in hands 350.00

21" h, large bisque head, blue glass sleep eyes, closed mouth, cloth body, celluloid lands, imp mark, 1920s, right hand repaired 460.00

Cameo Doll Co.

11" h, Kewpie, composition, molded and painted hair and features, jointed at shoulders, heart decal on chest, 1930s 230.00

12" h, Giggles, composition head, painted blues glancing to the side, closed smiling mouth, molded and painted hair, 5-pc composition body, yellow organdy dress, lace trimmed taffeta underclothing, orig shoes and socks, mkd "Kewpie Doll, design and copyright by Rose O'Neill" on top of box lid, "Copyright by Rose O'Neill, a Cameo doll" on cardboard wrist tag, orig box with Kewpie pictures on lid, unplayed-with condition.. 425.00

Chase, Martha, Pawtucket, RI, late 19th/early 20th C

13" h, painted head, arms, and legs, blond hair, blue eyes, cotton sateen body, period lawn outfit, stamped trademark left hip, slight paint loss at knees 800.00

16" h, oil painted stockinette head, painted blue eyes, heavy upper lashes, accented nostrils, closed mouth, molded and painted bobbed hair with side part, oil painted stockinette body tab jointed at shoulders and hips, applied thumbs, antique white dress trimmed with lace, replaced socks and shoes, unmarked, light wear, normal surface soil 425.00

21" h, blond hair, brown eyes, cotton sateen body, period cotton sailor dress, stamp on left hip, orig paper label on back, large pin holes on hair, face repainted, paint worn on hands and knee joints...... 635.00

China, 15-1/2" h, solid dome china shoulder head, pale pink tint, three sew holes, painted blue eyes, red accent line, single stroke brows, accented nostrils, closed mouth with white space between lips, orig human hair wig in orig style, replaced cloth body with china lower arms and lower legs, old rose taffeta dress with black overlay, black jet trim, unmarked 575.00

Cuno & Otto Dressel, 13-1/2" h, character, bisque head, sober face, painted blue eyes, orig blond mohair wig, pierced ears, open mouth, fully jointed composition body, navy blue sailor suit, imp "COD A2," c1910 .... 2,300.00

Dean's Rag Book, 14" h, Princess Margaret, papier-mâché over cloth swivel head, painted brown eyes, single stroke brows, painted upper lashes, closed mouth, orig mohair wig, cloth body jointed at shoulders and hips, stitched fingers, orig green felt coat and hat, mkd "Made in England by Dean's Rag Book Co., Ltd., London" on label on shoe, unplayed with condition 350.00

Effanbee

19" h, American Child, composition head, painted brown eyes, multi-stroke brows, painted upper lashes, closed mouth, orig human hair wig, 5-pc composition child body, orig blue flowered dress with pique bodice and collar, orig socks and white leather shoes with tassels, mkd "Effanbee, American Children" on back of head, ""Effanbee, Anne-Shirley" on back 1,000.00

19" h, Patsy Ann, composition head, brown sleep eyes with real lashes, single stroke brows, painted upper and lower lashes, closed mouth, molded and painted hair in bob, 5-pc composition child body, orig green dress with embroidered flowers, matching underclothing, old socks, new leather shoes, mkd "Effanbee, Patsy Ann, © Pat. #1283558" on back, fine crack in composition under each eye, normal wear at joints 300.00

Frozen Charlie, 10" h, deep pink tint china, unjointed, painted blue eyes, single stroke brows, accented nostrils, closed mouth with accents at corners, painted blond hair with brush strokes around face, arms extended in front with fingers in fist, unmarked 250.00

Gaulthier, Francois

14" h, fashion lady, bisque swivel head, pale blue paperweight eyes, multi-stroke brows, painted upper and lower lashes, accented nostrils, closed mouth with accented lips, pierced ears, orig mohair wig over cork pate, kid fashion body with gussets at hips and knees, individually stitched fingers, antique fashion dress, mkd "1" on back of head, "F. G." on left shoulder, "1" on right shoulder, light color wear on shoulder plate, finger missing from each hand, other fingers damaged. 1,000.00

22" h, Bebe, bisque socket head, large blue paperweight eyes with mauve blush over them, heavy feathered brows, painted upper and lower lashes, accented nostrils, open-closed mouth, pierced ears, orig mohair wig on cork pate, stockinette Gesland body over metal armature, composition shoulder plate, lower arms and lower legs, possible orig chemise trimmed with lace and pink ribbons, mkd "F. G." in scroll and "8" on back of head, "Bebe A. Gesland, Brevete, 5, Rue Beranger, Paris" on body, hairline at left repaired eye, light kiln dust, orig wig sparse and fragile, badly soiled body, composition arms and legs repainted, wear around neck edge and on shoulder plate 1,350.00

Gladdie, 17-1/2" h, painted bisque head, brown sleep eyes, feathered brows, open/closed mouth with molded tongue and 4 upper teeth, molded and painted hair, cloth body with composition arms and legs, blue sailor dress, mkd "Gladdie, Copyright by Helen J. Jensen, Germany" on back of head, light soil on orig finish, recovered cloth body badly discolored, body may not be orig to head, light crazing on arms, light wear and soil on legs...................... 425.00

Greiner, 23" h, papier-mâché shoulder head, painted blue eyes, single stroke brows, painted upper lashes, closed mouth, molded and painted black hair with 12 vertical curls, cloth body, brown kind lower arms, stitch joints at hips and knees, mkd "Greiner's Improved Patent Heads, Pat. March 30th '58" on label on rear shoulder plate, some touch-up 225.00

Halco, hard plastic head, blue flirty sleep eyes with real lashes, feathered brows, painted lower lashes, open mouth with 4 upper teeth and felt tongue, orig mohair wig in orig set, cloth body with composition arms and legs, orig white nylon dress with metallic dots, taffeta slip, underclothing, socks, and shoes. mkd "Superb Halco Brand, Beautiful Dolls, The Seal of Quality" on label on end of orig box, near mint in orig box 375.00

Handwerck, Heinrich

18-1/2" h, bisque socket head, set blue eyes, molded and feathered brows, painted lower lashes, open mouth with accented lips and 4 upper teeth, pierced ears, antique human hair wig, jointed wood and composition body, antique white dress with blue embroidered flowers, mkd "Germany, Heinrich Handwerck, Simon & Halbig, 1" on back of head, "W" on front at crown, "Heinrich Handwerck Germany, 1" stamped on lower left of back, eyes replaced and set, light rub on nose, lower arms and hands repainted 450.00

22-1/2" h, 99, bisque socket head, set brown eyes, feathered brows, painted upper and lower lashes, open mouth with accented lips and 4 upper teeth, pierced ears, synthetic wig, jointed wood and composition body, antique white dress, underclothes, and shows, mkd "11 1/2, 99, DEP Germany, H, 3" on back of head, "Germany, 3392" on right hip, small wig pulls, body repainted, repairs on both hip joints, normal wear at joints 325.00

23" h, bisque socket head, set blue eyes, molded and feathered brows, painted upper and lower lashes, open mouth with accented lips and 4 upper teeth, pierced ears, synthetic wig, jointed wood and composition body, nicely redressed, mkd "Germany, Heinrich Handwerck, Simon & Halbig" on back of head, very light rub on nose and right cheek, general wear and aging to body 375.00

24-1/2" h, 69, bisque socket head, blue sleep eyes, missing real lashes, painted lower lashes, molded and feathered brows, open mouth with accented lips and 4 upper teeth, pierced ears, orig mohair wig with long ropes, jointed wood and composition body, orig pink and white seersucker dress trimmed with ribbons, orig underclothing, socks, and leather shoes, mkd "69-12X, Germany, Handwerck Halbig, 4" on back of head, "Henrich Handwerck" stamped in red on right hip, small flake on left earring hole, minimal wear to body, 2 fingers missing 750.00

30" h, 109, bisque socket head, set brown eyes, molded and feathered brows, painted upper and lower lashes, open mouth, accented lips, 4 upper teeth, pierced ears, orig blond mohair wig, jointed wood and composition body, orig faded rose dress, white dotted Swiss pinafore, mkd "109-15, DEP, Germany, Handwerck, 6" on back of head, "Heinrich Handwerck, Germany" stamped on lower left back "6" on lower back, some repairs and touch-up around neck socket ... 750.00

Hertel, Schwab & Co., 11" h, 151 baby, solid dome bisque socket head, brown sleep eyes, feathered brows, painted upper and lower lashes, accented nostrils, open mouth with molded tongue and 2 upper teeth, lightly molded and brush-stroked hair, bent-limb composition baby body, antique baby dress, mkd "1, 151" on back of head, aged and discolored body, some toes missing........................ 250.00

Heubach, Ernst, 10" h, 399, brown bisque socket head, dark brown sleep eyes, painted upper and lower lashes, closed mouth, pierced

Left: Portrait Jumeau Fashion, bisque swivel head on bisque shoulder plate, kid body, dressed in antique clothes, 22" h, $2,200; **center:** F. G. Fashion Lady, bisque swivel head, kid fashion body, antique fashion dress, 14" h, $1,000; **right:** Jumeau Fashion, bisque socket head on bisque shoulder plate, kid body, 19" h, $1,000; **Photo courtesy of McMasters Doll Auction.**

ears with loop earrings, lightly molded and painted black hair, bent-limb composition baby body, orig grass red, brown, and white "grass"" skirt, mkd "Heubach•Koppelsdorf, 399•13/0 D.R.G.M. Germany" on back of head, light wear 360.00

Heubach, Gebruder, 8-1/2" h, 6969, pink bisque socket head, blue intaglio eyes, single stroke brows, closed pouty mouth, orig mohair wig, 5-pc composition body, antique sailor suit and matching hat labeled "Toulon" on black band, mkd "6969, 5, C (sunburst)" on back of head 500.00

Heubach Koppelsdorf, #320-116, 11" h, blue sleep eyes, mohair wig, composition body, redressed, slight damage to fingertips........ 280.00

Ideal

12" h, Fanny Brice, Baby Snooks, composition character head, painted blue eyes, single stroke brows, painted upper lashes, open/closed laughing mouth with teeth indicated, molded and painted hair with loop for bow, wood torso with flexible wire mesh arms and legs, composition hands, wood feet, orig blue print clothing, organdy collar and tie, mkd "Ideal Doll" on back of head.. 285.00

13" h, Shirley Temple, composition, hazel sleep eyes, orig blond mohair wig, open mouth, jointed at shoulders and hips, orig blue polka-dot dress, orig 15" h metal trunk with several orig dresses, accessories, plus hand made outfits, c1930 .... 700.00

18" h, Shirley Temple, composition head, hazel sleep eyes with real lashes, feathered brows, open mouth with 6 upper teeth, orig mohair wig, 5-pc composition child body, orig red and white dress from "Merrily Yours," orig underclothing, socks, and shoes, mkd "Shirley Temple, Cop. Ideal N & T Co." on back of head "Shirley Temple" on back, right heel cracked, general light crazing................................... 475.00

Jumeau

10-1/2" h, bisque head, blue paperweight eyes, open/closed mouth, pierced ears, cork pate, orig blond mohair wig, fully jointed composition body, orig bonnet and underclothes, tiny flake right ear . 4,830.00

13" h, light brown bisque head, Belton-type two hole solid pate, brown glass eyes, open/closed mouth, pierced ears, orig black mohair wig, straight wrist jointed composition body, tiny nicks right ear, restoration to body.. 2,300.00

14-1/2" h, child, bisque swivel shoulder head, brown paperweight eyes, open/closed mouth, pierced ears, ash blond human hair wig, jointed kid child body, bisque hands, period clothes, French shoes, imp "5" on head and shoulder, tiny chips right ear, clay blemish on forehead, left thumb missing 3,795.00

18" h, tinted brown bisque socket head, brown paperweight eyes, open mouth, pierced ears, black wooly mohair wig, fully jointed brown composition body, imp 1907 mark, tiny flakes to right ear, slight composition damage and paint wear 2,875.00

19" h, fashion, bisque socket head, bisque shoulder plate, bulbous blue paperweight eyes, heavy feathered brows, painted upper and lower lashes, closed mouth with accented lips, pierced ears, antique human hair wig, kid body with no gussets on arms or legs, blue antique fashion outfit with pleated skirt, antique undergarments, blue velvet hat, mkd "H5" in red, incised "7" on back of head, right earring pulled through, chip at left earring hole, kiln dusk on shoulder plate, body shows overall age and discoloration 2,025.00

22" h, portrait fashion, bisque swivel head, bisque shoulder plate, set pale blue eyes, feathered brows, painted upper and lower lashes, closed mouth with accented lips, pierced ears, orig human hair wig on cork pate, kid body with gussets at elbows, hips, and knees, individually stitched fingers, antique fashion dress, velvet hat, mkd "6" on back of head, some repairs to back, lower lid arm recovered 2,200.00

23" h, 1907, bisque socket head, blue paperweight eyes, feathered brows, painted upper and lower lashes, open mouth with 6 upper teeth, pierced ears, replaced human hair wig, jointed wood and composition French body with jointed wrists, antique white and pink dress and bonnet, mkd "1907, 10" on back of head, normal wear at joints, flaking and touch-up on hands, old repaint to lower legs 1,125.00

Kamkins, 18" h, oil painted muslin molded socket head, painted blue eyes, single stroke brows, closed mouth, orig mohair wig, muslin child body jointed at shoulders and hips, stitched fingers, orig organdy dress with bottom flowered panel, lace trimmed organdy

Kammer & Reinhardt, K*R 114, bisque socket head, orig dark mohair wig, orig Tryolean outfit, 7-1/2" h, $1,200. Photo courtesy of McMasters Doll Auctions.

teddy, socks, leatherette shoes, unmarked, evidence of missing heart label on front of torso, overall soiling to body, several water stains 775.00

Kämmer & Reinhardt

7-1/2" h, 114, bisque socket head, painted blue eyes, single stroke brows, closed pouty mouth, orig dark brown mohair wig, 5-pc composition body with molded and painted socks and shoes, orig Tyrolean outfit, mkd "K*R, 114, 19" on back of head, unplayed with condition ...1,200.00

15-1/2" h, 126, bisque socket head, blue sleep eyes, feathered brows, painted upper and lower lashes, open mouth with 2 upper teeth and spring tongue, orig mohair wig, bent limb composition baby body, well dressed in white baby dress, mkd "K * R, Simon & Halbig, 126" and "36"" on back of head, minor firing flaws 400.00

17" h, 717, celluloid socket head, flirty sleep eyes with thin lids, real lashes, feathered brows, painted upper and lower lashes, open mouth with accented lips and 4 upper teeth, orig mohair wig, jointed wood and composition flapper body with diagonal hip joints and high kneed joints, dressed in antique white dress, antique underclothing, socks, and shoes, mkd "K * R, 46/717 Germany" on back of head........325.00

18" h, 126 toddler, bisque socket head, brown sleep eyes, feathered brows, painted upper and lower lashes, open mouth with 2 upper teeth, spring tongue, orig human hair wig, toddler body ball jointed at shoulders, elbows, wrists, hips, and knees, antique dress, replaced socks and shoes, mkd "11, K * R, Simon & Halbig, 126, 42" on back of head, light wear to finish of arms and legs 800.00

22" h, 58 child, bisque socket head, brown sleep eyes, real lashes, molded and feathered browns, open mouth with 4 upper teeth, pierced ears, antique mohair wig, jointed wood and composition body, redressed, mkd "Simon & Halbig, K*R, 58" on back of head, "W" on forehead at crown, minor cheek rubs, kiln specks, wear to orig body finish 275.00

27" h, 126 baby, bisque sleep eyes with real lashed, feathered browns, painted upper and lower lashes, open mouth with 2 upper teeth, spring tongue, orig human hair wig, bent-limb baby body, antique baby dress, mkd "K*R, Simon & Halbig, 126, 62" on back of head, light wig pulls, some lashes missing, body repainted, 2 fingers missing, arms crazed 500.00

40" h, bisque socket head, set blue eyes with real lashes, molded and feathered brows, painted upper and lower lashes, open mouth with accented lips, 4 upper teeth, pierced ears, replaced human hair wig,

jointed wood and composition body, mkd "K*R, Simon & Halbig, 100" on back of head, dressed in antique child's dress, some surface cracks in finish, hands repainted 3,100.00

Kestner

10-1/2" h, baby, bisque socket head, blue sleep eyes, feathered brows, painted upper and lower lashes, open-closed mouth, orig skin wig, bent-limb composition baby body, orig factory chemise, mkd "J. D. K." on back of head below wig 550.00

11" h, 143, bisque socket head, brown sleep eyes, feathered brows, painted upper and lower lashes, open mouth with 2 upper teeth, orig blond mohair wig with orig plaster pate, jointed wood and composition Kestner body, antique white dress, mkd "Made in Germany 4, 143" on back of head, normal light wear and aging 600.00

12" h, Baby Jean, solid dome bisque socket head, blue sleep eyes, feathered brows, painted upper and lower lashes, open mouth with accented lips and 2 upper teeth, spring tongue, lightly molded and brush-stroked hair, composition bent-limb baby body, mkd "J. D. K made in 8 Germany" on back of head, minor mold flaw at mouth, repainted body 550.00

12-1/2" h, baby, solid dome bisque socket head, set blue eyes, feathered brows, painted upper and lower lashes, open-closed mouth with shading and accented lips, lightly molded and brush stroked hair, bent-limb composition Kestner baby body, redressed in yellow baby romper, mkd "J. D. K." on back of head, eyes have been set, orig body finish, light wear and soil on arms and legs 350.00

13" h, bisque socket head, blue sleep eyes, feathered brows, painted upper and lower lashes, open mouth with accented lips, 2 upper teeth, orig mohair wig, jointed wood and composition Kestner body, dressed in possibly orig white dress, lace and pink ribbon trim, matching hat, leatherette shoes, mkd "C made in Germany 7" on back of head "Germany O" stamped in red on right rear hip, some touch-up to body, repainted hands 675.00

13" h, tinted bisque socket head, Chinese baby, orig black mohair wig, glass eyes (fixed open), open mouth, bent limb tinted composition body, orig outfit, toy drum, imp "J. D. K. 243," hairline back of head....2,185.00

15" h, bisque socket head, brown sleep eyes, closed pouty mouth, synthetic wig, joined wood and composition body, antique white pique blouse, blue collar and cuffs, matching blue skirt, hairline on forehead, rubs to nose, cheeks, replaced right knee ball 500.00

17" h, 196, bisque socket head, blue sleep eyes with real lashes, fur brows, painted lower lashes, open mouth with accented lips and 4 upper teeth, orig mohair wig with orig plaster pate, jointed wood and composition body, orig white dress, factory chemise, and antique pants, old socks, blue leather shoes, mkd "B 1/2 made in Germany, 6-1/2, 196 on back of head, Germany, 1" stamped in red on lower right back, general light soil on body, two fingers missing........ 375.00

18" h, 257 baby, bisque socket head, brown sleep eyes with real lashes (some missing), feathered brows, painted upper and lower lashes, open mouth with accepted lips and 2 upper teeth, replaced wig, bent-limb composition baby body, new white lace trimmed baby dress, mkd "Made in Germany, J. D. K., 257, 46" on back of head, spring tongue loose, light wear on hands and feet................... 400.00

18" h, swivel head, bisque socket head on bisque shoulder plate, blue sleep eyes, heavy feathered brows, painted upper and lower lashes, closed mouth with accented lips, replaced human hair wig, kid body, bisque lower arms, gussets at elbows, hips, and knees, redressed, mkd "10" on back of head, body aged and lightly soiled, repairs at elbow and knees, tip of one finger missing 575.00

21" h, turned head, bisque shoulder head, brown sleep eyes, feathered brows, painted upper and lower lashes, open mouth with accented lips and 4 upper teeth, antique human hair wig, kid body with bisque lower arms and composition lower legs, rivet joints at hips and knees, antique red wool dress, trimmed in white fur, matching hat, mkd "J" at crown, "Made in Germany" on back of shoulder plate, normal wear and aging to body 315.00

23" h, celluloid, replaced composition arms and legs, burlap covered upper body, brown sleep eyes, replaced dark brown mohair wig, pink taffeta dress, broken fingers.. 110.00

34" h, 171, bisque socket head, set brown eyes, lightly molded and feathered brows, painted upper and lower lashes, open mouth with accented lips and 4 upper teeth, orig mohair wig, jointed wood and composition Kestner body, dressed in antique white child's dressmkd "N 1/2, made in Germany, 17 1/2, 171" on back of head, "Excelsior, Germany, 7-1/2" stamped on right hip, some kiln specks on nose, one eye repaired, general wear to body, hips poorly repaired, light cracks to hands 1,100.00

Kley & Hahn
12" h, character, bisque head, blue sleep eyes, open/closed mouth with tongue and teeth, orig ash blond mohair wig, fully jointed toddler body, imp "K + H 160-1," paint wear on hands, needs restringing 690.00

14-1/2" h, 161 baby, bisque socket head with cut-out on forehead at crown to hold crying mechanism, brown sleep eyes, feathered brows, painted upper and lower lashes, open-closed mouth with 2 upper teeth, human hair wig, bent-limb composition baby body, antique white baby dress, mkd "K & H (in banner), Germany, 161-6" on back of head, some surface cracks on torso, repairs to left arm socket 315.00

20" h, 546 character, bisque socket head, blue sleep eyes with real lashes, feathered brows, painted upper and lower lashes, closed mouth with accented lips, orig human hair wig in braids, jointed wood and composition body, possibly orig ethnic outfit, underclothing, socks, and shoes, mkd "K & H (in banner), 546, 8, Germany" on back of head, left hand replaced 2,100.00

Knickerbocker, 15" h, Mickey Mouse Clown, black and white cloth swivel head, black oilcloth pie eyes, black felt ears, string whiskers, painted smiling mouth, black cloth body, yellow cloth hands with 3 fingers and thumb, large orange flannel clown shoes with black pompoms, orig red and white polka dot clown suit, white neck ruffle, mkd "Licensed by Walt Disney Enterprises for the Exclusive Manufacture by the Knickerbocker Toy Co. Inc., New York," orig paper wrist tag, unplayed with condition.. 2,000.00

Konig & Wernicke, 23" h, baby, bisque head, blue sleep eyes, open mouth with molded tongue, orig light brown mohair wig, bent limb composition body with jointed wrists, imp "K + W," head restored, some paint wear to body 250.00

Kruse, Kathe
14" h, boy, brown hair and eyes, cotton and felt Bavarian outfit, leather shoes, c1949 .... 2,300.00

17" h, girl, light brown painted hair and eyes, narrow hips, thumb not separate, rayon dress, hat, and underwear, 1930s 1,840.00

20" h, hard plastic head, blond mohair wig, painted eyes, closed mouth, cloth body, jointed at shoulders and narrow hips, thumb not separate, period cotton outfit, leather sandals, partial tag, 1950s 750.00

Kuhnlenz, Gebruder, 29" h, 165, bisque socket head, set blue eyes, molded and feathered brows, painted upper and lower lashes, open mouth with accented lips and 4 upper teeth, synthetic wig, jointed wood and composition body, redressed, mkd "31, Gbr 165 K, 12, Germany" on back of head, "Germany, 6" on right lower back, normal wear to Kestner-type body, light wear on fingers 300.00

Lenci
8" h, Mascotte, pressed felt face, painted brown eyes, molded and single stroke brows, painted upper lashes, accented nostrils, mouth molded open, orig mohair wig, cloth torso and legs, felt arms and stitched fingers, orig regional type costume, orig underclothing, black felt shoes, mkd "Lenci, Torino, Made in Italy" on round paper tag, "Lenci, Made in Italy" on cloth tag, front of apron faded, light overall shelf soil 165.00

14" h, child, pressed felt swivel head, painted brown eyes to side, accented nostrils, closed mouth with two-tone lips, orig mohair wig, cloth torso, felt arms and legs, orig turquoise felt dress with white and yellow felt trim, orig organdy underclothing, knit socks, felt shoes, illegible marks on bottom of both feet, rub on nose and upper lip, pale facial coloring, overall light soil and aging 225.00

14" h, girl, pressed felt head, painted brown eyes, lightly molded and single stroke brows, painted upper and lower lasers, closed mouth with two-tone lips, applied ears, orig mohair wig in orig set, cloth torso with felt arms and left, orig ethnic costume, mkd "4" on bottom of right foot 550.00

16-1/2" h, golfer, all felt, mohair wig, patchwork outfit, wool stockings, leather shoes, tag missing 1,840.00

Madame Alexander
8" h, Scarlett, hard plastic, green sleep eyes, single stroke brows, closed mouth, orig wig, jointed walker body, orig white satin dress, straw hat, mkd "Alex" on body, "Scarlett O'Hara" by Madame Alexander, New York, U.S.A. on dress tag, 1965 .... 500.00

8" h, Wendy, hard plastic head, blue sleep eyes with molded lashes, orig wig in orig set with side part on right and rolled curl on left, hard plastic body with bent knees and walking mechanism, orig tagged white pique dress with blue flowers, orig socks and snap shoes, mkd "Alex" on body, "Alexander-kins, by Madame Alexander, Reg. U. S. Pat. Off, N.Y. U.S.A." on dress tag, mint condition, unusual hair style 500.00

8" h, Wendy, hard plastic head, blue sleep eyes with molded lashes, single stroke brows, closed mouth, orig red wig, hard plastic body with bent knees and walking mechanism, tagged red pleated dress, white felt jacket and hat, orig socks and red snap shoes, mkd "Alex" on back, "Alexander-kins" dress tag, 1956............................. 550.00

12" h, Lissy, hard plastic head, blue sleep eyes with molded lashes, single stroke brows, painted lower lashes, closed mouth, orig red wig in orig set, hard plastic child body joined at shoulders, elbows, hips, and knees, orig tagged green-yellow taffeta dress and white organdy pinafore, feather in hair, orig nylon socks and pink platform shoes, mkd "Lissy," "©Madame Alexander, New York, U.S.A." on dress tag, mint condition 500.00

15" h, Snow White, composition head, brown sleep eyes with real lashes, single stroke brows, painted upper and lower lashes, closed mouth, orig human hair wig in orig set, 5-pc composition body, orig tagged clothing, mkd "Princess Elizabeth, Alexander Doll" on back of head, "Snow White, Madame Alexander, NY All Rights Reserved" on dress tag, slight touch-up to one finger 600.00

18" h, Binnie Walker, hard plastic head, blue sleep eyes, real lashes, feathered brows, closed mouth, orig wig, hard plastic body with vinyl arms, jointed at shoulders, elbows, hips, and knees, orig tagged pink dress, white sweater, and hat, mkd "Alexander" on back of head, "Binnie Walker, ©Madame Alexander, Reg. U.S. Pat. Off., N.Y. U.S.A." on dress tag, orig box, unplayed with condition........ 1,800.00

Marseille, Armand
10" h, 351 black baby, solid dome brown bisque socket head, dark brown sleep eyes, painted upper and lower lashes, accented nostrils, open mouth with 2 upper teeth, lightly molded and painted hair, bent-limb composition brown baby body, orig red and white striped romper, mkd "A. M. Germany, 351/O.K." on back of head 375.00

16-1/2" h, 1894, bisque socket head, set brown eyes, feathered brows, painted upper and lower lashes, open mouth with 4 upper teeth, orig blond mohair wig, jointed wood and composition body with wood upper arms and legs, straight wrists, orig factory red dress with ecru silk bodice, matching hat, orig underclothing, damaged socks and shoes, mkd "1894, A. M. 4 DEP" on back of head, normal wear at joints, sparse wig, orig clothing fragile 310.00

26" h, Floradora, bisque socket head, brown sleep eyes with real lashes, molded and feathered brows, painted lower lashes, open mouth with accented lips and 4 upper teeth, antique human hair wig, jointed wood and composition body, antique pink dress, mkd "Made in Germany, Floradora, A. 11 . M." on back of head, chips to neck socket, general overall wear to body finish 375.00

31" h, child, bisque socket head, blue sleep eyes with real lashes, molded and feathered brows, painted upper and lower lashes, accented nostrils, open mouth with accented ,lips, 4 upper teeth, replaced human hair wig, jointed wood and composition French body, antique white child's dress, mkd "A. 14 M." on back of head, large chip out of rear rim, sliver off eye, repainted body, toes replaced, tip off one finger... 550.00

Mascotte, 11" h, bisque head, stationary blue paperweight eyes, closed mouth, pierced ears, cork pate, replaced wig, fully jointed composition body, imp "M2," tiny chips left ear, hands restored...................... 1,610.00

Ohlhaver, 26" h, Revalo, bisque socket head, blue sleep eyes, feathered brows, painted lower lashes, accented nostrils, open mouth with 4 upper teeth, orig human hair wig, jointed wood and composition body, yellow taffeta dress, mkd "Germany, Revalo, 8" on back of head, normal body wear, top of left foot crushed in 350.00

Papier-Mâché

9-3/4" h, lady, papier-mâché shoulder head, molded hairdo with long back curls, molded and painted features, kid body carved wood limbs, some paint wear, dress replaced 260.00

14" h, French type, papier-mâché shoulder head, dark pupiless eyes, painted upper and lower lashes, open mouth with 2 lower teeth, orig human hair wig with painted black hair underneath, shapely faded pink kid body with individually stitched fingers, orig gold dress with maroon velvet and gold braid trim, unmarked 650.00

14" h, French type, papier-mâché shoulder head, inset brown glass eyes, closed mouth, black painted pate, kid body, carved wood limbs, 1840s, wig missing, slight scuffing on nose and chin, damage to legs, left thumb missing 460.00

Parian, 27" h, man, untinted bisque shoulder head, painted blue eyes with red accent line, single stroke brows, closed mouth, molded and painted blond hair with exposed ears, molded shirt on shoulder plate, glazed collar and tie, cloth body with ceramic lower arms and lower legs, redressed in black jacket, black and gray striped pants, unmarked, worn gold dec, new cloth body 425.00

Poured Wax

14" h, wax shoulder head, blue glass eyes, partial brows, closed mouth, orig mohair inserted in wax, cloth body with wax arms and wax lower legs, orig pale blue dress trimmed with white organdy and organdy apron, orig underclothing and bonnet, unmarked 250.00

30" h, reinforced poured wax shoulder head, blue paperweight eyes with mohair lashes, feathered brows, well modeled eyelids, open mouth with accented lips, 4 upper teeth, pierced ears, orig mohair wig, kid body with gussets at elbows, hips, and knees, individually stitched fingers, ecru lace trimmed dress with bustle, orig underclothing, socks, and shoes, unmarked, cracks in wax on face and shoulder plate, some repairs to body 825.00

Schmidt, Franz, 10-1/2" h, 1295 toddler, bisque socket head, blue sleep eyes, feathered brows, painted upper and lower lashes, open mouth with 2 upper teeth, orig mohair wig, chubby 5-pc toddler body, antique blue shorts, white shirt, blue felt jacket and cap, mkd "1295, F. S. & C. Made in Germany, 25" on back of head, light wear to fingers 825.00

Schoenau & Hoffmeister, 22" h, Pansy, bisque head, blue sleep eyes, open mouth, light auburn mohair wig, fully jointed composition body, imp "Pansy III Germany," some paint wear, composition damage 320.00

Simon & Halbig

12" h, 1009, bisque socket head, blue sleep eyes, feathered brows, painted upper and lower lashes, open mouth with 4 upper teeth, pierced ears, orig mohair wig, jointed wood and composition child body, orig ornate ethnic outfit, mkd "1009, Simon & Halbig, Germany, S & H" on back of head, eyes loose, one eye socket slightly damaged, light rubs on cheeks 130.00

18" h, 929, character, lady, bisque swivel head, light blue paperweight eyes, replaced dark brown mohair wig, open/closed mouth, pierced ears, hand crafted outfit fashioned from antique fabrics, kid body and limbs, bisque arms, imp "929" 2,300.00

19" h, 1250, bisque shoulder head, brown sleep eyes, feathered brows, painted upper and lower lashes, open mouth with accented lips and triangular accent on lower lips, pierced ears, orig blond mohair wig, pink kid body with jointed wood and composition arms, rivet joints at hips and knees, orig lace trimmed dress, pink silk underdress, orig underclothing, socks, and satin shoes with silk rosettes, mkd "S & H 1250, DEP, Germany, 6-1/2" on back of head, light kiln specks in middle of forehead, lightly soiled body 525.00

26" h, 1079, bisque socket head, brown sleep eyes, molded and feathered brows, painted lower lashes, accented nostrils, open mouth with accented lips, 4 upper teeth, pierced ears, orig human hair wig, jointed wood and composition body, well dressed, mkd "S & H 1079, DEP, Germany, 13" on back of head, "68" stamped in red on bottom of feet, minor flake at earring hole, left thigh replaced, upper torso and lower arms repainted, both hip joints repainted 375.00

S.F.B.J.

19" h, Bebe Jumeau, Diplome d'Honneur, bisque socket head, set brown pupiless eyes, feathered brows, painted upper and lower lashes, open mouth with accented lips, 4 upper teeth, orig human hair wig, jointed wood and composition French body with jointed wrists, redressed, mkd "S.F.B.J., 60, Paris, -6-" on back of head, "Bebe Jumeau, Diplome d'Honneur" on label on lower back, tiny wig pulls, light kiln dust on forehead, body with wear at joints, light paint flaking, hands loose 325.00

19-1/2" h, toddler, composition socket head, blue flirty sleep eyes with real lashes, feathered brows, painted lower lashes, open mouth with 2 upper teeth, orig human hair wig, jointed wood and composition S.F.B.J.-type toddler body, modern knit baby outfit and cap, mkd "10" on back of head, "Shipped by Wingate & Johnston, ...Paris,...Made in France" on label on front of torso, wear at joints, 3 fingers repaired on left hand, crack in finish on right foot, break in back of left leg..575.00

Steiner, 24" h, "C" series, bisque head, brown glass sleeping eyes, wire mechanism, pierced ears, closed mouth, cork pate, replaced blond human hair wig, fully jointed composition body, bisque hands, imp mark, paint wear to body 6,900.00

Tete Jumeau, 28" h, bisque socket head, large blue paperweight eyes, heavy feathered brows, long painted upper and lower lashes, accented nostrils, closed mouth with shaded and accented lips, applied pierced ears, orig blond human hair wig on cork pate, jointed wood and composition marked Jumeau body, antique white dress, antique underclothing, orig socks and shoes, mkd "Depose, Tete Jumeau, 13" stamped in red, "HB" and artist mark, black "V" artist mark, "13" incised on back of head, "Made in France" on paper label on lower back, "Bebe Jumeau Bte. S.G.D.G. Depose" stamped in blue on lower back, "13 Paris (bee) Depose" on soles of shoes, tiny nose rub, light firing line on chin, normal body wear 4,100.00

Unis France, 27-1/2" h, 301, bisque socket head, blue sleep eyes with real lashes, feathered brows, painted lower lashes, accented nostrils, open mouth with 4 upper teeth, synthetic wig, jointed wood and composition French body with jointed wrists, redressed, mkd "Unis France, 71 301 149" on back of head, "12" on front of neck, hands repainted and flaking, general overall wear on finish and at joints 245.00

Vogue, 7" h, Toddles Dutch Boy and Girl, composition heads, blue eyes painted to side, single stroke brows, painted upper lashes, closed mouths, orig mohair wigs, 5-pc composition toddler bodies, boy dressed in blue outfit with matching hat, wooden shoes, girl dressed in blue dress, white organdy pinafore, white lace cap, wooden shoes, mkd "Vogue" on back of heads, "Doll Co." on backs, price for pr 300.00

Wax Over Composition, 23" h, shoulder head, blue sleep eyes, single stroke brows, open mouth with 2 lower teeth, orig blond mohair wig, cloth body stitch jointed at hips and knees, wax over composition hands, dressed in antique dress, unmarked, slight damage, water stain on foot... 200.00

DOORKNOBS and OTHER BUILDER'S HARDWARE

History: Man's home has always been his castle, whether grand and ornate, or simple and homey. The use of decorative doorknobs, back plates, door bells, knockers, and mail slots helped decorate and distinguish one's door. Creating a grand entrance was as important to our ancestors as it is today.

Before the advent of the mechanical bell or electrical buzzer and chime, a door knocker was considered an essential door ornament to announce the arrival of visitors. Metal was used to cast or forge the various forms; many cast-iron examples were painted. Collectors like to find door knockers with English registry marks.

Collectors of doorknobs and other types of builders hardware are growing as we learn to treasure the decorative elements of our past. Often old house lovers seek out these elements to refurbish their homes, adding to the demand.

Door Knob, bronze, plumed knight, mkd "Mfd By Metal Comp Cast Co.-R. E. Mfg Co. Sole Agt's" on reverse, $660. Photo courtesy of Web Wilson.

References: Ronald S. Barlow (comp.), *Victorian Houseware, Hardware and Kitchenware*, Windmill Publishing, 1991; Margarete Baur-Heinhold, *Decorative Ironwork*, Schiffer Publishing, 1996; Len Blumin, *Victorian Decorative Art*, available from ADCA (P.O. Box 126, Eola, IL 60519), n.d.; Maude Eastwood wrote several books about doorknobs which are available from P.O. Box 126, Eola, IL 60519; Constance M Greiff, *Early Victorian*, Abbeville Press, 1995; Philip G. Knobloch, *A Treasure of Fine Construction Design*, Astragal Press, 1995; Henrie Martinie, *Art Deco Ornamental Ironwork*, Dover Publications, 1996; James Massey and Shirley Maxwell, *Arts & Crafts*, Abbeville Press, 1995; Ted Menten (comp.), *Art Nouveau Decorative Ironwork*, Dover Publications, n.d.; *Ornamental French Hardware Designs*, Dover Publications, 1995; Ernest Rettelbusch, *Handbook of Historic Ornament from Ancient Times to Biedermeier*, Dover Publications, 1996; Alan Robertson, *Architectural Antiques, Chronicle Books*, 1987; Edward Shaw, *Modern Architect* (reprint), Dover Publications, 1996; *Turn of the Century Doors, Windows and Decorative Millwork*, Dover Publications, 1995 reprint; Web Wilson, *Antique Hardware Price Guide*, Krause Publications, 1999,—, *Great Glass in American Architecture*, E. P. Dutton, New York, 1986.

Periodical: *American Bungalow*, P.O. Box 756, Sierra Madre, CA 91204.

SPECIAL AUCTIONS

Web Wilson Antique Hardware Auction
P.O. Box 506
Portsmouth, RI 02871
(800) 508-0022

Collectors' Club: Antique Doorknob Collectors of America, Inc., P.O. Box 126, Eola, IL 60519.

Additional Listings: Architectural Elements, Stained Glass.

Advisor: Web Wilson.

Display Board, hardware store type, each has model, style, and finish mkd on back, built-in metal stand, set of 3 .... 50.00
Door Bell, Connell's Patent lever action, cast iron, good working order 60.00
Door Knob
    Emblematic, safe decorated with sailing ship, and carpenter squares in the background 170.00
    Entry size, Empire pattern by P. F. Corbin, features little critter with a foliate tail 90.00
    Entry, large "R" in raised circle 40.00
    Entry, Masonic, square, compass, and capital "G" 85.00
    Oval, large, emb queen bee 210.00
    Passage, bronze, Neo-Grec, knurled edge and mushroom foot, possibly MCCC/R&E 130.00
    Passage, Detroit Board of Education 55.00
    Passage, Gothic inspired design, high relief, fine color 25.00
Door Knocker, cast iron, figural, lion head 85.00
Figural Plate and Foliate Knob, Russell & Irwin, acanthus foliage, pair of full-bodied cherubs, passage size knob features grapes and cherries, R&E mark on plate reverse, shank bears patents dates of 1886 and 1896, knob shows wear 350.00
Hinges, pr, iron hinges, bronze finials, British patent mark 55.00

Door Knocker, cast iron, owl, brown, yellow eyes, green ribbon, wear to paint, $95.

Mortise Lock and Strike Plate, entry size mortise lock, Ekado pattern
by Sargent, c1885, good working order 130.00
Sash Lock, cast iron, Aesthetic dec, set of 7 .... 140.00

DOORSTOPS

History: Doorstops became popular in the late 19th century. They are either flat or three dimensional and were made out of a variety of different materials, such as cast iron, bronze, or wood. Hubley, a leading toy manufacturer, made many examples.

All prices listed are for excellent original paint unless otherwise noted. Original paint and condition greatly influence the price of a doorstop. To get top money, the piece must be close to mint original paint. Chipping of paint, paint loss, and wear reduce the value. Repainting severely reduces value and eliminates a good deal of the piece's market value, thereby reducing it's value. A broken piece has little value to none.

References: Jeanne Bertoia, *Doorstops*, Collector Books, 1985, 1996 value update; Douglas Congdon-Martin, *Figurative Cast Iron*, Schiffer Publishing, 1994.

Collectors' Club: Doorstop Collectors of America, 2413 Madison Ave., Vineland, NJ 08630.

Advisor: Craig Dinner.

Reproduction Alert: Reproductions are proliferating as prices on genuine doorstops continue to rise. A reproduced piece generally is slightly smaller than the original unless an original mold is used. The overall casting of reproductions is not as smooth as on the originals. Reproductions also lack the detail apparent in originals, including the appearance of the painted areas. Any bright orange rusting is strongly indicative of a new piece. Beware. If it looks too good to be true, it usually is.

Notes: Pieces described below contain at least 80% or more of the original paint and are in very good condition. Repainting drastically reduces price and desirability. Poor original paint is preferred over repaint.

All listings are cast-iron and flat-back castings unless otherwise noted.

Doorstops marked with an asterisk are currently being reproduced.

Basket, 11" h, rose, ivory wicker basket, natural flowers, handle with
bow, sgd "Hubley 121" 145.00
Bear, 15" h, holding and looking at honey pot, brown fur, black highlights 1,250.00
Bellhop
7-1/2" h, carrying satchel, facing sideways, orange-red uniform and
cap 400.00
8-7/8" h, blue uniform, with orange markings, brown base, hands at
side 300.00
Bobby Blake, 9-1/2" h, boy holding teddy bear, blue shirt, pink socks,
black pants, blond hair, Hubley 350.00
Bowl, 7" x 7", green-blue, natural colored fruit, sgd "Hubley 456" 125.00
Boy, 10-5/8" h, wearing diapers, directing traffic, police hat, red scarf,
brown dog at side 565.00
Caddie, 8" h, carrying brown and tan bag, white, brown, knickers, red
jacket* 525.00
Cat
8" h, black, red ribbon and bow around neck, on pillow* 125.00

Hubley series, left: Dolly, blue dress, white apron, pink bow in blond hair, holding doll, 9-1/2" h, $350; center: Little Red Riding Hood, basket at side, blond hair, red cape, tan dress with blue pattern, 9-1/2" h, $475; right: Bobby Blake, boy holding teddy bear, blond hair, blue shirt, black pants, pink socks, 9-1/2" h, $350. Photo courtesy of Craig Dinner.

10-3/4" h, licking paw, white cat with black markings, mkd "Sculpture Metal Studios" 425.00
Cat Scratch Fever, 8-3/4" h, girl in blue dress, blond hair, black cat at
side, scratches on arm, mkd "CJO 1271" 750.00
Child, 17" h, reaching, naked, short brown curly hair, flesh color .. 1,000.00
Clipper Ship, 5-1/4" h, full sails, American flag on top mast, wave base,
2 rubber stoppers, sgd "CJO" 65.00
Clown, 10" h, full figure, 2 sided, red suit, white collar, blue hat, black
shoes 700.00
Cosmos Flower Basket, 17-3/4" h, blue and pink flowers, white vase,
black base, Hubley 800.00
Cottage, 8-5/8" l, 5-3/4" h, Cape type, blue roof, flowers, fenced garden, bath, sgd "Eastern Specialty Mfg Co. 14" 150.00
Dancer, 8-7/8" h, Art Deco couple doing Charleston, pink dress, black
tux, red and black base, "FISH" on front, sgd "Hubley 270" .. 1,100.00
Dog
7" h, three puppies in basket, natural colors, sgd "Copyright 1932
M. Rosenstein, Lancaster, PA, USA" 350.00
9" h, Boston Bull, full figure, facing left, black, tan markings . 150.00
14" x 9", Sealyham, full figure, Hubley, cream & tan dog, red
collar 650.00
Dolly, 9-1/2" h, pink bow in blond hair, holding doll in blue dress, white
apron, yellow dress, Hubley 350.00
Doorman in Livery, 12" h, twin men, worn orig paint, mkd "Fish,"
Hubley 1,760.00
Drum Major, 12-5/8" h, full figure, ivory pants, red hat with feather, yellow baton in right hand, left hand on waist, sq base 275.00
Duck, 7-1/2" h, white, green bush and grass 245.00
Dutch Boy, 11" h, full figure, hands in pockets, blue suit and hat, red
belt and collar, brown shoes, blond hair 425.00
Elephant, 14" h, palm trees, early 20th C, very minor paint wear 210.00
Fisherman, 6-1/4" h, standing at wheel, hand over eyes, rain gear. 150.00
Frog, 3" h, full figure, sitting, yellow and green 60.00
Giraffe, 20-1/4" h, tan, brown spots, squared off lines to
casting 2,000.00
Girl, 8-3/4" h, dark blue outfit and beanie, high white collar, black
shoes, red hair, incised "663" 475.00
Golfer, 10" h, overhand swing, hat and ball on ground,
Hubley* 450.00
Halloween Girl, 13-3/4" h, 9-3/4" l, white hat, flowing cape, holding orange
jack-o-lantern with red cutout eyes, nose, and mouth* 2,000.00
Indian Chief, 9-3/4" h, orange and tan headdress, yellow pants, and
blue stripes, red patches at ankles, green grass, sgd "A. A. Richardson," copyright 1928 .... 295.00

Lighthouse, 14" h, green rocks, black path, white lighthouse, red window and door trim 285.00
Mammy
    8-1/2" h, full figure, Hubley, red dress, white apron, polka-dot bandanna on head 225.00
    10" h, white scarf and apron, dark blue dress, red kerchief on head* 325.00
Monkey
    8-1/2" h, 4 5/8" w wrap around tail, full figure, brown and tan 250.00
    14-3/8" h, hand reaching up, brown, tan, and white 600.00
Old Mill, 6-1/4" h, brown log mill, tan roof, white patch, green shrubs 325.00
Owl, 9-1/2" h, sits on books, sgd "Eastern Spec Co" 245.00
Pan, 7" h, with flute, sitting on mushroom, green outfit, red hat and sleeves, green grass base 150.00
Parrot, 13-3/4" h, in ring, two sided, heavy gold base, sgd "B & H" 250.00
Peasant Woman, 8-3/4" h, blue dress, black hair, fruit basket on head 250.00
Penguin, 10" h, full figure, facing sideways, black, white chest, top hat and bow tie, yellow feet and beak, unsgd Hubley 395.00
Policeman, 9-1/2" h, leaning on red fire hydrant, blue uniform and titled hat, comic character face, tan base, "Safety First" on front......650.00
Prancing Horse, 11" h, scrolled and molded base, "Greenlees Glasgow" imp on base, cast iron 175.00
Quail, 7-1/4" h, two brown, tan, and yellow birds, green, white, and yellow grass, "Fred Everett" on front, sgd "Hubley 459"* 265.00
Rabbit, 8-1/8" h, eating carrot, red sweater, brown pants 300.00
Rooster, 13" h, red comb, black and brown tail...........................325.00
Squirrel, 9" h, sitting on stump eating nut, brown and tan...........275.00
Storybook
    4-1/2" h, Humpty Dumpty, full figure, sgd "661" 350.00
    7-3/4" h, Little Miss Muffett, sitting on mushroom, blue dress, blond hair 175.00
    9-1/2" h, Little Red Riding Hood, basket at side, red cape, tan dress with blue pattern, blond hair, sgd "Hubley" 395.00
    12-1/2" h, Huckleberry Finn, floppy hat, pail, stick, Littco Products label 475.00
    Sunbonnet Girl, 9" h, pink dress...245.00
Tiger, 8-1/2" h, tan, black stripes, baseball bat on shoulder, black base 400.00
Whistler, 20-1/4" h, boy, hands in tan knickers, yellow striped baggy shirt, sgd "B & H" 2,250.00
Windmill, 6-3/4" h, ivory, red roof, house at side, green base* ...100.00
Woman, 11" h, flowers and shawl*...225.00
Zinnias, 11-5/8" h, multicolored flowers, blue and black vase, sgd "B & H" 185.00

DRESDEN/MEISSEN

History: Augustus II, Elector of Saxony and King of Poland, founded the Royal Saxon Porcelain Manufactory in the Albrechtsburg, Meissen, in 1710. Johann Frederick Boettger, an alchemist, and Tschirnhaus, a nobleman, experimented with kaolin from the Dresden area to produce porcelain. By 1720, the factory produced a whiter hard-paste porcelain than that from the Far East. The factory experienced its golden age from the 1730s to the 1750s under the leadership of Samuel Stolzel, kiln master, and Johann Gregor Herold, enameler.

The Meissen factory was destroyed and looted by forces of Frederick the Great during the Seven Years' War (1756-1763). It was reopened, but never achieved its former greatness.

In the 19th century, the factory reissued some of its earlier forms. These later wares are called "Dresden" to differentiate them from the earlier examples. Further, there were several other porcelain factories in the Dresden region and their products also are grouped under the "Dresden" designation.

Marks: Many marks were used by the Meissen factory. The first was a pseudo-Oriental mark in a square. The famous crossed swords mark was adopted in 1724. A small dot between the hilts was used from 1763 to 1774, and a star between the hilts from 1774 to 1814. Two modern marks are swords with a hammer and sickle and swords with a crown.

References: Susan and Al Bagdade, *Warman's English & Continental Pottery & Porcelain*, 3rd Edition, Krause Publications, 1998; Robert E. Röntgen, *The Book of Meissen*, revised ed., Schiffer Publishing, 1996.

Museums: Art Institute of Chicago, Chicago, IL; Cincinnati Art Museum, Cincinnati, OH; Dresden Museum of Art & History, Dresden, Germany; Gardiner Museum of Ceramic Art, Toronto, Canada; Meissen Porcelain Museum, Meissen, Germany; Metropolitan Museum of Art, New York, NY; National Museum of American History, Smithsonian Institution, Washington, DC, Robertson Center for the Arts and Sciences, Binghamton, NY; Schlossmuseum, Berlin, Germany; Stadtmuseum, Cologne, Germany; Wadsoworth Atheneum, Hartford, Ct; Woodmere Art Museum, Philadelphia, PA; Zwinger Museum, Dresden, Germany.

Dresden

Compote, 14-1/4" h, figural, shaped pierced oval bowl with applied florets, support stems mounted with 2 figures of children, printed marks, late 19th/early 20th C, pr..350.00
Cup, 3-1/2" d, white, relief prunus dec, two handles, attributed to Boettger, unmarked, 1715 ....265.00
Demitasse Cup and Saucer, blue ground, floral reserves...........275.00
Figural Group
    9" h, man, woman, and boy flower sellers surrounding cov urn, Thieme factory, late 19th C 690.00

Plate, cobalt blue and gold, 5-1/2" d, $80.

19" h, man and woman in fancy dress, holding flowers, late 19th C, restorations 750.00

Loving Cup, 6-1/2" h, 3 handles, woodland scene with nymph, gold trim 475.00

Miniature Portrait, 3-1/2" h, young boy in blue, sgd "F. Till(?) Dresden" 115.00

Plate, 8-1/4" d, enamel floral dec, c1900, 12 pc set....................600.00

Urn, cov, set of three, pair 6" h, one 12-1/2" h, figural panels alternating with floral panels, yellow ground 475.00

Vase, 13-1/4" h, alternating panels of figures and yellow floral bouquets, Thieme factory, late 19th C..115.00

Vase, cov, 14" h, alternating panels of lowers and turquoise ground floral bouquets, c1900, minor damage, pr 375.00

Whatnot Shelf, 13-1/2" w, 13-1/3" h, figural and foliate porcelain posts, mirrored back, shaped ebonized wood tiers, 20th C.............200.00

Meissen

Basket, 12" l, shaped oval, molded rococo cartouches, scrolling foliage, heavy gilt highlights, gilt bronze swing handles, late 19th/early 20th C, pr 850.00

Bowl, 11" d, molded flowering vine dec, molded cattail dec, gilt and white 200.00

Cabinet Plate, 9-5/8" d, enameled center with cupid and female in wooded landscape, gilt dec pink and burgundy border, titled on reverse "Lei Wiedergut"..490.00

Cake Basket, 12-3/8" l, oval, open lattice work body, applied flower and rococo cartouches, painted Deutsche Blumen, molded vine handles, gilt highlights, c1910..650.00

Chandelier, 23" h, baluster form shaft with handpainted flower and leaf motifs, similar applied motifs on white ground, 6 S-scroll arms with conforming applied floral dec, candlecups, suspending tassels with applied floral bouquets 900.00

Clock, 18-3/4" h, Rococo style, clock face surrounded by applied floral dec, 4 fully molded figures representing four seasons..........3,400.00

Compote, 11" d, 7" h, raised gilt dec, pr...................................425.00

Cup and Saucer
   Flower filled basket dec 90.00
   Forget-Me-Not 85.00
   Pink rose dec, snake form handle 110.00

Dessert Service, partial, pink floral dec, gilt trim, five 8" d plates with pierced rims, two 11-1/2" h compotes with figures of boy and girl flower sellers in center of dish, pierced rims, 20th C.............1,850.00

Dinner Service, partial
   Deutsche Blumen, molded New Dulong border, gilt highlights, 2 oval serving platters, circular platter, fish platter, 8-1/2" cov tureen with figural finial 2 sauce boats with attached underplates, 2 serving spoons, sq serving dish, 2 small oval dishes, cov jam pot with attached underplate and spoon, 20 dinner plates, 11 teacups and saucers, 9 salad plates, 10 bread plates, 10 soups, 74 pc set 8,500.00
   Pink and purple Indian painting with florals, coffee mug and saucer, cream jug, 10" h cov hot water pot, twelve 7" d plates, twelve 8-3/4" d plates, twelve 10" d plates, 14" l oval platter, 16-1/4" l oval platter, sauceboat, 9-7/8" d round serving bowl, 10-1/2" round serving bowl, 12-1/2" d round serving bowl, oval serving bowl, two sq serving bowls, twelve 9-1/2" d soup plates, cov sugar, ten teacups with twelve saucers, cov teapot, cov vegetable bowl..................4,890.00

Dish, 12" l, shaped oval, molded gilt and white foliate dec, floral sprays...325.00

Dish, cov, 6-5/8" h, female blackamoor, beside covered dish with molded basketweave and rope edge, modeled on freeform oval base with applied florets, incised #328, 20th C....................................575.00

Figure
   3-1/2" h, girl holding flower, incised #C.3, 19th C..................450.00
   3-3/4" h, boy with dog, mounted on sq base, incised #G.10, 19th C...635.00
   5-1/2" h, female representing Europe, late 19th/early 20th C ..400.00
   5-3/4" h, female and servant tending to bird, enamel and gilt dec, incised #2541, late 19th C 1,035.00
   6" h, lady with fan, incised #509, 20th C..............................230.00

6-1/4" h, female card player, modeled on circular base, incised #F.64, 19th C 1,380.00
6-3/8" h, lady, holding religious book, seated in armchair by spinning wheel, 19th C..1,095.00
6-1/2" h, children playing musical instruments, inscribed #B.24, late 19th C 3,450.00
6-1/2" h, five children in varying poses, small animals and flowers, inscribed #G.13, late 19th C 3,680.00
7-1/2" h, gardener, modeled on circular bases, incised #C.68 and #C.69, pr 1,100.00
8" h, male and female lovers and animals, incised #A.29, late 19th C, losses 1,725.00
8-3/4" h, Bacchus, modeled on wave-molded circular base, incised #2732...690.00
9-1/4" h, tailor on goat, mounted on rect base, incised #73011, 20th C 1,850.00
9-1/2" h, man, woman, and child picking fruits and flowers, mounted on acanthus molded circular base, incised #D94, late 19th/early 20th C 1,840.00
10" h four figures playing musical instruments, drapery swag dec circular base, late 19th/early 20th C 2,185.00
10-1/2" h, Bacchus, central figure modeled seated on wine barrel, surrounded by children and female figures, freeform base, incised #2202...1,495.00
10-3/4" h, wine makers, several figures playing musical instruments, holding grapes and drinking wine, late 19th C 5,175.00

Fish Set, 21-3/4" l platter, sauce boat and undertray, fish, coral, seaweed dec, cobalt blue rim with gilt scrolling design, damage to all pieces..150.00

Plate
   9" d, enameled female and cherubs, gilt foliate designs on pierced rim, 20th C, 8 pc set...4,485.00
   11-1/4" d, scalloped rim, three molded cartouches painted with floral sprays on border, molded details, heavy gilding, pr.......500.00
   11-3/4" d, floral dec, three molded gilt cartouches on rim......225.00

Tea and Coffee Service, Green Dragon, 10" h coffeepot, teapot, creamer, cov sugar...800.00

Teapot, 6" l, figural, rooster, enamel dec, late 19th/early 20th C 575.00

Tray, 17-3/8" l, oval, enameled floral sprays, gilt trim, 20th C.....400.00

Urn on Pedestal, 21" h, figural cartouches, scattered floral dec, 2 handles in form of pair of entwined snakes, mounted as lamps, pr 4,000.00

Vase
   7-1/2" h, campana form, floral filled cartouche, cobalt blue ground..300.00
   10-1/2" h, floral dec, bands of molded gilt dec, each handle molded as two entwined snakes, gilt highlights................................475.00
   15-1/2" h, scrolled snake handles, cobalt blue ground, gold and silver floral dec, 19th C, new gold trim to handles...............2,300.00

DUNCAN and MILLER

History: George Duncan, Harry B. and James B., his sons, and Augustus Heisey, his son-in-law, formed George Duncan & Sons in Pittsburgh, Pennsylvania, in 1865. The factory was located just two blocks from the Monongahela River, providing easy and inexpensive access by barge for materials needed to produce glass. The men, from Pittsburgh's south side, were descendants of generations of skilled glassmakers.

The plant burned to the ground in 1892. James E. Duncan, Sr., selected a site for a new factory in Washington, Pennsylvania, where operations began on Feb. 9, 1893. The plant prospered, producing fine glassware and table services for many years.

John E. Miller, one of the stockholders, was responsible for designing many fine patterns, the most famous being Three Face. The firm incorporated and used the name The

Centerpiece Bowl, Sanibel, pink opalescent, 13-1/2" l, $50.

Duncan and Miller Glass Company until the plant closed in 1955. The company's slogan was "The Loveliest Glassware in America." The U.S. Glass Co. purchased the molds, equipment, and machinery in 1956.

References: Gene Florence, *Elegant Glassware of the Depression Era*, 8th ed., Collector Books, 1998; Naomi L. Over, *Ruby Glass of the 20th Century*, Antique Publications, 1990, 1993-94 value update, *Book II*, 1999.

Collectors' Club: National Duncan Glass Society, P.O. Box 965, Washington, PA 15301.

Additional Listings: Pattern Glass.

Animal
  Goose, fat, crystal...275.00
  Heron, crystal 125.00
  Swan, 6-1/2" h, opal pink..115.00
Ashtray, Terrace, red, sq...35.00
Bowl, First Love, crystal, 11" d, scalloped.........................72.00
Bud Vase, First Love, crystal, 9" h.................................75.00
Candleholders, pr
  #30, 2-lite, crystal, removable bobeche and prisms,
    7-1/2" h, 8" w..275.00
  #30, 2-lite, First Love etch 125.00
Candy Box, cov, Canterbury, crystal, 3 part, 6" d...................70.00
Champagne, First Love, crystal 21.00
Coaster, Sandwich, crystal 15.00
Cocktail
  Caribbean, blue, 3-3/4 oz 45.00
  Sandwich, crystal , 3 oz...14.00
Cornucopia, #121, Swirl, blue opalescent, shape #2, upswept tail 75.00
Creamer and Sugar, Passion Flower, crystal..........................42.00
Cup and Saucer, Radiance, light blue................................22.00
Finger Bowl, Astaire, red...65.00
Goblet, water
  First Love, crystal10 oz...32.00
  Plaza, cobalt blue 40.00
  Sandwich, crystal , 9 oz...19.00
Ice Cream Dish, Sandwich, crystal , 4-1/4" d........................12.00
Juice Tumbler, Sandwich, crystal , 3-3/4" h, ftd 12.00
Nappy, Sandwich, crystal , 2 part, divided, handle 14.00
Oyster Cocktail, Canterbury, citrone 18.00
Plate
  Astaire, red, 7-1/2" d...15.00
  Radiance, light blue, 8-1/2" d.....................................17.50
  Spiral Flute, crystal, 10-3/8" d...................................15.00
  Terrace, cobalt blue, 7-1/2" d.....................................30.00

Relish, 5 part
  First Love, crystal, 10" d...65.00
  Terrace, crystal, gold trim 125.00
Sherbet, Language of Flowers, crystal 18.00
Sugar Shaker, Duncan Block, crystal.................................42.00
Whiskey, Seahorse, etch #502, red and crystal.......................48.00
Wine, Sandwich, crystal , 3 oz......................................20.00

DURAND

History: Victor Durand (1870-1931), born in Baccarat, France, apprenticed at the Baccarat glassworks where several generations of his family had worked. In 1884, Victor came to America to join his father at Whitall-Tatum & Co. in New Jersey. In 1897, father and son leased the Vineland Glass Manufacturing Company in Vineland, New Jersey. Products included inexpensive bottles, jars, and glass for scientific and medical purposes. By 1920, four separate companies existed.

When Quezal Art Glass and Decorating Company failed, Victor Durand recruited Martin Bach, Jr., Emil J. Larsen, William Wiedebine, and other Quezal men and opened an art-glass shop at Vineland in December 1924. Quezal-style iridescent pieces were made. New innovations included cameo and intaglio designs, geometric Art Deco shapes, Venetian Lace, and Oriental-style pieces. In 1928, crackled glass, called Moorish Crackle and Egyptian Crackle, was made.

Durand died in 1931. The Vineland Flint Glass Works was merged with Kimble Glass Company a year later, and the art glass line was discontinued.

Reference: Edward J. Meschi, *Durand: The Man and His Glass*, Glass Press, 1998.

Marks: Many Durand glass pieces are not marked. Some have a sticker with the words "Durand Art Glass," others have the name "Durand" scratched on the pontil or "Durand" inside a large V. Etched numbers may be part of the marking.

Bowl, 9-3/4" d, butterscotch, partial silver sgd 345.00
Candlesticks, pr, mushroom, red, opal pulled florals, pale yellow
  base 725.00
Decanter, 12" h, blue cut to clear, mushroom shaped stopper,
  unsigned...600.00
Jar, cov, 7-1/4" h, ginger jar form, King Tut, green, irid gold dec, applied
  amber glass dec on cov 3,100.00
Lamp Base, 12" h vase, blue, green, orange King Tut dec, opal
  ground, drilled 420.00
Table Torchieres, pr, 15-1/2" h, Egyptian crackle, trumpet form, green
  and white striated glass with irid gold crackle dec, bronze acanthus
  leaf electrified bases, c1926, pr 1,725.00
Vase
  5-3/4" h, flared rim, tapering to squatty base, gold irid int. and ext.,
    mkd "V" and "Durand 1990 6" across pontil 520.00
  6-3/8" h, broad ovoid, ambergris with peach-gold irid, applied gold
    spider web thread dec, cased to white flashed gold int., polished
    pontil, minor loss to threading.....................................500.00
  7" h, ovoid, flared rim, light blue ground with strong overall blue irid,
    polished pontil, sgd in silver "Durand 1710-7," c1925, scratches to
    irid surface 435.00
  7-1/4" h, ovoid, wide flared rim, irid blue, silvery blue threaded spi-
    der web glass overlay, unmarked, some loss to threading . 635.00
  7-3/4" h, Cluthra, ovoid, colorless ground with trapped bubbles and
    mottled blue and green rising to yellow at flared neck, obscured
    silver signature in polished pontil, c1930 ....635.00

9-1/2" h, vasiform, irid dark cobalt blue ground, silver heart and vine motif, silver-blue irid int. of flared mouth, polished pontil inscribed "Durand 1707" in silver 1,955.00

12-1/2" h, Lady Gray Rose, elongated neck, bulbous and ftd body, rose pink, coiled irid, cased to white-yellow flared int., silver enamel "Durand" over polished pontil 2,875.00

13" h, shape 1978, beehive, stepped form, amber ground, gold irid surface, polished pontil, unmarked, minor wear to irid surface, 1925 .... 920.00

EARLY AMERICAN GLASS

History: The term "Early American glass" covers glass made in America from the colonial period through the mid-19th century. As such, it includes the early pressed glass and lacy glass made between 1827 and 1840.

Major glass-producing centers prior to 1850 were Massachusetts (New England Glass Company and the Boston and Sandwich Glass Company), South Jersey, Pennsylvania (Stiegel's Manheim factory and many Pittsburgh-area firms), and Ohio (several different companies in Kent, Mantua, and Zanesville).

Early American glass was popular with collectors from 1920 to 1950. It has now regained some of its earlier prominence. Leading auction sources for early American glass include Garth's, Heckler & Company, James D. Julia, and Skinner, Inc.

References: William E. Covill, *Ink Bottles and Inkwells*, William S. Sullwold Publishing, out of print; George and Helen McKearin, *American Glass*, Crown, 1975; ——, *Two Hundred Years of American Blown Glass*, Doubleday and Company, 1950; Helen McKearin and Kenneth Wilson, *American Bottles and Flasks*, Crown, 1978; Dick Roller (comp.), *Indiana Glass Factories Notes*, Acorn Press, 1994; Jane S. Spillman, *American and European Pressed Glass*, Corning Museum of Glass, 1981; Kenneth Wilson, *American Glass 1760-1930*, 2 vols., Hudson Hills Press and The Toledo Museum of Art, 1994; ——, *New England Glass and Glassmaking*, Crowell, 1972.

Periodicals: *Antique Bottle & Glass Collector*, P.O. Box 187, East Greenville, PA 18041; *Glass Collector's Digest*, Antique Publications, P.O. Box 553, Marietta, OH 45750.

Collectors' Clubs: Early American Glass Traders, RD 5, Box 638, Milford, DE 19963; Early American Pattern Glass Society, P.O. Box 266, Colesburg, IA 52035; Glass Research Society of New Jersey, Wheaton Village, Glasstown Rd, Millville, NJ 08332; National Early American Glass Club, P.O. Box 8489, Silver Spring, MD 20907.

Museums: Bennington Museum, Bennington, VT; Chrysler Museum, Norfolk, VA; Corning Museum of Glass, Corning, NY; Glass Museum, Dunkirk, IN; Glass Museum Foundation, Redlands, CA; New Bedford Glass Museum, New Bedford, MA; Sandwich Glass Museum, Sandwich, MA; Toledo Museum of Art, Toledo, OH; Wheaton Historical Village Association Museum of Glass, Millville, NJ.

Additional Listings: Blown Three Mold; Cup Plates; Flasks; Sandwich Glass; Stiegel-Type Glass.

Bottle, 5-1/4" h, blown, globular, aqua, 30 swirled ribs, applied lip ...220.00
Bowl, 7-3/4" d, 3" h, blown, amber, flared rim, folded lip, Zanesville, OH 675.00
Candlesticks, pr
   6-3/4" h, colorless, flint, blown hollow sockets, hexagonal pressed base 275.00
   7-1/8" h, colorless, free blown sockets, lacy hairpin pattern base, Midwestern 5,250.00
   10" h, colorless, flint, hexagonal pressed base, hollow blown stem, hollow blown socket, all separated by wafers, minor chips on base 385.00

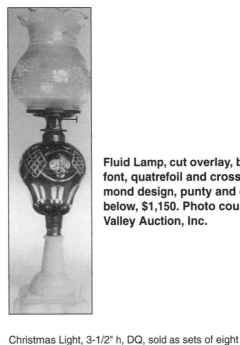

Fluid Lamp, cut overlay, blue cut to clear font, quatrefoil and cross-hatched diamond design, punty and oval band below, $1,150. Photo courtesy of Green Valley Auction, Inc.

Christmas Light, 3-1/2" h, DQ, sold as sets of eight
   Five amber, amethyst, green, and honey, chips 250.00
   Five shades of amber, two green, and blue, chips 265.00
   Three amber, amethyst, aqua, blue, green, and peacock green 180.00
Compote, 5-3/4" d, 3-1/4" h, blown, colorless, folded lip, applied flared foot with folded rim, Pittsburgh 350.00
Creamer, 5-7/8" h, cobalt blue, applied crimped foot, solid curled handle, tooled rim, South New Jersey, int. spall on side of spout .. 650.00
Curtain Tiebacks, 4-7/8" d, fiery opalescent, bow pewter posts, minor chips, set of 4 .... 100.00
Cuspidor, 5" d, 2-1/4" h, blown, deep amber, Midwestern 275.00
Flask, double eagle, yellow olive, sheared mouth, pontil scar, Coventry Glass Works 165.00
Fluid Lamp
   9-3/8" h, amethyst, heart, sawtooth, and thumbprint font, wafer, hexagonal base, brass collar 165.00
   9-1/2" h, colorless, globular form, drip catch, trapped bubble baluster form stem, round stepped base, minor surface wear, early 19th C 150.00
   9-3/4" h, colorless, flint, heart and thumbprint font, wafer, hexagonal base, brass collar, small chips on foot 220.00
   10-1/4" h, colorless, flint, Excelsior variant font, wafer, baluster stem, hexagonal foot, brass collar, pinpoint flakes on base 115.00
Jar
   6-5/8" h, blown, green-aqua, folded lip, ftd, Midwestern 260.00
   11-3/8" h, cylindrical, green, blown, applied flared foot with folded rim 115.00
Milk Pan, 16" d, 6-1/4" d, aqua, blown, molded top rim, pontil scar, America, early 19th C 800.00
Pan, colorless, blown
   6" d, folded rim with sapphire blue applied ring 150.00
   6-1/4" d, cobalt blue lip 150.00
Pitcher, 5-1/2" h, blown, aqua, lily pad design, applied handle and threading, New England, wear and scratches...................... 1,200.00
Salt
   2-1/2" d, sapphire blue, pattern molded, swirled ribs, tooled rim, applied circular foot, pontil scar, New England 395.00
   2-7/8" l, Neal EE1a, colorless, lacy, minor chips 150.00
   3-3/8" l, Neal SD3, colorless, lacy, minor chips 165.00
Sugar Bowl Base, 3-1/2" h, lacy, octagonal, dark violet blue, streaks of white, small chips 200.00
Sugar Bowl, cov, lacy, Peacock Feather pattern, one foot scallop chipped, Midwestern 500.00

Tumbler
  3-1/4" h, amethyst, eight panel, Pittsburgh............................150.00
  3-1/4" h, deep sapphire blue, eight panel, Pittsburgh, minor chip on
    base 95.00
  5-5/8" h, colorless, blown, molded ribs in base, copper wheel
    engraved band...175.00
Vase
  8-5/8" h, amethyst, hexagonal, ellipse bowl 580.00
  10-7/8" h, colorless, blown, pillar mold, eight rib bowl, scalloped
    rim, baluster stem, foot with ground pontil 200.00
Window Pane, 6-7/8" x 4-7/8", colorless, church type, Gothic Arch
  design, sgd "Bakewell" on reverse 2,200.00

ENGLISH CHINA and PORCELAIN (GENERAL)

History: By the 19th century, more than 1,000 china and porcelain manufacturers were scattered throughout England, with the majority of the factories located in the Staffordshire district.

By the 19th century, English china and porcelain had achieved a worldwide reputation for excellence. American stores imported large quantities for their customers. The special-production English pieces of the 18th and early 19th centuries held a position of great importance among early American antiques collectors.

References: Susan and Al Bagdade, *Warman's English & Continental Pottery & Porcelain*, 3rd Edition, Krause Publications, 1998; John A. Bartlett, *British Ceramic Art: 1870-1940*, Schiffer Publishing, 1993; Peter Bradshaw, *English Eighteenth Century Porcelain Figures, 1745-1795*, Antiques Collectors' Club, 1980; John and Margaret Cushion, *Collector's History of British Porcelain*, Antique Collectors' Club, 1992; Rachael Feild, *Macdonald Guide to Buying Antique Pottery & Porcelain*, Wallace-Homestead, 1987; Geoffrey A. Godden, *Godden's Guide to Mason's China and the Ironstone Wares*, Antique Collectors' Club, out of print; ——, *Godden's Guide to English Porcelain*, Wallace-Homestead, 1992; Pat Halfpenny, *English Earthenware Figures 1740-1840*, Antique Collectors' Club, 1992; R. K. Henrywood, *Relief Molded Jugs, 1820-1900*, Antique Collectors' Club; Llewellyn Jewitt, *Ceramic Art of Great Britain*, Sterling Publishing, 1985 (reprint of 1883 classic); Griselda Lewis, *Collector's History of English Pottery*, 5th ed., Antique Collectors' Club, 1999

Additional Listings: Castleford; Chelsea; Coalport; Copeland and Spode; Liverpool; Royal Crown Derby; Royal Doulton; Royal Worcester; Staffordshire, Historical; Staffordshire, Romantic; Wedgwood; Whieldon.

Bow
  Bowl, 4-1/2" d, blue trailing vine, white ground, c1770..........175.00
  Candlesticks, pr, two birds on flowering branches, dog and sheep
    on grassy base, wood stand, c1755 ....1,200.00
  Egg Cup, 2-1/2" h, 2 half flower panels, powder blue ground,
    pseudo Oriental mark, c1760...900.00
  Plate, 9" d, Turk's Cap Lily, dragonfly and moths, c1755 ......850.00
Caughley, coffeepot, cov, 8" h, underglaze blue floral and insects dec,
  floral finial, shaded crescent mark, 18th C, rim chips to cover. 980.00
Chelsea
  Bowl, 8-3/4" d, swirled ribs, scalloped, foliage and floral dec.....75.00
  Candlesticks, pr, 7-1/2" h, figural, draped putti, sitting on tree stump
    holding flower, scroll molded base, encircled in puce, gilt, wax
    pan..850.00

Stevenson and Hancock Derby, Blanc De Chine, figure of woman at trough, scrolling Rococo style base, late 19th C, 12-1/2" l, minor chips, glaze crazing, $200. Photo courtesy of Freeman\Fine Arts.

Cup and Saucer, multicolored exotic birds, white ground, gold
  anchor mark, c1765 ....750.00
Plate, 8-1/2" d, multicolored floral design, scalloped rim, gold
  anchor mark...475.00
Derby
  Figure, 8" h, 8-1/2" h, pastoral, boy resting against tree stump playing bagpipe, black hat, bleu-do-roi jacket, gilt trim, yellow breeches, girl with green hat, bleu-du-roi bodice, pink skirt, white apron with iron-red flowerheads, gilt centers, leaves, scroll molded mound base, crown and incised iron-red D mark, pr.....................2,200.00
  Jar, cov, 22" h, octagonal, iron-red, bottle green and leaf green, alternating cobalt blue and white grounds, gilding, grotesque sea serpent handles, now fitted as lamp with carved base, 19th C, pr...10,000.00
  Plate, 8" d, Imari palette, gilt trim, staining, early 19th C, set of
    12...350.00
Flight, Barr & Barr
  Crocus Pot, 9" w, 4" d, 6-1/4" h, D-form, molded columns and architrave, peach ground panels, ruined abbey landscape reserve, gilding 2,400.00
  Pastille Burner, 3-1/2" h, cottage, four open chimneys, mkd,
    c1815 ....425.00
Jackfield
  Creamer, 4-1/4" h, bulbous, emb grapes design, leaves, and tendrils, gilt highlights, 3 pr paw feet, ear shape handle..........175.00
  Pitcher, 6-1/2" h, applied handle, black, traces of enameling, bird, initials and "1763," wear, small flakes.................................125.00
  Sugar Bowl, cov, 4-1/2" h, 3-3/4" d, scalloped SS rims, SS mounted cov and ornate pierced finial..250.00
Lowestoft
  Coffeepot, cov, 9" h, dark blue, underglaze river scene, Chinese man fishing, trellis diaper border, c1770-75........................950.00
  Demitasse Cup and Saucer, blue underglaze dec 150.00
  Milk Jug, 3-1/4" h, dark blue underglaze, Chinese river scene, diaper border, brown rim, c1775...210.00
Masons
  Creamer, 4" h, Oriental style shape, mkd "Mason's Patent Ironstone"...85.00
  Jug, 8" h, octagonal, Hydra pattern, waisted straight neck, green enameled handle, lion head terminal, underglaze blue and iron-red flowers and vase, 2 imp marks and printed rounded crown mark, c1813-30..320.00
  Platter, 13-1/2" x 10-3/4", Double Landscape pattern, Oriental motif, deep green and brick red, c1883 ....265.00
  Potpourri Vase, cov, 25-1/4" h, hexagonal body, cobalt blue, large gold stylized peony blossom, chrysanthemums, prunus, and but-

Worcester, basket, blue and white printed floral dec, twist handles, flower encrusted exteriors, c1780, 9" l, chips, price for pair, $1,100. Photo courtesy of Freeman\Fine Arts.

terflies, gold and blue dragon handles, and knobs, trellis diaper rim border, c1820-25....................................... 1,750.00

New Hall

Creamer, Chinese figure on terrace, c1790........................... 190.00

Dessert Set, 2 oval dishes, 8 plates, printed and colored named views, lavender-blue borders, light blue ground, c1815...... 450.00

Tea Set, interwoven ribbon and leaf trails, blue and gilt oval medallion border, c1790, minor repairs, 44 pcs........................... 1,500.00

Woods

Cup and Saucer, handleless, Woods Rose 65.00

Dish, 8" l, 6" w, dark blue transfer of castle, imp "Wood"....... 165.00

Jug, 5-3/4" h, ovoid, cameos of Queen Caroline, pink luster ground, beaded edge, molded and painted floral border, c1820 ..... 425.00

Plate, 9" d, Woods Rose, scalloped edge 125.00

Stirrup Cup, 5-1/2" l, modeled hound's head, translucent shades of brown, c1760 .... 2,200.00

Whistle, 3-7/8" h, modeled as seated sphinx, blue accents, oval green base, c1770 .... 600.00

Worcester

Cream Jug, cov, 5" h, floral finial, underglaze blue floral and insect dec, shaded crescent mark, 18th C, cover possibly married, slight finial chips, shallow flake to cover....................................... 175.00

Deep Dish, 9-1/2" l, oval, underglaze blue Chantilly sprig pattern, shaded crescent mark, 18th C, footrim chips..................... 320.00

Sauce Boat, 5-1/4" l, molded body, panels of underglaze blue flowers, cell border, open crescent mark, 18th C 300.00

Teapot, cov, globular, 5-5/8" h, underglaze blue dec of Waiting Chinaman, floral finial, open crescent mark, 18th C, slight spout nick, chips to finial 865.00

Teapot, cov, globular, 5-3/4" h, underglaze blue flowers and insects, floral finial, shaded crescent mark, 18th C, cover married, chips to finial and collar.. 175.00

Tureen, cov, 10-1/2" l, oval, underglaze blue pine cone pattern, artichoke finial, shell handles, shaded crescent mark, 18th C, one handle restored, int. rim flake 800.00

ENGLISH SOFT PASTE

History: Between 1820 and 1860, a large number of potteries in England's Staffordshire district produced decorative wares with a soft earthenware (creamware) base and a plain white or yellow glazed ground.

Design or "stick" spatterware was created by a cut sponge (stamp), hand painting, or transfers. Blue was the predominant color. The earliest patterns were carefully arranged geometrics which generally covered the entire piece. Later pieces had a decorative border with a central

motif, usually a tulip. In the 1850s, Elsmore and Foster developed the Holly Leaf pattern.

King's Rose features a large, cabbage-type rose in red, pale red, or pink. The pink rose often is called "Queen's Rose." Secondary colors are pastels—yellow, pink, and, occasionally, green. The borders vary: a solid band, vined, lined, or sectional. The King's Rose exists in an oyster motif.

Strawberry China ware comes in three types: strawberries and strawberry leaves (often called strawberry luster), green featherlike leaves with pink flowers (often called cut-strawberry, primrose, or old strawberry), and relief decoration. The first two types are characterized by rust-red moldings. Most pieces have a cream ground. Davenport was only one of the many potteries which made this ware.

Yellow-glazed earthenware (canary luster) has a canary yellow ground, a transfer design which is usually in black, and occasional luster decoration. The earliest pieces date from the 1780s and have a fine creamware base. A few hand-painted pieces are known. Not every piece has luster decoration.

Because the base material is soft paste, the ware is subject to cracking and chipping. Enamel colors and other types of decoration do not hold well. It is not unusual to see a piece with the decoration worn off.

Marks: Marked pieces are uncommon.

Additional Listings: Gaudy Dutch; Salopian Ware; Staffordshire Items.

Creamware

Coffeepot, cov, 10" h, pear shape, polychrome dec black transfer of Tea Party and Shepherd prints, leaf molded spout, chips, restoration to body, attributed to Wedgwood, c1775 .... 350.00

Dish, 15" d, scalloped edge, late 18th C, rim chips 320.00

Figure, 2-1/2" h, monkey, brown sponging, base chips 250.00

Plate, 8-3/8" sq, red, blue, pink, green, and worn gilt 110.00

Platter, 18" l, 14-1/2" w, oval, scallop dec rim, chips, restorations.... 300.00

Sugar Bowl, 5-1/8" d, 2-3/4" h, int. with red and green enamel floral dec, purple luster and underglaze blue, ext. mkd "Be Canny with the Sugar" flanked by small flowers 385.00

Creamware, platter, basketweave, scroll, and lattice border, 16-5/8" x 13-3/8", $295.

Teapot
  4" h, floral dec, early 19th C, hairline along spout and handle 115.00
  4-3/4" h, molded acanthus spout, ribbed handle, small flakes....385.00
  6-1/2" h, flower knop, floral dec entwined reeded handle with touches of gilt, rim chip, restored spout, gilt loss, 19th C....230.00

Design Spatterware

Bowl, 7-1/2" d, 4" h, polychrome stripes 95.00
Creamer, 4-3/8" h, gaudy floral dec, red, green, blue, and black, mkd "Baker & Co., England" 75.00
Cup, oversize, gaudy floral dec, red, blue, and green, 6-1/8" d..200.00
Jug, 7" h, barrel shape, blue, rosettes and fern prongs 185.00
Miniature
  Cup and saucer, green and black, polychrome center flower 75.00
  Tea set, Five pieces, 5-3/4" h teapot, creamer, sugar, two handle-less cups and saucers, blue and white design spatter, teapot finial restored, chips 440.00
Mug, 4" h, octagonal, red, blue, and green stripes 135.00
Plate, 8-5/8" d, red, blue, green, and black, imp "Elsmore & Foster," minor wear and scratches, price for set of 6 ....385.00
Sugar Bowl, cov, 5" h, white, blue, and red flowers, green leaves, closed ring and shell handles..120.00

King's Rose

Bowl, 7-3/4" d, Rose, broken solid border, flakes 55.00
Cup and Saucer, handleless
  Oyster pattern, hairline cracks...40.00
  Rose, solid border 100.00
  Rose, vine border 150.00
Plate
  5-5/8" d, pink border, wear..55.00
  6-1/2" d, broken solid border, flakes 55.00
  6-1/2" d, vine border, wear...80.00
  7-3/8" d, some flaking 90.00
  8-1/4" d, scalloped borders and edges, some flakes, 6 pcs ..275.00
  8-1/4" d, pink border, wear...70.00
  8-1/4" d, vine border, 3 pcs 255.00
  9-3/4" d, scalloped border, 4 pcs 220.00
Soup Plate, 9-1/2" d, broken solid border, scalloped edges, some flakes, 3 pcs 360.00
Teapot, 5-3/4" h, broken solid border, some flakes.....................140.00

Pearlware

Bowl
  8-3/4" d, 3-7/8" h, blue and white Oriental transfer, yellow rim, wear and stains, chip on foot 145.00
  10-3/8" d, 4-1/8" h, interior with pink, green, red, and black floral enameled rim, mahogany stripes, minor wear....................250.00
  10-3/4" d, 4" h, polychrome enamel Oriental dec, minor wear and scratches 440.00
Coffeepot, cov, 9-1/4" h, blue Chinoiserie dec, early 19th C, chips to underside of cover...805.00
Cup and Saucer, handleless, 3-1/2" d cup, 5" d saucer, black transfer scene of horse-drawn chariot, flying putti set of 6 ....525.00
Figure
  3" l, sheep, brown, blue, and yellow ochre sponging, small edge flakes 275.00
  3-1/4" h, squirrel, nut and collar with ring, polychrome, orange coat, attributed to Derby, minor wear and small flakes on base .. 635.00

3-7/8" h, cat, seated, green base, yellow and brown polka dots, attributed to Wood, repairs, hairline in base, small flakes... 550.00
6-3/4" h, Autumn, molded base, green, brown, yellow, orange, black, and pink flesh tones, chips on base, old repair 330.00
Jar, cov, 12-1/4" h, blue transfer, willow pattern, gilt highlights, c1830 ....550.00
Pitcher
  6-5/8" h, gaudy floral dec, red, blue, green, and black, minor enamel wear, deteriorating professional repair...................110.00
  8-5/8" h, Leeds floral dec, green, brown, blue, and tan, later added row of peacocks, very flaked, stains, chips on spout..........275.00
Plate
  5-3/4" d, rose dec, molded luster rim, wear............................85.00
  7-3/4" d, blue and white Oriental dec, imp "Turner," minor wear 165.00
Platter, 20-3/4" l, blue feather edge, Leeds blue and white Oriental dec, wear, scratches, edge chips, old puttied repair 500.00
Teapot, 5-3/4" h, octagonal, molded designs, swan finial, Oriental transfer, polychrome enamel, attributed to T. Harley, some edge flakes and professional repair 425.00
Vase, 7" h, five finger type, underglaze blue, enameled birds and foliage, yellow ochre, brown, and green, silver luster highlights, chips and crazing, pr 500.00

Queen's Rose

Cream Pitcher and Sugar, cov, vine border, some flakes 250.00
Cup and Saucer, handleless, broken solid border 495.00
Plate
  6-1/2" d, broken solid border 50.00
  7-1/2" d, solid border 75.00
  8-1/4" d, vine border, scalloped edge 85.00
  10" d, vine border 110.00
Teapot and cov sugar, shell form, some flakes 420.00

Strawberry China

Bowl, 4" d 165.00
Cup and Saucer, pink border, scalloped edge 225.00
Plate, 8-1/2" d, Cut Strawberry 200.00
Sugar Bowl, cov, raised strawberries, strawberry knob 175.00
Tea Bowl and Saucer, vine border 250.00

Yellow Glazed

Child's Mug
  Floral leaf and vine dec 195.00
  Pious verse "My son if sinners entice thee consent thou not disgrace come upon thee"..250.00
  Silver luster foliate band 185.00
Pitcher, 4-3/4" h, transfer dec of foliate devices, reserve of shepherd with milk maid, hand painted dec, c1850 ....635.00
Plate, 8-1/4" d, brown transfer print, Wild Rose pattern, imp "Montread"...250.00
Soup Bowl, 8-1/4" d, molded border, Cabbage Rose pattern, iron-red and green dec 400.00
Sugar Bowl, cov, 5-1/2" h, printed transfer of The Tea Party, fishing scene, iron-red painted rims...1,250.00
Tea Bowl and Saucer, iron-red print of two cupids, mkd "Sewell"250.00
Teapot, 5-1/2" h, printed transfer of The Party, iron-red painted rims, minor hairline, spout damage...850.00

FAIRINGS

History: Fairings are small, charming china objects which were purchased or given away as prizes at English fairs in the 19th century. Although fairings are generally identified with England, they actually were manufactured in Germany by Conte and Boehme of Possneck.

Fairings depict an amusing scene, either of courtship and marriage, politics, war, children, or animals behaving as children. More than 400 varieties have been identified. Most fairings include a caption. Early examples, 1860-1870, were of better quality than later ones. After 1890, the colors became more garish, and gilding was introduced.

The manufacturers of fairings also made match safes and trinket boxes. Some of these were also captioned. The figures on the lids were identical to those on fairings. The market for the match safes and trinket boxes was the same as that for the fairings.

Reference: Janice and Richard Vogel, *Victorian Trinket Boxes*, published by authors (4720 S.E. Ft. King St., Ocala, FL 34470), 1996.

After The Race, cats in a basket	215.00
Five O'Clock Tea, group of cats	225.00
God Save the Queen, children singing around piano	350.00
Lets Us Do Business Together	95.00
Peep Through A Telescope, sailor and child	175.00
Present from Llangollen, china bootie, Elfin Ware, Dresden, 2" h, 2-1/2" l	75.00
The Welsh Tea Party, magenta dresses, striped aprons, black hats, gilt trim, c1870	95.00
Who Said Rats	95.00

FAIRY LAMPS

History: Fairy lamps, which originated in England in the 1840s, are candle-burning night lamps. They were used in nurseries, hallways, and dim corners of the home.

Two leading candle manufacturers, the Price Candle Company and the Samuel Clarke Company, promoted fairy lamps as a means to sell candles. Both contracted with glass, porcelain, and metal manufacturers to produce the needed shades and cups. For example, Clarke used Worcester Royal Porcelain Company, Stuart & Sons, and Red House Glass Works in England, plus firms in France and Germany.

Fittings were produced in a wide variety of styles. Shades ranged from pressed to cut glass, from Burmese to Nailsea. Cups are found in glass, porcelain, brass, nickel, and silver plate.

American firms selling fairy lamps included Diamond Candle Company of Brooklyn, Blue Cross Safety Candle Co., and Hobbs-Brockunier of Wheeling, West Virginia.

Two-piece (cup and shade) and three-piece (cup with matching shade and saucer) fairy lamps can be found. Married pieces are common.

Marks: Clarke's trademark was a small fairy with a wand surrounded by the words "Clarke Fairy Pyramid, Trade Mark."

References: Bob and Pat Ruf Pullin, *Fairy Lamps*, Schiffer Publishing, 1996; John F. Solverson (comp.), *Those Fascinating Little Lamps: Miniature Lamps Value Guide*, Antique Publications, 1988.

Periodical: *Light Revival*, 35 West Elm Ave., Quincy, MA 02170.

Collectors' Club: Night Light Club, 38619 Wakefield Ct., Northville, MI 48167.

Reproduction Alert: Reproductions abound.

Which is Prettiest, 3-1/2" x 2" x 4", $225.

Bisque, woman with flowers in flowing hair, Austria, 4-5/8" h, $225.

3-1/2" h, overshot, yellow swirl, cased, clear mkd Clarke candle
cup 125.00
3-7/8" h, peachblow, cream lining, acid finished rose shaded pink,
black lacy flower and leaf dec, clear mkd Clarke candle cup, gold
washed metal stand, attributed to Thomas Webb 350.00
4" h, bisque, figural, owl, cat, and dog, glass eyes, clear mkd Clarke
candle cup 265.00
4-1/4" h, colored lithophane, dome shade, gold accents, boy and girl in
garden, girl peering from window, another girl carrying basket and
pole, boy and dog, clear candle cup holder mkd "S. Clarke Patent
Trade Mark Fairy" 1,485.00
4-1/2" h, cranberry, crown shape, overshot shade, clear base, clear
mkd Clarke candle cup, c1887 ....220.00
4-5/8" h, sapphire blue, DQ, melon ribbed, clear mkd Clarke candle
cup 175.00
5" h, 5-1/2" d, ruby red Verre Moiré, bowl shaped base with fluted
edge, clear glass candle cup holder mkd "S. Clarke Patent Trade
Mark" 1,035.00
5-1/2" h, white spatter, chartreuse cased in crystal ground, swirled rib
mold, heavy applied crystal feet and base trim, clear mkd Clarke candle cup..550.00
5-1/2" h, 7-1/2" d pleated skirt, Burmese Criklite, clear candle cup mkd
"Clarke's Criklite Trade Mark" 1,085.00
5-3/4" h, 8-1/2" d, ruby red, profuse white loopings, bowl shaped base
with 8 turned up scallops, clear glass candle cup holder mkd "S.
Clarke Patent Trade Mark Fairy" 1,250.00
6" d, lavender satin ruffled dome top, 3 gold inset jeweled medallions,
ruffled base..350.00
6" h, blue and white frosted ribbon glass dome top shade, ruffled base,
clear mkd "S. Clarke" insert, flakes on shade......................490.00
6-1/2" h, 8" w, Verre Moiré, sweeping white loopings blend into delicate
blue background, done shaped shade, triangular shaped base with
pinch-in folds, clear glass cup holder with ruffled edge, mkd "S.
Clarke Patent Trade Mark Fairy" 950.00

FAMILLE ROSE

History: Famille Rose is Chinese export enameled porcelain on which the pink color predominates. It was made primarily in the 18th and 19th centuries. Other porcelains in
the same group are Famille Jaune (yellow), Famille Noire
(black), and Famille Verte (green).

Decorations include courtyard and home scenes, birds,
and insects. Secondary colors are yellow, green, blue,
aubergine, and black.

Rose Canton, Rose Mandarin, and Rose Medallion are
mid- to late 19th-century Chinese export wares which are
similar to Famille Rose.

Bowl
10" d, floral and scrolled border int., figural cartouche on gilt ground
on ext., 19th C 600.00
12" d, int. dec with alternating floral and figural reserves against
foliate pattern ground, floral dec ext., Ch'ing Dynasty 400.00
Box, cov, 4-1/2" d, figural and floral dec.....................................90.00
Bride's Lamp, 14" h, hexagonal form, reticulated panels,
electrified 345.00
Charger, 12" d, central figural dec, brocade border 265.00
Dish, 10-3/4" d, figural dec, Qing dynasty.................................65.00
Dish, cov, 11" d, figural dec, Qing dynasty................................200.00
Figure
13" h, peacocks, pr..275.00
16" h, cockerels, pr...550.00
Garden Set, 18-1/2" h, hexagonal, pictorial double panels, flanked and
bordered by floral devices, blue ground, 19th C, minor glaze
loss..1,100.00
Ginger Jar, cov, 10-1/2" h, ovoid, foo dog beside sea reserve, floral
and butterfly patterned ground, Famille Verte, Kangxi 420.00

**Dish, ogee shape, heron, peaches, symbols of longevity,
immortality, gold rim, Tongzhi seal, 6-1/2" d, $195.**

Jar, cov, 18" h, baluster, dec with female sprite figure emerging from
flower blossom, surrounded by floral devices, minor base chips,
19th C..750.00
Jardiniere, 9-3/4" h, flowering branches dec, Jiaqing 700.00
Lamp Base, 17" h, figural and crane dec, molded fu dog mask and ring
handles..175.00
Mug, 5" h, Mandarin palette, Qianlong, 1790 ....425.00
Pillow, 15-1/4", Phoenix and floral dec....................................225.00
Plate, 10" d, floral dec, ribbed body, Tongzhi mark, pr...............275.00
Platter, 16-3/4" l, chamfered corners, floral dec.........................150.00
Tea Caddy, 5-1/2" h, Mandarin palette, arched rect form, painted front,
figures and pavilion reserve, c1780 ....550.00
Tray, 8" l, oval, multicolored center armorial crest, underglaze blue diaper and trefoil borders, reticulated rim, late 18th C 550.00
Vase
15" h, painted to depict warriors, Qing dynasty 150.00
16" h, dragon, tiger, fu dog, and floral dec, molded fu dog and ball
handles, kylin dec, Qing dynasty, mounted as lamps, pr.1,200.00
17-1/2" h, Rouleau form, molded fu dog handles, scene of figures
picking fruit from large vines, verso with butterflies, traditional borders, late 19th C 250.00
Vase, cov, 26" h, shouldered ovoid, large cartouches with scenes of warriors on horseback, dignitaries holding court, molded fu dog handles,
conforming cartouches on lid, fu dog finial, c1850-70, pr 2,400.00

FENTON GLASS

History: The Fenton Art Glass Company began as a cutting shop in Martins Ferry, Ohio, in 1905. In 1906, Frank L.
Fenton started to build a plant in Williamstown, West Virginia, and produced the first piece of glass there in 1907.
Early production included carnival, chocolate, custard,
and pressed glass, plus mold-blown opalescent glass. In
the 1920s, stretch glass, Fenton dolphins, jade green,
ruby, and art glass were added.

In the 1930s, boudoir lamps, Dancing Ladies, and slag
glass in various colors were produced. The 1940s saw
crests of different colors being added to each piece by
hand. Hobnail, opalescent, and two-color overlay pieces
were popular items. Handles were added to different
shapes, making the baskets they created as popular then
as they are today.

Through the years, Fenton has beautified their glass by
decorating it with hand painting, acid etching, and copper-
wheel cutting

Marks: Several different paper labels have been used. In 1970, an oval raised trademark also was adopted.

References: Robert E. Eaton, Jr., (comp.), *Fenton Glass: The First Twenty-Five Years Comprehensive Price Guide 1998,* Glass Press, 1998; —, *Fenton Glass: The Second Twenty-Five Years Comprehensive Price Guide 1998,* Glass Press, 1998; *Fenton Glass: The Third Twenty-Five Years Comprehensive Price Guide, 1998,* Glass Press, 1998; William Heacock, *Fenton Glass: The First Twenty-Five Years (1978), The Second Twenty-Five Years (1980), The Third Twenty-Five Years (1989),* available from Antique Publications; Alan Linn, *Fenton Story of Glass Making,* Antique Publications, 1996; James Measell (ed.), *Fenton Glass: The 1980s Decade,* Antique Publications, 1996; Naomi L. Over, *Ruby Glass of the 20th Century,* Antique Publications, 1990, 1993-94 value update, —, *Book II,* Antique Publications, 1999; Ferill J. Rice (ed.), *Caught in the Butterfly Net,* Fenton Art Glass Collectors of America, Inc., 1991; John Walk, *The Big Book of Fenton Glass,* 1940-1970, Schiffer, 1998; Margaret and Kenn Whitmyer, *Fenton Art Glass 1907-1939,* Collector Books, 1996, 1999 value update; —, *Fenton Art Glass, 1939-1980,* Collector Books, 1996, 1999 value update.

Periodical: Butterfly Net, 302 Pheasant Run, Kaukauna, WI 54130.

Collectors' Clubs: Fenton Art Glass Collectors of America, Inc., P.O. Box 384, Williamstown, WV 26187; National Fenton Glass Society, P.O. Box 4008, Marietta, OH 45750; Pacific Northwest Fenton Association, 8225 Kilchis River Rd., Tillamook, OR 97141.

Videotape: *Making Fenton Glass, 1992,* Fenton Art Glass Co. Museum, 1992.

Museum: Fenton Art Glass Co., Williamstown, WV.

Advisor: Ferill J. Rice.

Additional Listings: Carnival Glass.

Ashtray
    Lincoln Inn, Aqua or Ruby 25.00
    #848 2 Ruby, three feet 20.00
Basket
    #1523 Aquacrest, 13" h 250.00
    #3830 10" Cranberry Opal, Hobnail 95.00
    #6137 Beatty Waffle, Green Opal 47.50
    #7237 7" h Rose Crest 45.00
    #7437 Burmese, Maple Leaf Decal 75.00
    #7437 DV Violets in the Snow on MI 75.00
Bell
    #7466 CV hp Christmas Morn 45.00
    #8466 OI Faberge, Teal Marigold 55.00
    #9463WS Nativity 55.00
Bon Bon
    #1621 Dolphin Handled, Green 32.50
    #8230 Rosalene Butterfly, two handled 35.00
Bowl
    Gold Crest, 8" d 40.00
    Peach Crest, Charleton dec 105.00
    #846 Pekin Blue, cupped 40.00
    #848 8 Petal, Chinese Yellow 45.00
    #1562 Satin Etched Silvertone, oblong bowl ... 55.00
    #7423 Milk Glass bowl, hp Yellow roses 65.00
    #8222 Rosalene, Basketweave 30.00

Candlestick, single
    #318 Pekin Blue, 3" h 40.00
    #951 Silvercrest Cornucopia 37.50
    #7272 Silver Crest 17.50
Candy Box, cov
    Hobnail, 6-1/2" sq, white, ... 40.00
    Ruby Iridized, Butterfly, for FAGCA 100.00
    #1980CG Daisy and Button 45.00
    #7380 Custard hp Pink Daffodils Louise Piper, dated March
      1975 .... 160.00
    #9394 UE 3 pc, Ogee, Blue Burmese 110.00
    #9394 RE 3 pc, Ogee, Rosalene 100.00
Comport
    #3728 PO Plum Opal Hobnail 5-1/2" 75.00
    #8422 Waterlily ftd, Rosalene 30.00
Cocktail Shaker, #6120 Plymouth, Crystal 55.00
Cracker Jar
    Lilac Big Cookies, no lid, handle 250.00
    #1681 Big Cookies, Jade 125.00
Creamer
    #1502 Diamond Optic, Black 35.00
    #1502 Diamond Optic, Ruby 30.00
    #6464 RG Aventurine Green w/Pink, Vasa Murrhina ... 45.00
Creatures (Animals and Birds)
    #5174 Springtime Green Iridized Blown Rabbit 45.00
    #5178 Springtime Green Iridized Blown Owl 45.00
    #5193 RE Rosalene Fish, paperweight 25.00
    #5197 Happiness Bird, Cardinals in Winter ... 32.50
    #5197 Happiness Bird, Rosalene 40.00
Cruet, #7701 QJ 7" Burmese, Petite Floral 175.00
Cup and Saucer, #7208 Aqua Crest 35.00
Epergne
    #3902 Petite Blue, Opal 4" h 125.00
    #3902 Petite French Opal, 4" h 40.00
    #7308 SC Silvercrest, 3 Horn 125.00
Fairy Light
    #1167 RV Rose Magnolia Hobnail 3 pc, Persian Pearl Crest, sgd
      "Shelly Fenton" 80.00
    #3380 CR Hobnail, 3 pc, Cranberry Opal 75.00
    #3680 RU Hobnail, 3 pc 55.00
    #3804 CA Hobnail 3 pc, Colonial Amber 25.00

Cruet, Hobnail, vaseline, clear stopper, 4-3/4" h, $35.

#3804 CG Hobnail 3 pc, Colonial Green 20.00
#8406 WT Heart, Wisteria 65.00
#8406 PE Heart, Shell Pink 25.50
#8408 VR Persian Medallion, 3 pc, Velva Rose - 75th
   Anniv. 75.00
#8408 BA Persian Medallion 3 pc, Blue Satin 35.00
Ginger Jar, #893 Persian Pearl w/base and top 150.00
Goblet, #1942 Flower Windows Blue 55.00
Hat, #1922 Swirl Optic, French Opal 110.00
Jug, #6068 Cased Lilac, Handled, 6-1/2" 50.00
Lamp
   #2606 Candy Stripe French Colonial, 20" 650.00
   #2700 Ruby Overlay Mariners 150.00
   #3782 CA Courting, Amber Hobnail, Kerosene 65.00
   #7312 BD Hurricane Candle Lamp, 5 Petal Blue
     Dogwood 75.00
   #7398 Black Rose, Hurricane, White Base, 9" h 100.00
Liquor Set, #1934 Flower Stopper, floral silver overlay, 8 pc,
   Set 250.00
Lotus Bowl, #849 Red 25.00
Nut Bowl, Sailboats, Marigold Carnival 50.00
Pitcher
   Amber Crest 115.00
   Christmas Snowflake, Cranberry Opal, water (L.G. Wright) .. 350.00
   Daisy & Fern, Topaz Opal, water (L.G. Wright) 200.00
   Plum Opal, Hobnail, water, 80 oz. 190.00
Powder Box, #6080, Wave Crest
   Blue Overlay 90.00
   Coral 225.00
Plate
   Lafayette & Washington, Light Blue Iridized, sample 80.00
   #107 Ming Rose 8" 30.00
   #1614 9-1/2" Green Opal w Label New World 65.00
   #1621 Dolphin Handled, Fenton Rose, 6" 25.00
   #5118 Leaf, 11" Rosalene, sample 120.00
Rose Bowl, #8954TH hanging heart 95.00
Salt & Pepper Shakers, pr, #3806 Cranberry Opal, Hobnail,
   flat 47.50
Sauce, Pinecone, 5" d, red 35.00
Sherbet
   #1942 Flower Windows, Crystal 35.00
   #4441 Small, Thumbprint, Colonial Blue 35.00
   #4443 Thumbprint, Colonial Blue 20.00
Sugar & Creamer, #9103 Fine Cut & Block (OVG) 20.00
Temple Jar, #7488 Chocolate Roses on Cameo Satin 25.00
Tumbler
   #1611 Georgian, Royal Blue, 5-1/2", ftd, 9 oz 18.00
   #1634 Diamond Optic, Aqua 6.00
   #3700, Grecian Gold, grape cut 15.00
   #3945MI Hobnail, 5 oz. 10.00
   #3945FO Hobnail, 2 oz. 15.00
Vanity Bottle, #3965MI 75.00
Vase
   Aristocrat Bud Vase, #98 cutting, Fenton Rose 45.00
   Butterfly & Berry, red, tightly crimped edge, 7" h 65.00
   Ivory Crest, 10" 65.00
   #847 Periwinkle Blue, Fan 62.50
   #3759 Plum Opal, Hobnail, swung 150.00
   #4454OR Thumbprint, swung 45.00
   #5858 Wild Rose, wheat 85.00
   #6457 GA Vasa Murrhina , fan 85.00
   #7460 Amberina Overlay crimped, 6-1/2" h 80.00
   #7547 Burmese, hp Pink Dogwood, 5-1/2" h 75.00
   #8457VE Grape, 3 toed 35.00

FIESTA

History: The Homer Laughlin China Company introduced Fiesta dinnerware in January 1936 at the Pottery and Glass Show in Pittsburgh, Pennsylvania. Frederick Rhead designed the pattern; Arthur Kraft and Bill Bensford molded it. Dr. A. V. Bleininger and H. W. Thiemecke developed the glazes.

The original five colors were red, dark blue, light green (with a trace of blue), brilliant yellow, and ivory. A vigorous marketing campaign took place between 1939 and 1943. In mid-1937, turquoise was added. Red was removed in 1943 because some of the chemicals used to produce it were essential to the war effort; it did not reappear until 1959. In 1951, light green, dark blue, and ivory were retired and forest green, rose, chartreuse, and gray were added to the line. Other color changes took place in the late 1950s, including the addition of a medium green.

Fiesta ware was redesigned in 1969 and discontinued about 1972. In 1986, Fiesta was reintroduced by Homer Laughlin China Company. The new china body shrinks more than the old semi-vitreous and ironstone pieces, thus making the new pieces slightly smaller than the earlier pieces. The modern colors are also different in tone or hue, e.g., the cobalt blue is darker than the old blue. Other modern colors are black, white, apricot, and rose.

References: Susan and Al Bagdade, *Warman's American Pottery and Porcelain*, Wallace-Homestead, 1994; Sharon and Bob Huxford, *Collector's Encyclopedia of Fiesta*, 8th ed., Collector Books, 1998; Ronald E. Kay and Kathleen M. Taylor, *Finding Fiesta: A Comprehensive Price Guide*, Fiesta Club of America, Inc., 1998 (P.O. Box 15383, Loves Park, IL 61132-5383); Jeffrey B. Snyder, *Fiesta, Homer Laughlin China Company's Colorful Dinnerware*, 2nd ed., Schiffer Publishing, 1999.

Collectors' Clubs: Fiesta Club of America, P.O. Box 15383, Loves Park, IL 61132-5383; Fiesta Collectors Club, 19238 Dorchester Circle, Strongsville, OH 44136; Fiesta Collector's Quarterly, P.O. Box 471, Valley City, OH 44280.

Reproduction Alert.

Additional Listings: See *Warman's Americana & Collectibles* for more examples.

After Dinner Coffeepot, cov, cobalt blue 550.00
After Dinner Cup and Saucer
   Charcoal 550.00
   Chartreuse 625.00
   Cobalt blue 95.00
   Gray 550.00
   Green 85.00
   Ivory 25.00
Ashtray, red 50.00
Bowl, 5-1/2" d
   Green 60.00
   Red 34.00
Cake Plate, green 1,950.00
Candlesticks, pr
   Bulb
     Ivory 125.00
     Turquoise 110.00
   Tripod
     Cobalt blue 950.00
     Turquoise 890.00
     Yellow 550.00
Carafe
   Turquoise 380.00
   Yellow 275.00

Casserole, cov
    Red 275.00
    Turquoise 135.00
Casserole, French
    Yellow 275.00
Chop Plate, 13" d
    Gray 95.00
    Ivory 45.00
Coffeepot, turquoise 235.00
Comport, 12" d, Ivory, mkd 225.00
Creamer, stick handle
    Ivory 75.00
    Red 75.00
    Turquoise 115.00
    Yellow 45.00
Cream Soup
    Gray 60.00
    Ivory 60.00
    Rose 95.00
Cup
    Cobalt blue 35.00
    Dark green 45.00
    Light green 25.00
    Medium green 70.00
    Turquoise 25.00
    Yellow 25.00
Dessert Bowl, 6" d
    Red 45.00
    Rose 45.00
Egg Cup
    Green 50.00
    Red 70.00
Fruit Bowl, 4-3/4" d
    Cobalt blue 25.00
    Medium green 550.00
Fruit Bowl, 11-3/4" d, cobalt blue 485.00
Gravy Boat
    Ivory 20.00
    Turquoise 30.00
Juice Pitcher, ivory 20.00

Lazy Susan, yellow base, blue, red, green, and turquoise sections, yellow center, 10-3/4" d, $200.

Juice Tumbler
    Cobalt blue 40.00
    Rose 65.00
    Yellow 40.00
Marmalade
    Turquoise 325.00
    Yellow 360.00
Mixing Bowl
    #1, cobalt blue 375.00
    #2, cobalt blue 195.00
    #2, yellow 140.00
    #4, green 195.00
    #5, ivory 275.00
    #7, ivory 580.00
Mug
    Dark green 90.00
    Ivory, marked 125.00
    Rose 95.00
Mustard, cov
    Cobalt blue 325.00
    Turquoise 275.00
Nappy, 5-1/2" d, turquoise 25.00
Onion Soup, cov
    Green 895.00
    Ivory 950.00
Pitcher, disk
    Chartreuse 275.00
    Turquoise 110.00
Pitcher, ice lip
    Green 135.00
    Turquoise 195.00
Plate, deep
    Gray 42.00
    Rose 42.00
Plate, 6" d
    Dark green 13.00
    Ivory 7.00
    Light green 9.00
    Turquoise 8.00
    Yellow 5.00
Plate, 7" d
    Chartreuse 13.00
    Ivory 10.00
    Light green 8.50
    Medium green 30.00
    Rose 14.00
    Turquoise 8.50
Plate, 9" d
    Cobalt blue 15.00
    Ivory 14.00
    Red 15.00
    Yellow 8.00
Plate, 10" d, dinner
    Gray 42.00
    Light green 28.00
    Medium green 125.00
    Red 35.00
    Turquoise 30.00
Plate, 15" d, cobalt blue 62.00
Platter, oval
    Gray 35.00
    Ivory 25.00
    Red 45.00
    Yellow 22.00
Relish
    Ivory base and center, turquoise inserts 285.00
    Red, base and inserts 425.00
Salt and Pepper Shakers, pr
    Red 24.00
    Turquoise 135.00

Saucer
    Light green..5.00
    Turquoise...5.00
Soup Plate
    Ivory...36.00
    Turquoise..29.00
Sugar Bowl, cov
    Chartreuse..65.00
    Gray..75.00
    Rose..75.00
Syrup
    Green...450.00
    Ivory...600.00
    Red...495.00
Sweets Compote, yellow................................65.00
Tea Cup, flat bottom, cobalt blue 100.00
Teapot, cov
    Cobalt blue, large 335.00
    Red
        Large...225.00
        Medium...250.00
    Rose, medium 350.00
Tumbler, cobalt blue.....................................75.00
Utility Tray, red...55.00
Vase
    8" h, green 595.00
    10" h, cobalt blue....................................850.00
    12" h, yellow...950.00

FIGURAL BOTTLES

History: Porcelain figural bottles, which have an average height of three to eight and were made either in a glazed or bisque finish, achieved popularity in the late 1800s and remained popular into the 1930s. The majority of figural bottles were made in Germany, with Austria and Japan accounting for the balance.

Empty figural bottles were shipped to the United States and filled upon arrival. They were then given away to customers by brothels, dance halls, hotels, liquor stores, and taverns. Some were lettered with the names and addresses of the establishment, others had paper labels. Many were used for holidays, e.g., Christmas and New Year.

Figural bottles also were made in glass and other materials. The glass bottles held perfumes, food, or beverages.

References: Ralph & Terry Kovel, *Kovels' Bottles Price List, 11th ed.*, Three Rivers Press, 1999; Kenneth Wilson, *American Glass 1760-1930*, 2 vols., Hudson Hills Press and The Toledo Museum of Art, 1994.

Periodical: *Antique Bottle and Glass Collector*, P.O. Box 187, East Greenville, PA 18041.

Collectors' Clubs: Federation of Historical Bottle Clubs, 88 Sweetbriar Branch, Longwood, FL 32750; New England Antique Bottle Club, 120 Commonwealth Rd, Lynn, MA 01904.

Museums: National Bottle Museum, Ballston Spa, NY; National Bottle Museum, Barnsley, S Yorkshire, England; Old Bottle Museum, Salem, NJ.

Bisque

Man, 4-1/" h, toasting, "Your Health," flask style, tree bark back..85.00
Sailor, 6-1/2" h, white pants, blue blouse, hat, high gloss front, mkd "Made in Germany" 115.00

The Nineteenth Hole, golfer wearing yellow suit, 3-5/8" h, 3-3/4" w, $120.

Turkey Trot, 6-3/4" h, tree trunk back, mkd "Made in Germany". 150.00

Glass

Ballet Dancer, 12" h, milk glass, pink and brown paint dec highlights, sheared mouth, removable head as closure, pontil scar, attributed to America, 1860-90 ....525.00
Barrel, 9-3/4" h, sapphire blue 750.00
Bear, 10-5/8" h, dense yellow amber, sheared mouth, applied face, Russia, 1860-80, flat chip on back 400.00
Big Stick, Teddy Roosevelt's, 7-1/2" h, golden amber, sheared mouth, smooth base, flat flake at mouth 170.00
Bull, John, 11-3/4" h, bright orange amber, tooled mouth, smooth base, attributed to England, 1870-1900, ...160.00
Cabin, 9" h, two story, Kellys Old Cabin Bitters, dark olive green 5,675.00
Cherub Holding Medallion, 11-1/8" h, blue opaque milk glass, sq collared mouth, ground pontil scar, attributed to America, 1860-90 ....120.00
Chinaman, 5-3/4" h, seated form, milk glass, ground mouth, orig painted metal atomizer head, smooth base, America, 1860-90 ....120.00
Crimean War, bust of Queen Victoria, Omar Pasha, Lord Raglan, Marshal St. Arnaud, open pontil 95.00
Ear of Corn, 12-1/2" h, National Bitters, light yellow amber........400.00
Fish, 11-1/2" h, Doctor Fisch's Bitters, golden amber, applied small round collared mouth, smooth base, America, 1860-80, some ext. high point wear, burst bubble on base 160.00
Garfield, James, President, 8" h, colorless glass bust set in turned wood base, ground mouth, smooth base, America, 1880-1900. 80.00
Indian Maiden, 12-1/4" h, Brown's Celebrated Indian Herb Bitters, yellow amber, inward rolled mouth, smooth base, America, 1860-80 ......600.00
Monkey, 4-1/2" h, sitting, opaque white milk glass................200.00
Pig, 10-3/8" l, Berkshire Bitters, golden amber 1,200.00
Queen Mary, ocean liner, c1936 ....155.00
Shoe, dark amethyst, ground mouth, smooth base 125.00
Washington, George, 10" h, Simon's Centennial Bitters, aquamarine, applied double collared mouth, smooth base, America, 1860-80 .650.00
Woman, 13-1/2" h, Victorian, frosted, painted head 900.00

Pottery and Porcelain

Book, 10-1/2" h, Bennington Battle, brown, tan, cream, and green flint enamel, minor chips................................850.00

Camel, 4" h, mother of pearl glaze, oz............................45.00
Canteen, painted bust of Lincoln, Garfield, and McKinley, half pint..375.00
Cucumber, 11-3/4" l, stoneware, green and cream mottled glaze....100.00
Fox, reading book, beige, brown mottled dec..............................85.00
Mermaid, 7-1/4" h, brown and tan Rockingham type glaze........125.00
Pig, 8-1/2" l, gray salt glaze, tan highlights, one ear chipped, other ear missing..470.00
Pretzel, brown..75.00
Wolf, 4-7/8" h, sitting, reading book, brown, beige glaze, mkd "Germany"..75.00

FINDLAY ONYX GLASS

History: Findlay onyx glass, produced by Dalzell, Gilmore & Leighton Company, Findlay, Ohio, was patented for the firm in 1889 by George W. Leighton. Due to high production costs resulting from a complex manufacturing process, the glass was made only for a short time.

Layers of glass were plated to a bulb of opalescent glass through repeated dippings into a glass pot. Each layer was cooled and reheated to develop opalescent qualities. A pattern mold then was used to produce raised decorations of flowers and leaves. A second mold gave the glass bulb its full shape and form.

A platinum luster paint, producing pieces identified as silver or platinum onyx, was applied to the raised decorations. The color was fixed in a muffle kiln. Other colors such as cinnamon, cranberry, cream, raspberry, and rose were achieved by using an outer glass plating which reacted strongly to reheating. For example, a purple or orchid color came from the addition of manganese and cobalt to the glass mixture.

References: Neila and Tom Bredenhoft, *Findlay Toothpick Holders*, Cherry Hill Publications, 1995; James Measell and Don E. Smith, *Findlay Glass: The Glass Tableware Manufacturers*, 1886–1902, Antique Publications, 1986.

Collectors' Club: Collectors of Findlay Glass, P.O. Box 256, Findlay, OH 45839.

Jar, gold ground, 3-7/8" h, $425.

Celery Vase, cream...450.00
Creamer, 4-1/2" h, Onyx, platinum blossoms, creamy white ground, clear handle..485.00
Dresser Box, cov, 5" d, cream................................675.00
Pitcher, 7-1/2" h, cream, applied opalescent handle, polished rim chip..800.00
Spooner, 4-1/2" h, satin surface, bright silver dec, few small rim flakes..485.00
Sugar, cov, 6" h, Onyx, platinum blossoms, cream white ground, silver medallion on base of bowl, rim chip and roughness to cover ..485.00
Sugar Shaker, raspberry...495.00
Syrup, 7" h, 4" w, silver dec, applied opalescent handle..........1,150.00
Toothpick Holder, cream 375.00

FINE ARTS

History: Perhaps it was first the cave man who decided to brighten his surroundings with paintings. At some point, some one cleverly decided paintings put onto canvas or other mediums could be moved from abode to abode as well as cherished for years. Today, we find paintings and all types of fine arts at almost every auction, antique show, and antique shop.

In any calendar year, tens, if not hundreds of thousands of paintings are sold. Prices range from a few dollars to millions. Since each painting is essentially a unique creation, it is difficult to compare prices.

Since an essential purpose of *Warman's Antiques And Collectibles Price Guide* is to assist its users in finding information about a category, this Fine Arts introduction has been written primarily to identify the reference books that you will need to find out more about a painting in your possession.

References: Artist Dictionaries: *1999 ADEC International Art Price Annual*, ADEC, 1999; E. H. H. Archibald, *The Dictionary of Sea Painters of Europe and America*, Antique Collectors' Club, 1999; Russell Ash, *Impressionists' Seasons*, Pavilion, 1999; Emmanuel Benezit, *Dictionnaire Critique et Documentaire des Peintres, Sculpteurs, Dessinateurs et Graveurs*, 10 volumes, Grund, 1999; John Castagno, *Old Masters: Signatures and Monograms*, Scarecrow Press, 1996; Ian Chilvers, *Concise Oxford Dictionary of Arts & Artists*, 2nd ed., Oxford University Press, 1996; Peter Hastings Falk, *Dictionary of Signatures & Monograms of American Artists*, Sound View Press, 1998; Mantle Fielding, *Dictionary of American Painters, Sculptors and Engravers*, Apollo Books, 1983; Franklin & James, *1988-1998 Decade Review of American Artists at Auction*, Franklin & James, 1999; Christine E. Jackson, *Dictionary of Bird Artists of the World*, Antique Collectors' Club, 1999; David Joel, *Charles Brooking and the 18th Century British Marine Painters*, Antique Collectors' Club, 1999; J. Johnson and A. Greutzner, *Dictionary of British Artists, 1880-1940: An Antique Collector's Club Research Project Listing 41,000 Artists*, Antique Collector's Club, 1976; Blake McKendry, *A to Z of Canadian Artists & Art Terms*, published by author, 1997.

Introductory information: Alan Bamberger, *Buy Art Smart*, Wallace-Homestead Book Company, 1990; ——, *How to Buy Fine Art You Can Afford*, Wallace-Homestead, 1994.

Walter E. Baum, Perkiomen Mill, oil on canvas, $19,250. Photo courtesy of Sanford Alderfer Auction Co.

Price Guide References, Basic: *Art at Auction in America*, 1998 ed., Krexpress, 1998; William T. Currier (comp.), *Currier's Price Guide to American Artists 1645-1945 at Auction*, 6th ed., Currier Publications, 1994; — (comp.), *Currier's Price Guide to European Artists 1545–1945 at Auction*, 4th ed., Currier Publications, 1994.

Price-guide references, advanced: R. J. Davenport, *1999-2000 Davenport's Art Reference & Price Guide*, Davenport Publishing, 1998; Peter Hastings Falk (ed.), *Art Price Index International '98*, Sound View Press, 1998; Richard Hislop (ed.), *Annual Art Sales Index*, 28th ed., Art Sales Index Ltd., 1996; Enrique Mayer, *International Auction Record*, Paris, Editions Enrique Mayer, since 1967; Judith and Martin Miller (comps. & eds.), *Miller's Picture Price Guide*, Millers Publications, 1994; Susan Theran

Henry Percy Gray, CA artist, watercolor landscape, 10" x 14", $5,880. Photo courtesy of Jackson's Auctioneers & Appraisers.

(ed.), *Leonard's Price Index of Art Auctions*, Auction Index, since 1980.

Museum Directories: *American Art Directory*, R. R. Bowker, 1995; American Association of Museums, *Official Museum Directory: United States and Canada*, R. R. Bowker, updated periodically.

Collectors' Club: American Art Collectors, 610 N. Delaware Ave., Roswell, NM 88201.

FIREARM ACCESSORIES

History: Muzzle-loading weapons of the 18th and early 19th centuries varied in caliber and required the owner to carry a variety of equipment, including a powder horn or flask, patches, flints or percussion caps, bullets, and bullet molds. In addition, military personnel were responsible for bayonets, slings, and miscellaneous cleaning equipment and spare parts.

During the French and Indian War, soldiers began to personalize their powder horns with intricate engraving, in addition to the usual name or initial used for identification. Sometimes professional hornsmiths were employed to customize these objects, which have been elevated to a form of folk art by some collectors.

In the mid-19th century, cartridge weapons replaced their black-powder ancestors. Collectors seek anything associated with early ammunition—from the cartridges themselves to advertising material. Handling old ammunition can be extremely dangerous because of decomposition of compounds. Seek advice from an experienced collector before becoming involved in this area.

References: Ralf Coykendall, Jr., *Coykendall's Complete Guide to Sporting Collectibles*, Wallace-Homestead, 1996; Jim Dresslar, *Folk Art of Early America—The Engraved Powder Horn*, Dresslar Publishing (P.O. Box 635, Bargersville, IN 46106), 1996; John Ogle, *Colt Memorabilia Price Guide*, Krause Publications, 1998; Nick Stroebel, *Old Gunsights, A Collector's Guide, 1850-1965*, Krause Publications, 1999.

Periodical: *Military Trader*, P.O. Box 1050, Dubuque, IA 52004.

Museums: Fort Ticonderoga Museum, Ticonderoga, NY; Huntington Museum of Art, Huntington, WV.

Reproduction Alert: There are a large number of reproduction and fake powder horns. Be very cautious!

Notes: Military-related firearm accessories generally are worth more than their civilian counterparts.

Belt, 36" l, 2" w, 30 nickel metal clips for holding shot shells, canvas shoulder straps, nickel plated buckle with Savage Arms logo cast into it, nickel plated hook 350.00

Canteen, 7" d, 2-5/8" deep, painted, cheesebox style, dark red paint overall, one side painted I gold with a large primitive eagle with shield breast, the top of the shield red with cream lettering "No. 37," other side painted in gold letters, "Lt. Rufus Cook," pewter nozzle, sq nail construction, strap loops missing 1,650.00

Cartridge Box

   3-7/8" x 2" x 1", Hall and Hubbard, .22 caliber, green and black label "100 No. 1/22-100/Pistol Cartridges," cov with molded cream and black paper, empty, missing about half green side label 300.00

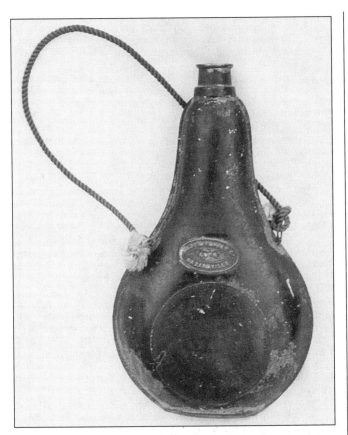

Powder Flask, tin, mkd "Indian Rifle Gun Powder," made by Hazard Powder Co., Hazardville, CT, 6-1/2" h, 4" w, $85.

3-7/8" x 2-1/8" x 1-1/4", Phoenix Metallic Cartridge Co., early green and black label, "50 Cartridges/32-100 Caliber Long," opened, but full 250.00

4" x 2-1/8" x 1-1/4", Union Metallic Cartridge Co., .32 caliber, cream and black label "Fifth .32 caliber/No. 2/Pistol Cartridges," engraving of Smith & Wesson 1st Model 3rd Issue, checked covering, orange and black side labels, unopened 210.00

Catalog, Stoeger Arms Corp., New York, NY, 1945, 512 pgs, 8" x 10", The Shooter's Bible, No. 36 .... 45.00

Dagger, Caucasian Kinjahl, Cossack, c1750 .... 750.00

Dirk, Naval, American, scabbard 600.00

Powder Flask
7-3/4" l, copper, emb shell 95.00
8-3/8" l, copper, hunt scene, swinging measure, stamped "Boche A. Paris" 145.00

Powder Horn
4-1/4" l, engraved spread eagle clutching American flag and arrows, ship under sail, various geometric and heart motifs, 19th C, losses, cracks 375.00
6-1/2" h, "E. K. B. 1831 Horn NH," dec foliate border, heats, star, and patriotic banner, rounded plug dec with hearts, centers inset brass button depicting eagle surrounded by stars 1,955.00
9" l, whale's tooth, engraved ship under sail, crosshatched diamond design, losses, cracks 350.00
13" l, "Daniel Chase his horn made in August ye 1786," dec with British coat of arms, townscape, hunt scene, reverse with gentleman, minor cracks and flaking 1,035.00
13" l, engraved fish, Indian hunting deer, fanciful figures and flowers, inscribed "John Mills his horn made at Crown Point, Ocf [sic] 4br 1758," minor insect damage, minor imperfections 2,000.00
13" l, engraved, initialed and dated "AB 1807," floral and geometric motifs 980.00

18-1/2" l, engraved coat of arms with dragons and crowns, soldier with kilt and feathers on helmet, officer tipping his hat, good patina, plug missing 660.00

Shot Flask, leather, 7" l, black pigskin body stamped "Sykes/Extra/lb/ 1," fitted with carrying ring, 2" German silver top with bright steel dispenser stamped "Skyes Extra" 85.00

Target Ball, 2-3/4" d, Bogardus, molded, amber glass, surface with overall net pattern, bottom with raised sunburst pattern, middle with 1/2" band "Bogardus Glass Ball Patd April '18 1877," chips at neck 200.00

Tinder Box, 4-3/8" d, tin, candle socket, inside damper, flint, and steel 330.00

Tinder Lighter, flintlock
5-1/2" l, rosewood pistol grip, tooled brass fittings 750.00
6-1/2" l, compartment for extra flint, taper holder 550.00

Uniform Button Mold, 9" l, brass, American, 18th C, casts 6 round buttons with central raised letter "I" for infantry, one 25 mm, one 18 mm, four 14.5 mm, each with eyelet, wooden handles missing 625.00

Water Keg, 9" x 7-1/2" x 9", wooden, American, late 18th/early 19th C, oval, flattened bottom, two Shaker style wide tongued wooden straps, large hand forged nail on each end for carrying cord, orig wood stopper 400.00

FIREARMS

History: The 15th-century Matchlock Arquebus was the forerunner of the modern firearm. The Germans refined the wheelock firing mechanism during the 16th and 17th centuries. English settlers arrived in America with the smoothbore musket; German settlers had rifled arms. Both used the new flintlock firing mechanism.

A major advance was achieved when Whitney introduced interchangeable parts into the manufacturing of rifles. Continued refinements in firearms continued in the 19th century. The percussion ignition system was developed by the 1840s. Minie, a French military officer, produced a viable projectile. By the end of the 19th century cartridge weapons dominated the field.

References: Robert W. D. Ball, *Mauser Military Rifles of the World*, Krause Publications, 1996; ——, Remington Firearms, Krause Publications; ——, *Springfield Armory Shoulder Weapons, 1795-1968*, Antique Trader Books, 1997; Ralf Coykendall, Jr., *Coykendall's Complete Guide to Sporting Collectibles*, Wallace-Homestead, 1996; Norman Flayderman, *Flayderman's Guide to Antique American Firearms And Their Values*, 7th ed., Krause Publications, 1998; *Gun Trader's Guide*, 15th ed., Stoeger Publishing, 1992; Herbert G. Houze, *Colt Rifles and Muskets from 1847–1870*, Krause Publications, 1996; ——, *History of Winchester Repeating Arms Company*, Krause Publications, 1994; Harold A. Murtz, *Guns Illustrated 2000*, 32nd ed., Krause Publications, 1999; ——, *Handguns 2000*, 12th ed., Krause Publications, 1999; John Ogle, *Colt Memorabilia Price Guide*, Krause Publications, 1998; Russell and Steve Quertermous, *Modern Guns Identification & Values*, 12th ed., Collector Books, 1998; Ned Schwing, *Browning Superposed*, Krause Publications, 1996; Ned Schwing, *Standard Catalog of Firearms*, 9th ed., Krause Publications, 1999; Jim Supica and Richard Nahas, *Standard Catalog of Smith & Wesson*, Krause Publications, 1996; John Taffin, *Action Shooting: Cowboy Style*, Krause Publications, 1999; ——, *Big Bore Sixguns*, Krause Publications, 1997; ——, *Modern Custom Guns*, Krause Publications, 1997; Tom

Turpin, *Custom Firearms Engraving*, Krause Publications, 1999; John Walter, *Rifles of the World*, Krause Publications, 1998; Ken Warner (ed.), *Gun Digest 2000*, 54th ed., Krause Publications, 1999.

Periodicals: *Gun List*, 700 E. State St., Iola, WI 54990; *Gun Report*, P.O. Box 38, Aledo, IL 61231; *Historic Weapons & Relics*, 2650 Palmyra Rd, Palmyra, TN 37142; *Man at Arms*, P.O. Box 460, Lincoln, RI 02865; *Military Trader*, P.O. Box 1050, Dubuque, IA 52004; *Sporting Gun*, P.O. Box 301369, Escondido, CA 92030; *Wildcat Collectors Journal*, 15158 NE. 6 Ave., Miami, FL 33162.

Collectors' Clubs: American Society of Military History, Los Angeles Patriotic Hall, 1816 S. Figuerora, Los Angeles, CA 90015; Winchester Arms Collectors Association, Inc., P.O. Box 6754, Great Falls, MT 59406.

Museums: Battlefield Military Museum, Gettysburg, PA; Museum of Weapons & Early American History, Saint Augustine, FL 32084; National Firearms Museum, Washington, DC; Remington Gun Museum, Ilion, NY; Springfield Armory National Historic Site, Springfield, MA; Winchester Mystery House, Historic Firearms Museum, San Jose, CA.

Notes: Two factors control the pricing of firearms—condition and rarity. Variations in these factors can cause a wide range in the value of antique firearms. For instance, a Colt 1849 pocket-model revolver with a 5-inch barrel can be priced from $100 to $700 depending on whether or not all the component parts are original, whether some are missing, how much of the original finish (bluing) remains on the barrel and frame, how much silver plating remains on the brass trigger guard and back strap, and the condition and finish of the walnut grips.

Be careful to note a weapon's negative qualities. A Colt Peterson belt revolver in fair condition will command a much higher price than the Colt pocket model in very fine condition. Know the production run of a firearm before buying it.

Flintlock Pistols-Single Shot

English

Blunderbuss, 29-1/2" overall, 14" round iron barrel with Birmingham proofs, fitted with 12-1/2" triangular snap bayonet, walnut full stock with lightly engraved brass furniture, 2 ramrod pipes, butt plate, trigger guard, small shield shaped wrist plate, 2 lock plate screw escutcheons, attributed to John White house, early 19th C, metal parts complete and orig throughout, missing sliver of wood along right side at muzzle 1,500.00

Tower, 60 caliber, 12" round barrel, full length military stock, brass trigger guard, butt cap and sidelined, lockplate mkd Tower behind hammer and crown over "GR" forward of hammer, proofed on left side of barrel at breech, crown on tang behind tang screw, good condition, re-browned and cleaned, replaced front sight, working order 700.00

European, blunderbuss, 70 caliber, 16" brass barrel, brass trigger guard and buttplate, full stock, lock plate mkd with crown over "R" under pan, good condition, mellow brass patina, working order, all orig 750.00

French Huguenot, dueling, sgd "Piereee Laffemand, Paris," c1640-80, 23" l, ivory stocks from pistol butt to barrel tip, barrels, butts, and trigger guards gold engraved with battle scenes, price for matched pr 122,000.00

French, military, 16" overall length, 9" round iron barrel, flat beveled lockplate with faceted pan fitted with flat beveled reinforced hammer, brass furniture, unmarked 800.00

Halsbach & Sons, Baltimore, MD, holster pistol, c1785 to early 1800s, 9" brass part round, part octagon barrel, 65 caliber, lock mkd "Halsbach & Sons," large brass butt cap with massive spread wing eagle (primitive) in high relief surrounded by cluster of 13 stars, large relief shell carving around tang of barrel, full walnut stock, pin-fastened 1,750.00

Kentucky, T. B. Cherington, 12-1/2" octagonal smoothbore barrel, stamped "T. P. Cherington" on barrel and lockplate, 45 caliber, brightly polished iron parts, walnut stock 2,500.00

U. S. Model 1805, 10" round iron barrel with iron rib underneath holding ramrod pipe, lockplate mkd with spread eagle and shield over "US" and vertically at rear "Harper's Ferry" over "1808," 54 caliber, walnut half stock with brass buttplate and trigger guard, Flayderman 6A-008.. 3,000.00

U. S. Model 1819, Simeon North, Middletown, CT, c1819-23, 10" round barrel, 54 caliber, smooth bore, barrel mkd at breech J//P//US, lock mkd ahead of hammer S. North over American eagle and shield motif with letters U and S at either side over bottom line MIDLTN CONN., date of production mkd at rear of lock below safety bolt, swivel type ramrod, iron mountings, sliding safety bolt, brass blade front sight, oval shaped rear sight on tang.. 850.00

Percussion Pistols-Single Shot

Note: Conversation of flintlock pistols to percussion was common practice. Most English and U. S. military flintlock pistols listed above can be found in percussion. Values for these percussion converted pistols are from 40 to 60% of the flintlock values as given.

Blunt & Syms side hammer, Blunt & Syms, NY, c1840-50, 6" octagon barrel, 44 caliber, barrel mkd "B & S New York," dec broad scroll engraving on frame, iron forend, ramrod mounted beneath, bag shaped handle, walnut grips 350.00

Caucasian Miguelet, extensive gold and silver inlay on stock, c1690-1720, butt had 1-1/2" split 5,000.00

German, dueling, sgd "A. J. Freund in Suhl," c1850.................. 700.00

John Dickson & Son, cased set, breech loading, under lever target pistols, 17-1/4" overall, 11" round barrel, caliber 45, flat matted ribs, sgd "John Dickson & Sons, 63 Princess Street, Eidenburgh," English scroll engraved steel but caps, actions, trigger guards, and locks fitted with sliding half cock safeties, well grained walnut stocks checkered at wrists, forends also checkered and fitted with horn tips, orig oak case, 20-1/4" x 11-1/2" x 3", heavy brass trimmed corners, orig accessories, complete with outer leather carrying case........ 7,500.00

Mule Ear, 9-1/4" overall, 5-1/8" octagonal rifled barrel, 44 caliber, large dovetailed brass front sight, open rear sight, simple mule ear lock with external mainspring, tiger striped full stock with simple brass forend cap and trigger guard, sear and corresponding notch of hammer restored, two small cracks in stock 500.00

Percussion Pistols-Multi-Shot

Belgian, side-by-side 4" round barrels, approx. .45 cal, double trigger boxlock percussion action and checkered bag grip, needs tuning 90.00

Colt

Navy, Model 1861, 7-1/2" round barrel, 36 caliber, 6 shot, creeping style

SPECIAL AUCTIONS

Sanford Alderfer Auction Company
501 Fairgrounds Rd.
Hatfield, PA 19440
(215) 393-3000
web site: http://www.alderfercompany.com

James D. Julia, Inc.
P.O. Box 830
Fairfield, ME 04937
(207) 453-7125

1861 Navy .58 cal., American, $375.

loading lever, barrel stamped "Address Co. Saml Colt New-York, U.S. America-.36 cal," cylinder roll scene depicts battle between Texas, Navy, and that of Mexico, one piece walnut grip 1,200.00

Paterson Belt Model, No. 2, 5-1/2" octagonal barrel, 31 caliber, 5 shot, barrel stamped "Patent Arms M'g Co. Paterson NJ Colt's Pt.," engraved cylinder, disappearing trigger, no trigger guard, flared walnut grips.. 5,000.00

Pocket, Model 1849, 3", 4", 5" and 6" barrel length, 31 caliber, 5 or 6 shot, octagon barrel with attached loading lever, barrel stamped "Address Co. Saml Colt New-York, U.S. America," cylinder engraved with stagecoach holdup scene, round trigger guard, walnut grips.. 600.00

Pocket, Model 1859, "6" barrel, 31 caliber, 6 shot cylinder, engraved stagecoach scene, "Address Col. Saml. Colt New York, U.S. America," mkd "Colt's Patent 12059," back strap engraved "Capt. R. B. Arms CoB. 16th Regt VT Vol." 6,325.00

Remington

Belt, New Model, 6-1/2" octagon barrel, 36 caliber, 6 shot, barrel stamped "Patented Sept 14, 1856/E. Remington & Sons, Ilion, New York U.S.A./New Model," round cylinder, threads visible at breech end, safety notches on cylinder shoulders between nipples 600.00

Navy, 1861, 7-3/8" octagon barrel, 36 caliber, 6 shot, barrel stamped "Patented Dec 17, 1861/Manufactured by Remington's Ilion, N.Y.," round cylinder, walnut grips................................... 675.00

Remington-Beals 3rd Model Pocket Revolver, cased, 4" octagon barrel, 31 caliber, 5 shot, barrel stamped "Beal's Patent 1856 7 57 758/Manufatured by Remington's Ilion, N.Y.," orig cardboard box with brass bullet mold, quantity of bullets, eagle and shield flask, mushroom shaped cleaning rod with screw-in type extension, extra pawl spring, can of Eley percussion caps.................................... 2,500.00

Revolvers

Colt

Cloverleaf, House Model, caliber 41 RF, 1-1/2" octagonal barrel stamped "Colt" on left side, 4 shot cylinder, walnut grips, hammer, trigger, and barrel with 98% orig blue, brass frame, orig light silver plate 2,450.00

1917 Military, 34 caliber, non-factory nickel finish, bottom of barrel mkd "United States Property," bottom of butt with normal markings, grips sanded and refinished 150.00

Flat Top, officer's model, target, .38 cal, 7-1/2" barrel, adjustable front and rear sights, silver medallion checkered walnut grips, 98% bright blue finish 400.00

Frontier Six Shooter, 44-40 caliber, nickeled finish, 7-1/2" roll marked barrel, black powder ram with rampant Colt black composition grips, accompanied by factory letter regarding 1893 shipment to Montgomery Ward in Chicago, 95% orig bright nickel, solid grips... 4,000.00

M.1901 Army, 38 caliber, blued finish, 6" barrel, half moon sight with smooth walnut grips, lanyard loop through butt, left side rear frame mkd with inspector initials "RAC" and "LEB," orig type commercial black flap holster 200.00

New Line 22, caliber 22RF, 7 shot cylinder, 2-1/4" barrel, varnished

rosewood grips, nickel plate finish, all orig, blued barrel with etched panel and even 75% blue, brass frame with 95% slightly dulled nickel plate 400.00

SAA, 32 caliber, standard blue and case color finish, 5-1/2" barrel, deluxe walnut medallion fleur-de-lis checkered grips, 97% bright orig bluing, orig case colors, bright bore 2,500.00

Harrington & Richardson, USRA target, 22 caliber, 7" barrel, checkered walnut grips, orig labeled carton with instructions on lid, 20% blue on forestrap only, balance 98% blue 750.00

Marlin No. 32 Standard, 32RF caliber, 3" round tip-up barrel, 5 shot fluted cylinder, steel frame with spur trigger, full factory engraved, fitted with DeGress grips, light grip with scroll and foliage relief, patent marking around screw hole, 1-1/2" h figure of standing woman surrounded by foliage, 95% of orig nickel plate 950.00

Smith & Wesson

M.686-3 DA, 357 caliber, 4-1/8" full lug barrel, red ramp, white outline sights, checked medallion magnum grips 200.00

M.1955, target, 45 caliber, blued finish, 6-1/2" barrel, partridge front sight, adjustable rear, target trigger and hammer and magnum checkered walnut grips, orig presentation box and paperwork 350.00

Walther Air Pistol MDL, LP3, .177 caliber, orig foam carton, tools and instructions, never used 350.00

Flintlock Long Arms

French, Model 1766 Charlesville Musket, 44-3/4" l orig barrel length, lockplate only partially legible, matching ramrod, top jaw and top screw period replacements 1,250.00

Kentucky, N. Beyer, 50 caliber, orig smooth bore, 58-1/2" overall, 42-1/2" part rounded barrel, orig front sight mounted on light engraved brass oval, sgd in script "N. Beyer" on top flat and secured to stock with incise carving on the forend to the faceted brass tailpipe, 2 faceted brass ramrod pipes and brass forend cap, beveled brass sideplate, raised scroll carving about tang with lightly engraved silver oval wrist escutcheon, incise carving at wrist on right side, left side with raised carved scrolls, a large raised carved scroll to rear of cheekpiece, engraved brass patch box with bird finial, typical Beyer beveled brass trigger guard, reconverted barrel and lock 3,650.00

Pennsylvania, attributed to W. Haga, Reading School, 50-1/2" l octagon to round barrel, maple stock, relief carving, incised details, brass hardware with flintlock, some age cracks, glued repair, good patina, replaced patch box lid 1,760.00

U. S. Model 1808, Thomas French, Canton, MA, Contract Musket, Harpers Ferry pattern, tail of lock stamped "Canton/1810," below the pan with the eagle and "US" over "FRENCH" (well struck with no trace of "T"), barrel stamped "US/V," with sunken eagle head CT proof (Flayderman 9A-131) 1,200.00

Virginia, curly maple stock with good figure, relief carving, old mellow varnished finish, brass hardware, engraved and pierced patch box, Ketland lock reconverted back to flint, silver thumb piece inlay, 41-1/2" l barrel and forend shortened slightly, small pierced repair at breech area, top flat engraved "H. B." 3,300.00

U. S. Model 1819, Hall, breech loading, second production type, Harpers Ferry Armory, John Hall's patents, 52 caliber, single shot, 32-5/8" round barrel, 3 barrel bands, brechblock deeply stamped 1,200.00

Percussion Long Arms

Note: Conversion of flintlock long arms to percussion was common practice. Most English, French, and U. S. military flintlock model long arms listed in the previous section can be found in percussion. Values of these percussion converted long arms are from 40 to 60% of the flintlock values previously noted.

English, 577 Rifled Musket, 39-1/4" barrel fitted with folding leaf long range sight, lockplate stamped with crown and "1863/Tower," walnut full stock with brass forend cap, trigger guard, and butt plate, orig nipple protector, complete with correct style English bayonet, excellent to mint condition 1,500.00

Kentucky Rifle, swivel breech, 51" overall, deeply rifled 38 caliber octagonal barrels, sgd "Jon Shuler/Liverpool PA," on both top flats, one side of the barrel group is a flat piece of steel, the other with four brass ramrod pipes, tiger stripped butt stock with engraved brass sideplate, light engraved brass trigger guard with double set triggers, engraved brass patchbox and toe plate, lightly engraved German silver escutcheon at right, 2" inlay on left side, back action lock sgd "N. Ashmore," old ramrod, probably not orig 1,200.00

Merrill, James H., Baltimore, MD, c1862-65, 54 caliber, breechloader, 33 round barrel, stamped with name and date forward of hammer, brass mountings and patchbox, full walnut stock, lug on right side of barrel at muzzle end for attaching saber type bayonet, complete and orig, 95% orig glossy brown finish 4,200.00

U. S. Model 1863, Rifle Musket, Type II (a.k.a. Model 1864), Springfield Armory, c1864-65, 58 caliber, single shot, muzzleloader, 40" round barrel, 3 barrel bands, lock stamped with eagle motif to right of hammer, "U. S./Springfield" beneath nipple bolster, "1864" at angle at rear section of lock, single leaf rear sight, walnut stock (Flayderman 9A-341) 850.00

Winchester, M.1866 musket, standard factory engraving, scrolls on right side of frame, similar scrolls on left side, standing stag within a round panel, light scroll engraving on top and bottom of frame with further scroll small area on top of buttplate, cleaning rod missing, accompanied by letter "...shipped from the warehouse on Mar h 24, 1877, with 345 other arms to order number 8365" 16,000.00

Rifles

Browning, safari grade, bolt action, cal. 257 Roberts, standard grade configuration, 22" pencil barrel on FN action, checkered wood with pistol grip Monte Carlo stock and engraved floor plate/trigger guard, high luster on wood, accompanied by 2 Browning letters stating this was special order 1,000.00

Harrington & Richardson Reising 60, semi-automatic, 45 caliber, blued 18-1/4" barrel, open rear sight, blade front sight, 12 shot detachable box, paint wood box, one pc semi pistol grip stock and forearm 450.00

Marlin

Model 94, lever action, cal. 38-40, standard grade, 24" octagon barrel, full magazine, straight drip stock with smooth steel buttplate, case colored receiver, 96% orig bluing, most orig varnish, brilliant shiny bore 350.00

Model 1893 SRC, cal. 38-55, standard carbine configuration, 20" barrel, full magazine, carbine ladder sight, plain wood with straight stock and carbine steel buttplate, 95% orig bluing, old refinish, shiny bore 400.00

Revolving percussion, underhammer, attributed to Elijah Jaquith, Brattleboro, VT, c1830, 52 caliber, 6 shot cylinder, 32" part round/part octagonal barrel, figured walnut stock with gothic pattern brass patchbox, hammer possibly replaced, some corrosion, split in stock 6,900.00

Winchester

M.67, single shot, 22 caliber, 27" tapered round barrel, open sights, nickeled bolt, blued trigger and trigger guard, 1 pc walnut stock, black composition buttplate, no serial number 125.00

M.68, single shot, 22 caliber, 27" tapered round barrel, ramp front sight with hood and Dockendorfer barrel mounted peep sight, nickeled bolt and trigger, 1 pc walnut stock, black logo composition buttplate, no serial number 165,99

M.75, target, 22 caliber, 28" round barrel, Lyman 17A front sight, Winchester rear peep sight, barrel mounted with scope blocks, receiver drilled and tapped 215.00

Model 94, deluxe factory presentation, 30 caliber, 26" part round barrel, ivory bead Lyman front sight, 3 leaf express sight, half magazine take down and 4-X pistol grip wood C-style carving and checkered in rare pattern, forearm with 90% coverage in 28 and 32 line checkering with scallops and florals with rect and circular patterns, pistol grip stock also carved and checkered with identical patterns having single major panel of 28 line and 3 smaller panels of 32 line checkering, adjacent to the receiver on either side are carved fleur-de-lis and half diamond patterns with scallops and modified lined carving at the pistol grip, left side of

receiver embellished "Compliments of/Winchester Repeating Arts Co.," upper tang equipped with Lyman style tang sight, buttplate is case colored crescent steel 13,500.00

Model 1890 case colored 2nd model pump, .22 cal, 24-1/2" tapered octagon barrel, fixed front sight, sight blank in the dovetail and Lyman tang sight installed, small ribbed forearm and straight drip stock with crescent steel buttplate, 95% bluing, 70% fading case colors, 90% orig varnish, shiny bore 1,000.00

Shotguns

Fox Sterlingworth, 16 ga, double barrel, 26" barrel, top lever break-open, hammerless, double trigger, blued, checkered walnut pistol grip stock and forearm 400.00

Ithaca, Grade 2E NID, 4-barrel set, cal. 10 ga, 32, 30, and two 28" barrels, all numbered to receiver and all fitted with ejectors and marked 3-1/2" chambers, one set of 28" barrels appears to be of later origin (mkd SB & Co.), all four sets mkd with Grade 2 designation, double beads, received fitted with single trigger and cocked indicators, typical Grade 2 engraved with standing quail on left side and woodcock on right with light coarse floral engraving to back and bottom, professional replacement wood with wide carved and checkered beavertail forearm, heavy carved and checkered cheekpiece buttstock, 14-7/8" over an Ithaca recoil pad, refinished trigger guard 2,000.00

Parker GHE, double barrel, cal. 28 ga, standard Parker configuration, 26" barrels on double "O" frame, double triggers and ejectors, splinter forearm, pistol grip stock, 14-3/8" over an ancient leather faced pad, receiver is game scene engraved with flying mallards, quail, and pheasants, surrounded by Arabesque patterns, 96% orig bright barrel blue, numerous small handing marks 6,250.00

Savage Model 720, 12 ga. 4-shot tubular, 30" cylinder bore, full coke, Browning patent, semi-automatic, hammerless, blued, checkered walnut pistol grip stock and forearm, plain receiver 200.00

Stevens, Model 970, 12 ga, single shot, 32" I round barrel with octagonal breech, top lever break-open, hammerless, automatic shell ejector, automatic safety, blued, case hardened frame, checkered walnut pistol grip stock and forearm 95.00

FIREHOUSE COLLECTIBLES

History: The volunteer fire company has played a vital role in the protection and social growth of many towns and rural areas. Paid professional firemen usually are found only in large metropolitan areas. Each fire company prided itself on equipment and uniforms. Conventions and parades gave the fire companies a chance to show off their equipment. These events produced a wealth of firehouse-related memorabilia.

References: Andrew G. Gurka, *Hot Stuff! Firefighting Collectibles*, L-W Book Sales, 1994; Ed Lindley Peterson, *First to the Flames: The History of Fire Chief Vehicles*, Krause Publications, 1999; James Piatti, *Firehouse Memorabilia: Identification and Price Guide*, Avon Books, 1994; Donald F. Wood and Wayne Sorensen, *American Volunteer Fire Trucks*, Krause Publications, 199_; —, *Big City Fire Trucks*, 1900-1950, Krause Publications, 1996 (Volume I), 1997 (Volume II).

Periodical: *Fire Apparatus Journal*, P.O. Box 141295, Staten Island, NY 10314, http://fireapparatusjournal.com; *Vintage Vehicle & Fire Engine Magazine*, Rt. 3, Box 425, Jasper, FL 32052, http://www.vintagevehicle.com/MASTOF97.htm.

Collectors' Clubs: Antique Fire Apparatus Club of America, 5420 S Kedvale Ave., Chicago, IL 60632; Fire Collectors Club, P.O. Box 992, Milwaukee, WI 53201; Fire Mark

Circle of the Americas, 2859 Marlin Dr., Chamblee, GA 30341; Gibson Road Antique Fire Association, 1545 Gibson Road, Crum Lynne, PA 19022, http://www.firefighting.com/grafa; Great Lakes International Antique Fire Apparatus Association, P.O. Box 2519, Detroit, MI 48231; International Fire Buff Association, Inc., 7509 Chesapeake Ave., Baltimore, MD 21219; International Fire Photographers Association, P.O. Box 8337, Rolling Meadows, IL 60008; Society for the Preservation & Appreciation of Motor Fire Apparatus in America, 5420 S. Kedvale Ave., Chicago, IL 60632, http://www.spaamfaa.org.

Museums: American Museum of Fire Fighting, Hudson, NY, http://www.firemumsumnetwork.org; Fire Museum of Maryland, Lutherville, MD; Hall of Flame, Phoenix AZ, http://www.halloflame.org; Insurance Company of North America (INA) Museum, Philadelphia, PA; New England Fire & History Museum, Brewster, MA; New York City Fire Museum, New York, NY, http://nyfd.com/museum.htlm; Oklahoma State Fireman's Association Museum, Oklahoma City, OK, http://tulsaweb.com/FIREMUS.HTM; San Francisco Fire Dept. Memorial Museum, San Francisco, CA; Smokey's Fire Museum, Chamblee, GA; Toledo Firefighters Museum, Toledo, OH, http://www.toledolink.com/~matgerke/~thm.

Additional Listings: See *Warman's Americana & Collectibles* for more examples.

Advertising
   Calendar, Quincy Mutual Fire Insurance Co., 1889, 3 rats playing with box of stick matches, burnt claws, coming to cat holding Quincy Fire policy, 9-3/4" x 6-1/2" 575.00
   Ink Blotter, Fireman's Fund 75th Year, Allendale, CA, fireman with little child, 1938, 4" x 9" 7.50
   Ledger Marker, Caisse General Fire Insurance, statue of Liberty illus, multicolored, tin litho, 12-1/4" l, 3" w 275.00
Alarm Box, mkd "Gamewell" and "Telegraph Station," 1880s 95.00

Whirligig, 2 firemen pumping, early paint, replaced base and post, $375.

Badge, brass
   Allison H. & L. Co., No. 2, pendant with 1" gray/black cello insert picture PA State Capitol Bldg, inscribed "Harrisburg, PA, State Fireman's Convention, PA, Oct. 3-4-5, 1923" 15.00
   C.B.F.D. No. 1/Cresson, PA, silvered, pale bronze luster over raised center relief image of fire fighting symbols, 1930s 20.00
Bell, 11", brass, iron back 125.00
Belt, red, black, and white, 43" l, mkd "Hampden" 85.00
Fire Bucket, painted leather
   12-1/2" h, green body, leaf dec banner "E. Sargent 1827," black painted rim and handle, some minor cracking to paint, pr 3,500.00
   13" h, inscribed "Garibaldi" in scrolled banner in gold, green, and black, red ground, leather handle, minor wear 3,080.00
   13" h, inscribed "Waltham Fire Club 1824 J. Hastings" in gilt on dark green ground, red band and int., handle missing, paint loss and abrasion 460.00
Fire Extinguisher
   Babcock, American La France Fire Engine Co., Elmire, NY, grenade, amber glass 500.00
   Hayward's Hand Fire Grenade, yellow, ground mouth, smooth base, 6-1/4" h, c1870 .... 85.00
   Red Comet, red metal canister, red glass bulb 50.00
Fire Mark, cast iron, oval
   8" x 11-1/2", relief molded design, pumper framed by "Fire Department Insurance," polychrome paint 495.00
   8" x 12", black, gold eagle and banner dec, mkd "Eagle Ins. Co. Cin O" 950.00
Helmet
   Leather, 4 comb type, painted red, black brim, gilt inscribed shield, " o. 3-EBD," orig padded straw liner, early 19th C 1,800.00
   Oil Cloth, blue, tin shield inscribed "Niagara 3 Brunswick," red underbrim, early 19th C 1,200.00
Lantern, Dietz, King Fire Dept., copper bottom 150.00
Magazine, *Blazes*, March-June issue, American-Lafrance-Foamite, Elmira, NY, 1950, 28 pgs, 8-1/2" x 11", articles and illus relating to fires, fire fighting 18.00
Nozzle, hose, 16" l, brass, double handle, mkd "Akron Brass Mfg. Co., Inc." 165.00
Parade Hat, 6-1/2" h, painted leather, polychrome dec, green ground, front with eagle and harp, banner above "Hibernia," back inscribed "1752" in gilt, "1" on top, red brim underside, some age cracks, small losses to brim edge 3,335.00
Presentation Trumpet, 16-1/4" h, coin silver, derby-style bell, inscribed "Presented by the City of Lowell to Mazeppa Engine Company No. 10 for the Third Best Horizontal Playing July 4, 1856" 1,500.00
Print, 9-1/2" x 13-1/2", hand colored lithograph, "Prairie Fires of the Great West," Currier and Ives, publishers, identified in inscriptions in matrix, period frame 320.00
Toy
   Arcade, fire chief car, cast iron, painted red, cast bell on hood, emb "Chief" on doors, orig decal on front hood, rubber tires, 5" l 1,650.00
   Arcade, fire pumper, 1941 Ford, cast iron, painted red, emb sides, cast fireman, hose reel on bed, rubber tires, repaired fender, 13" l 440.00
   Arcade, ladder truck, cast iron, painted red, two cast fireman, rubber tires, bed contains ladder supports, open frame design, 9-1/4" l 440.00
   Hubley, Ahrens Fox fire engine, cast iron, rubber tires, 7-1/2" l 475.00
   Hubley, Hubley Fire Dept., cast iron pumper, fire chief's car, hose reel truck, Harley Davidson with police driver, painted red, silver highlights, 9-1/2" x 14", orig box 2,750.00
   Kenton, fire pumper, cast iron, painted red, gold highlights on boiler, and ball, emb sides, disc wheels with spoke centers 615.00
   Kingsbury, horse drawn ladder wagon, sheet metal, pained red, wire supports, holding yellow wooden ladders, two seated drivers, pulled by two black horses, yellow spoke wheels, bell on frame rings as toy is pulled, 26" l 2,150.00

Williams, A. C., fire pumper, cast iron, painted red, gold highlights, cast driver, bell, and boiler, rear platform with railing, rubber tires, 7-1/2" l 315.00

FIREPLACE EQUIPMENT

History: In the colonial home, the fireplace was the gathering point for heat, meals, and social interaction. It maintained its dominant position until the introduction of central heating in the mid-19th century.

Because of the continued popularity of the fireplace, accessories still are manufactured, usually in an early-American motif.

References: John Campbell, *Fire & Light in the Home Pre 1820*, Antique Collectors' Club, 1999; Rupert Gentle and Rachael Feild, *Domestic Metalwork 1640-1820*, Revised, Antique Collectors' Club, 1994; George C. Neumann, *Early American Antique Country Furnishings*, L-W Book Sales, 1984, 1993 reprint.

Reproduction Alert: Modern blacksmiths are reproducing many old iron implements.

Additional Listings: Brass; Ironware.

Andirons, pr
   14" h, brass, belted ball top finials, turned baluster shafts, conforming log stops, sq strapped bases, sgd "John Molineaux, Boston," c1795, restorations 635.00
   17" h, wrought iron, gooseneck, rect stamp on arched legs, E. W. Wade, 19th C 320.00
   17-1/4" h, brass, belted urn finials, ring turned baluster shafts, spurred legs on ball feet, pair of similar tools, shove, and tongs, America, 19th C 550.00
   17-1/2" h, brass, double lemon top, early 395.00
   18" h, bell metal, belted ball top finials, short tapering shafts on sq plinths, engraved dec, conforming log stops, spurred legs with ball and claw feet, American, early 19th C 1,610.00
   18-1/2" h, brass urn finials, shaft through legs, knife blade, brass shield dec at bottom of shaft, sgd "J. C.," attributed to John Clark, late 18th C 1,100.00
   19-1/2" h, brass, faceted plinths, double belted lemon log stops, upturned spurs and pointed hoofed feet, America, early 19th C 1,100.00

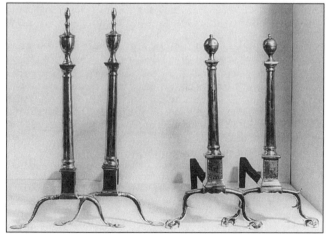

Andirons, left: brass, penny feet, Newburgh, NY, $1,800; right: claw and ball feet, plinth engraved with anchors and American eagle, $7,500.

Biscuit Oven, tin, $500.

   19-3/4" h, brass, classical, faceted and ring-turned finials and shafts, conforming log stops, bulbous turned legs on ball feet, America, mid-19th C 490.00
   22" h, brass, belted ball and urn-top finials, faceted plinths, conforming log stops, spurred legs on ball feet, New York, early 19th C 1,495.00
   22" h, brass, urn and belted ball finials above round plinths, spurred legs, ball feet, New York, early 19th C 1,265.00
   25-1/4" h, brass urn finials, shafts through top, iron knife blades, America, late 18th C 1,100.00
   25-1/2" h, brass, urn finials on tapering shafts above sq plinths, spurred legs, slipper feet, Philadelphia, late 18th C 1,380.00
   27" h, brass, urn finials on round tapering shafts, sq plinth, spurred legs, ball and claw feet, Philadelphia, early 19th C 4,715.00
Bellows
   15-1/4" l, turtle back, orig yellow paint, stenciled and freehand fruit and flowers, brass nozzle, old releathering, wear 365.00
   17-1/2" l, turtle back, orig white paint, smoked graining with yellowed varnish, stenciled and freehand red, green, black, and gold flowers and foliage, brass nozzle, professionally releathered 360.00
   18" l, orig red paint with stenciled and freehand gold, bronze, and black vintage dec, old worn releathering, brass nozzle 200.00
   18" l, turtle back, orig red paint, black, gold, and green cornucopia, brass nozzle, wear and touch-up repair, old releathering ... 385.00
   18" l, turtle back, worn orig red paint, black, gold, and green cornucopia, brass nozzle, deteriorated old leather 200.00
   18-1/4" l, turtle back, very work orig yellow paint with red, green, black, and gold cornucopia, brass nozzle, deteriorated old leather 150.00
Chestnut Roaster, 23" l, brass, reticulated detail, English 190.00
Coal Fire Grate, 24-1/2" l, 24" h, Georgian, iron, fire box with shell and scroll dec on to, brass reeded detailing to corners of box, serpentine front pierced and flanked by beading, front sq section tapered legs topped by urns, early 19th C 575.00
Fire Back, 22-1/2" x 27", cast iron, high relief design, anchors and fleur de lis arched crest, mkd "JFC," dated 1788 .... 1,250.00
Fire Basket, 15" w, 7-1/4" d, 15-1/2" h, cast iron, Neo-Gothic crocketed arcade, back plate with pierced floral crest surmounted by shell, French foundry plate, "Allez Freres," 19th C 225.00
Fire Fender, brass and wire, America or England, late 18th or early 19th C
   28-1/2" l, 9" d, 12-1/4" h, brass rim and bottom band, diamond pattern wire work 230.00
   29-3/4" l, 14-1/2" d, 9-1/2" h, brass top rim, vertical wire work, iron base 1,495.00
   31-1/2" l, 11-1/4" d, 12-1/4" h, brass rim and bottom band with four ball finials, diamond pattern wire work, iron base 1,265.00

35-1/2" l, 14-1/4" d, 12-1/2" h, wide ribbed brass rim and bottom band, two ball feet, intricately woven wire work, iron base 1,035.00

36-3/4" l, 15-3/4" d, 13-3/4" h, serpentine, brass top rim, three ball feet, vertical wire work and iron base, minor imperfections to base 1,495.00

39-3/4" l, 16-1/4" d, 17-3/4" h, brass top rim, scroll dec in vertical wire work 1,495.00

47-3/4" l, 15" d, 17" h, brass rim and bottom band with 4 ball feet, intricately woven wire work, iron base frame, some corrosion.......920.00

Fire Screen

49-1/2" w, 28" h, gilt-brass, three leaf, each with woven mesh panel in molded and beaded rect frame, incurved upper corners, surmounted by pierced, ribbon-tied berried-laurel crest, Belle Epoque, French, c1900 .... 250.00

53" w, 34-3/4" h, gilt-brass, four leaf, each arched leaf with tubular frame surmounted by bail handle, spherical terminals, Regency style 90.00

65" h, walnut and burl walnut, rect beadwork panel with foliate designs, incised gilt dec, cabriole legs, Renaissance Revival, c1875 .... 920.00

Footman, 9-3/4" d, 12" h, cast iron, round top with symbol of Isle of Man, outer belt lettered "Quocunque Jeceris Stabit," baluster standard, tripod base 175.00

Grate, 9" x 17-1/2", cast iron, mkd 19th C 90.00

Hearth Equipment, 12" h pr andirons, 12" d x 9" h trivet, 10-1/2" x 9-1/4" grill, wrought iron 490.00

Hearth Trivet, 11-1/4" x 13" x 11-1/2", shaped pierced top with heart handle, brass front leg, iron stretchers and rear legs, England, early 19th C...575.00

Kettle Shelf

7" x 13" x 12" h, turned wood handle, somewhat battered pierced brass shelf, wrought iron legs 330.00

10-1/2" x 16" x 10-3/4' h, brass, good detail, English, late 19th C 275.00

Log Box, 15" x 35" x 13", walnut, dovetailed case, hinged top ... 165.00

Pole Screen, 52-1/2" h, Hepplewhite, mahogany, acorn finial, turned suppressed ball column, adjustable oval screen, tripod base, spider legs, spade feet, old finish, PA, repairs to column, age crack in screen 1,980.00

Tools, 30" h stand, 3 brass tools, 19th C.................................... 125.00

FISCHER CHINA

History: In 1893, Moritz Fischer founded his factory in Herend, Hungary, a center of porcelain production since the 1790s.

Confusion exists about Fischer china because of its resemblance to Meissen, Sevres, and Oriental export wares. It often was bought and sold as the product of these firms.

Fischer's Herend is hard-paste ware with luminosity and exquisite decoration. Pieces are designated by pattern names, the best known being Chantilly Fruit, Rothschild Bird, Chinese Bouquet, Victoria Butterfly, and Parsley.

Fischer also made figural birds and animal groups, Magyar figures (individually and in groups), and Herend eagles poised for flight.

Museum: Victoria & Albert Museum, London, England.

Marks: Forged marks of other potteries are found on Herend pieces. The initials "MF," often joined together, is the mark of Moritz Fischer's pottery.

Cache Pot, 5" h, Rothchild Bird pattern, handled........................175.00

Charger, 13" d, multicolored enameled floral dec, gold grim 350.00

Ewer, 16-1/2" h, reticulated body, roe, blue, green, and gold enameled floral dec..295.00

Jar, cov, white ground, multicolored floral motif, raised relief medallions, reticulated fleur-de-lis, reticulated oval finial, 7-1/4" h, $275.

Jar, cov, 7-1/4" h, multicolored floral motif, raised relief medallions with reticulated fleur-de-lis, white ground, matching oval reticulated finial...275.00

Nappy, 4-1/2", triangular shape, Victoria Butterfly pattern, gold trim 150.00

Pitcher, 12" h, reticulated, multicolored floral dec 350.00

Plate, 7-1/2" d, Chantilly Fruit pattern 90.00

Sauce Boat, underplate, matching ladle, Parsley pattern 250.00

Tureen, cov, 8-1/2" l, Chantilly Fruit pattern, natural molded fruit finial, handles..350.00

Urn, 12" h, reticulated, blue floral dec, shield mark 250.00

Vase

13" h, 8" w, reticulated body, base, and neck, two winged serpent handles, blue, pink, and gold bands and accents, stamped in blue "Fischer J. Bugapest".. 395.00

15-1/4" h, 7-1/2" w, wide flaring shaped top, gold dec vine and fruit handles, turquoise background, front panel with pear shaped painting of birds in flowery landscape, back panel with flower spray on white ground, imp mark "C. F. 728," some loss to ruffled edge rim, pr.. 950.00

FITZHUGH

History: Fitzhugh, one of the most-recognized Chinese Export porcelain patterns, was named for the Fitzhugh family for whom the first dinner service was made. The peak years of production were 1780 to 1850.

Fitzhugh features an oval center medallion or monogram surrounded by four groups of flowers or emblems. The border is similar to that on Nanking china. Occasional border variations are found. Butterfly and honeycomb are among the rarest.

Reproduction Alert: Spode Porcelain Company, England, and Vista Alegre, Portugal, currently are producing copies of the Fitzhugh pattern. Oriental copies also are available.

Notes: Color is a key factor in pricing. Blue is the most common color; rarer colors are ranked in the following ascending order: orange, green, sepia, mulberry, yellow, black, and gold. Combinations of colors are scarce.

Basket, oval, reticulated, blue
    10-7/8" l 500.00
    11" l, matching undertray, handles 1,500.00
Bowl
    6-1/4" d, blue 220.00
    9-3/4" d, shallow, scalloped rim, blue 125.00
    10" w, sq, blue 325.00
Brush Box, cov, 7" w, 3-1/2" l, 2-1/4" h, blue, Nanking border, China,
    19th C, minor cracks 575.00
Creamer, 5-1/2" h, helmet shape, blue 450.00
Cup and Saucer, blue, set of 6 .... 395.00
Dish, 5-1/8" l, 5-1/4" w, scallop shell shape, c1770 .... 295.00
Gravy Boat, plain sides, blue 125.00
Jug, 12-1/2" h, blue 800.00
Pitcher
    6-7/8" h, blue 850.00
    7-1/2" h, blue 850.00
Platter
    13-1/4" l, blue, very minor chips 495.00
    17-1/4" l, blue, very minor chips 525.00
Rice Bowl, blue, pr 90.00
Soap Dish, 5-1/2" l, drain, blue 375.00
Sugar Bowl, cov, 5-1/4" h, blue 565.00
Teapot, cov, 5-1/2" h, drum shape, blue 1,200.00
Tureen, cov, undertray, blue, pr 2,750.00
Vase, 13-1/4" h, beaker shape, blue, teakwood stand 1,250.00
Vegetable Dish, cov
    12-1/2" l, rect, blue, liner 1,500.00
    13" l, cov, oval, liner 1,750.00
Wine Bottle, 10-3/4" h, blue 900.00

FLASKS

History: A flask, which usually has a narrow neck, is a container for liquids. Early American glass companies frequently formed them in molds which left a relief design on the front and/or back. Historical flasks with a portrait, building, scene, or name are the most desirable.

A chestnut is hand-blown, small, and has a flattened bulbous body. The pitkin has a blown globular body with a spiral rib overlay on vertical ribs. Teardrop flasks are generally fiddle-shaped and have a scroll or geometric design.

References: Gary Baker et al., *Wheeling Glass 1829-1939*, Oglebay Institute, 1994, distributed by Antique Publications; Ralph and Terry Kovel, *Kovels' Bottles Price List*, 11th ed., Three River Press, 1999; George L. and Helen McKearin, *American Glass*, Crown Publishers, 1941 and 1948; John Odell, *Digger Odell's Official Antique Bottle and Glass Collector Magazine Price Guide Series*, Vol. 3, published by author (1910 Shawhan Rd., Morrow, OH 45152), 1995; Michael Polak, Bottles, Avon Books, 1994; Kenneth Wilson, *American Glass 1760-1930*, 2 vols., Hudson Hills Press and The Toledo Museum of Art, 1994.

SPECIAL AUCTIONS

Norman C. Heckler & Company
Bradford Corner Rd
Woodstock Valley, CT 06282

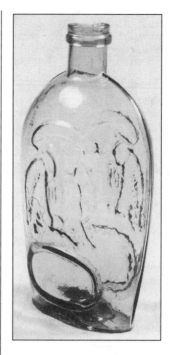

Eagle, pint, aqua, iron pontil mark, $90.

Periodical: *Antique Bottle & Glass Collector*, P.O. Box 187, East Greenville, PA 18041.

Collectors' Clubs: Federation of Historical Bottle Clubs, 88 Sweetbriar Branch, Longwood, FL 32750; The National Early American Glass Club, P.O. Box 8489, Silver Spring, MD 20907.

Notes: Dimensions can differ for the same flask because of variations in the molding process. Color is important in determining value—aqua and amber are the most common colors; scarcer colors demand more money. Bottles with "sickness," an opalescent scaling which eliminates clarity, are worth much less.

Glass

Chestnut, 4-3/4" h, Zanesville, OH, blown, 24 vertical ribs, amber, half
    pint, minor wear 250.00
Historical
    Double Eagle, Louisville Glass Works, Louisville, KY, 1955-60, vertically ribbed, pale blue green, sheared mouth, pontil scar, pint, McKearin GII-32A, manufacturer's mouth roughness, some int. haze 575.00
    Eagle-Cornucopia, early Pittsburgh district, 1820-40, light greenish-aquamarine, sheared mouth, pontil scar, pint, McKearin GII-6. 475.00
    Eagle-Stag, Coffin and Hay Manufacturers, Hammonton, NJ, 1836-47, aquamarine with pale yellowish green tint. Sheared mouth, pontil scar, half pint, McKearin GII-50 .... 325.00
    Eagle-Willington/Glass Co., Willington glass Works, West Willington, CT, 1860-72, bright medium yellowish-olive, applied double collared mouth, smooth base, half pint, McKearin GII-63 ... 210.00
    For Pike's Peak Prospector-Hunter Shooting Deer, attributed to Ravenna Glass Works, Ravenna, OH, 1860-80, aquamarine, applied mouth with ring, smooth base, quart, McKearin GXI-47, 1/4" shallow flake 325.00
    Masonic-Eagle, Keene Marlboro Street Glassworks, Keene, NH, 1815-30, pale bluish-green, tooled collared mouth, pontil scar, pint, McKearin GIV-7a 950.00
    Success to the Railroad, Keene Marlboro Street Glassworks, Keene, NH, 1830-50, light yellow amber with olive tone, sheared mouth, pontil scar, pint, McKearin GV-3 .... 250.00

Pattern Molded

4-5/8" l, Midwest, 1800-30, 24 ribs swirled to the right, golden amber, sheared mouth, pontil scar 190.00

7-3/8" l, Emil Larson, NJ, c1930, swirled to the right, amethyst, sheared mouth, pontil scar, some exterior high point wear. 250.00

Pictorial

Cornucopia-Urn, Lancaster Glass Works, NY, 1849-60, blue green, applied sloping collared mouth, pontil scar, pint, McKearin GIII-17, some minor stain 350.00

Flora Temple/Horse, Whitney Glass Works, Glassboro, NJ, 1860-80, cherry puce, applied collared mouth with ring, smooth base, pint, handle, McKearin GXIII-21 .... 170.00

Monument-Sloop, Baltimore Glass Works, Baltimore, MD, 1840-60, medium variated yellow green, sheared mouth, pontil scar, half pint, McKearin GVI-2, some exterior high point wear, overall dullness 1,100.00

Pitkin Type

Midwest, 1800-30, 6-1/4" l, ribbed and swirled to the right, 16 ribs, olive green with yellow tone, sheared mouth, pontil scar, some int. stain 300.00

New England, 1783-30, sheared mouth, pontil scar, 5-1/4" l, ribbed and swirled to the left, 36 ribs, light olive yellow 375.00

Portrait

Adams-Jefferson, New England, 1830-50, yellow amber, sheared mouth, pontil scar, half pint, McKearin GI-114 .... 325.00

General Jackson, Pittsburgh district, 1820-40, bluish-aquamarine, sheared mouth, pontil scar, pint, McKearin GI-68 .... 1,500.00

Lafayette-DeWitt Clinton, Coventry Glass Works, Coventry, CT, 1824-25, yellowish-olive, sheared mouth, pontil scar, half pint, 1/2" vertical crack, weakened impression, McKearin GI-82 2,100.00

Rough and Ready Taylor-Eagle, Midwest, 1830-40, aquamarine, sheared mouth, pontil scar, pint, McKearin GI-77 .... 1,200.00

Washington-Eagle, Kensington Glass Works, Philadelphia, PA, 1820-38, bright aquamarine, sheared mouth, pontil scar, pint, McKearin GI-14 .... 375.00

Washington-Sheaf of Wheat, Dyottville Glass Works, Philadelphia, PA 1840-60, medium yellow-olive, inward rolled mouth, pontil scar, half pint, McKearin GI-59 .... 9,000.00

Washington-Taylor, Dyottville Glass Works, Philadelphia, PA 1840-60, bright bluish-green, applied double collared mouth, pontil scar, quart, McKearin GI-42 .... 400.00

Gold, 7" l, 14kt, rect, rounded corners, vertical engine turning, flattened knop lid, monogrammed, R. Blackington & Co., early 20th C, 149.3 dwt.. 1,265.00

Majolica, 4-1/2" h, polychrome dec bulldog, landscape, and crest design, Italy, 19th C.. 200.00

Pewter, 14" h, Pilgrim, shaped figural handles, moon-shaped body, molded foliage, pierced base, losses, 16th C 345.00

Pottery, 3-1/2" h, shield shaped, eagle, brown glaze, "McKearin Collection of American Pottery" paper sticker, threaded neck repaired, screw cap missing.. 550.00

FLOW BLUE

History: Flow blue, or flown blue, is the name applied to china of cobalt and white china whose color, when fired in a kiln, produced a flowing or blurred effect. The blue varies from dark royal cobalt to a navy or steel blue. The flow may be very slight to a heavy blur where the pattern cannot be easily recognized. The blue color does not permeate through the body of the china. The amount of flow on the back of a piece is determined by the position of the piece in the sagger during firing.

Flow blue was first produced around 1830 in the Staffordshire area of England and credit is generally given to Josiah Wedgwood. He worked in the Staffordshire area of England. Many other potters followed, including Alcock, Davenport, Grindley, Johnson Brothers, Meakin, and New Wharf. Early flow blue, 1830s to 1870s, was usually of the ironstone. Variety. The later patterns, 1880s to 1900s, and modern patterns, after 1910, usually were made of the more delicate semi-porcelain. Approximately 90% of the flow blue was made in England, with the remainder made in Germany, Holland, France, Belgium, Wales and Scotland. A few patterns were also made in the United States by Mercer, Warwick, and the Wheeling Pottery companies.

References: Susan and Al Bagdade, *Warman's English & Continental Pottery & Porcelain*, 3rd Edition, Krause Publications, 1998; Mary F. Gaston, *Collector's Encyclopedia of Flow Blue China*, Collector Books, 1983, 1993 value update; ——, *Collector's Encyclopedia of Flow Blue China*, 2nd Series, Collector Books, 1994; Ellen R. Hill, *Mulberry Ironstone: Flow Blue's Best Kept Little Secret*, published by author, 1993; Norma Jean Hoener, *Flow Blue China, Additional Patterns and New Information*, Flow Blue International Collectors' Club, Inc. (P.O. Box 1526, Dickensen, TX 77539), 1996; Jeffrey Snyder, *Fascinating Flow Blue*, Schiffer Publishing, 1997; ——, *Flow Blue, A Collector's Guide to Pattern, History, and Values*, Schiffer, 1992; ——, *Historic Flow Blue*, Schiffer Publishing, 1994; Petra Williams, *Flow Blue China: An Aid to Identification*, revised ed. (1981), *Flow Blue China II* (1981), *Flow Blue China and Mulberry Ware: Similarity and Value Guide*, revised ed. (1993), Fountain House East (P.O. Box 99298, Jeffersontown, KY 40269).

Collectors' Club: Flow Blue International Collectors' Club, Inc., P.O. Box 1526, Dickenson, TX 77539.

Museum: The Margaret Woodbury Strong Museum, Rochester, New York.

Reproduction Alert: There are reproductions in flow blue and have been made since the mid-1950s. Many of these patterns look sloppy and blotched, with light blue allover background color. Some are plainly marked "flo blue" or "romantic flow blue" so the novice collector needs to be aware.

Acme, chocolate pot, cov, $550. Photo courtesy of Ellen G. King.

Advisor: Ellen G. King.

Acme, Hancock
    Cheese Dish, 2 pc. 350.00
    Chocolate Pot, cov 550.00
    Sardine Box, cov 275.00
Alaska, Grindley
    Butter Pat..45.00
    Plate, 10" d 95.00
    Relish Dish 220.00
Amoy, Davenport
    Creamer..400.00
    Cup and Saucer..165.00
    Pitcher, 5 1/2" h 325.00
    Plate, 10-1/2" d 175.00
    Potato Bowl, 12" d 1,000.00
    Razor Box, cov 550.00
Anemore, Minton, razor box, cov 295.00
Arabesque, Mayer
    Gravy Boat 250.00
    Teapot, cov, finial restored 500.00
Argule, Grindley
    Demitasse Cup and Saucer.....................................225.00
    Gravy Boat 175.00
    Oyster Bowl 250.00
    Sauce Tureen, top and bottom only........................500.00
    Soup Bowl, 7 1/2" d 70.00
Arundel, Doulton, ginger jar, cov 350.00
Aster & Grapeshot, Clementson, teapot, cov...................575.00
Athens, Adams, vegetable tureen, cov 400.00
Ayr, Corn
    Pitcher, 4 1/2" h 165.00
    Vegetable Bowl, open, 9-1/2" d 145.00
Avon, Furnivals, fruit compote, ftd 275.00
Bamboo, Alcock, soup tureen, top and bottom only 650.00
Basket, Godwin & Hackwood
    Child's creamer...500.00
    Child's sugar, manufacturing flaw on foot.............250.00
Belmont, Meakin, teapot, cov...425.00
Blue Danube, Johnson Bros.
    Butter Dish, 3 pcs. 450.00
    Butter Pat..48.00
    Plate, 10" d 95.00
    Soup Tureen, top and bottom only 750.00
Burleigh, Burgess & Leigh, butter pats, set of 12.............350.00
Campion, Grindley, pitcher and bowl wash set 1,300.00
Candia, Cauldon
    Punch Bowl..995.00
    Soup Bowl, 9" d, flanged 65.00

Candia, punch bowl, $995. Photo courtesy of Ellen G. King.

Clayton, soap dish, 3 pcs, $395. Photo courtesy of Ellen G. King.

    Tea Cup and Saucer...85.00
Carlton, Alcock, vegetable tureen, cov 475.00
Cashmere, Morley
    Cup and Saucer..195.00
    Soup Tureen, top and bottom only 2,250.00
    Teapot, cov 1,800.00
    Vegetable Bowl, 10-3/4" d, open 550.00
    Waste Bowl...500.00
Chatsworth, Myott, toothbrush holder, upright 200.00
Chen Si, Meir, relish dish, mitten shape............................250.00
Chusan, Clementson
    Cup Plate 150.00
    Sugar, cov...450.00
    Teapot, cov , small spot on spout 550.00
Chusan, Fell, creamer..350.00
Chusan, Morley, fruit compote, ftd 600.00
Clayton, Johnson Bros.
    Soap Dish, 3 pcs. 395.00
    Tea Cup and Saucer...80.00
Clayton Ware, W. & R., teapot, cov 365.00
Clover, Grindley
    Butter Dish, top and bottom only 225.00
    Platter, 16" l 275.00
    Tea Cup and Saucer...85.00
Coburg, Edwards
    Custard/punch cup 225.00
    Plate, 10-1/2" d 175.00
    Vegetable Bowl, 10 1/4" oval..................................150.00
Countess, Grindley, sugar, cov 275.00
Crumlin, Myott
    Creamer..250.00
    Milk Pitcher, 9" h 350.00
Delamere, Alcock
    Bone Dish 55.00
    Plate, 6" d 45.00
Doreen, Grindley, pitcher and bowl set 800.00
Dorothy, Johnson Bros.
    Bone Dish 50.00
    Butter Dish, top and bottom only 325.00
    Creamer..135.00
    Teapot, cov 450.00
Douglas, Till, platter, well and tree, 18" l 350.00
Duchess, Grindley
    Gray Boat, undertray 150.00
    Plate, 10" d 80.00
    Tea Cup and Saucer...95.00
    Vegetable Tureen, cov...275.00

Fairy Villas, plate, unusual edge gilding, 9" d, $135. Photo courtesy of Ellen G. King.

Eastern Plant, Wood & Baggaley, dessert set, 3 pcs................. 300.00
Eclipse, Johnson Bros.
    Creamer...250.00
    Dessert Dish, individual, 4 1/2" d..45.00
    Plate, 8" d..60.00
    Vegetable Tureen, cov...350.00
Excelsior, Fell
    Milk Pitcher..550.00
    Soup Bowl, 9"...90.00
    Waste bowl...100.00
Excelsior, Woods Well and tree platter, 20 1/4"....................650.00
Fairy Villas, Adams vegetable tureen, cov...................................375.00
    Creamer...250.00
    Plate, 9" d, unusual edge gilding..135.00
Festoon, Grindley, chamber pot to wash set..............................195.00
Florida, Johnson Bros., tea cup and saucer.................................95.00
Formosa, Mayer, plate, 9-3/4" d...100.00
Fulton, Maker unknown, sauce tureen, top, ladle, bottom,
    tray..255.00
Genoa, Meakin, pitcher, 6" h..175.00
Georgia, Johnson Bros.
    Butter Pat...50.00
    Creamer...265.00
Gironde, Grindley
    Gravy Boat, undertray...185.00
    Plate, 10" d...75.00
    Tea Cup and Saucer...85.00
Gothic, Furnivals
    Butter Dish, top and bottom only...425.00
    Milk Pitcher, 6" h..450.00
    Open Bowl, 9-3/4" oval..250.00
    Plate, 10-1/2" d..125.00
    Sauce tureen, top, bottom, tray (no ladle)..............................650.00
    Vegetable Tureen, cov...600.00
Granada, Alcock, milk pitcher..325.00
Hindustan, Maddock, plate, 8-3/4" d...125.00
Holland, Johnson Bros.
    Gravy Boat, with attached base...250.00
    Sugar, cov...350.00

Honc, Regout, bed pan...1,200.00
Hong Kong, Meigh
    Footbath, restored handle..4,500.00
    Pitcher and Bowl Wash Set..1,500.00
    Plate, 10-1/2" d..200.00
    Relish, shell shape..250.00
    Sauce Tureen, top, ladle, bottom, tray..............................1300.00
    Tea Cup and Saucer...195.00
    Vegetable Tureen, cov...400.00
Indian, Pratt, creamer...300.00
Indian Jar, Furnivals
    Open vegetable bowl, 9"..200.00
    Sauce Tureen, top and bottom only..375.00
Iris, Doulton, vase, 10" h, sponged gold....................................350.00
Iris, Royal Staffordshire, vegetable tureen, cov.........................275.00
Iris, Wedgwood, individual dessert/sauce dish..........................100.00
Iris and Bee, Doulton, chocolate pot, cov, 10 1/4" h..................375.00
Ivanhoe, Wedgwood, soup tureen, top, bottom, under tray
    (no ladle)...550.00
Janette, Grindley
    Pitcher, to wash set...495.00
    Vegetable Tureen, cov...315.00
Japan, Ridgways, vegetable tureen, cov.....................................275.00
Japan Flowers, Meigh, footbath, handle restored...................1,500.00
Kin Shan, Challinor, child's cup and saucer................................350.00
Kirkee, Meir, creamer..365.00
Kyber, Adams
    Plate, 10" d...125.00
    Soup Bowl, 9" d..65.00
La Belle, Wheeling
    Biscuit Jar, cov...475.00
    Bullion Cup with Saucer...950.00
    Demitasse Cup and Saucer...350.00
    Dresser tray, 8-1/2" x 12-1/4"...295.00
    Plate, 9-3/4" d...100.00
    Punch/Custard Cup...550.00
    Vegetable/Dessert Dish, individual, oval................................475.00
    Vegetable/Dessert Dish, individual, round..............................325.00
    Vegetable Tureen, cov..1,100.00
Lakewood, Wood
    Soup Tureen, top and bottom only..575.00
    Tea Cup and Saucer...110.00
Lonsdale, Ridgways, vegetable tureen, cov................................325.00
Lorne, Grindley, bone dish..65.00
Luton, Meakin
    Sauce Ladle, 8"...150.00
    Sugar, cov...135.00
    Teapot, cov...300.00
Manilla, Podmore Walker
    Cup Plate...125.00
    Teapot, cov...650.00
Marechal Neil, Grindley
    Platter, 12" l...155.00
    Soup Bowl, 9" d..45.00
Marlborough, Grindley
    Punch/Custard Cup...175.00
    Vegetable Bowl, open, round, 9" d..145.00
Melbourne, Grindley
    Soup Tureen, top and bottom only..495.00
    Vegetable Bowl, open, round, 9" d..225.00
    Vegetable Tureen, cov...325.00
Mongolia, Bros., plate, 10" d...120.00
Morrison, Doulton, ale pitcher, 10" d..265.00
Muriel, Upper Hanley, platter, 16" l..320.00
Neopolitan, Johnson Bros.
    Bone Dish...45.00
    Soup Tureen, top, ladle, bottom, tray.....................................500.00
Ning Po, Hall, platter, 15 1/2" l...575.00
Non Pariel, Burgess & Leigh
    Cake Plate, handled, 11" d..350.00

Creamer...295.00
Platter, 16" l 450.00
Normandy, Johnson Bros., sugar, cov 265.00
Oregon, Mayer
Plate, 10-1/2" d..175.00
Tea Cup and Saucer.......................................225.00
Teapot, cov 650.00
Oriental, Alcock, soup bowl, 10" d 150.00
Osborne, Ridgways
Platter, 17 1/2" l 325.00
Soup Tureen, top and bottom only...........................455.00
Oyama, Doulton
Plate, 10-1/2" d..175.00
Tea Cup and Saucer.......................................225.00
Teapot, cov 350.00
Pansey, Warwick
Candy Dish, fluted 125.00
Celery Dish, flat 150.00
Pekin, Dimmock
Plate, 9" d 70.00
Sauce Tureen, top, bottom, tray (no ladle) 450.00
Pelew, Challinoir
Pitcher and Bowl Wash Set 1,500.00
Platter, 18" l 1,000.00
Penang, Ridgways, teapot, cov 550.00
Persian Spray, Doulton
Humidor, cov..475.00
Jug, 6" h 180.00
Pitcher, 10" h 250.00
Pinwheel, Doulton, pitcher, 6 1/2" h 260.00
Portman, Grindley, platter, 18" l 450.00
Raleigh, Burgess & Leigh, plate, 9 1/2" d 65.00
Rebecca, Jones, plate, 8 1/2" d 125.00
Richmond, Johnson Bros., vegetable tureen, cov 355.00
Rhone, Furnivals, platter, 15" l 400.00
Rock, Challinor
Open Bowl, 10 1/2" d, octagon shape 265.00
Platter, 14" l 275.00
Rose, Bourne & Leigh, candlesticks, pr 375.00
Rose, Grindley
Platter, 16" 360.00

Pekin, plate, 9" d, $70. Photo courtesy of Ellen G. King.

Shanghae, teapot, cov, $875. Photo courtesy of Ellen G. King.

Vegetable Tureen, cov 250.00
Scinde, Alcock
Platter, 12 1/2" l 450.00
Platter, 16" l 500.00
Sauce Tureen, top, bottom, tray, restored edge to top 1,300.00
Teapot, cov 1,100.00
Vegetable Tureen, cov....................................795.00
Waste Bowl...400.00
Scinde, Walker, pitcher and bowl set, restoration to pitcher
spout 1,150.00
Shanghae, Furnivals, teapot, cov 875.00
Shanghai, Keeling, milk pitcher, polychrome, 8" h.........400.00
Shell, Challinor, cup plate 135.00
Sobraon, Alcock
Fruit Bowl, ftd, reticulated 1,000.00
Plate, 10-1/2" 225.00
Soup Tureen, top and bottom only 1,200.00
Temple, Podmore Walker
Creamer..350.00
Waste Bowl 250.00
The Holland, Grindley, butter dish, top and bottom only 325.00
Tonquin, Adams
Creamer..400.00
Platter, 12 1/4" l 375.00
Tonquin, Heath
Honey Dish, 4"...200.00
Tea Cup and Saucer.......................................325.00
Pitcher, to wash set 800.00
Touraine, Alcock
Butter Dish, top and bottom only 475.00
Butter Pat..65.00
Egg Cup 250.00
Soup Bowl, 9" flanged 90.00
Teapot, cov 950.00
Touraine, Stanley
Coffee Cup and Saucer...................................150.00
Plate, 10" d..200.00
Platter, 15" l 375.00
Udina, Clementson tea set, tea pot with lid, sugar with lid,
creamer 600.00
Unknown Patterns
Pitcher, blossoms, 9" h 425.00
Charger, Wedgwood, 16 1/2" d.........................650.00
Umbrella Stand...1,250.00

Vermont, Burgess & Leigh, soup tureen, top and bottom
  only 575.00
Versailles, Furnivals, vegetable tureen, cov 250.00
Victor, Rathbone, jardiniere, 9" tall 400.00
Vinranka, Sweden
    Milk Pitcher 325.00
    Tea Cup and Saucer 95.00
    Teapot, cov , sugar with lid, creamer 550.00
Wagon Wheel, maker unknown, creamer, 3 1/4" h 150.00
Waldorf, New Wharf
    Plate, 10" d 100.00
    Waste Bowl 275.00
Watteau, New Wharf
    Biscuit/Cracker Jar, cov 500.00
    Crepe Dish, cov, ftd 350.00
    Milk Pitcher 275.00
    Platter, 10 3/4" d 150.00
    Waste Bowl 185.00
Windmill, Warwick, chocolate pot with lid 425.00
Yedo, Ashworth, cake stand, ftd 325.00
York, Corn, cake stand, ftd 275.00

FOLK ART

History: Exactly what constitutes folk art is a question still being vigorously debated among collectors, dealers, museum curators, and scholars. Some want to confine folk art to non-academic, handmade objects. Others are willing to include manufactured material. In truth, the term is used to cover objects ranging from crude drawings by obviously untalented children to academically trained artists' paintings of "common" people and scenery.

References: Edwin O. Christensen, *Early American Wood Carvings*, Dover Publications, n.d.; Country Living Magazine, *Living with Folk Art*, Hearst Books, 1994; Catherine Dike, *Canes in the United States*, Cane Curiosa Press, 1995; Jim Dresslar, *Folk Art of Early America—The Engraved Powder Horn*, Dresslar Publishing (P.O. Box 635, Bargersville, IN 46106), 1996; Wendy Lavitt, *Animals in American Folk Art*, Knopf, 1990; Jack L. Lindsey, *Worldly Goods, The Arts of Early Pennsylvania, 1680-1758*, Pennsylvania Museum of Art, distributed by Antique Collectors' Club, 1999; Jean Lipman, *American Folk Art in Wood, Metal, and Stone*, Dover Publications, n.d. George H. Meyer, *American Folk Art Canes*, Sandringham Press, Museum of American Folk Art, and University of Washington Press, 1992; Donald J. Petersen, *Folk Art Fish Decoys*, Schiffer Publishing, 1996; Beatrix Rumford and Carolyn

SPECIAL AUCTIONS

Sanford Alderfer Auction Company
501 Fairgrounds Rd
Hatfield, PA 19440
(215) 393-3000
web site: http://www.alderfercompany.com

Garth's Auction Inc.
2690 Stratford Rd
P.O. Box 369
Delaware, OH 43015

Bag Stamp, gouge and chip carved, "William Peter 1834," PA, $280.

Weekly, *Treasures in American Folk Art from the Abby Aldrich Rockefeller Folk Art Center*, Little Brown, 1989.

Periodical: Folk Art Illustrated, P.O. Box 906, Marietta, OH 45750.

Museums: Abby Aldrich Rockefeller Folk Art Center, Williamsburg, VA; Daughters of the American Revolution Museum, Washington, DC; Landis Valley Farm Museum, Lancaster, PA; Mercer Museum, Doylestown, PA; Museum of American Folk Art, New York, NY; Museum of Early Southern Decorative Arts, Winston-Salem, NC; Museum of International Folk Art, Sante Fe, NM.

Birdhouse, 24" h, seacoast house shape, mansard roof and cupola, old red, gray, blue, white, and green paint, found in Kittery, Maine .. 1,815.00
Box, 2-3/4" x 4-1/4" x 2", wallpaper cov, poplar, dome top, tin hasp, traces of leather hinges, red, blue, and white wallpaper glued to light green, America, 19th C, int. staining, hinges missing 635.00
Calligraphy, 14-1/4" h, 8-1/2" w, watercolor and ink on paper, sgd and dated "George Macness, age 12, Salem, Massachusetts, October 24, 1812," framed, some toning and foxing 1,150.00
Checkerboard, 14-1/4" sq, wood, reverse painted with caricature of Zachary Taylor, mustard and dark brown paint, 19th C, minor paint wear 2,185.00
Figure, carved and painted wood
    2-3/4" h, bird, stylized, carved wig and head detail, serrated tail, painted green and brown, wire legs, domed sq base, Deco-Tex Carver, PA, 20th C 1,100.00
    5-1/4" h, rooster, pine, cross-hatched wing detail, orange, red, yellow, pink, and green, standing on grassy mound, Carl Snavely, Lititz, Lancaster County, PA, 20th C 400.00
    5-3/4" h and 6-3/4" h, hen and rooster, rooster in feeding position, head down and tail up, hen standing with head up, realistically carved, beige, black, red, and yellow, John Reber, Germansville, PA, early 20th C, pr 14,950.00
    6-5/8" h, gooney bird, stylized, chip-carved wings, black and orange paint, blue and yellow details, long legs, rect base, PA, early 20th C 520.00
    8-5/8" h, horse, standing, head up, carved mane flowing to one side, ears pricked, painted brown, black and white details, John Reber, Germansville, PA, early 20th C, small chip to ears 6,325.00

Figure, carved and painted pine oxen cart, orig painted surface, attributed to PA, early 20th C, 22" l, 5" h, $330.

10" h, fan-tailed rooster, standing, full bodied, head up, chip carved wing and tail detail, red, black, yellow, green, white, orange, and brown paint, domed mound, Schohaire County, NY, minor losses.. 1,380.00

13-1/2" h, elk, standing, head up and turned slightly left, ears priced, mottled brown and black paint, mounted on later rect wood base, John Reber, Germansville, PA, early 20th C 9,775.00

31-1/2" l, fox hunting group, 5 hunters astride horses, 12 hounds, figure of man holding a fox, snake, raccoon, and 2 birds in tree, mounted on rect base, George D. Wolfskill, Fivepointville, Lancaster County, PA, early 20th C 27,600.00

Glove Box, 4-5/8" h, 24" w, 7" d, bas relief carved mahogany, lid with foliate devices, stippled ground, centered initials "TW," rope twist borders, geometric designs, and "gloves" carved into sides, pale blue silk lining, 19th C, minor imperfections 300.00

Hanging Shelf, 16" w, 22" h, poplar, old dark finish, cut out floral crest, front molding on 2 shelves with punched zigzag design, minor damage and repairs 550.00

Lamp Base, 13-3/4" h, sewer pipe, tree and 4 stumps, naked lady, and lion, base incised "J. W. Moore, June 10, 1926, Uhrichsville, O. Evans Pipe Co." small chips 2,640.00

Rug, hooked, "Home Is Where The Heart Is," log cabin center, pine trees and fence 1,200.00

Scherenschnitte, (paper cutting)

6-1/4" sq, peacock in a tree, initialed and dated "MW 1805" lower right, period circular gilt gesso frame, American School, 19th C....... 460.00

12-1/4" x 11", image of Christ's face, done by Samuel Krauss, sgd in pencil lower center, Philadelphia, PA, Schwenkfelder, born in 1804.. 35.00

Sculpture

9-1/2" h, Indian head, buff colored sandstone, sgd "E. Reed" 525.00

40" l, rowing scull, painted tin and wood, composition articulated rowers, imperfections, America, c1920 .... 2,300.00

Theorem, American School, early 19th C

12" x 14-1/4", watercolor on paper, basket of flowers, unsigned, toning, fading, minor staining 575.00

12-1/2" h, 16-1/2" w, watercolor on velvet, roses and foliage, yellow, green, brown, and black, wear, selvage folded over and glued on board 85.00

15" h, 12" w, watercolor on paper, fruit and foliage, good detail, minor stains, gold painted frame.. 360.00

20" x 21", watercolor on velvet, ftd bowl with fruit, surrounded by birds and butterflies, sgd "Elizabeth Robinson, painted in 1810," unframed, creases, wear at edges, toning....................... 1,610.00

Watch Hutch, New England, early 19th C, carved and paint dec wood, tall case clock shape

8-1/4" h, foliate finials flanking central pediment, bracket feet .1,610.00

9-1/2" h, rounded finials flanking central peak, waisted case, wear to waist.. 550.00

12-1/2" h, scrolled bonnet, carved central rosette, losses, paint wear 1,840.00

Watercolor on Paper

4-3/4" h, 6" w, chicken, red, yellow, green, and blue, damage and water stains, matted and unframed 150.00

7-3/4" h, 5-3/8" w, graphite and gouache, Martha Barnes Aged 76 Years and 6 Months, partial family history inscribed on back, framed, minor staining and toning 1,725.00

11-1/2" h, 9-1/2" w, pen and ink, girl with flowering fabric dress, stylized tulips, and flowers, "Menta Chain 1846," green, teal blue, orange, brown, and black, old curly maple frame 1,100.00

11-1/2" h, 15-1/2" w, Bonaparte in Trouble, sgd "Executed by Jane R....ine," lower right, political cartoon with Napoleon on horseback being attached by lion and bear, lower margin inscribed "Explanation I the infernal spirit enticing Bonaparte with the Crown of Russia, 2 Bonaparte arrested ...in his progress by the Russian bear, 3 the British lion attacking him in the rear, having already wrestled from his power, the Crowns of Spain and Portugal and the Confederate Eagles of Austria and Prussia plucking the feathers of the Rhinish Confederation - The genius of Europe breaking the scepter of Bonaparte and loudly proclaiming Louis

the XVIII," framed, toning, minor scattered foxing, copied from etching by Amos Doolittle, published c1814 by CT firm of Shelton & Kensett 3,220.00

Whistle, pottery

4" h, bird with 3 baby birds, pink clay dog with yellow and black glaze 180.00

5" h, bird, white clay dog with red and black, chips, beak glued 150.00

5" h, goat, yellow and mottled black, wear and chips........... 285.00

5" h, sheep, pink and white clay, wear and chips 250.00

FOOD BOTTLES

History: Food bottles were made in many sizes, shapes, and colors. Manufacturers tried to make an attractive bottle that would ship well and allow the purchaser to see the product, thus giving assurance that the product was as good and as well-made as home preserves.

References: Ralph & Terry Kovel, *Kovels' Bottle Price List*, 11th ed., Three Rivers Press, 1999; John Odell, *Digger Odell's Official Antique Bottle and Glass Collector Magazine Price Guide Series*, Vol. 6, published by author (1910 Shawhan Rd, Morrow, OH 45152), 1995.

Periodical: *Antique Bottle and Glass Collector*, P.O. Box 187, East Greenville, PA 18041.

Collectors' Club: Federation of Historical Bottle Collectors, Inc., 88 Sweetbriar Branch, Longwood, Fl 32750.

Blueberry, 11" h, 10 lobed flutes, medium green, tooled rolled collared mouth 160.00

Catsup, 10" h, Cuyuga County Tomato Catsup, aqua, swirl design... 65.00

Celery Salt, 8" h, Crown Celery Salt, Horton Cato & Co., Detroit, yellow amber, smooth base, ground lip, orig shaker type cap 175.00

Codd, Lehigh & Sons, Salford, olive-amber, emb globe 50.00

Extract

Baker's Flavoring Extracts, 4-3/4" h, aqua, sq ring lip............. 15.00

L. C. Extract, label, orig box 180.00

Red Dragon Extract, emb dragon.. 20.00

Ginger, Sanford's orig label.. 12.00

Horseradish

As You Like It, pottery, clamp 25.00

Bunker Hill, aqua, label... 24.00

Lime Juice, 10-1/4" h, arrow motif, olive amber, smooth base, applied mouth 85.00

Milk

Cloverleaf Creamery Co., quart.. 85.00

Dellinger Dairy Farm, Jefferson, IN 25.00

Holsgern Farms Dairy, quart, tin top and closure 90.00

Purity Dairy, pint 60.00

Scott's Dairy, quart, emb 30.00

Wonsidlers Dairy, quart 25.00

Mustard

Blossom Brand Prepared Mustard, wire bale, orig label 22.00

Giessen's Union Mustard, 4-3/8" h, clear, eagle..................... 85.00

Olive Oil

7-1/2" h, Bertin Brand Pure Olive Oil, dark green................... 18.00

11" h, Elwood Cooper Pure Olive Oil, aqua............................ 45.00

Peanut Butter, 5" h, Bennett Hubba....................................... 20.00

Pepper Sauce

8" h, S & P Pat. Appl. For, teal blue, smooth base, tooled lip 50.00

8-7/8" h, W & E Peppersauce, sq, aqua 165.00

Pickle, cathedral, America, 1845-80, sq, beveled corners

10-5/8" h, 4 fancy cathedral arch designs, medium green, tooled rolled mouth, smooth base 650.00

11-1/2" h, 3 fancy cathedral designs, greenish-aqua, tooled rolled mouth, smooth base 150.00
11-3/4" h, 4 different fancy cathedral arch designs, protruding irregular panels, aquamarine, tooled sq mouth, iron pontil mark170.00
13-5/8" h, sq, medium green, tooled collared mouth, pontil scar, Willington Glass Works, CT 2,200.00
Syrup, 12-1/4" h, Boston Cooler, clear, blue and gold label, tooled mouth, metal cap, smooth base, c1900 .... 350.00
Vinegar, Weso Biko Co. Cider Vinegar, jug shape 45.00

FOOD MOLDS

History: Food molds were used both commercially and in the home. Generally, pewter ice cream molds and candy molds were used commercially; pottery and copper molds were used in homes. Today, both types are collected largely for decorative purposes.

The majority of pewter ice cream molds are individual serving molds. One quart of ice cream would make eight to ten pieces. Scarcer, but still available, are banquet molds which used two to four pints of ice cream. European-made pewter molds are available.

Marks: Pewter ice cream molds were made primarily by two American companies: Eppelsheimer & Co. (molds marked "E & Co., N.Y.") and Schall & Co. (marked "S & Co."). Both companies used a numbering system for their molds. The Krauss Co. bought out Schall & Co., removed the "S & Co." from some, but not all, of the molds, and added more designs (pieces marked "K" or "Krauss"). "CC" is a French mold mark.

Manufacturers of chocolate molds are more difficult to determine. Unlike the pewter ice cream molds, makers' marks were not always used or were covered by frames. Eppelsheimer & Co. of New York marked many of their molds, either with their name or with a design resembling a child's toy top and the words "Trade Mark" and "NY." Many chocolate molds were imported from Germany and Holland and were marked with the country of origin and, in some cases, the mold-maker's name.

Reference: Judene Divone, *Chocolate Moulds*, Oakton Hills Publications, 1987.

Museum: Wilbur's American Candy Museum, Lititz, PA.

Additional Listings: Butter Prints.

Chocolate Mold

Basket, 3-1/2" x 6", one cavity 50.00
Boy on bicycle, 8-1/4" h, 2 parts 395.00
Catalog, Anton Reich, 13" x 17", 86 pgs 2,420.00
Chick and egg, 3-1/2" h, two parts, folding, mkd "Allemagne," Germany 65.00
Easter Rabbit, 18-1/2" h, standing, two part mold, separate two part molds for ears and front legs, "Anton Reiche, Dresden, Germany"..........220.00
Elephant, tin, 3 cavities 95.00
Fish 95.00
Heart, 6-1/2" x 6", 2 cavities 70.00
Hen on basket, 2 pcs, clamp type, mkd "E. & Co./Toy"............... 60.00
Pig 95.00
Rabbits, 10-1/2" l, 3 cavities, sitting, tin plated steel, folding, two part mold 70.00
Skeleton, 5-1/2" h, pressed tin 60.00
Teddy Bear, 2 pcs, clamp type, mkd "Reiche"....................... 295.00
Turkey, 14" x 10", tray type, 8 cavitities 65.00
Witch, 4-1/2" x 2", 4 cavities 75.00

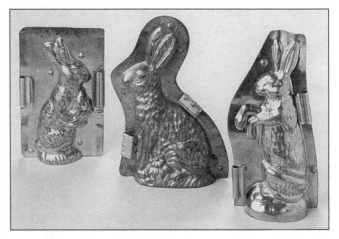

Chocolate Mold, tin, each 2 part, orig clamps, rabbits, $95 to $125 each.

Food Mold

Butter, 4-1/2" x 6-7/8", rect cased, cherry, deep carved geometric design.. 125.00
Cake, rabbit, Griswold.. 265.00
Cheese, 5" x 13", wood, relief carved design and "Bid," pinned, branded "Los," carved scratch date 1893 .... 60.00
Pudding, tin and copper
    4-1/2" d, round, star, ribbed sides.......................... 175.00
    5" x 5" x 6-1/2", oval, pineapple............................ 95.00
    6" l, oval, trimmed copper eagle 195.00
    6-1/2" d, round, fruit design 125.00
    8" l, oval, lion.. 220.00
    9" l, rect, oval sheaf...................................... 175.00

Ice Cream Mold, pewter

Asparagus, 3-5/8" h 35.00
Basket, replaced hinge pins... 25.00
Camel, pewter, mkd "E & Co. NY, #681"............................... 75.00
Cherub riding Easter Bunny, 4" h.................................... 45.00
Circle, mkd "Kiwanis Club" and "E & Co. NY"......................... 25.00
Easter Lily, 3 part 75.00
Egg, 2-3/4" d, mkd "E & Co. NY" 35.00
Flag, 13 stars 95.00
Fruit, 2-3/4" d, mkd "E & Co. NY"................................... 30.00
Heart with Cupid, 4" h.. 65.00
Hen, 3-3/4" h... 85.00
Man in the Moon, 5-1/2" h, mkd "E & Co. copyright 1888" 95.00
Naked lady with drape, 3 part, 5-1/4" h............................. 275.00
Owl, banquet size, 4 pints, mid "S & Co. 7"........................ 600.00
Pear, banquet size, mkd "S & Co. 17"................................ 325.00
Potato, 4" h, pewter 70.00
Rose, two part, 3-1/2" d.. 125.00
Ship, banquet size, 2 quarts 265.00
Steamboat... 115.00
Tulip, 4-1/8" h, mkd "E. & Co. NY".................................. 45.00

FOSTORIA GLASS

History: Fostoria Glass Co. began operations at Fostoria, Ohio, in 1887, and moved to Moundsville, West Virginia, its present location, in 1891. By 1925, Fostoria had five furnaces and a variety of special shops. In 1924, a line of colored tableware was introduced. Fostoria was purchased by Lancaster Colony in 1983 and continues to operate under the Fostoria name.

References: Frances Bones, *Fostoria Glassware; 1887-1982*, Collector Books, 1999; Gene Florence, *Elegant Glassware of the Depression Era*, 8th ed., Collector Books, 1998; Ann Kerr, *Fostoria: An Identification and Value Guide of Pressed, Blown, & Hand Molded Shapes* (1994, 1997 values), *Etched, Carved & Cut Designs* (1996, 1997 values) Collector Books; Milbra Long and Emily Seate, *Fostoria Stemware*, Collector Books, 1995, ——, *Fostoria Tableware, 1924-1943*, Collector Books, 1999; ——, *Fostoria Tableware 1944-1986*, Collector Books, 1999; Gary Schneider, Melanie Hildreth, Therese Ujfalusi and Irene Gardner, *Navarre by Fostoria, Past Reflections*, 1998.

Periodical: *The Daze*, P.O. Box 57, Otisville, MI 48463.

Collectors' Clubs: Fostoria Glass Collectors, Inc., P.O. Box 1625, Orange, CA 92856; Fostoria Glass Society of America, P.O. Box 826, Moundsville, WV 26041.

Museums: Fostoria Glass Museum, Moundsville, WV; Huntington Galleries, Huntington, WV.

Ashtray
    Century, individual size 12.00
    Coin, crystal 30.00
    June, blue 75.00
Basket, American, reeded handle 210.00
Berry Bowl, June, blue, 5" d 50.00
Bowl
    Baroque, blue, 4" sq, 1 handle 22.00
    Century, 10-1/2" d 35.00
    Coin, emerald, 8" d 110.00
    June, 12" d, blue 125.00
Bud Vase, Coin, crystal, 8" h 17.00
Cake Salver
    Century, crystal 60.00
    Coin, crystal 98.00
    Corsage, 10-1/2" d 32.00
Candleholders, pr
    Baroque, 4" h, 1-lite, silver deposit Vintage dec on base, #2496 .... 75.00
    Baroque, 8-1/2" h, 10" w, 2-lite, removable bobeche and prisms, #2484 .... 375.00
    Buttercup, 8" h, 8" w 150.00
    Coin, red, tall 150.00
    Meadow Rose 185.00
    Midnight Rose, #2472, etched, 5" h, 8" w 150.00
    Navarre, #2496 .... 185.00
    Trindle, #2594, 3-lite, Buttercup etch, 8" h, 6-1/2" w 250.00
Candy Dish, cov
    Baroque, crystal 40.00
    Coin, amber, 6-1/2" d 20.00
    June, yellow 370.00
    Navarre, 3 part 175.00
    Versailles, blue, 3 part 345.00
Card Tray, Brocaded Daffodil, 2 handles, pink, gold trim 40.00
Celery Tray, 5 part
    Lido 100.00
    Navarre 175.00
Champagne
    Chintz 20.00
    Navarre 22.00
Cheese and Cracker
    Chintz 70.00
    Colony 55.00
Cigarette Box, cov
    Morning Glory etching 65.00
    Oriental 170.00

Claret
    Camelia 30.00
    June, pink 175.00
    Navarre 80.00
    Trojan, yellow, 6" h 100.00
Cocktail, Baroque, yellow 15.00
Compote
    Baroque, crystal, 6" 18.00
    Century, 4-1/2" 20.00
Condiment Set, American, pr salt and pepper shakers, pr, cloverleaf tray, pr cruets 200.00
Console Set
    Brocaded Palms, 14" oval console bowl, pr candlesticks, white 70.00
    Chintz, 12" oval flame bowl, pr double candlesticks 185.00
Cordial, Holly 30.00
Courting Lamp, Coin, amber 150.00
Creamer, individual size
    Century 9.00
    Raleigh 8.00
Creamer, table size
    Chintz 20.00
    Raleigh 10.00
Creamer, Sugar, Tray, individual size
    Camelia 45.00
    Century 30.00
Cream Soup
    Colony 95.00
    Versailles, pink 65.00
    Vesper, amber 30.00
Cruet, June, yellow 700.00
Cup and Saucer
    Baroque, blue 35.00
    Buttercup 21.00
    Camelia 20.00
    Fairfax, crystal 7.00
    Raleigh 6.50
    Rose 25.00
Dinner Plate
    American 20.00
    Colony, slight use 18.00
    June, pink, 10-1/4" d 160.00
    Lido 45.00
Float Bowl, Century, 8-1/2" d 35.00
Goblet, water
    Baroque, crystal 12.00
    Captiva, light blue 12.00
    Century 22.00
    Chintz 33.00
    Coin, red 105.00
    Jamestown, blue 20.00
    June, yellow 55.00
    Meadow Rose 30.00
    Navarre 40.00
Grapefruit, Coronet 9.00
Gravy Boat, liner, Kasmir, blue 180.00
Ice Bucket
    Brocaded Palms, ice green, irid, gold trim 110.00
    Shirley 50.00
    Sunray 50.00
Iced Tea Tumbler, Jamestown, brown 10.00
Jelly, cov
    Coin, amber 30.00
    Meadow Rose, 7-1/2" d 90.0
Juice Tumbler
    Captiva, light blue 12.00
    Jamestown, blue 25.00
    Navarre 27.00
Lily Pond, Buttercup, 12" d 55.00

Pitcher, American pattern, straight sides, ice lip, 8-1/4" h, $165.

Marmalade, cov, American, 125.00
Mayonnaise, liner, Navarre 90.00
Milk Pitcher, Century 60.00
Muffin Plate, Century, 9-1/2" d 30.00
Nappy, handle
    Century, 4-1/2" d 12.00
    Coin, blue, 5-3/8" d 30.00
Nut Cup, Fairfax, amber 15.00
Oil Cruet
    Century 50.00
    Versailles, yellow 550.00
Old Fashioned Tumbler, Coin, crystal 30.00
Oyster Cocktail
    Colony 12.00
    Holly 15.00
Parfait, June, pink 180.00
Pickle
    Century, 8-3/4" 15.00
    Colony, 2 part 16.00
Pitcher, Lido, ftd 225.00
Plate
    Baroque, blue, 7-1/2" d 15.00
    Century, 9-1/2" d 30.00
    Rose, 9" d 15.00
Platter, Versailles, pink, 15" l, oval 350.00
Punch Bowl, ftd, Baroque, crystal, orig label 425.00
Relish Dish, cov, Brocaded Summer Gardens, 3 sections, white . 75.00
Relish Dish, open
    American, divided, small.. 18.00
    Baroque, blue, 4 part 225.00
    Corsage, 5 part 58.00
    Fairfax, yellow, 3 part, 11-1/2" l............................... 15.00
    Romance, 2 part, 8-1/2" l 25.00
Rose Bowl, American, small 18.00
Salad Plate
    Buttercup 12.00
    June 14.00
Salt and Pepper Shakers, pr
    Century 20.00
    Coin, red.. 60.00
    Coronet 15.00
    Virginia, amber 20.00
Sauce Boat, Versailles, green....................................... 240.00
Sherbet
    Baroque, blue 25.00
    Buttercup, low 18.00
    Chintz 22.00
    Holly, tall 12.00

    Jamestown, amber 6.00
    Seville, amber, high 10.00
    Sunray, blue... 19.00
Snack Plate, Century, 8" d 25.00
Sugar, individual size
    Baroque, blue 4.00
    Raleigh 8.00
Sugar, cov, table size
    Chintz 20.00
    Fairfax, orchid, ftd 10.00
    Lido.. 9.00
Syrup, cov, matching underplate, Mayfair, yellow 125.00
Tidbit, 12" d, six-sided, Brocaded Summer Garden, white 45.00
Torte Plate
    Century, 14" d 30.00
    Colony, 15" d 80.00
    Heather, 13" d 45.00
Tray, Navarre, 8" l 100.00
Tumbler, water
    Chintz 33.00
    Colony 18.00
Urn, cov, Coin, amber, 12-3/4" h 68.00
Vanity Set, #2276, pink 125.00
Vase
    Century, 8-1/2" h.. 125.00
    June, yellow, 8" h.. 575.00
    Meadow Rose, 9-1/2" h 260.00
    Minuet, yellow, 6-3/4" h 250.00
    Versailles, yellow, 8" h, flip 395.00
Whipped Cream Pail, Versailles, blue............................ 270.00
Whiskey, June, yellow 85.,00
Wine
    Chintz 40.00
    Coin, red 90.00
    Jamestown, green 20.00
    June, pink 118.00

FRAKTUR

History: Fraktur, the calligraphy associated with the Pennsylvania Germans, is named for the elaborate first letter found in many of the hand-drawn examples. Throughout its history, printed, partially printed/partially hand-drawn, and fully hand-drawn works existed side by side. Frakturs often were made by schoolteachers or ministers living in rural areas of Pennsylvania, Maryland, and Virginia. Many artists are unknown.

Fraktur exists in several forms—geburts and taufschein (birth and baptismal certificates), vorschrift (writing examples, often with alphabet), haus sagen (house blessings), bookplates and bookmarks, rewards of merit, illuminated religious texts, valentines, and drawings. Although collected for decoration, the key element in fraktur is the text.

References: Donald A. Shelley, *Fraktur-Writings or Illuminated Manuscripts of the Pennsylvania Germans*, Pennsylvania German Society, 1961; Frederick S. Weiser and

SPECIAL AUCTIONS

Sanford Alderfer Auction Company
501 Fairgrounds Rd
Hatfield, PA 19440
(610) 368-5477

Howell J. Heaney (comps.), *Pennsylvania German Fraktur of the Free Library of Philadelphia*, 2 vols., Pennsylvania German Society, 1976.

Museum: The Free Library of Philadelphia, Philadelphia, PA.

Notes: Fraktur prices rise and fall along with the American folk-art market. The key marketplaces are Pennsylvania and the Middle Atlantic states.

Account Book, 12-1/2" x 7-3/4", watercolor, pen and ink on paper, marbled covers, leather binding, several pages of full color drawings, sums, and ornamental calligraphy of David Schultz, tinsmith, Schwenkfelder, dated 1834 .... 1,955.00

Birth Certificate (Geburts and Taufschein)

5" h, 8-1/4" w, pen and ink, wove paper, brown, black, and green flourishes and German inscription, "Marie Grager, 1850, born June 4th, AD 1833 in State of Ohio," minor paper damage, 6-1/2" x 9-1/2" w frame... 825.00

6-3/8" h, 8" w, watercolor, pen and ink on paper, sgd "Martin Brechall," Linn Township, Northampton County, PA, paired tulips, red and yellow blossoms, for Lea Claus, dated March 7, 1808 ....1,035.00

7-1/2" h, 8" w, Jesse Snyder, Towamencin Twp, PA, born in 1812, Schwenkfelder, 1873, orange, yellow, and green, two birds on branches 275.00

7-3/4" h, 12-1/2" w, watercolor, pen and ink on paper, red and yellow blossoms, pale green vines, for Christian Heft, Springfield Township, Bucks County, PA, dated March 10, 1816 ...... 2,875.00

9" h, 11" w, watercolor, pen and ink on paper, heart with vintage, birds, flowers, orange, green, blue, black, and yellow, penciled birth entries for 1878 and 1886, edge sgd "Henry E. Witmer," stains and minor edge damage, framed 220.00

12" h, 15"w, hand-colored printed form, Frederick Krebs, watercolor elements, red and green parrots, tulips, sun faces and crown, for Henrich Ott, Bucks County, Bedminster Township, PA, dated Oct 29, 1800 .... 980.00

12" h, 15-1/2" w, hand colored printed form, S. Baumann, for Joseph Raub, Berks County, Bern Township, PA, dated July 8, 1809 .460.00

12-1/4" h, 15-1/2" w, watercolor, pen, and ink on paper, Berks County artist, winged angels, paired birds and mermaids, for Frederick Heverling, dated 1784 .... 2,100.00

12-3/4" h, 15-1/2"w, watercolor, pen, and ink on paper, Flat Parrot artist, for Susana Gensemer, dated 1811 .... 1,265.00

13" h, 15-7/8" w, hand colored printed form, printed by Gottlieb

Jungmann, Reading, 1795, Friedrich Krebs imprint, paired parrots, blossoms, and sun faces, for Johannes Ries, Paxton Township, Dauphin County, PA, dated Aug 28, 1799 .... 2,185.00

13" h, 16" w, hand colored printed form, watercolor elements, Frederick Speyer, paired angels, parrots, blossoms, and mermaids, for Sarra Grill, Lehigh County, PA, dated April 18, 1789 .. 1,380.00

13" h, 17" h, watercolor, pen and ink on wove paper, heart with parrots, tulips, corner fans, crown and birds, red, blue, brown-yellow, and green, 1820 Columbia County, OH, birth, worn and wrinkled, edge damage, old newspaper backed repair along one tear, framed.. 2,530.00

15-1/2" h, 12-1/4" w, watercolor, pen and ink on paper, gilded decoupage elements, Frederick Krebs, pair of certificates for brothers Daniel Raup (1784) and Peter Raup (1791), pr. 3,800.00

18-1/4" h, 16" w, printed by Blumer and Busch in 1846, records 1835 Montgomery County, PA, birth, hand colored maroon, blue, green, and yellow, glued down, minor damage, framed 220.00

Bookplate, pen, ink, and watercolor

3" h, 5" w, two birds on branches of potted tulip plant, leather bound book cover detached from book 110.00

3" h, 5-1/4" w, book plate, pen and ink and watercolor on wove paper, "Christina Yoder 1828," red, black, and green, PA German, stains and edge damage, new curly frame 425.00

5-7/8" h, 3-3/4" w, wove paper, red, orange, blue, olive, and yellow stylized flowers and "1830," edge wear, stains, tape stain, 9" h x 6-1/2" w frame.. 660.00

6-3/8" h, 4" w, Rebecka Meuer the Testament 1850, very minor foxing 230.00

6-1/2" h, 3-1/2" w, The Serpent and the Apple from Garden of Eden, attributed to Berks County, PA................................. 495.00

6-1/2" h, 4" w, Esther Hoch, Hereford Township, Berks County, (PA), January 25, 1808, hearts and tulips, drawn in red, yellow, and brown, inside first edition Germantown printed leather bound song book 1,100.00

Child's Book of Moral Instruction (Metamorphis), watercolor, pen and ink on paper

5-3/4" x 7-1/2", dec on both sides of 4 leaves, each with upper and lower flaps showing different versus and color illus, unknown illustrator 345.00

6" x 7", printed form on paper, hand colored elements, The Great American Metamorphosis, Philadelphia, printed by Benjamin Sands, 1805-06, printed on both sides of 4 leaves, each with upper and lower flaps, engraved collar illus by Poupard 420.00

6-1/4" x 7", dec on both sides of 4 leaves, when folded reveals different versus and full-page color illus, executed by Sarah Ann Siger, Nazareth, PA, orig string hinges 575.00

Confirmation Certificate, 6" x 7-3/4", watercolor, pen and ink on paper, David Schumacher, paired tulips and hearts, for Maria Magdalena Spengler, dated 1780 .... 4,600.00

Drawing, watercolor, pen and ink

4" h, 2-3/4" w, red yellow and blue rooster with bushy tail, American School, 19th C 865.00

5-3/8" h, 7-3/4" w, pen and ink and watercolor on heavy paper, Daniel Sehaey, Smithville, Wayne County, OH, Oct 11th, A.D. 1854, written by T.H.C.B., black, red, and greenish yellow, 8-3/4" h, 10-3/4" w walnut beveled frame..................................... 590.00

9-1/2" h, 7-1/8" w, red, green and black interlaced calligraphic figure eight with 4 angel heads in corners, attributed to Gottschall family, PA, early 19th C.. 3,800.00

House Blessing (Haus Segen)

15-1/2" h, 11-3/4" w, printed by Johann Ritter, Reading, hand colored, orange, green, blue, yellow, brown, and black, professionally repaired and rebacked on cloth, 18-1/4" h, 14-3/8" w old stenciled dec frame... 500.00

16-1/2" h, 13" w, printed and handcolored, red, blue, green, and yellow, dated 1785, damage and portions missing, framed 385.00

Marriage Certificate, 8" x 12-1/2", watercolor, pen and ink on paper, Daniel Schumacher, paired red, yellow and green birds flanking an arch with crown, for Johannes Haber and Elisabeth Stimmess, Windsor Township, Berks County, PA, dated 1777 .... 1,035.00

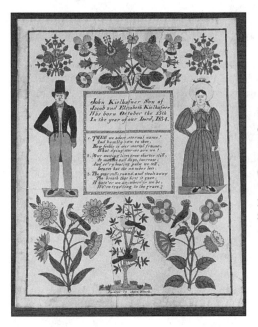

Birth Certificate, John Kielhafner, Lancaster County, PA, 1834, 7-15/16" x 10-1/8", $3,600.

Reward of Merit, American School, early 19th C, watercolor, pen, and ink on paper
    3-5/8" x 3-1/8", red, yellow, and blue-tailed bird perched on flowering branch 1,092.00
    4-1/8" x 3-1/4", red and yellow birds, green and yellow pinwheel flower 345.00
Song Book, 4-1/8" x 6-3/4", watercolor, pen, and ink on paper, marbled covers, leather binding, several handwritten and calligraphy pages, illuminated bookplate, David Hiestand, dated Feb 8, 1823, Macungie Township, Lehigh County, PA 1,380.00
Writing Book (Schreibbuch)
    Catharine Rohr, New Britain Township, Bucks County, PA, legal size, soft cover manuscript, dating from 1784 to approx. 1824, written in German script, 45 pgs of text, 5 full page fraktur inscriptions by unidentified hand, family records, tailoring records 4,400.00
    Ella M. Eisenbach, full page ink drawings, biblical quotes, Nov 25, 1898 .... 150.00

FRANKART

History: Arthur Von Frankenberg, artist and sculptor, founded Frankart, Inc., in New York City in the mid-1920s. Frankart, Inc., mass produced practical "art objects" in the Art Deco style into the 1930s. Pieces include aquariums, ashtrays, bookends, flower vases, and lamps. Although Von Frankenberg used live female models as his subjects, his figures are characterized by their form and style rather than specific features. Nudes are the most collectible; caricatures of animals and human figures were also produced, no doubt, to increase sales.

Pieces were cast in white metal in one of the following finishes: cream—a pale iridescent white; bronzoid—oxidized copper, silver, or gold; french—medium brown with green in the crevices; gunmetal—iridescent gray; jap—very dark brown, almost black, with green in the crevices; pearl green—pale iridescent green; and verde—dull light green. Cream and bronzoid were used primarily in the 1930s.

Marks: With few exceptions, pieces were marked "Frankart, Inc.," with a patent number or "pat. appl. for."

Note: All pieces listed have totally original parts and are in very good condition unless otherwise indicated.

Ashtray
    5" h, stylized duck with outstretched wings supports green glass ash receiver 120.00
    6" h, nude figure kneels on cushion, holding 3" d removable pottery ashtray 225.00
Bookends, pr, modernistic lady heads 275.00
Candlesticks, pr, 12-1/2" h, nude figures standing on tiptoes, holding candle cup over head 395.00
Cigarette Box, 8" h, back to back nudes supporting removable green glass box 450.00
Lamp
    11" h, 8-1/4" w, 4" d, frosted amber crackle glass shade, metal base, worn patina 345.00
    13" h, two back to back dancing nude figures support 11" sq glass cylinder satin finished shade 775.00
    18" h, standing nude figure holds 6" d round crackled rose glass globe 425.00
Wall Pocket, 12" h, seated nude figure supported by wrought iron metal frame work, metal pan for flowers 350.00

FRATERNAL ORGANIZATIONS

History: Benevolent and secret societies played an important part in America from the late 18th to the mid-20th centuries. Initially, the societies were organized to aid members and their families in times of distress. They evolved from this purpose into important social clubs by the late 19th century.

In the 1950s, with the arrival of the civil rights movement, an attack occurred on the secretiveness and often discriminatory practices of these societies. Membership in fraternal organizations, with the exception of the Masonic group, dropped significantly. Many local chapters closed and sold their lodge halls. This resulted in the appearance of many fraternal items in the antiques market.

Museums: Iowa Masonic Library & Museum, Cedar Rapids, IA, http://www.gl-ia.org/museums.htlml; Knights of Columbus Headquarters Museum, New Haven, CT, http://www.kofc-supreme-council.org; Masonic Grand Lodge Library & Museum of Texas, Waco, TX, http://www.gltexas.org; Museum of Our National Heritage, Lexington, MA, http://www.mnh.org; Odd Fellows Historical Society, Caldwell, ID.

Additional Listings: See *Warman's Americana & Collectibles* for more examples.

Benevolent & Protective Order of the Elks, (BPOE)
    Badge, 1920 Chicago 56th Annual Reunion 20.00
    Beaker, 5" h, cream, black elk head, mkd "Mettlach, Villeroy & Boch" 110.00
    Book, *National Memorial*, 1931, color illus 35.00
    Bookends, pr, bronzed cast iron, elk in high relief 75.00
    Plate, tin, litho, Elk Lodge, Mt. Hood and elk by river scene, 1912 .... 85.00

Ashtray, chrome Scottie, black enamel base, mkd "Frankart Inc./Pat Appld For," $115.

Foresters of America, badge, red, white, and blue ribbon, $7.50.

Shaving Mug, pink and white, gold elk head, crossed American flags and floral dec, mkd "Germany" on bottom....................90.00

Eastern Star

Demitasse Cup and Saucer, porcelain 25.00
Pendant, SP, rhinestones and rubies 45.00
Ring, gold, Past Matron, star shape stone with diamond in center...150.00

Independent Order of Odd Fellows (I.O.O.F)

Badge, 1-3/4" d celluloid pinback, striped red, white, and blue fabric ribbon suspending 1-1/2" brass pendant with Odd Fellow symbols, headquarters, bale of cotton, Negro man, plus draped US flags, 1912 ....45.00
Goblet...48.00
Sign, 29-1/2" h, 100" l, Phillipstown Lodge 815, carved, painted, gilt lettering, 3 interlacing ropes, c1930...............................2,750.00
Watch Fob, 94th Anniversary, April 12, 1913 ....30.00

Knights Templar

Business Card, Reynolds, J. P., Columbia Commandery No. 18 (K of P) Sturgis, MI, color logo, c1890 ....6.00
Plate, 9" d, Pittsburgh Commandry, 1903, china.....................50.00
Tumbler, 4" h, 36th Conclave, glass 75.00

Masonic

Apron

14" x 12", leather, white, blue silk trim, white embroidery, silver fringe 35.00
18" x 17", satin, ivory, red fringe, polychrome painted insignia 65.00

Book, *Freemasonry in Roxborough (Pennsylvania), The History of Roxborough Lodge #135*, 1813-1913, Platt & Lawson Pub., 299 pgs, color and black and white illus 35.00
Box, cov, 5" x 16-1/4" x 12-1/2", Chinese Export black lacquer, molded top with mother-of-pearl and lacquer Masonic devices, sides with floral dec, top loose, lock mechanism missing, minor lacquer loss...920.00
Catalog, Ihling Bros. Everard Co., Kalamazoo, MI, 72 pgs, 7" x 12", Cat. #82, Masonic costumes, paraphernalia, etc.................48.00

Certificate, Third Degree Freemason, Penobscot Lodge, dated Aug. 8, 1863 ....175.00
Chocolate Pot, cov, china, lodge name and officer roster dec, platinum color trim 125.00
Goblet, St Paul, 1908 ....70.00
Ice Cream Mold, 3-3/4" d, pewter, symbol, mkd "E & Co, NY" 30.00
Jug, 5-5/8" h, lusterware, transfer printed and painted polychrome enamels, horseman, inscribed "James Hardman 1823," Masonic dec, royal coat of arms, minor wear.....................................410.00
Match Holder, 11" h, wall type, walnut, pierce carved symbols75.00
Painting, 23-1/4" h, 20" w, oil on canvas, "Our Motto," framed, retouched, craquelure...2,645.00
Pendant, moonstone and tiger's claw, claw set in crescent design, centered by carved moonstone in full relief, depicting pharaoh's head surrounded by white enameled headdress, rose-cut diamond accents, verse engraved with Masonic symbols, 10kt yg mount, nose chipped 300.00
Shield, 19-1/2" x 17-1/2", carved walnut, figural, square and compass framing arm and gavel, mounted on shield, upper end of rim incised "March 6, 1902" 230.00
Watch Fob, 10K yg, raised emblem, chain and ring................90.00

Shrine

Cup and Saucer, Los Angeles, 1906....................................70.00
Dinnerware, Rajah, partial set, various marks, 52 pcs 150.00
Goblet, St Paul, 1908, ruby stained, pedestal foot 70.00
Ice Cream Mold, 4-1/4" d, pewter, crescent with Egyptian head, mkd "E & Co, NY" 30.00
Mug, Syria Temple, Pittsburgh, 1895, Nantasket Beach, gold figures 125.00
Shot Glass, cranberry and clear, symbols and officers' names, St. Louis, 1909 ....300.00

FRUIT JARS

History: Fruit jars are canning jars used to preserve food. Thomas W. Dyott, one of Philadelphia's earliest and most innovative glassmakers, was promoting his glass canning jars in 1829. John Landis Mason patented his screw-type canning jar on Nov. 30, 1858. This date refers to the patent date, not the age of the jar. There are thousands of different jars and a variety of colors, types of closures, sizes, and embossings.

References: Douglas M. Leybourne, Jr., *Red Book No. 8*, published by author (P.O. Box 5417, N. Muskegon, MI 49445), 1997; Jerry McCann, *Fruit Jar Annual*, published by author (5003 W. Berwyn Ave., Chicago, IL 60630), 1995; Dick Roller (comp.), *Indiana Glass Factories Notes*, Acorn Press, 1994; Bill Schroeder, *1000 Fruit Jars: Priced and Illustrated*, 5th ed., Collector Books, 1987, 1996 value update.

Periodical: *Fruit Jar Newsletter*, 364 Gregory Ave., West Orange, NJ 07052.

Collectors' Clubs: Ball Collectors Club, 22203 Doncaster, Riverview, MI 48192; Federation of Historical Bottle Collectors, Inc., 88 Sweetbriar Branch, Longwood, FL 32750; Midwest Antique Fruit Jar & Bottle Club, P.O. Box 38, Flat Rock, IN 47234.

Additional Listings: See *Warman's Americana & Collectibles* for more examples.

Adams, Allison & Co., Middlebury., tan to brown chestnut, wax seal, 7-3/4" h..100.00
Advance, Pat. Appl'd For, aqua, ground lip, qt............................95.00
A. Stone & Co/Philada, aquamarine, applied collared mouth, glass lid, smooth base, half gallon, 2 mouth chips, L #2747..................175.00
Atlas Mason's Patent, medium yellow green, ABM lip, qt.............50.00

Crown Imperial, quart, aqua, glass insert top, zinc screw band, $17.50.

Ball, mason, yellow green, amber striations, qt 75.00
B. B. Wilcox, aquamarine, ground mouth, glass lid, wire bale, smooth base, half gallon, L #3000 .... 100.00
Belle, Pat. Dec 14th 1869, aqua, 3 raised feet, ground lip, metal neck band, wire bail, qt 75.00
Canton Domestic, Patent 1889, clear 85.00
Clarke Fruit Jar Co., Cleveland, OH, aqua, ground lip, lid, metal cam lever closure, 1-1/2 pt 165.00
Crystal Jar, Patd dec 17, 1878, clear, ground lip 70.00
Dillion G. Co., Fairmont, IN, green, quart, wax seal, long crack ... 12.50
Dodge Sweeney & Co.'s California, aqua, ground lip, glass insert, zinc band, 1-1-2 qt 425.00
Eagle, deep aquamarine, applied collared mouth, glass lid, iron yoke, smooth base, half gallon, # 872 .... 160.00
Excelsior, aqua, ground lip, insert, zinc band, qt................... 575.00
Fahnestock Albree & Co., aqua, applied mouth, qt 35.00
Franklin Fruit Jar, aqua, ground lip, zinc lid, qt 225.00
Friedley & Cornman's Patent Oct 25th 1958, Ladies Choice, aquamarine, ground mouth, iron rim, gutta percha or leather insert, smooth base, half gallon, iron rim lid rusty, L #1039 .... 1,200.00
Gilberds Improved Jar, aqua, ground lip, wire band, qt 160.00
Green Mountain, CA, clear 10.00
Helmen's Railroad Mills, amber, ground lip, insert, zinc band, pt . 70.00
High Grade, aqua, ground lip, zinc lid, qt................................... 150.00
Johnson & Johnson, New York, cobalt blue, ground lip, orig insert, screw band, qt........................ 325.00
Keystone Mason, Patent Nov 3, 1858, quart, aqua 50.00
Lafayette, aqua, tooled lip, orig 3 pc glass and metal stopper, qt.....200.00
Mason Crystal Jar, clear, ground lip, zinc lid................................ 65.00
Mason's Kempton, 1858 .... 4.25
Mason's Patent Nov 30th, 1858, light green, profuse amber striations, machined mouth, zinc lid, smooth base, half gallon, some int. stain, L#1787 .... 325.00
Midget, T. M. Improved, pint, green-aqua 20.00
Moore's Patent Dec 3d 1861, aquamarine, applied collared mouth, glass lid, iron yoke clamp, smooth base, qt, L #2204 .... 120.00
Peerless, aqua, applied mouth, iron yoke, half gallon 85.00
Pet, aqua, applied mouth, qt.............................. 55.00
Protector, aquamarine, ground mouth, unmarked tin lid, smooth base, qt, L #2420 .... 70.00
Star, aqua, emb star, ground lip, zinc insert and screw band, qt 300.00

Sun, aquamarine, ground mouth, glass lid, iron clamp, smooth base, qt 130.00
The Magic (star) Fruit Jar, greenish-aqua, ground mouth, glass lid, iron clamp, smooth base, half gallon, chips to mouth, L #1606 ...... 180.00
The Pearl, aqua, ground lip, screw band, qt 40.00
The Van Vilet Jar of 1881, aqua, ground lip, orig wire and iron yoke, qt 365.00
Union N1, Beaver Falls Glass Co., Beaver Falls, PA, aqua, applied wax seal ring, half gallon......................... 45.00
Whitmore's Patent, Rochester, NY, aqua, ground lip, wire closure, qt 425.00
Woodbury Improved (monogram), aquama4rine, ground mouth, quart, L #3029 .... 40.00

FRY GLASS

History: The H. C. Fry Glass Co. of Rochester, Pennsylvania, began operating in 1901 and continued in business until 1933. Its first products were brilliant-period cut glass. It later produced Depression glass tablewares. In 1922, the company patented heat-resisting ovenware in an opalescent color. This "Pearl Oven Glass," which was produced in a variety of pieces for oven and table, included casseroles, meat trays, and pie and cake pans.

Fry's beautiful art line, Foval, was produced only in 1926 and 1927. It is pearly opalescent, with jade green or delft blue trim. It is always evenly opalescent, never striped like Fenton's opalescent line.

Marks: Most pieces of the oven glass are marked "Fry" with model numbers and sizes. Foval examples are rarely signed, except for occasional silver-overlay pieces marked "Rockwell."

Reference: Fry Glass Society, *Collector's Encyclopedia of Fry Glass*, Collector Books, 1989, 1998 value update.

Collectors' Club: H. C. Fry Glass Society, P.O. Box 41, Beaver, PA 15009.

Reproduction Alert: In the 1970s, reproductions of Foval were made in abundance in Murano, Italy. These pieces,

Hot Water Server, Foval, green handle and finial, 5-3/4" h, $250.

including items such as candlesticks and toothpicks, have teal blue transparent trim.

Bowl, 8" d, cut glass, pineapple design, wheel cutting, sgd........ 120.00
Butter Dish, cov, Pearl Oven Ware 75.00
Canapé Plate, 6-1/4" d, 4" h, cobalt blue center handle,
    Foval 165.00
Candlesticks, pr, 12" h, Foval, pearl white candlesticks, jade green
    threading and trim 1,380.00
Creamer and Sugar, Set 200, Foval, delft blue handles 175.00
Cruet, Foval, cobalt blue handle, orig stopper 125.00
Cup and Saucer, Foval, blue handles 65.00
Decanter, 9" h, ftd, Foval, applied Delft blue handle.................. 195.00
Fruit Bowl, 9-7/8" d, 5-1/4" h, Foval, pearl white, ridged, delft blue
    foot 520.00
Ice Cream Tray, 14" l, 7" w, cut glass, Nelson pattern variation, all over
    cutting, sgd "Fry".. 290.00
Lemonade Pitcher, 10-1/2" h, 5" w, tankard, applied Delft Blue large
    loop handle and foot, strong pearlescence 675.00
Nappy, 6" d, cut glass, pinwheel and fan with hobstar center, sgd60.00
Platter, 17" l, Oven Ware.. 65.00
Punch Cup, Crackle, clear, cobalt blue ring handle 45.00
Sherbet, 4" h, cut glass, Chicago pattern...................................... 75.00
Teacup and Saucer, Foval, delft blue handles 95.00
Tea Set, 6-1/2" h teapot, 3-1/2" d cup, Foval, pearl glass, silver overlay
    rims, teapot, creamer, sugar, six cups and saucers 875.00
Trivet, 8", Oven Ware.. 20.00
Tumbler, cut glass, pinwheel, zipper, and fan motifs, sgd, 6 pc
    set 180.00
Vase, 7-1/2" h, Foval, jade green, rolled rim and foot................. 200.00

FULPER POTTERY

History: The Fulper Pottery Company of Flemington, New Jersey, made stoneware pottery and utilitarian ware beginning in the early 1800s. It switched to the production of art pottery in 1909 and continued until about 1935.

The company's earliest artware was called the Vasekraft line (1910-1915), featuring intense glazing and rectilinear, Germanic forms. Its middle period (1915-1925) included some of the earlier shapes, but it also incorporated Oriental forms. Fulper's glazing at this time was less consistent but more diverse. Its last period (1925-1935) was characterized by water-down Art Deco forms with relatively week glazing.

Pieces were almost always molded, though careful hand-glazing distinguished this pottery as one of the premier semi-commercial producers. Pieces from all periods are almost always marked.

Marks: A rectangular mark, FULPER, in a rectangle is known as the "ink mark" and dates from 1910-1915. The second mark, as shown, dates from 1915-1925, it was incised or in black ink. The final mark, FULPER, die-stamped, dates from about 1925 to 1935.

References: Susan and Al Bagdade, *Warman's American Pottery and Porcelain*, Wallace-Homestead, 1994; Ralph and Terry Kovel, Kovels' *American Art Pottery*, Crown Publishers, 1993; David Rago, *American Art Pottery*, Knickerbocker Press, 1977; —, Fulper Pottery, *Arts & Crafts* Quarterly Press, n.d.

Collectors' Clubs: American Art Pottery Association, P.O. Box 834, Westport, MA 02790-0697, http://www.amart-pot.org;; Stangl/Fulper Collectors Club, P.O. Box 538, Flemington, NJ 08822.

Advisor: David Rago.

Bowl
    8-1/2" d, 4-1/4" h, semi-spherical, 4 ftd base, mahogany and ivory
        flambé glaze, matte mustard base, unmarked.................... 425.00
    13" d, 3" h, roped border, matte blue glaze, int. cov in Chinese Blue
        flambé, ink racetrack mark.. 300.00
Candle Sconce, 10-1/2" h, 5-1/2" d, 3 inset leaded glass pieces,
    Cucumber Crystalline glaze, incised racetrack mark 2,000.00
Centerpiece Bowl
    11-1/4" d, 5" h, 3 ftd, Rose Famille glaze, paper label........... 375.00
    13" d, 3-1/4" h, ext. Chinese Blue flambé, int. fine green crystalline
        glaze, ink rect mark.. 700.00
Effigy Bowl, 10" d, 7-1/2" h, int. and gargoyles cov in Café-au-lait and
    yellow crystalline glaze, matte mustard ext., rect ink mark 500.00
Inkwell and Pen Tray, 4" l, 4-3/4" d, 5" h, Vasekraft, matte ochre glaze,
    ink racetrack mark 500.00
Jug, 10-1/2" h, 5-1/2" d, mahogany, green, and ivory flambé glaze, rect
    ink mark 475.00
Lamp, table, 16-1/2" h, 14" d mushroom shaped shade inset with blue,
    green, and purple leaded glass pcs, Chinese Blue flambé glaze, rect
    ink mark.. 12,000.00
Urn
    9-1/4" h, 8-3/4" d, classical shape, flat shoulder, Chinese Blue crys-
        talline to Famille Rose glaze, raised racetrack mark, burnt glaze
        bubbles at base.. 375.00
    10-1/4" h, 5-3/4" d, 2 buttressed handles, rare speckled matte
        green glaze, incised racetrack mark 750.00
    11-1/2" h, 8-1/2" d, bulbous, tapering base, collared rim, blue, green,
        and cobalt flambé mirrored glaze, raised racetrack mark........ 900.00
    11-3/4" h, classical shape, glossy rose to crystalline taupe flambé
        glaze, raised racetrack mark.. 500.00
    13" h, 8" d, Mirror Black glaze, incised racetrack mark 425.00
    16-1/4" h, 5-1/2" d, Café-Au-Lait glaze, 4 faceted feet, incised race-
        track mark, bruise to one foot 700.00
Vase
    4" h, 3" d, barrel shape, frothy Chinese Blue over Mirror Black
        flambé glaze, vertical mark, 2 short opposing hairlines 150.00
    6" h, 7" d, spherical, frothy Cucumber Crystalline matte glaze,
        incised racetrack mark.. 750.00

Left: urn, Leopard Skin Crystalline glaze, ink racetrack mark, 12" h, 11" d, $2,300; right: vase, flowing matte green crystalline glaze, incised racetrack mark, stilt pull to base, 17" h, 8" d, $1,900. Photo courtesy of David Rago Auctions, Inc.

6" h, 7" d, spherical, Leopard Skin Crystalline glaze, rect ink mark 650.00
8" h, 5-3/4" d, tapered, 4 buttressed handles, Flemington Green glaze, rect ink mark 475.00
8" h, 5-3/4" d, tapered, 4 buttressed handles, Mirror Black and Ivory flambé glaze, rect ink mark 750.00
8" h, 6" d, bulbous, Cucumber Crystalline, incised racetrack mark 350.00
8-1/4" h, 5-1/4" d, closed-in rim, Elephant's Break to Leopard Skin Crystalline flambé glaze, stamped "Prang".........................450.00
9" h, 4" d, bottle shape, mahogany mottled glaze, ink rect Prang mark 550.00
9" h, 5-1/4" d, ovoid, 2 scrolled handles, Cat's Eye flambé, ink racetrack mark 175.00
9-1/2" h, 6" d, classical shape, Leopard Skin Crystalline glaze, ink racetrack mark 900.00
9-1/2" h, 7" d, corseted, buttressed handles, Copperdust Crystalline to Flemington Green flambé glaze, incised racetrack mark, remnant of paper label, stilt pull to base 450.00
9-1/2" h, 7" d, corseted, 2 angular buttressed handles, Chinese Blue and Elephant's Breath flambé glaze, raised racetrack mark....450.00
10" h, 5-1/4" d, faceted, blue, mahogany, and ivory flambé glaze, incised racetrack mark 475.00
10" h, 7-1/2" d, corset, 2 buttressed handles, frothy Copperdust Crystalline over Flemington Green flambé glaze, raised racetrack mark 425.00
10" h, 7-1/2" d, pillow, curled handles, Flemington Green to Cat's Eye flambé mirror glaze, rect ink mark 500.00
10-3/4" h, 3-1/4" d, cylindrical, curdled Flemington Green microcrystalline glaze, ink rect mark, stilt-pull at base..................400.00
12" h, 4-1/2" d, baluster, butterscotch flambé glaze, incised racetrack mark 500.00
12-1/2" h, 6" d, Leopard Skin Crystalline glaze, rect ink mark, jagged firing base chip 850.00
12-1/2" h, 7" d, bullet shape, frothy green and mauve flambé glaze, incised racetrack mark 1,500.00
13-1/4" h, 5-3/4" d, classical shape, bright Chinese Blue to Flemington Green flambé glaze, incised racetrack mark...........700.00
17" h, 9" d, rare mottled brown, green, and ivory flambé mirror glaze, raised racetrack mark, restored rim chip.................450.00

Vessel
5-3/4" h, 8-1/2" d, squat, leathery Famille Rose matte glaze, ink racetrack mark 325.00
5-3/4" h, 8-3/4" d, squat, small opening, Leopard Skin Crystalline glaze, ink racetrack mark...500.00
6-1/2" h, 9-1/4" d, squat, scalloped, two handles, Mirrored Black glaze, horizontal stamp mark 175.00
13" h, 10-1/2" d, buttressed, Chinese Blue to Cat's Eye flambé, underglaze showing thru on handles, unmarked, drill hole near base 3,250.00

FURNITURE

History: Two major currents dominate the American furniture marketplace—furniture made in Great Britain and furniture made in the United States. American buyers continue to show a strong prejudice for objects manufactured in the United States. They will pay a premium for such pieces and accept them above technically superior and more aesthetically appealing English examples.

Until the last half of the 19th century, formal American styles were dictated by English examples and design books. Regional furniture, such as the Hudson River Valley (Dutch) and the Pennsylvania German styles, did develop. A less-formal furniture, often designated as "country" or vernacular style, developed throughout the 19th and early 20th centuries. These country pieces deviated from the

accepted formal styles and have a charm that many collectors find irresistible.

America did contribute a number of unique decorative elements to English styles. The American Federal period is a reaction to the English Hepplewhite period. American designers created furniture which influenced, rather than reacted to, world taste in the Gothic Revival style and Arts and Crafts, Art Deco, and Modern International movements.

FURNITURE STYLES APPROX. DATES

William and Mary	1690-1730
Queen Anne	1720-1760
Chippendale	1755-1790
Federal (Hepplewhite)	1790-1815
Sheraton	1790-1810
Empire (Classical)	1805-1830
Victorian	
French Restoration	1830-1850
Gothic Revival	1840-1860
Rococo Revival	1845-1870
Elizabethan	1850-1915
Louis XIV	1850-1914
Naturalistic	1850-1914
Renaissance Revival	1850-1880
Néo-Greek	1855-1885
Eastlake	1870-1890
Art Furniture	1880-1914
Arts and Crafts	1895-1915
Art Nouveau	1896-1914
Art Deco	1920-1945
International Movement	1940-Present

Reproduction Alert: Beware of the large number of reproductions. During the 25 years following the American Centennial of 1876, there was a great revival in copying furniture styles and manufacturing techniques of earlier eras. These centennial pieces now are more than 100 years old. They confuse many dealers as well as collectors.

References: *Antique Wicker from the Heywood-Wakefield Catalog*, Schiffer Publishing, 1994; Edward Deming Andrews and Faith Andrews, *Masterpieces of Shaker Furniture*, Dover Publications, 1999; John Andrews, *British Antique Furniture Price Guide and Reasons for Values*, Antique Collectors' Club, 1999; —, *Victorian and Edwardian Furniture Price Guide and Reasons for Values*, Antique Collectors' Club, 1999; Joseph T. Butler, *Field Guide to American Furniture*, Facts on File Publications, 1985; Victor Chimnery, *Oak Furniture, The British Tradition*, Antique Collectors' Club, 1999; Frances Collard, *Regency Furniture*, Antique Collectors' Club, 1999; Bernard D. Cotton, *The English Regional Chair*, Antique Collectors' Club, 1999; Eileen and Richard Dubrow, *Styles of American Furniture*, 1860-1960, Schiffer Publishing, 1997; Nancy Goyne Evans, *American Windsor Chairs*, Hudson Hills Press, 1996; —, *American Windsor Furniture: Specialized Forms*, Hudson House Press, 1997; *Fine Furniture Reproductions*, Schiffer Publishing, 1996; Tim Forrest, *Bulfinch Anatomy of Antique Furniture*, Bulfinch Press, 1996; Don Fredgant, *American Manufactured Furniture*, revised and updated ed., Schiffer

Publishing, 1996; Phillipe Garner, *Twentieth-Century Furniture*, Van Nostrand Reinhold, 1980; Bruce Johnson, *The Pegged Joint*, Knock on Wood Publications, 1995; Edward Joy, *Pictorial Dictionary of British 19th Century Furniture Design*, Antique Collectors' Club, 1999; John Kassay, *The Book of American Windsor Furniture: Styles and Technologies*, University of Massachusetts Press, 1998;Myrna Kaye, *Fake, Fraud, or Genuine*, New York Graphic Society Book, 1987; —, *There's a Bed in the Piano: The Inside Story of the American Home*, Bullfinch Press, 1998; William C. Ketchum, Jr., *American Cabinetmakers*, Crown, 1995; Ralph Kylloe, *History of the Old Hickory Chair Company and the Indiana Hickory Furniture Movement*, published by author, 1995; —, *Rustic Traditions*, Gibbs-Smith, 1993; David P. Lindquist and Caroline C. Warren, *Colonial Revival Furniture with Prices*, Wallace-Homestead, 1993; —, *English & Continental Furniture with Prices*, Wallace-Homestead, 1994; —, *Victorian Furniture with Prices*, Wallace-Homestead, 1995, distributed by Krause Publications; Jack L. Lindsey, *Worldly Goods, The Arts of Early Pennsylvania, 1680-1758*, Pennsylvania Museum of Art, distributed by Antique Collectors' Club, 1999; Robert F. McGiffin, *Furniture Care and Conservation*, revised 3rd ed., American Association for State and Local History Press, 1992; *Herman Miller 1939 Catalog, Gilbert Rohde Modern Design*, Schiffer Publishing, 1998; Marie Purnell Musser, *Country Chairs of Central Pennsylvania*, published by author, 1990; Milo M. Naeve, *Identifying American Furniture*, W. W. Norton, 1998; John Obbard, *Early American Furniture, A Practical Guide for Collectors*, Collector Books, 1999; Peter Philip, Gillian Walkling, and John Bly, *Field Guide to Antique Furniture*, Houghton Mifflin, 1992; Leslie Piña, *Fifties Furniture*, Schiffer Publishing, 1996; Rudolf Pressler and Robin Staub, *Biedermeier Furniture*, Schiffer Publishing, 1996; Don and Carol Raycraft, *Wallace-Homestead Price Guide To American Country Antiques, 156th Edition*, Krause Publications, 1999; Steve and Roger W. Rouland, *Heywood-Wakefield Modern Furniture*, 1995, 1997 value update, Collector Books; Paul Royka, *Mission Furniture ,from the American Arts & Crafts Movement*, Schiffer Publishing, 1997.

Albert Sack, *New Fine Points of Furniture*, Crown, 1993; Harvey Schwartz, *Rattan Furniture*, Schiffer Publishing, 1999; Klaus-Jurgen Sembach, *Modern Furniture Designs, 1950-1980s*, Schiffer Publishing, 1997; Nancy A. Smith, *Old Furniture*, 2nd ed., Dover Publications, 1990; Robert W. and Harriett Swedberg, *Collector's Encyclopedia of American Furniture*, Vol. 1 (1990, 1996 value update), Vol. 2 (1992, 1999 value update), Vol. 3 (1998), Collector Books; —, *Furniture of the Depression Era*, Collector Books, 1987, 1999 value update; —, *Swedberg's Price Guide to Antique Oak Furniture*, 1st Series, Collector Books, 1994; Thonet Co., *Thonet Bentwood and Other Furniture* (1904 catalog reprint), Dover Publications, 1980; Elizabeth White, ed., *Pictorial Dictionary of British 18th Century Furniture Design*, Antique Collectors' Club, 1999; S. Whittington & C. Claxton Stevens, *18th Century Furniture*, Antique Collectors' Club, 1999; Eli Wilner, *Antique American Frames*, Avon Books, 1995; Ghenete Zelleke, Eva B. Ottillinger, and Nina Stritzler, *Against the Grain*, The Art Institute of Chicago, 1993.

There are hundreds of specialized books on individual furniture forms and styles. Two of note are: Monroe H. Fabian, *Pennsylvania-German Decorated Chest*, Universe Books, 1978, and Charles Santore, *Windsor Style In America*, Revised, vols. I and II, Dover Publications, n.d.

Additional Listings: Arts and Craft Movement; Art Deco; Art Nouveau; Children's Nursery Items; Orientalia; Shaker Items; Stickley.

Notes: Furniture is one of the types of antiques for which regional preferences are a factor in pricing. Victorian furniture is popular in New Orleans and unpopular in New England. Oak is in demand in the Northwest, not as much so in the Middle Atlantic states.

Prices vary considerably on furniture. Shop around. Furniture is plentiful unless you are after a truly rare example. Examine all pieces thoroughly—avoid buying on impulse. Turn items upside down; take them apart. Price is heavily influenced by the amount of repairs and restoration. Make certain you know if any such work has been done to a piece before buying it.

The prices listed below are "average" prices. They are only a guide. High and low prices are given to show market range.

Beds

Art Deco, designed by Gilbert Rhode, c1933, manufactured by Herman Miller, Zeeland, MI, suite with tall 47" h dresser, mirrored 33" h dresser with catalin pulls, 56" w bed with curvilinear foot board, 14-1/2" d circular night stand, blond finish, some tubular metal supports, sgd by designer and manuf.. 4,890.00

Arts & Crafts
  Gustav Stickley, no. 923, full size, tapered posts, rounded top rail, 5

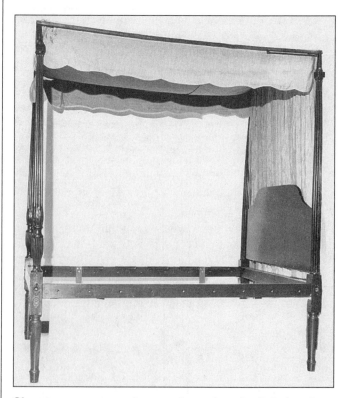

Sheraton, canopy, mahogany, turned posts, fluted and carved, $4,850.

broad vertical slats to head and footboard, fine orig finish, branded mark, 56-3/4" w, 78-1/2" l, 48" h 6,500.00

L. and J. G. Stickley, three-quarter size, tall tapering posts, 6 vertical slats to head and foot boards, orig finish, marked, 51-3/4' w, 84-3/4' l, 54" h 3,000.00

Chippendale, Rhode Island, 18th C, tall post, mahogany, octagonal head posts with lamb's tongue detail continue to sq legs flanking angled headboard joined to fluted and stop-fluted foot posts which include lamb's tongued detailing above sq legs joined by rails fitted for roping, accompanying tester frame and bed bolts, old refinish, imperfections, 85" l, 55" w, 79" h.............................2,300.00

Classical, mid-Atlantic states, c1820, post, tall, spiral carved footposts with classical acanthus leaves and beading above dies and turned feet, rd painted headposts flank similarly painted scrolled headboards, orig rails with minor additions, tester missing, 55-7/8" w, 78-3/4" l, 81-3/4" h 2,500.00

Country
Pencil Post, walnut, scalloped head and footboards, orig rails and canopy frame, 46-1/2" x 65" mattress size, 76-1/2" h......4,200.00

Rope, curly maple, light natural refinishing, replaced side rails, 47" x 74" mattress size, 54-1/2" h 1,600.00

Rope, popular, turned posts, peaked headboard, pine side rails, red stain, 41-1/2" h, 52-1/2" x 70-1/2" mattress 195.00

Federal, Southern, 19th C, tall post, carved mahogany, 4 reeded tapering tall posts with tapering tall posts with carved wrapped leafage above stylized pineapple carving flanking serpentine headboard, sq tapering fluted and stop fluted legs joined to front posts by molded rails fitted for roping, accompanying tester and bolt covers, old surface, minor imperfections, added angle irons and mattress supports, 52-1/4" w, 78" l, 90" h............................9,200.00

Louis XVI Style, painted and partially gilt, carved, gilt, and shaped headboard crest flanked by acorn finials over fluted and acanthus leaves capped columns, similar footboard, reeded toupie feet, twin size, pr..900.00

Low Post
New England, early 19th C, shaped headboard with orig rails, hinged for folding, attached to footposts with conforming carving, turned finials and legs, orig red paint, rails fitted for roping, very minor imperfections, 49-3/4" w, 74" l, 35-1/2" h 800.00

PA, late 18th or early 19th C, walnut, cylindrical turned short headposts, ball turned finials, center arched headboard, turned tapering legs, conforming footposts and footboard, rails, 73-1/4" x 49-3/4" w, 31" h, later hardware added to support box spring . 725.00

Sheraton, c1825, rope, maple, goblet finials, side rails, 57" h, 54" w 425.00

Tall Post, New England, early 19th C
Birch, 4 rect tapering posts continuing to sq legs joined by molded peaked headboard and flat tester frame, old surface, 51" w, 71" h, 81" h..17,250.00

Cherry, 4 octagonal tapering pencil posts continuing to sq tapering feet, joined by flat tester frame, shaped headboard, old finish, 40-1/2" w, 70-1/2" l, 81-3/4" h 4,200.00

Benches

Arts & Crafts, settle
Limbert, open-arm, vertical back slats, corbels, new upholstered drop-in seat cushion, 2 loose pillows, new finish, branded mark, 74-1/4" l, 26-1/2" d, 37" h.............................2,000.00

Mission Oak, curved crest rail over 13 vertical slats, shaped arms over 4 vertical side rails, arched front seat rail, mortise and tenon construction, medium brown finish, replaced cushion, one broken arm tenon, roughness and scratches, 59-1/2" l, 23-1/2" d, 37-3/4" h 750.00

Unknown Maker, oak, rect top with raised edge, pierced and arched apron supported by side slabs, scrolled cut-outs at base, refinished top, orig finish to base, 42" w, 14" d, 18" h............. 1,600.00

Classical, window
Boston, 1835-45, carved mahogany veneer, upholstered seat, veneered rail, leaf-carved cyma curved ends, joined by ring-turned medial stretcher, 48" w, 16-1/4" d, 17-1/2" h.........2,185.00

Primitive, pine, hand made, $75.

New York, 1815-25, mahogany veneer, curving upholstered seat flanked by scrolled ends, scrolled base, old refinish, some veneer cracking and loss, 20th C olive green velvet upholstery, 39-1/2" w, 14" d, 23-5/8" h 3,500.00

New York, c1820, mahogany and mahogany veneer, upholstered slip seat, veneered rect frame, beaded curule legs joined by vase and ring-turned stretcher, old finish, 24-1/4" w, 15" d, 19" h........1,035.00

Classical Revival, mahogany, carved paw feet and lion's heads, maroon velvet cushion, old finish, 16-1/2" l, 29-1/4" w, 23" h...600.00

Country
68-1/2" l, Canadian, settle, pine, paneled construction, shaped arms, turned spindles, shaped crest, folds open into bed, old worn finish, traces of paint 600.00

96" l, 18-1/4" w, 13" h, pine, orig red paint, PA, early 19th C. 750.00

104" l, 13-1/2" w, pine, old worn and weathered green repaint, one board top with rounded front corners, beaded edge apron, cut-out feet mortised through top, age crack in one end of top 325.00

Federal
New England, c1810, window, mahogany, upholstered seat and rolled arms, sq tapering legs, H-form stretchers, refinished, minor repair to one leg, 39-1/2" l, 16" d, 29" h 900.00

New York, c1825, window, figured mahogany, each end with rect crotch-figured crest centering removable slip seat, matching seat rail, saber legs, 40-1/2" l 3,500.00

George III, English, mid-18th C, window, mahogany, rect seat, scrolling arms, later velvet cov, straight legs, blind fret craved, H-form stretcher, pr, 38" l 4,750.00

Gothic Revival, American, c1820-40, carved mahogany, angled over-upholstered seat, carved seat rails centering quatrefoil, facet lancet-carved legs, molded faceted feet, 65" l, 20" d, 15-1/2" h 1,750.00

Jacobean Style, late 19th C, joint, oak, rect molded top over molded and carved frieze, turned legs joined by stretchers, plain feet, 46" w, 12" d, 19-1/2" h 700.00

Louis XVI-Style, window
Carved cherry, overstuffed seat, channeled rails, flanked by molded, overscroll arms carved with be-ribboned foliate sprays, turned, tapered, and leaf-capped legs 200.00

Mahogany, out-curved overscroll arms with X-splats, close-nailed, horsehair upholstered seat, sabre legs with castors, frame reeded and carved with paterae, brass plaque reading, "...Colonial Mft Co., Zeeland, Michigan"....................................550.00

Neoclassical-Style, Italian, 19th C, giltwood, worn leather top, 44-1/2" w, 20" d, 21" h 2,530.00

Wagon Seat, New England, late 18th C, painted, two pairs of arched slats joining three turned stiles, double rush seat flanked by turned arms ending in turned hand-holds, tapering legs, old brown paint over earlier gray, 15" h seat, 30" l 1,200.00

Water, American, 19th C, pine and birch, rect top, plain rails raised on stile ends, bi-furcated feet, as found condition, 42-1/4" l..........100.00

Wicker, painted white, hooped crest rail flanked by rows of dec curlicues, spiral wrapped posts and six spindles, pressed-in oval seat, dec curlicue apron, wrapped cabriole legs, X-form stretcher, 35" w, 31" h 500.00

Windsor

Country, kneeling, gray over olive green and red paint, reeded edge top, bamboo-turned legs, splayed base, 36-3/4" l, 6-3/4" d, 6" h 350.00

Mammy, painted black over red, gold stenciling, back crest with stenciled flowers, removable front gate, bench fitted with orig rockers, light brown painted scrolled arms, 48" w, 29-1/4" h 1,000.00

Pennsylvania-Style, deep seat, white cushion, half spindle back, shaped top crest, curved and scrolled arms, eight legs, box stretchers, medium to light brown finish, 19-1/2" d seat, 34" h 1,200.00

Bentwood

In 1856, Michael Thonet of Vienna perfected the process of bending wood using steam. Shortly afterward, Bentwood furniture became popular. Other manufacturers of Bentwood furniture were Jacob and Joseph Kohn; Philip Strobel and Son; Sheboygan Chair Co.; and Tidoute Chair Co. Bentwood furniture is still being produced today by the Thonet firm and others.

Box

6-3/4" h, oval, Shaker, Harvard type, finger construction, steel tacks, presentation inscription on inside of lid, old varnish finish, lid has some damage..175.00

8" d, 7" h, round, worn orig paint resembles wallpaper, yellow and black foliage scrolls on blue ground, some edge damage to lid........750.00

12" d, round, old dark finish, swivel handle, minor lid edge damage 200.00

14" l, oblong, ash and poplar, orig white, red, and black floral dec, natural ground, lapped seams with tin lacing, some wear and edge damage..2,090.00

14-3/4" l, oblong, pine, laced seams, old blue paint, edge damage 250.00

17-1/4" l, band, pine, orig blue paint, unusual decoupage paper scene of black man, woman, and child, foreign inscription, wear and loose bottom board 550.00

Chair

Austrian, Vienna Secession-style, c1910, side, back splat with three circular perforations, three slender spindles, painted black, set of eight 5,500.00

Thonet, arm, c1935, lacquered, pine frame, upholstered back and seat, 43" h..600.00

Thonet, side, Model #17, designed by Michael Thonet, tall arched patterned wood back with caned back and seat, 46-1/4" h, caning damage 750.00

Cradle, 41" l, 39" h, ivory fittings 440.00

Hall Tree, Thonet, c1910, bentwood frame, contrasting striped wood inlay, coat hooks with central beveled mirror above one door, metal drip pan, orig label, 57" w, 13" d, 76" h 2,750.00

Rocker

Bent Twig, early 20th C, mixed woods, seat and back of curved bent slats, bent twig arms and cross bracing, 37-1/2" h and 41-1/2" h, pr..920.00

Thonet, arched twined top rail, cut-velvet fabric fitted back, armrests, and seat, elaborate scrolling frame, curved runners, 53" l.......750.00

Stool, Thonet, attributed to Marcel Kammerer, Austria, 1901, beech, sq seat, four legs, U-shaped braces forming spandrels, shaped bronze sabot feet, 14-1/4" sq, 18-1/2" h..............................1,500.00

Table, Josef Hoffman, c1905, circular top, wooden spheres dec below rim, 21-1/4" h..500.00

Blanket Chests

Chippendale, miniature, PA, attributed to Octarora Valley, Chester County, walnut, pine and poplar secondary woods, old finish (possibly orig), applied edge molding on top, dovetailed case with paneled facade and 2 overlapping dovetailed drawers, arch pillars have inlaid diamonds, band of maple Greek key molding over drawers, raised panels and orig brasses on drawers, wrought strap hinges, bracket

Grain Painted, Lancaster County, PA, dec after Henrich Otto, green and black paint, two front panels with potted plants with stylized flowers and date "1786," side panels with lion and tulip dec, bracket feet, orig crab lock and keys, glove box int., hinges refastened, damage to feet, 49" w, 21" d, 21" h, $22,200. Photo courtesy of Alderfer Auction Co.

feet, interior till with lid, 26-3/4" w, 15-3/4" d, 16-3/4" h 34,100.00

Chippendale, walnut, poplar secondary wood, dovetailed case, 2 dovetailed overlapping low drawers, dovetailed bracket feet, molded edge till with lid, wrought iron bear trap lock and strap hinges, replaced drawer brasses, refinished, repairs, 48-1/2" w, 23-5/8" d, 26" h 3,300.00

Country, New England, early 19th C, pine, six board, dovetail construction, hinged top, opening to int. with till and drop panel and drawer, bracket feet, old surface, 39-1/4" w, 21" d, 21-1/4" h 500.00

Decorated, Berks County, PA, early 19th C, pine and poplar, lift top, two drawers in base, four bracket feet, old green ground paint striped with red, three tablets, center one with uniform, tulips and vines dec on drawers, later paint, flaking, 43-1/2" w, 18-1/2" d, 38-1/2" h 1,265.00

Dowry, Mahantango Valley, Pennsylvania, "Samuel Grebiel 1799," orig paint dec, red, blue, mustard, black, and white, two shaped polygons painted in blue grain painting, identical polygons on each side, two in front with banner above with name and date, int. lidded till, black painted dovetailed bracket base, off-set strap hinges, orig lock, 48-1/2" w, 21" d, 23-1/2" h....................................3,000.00

Grain Painted, New York sate, c1830, molded hinged lift top, lidded till, molded bracket black painted base, orig fanciful ochre and raw umber graining, 48" w, 22" d, 29" h 1,265.00

Jacobean, oak, paneled construction with relief carving, drawer and feet replaced, repairs to lid and molding, old dark finish, 44-1/2" w, 19-1/2" d, 31-3/4" h 825.00

Italian Renaissance-Style, walnut, antique elements, 60-1/2" d, 20" d, 21-3/4" h..4,000.00

Mule, America, pine, thumb-molded top, two overlapping dovetailed drawers, bracket feet, old dark finishing, int. lined with 1875 Boston newspaper, pierced repairs to feet and drawer fronts, 40" w, 18" d, 34-3/4" h 700.00

Painted

Massachusetts, western, 18th C, pine, hinged top with molded edge, lidded molded till, single base drawer, molded bracket feet, old green paint over red, old replaced glass pulls, paint wear on top, 45" w, 17" d, 31-5/8" h 2,650.00

Milford, Connecticut, early 18th C, yellow pine, six board construction, vestiges of painted dec, replaced ball feet, imperfections, 42-1/2" w, 20" d, 26-1/2" h 950.00

New England, early 19th C, painted poplar, six board, rect molded hinged top, dovetail constructed box and bracket feet, center triple arch pendant, painted old apple green over earlier paint, imperfections, 38" l, 18" d, 21-1/2" d................................575.00

New England, painted, six board, molded hinged lid opens to cavity with lidded till, molded straight skirt with shaped sides, early blue-green paint, minor surface imperfections, 50" w, 19-3/4" d, 25" h... 1,725.00

Pennsylvania, attributed to Lehigh County, pine and poplar, orig painted decoration, top and ends with brown vinegar graining, blue panel and red trim, blue front panel with stylized flowers and wreath in red and white, "Jong Breing 1776," brown feet and lid edge moldings, dovetailed case, dovetailed bracket feet, till with lid, wrought iron bear trap lock, strap hinges, 50" w, 23" d, 23-1/4" h 30,250.00

Pilgrim Century, attributed to Peter Blin, Wethersfield, CT, 1675-1710, carved, painted, and ebonized oak, rect hinged lid, storage well with till, front carved with two rect inset panels of stylized tulips and leaves, center octagonal panel carved with sunflowers, ebonized splint balusters, mid molding, two long drawers with egg appliqués, stiles continue to form feet, replaced lid, reduced feet, traces of orig red and black pigment, 47-1/2" w, 20-3/4" d, 34-1/4" h 12,000.00

Queen Anne, New England, c1750, marriage chest, pine, hinged rect lift lid, upper half faced with faux drawer fronts, brown paint, 35"....4,000.00

Sheraton, country, pine and poplar, orig red paint, molded edge top, paneled front and ends, sq corner posts, mortised and pinned frame, scalloped apron, turned feet, 44" w, 19-1/2" d, 25-1/2" h 900.00

William and Mary, New England, c1700, oak and yellow pine, joined, drawer base, old finish, minor imperfections, 48-1/2" w, 22" d, 32-3/4" h 4,500.00

Bookcases

Arts & Crafts

L. & J. G. Stickley, Fayetteville, NY, c1910, No. 645, gallery top, double pegged through tenons, 2 doors each with 12 panes, copper pulls, red Handcraft decal, 53" w, 12-1/2" d, 55-1/2" h....................6,900.00

Unknown Maker, c1916, oak, gallery top over 4 shelves, single door with 16 panes, unsgd, 35" w, 13" d, 56" h, door stripped, hinge hardware incomplete, roughness.......................... 1,380.00

Biedermeier-Style

Inlaid cherry, outset molded cornice with ebonized bead, front with two recessed glazed doors, four shelves, outset molded base raised on black feet, burr poplar panels, ebonized stringing, 53-1/2" w, 21" d, 72".. 700.00

Mahogany, outset molded top, front with two glazed doors, three shelves, sq section stile feet, 35-3/4" w, 15" d, 52" h............... 375.00

Chippendale, Maryland or Pennsylvania, 1765-65, mahogany, three sections, upper: dentiled triangular pediment, plinth with contemporary bust of William Shakespeare, plain veneered frieze; center: bookcase with double glazed cupboard doors, astragal mullions, Chinoiserie pattern, molded base; lower: chest with short thumb-molded central drawer flanked by two similar box drawers, two graduated long box drawers, two graduated long drawers, flanked by fluted quarter columns, ogee bracket feet, 44-3/4" d, 25-1/4" d, 106-1/4" h. 18,500.00

Chippendale-Style, New England, mahogany, broken arch pedestal over two arched panele3d doors, fitted secretary int. with pigeonholes, six small drawers, lower section with fall front, stepped fitted int., straight front, two small and two wide drawers, brass bail handle, escutcheons, lock plates, straight bracket feet, 42" w, 24" d 93-3/4" h 3,200.00

Classical, New York, 1810-30, mahogany, three-part construction, upper: deeply projecting rect cornice over arched frieze; middle: conforming case fitted with pair of geometric glazed cupboard doors, two int. shelves; lower: rect white marble top above bolection-molded frieze drawer, pair of paneled cupboard doors enclosing shelf, centered by engaged colonettes, foliate-carved and gadrooned bun feet, 47-1/2" w, 24-1/4" d, 92-1/4" h 3,500.00

Eastlake, America, c1880, cherry, rect top, flaring bead trimmed cornice, pair of single-pan glazed cupboard doors, carved oval paterae and scrolls across top, adjustable shelved int., stepped base with line-incised drawers, bail handles, 47-1/2" w, 15-1/4" d, 69-1/4" h .1,200.00

Empire, crotch mahogany veneers, top section: large architectural type cornice, two large glass doors with cathedral top muttons, three adjustable shelves; base: eleven drawers, oval brass knobs, applied base molding, two panes of glass cracked, 66" w, 83" h 5,500.00

Empire-Style, late 19th C, gilt bronze mounted mahogany, rect marble top over drawer, pair of glazed doors enclosing shelves, hairy paw feet, damage to marble, 36" w, 15" d, 53-1/4" h....................1,850.00

Federal, Philadelphia, 1790-1810, mahogany veneered, four part construction: long rect top with detachable molded cornice; two book-case sections each with pairs of glazed cupboard doors, twelve rect panes below top row of arched panes, adjustable shelves int.; lower: center butler's fall-front desk drawer, kneehole area flanked by bands of three cockbeaded short drawers, large paneled cupboard doors, molded base, 119" w, 17-1/2" d, 105-3/4" h 27,500.00

George III, English, mahogany, dentil molded cornice over 3 glazed doors enclosing shelves above 3 drawers, associated base with drawer fitted with pull-out leather topped writing surface, fitted drawer over kneehole fitted with 3 drawers flanked by cupboards, ogee bracket feet, 52-1/4" w, 24-1/4" d, 35" h 5,750.00

George III-Style

Mahogany, stepped dentiled cornice, four glazed lattice doors, shelves int., lower section with two small over two wide cockbeaded drawers flanked by twin panel doors, ogival bracket feet, 74-3/4" w, 17-1/2" d, 77-1/2" h 2,500.00

Pine, revolving, four circular tiers, simulated books for supports, quadruped base, 26" d, 60" h, pr 6,000.00

Georgian-Style, mahogany, outset molded cornice, front with three glazed doors, each with simulated eighteen-pane tracery, adjustable shelves, molded plinth base, bracket feet, 71-1/4" w, 15" d, 54-1/4" h.. 600.00

Italian Renaissance-Style, 19th C, walnut, molded cornice above 2 pairs of wrought iron fronted doors enclosing wooden shelves, 4 short drawers, molded bracket base, 80-1/4" w, 21" d, 98" h 4,890.00

Louis XVI-Style, 19th C, inlaid mahogany, parquetry top, low three-quarter gallery and center oval panel inlaid with fleur-de-lis, open shelf raised on sq-section tapered legs, conforming sabots, 24" w, 8-1/4" d, 27-1/4" h, pr 900.00

Regency, mahogany, projecting molded cornice over two mullion glazed doors, two lower cupboard doors, int. shelves, bracket feet, 56" w, 22" d, 89"..9,000.00

Revolving, American, second half 19th C, oak, molded rect top, five compartmentalized shelves with slatted ends, quadruped base with castors, stamped "Danners Revolving Book Case...Ohio," 24" w, 24" d, 68-1/4" h 1,100.00

Victorian

Globe-Wernicke, barrister type, stacking, oak, glass fronted drawers, drawer in base, metal bands, orig finish 700.00

Macey, barrister type, stacking, oak, leaded glass door, drawer in base, three sections of varying height, needs regluing, 34" w, 11" d.. 400.00

Boxes

Band, pine, orig polychrome floral dec

Black, white, and red, natural ground, laced seams, edge damage, age cracks, repairs, revarnished, 9-1/2" x 15-1/4" 400.00

Blue ground, laced seams, edge damage, poorly glued repairs, 8-3/4" x 13-3/4" 220.00

Bride's, decorated, pine, orig polychrome floral dec

Blue ground, youth pushing girl on swing, German inscription on lid, laced seams, partial decal on lid "Nederland...," age cracks. 2,035.00

Brown ground, figure on lid, laced seams, some edge damage, repair, 10-1/4" x 16-3/4" 495.00

Candle, hanging, pine and chestnut, traces of old red, carved compass designs on front boards, scratched carved compass design on crest, 12" w, 8-1/2" d, 15-1/4" h... 1,100.00

Cave-A-Liqueur, Napoleon III, brass and ebonized wood, rect, shaped front and top, front inlaid with central cartouche surrounded by flower buds within scrolling borders, wide border with conforming floral inlay, hinged top and sides open to reveal ormolu mounted removable tray fitted with 16 cordials and 4 decanters, 13-1/4" x 10" x 10-1/4"... 1,100.00

Chess and Backgammon, Victorian, lacquered, rect, Chinoiserie gilt-dec on sides with figures and foliate borders, chess board on outside with various figures on each black sq, int. of backgammon board with

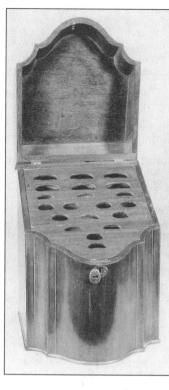

Knife Box, mahogany, inlay, 20 slots, brass escutcheon, 13" h, $650.

central gilt foliate and red polychromed details, associated backgammon pieces, 19-1/2" x 9-3/4" x 3-3/8" closed 400.00
Chocolate, Victorian, lacquered wood, rect, applied enameled brass dec at corners, hinged lid cornered with conforming applied decorations, centered by domed medallion, 8-1/2" l, 5-3/4" d, 4" h 200.00
Cigar, Edwardian
   Continental, kingwood and inlaid, architectural structure, 2 upper doors, central turn handle, fitted int., small sliding trap door for cigar cutter over a drawer, plinth base, c1860, 8-3/4" w, 13-1/2" h 2,000.00
   English, mahogany and ormolu mounted, hexagonal, body with light mahogany flanking each door, coiled handle at top turns to open each of 6 doors revealing cigar compartments, base with applied floral border, 8-1/2" h 450.00
Cutlery Tray
America, mid 19th C
   Handmade, worn varnish finish, divider with cutout handle, 16" l, 11" w 140.00
   Painted wood, two compartments, divider with shaped cutout and curved handle, molded edge and base, repainted blue, traces of old red paint, minor age splits, 13-1/2" l, 9-1/2" w, 4-3/4" h 980.00
   Walnut, dovetailed drawer in base, divider with heart shaped cutout, old finish, 22" l, 12-3/4" w, 11-1/2" h 1,375.00
Dome Top, decorated
   Beech, orig blue paint, white striping, white, red, and yellow flowers, birds, and garlands, staple hinges, wrought iron lock and hasp, wear 1,200.00
   Pine, orig brown paint and striping, red and white flowers and birds, wire staple hinges, wear, and minor edge damage, hasp missing, 10" l 1,980.00
   Pine, orig orange-red paint, yellow striping, red, white, green, and mahogany flowers, wire and tin hinges, tin hasp, attributed to Heinrich Bucher, wear, some edge damage 7,700.00
Dough, country, poplar, cherry finish, turned splayed legs with button feet, one board top, 20-3/4" w, 35-3/4" l, 27-1/2" h 420.00
Games, English, late 19th C, walnut veneer, rect, ebonized detailing, lid opens to fitted int., removable trays holding period dice, dice throwers, game cards, cribbage board with ivory inlay, bone dominoes, int. of lid with removable leather gaming board, lower section

with drawer released by button underneath lid, holding wooden checkers and chess pieces, 10-1/4" l, 9-3/4" d, 6-1/4" h 1,610.00
Knife
   Country, walnut, old finish, dovetailed drawer in base, divider with heart-shaped cut out, 12-3/4" w, 22" l, 11-1/2" h 1,375.00
   Federal, England or America, early 19th C
      Inlaid mahogany and mahogany veneer, serpentine front, slant lid top with silver fittings, fitted int. with inlaid dec, repairs, imperfections, 9" w, 11" d, 15" h 1,100.00
      Inlaid mahogany and mahogany veneer, shaped front slant lid to, silver fittings, fitted int. with inlaid dec, missing lock plate, veneer damage, 8-1/2" w, 13" d, 14-3/4" h 690.00
      Inlaid maple, serpentine front, slant lid top with shell inlay, fitted int. with inlaid dec, age cracks, warping to lid, 8-1/2" w, 11-1/2" d, 15-1/2" h 690.00
   Hepplewhite, mahogany veneer with inlay, convoluted serpentine facade with segmented edge inlay, int. baffles (old replacements) have inlaid design, veneer damage, price for pair, 9-1/2" w, 11-3/4" d, 15" h 2,310.00
Pantry, American, mid 19th C, round, staved construction, fastened with 2 woven lap hoops, carved initials on cover "R. P. F.," minor paint loss to green paint, 14-1/2" d, 6-1/2" h 865.00
Pipe, hanging type
American, early 19th C
   Cherry, chestnut and pine secondary wood, scrolled top rim and crest, one dovetailed overlapping drawer, molded bottom edge, old refinishing, orig gray paint on int., incomplete drawer bottom, 19-1/4" h 3,850.00
   Cherry, pine secondary wood, scrolled top edge with lollipop crest, molded corners, one dovetailed drawer, molded edge base, turned pull, old finish, some edge damage, age cracks, 18-1/2" h 2,950.00
   Mahogany, pine secondary wood, scrolled top edge with tulip crest, one dovetailed drawer, molded edge base, turned pull, old varnish finish, minor edge damage, small old repair, 20-3/4" h 2,200.00
   Mahogany stained poplar, nailed construction, shaped top edges at front, sides and extended backboard, thumb-molded drawer front, brass knob, molded base, minor wear, 4-3/4" w, 5" d, 22" h 2,645.00
   Pine with orig dark reddish brown paint, one drawer with dovetailed and nailed construction, front board has decorative circle designs forming initials "I. S.," and edging carved medallion, deeply scrolled top edges with lollipop rest, minor edge damage, some old renailing, 17-1/4" h 5,225.00
   Pine with orig red paint, chip carved edge on open top and fish tail crest with compass star designs, one drawer with molded edge, bracket feet, early wide dovetailing, minor edge damage, 18-1/2" h 8,800.00
   Pine with red stain, three cut-out hearts and elaborately scrolled crest, one dovetailed drawer, two compartments with finely cut scalloped edge, molded bottom edge, back of drawer scratch carved inscription "January 13, 1813, John ___," minor repairs, small hanging hole added above top heart, 16-3/4" h 4,950.00
American, early 19th C, poplar, old gray-blue over red paint, well detailed scalloped backboard and crest, one nailed drawer, 19-1/2" h 16,500.00
Connecticut, cherry, old finish, applied carved heart, scrolled edges and crest with applied pinwheel-like flower, one dovetailed overlapping drawer in base, minor edge damage, wear at hanging hole in crest, 20" h 3,850.00
Salt, hanging type, mahogany, old finish, applied base molding, hinged slant front lid and shaped crest, old replaced pine bottom board, attributed to PA, 7-3/4" w, 6-1/2" d, 10" h 440.00
Sewing
   America, mid 19th C, painted red and black, attached lid, molded edge, landscape scene with 2 large buildings, trees in background, 9-1/4" w, 6-1/2" d, 2-3/4" h 5,175.00
   Chinese Export, 19th C, lacquer and gilt, 8-sided ftd box, dragons

and figural motifs, fitted compartments with ivory sewing implements, lower drawer and brass handles, minor wear, one broken handle, 14-1/4" l, 11" d, 6-3/4" h 1,735.00
Spice Chest, American, 19th C, pine, 6 drawer, three tiered construction, overhanging molded edges, shaped backboard, round wooden pulls, painted red, minor wear, 15-1/2" w, 6-1/2" d, 12-3/4" h 1,840.00
Storage
   America, mid 19th C, grain painted pine, yellow striping, iron lock and hasp, int., lined with remnants of early fabric, minor paint loss, 28" l, 12-1/2" d, 9-1/2" h 350.00
   Massachusetts, early 19th C, carved and painted dec, rect hinged top with applied carved crouching cat handle, box carved in relief with full figure of woman wearing lace cap, white ruffled collar, yellow dress trimmed in red-orange, holding yellow flower on leafy stem, flanked by large tree with red fruit, gray dog stands to right, red and green bird in flight, 16-1/4"w, 8-3/4"d, 11-1/2" h 26,450.00
Tantalus
   Continental, mahogany, rect, inlaid borders, hinged sides fitted with 16 cordials, int. with four decanters and stoppers, 12" x 8-3/4" x 8-1/2" 900.00
   Viennese, c1850-70, ebonized wood, rect case, applied brass mounted hardstone panels, top and front of hinged lid with cast armorials applied to rouge hardstone medallions, shield shaped lockplate, velvet lined int. fitted with glass decanter and stopper, box stamped "Frid. Strobl. K. K. Priv., Wien," 4-3/4" x 6" x 6-3/4" ...800.00
Tobacco, Viennese, c180, rect, cornered by pewter bands, lid with central inlaid hardstone mosaic style panel with "Karlsbad," vacant int. with painted glass panels, 6-1/2" x 5" x 4-5/8" 600.00
Wall
   PA or CT, c1830-40, carved and painted walnut, arched cornice molding flanks carved device, tasseled pendants, curving sides continuing to form box with carved vines and leaves flanked by cross-hatching, arched mirror back, dark red-brown stain, old black paint, minor imperfections, 12" w, 4-1/8" d, 20-1/4" h 1,955.00
Wedding, Charles X, calamander, tapering rect, stepped lid, ormolu mounted lock platen cast with flowering cornucopia, cast claw feet, silk lined int., 17-1/4" x 12-1/2" x 10" 1,500.00
Work, Chinoiserie, wood with black lacquer and worn gilded dec, octagonal case, fitted int. with six boxes, carved low feet, one int. lid missing, one foot replaced, wear, damage, 15" l 275.00
Writing
   Mahogany, old finish, dovetailed drawer in base, one external dovetailed drawer, brass bale handles, 16" w, 10" d, 6" h ..385.00
   Mahogany, old finish, dovetailed case, tambour top made to open when dovetailed drawer is pulled out, lift-top lid, partial paper label "Mrs. Anna M. McIntosh...New York," orig brass bales on ends, repairs to hinge rail, cloth backing of tambour deteriorated, 16" w, 10" d, 6-3/4" h 700.00
   Mahogany, old finish, one dovetailed drawer in end, orig brass bale, fitted int. with 2 old inks and pen, writing surface recovered with green felt, 9-1/2" w, 15-3/4" l 600.00
   Mahogany, old finish, fitted interior with one external dovetailed drawer, brass bale handles, 16" w, 10" d, 6" h 385.00
   Pine, old worn olive brown graining over red, dovetailed case, fitted int. with 4 pigeon holes, 2 drawers, orig brass bales, hinges and lock replaced, age crack in lid, edge damage, 20" w, 10-1/4" d, 9" h 275.00

Cabinets

Art Deco, vitrine, teak
   Continental, molded rect top, rounded corners, 2 glazed cupboard doors, shelved int., above 2 paneled cupboard doors, stepped block feet, 36" w, 17-1/2" d, 69-1/2" h 400.00
   Dutch, shaped and molded cornice, carved sq geometric designs over single glazed paneled door with serpentine edge, shelved int., 2 small drawers, molded and shaped plinth base, 36-1/2" w, 17-1/2" d, 75" H 450.00
Arts & Crafts
   Cellarette, c1905, oak, drop front inlaid with copper, int. fitted with racks and porcelain cylinder, single door, hammered brass hard-

Humphrey's Veterinary Specific, oak cabinet, composition front, 4 int. shelves, 21" w, 10" d, 27-1/2" h, $1,650.

ware, int. of lower door fitted with insulating metal, 21-3/4" w, 13-3/4" d, 43-1/2" h 550.00
   Display, 2 display sections, recessed beveled mirror, 2 drawers between 2 glazed display sections, over 2 larger paneled base doors, sq faceted wooden pulls, overcoated finish, unmarked, 49-1/2" w, 20-1/2" d, 62-1/2" h 2,100.00
Classical, server, Boston, c1926, mahogany and mahogany veneer, rect top, ogee molded drawer, 2 cupboard doors with flat mitered borders, flanking scrolls, scrolled legs, old finish, minor imperfections, 40" w, 18-1/2" d, 34" h 1,725.00
Colonial Revival, Chippendale Style, c1940, china, walnut veneer, breakfront, scrolled broken pediment, center urn finial, pr of glazed doors and panels, long drawer over 2 cupboard doors, 44" w, 15" d, 76" h 600.00
Country, spice, pine, orig cream colored paint, red striping, stepped case with 12 drawers with porcelain pulls, repaired break on scrolled crest, 20" w, 11-1/2" d, 16-1/2" h 2,860.00
Empire, c1825, pedestal, mahogany, circular gray marble top, cylindrical body, door enclosing shelves, plinth base, 16" d, 29" h...... 800.00
French Style, vitrine, Paines Furniture Co., late 19th C, gilt bronze, kingwood, and marquetry, galleried bowed top, glazed front and sides, 2 glass shelves, cabriole legs, orig paper label, 28" w, 17" d, 61" h 2,645.00
George II Style, corner, oak, incorporating period elements, cavetto molded triangular top, front with pair of bi-paneled doors opening to 2 shaped shelves, outset molded base with bracket feet, 37" w, 20-1/2" d, 46-3/4" h.. 800.00
George IV, library, English, c1825, mahogany, superstructure of 4 graduated bookshelves on either side, stand with 2 frieze drawers on one side, false drawers on reverse, trestle support with concentric bosses, down swept legs joined by turned cylindrical stretcher, casters, 36" w, 59" h 5,225.00
Gothic-Revival, side, first quarter 20th C, carved oak, molded rect hinged top over paneled door carved with Gothic tracery, flanked by columnar stiles surmounted by mediaeval statues, sides and back similar, columnar legs joined by platform stretcher, fitted with phonograph, 19-1/4" w, 19-1/4" d, 51-1/4" h 900.00
Hepplewhite, china, inlaid mahogany, leaded glass, velvet lined int., 643" w, 21" d, 75-1/2" h 700.00
Louis XVI Style, side, amaranth and satinwood, porcelain and gilt metal mounted, superstructure surmounted by rect top with convex ends, pierced three-quarter gallery, front with pair of paneled doors, porcelain panels painted with floral urns, opening to shelves, all flanked by conforming open shelves, outset lower section with similarly rounded ends, conforming frieze centered by a drawer inset with 3 further porcelain plaques painted with floral sprays and garlands,

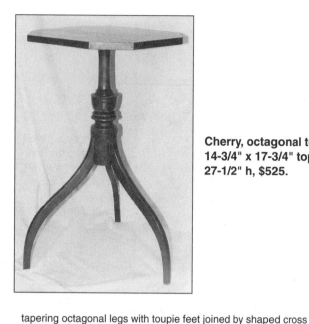

Cherry, octagonal top, 14-3/4" x 17-3/4" top, 27-1/2" h, $525.

tapering octagonal legs with toupie feet joined by shaped cross stretcher, gilt metal mounts, 41-1/2" w, 12-3/4' d, 51-1/2" h..2,600.00
Napoleon III, display, gilt bronze mounted walnut, upper part with molded frame over gilt-bronze mounted frieze, glazed panel door opening to int. fitted with one shelf, flanked by 2 tapering columns mounted with lions heads, outset lower part centered with single drawer, supported by pr of double turned columns, platform base, toupie feet, 29" w, 21" d, 80" h 1,200.00
Victorian
China, oak, bow front, leaded glass, amber glass diamonds in top panels, 37-1/2" w, 14-1/2" d, 61-3/4" h 600.00
Side, last quarter 19th C, Asian taste, stained pine, rect top with heavily carved and reticulated iris gallery, drawer and cabinet door enclosing shelves, all with similar carved reticulated paneling, 35-1/2" w, 16" d, 66-1/2" h 700.00

Candlestands

Chippendale
American
Cherry, round one board top, urn turned column, tripod base, snake feet, old finish, old repairs to base of column, 17-1/2" d, 27-1/2" h 990.00
Mahogany, one board dish turned top, turned column, tripod base, snake feet, old finish, 15-1/2" d, 26" h 2,860.00
England or America, c1780, mahogany, tilt-top, dished circular top, spiral carved base and ring turned support, tripod cabriole legs, pad feet on platforms, old refinish, imperfections, 21" d, 27" h 1,380.00
Empire, Continental, first quarter 19th C, circular cockbeaded top, twist-turned standard, triangular platform base with concave sides, paw feet, 12-3/4" d, 27-1/2" h 250.00
Federal
Connecticut, c1790, cherry, circular top, vase and ring-turned support, tripod cabriole leg base, pad feet, old finish, minor imperfections, 21" d, 28" h 1,495.00
Connecticut, c1790, cherry, sq top, applied beaded edge, vase and ring-turned post, tripod cabriole leg base, pad feet, refinished, 18" w, 17" d, 27-1/2" h 1,380.00
Connecticut, c1790, cherry, sq top with ovolo corners, vase and ring-turned post and tripod cabriole leg base, pad feet on platforms, refinished, minor imperfections, 16-1/2" w, 16-1/4" d, 28" h 1,495.00
Connecticut, c1815-20, cherry, rect top, single drawer, straight sides, joined by corner drops on vase and ring-turned post and arris cabriole legs, pad feet on platforms, refinished, 19" w, 19-1/2" d, 25-1/2" h 750.00
Massachusetts, c1800, tilt-top, mahogany, serpentine top, square corners, vase and ring turned post and tripod cabriole leg base,

pad feet on platforms, refinished, minor imperfections, 19-1/2" w, 19-1/2" d, 25-1/2" h 2,300.00
Massachusetts, c1815-25, birch, octagonal top, vase and ring-turned support, tripod cabriole leg base, pad feet, old finish, imperfections, 14-1/2" w, 18-1/2" d, 28-3/4" h 920.00
New England, c1825, mahogany, shaped tilt top, vase and ring-turned post, tripod spider leg base, old finish, imperfections 400.00
Rhode Island, c1790, mahogany inlaid, sq top with string inlaid edge, vase and ring turned support on tripod cabriole leg base, ending in pad feet, refinished, 17-3/4" w, 17-3/4" d, 28" h1,265.00
Western Massachusetts, late 18th C, cherry, octagonal top, vase and ring-turned post, tripod cabriole leg base, old varnish, 15-1/4" w, 15-1/8" d, 25" h 2,300.00
Hepplewhite
Cherry and maple, one board top with cut corners, turned column, tripod base with spider legs, refinished, 16-1/4" x 17-3/4" top, 27-3/4" h 350.00
Mahogany with inlay, cut-corner top with banded beaded edge and conforming inlay medallion, turned column, tripod base with spider legs, stringing on edge of top and legs, old finish with wear, 13-1/2" x 19-3/4" top, 27" h 1,375.00

Chairs

Aesthetic Movement, late quarter 19th C
American, arm, heart shaped back surmounted by carved and pierced crest, scrolling half-upholstered arms, turned and tapered legs, casters, 24" w, 23-1/2" d, 41" h, pr 550.00
American, side, walnut, upholstered back above foliate carved panel, over-upholstered seat, ring-turned legs ending in casters, gold velvet upholstery, restorations, 33-1/2" h, pr 460.00
Bedford, MA, side, cherry, foliate carved back, twisted slender splats, caned seat, slender tapered legs, partial paper label "The Marble & Shattuck Chair Mfg...Bedf.," pr, 34-1/4" h 230.00
Art Deco
Arm, Paimio, designed by Alvar Aalto, c1932, birch plywood seat suspended in continuous laminated wood frame, 24-1/2" w, 34-1/2' d, 25" h 3,500.00
Side, shaped over-scrolling top rail, padded rect curved backrest, overstuffed seat, sabre legs, set of 6 .... 750.00
Art Moderne
Arm and side chairs, Luigi Tagliabue, light wood, vertical ebony stripes, black seats, 39" h, pr 600.00
Lounge, black wire frame seat and back, dec wooden arm rests, coiled spring seat support, 4 prong shaped splayed legs, c1955, 32-1/4" h, pr 1,200.00
Side, Charles Eames, manufactured by Herman Miller, natural finish laminated wood, back rest on metal frame, rod shape legs, paper label, 17-1/2" w, 30" h, set of 6 .... 600.00
Arts & Crafts
Arm, David Wolcott Kendall, oak, caned back and seat, flat arms with sq vertical supports to the floor, 29-3/8" w, 34-1/4" h, caning damage, minor wear, pr 1,850.00
Arm, Limbert, 2 sq cut-outs to back slats, flat tapered arm rests, new black leather drop-in seat cushion, orig finish, branded mark, small repair to back leg, 27-1/2" w, 24-1/4" d, 38-1/2" h .. 4,250.00
Arm, L. and J. G. Stickley, ladderback, arched apron, corbels, and new upholstered drop-in spring seat, new finish, "The Work of..." label, 27-3/4" w, 22" d, 40-1/2" h 425.00
Arm, unknown maker, oak, wide crest rail over 3 back slats, spring cushion seat, orig dark finish, marring, roughness, 29-1/4" w, 24-1/4" d, 34-1/2" h 200.00
Desk, Limbert, Michigan, c1912, horizontal H-back over single slat, orig leather seat, branded mark, 35" h 550.00
Dining, L. & J. G. Stickley, 3 vertical back slats, arched front rail, new rush seats, orig dark finish, Handcraft label, 20" w, 16-1/2" d, 36" h, set of 4 .... 3,000.00
Dining, unmarked, tall back, 3 vertical back slats, drop-in seats cov in new brown leather, new finish, wear to back legs, 19-1/4" w, 19" d, 46" h, pr 600.00

Ladder Back, wavy slats, woven rush seat, English, country, late 18th C, $385.

Folding, church, Boston, c1895, back and sides carved with stylized flowers and leaves, 8 keyed through-tenon joints on X-shaped base, orig finish, unmarked, 27" w, 22" d, 5" h.... 1,500.00

Morris, lady's, similar to Gustav Stickley no. 367, NY, c1907, spindle-sided, flat arm with corbel support over 20 sq spindles, rails with through tenons, unsigned, 34-1/2" d, 27-1/2" h........ 5,750.00

Morris, L. & J. G. Stickley, Fayetteville, NY, flat arm with corbel supports over 5 long vertical slats, 27-1/2" w, 30-1/2" d, 39" h ...2,415.00

Recliner, L. & J. G. Stickley, Fayetteville, NY, #830, c1912, oak, orig leather upholstery, box spring and cushion, remnants of "The Work of..." decal, 29-1/4" w, 40" h 1,250.00

Set, No. 354-1/2, oak, one arm chair, 4 side chairs, V-shaped crest rail over 5 vertical slats, leather seat with copper tacks, some with paper labels, NY, c1907, 36" h, set of 5 .... 6,325.00

Side, L. & J. G. Stickley, Fayetteville, NY, oak, slightly curved crest rail over 3 vertical slats, leather seat, Handcraft decal, 15-3/4" w, 18" d, 37-1/4" h 350.00

Side, Turner & Co., England, c1910, oak, shaped crest rail over 4 vertical slats continuing to lower stretcher, plank seat, maker's tag, 13-1/4" w, 12-1/2" d, 21-1/4" h 520.00

Belle-Epoque, French, last quarter 19th C, salon, painted and parcel-gilt beechwood, open rect back with arched crest rail over pierced cross-bar, serpentine front over-stuffed seat, turned, tapered, and leaf-capped legs, frame carved with foliate motifs 125.00

Chinese Export, early 19th C, arm, bamboo, rect back, down swept arms, caned seat, columnar legs joined by stretchers, fitted with cushion, minor losses, 34" h 850.00

Chippendale

American, c1775, side, carved mahogany, splayed rect back, tri-arched crest rail over pierced gothic tracery splat, over stuffed seat with shaped and molded rails, cabriole legs, claw and ball feet, claws with back-swept talons, frame molded throughout, crisply carved with acanthus foliage 1,300.00

American, c1780, side, carved mahogany, fluted back posts with pierced and carved splat, crest with carved ears and relief carved center medallions, molded edge seat frame with shaped apron, orig slip seat frame, cabriole legs, carved knees, ball and claw feet, orig finish, reupholstered seat, repairs to one back foot, corner crack in seat frame, 39-5/8" h 5,500.00

Boston or Salem, MA, area, 1750-1800, side, carved mahogany, serpentine crests include central shells with flanking chip carving, terminating in raking molded ears, strapwork patterns splats ending in scrolls, trapezoidal slip seats, molded frames, cabriole legs with arris knees, frontal ball and claw feet joined to rear raking sq legs by block ended turned stretchers, old refinish, imperfections, 16-1/2" h seat, 37-1/2" h, pr.. 27,600.00

Boston or North Shore, MA, 1755-85, side, mahogany, serpentine crest terminates in raked molded ears, pierced splats, trapezoidal over-upholstered seats, cabriole legs with arris knees ending in paw feet, joined to sq chamfered rear legs by block ended side stretchers, old refinish, very minor imperfections, 18" h seat, 38" h, set of 3 .... 5,500.00

Concord, MA, last quarter 18th C, side, dark stain, serpentine crest, raked molded terminals, pierced splat, upholstered slip seat, sq legs, front legs with molded outside edges, jointed by sq molded stretchers, imperfections, 17-3/8" h seat, 39" h 885.00

English, dining, two armchairs, six side, mahogany, rect back with shaped crest rail over pierced tracery splat, drop-in seat with molded rails, molded sq section legs joined by U stretcher, set of 8 .... 6,000.00

Massachusetts, 1770-1800, roundabout, walnut, shaped crest on scrolled arms, shaped splats, slip seat in molded frame, frontal cabriole leg ending in pad feet, 3 turned legs ending in small turned feet, old refinish, repairs, 17" h seat, 30" h 10,350.00

Pennsylvania, 1760-80, side, carved mahogany, serpentine crest rails with central carved shells terminating in scrolled back notched ears above interlaced splats, scrolled volutes flanked by fluted stiles, rounded backs, molded trapezoidal seat frames, central carved shells above cabriole legs embellished with foliate and leaf carving, ball and claw feet, old dark surface, imperfections, 17-3/4" h seat, 39-1/2" h, pr 80,600.00

Philadelphia, PA, 1750-80, side, carved mahogany, serpentine crests end in scrolled back ears, carved central shells and beaded edges, reverse curved interlaced scroll splats flanked by similarly spooned stiles with beaded edges and rounded backs, shaped molded trapezoidal seat frames with carved applied central shells over shell carved cabriole legs with scrolled knee brackets, ball and claw feet, old dark surface, 17-1/2" h seat, 40-1/2" h, pr 47,150.00

Philadelphia, PA, c1780, side, carved mahogany, open rect back, tri-arched crest rail over Gothic tracery splat, drop-in seat with molded rails, sq section legs joined by H stretcher............. 850.00

Renaissance Revival, finger molded, carved crest, upholstered, $425.

Philadelphia, PA, c1785, side, carved mahogany, open rect back with tri-arched crest rail surmounting pierced vasiform splat, drop-in seat with molded rails, molded sq section legs with pierced brackets 400.00

Rhode Island, c1780, side, mahogany, serpentine crest rail centering scratch carved punchwork quarter fan above pierced vase splat, square raked stiles, trapezoidal upholstered slip seat on sq legs joined by stretchers, old refinish, 17-1/2" h seat, 39" h 1,380.00

Chippendale Style, early 20th C

Dining, two arm chairs, six side chairs, hardwood with old brown finish, carved ribbon back slats, needlepoint upholstered slip seats, molded legs, 19" h, 37" h, set of 8 .... 1,150.00

High, mahogany, pierced splat, shaped crest, slip seat, shaped arms, cabriole legs, ball and claw feet, hinged tray, old finish, 38-1/2" h 550.00

Wing, mahogany, canted back with shaped crest flanked by outward flaring wings and scrolled arms, cabriole legs, claw and ball feet, upholstered in yellow fabric, 28" w, 23-1/2" d, 43-1/2" h 125.00

Wing, mahogany, tall back with shaped crest flanked by wings and outscrolled arms, sq legs joined by H-stretcher, light blue damask upholstery, 24" w, 23" d, 48" h 250.00

Classical

Boston, c1920, side, children's, mahogany, paneled concave crests, horizontal splat joining raked stiles, upholstered slip seats, sabre legs, refinished, 14-1/2" h seat, 28" h, pr 550.00

New York State, c1835, dining, tiger and bird's eye maple, lyre shaped splat, caned seat, refinished, repairs, 17" h seat, 33-1/4" h back, set of 8 .... 2,400.00

Directorie, French, second half 19th C

Bergere, fruitwood, caned barrel back, serpentine seat, baluster turned arms, circular tapering legs 750.00

Fauteil, mahogany, rect upholstered back and seat, turned tapering legs 750.00

Eastlake

American, c1870, lady's, walnut, Minerva head carving on crest, incised lines, applied burl veneer panels and roundels dec, shaped hip brackets with conforming dec, shaped reupholstered back and seat, turned front legs, 36" h 475.00

English, open arm, mahogany, arms resting on carved eagle supports rising into rolled upholstered back, resting on stretcher base, 27" w, 34" d, 34" h 450.00

Edwardian, English, c1900, side, rect pierced carved splat with Gothic arches, rect figural painted panel, foliate and fluted circular stiles, rect caned seat, turned tapering legs, pr 700.00

Empire, America, first quarter 19th C

Arm, mahogany, upholstered rect back, bowed seat, sq tapering legs, 23" w, 20-1/2" d, 35" h, pr 2,750.00

Dining, mahogany, carved crest rail, shaped splat, needlepoint seats, shaped legs, set of 4 .... 600.00

Side, tiger-maple, open rect back with curved over-scroll crest rail, pierced foliate cross-bar, seat with convex rails, turned and ring-turned legs, splayed feet, turned box stretcher, set of four 1,200.00

Federal

Arm, New England, 1775-1800, curving crest above raked terminals, vasiform splat, downward scrolling arms, block and baluster turned front legs ending in Spanish carved feet, joined by boldly turned front medial stretcher, old splint seat, old red paint, imperfections, 17-1/4" h seat, 35-1/2" h 8,050.00

Dining, Massachusetts, 1790-1900, 2 arm chairs, 6 side chairs, mahogany, inlaid, shield back with rays terminating in sunset type carving, upholstered seats with decorative tacks, straight tapered legs and cross stretchers, 17" h, set of 8 .... 15,000.00

Dining, Rhode Island or Salem, MA, c1795, mahogany carved, set of four side and matching arm chair, shield back with molded crest and stiles above carved kylix with festoons draped from flanking carved rosettes, pierced splat terminating in carved lunette at base above molded rear seat rail, seat with serpentine front rail, sq tapering legs joined by stretchers, over-upholstered seats covered in old black horsehair with scalloped trim, old surface, 16-1/2" h seat, 37-3/4" h 23,000.00

Side, Massachusetts or Rhode Island, c1780, mahogany inlaid, shield back, arched molded crest above five molded spindles and inlaid quarter fan, overupholstered seats with serpentine fronts, molded tapering legs joined by stretchers, 17-1/2" h seat, 37" h, pr 5,475.00

Side, New Hampshire, Portsmouth, attributed to Langley Boardman, 1774-1833, mahogany, sq back, reeded on rest rail, stiles, and stay rail, over upholstered serpentine seat, molded sq tapering front legs, sq stretchers and rakes rear legs, refinish, minor imperfections, 18" h seat, 36" h 1,035.00

Side, Philadelphia, c1805, carved and satinwood inlaid mahogany, molded shield back, pierced flower head and bellflower carved splat, satinwood inlaid fan, over upholstered seat, sq molded tapering legs, feet extended, pr 4,500.00

George I Style, arm, open waisted back with inset acanthus and tassel carved vase form splat, shepherd's crook arms, balloon seat, acanthus carved molded legs, claw and ball feet 800.00

George II Style, bar, carved walnut, over-scroll crest rail raised on continuous out-curved arm with 3 curved supports interspersed with 2 pierced splats, serpentine-front drop-in seat with conforming rails, raised on leaf-capped cabriole legs, claw and ball feet, joined by composite stretcher, pr 1,200.00

George III

English, attributed to Thomas Chippendale, c1773, arm, giltwood, oval backrest carved with guillouche and husk wreaths, similar carved arms, bowed seat rail, leaf carved circular fluted tapering legs ending in gadrooned ball feet 25,300.00

English, late 18th C, dining, 6 side, mahogany, rect carved back, upholstered seat, sq tapered molded legs, restorations, set of 6, 36-1/2" h 1,380.00

English, late 18th/early 19th C, side, mahogany, shield back with sheaf of wheat carved splat, bowed upholstered seat, circular tapering stop-fluted legs, damages, restorations, pr, 37" h. 690.00

George III Style, English, late 19th C

Dining, two armchairs, six side chairs, mahogany, ribbon back, pale blue upholstery, restorations, set of 8, 37-1/2" h 3,750.00

Side, paint dec mahogany, shaped backs with urn-form splats, upholstered seat, sabre legs, exotic birds and foliage dec, restorations, set of 4, 34" h 4,600.00

Hitchcock, Hitchcockville, CT, c1825-30, black painted, stencil dec, gilt and polychrome dec, turned crest rails, horizontal splats with fox hunting scenes, flanked by raked tiles, rush seats, ring turned legs joined by stretchers, imperfections, pr, 18" h, 33-1/2" h 1,150.00

International Movement

Dining, designed by Hans Wegner, Denmark, c1950, walnut, bent back and arm rail, plank seat raised on tapered circular legs, 30-1/2" h, set of six 900.00

Lounge, Charles and Ray Eames, c1956, manufactured by Herman Miller, bent and laminated wood, black leather upholstery, meal tag, 32" w, 32" h matching 26" h ottoman, some wear and abrasion 1,265.00

Ladderback, America, country, side, sausage turned posts, 4 arched slats, turned finials, turned legs and stretchers, feet ended out, wear to rush seats, old finish, pr 275.00

Louis Phillipe, c1830, fauteuils, walnut, molded top rail continuing to downswept arms, stuffed back and bowfront seat with nail head detail, carved tapering legs, toupie feet, 23" w, 21-1/2" d, 41" h, pr 3,750.00

Louis XVI, last quarter 18th C, child's fauteuil en cabriolet, painted gray, padded and splayed rect back flanked by fluted columnar posts, out-curved arms with padded elbow rests, baluster form supports, bow-front over-stuffed seat with conforming rails, turned tapered and fluted legs, frame channeled throughout and carved with piastres, guilloche banding, paterae and lotus banding 2,600.00

Louis XVI Style

Bergeres, carved and molded top rail continuing to half upholstered downswept arms and pads, overstuffed seat with loose cushion, carved and molded rail on turned, tapered, and fluted legs, toupie feet, neoclassical motifs tapestry covering, set of 4 .... 3,000.00

Fauteuils a la Reine, giltwood, padded rect back within conforming frame surmounted by floral crest, downswept arms with padded elbow rests, scroll terminals on back-curved supports, bow-fronted over-stuffed seat with conforming rails, turned, tapered, and fluted legs headed by paterae, cared throughout with fucillage and ruban enroule, pr...2,500.00

Napoleon III, third quarter 19th C, Fauteils a la Reine, giltwood, cartouche-form padded back, conforming frame surmounted by carved foliate crest, center espagnolette, downswept arms with padded elbow rests and scrolled terminals, back-curved supports, serpentine front over-stuffed seat with conforming shaped rails centering further espagnolettes, cabriole legs with scrolled toes, frame channeled throughout and crisply carved with feuillage, coquillage, trailing husks and beading, pr...4,750.00

Queen Anne

Boston, MA, 1740-60, side, maple, shaped crest above vasiform splat, slip seat over scrolled seat rail, cabriole legs ending in pad feet, joined to raked rear legs by block and baluster turned stretchers, old refinish, repairs, 16-3/4" h, 40" h..............5,100.00

Boston, MA, 1740-65, side, walnut, double arched crest, central carved shell above vasiform splat, balloon shaped over-upholstered seat, cabriole legs joined by block and baluster turned H-stretchers, padded disc front feet, old surface, imperfections, 17" h seat, 40-1/2" h...8,050.00

Boston, MA, 1750, side, walnut, vase splat and curved back posts with yoke crest, balloon seat, cabriole legs with duck feet, turned stretchers, old refinishing, reupholstered slip seats, price for pr, 39-1/2" h 11,500.00

English, 18th C, side, mahogany, yoke back and vasiform splat, slip seat, cabriole legs joined by stretchers, pad feet, set of 4, 39-1/2" h 950.00

New York, attributed to Jacob Smith, 18th C, side, cherry and ash, shaped crest rail above vase splat, arched stay rail, flanked by vase and ring-turned stiles, rush seat on vase and ring-turned tapering legs ending in pad feet on platforms, joined by bulbous turned front stretchers and plain turned double side stretchers, old refinish, 18" h seat, 41-1/2" h...750.00

Portsmouth, NH, attributed to, 1730-70, side, maple yoke crests, vasiform splats flanked by stiles, rear chamfering above trapezoidal over-upholstered seats, cabriole legs with arris knees, pad feed, joined by block ended stretchers, old refinish, minor surface imperfections, 18" h, 37-1/2" h, pr..............................4,890.00

SE New England, c1740-60, roundabout chamber chair, cherry, shaped crest rail continues to scrolled arms, vase and ring turned supports, shaped splats on molded shoes, upholstered slip set and 3 block and turned tapering legs, button feet, joined by deep skirt, front cabriole leg ends in high pad foot, old finish, 16-1/2" h seat, 28" h...4,325.00

Queen Anne Style, America, dining, two armchairs, six side chairs, dipped crest rail over vasiform splat, needlepoint overstuffed seat with shaped rails, cabriole legs with hairy-paw feet, carved flower heads and foliage, set of 8 ....3,000.00

Regency, dining, inlaid mahogany, open rect back with curved, scroll crest rail inset with flame mahogany panel, curved crossbar, slip seat, molded sabre legs, set of 6....................................2,200.00

Regency Style, arm, painted, slightly curved pierced rect top rail with hand painted figures above pierced and carved splat, downswept arms, flared bow front rect carved seat with cushion, tapering turned legs with paw feet...225.00

Renaissance Style, arm, walnut, needlepoint upholstered backrest centered by bouquet of flowers, curved arms, padded seat on turned legs joined by double "C" stretcher 300.00

Rococo Revival, third quarter 19th C, side, laminated rosewood, arched back with foliage and scroll dec upholstered serpentine seat, cabriole legs on casters, 35-1/4" h 575.00

Sheraton, dining, two arm chairs, six side chairs, old worn cream colored paint with gold and black, turned legs and posts, outward curving feet, balloon seats, shaped arms and ladderbacks, replaced paper rush seats, minor repairs, 33-1/2" h 1,980.00

Victorian

America, 19th C, invalid, walnut, rounded top rail continuing into half-upholstered arms mounted with swiveling directional knobs, shaped legs flanked by 2 front and one back wheel, folding foot rest, 26-1/2" w, 26" d, 43" h 1,100.00

America, third quarter 19th C, arm, carved mahogany, cartouche-shaped padded back within conforming frame surmounted by flower carved crest, out-curved scroll arms with padded elbow rests, serpentine-fronted overstuffed seat with shaped conforming rails continuing into cabriole legs with scroll feet, frame carved throughout with flowers and foliage, pr 700.00

English, c1880, easy, walnut and green leather upholstery, scrolled back, padded neck, loose bowed seat, short turned legs on casters, scuffing, 37" h 2,185.00

William IV, English, second quarter 19th C, revolving library armchair, mahogany and black leather upholstery, high buttoned back, over out-scrolled arms, plain seat, short turned legs ending in brass caps and casters, restorations, 39" h...2,100.00

Windsor

Birdcage, side, painted bamboo turned, Daniel Abbot, Newburyport, MA, 1809-11, 6 spindles and bamboo turnings, painted black, branded "D. Abbot & Co.," 16-1/2" h seat, 33" h 230.00

Bow Back

Arm, reeded bow, scrolled arms and spindle back, bamboo turnings, shaped seat with edge carving, turned arm posts, splayed base and rungs, old worn black paint, repairs, 18-1/2" h seat, 36" h 475.00

Arm, shaped arms and spindle back, turned arm supports, shaped seat, splayed base, bulbous turned legs, "H" stretcher, worn old black over green paint, arm posts don't match leg turnings, one doweled repair, 17" h seat, 34-1/2" h.......990.00

Side, adult's, Boston, 1790, maple and ash, branded "S. J. Tuck," bowed beaded crest above 9 tapering incised singles, incised shaped seat, swelled splayed legs joined by H-stretchers, refinished, 18-1/2" h, 38" h 1,100.00

Side, child's, New England, early 19th C, bowed crest and spindles, plank shaped seat, swelled legs joined by H stretchers, old black paint, cracks in seat, paint loss, 8-1/4" h seat, 20-1/2" h...800.00

Brace Back, New York, c1770-90, arm, black paint, yellow dec, oak scrolled crest rail, hickory back posts and five spindles, maple arms, legs, and stretcher, poplar seat, 26" w, 19-1/2" d, 17-1/4" h seat, 43" h 9,500.00

Braced continuous arm, CT, 1780-1803, chestnut and maple, branded "E. B. Tracy," crest with beaded edge continues to shaped hand-holds over shaped seat with extended piece to receive bracing above deeply incised splayed legs joined by H stretchers, 17" h seat, 37" h..1,100.00

Comb Back, New England, early 19th C

Continuous arm, pine and maple, remnants of old resin varnish surface, rockers added, height loss, 15" h seat, 44" h ..750.00

Writing arm, painted, shaped crest rail, five spindles, shaped back, writing surface with two drawers beneath, shaped seat with drawer, splayed bamboo turned legs joined by stretchers, old black paint, restoration to drawers, 17" h seat, 42-1/2" h..4,025.00

Continuous Arm, New England, early 19th C, pine and maple, shaped incised seats, turned splayed legs, refinished, 35" h, price for pr 1,100.00

Fan Back, New England, early 19th C, painted, curving crests, tapering spindles, shaped seats, splayed legs, repainted dark red, 35-1/2" h, price for set of four 3,200.00

High Back, Pennsylvania, 1770-80, arm, painted, serpentine crest terminates in carved scrolls above spindles, open arms ending in carved knuckles, shaped incised seat, bulbous turned legs joined by swelled stretchers, old red paint, 18-1/2" h seat, 39-3/4" h...6,325.00

High Chair, child's, rod-back, New England, early 19th C, painted, incised tapering spindles, 21-3/4" h seat, 33-1/2" h............980.00

Hoop Back, American, early 19th C, side, bamboo-turned spindle back, saddle seat, rakish legs, H-form stretcher, painted green........700.00

Rod Back, William Dalton, Boston, c1800, side, slightly concave crest rail, seven spindles, bamboo-turned stiles, shaped incised seat, splayed legs joined by stretchers, old dark brown surface, branded "W. Dalton," 17" h, 33" h, set of six 4,325.00
Sack Back
New England, c1780, maple and ash, bowed crest rail above seven spindles, shaped arms, vase and ring-turned supports, shaped saddle seat, splayed vase and ring-turned legs joined by stretchers, old varnish, repair to crest rail, 16-1/2" h seat, 38" h 2,185.00
New England, late 18th C, painted, bowed crest rail above seven spindles, shaped arms, vase and ring-turned supports, shaped saddle seat, splayed vase, ring-turned legs joined by swelled stretchers, old black paint, 17" h seat, 35-1/4" h 2,300.00
Southern New England, late 18th C, later rosewood graining and yellow outlines, old surface, 17-5/8" h seat, 38" h 1,500.00
Side, New England, 1820-30, painted yellow ground, green and red stenciled leaf and berry dec, green accents, shaped plank seats, splayed bamboo turned legs, some repaint, 17" h seat, 33-1/4" h, set of four 900.00

Chests of Drawers

Art Deco, Quigley, France, c1925, parchment covered, rect top, three tapering drawers, pyramid mirrored stiles, bracket feet, back branded, 44-1/2" x 35"..2,750.00
Chippendale
Boston, MA, c1780, mahogany, serpentine front, molded edge top, 4 dovetailed drawers, beaded frame, base edge molding and apron drops, ogee feet, old brasses, old finish, 42" w, 24-1/4" d, 31-1/2" h 7,150.00
Boston, MA, c1780, mahogany, serpentine front, thumb-molded top, 4 dovetailed drawers, beaded frame, high bracket feet with well-shaped scroll work, old replaced period brasses, old finish, minor repairs to feet, 20-1/2" x 37-3/4" top, 34-3/4" w, 32-1/2" h . 23,100.00
Connecticut River Valley, birch, pine secondary wood, serpentine front, thumb-molded top, 4 dovetailed drawers set in beaded frame, well shaped bracket feet, replaced brasses, refinished, age crack, repaired breaks in top, 34" w, 22-1/2" d, 32-3/4" h 8,800.00
Massachusetts, c1770-80, cherry, rect molded top, case of 4 thumb-

molded graduated drawers flanked by engaged turned and reeded quarter columns, ogee bracket feet, replaced brasses, refinished, restorations, 38" w, 20" d, 34" h.. 2,990.00
Massachusetts, c1770-80, maple, flat molded cornice, case of 2 thumb-molded graduated short drawers over 4 graduated long drawers, bracket feet, most brasses orig, old refinish, 36-3/4" w, 18" d, 44-1/2" h 4,025.00
Massachusetts, c1775, mahogany, pine secondary wood, block front, thumb-molded top, 4 dovetailed drawers set in beaded frame, conforming base molding, apron drop with carved fan, ogee feet, orig brasses, old finish, minor base repairs, 33" w, 21" d, 30" h 25,300.00
Massachusetts, c1780, mahogany, carved bowfront, overhanging top with inlaid edge, cockbeaded case, 4 graduated drawers, carved claw and ball feet, old refinish, replaced brasses, imperfections, 37-3/4" w, 22" d, 34-1/2" h 5,500.00
Massachusetts, c1790, mahogany, pine secondary wood, serpentine, thumb-molded top, 4 dovetailed drawers with edge beading, base moldings, ogee feet, orig brasses, old finish, old repairs, 35-1/2" w, 32" h 14,300.00
Massachusetts, c1780, maple, rect overhanging molded top, case of 4 graduated thumb-molded drawers, ogee bracket feet on casters, old brasses, old refinish, restoration, 36" w, 19-1/2" d, 31-1/2" h 2,300.00
New Hampshire, 1760-80, maple, flat molded cornice, case of 5 thumb-molded graduated drawers, bracket feet, center pinwheel carved pendant, brasses missing, old refinish, minor imperfections, 38-1/2" w, 18" d, 49-1/4" h.................................. 4,000.00
Pennsylvania, c1770-80, carved cherry, rect molded top, case with 4 thumb-molded graduated drawers flanked by fluted lamb's tongue corners, bracket feet, replaced brasses, refinished, minor imperfections, 41-1/2" w, 19-1/4" d, 34" h........................ 4,140.00
Pennsylvania, c1780, carved mahogany, rect molded top, case with 4 cockbeaded graduated drawers, flanked by fitted quarter columns, ogee bracket feet, replaced brasses, old refinish, restoration, 40" w, 19-1/2" d, 35" h.. 6,325.00
Rhode Island, c1770-80, cherry, overhanging molded top, case with 2 thumb-molded short drawers and 4 graduated long drawers, ogee bracket feet, replaced brasses, old refinish, restorations, 36-1/2" w, 18-1/2" d, 42" h.................................... 2,415.00
Rhode Island, c1780, maple, molded cornice, case with 2 thumb-molded short drawers and 6 graduated long drawers, bracket feet, old brasses, old refinish, restored, 36" w, 19" d, 53-1/2" h....3,450.00
Chippendale Style, mahogany, molded top, 4 graduated long drawers, bracket feet, some 18th C components, 37" w, 19-3/4" d, 31-3/4" h... 500.00
Classical, northshore MA, c1825, carved mahogany and mahogany veneer, scrolled backboard over three short drawers on projecting case of two half drawers over three long drawers, flanked by recessed panels and pineapple, acanthus leaf and spiral carved columns continuing to turned feet, replaced glass pulls, refinished, imperfections, 42-3/4" w, 22" w, 45" h 1,000.00
Eastlake, curly walnut, burl veneer, carved detail, scrolled crest, four dovetailed drawers, two handkerchief drawers, well detailed molded panel fronts, refinished, 39" w, 17-1/2" d, 46" h 750.00
Empire, America, second quarter 19th C, mahogany, rect mirror plate on chamfered swing-frame suspended between obelisk form posts, base with 2 drawers, outset chest with rect marble top over outset ogee molded drawer raised on scrolled pilasters flanking 2 long drawers, scroll feet, 42-1/2" w, 22" d, 80-1/2" h 550.00
Empire, late, America, second quarter 19th C, cherry and pine, rect top, 4 drawers, upper drawer molded en arbalette, turned short feet, as found condition, 43-1/4" w, 18-1/4" d, 43-1/2" h 250.00
Federal
Massachusetts, Salem, c1810, mahogany and flame birch veneer, bowfront, birch bowed top, case with 4 graduated drawers veneered with flame birch surrounded by mahogany crossbanded veneer, flanked by colonettes and reeding, terminating in ring turned feet, shaped skirt outlined with starts burned into the wood,

Chippendale, MA, c1780, serpentine front, mahogany, rect molded top, applied undermolding, 4 graduated drawers, ogival bracket feet, 36" w, 21" d, 32-1/4" h, $36,000. Photo courtesy of Freeman\Fine Arts.

replaced brasses, old refinish, minor imperfections, 36-3/4" w, 20-1/4" d, 37" h 14,950.00

Massachusetts, c1825, carved mahogany and mahogany veneer, scrolled backboard, 2 cockbeaded short drawers flanked by quarter-engaged vase and ring-turned columns, projecting bowfront case with cockbeaded graduated drawers, flanked by ovolo corners and quarter-engaged vase and ring-turned spiral-carved posts, turned legs, wooden pulls, old finish, imperfections, 37-1/2" w, 17-1/4" d, 44-1/2" h 1,495.00

New England, southeastern, c1800-10, cherry, overhanging rect top, case of 4 cockbeaded graduated drawers, flaring French feet, old brass pulls, old finish, 36-3/4" w, 19" d, 36-1/2" h 4,600.00

New England, 1815-25, carved mahogany and mahogany veneer, rect top with ovolo corners, case of 4 cockbeaded graduated drawers flanked by quarter engaged ring-turned reeded posts continuing to vase and ring-turned legs, replaced brass pulls, old refinish, 42-3/4" w, 19-3/4" d, 43-1/4" h 1,035.00

New Hampshire, early 19th C, mahogany and bird's eye maple veneer, bowfront, bowed top with inlaid edge, case of 4 cockbeaded drawers, bird's eye maple veneer surrounded by crossbanded mahogany veneer, scrolled front skirt with side shaping, curving feet, orig brasses, old refinish, minor imperfections, 39-3/4" w, 22" d, 37" h..9,775.00

Rhode Island, c1815-20, mahogany inlaid, rect top with ovolo corners, case of 4 graduated cockbeaded drawers flanked by quarter engaged ring-turned reeded columns ending in vase and ring-turned legs, ball feet, joined by shaped skirt, brasses may be original and include portrait likeness of Napoleon, old refinish, imperfections, 44" w, 23-3/4" d, 38-1/4" h 2,185.00

Federal, late, American

Mahogany, rect top, open molded splashboard, 4 long drawers, turned legs, 41" w, 22" d, 52" h 475.00

Walnut, rect molded top, 4 long drawers, turned tapering legs, replaced brasses, 46" w, 21" d, 44" h 400.00

Federal Style, Kittinger, Old Dominion, pattern 2023 HC, molded top, 4 serpentine form long drawers, burl inlaid shaped skirt continuing into shaped legs, 37" w, 22" d, 34" h.......................................500.00

George III, late, English, early 19th C

Mahogany and inlay, rect molded to, 2 short drawers, central secret drawer over 3 graduated drawers, bracket feet, 52-1/4" w, 21-3/4" d, 39-1/2" h 4,350.00

Mahogany, bowfront, bowed top over 4 graduated cockbeaded drawers, French feet, restorations, 41" w, 23" d, 34" h 1,035.00

Hepplewhite, cherry, poplar secondary wood, bowfront, front edge of bowed top has curly maple banding, 4 dovetailed drawers, shaped apron, high French feet, oval medallion on apron, stringing, and invected corners on drawers inlay, orig oval brasses with emb flowers and foliage, old varnish finish, edge damage and age cracks in apron, old repair, 36" w, 20-3/4" d, 43-1/4" h.......................3,300.00

Sheraton

Country, cherry and curly maple, 4 dovetailed drawers with edge beading, pine end panels, turned feet, refinished, 47" w, 18-1/2" d, 45-1/4" h 750.00

Country, cherry, poplar and walnut secondary wood, 4 dovetailed drawers with cock beading, paneled ends, scrolled apron, turned feet, refinished, 39-1/4" w, 19-3/4' d, 39-1/2" h 800.00

Pennsylvania, cherry, inlay, poplar and oak secondary wood, top section with rounded top and 5 dovetailed drawers, center doors with star inlay and 3 interior drawers, base with 7 dovetailed drawers, paneled ends, scrolled apron, turned feet, brass pulls, old finish, some edge damage to feet, repairs to base, mismatched top, 41-1/2" w, 21" d, 69-3/4" h 3,025.00

Chest of Drawers, Other

Chest on Chest

Chippendale

Connecticut, attributed to London County, cherry, pine secondary wood, bonnet top, top: carved rosettes, flame finial on shell plinth, 7 drawers, carved shells on drawers in top and base. base: 5 dovetailed overlapping drawers, scrolled and carved apron that

Chippendale, c1770, walnut, rect molded top, straight front, 5 small over 4 wide graduated thumb molded drawers, brass bail handles, escutcheons, and lock plates, molded base, straight bracket feet, 40" w, 22" d, 60" h, $5,100. Photo courtesy of Freeman\Fine Arts.

conforms to curve of 4 cabriole legs, ball and claw feet, replaced brasses, old mellow finish, sgd "A. H. Landon," on upper right hand drawer, 37-1/4" w, 21" x 40" cornice, 84" h 49,500.00

Lancaster County, PA, walnut, boldly detailed, molded cornice, top case with 7 dovetailed overlapping drawers, fluted quarter columns on top and base, one dovetailed drawer in base, base moldings, ogee feet, old finish, some edge damage, wear, 47-3/4" w, 21" d, 65" h 14,300.00

George III, English, late 18th C, scarlet japanned and Chinoisiere dec, broken swan's neck cornice over pair of short drawers over 3 graduated drawers, base with 3 graduated drawers, bracket feet, restoration o paint, 38-1/4" w, 21" d, 77" h 7,000.00

Chest on Frame, Queen Anne, country, walnut, dovetailed chest, 7 dovetailed overlapping drawers, inlaid initials "M. E." on top drawer, base with scalloped apron, cabriole legs, and duck feet, repairs to drawers, cornice replaced, brasses replaced, replaced base, refinished, 20-1/4" x 40-1/2", 58-1/2" h 1,650.00

Chest on Stand, Flemish Baroque Style, late 19th C, ivory inlaid ebony, rect chest with 18 drawers and handles on sides, raised on short turned feet, base with baluster turned legs joined by shaped stretcher, whole with intricate foliate and figural inlay, losses, damage, 38-3/4" w, 14-1/4" d, 55-1/4" h 2,650.00

Commode

Louis XV Style, molded rect top with serpentine front and sides, conforming front with 2 short drawers over 2 long drawers flanked by keeled stiles continuing into splayed feet, joined by shaped skirt, painted pale green ground with floral sprays in scrolled reserves, 45-1/2" w, 21-3/4" d, 36-3/4" h 2,750.00

Louis XV Style, serpentine brocatelle marble top, 2 long drawers, serpentine sides, short cabriole legs with acanthus sabots, 51-1/2" w, 21-1/4" d, 33-1/2" h..1,500.00

Rococo, Italian, mid 18th C, walnut, molded rect top with serpentine front edge, conforming bombe front with 3 molded drawers veneered in burl walnut, paneled bombe stiles continuing to splayed sq section legs joined by shaped skirt, 50-1/2" w, 24-1/2" d, 33-1/4" h...2,500.00

Transitional Louis XV/Louis XVI, amaranth and parquetry, molded beche d'Alep rect marble top with serpentine front and sides, conforming front with 3 drawers flanked by convex stiles continuing into keeled cabriole legs joined by shaped skirt, 48" w, 20-3/4" d, 32" h...700.00

Highboy
Chippendale, New England, 18th C, carved cherry, serpentine cove molding above upper case of thumb-molded drawers, single one fan carved, lower case with similar drawers, central fan carved drawer, skirt with front and side shaping, cabriole legs, pad feet, some replaced brasses, refinished, repairs, missing finials and pendants, 38" w, 19-1/2" d, 84" h 37,950.00
Queen Anne
Massachusetts, cherry and maple, molded cornice, nine dovetailed overlapping drawers in top, four in base, scrolled apron with block carving that conforms to carved fan on center drawer, cabriole legs with duck feet, replaced Ball & Ball brasses, refinished, several repairs, two sets of apron drops included, 35-1/2" w, 76-3/4" h 8,525.00
New Hampshire, walnut and birch, 2 sections, upper: dovetailed case with 8 overlapping dovetailed drawers with carved shells, turned finials, molded cornice, base: 5 overlapping drawers with carved shells, scrolled apron, cabriole legs with duck feet, orig brasses, old finish, some old repairs, 36" w, 20" d, 84" h 15,400.00
Pennsylvania, walnut, pine secondary wood, bonnet top with seven dovetailed overlapping drawers with carved fan and flame carved finials, 4 dovetailed overlapping drawers with carved fan, scrolled apron with acorn drops, cabriole legs with duck feet, old replaced engraved brasses, old finish, repairs to bonnet top, 36" w, 83-1/2" h 18,700.00
Lowboy
Queen Anne
Massachusetts, cherry, poplar secondary wood, carved fan and thumb molded top with cut-out corners, 4 dovetailed overlapping drawers, scrolled apron with acorn drops, cabriole legs, duck feet, orig brasses, old finish, pristine condition, 20-3/4" x 34-3/4" top, 30-1/4" h 34,100.00
Massachusetts, attributed to North Shore, walnut, pine secondary wood, thumb-molded two board top, 6 dovetailed drawers with banded inlay, center drawer with concave blocking with inlaid compass star, scrolled apron with turned drops, cabriole legs with duck feet, replaced brasses, old mellow finish, age cracks in top, interior stains, back painted black, 34-1/2" x 25" top, 32" h 15,400.00
Pennsylvania, figured walnut, pine and oak secondary woods, thumb-molded one board top with cut corners, case with scrolled apron with carved shell, quarter columns with carved foliage, 4 dovetailed drawers, cabriole legs with carving on knees, stocking legs, trifid feet, orig brasses, old finish, age crack in top, possible reshaping to apron, 33-1/4" x 20" top, 29-3/4" h 19,800.00
Mule, country
Decorated, pine, old red repaint, black combed graining, lift top lid, 2 early dovetailed drawers, bracket feet, early brasses, repairs to feet, some side scratches, 41-1/2" w, 17-1/2" d, 44-1/2" h . 825.00
Oak and pine, hinged lid with six false drawer fronts, 2 dovetailed overlapping drawers, scrolled apron, bandy feet, replaced brasses, refinished, repairs to feet, apron, and lid, 47-3/4" w, 21" x 50-1/2", 42-1/2" h 2,200.00
Semanier, transitional Louis XV/Louis XVI style, kingwood and parquetry, rect sienna marble top with breakfront edge, canted corners, conforming front with 7 parquetry drawers flanked by canted and crossbanded stiles, short keeled cabriole legs joined by shaped skirt, 29" w, 15-1/4" d, 57-3/4" h 1,200.00
Sugar, Sheraton, walnut, fine turned legs, single drawer in base, int. divided into 3 sections, fine dovetailed construction, sgd "Read Atlanta GA" old refinish, 29" w, 18-3/4" d, 39" h 3,200.00
Tall
Chippendale
Massachusetts, late 18th C, cherry, flat molded cornice, 5 thumb-molded graduated drawers, bracket feet, replaced brasses, refinished, stained to resemble tiger maple, 36-1/2" w, 17" d, 52" h 4,600.00

Massachusetts or New Hampshire, 18th C, maple and birch, flat molded cornice over case with 5 thumb-molded graduated drawers, top drawer with faux three drawer facade with center carved fan, tall bracket feet, replaced brasses, refinished, imperfections, 38-1/4" h, 19-1/4" d, 49-3/4" h 1,955.00

Cradles

Chippendale Style, birch, canted sides, scalloped headboard, turned posts and rails, refinished, 37-1/2" l 400.00
Country
American, hooded, mahogany, dovetailed case, scrolled detail on foot and hood, cutout rockers, pine bottom board, brass end handles, old, possibly orig finish, minor old repair, 44" l 1,210.00
New England, 18th C, painted pine, arched hood continuing to shaped and carved dovetailed sides, rockers, old light green paint, old repairs, 40" l 300.00
Pennsylvania, late 18th C, dovetailed, refinished curly maple, cut-out hearts, age cracks and shrinkage, 41" l550.00
Pennsylvania, 19th C, walnut, scrolled back and sides, shaped rockers, old refinish, repaired crest, 39" l, 18-1/4" d, 21" h 250.00
Eastlake, 1875, walnut, paneled headboard, footboard, and sides, scrolling crest above short turned spindles, platform support, orig finish, dated 495.00
Rustic, twig construction, rocker base, unsigned, 33" l, 22" d, 22" h 100.00
Victorian, cast iron, painted black, wooden slat bottom, finial missing, 37" l, 21" d, 36" h 200.00
Windsor, New England, c1800-20, bamboo turned spindles, worn finish 850.00

Cupboard

Armoire
Art Deco, teak, architectural form cornice, ebonized trim, center applied ebonized stepped plaque, 2 raised paneled doors with ebonized trim, 2 drawers over geometrically shaped apron with ebonized trim, small ebonized stepped block feet, 39" w, 21-1/2" d, 79" h 650.00
Art Nouveau, teak, molded arched crest over plain frieze, pair of paneled doors, glazed panels at top, plinth base, 46" w, 16-1/2" d, 85" h 750.00
Empire Style, America, mahogany, rect outset top over front with pair of outset frieze drawers surmounting pr of paneled doors,

Country, one piece, corner, molded cornice, 12 panes in top door, paneled door, scrolled apron, cut-out feet, refinished walnut, cut down, feet replaced, repairs, 37-1/4" w, 74" h, $1,540. Photo courtesy of Garth's Auctions.

sliding shelves, plinth base, turned short feet, 43" w, 27-1/2" d, 60" h...650.00

French Colonial, 19th C, rosewood, triple arched crest with berry and vine dec, three mirrored doors, sides with reverse paintings of deer amidst trees, cabriole legs, scrolled toes, 70-1/2" w, 19-3/4" d, 91" h...1,725.00

French Provincial, 18th C, arched cornice over carved frieze with finely carved floral basket, pair of conforming raised and fielded panel doors with floral carving, shaped apron continuing to short cabriole legs, scroll feet, 51-1/2" w, 20-1/2" d, 93" h........3,250.00

French Provincial Style, oak, arched, molded cornice over 2 paneled cupboard doors, shaped apron, raised on shaped ball feet, 44-1/2" w, 22" d, 78-1/2" h...1,800.00

Provincial Louis XV, carved pine, arched cavetto cornice surmounted by scrolls, conforming paneled frieze centering circular cartouche, front with pair of doors, each with 2 shaped panels, opening to shelves, trays, and hanging space, flanked by rounded stiles continuing into short cabriole legs with scroll toes joined by shaped skirt, 58-3/4" w, 27-1/2" d, 92-3/4" h 1,500.00

Louis XIV, French, late 17th C, walnut, rect molded cornice above finely scroll carved frieze centering half-shell, 2 irregularly fielded panel doors, central rect reserves, later block feet, restoration and replacements, 60" w, 26" d, 94" h 6,000.00

Chifforobe, Art Deco, 1935, herringbone design waterfall veneer, arched center mirror, dropped center section, four deep drawers flanked by tall cupboard doors, shaped apron 450.00

Corner

Chippendale, Pennsylvania, attributed to Lancaster County, two piece, cherry, pine and poplar secondary wood, upper: broken arch pediment with carved foliage and shell and carved rosettes, carved finials on fluted plinths, door with 12 panes, arched to rail, base: raised panel doors, 3 dovetailed drawers, ogee feet, replaced brasses and hardware, old mellow finish, repairs and restoration, 44-1/4" w cornice, 102" h 9,350.00

Empire, Ohio, attributed to Perry or Fairfield County, cherry, burl veneer and figured veneer, poplar secondary wood, bowfront, elaborate molded cornice with applied moldings, arched double doors each with 10 panes of old glass, paneled doors, one nailed drawer, turned pilasters with rope, pineapple and herringbone carving, paw feet, replaced brasses, old mellow finish, butterfly shelves in top, 55" w, 103" h 8,250.00

Federal, Perry County, Ohio, cherry and curly maple, ebonized trim, 6 dovetailed drawers with turned pulls, paneled doors, turned quarter columns, bracket feet, old varnish finish, 46" w, 50" h...3,300.00

Hepplewhite, Southern, attributed to VA or the Piedmont, one piece, walnut, yellow pine and polar secondary wood, inlay, broken arch pediment with molded cornice, double top doors each with 8 panes of glass, paneled doors, scrolled apron, bracket feet, stringing, diamonds, and vining foliage with fan in cornice and geometric design in rosettes, old soft finish, scrolled front shelves in top section, minor edge damage, 48-5/8" w, 94" h.....18,700.00

Hanging, George III, last quarter 18th C, inlaid mahogany, corner, outset molded cornice with canted ends, front with crossbanded frieze, similarly banded tracery door with 12 panes, glazing bars with boxwood stringing, interior with 3 shelves, raised on outset molded base, 31-1/4" w, 19" d, 44-1/2" h...1,800.00

Jelly, country, refinished poplar, molded edge top with crest, two dovetailed drawers, paneled doors, paneled ends, turned feet, minor edge damage, age cracks, 39-1/2" w, 20-1/2" x 42" top, 53" h 625.00

Kas, Long Island, NY, c1730-80, cherry, pine, and polar, architectural cornice molding, two raised panel thumb-molded doors flanked by reeded pilasters, applied moldings, single drawer, painted detachable disc and stretcher feet, replaced hardware, refinished, restored, 65-1/2" w, 26-1/4" d, 77-1/4" h 4,500.00

Kitchen (Hoosier), American, early 20th C, oak, scalloped cornice over three cupboard doors, two glazed over two larger paneled doors, outset lower section with aluminum-lined work surface, over cupboard door flanked by three graduated drawers, 39-1/2" w, 28" d, 71-3/4" h...650.00

Linen Press, George III, late 18th/early 19th, mahogany, rect dentil molded cornice over pair of plaint doors, shelved int., base with 3 cockbeaded drawers, bracket feet, some restoration, 48-1/4" w, 23" d, 82-1/2" h 2,300.00

Pewter, two part, top: cornice molding, two six glass pane doors, two shelves, open pie shelf; base: two drawers over raised panel doors, one shelf int., short turned feet, 56" w, 20" d, 87" h 2,250.00

Pie Safe, country

Butternut and poplar, dovetailed case, corner and base moldings, tin paneled doors with star flower and bird dec, old worn green over red paint, orig cast iron latch, porcelain knob, removable batten, insect damage, 48-1/2" w, 72" h 900.00

Poplar, attributed to east Tennessee, worn old red paint, tin panel on each side, two pairs on each door with soldered seams, stylized urns of flowers and oak leaves, turned feet, 53" w, 48" h .. 1,650.00

Poplar, attributed to Zanesville, OH, area, 12 punched tins with snowflake designs, joined with solderless crimped seams, stripped of orig paint, later red wash...............................1,980.00

Slant Back, New England, late 18th C, pine, flat molded cornice above beaded canted front flanking shelves, projecting base with single raised panel door, old refinish, doors missing from top, imperfections, 37-1/2" w, 18" d, 73" h 2,300.00

Spice, oak, maple, mahogany, and walnut, molded cornice with Greek key frieze, paneled door with inlaid sunburst, dovetailed interior drawers, bracket feet, hinges replaced, repairs, 13-3/8" w, 19-1/2" h 6,875.00

Step Back

New England, 18th C, primitive, two pc, top: three shelves with plate groove; lower: two drawers, two panel doors, traces of orig red paint, 56-1/2" w, 23-1/2" d, 81" h 1,700.00

Pennsylvania, two piece, pine and poplar, upper: flat top with dove molded cornice, two paneled doors, shelf int., turned quarter columns, pie shelf; lower: three small dovetailed overlapping drawers, two paneled cupboard doors, turned quarter columns, straight apron, bracket feet, wood knob handles, brownish-red paint traces, repainted black trim, 55" w, 22" d, 84" h......4,500.00

Wall

Federal, PA or Ohio, c1830, cherry, molded top above 2 beaded small drawers, similar glazed door opens to int. space flanked by recessed panel sides, turned legs ending in small ball feet, refinished, imperfections, 28" w, 13-1/2" d, 25" h 1,850.00

Queen Anne Style, English, late 19th/early 20th C, walnut, burl walnut, and polychrome dec, molded cornice over shelves, central cabinet door and drawer, base with drawers, cabriole legs, pad feet, shrinkage, wear to polychrome, 42-3/4" w, 17-1/2" d, 70-1/2" h 4,900.00

Shaker, New Lebanon, NY, 19th C, painted pine, 2 doors, numbered and labeled shelved int., old light green paint, int. unpainted, some shelves missing, 23-3/4" w, 7-1/2" d, 40-1/2" h 1,610.00

Wardrobe, Ohio, attributed to Delaware County, walnut, molded cornice, one paneled door, scrolled apron, cutout feet, one int. shelf, orig hooks removed, brass latch added, old soft finish, one end of cornice cut to fit corner, 41-3/4" w, 77-1/2" h 1,870.00

Desks

Art Nouveau, style of Louis Majorelle, c1900, rect top, leather inset over central drawer flanked by double drawers with brass mounts, stylized pine cone motifs, molded legs, 51" l, 29-1/2" w, 29" 6,900.00

Arts & Crafts

American

c1912, oak, drop front, floriform strapwork, int. fitted with drawers and letter compartments, 2 split drawers over 2 long drawers, refinished, 36-1/4" w, 17-1/2" d, 45-3/4" h 1,840.00

c1916, oak, rect top, through posts over single drawer, round wood pulls flanked by book compartments with vertical slats, round revealed plugs, unsigned, 48" w, 28" d, 29" h....................800.00

Limbert, Michigan, c1912, No. 718, central pen tray, flanked by letter holders over 2 drawers with "V" pulls, median shelf, branded mark, 36" w, 20" d, 37-3/4" h, stains, joint separation 1,100.00

Stickley, L. and J. G., Onondaga Shops, chestnut, drop-front, full gallery int., chamfered back, lower shelf area with open sides, shoe feet, new ebonized finish, unmarked, 32-1/2" w, 14-1/2" d, 48" h 700.00

Eastlake, cylinder top, lady's, fitted int., carving, $850.

Chippendale

Boston, MA, c1770-80, slant lid, mahogany, int. with central concave fan carved prospect door opening to 3 concave drawers, flanked by baluster fronted document drawers, 3 valanced compartments, blocked drawers, fan carved drawer above 2 concave drawers, case with 4 thumb-molded graduated drawers, bracket feet, replaced brasses, old refinish, imperfections, 39-1/2" w, 19-1/2" d, 42-1/4" h 37,600.00

Concord, MA, c1780-90, slant lid, maple, 3 thumb-molded drawers over case with slant lid, int. with valanced small compartments, 2 document drawers, 5 small drawers, case with 4 graduated thumb-molded drawers, molded base , high shaped bracket feet, old refinish, imperfections, inscribed "the property of Merriam, the first settlers of Concord," 35" w, 18" d, 47-1/2" h 17,250.00

Country, maple, slant front, dovetailed case, 4 dovetailed overlapping drawers, fitted int. with 13 dovetailed drawers, ogee feet, orig brasses, refinished, replaced int., repairs to feet and drawers, 40" w, 19-1/2" d, 43-1/2" h 1,100.00

Massachusetts, c1780, slant lid, birch, lid opens to shaped into with 10 compartments and small drawers, cockbeaded case with 4 graduated drawers, bracket feet, replaced brasses, old refinish, imperfections, 40" w, 21-1/4" d, 44-1/4" h 1,955.00

Rhode Island, c1770-80, slant lid, mahogany, int. of 8 valanced drawers above compartments, 4 small drawers with central shell carved prospect door enclosing 2 valanced compartments and 2 blocked drawers, case with 4 thumb-molded graduated drawers, ogee bracket feet, replaced brasses, 38" w, 19" d, 41-1/4" h.........2,415.00

Classical, New England, 1825-35, mahogany veneer, projecting cornice above veneered frieze and glazed doors, opens to two adjustable shelves over 3 small drawers, fold-out fitted writing surface lists to well with two drawers and open compartments, 2 recessed panel doors open to single shelved int. flanked by scrolled supports which end in leaf and paw carved front feet, replaced brasses, refinished, restoration, 40" w, 23-1/4" d, 81" h 1,380.00

Colonial Revival

Chippendale Style, c1930, block front, solid walnut case, walnut veneered slant front, fitted int., secret drawer, paw feet, 32" w, 18" d, 42" h 750.00

Governor Winthrop Style, c1920, serpentine front, mahogany veneer, solid mahogany slant front, fitted int. with 2 document drawers, shall carved center door, 4 long drawers, brass pulls and escutcheons... 800.00

Eastlake, lady's, walnut, two part, top section sits on pegs, top: mirror with two columns supported shelves, fancy carving, pressed dec; base section: double hinged writing surface with dec floral carving, writing surface with two panels of green felt, lifts to reveal compartment desk int. with two drawers, one side fitted with two long drawers, gallery shelf in base, dec applied pieces, shoe foot base, metal asters, 31-1/2" w, 19" d, 57" h 1,150.00

Edwardian, c1900, kneehole, mahogany, rect crossbanded top with central oval medallion, front canted corners, long frieze drawer, two banks of three drawers, center cupboard door, foliate marquetry dec, 37-1/2" w, 31" h 600.00

Empire, America, first quarter 19th C, butler's, various woods, rect top with outset paneled frieze drawer, fall-front, fitted int. with small drawers, valanced pigeon holes and writing surface, 3 long cockbeaded drawers flanked by split spindles, turned short legs, repairs, wear, 41" w, 21-1/4" d, 47" h 425.00

Federal

Central Massachusetts, early 19th C, lady's, mahogany inlaid, cove-molded top above three drawers with inlaid floral vines, checkered veneer banding opening to three-section int., end sections each with three drawers above openings flanking two central compartments over fold-out writing surface, cockbeaded bird's eye maple and mahogany veneer drawers flanked by colonettes above spiral carved engraved columns ending in turned feet, replaced brass, old surface, door inscribed "F. A. Butler, Deerfield, March 1864," legs pieced, other repairs, 40-3/4" w, 20-1/2" d, 54" h 4,325.00

New England, early 19th C, mahogany and mahogany veneer inlaid, top section shaped gallery above flat molded cornice, two glazed doors enclosing compartments and drawer, flanking door and small drawer; projecting base with fold-out writing surface, two cockbeaded short drawers, two graduated long drawers, four sq tapering legs, inlaid cross-banding, old refinish, some restoration, inscribed "22 Geo. L. Deblois Sept 12th 1810," 37-1/8" w, 20" d, 51-1/2" h 3,000.00

New York State, early 19th C, mahogany veneer inlaid, slant lid and three graduated drawers outlined in stringing with ovolo corners, int. of veneer and outline stringing on drawers, valanced compartments, prospect door opening to inner compartments and drawers, flanking document drawers, orig brasses, old surface, veneer cracking loss and patching, other surface imperfections, 41-1/2" w, 21-1/2" d, 44" h 2,550.00

Pennsylvania, early 19th C, walnut inlaid, slant front, lid and cockbeaded drawers outlined in stringing, base with band of contrasting veneers, int. of small drawers above valanced compartments, scrolled dividers flanking prospect door which opens to two small drawers, three drawers, old refinish, repairs, 40" w, 20" d, 44-1/2" h 3,550.00

Southern New England, c1780-1800, slant lid, wavy birch, lid opens to valanced multi-drawer int., case of 4 gradated drawers with incised cockbeading on cutout base, replaced brasses, old refinish, minor imperfections, 39-1/4" w, 19-1/2" d, 43-1/2" h 2,550.00

George III, English, late 18th/early 19th C

Partner's, mahogany, rect molded top divided into 4 sections, all inset with lifting panels of tooled green leather, pedestals with drawers on one side, cupboard doors on reverse, restoration, 68-1/2" l, 48" d, 31" h 8,100.00

Slant front, mahogany, lid enclosing fitted writing compartment above 4 graduated cockbeaded drawers, shaped bracket feet, some restoration, 38-1/2" w, 18-1/2" d, 42-1/4" h 1,000.00

George III, late, English, burl elmwood, slant front with rect crossbanding, fitted int. of pigeonholes and drawers, three graduated crossbanded drawers, serpentine apron, bracket feet, restorations, 30-1/2" w, 38" h 1,800.00

George III Style, partner's, third quarter, 19th C, burl elm, rect top, gold tooled green leather writing surface, molded edge, four crossbanded cockbeaded frieze drawers, two banks of three crossbanded cockbeaded and opposing cupboard doors, plinth base, 72" w, 31" h 2,875.00

Hepplewhite
American, cherry, slant front, dovetailed case, four dovetailed drawers with edge beading, fitted int. with eight dovetailed drawers, two letter drawers and center door, scrolled apron, French feet, replaced brasses, old mellow refinishing, old pieced repairs, 41-1/2" w, 19" d, 35" h writing surface, 46" h 3,350.00

Pennsylvania, early 19th C, walnut, rect top, thumb molded edge, string and quarter fan inlaid hinged slant front, fitted int., four line inlaid graduated long drawers, oval brass handles, shaped skirt with banded inlay, French feet, 42" w, 45" h 3,000.00

Napoleon III, Bouille Bureau de Dame, sgd "P. Sorman/10, R. Charlot/ Paris," third quarter 19th C, red tortoise shell, serpentine superstructure with pierced three-quarter gallery over 2 small drawers, bombe shape opening to fitted int. with leather-lined writing surface, open shelf over 3 serpentine-fronted, bombe drawers veneered with cube parquetry, int. lined with bois de violette, shaped serpentine frieze with drawer, sq section cabriole legs with sabots, sides also bombe, ebonized throughout, gilt-brass stringing, inlaid with foliate panels of premiere partie brass, 29-1/4" w, 18" d, 39-1/2" h.................4,500.00

Queen Anne, Pennsylvania, c1740-60, table top, walnut, lid opens to int. of valanced compartments above 2 drawers and well, case with trunnels on molded dovetailed bracket base, centering shaped pendant, refinished, restoration, 23-1/2" w, 14-1/2" d, 16-1/2" h.2,530.00

Queen Anne Style, English, late 19th/early 20th C, lady's, walnut, molded top, slant top, fitted writing compartment, faux leather book fronted doors, cabriole legs, pad feet, 25-1/4" w, 13" d, 39" h .1,850.00

Regency, English, first half 19th C, Davenport, rosewood, brass galleried top over leather inset writing slope, fitted compartment above drawers, pen drawer to side, turned feet on casters, restorations, 18-3/4" w, 19-3/4" d, 32-3/4" h 1,500.00

William and Mary, attributed to Connecticut, early 18th C, slant lid, walnut veneer, valanced int. with 2 document drawers with columns above 4 drawers with burl veneer and well below, double arch molded case with 2 short drawers and 2 long drawers, molded base, turned feet, replaced engraved brasses, old refinish, 35" w, 19-1/2" d, 40-1/2" h 5,175.00

Renaissance Revival, walnut, beveled mirror, brown marble insert, 80" h, $500.

Hall Trees and Hat Racks

Arts & Crafts, early 20th C
Coat Rack, copper and metal, rect patinated lattice strapwork with 8 coat hooks, pierced copper riveted frame on beveled mirror, 48" w, 26-3/4" h...490.00
Costumer, 4 tall bent vertical slats, joined by 3 graduated clip-cornered medial shelves, 4 angular and reticulated double brass hooks, orig drip pan missing from lower shelf, 12-3/4" w, 72" h.................290.00

Black Forest, foyer etagere, carved and polychrome, shaped mirror plate surmounted by carved winged dragon over jardiniere, flanked on one side by plant stand raised on columnar supports, other side with winged dragon over etagere with 3 open shelves, 2 with spindle galleries, one supported by twisted column, other with carved dragon, resting on carved cabriole leg in shape of mythological beast, reeded toupie form leg, polychrome dec, 45" w, 16-1/2" d, 92" h 3,500.00

Colonial Revival, Baroque-Style, American, 1910, cherry, shell carved crest over cartouche and griffin carved panel back, lift seat, high arms, mask carved base, paw feet, 39-1/2" w, 21-1/2" d, 51" h 700.00

Streamline, design attributed to Jean Lucien, c1935, chromed aluminum structure, hat rack and disc shaped hat pegs over center mirror and umbrella rack, 37-1/2" w, 8" d, 70" h 800.00

Victorian, American, burl walnut, ball finials above paneled and shaped cornice, rect mirror flanked by turned garment holders, marble top drawer supported by turned legs, shaped base, painted metal plant holders, 29" w, 14" d, 93" h 1,400.00

Windsor, American, pine, bamboo turned, six knob like hooks, orig yellow varnish, black striping, 33-3/4" w 200.00

Mirrors

Art Nouveau, wrought iron, octagonal reticulated internal edge, upper part mounted by stylized fountain and floral ground, beveled edge mirror, stamped "E. Brandt" lower right corner, 43" l, 38-1/2" w..64,000.00

Arts & Crafts, early 20th C
Cheval, attributed to CA, c1912, oak, inverted V-shaped crest rail with circular wavy line cutout, rect swivel mirror, 27" w, 75" h 1,725.00

Left: Chippendale, scroll, mahogany, molded frame, gilded liner, composition eagle in crest with old gilding, orig mirror glass, minor wear to silvering, orig finish, 40-1/2" h, 19-3/4" w, $3,575; right: mahogany with gilded gesso detail, eagle finial, repairs, old gold repaint, age but probably not period, 36" h, $550. Photo courtesy of Garth's Auctions.

Wall, oak, rect frame, unsigned, 31" w, 3/4" d, 40" h 175.00
Biedermeier, c1830, wall, walnut, rect plate within conforming frame, out-set deep upper and lower rails, surmounted by cavetto-molded cornice, indecipherable maker's stamp on reverse, 17" w, 24" h 600.00
Chippendale
America, mid 18th C, wall, walnut, rect plate within ogee-molded crossbanded frame surmounted by pierced scroll fretted crest with center rosette, corners issuing further scrolls, suspending similarly fretted skirt, 20" w, 36-1/4" h 950.00
Country, scroll, mahogany veneer on pine, crown ornament and liner have gold repaint, considerable old repair, 31-3/4" h, 17-1/4" w 200.00
England, late 18th C, wall, walnut and parcel gilt, scrolled frame center-ing feathered plume, pierced crest above inlaid gilt incised liner, refinished, imperfections, 24-3/4" w, 43-3/4" h 2,415.00
New England, c1780, inlaid mahogany, scrolled frame with pierced crest of gilt carved phoenix bird above string inlaid liner, 22-3/4" w, 46-1/4" h 2,300.00
New England, 1790-1810, mahogany and carved gilt, scrolled frame, pierced crest and carved phoenix bird above molded gilt incised liner, old finish, minor repairs, 17-1/2" w, 33-1/2" h. 750.00
New England, 1790, mahogany on pine, gilded liner, gilded phoe-nix, good detail, molded mirror frame, minor repairs, replaced glass, 14-1/2" w, 26" h 3,375.00
Chippendale Style
Over Mantel, Chinese, late 19th/early 20th C, giltwood, topped by stylized columns, shaped surround with scrolls, acanthus, and rocaille throughout, Chinese-style birds on each side, 47-1/2" x 52" 2,415.00
Scroll, mahogany veneer, poplar secondary wood, old varnish fin-ish, old repairs, backboard from clock, partial paper label, 19th C, 20-1/2" w, 38" h 550.00
Classical
America, 1830-40, giltwood, 4 sq corners elaborated with foliate devices, repairs, losses, some regilding, 30" w, 26-1/2" h .. 460.00
England, early 19th C, giltwood, girandole, circular convex glass, reeded ebonized surround, carved eagle in flight on crest, carved acanthus leaves and floral pendant device, reglued, restored, 19" w, 39" h 2,645.00
Empire
Architectural, mahogany, acorn drop cornice, turned and acanthus carved pilasters, reeded trim, orig reverse painting of house, trees, and sailboat, old finish, one brass corner rosette missing, 18" w, 32-1/4" h 300.00
Dressing, 1820, swing, mahogany, rect, shaped cornice, half col-umns on sides, fitted single drawer, 17-1/2" w, 10" d, 29" h .. 275.00
Two part, mahogany veneer, ebonized half columns with gold sten-ciled foliage, shiny varnish, replaced glass, 26" h, 13-1/2" w ... 220.00
Federal, America, 19th C
Architectural, double spiral columns sides, flower heads and ribbon swag with bows on top, gilded, 56-1/2" h 3,000.00
Split baluster, eglomise fruit panel, orig gilding, one corner block missing, imperfections, paint loss, 30-1/4" h 300.00
George III Style, English, 19th C
Giltwood, oval, topped by acanthus flanked by spirals, suspending drapery swag looped through spiral suspending husks, bellflower drop to base, 23-1/2" w, 39" l 350.00
Ward, Charles, London, giltwood, swan's neck cresting centered by sea serpent, architectural frame modeled with foliage, shell pen-dant, orig Charles Ward label, flaking, 34" w, 53" h 3,450.00
Henri II Style, French, walnut, architectural molded cornice, shaped finials over frieze fitted with spindle gallery, beveled plate flanked by turned columns, Corinthian capitals, 33-1/2" w, 62" h 450.00
Hepplewhite
Scroll, mahogany veneer on pine, banded inlay, refinished, veneer repairs, old glass with some edge wear to silvering, back boards renailed, 24" w, 47" h 1,155.00
Shaving, mahogany with figured veneer
Bowfront, shield shaped mirror, 3 dovetailed drawers, ogee feet, old finish, orig glass with some silvering wear, orig ivory knobs

and ornaments with some wear, minor edge damage and veneer repair, 17-3/4" w, 8" d, 23-3/4" h 880.00
Serpentine front, figured veneer facade and inlay, oval mirror with shaped posts, 3 dovetailed drawers, ogee feet, inlay con-sists of herringbone banding around drawer, mirror frame, and edge of case, inlaid ivory shield shaped key escutcheon, replaced brass pulls, minor repairs, feet replaced, 17-1/2" w, 8-1/2" d, 23-1/2" h 1,320.00
Italian, Trumeau, mid 18th C, giltwood, rect, divided plate within ogee molded composite frame carved with strap-work, paterae and wheat husks, 23" w, 46-1/4" h 850.00
Modern Gothic, manner of Isaac Scott, c1870, over mantel, walnut and maple, arched crest with five finials, frame chip carved dec, side pan-els with aesthetic foliate dec, 60-1/4" l, 31" h 750.00
Napoleon III, mid 19th C, giltwood, composition, and gray pained, upper panel with pine cone filled urn, lower section with two-part mir-rored plate and foliate frame, 31" w, 72-1/2" h 2,645.00
Neoclassical
Girandole, England, c1790, carved giltwood, circular convex mirror surrounded by delicately executed ornaments, flanked by double, intertwined and leaf carved candlearms with gilt bobeche, candle-cups and cut glass pendants, mirror frame, outlined in leafage and neoclassical spherules has ebonized molded liner, sur-mounted by carved veined Prince of Wales' feathers above crest of carved bow know flanked by cascading laurel leaves, conform-ing pendant attached by 2 lion's heads, old re-gilding, minor imperfections, 41-1/4" x 40-1/4" 26,450.00
Pier, attributed to Boston, c1815, carved giltwood, shell above leafage and cat o'nine tails crest, spiral and acanthus leaf carved ring turned columns punctuated by leaf carved squares at each corner, molded black liner, orig gilding, old glass, 36" w, 71" h 21,850.00
Queen Anne, walnut veneer, pine secondary wood, applied gilded carv-ings, scrolled crests and open frame with gilded liner, old mirror with some wear and flaking to silvering, age cracks in veneer, 13-1/4" w, 31-1/2" h 1,875.00
Queen Anne Style, 19th C, japanned, rocaille carved cresting, serpen-tine front painted with Chinoiserie symbols, 18" w, 39" h 500.00
Renaissance Revival, third quarter 19th C, giltwood, over mantel, fig-ural cresting with female face, floral and acanthus carving, 64" w, 74" h 1,725.00
Rococo Style, English, late 19th/early 20th C, carved giltwood, sur-round carved with continuous scrolling acanthus, 19" w, 38-1/2" h, pr 3,450.00
Sheraton Style, country, early 20th C, shaving, bowfront, cherry, inlay, turned posts and adjustable mirror, 2 dovetailed drawers, turned feet, old mellow refinishing, 16" w, 7-1/2" d, 19-3/4" h 250.00
Victorian, over mantel, giltwood, domed cresting, frame carved with foliate swags, ribbons, and corbels, early 20th C, 43" w, 68" h 1,035.00

Rockers

Art Deco, platform, late 19th C, oak and leather, allover geometric forms, sq crest rail over trapezoid-shaped back with leather insert, flat arm over vertical down shaped supports, conforming seat with leather insert, rocks on cross-braced wire supports, 24-1/2" w, 23" d, 40-3/4" h 865.00
Arts & Crafts
Harden and Co.
Oak, curved crest rail over 4 narrow and one wide vertical back slat, open arm with 2 side corbels, spring cushion leather seat, paper label, some stains and roughness, 27-1/4" w, 31-1/2" d, 37" h.. 550.00
Wave, 2 horizontal crest rails, wide central vertical slat flanked by 2 narrower slats, curved arms over 4 vertical side slats, skirt with through tenons, unsigned, seat missing, 29-1/2" w, 31-1/2" h, 36-1/4" h 1,495.00
Sewing, c1912, oak, curved crest rail over 3 vertical slats, shaped seat over lower side stretchers, some wear, 17" w, 24" d, 32" h...... 115.00
Stickley, L. & J. G., c1912, oak
Curved crest rail over 5 vertical slats, straight sides with spring cushion seat, arched seat rail, minor wear, 18-1/4" w, 33-3/4" h 375.00

Stenciled, mixed woods, 7 spindle back, orig paint, $225.

No. 451, concave crest rail over 6 vertical slats, shaped flat arm with corbels over 6 vertical slats, branded "The Work of L. & J. G. Stickley," 28" w, 31-1/2' d, 38-1/2" h, scratches on arm... 1,380.00

Unsigned, c1912, oak, curved crest rail over 4 vertical slats, flat open arms, spring cushion seat, upholstery missing, 39" h 375.00

Unsigned, c1916, oak, adjustable back, 4 horizontal back slats, flat arms over 4 side slats, orig dark finish, reupholstered back and seat cushions, 26-5/8" w, 34" d, 42-1/8" h 990.00

Young, J. M., c1910, oak, 4 curved horizontal crest rails, flat arm with short corbel supports, leather spring cushion seat, 28" w, 35" h............ 250.00

Boston, American, 19th C, maple, spindle back 200.00

Colonial Revival, Windsor-style, Colonial Furniture Co., Grand Rapids, MI, comb back, birch, mahogany finish, turned legs, 21" w, 17" d, 27-1/2" h.. 200.00

International Movement, Charles Eames, manufactured by Herman Miller, salmon fiberglass zenith shell, rope edge, black wire struts, birch runners, c1950, 25" w, 27" d, 27" h 1,400.00

Renaissance Revival, George Huntzinger, NY, 1876, walnut, ring turned armrests and stretchers, cloth wrapped wire seat and back, dated, 21" w, 33" h 400.00

Wicker, painted white, sq back, basket weave pattern over openwork back, rect armrests with wrapped braces, openwork sides, braided edge on basketweave seat and skirt, X-form stretcher, 32" w, 33" h......200.00

Windsor, comb back, crusty black repaint, yellow design on crest, alligatored finish, bamboo turnings, scrolled arms, step down crest, repairs to crest, 43-3/4" h 200.00

Secretaries

Arts & Crafts, English, oak, 2 leaded glass doors, inlaid front, 2 small drawers suspended from writing surface, cut-out sides, orig finish, 32" w, 18-1/2" d, 60-1/4" h.. 2,100.00

Biedermeier, German, secretaire a abattant, walnut, rect top over long drawer, hinged fall front, fitted int., over 3 long drawers, block feet, 34" w, 17-1/2" d, 60-1/2" h.. 2,200.00

Centennial, inlay mahogany, two part: top with four drawers over six cubbyholes center, line inlay door opening to reveal two cubbyholes and large drawer, sliding tambour doors flanked by inlay panels with simulated columns; lower: fold-over line inlay lid, two drawers with line inlay, diamond inlay on legs, some lifting to veneer, replaced cloth writing surface, 37-1/4" w, 19-3/4" d, 46" h 800.00

Chippendale

American, 18th C, mahogany, two pieces, upper: molded cornice, paneled doors with scrolled stiles and rails, 1 adjustable shelf, base: slant front lid, fitted int. consisting of 11 dovetailed drawers, 3 with carved fans, 2 pull-out letter drawers with half columns and turned finials, 4 dovetailed drawers with applied edge beading, serpentine apron and drop with central carved fan, ogee feet, orig brasses, old finish, minor repairs to feet, 40-1/2" w, 14" d, 66-1/2" h 35,750.00

Connecticut, 18th C, cherry, molded scrolled cornice with carved pinwheels above applied central ornament and recessed panel doors, int. with 2 shelves and scrolled dividers above desk int. of small valanced compartments with scrolled dividers flaking pinwheel carved drawer and small drawers arranged in two-step interior, case of graduated thumb-molded drawers flanked by fluted quarter engaged columns, bracket feet on platforms, some old brass, refinished, restoration, 39" w, 20-1/2" d, 91-1/2" h 35,650.00

Pennsylvania, cherry, two piece, upper: broken arch pediment, boldly carved floral rosettes, turned and carved finials, double doors each with 7 panes of glass in geometric arrangement, fluted quarter columns, applied reeded detail, base: slant top lid with fully developed fitted int. of 8 dovetailed drawers with serpentine fronts, center door with blocking and carved fan with 5 graduated drawers with serpentine fronts, 8 pigeonholes each with hidden drawers and fan carving, 2 letter drawers with fluted columns and reeding, 4 overlapping dovetailed drawers, fluted quarter columns, ogee foot, orig eagle brasses, "H" hinges, and latches, orig finish, minor repairs to feet and some replaced glue blocks, 38-1/4" w, 20-3/4" d, 90" h 88,000.00

Classical, Boston, 1820-25, secretaire a'abattant, carved mahogany and mahogany veneer, marble top above cove molding, mahogany veneer facade flanked by veneered columns topped by Corinthian capitals, terminating in ebonized ball feet, recessed panel sides, fall front opens to desk int. over two cupboard doors, old refinish, 35" w, 17-1/2" d, 57-1/2" h 16,100.00

Colonial Revival, Colonial Desk Co., Rockford, IL, c1930, mahogany, broken arch pediment, center finial, two glazed mullioned doors, fluted columns, center prospect with acanthus carving flanked by columns, four graduated drawers, brass eagle, carved claw and ball feet, 41" w, 21" d, 87" h 1,000.00

Eastlake, American, burl walnut and mahogany, shaped cornice, pair of glazed cabinet doors, cylinder front, writing surface, two doors in base, shaped apron, 27" w, 22" d, 66" h 1,500.00

Empire, early 19th C, Secretarie Abbatant, mahogany, granite top, fall front enclosing later fitted compartment, gilt bronze mounts, veneer loss, 32-1/4" w, 18-1/4" h, 54-3/4" h 1,150.00

Empire-Style, late 19th C, gilt bronze mounted mahogany, rect top, fall front with fitted int., over pr of recessed cupboard doors, flanked by columns, paw feet, 44-1/4" w, 23-1/2" d, 49-1/4" h 1,955.00

Federal, Boston or North Shore, MA, early 19th, mahogany inlaid, top section: central panel of bird's eye maple with cross-banded mahogany veneer border and stringing joined to the plinths by a curving gallery above flat molded cornice, glazed beaded doors with Gothic arches and bird's eye maple panels and mahogany cross-banding and stringing enclosing shelves, compartments, and drawers; lower: projecting section with fold-out surface inlaid with oval bird's eye maple panel set in mitered rect with cross-banded border and cockbeaded case, two drawers veneered with bird's eye maple panels bordered by mahogany cross-banding and stringing, flanked by inlaid panels continuing to sq double tapered legs, lower edge of case and leg cuffs with lunette inlaid banding, old finish, replaced brasses, imperfections, 41" w, 21-3/4" d, 74-1/2" h 9,775.00

George III, English, early 19th C, japanned, swan neck pediment, rosette carved terminals, two glazed cupboard doors, fitted int. of compartments and small drawers, fall front writing surface with cubbyholes and drawers, four graduated drawers, shaped apron, bracket feet, gilt and polychrome warrior and figural landscape scenes, birds, and flowering trees, green ground, over painting and minor reconstruction, 40-1/4" w, 21-1/2" d, 96-1/2" h............ 5,000.00

Hepplewhite Style, lady's, two piece, mahogany with inlay, top: cornice with brass finials, tambour section with fitted interior with dovetailed drawers, double doors with geometric arrangement of glass, base: fold-down writing shelf, 3 dovetailed drawers, considerable restoration, 39-1/4" w, 18-1/2" d, 74-3/4" h....................................... 1,800.00

Modern Gothic, c1870, walnut, galleried top over slant lid, int. fitted writing compartment over drawer over cabinet doors and drawers, molded base, 36" w, 20-1/4" d, 63-1/2" h 2,415.00

Regency, English, early 19th C, mahogany and part ebonized, scroll crest above pair of glazed mullioned doors enclosing shelves, flanked by spiraled and reeded columns, base with drawer fitted for writing compartments above pair of cabinet doors, French feet, restorations, 36-3/4" w, 20-1/2" d, 87-1/2" h 7,475.00

Renaissance Revival, American, c1865, walnut, two sections, upper: bookcase section, S-curved pediment with center applied grapes and foliage carving, two arched and molded glazed doors, shelved int., three small drawers with applied grapes and foliage carved pulls; lower: fold-out writing surface, two short drawers over two long drawers with oval molding and applied grapes and foliage carved pulls, matching ornamentation on skirt, 48" w, 21" d, 95" h 5,000.00

Settees

Art Deco, attributed to Warren McArthur, c1930, tubular aluminum frame, sheet aluminum seat and back supports, removable vinyl cushions, 68" l 5,750.00

Arts & Crafts
    Limbert, #939, oak, eleven back slats, corbels under arm, recovered orig drop-in cushion, branded, refinished, 75" w, 27" d, 40" h 800.00
    Stickley, L. & J. G., oak, drop-arm form, twelve vertical slats to back and drop-in orig spring cushion, recovered in brown leather, refinished, unsigned, 65" w, 25" d, 36" h 1,800.00

Baroque Revival, Flemish, scroll, mahogany, old cane in back medallion, cane seat has been upholstered, old dark finish, 66" w, 50" h 750.00

Biedermeier-Style, beechwood, curved open back, three vasiform splats, out-curved arms, caned seat raised on six sq-section sabre legs 650.00

Chippendale Style, English, 19th C, mahogany, upholstered seat, old finish, repairs, 61" w, 37" h 2,000.00

Classical, American, c1850, mahogany, serpentine front, carved crest, transitional rococo design elements, 82" l 600.00

Colonial Revival, William and Mary style, American, c1930, loose cushions, turned baluster legs and stretcher, 48" l 750.00

Empire-Style, late 19th/early 20th C
    Mahogany and parcel-gilt, two seat canapé, curved and padded back, reeded frame continuing into arms with swan-form supports, overstuffed seat, sabre legs 400.00
    Mahogany, two seat, curved backs, each armrest ending on ram's head, hoof-foot feet 2,100.00

French Restauration, New York City, c1840, rosewood, arched upholstered back, scrolled arms outlined in satinwood terminating in volutes, rect seat frame with similar inlay, bracket feet, 80" l, 27" d, 33-1/2" h 1,200.00

Gothic Revival, American, c1850, carved walnut, shaped crest rail surmounted by center carved finial, stiles with arched recessed panel and similarly carved finials, upholstered back and seat, open arms with padded armrests and scrolled handholds, carved seat rail, ring turned legs, ball feet, 67-1/2" w, 23-1/2" d, 49-3/4" h 800.00

Louis XVI-Style, third quarter 19th C
    Gilt bronze mounted ebonized maple, Leon Marcotte, New York City, c1860, 55-1/2" l, 25" d, 41-1/2" h 2,185.00
    Giltwood, two-seat canapé, upholstered with Fortuny fabric, flaking, 55" l, 36" h 1,610.00

Renaissance Revival, America, c1875, carved walnut, triple back, each having carved crest and ebonized plaque inlaid with musical instruments, red floral damask upholstery 1,200.00

Rococo Revival, rosewood, laminated curved backs, Stanton Hall pattern, attributed to J. & J. Meeks, rose crest in scrolled foliage and vintage, tufted gold velvet brocade reupholstery, age cracks and some edge damage, 65-1/2" l 5,500.00

Victorian
    Carved rosewood, c1870, shaped and padded back, two arched end sections joined by dipped section, each with pierced foliate crest,

Victorian, walnut, marble top, carved game birds and fish, $900.

over upholstered serpentine front seat, flanked by scroll arms, conforming rail continue to cabriole legs, frame leaf carved 850.00
    Wrought and cast brass, lion finials on back posts, red and gold brocade seat cushions and upholstered back, 48-1/2" l 825.00

Wicker, tightly woven rect back, inverted triangle-dec, tightly woven arms, rect seat with woven diamond herringbone pattern, continuous braided edging from crest to front legs, turned spindle apron, 43" w, 36" h 500.00

Sideboards

Art Deco, French, Macassar, stepped rect marble top over 2 leaf-cast silvered bronze mounted tambour cupboard doors, flanked by D-shaped marble top over 2 drawers and open shelf, ebonized ball feet 700.00

Art Nouveau, Louis Majorelle, 1900, oak and mahogany, rect, bowed front, inset marble top, tow long drawers, undulating brass pulls cast with sheaves of wheat, tow cupboard doors with large applied brass sheaves of wheat and undulating leaves, molded apron, four lug feet, 65" w, 39-1/8" h 6,000.00

Arts and Crafts
    Limbert, Grand Rapids and Holland, MI, c1907, No. 1453-3/4, rect plate rack over central mirror, conforming rect top, 2 central drawers flanked by cabinet doors over long drawer, branded mark, 48" w, 19" d, 52-5/8" h 2,500.00
    Shop of the Crafters style, c1915, oak, whole rect canted form, long mirror with arch, rect top, 2 short drawers above 2 cabinet doors over single long drawer, unsigned, 42" w, 19-1/4" d, 37-1/2" h, some damage 1,265.00
    Stickley, L. and J. G., plate rack, 6 small drawers, 2 cabinet doors over linen drawer, arched apron, orig medium finish, Handcraft label 4,250.00
    Unknown American Maker, c1916, oak, gallery shelf with mirror, 2 half drawers, 2 doors over central long drawer, orig finish, unsigned, 54" l, 20" d, 55-1/4" h, some stains and roughness to veneer 500.00

Centennial, Chippendale-Style, America, late 19th C, mahogany, block front with shell carving, four drawers, front cabinet doors, gadrooned apron, cabriole legs, claw and ball feet, 68" w, 24" d, 40" h 950.00

Classical
    New York, c1825, mahogany carved and mahogany veneer, rect top, case with 2 cockbeaded short drawers and long drawer with banded borders flanked by applied gothic panels above vase and ring turned spiral carved legs joined by medial shelf, cast brass

castors, replaced pulls, old refinish, minor imperfections, 30" w, 16-1/4" d, 33-1/2" h 2,100.00

Empire, American, mid 19th C

Mahogany, molded backsplash over rect top, 3 drawers and 3 recessed cupboard doors flanked by columns, ball feet, 59-1/4" w, 21-3/4" h, 48" h 2,415.00

Mahogany, rect faux-marble top surrounded by brass gallery, 3 short drawers above 2 paneled doors centered by 2 small drawers, flanked by pineapple carved columns, paw feet, 54" w, 22" d, 56" h 850.00

Federal

Boston, 1785-1810, mahogany inlaid, D-shaped top with banded edge, mahogany veneer between maple stringing, case with 3 cockbeaded drawers, 4 cupboard doors, flanked by turned and reeded legs topped by stringing in outline, old surface, replaced brasses, imperfections, 61-1/4" l, 23-1/4" d, 29" h 8,625.00

New England, c1800, mahogany inlaid, shaped top with inlaid edge, conforming case with single central drawer flanked by 2 small end drawers over 4 cupboard doors and 2 sectioned bottle drawers, facades outlined in stringing with ovolo corners, 6 sq tapering legs with cuff inlays, replaced hardware, refinished, some restoration, 67-1/2" w, 21" d, 41" h 11,500.00

New York City, 1780-1800, mahogany inlaid, straight front, recessed central cupboards and bowed ends, conforming top with veneered edge, 3 drawers with stringing in outline, each front leg topped by book inlay, outlined in stringing to cuff inlays, oval inlays in double-line stringing, replaced brasses, refinished, imperfections, 71-1/2" l, 26-1/4" d, 41-1/2" h 23,000.00

Federal Style, mahogany, top with outset rounded corners, shaped splashboard with ebonized accents, 2 frieze drawers, turned tapered legs, 51" w, 19-1/2" d, 44-3/4" h 800.00

French Provincial, mid 18th C, walnut, buffet, carved body, molded stiles and carved ogee detail on top, 2 centered drawers with orig hardware, surrounded by molded, serpentine, and shell detail open shelf, 2 carved doors with foliage and rosette detail, cabriole legs, 50-1/2" l, 18-1/2" d, 53-1/2" h 2,000.00

George III, English, 19th C, mahogany, bowfront, bowed and cross-banded top over conforming case, narrow central drawer flanked by deep drawers, sq tapering legs ending in space feet, restorations, 58" w, 24" d, 35-1/4" h 5,175.00

Hepplewhite

America, mahogany with figured mahogany veneer with inlay, 4 doors and 3 dovetailed drawers, stringing and banding with foliage designs on posts and banding around edge of doors, drawers, and top, sq slightly tapered legs, replaced eagle brasses, minor repairs, 54" w, 18-3/8" d, 38" h 11,000.00

New York, mahogany and figured mahogany veneer with inlay, serpentine case, 5 dovetailed drawers, double doors, stringing and banding with husk and bookend inlay on tapered legs, diamond escutcheons, old brasses, minor veneer repairs, drawers lined with green felt, 71" w, 30-1/4" d, 40-1/4" h 12,650.00

International Movement, George Nakashima, New Hope, PA, c1960, walnut, rect top, 3 sliding doors, int. fitted with 2 compartments flanking 4 central drawers, right hand compartment drilled for stereo, 75" w, 24" d, 30-1/2" h 6,900.00

Regency, English, early 19th C, mahogany and inlay, shaped top above frieze fitted with drawers, two tapered pedestals with cupboard doors enclosing drawers, brass hairy paw feet, restoration, 51-3/4" w, 24" d, 38-3/4" h.. 4,890.00

Renaissance Revival, third quarter 19th C

Walnut, burl walnut, marquetry, and gilt incised, shaped backsplash with oval marquetry panel, shaped case with drawer over door enclosing shelf, molded base, turned feet, 49-1/2" w, 19" d, 57" h.. 4,025.00

Walnut, marquetry, and panel gilt, shaped top with removable statuary stand, cabinet door with floral marquetry, plinth base with shaped feet, minor damage, 50-1/4" w, 22" d, 51-3/4" h . 3,750.00

Victorian, English, third quarter 19th C, carved mahogany, reverse breakfront, rect top with rounded corners, recessed serpentine central section, arched and molded back board, carved with scrolling foli-

ate and flower heads, center pierced rocaille, conforming frieze drawer flanked on each side by pedestal, each with paneled door, shaped panel carved with fruit sag, opening to drawer and shelf, outset molded plinth, 90-1/4" w, 29-1/2" d, 65-4/5" h 2,000.00

Sofas

Aesthetic Movement, America, late 19th C, top rail centered by carved cartouche, flanked by finials, scrolled armrests, half-scroll legs, casters, as found condition, 61" w, 23-1/2" d, 41" h........................ 650.00

Art Nouveau, Carlo Bugatti, 1900, ebonized wood, rect back, mechanical seat, slightly scrolling rect arms, parchment upholstery, painted swallows and leafy branches, hammered brass trim, four block form feet, 68-3/8" l 1,900.00

Centennial, Chippendale-style, American, late 19th C, mahogany, shaped back, rolled arms, yellow velvet upholstered seat, gadrooned apron, cabriole legs with carved knees, claw and ball feet, 62" l 1,500.00

Chippendale, country, step down back with step down arms, bowed front with large down filled cushions, eight molded carved legs, cup caster feet, reupholstered, 76" w, 32" d, 36" h 3,000.00

Chippendale Style, mahogany, arched back flanked by scrolled arms, sq molded legs, upholstered in ivory silk, 78" l, 29" d, 35" h 250.00

Classical

Mid Atlantic States, 1805-20, carved mahogany and bird's eye maple veneer, Grecian style, scrolled and reeded arm and foot, punctuated with brass rosettes, continuing to similar reeded seat rail with inlaid dies, reeded saber legs flanked by brass flowerettes, brass paw feet on castors, old surface, 75" l, 14-1/2" h seat, 35" h 3,680.00

Duncan Phyfe Style, Centennial, mahogany, reeded lyre frame, carved crest with foliage, cornucopia, etc., reeded legs, paw feet, old finish, old reupholstery, 78" l 1,430.00

Hepplewhite Style, mahogany, boldly banded inlay in two colors, lyre arms with brass rosettes, rounded edge stretchers, sq tapered legs, reupholstered in floral stripe brocade, 79" l............................ 1,870.00

Regency, mahogany reclining arms form chaise, black and white striped upholstery, carved, 58-1/2" l 1,700.00

Restauration, American, NY, c1835-40, carved mahogany, scrolling back extends to form arms, orig upholstery removed 1,400.00

Victorian, American, mid 19th C, carved mahogany, shaped crest rail, arched pediment, acanthus carved arm supports, later velvet upholstery... 1,200.00

Stands

Book, Victorian, walnut veneer, end pieces set with pate-sur-pate

Shaving, Queen Anne-style, mahogany, 2 drawers, tripod foot, $295.

plaques of cupids playing badminton, Bettemann's patent, sold by Shreve Crump and Low, 16" l....................600.00

Center, Rococo Revival, Italian, gray veined carrara marble top, resting on sectioned berry leaf design supported by trifid base with dragons and acanthus leaves, gilt and silver gesso, carved wood, 17" d, 31-1/2" h....................800.00

Chamber

Classical

New England, 1825-35, mahogany veneer, scrolled supports, attached dressing glass over two small drawers above long drawer, 4 ring-turned tapering legs, restoration, 36-1/2" w, 19-1/4" d, 63-1/2" h....................2,645.00

Vermont, attributed to, c1825, paint dec and gilt stenciled, scrolled splashboard above pierced top with bowfront and sq corners, conforming skirt with 2 flanking small drawers painted black with gilt cornucopia and Greek key dec, scrolled sides joining medial drawers with vase and ring turned legs, orig lighter blue-green paint, apple green striped borders, 18-1/2" w, 15" d, 37-1/4" h....................2,300.00

Federal

New England, c1815-25, mahogany, shaped splash-back flanking quarter round shelves, pierced top, turned supports joining valanced skirt and medial shelf with drawer, vase and ring-turned legs, old brass pull, refinished, 20-1/2" w, 16" d, 47" h....2,100.00

New York, c1820, mahogany and mahogany veneer, shaped gallery above rect top, 4 vase and ring-turned legs joined by medial shelf with 2 short drawers, brass pulls, refinished, 33-1/2" l, 16-3/4" d, 34" h....................1,100.00

Crock, country, American, primitive, 5 stepped shelves, old green repaint, late wire nail construction, 38" w, 30" d, 31" h....................195.00

Display, Art Nouveau, Majorelle, France, c1900, 3 tiers, fruitwood and marquetry, 2 rear legs with conjoined front support, 2 open shelves in stylized floral designs, sgd "L. Majorelle," 21-1/2" w, 16' d, 48-3/4" h, repair, veneer wear....................3,790.00

Dressing. Tramp Art, America, 19th C, 5 tiers, swivel mirror at top, 4 drawers, lift-top compartment, allover chip-carved raised panel dec, shaped mirror inserts, minor wear, 30-1/2" h....................1,150.00

Drink, L. and J. G. Stickley, circular top and shelf, cross-stretchers, "Work of …" decal, skinned orig finish, old stains, filled holes on top, 18" d, 29" h....................950.00

Easel

Aesthetic Movement, American, c1875-80, attributed to Kimbel and Cabus, NY, ebonized, damage to one foot, 70-1/2" l....................1,800.00

Victorian, Gothic style, American, c1872, oak, swiveling pierced stand, tracery-carved to rail, rotating on platform base, molded sq legs joined by stretchers, adjustable racks missing, stamped "1738," 31" w, 87" h, pr....................5,500.00

Lamp, Arts & Crafts

Limbert, No. 260, rect top, lower shelf, 4 drawers with hammered copper pulls, orig finish, paper label, minor buckling to veneer at side bottom, 17" w, 15-1/2" d, 36" h....................2,900.00

Unsigned, c1916, circular top, 4 legs, lower cross stretcher with through tenons, 13" d, 30-1/8" h, top water damage and wood separation....................990.00

Music, Victorian, oak and mahogany, checkered line inlaid lip, tapered reeded standard, circular platform, 4 stylized animal legs, 19th C....................1,700.00

Night, Arts & Crafts, unmarked

17" w, 16" d, 29-3/4" h, one drawer over open space over small cabinet, sq faceted wooden pulls, tapered legs, new dark finish, repair to top....................850.00

18" sq top, 28-1/2" h, flush top, 2 short drawers over 2 full width drawers, sq faceted wooden pulls, open space above lower sq shelf....................1,100.00

Sewing, Federal, MA, c1790, bird's eye and tiger maple veneer, rect bird's eye veneered top outlined with mahogany veneer and half-round molding, 2 bird's eye maple veneered drawers with bone escutcheons, ring-turned tiger maple tapering legs, small turned ball feet, imperfections, veneer cracks and losses, 20-1/2" w, 16-3/4" d, 30-1/4" h....................2,990.00

Side

Classical, French, early 20th C, sq onyx top with cloisonné rim, four bronze columns, sq base, paw feet....................3,220.00

Federal, Rhode Island, c1825, cherry, bird's eye maple, and mahogany veneer, rect overhanging top with applied beaded edge, drawer with bird's eye maple veneer and mahogany cross-banding, 4 vase and ring-turned legs continuing to tapering feet, old finish, imperfections, 20" w, 19" d, 27-3/4" h....................690.00

Table-A-Ecrire, Provincial Louis XV/Louis XVI, elmwood, rect top, three-quarter gallery, serpentine front edge, shaped frieze with drawer, sq section restrained cabriole legs, 27" l, 17-1/4" d, 24-3/4" h....................450.00

Telephone, Arts & Crafts, drawer, small cabinet, paneled sides, sq copper Limbert pulls, new finish, unmarked, 17-1/2" sq, 36' h....1,300.00

Tilt Top, Federal, New York, refinished mahogany top and legs, rect top with cut corners, curly maple column, tripod base with scimitar legs, turned button feet, 17" x 23" x 26" h....................715.00

Wash

Empire, American, first quarter 19th C, cherry and bird's eye maple, corner, molded convex top with scalloped backboard supporting small corner shelf, baluster turned supports, conforming undertier with two small drawers flanked by central dummy drawer, ring and twist-turned legs, bun feet, 24-1/2" w, 18" d, 38-1/2" h 550.00

Sheraton, decorated pine, orig white paint, red and green striping, turned legs and posts, dovetailed drawer, crest with corner shelves, hole for bowl, white porcelain knobs, 20-1/4" x 16-1/4" x 32-3/4" h....................250.00

Wig, Queen Anne, English, washbowl holder, mahogany, pine and oak secondary woods, turned ring supporting blue transfer Copeland Spode bowl, turned and carved columns, 2 dovetailed drawers, tripod base, snake feet, 31-1/2" h....................750.00

Steps

Bed, Victorian, English, third quarter 19th C, mahogany, each tread with leather-lined molded top, uppermost hinged and opens to storage well, middle tread hinged and slides open, short turned and tapered legs....................1,700.00

Chair, George III, English, c1811, mahogany and caning, metamorphic, open armchair hinged at seat rail, back turning over to form set of library steps, damage to caning, minor losses, 36" h....................8,625.00

Library

George III, English, late 18th C, mahogany, rect molded hinged top, eight steps, 49-1/2" w, 53-1/2" h....................2,500.00

Regency, English, early 19th C, mahogany, three steps, inset green leather treads, scrolling banister, sq balusters, feet with brass casters, 46" w, 27" w, 56" h....................2,400.00

Stools

Bar, International Movement, Alvar Aalto, designed for Artek, c1954, "X," each leg of 5 laminated ash pieces jointed at seat, leather upholstery, traces of orig label, 18-1/2" w, 18" h, pr....................450.00

Child's, carved and painted wood, mushroom, tree trunk pedestal, tripod legs, 7-1/2" d, 9" h....................375.00

Choir, Louis XV, Provincial, oak, molded D-shaped top, sq legs joined by stretchers, 25-1/4" h, pr....................500.00

Foot

Continental, mahogany, loose cushion top, sq top with canted corners, shaped frieze, sq tapering legs, 18" w, 18" d, 13-1/2" h, pr....................800.00

Decorated, splayed turned legs, rect top, old dark green paint, yellow and green, "F" and flowers, 7-1/2" x 13-1/2'....................85.00

Empire, America, second quarter 19th C, mahogany, overstuffed tapestry top, serpentine sides, molded conforming rails, scrolled feet with castors....................150.00

George I, c1740, walnut, rect, cabriole legs, pad feet, needlepoint seat, 20" l, 17" w, 14-1/2" h....................1,500.00

Victorian, walnut, finger carved, green velvet upholstery......250.00

Windsor, oval, splayed base, old dark green repaint, 10" x 14 x 10-3/4" h....................250.00

Joint

William and Mary, attributed to MA, early 18th C, rect molded overhanging top, 4 splayed block vase and ring turned legs, turned

feet joined by molded skirt and stretcher, old refinish, minor imperfections, 24" w, 16" d, 23" h 8,050.00
Ottoman, Victorian, tufted rect seat, mahogany turned and tapered legs, 26" w, 19" d, 16-1/2" h 200.00
Piano, Classical, late, American, c1840, rosewood, columnar, swivel top 275.00
Thebes, Aesthetic Movement, attributed to Liberty & Co., c1884, mahogany, sq slatted top, turned legs joined by spindle supports, scuffing, 17" w, 17" d, 14-1/2" h 3,450.00
George II, English, mahogany, cabriole legs, hoof feet, reupholstered, pair, 16-1/2" x 22" top, 16-1/2" h 3,850.00

Tables

Breakfast

Empire, America, second quarter 19th C, carved mahogany, circular tilt-top, molded segmented veneered top with crossbanded frieze, elaborately turned baluster form standard carved with bands of foliage, rect platform base with concave sides, cased corners, raised on winged lion-paw feet with castors, 43" d, 31" h 2,300.00

Federal

America, first quarter 19th C, mahogany, molded rect top with rounded front corners, single drop leaf, baluster turned standard, quadruped base, reeded downswept legs, lion paw caps with castors, 54" l, 44-1/2" d, 28-1/2" h 850.00
Charleston, SC, 1790-1800, mahogany and kingwood inlaid, top with large oval veneered central reserve banded in kingwood veneer and stringing, outlined with meandering inlaid vine with leaves and berries, skirt with one faux and one working drawer inlaid with flowerette at each corner, two others flanking central lozenge of stringing over front sq tapering legs topped with twelve-point paterae above three-point husks which descent toward cuff inlays over brass casters, old refinish, missing or replaced brass, veneer loss and imperfections, 31-1/4" w, 19-5/8" d, 10" d leaves, 28-12" h 266,500.00
Federal, late, America, c1800, mahogany, drop-leaf, rect top with rule-jointed leaves, sq section tapering legs, 40-1/2" l, 39-1/4" w, 28-1/4" h 450.00

Card

Classical, American, mahogany, rect molded top, carved and molded frieze, carved baluster form supports, 4 paw feet, casters, as found condition, 36" w, 17-1/2" d, 29" h 800.00
Classical, Philadelphia area, c1825, mahogany carved and veneer, rect folding top, conforming frieze with beaded edge, carved support with acanthus leaves and basket of fruit, shaped concave platform and acanthus leaf scroll and paw carved feet, refinished, 38" w, 18-1/2" d, 30-1/4" h 4,900.00

Federal

Boston, MA, 1790, mahogany and bird's eye inlaid, serpentine top with outset corners, conforming bird's eye maple veneered skirt with central flame birch veneer oval reserve, mahogany veneered panel flanked by reeded front legs stopped by colonettes, ending in ring-turned swelled feet, old refinish, minor surface blemish, 36" w, 17-3/4" d, 28-1/2" h 4,900.00

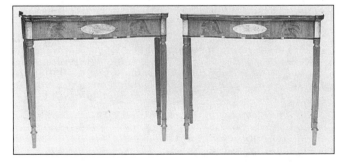

Pair of card tables, Sheraton, attributed to Salem, MA, mahogany, serpentine from, flaming birch oval panels, banded inlay and reeded legs, $15,000.

Massachusetts, c1790, mahogany inlaid, folding top, half serpentine ends elliptic front and sq corners, conforming base centering an inlaid panel bordered by geometric stringing and cross-banding with cross-banded lower edge joining 4 sq tapering legs, cross-banded panels in the dies continuing to inlaid cuffs, refinished, minor imperfections, 35-3/4" w, 17" d, 30" h 2,875.00
Massachusetts, c1800, tiger maple, folding top with half serpentine ends, elliptic front and sq corners above conforming skirt joining four sq tapering legs, old refinish, minor imperfections, 36" w, 16-3/4" d, 28-1/2" h 1,840.00
Massachusetts, c1810-15, mahogany inlaid and carved, top with half-serpentine ends, sq corners, elliptical front and crossbanded edge above conforming crossbanded skirt joining 4 vase and ring-turned reeded legs ending in turned tapering feet, old refinish, imperfections, 36" w, 17-1/2" d, 27-3/4" h 3,220.00
Newburyport, MA, c1790, mahogany inlaid, shaped top above skirt with central veneered oval patera in rect panel flanked by sq double tapering legs topped by rect dies bordered by patterned inlay, cuff inlays, refinished, 36" w, 17-1/2" d, 28-1/4" h 3,565.00
North Shore, MA, c1800, mahogany and flame birch veneer, serpentine top outlined in patterned inlay, ovolo corners above skirt with 2 rect inlaid panels, flanking central oval above reeded and ring-turned legs with carved and veined leafage, old refinish, very minor imperfections, 36" w, 16-7/8" d, 30" h 7,475.00
Rhode Island, c1760, mahogany inlaid, hinged top, elliptical front, sq corners, crossbanded edge, conforming frieze of central oval panel flanked by shaped panels defined in stringing, 4 sq tapering legs, dies with contrasting panels above banding, leaf device and stringing, old refinish, restorations, 34-3/4" w, 17-1/2" d, 28-3/8" h.............2,300.00

Hepplewhite

America, mahogany and figured mahogany veneer with inlay, exaggerated serpentine apron with ovolo corners, sq tapered legs, 2 swing legs support hinged lid, stringing and bell flower inlay in legs, banding and stringing on apron and posts, stringing on edge of top, old finish, some loss of height to feet, added brass castors, minor repairs at hinges, initials "W. P." carved inside apron, 35-1/2' w, 17-1/2" d, 27" h 3,850.00
America, mahogany with inlay, chestnut secondary wood, serpentine top, serpentine apron, sq tapered legs, banding and stringing inlay on legs, figured veneer apron with banding, stringing and inlaid eagle in oval, banded inlay on top edge, refinished, opaque red stain on underside of top and apron, 35-3/4" w, 18-3/8" d, 28-1/2" h 4,675.00
America, mahogany with inlay, serpentine top, conforming apron, sq tapered legs, stringing and banding around apron and rectangles with invected corners dissected by stringing on flame figure veneer, stringing on top edge, sgd "J. Wilson," three board leaf replaced, veneer repair, 35-3/4" w, 28-3/4" h...................3,025.00
Newport, RI, demilune, inlaid mahogany, pine secondary wood, figured veneer apron with banded inlay forming rectangles with pattern in center of each, top edge with matching banded inlay, sq tapered legs with banded inlay, 2 swing legs, 2 secret drawers in back of apron, old finish, some loss of height to feet, 36" w, 17-3/4" d, 26-1/2" h 2,640.00

Center

Aesthetic Movement, manner of E. W. Goodwin, late 19th C, mahogany, circular overhanging top, lower hexagonal median shelf, 6 hexagonal legs, 38-1/4" d, 28-3/4" h 1,840.00
Federal Style, mahogany, circular quarter veneered top, paneled frieze with drawer, baluster-form standard, tripod base with downswept legs, block feet, castors, 30-1/2" d, 27-1/2" h 650.00
German, mid 19th C, carved and inlaid walnut, circular, segmentally veneered top with molded serpentine edge, inlaid band of scrolling foliage in boxwood on kingwood ground, baluster-carved standard with cabochons, quadruped base with leaf-capped, downswept scroll legs and castors, similarly scrolled and carved secondary supports, 43-1/2" d, 28-1/2" h 750.00
Renaissance Revival, third quarter 19th C, walnut, burl walnut, marquetry, part ebonized, shaped molded top above conforming

frieze, carved trestle supports joined by stretcher, 45" w, 26" d, 28-1/2" h 3,750.00

Chair, New England, 18th C, red painted pine, scrubbed top tilts above base, shoe feet, top has been squared at ends, other minor imperfections, 42-1/2" w, 43-1/4" d, 26-1/2" h 1,380.00

Console

Arts & Crafts, Lifetime, narrow bow-front top, single center drawer, six legs, long corbels, orig finish with minor wear, paper label, 67" l, 22" d, 31" h 7,500.00

Empire, French, late 19th C, painted and parcel-gilt, rect white onyx top over frieze carved with swan forms, foliate arabesques centered by urn, end supports in form of winged female monopodi terminating in lion paw feet, backed by rect mirror flanked on each side by carved panel, U-shaped plinth with petal molding, painted sage green, gilt highlights, 62-1/2" l, 17-3/4" w, 37-3/4" h ..7,000.00

Dining

Art Deco, Palisanderwood, rect top with bowed ends, conforming frieze, oval pedestal with ebonised molding, spreading foot capped with hammered brass, 43-1/4" w, 90" l extended, 31-3/4" h 300.00

Arts & Crafts

Limbert, #403, cut-corner top over intricate base, slab supports with three spindles in an oval cut-out keyed stretchers connecting to a center leg, one leaf, orig finish, numbered, 50" w, 50" d, 30" h 2,500.00

Limbert, No. 1480-C-54, circular flush top, central pedestal, 4 through-tenon trestle legs, 2 12' leaves, skinned finish, veneer patch to section of apron, branded mark, 54" d, 28" h 3,250.00

Stickley Brothers, c1916, oak, round top with 5 leaves in orig box, corbeled pedestal base, metal label, refinished, 54" d, 11" w leaves, 29-1/2" h 4,025.00

Empire-Style, Continental, 19th C, walnut, quarter-veneered top with crossbanded border, conforming frieze, canted scroll supports, rect platform stretcher with concave sides, gilt lion-paw feet, octagonal center support, one leaf, 46-1/4" w, 94-3/4" l extended, 31-1/4" h....2,300.00

Federal

America, first quarter 19th C, mahogany, rect top with rounded corners, conforming molded frieze, turned, tapered, and reeded legs headed by acanthus carved panels ending in brass caps with castors, 48" l, 42-1/2" w, 29" h 850.00

New England, c1820-25, cherry and bird's eye maple, two part, two rect ends each with hinged drop-leaf, ring-turned tapering legs ending in ball feet, orig surface, minor surface marks, 82" w, 44-1/2" d, 28-3/4" h 1,725.00

Federal, late, early 19th C, America, various woods, rect top with rule-jointed leaves, plain frieze with single drawer, turned legs with tulip-turned feet, 62-1/2" l, 46-3/4" w, 29-3/4" h 350.00

Federal Style, mahogany, molded rect top with rounded corners, each end support with molded downswept legs terminating in brass caps, joined by turned pole stretchers, 130-1/4" l, 42" w, 28" h 400.00

George III-Style, mahogany, D-shaped top with rounded corners and reeded edge, twin pedestal bases of column raised on tripod base, downswept legs, brass toe caps and castors, 120" l, 44" w, 29-1/4" h.. 2,100.00

International Movement, designed by Hans Wegner, Denmark, c1950, walnut, rect top, semi-circular drop leaves, wide rect drop leaf insert 865.00

Italian Rococo, late 19th C, walnut, burl walnut, and mahogany, top with serpentine molded edge, cabriole legs, stylized feet, restoration, 78" l, 38-1/2" d, 31-1/4" h 2,300.00

Neoclassical, NY, c1805, mahogany, 3-part, center section with 2 hinged leaves, shaped veneered platform with 4 reeded curving legs ending in brass paw feet on casters, 4 spiral curved and ring turned columns, 2 flanking sections each with D-end with single hinged drop leaf above pedestal form conforming to center section, skirt punctuated by rect dies above turned pendants, bottom edge outlined in veneer, refinished, minor patch in top, 53-3/4" w, 163-1/2" l, 30" h....................... 68,500.00

Queen Anne, New England, late 18th C, mahogany, sq overhanging drop leaves, 4 cabriole legs with arris knees, pad feet, cutout apron, old refinish, imperfections, 47" w, 46" d, 27-3/8" h 2,760.00

Queen Anne Style, America, walnut, oval, molded circular top extends with 2 leaves, molded conforming frieze, cabriole legs with pad feet, 88" l, 44" w, 28-3/4" h 650.00

Regency, English, first quarter 19th C, mahogany, rect reeded top with rounded ends, extending frieze, curved support, four splayed legs ending in brass caps and casters, restorations, 2 additional 48" l leaves, 64" l, 21-1/2" d, 28-1/4" h 11,500.00

Rustic, 18th C Style, French, quartered oak, rect top with rounded corners, frieze with 2 drawers, 2 opposing drawers, sq section chamfered legs joined by H-stretcher, 79" l, 32-1/4" w, 29" h 1,300.00

Victorian

America, c1875, carved walnut, molded rect top with rounded corners, molded conforming frieze, baluster-turned legs, acanthus scroll feet joined at each end by molded U-stretcher, seven leaves, 53-1/2" w. 140-3/4" l extended, 30-1/4" h 2,500.00

Morris & Co., designed by George Jack, c1890, mahogany and inlay, rect top with ebony and holly herringbone inlay on sides, shaped legs with stylized foliage inlay, joined by hayrake stretcher, tapered feet, 96" l, 37" w, 28-3/4" h 19,550.00

Dressing

Aesthetic Movement

American, c1890, maple, rect mirror above rect molded top, 3 drawers with silvered Art Nouveau hardware, sq tapering legs joined by shaped shelf stretcher, 38" w, 19" d, 55" h 900.00

Herter Brothers, molded edge cherry top, chest with orig frame, feet, and top drawer with orig hardware and marquetry inlaid garland of flowers ending in bows, side posts have incised lines, large button feet, fine-grained mahogany panels, later fitted with 3 drawers where orig open space with shelf was, matching rect mirror with beveled edge, originally supported by two arms that attached to top of dressing table (now missing), holes plugged, from commission for furniture by Hon. William Drew Washburn, for his Greek Revival house in Minneapolis, MN, copy of orig bill, 30-3/4" w, 17" d, 29" h 2,350.00

Federal, New York state, c1825, carved mahogany and mahogany veneer, brass inlaid, cockbeaded rect mirror, scrolled acanthus leaf carved supports with brass emb rosettes above three short drawers, projecting case of two short drawers, one long drawer joining four vase and ring-turned acanthus carved legs, castors, refinished, repaired, 36-1/4" w, 21-1/2" d, 55" h 1,725.00

Painted and Decorated, New Hampshire or Massachusetts, early 19th C, shaped splashboard, table top with single drawer below, ring-turned legs, orig yellow ground, green and gold stencil dec, gold striping, replaced brasses, paint loss and wear, 34-1/4" w, 17-1/2" d, 37" h 1,150.00

Queen Anne

American, walnut, pine secondary wood, two board top with thumb-molded edge, mortised and pinned apron, two dovetailed overlapping drawers, round tapered legs, duck feet, old finish, edge damage to replaced top and drawer fronts, some damage to period brasses, 21-1/2" x 36" x 30-1/2" h 7,700.00

Boston, MA, 1730-50, walnut, thumb-molded overhanging top with shaped front corners, case with one long drawer over 3 small drawers, central one with lunette, flat arched skirt, drop pendants, four cabriole legs, high pad feed, replaced brass, old refinish, repairs, 34-1/2" w, 21" d, 30-1/2" h 10,350.00

Rhode Island, 1790s,. mahogany, shaped hinged leaves, straight skirt, turned cabriole legs ending in small high pad feet, refinished, repaired, 48-1/2" w, 35-1/2" d, 28" h 2,100.00

Sheraton, Vermont, 1835-45, bird's eye and tiger maple veneer, dressing mirror with tiger maple frame flanked by scrolled supports above 2 short drawers, projecting base with single long drawer on 4 ring turned sq legs ending in turned feet, replaced pulls, refinished, imperfections, 36-3/4" w, 19" w, 58" h 1,100.00

Sheraton Style, English, 19th C, lady's, painted satinwood, rect top with serpentine front edge, outset rounded corners, conforming front with central drawer over arched kneehole, flanked on each side by 2 further drawers, interspersed by outset columnar stiles with gilt foliate capitals continuing into turned, tapered, and fluted legs with casters, painted with floral arabesques, inlaid rosewood crossbanding, 47-3/4" w, 22" d, 30-1/2" h 4,500.00

Transitional, New England, early 19th C, painted and dec, shaped backsplash, gold and green stenciled dec, green and mustard grained surface, single drawer, ring-turned tapering legs, old replaced opalescent drawer pulls, 32-1/4" w, 15" w, 34" h 1,380.00

Drop Leaf

George III, Irish, mid 18th C, mahogany, molded top with deep D-shaped leaves, foliate carved cabriole legs ending in heavily carved paw feet, imperfections to top, 45-1/2" w, 17-1/4" d, 28-1/2" h 10,925.00

Queen Anne

Country, maple and other hardwoods, tapered legs with duck feet, swing legs, refinished, repairs, top reattached, 41-3/4" l, 14-3/4" leaves, 26-1/4" h 2,450.00

Country, maple with curly top, cabriole legs with curved ankles, small duck feet, swing legs, top rubbed down to old soft finish, edge damage and wear, hinges replaced, traces of old red on underside, leaves warped, 1-3/4" w, 13-3/4" l leaves, 26" h 3,850.00

Massachusetts, maple, one board top, leaves open to form enlarged oval, slender tapered legs with duck feet, two swing legs, old mellow refinishing, some damage and repairs to rule joints, stains on top, 41" l, 14-3/4" leaves, 25-3/4" h 2,420.00

Rhode Island, late 18th C, maple, painted, hinged leaves fall to flank straight skirt, ring-turned tapering legs end in turned feet, orig surface, scrubbed top, faint gray-green painted surface, rough condition, 42" l, 14-1/2" d, 26-3/4" h 5,465.00

Games

Empire, tilt top, ebonized veneer, inlaid checker board top with brass edging, ivory segments in turned, reeded, and rope carved column, ivory inlay on trefoil foot, 18-1/4" x 18-1/2" x 30" h, some edge damage and repairs 1,430.00

Hepplewhite, American, 19th C, inlaid cherry, hinged demilune to, conforming apron, sq tapering legs 400.00

Louis XVI Provincial, late 18th/early 19th C, fruitwood, demilune, hinged top, plain frieze raised on sq tapering legs, restoration, feet tipped, 40-1/2" w, 20-1/4" d, 30" h 2,530.00

Renaissance Revival, A. Cutler & Son, Buffalo, NY, c1874, ebonized and parcel-gilt, drop leaf, orig paper label, wear to baise, 36" w, 13-3/4" d, 28-3/4" h 700.00

William IV, second quarter 19th C, mahogany and inlay, rect top with chess/checkers board on top, felt lined verso, base enclosing backgammon board, plain frieze with egg and dart molding, pedestal base, foliate collar, quadripartite base on carved turned feet on casters, shrinkage, minor veneer loss, 24-1/2" w, 24-1/2" d, 28-1/4" h 2,100.00

Gate Leg, William and Mary, Massachusetts, early 18th C, maple, oval drop leaf top, six block vase and ring turned legs joined by molded apron with drawer and block, vase and ring turned stretchers, refinished, imperfections, 41-1/2" w, 52-1/4" d, 22" w 9,775.00

Gueridon

Empire Revival, Russian, late 19th C, malachite and gilt bronze, round malachite veneer top, fluted baluster form support, trifid base cast with anthemion and paw feet, 24" d, 30" h 3,000.00

Restoration, mahogany, gray round marble top, simple frieze with gilt bronze mounting, faceted baluster columns with gilt bronze mountings, mkd "Pietement Tripode a Console," 32" d, 29-1/2" h .. 2,500.00

Hutch, country, pine, two board top, old worn yellow and brown graining, black striping, paneled edges, hinged seat in base, 56" l, 30" h. 1,870.00

Lamp, Arts & Crafts, attributed to Stickley Bros., circular, orig tacked-on burgundy leather top with floral tacks, lower clip-cornered shelf, cross stretchers, new finish to base, unmarked, 26" d, 29-1/2" h 1,400.00

Library

Arts & Crafts, Imperial Furniture Co., #981, two drawers, elaborate copper hardware, cleaned orig finish, remnant of decal, 54" w, 30" d, 29" h 1,600.00

Arts & Crafts, Limbert, #132, rect top, single drawer, orig brass pulls flanked by book shelves opening at sides, branded signature, orig red brown finish, 45" w, 28" d, 29" h 850.00

Arts & Crafts, Limbert, #153, turtle-top, overhanging contoured top, single blind drawer, lower shelf mortised through trestle legs, 4 sq cut-outs, fine orig finish, branded mark, 47-3/4" l, 30" d, 29-1/2" h 9,500.00

Arts & Crafts, Limbert, #999, rect top, two drawers, orig hardware, long corbels on legs, six wide slats on each side, orig finish, paper label, some veneer restoration, 54" w, 30" d, 30" h 900.00

Arts & Crafts, L. and J. G. Stickley, two drawers, copper pulls, lower shelf, orig dark finish, Handcraft decal, 3 small drilled homes in one leg, some splits to lower shelf and leg top, 48" l, 30-1/4" d, 29-1/2" h 1,600.00

George III, c1800, mahogany and inlay, circular drum top, alternating working and faux drawers, inset gilt tooled green leather top, 42" d, 31" h 8,625.00

George III Style, second half 19th C, mahogany, drum, circular top with inset gilt tooled brown leather, working and faux drawers, quadripartite splayed legs ending in brass caps on casters, 44-3/4" d, 29-1/2" d 4,325.00

Regency, English, first quarter 19th C, mahogany and ebony inlaid, drum, circular top with inset green gilt tooled leather over frieze fitted with drawer, 3 faux drawers, turned and reeded pedestal, tripartite base on casters, restorations, damage, 26-1/2" d, 30-3/4" h 2,185.00

Renaissance Revival, American, late 19th C, mahogany, oblong top, carved edge, gadroon carved apron, trestle base with caryatid supports at each side joined by flat stretcher shelf, acanthus carved wide scroll feet, 60" l 30" h 3,500.00

Occasional

Federal, first quarter 19th C, cherry, outset rect top, frieze with drawer, turned, tapered, and reeded legs, 17-1/4" w, 17-1/4" d, 28-1/2" h 1,000.00

Louis XVI Style, giltwood and marble top, gray veined white marble oval top, pierced foliate frieze suspending floral swags, turned and fluted legs joined by X-form stretcher, 29-1/2" l, 22" w, 23" h ... 200.00

Parlor, Victorian

American, walnut, molded detail, white marble turtle top, carved dog on base shelf, old dark finish, old repairs, top cracked, 23" x 3" x 29" h 770.00

Gothic Revival, walnut, rosewood veneer apron, replaced top, 20" x 36" x 29-1/4" h 500.00

Pedestal

Biedermeier-Style, cherry and burr poplar, circular top with crossbanded edge, conforming apron, hexagonal support rising from triangular platform base with concave sides, three scroll supports, 29-1/2" d, 27-1/2" h 600.00

Second Empire-Style, walnut, marquetry, and parcel-gilt, quarter-veneered circular top, polychrome floral marquetry, gilt-metal gadrooned edge, sq section tapered pedestal with concave sides and canted corners, gilt hairy-paw feet, 33-1/2" d, 28-1/4" h 1,000.00

Pembroke

Chippendale

Cherry, poplar secondary wood, one dovetailed drawer, drop leaf top with cut ovolo corners on leaves, sq molded legs, orig brass bale, old mellow refinishing, 34-1/2" l, 8-1/2" leaves, 28-1/2" h 2,310.00

Mahogany, drop leaf top, one dovetailed drawer, sq tapered legs with inside chamfer, cross stretcher base, old finish, replaced brasses on drawer, repair to cross stretcher, 20" w, 33" l, 9-1/2" l leaves, 28" h 1,550.00

Federal

....New England, c1810-15, mahogany inlaid, rect overhanging top, rounded leaves, straight skirt with drawer, lower inlaid edge continuing to 4 vase and ring-turned reeded tapering legs, old refinish, imperfections, 36" w, 18-3/4" d, 28-1/2" h 1,955.00

New York, c1790-1800, mahogany inlaid, rect top, shaped drop leaves bordered by stringing, crossbanded skirt, working and faux birch veneered drawers, bordered by stringing, 4 sq tapering legs inlaid with wavy birch panels in the dies above stringing and inlaid legs, refinished, some fading, 20-1/2" w, 30-1/2" d, 28-1/2" h 2,300.00

Hepplewhite, mahogany with inlay, pine and poplar secondary woods, curved end aprons and conforming top, one dovetailed drawer in apron, sq tapering legs, restored banding and stringing inlay, orig ring brasses, old finish, 31-5/8" l, 10-1/2" l leaves, 28-1/2" h 6,100.00

Refractory, Italian Renaissance-Style, late 19th C

Walnut and inlay, molded top, carved trestle supports, molded base, imperfections to top, 90-1/2" l, 37-1/2" w, 32-1/2" h 575.00

Walnut, rect top with curved molded edge, carved trestle supports, stretcher base, on casters, 85" l, 40" d, 31-1/4" h 2,990.00

Side

Federal, New England, c1790-1800, mahogany and birch, figured mahogany overhand, figured birch drawer, 4 sq tapering legs, straight skirt with drawer, old refinish, minor imperfections, 17" w, 17-1/2" d, 27-3/4" h 2,875.00

Late Federal, 20-3/4" w, 29" h, c1800-1825, cherry, poplar secondary wood, molded rect top, frieze drawer, turned and ring-turned legs, bun feet 250.00

Sofa

Classical, Boston, c1825, mahogany and mahogany veneer, rect overhanging top with rounded leaves, straight skirt with 2 short drawers and sq tapering support, serpentine platform with canted corners, suppressed ball feet, old turned wooden pulls, refinished, minor imperfections, 57" w, 24" d, 30" h 1,850.00

Regency-Style, English, satinwood, rosewood crossbanded, ebony inlaid, silvered hardware, trestle supports ending in caps on casters, 37-1/2" w, 23" d, 29-1/2" h 2,990.00

Tavern, Queen Anne, country, maple, oval two board top, mortised and pinned apron, cut-out detail, tapered legs with duck feet, old reddish stain on base, wear and repair to feet, old repairs, 30-1/2" x 22" top, 26-3/4" h 3,355.00

Tea

Chippendale

America, mahogany, quatrefoil shaped two board tilt top with thumb-molded edge, turned column, tripod base with cabriole legs and snake feet, refinished, sun bleached finish, refastened cleats, 31-1/2" x 33-1/4" top, 28-3/4" h 1,925.00

America, mid 18th C, mahogany, circular tilt top, single plant top with molded edge, baluster turned standard, molded downswept tripod legs, pointed pad feet, reduced in height, 34" d, 21-1/4" h 325.00

England, late 18th C, carved mahogany, circular top supported on dovetailed mahogany box open at both ends, rotated above pedestal with carved diamonds enclosing scratch carving details, tripod base with acanthus leaf carving on knees, ball and claw feet, old surface, repairs, 32-1/4" w, 31-3/4" d, 29" h 2,415.00

Newport, Rhode Island, Santo Domingo mahogany, two board top, turned column, tripod base, carved knees, elongated ball and claw feet, old finish, repairs to hinge block, 33-1/2" d, 27-1/2" h ...8,250.00

Pennsylvania, c1760, mahogany, birdcage tilt-top, swelled pedestal over cabriole legs, pad feet, refinished, imperfections, 21-3/4" d, 27-3/4" h 2,185.00

Pennsylvania, c1770, walnut, bird cage with turned posts, one board top, piecrust edge, turned column, tripod base, carved walnut knees with oval and bellflower, claw and diamond shaped ball feet, old finish, repairs to base of column where legs join, repairs to bird cage, minor age cracks, 26" d, 28" h 4,400.00

Rhode Island, c1780, cherry, circular tilt-top, urn turned support, tripod cabriole leg base ending in pad feet, old refinish, some imperfections, 31-1/2" d, 28" h 650.00

Federal Style, inlaid walnut, fold-over, rect top with inset rounded corners, conforming frieze raised on sq section tapering legs, boxwood stringing, 36-1/2""l,. 25-3/4""w, 30-1/4" ", pr 800.00

Queen Anne

Mahogany, two board porringer top with candle shelves, mortised and pinned apron with simple cutout detail, slender tapered legs terminate in slightly curved ankle with duck feet, old dark finish, repairs, top and pullout candle shelves are old replacements, 25-1/2" x 32-1/2" top, 26-1/2" h 4,125.00

Maple, oval overhanging top, 4 block turned tapering legs, pad feet, straight skirt, old refinish, minor imperfections, 32-1/2" w, 26" d, 25-3/4" h 3,250.00

Federal, Massachusetts, c1800, mahogany inlaid, octagonal tilt-top bordered with inlaid geometric stringing and crossbanding, vase and ring-turned post and three shaped legs inlaid with geometric banding, old refinish, imperfections, 23-1/4" w, 16-1/4" d, 29" h ...2,990.00

Vitrine, transitional Louis XV/Louis XVI, walnut and parquetry, hinged rect top with serpentine edges, glazed conforming panel opening to reveal velvet-lined int., shaped concave frieze continuing into sq section cabriole legs, inlaid with foliage and floral arabesques, gilt-metal mounts, 24" w, 16-1/4" d, 24-1/4" h 600.00

Work

Federal

Massachusetts, c1815, mahogany veneer, rect top, case with 3 graduated drawers flanked by reeded panel legs, casters, replaced brasses, refinished, restored, 22-1/4" w, 18-1/4" d, 32-1/2" h 2,875.00

New England, c1820, mahogany and mahogany veneer, rect top, 2 cockbeaded graduated drawers and straight cockbeaded skirt joining front delicate vase and ring-turned legs, ball feet, old refinish, minor imperfections, 18" w, 15-1/2" d, 28-1/4" h 2,100.00

New York or Philadelphia, c1815, carved and veneered mahogany, projecting rect case with flanking hinged tops, astragal ends, cockbeaded compartment drawer, deep drawer below on vase and ring turned legs, tapering feet, refinished, replaced brasses, minor imperfections, 24-1/2" w, 13-1/4" d, 28-1/2" h 2,530.00

Federal, late, c1800-25

23-1/2" w, 18-1/2" d, 26-3/4" h, cherry and tiger maple, outset rect top over front with 2 drawers, spiral-turned legs, tulip form feet 650.00

37-1/4" l, 22-1/2" w, 28-3/4" h, cherry and bird's eye maple, drop leaf, rect top, rule-jointed leaves, plain frieze with drawer, turned sq section legs, turned and tapering feet 400.00

37-1/4" l, 23-3/4" w, 26-1/2" h, cherry and bird's eye maple, rect top with rounded corners, rule-joined leaves, frieze with 2 drawers, lower drawer with fitted int., turned and tapering legs 600.00

Sheraton, mahogany, figured mahogany veneer, 2 dovetailed drawers with third drawer front that holds work bag frame, turned and rope carved legs with spool turned posts, replaced brasses, old finish, top drawer fitted, lift-up writing surface, old replaced legs, 17" x 18-1/4" top, 8-1/4" leaves, 29-3/4" h 725.00

Writing, Regency, English, first quarter 19th C, rosewood, part ebonized and brass inlaid, rect top with rounded corners, inset with green gilt-tooled leather, 2 drawers opposed by faux drawers, trestle supports with turned stretcher, splayed legs with cast brass caps on casters, locks stamped "I & C Cope," restorations, 53-3/4" w, 28" d, 28-1/2" h 11,500.00

GAME PLATES

History: Game plates, popular between 1870 and 1915, are specially decorated plates used to serve fish and game. Sets originally included a platter, serving plates, and a sauce or gravy boat. Many sets have been divided. Today, individual plates are often used as wall hangings.

Birds
Plate
- 9-1/2" d, bird, scalloped edge, mauve ground, gold trim, sgd "Vitet Limoges" 140.00
- 9-1/2" d, duck, pastel pink, blue, and cream ground, duck flying up from water, yellow flowers and grasses, sgd "Laury," mkd "Limoges," not pierced for hanging 125.00
- 10" d, pheasant, Limoges, sgd "Max" 95.00
- 10-1/2" d, game bird and two water spaniels, crimped gold rim, sgd "RK Beck" 125.00
- 13-1/4" d, game bird and pheasant, heavy gold, scalloped emb rococo border, mkd "Coronet Limoges, Bussilion" 250.00
- Platter, 16" l, 2 handles, quail, hp gold trim, Limoges 150.00

Set
- 7 pcs, wild game birds, pastoral scene, molded edges, shell dec, Fazent Meheim, Bonn, Germany 250.00
- 12 pcs, 10-1/2" d plates, game birds in natural habitat, sgd "I. Bubedi" 3,500.00

Deer
- Plate, 9" d, buck and doe, forest scene 65.00
- Set, 13 pcs, platter, 12 plates, deer, bear, and game birds, yellow ground, scalloped border, "Haviland China," sgd "MC Haywood" 3,200.00

Fish
Plate
- 8" d, bass, scalloped edge, gray-green trim, fern on side of fish, Limoges 75.00
- 8-1/2" d, colorful fish swimming on green shaded ground, scalloped border, gold trim, sgd "Lancy," "Bairritz, W. S. or S. W. Co. Limoges, France," pierced for hanging 60.00

Platter
- 14" l, bass on lure, sgd "RK Beck" 125.00
- 23" l, hp, Charoone, Haviland 200.00

Set
- 8 pcs, 4 plates, 24" l, platter, sauce boat with attached plate, cov tureen, Rosenthal 395.00
- 11 pcs, ten 9" d plates, 23" l platter, sauce boat with attached underplate, scalloped and ridged, gilt trim, underwater scene, salmon colored fish, seaweed and gilt clam, Limoges 500.00
- 13 pcs, 11 plates, 25" l platter, sauce boat, Continental, ... 475.00
- 15 pcs, 12 9" plates, 24" platter, sauce boat with attached plate, cov tureen, hp, raised gold design edge, artist sgd, Limoges ... 800.00

GAMES

History: Board games have been commercially produced in this country since at least 1822, and card games since the 1780s. However, it was not until the 1840s that large numbers of games were produced that survive t this day. The W. & S. B. Ives Company produced many board and card games in the 1840s and 1950s. Milton Bradley and McLoughlin Brothers became major producers of games starting in the 1860s, followed by Parker Brothers in the 1880s. Other major producers of games in this period were Bliss, Chaffee and Selchow, Selchow and Righter, and Singer.

Today most games from the 19th century are rare and highly collectible, primarily because of their spectacular lithography. McLoughlin and Bliss command a premium because of the rarity. The quality of materials, and the extraordinary art that was created to grace the covers and boards of their games.

In the 20th century, Milton Bradley, Selchow and Righter and Parker Brothers became the primary manufacturers of boxed games. They have all now been absorbed by toy giant Hasbro Corporation. Other noteworthy producers were All-Fair, Pressman, and Transogram, all of which are no longer in business. Today the hottest part of the game collecting market is in rare character games from the 1960s. Parker Brothers and All-Fair games from the 1920s to 1940s also have some excellent lithography and are highly collectible.

References: *Board Games of the 50's, 60's & 70's with Prices*, L-W Books, 1994; Lee Dennis, *Warman's Antique American Games, 1840-1940*, Wallace-Homestead, Krause Publications, 1991; *Dexterity Games and Other Hand-Held Puzzles*, L-W Book Sales, 1995; Alex G. Malloy, *American Games*, Antique Trader Books, 1998; Jack Matthews, *Toys Go to War*, Pictorial Histories Publishing, 1994; Rex Miller, *The Investor's Guide to Vintage Character Collectibles*, Krause Publications, 1999; Rick Polizzi, *Baby Boomer Games*, Collector Books, 1995; Rick Polizzi and Fred Schaefer, *Spin Again*, Chronicle Books, 1991; Bruce Whitehill, *Games: American Boxed Games and Their Makers*, Wallace-Homestead, Krause Publications, 1992.

Periodicals: *The Games Annual*, 5575 Arapahoe Rd, Suite D, Boulder, CO 80303; *Toy Shop*, 700 E. State St., Iola, WI 54990; *Toy Trader*, P.O. Box 1050, Dubuque, IA 52004.

Collectors' Clubs: American Game Collectors Association, P.O. Box 44, Dresher, PA, 19025; Gamers Alliance, P.O. Box 197, East Meadow, NY 11554.

Museums: Checkers Hall of Fame, Petal, MS; Essex Institute, Salem, MA; Margaret Woodbury Strong Museum, Rochester, NY; University of Waterloo Museum & Archive of Games, Waterloo, Ontario, Canada; Washington Dolls' House and Toy Museum, Washington, D.C.

Additional Listings: See *Warman's Americana & Collectibles*.

Notes: While people collect games for many reasons, it is strong graphic images that bring the highest prices. Games which are collected because they are fun to play or for nostalgic reasons are still collectible but will not bring high prices. Also, game collectors are not interested in common and "public domain" games such as checkers, tiddley winks, Authors, Anagrams, Jackstraws, Rook, Pit, Flinch, and Peter Coodles. The game market today is characterized by fairly stable prices for ordinary items, increasing discrimination for grades of condition, and continually rising prices for rare material in excellent condition. Whether you are a dealer or a collector, be careful to buy games in good condition. Avoid games with taped or split corners or other box damage. Games made after about 1950 are difficult to sell unless they are complete and in excellent condition. As games get older, there is a forgiveness factor for condition and completeness that increases with age.

These listings are for games that are complete and in excellent condition. Be sure that the game you're looking to price is the same as the one described in the listing. The 19th century makers routinely published the same title on several different versions of the game, varying in size and graphics. Dimensions listed below are rounded to the nearest half inch.

After Dinner, Frederick H. Beach, 1933, 8" x 11" 70.00
Big Chief, Milton Bradley, 1938, 8" x 17" 125.00
Big Trail Game, Parker Brothers, c1930, 13-1/2" x 17"...............250.00
Bugs Bunny Adventure Game, Milton Bradley, c1961, 9-1/2" x 19"...35.00
Bull In A China Shop, Milton Bradley, 1937 ....100.00
Bullwinkle and Rocky Role Playing Party Game, TSR, c1988......20.00
Chiromagia Game, McLoughlin, 3 answer sheets, 2 question discs, lid
   missing 100.00
Clue, Parker Brothers, c1949, separate board and pieces box 25.00
Dixie Pollyana, Parker Brothers, c1952, 8" x 18", all wooden pcs, 4 orig
   dice and dicecups 100.00
Eldorado, Parker Brothers, c1941, 15" x 24-1/2" 125.00
Fish Pond, McLoughlin Bros., c1898, 8" x 18", children on cover....125.00
Fish Pond, Milton Bradley, c1910, 10" x 20", fisherman on cover. 75.00
Flap Jacks, Alderman-Fairchild, c1931, toss game, 15-1/2" x 12-1/2" 75.00
Funny Sentences, A Party Game, AllFair, 5" x 7" 58.00
Game of Battles or Fun For Boys, McLoughlin Bros., c1900, 23" x 23",
   cardboard soldiers and cannons 2,500.00
Game of Billy Possum, c1910, 8" x 15" 600.00
Game of Bo Peep, J. H. Singer, 8-1/2" x 14" 275.00
Game of Goose, by Mary D. Carrol, made by Charles Akerman, dated
   1855, 20" w opened 230.00
Game of Moon Tag, Parker Brothers, c1950, 10-1/2" x 20"..........50.00
Game of Oasis, Milton Bradley, c1937, 9-1/2" x 19-1/2" 150.00
Game of Rival Policeman, McLoughlin Brothers, c1898, 12" x 21",
   comic style cover art, lead figural playing pieces 4,000.00
Gilligans Island Game, Game Gems, c1965, 9-1/2" x 18-1/2"......350.00
Going to Jerusalem, Parker Brothers, c1955, 10-1/2" x 20" 75.00
Hit That Line, The All American Football Game, La Rue Sales, Lynn,
   MA, 6" x 8" box, orig instructions..65.00
Jolly Darkie Target Game, Milton Bradley, c1900, 10-1/2" x 19". 750.00
Jumpy Tinker, Toy Tinkers, 5" x 11" 70.00
Mail Coach Game, Whitman, 13" x 13".......................................165.00
Mickey Mantle's Big League Baseball Game, Gardner Games.. 175.00
Midget Auto Race, Samuel Lowe, 5" x 7" 70.00
Monopoly, Parker Brothers, c1935, white box edition #9, metal playing
   pieces and embossed hotels..150.00
Monopoly, Parker Brothers, 1946 Popular Edition, separate board and
   pieces box 25.00
Motorcycle Game, Milton Bradley, c1905, 9" x 9" 250.00
New Board Game of the American Revolution, Lorenzo Borge, 1844,
   colored scenes and events, 18-1/2" w opened 690.00
One Two, Button Your Shoe, Master Toy Company, 11" x 12".... 145.00
Peter Coddles Trip to New York, Milton Bradley, orig instruction sheet,
   6" x 8-1/2" 65.00
Pike's Peak or Bust, Parker Brothers, 1895, 7" x 7" 145.00
Race To The Moon, All-Fair, c1932, early space target game,
   10" x 19" 600.00
Radio Amateur Hour Game, 10" x 13" 145.00
Ralph Edwards This Is Your Life, Lowell, c1955, 13" x 19".........125.00
Razzle Dazzle Football Game, Texantics, 1954, 10" x 17" 225.00
Rose Bowl Action Filled Football Game, E. S. Lowe, 11" x 15",
   masonite board 90.00
Star Reporter, Parker Brothers, c1950, 10-1/2" x 20" 65.00
Strange Game of Forbidden Fruit, Parker Brothers, c1900, 4" x
   5-1/2"..35.00
The Boy Hunter, shooting game, metal cork firing gun, 16" x 6". 185.00
The Game of the Wizard of Oz, Whitman, c1939, 7" x 13-1/2"... 300.00
The Limited Mail and Express Game, Parker Brothers, c1894, 14" x
   21", metal train playing pieces 250.00
The Mansion of Happiness, W. & S. B. Ives, c1843 ....950.00
The Wonderful Game of Oz, Parker Brothers, 1921, 10" x 19"... 275.00
Tom Swift, Parker Brothers, c1966, 9-1/2" x 19-1/2 ....250.00

Truth of Consequences, Gabriel, c1955, 14" x 19-1/2" 75.00
Whirlpool, McLoughlin Brothers, 1899, #408, 7-1/4" sq, instructions on
   cover 40.00
Who Do You Love Best, J. Jay Gould, 1876, 7-1/2" x 5" 35.00

GAUDY DUTCH

History: Gaudy Dutch is an opaque, soft-paste ware made between 1790 and 1825 in England's Staffordshire district.

The wares first were hand decorated in an underglaze blue and fired; then additional decorations were added over the glaze. The over-glaze decoration is extensively worn on many of the antique pieces. Gaudy Dutch found a ready market in the Pennsylvania German community because it was inexpensive and extremely colorful. It had little appeal in England.

Museums: Henry Ford Museum, Dearborn, MI; Philadelphia Museum of Art, Philadelphia, PA; Reading Art Museum, Reading, PA.

Marks: Marks of various potters, including the impressed marks of Riley and Wood, have been found on some pieces, although most are unmarked.

References: Susan and Al Bagdade, *Warman's English & Continental Pottery & Porcelain*, 3rd Edition, Krause Publications, 1998; Eleanor and Edward Fox, *Gaudy Dutch*, published by author, 1970, out of print; John A. Shuman, III, *Collector's Encyclopedia of Gaudy Dutch & Welsh*, Collector Books, 1990, 1998 value update.

Collectors' Club: Gaudy Collector's Society, P.O. Box 274, Gates Mills, OH 44040.

Reproduction Alert: Cup plates, bearing the impressed mark "CYBRIS," have been reproduced and are collectible in their own right. The Henry Ford Museum has issued pieces in the Single Rose pattern, although they are porcelain rather than soft paste.

Advisor: John D. Querry.

Butterfly
   Bowl, 11" d..3,900.00
   Coffeepot, 11" h...4,500.00
   Cup and Saucer, handleless, minor enamel flakes, chips on table
      ring 645.00
   Plate, 7 1/4" d...775.00
   Soup Plate, 8 1/2" d, wear and scratches, rim
      hairline 615.00
   Sugar Bowl, cov...900.00
   Teapot, 5" h, squat baluster form 1,400.00
   Waste Bowl...1,275.00
Carnation
   Bowl, 6-1/4" d...750.00
   Creamer, 4-3/4" h...700.00
   Pitcher, 6" h..675.00
   Plate, 8" d...850.00
   Teabowl and Saucer..575.00
   Teapot, cov...1,275.00
   Toddy Plate...525.00
   Waste Bowl...450.00
Dahlia
   Bowl, 6-1/4" d...675.00
   Plate, 8" d..1,100.00
   Teabowl and Saucer..700.00

Double Rose
    Bowl, 6-1/4" d 545.00
    Creamer.. 650.00
    Gravy Boat.. 575.00
    Plate
        8-1/4" d 675.00
        10" d 935.00
    Sugar Bowl, cov.. 750.00
    Teapot, cov 800.00
    Toddy Plate, 4-1/2" d 425.00
    Waste Bowl, 601/2" d, 3" h 550.00
Dove
    Creamer.. 675.00
    Plate
        7-1/2" d 770.00
        8 1/8" d, very worn, scratches, stains............ 245.00
    Waste Bowl 650.00
Flower Basket, plate, 6-1/2" d 375.00
Grape
    Bowl, 6-1/2" d, lustered rim 475.00
    Plate, 6-1/4" d 580.00
    Sugar Bowl, cov.. 675.00
    Teabowl and Saucer 475.00
    Toddy Plate, 5" d 475.00
Leaf, bowl, 11-1/2" d, shallow 4,800.00
Oyster
    Bowl, 5-1/2" d 300.00
    Coffeepot, cov, 12" h 3,000.00
    Plate, 9-1/2" d 575.00
    Soup Plate, 8-1/2" d 550.00
    Teabowl and Saucer 400.00
    Toddy Plate, 5-1/2" d 425.00
Single Rose
    Bowl, 6" d 275.00
    Coffeepot, 10-3/4" h, double-gourd form 850.00
    Cup and Saucer, handleless, pr 850.00
    Plate, 8-1/4" d 650.00
    Quill Holder, cov 2,500.00
    Sugar Bowl, cov.. 700.00
    Toddy Plate, 5-1/4" d 250.00

Plate, Oyster pattern, 9-1/2" d, $575.

Waste Bowl, 5 1/2" d, wear, hairlines, stains, flake on table rim, glaze
    rim flakes.. 365.00
Sunflower
    Bowl, 6-1/2" d 900.00
    Coffeepot, cov, 9-1/2" h 6,500.00
    Creamer.. 850.00
    Cup and saucer, handleless, wear, chips 575.00
Urn
    Creamer.. 475.00
    Cup and Saucer, handleless, wear and scratches 375.00
    Plate
        8-1/4" d 910.00
        9 7/8" d, very worn, scratches, stains, rim chips 225.00
    Sugar Bowl, cov, 6-1/2" h, round, tip and base
      restored.. 295.00
War Bonnet
    Bowl, cov 225.00
    Coffeepot, cov 9,500.00
    Cup and Saucer, handleless................................ 575.00
    Plate, 8-1/8" d, pinpoint rim flake, minor wear 880.00
    Teapot, cov 2,400.00
    Toddy Plate, 4-1/2" d 525.00

GAUDY IRONSTONE

History: Gaudy Ironstone was made in England around 1850. Ironstone is an opaque, heavy-bodied earthenware which contains large proportions of flint and slag. Gaudy Ironstone is decorated in patterns and colors similar to those of Gaudy Welsh.

Museums: Henry Ford Museum, Dearborn, MI; Philadelphia Museum of Art, Philadelphia, PA; Reading Art Museum, Reading, PA.

Marks: Most pieces are impressed "Ironstone" and bear a registry mark.

Chop Plate, 12-3/4" d, 9 rabbits, 4 frogs and flowers, circular center,
    black transfer, red, blue, green, and yellow dec 990.00
Creamer, Morning Glory, 6-1/2" h, paneled, foliage handle 175.00
Cup and Saucer, handleless
    Floral 85.00
    Morning Glory 90.00
    Rose 80.00
    Strawberry 85.00
    Urn 115.00
    Urn and Flowers 135.00
Pitcher
    7-1/2" d, lion head snake handle, red, blue, and green, Mason's,
      mkd "Patent Ironstone China".......................... 330.00
    9" h, molded design, floral dec, underglaze blue, red, and green
      enamel, luster trim, firing flaw near handle, some flaking to
      green.. 475.00
Plate
    9-3/8" d, 6 rabbits, 3 frogs and flowers, black transfer, red, blue,
      green, and yellow dec.................................... 470.00
    9-3/8" d, 9 rabbits, 3 cabbages, 3 frogs, 3 trees, black transfer, red,
      blue, green, and yellow dec 420.00
    9-1/2" d, 8 rabbits, black transfer, red, blue, green, and yellow dec,
      stains and crazing.. 360.00
    9-3/4" d, twelve-sided, Urn and Flowers, blue, red, pink, and green,
      minor enamel flaking.................................... 140.00
Platter
    14-7/8" l, 8 rabbits, 4 frogs and flowers, black transfer, red, blue,
      green, and yellow dec, stains and crazing........ 1,100.00
    22-1/4" l, polychrome floral enameling, underglaze blue, minor flaking, Staffordshire... 770.00
Sugar Bowl, cov
    Floral, 7-1/4" h, luster trim 125.00

Morning Glory, 8" h, paneled, underglaze blue, foliage handles.195.00
Teapot, cov, 10" h, Blackberry, paneled, underglaze blue and black, yellow and red enamel and luster, cock's comb handle and final glued, chips on rim and spout 880.00
Toddy Plate, Urn, 4-3/4" d 200.00
Vase, 9-3/4" h, bulbous, flared mouth, banded cobalt blue dec, gilt and floral dec, pr 975.00
Waste Bowl, Strawberry, 5-3/8" h 185.00

GAUDY WELSH

History: Gaudy Welsh is a translucent porcelain that was originally made in the Swansea area of England from 1830 to 1845. Although the designs resemble Gaudy Dutch, the body texture and weight differ. One of the characteristics is the gold luster on top of the glaze.

In 1890, Allerton made a similar ware from heavier opaque porcelain.

Museums: Royal Institution of South Wales, Swansea Mills; St. Fagen's Welsh Folk Museum, Cardiff, Wales; Welsh National Museum, Cardiff, Wales.

Marks: Allerton pieces usually bear an export mark.

References: Susan and Al Bagdade, *Warman's English & Continental Pottery & Porcelain*, 3rd Edition, Krause Publications, 1998; John A. Shuman, III, *Collector's Encyclopedia of Gaudy Dutch and Welsh*, Collector Books, 1990, 1991 value update, out-of-print; Howard Y. Williams, *Gaudy Welsh China*, Wallace-Homestead, out-of-print.

Collectors' Club: Gaudy Collector's Society, P.O. Box 274, Gates Mills, OH 44040.

Columbine
    Bowl, 10" d, 5-1/2" h, ftd, underglaze blue and polychrome enamel floral dec 410.00
    Plate, 5-1/2" d 75.00
Daisy and Chain
    Creamer 185.00
    Cup and Saucer 95.00
    Sugar Bowl, cov 195.00
    Teapot, cov 225.00
Flower Basket
    Bowl, 10-1/2" d 195.00
    Mug, 4" h 95.00
    Plate 65.00
    Sugar Bowl, cov, luster trim 175.00
Grape
    Bowl, 5-3/4" d 50.00
    Cup and Saucer 75.00
    Mug, 2-1/2" h 70.00

Grape Pattern #1, tea service, $1,850.

Plate, 5-1/4" d 65.00
Oyster
    Bowl, 6" d 85.00
    Child's Tea Set, 4-3/4" h teapot, two 3" h creamers, two 4" h cov sugar 480.00
    Cream Pitcher, 4" h 115.00
    Cup and Saucer, set of 12, minor chips and hairlines 385.00
    Pitcher, 7" h 200.00
    Plate
        5-1/2" d 80.00
        6" d, set of 22, some damage 525.00
        8-1/2" d, sq, patterned border, set of 4, some chips 275.00
        9-1/4" d, set of 8, some wear 250.00
    Shaving Mug 215.00
    Sugar, cov, 5-1/2" h 275.00
    Waste Bowl, hairline 50.00
Strawberry
    Creamer 90.00
    Cup and Saucer 80.00
    Plate, 8-3/4" d 150.00
Tulip
    Bowl, 6-1/4" d 60.00
    Cake Plate, 10" d, molded handles 125.00
    Creamer 100.00
    Sugar, cov, 6-3/4" h 115.00
    Teapot, 7-1/4" h 195.00
Wagon Wheel
    Cup and Saucer 85.00
    Mug, 2-1/2" h 95.00
    Pitcher, 8-1/2" h 200.00
    Plate, 8-3/4" d 90.00

GIRANDOLES and MANTEL LUSTRES

History: A girandole is a very elaborate branched candleholder, often featuring cut glass prisms surrounding the mountings. A mantel lustre is a glass vase with attached cut glass prisms.

Girandoles and mantel lustres usually are found in pairs. It is not uncommon for girandoles to be part of a large gar-

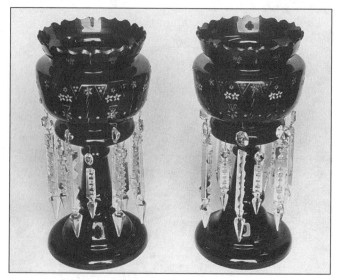

Ruby glass, enameled floral dec, 14" h, $450.

niture set. Girandoles and mantel lustres achieved their greatest popularity in the last half of the 19th century both in the United States and Europe.

Girandoles, pr

13" h, Bohemian, tulip shape, cranberry, rect prisms, gilt dec, circular foot, c1875 .... 325.00
14" h, SP and cut glass, three tiers hung with faceted drops, scrolled candle arms, c1900 .... 165.00
15" h, Victorian, pink, enameled and colored wild flowers, notched prisms 275.00
15-1/2" h, candlesticks, marble bases, figural brass stems, clear cut prisms 140.00
15-1/2" h pr candlesticks, 17-1/2" d center 3 light girandole, stepped marble base, gilded brass stems, child, deer, dog, and vintage prism bands with clear cut prisms 525.00
16-3/8" h, three arms, clear cut prisms, cast brass frame, marble base with brass boy and dog 145.00
18" h, courting couple, brass relief, triple branch with prisms, marble base 125.00
20-1/2" h, pierced and shaped rect frame, orig glass, crest, Italian Rococo, 18th C 450.00
35-1/2" h, bronze, 7 light glass drops suspended from pressed glass stars 600.00
40" h, Regency, giltwood, eagle on rockwork cresting, foliate pendant, four scrolled candle arms and spherules, early 19th C 1,725.00

Mantel Lusters

6-1/4" h, 8" w, cornucopia style, opaline glass horns, alternating with gilt-bronze female hand, white marble base, French, 19th C, pr 250.00
9" h, blue, enameled florals, gold trim, white beading, Waterford crystal prisms 240.00
10-1/2" h, green, cut to crystal, ten cut glass prisms 295.00
12" h, opaline, green fold over top, white satin glass bodies, gold trim 250.00
14" h, double cut overlay, white to emerald green, prisms of alternating lengths 250.00
15-3/4" h, Bohemian, cobalt blue, gilt scrollwork dec, colored floral springs, 2 rows of crystal prisms, late 19th C 350.00

GOLDSCHEIDER

History: Friedrich Goldscheider founded a porcelain and faience factory in Vienna, Austria, in 1885. Upon his death, his widow carried on operations. In 1920, Walter and Marcell, Friedrich's sons, gained control. During the Art Deco period, the firm commissioned several artists to create figural statues, among which were Pierrettes and sleek wolfhounds. During the 1930s, the company's products were mostly traditional.

In the early 1940s, the Goldscheiders fled to the United States and re-established operations in Trenton, New Jersey. The Goldscheider Everlast Corporation was listed in Trenton City directories between 1943 and 1950. Goldscheider Ceramics, located at 1441 Heath Ave., Trenton, New Jersey, was listed in the *1952 Crockery and Glass Journal Directory* but was not listed in 1954.

Reference: Susan and Al Bagdade, *Warman's English & Continental Pottery & Porcelain*, 3rd Edition, Krause Publications, 1998.

Bust, 26" h, finely molded face, downcast eyes, long light brown hair looped into chignon, narrow mauve head band and straps with oval irid glass jewels, gilt draped gown, incised "Montenave, Goldschneider seal molded in relief" 2,800.00
Figure, terra cotta, polychrome dec, late 19th/earlyb 20th C

Bust, black woman, blue hair, orange highlights, sgd "Goldschieder, Vienna, 1927," pedestal base, $310.

21-1/2" h, Sitting Tunsian Boy, boy sitting on blanket, arms resting on bent legs, inscribed artist's name "Rokel," and "Reproduction Reserve," cast numbers "1415-5" 3,700.00
23-1/4" h, Nubian Maiden with Basket, inscribed "Fr. Goldscheider Wien/Reproductione Reserve," cast numbers "845/4580" in base 2,750.00
26-1/4" h, Slave Girl, young woman with drapery falling from belt at her waist, hands tied behind and around naturalistically cast tree trunk, inscribed "Fr. Goldscheider Wien/Reproductione Reserve," cast numbers "1065" in base 2,950.00
Plaque, 13-1/2" w, 25-1/8" h, earthenware, rect, molded maiden profile, garland of blossoms and berries in hair, large blossom and cluster on left, earth tones, designer sgd "Lamassi," c1900 .... 1,100.00
Plate, mermaid pattern, multicolored 175.00
Wall Mask, 11-1/4" h, Art Deco, curly brown haired girl, red lips, aqua scarf 400.00

GONDER POTTERY

History: Lawton Gonder established Gonder Ceramic Arts, Inc., at Zanesville, Ohio, in 1941. He had gained experience while working for other factories in the area. Gonder experimented with glazes, including Chinese crackle, gold crackle, and flambé. Lamp bases were manufactured under the name "Eglee" at a second plant location. The company ceased operation in 1957.

Marks: Pieces are clearly marked with the word "Gonder" in various forms.

References: Susan and Al Bagdade, *Warman's American Pottery and Porcelain*, Wallace-Homestead, 1994; Ron Hoppes, *Collector's Guide and History of Gonder Pottery*, L-W Book Sales, 1992.

Collectors' Club: Gonder Collectors Club, 917 Hurl Drive, Pittsburgh, PA 15236.

Bowl
    6-1/2" d, ribbed, yellow 10.00
    8" d, H-29, gray, pink int. 20.00
Candlesticks, pr
    4-3/4" h, turquoise ext., pink-coral int., mkd "E-14, Gonder" ... 25.00
    5" h, cornucopia, light gray, pink highlights, mkd "Gonder USA
    #552" 32.00
Creamer and Sugar, dark brown drip and brown
    spatter 30.00
Ewer
    6" d, mottled blue, pink int. 24.00
    13" h, Shell and Star pattern, green 50.00
Figure
    7" h, swan, shaded blue 18.00
    10-1/2" h, elephant, raised trunk, rose and gray 45.00
Flower Frog, 7-3/4" x 7", Swirl pattern, blue and brown glossy glaze 25.00
Planter, 7" l, light brown 25.00
Vase
    6" h, E-68, yellow, applied leaf 25.00
    6-1/4" h, E-64, twisted, blue-gray ext., gray-pink int. 25.00
    7" h, E-3, dogwood flower shape, pink and mottled blue glaze 35.00
    7" h, E-5, light gray to pink, upright cornucopia 30.00
    7" h, 2-3/4" d, turquoise 15.00
    9" h, H-14, upright cornucopia, blended green, brown, and pink,
    mkd "Gonder USA H-14" 60.00

GOOFUS GLASS

History: Goofus glass, also known as Mexican ware, hooligan glass, and pickle glass, is a pressed glass with relief designs that were painted either on the back or front. The designs are usually in red and green with a metallic gold ground. It was popular from 1890 to 1920 and was used as a premium at carnivals.

It was produced by several companies: Crescent Glass Company, Wellsburg, West Virginia; Imperial Glass Corporation, Bellaire, Ohio; LaBelle Glass Works, Bridgeport, Ohio; and Northwood Glass Co., Indiana, Pennsylvania, Wheeling, West Virginia, and Bridgeport, Ohio.

Goofus glass lost its popularity when people found that the paint tarnished or scaled off after repeated washings and wear. No record of its manufacture has been found after 1920.

Marks: Goofus glass made by Northwood includes one of the following marks: "N," "N" in one circle, "N" in two circles, or one or two circles without the "N."

Periodical: *Goofus Glass Gazette*, 9 Lindenwood Ct., Sterling, VA 20165.

Bowl
    9" d, carnations 30.00
    10-1/2" d, red roses, molded, gold ground 45.00
Cake Plate
    10-1/2" d, Cabbage Roses, red dec, gold foliate
    ground 35.00
    11" d, Dahlia and Fan, red dec, gold ground 40.00
Candle Holder, red and gold 20.00
Compote, 9-1/2" d, strawberries and leaves, red and green dec, gold
    ground, ruffled 50.00
Dish, 11" d, chrysanthemum sprays, rd and gold, scalloped
    rim 75.00
Pickle Jar, aqua, molded, gold, blue, and red painted floral design 50.00
Pitcher, red rose bud dec, gold leaves 70.00
Plate
    8-3/8" d, apples, red dec, gold ground 20.00

Plate, Old Rose Distilling Co., Chicago, advertising emb in center, gold ground, 8-1/4" d, $65.

    11" d, roses, red and gold, scalloped rim 45.00
Salt and Pepper Shakers, pr, Poppy 40.00
Serving Plate, 13" d, colorless ground, gold leaves, red grapes,
    scalloped 35.00
Vase
    7" h, Cabbage Rose, gold ground, red roses 25.00
    7-1/2" h, brown, red bird 30.00
    12" h, red roses, molded, gold ground 60.00

GOUDA POTTERY

History: Gouda and the surrounding areas of Holland have been principal Dutch pottery centers for centuries. Originally, the potteries produced a simple utilitarian tin-glazed Delft-type earthenware and the famous clay smoker's pipes.

When pipe making declined in the early 1900s, the Gouda potteries turned to art pottery. Influenced by the Art Nouveau and Art Deco movements, artists expressed themselves with free-form and stylized designs in bold colors.

References: Susan and Al Bagdade, *Warman's English & Continental Pottery & Porcelain*, 3rd Edition, Krause Publications, 1998; Phyllis T. Ritvo, *The World of Gouda Pottery*, Font & Center Press, 1998.

Periodical: *Dutch Potter*, 47 London Terrace, New Rochelle, NY 10804.

Reproduction Alert: With the Art Nouveau and Art Deco revivals of recent years, modern reproductions of Gouda pottery currently are on the market. They are difficult to distinguish from the originals.

Bowl
    6-3/4" d, 4" h, , rust, gold flowers, sage leaves, variegated black, blue,
    yellow, cobalt blue, green, and white int., sgd "Regina" 290.00

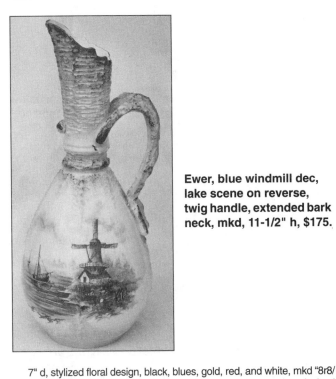

Ewer, blue windmill dec, lake scene on reverse, twig handle, extended bark neck, mkd, 11-1/2" h, $175.

until the 1860s. At the start of World War I, when European companies turned to manufacturing war weapons, American producers took over the market.

Gray and white were the most common graniteware colors, although each company made their own special color in shades of blue, green, brown, violet, cream, or red.

Older graniteware is heavier than the new. Pieces with cast-iron handles date between 1870 to 1890; wood handles between 1900 to 1910. Other dating clues are seams, wooden knobs, and tin lids.

References: Helen Greguire, *Collector's Encyclopedia of Granite Ware: Colors Shapes and Values*, Book 1 (1990, 1994 value update), Book 2 (1993, 1998 value update), Collector Books; David T. Pikul and Ellen M. Plante, *Collectible Enameled Ware: American & European*, Schiffer Publishing, 1998.

Collectors' Club: National Graniteware Society, P.O. Box 10013, Cedar Rapids, IA 52410.

Reproduction Alert: Graniteware still is manufactured in many of the traditional forms and colors.

Additional Listings: See *Warman's Americana & Collectibles* for more examples.

Berry Pail, cov, 7" d, 4-3/4" h, gray and black mottled 50.00
Bowl
    7-1/2" d, mottled dark brown and white, Onyxware 40.00
    11-3/4" d, 3-3/4" h, green and white 50.00
Bread Riser, cov, blue and white swirl, tin lid, large 175.00
Cake Pan, 7-1/2" d, robin's egg blue and white
    marbleized 45.00
Child's Feeding Set, cup and dish, white, chickens dec, worn 35.00
Coffee Boiler, cov, blue and white swirl 100.00
Coffeepot, cov
    Blue and white, 9-1/2" h 225.00
    Dark green and white swirl 250.00
    Red swirl 235.00
Colander, 12" d, gray, pedestal base 30.00
Cream Can, Crystallite, green 2,500.00
Creamer, 5" h, turquoise swirl 18.00
Cup, 2-3/4" h, blue and white medium swirl, black trim and handle ... 50.00

7" d, stylized floral design, black, blues, gold, red, and white, mkd "8r8/ GABY/house logo/Gouda/Made in Holland/4239," other incised marks 200.00
Box, cov, 4-1/4" l, carved, black, gold, and white, glazed, Regina mark 175.00
Butter Pats, set of six, sgd "Favorite Distel" 85.00
Candleholders, pr, 6-1/2" h, one damaged 150.00
Chamberstick, 11-1/2" h, attached bobeche, side handle, black ground, green, brown, and rust dec 195.00
Charger, 12" d, white magnolias, teal petals, black stems, orange and amber speckled ground, mkd "NV Kon Pazuis Unique Gouda Holland," artists monogram "JVS," (J. W. Van Schaik), c1930 ...... 450.00
Clock, 9" d, 3" d, dark blue high glaze, stylized blue, mauve and yellow irises and green, rust foliage, gilded metal clock in center, works mkd "J. Unghams," c1900, crazing, clock not working 800.00
Decanter, 10-1/2" h, Nadra pattern, orange, brown, and ochre floral dec, black base, handle, stopper 165.00
Jar, cov, 5-1/2" h, Aero pattern, glossy finish, Royal Zuid mark 65.00
Lantern, 6" h, Art Nouveau dec, Palzuid house mark 165.00
Pitcher
    5" h, 3" d, brown, blue, orange, and white, mkd "ROSEVOL/Gouda/ X195/house logo/AB/Made in Holland" 125.00
    5" h, 3-1/2" w, stylized flowers 90.00
Planter, 6" d, 4" at base, white, orange, blue, yellow, and black, dark blue int. 125.00
Plate, 12" d, Nadra pattern 115.00
Tobacco Jar, cov, 5" h, Vernon pattern 115.00
Trivet, 4" w, Damascus, c1895 .... 195.00
Vase
    5-1/2" h 275.00
    8-1/4" h, 4-1/2" h, four buttress handles, deep green and purple stylized flowers, factory symbol "A to H" and "Zuid, Holland" 345.00
Wooden Shoe, 6" l, 2-1/2" w, 2-1/4" h, purple, yellow, orange, brown, and turquoise 90.00

GRANITEWARE

History: Graniteware is the name commonly given to enamel-coated iron or steel kitchenware.

The first graniteware was made in Germany in the 1830s. Graniteware was not produced in the United States

Teapot, Perfection Granite Ironware, pewter handle, lid, and spout, made by Manning Bowman & Co., West Meriden, CT, c1876, $325. Photo courtesy of Tina Carter.

Double Boiler, red swirl 3,600.00
Frying Pan, 10-1/4" d, blue and white mottled, white int. 135.00
Funnel, cobalt blue and white marbleized, large...........................50.00
Grater, medium blue 115.00
Hotplate, 2 burners, white graniteware, Hotpoint.......................165.00
Kettle, cov, 9" h, 11-1/2" d, gray mottled 50.00
Measure, 1 cup, gray 45.00
Milk Pan, blue and white 35.00
Mixing Bowls, red and white, nested set of 4, 1930s.................155.00
Mold, ftd, melon, speckled blue 185.00
Muffin Pan, blue and white mottled, 8 cups 250.00
Pail, cobalt blue swirl, 9" h, 10-3/4" d..195.00
Pan, 11" x 6", mottled gray, handle 40.00
Pie Pan, 6" d, cobalt blue and white marbleized.........................25.00
Pitcher, 11" h, gray, ice lip 110.00
Pudding Pan, 8" d, cobalt blue and white swirl 40.00
Refrigerator Bowls, red swirl, 4 pc set 585.00
Roaster, cov
    Cobalt blue, emb "Savory," 11-1/2" w, 17-1/2" l, 8" h, used 60.00
    White lid, black base, 12" w, 18-1/2" l, 5" h, used...................75.00
Skimmer, 10" l, gray mottled 25.00
Sieve, triangle shape, cream, blue trim.......................................30.00
Soap Dish, hanging, blue and white swirl 120.00
Spittoon, blue and white swirl 325.00
Syrup
    Gray, some wear 125.00
    White, some wear 65.00
Tea Kettle, dark blue, white specks, stationary handle 70.00
Teapot, cov, red, cobalt blue, orange, and black swirls, early 1900s325.00
Tube Pan, octagonal, gray mottled 45.00
Vegetable Bowl, oblong, blue and white 90.00
Wash Basin, 11-3/4" d, blue and white swirl, Blue Diamond Ware...150.00
Water Pail, lime green, brown, and white swirl, early 1900s.......225.00

GREENAWAY, KATE

History: Kate Greenaway, or "K.G." as she initialed her famous drawings, was born in 1846 in London. Her father was a prominent wood engraver. Kate's natural talent for drawing soon was evident, and she began art classes at the age of 12. In 1868, she had her first public exhibition.

Her talents were used primarily in illustrating. The cards she decorated for Marcus Ward are largely unsigned. China and pottery companies soon had her drawings of children appearing on many of their wares. By the 1880s, she was one of the foremost children's book illustrators in England.

Reference: Ina Taylor, Art of Kate Greenaway: A Nostalgic Portrait of Childhood, Pelican Publishing, 1991.

Collectors' Club: Kate Greenaway Society, P.O. Box 8, Norwood, PA 19074.

Reproduction Alert: Some Greenaway buttons have been reproduced in Europe and sold in the United States.

Book, *Kate Greenaway*, M. H. Spielmann and G. S. Layard, Black, London, 1905
    Large 8vo, illus, blue levant gilt by Bayntun, vari-colored morocco inlaid panel on front cover of Greenaway dwg of girl opening door, spine faded, cloth slipcase................................575.00
    Thick 4to, first edition, 53 color plates, lettered tissue guards, 90 black and white illus, thick 4to, gilt lettered cream cloth covers, overall light soiling, 1 of 500 numbered copies, sgd by John Greenaway, orig pencil sketch by Kate of young girl with bonnet holding pencil, smaller study of her hand in margin........1,055.00
Butter Pat, transfer print of boy and girl 35.00

Napkin Ring, little girl and cat, mkd "Meridan 199," 3-1/4" h, 3-1/4" l, $275.

Button, 3/4" d, girl with kitten on fence..15.00
Children's Book, Greenaway illus
    A Day In A Child's Life, London, 1881, first edition, 4to, cloth backed pictorial boards, rubbed, hinges cracked 80.00
    Marigold Garden: Pictures and Rhymes, London, 1885, first edition, first issue, 4to, cloth backed pictorial boards, edges lightly rubbed...165.00
    Under the Window, Routledge, London, 1878, first edition, 4to, cloth backed pictorial glazed boards....................................75.00
Children's Play Dishes, tea set, multicolored scenes, gold trim, 15 pc set 450.00
Cup and Saucer, transfer print of girl doing laundry in wooden tub....35.00
Dish, 11" l, oval, transfer print of Jack Sprat and Sunbonnet girl ..50.00
Figure, 8-1/2" h, boy with basket, satin, gold, pink, and blue trim, mkd "1893"..525.00
Hat, bisque, 3 girls sitting on brim, flowers 120.00
Inkwell, bronze, emb, 2 children 200.00
Match Safe, SP, emb children..50.00
Napkin Ring, SS, girl feeding yearling 160.00
Perfume Bottle, 2" l, SS, low relief of girls, orig stopper...200.00
Plate, 7" d, transfer print of boy chasing rabbits 65.00
Stickpin, figural, bronze, children playing ring around the rosy, c1900...35.00
Tape Measure, figural, girl holding muff......................................45.00
Teaspoon, SS, figural, girl handle, bowl engraved with Lucy Locket verse 50.00
Thimble Holder, SP, Kate Greenaway-type girl sitting on rect base, holding thimble, base imp "My Favorite Thimble" 200.00
Tile, each 6-3/8" d, transfer print, 4 seasons, one spacer, brown and white dec, blue border, stamped mark, produced by T & R Boote, 1881, framed, 5 pc set 375.00

GREENTOWN GLASS

History: The Indiana Tumbler and Goblet Co., Greentown, Indiana, produced its first clear, pressed glass table and bar wares in late 1894. Initial success led to a doubling of the plant size in 1895 and other subsequent expansions, one in 1897 to allow for the manufacture of colored glass. In 1899, the firm joined the combine known as the National Glass Company.

In 1900, just before arriving in Greentown, Jacob Rosenthal developed an opaque brown glass, called "chocolate," which ranged in color from a dark, rich chocolate to a lighter coffee-with-cream hue. Production of chocolate glass saved the financially pressed Indiana Tumbler and Goblet Works. The Cactus and Leaf Bracket patterns were made almost exclusively in chocolate glass. Other popular chocolate patterns include Austrian, Dewey, Shuttle, and Teardrop and Tassel. In 1902, National Glass Company bought Rosenthal's chocolate glass formula so other plants in the combine could use the color.

In 1902, Rosenthal developed the Golden Agate and Rose Agate colors. All work ceased on June 13, 1903, when a fire of suspicious origin destroyed the Indiana Tumbler and Goblet Company Works.

After the fire, other companies, e.g., McKee and Brothers, produced chocolate glass in the same pattern designs used by Greentown. Later reproductions also have been made, with Cactus among the most-heavily copied patterns.

Reference: James Measell, *Greentown Glass*, Grand Rapids Public Museum, 1979, 1992-93 value update, distributed by Antique Publications.

Collectors' Clubs: Collectors of Findlay Glass, P.O. Box 256, Findlay, OH 45839; National Greentown Glass Association, P.O. Box 107, Greentown, IN 46936.

Videotape: *Centennial Exhibit of Greentown Glass and Reproductions of Greentown Glass*, National Greentown Glass Association, P.O. Box 107, Greentown, IN 46936.

Museums: Grand Rapids Public Museum, Ruth Herrick Greentown Glass Collection, Grand Rapids, MI; Greentown Glass Museum, Greentown, IN.

Additional Listings: Holly Amber; Pattern Glass.

Reproduction Alert.

Animal Covered dish
    Dolphin, chocolate, chip off tail 195.00
    Rabbit, dome top, amber 250.00
Bowl, 7-1/4" d, Herringbone Buttress, green 135.00
Butter, cov, Cupid, chocolate 575.00
Celery Vase, Beaded Panel, clear 100.00
Compote, Geneva, 4-1/2" d, 3-1/2" h, chocolate 150.00
Cordial, Austrian, canary 125.00

Butter Dish, Geneva pattern, chocolate, tripod feet, $475.

Creamer
    Cactus, chocolate 85.00
    Cupid, Nile green 400.00
    Indian Head, opaque white 450.00
Cruet, orig stopper, Leaf Bracket, chocolate 275.00
Goblet
    Overall Lattice 40.00
    Shuttle, chocolate 500.00
Mug, outdoor drinking scene, Nile green 200.00
Mustard, cov, Daisy, opaque white 75.00
Nappy, Masonic, chocolate 85.00
Paperweight, Buffalo, Nile green 600.00
Plate, Serenade, chocoalgeq85.00
Punch Cup, Cord Drapery, clear 20.00
Relish, Leaf Bracket, 8" l, oval, chocolate 75.00
Salt and Pepper Shakers, pr, Cactus, chocolate 150.00
Sugar, cov, Dewey, cobalt blue 145.00
Syrup, Indian Feather, green 175.00
Toothpick, Cactus, chocolate 75.00
Tumbler
    Cactus, chocolate 60.00
    Dewey, canary 65.00

GRUEBY POTTERY

History: William Grueby was active in the ceramic industry for several years before he developed his own method of producing matte-glazed pottery and founded the Grueby Faience Company in Boston, Massachusetts, in 1897.

The art pottery was hand thrown in natural shapes, hand molded, and hand tooled. A variety of colored glazes, singly or in combinations, were produced, but green was the most popular. In 1908 the firm was divided into the Grueby Pottery Company and the Grueby Faience and Tile Co. The Grueby Faience and Tile Company made art tile until 1917, although their pottery production was phased out about 1910.

Minor damage is acceptable to most collectors of Grueby Pottery.

References: Paul Evans, *Art Pottery of the United States*, 2nd ed., Feingold & Lewis Publishing, 1987; Ralph and Terry Kovel, *Kovels' American Art Pottery*, Crown Publishers, 1993; Susan Montgomery, *The Ceramics of William H. Grueby*, Arts and Crafts Quarterly Press, 1993; David Rago, *American Art Pottery*, Knickerbocker Press, 1997.

Advisor: David Rago.

Cabinet Vase, 3" h, 3-1/4" d, squat, leathery oatmeal matte glaze,
    ground bottom, unmarked 750.00
Candlestick, 9-3/4" h, 4" d, tooled leaves, leathery dark blue matte
    glaze, unmarked 1,500.00
Fireplace Surround, 29" h, 45" w (int. measurement), 7 rect tiles,
    cuenca dec, landscape frieze, unmarked, restored, from Dream-
    mwold Mansion, Scituate, MA, c1902, design attributed to Addison
    LeBoutiller 22,500.00
Floor Vase
    15-1/2" h, 10" d, tooled and applied broad leaves alternating with
        yellow buds, leathery matte green glaze, circular pottery mark,
        incised "WP," Wilhemina Post 60,000.00
    23-1/4" h, 8-1/2" d, tall stovepipe neck, tooled and applied yellow
        buds alternating with leaves, fine matte green glaze, factory label,
        minor glaze chips to base, edge nicks to leaves 25,000.00
Frieze, 6" h, 18" d, three horizontal tiles, cuenca, ivory and yellow
    waterlilies, light green leaves, dark green ground, stamped
    "GRUEBY BOSTON/63," framed 4,250.00
Jardiniere, 5-3/4" h, 8-3/4" d, curdled matte green glaze, stamped
    "Grueby Pottery," minor rim touch-up 1,600.00

Floor Vase, stovepipe neck, tooled and applied yellow buds alternating with leaves, matte green glaze, factory label, minor glaze chips to base, nicks to edges of leaves, 23-1/4" h, 8-1/2" d, $25,000. Photo courtesy of David Rago Auctions, Inc.

Lamp, table

9-1/2" h x 10" d Grueby sq base with cylindrical neck, applied and modeled leaves alternating with yellow trefoils, leathery matte green glaze, circular pottery mark, incised "I.E.H./187-1" with 4 paper labels; 6-1/2" h x 15-3/4" d Tiffany leaded glass Acorn pattern shade, green grid, band of yellow acorns, die-stamped "Tiffany Studios, New York/1435-39," Tiffany patinated bronze lamp fixture mkd "Bailey, Banks, & Biddle," few hairlines to glass 25,000.00

11" h, 7-3/4" d Grueby double gourd shaped base by Wilhelmina Post, leathery cobalt blue matte glaze, orig bronze lamp inserted, 7" h, 12-1/2" d leaded cobalt blue and green slag glass period shade, circular pottery mark and "228," paper label, incised "W.P.," orig order label with instructions for shade...........9,000.00

12-1/2" h, 10" d Grueby Kendrick base with 7 handles and tooled leaves, 7" h, 18" d leaded glass Tiffany turtle back shade with halo of lustered tiles on green slag glass, matte green glaze, orig oil lamp retro fitted to electric at Grueby factory, two paper labels on base "Change to electric, 3 lights, chain sockets/bronze band at foot of base/cord to come thru here," and "Do not make a shade, Sold with turtleback sh.(sic)," Grueby price tag "$125," Grueby label, and stamp, shade and font stamped "Tiffany Studios/New York," Tiffany bronze beading at base complete by loose 26,000.00

Paperweight, scarab, circular Faience mark

3-1/4" h, 2-1/4" l, blue matte glaze, restored 300.00

4" h, 2" l, matte green glaze, restoration to small chip 475.00

Tile, cuenca seca

3" h, 6" l, frieze of purple berries and green leaves, blue ground, pr, unmarked, chips to edge of one 450.00

4" sq, Alice in Wonderland Chesire Cat, raised architectural and artist's initials, Pardee, 1/2" glaze chip on front 700.00

4" sq, polychrome fountain and hedgerow, restoration to break at corner, unmarked..300.00

5-1/2" sq, haystacks in landscape, unmarked, set of 4, one with chips, from Dreammwold Mansion, Scituate, MA, c1902, design attributed to Addison LeBoutiller......................................6,000.00

6" sq, stylized waves, white flying seagulls, sea blue ground, mounted in Arts & Crafts frame 1,400.00

8" sq, ochre and ivory tall ship, green sea, blue sky, dead-matte leather glaze, stamped "92" 900.00

8-1/2" h, 12-3/4" l, scalloped architectural faience, yellow, black, and white oriole, white and blue floral ground, sgd "ES" in slip, c1917 ....700.00

Vase

5-1/2" h, 4" d, ovoid, collared rim, matte green glaze, Marie Seaman initials, glaze miss to rim, shaved bottom 650.00

5-1/2" h, 4" d, ovoid, tooled and applied full length leaves, light green matte glaze, stamped mark 1,400.00

6-1/2" h, 4-1/2" d, squat base, cylindrical neck, leathery matte green glaze, unmarked..900.00

7-1/2" h, 4-1/2" d, bulbous, lobed opening, tooled and applied leaves alternating with buds, matte blue-green glaze, circular Faience stamp, minor rim nick, restoration to chip 1,880.00

9" h, 5-3/4" d, bottle shape, tooled and applied leaves, medium green matte glaze, circular pottery 10,000.00

11-1/4" h, 6" d, three-color, tooled and applied daffodils in profile, yellow, red, and green, ochre centers, body cov in exceptional leathery matte green glaze, pottery stamp mark, restoration to rim chips 10,000.00

11-1/4" h, 6" d, full height tooled and applied leaves alternating with scrolled handles, thick curdled matte green enamel, circular mark under glaze, several small rim chips, glaze slippage in several areas...2,200.00

11-1/2" h, 5" d, ovoid, tooled and applied leaves and daffodils, leathery matte green ground, stamped pottery mark and "MS," Marie Seaman, minor nicks to leaf edges........................6,500.00

11-1/2" h, 5" d, tooled and applied leaves alternating with scrolled handles, feathered matte green glaze, stamped Faience mark, few chips to handles 7,250.00

13-1/4" h, 8" d, bottle shape, leathery matte green glaze, stamped pottery mark , "No. 166," rim chip 4,200.00

Vessel

7" h. 11-1/2", squat, tooled and applied leaves alternating with yellow buds, pulled matte green glaze, stamped Faience mark, several nicks to leaf edges, couple of flat stilt pull chips to base 8,500.00

11-3/4" h, 5-1/2" d, closed-in rim, alternating full length tooled and applied buds and leaves, leathery matte green glaze, stamped mark..6,500.00

HAIR ORNAMENTS

History: Hair ornaments, among the first accessories developed by primitive man, were used to remove tangles and keep hair out of one's face. Remnants of early combs have been found in many archaeological excavations.

As fashion styles evolved through the centuries, hair ornaments kept pace with changes in design and usage. Hair combs and other hair ornaments are made in a wide variety of materials, e.g., precious metals, ivory, tortoiseshell, plastics, and wood.

Combs were first made in America during the Revolution when imports from England were restricted. Early American combs were made of horn and treasured as toiletry articles.

References: Mary Bachman, *Collector's Guide to Hair Combs, Identification and Values,* Collector Books, 1998; Evelyn Haetig, *Antique Combs and Purses,* Gallery Graphics Press, 1983.

Collectors' Club: Antique Comb Collectors Club International, 8712 Pleasant View Road, Bangor, PA 18013; Antique Fancy Comb Collectors Club, 3291 N. River Rd, Libertyville, IL 60048; National Antique Comb Collectors Club, 3748 Sunray Dr., Holiday, FL 34691.

Museums: Leominster Historical Society, Field School Museum, Leominster, MA; Miller's Museum of Antique Combs, Homer, AK.

Back Comb, celluloid
  5" l, 4" w, carved openwork, purple and lavender rhinestones 70.00
  5-1/2" l, 4-1/4" w, imitation tortoiseshell, swirled mauve, 110 red rhinestones 65.00
  5-3/4" l, 6" w, imitation tortoiseshell, 109 gold rhinestones 85.00
  6" l, 5 prongs, translucent pearlized amber, fan shaped back, flying bird, blue rhinestone feathers 85.00
  7" l, 5 prongs, translucent green, Spanish Revival, filigree, trefoil design, c1925 .... 45.00
  Barrette, 4" l, Mexican silver, inlaid abalone shell in flower design, black background, mkd "Alpaca Mexico" 24.00
Comb
  2-1/2" l, 4-1/2" w, celluloid, imitation tortoiseshell, flower motif, rhinestone accents 20.00

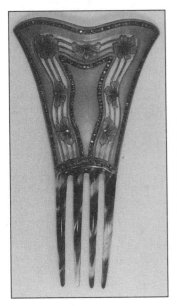

Ornament, celluloid, frosted amber, flowing floral dec, trimmed with blue rhinestones, 4 prong imitation tortoise comb, late 1920s, 6" h, $75. Photo courtesy of Julie P. Robinson.

3-1/8" h, 2-1/4" w, celluloid, imitation tortoiseshell, openwork spider motif 30.00
3-3/4" h, 4-1/2" w, celluloid, emb "Samoa" in gold 45.00
4-1/2" l, Mexican silver, flower and leaf design, blue-green abalone, white background, mkd "Alpaca Mexico" 24.00
6-1/4" l, Art Deco, teal blue celluloid, swirled pearlescence, matching blue rhinestones 80.00
Hair Ornament
  7/8" l, double prong, imitation tortoise ornament, triple row of topaz rhinestones, three-prong imitation tortoise comb, Art Deco styling, topaz colored rhinestones 50.00
  16" l, 9" w, pale pink, dangling pearl and flower ornaments, soft pink flowers outlined in silver with tiny pearls at top center, pale pink brocade leaves 40.00
Hair Pick, 7" l, single prong hair ornament, imitation ivory, gracefully twisted top, diecut filigree 35.00
Side Comb
  1-1/2" l, 3" w, tiara, rhinestones 35.00
  4-1/2" l, celluloid, imitation amber, shaped like long hair pins, delicate hand painted floral motif, pr 35.00

HALL CHINA COMPANY

History: Robert Hall founded the Hall China Company in 1903 in East Liverpool, Ohio. He died in 1904 and was succeeded by his son, Robert Taggart Hall. After years of experimentation, Robert T. Hall developed a leadless glaze in 1911, opening the way for production of glazed household products.

The Hall China Company made many types of kitchenware, refrigerator sets, and dinnerware in a wide variety of patterns. Some patterns were made exclusively for a particular retailer, such as Heather Rose for Sears.

One of the most popular patterns was Autumn Leaf, a premium designed by Arden Richards in 1933 for the exclusive use of the Jewel Tea Company. Still a Jewel Tea property, Autumn Leaf has not been listed in catalogs since 1978 but is produced on a replacement basis with the date stamped on the back.

References: Susan and Al Bagdade, *Warman's American Pottery and Porcelain,* Wallace-Homestead, 1994; Harvey Duke, *Hall China: Price Guide Update Two,* ELO Books, 1995; ——, *Official Price Guide to Pottery and Porcelain,* 8th ed., House of Collectibles, 1995; C. L. Miller, *Jewel Tea Grocery Products with Values,* Schiffer Publishing, 1996; ——, *Jewel Tea: Sales and Housewares Collectibles,* Schiffer Publishing, 1995; Jim and Lynn Salko, *Halls Autumn Leaf China and Jewel Tea Collectible,* published by authors (143 Topeg Dr., Severna Park, MD 21146); Margaret and Kenn Whitmyer, *Collector's Encyclopedia of Hall China,* 2nd ed., Collector Books, 1994, 1997 values update.

Periodicals: *The Daze,* P.O. Box 57, Otisville, MI 48463; *Hall China Encore,* 317 N. Pleasant St., Oberlin, OH 44074.

Collectors' Clubs: Hall Collector's Club, P.O. Box 360488, Cleveland, OH 44136, http://www.chinaspecialities.com/hallnews.html; National Autumn Leaf Collectors Club, P.O. Box 162961, Fort Worth, TX 76161-0961.

Additional Listings: See *Warman's Americana & Collectibles* for more examples.

Kitchen Ware
Bean Pot, New England, #1, Orange Poppy 100.00
Coffeepot, Great American, Orange Poppy 65.00

Autumn Leaf, coffeepot, mkd "Hall's Superior Quality Kitchenware, Tested and Approved by Mary Dunbar, Jewel T Homemakers Institute," $90.

Creamer, Lazy Daisies, Kraft 15.00
Cup and Saucer, Lazy Daisies, Kraft 15.00
Fork, Feather, experimental pattern, blue 200.00
Jug, Primrose, rayed 20.00
Reamer, lettuce green 450.00
Spoon, Feather, experimental pattern, yellow 300.00
Watering Can, lilac 850.00

Patterns

Autumn Leaf
Baker 100.00
Bread and Butter Plate 8.00
Casserole 65.00
Coffeepot, cov 95.00
Creamer 30.00
Cup and Saucer 20.00
Dessert Bowl 12.00
Dinner Plate 16.00
Drippings Bowl 40.00
Jug, ball 65.00
Milk Pitcher, 5-3/4" h 50.00
Pitcher 90.00
Salad Plate 12.00
Sugar Bowl, cov 45.00
Teapot, cov 90.00
Vegetable Bowl
    Divided 125.00
    Oval, open 65.00
    Round, open 70.00
Banded Indian Red, cookie jar 100.00

Blue Bouquet
Creamer, Boston 20.00
Cup and Saucer 25.00
French Baker, round 25.00
Platter
    13" l 35.00
    15" l 40.00
Soup, flat 30.00
Spoon 100.00
Vegetable, open, round 30.00

Cameo Rose
Bowl, 5-1/4" d 3.00
Butter Dish, 3/4 lb 30.00
Casserole 25.00
Creamer and Sugar 10.00
Cream Soup, 6" d 7.00
Cup and Saucer 9.00
Luncheon Plate, 8" d 2.50
Teapot, cov, 6 cup 35.00

Tidbit, 3 tier 40.00
Crocus
Coffeepot, cov 65.00
Cup and Saucer 15.00
Luncheon Plate 18.00
Platter
    Medium 40.00
    Small 30.00
Salad Plate 15.00
Vegetable Bowl, cov 50.00
Vegetable Bowl, open, round 30.00
Fuji
Coffee Server 40.00
Creamer and Sugar 25.00
Hallcraft, vegetable, oval, open, white 30.00
Highlander, #3909, cup and saucer 15.00
Holiday, gravy boat 25.00
Mount Vernon
Coffeepot 125.00
Creamer 10.00
Cup 8.00
Dinner Plate, 10" d 15.00
Fruit Bowl 9.00
Gravy Boat 20.00
Saucer 3.00
Soup Bowl, 8" d, flat 6.50
Vegetable Bowl, 9-1/4" l, oval 10.00
Red Poppy
Bowl, 5-1/2" d 5.00
Cake Plate 17.50
Cake Server 65.00
Casserole, cov 25.00
Coffeepot, cov 12.00
Creamer and Sugar 15.00
Cup and Saucer 8.00
French Baker, fluted 15.00
Jug, Daniel, radiance 28.00
Luncheon Plate 20.00
Salad Bowl, 9" d 14.00
Teapot, New York 90.00
Vegetable Bowl, round, open, platinum edge 25.00
Serenade Gravy Boat 40.00
Silhouette
Bean Pot 50.00
Bowl, 7-7/8" d 50.00
Coffeepot, cov 30.00
Mug 32.00
Pretzel Jar 75.00
Tulip
Bowl, 10-1/4" l, oval 36.00
Coffee Maker, drip, Kadota, all china 115.00
Condiment Jar 165.00
Creamer 15.00
Cup and Saucer 15.00
Fruit Bowl, 5-1/2" d 10.00
Luncheon Plate, 9" d 16.00
Mixing Bowl, 6" d 27.00
Platter, 13-1/4" l, oval 42.00
Shakers
    Bulge-type, price for pr 110.00
    Set, salt, pepper, flour, and sugar, handles 240.00
Sugar, cov 25.00

Teapots
Baltimore, ivory and gold, gold label 200.00
Blue Blossom, airflow 950.00
Cadet, Radiance 350.00
Chinese Red, 3 cup 40.00
Cleveland, turquoise and gold 165.00
Los Angeles, cobalt blue 160.00

Philadelphia, ivory, gold label...115.00
Surfside, emerald and gold 250.00
Windshield, rose 90.00

HAMPSHIRE POTTERY

History: In 1871, James S. Taft founded the Hampshire Pottery Company in Keene, New Hampshire. Production began with redwares and stonewares, followed by majolica in 1879. A semi-porcelain, with the recognizable matte glazes plus the Royal Worcester glaze, was introduced in 1883.

Until World War I, the factory made an extensive line of utilitarian and art wares including souvenir items. After the war, the firm resumed operations but made only hotel dinnerware and tiles. The company was dissolved in 1923.

References: Susan and Al Bagdade, *Warman's American Pottery and Porcelain,* Wallace-Homestead, 1994; Ralph and Terry Kovel, *Kovels' American Art Pottery,* Crown Publishers, 1993.

Bowl, 9" d, raised tulips and leaves, half matte and half glossy green glaze, imp "Hampshire Pottery," circled "M" and "57" 300.00
Candeholder, 6-1/2" h, shield back with handle, matte green glaze...250.00
Inkwell, 4-1/8" d, 2-3/4" h, round, large center well, 3 pen holes..175.00
Lamp Base, 19-1/4" h, oval, alternating bud on stem and lotus leaves in relief, dark matte blue glaze, carved Oriental-style wood base, green glass and brass finial, imp "Hampshire Pottery 42," Cadmon Robertson cipher, minor glaze bursts.....................575.00
Vase
    2-1/2" h, 5-1/2" d, incised geometric design under matte green glaze, incised "Hampshire Pottery" with "Hampshire Pottery Keene, New Hampshire" printed in red, "M" cipher inside circle, modeled by Cadmon Robertson 350.00
    2-7/8" h, flattened sq form, inverted rim, brown over green curdled matte glaze, imp "Hampshire Pottery M" within a circle, artist Cadmon Robertson cipher, and "149" on base, glaze burst on rim 290.00
    6-1/4" h, 3-1/2" d, incised foliate design, matte green glaze, frothy white highlights, incised "Hampshire Pottery 52/2" 400.00

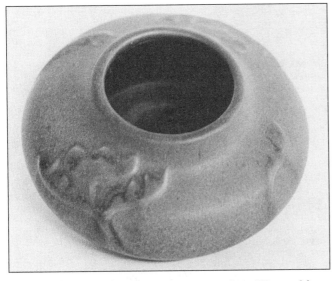

Vessel, relief floral design, green matte, imp "Hampshire Pottery," 5-3/4" d, $135.

6-3/4" h, 3-3/4" d, ovoid, closed-in rim, emb broad leaves, green and blue glaze, incised "Hampshire Pottery" 750.00
9" h, lobed circular body, matte green glaze, imp "Hampshire" and "M" within a circle, "900," designed by Cadmon Robertson, c1907, hairline 865.00

HATPINS and HATPIN HOLDERS

History: When oversized hats were in vogue, around 1850, hatpins became popular. Designers used a variety of materials to decorate the pin ends, including china, crystal, enamel, gem stones, precious metals, and shells. Decorative subjects ranged from commemorative designs to insects.

Hatpin holders, generally placed on a dresser, are porcelain containers which were designed specifically to hold these pins. The holders were produced by major manufacturers, among which were Meissen, Nippon, R. S. Germany, R. S. Prussia, and Wedgwood.

Reference: Lillian Baker, *Hatpins & Hatpin Holders: An Illustrated Value Guide,* Collector Books, 1983, 1997 value update.

Collectors' Clubs: American Hatpin Society, 20 Montecillo Drive, Rolling Hills Estates, CA 90274; International Club for Collectors of Hatpins and Hatpin Holders, 1013 Medhurst Rd, Columbus, OH 43220.

Museum: Los Angeles Art Museum, Costume Dept., Los Angeles, CA.

Reproduction Alert: Many reproduction hatpins and hatpin holders are currently being made and offered for sale. Look for signs of age and wear, as well as mellowed colors and vintage designs.

Hatpins

3" l, 1/2" w, celluloid, pearlesence, one end with circle of rhinestones, other end with 2 accent rhinestones on side, c1930 .... 40.00
3-1/2" x 1-1/2", Art Deco, small glittering stones, black details, c1920 ....45.00
5-5/8" l, 2-1/4" x 1-1/4" x 3/4" head, black faceted glass 150.00
6" l, ball, mkd "Sterling"...60.00
6" l, 9/16" d, gold ball, mkd "10K".......................................75.00
6-1/8" l, 1/2" d head, pink swirl pearlized, large center rhinestone 45.00
6-3/8" l, 1/2" x 3/8" d head, pearl surrounded by 7 rhinestones.... 45.00
6-3/4" l, 1-1/8" l head, sword, sterling silver.................................95.00
6-3/4" l, 2-1/8" l silver colored metal column................................55.00
6-7/8" l, 1-1/8" d head, swooping bird, freeform design head, hallmarked 95.00
7" l, faceted amber glass head, c1920, matched pair.................125.00
7" l, 1" x 5/8" d filigree head with prong set amethyst faceted glass stone, Victorian 125.00
7" l, 2-1/2" l x 1-3/8" d head, black glass, bird foot design, Victorian 125.00
7-1/8" l, 2-1/8" black faceted glass head......................................75.00
7-3/8" l, 3/8" l x 3/8" d head with single large rhinestone.............45.00
7-5/8" l, 3/4" l teardrop shaped filigree head................................65.00
7-3/4" l, 1-3/4" w head, Czechoslovakian rhinestones..................85.00
7-7/8" l, 1-1/4" d amethyst colored stone in sq brass head, cross bar finding..130.00
8" l, 1-1/8" l clover bud with amethyst faceted colored stone 95.00
8" l, 1-5/8" x 1-1/4" emb copper head, bezel set coral colored stone 95.00
8-1/4" l, 3/8" d ball with 12 clear rhinestones.............................45.00

Woven celluloid hatpin holder, conical, weighted base, $145; celluloid hatpins range in price between $45 and $85. Photo courtesy of Julie P. Robinson.

8-1/2" l, 1-1/4" l x 15/16" d, oval, made from half dollar 60.00
8-1/2" l, 1-5/8" l head, double faced, brass 110.00
8-3/4" l, 1-3/8" l x 1" d shell head, metal holder 75.00
8-7/8" l, 1" l x 7/8" clear glass, faceted acorn shape 65.00
9-1/2" l, 2" d head, early military emblem 125.00
9-5/8" l, 1-1/4" d head with 37 rhinestones 65.00
10" l, 3-1/4" l full figural Buddha on filigree floral head, brass shank 125.00
11-1/4" l, 1-3/4" d, irid, metal head with smooth ring around
   faceted dome 125.00
11-1/4" l, 1" d filigree head, 8-point floral design, 9 clear prong set
   rhinestones 75.00
11-3/8" l, 1-1/4" d, amethyst colored stone in sq brass setting, cross
   bar finding 130.00
11-1/2" l, 2-3/4" l head, black ebonized wood, metal separator .. 100.00
11-3/4" l, 1-7/8" d filigree top, 11 rhinestones, rust colored center
   stone 120.00
12-1/8" l, 1-7/8" d filigree head, 22 rhinestones, cross bar finding, Victorian 145.00
12-3/4" l, 1-1/4" round ebonized wood ball, japanned shaft 95.00
13-1/4" l, 2" l amber faceted head, japanned shaft 125.00
13-3/4" l, 1-3/4" l four-sided head with fired gold bamboo plants, white
   and gold mottled background 135.00

Hatpin Holders

Austria, 5" h, hand painted blue forget-me-nots 45.00
Bavarian, mother-of-pearl dec, mkd "H & C Bavaria" 85.00
Carnival Glass, Formal pattern, Dugan, marigold 525.00
Limoges, 5" h, hand painted, floral dec, holes for 13 hatpins 20.00
Nippon
   4" h, pink ground, mauve and lavender flowers, green leaves, gold trim,
     c1900, mkd "Hand Painted Nippon The Jonroth Studios" 195.00
   4-3/4" h, hand painted, gold trim, wear to dec 95.00
   4-7/8" l, blue daisies, mkd "Hand Painted Nippon E OH China" .185.00
   RS Prussia, 4-1/2" h, bulbous, ivory ground, rose, pink, lavender,
     green, and yellow flowers, gold trim 40.00

HAVILAND CHINA

History: In 1842, American china importer David Haviland moved to Limoges, France, where he began manufactur-

ing and decorating china specifically for the U.S. market. Haviland is synonymous with fine, white, translucent porcelain, although early hand-painted patterns were generally larger and darker colored on heavier whiteware blanks than were later ones.

David revolutionized French china factories by both manufacturing the whiteware blank and decorating it at the same site. In addition, Haviland and Company pioneered the use of decals in decorating china.

David's sons, Charles Edward and Theodore, split the company in 1892. In 1936, Theodore opened an American division, which still operates today. In 1941, Theodore bought out Charles Edward's heirs and recombined both companies under the original name of H. and Co. The Haviland family sold the firm in 1981.

Charles Field Haviland, cousin of Charles Edward and Theodore, worked for and then, after his marriage in 1857, ran the Casseaux Works until 1882. Items continued to carry his name as decorator until 1941.

Thousands of Haviland patterns were made, but were not consistently named until after 1926. The similarities in many of the patterns makes identification difficult. Numbers assigned by Arlene Schleiger and illustrated in her books have become the identification standard.

References: Susan and Al Bagdade, *Warman's American Pottery and Porcelain,* Wallace-Homestead, 1994; Mary Frank Gaston, *Haviland Collectibles & Art Objects,* Collector Books, 1984; Charles E. & Carol M. Ulrey, *Matching Services for Haviland China,* published by author, (P.O. Box 15815, San Diego, CA 92175); Arlene Schleiger, *Two Hundred Patterns of Haviland China,* Books I-V, published by author, 1950-1977; Nora Travis, *Haviland China,* Schiffer Publishing, 1997, 1998 value update.

Collectors' Club: Haviland Collectors International Foundation, P.O. Box 802462, Santa Clarita, CA 91380.

Celery Dish, scalloped edge, green flowers, pale pink scrolls 48.00
Chocolate Set, chocolate pot, six cups and saucers, Baltimore Rose
   pattern 1,600.00
Cup and Saucer
   3" w, light coral flowers, translucent porcelain, mkd "Haviland Limo-
     ges," c1888, minor gilt wear on handle 40.00
   3-1/4" w x 2" h cup, 5-1/4" w saucer, over painted roses, gilt trim,
     gilt ribbon handle, mkd "Haviland Limoges," c1893-1930 ..... 40.00
Demitasse Cup and Saucer
   2-1/2" w cup, pastel flowers, gilt trim, beaded loop handle, scal-
     loped saucer, mkd "Haviland Limoges," c1893-1930 .... 45.00
   2-1/2" w x 2" h cup, 4-3/4" d saucer, purple flowers, cream ground,
     mkd "Haviland Limoges" 25.00
Dinner Service
   Blue Garland, 81 pcs 295.00
   Rosalinda, 75 pcs 695.00
   Vieux Paris Green, 60 pcs 2,350.00
Fish Set, twelve 8-1/4" d plates, 19-1/2" l tray, underglaze cobalt blue
   banded borders, enamel dec transfer fish prints, France, 1880 ....
   1,250.00
Ink Blotter, hp violets and foliage, mkd "Haviland" 45.00
Oyster Plate, 8-3/4" d, printed leaf and floral dec branches, gilt trim,
   mkd "Haviland, Limoges," c1900, set of 12 .... 635.00
Teacup and Saucer, 2-1/2" h, Amstel Hotel, rose transfer, angular lop
   handle with gilt dots and feathers, mkd "Haviland Limoges" 40.00
Tete-A-Tete, 3-1/2" h teapot, creamer, cov sugar, two cups and saucers,
   tray, molded and polychromed butterfly handles, gilt highlights .1,100.00
Vase, 4-1/2" h, 8" w, rect, slip painted village scene, 2 figures under

bridge, cream, pink, blue, brown, and green, sgd "YM," imp "Haviland & Co., Limoges, S6, 3," decorated by Yefgheni Morand, repairs to base, rim chip 460.00

Selected Dinnerware Pattern Prices

Bread and Butter Plate
    Autumn Leaf, Schleiger #060 ....15.00
    Delaware 10.00
    Laserre 18.00
    Lorraine, Schleiger #686 ....16.00
    Mount Vernon 12.00
    Rosalinde 27.00
    Troy...5.00
Cake Plate, Mount Vernon 45.00
Chop Plate, Mount Vernon 45.00
Creamer
    Greek Key 24.00
    Rosalinde 35.00
Cream Soup and Saucer
    Mount Vernon 35.00
    Rosalinde 63.00
Cup and Saucer
    Autumn Leaf, Schleiger #060 ....30.00
    Delaware 35.00
    Greek Key 24.00
    Laserre 25.00
    Lisbon, Schleiger #569 ....28.00
    Mount Vernon 32.00
    Rosalinde 48.00
    Troy...30.00
Dinner Plate
    Ambazar 20.00
    Delaware 35.00
    Laserre 40.00
    Mount Vernon 31.00
    Rosalinde 48.00
    Troy...20.00
Fruit or Dessert Bowl
    Mount Vernon 15.00
    My Garden 25.00
    Rosalinde 34.00
    Troy...15.00
Gravy Boat
    Delaware 50.00
    Mount Vernon 65.00
    Rosalinde 135.00
    Troy...90.00
Platter
    Greek Key, small 40.00

Cup and Saucer, Delaware pattern, $17.50.

    Laserre, medium 60.00
    Mount Vernon, medium 75.00
    Rosalinde, large 145.00
    Rosalinde, small 125.00
    Troy, medium 85.00
    Troy, large 95.00
    Troy, small 75.00
Salad Plate
    Autumn Leaf, Schleiger #060 ....14.00
    Delaware 20.00
    Laserre 28.00
    Rosalinde 30.00
    Troy...18.00
Saucer, Ranson 5.00
Soup Bowl
    Autumn Leaf, Schleiger #060 ....20.00
    Lisbon, Schleiger #569 ....12.00
    Mount Vernon 30.00
Sugar Bowl, cov, Rosalinde 75.00
Vegetable, covered
    Greek Key 125.00
    My Garden 150.00
    Troy 210.00
Vegetable, open, oval
    Laserre 50.00
    Mount Vernon 45.00
    Rosalinde 115.00

HEISEY GLASS

History: The A. H. Heisey Glass Co. began producing glasswares in April 1896, in Newark, Ohio. Heisey, the firm's founder, was not a newcomer to the field, having been associated with the craft since his youth.

Many blown and molded patterns were produced in crystal, colored, milk (opalescent), and Ivorina Verde (custard) glass. Decorative techniques of cutting, etching, and silver deposit were employed. Glass figurines were introduced in 1933 and continued in production until 1957 when the factory closed. All Heisey glass is notable for its clarity.

Marks: Not all pieces have the familiar H-within-a-diamond mark.

References: Neila Bredehoft, *Collector's Encyclopedia of Heisey Glass,* 1925-1938, Collector Books, 1986, 1999 value update; Lyle Conder, *Collector's Guide to Heisey's Glassware for Your Table,* L-W Books, 1984, 1993-94 value update; Gene Florence, *Elegant Glassware of the Depression Era,* 8th, Collector Books, 1998; Frank L. Hahn and Paul Kikeli, *Collector's Guide to Heisey and Heisey by Imperial Glass Animals,* Golden Era Publications, 1991, 1998 value update.

Collectors' Clubs: Bay State Heisey Collectors Club, 354 Washington St., East Walpole, MA 02032; Heisey Collectors of America, 169 W. Church St., Newark, OH, 43055; National Capital Heisey Collectors, P.O. Box 23, Clinton, MD 20735.

Videotape: Heisey Glass Collectors of America, Inc., *Legacy of American Craftsmanship: The National Heisey Glass Museum,* Heisey Collectors of America, Inc., 1994.

Museum: National Heisey Glass Museum, Newark, OH.

Reproduction Alert: Some Heisey molds were sold to Imperial Glass of Bellaire, Ohio, and certain items were reissued. These pieces may be mistaken for the original Heisey. Some of the reproductions were produced in colors which were never made by Heisey and have become collectible in their own right. Examples include: the Colt family in Crystal, Caramel Slag, Ultra Blue, and Horizon Blue; the mallard with wings up in Caramel Slag; Whirlpool (Provincial) in crystal and colors; and Waverly, a 7-inch, oval, footed compote in Caramel Slag.

Almond Dish, Greek Key 38.00
Ashtray
    Diamond Point, 2-1/2" d 20.00
    Mahabar, 3" sq 12.00
    Wampum 22.00
Basket, Octagon, Hawthorne orchid, etching, 5" h 125.00
Bon Bon, Fern, zircon, 6" d 65.00
Bookends, pr, horse heads 150.00
Bowl
    Empress, Sahara, 6" d 30.00
    Rococo, 8" d 85.00
Butter Dish, cov, Orchid 235.00
Candleholders, pr
    Trident, 2-lite, Sahara 300.00
    Warwick 135.00
Candlesticks, pr, Rose, 3 lite 300.00
Candy Dish, cov, Lariat, caramel 75.00
Celery Tray, Ridgeleigh, 12" d 40.00
Champagne
    Carcassonne, #3390, Sahara 35.00
    Orchid, sq foot 100.00
    Rose 30.00
Cheese Dish, cov, Lariat, 5" d 50.00
Cigarette Holder, Orchid, sq foot 100.00
Cocktail
    Carcassonne, #3390, Sahara 35.00
    Lariat, moonglow cut 25.00
    Pheasant 75.00
Compote, low, ftd, Orchid 50.00
Creamer
    Empress, pink 50.00
    Ridgeleigh 30.00
Creamer and Sugar, individual size, Empress, Sahara 70.00
Cruet
    Pleat and Panel, pink 125.00
    Rose 225.00
Cup, Waverly 12.00
Decanter, Orchid, etched "Sherry" 360.00
Deviled Egg Plate, Lariat 140.00
Dinner Plate
    Lariat 115.00
    Orchid 235.00
Egg Cup
    Greek Key 48.00
    Yeoman, flamingo pink 30.00
Gardenia Bowl
    Orchid, 9" d 80.00
    Rose, 13" d 85.00
Goblet
    Carcassonne, #3390, Sahara 50.00
    Diamond Optic, flamingo pink 30.00
    Lariat 22.00
    Rose 35.00
    Victorian 25.00
Hors D'oeuvre Plate, Octagon, flamingo pink, 13" d 30.00
Iced Tea Tumbler
    Lariat, moonglow cut 32.00
    Orchid, flat, 5" h 65.00
    Twentieth Century, Dawn 80.00

Ice Tub
    Octagon, Hawthorne orchid, etching 75.00
    Twist, moongleam green, silver handles 80.00
Ivy Vase, #4224, tangerine, 4" h 275.00
Jug
    Greek Key, 1 pint 320.00
    Queen Ann, Olympiad etch 125.00
Juice Tumbler, Carcassonne, #3390, Sahara 40.00
Marmalade Jar, cov, Plantation, pineapple shape, orig sgd spoon .. 125.00
Mayonnaise and Underplate, Crystolite 80.00
Mint Dish, Chintz, Sahara yellow 35.00
Nut Dish
    Empress, Sahara 30.00
    Flat Panel, flamingo pink, ruffled 31.50
Oil Bottle, Lariat 75.00
Parfait, Yeoman 9.00
Pitcher
    Orchid 535.00
    Plantation 500.00
    Rose, 76 oz 895.00
Plate
    #393, crystal, 6" d 5.00
    #1230, crystal, 7-1/4" d 8.00
    Empress, Sahara, 8" d, sq 22.00
    Empress, tangerine, 7" d 185.00
Punch Bowl Set, Banded Flute, 14" d punch bowl, high base, 5 punch cups 275.00
Punch Cup
    Colonial 15.00
    Lariat 6.00
Relish
    Plantation, 3 part, 11-1/4" d 90.00
    Rose, 3 part, 11" d 80.00
Salad Plate, Crystolite 15.00
Salt and Pepper Shakers, pr, Waverly 32.00
Sandwich Plate, Rose 220.00
Sherbet
    Carcassonne, #3390, Sahara 40.00
    Lariat, moonglow cut 20.00
    Victorian 15.00
Sherry, Orchid, #5025 .... 125.00
Sugar, cov
    Lariat 20.00
    Orchid 38.00
    Victorian 30.00
Torte Plate, Rose, 14" d 85.00

Sherbet, Victorian, crystal, ftd, sgd, $18.

Tumbler
    Duquesne, tangerine, 5-1/4" h...............................155.00
    Greek Key, 10 oz, flat 100.00
    Orchid, 12 oz, 7-3/4" h...60.00
Vase
    Lariat, 7" h 25.00
    Waverly, fan shape 40.00
Wine
    Lariat...20.00
    Minuet..72.00
    Plantation..28.00
    Provincial...25.00
    Rose..38.00
    Victorian..30.00
    Wabash...20.00

HOLLY AMBER

History: Holly Amber, originally called Golden Agate, was produced by the Indiana Tumbler and Goblet Works of the National Glass Co., Greentown, Indiana. Jacob Rosenthal created the color in 1902. Holly Amber is a gold-colored glass with a marbleized onyx color on raised parts.

Holly (No. 450), a pattern created by Frank Jackson, was designed specifically for the Golden Agate color. Between January 1903 and June of that year, when the factory was destroyed by fire, more than 35 different forms were made in this pattern.

Reference: James Measell, *Greentown Glass, The Indiana Tumbler & Goblet Co.,* Grand Rapids Public Museum, 1979, 1992-93 value update, distributed by Antique Publications.

Collectors' Club: National Greentown Glass Association, 19596 Glendale Ave., South Bend, IN 46637.

Museums: Grand Rapids Public Museum, Ruth Herrick Greentown Glass Collection, Grand Rapids, MI; Greentown Glass Museum, Greentown, IN.

Additional Listings: Greentown Glass.

Berry Bowl, 8-1/2" d 375.00
Butter, cov, 7-1/4" x 6-3/4" d 1,200.00
Cake Stand 2,000.00
Compote, cov, 8-1/2" d, 12" h 1,800.00

Compote, open, 7-3/8" d, 6-3/4" h, $875.

Creamer and Sugar 1,550.00
Cruet, 6-1/2" h, orig stopper...................................2,100.00
Jelly Compote, 4-3/4" d..450.00
Match Holder...400.00
Mug, 4-1/2" h 450.00
Nappy..375.00
Parfait..575.00
Relish, oval 275.00
Salt and Pepper Shakers, pr.....................................500.00
Sauce Dish..225.00
Spooner 425.00
Syrup, 5-3/4" h, SP hinged lid................................2,000.00
Toothpick, 2-1/2" h 585.00
Tumbler..350.00

HORN

History: For centuries, horns from animals have been used for various items, e.g., drinking cups, spoons, powder horns, and small dishes. Some pieces of horn have designs scratched in them. Around 1880, furniture made from the horns of Texas longhorn steers was popular in Texas and the southwestern United States.

Additional Listings: Firearm Accessories.

Calling Card Case, horn and ivory, floral dec...............75.00
Chair, arm, curled horn crest, arms, and legs, black leather upholstery,
    29-1/2" w, 41" h 500.00
Ladle, George III sterling bowl, twist-turned horn handle, London sil-
    versmith's mark "EM," c1805......................................150.00
Shoehorn, scratch dec, 1756.......................................75.00
Snuff Box, carved
    2-3/4" l, 2" w, eye of God dec on lid, Saint on bottom "S Antoni,"
      inscription on side, European, late 18th/early 19th C 100.00
    3-1/4" l, 1-3/4" w, rect, lid carved in low relief, scene of man on
      deathbed, Continental, 19th C....................................395.00
    3-3/4" l, 2" w, horn and hardwood, multiple top, European,
      18th C 200.00
    3-3/4" l, 2-1/2" w, green and red wax inlay, English, late 19th C.300.00
    3-3/4" l, 3-1/4" w, coat of arms and "Trust is in God," initials "R. K.,"
      wood and horn, English, 18th C.................................1,550.00
    4" l, western motif, American, early 20th C 45.00
Snuff Mull, 11" w, 6" h, ram horn fitted with pewter hinged lid, small
    snuff storage area, tip fitted with pewter finial, mellow patina, late
    18th C/early 19th C 475.00
Spoon, 5-1/2" l, silver thistle on end, monogrammed "MBL, 1907," hall-
    marked 48.00
Tea Caddy, cov, 14-1/2" w, 8" d, 7-1/2" h, Anglo-Indian, Visapatnam,
    early 19th C, antler veneer, steer horn, ivory, int. cov compartments,
    etched scrolling vines, restorations 1,950.00
Tumbler
    3-3/8" h, engraved scene of coach and four with houses, etc., some
      rim damage 165.00

Hat Rack, natural steer horn and leather, $145.

3-1/2" h, silver rim, engraved scene of fox hunt, wear and surface damage 200.00

HULL POTTERY

History: In 1905, Addis E. Hull purchased the Acme Pottery Company, Crooksville, Ohio. In 1917, the A. E. Hull Pottery Company began making art pottery, novelties, stoneware, and kitchenware, later including the famous Little Red Riding Hood line. Most items had a matte finish with shades of pink and blue or brown predominating.

After a disastrous flood and fire in 1950, J. Brandon Hull reopened the factory in 1952 as the Hull Pottery Company. New, more-modern-style pieces, mostly with glossy finish, were produced. The company currently produces wares for florists, e.g. the Regal and Floraline lines.

Marks: Hull pottery molds and patterns are easily identified. Pre-1950 vases are marked "Hull USA" or "Hull Art USA" on the bottom. Many also retain their paper labels. Post-1950 pieces are marked "Hull" in large script or "HULL" in block letters.

Each pattern has a distinctive letter or number, e.g., Wildflower has a "W" and a number; Waterlily, "L" and number; Poppy, numbers in the 600s; Orchid, in the 300s. Early stoneware pieces are marked with an "H."

References: Joan Hull, *Hull, The Heavenly Pottery,* 6th ed., published by author (1376 Nevada, Huron, SD 57350), 1999; ----, *Hull, The Heavenly Pottery Shirt Pocket Price List,* published by author, 1998; Brenda Roberts, *The Ultimate Encyclopedia of Hull Pottery,* Collector Books, 1995, 1999 value update; Mark and Ellen Supnick, *Collecting Hull Pottery's Little Red Riding Hood, Revised Edition,* L-W Books, 1998.

Periodicals: *Hull Pottery Association,* 11023 Tunnel Hill NE, New Lexington, OH 43764; *Hull Pottery Newsletter,* 7768 Meadow Dr., Hillsboro, MO 60350.

Tea Set, B20-6 teapot, B22-4 sugar bowl, B21-4 creamer, $350.

Additional Listings: See *Warman's Americana & Collectibles* for more examples.

Advisor: Joan Hull.

Pre-1950 Matte

Bowknot
B-4 6-1/2" h vase 470.00
B-7 cornucopia 265.00
B-11 10-1/2" h vase 500.00
B-12, 10-1/2" h basket 750.00
B-16 console bowl 325.00
B-17 candleholders, pr 325.00

Calla Lily
500-32 bowl 200.00
520-33, 8" h vase 250.00

Dogwood (Wild Rose)
501, 8-1/2" h basket 300.00
508 10-1/2" window box 525.00
513, 6-1/2" h vase 125.00

Little Red Riding Hood
Creamer and Sugar, side pour 600.00
Dresser or Cracker Jar 800.00
Lamp 2,500.00
Matchbox for wooden matches 900.00
Salt and Pepper Shakers, pr, small 120.00
Teapot, cov 395.00
Wall Pocket Planter 620.00

Magnolia
3 8-1/2" h vase 115.00
9 10-1/2" h vase 175.00
14 4-3/4" h pitcher 50.00
20 15" floor vase 425.00

Open Rose/Camellia
106 13-1/2" h pitcher 575.00
114 8-1/2" h jardiniere 375.00
119 8-1/2" h vase 175.00
127 4-3/4" h vase 75.00

Orchid
301 4-3/4" h vase 165.00
302 6" h vase 150.00
303 8" h vase 195.00
304 10-1/2" h vase 325.00
310 9-1/2" jardiniere 450.00

Poppy
601 9" h basket 750.00
607 10-1/2" h vase 425.00
610 13" pitcher 1,350.00
6112 6-1/2" h vase 300.00

Rosella, vase
R-2 5" h vase 75.00
R-6 6-1/2" h vase 115.00
R-15 8-1/2" h vase 125.00

Tulip
101-33 9" h vase 245.00
103-33 6" h vase 250.00
107-33 6" h vase 125.00
109-33-8" pitcher 235.00

Waterlily
L-14, 10-1/2" basket 350.00
L-16, 10-1/2" vase 395.00
L-20-15" floor vase 500.00

Wild Flower, No. Series
53 8-1/2" h vase 295.00
61 6-1/2" h vase 160.00
66 10-1/4" h basket 2,000.00
71 12" h vase 395.00

Woodland
W9 8-3/4" h basket 345.00
W11 5-1/2" flower pot and saucer 175.00

W13 7-1/2" l wall pocket, shell 165.00
W14 10-1/2" window box 195.00

Post 1950

Blossom Flite
T4 8-1/2" h basket..125.00
T13 12-1/2" h pitcher 150.00
Butterfly
B9 9" h vase...55.00
B13 8" h basket 150.00
B15 13-1/2" h pitcher 185.00
Continental
C29 12" h vase 95.00
C55 12-1/2" basket 150.00
C62 8-1/4" candy dish..45.00
Ebb Tide
E-1 7" h bud vase 95.00
E-8 ashtray with mermaid 225.00
E-10 13" h pitcher 250.00
Parchment and Pine
S-3 6" h basket..75.00
S-11 and S-12 tea set 150.00
S-15 8" h coffeepot 155.00
Serenade
S1 6" h vase...50.00
S-15 11-1/2" d fruit bowl, ftd...110.00
S11 10-1/2" h vase...95.00
S17 teapot, creamer and sugar 250.00
Sunglow
53 grease jar..35.00
82 wall pocket, whisk broom 65.00
85 8-3/4" h vase, bird...45.00
Tokay/Tuscany
3 8" h pitcher...95.00
8 10" h vase 125.00
10 11" l cornucopia..65.00
12" h vase 110.00
Tropicana
T53 8-1/2" h vase 500.00
T55, 12-3/4" h basket..750.00
Woodland (glossy)
W1 5-1/2" h vase 45.00
W15 8-1/2" h vase, double 75.00
W19 14" d console bowl...100.00

HUMMEL ITEMS

History: Hummel items are the original creations of Berta Hummel, who was born in 1909 in Massing, Bavaria, Germany. At age 18, she was enrolled in the Academy of Fine Arts in Munich to further her mastery of drawing and the palette. Berta entered the Convent of Siessen and became Sister Maria Innocentia in 1934. In this Franciscan cloister, she continued drawing and painting images of her childhood friends.

In 1935, W. Goebel Co. in Rodental, Germany, began producing Sister Maria Innocentia's sketches as three-dimensional bisque figurines. The Schmid Brothers of Randolph, Massachusetts, introduced the figurines to America and became Goebel's U.S. distributor.

In 1967, Goebel began distributing Hummel items in the U.S. A controversy developed between the two companies, the Hummel family, and the convent. Law suits and counter-suits ensued. The German courts finally effected a compromise: the convent held legal rights to all works produced by Sister Maria Innocentia from 1934 until her death

in 1946 and licensed Goebel to reproduce these works; Schmid was to deal directly with the Hummel family for permission to reproduce any pre-convent art.

Marks: All authentic Hummel pieces bear both the signature "M. I. Hummel" and a Goebel trademark. Various trademarks were used to identify the year of production:

Crown Mark (trademark 1) 1935 through 1949
Full Bee (trademark 2) 1950-1959
Stylized Bee (trademark 3) 1957-1972
Three Line Mark (trademark 4) 1964-1972
Last Bee Mark (trademark 5) 1972-1979
Missing Bee Mark (trademark 6) 1979-1990
Current Mark or New Crown Mark (trademark 7) 1991 to the present

References: Ken Armke, *Hummel: An Illustrated History and Price Guide,* Wallace-Homestead, 1995; Carl F. Luckey, *Luckey's Hummel Figurines and Plates: A Collector's Identification and Value Guide,* 11th ed., Krause Publications, 1997; Robert L. Miller, *No. 1 Price Guide to M. I. Hummel: Figurines, Plates, More...,* 6th ed., —, *Hummels 1978-1998: 20 Years of "Miller on Hummel" Columns,* Collector News, 1998; Portfolio Press, 1995.

Collectors' Clubs: Hummel Collector's Club, Inc., 1261 University Dr., Yardley, PA 19067; M. I. Hummel Club, Goebel Plaza, Rte 31, P. O. Box 11, Pennington, NJ 08534.

Museum: Hummel Museum, New Braunfels, TX.

Additional Listings: See *Warman's Americana & Collectibles* for more examples.

Bookends, pr
Chick Girl, #618, full bee, trademark-2 ....325.00
Playmates, #61A, full bee, trademark-2..325.00
Calendar, 16" x 21", Sunny Weather, canvas, limited edition, 1981, #4,545 of 15,000, orig certificate of authenticity, wall hanging, walnut finished cross pcs, decorative top hanger, orig tube 125.00
Candleholder
Silent Night, #54, trademark 5 ....175.00

#311, girl and doll, three line bee mark, 6-1/8" h, $30.

Watchful angel, #194, trademark 2 .... 400.00

Candy Box, cov

Happy Pastime, #III/169, trademark 4 .... 125.00

Joyful, #III/53, trademark 4 .... 115.00

Christmas Angel

Boy, #117, trademark 3 .... 45.00

Girl, #116, fir tree, 3" h, trademark 3 .... 40.00

Figure

Adventure Bound, trademark 6 .... 2,200.00

Apple Tree Boy, #142, 6" h, trademark 5 .... 335.00

Apple Tree Girl, #141, 6" h, trademark 5 .... 335.00

Baker, #128, 5" h, trademark 3 .... 200.00

Band Leader, #129, trademark 5 .... 120.00

Be Patient, #197, trademark 4 .... 400.00

Boots, #143, 5-1/2" h, trademark 3 .... 300.00

Chimney Sweep, #122/10, trademark 5 .... 70.00

Congratulations, #17/0, 1971, MIB 150.00

Doctor, #127, 5" h, trademark 3 .... 165.00

Farm Boy, #66, 5-3/4" h, trademark 3 .... 350.00

For Father, #87, 5-1/2" h, trademark 3 .... 350.00

Happiness, #85, 5" h, trademark 3 .... 175.00

Heavenly Angel, #21/0, trademark 3 .... 100.00

Joyful, #53, trademark 5 .... 90.00

Just Resting, #112/13/0, trademark 4 .... 90.00

Kiss Me, #311, trademarkn3 .... 150.00

Little Bookkeeper, #306, trademark 4 .... 220.00

Little Scholar, #80, 5-3/4" h, trademark 5 .... 275.00

Merry Wanderer, #7, 7" h, trademark 3 .... 700.00

Photographers, #178, trademark 4 .... 215.00

Postman, #119, trademark 3 .... 175.00

Prayer Before Battle, #20, 4-1/2" h, trademark 3 .... 250.00

Sensitive Hunter, #640, trademark 4 .... 150.00

Soldier Boy, #332, trademark 4 .... 300.00

Strolling Along, #5, 5-3/4" h, trademark 2 .... 550.00

The Lost Sheep, #68, 5-1/2" h, trademark 3 .... 250.00

Wash Day, #321/4/0, 3-1/4" h, trademark 6 .... 80.00

Font

Angel Cloud, #206, trademark 5 .... 45.00

Child Jesus, #26/0, MK 4 .... 35.00

Guardian angel, #248, trademark 4 .... 60.00

Holy Family, #246, trademark 2 .... 85.00

Seated Angel, #10/1, trademark 3 .... 420.00

Plaque

Madonna, #48/0, trademark 7 .... 250.00

Mail Coach, #140, trademark 5 .... 145.00

IMARI

History: Imari derives its name from a Japanese port city. Although Imari ware was manufactured in the 17th century, the pieces most commonly encountered are those made between 1770 and 1900.

Early Imari was decorated simply, quite unlike the later heavily decorated brocade pattern commonly associated with Imari. Most of the decorative patterns are an underglaze blue and overglaze "seal wax" red complimented by turquoise and yellow.

The Chinese copied Imari ware. The Japanese examples can be identified by grayer clay, thicker glaze, runny and darker blue, and deep red opaque hues.

The pattern and colors of Imari inspired many English and European potteries, such as Derby and Meissen, to adopt a similar style of decoration for their wares.

Reference: Nancy N. Schiffer, *Imari, Satsuma, and Other Japanese Export Ceramics*, Schiffer Publishing, 1997.

Reproduction Alert: Reproductions abound, and many manufacturers continue to produce pieces in the traditional style.

Bowl, 13-1/2" l, oval, scalloped rim, central reserve of butterflies and scrolls, wide ornate border with conforming dec, centered at each end by reserves of bird, blue and white foliate detail ext., sgd, c1850-70, pr 1,500.00
Charger
    14-1/2" d, scalloped, alternating floral and foliage panels, basket reserve, 19th C 200.00
    18" d, central floral medallion flanked by fan shaped panels alternating with figural and floral dec, Japanese 425.00
    24" d, figural panel, 2 panels of phoenix birds, foliate ground, Chinese, late 19th C 750.00
Creamer and Sugar, 5-1/2" h creamer, 5-7/8" cov sugar, ovoid, dragon form handles, gilt and bright enamels, shaped reserves, dragon-like

beasts, stylized animal medallions, brocade ground, high dome lid, knob, cipher mark of Mount Fuji, Fukagama Studio marks, Meiji period 500.00
Dish
    8-3/8" d, central scene with fence and flowering tree dec, shaped cartouches enclosing flowers and hares on crackle blue ground at rim, gilt highlights, Meiji period, price for pr 650.00
    9-1/2" d, shaped rim, allover flowering vine dec, gilt highlights ..150.00
Food Box, 6" h, 3 section, ext. and lid with phoenix and floral design, underglaze blue, iron-red, and gilt enamels, 19th C 400.00
Jardiniere, 10" h, hexagonal, bulbous, short flared foot, alternating bijin figures and immortal symbols, stylized ground 250.00
Plate
    9" d, central reserve of iron-red chrysanthemums, iron-red and black rim, gilt highlights, Qianlong, pr 700.00
    14-3/4" d, scalloped, floral dec, 16-1/2" h fitted wooden table form stand 375.00
Platter, 18" d, alternating panels of figures and foliage, trelliswork ground, Japanese, late 19th C 475.00
Punch Bowl, 11" d, red and blue floral dec, scalloped rim, 19th C ... 395.00
Teabowl and Saucer, 5" d, floriform, floral spray dec, gilt highlights on saucer 200.00
Umbrella Stand, 24" h, cobalt blue band dividing phoenix, dragons, medallions, and floral dec 1,500.00
Urn, 21" h, gilt bronze mounts, deep bowl, red, blue, and gilt floral dec, everted pierced collar, S-scroll arms of leaves and cattails, mid band of plaited reeds, flaring porcelain base banded in bronze, pierced skirt interspersing 4 foliate clasps, pr 14,000.00
Vase
    9-1/4" h, Louis XV/XVI style, sectioned vase with foliate dec, reserves of birds, applied female mask handles and acanthus cast rim border, three ftd cast ormolu base, late 19th C, some restoration 350.00
    11" h, double gourd form, Japanese, Meiji period, pr 800.00
Vegetable Tureen, cov, 11-3/4" l, ironstone, enamel dec, England, 19th C 230.00

IMPERIAL GLASS

History: Imperial Glass Co., Bellaire, Ohio, was organized in 1901. Its primary product was pattern (pressed) glass. Soon other lines were added, including carnival glass, Nuart, Nucut, and Near Cut. In 1916, the company introduced Free-Hand, a lustered art glass line, and Imperial Jewels, an iridescent stretch glass that carried the Imperial cross trademark. In the 1930s, the company was reorganized into the Imperial Glass Corporation, and the firm is still producing a great variety of wares.

Imperial recently acquired the molds and equipment of several other glass companies—Central, Cambridge, and Heisey. Many of the retired molds of these companies are once again in use.

Marks: The Imperial reissues are marked to distinguish them from the originals.

References: Margaret and Douglas Archer, *Imperial Glass*, Collector Books, 1978, 1998 value update; Gene Florence, *Elegant Glassware of the Depression Era*, 8th ed., Collector Books, 1998; Myrna and Bob Garrison, *Imperial's Boudoir, Etcetera*, 1996; National Imperial Glass Collectors Society, *Imperial Glass Encyclopedia: Volume I, A–Cane*, Antique Publications, 1995; ——, Vol. II: Cape Code- L, Antique Publications, 1998; ——, *Imperial Glass 1966 Catalog*, reprint, 1991 price guide, Antique Publications; Virginia R. Scott, *Collector's Guide to Imperial Candlewick*, published by

Plate, blue, orange, and yellow marine motif, c1870, 10" d, $395.

author (275 Milledge Terrace, Athens, GA 30606); Mary M. Wetzel-Tomlka, *Candlewick: The Jewel of Imperial Books I and II*, published by author (P.O. Box 594, Notre Dame, IN 46556-0594); ——, *Candlewick The Jewel of Imperial, Personal Inventory & Record Book*, published by author, 1998; ——, *Candlewick The Jewel of Imperial, Price Guide 99 and More*, published by author, 1998.

Collectors' Clubs: National Candlewick Collector's Club, 275 Milledge Terrace, Athens, GA 30606, plus many regional clubs; National Imperial Glass Collectors Society, P.O. Box 534, Bellaire, OH 43906.

Periodicals: *Glasszette*, National Imperial Glass Collector's Society, P.O. Box 534, Bellaire, OH 43528; *Spyglass Newsletter*, Michiana Association of Candlewick Collectors, 17370 Battles Rd, South Bend, IN 46614; *The Candlewick Collector Newsletter*, National Candlewick Collector's Club, 6534 South Ave., Holland, OH 43528; *TRIGC Quarterly Newsletter*, Texas Regional Imperial Glass Collectors, 2113 F. M. 367 East, Iowa Park, TX 76367.

Videotapes: National Imperial Glass Collectors Society, Candlewick: At Home, In Any Home, Vol. I: Imperial Beauty, Vol. II: Virginia and Mary, RoCliff Communications, 1993; ——, Glass of Yesteryears: The Renaissance of Slag Glass, RoCliff Communications, 1994.

Additional Listings: See Carnival Glass; Pattern Glass; and *Warman's Americana & Collectibles* for more examples of Candlewick Pattern.

Art Glass

Candlesticks, pr, 10-3/4" h, cobalt blue luster, white vine and leaf dec 325.00
Hat, 9" w, ruffled rim, cobalt blue luster, embedded irid white vines and leaves 120.00
Vase
    5-3/4" h, free-hand ovoid form, dark blue ground, orange leaves on vines, overall irid surface, white rim wrap to flared neck, gold foil label, polished pontil 1,265.00
    6-3/4" h, baluster, flared neck, gold ground, blue pulled loop dec, white int. neck flashed irid orange-gold, polished pontil......950.00

Cup and Saucer, Candlewick, 400/35, $12.

    9-1/2" h, bulbous, wide flared neck, white glass cased to cobalt blue ext., int. rim flashed with irid orange, polished pontil ..575.00
    10-1/2" h, heavy walled body swelling to top, cream colored glass, strong gold irid dec, on ext., 3 branches of holly leaves rising from base, polished pontil 575.00

Carnival

Basket, 10", Plain Jane, teal 85.00
Bottle, 5" h, Corn, smoke 300.00
Bowl, sq, ruffled, dark marigold, stretch irid 35.00
Candlesticks, pr
    Hex shape, irid smoke 75.00
    Premium pattern, irid smoke 100.00
Nappy, 5" d, handle, Heavy Grape, electric purple 110.00
Rose Bowl, purple, iron cross mark 500.00
Salad Set, Optic & Button, light marigold, iron cross mark, 2 pcs. 50.00
Sugar, Flute, electric purple 75.00
Vase
    5" h, Thin Rib & Drape, marigold 40.00
    5-1/2" h, 6" w, turned in top, purple, iron cross mark.....500.00
    6-1/2" h, Morning Glory, olive green 60.00
    6-1/2" h, 4" d flare at top, Morning Glory, smoke..........50.00
    6-1/2"h, 4" d, flare at top, Morning Glory shape, irid stretch body, smoke ground.................................50.00

Engraved or Hand Cut

Bowl, 6-1/2" d, flower and leaf, molded star base 25.00
Candlesticks, pr, 7" h, Amelia 35.00
Celery Vase, 3 side stars, cut star base............................25.00
Pitcher, tankard, Design No. 110, flowers, foliage, and butterfly cutting 60.00
Plate, 5-1/2" d, Design No. 12 ....15.00
Jewels
Bowl, 6-1/2" d, purple Pearl Green luster, mkd 75.00
Compote, 7-1/2" d, irid teal blue 65.00
Rose Bowl, amethyst, green irid 75.00
Vase, 7-3/4" h, classic baluster, white body, mirror bright tray-blue surface, deep orange irid int. rim 320.00
Nuart
Ashtray 22.00
Lamp Shade, marigold...50.00
Vase, 6" h, green, polished pontil, tucked in top 275.00
Nucut
Berry Bowl, 4-1/2" d, handles 18.00
Celery Tray, 11" l 20.00
Creamer 20.00
Fern Dish, 8" l, brass lining, ftd 30.00
Orange Bowl, 12" d, Rose Marie 48.00
Pressed
Birthday Cake Plate
Cape Cod..295.00
Tradition 125.00
Bowl
    6-1/2" d, Beaded Block, blue opalescent 75.00
    9" d, Cape Cod, ftd 95.00
Butter Dish, cov, Candlewick, quarter pound 32.00
Candlesticks, pr, Candlewick, #207, 3 toes 260.00
Candy Dish, cov, Candlewick, 3 part 180.00
Champagne, Cape Cod, azalea..24.00
Cheese and Cracker, Candlewick 65.00
Compote, cov, Cape Cod, ftd 85.00
Cup and Saucer, Pillar Flutes, light blue 28.00
Figure, cygnet, light blue 35.00
Goblet, Cape Cod, red 135.00
Gravy Boat, liner, Candlewick 190.00
Ivy Ball, 4" h, crystal foot, spun red...................................65.00
Plate, Windmill, glossy, green slag, IG mark......................48.00
Relish, Candlewick, floral cutting 60.00
Salad Fork and Spoon, Candlewick....................................45.00
Tumbler, Candlewick, 12 oz 16.00
Vase, Cape Cod, flip 85.00

INDIAN ARTIFACTS, AMERICAN

History: During the historic period there were approximately 350 Indian tribes grouped into the following regions: Eskimo, Northeast and Woodland, Northwest Coast, Plains, and West and Southwest.

American Indian artifacts are quite popular. Currently, the market is stable following a rapid increase in prices during the 1970s.

References: C. J. Brafford and Laine Thom (comps.), *Dancing Colors: Paths of Native American Women*, Chronicle Books, 1992; Harold S. Colton, *Hopi Kachina Dolls*, revised ed., University of New Mexico Press, 1959, 1990 reprint; Gary L. Fogelman, *Identification and Price Guide for Indian Artifacts of the Northeast*, Fogelman Publishing, 1994; Lar Hothem, *Arrowheads & Projectile Points*, Collector Books, 1983, 1997 value update; —, *Collector's Guide to Indian Pipes*, Collector Books, 1999; —, *Indian Artifacts of the Midwest*, Book I (1992, 1996 value update), Book II (1995), Book III (1997), Collector Books; —, *Indian Axes & Related Stone Artifacts*, Collector Books, 1996; *North American Indian Artifacts*, 6th ed., Krause Publications, 1998; Preston E. Miller and Carolyn Corey, *The Four Winds Guide To Indian Trade Goods and Replicas*, Schiffer, 1998; Karen and Ralph Norris, Northwest *Carving Traditions*, Schiffer Publishing, 1999; Robert M. Overstreet, *Overstreet Indian Arrowheads Identification and Price Guide*, Avon Books, 1997; Lillian Peaster, *Pueblo Pottery Families*, Schiffer Publishing, 1997; Dawn E. Reno, *Native American Collectibles*, Avon Books, 1994; Nancy N. Schiffer, *Indian Dolls*, Schiffer Publishing, 1997; Peter N. Schiffer, *Indian Jewelry on the Market*, Schiffer Publishing, 1996; Lawrence N. Tully & Steven N. Tully, *Field Guide to Flint Arrowheads & Knives of North American Indians*, Collector Books, 1997; Sarah Peabody Turnbaugh and William A. Turnbaugh, *Indian Baskets*, Schiffer Publishing, 1997.

Periodicals: *American Indian Art Magazine*, 7314 E. Osborn Dr., Scottsdale, AZ 85251; *American Indian Basketry Magazine*, P.O. Box 66124, Portland, OR 97266; *Indian-Artifact Magazine*, RD #1 Box 240, Turbotville, PA 17772; *Indian Trader*, P.O. Box 1421, Gallup, NM 87305; *Whispering Wind Magazine*, 8009 Wales St., New Orleans, LA 70126.

Collectors' Club: Genuine Indian Relic Society, Int., 8117 Preston Road, Dallas, TX 75225-6324; Indian Arts & Crafts Association, Suite B, 122 Laveta NE, Suite B, Albuquerque, NM 87108.

Museums: Amerind Foundation, Inc., Dragoon, AZ; The Heard Museum, Phoenix, AZ; Colorado River Indian Tribes Museum, Parker, AZ; Favell Museum of Western Art & Indian Artifacts, Klamath Falls, OR; Field Museum of Natural History, Chicago, IL; Grand Rapids Public Museum, Grand Rapids, MI; Indian Center Museum, Wichita, KS; Institute of American Indian Arts Museum, Sante Fe, NM; Maryhill Museum of Art, Goldendale, WA; Museum of Classical Antiquities & Primitive Arts, Medford, NJ; Museum of the American Indian, Heye Foundation, New York, NY; US

SPECIAL AUCTIONS

W. E. Channing & Co.
53 Old Santa Fe Trail
Santa Fe, NM 87501
(505) 988-1078

Garth's Auction, Inc.
2690 Stratford Rd.
P.O. Box 369
Delaware, OH 43015
(614) 362-4771

Old Barn Auction
10040 St. Rt. 224 West
Findlay, OH 45840
(419) 422-8531

Dept. of the Interior Museum, Washington, DC; Wheelwright Museum of the American Indian, Sante Fe, NM.

Note: American Indian artifacts listed below are prehistoric or historic objects made on the North American continent.

Amulet, Northwest Coast, attributed to Tlingit, 3-1/2" l, carved Orca whale's tooth, carved motifs of 2 seated humans and avian form 1,725.00

Axe, Missouri
    4-3/4" l, hematite, full groove 55.00
    23-1/4", war type, old handle 1,320.00

Bandolier Bag, Great Lakes, Ojibwa, c1880, 34" l, loom cloth, backed in black wool felt, bound in black cotton tape, shoulder strap beaded n bilateral geometric devices, white heart red, pumpkin, bottle green, greasy yellow, and various blue beads on white field, top of bag beaded in crystal in double zigzag pattern, crystal bead edging and red rickrack, central panel of loom beaded bilateral bead work in geometrical and heart devices, white heart red, amber, and various blues on crystal field, loom beaded suspensions with yarn tassels, some restoration 920.00

Bandolier Strap, Great Lakes, c1890, 43" l, loom beaded, bilateral geometric motif, translucent green and red, greasy yellow, medium and dark blue beads on white field, mounted on muslin, backed with hide strap bound with olive green finishing cloth 260.00

Banner Stone
    4-3/4" l, Nodular Eye, Glacial Kame, tally marks on head, found east of Tittin, Seneca Co., OH 2,970.00
    4-7/8" l, Grant Co., IN, 4-5/8" single notch, found 1939 .... 1,230.00
    5-1/2" l, Ashland Co., OH, shown in Prehistoric Artifacts, Vol. 20, #4 .... 1,705.00
    5-7/8" l, Kent Co., MI, pick 1,540.00

Basket, cov
    3-1/4" d, Inuit, coiled baleen, slightly flaring form, pierced ivory disc base, lid with disc finial and carved pinniped head, 2 small carved ivory avian trinkets 1,495.00
    5-1/4" d, Northwest Coast, Tlingit, late 19th C, polychrome twined rattle top, twined spruce root dyed orange, sienna, and brown, stepped motifs on body, radiating devices on lid, split at rim 690.00
    6-1/2" l, Northwest Coast, Aleut, early 20th C, polychrome, closed twined grass woven with trade yard, multicolored lineal devices, lid handle finely woven of polychrome trade wool, losses to yarn 980.00

Basket, open
    11-3/4" d, 11-1/4" w, Canada, Great Lakes, Six Nation Reserve, grain type 125.00
    16-1/2" d, 8" h, Northwest, Klekitat, coiled, black stepped motif, some rim coils missing 275.00

Belt
    Plateau, c1900, 30" l, harness leather, beaded panels of geometric

devices and panels of linear tacked motifs, pumpkin, cut black, apple green, light and medium blue beads 490.00

Woodlands, attributed to Cree, third quarter 19th C, 26-7/8" l, woven quills, natural and commercial dyed quills, finely woven in zigzag design, white beaded edge, tartan cotton and buffalo hide backing 400.00

Bidarka, Eskimo, 31-1/2" l, three-man, wood and seal skin, paint and trade beads, later carved head gear 1,725.00

Blanket Strip, Central Plains, Lakota, c1880, 58" l, beaded hide, sinew sewn strip, roundels with Maltese crosses, linear, chevron, and zig-zag dec, medium green, cobalt blue, and white heart red beads, white field, some bead loss 1,380.00

Bow Case and Quiver, child's, 25" l, Central Plains, Lakota, late 19th C, beaded, sinew sewn hide forms cotton twill binding, beaded motif of bars and boxes, light and medium blue, greasy yellow, and dull pink.................. 3,450.00

Bowl, basketry
  4-1/2" d, Northern California, Karuk, twined in half-twist overlay of beargrass, dyed yellow beargrass, maidenhair fern, and conifer root, stepped geometric devices 750.00
  11-3/4" d, California, Mission, c1900, polychrome, coiled, brown and yellow radiating stepped motif 1,100.00
  11-3/4" d, California, Yokuts, mid to third quarter 19th C, poly-chrome, tightly coiled flat base with flaring sides, pattern of abstracted hour glass motif in four radiating rows, some rim stitch loss 2,185.00
  12" d, Californian, attributed to Yokuts or Tubatulatal, 19th C, poly-chrome, finely coiled flat bottom, gentle flaring high sides, pattern woven in willow and devil's claw, trace remains of redbud, small stepped geometric devices, 2 bands of repeating zigzag devices above, wear at base, minor stitch loss................................. 800.00
  13" d, Southwest, Apache, early 20th C, high sided, central star motif surrounded by radiating rosettes encompassing row of cross devices, inverted repeated stepped triangular motifs at rim..1,265.00
  16" d, California, Yokuts, early 20th C, coiled form, flaring sides, redbud and bracken fern abstracted hour glass devices, minor stitch loss at rim 865.00
  18-1/2" d, California, Cahuilla, attributed to Ramona, woven on varie-gated ochre rush ground with devil's claw, central 4 directional arrows radiating out of rosette pattern, 4 eagle devices above double chevron motifs separated by urn- like devices with repeating cross motifs, accompanied by letter from orig owner 23,000.00

Bowl, carved wood, Northwest Coast
  14-1/2" d, carved wood, pinniped form, open mouth, inset ivory peg teeth, abalone eyes and nostrils, sides incised with octopus forms, small white beads inset, similar inlay on back flippers, series of bone inlay at rim................................ 1,100.00
  15-3/4" d, attributed to Nootka, 20th C, carved puffin form, incised geo-metric devices at face, chest, and tail, inlaid abalone at rim 300.00

Bowl, pottery, Southwest
  4-1/4" h, Zuni, c1920, globular form, carved stepped rim, cream slip, brown tadpole devices on int., frog-like motifs on ext.. 550.00
  6" d, Santa Clara, Red Ware, globular, deeply carved Avanyu device below lip, sgd "Teresita Naranjo," abrasion to slip 300.008-1/2" d, San Idefonso, deep bowl form, high polished plain finish, sgd "Santana and Adam," abrasions, scratches 350.00
  9" d, Nampeyo, 1915, shallow, lug on one side, int. painted in two panels, one of black slip feather devices on red ground, other black and red slip wing or bird motif on creamy orange ground, Fred Harvey tag "Made by Nampeyo-Hopi-??1.25" and "3628, HopiWare bought at San Diego Exposition," small rim chips, minor slip loss 12,650.00

Bracelet, Northwest Coast, Tlingit, 1/4" d, silver, incised, tooled raven form 290.00

Box, cov
  Northwest Woodlands, MicMac, mid 19th C, polychrome quilled birch bark, lower box of soft wood, lid and bottom overlaid in birch bark with polychrome embroidery, top and bottom sides quilled in repeated geometric motifs 230.00

Southwest, Zuni, c1940, 3-1/2" d, silver, cylindrical, scalloped edge, central inlaid stone motif of knifewingman, stamped tomahawk mark................................ 1,265.00

Burden Basket, Southwest, Apache, early 20th C, 15" d rim, poly-chrome, twined cone form, hide bottom, fringe with tin cone suspen-sions, red trade cloth trim, red and green over paint on ext.. 1,100.00

Cradle Board
  6-1/2" l, Southwest, attributed to Piute, 1920s, hide wrapped wood, bead work at crown and chest, wicker hood, cotton print bedding.......................... 225.00
  35-1/2" l, Southwest, Apache, 20th C, bent wood and willow form, muslin wrap, hood, and ties, faceted bead dangler from hood with crescent moon cut out 290.00

Cuffs, pr, Ojibwa, c1920-30, 8" l, beaded hide, overlay bead work of meandering floral design with butterflies, lavender, squirt-gun green, and orange faceted beads on white field, fringe 175.00

Dance Wand Mirror, 18" l, attributed to Shoshone, late 19th C, sal-vaged carved wood handle and mirror frame, painted red and blue, tacked throughout, paper roundel mounted on back with period illus of woman looking in cherub-held mirror 1,150.00

Doll, Central Plains, Lakota, c1880, 10-1/2" h, beaded hide, cotton tick-ing form, dressed in buckskin, linear and zigzag beadwork trim on dress, leggings, and moccasins, bead loss to face 920.00

Dough Bowl, Polacca, Hopi, c1860, 9-1/8" d, polychrome dec, triangu-lar shaped volute.................. 910.00

Dress, woman's, Plains, c1910, 52" l, beaded yoke, fringe dec 2,035.00

Face Mask, Northwest Coast, attributed to Tlingit, mid 19th C, 8" l, carved cedar, white, black, red, and blue-green polychrome, brown patina to unpainted surface, stylized wrinkles at mouth and brown, peg remains at chin and upper lip, cracks and loss 18,400.00

Fetish, Plains, 6-1/2" l, beaded 110.00

Flint Ridge
  3-3/8", Adena, Athens Co., OH 125.00
  4" l, dovetail, found near Defiance, OH 1,320.00
  4" l, Hopewell Pt., Ross Co., OH 90.00
  4" l, Seneca Co., OH 100.00
  5" l, Adena, Van Wert Co., OH 110.00

Fish Club, Northwest Coast, 23" l, carved yew wood, cylindrical pom-mel of seal or sea lion head, round concentric eye and carved mouth, slightly recessed grip, dark brown patina 490.00

Gauntlets, Plateau, early 20th C, 14-1/2" l, meandering floral design bead-work, amber, translucent green, and blue beads, fringed cuff....... 490.00

Gorget
  4-1/4" l, McComb Co., MI, reddish slate 165.00
  5" l, Sandusky Co., OH, quartz Adena, partial drilling 770.00

Hair Drop, Central Plains, Lakota, last quarter 19th C, 29" h, parfleche stripe, trade mirrors, brass beads, trade shells, commercially dyed quill wrapped suspensions, horsehair, beaded buffalo hide strip, edged in white heart red beads, panel beaded in repeated linear and geometric motifs, apple green, white heart red, and navy beads on white field 2,650.00

Hat, basketry
  6-1/2" d, Northern California, Hupa, polychrome, finely twined form, pinwheel device at crown, concentric stripes, middle panel of interlocking parallelograms 490.00
  7" d, California, Hupa, c1915, brown and yellow woven twine, repeated stepped and interlocking geometric devices, labeled "skull cap basket made by Mission Indians at San Diego" . 350.00

Jacket, chief's, Athabascan, c1890, smoked caribou hide, sinew and thread sewn, shirt-style, fringe at collar, yoke, and shoulders, appli-quéd red wool trade cloth beaded in bilateral flora pattern, zigzag tendrils, mother-of-pearl commercial buttons, various blues, greasy yellow, light pink, amber, and white beads, two int. pockets . 1,840.00

Jar, basketry
  8-1/2" d, California, Yokuts, late 19th/early 20th C, flat base, flaring side and flat shoulder, coiled with 5 panels of abstracted repeat-ing quail top knots running from base to rim 3,110.00
  11" d, 10-1/2" h, Pima, few coils missing.............................. 635.00

Jar, pottery, Southwest
  6-1/2" h, Zia, c1930-40, globular form, painted orange and black, cream ground with birds in medallions.................290.00
  6-1/2" h, Zuni, early 20th C, 3 applied frogs at neck, painted stepped geometric devices, scroll like devices, deer with heart lines, brown and orange, cream ground 1,495.00
  7" h, Acoma, c1930, high shoulder form with indented base, brown and orange slip painted in 4 geo-linear medallions 435.00
  8-1/2" h, San Ildefonso, polished gun metal finish, band of matte painted in repeated feather devices, geometric motif, sgd "Marie and Julian," abrasions to surface 1,035.00
  8-3/4" h, San Idefonso, first quarter 20th C, high shoulder form, red, orange-red, and black slip, cream ground, repeated scallop forms, linear devices, abstracted floral motifs, dark red stripe at bottom, indented base, loss to rim, airline cracks...........1,265.00
  9" h, 7-1/2" d, Zia, polychrome, bird motif 375.00
Kachina
  11" h, Southwest, Navajo, c1920, polychrome, carved cottonwood form, lively colors 115.00
  15-1/2" h, Southwest, Hemis, Hopi, c1950, carved wood, sgd on right foot, carved cottonwood form, painted kilt and sash, body painted black with articulated arms, head with mask and tablita 435.00
Knife, Inuit, late 19ty C, 6-3/4" l, carved ivory, handle of 2 facing walruses, inlaid bead eyes, small spade-like blade (cut down) stamped "George Wostenholm 1KL Cutlery Sheffield" 460.00
Knife Scabbard, child's, Central Plains, Lakota, c1890, 10" l, sinew sewn native tanned hide roll-beaded down edge, roll-beaded drop, white, heart red, light green, and pumpkin, salt and pepper checkerboard pattern, tin cone suspensions at top and bottom 575.00
Moccasins, pr, native tanned hide form
  Central Plains, Lakota, c1900, 11" l, vamp and heel of pink, blue, and pumpkin dyed quill work surrounded by 3 rows of white, brass faceted and dark blue beads, medium blue field, hard soles 1,955.00
  Central Plains, late 19th C, 8-1/4" l, sinew sewn with vamps beaded in buffalo track pattern, single lane of bead work around heel, bottle and apple green, greasy yellow, white heart red, and white beads 435.00
  Central Plains, late 19th C, 11" l, bifurcated tongues with tin cone danglers, tops worked with geometric multicolor quilled pattern surrounded by row of lazy stitch beadwork of apple green, light and medium blue beads, white field, hard buffalo hide soles.......1,725.00
  Eastern Sioux, late 19th C, 10-1/2" l, pink, red, and teal dyed quills, bilateral floral pattern, tongue and sides lined with muslin.. 350.00
  Plateau, late 19th C, 10" l, vamps beaded in bilateral floral design, brick red, black, lavender, and light blue beads outlined in white 865.00
  Southern Plains, Kiowa, c1910, 9-1/2" l, sinew sewn and painted yellow, stylized geometric device at vamp, single lane of bead work around whole..................490.00
Octopus Bag, beaded cloth
  Lower Canadian, attributed to Cree, c1880, 17-1/2" l, navy blue stroud cloth, lined in cotton and early red trade cloth, top panel beaded in meandering floral motif, multicolored and metallic faceted beads, tabs outlined in single land of beadwork with meandering floral devices, fringed wool beaded suspensions.. 2,645.00
  Northern Plains, Cree, last quarter 19th C, 13" l, blue stroud cloth form, lined with cotton, ribbon handle, bound and formerly edge beaded, top panel beaded in slightly meandering floral pattern, various green and white heart red, dull pink, crystal and metallic beads, bilateral tentacles of floral and foliate motifs 2,185.00
  Northwest Coast, attributed to Tlingit, c1890, 19-1/2" l, red trade cloth top with bilateral floral design, 4 tab suspension, checked cotton cloth lining, dark navy trade cloth back, edge beaded in white, greasy yellow, bottle green, medium and navy blue beads 1,380.00
Olla, basketry, Southwest, coiled, early 20th C
  13-1/2" h, stout, slightly flaring neck, central dark circle motif at base, radiating rhombic devices, myriad of human, quadruped, whirling log, and cross devices articulated in positive/negative designs, some stitch loss, repair.....................2,645.00
  16-1/2" h, flat bottom, slightly flaring sides, high shoulder, slightly flaring neck, woven willow and devil's claw, 5 radiating double line bor-

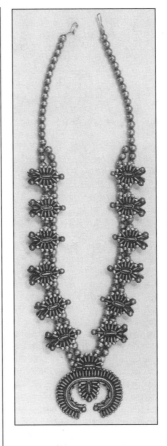

Necklace, Zuni, squash blossom, turquoise, 13-3/4" l, $2,200.

ders, separating various dec devices including quadrupeds, human figures, zigzags, rectilinear devices, old rim repair................3,335.00
Painting, George Ahgopak, Inuit, 20th C, Tundra Village Life, pen and wash on skin, scenes of caribou round-up, 34" x 17-1/2", framed 550.00
Photograph
  4-1/8" x 2-1/2", Sitting Bull portrait, carte-de-viste, labeled "TA-TON-KA-I-YO-TON-RA, Sitting Bull, the Chief in Command at the Custer Massacre," back mkd "photographed by W. R. Cross, Niobrara, Neb. Publisher of wild Indian and Badland Scenery…"....................690.00
  4-1/4" x 6-1/2", Curley, Crow scout for Custer, back labeled "Cabinet Series of Noted Indian Chiefs…," published by F. Jay Haynes, Fargo, D. T. 1,495.00
  5-1/2" x 4", Sun Boy wearing cavalry jacket, holding bow, labeled "Son of the Sun, Kiowa Chief," W. S. Soule.......................550.00
  6-1/2" x 4-1/4", studio portrait of youth in native garb, holding hoop, mounted on cabinet card, stamped "Mystic Studios, Ponca City Okla" on front 690.00
  7-1/2" x 5-1/2", native people in front of tepee, sgd in plate lower left "Soule," labeled on card "Arapaho Lodge"...............1,100.00
  7-3/4" x 5-1/2", woman and child, labeled "Copyright, B. A. Gifford the Dalles Ore," framed 60.00
  8-1/4" x 6-1/2", camp scene, young people, tepees, and dogs, labeled "Dept. of Interior U. S. Geological Survey of the Territories…," sgd "Bancocks" in pencil, William H. Jackson, some pencil marks.........................230.00
  11" x 6-3/4", chief Gall, mounted on card, back labeled "D. F. Barry, photographs of all noted Indian Chiefs…Superior Wisconsin," stamped on front "copyright D. F. Barry, Barry"...................230.00
  13 x 10-1/2", "The Scout," image of scout on horse back in desert, sgd "Curtis" lower left (Edward Curtis), oratone, orig back wing frame.................6,900.00
Pick, hardstone, Fairfield Co., OH, 11-3/4" l, curved..................715.00
Pipe and Stem, Central Plains, last quarter 19th C, red stone, carved T-bowl, carved concentric rings at bowl and near stem, ask stem

incised with repeated lineal and cross motif, trace pigment..... 350.00

Pipe and Stem, miniature, Central Plains, attributed to Lakota, early 20th C, 9" l, black pipe stone, T-shaped bowl, carved ash stem, 4 carved turtles, red stem............ 375.00

Pipe Bag, beaded hide

Central Plains, Lakota, 29" l, reconstructed from woman's legging, cloth fringe............ 350.00

Central Plains, Lakota, c1880, 33" l, beaded buffalo hide, sinew sewn, edge beading at opening, single lane of beads around top and down side, lower panel topped by abstract devices on one side, coup feathers on reverse, stepped geometric and bar and box motif, linear and stepped rhomboid devices on reverse, commercially dyed quill wrapped slats with hide fringe, greasy yellow, medium green, blues, and white heart red beads, multiple repairs, holes, bead loss............ 2,645.00

Northern Plains, Cree, c1870, 21" l, smoked native tanned hide, top 4 tabs and side edge beaded in white, metal tack closure, lower panel of bilateral floral motif on one side, slightly meandering on other side, white heart red, pumpkin, dull pink, light and medium blue, various green beads, white field, buffalo hide fringe..1,035.00

Northern Plains, mid 19th C, 21" l, six tab top, white edging, white heart red pony beads, buckskin form sinew sewn, 2 feather devices on each side above beaded panel, lower panel with bar design, amber, dull pink, pony trader blue, and Kiowa red, twisted fringe finish 8,625.00

Plate, pottery, Southwest, San Ildefonso

6-5/8" d, highly polished gun metal finish, Avanyo motif, sgd "Maria and Popovi" 1,610.008" d, highly polished black on black surface, central dec motif of oval form, radiating and stepped geometric devices, sgd "Marie" 2,185.00

Quiver, child's, Plains, Parfleche, 19" l, fringe and lid 965.00

Sash, child's, Prairie, attributed to Osage, late 19th C, 39" l, woven and beaded, finger woven commercial blue-green and maroon yarn, zigzag pattern, white beads bordering colors, drop ties with knotted tassel finials 350.00

Seed Jar, pottery, Southwest, Hopi, possibly Nampeyo, c1915, 9-1/2" d, cream slip, 2 brown and red bird motifs painted on shoulder, labeled "Hopi Ware bought at San Diego Exposition" 10,925.00

Shirt, child's, Southwest, Navajo, c1930, 22" l, burnt orange velvet, silver button dec at cuffs, elbow, shoulders, collar, and plaque ... 260.00

Spoon, wood, Northwest Coast, Tlingit, late 19th C, 5-1/2" l, carved handle with avian and wolf's head, inlaid eyes, smoothly carved orb, chipped............ 700.00

Storyteller Bear, pottery, Southwest, Cochiti, 9" h, black bear form, jar on her lap, 4 cinnamon cups on her lap and shoulders, sgd "Louis Naranjo" 490.00

Totem Pole, Northwest Coast

12-3/4" h, attributed to Haida, carved argalite, slightly concave back, bear forms, topped with human form, mended hairline crack 1,100.00

13-1/2" h, early 20th C, abalone inlaid, hollowed back, carved human head, bird of prey atop............ 800.00

19" h, Tlingit, early 20th C, polychrome carved wood, hollowed cedar back, human, avian, and worm, commercial paint on front ..1,150.00

22-1/2" h, polychrome wood, animals forms, human, bear, and avian 750.00

23-1/2" h, attributed to Bela Coola, c1900, polychrome carved wood, incised human and animal forms, illegible old tags 1,100.00

25" h, polychrome wood, cedar wood pole, carved concave back, towering Shaman, bear, and frog motifs, commercial pigments ...865.00

26" h, attributed to Haida, early 20th C, polychrome carved wood, animal, human, and avian forms, commercial paints, back labeled "The Nugget Shop, Juneau, Alaska," sgd "Crow" at base . 2,990.00

58" h, attributed to Haida, late 19th C, carved cedar, concave back, front and base painted with commercial pigments, myriad towering fantastic creatures, commercial wood crate............ 6,325.00

Tray, basketry

14-3/4" d, Southern California, Mission, 19th C, finely coiled shallow form, large central motif of pinwheel, rim dec with repeated inverted triangular devices, minor fading, rim loss........... 2,760.00

17" d, Southwest, Apache, early 20th C, shallow form, dark center and radiating checkerboard pattern surrounded by interlocking rhombic devices, row of cross motifs surmounted by row of dog motifs 2,415.00

Tunic, Northwest Coast, Tlingit, c1900, 40" l, black wool trade cloth, red wood trade cloth accent, calico and unbleached muslin lining, edge beaded red accents at hem, cuffs, yoke, and collar, pocket and front plaquette with bi-lateral abstract linear bead work, blue, white, black, and greasy yellow beads 2,530.00

Vest, man's, beaded canvas, Plateau, early 20th C, 21-3/4" l, bilateral floral design, multicolored beads, robin's egg blue field, calico lining, black cotton back with sequins............ 920.00

Wadelow Blade, St. Louis Co., MI, 6-3/4" l 360.00

Water Bottle, Mississippian, Fulton Co., KY, 6-1/4" h, hooded ... 330.00

INDIAN TREE PATTERN

History: Indian Tree pattern is a popular pattern of porce-

Pot, Acoma type, geometric earthtones, 4-1/2" h, $195.

Soup Plate, mkd "Maddock/England," 9" d, $40.

lain made from the last half of the 19th century until the present. The pattern, consisting of an Oriental crooked tree branch, landscape, exotic flowers, and foliage, is found predominantly in greens, pinks, blues, and oranges on a white ground. Several English potteries, including Burgess and Leigh, Coalport, and Maddock, made wares in the Indian Tree pattern.

Bowl, 8-1/2" d, ftd, Minton	45.00
Butter Dish, cov Johnson Bros.	48.00
Cake Plate, 10-1/2" d, Coalport	45.00
Creamer and Sugar, scalloped, Coalport	60.00
Cup and Saucer, scalloped, Coalport	30.00
Egg Cup, 4" h, Maddock & Sons	25.00
Gravy Boat, Brownfield & Sons, c1856	35.00
Plate, 9-1/2" d, KPM	15.00
Sauce Dish, 5" d, Johnson Bros.	9.50
Soup Plate, 7-1/2" d, Coalport	22.00
Vegetable Bowl, oval, smooth edge, Coalport	60.00

INK BOTTLES

History: Ink was sold in glass or pottery bottles in the early 1700s in England. Retailers mixed their own formula and bottled it. The commercial production of ink did not begin in England until the late 18th century and in America until the early 19th century.

Initially, ink was supplied in often poorly manufactured pint or quart bottles from which smaller bottles could be filled. By the mid-19th century, when writing implements had been improved, emphasis was placed on making an "untippable" bottle. Shapes ranging from umbrellas to turtles were tried. Since ink bottles were usually displayed, shaped or molded bottles were popular.

The advent of the fountain pen relegated the ink bottle to the back drawer. Bottles lost their decorative design and became merely functional items.

References: Ralph & Terry Kovel, *Kovels' Bottles Price List*, 11th ed., Three Rivers Press, 1999; John Odell, *Digger Odell's Official Antique Bottle and Glass Collector Magazine Price Guide Series*, Vol. 4, published by author (1910 Shawhan Rd., Morrow, OH 45152), 1995.

Periodical: *Antique Bottle and Glass Collector*, P.O. Box 187, East Greenville, PA 18041.

Additional Listings: See *Warman's Americana & Collectibles* for more examples.

Cylindrical, 5-5/8" h, America, 1840-60, "Harrison's Columbia Ink," cobalt blue, applied flared mouth, pontil scar, 3" crack, mouth roughness, C #764 .... 150.00
Figural, America, 1860-90
  2" h, house, domed offset neck for, emb architectural features of front door and 4 windows, colorless, sheared mouth, smooth base, Carter's Ink, some remaining int. ink residue, C #614 .... 650.00
  2" h, locomotive, aquamarine, ground mouth, smooth base, C #715 .... 800.00
  2-3/8" h, log cabin, rect, colorless, tooled sq collared mouth, smooth base, pinhead sized hole in one base corner, some int. haze, C #680 .... 200.00
  2-5/8" h, house, 1-1/2 story cottage form, full label on reverse "Bank of Writing Fluid, Manuf by the Senate Ink Co Philadelphia," aquamarine, tooled sq collared mouth, smooth base, small area of label slightly faded, C# 682 .... 300.00

Pottery, cone style, brown glaze, 2-5/8" h, $15.

Hexagonal, 9-7/8" h, America, 1900-20, "Carter," cathedral panels, colorless with pale yellow cast, machined mouth, smooth base, similar to C #820 .... 700.00
Inverted Concial
  2-3/8" h, Stoddard, NH, 1846-1860, deep yellow-olive, sheared mouth, pontil scar, pinhead flake on mouth edge, C #15 .... 170.00
  2-1/2" h, America, 1840-60, medium cobalt blue, tooled mouth, tubular pontil scar, C #23 .... 800.00
  2-1/2" h, America, 1840-60, "Woods/Black Ink/Portland," aquamarine, inward rolled mouth, pontil scar, C #12, unearthed with some remaining stain 170.00
Octagonal
  G. H. Gilbert Co., West Brookfield, MA, orig label 150.00
  Harrison's Columbian Ink, light green 65.00
  Laughlin's And Bushfield Wheeling Va., 2-7/8" h, aquamarine, inward rolled mouth, pontil scar 300.00
Umbrella, America, 1840-60
  2-1/8" h, twelve-sided, sapphire blue, inward rolled mouth, pontil, scar, C #182, professionally cleaned 950.00
  2-1/4" h, New England, 1840-60, octagonal, golden amber, sheared mouth, C #145 .... 160.00
  2-3/8" h, octagonal, sapphire blue, inward rolled mouth, pontil, scar, C #141 .... 700.00
  2-5/8" h, octagonal, lime green, labeled "Williams/Black/Empire/Ink/New York," tooled mouth, smooth base, label 95% intact, C #173 .... 160.00
  2-5/8" h, octagonal, sapphire blue, inward rolled mouth, pontil, scar, C #129 .... 950.00

INKWELLS

History: Most of the commonly found inkwells were produced in the United States or Europe between the early 1800s and the 1930s. The most popular materials were glass and pottery because these substances resisted the corrosive effects of ink.

Inkwells were a sign of the office or wealth of an individual. The common man tended to dip his ink directly from the bottle. The years between 1870 and 1920 represent the golden age of inkwells when elaborate designs were produced.

References: Veldon Badders, *Collector's Guide to Inkwells: Identification and Values*, Book I (1995), Book II, 1997, Collector Books; William E. Covill, Jr., *Inkbottles and Inkwells*, William S. Sullwold Publishing, out of print.

Collectors' Clubs: St. Louis Inkwell Collectors Society, P.O. Box 29396, St. Louis, MO 63126; The Society of Inkwell Collectors, 5136 Thomas Ave. So., Minneapolis, MN 55410, http://www.soic.com.

Additional Listings: See *Warman's Americana & Collectibles* for more examples.

Blown Three Mold, glass
    1-5/8" h, Mount Vernon Glass Works, Vernon, NY, 1820-40, dense olive amber, tooled disc mouth, pontil scar, McKearin GII-15 ..150.00
    1-3/4" h, Boston and Sandwich Glass Works, Sandwich, MA, 1860-90, cylindrical, vertical flues, fiery opalescent milk glass, crudely sheared mouth, smooth base, small areas of roughness and flaking, C #1173.................200.00
Brass, figural rose, color wash, pink/red petals, green stem 250.00
Bronze
    9-3/4" l, patinated, Zodiac pattern, sexagonal inkwell with glass liner, sq pen tray, imp "Tiffany Studios, New York/1073"..1,000.00
    12" w, 6-7/8" h, gilt bronze, 2 nude women in surf, inkwell lid in form of crab, brown composition base, Vve Leonie Ledru, France, c1900 ....525.00
Figural
    3-7/8" h, painted metal, howling cat, paint wear, minor corrosion, 19th C 175.00
    5-1/2" h, 7-3/4" w, Putti and Drum, playful figure with drumsticks, seated between two covered inkwells, gilt bronze, French, late 19th C 490.00
Folk Art, 4" x 4-1/2", cast iron and glass insert, old blue paint, red inscription "Osgood" and "Napoleon" 300.00
Freeblown Glass, 1-3/4" h, attributed to America, 1840-60, sq, opaque electric blue, flared mouth, pontil scar.................120.00

Porcelain, sq, "Runelle, Nivernaix, D. Dugnas. Nevers," mkd "Depost," Triple Sac/Dianout/C. Dugnas, Nevers," 3-1/4" sq, 1-5/8" h, $80.

Gilt Metal, 11" l, 4-1/2" h, double, Moorish pattern, cast brass, two hinged-top inkwells with hooks to hold pen, base imp "Tiffany & Co," foot restored, pen missing.................345.00
Heintz, 4" d, bronze with silver overlay, patented Aug 12, 1912, #1182 ....90.00
Majolica, 6-1/2" h, dolphin molded base supporting circular form inkwell, relief masks, Italy, 19th C.................300.00
Paperweight, 6-1/4" h, 4-1/2" d, multicolored concentric millefiore, base with 1848 date canes, Whitefriars 175.00
Pattern Molded Glass, 2" h, America, 1840-60, cylindrical, vertical ribs, cobalt blue, sheared rim, pontil scar, C #1066 ....140.00
Pearlware, 5-1/2" h, gilt highlights, imp "By F. Bridges, Phrenologist," and "EM" on base, England, 19th C, very minor chips, gilt wear.........520.00
Pitkin Type, 1-7/8" h, New England, 1780-1830, 36 ribs swirled to left, cylindrical, deep yellow-olive, tooled mouth, pontil scar, C #1160 .400.00
Teakettle, ceramic
    2-1/8" h, France, 1830-60, hexagonal, mottled ruby red and white glazes 80.00
    2-1/2" h, attributed to America, 1830-60, hexagonal, blue glaze, transfer scene on top, gilt dec highlights, ground mouth with brass collar and cap, smooth base, C #1240 ....450.00
Teakettle, glass, attributed to America, 1830-60, cut and polished octagonal form
    1-5/8" h, orange amber, ground mouth, applied brass collar, smooth base, brass cap missing, C #1268.................325.00
    2" h, opalescent electric blue, ground mouth, smooth base, C #1255 ....400.00
    2-1/8" h, canary, ground moth, smooth base, missing closure, C #1268 ....250.00
    2-5/8" h, brick red and burgundy slag glass, ground mouth with brass cap, smooth base, two small chips, C#1261 ....110.00
    3-1/4" h, additional applied ink reservoir on top, opaque blue, gilt highlighted dec, ground mouth, smooth base, no collar and cap, wear to gilt 350.00
Traveling, 2-1/4" l, 2-1/4" w, 1-1/2" h, silver, made by Gorham, retailed by Black, Starr & Frost, sq, rounded corners, hinged lid engraved with leafy scrolls and flowerheads, central monogram, lid opening with front latch, int. with further cover over fitted glass well, int. lid engraved with presentation inscription, 3 troy oz 350.00
Wedgwood & Bentley, 6-1/4" l, black basalt, oblong, central candle holder, removable sander, imp mark, c1775, foot rim flake, inserts missing 800.00

IRONS

History: Ironing devices have been used for many centuries, with the earliest references dating from 1100. Irons from the medieval, Renaissance, and early industrial eras can be found in Europe but are rare. Fine engraved brass irons and hand-wrought irons predominated prior to 1850. After 1850 the iron underwent a series of rapid evolutionary changes.

Between 1850 and 1910, irons were heated in four ways: 1) a hot metal slug was inserted into the body, 2) a burning solid, e.g., coal or charcoal, was placed in the body, 3) a liquid or gas, e.g., alcohol, gasoline, or natural gas, was fed from an external tank and burned in the body, or 4) conduction heat, usually drawing heat from a stove top.

Electric irons are just beginning to find favor among iron collectors.

References: Dave Irons, *Irons by Irons*, published by author (223 Covered Bridge Rd, Northampton, PA 18067), 1994; ——, *More Irons by Irons*, published by author, 1997; ——, *Pressing Iron Patents*, published by author, 1994.

Periodical: *Iron Talk*, P.O. Box 68, Waelder, TX 78959.

Collectors' Clubs: Club of the Friends of Ancient Smoothing Irons, P.O. Box 215, Carlsbad, CA 92008; Midwest Sad Iron Collectors Club, 24 Nob Hill Dr., St. Louis, MO 63138.

Museums: Henry Ford Museum, Dearborn, MI; Shelburne Museum, Shelburne, VT; Sturbridge Village, Sturbridge, MA.

Additional Listings: See *Warman's Americana & Collectibles* for more examples.

Advisors: David and Sue Irons.

Charcoal
Brass Dutch, tall sides with cut work, latch in front many
  sizes 400.00
Dragon Head, tall chimney, German, a dragon head is the chimney,
  6-5/8" 600.00
Eclipse, 1903, top lifts off, 6-3/4"...................................... 120.00
Tall chimney, Cummings & Bless 1852, Vulcan Face Damper ... 130.00
Children's
Amzoc, Mexican, engraved with leaves and flowers, 3" 250.00
Dover Sad Iron No. 812, 4", 2 piece iron 45.00
Enterprise Mfg Co Phila No 115, holes through handle, 3-7/8"... 110.00
Ober, Chagrin Falls O., sleeve, 4 1/2"............................. 250.00
Our Pet, 3-1/2" wood handle....................................... 125.00
Swan, cast in sizes 1-1/4" to 3", some painted
    Not painted 130.00
    Painted red with white highlightings for feather 250.00
Electric
Hot Point, early 1900 style 80.00
Pelovze, "L" handle Chicago...................................... 70.00
Petipoint, Model No. 410, Art Deco style, fins on side 260.00
Saunders Silver Streak, all glass , Pyrex, red color 900.00
Flat
Cast, anchor symbol #7, 6-1/8"...................................... 40.00
Cold Handle
    Bless and Drake, bentwood removeable handle 160.00
    Slant handle, 7 3/8" 190.00
Dover Sad Iron, 2 piece, 6-5/8".................................... 40.00
Enterprise, boxed set of three-one handle, 3 bases 250.00
French, low profile, Le Caiffa 70.00
P. W. Weida's, 1870 Phila., PA., handle folds back.................... 200.00
Fluters
Charcoal Iron with fluter attachment
    Acme 180.00
    Combination , fluter inside, wire clip to hold together, 7"....... 150.00
Machine, Dudley 1876, painted and pin striped......................... 400.00

Flat, Gothic, 1480-1520, $11,500. Photo courtesy of Auction Team Breker.

Sad, removable wooden handle, 3-3/4" l, $75.

Machine, Crown, Am. Machine Co., Phila. PA............................ 150.00
Roller Type, Shepard Hardware 1879............................... 150.00
Rocker Type, The Best, C. W. Whitfield.............................. 100.00
Rocker Type, Geneva Hand Fluter 1866 .... 70.00
Goffering
Double Barrel, cast base, elegant................................ 750.00
Single Round Base, "S" post, most common 90.00
Wrought, single barrel, tripod feet................................ 300.00
Liquid Fuel
Beetall, English Natural Gas, "L" handle, 6-1/4" 250.00
Clarks Fairy Prince, English, Blue Porcelain......................... 220.00
Coleman, Model 5, Green, 7-3/8" 250.00
Jubilee Iron, Gasoline 1904, 6-5/8"................................ 150.00
Uneedit Gas Iron, natural gas, 6-1/2" 150.00
Acetylene Stove Mfg. Co., natural gas, 6" 85.00
Miscellaneous
Centennial Heater 1876, mechanical type, holds one iron 500.00
Mini Taylors Iron, advertising give-away 300.00
Slug
Bless-Drake Salamander Brac Uron, top lifts off, 6" 250.00
Brass, box, Austrian, Liftup Gate, 7-1/4"........................... 160.00
Handmade Bag, French, Early Construction, 7" 350.00
Sensible, Groton, NY, top lifts off 275.00
Smoothing Mangle Boards
Horse Handle, decorated with chip carving in geometric designs, paint
    decorated, 27" 900.00
Turned Handle, dated 1890, 26" 150.00
Special Purpose
Egg, Hand Held.. 90.00
Enterprise, Star Polisher 5-1/2" 120.00
Leather Press, two handles, swingtype 450.00
Mabs Cooks, Polisher, rounded edges, 4-3/4"........................ 140.00
Round Bottom, Carron #2, 4-5/8" 130.00
Sleeve, Guelph, Canadian, 7".................................... 80.00

IRONWARE

History: Iron, a metallic element that occurs abundantly in combined forms, has been known for centuries. Items made from iron range from the utilitarian to the decorative. Early hand-forged ironwares are of considerable interest to Americana collectors.

References: *Collectors Guide to Wagner Ware and Other Companies*, L-W Book Sales, 1994; Douglas Congdon-

Martin, *Figurative Cast Iron*, Schiffer Publishing, 1994; Griswold Cast Iron, L-W Book Sales, 1997; Jon B. Haussler, *Griswold Muffin Pans*, Schiffer Publishing, 1997; Kathryn McNerney, *Antique Iron Identification and Values*, Collector Books, 1984, 1998 value update; George C. Neumann, *Early American Antique Country Furnishings*, L-W Book Sales, 1984, 1993 reprint.

Periodicals: *Cast Iron Cookware News*, 28 Angela Ave., San Anselmo, CA 94960; *Kettles 'n Cookware*, Drawer B, Perrysburg, NY 14129.

Collectors' Club: Griswold & Cast Iron Cookware Association, P.O. Drawer B, Perrysburg, NY 14129-0301.

Reproduction Alert: Use the following checklist to determine if a metal object is a period piece or modern reproduction. This checklist applies to all cast-metal items, from mechanical banks to trivets.

Period cast-iron pieces feature well-defined details, carefully fitted pieces, and carefully finished and smooth castings. Reproductions, especially those produced by making a new mold from a period piece, often lack detail in the casting (lines not well defined, surface details blurred) and parts have gaps at the seams and a rough surface. Reproductions from period pieces tend to be slightly smaller in size than the period piece from which they were copied.

Period paint mellows, i.e., softens in tone. Colors look flat. Beware of any cast-iron object whose paint is bright and fresh. Painted period pieces should show wear. Make certain the wear is in places it is supposed to be.

Period cast-iron pieces develop a surface patina that prevents rust. When rust is encountered on a period piece, it generally has a greasy feel and is dark in color. The rust on artificially aged reproductions is flaky and orange.

Additional Listings: Banks; Boot Jacks; Doorstops; Fireplace Equipment; Food Molds; Irons; Kitchen Collectibles; Lamps; Tools.

Apple Roaster, 34-1/4" l, wrought, hinged apple support, pierced heart end on slightly twisted projecting handle, late 18th C 1,750.00

Hitching Post, horse head, 28-1/2" h, $525.

Boot Scraper, cast
    12" l, scroll ends, green granite base 120.00
    14" l, 9" h, pecking rooster, molded, traces of red polychrome paint, 19th C 1,600.00
Branding Iron, 17" h, wrought iron, ferule end as candlestick....... 65.00
Candle Bracket, 25" l, wrought iron, 5 jointed arms, attached to vertical sliding carrier, ending in 2 spikes, 18th C................................ 920.00
Candlestand, wrought iron
    48-1/4" h, two arms, two brass cups and drip pans fitted to horizontal sliding carrier, tripod base, brass finial and standard dec, wear, 18th C 3,150.00
    56" h, post with twisted detail and threaded finial, adjustable five segment candle arm with brass socket, tripod base with penny feet, finial may be replacement...................................... 1,375.00
Coal Hod, 31" l, wrought, sliding lid 245.00
Dipper, wrought iron and brass, mkd "F. B. S. Canton"................. 85.00
Doormat, 35-1/2" x 22", sheet iron, shaped hearts connected by wire rod running through shoulders and lower point of each heart, America, late 19th C/early 20th C 260.00
Fire Dogs, pr, 7" h, miniature, wrought, penny feet, gooseneck finials, tooled detail.. 715.00
Hat Rack, 40-1/2" h, 33" w, cast, painted, flower basket form, late 19th C.. 800.00
Kettle Stand, 8-1/2" d, 12" h, wrought, rotating, round top, tripod base, penny feet, brass trim.. 300.00
Lighting Device, 13" h, primitive, candle socket, spring clip rush holder, brown base.. 115.00
Lock, 10" l, wrought, simple dec detail.. 55.00
Match Holder, cast iron, two donkeys facing each other, motto in between "When shall we three meet again," orig paint 145.00
Paperweight, 4-3/4" l, cast, cat, oval base, old black paint 300.00
Pedestal, 14-1/2" w, 14-1/2" d, 38-1/2" h, wrought iron, Gothic-Revival, French, third quarter 19th C, rect tile top set with conforming molded frame, splayed, twist-turned legs terminating above in volutes and below on paw feet, sides filled with lattice work panels of flowering vines.. 2,500.00
Pipe, 18" l, cast iron, worn bowl with 2 holes............................. 715.00
Pipe Tongs, 21" l, wrought iron 1,155.00
Potbellied Stove, 25-1/2" d, 46-1/2" h, cast, Station Agent, Union Stove Works, NY, name emb on circular top rim 400.00
Sewing Machine, child's, cast.. 150.00
Shelf Brackets, pr, 5-1/2" h, wrought, painted............................. 20.00
Shooting Gallery Target, cast iron, figural
    3-1/4" h, bird 35.00
    5-1/4" l, bear, mkd "H. C. Evans & Co"............................... 110.00
Skimmer, wrought iron and brass, mkd "F. B. S. Canton"............. 90.00
Splint Holder
    9-1/4" h, candle socket counterweight, wrought iron, worm eaten wood base 270.00
    11-3/4" h, knob counterweight, wrought iron turned wood base.. 200.00
Stove, 22" h, cast, emb "Bellaire Stove Co., Bellaire, O. Scout No. 8," complete... 55.00
Table, 36" d, 29-3/4" h, cast, Neoclassical-style, circular carrara marble top, base cast with ram's heads, ribbons, and foliage, stylized hoof feet, late 19th/early 20th C 230.00
Utensil Rack, 26" l, wrought iron, scrolled detail......................... 250.00
Windmill Weight, 13-1/2" h, cast iron, figural rooster, Hummer E184, Elgin Wind, Power & Pump Co., Elgin, IL, pitted finish, rect base.......... 330.00

IVORY

History: Ivory, a yellowish white organic material, comes from the teeth or tusks of animals and lends itself to carving. Many cultures have used it for centuries to make artistic and utilitarian items.

A cross section of elephant ivory will have a reticulated crisscross pattern. Hippopotamus teeth, walrus tusks, whale teeth, narwhal tusks, and boar tusks also are forms of ivory.

Crucifix, carved, 18th C, 7" h, $1,760. Photo courtesy of Jackson's Auctioneers & Appraisers.

Vegetable ivory, bone, stag horn, and plastic are ivory substitutes which often confuse collectors. For information on how to identify real ivory, see Bernard Rosett's "Is It Genuine Ivory" in Sandra Andacht's *Oriental Antiques & Art: An Identification and Value Guide* (Wallace-Homestead, 1987).

References: Edgard O. Espinoza and Mary-Jacque Mann, *Identification for Ivory and Ivory Substitutes*, 2nd ed., World Wildlife Fund, 1992; Gloria and Robert Mascarelli, *Oriental Antiques*, Wallace-Homestead, out of print.

Periodical: *Netsuke & Ivory Carving Newsletter*, 3203 Adams Way, Ambler, PA 19002.

Collectors' Club: International Ivory Society, 11109 Nicholas Dr., Wheaton, MD 20902.

Note: Dealers and collectors should be familiar with The Endangered Species Act of 1973, amended in 1978, which limits the importation and sale of antique ivory and tortoiseshell items.

Bobbin Winder, carved as woman with spinning wheel, Continental, late 19th C 250.00
Box, cov
    2-3/4" h, oval, side carved with relief medallions of putti, top with pierced carving, central cabochon stone, Russian, late 19th C 375.00
    3-5/8" x 2-3/4" x 1-1/2", rect, sides polychromed with bands entwined ribboned garlands, lid with city scene and figures, sgd

"Eailus," Continental, late 18th/early 19th C 300.00
Brush Pot, 4" h, carved, figures and pavilions, Chinese, c1885 .... 1,200.00
Chess Set, 2-7/8" h king, carved, natural ivory and stained brown pieces, fitted case and board 400.00
Cribbage Board, 9" l, engraved salmon, walrus, and "Nome Alaska," Eskimo, several orig pins 330.00
Cup, cov, foliate finial, oval body, carved frieze of putti with hound, mask and acanthus baluster stem, round foot, Continental, early 18th C 1,200.00
Dresser Set, mirror, 3 brushes, glove stretcher, shoe horn, 3 jars, brush rest, monogrammed 350.00
Fan, 10" l, carved, Chinese Export, Chinoiserie dec lacquer box, late 19th C 260.00
Figure
    2-1/4" h, merchant, Japanese 175.00
    7-1/4" h, Christ, brass crucifix, Continental, dated 1922 .... 550.00
    7-1/8 h, emperor and empress, seated on throne, traditional costume, wood bases, pr 700.00
    7-3/4" h, woman with parasol, titled "Merveilleuse," lace edged parasol and bonnet, laced bodice with ruched skirt, holding reticule, ivory socle, French, late 19th C 1,300.00
    8-1/2" h, fisherman, standing, bamboo pole and catch, whimsical expression, leaf-form hat, carved wood base 350.00
    11-3/8" and 11-1/2", Renaissance lady and gentleman, lady with turban and long gown, holding book, man with plumed hat, lace collar, cape, and sword, each on wooden base, traces of gilt detailing, Continental, late 19th C, pr 11,500.00
    11-1/2" h, warrior, elaborately carved costume, jeweled head piece, bearded figure, holding musical instrument, carved wood base 825.00
Gavel, 8-1/4" l, engraved scribe lines 250.00
Jewelry Box, 6-1/2" w, 4-1/2" h, relief carved lid, procession of Mandarins in landscape with pagodas and animals, sides with conforming carved reserves, beast form feet, Chinese, 19th C 1,450.00
Mask, 7" h, Samurai, carved frieze expression, wood mount 600.00
Miniature, 3-3/4" h, carved carriage with figures and driver, pulled by 2 oxen, Continental, late 19th C 325.00
Panel, 7-3/4" x 2-3/4", one side carved with birds among flowers, other side with incised seal and floral design, fitted wood stand, Chinese, 19th C 995.00
Plaque, 15-3/4" h, Roman battle scene, enthroned emperor, Continental, minor damage 2,000.00
Powder Box, cov, cylindrical, domed lid, int. fitted with inner lid, ivory handled puff, Continental, late 19th C, retailed by Bailey, Banks & Biddle Co., monogrammed 375.00
Seal, 2-1/8" h, carved as closed fist, knopped stem, mounted to engraved brass seal, Continental, late 19th C 200.00
Sewing Case, 2-1/2" x 1-1/2" x 3/4", rect, rounded corners, fitted int. with thimble, gilt scissors, thread pull, Continental, late 19th C 275.00
Snuff Box, 3-3/8" d, circular, high relief silver medallion of wild boar in woods, foliate details, gold border, tortoiseshell bottom, int. of lid with tortoiseshell, sgd "Kirsten of Strasbourg," late 18th C 950.00
Stand, 7" h, pierced relief, pink and cream flowers, peony and lotus flowers, green stones 425.00
Vase, 18-1/2" h, flattened cylindrical, indented neck, raised rect panel with figures above continuous scenes of women and children in garden, domed cov with fu lion finial, ring handles, China, c1900, pr 1,400.00
Watch Hutch, 14" h, 8-1/4" x 5" w at base, carved whale ivory, whale bone, and ebonized wood, extended back of 3 pierced and carved staves with rounded window cut out beneath a shaped crest, dec with heart and urn finials, double tiered balcony with carved railings and balusters topped with urn finials, lower tier centered at back with vase and sunflower, double stepped base with shaped skirt, applied beads and ebonized wood frame, secret compartment, attributed to prisoner of war carving, America, 19th C 4,025.00

JADE

History: Jade is the generic name for two distinct minerals: nephrite and jadeite. Nephrite, an amphibole mineral from Central Asia that was used in pre-18th-century pieces, has a waxy surface and hues that range from white to an almost-black green. Jadeite, a pyroxene mineral found in Burma and used from 1700 to the present, has a glassy appearance and comes in various shades of white, green, yellow-brown, and violet.

Jade cannot be carved because of its hardness. Shapes are achieved by sawing and grinding with wet abrasives such as quartz, crushed garnets, and carborundum.

Prior to 1800, few items were signed or dated. Stylistic considerations are used to date pieces. The Ch'ien Lung period (1736-1795) is considered the golden age of jade.

Periodical: *Bulletin of the Friends of Jade,* 5004 Ensign St., San Diego, CA 92117.

Museum: Avery Brundage Collection, de Young Museum, San Francisco, CA.

Bookends, pr, 7" h, carved, brass trim, pierced foliate motif,
    Chinese 265.00
Bowl, 3" d, blue foliate Peking enamel ground, jade serpent
    handle 125.00
Bracelet, bangle, white jadeite, hololith bracelet, 7-1/2" d 460.00
Button, Mandarin, oval, gold fill loop 275.00
Censer, cov, 7-3/4" h, compressed globular form, high relief carved
    sides and cov, 3 short feet, carved hardwood stand, Chinese . 200.00
Cup, 2-3/4" h, handle, Chinese 200.00
Earrings, pr, carved, suspended on fine gold chain, pearl accent, European hallmarks 460.00
Figure
    Fu Dog, 4-1/2" h, carved wood base, pr 225.00
    Hotei, round face, seated position 275.00
    Man carrying vase of flowers, wood base 300.00
Handle, cylindrical, carved, spiraling linear design, cup attached with
    ext. petal motif, pointed knop at base, celadon green stone, Moghul
    style, 19th C 250.00
Pendant, carved
    Jade, foliate carved plaque, gold scrolled cap, topped by tumbled
        oval pink tourmaline, beaded gold bale, 18K yg 2,100.00

Jadeite, rabbit on gourd form, suspended from red silk cord 2,100.00
Plaque, 6" l, dragon form, pale celadon color, russet rivering throughout,
    shaped into S-curve with hind legs tucked between tail and back,
    comma scrolls, key fret border, scrolling tail and mane, 18th C . 1,200.00
Snuff Bottle
    3" l, flattened oval, carved kaylin, Chi'ing Dynasty, Chinese ... 65.00
    3-1/4" l, silver mounted, repousse dec, Chinese 95.00
Vase, 7" h, carved jade and lapis, cylindrical form, stepped feet, green
    stones at back knee, Chinese 375.00
Vase, cov, 5-3/8" h, white, ftd ovoid, shouldered by animal masks holding loose rings, domed stopper, fu lion finial, wood base 250.00

JASPERWARE

History: Jasperware is a hard, unglazed porcelain with a colored ground varying from the most common blues and greens to lavender, yellow, red, or black. The white designs, often classical in nature, are applied in relief. Jasperware was first produced at Wedgwood's Etruria Works in 1775. Josiah Wedgwood described it as "a fine terracotta of great beauty and delicacy proper for cameos."

In addition to Wedgwood, many other English potters produced jasperware. Two of the leaders were Adams and Copeland and Spode. Several Continental potters, e.g., Heubach, also produced the ware.

References: Susan and Al Bagdade, *Warman's English & Continental Pottery & Porcelain,* 3rd Edition, Krause Publications, 1998; R. K. Henrywood, *Relief-Moulded Jugs,* 1820-1900, Antique Collectors' Club.

Museums: British Museum, London, England; Memorial Hall Museum, Philadelphia, PA; Museum of Fine Arts, Boston, MA; Victoria & Albert Museum, London, England.

Reproduction Alert: Jasperware still is made today, especially by Wedgwood.

Note: This category includes jasperware pieces which were made by companies other than Wedgwood. Wedgwood jasperware is found in the Wedgwood listing.

Bookcase, 3-3/8" w, 8-1/4" l, 5" h, rect oak case, brass hardware, 7
    light blue jasper medallions with applied white portraits or classical
    subjects, 5 leather bound journals, hardware mkd "Howell, James &
    Co, Regent Street, London" 1,610.00
Bottle, 11-3/4" h, solid black dip, glazed surface, applied white foliage
    and fruiting grapevine swags between lion masks, unmarked, one
    handle restored, pr 375.00
Candlestick, 8-3/4" h, dark blue, applied white classical relief, mkd
    "Dudson Brothers," 19th C 200.00

Snuff Bottle, mottled brown jade body, green jade stopper, incised animal design, hand carved, 3" h, $420.

Tea Set, Wedgwood, Jasperware, unglazed porcelain with decoration in white relief, modern set includes creamer and sugar, mark, Wedgwood, England, set, $295. Photo courtesy of Tina Carter.

Cheese Dish, cov

7-1/2" h, dark blue dip, applied white classical figures and oak leaves relief, mid 19th C, restored finial.............................300.00

9-1/2" h, dark blue dip, applied white classical figures and oak leaves relief, mid 19th C 520.00

Drum Base, 3-3/8" d, 4" h, light blue dip, applied white classical and foliate relief, unmarked, late 18th C, both with slight relief losses, pr.......375.00

Hanging Pot, 6-1/2" h, dark blue dip, applied white classical and foliate relief, unmarked, late 19th C 400.00

Inkwell, 4-1/8" l, oval, solid pale blue ground, lavender medallion, white relief classical figures and foliate design, early 19th C.............920.00

Jardiniere, 7-1/4" h, dark blue, applied white classical relief, mkd "Adams"...200.00

Jug

5" h, dark blue dip, adv for "Ross's Belfast Ginger Ale," imp "Adams" 195.00

5-3/4" h, solid blue, applied white classical and foliate relief, imp "Adams & Co," late 18th C, restoration to handle and tip of spout 920.00

8-1/4" h, dark blue dip, bottle form, applied white relief classical figures and foliate dec, unmarked, 19th C 230.00

Medallion, 3-1/4" h, 4" w, solid blue, oval, white classical figure, Wedgwood & Bentley, c1775, slight surface crazing 1,100.00

Plaque

1-1/8" h, 1-3/8" w, black, oval, applied white classical figures, imp "Wedgwood & Bentley," c1775, pr 490.00

4" h, 5" w, dark blue dip, oval, applied white classical subject, imp "Adams," 19th C, surface chips to back edge 320.00

Salad Bowl, 6-7/8" d, dark blue dip, applied fox hunting scene, imp "Adams," 20th C 150.00

Scent Bottle, 3-1/4" l, dark blue dip, oval, applied white classical relief, early 19th C 1,035.00

Sugar Bowl, cov, 4-1/2" h, solid blue, oval, applied white classical and foliate relief, swan finial, engine-turned band to foot, imp "Adams," late 18th C, slight rim chip 1,495.00

Tea Kettle, cov, 7" h, light blue dip, applied white classical and foliate relief, 3 paw feet, unmarked, 19th C, chips to feet 200.00

Tobacco Jar, cov, 5-5/8" h, dark blue, applied fox hunting relief scene, unmarked, 19th C..325.00

Vase

2-7/8" h, dark blue dip, applied white classical figures, imp "Adams" 100.00

4-7/8" h, dark blue ground, applied white classical figures, green acanthus and bell flowers in relief, imp "Adams," early 19th C, rim hairlines 115.00

10" h, three color, blue ground, lavender medallions, applied white portraits, fruiting grapevine festoons, and foliate borders, unmarked, attributed to Adams & Bromley, c1875, cov missing 260.00

10-3/4" h, dark blue dip, applied white classical relief, scrolled handles, unmarked, mid 19th C 320.00

12" h, dark blue dip, applied white classical and foliate relief, unmarked, mid 19th C 375.00

14" h, solid pale blue, applied white classical and foliate relief, snake handles, imp mark, late 18th C, restored handles, socle and plinth 2,415.00

Vase, cov

8-3/8" h, solid dark blue, applied white acanthus and floral relief, pierced cover, imp "Adams," c1800, rim chips to cover, minor relief loss, int. restoration 175.00

10" h, dark blue dip, applied white Roman figures with horses and chariot, foliate borders, female mask handles, imp "Adams," 20th C 350.00

17-3/4" d, light blue ground, applied white relief of fruiting grapevine festoons, oval portrait medallions with lavender ground, imp "Adams and Bromley" mark, c1880, cover restored, inner lid missing 690.00

Vase, pedestal, dark blue, applied white classical and foliate relief, scrolled handles, mounted on sq pedestal, imp "Adams," 19th C, cover missing, restored handle and rim chips 750.00

Wall Pocket, 11-1/4" l, solid light blue, cornucopia, applied white classical relief, imp "Adams," late 18th C 250.00

Wine Cooler, 6-3/8" h, dark blue, applied white classical portraits and scrolled handles, mid 19th C, handles restored 175.00

JEWEL BOXES

History: The evolution of jewelry was paralleled by the development of boxes in which to store it. Jewel-box design followed the fashion trends dictated by furniture styles. Many jewel boxes are lined.

3-5/8" l, 2-5/8" w, gold and enamel, 22kt marks for London, c1795, French petite guarantee mark for 1819-38, octagonal, lid with central stippled gold ground set with seed pearls in depiction of an Ottoman tugras, flanked to upper corners with blue, red, green, and clear rose-cut stones set as floral sprays, center portion of lid surrounded by enameled flower-filled border, upper of edge of lid on three sides of curved lappet form, engraved gold scrolls offset with enamel roundels on blue ground, all four sides further enameled with cartouches depicting landscape scenes, fruit, flowers, tools, instruments, and arms, underside of box with central octagonal enamel rending of Dutch-style vase of flowers, surrounded by enamel roundels linked by engraved gold swags on blue ground, box opening to enameled landscape scene in lint. Of lid, with city, possibly Istanbul, harbor, mosque in foreground, sky with translucent enamel over engine-turned gold giving sunset effect, scene framed with molded as draper proscenium, fully marked, minor enamel loss to one side landscape panel 40,250.00

4-7/8" l, 2-3/4" w, 2-3/4" h, Continental silver, rect, sides chased and emb with scenes of courting couples surrounded by foliate scrolls, top with satyr and female Bacchante, int. with lock, green velvet lining, lid int. gold washed, engraved "Ruth" on lid, inscription engraved on bottom, some preservation, 9 troy oz...............................550.00

5" l, rect cut-corner blue jasper plaque with applied white classical relief, hand hammered pewter box, plaque attributed to Wedgwood, early 20th C 165.00

5-1/8" d, 2" h, silver, round, curved vertical reeding to sides, plain lid, blue velvet int., mkd "Pr. S. Denmark," 10 troy oz...................200.00

5-1/2" w, 3-1/4" d, 1" h, gilt, silver plated, rect, double headed eagle inset with amethyst, cobalt blue enameled ground, Continental 2,750.00

Art Nouveau style, gilded pot metal, rose dec, padded lining, 6" l, 5" h, $60.

6-1/4" h, Viennese enamel and ebony, equestrian finial, fitted allover with figural and landscape plaques, int. similarly dec, 2 drawers, late 19th C..2,415.00

7" l, gilt bronze and malachite, quatrefoil shape, mounts elaborately modeled with foliage, velvet lined int., sgd "Tajan Freres of Paris" 2,185.00

7" l, gilt bronze, French porcelain plaques with putti at various pursuits, bronze mounts modeled with masks, figures, and foliage, stamped "Tajan Freres," third quarter 19th C..2,070.00

7-1/4" l, 2-1/2" h, silver, .800 fine, lid engraved with leafy scrolls, beaded edge, squat bombe form, 4 scroll feet, Continental, early 20th C, 16 troy oz..350.00

7-1/2" l, 4-3/4" h, gilt metal mounted porcelain, scrolled gilt trim, enameled floral designs, Germany, 19th C..875.00

9" w, 5" d, 6" h, burl walnut and satinwood, domed cov, rect case, banded geometric inlay, Victorian..200.00

9" w, 8" d, 10-1/2" h, domed top casket, ebonized wood, 4 figural finials, 2 doors open to 6 small drawers over long drawer, case flanked by gilt bronze columns, inset enameled panels of neoclassical figures, bracket feet, Italian, late 19th C..................................3,500.00

9-1/8" l, 6-1/8" d, 3-3/8" h, marquetry inlaid, rect, central inlay of musical instruments surrounded by ribboned laurel swag, brass borders, silk-lined int., Continental, late 19th C..400.00

10-1/2" l, 5-1/2" w, 4" h, metal, rect, painted riveted strapwork, tooled and enameled Celtic-style motifs, glass jewel-like inserts, lock and key, raised mark "Alf Daguet Paris" on base..........................1,265.00

12-3/4" l, 9-1/4" w, 7" h, burl walnut veneer, ebonized detailing, hinged lid inset with central metal shield, velvet and leather-lined fitted int., inside of lid fitted with leather document file, lower section fitted with drawer, England, mid 19th C..260.00

14-1/2" w, 14" h, covered allover with needlework figural and foliate panels, hinged top, fitted int., front fitted with door enclosing int. of drawers, Continental, late 17th C..635.00

JEWELRY

History: Jewelry has been a part of every culture. It is a way of displaying wealth, power, or love of beauty. In the current antiques marketplace, it is easiest to find jewelry dating after 1830.

Jewelry items were treasured and handed down as heirlooms from generation to generation. In the United States, antique jewelry is any jewelry at least 100 years old, a definition linked to U.S. Customs law. Pieces that do not meet the antique criteria but are at least 25 years old are called "period" or "heirloom/estate" jewelry.

The names of historical periods are commonly used when describing jewelry. The following list indicates the approximate dates for each era.

Georgian	1714-1830
Victorian	1837-1901
Edwardian	1890-1920
Arts and Crafts	1890-1920
Art Nouveau	1895-1910
Art Deco	1920-1935
Retro Modern	1935-1945
Post-War Modern	1945-1965

References: Lillian Baker, *Art Nouveau & Art Deco Jewelry,* Collector Books, 1981, 1994 value update; ——, *100 Years of Collectible Jewelry,* 1850-1950, Collector Books, 1978, 1997 value update; Howard L. Bell, Jr., *Cuff Jewelry,* published by author (P.O. Box 11695, Raytown, MO 64138), 1994; C. Jeanenne Bell, *Answers to Questions about Old Jewelry,* 4th ed., Books Americana, 1996; ——, *Collector's Encyclopedia of Hairwork Jewelry: Identification and Values,* Collector Books, 1998; David Bennett and Daniela Mascetti, *Understanding Jewellery,* Antique Collectors' Club, 1999; France Borel, *Splendor of Ethnic Jewelry,* Harry N. Abrams, 1994; Shirley Bury, *Jewellery 1789-1910,* Vols. I and II, Antique Collectors' Club, 1991; Deanna Farneti Cera, *Costume Jewellery,* Antique Collectors' Club, 1999; —— *The Jewels of Miriam Haskell,* Antique Collectors' Club, 1999; Monica Lynn Clements and Patricia Rosser Clements, *Cameos: A Pocket Guide,* Schiffer Publishing, 1999; Franco Cologni and Eric Nussbaum, *Platinum By Cartier, Triumphs of the Jewelers' Art,* Harry N. Abrams, 1996; Genevieve Cummins and Neryvalle Taunton, *Chatelaines,* Antique Collector's Club, 1994.

Lydia Darbyshire and Janet Swarbrick (eds). *Jewelry, The Decorative Arts Library,* Chartwell Books, 1996; Ginny Redington Dawes and Corinne Davidov, *Victorian Jewelry,* Abbeville Press, 1991; Ulysses Grant Dietz, Janet Zapata et. al., *The Glitter & the Gold, Fashioning America's Jewelry,* The Newark Museum, 1997; Janet Drucker, *Georg Jensen, A Tradition of Splendid Silver,* Schiffer Publishing, 1997; Alastair Duncan, *Paris Salons 1895–1914,* Jewelry, 2 vols., Antique Collectors' Club, 1994; Martin Eidelberg, (ed.), *Messengers of Modernism, American Studio Jewelry 1940-1960,* Flammarion, 1996; Lodovica Rizzoli Eleuteri, *Twentieth-Century Jewelry,* Electa, Abbeville, 1994; Martha Gandy Fales, *Jewelry in America 1600-1900,* Antique Collectors' Club, 1999; Fritz Falk, *Lalique and His Circle,* Arnoldsche, distributed by Antique Collectors' Club, 1999; Charlotte Gere and Geoffrey Munn, *Pre-Raphaelite to Arts & Crafts Jewelry,* Antique Collectors' Club, 1999; Stephen Giles, *Jewelry, Miller's Antiques Checklist,* Reed International Books Ltd., 1997; Geza von Habsburg, *Fabergé in America,* Thomas and Hudson, 1996; S. Sylvia Henzel, *Collectible Costume Jewelry,* Third Edition, Krause Publications, 1997; Helmet Kahlert, Richard Mühe, Gisbert L. Brunner, *Wristwatches: History Of A Century's Development,* Schiffer Publishing, 1999; George Frederick Kunz and Charles Hugh Stevenson, *Book of the Pearl,* Dover Publications, 1973; David Lancaster, *Art Nouveau Jewelry,* Christie's Collectibles, Bulfinch Press, Little Brown and Co., 1996.

Daniel Mascetti and Amanda Triossi, *Bulgari,* Abbeville Press, 1996; Daniel Mascetti and Amanda Triossi, *The Necklace, From Antiquity to the Present,* Harry N. Abrams, Inc., 1997; Antionette Matlins, *The Pearl Book,* GemStone Press, 1996; Patrick Mauries, *Jewelry by Chanel,* Bulfinch Press, 1993; Anna M. Miller, *Cameos Old and New,* Van Nostrand Reinhold, 1991; ——, *Illustrated Guide to Jewelry Appraising: Antique Period & Modern,* Chapman & Hall, 1990; Penny C. Morrill, *Silver Masters of Mexico,* Schiffer Publishing, 1996; Penny Chittim Morrill and Carol A. Beck, *Mexican Silver: 20th Century Handwrought Jewelry and Metalwork,* Schiffer Publishing, 1994; Gabriel Mourey et al., *Art Nouveau Jewellery & Fans,* Dover Publications, n.d.; Karima Parry, *Bakelite Bangles, Price & Identification Guide,* Krause Publications, 1999; Clare Phillips, *Jewelry, From Antiquity to the Present,* Thames and Hudson, 1996; Michael Poynder, *Jewelry, Reference & Price Guide,* Antique Collectors' Club, 1999; ——, *Price Guide to Jewel-*

lery 3000 B.C.-1950 A.D., Antique Collectors' Club, 1990 reprint; Penny Proddow and Marion Fasel, *Diamonds, A Century of Spectacular Jewels,* Harry N. Abrams, 1996; Penny Proddow, Debra Healy, and Marion Fasel, *Hollywood Jewels,* Harry L. Abrams, 1992; Dorothy T. Rainwater, *American Jewelry Manufacturers,* Schiffer Publishing, 1988; Christie Romero, *Warman's Jewelry,* 2nd ed., Krause Publications, 1998; Judy Rudoe, *Cartier 1900-1939,* Harry N. Abrams, 1997; Nancy N. Schiffer, *Silver Jewelry Designs,* Schiffer Publishing, 1996; —, *The Best of Costume Jewelry,* 3rd ed., Schiffer Publishing, 1999; Sheryl Gross Shatz, *What's It Made Of? A Jewelry Materials Identification Guide,* 3rd ed., published by author (10931 Hunting Horn Dr., Santa Ana, CA 92705), 1991; Doris J. Snell, *Antique Jewelry with Prices, Second Edition,* Krause Publications, 1997; Ralph Turner, *Jewelry in Europe and America, New Times, New Thinking,* Thames and Hudson, 1995; Fred Ward, Opals, Gem Book Publishers, 1997; Janet Zapata, *Jewelry and Enamels of Louis Comfort Tiffany,* Harry N. Abrams, 1993.

Periodicals: *Auction Market Resource for Gems & Jewelry,* P.O. Box 7683, Rego Park, NY 11374; *Gems & Gemology,* Gemological Institute of America, 5355 Armada Drive, Carlsbad, CA 92008; *The Estate Jeweler,* Estate Jewelers Association of America, 209 Post St., Suite 718, San Francisco, CA 94108; *Professional Jeweler,* Bond Communications, 1500 Walnut St., Suite 1200, Philadelphia, PA 19102.

Collectors' Clubs: American Hatpin Society, 2101 Via Aguila, San Clemente, CA 92672; American Society of Jewelry Historians, Box 103, 133A North Avenue, New Rochelle, NY 10804; Leaping Frog Antique Jewelry and Collectable Club, 4841 Martin Luther Blvd., Sacramento, CA 95820; National Antique Comb Collectors Club, 3748 Sunray Rd., Holiday, Fl 34691; National Cuff Link Society, P.O. Box 346, Prospect Heights, IL 60070; Society of Antique & Estate Jewelry, Ltd., 570 7th Ave., Suite 1900, New York, NY 10018.

Videotapes: C. Jeanne Bell, *Antique and Collectible Jewelry Video Series, Vol. I: Victorian Jewelry, Circa 1837-1901, vol. II: Edwardian, Art Nouveau & Art Deco Jewelry, Circa 1887–1930's,* Antique Images; Leigh Leshner and Christie Romero, *Hidden Treasures,* Venture Entertainment (P.O. Box 55113, Sherman Oaks, CA 91413).

Notes: The value of a piece of old jewelry is derived from several criteria, including craftsmanship, scarcity, and the current value of precious metals and gemstones. Note that antique and period pieces should be set with stones that were cut in the manner in use at the time the piece was made. Antique jewelry is not comparable to contemporary pieces set with modern-cut stones and should not be appraised with the same standards. Nor should old-mine, old-European, or rose-cut stones be replaced with modern brilliant cuts.

The pieces listed here are antique or period and represent fine jewelry (i.e., made from gemstones and/or precious metals). The list contains no new reproduction pieces. Inexpensive and mass-produced costume jewelry is covered in Warman's Americana & Collectibles.

SPECIAL AUCTIONS

Beverly Hills Auctioneers
9454 Wilshire Blvd., Suite 202
Beverly Hills, CA 90212
(310) 278-8115

Butterfield & Butterfield
220 San Bruno Ave.
San Francisco, CA 94103
(415) 861-7500

Christie's
502 Park Ave.
New York, NY 10022
(212) 546-1000

Dunning's Auction Service
755 Church Rd.
Elgin, IL 60123
(847) 741-3483

Phillips Fine Art Auctions
406 E. 79th St.
New York, NY 10021
(212) 570-4830

Skinner, Inc.
The Heritage on the Garden
63 Park Plaza
Boston, MA 02116
(617) 350-5400

Sotheby's
1334 York Ave.
New York, NY 10021
(212) 606-7000

Bar pin
Art Deco, diamond and emerald, centered bead-set round diamond (0.45 cts), flanked by 12 calibre-cut emeralds, 40 smaller diamonds, pierced and millegrained platinum mount, findings for pendant or watch pin, sgd "JW, no. 26563" 3,450.00
Victorian, onyx, gold, and pearl, 5 seed pearls in sq millegrained mounts, suspending shield shaped onyx plaque centered by circlet of seed pearls, black enamel accents, 14K yg, hallmark for S. B. Champlin Co., Providence, RI 460.00

Bracelet
Art Deco
Diamond, geometric design, center marquise-cut diamond (0.50 cts), surrounded by hinged plaques set with round diamonds, mesh strap set at intervals with pairs of diamonds (2.50 cts total), accented by buff-top green stones, platinum mount, 6-1/2" l 5,300.00
Diamond and onyx, line, alternating rows of 4 bead-set old European-cut diamonds and faceted sq-cut onyx, 20 diamonds (2.00 cts total), millegrained platinum mount, engraved gallery, hallmark, 7-1/8" l 4,025.00
Jade and enamel, 3 carved jade plaques separated by openwork red and black enamel spacers, 14K yg mounting, hallmark for Cartier, Gough & Co., Newark, inscribed and dated 1932, 7" l, very minor enamel loss 2,415.00
Platinum and diamond, 72 round continuously set diamonds (10.0 cts total), engraved gallery, obliterated French hallmarks 9,200.00

Art Nouveau, bangle, pierced and chased foliate design, 14K yg, 18.4 dwt, 7-1/2" l 1,035.00

Arts & Crafts, cuff, sterling silver and amethyst, 3 bezel set faceted round amethysts, pierced geometric design, hand hammered finish, sgd "Kalo" 920.00

Edwardian, gold, lion's head, holding diamond in mouth, red stone eyes, oval and baton links, 10K yg, 7-1/2" l, 7.8 dwt 400.00

Post-War Modern

Castillos, Los, Taxco, Mexico, 8 half dome rect segments, each segment composed of 3 horizontal bands relief dec with braided line and bead dec, pin clasp, imp marks, 2-1/4" d 175.00

Jensen, Georg, sterling silver, cuff style, etched linear outline, mkd "Georg Jensen" in oval, "Sterling Denmark 85 A," 6-5/8" l.. 520.00

Retro, flexible 14K yg, brickwork style mesh, pave diamond clasp, 0.55 cts, channel-set calibre-cut ruby accents, 2.50 total ruby wt, 1940s .. 2,415.00

Victorian

Bangle, center oval bezel set white agate, accented by round cut Persian turquoise in floral motif, scroll and engraved work on bangle, 16K yg 1,750.00

Bangle, hinged, black enamel tracery, inscribed "Lillie from Gus/dec 25th '82," pr, hinge broken on one 635.00

Bangle, hinged, gold and Pietra Dura, oval hardstone plaque inlaid with bouquet of flowers, flanked by gold leaves, 10K rose gold mount 575.00

Buckle, gold mesh, woven links dec with tiny beading, applied wiretwist and beading to buckle clasp, suspending beaded tassel fringe, 14K yg, adjustable, 40.6 dwt 1,265.00

Cameo, gold and coral, prong set in octagonal frame flanked by tapered rectangles, foliage engraved details, fancy link bracelet, monogrammed clasp, safety chain, 6-1/2" l 700.00

Mesh, 14K yg and pearl central ovoid plaque set with 4 seed pearls, suspending foxtail tassels, adjustable, black enamel detailing, adjustable to 8" l, pr 1,100.00

Brooch/Pin

Art Deco

Diamond and emerald, openwork geometric design, old mine-cut and rose-cut diamonds, 8 bezel-set emeralds, platinum and white gold mount, French hallmarks, gold solder 3,450.00

Diamond and sapphire, bow, centered collet-set old European-cut diamond (0.35 cts,) surrounded by smaller bead-set old European-cut diamonds, edged with channel-set calibre-cut sapphires, silver mount, gold pin stem, European hallmarks 2,415.00

Star sapphire and demantoid, 7 star sapphires, accented by green garnets, top hinged section in trefoil design, suspending sq plaque with locket compartment, 3 flexibly-set drops, black

Brooch, Victorian, cameo, Persaphone motif, oval gold frame, artist sgd, $2,000.

enamel and gold beading, verso engraved, stippled 14K yg mount, sgd "M & Co." for Marcus & Co. 3,795.00

Star sapphire and diamond, bezel-set star sapphire (19.47 x 17.40 x 13.02 mm) framed in old European-cut diamonds (2.97 cts total), platinum mounts, sgd "M & Co" for Marcus & Co. .. 9,200.00

Art Nouveau

Crane, set with rose-cut diamonds, silver and gold mounting, wings etched orange and yellow stones, minor lead solder 2,415.00

Veiled head of woman wearing plumed hat, attributed to Unger Bros., Newark, NJ, sterling, imp "Sterling Top," 2-3/8" l 920.00

Arts & Crafts

Calla Lily Blossom, SS, stamped "Sterling," 2-3/4" x 1-1/2" .. 290.00

Carved jade center flanked by 2 pear-shaped jades, highlighted by prong-set round rubies, emeralds, and seed pearls, mounted in silver, gilt scroll and bead accents, attributed to Dorrie Nossiter. 750.00

Danish, SS and garnet, figural fish and spray of water, hammered finish on body, cabochon garnet in collet setting, imp "Sterling Denmark 10 925 GJ," 1-1/4" d 435.00

Diamond Shape, SS, pansy blossom and leaves, stamped "Sterling," 2-7/8" x 1-7/8" 250.00

Floral Spray, prong-set, various colored gems, lilac, yellow, pink, and green, sapphires, kunzite, emerald, and amethyst, seed pearl accents, gilt silver mount, Dorrie Nossiter 2,760.00

Gold and lapis, oval bezel set lapis, 18K yg, ropetwist frame with scrollwork, floral and beaded accents, 14K clasp 320.00

Edwardian

Diamond, stylized heart, central floral motif, openwork design flanked by scrolls, bead-set rose-cut diamonds, collet-set old European-cut diamonds, platinum topped gold mount, approx 75 diamonds 1,150.00

Diamond and pearl, circle, pierced and millegrained design of flower basket, rose-cut diamonds, seed pearl accents, retractable bail, platinum mount, gold pin stem sgd "Tiffany & Co." .. 1,495.00

Diamond and pearl, old mine and rose-cut diamonds (4.27 cts), platinum topped gold mount, lead solder event 3,750.00

Gold and diamond, pavé-set old mine-cut diamonds, suspending collet-set diamond drop, knife-edge bar, mounted in 18K white gold, French hallmarks, clasp replaced 2,415.00

Post-War Modern, Georg Jensen, SS

Bird within wreath, imp "Georg Jensen" in beaded oval, "Sterling Denmark 123," 1-3/4" d 325.00

Oval form, leaf and bead dec, imp "Georg Jensen" in beaded oval, "Sterling Denmark 101," 1-3/4" d 320.00

Rect, flowers and leaves, mkd with stamped dots in oval surrounding "Georg Jensen, Sterling, Denmark 66," 1-3/4" d 350.00

Retro Modern

Gold and diamond, 14K yg bow interlaced with ribbon of rose-cut diamonds set in white gold, repair to top 635.00

Gold and diamond, large pink gold bow, center diamond and sapphire accent, set in platinum, sgd "Tiffany & Co.," hallmark for Eckfeldt & Ackley, Newark 2,300.00

Gold and garnet, openwork quatrefoil design, 8 bezel set sq-cut garnets, 14K yg, black inscribed and dated Jan 3, 1942, sgd "Tiffany & Co" 1,380.00

Large central oval green stone flanked by 2 small round green stones, silver plated setting dec with stylized branches, unmarked, 1-1/2" x 1-1/8" 250.00

Victorian

Gold and garnet, top set with oval foil backed garnet, suspending pear-shaped garnet drop, Rococo Revival frames, 18K yg 575.00

Gold and topaz memorial, centered by oval topaz (11.65 x 9.76 mm), Rococo Revival frame, 14K yg, reverse locket compartment.. 260.00

Micromosaic, oval floral mosaic, some relief flowers, 18K yg frame, vine tendrils and scrollwork, verso locket compartment .. 1,725.00

Victorian, Etruscan Revival, central faceted foil backed purple stone, gold filled mount, ropetwist accents 300.00

Cameo (Brooch)

Classical Revival, shell, two warrior profiles with putto, 14K yg oval frame with wiretwist detail, minor hairlines to shell 550.00

Edwardian, agate, woman in Elizabethian dress, framed in seed pearls, 4 round diamond accents, millegrained platinum and 14K gold mount, 0.20 cts, hallmark for D. de W. Brokaw, NY....... 1,035.00

Victorian

Agate, depicting Jerome Augustus Bacon, Bedford, MA, owner of Bacon Paper Co., framed with 26 faux pearls, mounted in 18K yg, cameo sgd "Bernard Bonet/NY, 1868," pearls replaced, lead solder to clasp 500.00

Gold and shell, high-relief carved female profile, grapes entwined with leaf motif, 18K yg rope-turned and beaded frame, hairlines, shell loose 1,100.00

Gold, pearl, and onyx, female bust framed in split pearls, inscribed and dated 1866, 14K yg, clasp replaced 1,380.00

Chain

Art Nouveau

Gold, 18K yg fancy links, 14K swivel hook, 58" l, 46.5 dwt 1,725.00

Silver plated, double sided circular plaques depicting female profile, 42-1/2" l.. 460.00

Edwardian, 14K yg, rounded box-link, swivel hook, 25" l............ 200.00

Victorian

14K yg, reeded fancy links, each surmounted by stylized flower, 19" l, 27.1 dwt 750.00

Rose Gold, alternating reeded and round links, 10K rose gold, 14K yg clasp, 42-1/2" l, 66.2 dwt.. 700.00

Cigarette Case, Art Deco, 3-5/8" l, 3-1/8" w, 14K gold, rect, rounded corners, engine-turned patterning, monogrammed lid, engraved int. with presentation inscription dated 1926, R. Blackington & Co., early 20th C 575.00

Cloak Pin, Edwardian, ruby and diamond, sword, hilt set with old mine-cut diamonds, ruby accents, pearl terminals, 14K yg mount, 6" l........ 750.00

Cuff Buttons, pr, Victorian, gold, bird and nest in circle frame, sq plaque with beaded accents, bicolor 14K gold, 7.5 dwt 635.00

Cufflinks, pr

Art Deco, sapphire and diamond, disc set with 5 fancy-cut sapphires, cross motif of bead-set round diamonds, numbered, 2 links converted to earrings with removable diamond studs (0.33 cts each), one link converted to ring, sgd "C. B. Stark," other single vest button (missing 2 stones) 1,495.00

Art Nouveau, 14K yg, oval, hand chased engraved floral motif borders, approx 7.20 dwt... 230.00

Post-War Modern, Georg Jensen, SS, inverted dome form, "Georg Jensen" in beaded oval, "Sterling Denmark 74A," 1" d 245.00

Dress Clip, SS, lily pad form, silver beads, wire work, imp "Mary Gage Sterling," 1-3/4" d 290.00

Earrings, Pr

Arts & Crafts, cluster design, prong-set amethysts and blue zircons, each suspending 5 cultured pearl drops, gilt silver mounts, clip backs, Dorrie Nossiter.. 1,265.00

Edwardian, diamond, cascade of flexibly-set crescents set with old European-cut diamonds (3.15 cts), millegraining, platinum mounts, later yg plating, 1-1/4" l... 3,910.00

Post-War Modern, Georg Jensen, Denmark, SS

Round convex form centered by channel that flares at each end, imp "Georg Jensen" in beaded oval, "Sterling Denmark 270," 1" d 290.00

Screw back, open petal and bead design, imp "Georg Jensen" in beaded oval, "Sterling Denmark 106," 7/8" x 3/4" 230.00

Victorian

Gold and coral, 14K yg ball top suspending faceted coral drop, 18K gold foliate cap, gold bead terminal, dent on gold ball........ 290.00

Gold, circular tops suspending shield shape, tasseled drops, black enamel tracery, 14K yg, 2-3/4" l, minor enamel loss, lead solder to fittings 825.00

Victorian, Etruscan Revival

Lapis, bezel set round lapis, surrounded by applied wiretwist and beaded accents, 18K yg mounts 800.00

Micromosaic, angel set into oval malachite plaque, 18K yg floral frame, cracks to malachite, losses to one mosaic, repairs . 865.00

Lavaliere, Arts & Crafts, rect, center cushion cut synthetic sapphire, suspending pear shaped drop with rect synthetic sapphire, openwork foliate frames, 14K yg, ropetwist chain, 15" l 300.00

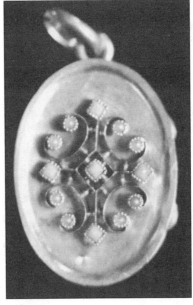

Locket, Victorian, 18K gold, pearl and turquoise center, $850.

Locket

Art Nouveau, gold and diamond heart shape, repoussé lid with female bust, 4 old European-cut diamond accents, 10K yg................. 460.00

Victorian, gold, shield shape

Beaded accents, hinged top, applied wiretwist, 14K yg, minor dents 330.00

Center 3 seed pearls, ropetwist and bead detailing throughout, reverse with hinged locket compartment 350.00

Seed pearl, blue stone accents, applied wiretwist, initialed locket compartment on reverse, 14K yg...................................... 520.00

Necklace

Art Deco, jade, diamond, and onyx, pendant centered by carved rect jade plaque in geometric frame, bead-set round diamonds and onyx, suspended from chain with fancy engraved links, platinum topped gold, 17-1/2" l, one small onyx missing 2,415.00

Art Nouveau, freshwater pearl and gold, 14K yg trace links, swivel hook, 56" l 500.00

Edwardian

Festoon, 11 strands of 14K yg 2.75 mm beads, rigid gold bead spacers, 14" l, 41.5 dwt, 4 beads replaced 1,725.00

Festoon, floral center highlighted by seed pearls, bezel set garnet and glass doublets, 10K yg, 15-1/2" l 400.00

Foliate swag, bead-set seed pearls, 6 collet-set round amethysts, 18K gold mount, English gold mark, 15-3/4" l, orig box... 2,300.00

Fringe, gold and seed pearls, trace-link chain suspending 72 graduated strands of pearl and gold links ranging from 4-3/4", 18K yg, 13-1/2" l 1,610.00

Natural pearls, graduated strand of 83 pearls, ranging from 6.60 to 4.85mm, modified octagonal clasp centered by bezel set marquise-cut diamond (0.25 cts) surrounded by smaller round diamonds, pierced and millegrained platinum mount, 17" l, accompanied with GIA Report stating natural pearls....... 3,450.00

Victorian

Gold and garnet, memorial, woven gilt chain, suspending 3 foil-backed oval cabochon garnet drops in 18K yg foliate frames, center drop accented with pale blue enamel, reverse locket compartment containing intricate hairwork 700.00

Gold and hardstone, central oval blue chalcedony in ropetwist frame, reeded curves, freshwater pearl accents, suspending 3 pear shaped stones, fine curb link chain with 4 oval chalcedony spacers, 14K yg chain, 19-1/2" l 650.00

Gold and turquoise, snake, interlocking gold petal links, shake's head terminal encrusted with turquoise, pearls and green stone eyes, old mine cut-diamond in mouth, 14K yg, 15" l, lead solder to diamond mount 1,265.00

Gold chain and pendant, fancy link chain suspending shield-shaped pendant, seed pearl accents, bicolor gold acorn and oak tree motifs, tasseled drops, 14K yg, 16" l, 24.0 dwt............ 920.00

Onyx, shield shaped pendant surmounted by foliate design in seed pearls, black enamel bail, suspended from onyx link chain with pearl accents, 14K yg mount, 24" l 920.00

Pendant

Art Deco, jade and diamond

Carved and pierced floral design, accented with collet-set diamonds, surmounted by diamond-set cap, cabochon sapphire accent, suspended from rose-cut diamond bail and black cork with rose-cut diamond terminals, pendant sgd "Cartier, New York," clasp sgd "Cartier," obliterated numbers, 7" l......... 8,100.00

Center pierced and carved jadeite gourd pendant, surrounded by oval platinum frame set with round diamonds, channel-set faceted onyx, diamond-set bail and slide, suspended from black cord, boxed, 19" l 5,465.00

Art Moderne, style of Fouquet, geometric sections, faceted citrine, carved aquamarine, black glass baguettes, accented with roundels, suspending large reeded amazonite sphere, SS mount, black cord, 16-1/2" l, one citrine loose... 1,265.00

Edwardian, pearl and diamond, four leaf clover and stem, pavé-set with seed pearls, centered by old European-cut diamond (0.25 cts), 14K yg mount, retractable bail 400.00

Victorian

Flower, each petal and leaf set with round cut pieces of Persian turquoise, accented by 4 natural pearls, center with 1 European cut diamond, 10K yg setting 1,200.00

Flower, gold, diamond, and pearl, flower-form cluster of 17 prong and collet-set old-European diamonds (1.08 cts), 18K yg .. 800.00

Victorian, Etruscan Revival, centered carnelian scarab seal, swivel setting, ropetwist and beaded accents, 18K yg mount, 14K clasp, boxed, repair to bezel, c1880.. 1,150.00

Ring

Art Deco

Blister pearl and diamond, 11.00 mm pearl, shoulders bead-set with 4 round diamonds (0.16 cts), engraved platinum mount, sgd "Relais," crack to shank 520.00

Cat's eye and diamond, center cabochon cat's eye chrysoberyl (10.25 x 9.51 x 7.75 mm), single-cut diamonds mounted in scalloped border, platinum setting, obliterated hallmark, surface abrasions to chrysoberyl 1,850.00

Coral, enamel, and diamond, center sugarloaf coral within black enamel bezel, foliate motif diamond shoulders (0.20 cts), platinum mounting, 18K yg, enamel loss, coral reglued......... 2,760.00

Diamond, 1 round cut 1.00 carat diamond, accented by 12 round cut diamonds, 6 channel set sq cut blue sapphires, 2 trillion cut blue sapphires, platinum setting 4,200.00

Diamond, 3 old mine-cut diamonds (1.15, 1.18 and 1.19 cts), oval pavé diamond setting, diamond set shoulders, pierced gallery, platinum mount, Jung & Klitz, NY, hallmark 9,775.00

Ring, 18K rose gold, emerald cut natural blue topaz, prong set, flanked by two flowerheads with synthetic rubies centers, splint shank, c1940, $750.

Diamond, solitaire, center prong-set old European-cut diamond (1.00 cts), pierced and engraved platinum mount set with round diamonds, millegraining, inscribed, dated 1928, Shreve, Crump & Low box 2,760.00

Diamond, solitaire, old European-cut diamond (1.65 cts), shoulders set with French-cut diamonds, pierced and engraved gallery, platinum mount, inscribed, dated 1926.............................. 6,900.00

Diamond and sapphire, pierced and millegrained plaque design set with old European-cut diamonds, triangular-cut sapphires, channel-set sq-cut sapphires, platinum mount, orig box 1,150.00

Diamond, emerald, and sapphire, octagonal, centered bezel-set old European-cut diamond (1.15 cts), surrounded by 14 smaller round diamonds, bordered by alternating calibre-cut emeralds and sapphires, millegrained platinum mount, French hallmarks..... 6,325.00

Platinum and diamond, center bezel-set old European cut (1.16 cts), flanked by diamond baguettes, surrounded by 18 round diamonds (0.57 cts) 2,650.00

Platinum and diamond, geometric design, old European cut and full cut diamonds, 1.35 cts 980.00

Platinum and diamond, geometric design, old European cut and single-cut diamonds, 0.80 cts 700.00

Platinum and diamond, oval millegrained mount pierced with stylized flowers, center round collet-set diamond, flanked above and below with prong-set round diamonds in sq settings, set allover with small prong-set round diamonds, 1.67 cts 1,100.00

Star sapphire, 17.00 x 12.60 x 10.55 mm sapphire, shoulders each set with baguette-cut diamond and bead-set round diamonds, platinum mount, hallmark... 1,220.00

Art Nouveau

Bacchus intaglio, bezel set yellow-brown stone, bust of Roman god of wine, hand chased design of grapevines, 18K yg, sgd "F.W.L.," minor chips to intaglio, split shank 750.00

Snake, gold and diamond, 2 snakes entwined in sinuous loops, heads each with rose-cut diamond, 18K white and yellow gold mount, French hallmark 300.00

Arts & Crafts, diamond and sapphire, center bezel set old European-cut diamond (1.15 cts), surrounded by 12 round sapphires, pierced foliate design within oval frame, foliate shoulders and gold bead accents, 14kt yellow gold, attributed to Edward Oakes......... 2,645.00

Retro Modern, gold, cat's eye, and diamond, bypass style, clipped flared edges, 3 central prong-set round chrysoberyls, offset with 4 small brilliant-cut prong-set diamonds, stones accented with central ropetwist detailing, 14K yg, 0.20cts.. 700.00

Victorian, gold and diamond, center old mine-cut diamond in crimped collet setting, surrounded by 12 old mine-cut diamonds, silver topped 18K yg mount 635.00

Seal Fob, Victorian, spherical, foliage engraving, beaded band, hinged base with bloodstone intaglio seal swivel, 14K yg 400.00

Slide Chain, Victorian, 18K yg trace link chain, 14K gold engraved ovoid slide, suspending gold filled charm of lady's high button shoe, 29-3/4" l, 17.4 dwt, dents to chain 425.00

Suite

Classical Revival, agate cameo, brooch, matching earrings, female figures, gold scrollwork and seed pearl drops, brooch with rose cut diamonds, set in silver, 18K yg mount 2,415.00

Edwardian, brooch, matching bracelet, light blue enamel flowers, diamond accent, Krementz hallmark, curb-line bracelet with pale pink and blue enamel flowers, heart padlock closure, 14K yg, 6" l, clasp missing on bracelet 490.00

Victorian

Bar Pin, bracelet, 14K yg, quatrefoil gold knot centered by prong-set round diamond, pale pink and blue enamel flowers, 7-1/4" l foliate half-moon links bracelet, minor enamel loss 920.00

Brooch, matching earrings, gold, grapevine, 14K yg repousse leaves, seed pearl accents, repairs 550.00

Brooch, matching earrings, gold, shield shape, surmounted by silver doves and leaves with nest, blue stone, and pearl accents, suspending 3 teardrops, matching earrings with 10K tricolor gold mounts 700.00

Vinaigrette, Victorian, gold, both sides with Asian landscape with sailboat, diamond accent, applied beaded detail in multicolor 14kg gold, minor discoloration to beading 865.00

Watch Chain, Victorian
    Curb-link chain, slide, 14K yg, hallmark for Allard & Finkel, NY, 20-1/2" l, 16.3 dwt 370.00
    Reeded tubular fancy link chain, suspending oval locket centered by small round diamond, ribbed slide, 18K rose gold, European hallmark, 20" l, 33.7 dwt... 920.00

Watch, Pendant, Art Deco, L. & S. L. Nerny, Swiss 16 jewel movement, 3 adjustments, pierced and engraved rect case set throughout with round diamonds, triangular blue stone accents, cream colored dial with black Arabic numerals, sterling silver curb-link chain, 20" l......1,265.00

Watch, Ring, Art Deco, Tiffany & Co., platinum and diamond, silvertone dial with black Arabic numerals, 18 jewel movement, sgd "C. H. Meylan," 5 adjustments, diamond set bezel and foliate shoulders, case hallmarked for Dreseaux, size 3-1/2 .... 3,565.00

JUDAICA

History: Throughout history, Jews have expressed themselves artistically in both the religious and secular spheres. Most Jewish art objects were created as part of the concept of Hiddur Mitzva, i.e., adornment of implements used in performing rituals both in the synagogue and home.

For almost 2,000 years, since the destruction of the Jerusalem Temple in 70 a.d., Jews have lived in many lands. The widely differing environments gave traditional Jewish life and art a multifaceted character. Unlike Greek, Byzantine, or Roman art which have definite territorial and historical boundaries, Jewish art is found throughout Europe, the Middle East, North Africa, and other areas.

Ceremonial objects incorporated not only liturgical appurtenances, but also ethnographic artifacts such as amulets and ritual costumes. The style of each ceremonial object responded to the artistic and cultural milieu in which it was created. Although diverse stylistically, ceremonial objects, whether for Sabbath, holidays, or the life cycle, still possess a unity of purpose.

References: Anton Felton, *Jewish Carpets,* Antique Collectors' Club, 1999; Penny Forstner and Lael Bower, *Collecting Religious Artifacts (Christian and Judaic),* Books Americana, 1996; Eric and Myra Outwater, *Judaica,* Schiffer Publishing, 1999.

Collectors' Club: Judaica Collectors Society, P.O. Box 854, Van Nuys, CA 91408.

Museums: B'nai B'rith Klutznick Museum, Washington, DC; H.U.C., Skirball Museum, Los Angeles, CA; Jewish Museum, New York, NY; Yeshiva University Museum, New York, NY; Judah L. Magnes Museum, Berkeley, CA; Judaic Museum, Rockville, MD; Spertus Museum of Judaica, Chicago, IL; Morton B. Weiss Museum of Judaica, Chicago, IL; National Museum of American Jewish History, Philadelphia, PA; Plotkin Judaica Museum of Greater Phoenix, Phoenix, AZ.

Notes: Judaica has been crafted in all media, though silver is the most collectible.

Bible
    English and Hebrew, *The Pentateuch and the Haftaroth Newly Translated, Dr. A. Benisch,* S. Lehrberger & Co., 1904, Rodelheim, gilt stamped red morocco.. 175.00
    German, *Die Heilige Schrift Der Israeliten,* Stuttgart, 1854, numerous illus by Gustav Dore, folio, gilt-stamped cloth, gilt edges, scuffing 230.00
Book
    Fuchs, Eduard, *Die Juden in Der Karikatur,* Albert Langen, 1921, Munich, illus, orig cloth with color pictorial label on front cover 200.00
    Gorion, Ben, *The Wonderful and Most Deplorable History of the Latter times of the Jews,* Adams & Wilder, 1803, leather binding, some foxing 90.00
    Grossinger, Jennie, *The Art of Jewish Cooking,* Random House, 1958, NY, first printing, color pictorial boards, dust jacket, chips 115.00
Buckle, 3-1/4" h, copper, deer among foliage, central clasp formed as tree with perching birds, sgd on reverse "I. Schor" with bird device, traces of gilding, Ilya Schor, NY, c1946 .... 2,990.00
Bust, 10-3/4" h, Nathan the Wise, alabaster and marble, depicting actor Adolph Ritter Von Sonnethal, back sgd "A. Jahn," (Adolph Jahn,) late 19th C, presentation plaque on marble base 600.00
Candleholder for Gathering Chametz, 9" h, silver repousse, candleholder with tray, appropriate Hebrew text, foliage, and scrollwork, Continental 3,105.00
Charity Container, 13" h, metal, modeled as building with coin slot in top, hinged door, manuscript ink on parchment panel, Palestine, early 20th C... 2,875.00
Circumcision Knife, 6-1/2" l, double edge steel blade, silver mounted agate handle, rose quartz finial, Continental, late 18th/early 19th C, fitted case... 980.00
Ephemera
    Charter for Hebrew Ladies' Benevolent Society of K. K. Adat Israel,

SPECIAL AUCTIONS

Phillips Fine Art Auctions
406 E. 79th St.
New York, NY 10021
(212) 570-4830

Skinner, Inc.
The Heritage on the Garden
63 Park Plaza
Boston MA 02116
(978) 350-5429
web site: http://www.skinnerinc.com

Diecut, Salomo's Urteil, copyright Fuld & Co., NY, 3-1/2" w, 3" h, $18.

Cincinnati, Ohio, c1864, printed paper, scene of Rebecca at the Well, listing organization officers, orig frame, minor discoloration, 17-3/4" h 1,725.00

Diary, Hungarian peddler's, c1884-85, recording travels, cloth, 48 pgs, printed text, stamps, handwritten entries, worn 260.00

Invitation, Jews Hospital Charity Ball Invitation, NY, c1858, litho card, admitting named gentleman and ladies, 3" x 4-1/2" 635.00

Etrog Box, 6-1/2" h, German silver and silver gilt, ring finial, domed hinged lid, body with scrolled foliate designs, cast feet, dedicatory inscription on reverse from Cincinnati, 1890 .... 345.00

Etrog Container

5" h, Russian silver and silver-gilt, hinged ribbed fruit form, etrog finial, loop handles, 4 leaf-shaped feet, 1908-17 .... 1,955.00

7" l, olivewood, hinged lid with applied fruit form dec, relevant printed Hebrew text, Palestine, 20th C 290.00

Greggor, Purim Noisemaker

3-3/4" h, litho tin, second quarter 20th C, cylindrical, yellow ground, black dec of relevant characters and text in Hebrew and English, wooden handle 400.00

6-3/4" h, walnut, Continental, late 19th/early 20th C 375.00

Hanukkah Lamp

4-3/4" h, silver, arched back pate with cut-out birds among branches, removable servant light, base with candleholders, domed circular foot, hallmarked, Austrian, early 20th C 635.00

5-3/4" h, cast bronze, slightly arched back plate cast and chased allover with foliage motifs, removable servant light to right side, base with oil font, plain feet, sgd in Hebrew, Palestine, early 20th C 635.00

6-1/2" h, bronze, back plate with stylized foliage and birds, similar sides with candle-arm, base with cast oil fonts, flattened circular feet, Polish, late 18th/early 19th C, old repairs, losses 1,840.00

9-1/2" h, silvered brass, arched back plate with crown, lions holding candelabra, two detachable candleholders, base with removable silvered copper oil holders with lids, mkd "W.M.F.," Warsaw, late 19th C, surface wear, lacking one cover 460.00

11" l, cast bronze, arched reticulated back plate with double headed eagle, crown, and recumbent lions, deer form supports, row of 8 oil fonts, Continental, late 19th/early 20th C, lacking servant lamp, minor losses 350.00

Ketubah, marriage contract, 16-1/4" x 12-3/4", Persian, rect form, text in ink on parchment, surrounded by polychrome birds, foliage, and Star of David devices, 1860s, framed 460.00

Kiddish Cup

2-1/2" h, Russian silver, flared rim, tightly etched floral designs and bands, rampant lion, shield and anchor, inscribed in Hebrew, third quarter 19th C, mkd "84" 400.00

4" h, Bohemian ruby flashed and etched glass, tapered bowl, spreading circular foot, traces of Hebrew gilt inscription, late 19th C 230.00

4" h, German Baroque silver and silver-gilt, cast bold foliate motifs, 3 ball feet, hallmarked, 18th C 1,725.00

5-1/2" h, Italian silver, flared rim, cast body with baroque-style dec, crown, and tablets, spreading circular foot, hallmarked, late 19th/early 20th C 3,220.00

Marriage Belt, silver and niello, inscribed in Hebrew "mazel tov," Near Eastern, late 19th/early 20th C 690.00

Marriage Bowl, 5-1/4" d, silver, silver-gilt, and niello, inscribed with text relating to 7 benedictions of marriage, Buchara, dated "1683," fitted box 4890.00

Matzah Cover, 18" d, embroidered silk, magenta ground with satin Hebrew text and foliage designs, gilt metal thread fringe, Continental, attributed to eastern Europe, 1906 .... 290.00

Medallion, 2-1/2" d, bronze, Second Zionist Conference, depicting allegorical scene of family beholding standing woman crowned with halo of 7 stars, pointing to rising sun, reverse with Hebrew text, sgd lower right "Beer, Paris, 1898," rim stamped "Bronze," orig red leather case 400.00

Megillahy, Esther Scroll

12" h, Bezalel silver and silver filigree, Jerusalem, c1940, crown set with green stones, inscribed in Hebrew "Megillah Esther," applied plaque relating to Purim story, "Bezalel Jerusalem" mkd on thumb piece in Hebrew, hand written ink on parchment scroll.... 7,475.00

17-1/2" h, Near Eastern, late 19th/early 20th C, attributed to Morocco, handwritten ink on calfskin, fruitwood rollers 350.00

Mezuzah, 3-1/2" h, silver, cast foliage and cherubs, later hinged cover with etched motifs of Adam and Eve, Italian, indistinctly mkd .. 980.00

Passover Flatware Set, traveling, German Baroque silver-gilt, knife with steel blade, fork, and spoon, orig fitted leather covered case, Andreas Wickhardt maker, Augsburg, early 18th C 1,955.00

Passover Seder Plate, porcelain, polychrome dec

9-1/4" d, opalescent porcelain, green rim, divided compartments Hebrew gilt lettering, mkd "Karlsbad," early 20th C 490.00

10" d, pale green ground, leaf dec rim, reserves with Hebrew text, foliage center design, Herend, early 20th C 1,725.00

Pocket Watch, 2-1/2" h, silvered metal, white enameled dial with Hebrew characters and coat of arms, silvered bronze case, Continental, early 20th C 1,955.00

Poster, Jewish National Fund, Ben Uri, printed by Graifica, Jerusalem, c1936, text from Isaiah 45:22, mounted to linen 690.00

Purim Plate, 13-1/4" d, oval, shaped edge and handles, polychrome dec, Hebrew text relating to Purium, center painted with figures outside house, Continental, 20th C 1,100.00

Rimonium, Torah Finials, pr

10" h, silver, crown finial above cylindrical open work body hung with bells, narrow tapered base, mkd "12," Continental, late 19th/early 20th C, bell missing.. 3,565.00

12" h, repousse silver, crown finial, 2 floral repousse knops with foliate and animal motifs, deer and bells, plain shaft with Hebrew inscription, hallmarked, Continental, late 19th C, several bells missing.. 800.00

16" h, silver, leaf and berry finial over reeded ball, hexagonal paneled body reticulated with stylized arches and bells, tapered shaft, mkd "Sterling," Italian, some bells missing 800.00

Sabbath Candlesticks, pr

6-3/4" h, silver, candle socket with Hebrew text, each with central band of figures in traditional Jewish costume performing Sabbath and festival rituals, scroll0work and foliage circular domed bases with Hebrew text and cut-work dec, mkd "Ilya Schor" in English and Hebrew with bird device, dated 1953, further dec with stylized floral motifs 27,600.00

8-1/2" h, silver, removable bobeche over baluster shaft, heavily case with flliage, spreading circular base on sq foot, fully marked, Warsaw, first half 19th C.. 2,070.00

13" h, cast bronze, turned form, dished midsection drip pan, domed circular foot, North Africa, early 20th C............................... 460.00

13" h, silver plated, baluster form, emb and chased with lions, Star of David motifs, and foliage, sq bases, B. Nenneberg, Warsaw, c1908 .... 800.00

Sabbath Lamp, 20" h, hanging, brass, ratchet, turned bulbous stem, star-shaped oil font, attached drip pan, German, 19th C 400.00

Shabbat Knife, 5-1/2" l, metal and mother-of-pearl, relevant Hebrew inscription, mkd "Karlsbad,"" early 20th C 290.00

Spice Container

2" h, silver, nutmeg form, hinged nut, opens to reveal grater, unmkd, late 18th/early 19th C.. 175.00

4" h, brass, formed as Rachel's Tomb, applied blessing for spices, door to left side, Palestine, 20th C..................................... 460.00

5" h, silver, bird finial over circular pierced hinged lid, chased foliate motifs, turned stem, spreading circular foot, Continental, late 19th C 800.00

5-1/2" h, silver and silver filigree, tower form, pendant flags over rect body, door and foliate appliqués, curved wire supports jointed by box-form base, Continental, late 19th/early 20th C........ 800.00

6-1/4" h, German silver, tower form, central spire and turrets, cylindrical body with brickwork, windows, and central door, foliage designs throughout, turned support, domed circular foot, early 20th C 1,265.00

10" h, silver, removable lid with foliate finial, circular body with Hebrew inscription, turned stem, spreading circular foot with incised foliate designs, import marks for Netherlands, post 1953 ....1,265.00

11" h, carved ivory, Sabbath candelabra finial above octagonal body, reticulated with foliage, hinged door, dec with lions, birds among branches, grape clusters, temple columns, short cabriole legs, sgd in Hebrew on base, mid 20th C 8,050.00

11-1/2" h, German silver and silver filigree, tower form, pendant flag over tapered spire, stepped filigree box form compartment with flags, tapered support, circular stepped foot, Berlin, mid 19th C 865.00

Tefilin Bag, 8" l, embroidered blue, polychrome foliate designs and Hebrew text, Chinese, late 19th C 230.00

Torah Breast Plate, suspension chain

8" h, brass, curved rect form, engraved names of twelve tribes of Moses, mounted with hardstones, attributed to England, 20th C 460.00

11" h, silver plated, rect form, crown surmounted festival plaque, columns, and tulips, foliate border, pendant bells, unmkd, Continental, 20th C 575.00

14" h, silver, cartouche form, crown flanked by griffins above lions flanking decalogue and festival plates, floral devices, scroll work throughout, edges engraved with Hebrew text, c1870, mkd "J. Z.," Austro-Hungarian, loses, repairs 635.00

Vase, 7" h, Bezalel shell case, etched dec of circle depicting Rachel's tomb, Hebrew text, reverse with Star of David device and tablets, mkd with monogram "R.A.S." in Hebrew, Jersualem, after 1918 ....460.00

Wall Pocket, 23" l, Victorian, scroll-cut walnut, foliage and figures, inscribed "Newspapers," dated in Hebrew 1902, American, losses, restorations 800.00

Yad, Torah Pointer

8" l, silver plated, reeded ball finial, spiral turned support with wire midsection, curved to terminate in hand with pointed index finger, unmkd, Continental, 20th C 980.00

12" l, silver, rampant lion with shield and Star of David, knop, reeded shaft, cuffed sleeve, pointed hand, suspension chain, Bohemianstyle, late 19th/early 20th C, mkd "800," hallmarked 460.00

JUGTOWN POTTERY

History: In 1920, Jacques and Julianna Busbee left their cosmopolitan environs and returned to North Carolina to revive the state's dying pottery-making craft. Jugtown Pottery, a colorful and somewhat off-beat operation, was located in Moore County, miles away from any large city and accessible only "if mud permits."

Ben Owens, a talented young potter, turned the wares. Jacques Busbee did most of the designing and glazing. Julianna handled promotion.

Utilitarian and decorative items were produced. Although many colorful glazes were used, orange predominated. A Chinese blue glaze that ranged from light blue to deep turquoise was a prized glaze reserved for the very finest pieces.

Jacques Busbee died in 1947. Julianna, with the help of Owens, ran the pottery until 1958 when it was closed. After long legal battles, the pottery was reopened in 1960. It now is owned by Country Roads, Inc., a nonprofit organization. The pottery still is operating and using the old mark.

Bowl

8-1/2" d, 5-1/2" h, 3 applied shoulder handles, blue pebbly finish, not marked, chips 55.00

10-1/2" d, 4-1/2" h, ribbed, flaring, Frogskin glaze, circular stamp 350.00

11" d, flared shape, light gray mottled glaze.........................125.00

Cabinet Vase, 4" h, 3" d, Chinese Blue glaze, circular stamp.....750.00

Creamer, 3-1/2" h, intertwined incised lineal design, salt glaze finial, cobalt blue accents on handle and rim, imp "Jugtown Ware"...300.00

Pitcher, 10-1/2" h, redware, pumpkin-orange glaze, imp mark ...325.00

Sugar Bowl, cov, tobacco spit glaze, imp stamp mark................300.00

Vase

5-1/4" h, 4" d, ovoid, Chinese Blue glaze, circular stamp 700.00

14-1/2" h, 6-1/4" d, milk can shape, two medallions emb at shoulder, mottled semi-matte white glaze, stamped "Jugtown Ware," 3 hairlines to rim 1,000.00

KPM

History: The "KPM" mark has been used separately and in conjunction with other symbols by many German porcelain manufacturers, among which are the Königliche Porzellan Manufactur in Meissen, 1720s; Königliche Porzellan Manufactur in Berlin, 1832-1847; and Krister Porzellan Manufactur in Waldenburg, mid-19th century.

Collectors now use the term KPM to refer to the high-quality porcelain produced in the Berlin area in the 18th and 19th centuries.

Cup and Saucer, hunting scene, filigree, 18th C............................65.00
Dish, 9-1/2" l, leaf shape, painted, birds on flowering branch, burgundy border, gilt drapery, blue scepter, lion red KPM and orb mark, c1860 . 270.00
Plaque, enamel dec
    6" x 8", St Jerome, artist sgd "Knoeller Dresden," imp "KPM," giltwood frame 1,265.00
    6" x 9", rect, boy smoking, sgd "O. Liebmann nach E. V. Blass," imp "KPM," giltwood frame 900.00
    6-1/4" x 9", female figure in wooded landscape, standing by tree, imp "KPM," giltwood frame 1,840.00
    7-1/4" x 9-1/2", polychrome printed tavern scene with card players, giltwood frames, c1900, pr.. 550.00
    7-1/2" x 10", rect, figural scene with woman kneeling by small girl holding water ewer, imp "KPM," giltwood frame............... 3,680.00
    10" x 12-1/2", rect, Return from His First Voyage, imp "KPM," giltwood frame 9,200.00
    13" sq, mother holding child, surrounded by red and blue glass border, incised sword mark over "KPM/265/Z".........................300.00
    15-1/2" x 10", Ruth, sgd "Ch. Landell," imp marks, giltwood frame.. 4,890.00
    17-1/2" x 21", exotic East Indian nude woman holding feather fan, multicolored leaded glass border, incised sword mark over "KPM/268/St.," some damage glass border.................................. 470.00
Scent, molded scrolls, multicolored painted bouquets of flowers, gilt trim, gilt metal C-scroll stopper, mkd, mid 19th C..................... 200.00
Urn, cov, cobalt blue and gilt, floral and cherub dec, pr 400.00
Vase, 7" h, shouldered ovoid, molded acanthus and ram's masks, gilt highlights 225.00

Plate, pink band, fruit, pear, and plum dec, worn gold trim, 8-1/4" d, $45.

KAUFFMANN, ANGELICA

History: Marie Angelique Catherine Kauffmann was a Swiss artist who lived from 1741 until 1807. Many artists who hand-decorated porcelain during the 19th century copied her paintings. The majority of the paintings are neoclassical in style.

References: Susan and Al Bagdade, *Warman's English & Continental Pottery & Porcelain*, 3rd edition, Krause Publications, 1998; Wendy Wassying Roworth (ed.), *Angelica Kauffmann*, Reaktion Books, 1993, distributed by University of Washington Press.

Bowl, scenic portrait, gold, jeweled enamel edge, sgd, Limoges.. 90.00
Box, cov, 2-3/4" x 4-1/2", lilac, 2 maidens and child in woods on cov, brass hinges 70.00
Cake Plate, 10" d, ftd, classical scene, 2 maidens and cupid, beehive mark 90.00
Compote, 8" d, classical scene, beehive mark, sgd 85.00
Cup and Saucer, classical scene, heavy gold trim, ftd.................. 90.00
Inkwell, pink luster, classical lady... 80.00
Pitcher, 8-1/2" h, garden scene, ladies, children, and flowers, sgd.. 100.00
Plate, 8" d, cobalt blue border, reticulated rim, classical scene with 2 figures 65.00
Portrait Plate, portrait with cherubs, dark green and cream ground, gold trim, sgd "Carlsbad, Austria, Kaufmann," 4 pc set............ 495.00
Print, 10-3/4" x 9-1/2", set of engravings, Charlotte, Werter Contemplating on Charlotte's Wedding Ring, The Last Interview of Werter and Charlotte, and Charlotte at the Tomb of Werter, identified in margin, framed, some damage, price for 4 pc set......................... 400.00
Tobacco Jar, classical ladies and cupid, green ground, SP top, pipe as finial.. 415.00

Clock, porcelain case, multicolored dec, $125.

Tray, 16-1/2" d, round, classical figures in reserve, sgd, beehive mark 200.00

KEW BLAS

History: Amory and Francis Houghton established the Union Glass Company, Somerville, Massachusetts, in 1851. The company went bankrupt in 1860, but was reorganized. Between 1870 and 1885, the Union Glass Company made pressed glass and blanks for cut glass.

Art-glass production began in 1893 under the direction of William S. Blake and Julian de Cordova. Two styles were introduced: a Venetian style, which consisted of graceful shapes in colored glass, often flecked with gold; and an iridescent glass, called Kew Blas, made in plain and decorated forms. The pieces are similar in design and form to Quezel products but lack the subtlety of Tiffany items.

The company ceased production in 1924.

Museum: Sandwich Glass Museum, Sandwich, MA.

Bowl, 14" d, pulled feather, red ground, sgd 1,400.00
Candlesticks, pr, 8-1/2" h, irid gold, twisted stems 750.00
Compote, 4-1/2" d, 3-1/2" d, gold irid, flared rim, applied pedestal foot with folded edge, inscribed "Kew Blas" on base 460.00
Decanter, 14-1/2" h, 4-3/4" d base, gold irid, ribbed and painted stopper, purple-pink highlights, sgd on base 1,450.00
Finger Bowl and Underplate, 5" d bowl, 6" d, plate, ribbed, scalloped border, metallic luster, gold and platinum highlights 475.00
Pitcher, 4-1/2" h, green pulled feather pattern, deep gold irid int., applied swirl handle, sgd "Kew-Blas" 900.00
Rose Bowl, 4" d, scalloped rim, cased glass sphere, green vertical zipper stripes, orange irid int., inscribed "Kew Blas" on base 690.00
Salt, irid gold 220.00
Tumbler, 4" h, pinched sides, irid gold, sgd 225.00
Vase
   6-1/4" h, cylinder, rolled rim, gold and green swags, pale orange ground, early 20th C, sgd, orig paper label 950.00

Bowl, green dec on cream ground, irid int., pedestal base, sgd, 4-7/8" d, 4-1/4" h, $575.

6-1/2" h, 7" w, bulbous, oyster white ground, deep green hooked and pulled feathering, gold irid feathers, gold irid rim on neck, sgd 1,450.00
12" h, trumpet form, lightly flared, amber body, bulbed applied disk foot, strong irid, int. with stretched gold irid, sgd "Kew Blas" within polished pontil 900.00
Wine Glass, 4-3/4" h, curving stem, irid gold 250.00

KITCHEN COLLECTIBLES

History: The kitchen was the focal point in a family's environment until the 1960s. Many early kitchen utensils were handmade and prized by their owners. Next came a period of utilitarian products made of tin and other metals. When the housewife no longer wished to work in a sterile environment, enamel and plastic products added color, and their unique design served both aesthetic and functional purposes.

The advent of home electricity changed the type and style of kitchen products. Fads affected many items. High technology already has made inroads into the kitchen, and another revolution seems at hand.

References: E. Townsend Artman, *Toasters: 1909-1960*, Schiffer Publishing, 1996; Ronald S. Barlow, *Victorian Houseware*, Windmill Publishing, 1992; Ellen Bercovici, Bobbie Zucker Bryson and Deborah Gillham, *Collectibles for the Kitchen, Bath and Beyond*, Antique Trader Books, 1998; *Collector's Digest Price Guide to Griswold Mfg. Co. 1918 Catalog Reprint*, L-W Book Sales, 1996; *Collectors Guide to Wagner Ware and Other Companies*, L-W Book Sales, 1994; Linda Fields, *Four & Twenty Blackbirds: A Pictorial Identification and Value Guide for Pie Birds*, published by author, 1998, (158 Bagsby Hill Lane, Dover, TN 37058); Gene Florence, *Kitchen Glassware of the Depression Years*, 5th ed., Collector Books, 1999; Linda Campbell Franklin, *300 Years of Housekeeping Collectibles*, Books Americana, 1992; ——, *300 Hundred Years of Kitchen Collectibles*, 4th ed., Krause Publications, 1997; Ambrogio Fumagalli, *Coffee Makers*, Chronicle Books, 1995; Michael J. Goldberg, *Collectible Plastic Kitchenware and Dinnerware*, Schiffer Publishing, 1995; ——, *Groovy Kitchen Designs for Collectors*, Schiffer Publishing, 1996; Helen Greguire, *Collector's Guide to Toasters & Accessories*, Collector Books, 1997; Susan E. Grindberg, *Collector's Guide to Porcelier China*, Collector Books, 1996; Jon B. Haussler, *Griswold Muffin Pans*, Schiffer Publishing, 1997; *Griswold Cast Iron*, L-W Book Sales, 1997; Frances Johnson, *Kitchen Antiques*, Schiffer Publishing, 1996; Jan Lindenberger, *Black Memorabilia for the Kitchen*, 2nd ed., Schiffer Publishing, 1999; ——, *The 50s & 60s Kitchen*, Schiffer Publishing, 1994; ——, *Fun Kitchen Collectibles*, Schiffer Publishing, 1996; Barbara Mauzy, *Bakelite in the Kitchen*, Schiffer Publishing, 1998; ——, *The Complete Book of Kitchen Collecting*, Schiffer Publishing, 1997; Gary Miller and K. M. Mitchell, *Price Guide to Collectible Kitchen Appliances*, Wallace-Homestead, 1991; Jim Moffett, *American Corn Huskers*, Off Beat Books (1345 Poplar Ave., Sunnyvale, CA 94087), 1994; Don and Carol Raycraft, *Wallace-Homestead Price Guide to American Country Antiques*, 16th ed., Krause Publications, 1999; James Rollband, *American Nutcrackers*, Off Beat Books (1345 Poplar

Ave., Sunnyvale, CA 94087), 1996; David G. Smith and Charles Wafford, *Book of Griswold & Wagner*, Schiffer Publishing, 1996; Diane Stoneback, *Kitchen Collectibles*, Wallace-Homestead, 1994; Don Thornton, *Apple Parers*, Off Beat Books, (1345 Poplar Ave., Sunnyvale, CA 94087) 1997; —, *Beat This: The Eggbeater Chronicles*, Off Beat Books, 1994; *Toasters and Small Kitchen Appliances*, L-W Book Sales, 1995; April M. Tvorak, *Fire-King Fever '96*, published by author, 1995.

Periodicals: *Cast Iron Cookware News*, 28 Angela Ave., San Anselmo, CA 94960; *Kettles 'n' Cookware*, P.O. Box B, Perrysburg, NY 14129; *Kitchen Antiques & Collectible News*, 4645 Laurel Ridge Dr., Harrisburg, PA 17110; *Piebirds Unlimited*, 14 Harmony School Rd., Flemington, NJ 08822.

Collectors' Clubs: Cook Book Collectors Club of America, P.O. Box 56, St. James, MO 65559-0056; Cookie Cutter Collectors Club, 1167 Teal Rd, SW, Dellroy, OH 44620; Eggcup Collectors' Corner, 67 Steven Ave., Old Bridge, NJ 08857; Glass Knife Collectors' Club, 4448 Ironwood Ave., Seal Beach, CA 90740; Griswold & Cast Iron Cookware Association, 3007 Plum St., Erie, PA 16508; International Society for Apple Parer Enthusiasts, 17 E. High, Mount Vernon, OH 43050; Jelly Jammers, 6086 W. Boggstown Rd, Bottstown, IN 46110; Kollectors of Old Kitchen Stuff, 501 Market St., Mifflinburg, PA 17844; National Cookie Cutters Collectors Club, 2763 310th St., Cannon Falls, MN 55009; National Reamer Collectors Association, 47 Midline Court, Gaithersburg, MD 20878; Pie Bird Collectors Club, 158 Bagsby Hill Lane, Dover, TN 37058.

Museums: Corning Glass Museum, Corning, NY; Kern County Museum, Bakersfield, CA; Landis Valley Farm Museum, Lancaster, PA.

Additional Listings: Baskets; Brass; Butter Prints; Copper; Fruit Jars; Food Molds; Graniteware; Ironware; Tinware; Woodenware. See *Warman's Americana & Collectibles* for more examples including electrical appliances. See *Warman's Flea Market Treasures* also.

Apple Butter Kettle, copper, flat bottom, iron handles, 40 gallons, 19th C..550.00
Apple Peeler, cast iron, Reading Hardware Co. 90.00
Bill Hook, celluloid cov, Carey Salt Co., 8-1/2" h, 2" w...............100.00
Boiler, cov, oval, copper, turned wood handles...........................145.00
Bowl, 16" d, 6" h, ash burl, fissures in figure, old finish..1,210.00
Butter Churn, 49" h, old blue paint, America, 19th C, minor imperfections..345.00
Butter Paddle, 12-1/4" l, curl and circle end handle, old finish.... 165.00
Catalog
  Armour & Co., Chicago, IL, 32 pgs, 3-1/2" x 8", illus of ham, bacon, etc. 16.00
  Badger Aluminum Ware, Louisville, KY, c1930, 24 pgs, 8-1/2" x 11", kettles, pots, roasters, etc................................24.00
  Decatur Extract Co., Decatur, IL, 64 pgs, 5-3/4" x 8-1/2", "Purity Household Guide,"..18.00
  Lamson & Goodnow Mfg. Co., Shellburne Fall, MA, 19 pgs, 3-1/2" x 6-1/2", 1922, Anchor Brand cutlery......................................24.00
  McDougall & Son., G. P., Indianapolis, IN, 48 pgs, 6-1/2" x 8", 1906, kitchen cabinets 75.00
  Midland Specialties Co., Chicago, IL, 1930, 12 pgs, 8-1/2" x 11", Cat. No. 15, Midland Improved Products, funnels, measures, etc. ...28.00

Apple Slicer, Davis, patented March 13, 1834, $1,200.

  Montgomery Ward & Co., Chicago, IL, 1898, 24 pgs, 10" x 13", Price List No. 430 of Groceries, furnishings, folded in center 21.00
  Sherer-Gillet Co., Chicago, IL, 1928, 4 pgs, 12-1/4" x 18-1/2", Departmentalized Food Store, orig mailing envelope.............9.00
Cheese Sieve, 8" d, 7-1/2" h, wood, stave construction, iron band....25.00
Cherry Stoner, 8-1/2" h, hand crank, mkd "Pat'd Nov 17, 1863"...65.00
Colander, 10-3/4" d, 3" h, copper, punched star design................70.00
Cookie Board
  5" x 7", floral oval wreath with rooster on one side, other with double strawberry, black finish..450.00
  6-3/4" x 11", oak, relief carved man and woman figures, brown patina 275.00
Dipper, 14-1/4" l, brass and wrought iron, polished 175.00

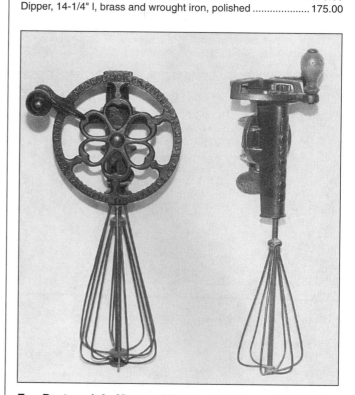

Egg Beaters, left: Monroe Mfg. Co., Fitchburg, MA, $900; right: Monitor Beater, patented by Moses G. Crane, Boston, $1,300.

Dough Box, pine and turned poplar, PA, 19th C, rect removable top, tapering well, splayed ring-turned legs, ball feet, 38" w, 19-1/4" d, 29-1/2" h 425.00

Egg Cup, 2-3/4" h, Lehneware, turned wood, ftd, orig red, green, black, and yellow strawberry dec, salmon pink ground 525.00

Flour Sifter, 14" h, 12" w, Tilden's Universal, wood, partial intact paper label 335.00

Food Chopper, 7" w, wrought iron, scalloped edge blade, turned wood handle 270.00

Fork, 11-3/8" l, wrought iron 60.00

Grain Measure, 11-3/4" d, bentwood, round 65.00

Griddle, cast iron, Griswold, No. 10 .... 70.00

Ice Shaver, nickel plated steel, mkd "Enterprise," July 4, 1893 patent 42.00

Kettle, cast iron, Griswold No. 4 .... 85.00

Kraut Cutter, 19" l, walnut, worn patina, heart cutout in handle ..220.00

Ladle, 15" l, wood, pot hook handle 50.00

Lemon Squeezer, iron, glass insert, mkd "Williams" 50.00

Meat Tenderizer, 9-1/2" l, stoneware, wood handle, mkd "Pat'd Dec 25, 1877" 95.00

Nutmeg Grater, 7" l, Champion, brass and wood 635.00

Pantry Box, cov, 11-1/2" d, 6-1/2" h, oak, bail handle 175.00

Pastry Board, wood, 3 sided 32.00

Potato Masher, 9" l, turned maple 40.00

Raisin Seeder, 5" h, Ezy Raisin Seeder, removable cup, clamp grip, patent date May 21, 1895 .... 125.00

Recipe Booklet

    Best War Time Recipes, Royal Baking Powder Co., NY, 1917, 6 pgs 5.00

    Blue Ribbon Malt Extract, 1951, 20 pgs 6.50

    Carefree Cooking with Frigidaire Electric Range, 1937, General Motors Sales Corp., Dayton, OH 8.00

    Kerr Glass Mfg., Portland, OR, 1909, 20 pgs, 3-1/4" x 8-1/2", Economy Jar Home Recipes 21.00

Recipe File, California Prune Recipe File, 1942, 5" x 3-1/2" envelope with 15 recipe sheets 10.00

Rolling Pin

    15-3/4" l, blown glass, deep amber knopped handles, 19th C....150.00

    22" l, milk glass, cylindrical, turned wood handles, mkd "Imperial Mfg., Co. July 25, 1921" 90.00

    23-1/2" l, curly maple 80.00

Sausage Stuffer, 17-1/2" l, turned wood plunger 30.00

Spatula, 17-3/4" l, brass and wrought iron, polished................... 175.00

Sugar Bucket, 5-3/4" h, 6-1/2" d, stave construction, iron bands, swivel handle, old dark finish, bands pitted, replaced pins 115.00

Sugar Hammer, 8" l, brass and steel, curly maple handle 1,155.00

Taster, 7" l, brass and wrought iron, polished 150.00

Tin

    Dining Car Brand, Norwine Coffee Co., St. Louis, Ground Black Pepper, fancy int. of train's dining car front and back, cardboard sides, 6-5/8" h, 3-3/4" w, 2-1/2" d.. 825.00

    Donovan's Baking Powder, Mt. Morris, NY, 1 lb, paper label, 5-1/4" h, 3" d.. 475.00

    Egg-O Brand Baking Powder, paper label, 2-3/4" h, 1-1/4" d 110.00

    Fairy Queen Marshmallow, Loose-Wiles, 14 x 10 x 8" 90.00

    Fulford Powder, multicolored 25.00

    Kavanaugh's Tea, 1 lb, little girl on porch in dress, talking to doll, mother sipping tea in window, cardboard sides, tin top and bottom, 6" h, 4-1/2" w, 4-1/2" d 500.00

    Maltby's Cocoaut, slip top 40.00

    Miller's Gold Medal Breakfast Cocoa, red and black, c1890, 2" h, 1-5/8" w, 1-1/8" d.. 250.00

    Opal Powdered Sugar, Hewitt & Sons, Des Moines, 8" h, 4-1/2" w, 3-1/4" d 180.00

    Parrot and Monkey Baking Powder, 4 oz, full, 3-1/4" h, 2-1/8" d 375.00

    Sunshine-Oxford Fruit Cake, early 1900s, sq corners............. 20.00

    Three Crow Brand Cream of Tartar, early, #1 .... 45.00

    Towle's Log Cabin Brand Maple Syrup, cabin shaped, woman and girl in doorway, 4" h, 3-3/4" l, 2-1/2" d.................................. 110.00

Trivet, 12" l, lyre form, wrought iron frame and turned handle, brass top, replaced foot, stamped maker's mark 45.00

Vegetable Cutter, 16-1/2" h, cast iron and tin, worn orig black paint with striping, "Enterprise Mfg. Co. Phila., Vegetable Cutter, Pat. June 5, 1888," rust 220.00

Wafer Iron, cast iron, octagonal, church with steeple and trees dec on one side, pinwheel with plants and star flowers on reverse, wrought iron handles.. 400.00

KUTANI

History: Kutani originated in the mid-1600s in the Kaga province of Japan. Kutani comes in a variety of color patterns, one of the most popular being Ao Kutani, a green glaze with colors such as green, yellow, and purple enclosed in a black outline. Export wares made since the 1870s are enameled in a wide variety of colors and styles.

Beaker, 4-1/2" h, hp flowers and birds, red, orange, and gold, white ground, mkd "Ao-Kutani" 95.00

Biscuit Jar, cov, Geisha Girl, c1890 .... 190.00

Bottle, 18" h, raised foot, elongated neck, patterned strips swirling around body, sgd, Japanese, 20th C 575.00

Bowl, 6-3/8" d, gilt and bright enamel design, figural, animal, and floral reserves, kinrande ground, base inscribed "Kutani-sei," set of 10 400.00

Charger, 18-3/8" d, pomegranate tree, chrysanthemums, and 2 birds on int., birds and flowers between scrolling foliate bands, irregular floral and brocade border, 11 character inscription 600.00

Cup, 3-1/4" d, continual design of phoenix surrounded by floral scroll, ruyi lappet borders around int. rim and foot, underglaze blue, iron red, and gilt Fukagawa mark, 19th C 60.00

Dish, 10-1/2" d, central scene, magpies in bamboo forest 275.00

Figure

    12" h, Bodhidhama, standing, long red rope, flywisk in right hand 225.00

    14-1/4" h, Kannon, polychrome and gilt dec, standing, dragon mount, high coiffure, wind-swept rope, inscribed "Kutani-sei"............ 600.00

Garden Set, 19" h, barrel shape, 2 large circular reserves with florals and landscape scenes, spiraling brocade ground, top pierced with circular florets, pr.. 2,100.00

Plate, 8-1/2" d, $45.

Jar, cov, 20-1/2" h, ovoid, fan shaped reserves of warriors, molded ribbon tied tasseled ring handles, shippo-tsunagi ground, multicolored brocade patterned dome lid, pr 1,400.00

Mustard Pot, attached saucer, Nishikide diapering, figural raised gold serves, mkd 125.00

Tea Caddy, 6" h, bulbous, hexagonal, Nishikide diapering, figural raised gold reserves of children, red script mark...................... 165.00

Teapot, cov, bulbous, One Thousand Faces............................. 250.00

Tray, 14" l, polychrome and gilt dec, figural scene, red, orange, and gold border 340.00

Vase

9-3/4" h, ovoid, waisted neck, recessed ring foot, upper portion with enameled reddish-brown wave pattern, underglaze blue wide band of archaistic keyfret design, raised borders, lower section with gilt painted stylized lotus blossoms, green enamel scrolling leafy tendrils, bluish-black ground 395.00

11" h, painted procession of deities, Japanese, late 19th C, mounted as lamp 250.00

LACE and LINENS

History: Lace, lacy linens, embroidery, and hand-decorated textiles are different from any other antique. They are valued both as a handmade substance and as the thing the substance is made into. Thread is manipulated into stitches, stitches are assembled into lace, lace is made into handkerchiefs, edgings, tablecloths, bedspreads. Things eventually go out of style or are damaged or worn, and just as the diamonds and rubies are taken from old jewelry and placed into new settings, fine stitchery of embroidery and lace is saved and reused. Lace from a handkerchief is used to decorate a blouse, fragments of a bridal veil are made into a scarf; shreds of old lace are remounted onto fine net and used again as a veil.

At each stage in the cycle, different people become interested. Some see fragments as bits and pieces of a collage, and seek raw materials for accent pieces. Others use Victorian whites and turn-of-the-century embroidered linens to complement a lifestyle. Collectors value and admire the stitches themselves, and when those stitches are remarkable enough, they will pay hundreds of dollars for fragments a few inches square.

Until the 1940s, lace collecting was a highly respected avocation of the wealthy. The prosperity of the New World was a magnet for insolvent European royalty, who carried suitcases of old Hapsburg, Bourbon, Stuart, and Romanov laces to suites at New York's Waldorf hotel for dealers to select from. Even Napoleon's bed hangings of handmade Alencon lace, designed for Josephine and finished for Marie Louise, found their way here. In 1932, *Fortune* magazine profiled socially prominent collectors and lace dealers. For the entire first half of this century, New York City's Needle and Bobbin Club provided a forum for showing off acquisitions.

Until 1940, upscale department stores offered antique lace and lacy linens. Dealers specializing in antique lace and lacy linens had prominent upscale shops, and offered repair, restoration, remodeling, and cleaning services along with the antique linens. In addition to collecting major pieces—intact jabots from the French Ancient Regime, Napoleonic-era Alencon, huge mid-Victorian lace shawls, Georgian bed hangings appliquéd with 17th-century needle lace—collectors assembled study collections of postcard-size samples of each known style of antique lace.

When styles changed round the 1940s and 1950s and the market for antique lace and linens crashed, some of the best collections did go to museums; others just went into hiding. With renewed interest in a gracious, romantic lifestyle, turn-of-the-century lacy cloths from the linen closets of the barons of the industrial revolution are coming out of hiding. Collectors and wise dealers know that many of the small study-pieces of irreplaceable stitchery—fragments collectors will pay ten to hundreds of dollars for—still emerge in rummage and estate sales.

Very large banquet-sized lace tablecloths, especially those with napkins, continue to be especially popular. Appenzell, a white-on-white embroidered lacework of 19th C Switzerland, has become one of the hottest collector's items. Strong interest continues in patterned silk ribbons, all cotton lace yardage, and other lacy materials for heirloom sewing and fashion.

The market for antique lace definitely is changing. Interest is still rising for elaborate lace for home decorating and entertaining, and interest in fine quality lace collars is increasing. Large lace shawls and veils, especially for bridal wear, continue to be in demand. Internet auctions and chat groups make it possible for a dealer in Wyoming to link up with a collector in Louisiana, and find a home for an interesting piece. Those interested in fine quality lace are realizing they need to start buying at market prices instead of waiting for that lucky find that they alone recognize. Current market prices, although rising, still are usually far below what the pieces would have cost when new, or during the early twentieth century heyday of lace collecting.

As prices rise, buyers more often want an accurate identification: what is it, where was it made, how old is it? What makes it worth the price? Word spreads quickly over the Internet when it is obvious a dealer has mislabeled something, especially labeling something as handmade that is obviously machine. Lace has long been a sideline for most dealers, and they did not bother to learn to identify it. As long as they could turn it over quickly for a small markup, they were satisfied. That is changing. More sophisticated buyers won't put up with that without comment.

The basic techniques are bobbin lace, needle lace, crochet, tatting, knitting, knotting, and needleweaving. Identifying how a piece was made is the easy part, and there is no excuse for a dealer not being able to separate crochet from bobbin lace. Anyone can identify the technique after just a weekend workshop, or by comparing a piece to pictures in a good textbook. The technique, plus the quality of the design, and the condition, provides nearly all the information anyone needs to decide what a piece is worth.

After identifying the technique, many like to apply a name to the style (Duchesse bobbin lace, Point de Gaze needle lace, Irish crochet). This serves as a useful shorthand in talking about lace, but adds nothing to the value of the piece. This is often the confusing part. Unlike most antiques, there is no uniformity in labeling styles of lace. Names changed at different points in time, different names were used for similar products made in different countries, and foreign names often were translated differently. Any dealer should be expected to be able to explain why they chose to use any specific style name.

The Internet offers a unique access to a wide variety of kinds of lace and lacy linens. The small pictures available on the Internet, however, rarely show enough detail to know just what you are buying. Insist on a return policy for any lace purchased sight unseen on the Internet. Even well intentioned dealers may miss details that significantly affect the value of lace. Handmade meshes cannot be positively identified without high powered magnification. Repairs often go unnoticed and unreported. Color and texture make a great deal of difference in determining whether a piece of lace is attractive or not.

Whether purchasing fine quality collector's study samples, or boxes and bags of recyclable fragments for sewing, it is worth taking a close look at all the details. It is not uncommon for good quality study samples that a collector will pay $10 to $100 for in the "rag bags."

Those who learn to recognize the artistry and value of old stitchery will not only enhance their lives with beauty, they may find a windfall.

References: Pat Earnshaw, *Identification of Lace,* Lubrecht and Cramer, 1989; Frances Johnson, *Collecting Antique Linens, Lace, and Needlework,* Wallace-Homestead, 1991; –, *Collecting More Household Linens,* Schiffer Publishing, 1997; Elizabeth Kurella, *Guide To Lace and Linens,* Antique Trader Books, 1998; —, *Secrets of Real Lace,* The Lace Merchant (P.O. Box 222, Plainwell, MI 49080), 1994; —, *Pocket Guide to Valuable Old Lace and Lacy Linens,* The Lace Merchant (P.O. Box 222, Plainwell, MI 49080), 1996; —, *The Complete Guide To Vintage Textiles,* Krause Publications, 1999; Marsha L. Manchester, *Vintage White Linens A to Z,* Schiffer Publishing, 1997; Elizabeth Scofield and Peggy Zalamea, *Twentieth Century Linens and Lace,* Schiffer Publishing, 1997.

Collectors' Club: International Old Lacers, P.O. Box 554, Flanders, NJ 07836, http://members.aol.com/iolinc/ioli.html.

Museums: Chicago Art Institute, Chicago, IL; Cooper Hewitt (Smithsonian), New York, NY; Metropolitan Museum of Art, New York, NY; Museum of Early Southern Decorative Arts (MESDA), Winston-Salem, NC; Museum of Fine Arts, Boston, MA; Rockwood Museum, Wilmington, DE; Shelburne, Museum, Shelburne, VT; Smithsonian Institution, Washington, DC.

Advisor: Elizabeth M. Kurella.

Bedspread

Crochet, double size, filet crochet grid-style design, scrolling leaves design 85.00
Embroidered, double size, white cloth with red "turkey work" embroidery, cartoon character designs, c1930 .... 150.00
Princess Lace (machine tapes appliquéd to machine net) scrolling flower and leaves design 350.00

Bridal Veil

Point De Gaze needle lace in rose and leaf design with scrolls and medallions in 12" edge border on 7' long teardrop shape veil 1,500.00
Princess Lace, 65 x 48" oval, machine net decorated with floral and scroll design 325.00
Bridge Set, linen, embroidered in red and black motifs of playing-card suits, matching napkins 85.00

SPECIAL AUCTIONS

Christies South Kensington
85 Old Brompton Road
London, England SW7 3LD
011-44-171-581-7611

William Doyle Galleries
175 East 87th St.
New York, NY 10128
(212) 427-2730

Phillips
Blenstock House
Blenheim Street
101 New Bond St.
London, England W1Y OAS
011-44-171-629-6602

Collar

Berthe-style, Brussels mixed lace, floral and scroll work of Duchesse bobbin lace with rose inserts of Point de Gauze, many exotic filling stitches of needle lace, 6" deep, 38" l 625.00
Duchesse bobbin lace, c1870, roses, daisies, and scrollwork design, 5" at center back, 32" l 125.00
Point de Grace, 19th C Belgian needle lace, roses with shaded petals and leaves design, pr of 10" l labels, price for pr 75.00

Curtains

Hand-embroidered machine net, c1900, iris, roses, and filigree elaborate designs, 48" x 96", pr 50.00
Machine lace, ecru, 36" x 72" 75.00

Doily

Crochet, roses, raised petals, 8" d round 10.00
Flemish bobbin lace, c1900, goldfish design in Petit de Paris ground, 10" d round, 3" deep lace 75.00
Needle lace, rose design, 6" d round 20.00

Dresser Scarf

Drawnwork, Victorian, white geometric design, 28 x 48" 45.00
White cotton, flower basket embroidered in bright colors, white crochet edging, c1930, 24" x 38" 10.00

Fragments of Collector's Lace

Gros Point de Venise, c1650, stylized scrolling floral design, motifs defined by raised and padded outlines dec with many styles of picots, 2" x 12" 285.00
Point de Neige, c1680, needle lace with minute stylized design and layers of raised picots, 10" x 18" 285.00
Point de Venise, design of cupid with quiver of arrows, medallions, and scrolling flowers, c1900, 12" x 16" 75.00
Point de Venise a Reseau, stylized floral design, Alencon mesh background, no cordonnet, 3" x 6" fragment of edging 185.00

Handkerchief

Linen
   Edged with colored crochet scallop design, 12" sq 2.00
   Edged with half inch of white tatting, 12" sq 6.00
   4" of Irish Youghal needle lace with stylized shamrocks design, background of stitched bars dec with picots, 16" sq 375.00
Whitework, French, 1870s, edged with embroidery, drawnwork, and needle-lace inserts 95.00

Napkin

Cocktail, white, edge with single scallop of needle lace, 1" sq corner inserts of needle lace worked in stylized animal design, price for 6 pc set 45.00
Dinner, linen with needle-lace edging, corner insert, c1900, 24" sq, price for 6 pc set 185.00

Crocheted Picture, woodland scene, children on swing, 29" x 22", $65.

Pillowcase

Cotton, embroidered multicolored flower-basket design, crochet edge, c1930, pr 15.00

Linen, white, figural designs in needle-lace inserts, floral design in needle-lace edging, pr 125.00

Maderia, white cotton, flower silhouetted in cutwork, embroidered with satin stitch, pr 15.00

Pillow Cover, linen, white, dec with inserts of needle lace, scrolling floral designs, embroidered in satin stitch, Cluny bobbin lace edging, 18" d round 125.00

Pincushion, white satin, top cov with sq of white Italian drawn work in heavy linen, embroidered raised flower and tendril design, corners dec with whimsical knotted tassels, 4" sq, 1" deep 65.00

Runner, Normandy work, patchwork of handmade Vaienciennes bobbin lace and other laces, mostly handmade, central motif of French embroidered whitework with birds and flowers, oval, 24" x 18" 145.00

Shawl

Chantilly, flowers, ferns, and scrolls design, 4' x 8' triangle
    Handmade, bobbin lace 385.00
    Machine, black 75.00

Machine-made net cov with bouquets and garlands of Brussels bobbin lace and Point de Gaze needle lace, white, c1865, 4' x 8' triangle 675.00

Tablecloth

Crochet, round medallions design, 48" x 68" 75.00

Cutwork
    Floral and scrollwork satin-stitch embroidery, needle-lace inserts, 8" deep border of filet in figural designs, Italian, c1900, 42" sq 175.00
    Floral designs in satin-stitch embroidery, inserts of needle lace with rose designs, 68" x 140", twelve matching napkins, price for set 975.00

Filet, geometric design darned over knotted network, 48" x 72" 125.00

Linen, natural color, Richelieu, all handmade cutwork and embroidery, floral and scroll motif, early 20th C, 68" x 100" 575.00

Swiss Appenzell whitework, with designs of cherubs, and a lady with a parrot dressed in 18th C costume, 120" x 85", eight napkins, price for set 2,500.00

Yardage

Crochet, white, pinwheel design, 4" deep, per yard 12.00

Ribbons, silk embroidered with floral pattern, 2" wide, still on reel with paper leaf, per yard 10.00

Tatting, white, half inch deep, design of round medallions with picots, per yard 5.00

Valenciennes
    Handmade bobbin lace, strawberries and blossoms design, 4" deep, 4 yards long 850.00
    Machine made, all cotton, floral and scrollwork design, 4" deep, per yard 10.00

LALIQUE

History: René Lalique (1860-1945) first gained prominence as a jewelry designer. Around 1900 he began experimenting with molded-glass brooches and pendants, often embellishing them with semiprecious stones. By 1905, he was devoting himself exclusively to the manufacture of glass articles.

In 1908, Lalique began designing packaging for the French cosmetic houses. He also produced many objects, especially vases, bowls, and figurines, in the Art Nouveau and Art Deco styles. The full scope of Lalique's genius was seen at the 1925 Paris l'Exposition Internationale des Arts Décorative et Industriels Modernes.

Marks: The mark "R. LALIQUE FRANCE" in block letters is found on pressed articles, tableware, vases, paperweights, and automobile mascots. The script signature, with or without "France," is found on hand-blown objects. Occasionally, a design number is included. The word "France" in any form indicates a piece made after 1926.

The post-1945 mark is generally "Lalique France" without the "R," but there are exceptions.

Reference: Fritz Falk, *Lalique and His Circle,* Arnoldsche, distributed by Antique Collectors' Club, 1999.

Periodicals: *Lalique Magazine,* 400 Veterans Blvd., Carlstadt, NJ 07072; T & B, P.O. Box 1555, Plantation, FL 33318.

Collectors' Club: Lalique Collectors Society, 400 Veterans Blvd., Carlstadt, NJ 07072; Lalique Society of America, 400 Veterans Blvd., Carlstadt, NJ 07072.

Reproduction Alert: The Lalique signature has often been forged, the most common fake includes an "R" with the post-1945 mark.

Bar Pin, 2-3/8" l, flowering branch, electric blue, gilt-metal mount, mkd "R. (cross) Lalique," Marcilhac 1354, c1912 .... 460.00

Box, cov
    3-1/8" d, 2" h, Quatre Papillions, 4 butterflies, delicate floral motif on sides, faint molded "Lalique Depose" on base, Marcilhac 14 ..575.00
    4-1/4" d, colorless and frosted 225.00

Bowl
    5-1/4" h, molded with bird and foliate dec, colorless and frosted 300.00
    7" d, Vessels, press-molded, colorless, repeating dec vases of flowers, light brown patina, foliate pattern on base, sgd "R. Lalique, France," Marcilhac 3024, 1921, mold imperfections 115.00
    7-3/4" d, 3-1/8" d, Ondines Refermee, molded opalescent, blue-opal inverted rim, 6 nude mermaids on ext., lower edge engraved block sgd "R. Lalique/France No. 381" 1,870.00
    8-5/8" h, 2-1/8" h, Nonetes, press-molded circular shallow bowl, 3 pairs of opalescent marsh-tits in flight, colorless ground, molded "R. LALIQUE" on base, Marcilhac 398 .... 290.00
    9-3/8" d, Fishes, intaglio fishes spiraling out from center of bubbles, "V. D.A." on int. base, base inscribed "R. Lalique France," Marcilhac 3212, c1931, mold imperfections 400.00
    9-3/4" d, 1-3/4" h, Eglantine, shallow circular press-molded dog-rose flower sprays, blue ground, acid stamped "R. LALIQUE FRANCE" on base, Marcilhac 415, scratch 350.00
    11-1/2" d, shallow, Fishes, intaglio fishes spiraling out from center of bubbles, mold mark "R. Lalique," Marcilhac 3212, c1931, slight int. wear 260.00
    13-3/4" d, scalloped edge, fish and water droplet dec, mkd "Lalique France" 350.00

Clock, 13-1/2" l, 13-1/4" h, two etched figures in frosted and colorless glass, central clock, mounted on rect metal base, bottom light, attributed to Rene Lalique, Marcilhac 726, 1926, slight wear and abrasions to base 6,900.00

Dresser Jar, 3-1/2" h, Epines, sepia patina on colorless molded thorny bramble motif, round bottle, conforming cov, raised "R. Lalique" and "France" on base 350.00

Figure
    3-1/8" h, toad, frosted and polished colorless ground 230.00
    9-1/2" l, 4" h, cat, head forward, frosted colorless, inscribed "Lalique France" 690.00
    10" l, 5-1/2" h, pigeon, press-molded, colorless, script sgd "R. Lalique France" on base, Marcilhac 1204 .... 700.00

Mascot
    4" h, 8" l, star with trail, circular metal base, mounted to rect display platform, mkd "R. Lalique," chip 5,175.00
    5-1/4" h, Chyrsis, frosted, reclining nude, hair outstreched, mkd "R. Lalique France" 4,025.00
    7-3/4" l, greyhound, press-molded ovoid disc, colorless ground, frosted intaglio form of running greyhound, mold mark "R. Lalique France" at lower edge, Marcilhac 1145, c1928 .... 1,725.00

8" l, 8-1/4" h, dragonfly, colorless ground, upright wings, frosted design, sgd in mold, inscribed "R. Lalique France," Marcilhac 1141, c1928, pr, chips 4,945.00

Paperweight

5" l, 2-1/2" h, press-molded sparrow, colorless frosted glass, sgd in script "R. Lalique France" on base, Marcilhac 1166............150.00

5-1/4", Chrysis, woman kneeling, frosted colorless, base inscribed "Lalique France"..375.00

5-1/2" l, 4-1/2" h, eagle head, frosted polished colorless ground...350.00

Pendant, suspended on black silk knotted cord attached black silk tassel

1-1/8" l, Marguerite, aquamarine disk, press-molded flower, gold enamel petals, sgd "R. Lalique" on reverse, Marcilhac 1626...350.00

2-1/4" l, Wasp, amethyst glass disk, press-molded circle of wasps, Marcilhac 1650, 1920 ....700.00

Perfume Bottle

4-1/4" h, Dans La Nuit, Worth, sphere, blue, star motif, quarter moon stopper, sgd 725.00

5-1/2" h, Fleurs de Pommier, molded, scalloped, reticulated apple blossoms in tiara stopper, molded signature "L. Lalique," stress lines, tiny chip 4,500.00

Perfume Burner, 6-3/4" h, Sirenes, Brule, opal, allover green patina, 10 full length mermaids, ocean wave motif on cov 1,450.00

Plate, 11" d, Sea Anemone, swirled tendril design, opalescent glass, acid stamp "R. Lalique France," Marcilhac 10-391....................290.00

Sauce Bowl, 5-1/8" d, 1-7/8" h, Dandelion, colorless, externally dec, recessed dandelion leaves, frosted, int. sgd "R. Lalique France No. 3104," Marcilhac 3104, flake, mold roughness, set of 6...........400.00

Statuette, 9-1/4" h, nude female, frosted colorless, inscribed "Lalique France," designed by Marc Lalique, c1960, orig paper label ...375.00

Vase

6" h, Renoncules, press molded flowers on bulbous body, flared rim, frosted colorless body, blue patina, engraved "R. Lalique France" on base, Marcilhac 1044 ....635.00

6-1/2" h, Mistletoe, emerald green, mold-blown interwoven sprigs, frosted and polished, base inscribed "R. Lalique France no. 948," Marcilhac 948, two shallow base chips..........................2,185.00

7" h, 6" d, cylindrical, flared rim, colorless frosted body, lower half surrounded by stack of 3 octagonal sided clear glass rings, base inscribed "R. Lalique France"..260.00

9-3/8" h, Ceylon, opalescent, repeating parakeet motif, stylized vines, base engraved "R. Lalique" in block letters, Marcilhac 905, c1924, chips to base, flake to one tail...............................4,025.00

10" h, Perruches Parrot, brilliant blue, 14 pairs of lovebirds perched

Vase, clear and frosted, flaring, molded stylized bird head handles, inscribed "R. LALIQUE," 6-3/4" h, $620.

on flowering branches, frosted and polished to enhance design, mkd "R. Lalique" in mold, Marcilhac 876, small rim nick.. 8,000.00

LAMP SHADES

History: Lamp shades were made to diffuse the harsh light produced by early gas lighting fixtures. These early shades were made by popular Art Nouveau manufacturers including Durand, Quezal, Steuben, and Tiffany. Many shades are not marked.

Aladdin, satin, white, dogwood dec................................65.00

American, 28-1/2" d, leaded glass, chandelier type, parasol form, irregular border, multicolored flowering vine with trellis of green and olive, mottled blue-green ground, some cracked segments 4,890.00

Bigelow Kennard, 21-3/4" d, leaded, domed, irregular border, trailing yellow and amber rippled glass roses, striated green leaves, blue slag glass ground, emb metal tag at rim "Bigelow Kennard Boston" 14,950.00

Duffner & Kimberly, 22-1/2" d, leaded slag glass, domed, light turquoise slag glass segments, intricately leaded dropped apron of turquoise and amber fleur-de-lis and foliate motif on deep maroon and navy striated glass ground, few cracked segments 9,775.00

Fenton, Dragon's Tongue, marigold carnival over moonstone ground 35.00

Fostoria, 5-1/2" d, zipper pattern, green p8lled dec, opal ground, gold lining 185.00

Handel, 5-1/4" h, six-panel petal form, frosted, textured yellow-green shade, repeating stenciled red and green leaf and flower motif painted on ext., sgd "Handel 3382"..275.00

Loetz, 6" h, bell form, fluted and scalloped rims, amber, irid gold spot dec, pr 800.00

Monart Glass, 6-1/2" d, white opal.................................90.00

Northwood, Pillar and Drape pattern, marigold carnival on moonstone ground 25.00

Pairpoint, 7" h, puffy, flower basket, reverse painted pink and yellow poppies and roses...400.00

Quezal, feather pattern, irid gold ground, sgd............................125.00

Tiffany, Favrile

7" d, ruffled, gold irid, highlighted by green pulled an coiled dec, stretch irid at lower rim, inscribed "L. C. T.," small chips to top rim, pr..1,495.00

7" d, 3-1/2" h, ten ribbed cone, white ex., green swirls highlighted with trailing gold irid ribbons, rim inscribed "L. C. T. Favrile," rim chips, wear to irid...3,740.00

7-1/2" d, ruffled, amber, honeycomb, strong gold irid, onion skin at rim, top rim sgd "L.C. T.," pr 1,150.00

Carnival Glass, marigold, ribbed, 2" d fitter ring, $30.

LAMPS and LIGHTING

History: Lighting devices have evolved from simple stone-age oil lamps to the popular electrified models of today. Aimé Argand patented the first oil lamp in 1784. Around 1850, kerosene became a popular lamp-burning fluid, replacing whale oil and other fluids. In 1879, Thomas A. Edison invented the electric light, causing fluid lamps to lose favor and creating a new field for lamp manufacturers. Companies like Tiffany and Handel became skillful at manufacturing electric lamps, and their decorators produced beautiful bases and shades.

References: James Edward Black (ed.), *Electric Lighting of the 20s-30s* (1988, 1993 value update), *Volume 2 with Price Guide* (1990, 1993 value update), L-W Book Sales; John Campbell, *Fire & Light in the Home Pre 1820,* Antique Collectors' Club, 1999; J. W. Courter, *Aladdin Collectors Manual & Price Guide* #18, published by author (3935 Kelley Rd., Kevil, KY 42053), 1998; —, *Aladdin, The Magic* Name In Lamps, Revised Edition, published by author, 1997; *Electric Lighting of the 20s-30s,* Vol. 1 (1994, 1998 value update), Vol. 2, (1994), L-W Book Sales, Carole Goldman Hibel, John Hibel, John Fontaine, *The Handel Lamps Book,* Fontaine Publishers, 1999; Marjorie Hulsebus, *Miniature Victorian Lamps,* Schiffer Publishing, 1996; Jan Lindenberger, *Lamps of the 50s & 60s,* Schiffer Publishing, 1997; L-W Book Sales, *Better Electric Lamps of the 20s & 30s,* L-W Book Sales, 1997; Calvin Shepherd, *50s T. V. Lamps,* Schiffer Publishing, 1998; Richard Miller and John Solverson, *Student Lamps of the Victorian Era,* Antique Publications, 1992, 1992-93 value guide; Bill and Linda Montgomery, *Animated Motion Lamps 1920s to Present,* L-W Book Sales, 1991; Denys Peter Myers, *Gaslighting in America,* Dover Publications, 1990; Henry A. Pohs, *Miner's Flame Light Book,* Hiram Press, 1995; Sam and Anna Samuelian, *Collector's Guide to Motion Lamps,* Collector Books, 1998; Tom Santiso, *TV Lamps,* Collector Books, 1999; Jo Ann and Francis Thomas, *Early Twentieth Century Lighting Fixtures,* Collector Books, 1999; Catherine M. V. Thuro, *Oil Lamps,* Wallace-Homestead, 1976, 1992 value update; —, *Oil Lamps II,* Collector Books, 1983, 1994 value update; John J. Wolfe, *Brandy, Balloons & Lamps: Ami Argand,* 1750-1803, South Illinois University Press, 1999.

Periodical: *Light Revival,* 35 West Elm Ave., Quincy, MA 02170.

Collectors' Clubs: Aladdin Knights of the Mystic Light, 3935 Kelley Rd, Kevil, KY 42053; Coleman Collector Network, 1822 E Fernwood, Wichita, KS 67216; Historical Lighting Society of Canada, P.O. Box 561, Postal Station R, Toronto, Ontario M4G 4EI, Canada; Incandescent Lamp Collectors Association, Museum of Lighting, 717 Washington Place, Baltimore, MD 21201; International Coleman Collectors Club, 2710 Nebraska St., Amarillo, TX 79106; International Colmean Collector's Network, 3404 West 450 North Rochester, IN 46975-8370; Night Light, 38619 Wakefield Ct., Northville, MI 48167; Rushlight Club, Inc., Suite 196, 1657 The Fairway, Jenkintown, PA 19046.

Museums: Kerosene Lamp Museum, Winchester Center, CT; Pairpoint Lamp Museum, River Edge, NJ.

SPECIAL AUCTIONS

Fontaine's Auction Gallery
1485 W. Housatonic St.
Pittsfield, MA 01201
(413) 488-8922

Green Valley Auctions, Inc.
Rte 2, Box 434
Mt. Crawford, VA 22841
(540) 434-4260

James D. Julia, Inc.
P.O. Box 830
Fairfield, ME 04937
(207) 453-7125

Reproduction Alert: The following is a partial list of reproduction kerosene lamps. Colors in italics indicate a period color:

Button & Swirl, 8" high—*clear, cobalt blue,* ruby
Coolidge Drake (a.k.a. Waterfall), 10" high—*clear, cobalt blue, milk glass,* ruby
Lincoln Drape, short, 8-3/4" high—*amber, clear, green, and other colors*
Lincoln Drape, tall, 9-3/4" high—*amber, clear, cobalt blue, moonstone, ruby*
Shield & Star, 7" high—*clear,* cobalt blue
Sweetheart (a.k.a. Beaded Heart), 10" h—clear, milk glass, pink, pink cased font with clear base

General clues that help identify a new lamp include parts that are glued together and hardware that is lacquered solid brass.

Boudoir, Roycroft, designed by Dard Hunter, leaded slag glass shade with band of pink stylized dogwood blossoms on yellow ground over band of 4 curled flat bands, orig patina, imp orb and cross mark, 14-3/4" h, 7" d, small cracks to some panes, replaced copper cap, $4,750. Photo courtesy of David Rago Auctions, Inc.

Boudoir

Aladdin, 14-1/2" h, 8" d, reverse painted bell shade, pine border, floral molded polychromed metal base 225.00

Cut Glass, 9" h, mushroom shade, flared base, sunburst design 400.00

French, 11" d, 6" d, weighted brass base, crystal glass paneled insert, brass emb leaves and berries, rod curving upward holding night light, brass chains, and mounts, glass night light, holds candle 215.00

Handel, 14-1/2" h, 8" d ribbed glass domed shade with squared scalloped rim, obverse painted with snowy winter scene, pastel yellow orange sky, sgd "Handel 5637" on rim, raised on bronzed metal tree trunk base, threaded Handel label 3,335.00

Heintz, sterling on bronze

10" h, 6-1/2" d helmet shade, pierced vertical motif in Moorish style, acid-etched, new mica lining, orig patina 2,200.00

10" h, 8-1/2" d conical shade pierced with poppy panels, lined with new mica, spherical base overlaid with poppies, orig verdigris patina 2,000.00

McKenny and Waterbury Co., 13-3/4" h, 8" d domed reverse painted shade with daffodils on amber ground, patinated metal slender standard flaring to round base, woven label on base 1,150.00

Pairpoint

14" h, Portsmouth shade, reverse painted roses, pale yellow and white ground, black enamel highlights on ext., bronzed metal base, shade mkd "The Pairpoint Corp'n," base mkd "Pairpoint" and logo 2,100.00

14" h, 9" d heavily molded shade, obverse painted yellow, pink, and blue blossoms, 3 arm spider above gilt-metal base, imp "Pairpoint P B3048" 1,035.00

14-1/2" h, 9-3/4" d domed shade flaring to rim, surface dec autumn leafed trees, green flowers, butterflies, frosted glass ground, patinated metal base, raised Pairpoint mark and "C3064" on base 1,265.00

Pittsburgh Lamp Co., 15" h, 7" d shade, reverse painted, 4 flared ribbed panels, metal shade framework and base enamel dec with raised Oriental motif, c1920, worn finish 230.00

Chandelier

Art Glass, Italy, mid 20th C, 29" h, trumpet and baluster shaped shaft, 32 branching floral and leaf glass armatures, white, yellow, transparent green, and colorless glass, one branch missing, minor loss to glass 865.00

Belle Epoque, French, late 19th C, gilt brass and painted porcelain, 8 light, stamped "G. D. 4310," circular Serves-style bowl painted with figural vignettes of the seasons, pierced rocaille frame issuing foliate candle branches, foliate nozzles and drip pans, suspended by chains from foliate corona, 22-1/2" d, 23" h 900.00

Bradley & Hubbard, 25" d, hand beaten curled heavy brass frame, six caramel colored bent slag glass panels, 19" of heavy brass chain and mounting 980.00

18th C Style, gilt and enamel, 7-light, arched cage form corona suspending delicate rush bush terminating below in 6 sconces surrounded by galleried circlet, all hung with prismatic drops, 14" d, 31" h 800.00

French Empire Revival Style, gilt bronze, patinated bronze bowl, internally fitted with 4 lights, cast with gilt bronze anthemion and acorn finial, 4 scroll arms, held to similarly cast corona by strapwork with cast anthemion and tied ribbons, 26-1/2" d, 40" h 1,750.00

Gilt bronze and cut crystal, gilt bronze circles issuing 4 gilt bronze scroll arms with candlecups hung with prisms above 5 decreasing rows of prismatic drops, surmounted by gilt bronze corona hung with swags of glass drops, 36" h 1,400.00

Leaded Glass, 34" h, 45" d, two part fixture, domed shaded with radiating bent panels of caramel and white slag glass ending in ring with fleur-de-lis motif suspending from large circular radiating patinated metal strapwork, border of raised enameled grape cluster and leaf motifs with bent panels of caramel slag and red leaded glass segments 4,890.00

Louis XV Style, molded glass, twelve-light, boldly scrolled candle arms, decorative stems, hung allover with chains and faceted prisms, electrified, French 3,450.00

Regency Style, 45" d, 42" h, gilt bronze, 18-light, c1900 .... 6,800.00

Rustic, lodge-style, six-light, formed from antlers, electrified, 50-1/2" w, 44" h 2,070.00

Victorian, shaft surrounded by icicles and prismatic beads, four "C" scroll arms supporting frosted glass shades hung with icicles, 41" h, 31" d 850.00

Desk

Arts and Crafts, student, 20-3/4" h, 20" w, two patinated metal conical shades, each with 4 medallions of caramel and white slag glass, cast patinated metal base with hammered and studded strapwork detail on flared ftd sq base 1,035.00

Bradley & Hubbard, 13" h, 8-1/2" d adjustable tilt shade, narrow ribbed panels, reverse painted green, blue, and brown Arts and crafts border motif, single socket metal base 460.00

Charles V, 3 foliate cast C-scroll candle branches, fluted vase shaped support, circular base, adjustable green tôle shade, electrified 650.00

Continental, 20" h, carved alabaster, two dolphins supporting open scallop shell, wide gilt borders, shaped base, mounted at back with 2 light arm 750.00

Handel, 16-1/4" h, 18" d, bronze, Art Nouveau style, 2 green leaded slag glass shades, 2 leaded glass pods, lilypad base, sinuous stems, orig verdigris finish, die-stamped mark 1,700.00

Heintz, 12-1/2" h, 11" d, acid-etched, gold dore finish, bulbous base overlaid with dancing maidens, shade pierced in Moorish motif, lined in silk, orig condition, paper label 2,600.00

Modern, France, c1935, designed by Jean-Michel Frank, 15-1/4" h, 19" w, staff composition double lamp, arched U-form, rect felted base, cream, pr 3,750.00

Student

22" h, double, brass frame, electrified, cased green shades 605.00

23-1/2" h, brass frame and adjustable arm, white glass shade, early 20th C 260.00

Tiffany

13-1/2" h, 7" d swirl dec irid green ribbed dome Damascene shade cased to white, mkd "L.C.T" on rim, swivel-socket bronze harp frame, rubbed cushion platform, five ball feet, imp "Tiffany Studios New York 419" 3,740.00

17-1/2" h, 7" d swirl dec irid green cased dome Damascene shade, mkd "L.C.T. Favrile," swivel-socket dark patina bronze harp frame with baluster shaft, ribbed cushion platform, five ball feet, imp "Tiffany Studios New York 7907" 4,025.00

18" h, 10-1/2" d gold irid Steuben bell shade, swivel socket dark etched bronze wide harp frame, adjustable shaft above leaf and petal base, imp "Tiffany Studios New York 569" 1,100.00

Early American

Astral

13-3/4" h, brass font, replaced collar, stem with pierced and ribbed brass collar over red glass insert, stepped marble base 220.00

21" h, gilded brass, prism ring with clear cut prisms, frosted shade with cut to clear floral designs, electrified, marble base may be replacement, small chips on prisms 250.00

Betty Lamp

3-1/2" h wrought iron lamp, stamped "M," 4-1/4" h redware stand with incised wavy lines, minor rim chips 440.00

4-1/4" h, wrought iron, hanger, and pick 300.00

Blown, colorless, 10" h, drop burners, pressed stepped base, chips on base, pr 385.00

Boston, mid 19th C, 12" x 9", painted tin and cast iron, trunnion, lard, brass label stamped "S. N. & H. C. Ufford 117 Court St. Boston Kinnear Patent Feb 4, 1851," tin lozenge shaped font with 2 wick tubes suspended from cast iron foliate frame and base, gilt, green, and red dec on yellow ground, minor paint loss 490.00

Cage Lamp, 6" d, wrought iron, spherical, self righting gyroscope font, two repaired spout burners 500.00

Candle Holder, 19" h, wrought iron, hanging type, primitive twisted arms and conical socket 385.00

Candle Stand, 57-1/4" h, 24-1/2" w, wrought iron, double arms, brass candleholders and drip pans, attributed to PA, 18th C, pitting, losses to drip pans 8,100.00

Hour Glass, 7" h, clear blown glass, pine and oak frame, whittled baluster posts, old brown finish, glued break in bottom plate 275.00
Loom Light, 14-3/4" h, wrought iron, candle socket, trammel 500.00
Miner's Lamp, 7-3/8" h, cast and wrought iron, chicken finial, replaced hanger 110.00
Rush Light Holder
   9" h, wrought iron, turned wooden base, pitted iron 225.00
   9-1/2" h, wrought iron, candle socket counter weight, tripod base, penny feet, tooled brass disk at base of stem, simple tooling ..470.00
Skater's Lamp, 6-3/4 h, brass, clear glass globe mkd "Perko Wonder Junior," polished, small splint in top of brass cap 160.00
Splint Holder
   9-1/2" h, wrought iron, candle socket counter weight, tripod base, diamond shaped feet 415.00
   12-1/2" h, wrought iron, tripod base, penny feet, one leg brazed, later added candle socket 250.00
Taper Jack, 5" h, Sheffield silver on copper, old repairs 195.00

Floor

53" h, 9" d leaded glass shade, red, green, and amber stylized tulip design, adjustable cast metal frame, ribbed shaft, weighted foliate platform base 600.00
58-1/2" h, 21" d bent panel shoulder shade, creamy caramel textured slag glass, wide scalloped slag glass band of light blue and red blossoms, green heart-shaped leaves and orange border, 3 socket, 3 ftd patinated metal standard, metal tag on shade stamped "Miller," base stamped "Miller" 1,150.00
50" h, 10" d, Tiffany/Aladdin, spun bronze shade, reflective white int., mkd "Tiffany Studios New York," adjustable bridge lamp base with Arabian Nights motif, orig dark bronze patina, elaborate platform base, stamped "Tiffany Studios New York 576" 2,990.00
56" h, 7" d, Bradley and Hubbard, small domed leaded glass shade, green slag glass, gold key border, open framework adjustable standard, domed circular foot 400.00
Handel, harp base, bronze finish, 2 parrots on yellow ground shade, sgd "Handel #7073 G A" 8,000.00
64-1/2" h, 24" d umbrella shade with broad irregular drop apron, leaded trailing grapevines, purple and red glass jewel grape clusters, pink and yellow slag flowers, green slag ground, tree-form base ribbed and grapevine tendrils and leaves, dark green patina.................... 23,000.00
68" h, torchiere, modeled with foliate motifs, brass inlaid marble base, pr 1,610.00
76-1/2" h, Crest, paneled mica shades designed as stylized sunflowers, centered by metal plate dec in armor motif, mixed metal patinated black, silver, and gold, supported on mixed metal stands of 2 rectilinear segmented shafts around third rod, scrolled and ball finials, claw feet, shaped, sq bases, mkd "Crest," 20th C, slight loss to varnish over mica, pr........................ 6,900.00

Fluid

Boston and Sandwich
   11" h, clear blown molded font, shell pattern with band of etched foliate dec at shoulder, brass collar and connector, translucent green pressed Baroque pattern base, minor imperfections.............920.00
   11-1/2" h, double overlay, cranberry and white cut to clear font, stars, quatrefoil, elongated ovals, punties, pointed ovals, brass collar, reeded standard, sq stepped marble base, minor imperfections 3,800.00
   12-3/4" h, light emerald green cut to clear font with stars, quatrefoil, ovals, punties, and pointed ovals, brass collar, reeded standard, sq stepped marble base, minor imperfections 1,150.00
   13-3/4" h, cobalt blue to clear Washington cut font, brass collar and connector, opalescent white columnar standard, sq base with gilt highlights, mold imperfections 750.00
   14-1/2" h, colorless pear-shaped font with Bull's Eye pattern, foliate etching on shoulder, translucent blue Baroque pattern base, brass collar and connector, int. crack on standard 290.00
New England, 19-1/4" h, colorless, free-blown, cut punty and flute dec, bulb-form, ruffled acid etched lacy pattern shaded yellow to clear shades, brass kerosene burner and chimneys, chip, restoration, pr........... 800.00

Hanging, parlor, 15" d blue satin opalescent quilted shade, ornately emb ring with matching glass font, scrolled side frame with jeweled ruby mounts, working pull-down mechanism, orig smoke bell, 2 pc cut crystal pendants, 36" h, $4,480. Photo courtesy of Jackson's Auctioneers & Appraisers.

Ripley, marriage, 11-3/8" h, opaque white base, blue fonts, back holder, mkd "D.C. Ripley & Co. Pat. Pending," gilded brass connector and collars, chips, in-the-making base flaws........................... 660.00

Hanging

American, 19th C
   18" h, patinated metal and cut glass, hall type, candle socket, Gothic arches, diamonds and flowerheads dec.............. 1,380.00
   23" h, clear blown glass, hall type, elaborate wheel cut dec of birds and deer in landscape, foliate devices, pressed brass mounts 2,415.00
Arts and Crafts, brass washed metal, 4 lanterns, hammered amber glass........................ 1,000.00
Handel, 10" d, hall type, spherical form, acid cut, translucent white, brown, vase and foliate dec, ornate orig hardware 4,200.00
Perzel, 40-1/4" d, chrome, metal, and glass 1,225.00
Tiffany, 18" l, 15" d, attributed to Tiffany Glass and Decorating Co., late 19th C, square green and opalescent diamond-shaped glass jewels arranged as central pendant chandelier drop, twisted wire frame.............. 2,990.00

Table

Bigelow Kennard, Boston, 26" h, 18" d domed leaded shade, opalescent white segments in geometric progression border, brilliant green leaf forms repeating motif, edge imp "Bigelow Kennard Boston/Bigelow Studios," three socket over Oriental-style bronze base cast with fu dog handles, Japonesque devices 2,875.00
Bradley & Hubbard
   15" sq octagon shade, 21-1/2" h, Prairie School, shade with geometric overlay on green and white slag glass panels with red squares, sgd on base and shade.................................... 1,150.00
   21-1/2" h, 18" d bent panel ribbed shade, water lily border, reverse painted olive and tan, 3-socket flared patinated metal standard, raised grapes and leaves, triangular Bradley & Hubbard stamp near socket, married shade and base, finial missing.......... 865.00
Daum, 11-1/2" h, mushroom shaped shade of mottled white, cobalt blue, and yellow-green glass, acid mark "Daum Nancy (cross)," sq wrought iron pillar base with beaded details, sunburst base, hammered style ball feet, replaced rivet, rewired, c1920............. 1,265.00
Duffner and Kimberly, New York
   24" h, 21" d conical leaded glass shade, amber slag background panels, three repeating intricate heraldic elements of lavender-amethyst glass superimposed on crimson red medial band, lower border glass in chevron motif, amber granite and mauve ripple accent colors, three-socket bronzed shaft with cast foliate devices............. 4,600.00

26" h, 24-1/2" d dome leaded glass shade with tuck-under irregular rim, multicolored blossoms with yellow centers, green leaves, long stemmed flowers extending to top on segmented white background, three socket bronze lobed shaft with quatraform shaped base 7,435.00

H. A. Best Lamp Company, Chicago, 19-1/2" h, 14" d domed leaded shade, repeating panels of floral and geometric slag glass segments, pink, green, and blue separated by stripes of textured red glass segments, 2 socket patinated metal base, raised "H. A. Best Lamp Co." on base 1,725.00

Handel
23" h, 16-1/2" d 6-panel green slag glass shade, band of stylized flowers, bronze faceted base and shaft, No. 5081, both shade and base mkd 2,500.00

23-1/4" h, 16-1/2" d domed patinated metal framework shade, painted fleur-de-lis border over caramel slag glass panels, 3 socket shaped slender standard with raised lapped leaf patinated metal circular base, wood base with 4 shaped bracket feet, metal "Handel" tag on top rim of shade 2,100.00

24" h, 17-1/4" d domical reverse painted textured shade, continuous band of trees silhouette against shaded pink sky, pools of blue water, blossoming foliate and vines, yellow, orange, black, and blue, shade sgd "Handel 7202," initials "PAL," wear to patina.................. 6,325.00

24-1/2" h, 18" d reverse painted frosted and textured domed shade, wide border of repeating flowers, birds, and scrolls, brown-green, blue, pink, and yellow, mottled amber ground, three-socket scrolled tripod standard, stepped circular base, imp mark "Handel Lamps" on top of shade, woven tag on felted base, patination loss........ 4,890.00

26" h, 20" d domed shade with lapped petal design, amber and cream slag glass, 4 socket flared patinated copper shaft, raised lapped lily pad base, raised "Handel" mark on shade and base, wear to patina, crack to one petal 3,335.00

Jefferson, 16" h, 21" flared dome shade, reverse painted lakeside landscape, summer trees, lower edge inscribed "1972 Jefferson Co.," assembled lamp base, new wiring and sockets 1,265.00

Miller, 17-1/4" h, Mission style, 4 green slag panels set in black scrolled metal framed shade, rect black metal base with raised and curved armature, 4 applied lion motifs, electrified oil canister stamped "Miller - the Juno Lamp, Made in USA," black over-painting.................... 550.00

Pairpoint
20-1/2" h, 11-1/2" d domed closed top mushroom-cap glass shade, Vienna, coralene yellow int., painted stylized olive green leaves and red berries, gold outline on ext., ball-decorated ring supported by four arms, quatraform base molded with foliate devices, imp "Pairpoint Mfg. Co., 3052" 2,070.00

22-1/2" h, 16-1/2" d reverse painted ribbed quatrefoil blown-out shade, gold and black striped butterflies at each corner, blue and pink floral design, white ground, stamped "The Pairpoint Corp.," raised gilt metal two-socket base with relief lapped leaf pattern, imp "Pairpoint Mfg. Co., C3066," trademark on base, crack to shade, worn patina on base... 2,300.00

23" h, 16-1/2" d scenic reverse painted lightly textured Exeter shade, pastoral scene with trees and grassy hillsides, shaded blue sky, yellow band about shoulder with brown repeating windmill motifs, sgd "C. Durand," 3 socket gilt metal, scrolled three-part base, imp "Pairpoint D 3070,"logo on base, wear to gilt..................... 2,990.00

Pittsburgh Lamp, Brass & Glass Co.
9-1/4" h, 14" d hp domed shade, evening tree lined shore scene, amber, rust, and green, 2 socket patinated metal base ... 1,150.00

23" h, 14" d frosted amber glass shade, shirred drapery style, 2 socket patinated metal base, raised leaf blade and floral dec, circular, flared, weighted base 1,100.00

Riviere Studios, 25-1/2" h, 14" d six-panel reticulated metal overlay shade, flowering vine pattern, swirled purple, blue, and green slag glass, 2 socket, hexagonal sided illuminated base in same overlay and slag glass pattern, early 20th C.................................... 1,380.00

Secessionist-Style, 17-3/4" h, 10-1/2" d bejeweled helmet shade, brass, 3 stylized claw feet, unmarked 600.00

Steuben, Carder, 23" h, 11" h moss agate angular shouldered oval glass shaft, purple and lavender with mica flecks, green aventurine,

amber, red, and blue swirls, gilt metal two socket lamp fittings, catalog #8026 .... 1,610.00

Suess, 23-1/2" h, 24-1/4" parasol shaped leaded shade, branching striated pink and yellow apple blossoms descending from top rim to green ground, three-socket slender standard, wide circular base with etched wave border, c1906, spotting to base........................ 9,775.00

Tiffany
22" h, 16" d dome leaded shade, Bellflower, Favrile glass segments leaded as clusters of vivid red and red-orange bellflowers, yellow and fiery-amber scrolling foliate devices against green shaded background, stamped "Tiffany Studios New York" on rim, dark bronze urn-form lamp base set into three-arm shaft above sq platform, early TS circular imp mark 12,075.00

22-1/2" h, 12" d dome shade, irid swirl dec green Damascene shade cased to reflective white and amber, dark bronze three-arm spider and fluid unit, four-legged base, imp "S1089" on frame and font, also stamped "Tiffany Studios New York" with TG&D Co. logo 5,175.00

Wilkinson Co., 27-1/2" h, 20" d scalloped conical leaded glass shade, yellow centered pink and peach colored blossoms, green leaves bordering amber and green slag glass segments arranged in ladderwork progression, locking mechanism with three baluster shaft, bulbed turnings, stepped platform base, imp "Wilkinson Co/Brooklyn, NY"......... 3,220.00

Williamson, Richard, & Co, Chicago, 25" h, 20" d peaked leaded glass dome, amber slag bordered by red tulips, pink and lavender-blue spring blossoms, green leaf stems, carved glass, mounted on four-socket integrated shaft with stylized tulip blossoms above leafy platform, imp "R. Williamson & Co./Washington & Jefferson Sts./Chicago, Ill," restored cap at top rim... 3,220.00

Wall

French, gilt-bronze, Paris, c1880, early 18th C Regency manner, 3 elaborate scrolling acanthus candle arms, surmounted by sphinx's head, pr 2,750.00

LANTERNS

History: A lantern is an enclosed, portable light source, hand carried or attached to a bracket or pole to illuminate an area. Many lanterns have a protected flame and can be used both indoors and outdoors. Light-producing materials used in early lanterns included candles, kerosene, whale oil, and coal oil, and, later, gasoline, natural gas, and batteries.

References: *Collectible Lanterns,* L-W Book Sales, 1997; Anthony Hobson, *Lanterns That Lit Our World,* Hiram Press, reprinted 1996; Neil S. Wood, *Collectible Dietz Lanterns,* L-W Book Sales, 1996.

Collectors' Club: Coleman Collectors Network, 1822 E. Fernwood, Wichita, KS 67216.

Arts and Crafts, 20" sq, 30" h, carved oak, 4 sided, peaked top, panels of leaded amber slag glass within arched windows, heavy iron link chain, nicks to wood, some cracks in glass panels............... 1,265.00

Astronomical, 12" l, tôle ware, orig black and gold paint, 2 candle sockets, frosted glass, 13 cards punched with constellations, orig wooden box, labeled "Clarke's Astronomical Lantern, Manufactured by D. C. Heaty & Co., Boston," unused... 400.00

Barn, 11" h, wood, 4 glass sides, hinged door 150.00

Candle, 7" w, 15" h, hanging, sq form, conical top, loop handle, 3 glass panels with horizontal wire guards, tin rear opening panel, one cracked glass, wire missing 375.00

Dark Room, 17" h, Carbutt's Dry Plate Lantern, orig black paint, white striping, tin kerosene font and burner, name and patent date of April 25, 1882 on label.. 95.00

Hall, patinated bronze and green glass, corona with 3 branches supporting circlet mounted with beribboned laurel leaves, suspending basket covered with green glass flowerheads with pearl centers 375.00

Masthead, copper and brass, oil fired, orig burner, intricate label for Ellerman, Wilson Line, mid 19th C, 23" h, $285.

Kerosene, 24-1/2" h, orig black paint and kerosene burner, mercury reflector, stenciled label "C. T. Ham Mfg. Co.'s New No. 8 Tubular Square Lamp, Label Registered 1886" 185.00
Miner's tin, 3 part, leather fitting for head, adapter with brass plate for pole, 2 wire loop handles, adjustable reflector, hinged tin door, emb "Ferguson NY 1878" 165.00
Skater's, tin
    6-1/4" h, clear globe with red stain 110.00
    6-3/4" h, cobalt blue globe, top threads of globe chipped...... 275.00
Töle, painted, pierced hexagonal cage surmounted by turret with applied cast leaves, verde finish, Venetian, pr 500.00

LEEDS CHINA

History: The Leeds Pottery in Yorkshire, England, began production about 1758. Among its products was creamware that was competitive with that of Wedgwood. The original factory closed in 1820, but various subsequent owners continued until 1880. They made exceptional cream-colored wares, either plain, salt glazed, or painted with colored enamels, and glazed and unglazed redware.

Marks: Early wares are unmarked. Later pieces are marked "Leeds Pottery," sometimes followed by "Hartley-Green and Co." or the letters "LP."

Reproduction Alert: Reproductions have the same marks as the antique pieces.

Bowl, cov, floral panels dec, swan finial 185.00
Butter Pat, 3-3/4" d, blue feather edge dec, imp border 65.00
Candlestick, 10" h, spreading sq pedestal pierced shaft, stylized flowers, balustrade nozzle, sq leaf sprig molded bobeche, sq coved leaf spring molded and foliate reticulated base, imp "Leeds Pottery" 250.00

Teapot, blue and green stylized floral dec, c1820-40, 8-1/2" w, 4-7/8" h, $225.

Charger, 15-3/8" d, multicolored urn of flowers, blue feather edge 450.00
Chop Plate, 14-1/4" d, blue and white floral dec, blue feather edge, wear, hairline 220.00
Creamer and Sugar, cov, 4-3/4" h and 5" h, Granite, white dec band, handles, foot, and finial, 19th C, imperfections, edge repair to sugar.. 550.00
Egg Cup, 2-3/4" , creamware, reticulated 150.00
Mug, 5" h, multicolored polychrome floral dec 250.00
Pitcher
    6" h, molded soft paste, large spout, scroll type handle, vertical leaves on body, panels at neck, rust colored flowers with blue stems, other blue highlights around neck, spout, and handle 250.00
    6-3/4" h, Agate, early 19th C, repaired spout and rim, hairlines . 805.00
Plate
    8" d, scalloped rim, green feathered edge, eagle and shield center 770.00
    8-1/8" d, pierced edge, mkd on base, early 19th C, minor chips and staining, 6 pc set 805.00
    9-1/2" d, blue feather edge, mkd "Wedgwood," 19th C, minor discoloration 145.00
    9-1/2" d, creamware, painted with departure and return of prodigal son, floral border, c1780, pr 700.00
    9-1/2" d, Chinoiserie design, 19th C, minute rim chips.......... 200.00
    10" d, creamware, molded flutes and edge design, reticulated rim, two imp "Leeds Pottery," some chips, 8 pcs 1,100.00
Sauce Boat, 3" h, bands of blue dec... 200.00
Tureen, 4-1/2" h, bands of blue dec, raised dec, blue floral finial, married lid... 150.00
Teapot, cov, creamware
    4-3/4" h, intertwined ribbed handle, molded floral ends and flower finial, polychrome enameled rose, ... 3,025.00
    5" h, molded spout, intertwined ribbed handle, polychrome enameled portraits of Prince of Orange, completely restored mismatched lid, some flakes, enamel wear............................ 440.00

LEFTON CHINA

History: China, porcelain, and ceramic with that now familiar "Lefton" mark has been around since the early 1940s and is highly sought by collectors in the secondary marketplace today. The company was founded by George Zoltan Lefton, a Hungarian immigrant who arrived in the United States in 1939. In the 1930s, he was a sportswear designer and manufacturer, but his hobby of collecting fine china and porcelain led him to a new business venture.

After the bombing of Pearl Harbor in 1941, Mr. Lefton aided a Japanese-American friend by helping him to protect his property from anti-Japanese groups. As a result, Lefton came in contact with and began marketing pieces from a Japanese factory owned by Kowa Toki KK. At this time he embarked on a new career and began shaping a business that sprang from his passion for collecting fine china and porcelains. Though his funds were very limited, his vision was to develop a source from which to obtain fine porcelains by reviving the postwar Japanese ceramic industry, which dated back to antiquity. As a trailblazer, George Zoltan Lefton soon earned the reputation of "The China King."

Figurines and animals, plus many of the whimsical pieces such as the Bluebirds, Dainty Miss, Miss Priss, Angels, Cabbage Cutie, Elf Head, Mr. Toodles, and the Dutch Girl, are popular with collectors. All types of dinnerware and tea-related items are eagerly acquired by collectors. As is true with any antique or collectibles, prices vary, depending on location, condition, and availability.

Marks: Until 1980, wares from the Japanese factory include a "KW."

Reference: Loretta DeLozier, *Collector's Encyclopedia of Lefton China,* Vol. 1 (1995), Vol. 2 (1997), Vol. 3 (1999), Collector Books; *1998 Lefton Price Guide.*

Collectors' Club: National Society of Lefton Collectors, 1101 Polk St, Bedford, IA 50833.

Advisor: Loretta DeLozier.

Angel, 4-1/4", Cherub busts, #1415, pr 70.00
Animal
    3-1/2", rabbit with tulips, #5469 .... 10.00
    4", Reindeer, green holly, #1187 .... 40.00
    4-1/2", Blue Gill, #1072 .... 38.00
Ashtray, 6" l, kidney shaped china with roses or violets, #4229 .... 30.00
Bank, 8", Devil "Root of All Evil," #4923 .... 60.00
Bird, 6"
    Angel On Leaves with blue bird, #852 .... 60.00
    Peacock, tail spread, #2336 .... 55.00
Bone Dish, 6-1/2", "To a Wild Rose," #2598 .... 10.00

Bird, Bohemian Waxwing, #1283, 6-1/2" h, $55. Photo courtesy of Loretta DeLozier.

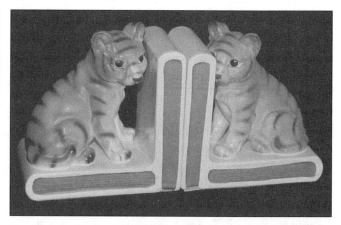

Bookends, tigers, #6663, $35. Photo courtesy of Loretta DeLozier.

Bookends, pr, Tigers, #6663 .... 35.00
Candy Box, 4-3/4" heart shaped, with doves, #5597 .... 22.00
Chip & Dip, 10-1/4", Rose Chintz, #2282, set 55.00
Cigarette Set
    Three pieces, 7", Santa Claus, #2735, set 50.00
    Seven pieces, French Rose, #3835, set 35.00
Compote, Lilac Chintz, #130 .... 28.00
Cookie Jar, 11", Monkey Chef with spoon, #7794 .... 150.00
Creamer and Sugar
    Bloomer Girl, #3967 .... 60.00
    Bluebirds, #290 .... 95.00
    Pink Cotillion, #3187 .... 30.00
    Wheat Poppy, #1454 .... 20.00
    White with floral design, #292 .... 45.00
Demitasse Cup & Saucer, Pine Cone, #354 .... 20.00
Dish, 2 compartment, Miss Priss, #1507 .... 155.00
Dish, white, with violets, gold trimmed, #2334 .... 38.00
Egg Cup, Elegant Rose, #2048 .... 35.00
Figurine
    3-1/4" h, bow girl, pink, #8267 .... 45.00

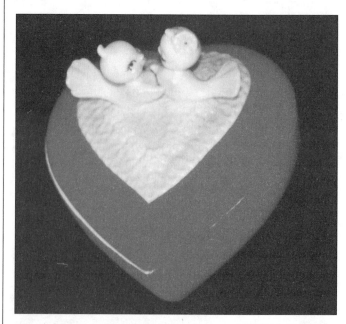

Candy Box, cov, heart shaped, doves, red, #5597, 4-3/4" w, $22. Photo courtesy of Loretta DeLozier.

Figurines, Colonial Couple, Brian and Gwendolyn, #337, 10" h, $350. Photo courtesy of Loretta DeLozier.

4" h, Little Red Riding Hood, 3 kinds, #471 ....20.00
4" h, nurse with tray, #4704 ....45.00
5-1/4" h, Bride & Groom, ring bearer & flower girl, #715, set 100.00
6" h, Dutch Girl, #5096 ....20.00
6" h, girl touching bonnet, #1927 ....85.00
6" h, Sing A Long of Six Pence, #1254 ....150.00
6-1/4" h, girls, 4 seasons, #4834 ....175.00
6-1/2" h, Marilyn Monroe, #411 ....175.00
6-1/2" h, Provincial Boy & Girl, #364, pr 150.00
6-3/4" h, Old Shoemaker, #4718 ....85.00
7-1/2" h, Madeline, #5745 ....125.00
8" h, Calypso Dancers, #021, pr 125.00
8" h, Colonial Marguerite & Edward, #345, pr 150.00
8" h, George Washington, #1108 ....85.00
8" h, lady in green dress, #4494 ....80.00
8" h, man & woman "Le Pas De Fantaisie," #3508, pr 150.00
8" h, man & woman on Stand, #5752, pr.................................120.00
8-1/2" h, Madonna & Child, #543 ....75.00
8-1/2" h, Siamese Dancers with stones, #10293, pr..............250.00
14" h, Colonial man & woman, #1065, pr 450.00
Frame, 4-3/4", house shape, bride & groom, Heavenly Hobo, #04638 ....30.00
Gravy Boat, 8-1/2" l, Americana, #962....................................55.00
Head Vase, lady with necklace, #6638 ....65.00
Jam Jar, Cuddles, #4451 ....30.00
Jam Jar, Dish with saucer, Ruffled Rim, Floral Mood, #5209 ....30.00
Lamp, 7-3/4" oil, floral bisque bouquet, #4208.......................45.00
Nappy, Misty Rose, #5517 ....18.00
Night Light, 6" girl, dressed in pink dress with hat, #486 ....40.00
Pansy Ring, centerpiece, white with flowers, #8078..................120.00
Pitcher & Bowl, 6", floral design, #7643.................................45.00 set
Planter
    4" h, clown, #4498 ....45.00
    5-1/2" h, girl, #056 ....65.00
    5" h, bird house, "Home Tweet Home," #50261 ....40.00
    6" h, boy & girl, Valentine, #2772...22.00
    8" h, bicycle with boy & girl, #50517 ....65.00
Plate
    7 1/4" d, white Pear N Apple, #4256......................................12.00

Teapot, To A Wild Rose, #2561, $165. Photo courtesy of Loretta DeLozier.

9" Rose Chintz, #659..30.00
Salt and Pepper Shakers, pr
    3-1/2" h, Puppies .... 20.00 check on number
    Mammy & Chef, #2046 ....30.00
Salt Box, pink clover, #2497..40.00
Shoe, 3-1/2" Mardi Gras, with stones, #50430 ....45.00
Snack Set, Festival, #2619 ....20.00
Teabag Holder, Miss Priss, #1506 ....55.00
Teapot
    Brown Heritage Floral, #3112 ....185.00
    Brown Heritage Fruit, demi 478..65.00
    Elf Head, #3973 ....185.00
    Heirloom Elegance, #5394 ....150.00
    Holly, red candy cane, #742 ....115.00
    To A Wild Rose, #2561 ....165.00
Teapot, sugar, and creamer, stacked, Heavenly Rose, #20596, set 195.00
Tidbit Tray, 2 tiers, Sweet Violets, #2850 ....45.00
Tumble-Up, Green Heritage, #1266...125.00
Vase
    3-1/2" h, bud, white with gold swirl, #70448, pr 32.00
    6-1/4" h, Christy, #438 ....15.00
    7" h, lavender with phlox, #7633 ....65.00
Wall Plaque
    7", fish with 3 babies, green, #60419, set............................75.00
    7", roosters, #397, pr 30.00
    8", Madonna with Child, #578..75.00
Wall Pocket, 7" h, girl with basket, #50264 ....135.00

LENOX CHINA

History: In 1889, Jonathan Cox and Walter Scott Lenox established The Ceramic Art Co. at Trenton, New Jersey. By 1906, Lenox formed his own company, Lenox, Inc. Using potters lured from Belleek, Lenox began making an American version of the famous Irish ware. The firm is still in business.

Marks: Older Lenox china has one of two marks: a green wreath or a palette. The palette mark appears on blanks supplied to amateurs who hand painted china as a hobby. The Lenox company currently uses a gold stamped mark.

References: Susan and Al Bagdade, *Warman's American Pottery and Porcelain,* Wallace-Homestead, 1994; Richard E. Morin, *Lenox Collectibles,* Sixty-Ninth Street Zoo, 1993.

Additional Listings: Belleek.

Ashtray, cream, gold edge, turned up edges 30.00
Bouillon Cup and Saucer, Detroit Yacht Club, palette mark.......... 85.00
Bowl, 9" d, acanthus leaf dec, cream, gold edge 48.00
Candy Bowl, 6-1/2" h, 5" w, cream ground, holly leaves dec, 24K gold edge 65.00
Chop Plate, 14" d, ivory flower, cobalt blue border stripe, gilt and sterling silver rim 160.00
Chocolate Set, cov chocolate pot, 6 cups and saucers, Golden Wheat pattern, cobalt blue ground, 13 pc set 275.00
Cigarette Box, white apple blossoms, green ground, wreath mark 40.00
Compote, 2" h, 5" d, brown rim, white ground, black hp insignia, pre-1930 .... 40.00
Cup, 4-5/8" d, 2-5/8" h, cream, scene of man fishing in river, inside mkd "Reserved For A Wonderful Guy," gold mark 22.00
Demitasse Cup and Saucer, 2-1/4" w, 1-1/2" h, stick handle, gold trim, c1930 .... 35.00
Figure, 7-1/4" h, 7" w, Wind Dancers, pr of swallows, white, gold eyes 100.00
Honey Pot, 5" h, 6-1/4" d underplate, ivory beehive, gold bee and trim 85.00
Jug, 4" h, hp, grapes and leaves, shaded brown ground, sgd "G. Morley" 250.00
Mug, 6-1/4" h, monk, smiling, holding up glass of whine, shaded brown ground, SS rim 170.00
Perfume Lamp, 9" h, figural, Marie Antoinette, bisque finish, dated 1929 .... 650.00
Pitcher, 7-1/2" h, 6" w, cream ground, gold handle and rim, mkd "Made for Frederick Keer's Sons, Newark, NJ," c1924-30 .... 250.00
Salt, 3" d, creamy ivory ground, molded seashells and coral, green wreath mark 35.00
Salt and Pepper Mill Set, 8" h, Lido, enameled dec.................... 145.00
Swan, 9" l, open back 100.00
Tea set, cov teapot, creamer, cov sugar, Hawthorne pattern, silver overlay... 225.00
Tea Strainer, hp, small pink roses 70.00
Vase
   6" h, pink and roses dec, green leaves, sgd "W. Morley" 195.00
   11-1/2" h, 6-3/4" d, Presidential Garden Series, Jefferson, cream ground, brown, black, and yellow birds, pink and lavender flowers, medium green foliage, brown tree limbs, gold trim, wreath mark 325.00
   11-5/8" h, 4-5/8" d, cylindrical, daisies in columns, gold rims, gold mark 95.00

Dinnerware

Bread and Butter Plate
   Alaris A501 .... 27.00
   Belvidere S314 .... 27.00
   Buchanan 27.00
   Caribbee X444... 27.00
   Cinderella (platinum) 27.00
   Country Garden W302.. 27.00
   Cretan O316 .... 27.00
   Empress O389.. 27.00
   Fairfield T428... 25.00
   Flirtation 27.00
   Golden Wreath 27.00
   Jefferson 27.00
   Kingsley 34.00
   Kingsley X445... 18.00
   Olympia 303 (platinum) 13.00
   Rhodora 27.00
   Rose 25.00

   Tuscany 41.00
   Wheat R442... 27.00
   Wyndcrest A500 .... 30.00
Chop Plate
   Olympia 303, (platinum) 185.00
   Tuscany 185.00
Compote, Rose, small.. 175.00
Creamer
   Cretan O316 .... 100.00
   Starlight X302 .... 61.00
   Tuscany 125.00
Cup
   Olympia 303 (platinum) 26.00
   Rosedale 35.00
   Sky Blue Blossoms 12.00
Cup and Saucer
   Alaris A501 .... 48.00
   Beacon 54.00
   Belvidere S314 .... 52.00
   Biltmore 54.00
   Blue Ridge P316 .... 54.00
   Brookdale 52.00
   Buchanan 41.00
   Caribbee X444... 57.00
   Cinderella (platinum) 52.00
   Country Garden W302.. 52.00
   Cretan O316 .... 54.00
   Empress O389.. 54.00
   Flirtation 54.00
   Golden Wreath 52.00
   Jefferson 41.00
   Kingsley 54.00
   Lowell P67, green 95.00
   Mandarin 68.00
   Mansfield 48.00
   Rhodora 52.00
   Rose, oversized 68.00
   Sachet 48.00
   Springdale 54.00
   Tuscany 81.00
   Tuxedo 65.00
   Wheat R442... 48.00
   Wyndcrest A500 .... 48.00
Demitasse Cup and Saucer, Starlight X302........................... 48.00
Dinner Plate
   Alaris A501 .... 52.00
   Autumn 68.00
   Beacon 52.00
   Belvidere S314 .... 54.00
   Blue Ridge P316 .... 54.00
   Brookdale 48.00
   Buchanan 38.00
   Caribbee X444... 52.00
   Cinderella (platinum) 48.00
   Country Garden W302.. 48.00
   Cretan O316 .... 54.00
   Empress O389.. 48.00
   Fairfield T428... 41.00
   Golden Wreath 54.00
   Jefferson 38.00
   Kingsley 61.00
   Kingsley X445... 50.00
   McKinley 32.00
Meadow Song 52.00
   Poppies on Blue 20.00
   Repertoire 52.00
   Rhodora 48.00
   Rose 41.00
Snow Flower 52.00
   Springdale 50.00

Tuscany	88.00
Wheat R442	41.00
Wyndcrest A500	41.00
Dinner Service, partial, Lowell, 48 pcs	600.00

Fruit or Dessert Bowl

Cretan O316	55.00
Empress O389	41.00
Jewel	34.00
Olympia 303, (platinum)	41.00
Starlight X302	42.00

Gravy Boat

Kingsley	215.00
Tuscany	250.00
Mug, Tulips	30.00
Pie Plate, Lowell P67, green	41.00

Platter

Cretan O316, small	170.00
Empress O389, large	200.00
Golden Wreath, medium	185.00
Kingsley, small	200.00
Rose, small	185.00
Wyndcrest A500, large	185.00

Salad Plate

Alaris A501	34.00
Autumn	34.00
Belvidere S314	34.00
Buchanan	34.00
Cinderella (platinum)	34.00
Country Garden W302	34.00
Cretan O316	38.00
Empress O389	34.00
Fairfield T428	27.00
Flirtation	34.00
Fresh Meadow	34.00
Golden Wreath	34.00
Jefferson	34.00
Kingsley	41.00
Kingsley X445	24.00
Rhodora	34.00
Rose	27.00
Springdale	34.00
Tuscany	52.00
Wheat R442	48.00
Wyndcrest A500	34.00
Soup Bowl, Tuscany	110.00

Sugar Bowl, cov

Cretan O316	115.00
Kingsley	130.00
Starlight X302	65.00
Tuscany	165.00

Vegetable, open, oval

Cretan O316	130.00
Kingsley	185.00
Rose	130.00
Olympia 303, (platinum)	115.00
Starlight X302	115.00
Tuscany	185.00
Wyndcrest A500	100.00

LIBBEY GLASS

History: Edward Libbey established the Libbey Glass Company in Toledo, Ohio, in 1888 after the New England Glass Works of W. L. Libbey and Son closed in East Cambridge, Massachusetts. The new Libbey company produced quality cut glass which today is considered to belong to the brilliant period.

In 1930, Libbey's interest in art-glass production was renewed, and A. Douglas Nash was employed as a designer in 1931.

The factory continues production today as Libbey Glass Co.

References: Bob Page and Dale Frederickson, *Collection of American Crystal,* Page-Frederickson Publishing, 1995; Kenneth Wilson, *American Glass 1760-1930,* 2 vols., Hudson Hills Press and The Toledo Museum of Art, 1994.

Banana Boat, 13" x 7" x 7", cut glass, scalloped pedestal base, 24 point hobstar, hobstar, cane, vesica, and fan motifs, sgd 1,500.00

Bell, 5-3/4" h, colorless, acid etched dec "1893 World's Fair," circular logo surrounded by acid-etched florals and banners, shoulder int. molded "1893 World's Columbian Xposition" (sic), twisted frosted handle with star at top, metal clapper 25.00

Bowl

8" d, cut glass, hobstar, bands of strawberry diamond and fans, sgd 110.00

9" d, cut glass, Somerset pattern, sgd 150.00

Celery Vase, 9-3/4" h, 6-1/2" d, notched edges, ABP 125.00

Charger, 14" d, cut glass, hobstar, cane, and wreath motifs, sgd 300.00

Cologne Bottle, 5-1/4" h, alternating bull's eye and cross-cut squares, faceted cup stopper, sgd "Libbey" 325.00

Compote, 10-1/2" w, 4" h, colorless, pink Nailsea-type loops, flaring top, sgd "Libbey" 595.00

Creamer and Sugar, Zenda, sgd "Libbey" 90.00

Dessert and Underplate, 5-1/2" h, 8-1/2" d plate, amberina, c1917. 975.00

Pitcher, 9-1/2" h, 4-1/2" d top, bulbous petticoat shape, notched edges and handle, ABP, sgd 145.00

Rose Bowl, 3-1/2" w, 2-1/2" h, melon ribbed bowl, beige ground, two pansies and leaves, white beads, sgd "Libbey Cut Glass" 550.00

Salad Bowl and Underplate, 10" d, 6" h bowl, 11-1/2" d underplate, Spilane (Trefoil & Rosette) pattern, cross-cut vesicas, notched prism, hobstars and fans, sgd "Libbey" 2,200.00

Sherbet, silhouette stem, black rabbit, sgd 185.00

Toothpick Holder, 2-1/2" h, Little Lobe, tiny blue flowers, ivy leaves, lower half tinted pink, sgd "Libbey Cut Glass Toledo O" 300.00

Jack-In-The-Pulpit Vase, amberina, gold lettering "World's Fair 1893," painted floral motif, 7" h, $495.

Tumbler, 4" h, Maize, pale green, golden molded leaves with brushed gold highlights 265.00
Vase
  10" h, 6-1/2" w, cut glass, corset shape, notched edges, ABP, sgd 125.00
  11-1/4" h, amberina, flared rim, slender neck, intense shading color, shape #3004, sgd 1,200.00
Water Carafe, Wedgemere pattern, Libbey, 9" h, ABP 1,200.00

LIMOGES

History: Limoges porcelain has been produced in Limoges, France, for over a century by numerous factories in addition to the famed Haviland.

Marks: One of the most frequently encountered marks is "T. & V. Limoges," which is on the wares made by Tressman and Vought. Other identifiable Limoges marks are "A. L." (A. Lanternier), "J. P. L." (J. Pouyat, Limoges), "M. R." (M. Reddon), "Elite," and "Coronet."

References: Susan and Al Bagdade, *Warman's English & Continental Pottery & Porcelain,* 3rd Edition, Krause Publications, 1998; Mary Frank Gaston, *Collector's Encyclopedia of Limoges Porcelain,* 2nd ed., Collector Books, 1992, 1998 value update.

Additional Listings: Haviland China.

Bacon Platter, 9-1/2" x 8", hp flowers, c1876-89............................ 75.00
Butter Pat, 3" d, white ground, ring of green leaves, set of 6 .... 15.00
Cabinet Plate, 9-1/2" d, central printed scene of lovers in wooded setting, scrolled gilt trim with enameled floral cartouches, gilt wood frame 175.00
Cache Pot, 7-1/2" w, 9" h, male and female pheasants on front, mountain scene on obverse, gold handles and 4 ball feet 225.00
Charger
  10" d, hp, two seagulls, gold rococo border, artist sgd "L R L," c1920 .... 250.00
  10" d, hp, swan in lake, green ground, sgd "B & H," c1890... 115.00
  11-1/2" d, boy fishing in lake, dec by Klingenberg & Dwenger, c1900-10.. 295.00
  11-1/2" d, roses, gold rococo on dark green border, mkd "T & V Limoges," c1907-19 .... 350.00
  12-1/4" h, hp ears of corn, sgd "C. L. Olmsted," c1912 .... 95.00

Platter, white ground, pink flowers, dated January 1911, mkd "T & V Limoges, Depose," 16-1/2" l, 9" w, $90.

12-1/2" d, hp, pink and purple clover, green border, white center, gold rococo border... 195.00
13-3/4" d, hp poppies, gilt border, designed by Charles Martin, artist sgd "E. Hamm," c1891 .... 250.00
Demitasse Cup and Saucer, Eiffel Tower on front, white ground, gold trim, green ink mark "Limoges France," gold ink mark "Edite Par Goutde Ville Limoges Made in France" 20.00
Dessert Service, scrolling foliate and swag border, gilt rims and handles, 10-1/4" h coffeepot, six dessert plates, seven cups and saucers, cov sugar, creamer, serving plate.................................. 300.00
Dinner Service, partial
  Foliate and floral swag border, gilt rim, twenty 9-3/4" d dinner plates, 25 large soup plates, 17 smaller soup plates, 19 salad plates, 8 dessert plates, 3 rim soups, large serving bowl, handled sectional serving dish, two-handled charger, 95 pcs 600.00
  Shaped rim, berried-laurel border flanked by decorative gilding, molded and gilt foliate handles, 16" l cov tureen, 3 circular chargers, 46 dinner plates, 35 salad plates, 24 soups, ftd serving bowl, 4 shaped oval dishes, small cov vegetable dish, large oval platter, small oval platter, sauce boat with attached underplate, sauce tureen, ftd cake plate, 2 compotes, 123 pcs 2,500.00
Dresser Box, 3" w, transfer dec sgd "Fragonard," white ground, blue and gold trim 30.00
Game Platter, 17-3/4" l, 12-7/8" w, fish dec, Guerin Mark 3, c1900 . 985.00
Hair Receiver, blue flowers and white butterflies, ivory ground, gold trim, mkd "JPL".. 80.00
Lemonade Pitcher, matching tray, water lily dec, sgd "Vignard Limoges" 350.00
Pitcher, 10" h, 5-1/4" d, hp, purple wisteria blossoms, green leaves, gold trim, gold handle 315.00
Oyster Plate, 9" l, crescent shape, gilt foliate designs, blue, pink, green, and yellow ground, c1900, set of 18 .... 2,100.00
Plaque, 5-5/8" w, 7-5/8" h, scenic, cottages and trees near water, blue and brown, glossy glaze, framed, stamped in green "T & V Limoges France" 520.00
Plate
  8-1/2" d, hp, green, purple, and white flowers, mint green border, mkd "B & G Co. France," c1910-14 .... 135.00
  9-1/4" d, hp roses on pale green ground, daisies on black ground, gilt dec, mkd "B & H Decorating Studio," c1890 .... 150.00
  9-1/2" d, pink roses, blue border, white ground, green crown mark, set of 6 .... 120.00
Tea Service, peacock on flowering branch, shades of green, blue, and red, gilt highlights, 7-3/4" h teapot, creamer, cov sugar, 12 cups and saucers.. 600.00
Tray, 12" l, 5-1/2" w, 1-1/2" h, pink wild roses, worn gold trim 120.00

LIMITED EDITION COLLECTOR PLATES

History: Bing and Grondahl made the first collector plate in 1895. Royal Copenhagen issued its first Christmas plate in 1908.

In the late 1960s and early 1970s, several potteries, glass factories, mints, and artists began issuing plates commemorating people, animals, and events. Christmas plates were supplemented by Mother's Day plates and Easter plates. Speculation swept the field, fostered in part by flamboyant ads in newspapers and flashy direct-mail promotions.

References: Jay Brown, *The Complete Guide To Limited Edition Art Prints,* Krause Publications, 1999; *Collectors' Information Bureau Collectibles Market Guide & Price Index,* 17th ed., Krause Publications, 1999; Beth Dees, *Santa's Price Guide To Contemporary Christmas Collectibles,* Krause Publications, 1997; Carl Luckey, *Luckey's*

Hummel Figurines & Plates, 11th Edition, Krause Publications, 1997; Mary Sieber (ed.), *2000 Price Guide to Limited Edition Collectibles,* Krause Publications, 1999.

Periodicals: Collector Editions, 170 Fifth Ave., 12th Floor, New York, NY 10010; Collectors Mart Magazine, 700 E. State St., Iola, WI 54990; Collectors News, 506 Second St., P.O. Box 156, Grundy Center, IA 50638; Insight on Collectibles, 103 Lakeshore Rd, Ste 202, St. Catharines, Ontario L2N 2T6 Canada; International Collectible Showcase, One Westminster Place, Lake Forest, IL 60045; Plate World, 9200 N. Maryland Ave., Niles, IL 60648; Toybox Magazine, 8393 East Holly Rd, Holly MI 48442.

Collectors' Clubs: Franklin Mint Collectors Society, US Route 1, Franklin Center, PA 19091; Hummel Collector's Club, Inc., P.O. Box 257, Yardley, PA 19067; International Plate Collectors Guild, P.O. Box 487, Artesia, CA 90702; M. I. Hummel Club, Goebel Plaza, Rte. 31, P.O. Box 11, Pennington, NJ 08534.

Museum: Bradford Museum of Collector's Plates, Niles, IL.

Additional Listings: See *Warman's Americana & Collectibles* for more examples of collector plates plus many other limited edition collectibles.

Notes: The first plate issued in a series (FE) is often favored by collectors. Condition is a critical factor, and price is increased if the original box is available.

Limited edition collector plates, more than any other object in this guide, should be collected for design and pleasure and only secondarily as an investment.

Bing and Grondahl (Denmark)

Christmas Plates, various artists, 7" d
1895 Behind the Frozen Window......................................3,450.00
1896 New Moon over Snow Covered Trees 1,975.00
1897 Christmas Meal of the Sparrows...................................725.00
1898 Christmas Roses and Christmas Star.............................700.00
1899 The Crows Enjoying Christmas.....................................900.00
1900 Church Bells Chiming in Christmas 800.00
1901 The Three Wise Men from the East................................450.00
1902 Interior of a Gothic Church...285.00
1903 Happy Expectation of Children 150.00
1904 View of Copenhagen from Frederiksberg Hill 125.00
1905 Anxiety of the Coming Christmas Night 130.00
1906 Sleighing to Church on Christmas Eve 95.00
1907 The Little Match Girl..125.00
1908 St Petri Church of Copenhagen 85.00
1909 Happiness over the Yule Tree 100.00
1910 The old Organist 90.00
1911 First It Was Sung by Angels to Shepherds in the Fields 80.00
1912 Going to Church on Christmas Eve 80.00
1913 Bringing Home the Yule Tree 85.00
1914 Royal Castle of Amalienborg, Copenhagen.....................75.00
1915 Chained Dog Getting Double Meal on Christmas Eve.......120.00
1916 Christmas Prayer of the Sparrows.................................85.00
1917 Arrival of the Christmas Boat 75.00
1918 Fishing Boat Returning Home for Christmas 85.00
1919 Outside the Lighted Window 80.00
1920 Hare in the Snow 70.00
1921 Pigeons in the Castle Court 55.00
1922 Star of Bethlehem 60.00
1923 Royal Hunting Castle, The Hermitage 55.00
1924 Lighthouse in Danish Waters 65.00
1925 The Child's Christmas 70.00
1926 Churchgoers on Christmas Day.....................................65.00

1927 Skating Couple..110.00
1928 Eskimo Looking at Village Church in Greenland................60.00
1929 Fox Outside Farm on Christmas Eve..............................75.00
1930 Yule Tree in Town Hall Square of Copenhagen 85.00
1932 Lifeboat at Work...95.00
1934 Church Bell in Tower 70.00
1936 Royal Guard Outside Amalienborg Castle in Copenhagen..75.00
1938 Lighting the Canles 115.00
1940 Delivering Christmas Letters......................................175.00
1942 Danish Farm on Christmas Night..................................150.00
1944 Sorgenfri Castle 125.00
1946 Commemoration Cross in Honor of Danish Sailors Who Lost
    Their Lives in World War II 90.00
1948 Watchman, Sculpture of Town Hall, Copenhagen 80.00
1950 Kronborg Castle at Elsinore.......................................145.00
1952 Old Copenhagen Canals at Wintertime with Thorvaldsen
    Museum in Background...90.00
1954 Birthplace of Hans Christian Andersen, with Snowman.....110.00
1956 Christmas in Copenhagen..150.00
1958 Santa Claus 110.00
1960 Danish Village Church 175.00
1962 Winter Night 85.00
1964 The Fir Tree and Hare 60.00
1966 Home for Christmas 55.00
1968 Christmas in Church 50.00
1970 Pheasants in the Snow at Christmas 25.00
Mother's Day Plates, Henry Thelander, artist, 6" d
1969 Dog and Puppies 400.00
1971 Cat and Kitten 20.00
1973 Duck and Ducklings 20.00
1975 Doe and Fawns 20.00
1977 Squirrel and Young 25.00
1979 Fox and Cubs 30.00
1981 Hare and Young 40.00
1983 Raccoon and Young 45.00
1985 Bear and Cubs 40.00
1987 Sheep with Lamps 40.00
1989 Cow with Calf 45.00
1990 Hen with Chicks 65.00

Reed & Barton (United States)

Audubon Series, various artists
1970 Pine Siskin, FE..165.00
1971 Red-Shouldered Hawk...75.00
1972 Stilt Sandpiper...70.00
1974 Boreal Chickadee 60.00
1975 Yellow-Breasted Chat 60.00
1977 Purple Finch..65.00
Christmas Series, Damascene silver, 11" d through 1978, 8" d 1979 to present
1970 A Partridge in a Pear Tree, FE....................................200.00
1971 We Three Kings of Orient Are.......................................65.00
1973 Adoration of the Kings..75.00
1975 Adoration of the Kings..65.00
1977 Decorating the Church..60.00
1979 Merry Old Santa Claus..65.00
1981 The Shopkeeper at Christmas......................................75.00

Rosenthal (Germany)

Christmas Plates, various artists, 8 1/2" d
1910 Winter Peace 550.00
1911 The Three Wise Men..325.00
1912 Shooting Stars 250.00
1913 Christmas Lights 235.00
1915 Walking to Church..180.00
1917 Angel of Peace 200.00
1919 St Christopher with the Christ Child...............................225.00
1920 The Manger in Bethlehem...300.00
1922 Advent Branch 210.00
1924 Deer in the Woods 200.00

1926 Christmas in the Mountains 175.00
1928 Chalet Christmas 185.00
1930 Group of Deer under the Pines 190.00
1932 Christ Child 200.00
1934 Christmas Peace..210.00
1936 Nurmberg Angel 185.00
1940 Marien Church in Danzig 250.00
1942 Marianburg Castle..300.00
1944 Wood Scape 275.00
1946 Christmas in an Alpine Valley 250.00
1948 Message to the Shepherds 875.00
1950 Christmas in the Forest...190.00
1952 Christmas in the Alps 195.00
1954 Christmas Eve...190.00
1956 Christmas in the Alps 190.00
1958 Christmas Eve...185.00
1960 Christmas in Small Village 210.00
1962 Christmas Eve...185.00
1964 Christmas Market in Nurmberg 220.00
1966 Christmas in Ulm 250.00
1968 Christmas in Bremen 200.00
1970 Christmas in Cologne..175.00

Royal Copenhagen (Denmark)

Christmas Plates, various artists, 6" d 1908, 1909, 1910; 7" 1911 to
    present
1908 Madonna and Child..1,750.00
1909 Danish Landscape 150.00
1910 The Magi 120.00
1911 Danish Landscape 135.00
1912 Elderly Couple by Christmas Tree 120.00
1913 Spire of Frederik's Church, Copenhagen...........................125.00
1914 Sparrows in Tree at Church of the Holy Spirit,
    Copenhagen..100.00
1915 Danish Landscape 150.00
1916 Shepherd in the Field on Christmas Night 85.00
1917 Tower of Our Savior's Church, Copenhagen 90.00
1918 Sheep and Shepherds 80.00
1919 In the Park...80.00
1920 Mary with the Child Jesus 75.00

Royal Copenhagen, Christmas, 1963, Windmill, $85.

1921 Aabenraa Marketplace...75.00
1922 Three Singing Angels...70.00
1923 Danish Landscape 70.00
1924 Christmas Star Over the Sea and Sailing Ship 100.00
1925 Street Scene from Christianshavn, Copenhagen.................85.00
1926 View of Christmas Canal, Copenhagen 75.00
1927 Ship's Boy at the Tiller on Christmas Night 140.00
1928 Vicar's Family on Way to Church.....................................75.00
1929 Grundtvig Church, Copenhagen 100.00
1930 Fishing Boats on the Way to the Harbor 80.00
1931 Mother and Child...90.00
1932 Frederiksberg Gardens with Statue of Frederik VI...............90.00
1933 The Great Belt Ferry 110.00
1934 The Hermitage Castle 115.00
1935 Fishing Boat off Kronborg Castle 145.00
1936 Roskilde Cathedral...130.00
1937 Christmas Scene in Main Street, Copenhagen..................135.00
1938 Round Church in Osterlars on Bornholm 200.00
1939 Expeditionary Ship in Pack-Ice of Greenland 180.00
1940 The Good Shepherd 300.00
1942 Bell Tower of Old Church in Jutland 290.00
1944 Typical Danish Winter Scene 150.00
1946 Zealand Village Church...175.00
1948 Nodebo Church at Christmastime....................................160.00
1950 Boeslund Church, Zealand 175.00
1952 Christmas in the Forest...125.00
1954 Amalienborg Palace, Copenhagen 160.00
1956 Rosenborg Castle, Copenhagen.....................................170.00
1958 Sunshine over Greenland 145.00
1960 The Stag 150.00
1962 The Little Mermaid at Wintertime 220.00
1964 Fetching the Christmas Tree...80.00
1966 Blackbird at Christmastime 60.00
1968 The Last Umiak..45.00
1970 Christmas Rose and Cat...115.00
Mother's Day Plates, various artists, 6 1/4" d
1971 American Mother...125.00
1973 Danish Mother...60.00
1975 Bird in Nest 50.00
1977 The Twins 50.00
1979 A Loving Mother 30.00
1981 Reunion...40.00

Wedgwood (Great Britain)

Christmas Series, jasper stoneware, 8" d
1969 Windsor Castle, FE 225.00
1970 Christmas in Trafalgar Square 30.00
1971 Piccadilly Circus, London 45.00
1972 St Paul's Cathedral 40.00
1973 The Tower of London 45.00
1974 The Houses of Parliament 40.00
1975 Tower Bridge...50.00
1976 Hampton Court...45.00
1977 Westminster Abbey...55.00
1978 The Horse Guards 55.00
1979 Buckingham Palace 60.00
1980 St James Palace 70.00
1982 Lambeth Palace 80.00
1981 Marble Arch...75.00
1983 All Souls, Langham Palace 80.00
1984 Constitution Hill 80.00
1985 The Tate gallery 80.00
1986 The Albert Memorial..80.00
1987 Guidhall 80.00
1988 The Observatory/Greenwich 90.00
1989 Winchester Cathedral 85.00
Mothers Series, jasper stoneware, 6 1/2" d
1971 Sportive Love, FE 25.00
1972 The Sewing Lesson 20.00
1973 The Baptism of Achilles 30.00

LITHOPHANES

History: Lithophanes are highly translucent porcelain panels with impressed designs. The designs result from differences in the thickness of the plaque; thin parts transmit an abundance of light while thicker parts represent shadows.

Lithophanes were first made by the Royal Berlin Porcelain Works in 1828. Other factories in Germany, France, and England later produced them. The majority of lithophanes on the market today were made between 1850 and 1900.

Collectors' Club: Lithophane Collectors Club, 2030 Robinwood Ave., P.O. Box 4557, Toledo, OH 43620.

Museum: Blair Museum of Lithophanes and Carved Waxes, Toledo, OH.

Candle Shield, 9" h, panel with scene of 2 country boys playing with goat, castle in background 275.00
Cup and Saucer, blue Oriental lady with nude lady 175.00
Fairy Lamp, 9" h, 3 panels, lady leaning out of tower, rural romantic scenes...1,250.00
Lamp, oil
5" d, 4" h, circular, 4 convex colored lithophane sides with landscapes, pierced gallery and lid 350.00

Lamp, wall type, brass, lithophane woodland scene, $170.

5-1/4" h, 5-1/4" w, lithophane sides of landscapes, star punched brass frame, scrolled front, single wired handle, electrified, orig burner, some damage to frame..225.00
Night Lamp, 5-1/4" h, sq, 4 scenes, irid green porcelain base, gold trim, electrified..650.00
Panel
  KPM
    2-1/2" x 3-1/4", view from West Point............................195.00
    3-7/8" x 5-1/4", lake setting, ship and windmill 175.00
  PPM
    3-1/4" x 5-1/4", view of Paterson Falls 200.00
    4" x 6", woman and children with hay cart, incised "PPM. 553"..125.00
  PR Sickle, 4-1/4" x 5"
    Cupid and girl fishing...180.00
    Scene of 2 women in doorway, dog and 2 pigeons, sgd, #1320 ....150.00
  Unmarked, 6" x 7-1/2", Madonna and Child 175.00
Pitcher, puzzle type, Victorian scene, nude on bottom 175.00
Stein, lithophane in bottom, German porcelain, transfer dec
  11" h, Neuschwanstein Castle, Bavaria, hp gold borders, ornamental pewter lid...100.00
  12-3/4" h, Technical Troops Regimental, detailed infantry multicolor motif framed with relief pearl borders, gold leaf bands, ornamental pewter lid with soldier finial, eagle thumb-lift 120.00
  13" h, transfer dec, Navy Regimental, detailed nautical multicolor motif framed with relief pearl borders, gold leaf bands, ornamental pewter lid with sailor finial, eagle thumb-lift 120.00
Tea Warmer, 5-7/8 h, one pc cylindrical panel, 4 seasonal landscapes with children, copper frame, finger grip and molded base 250.00
Wall Plaque, 14" x 15-1/4", int. scene with Arabian man and woman, multicolored geometric slag glass border, unmarked, imperfections in porcelain..125.00

LIVERPOOL CHINA

History: Liverpool is the name given to products made at several potteries in Liverpool, England, between 1750 and 1840. Seth and James Pennington and Richard Chaffers were among the early potters who made tin-enameled earthenware.

By the 1780s, tin-glazed earthenware gave way to cream-colored wares decorated with cobalt blue, enameled colors, and blue or black transfers.

The Liverpool glaze is characterized by bubbles and frequent clouding under the foot rims. By 1800 about 80 potteries were working in the town producing not only creamware, but soft paste, soapstone, and bone porcelain.

References: Susan and Al Bagdade, *Warman's English & Continental Pottery & Porcelain,* 3rd Edition, Krause Publications, 1998; Robert McCauley, *Liverpool Transfer Designs on Anglo-American Pottery,* Southworth-Anthoensen Press; Bernard M. Watney, *Liverpool Porcelain of the Eighteenth Century,* Antique Collectors' Club, Ltd., 1997.

Museums: City of Liverpool Museum, Liverpool, England; Henry Ford Museum, Dearborn, MI; Potsdam Public Museum, Potsdam, NY.

Reproduction Alert: Reproduction Liverpool pieces were documented as early as 1942. One example is a black transfer-decorated jug which was made in the 1930s. The jugs vary in height from 8-1/2 to 11 inches. On one side is "The Shipwright's Arms"; on the other, the ship Caroline flying the American flag; and under the spout, a wreath with the words "James Leech."

Jug, The Farmer's Arms, multicolored, c1810, 7-3/4" h, $850.

A transfer of the *Caroline* also was used on a Sunderland bowl about 1936 and reproduction mugs were made bearing the name "James Leech" and an eagle.

The reproduction pieces have a crackled glaze and often age cracks have been artificially produced. When compared to genuine pieces, reproductions are thicker and heavier and have weaker transfers, grayish color (not as crisp and black), ecru or gray body color instead of cream, and crazing that does not spiral upward.

Cup and Saucer, handleless, black transfer, bust of Washington and other gentleman on cup, "Washington, His Country's Father" on saucer, hairlines in cup 330.00
Jug, creamware, transfer print
   7-3/4" h, reserve of ships *L'Insurgent and Constellation,* reserve of ship yard, cracks, chips, minor losses, transfer imperfections 1,265.00
   8-3/4" h, "The Greenwich Pensioner," text underneath, ship on reverse, repairs 460.00
   9-1/2" h, "Representation of the British defeat of the French Fleet of Brest by Earl Howe, 1794," reverse "The Flowing Cann," picture of drinking and dancing, descriptive text, minor glaze wear 815.00
   9-5/8" h, English hunting scenes "Jos Edge Caldon Grange" inscribed under spout, extensive repairs 345.00
   9-3/4" h, oval medallion portrait of John Adams, surrounded by Plenty, Justice and Cupid, circular panel "Peace Plenty and Independence" on reverse flanked by Plenty and Peace destroying the implements of war, surmounted by spread eagle, chips, scratches, minor transfer wear 4,025.00
   9-3/4" h, reserves of Thomas Jefferson and James Monroe, misidentified as "Hancock," hp foliate gilt highlights, repairs, hairlines, minor chip, gilt, and enamel wear 20,700.00
   10" h, portrait of Thomas Jefferson, American eagle on reverse, chips, glaze wear to handle 21,850.00
Mug
   3-3/4" h, dark brown transfer, Hope, allover luster trim, c1829-30 .... 200.00
   6" h, creamware, transfer printed three masted ship under sail, figure of Hope, "Jennett Lawson," hairline on base 750.00
Pitcher
   8" h, red transfer dec, creamware, American eagle, reverse with figural panel, wear to transfer, chips, hairline to base 980.00
   10" h, transfer dec, obverse with oval reserve of military scene, conquering hero and symbolic fallen lion, bordered by American flags, wreath of peace, cannon, banner "By virtue and valor, we have freed our country, extended our commerce, and laid the foundation of a great empire," reverse with American warship *The John,* polychrome monogram above great seal of US under spout, floral device under handle, band of grapes and flowers top

band, damage, restoration, discoloration........................... 690.00
Trinket Pot, cov, 5-1/4" d, Delft, blue and white, two handles, chips and hairline in bottom 495.00

LOETZ

History: Loetz is a type of iridescent art glass that was made in Austria by J. Loetz Witwe in the late 1890s. Loetz was a contemporary of L. C. Tiffany's, and he had worked in the Tiffany factory before establishing his own operation; therefore, much of the wares are similar in appearance to Tiffany products. The Loetz factory also produced items with fine cameos on cased glass.

Marks: Some pieces are signed "Loetz," "Loetz, Austria," or "Austria."

Reference: Robert and Deborah Truitt, *Collectible Bohemian Glass:* 1880-1940, R & D Glass, 1995.

Bowl, 9" w, 6-1/2" d, 5" h, rect amber glass bowl, papillon and swirled irid, crimped rim, polished pontil, Art Nouveau gilded and enameled bronze mount of entwined snakes and flowering tulip bulbs, c1900 ...... 1,725.00
Bulb Vase, 4-3/4" h, mold blown, green, pulled magenta and pearl irid, rising to green bulbous top, small inside rim chips 1,035.00
Compote, 11" d, 10-1/2" h, ruffled rim, hobnailed bowl, mottled irid rose red and pale green, gilt metal Vienna Secessionist style tripart frame . 265.00
Decanter, 11-1/4" h, bottle form, cobalt blue ground, silver blue luster, silver overlay, carved as foliate and scrolling dec, monogrammed, conforming silver overlaid stopper 2,500.00
Ewer, 10-1/2" h, flared cylindrical form, brilliant blue papillon dec, silver overlay engraved as entwined grapes on vines, applied silver handle, polished pontil 8,050.00
Inkwell, 3-1/2" h, amethyst, sq, irid, web design, bronze collar ..125.00
Jack-In-The-Pulpit Vase, 13-1/2" h, freeblown floriform, colorless, striated gold amber pulled feather dec, gold and blue irid surface 1,500.00
Lamp, desk, 17-1/4" h, double socket, raised gold irid festoons on linen-fold style shades, mounted on adjustable standard, ring-shaped finial, oval hammered brass base............................ 1,495.00
Lamp Shade, mushroom shape, creamy irid ground, irid violet wavy swirled oil spot bands, pr...................... 1,380.00
Pitcher, 8-1/2" h, pinched bulbous body, purple-green irid, applied handle, gilt metal mount with cast foliate motif............................... 600.00
Rose Bowl, 6-1/2" d, ruffled purple irid raindrop dec................... 220.00

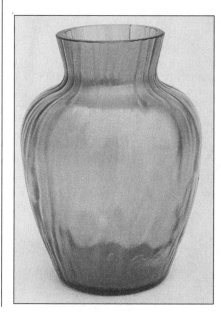

Vase, irid green, tree bark pattern, acid etched sgd "Loetz, Austria," 4-1/4" h, $200.

Sweetmeat Jar, cov, 5" h, irid silver spider web dec, green ground, sgd 400.00
Vase
4-1/4" h, pinched oviform, raised rim, semi-opaque pink body, pulled purple swirls, silver spots, overall irid surface, spurious acid stamp in polished pontil, c1900 ....2,645.00
4-1/4" h, pinched oviform, tricorn rim, light blue body, surface dec with knotted wood texture, overall light blue luster, polished pontil, few dark inclusions 375.00
4-1/2" h, flared oval body, green glass, silver-blue oil spot irid, silver overlay of Art Nouveau styled clover, polished pontil..........815.00
5" h, pinched oval, amber ground, pulled irid gold threads in scalloped drapery pattern, opalescent blue luster highlights, polished pontil, c1900 ....575.00
5-1/2" h, oviform, raised and flared rim, pale pink body, pulled and swirled silver irid threads and oval dots over gold oil spot luster surface, polished pontil 1,495.00
6" h, double bulbed and pinched form, pale green ground with irid gold papillon dec, polished pontil 350.00
6" h, waisted form, flattened rim, cobalt blue, silver papillon irid, polished pontil 675.00
6-1/2" h, tapered form, cased glass with swirled irid green rising to pearly blue, Art Nouveau stylized silver overlay, polished pontil, rubbed marks on overlay, c1905 ....750.00
7" h, broad shouldered form, ruffled rim, colorless body with light blue papillon dec on dark gold luster surface, allover stylized iris silver overlay dec, c1900, burst bubble, loss to silver overlay 1,725.00
7-3/4" h, tricorn rim flaring to wide pinched base, irid green, pulled blue, purple, and green dec, polished pontil, sgd "Loetz Austria"... 1,035.00
8" h, oviform, raised rim, colorless cased to olive green, broad leaves of irid papillon dec, sgd "Loetz Austria" in polished pontil......1,265.00
9" h, Persian bottle form, salmon pink, pulled silver blue leaves rising from base, descending from mouth, band of blue, amber, and white pulled swirls at base, polished pontil inscribed "Loetz Austria," c1900 ....2,750.00
10" h, three-sided double bulbed body, translucent green mold blown glass, knotted wood grain surface, light irid, ruffled rim, polished pontil 350.00
10" h, waisted, colorless glass with veils of gold irid papillon dec, over reddish gold irid surface, polished pontil, c1900 ....2,200.00

LUSTER WARE

History: Lustering on a piece of pottery creates a metallic, sometimes iridescent, appearance. Josiah Wedgwood experimented with the technique in the 1790s. Between 1805 and 1840, lustered earthenware pieces were created in England by makers such as Adams, Bailey and Batkin, Copeland and Garrett, Wedgwood, and Enoch Wood.

Luster decorations often were used in conjunction with enamels and transfers. Transfers used for luster decoration covered a wide range of public and domestic subjects. They frequently were accompanied by pious or sentimental doggerel as well phrases which reflected on the humors of everyday life.

Copper luster was created by the addition of a copper compound to the glaze. It was very popular in America during the 19th century, and collecting it became a fad from the 1920s to the 1950s. Today it has a limited market.

Pink luster was made by using a gold mixture. Silver luster pieces were first covered completely with a thin coating of a "steel luster" mixture, containing a small quantity of platinum oxide. An additional coating of platinum, worked in water, was then applied before firing.

Sunderland is a coarse type of cream-colored earthenware with a marbled or spotted pink luster decoration which shades from pink to purple. A solution of gold compound applied to the white body developed the many shades of pink.

The development of electroplating in 1840 created a sharp decline in the demands for metal-surfaced earthenware.

Reference: Michael Gibson, *19th Century Lustreware,* Antique Collectors' Club, 1999.

Reproduction Alert: The market for copper luster has been softened by reproductions, especially creamers and the "polka" jug, which fool many new buyers. Reproductions are heavier in appearance and weight than the earlier pieces.

Additional Listings: English Soft Paste.

Copper
Creamer
4" h, blue bands dec...90.00
4-1/2" h, leaf band dec 85.00
Figure, 8" h, spaniels, pr...125.00
Goblet, 4-1/2" h, 3-1/2" d, pink luster band, floral resist dec, copper luster int. 50.00
Jug, 8" h, 3 transfers of mother and child playing badminton and writing letters on canary yellow band...185.00
Milk Jug, light blue bands, 2 white dogs 160.00
Milk Pitcher, brown base 130.00
Mug, 4-3/4" h, leaves and berries on orange luster band...60.00
Pepper Shaker, 4-1/4" h, cream colored band.............................45.00
Pitcher
4-1/4" h, molded and applied vintage band and classical scenes with cherubs and eagle, blue band with white and worn pink luster, wear, crazing, and short hairline in spout 165.00
7-1/2" h, Adam Buck style, two reserves of genre scenes, yellow ground, England, 19th C, minor base chip 175.00
10" h, wide blue band around body, emb greyhound, bull, and urn of flowers in polychrome enamel, pink and purple luster....210.00
Teapot, 6" h, emb ribs, polychrome enameled floral dec 125.00

Pink
Child's Mug, 2" h, pink luster band, reddish hunter and dogs transfer, green highlighted foliate transfer...85.00

Bowl, copper luster ground, blue band, applied multicolored pastoral and floral dec, pedestal base, 6-3/8" d at top, 3-3/4" h, $115.

Creamer, 4-3/8" h, stylized flower band, pink luster highlights and rim, ftd 75.00
Cup and Saucer, magenta transfers, Faith, Hope, and Charity, applied green enamel highlights, pink luster line borders 60.00
Figure, 4-1/2" h, dogs, white, luster gilt collar, cobalt blue base with gilt trim, Staffordshire, pr....................................620.00
Pitcher
  5-1/2" h, House pattern, ornate pink luster dec 120.00
  5-3/4" h, emb ribs, eagle, and flowers in pink and purple luster 150.00
Plate
  6-1/4" d, relief figures of dogs running on rim, highlighted with green, red, and pink luster, red, green, and blue stylized floral dec in center 55.00
  7-3/4" d, green transfer of "Employ time well," emb floral border with polychrome enamel and luster trim 75.00
  9-3/4" d, painted flowers and leaves, pink, purple, and yellow, green and red overglaze...45.00
Plaque, 9-3/8" l, 8-3/8" h, rect, "The Great Eastern Steam Ship," black transfer with polychrome, pink luster shaped border................450.00
Posset Cup and Saucer, Tray, 5" h, wide luster bands flanked by 2 red bands, 19th C 295.00
Teapot, 12" h, House pattern, Queen Anne style, repaired finial on lid...285.00
Toddy Plate, 5-1/16" d, pink luster House pattern, emb floral sprigs border..45.00
Waste Bowl, 6" d, House pattern 125.00

Silver

Coffee Service, 7-3/8" h cov coffeepot, cov sugar bowl, 6 coffee cans and saucers, silver luster grape and leaves, rust enamel accents, yellow ground 450.00
Creamer, 4" h, 5" w, ribbed loop base, incised band near top, shaped handle 85.00
Cup and Saucer, handleless, overall floral band on cup, scattered florals on saucer 45.00
Figure, 11-7/8" l, standing lion, paw on globe, rect base, early 19th C, repaired 900.00
Goblet, 4-3/8" h, silver luster grapes and vines, white ground, lustered foot 220.00
Jug
  4-1/2" h, village scene 100.00
  5-1/2" h, blue printed hunting scene, border of flowers and leaves, luster ground, Staffordshire, c1815...................................975.00
  6-1/2" h, shell detail, minor wear 100.00
Miniature Pitcher, 2-1/4" h, Sandland Ware, silver accents and leaves, mkd "LLE"...30.00
Pitcher, 5-1/2" h, squatty body, wide lip, overall silver luster, 19th C 95.00
Spill Vase, 4-1/8" h, gray marbleized applied vines and fruits, silver luster accents, white int., pr 95.00
Teapot, 5-1/4" h, reeded detail...140.00
Trivet, Sadler...30.00

Sunderland

Bowl, 8-1/4" d, polychrome highlighted black transfers of ship and verse, pink marble luster, mid 18th C....................................265.00
Creamer, 5" h, "The Sailor's Tear," outlined in florals, verse with sailing ship and "May Peace and Plenty...," luster trim........................275.00
Jug
  7-1/2" h, transfer printed, painted polychrome enamels, Iron Bridge in Sunderland on one side, ship on reverse, chips, some wear ..300.00
  8-3/8" h, transfer printed, painted polychrome enamels, two marine rhymes, chips, some wear 245.00
Salt, master, Cloud pattern, ftd 50.00

Finger Bowl and Underplate, colorless body, aquamarine twist bands, gold borders, 4-1/2" d bowl, 6-3/4" d underplate, $165.

Mug
  4-3/4" h, two polychrome dec transfers, "Success to the Fisherman" and "Love," motto, two luster ovals, frog figure inside, staining, wear to rim 690.00
  5-5/8" h, transfer dec, Sailor's Farewell on one side, Sailor's Prayer on reverse, two handles, frog figure inside, hairline 600.00
Mustard Pot, 4" h, loop handle..160.00
Pitcher, 7-1/8" h, hex panels, black transfers of John Wesley on one side, verse on other, pink marble luster, c1850........................185.00
Plaque, 8-1/2" l, 7-1/2" w, "Thou God Seeist Me," luster trim, Dixon mark 175.00

LUTZ-TYPE GLASS

History: Lutz-type glass is an art glass attributed to Nicholas Lutz. He made this type of glass while at the Boston and Sandwich Glass Co. from 1869 until 1888. Since Lutz-type glass was popular, copied by many capable glassmakers, and unsigned, it is nearly impossible to distinguish genuine Lutz products.

Lutz is believed to have made two distinct types of glass: striped and threaded. The striped glass was made by using threaded glass rods in the Venetian manner, and this style is often confused with authentic Venetian glass. Threaded glass was blown and decorated with winding threads of glass.

Bowl, 3-1/4" d, 3" h, white, amethyst, and yellow latticino, colorless ground, goldstone border 55.00
Compote, 8-7/8" x 6-1/2", DQ, threaded, amberina, colorless hollow stem 500.00
Epergne, 3 pcs, pink threads 275.00
Finger Bowl and Underplate, 7" d, ruffled edge, amber swirls, amethyst latticino, gold metallic borders...165.00
Lamp Shade, 8" sq, 20-1/2" fitter ring, opaque white loopings, applied cranberry threading, ribbon edge 180.00
Punch Cup, 3" x 2-5/8", cranberry threading, colorless ground, circular foot, applied colorless handle...85.00
Tumbler, 3-3/4" d, white and amethyst latticino goldstone highlights 75.00
Vase, 8" h, bulbous, white latticino, colorless ground, applied colorless handle 150.00

MAASTRICHT WARE

History: Petrus Regout founded the De Sphinx Pottery in 1836 in Maastricht, Holland. The firm specialized in transfer-printed earthenwares. Other factories also were established in the area, many employing English workmen and adopting their techniques. Maastricht china was exported to the United States in competition with English products.

Bowl
    6" d, Sana pattern, black Oriental transfer dec, orange wash, mkd "Petrus Regout Maastricht Sana" 75.00
    7-1/2" d, 4" h, PaJong, mkd "Petrus Regout & Co., Holland"...... 120.00
Creamer and Sugar, 2-1/4" h, yellow, green, and blue gaudy stick spatterware floral dec, mkd "Maastricht" 175.00
Pitcher, 5" h, red transfer rooster, iris, and leaves, mkd "Regout & Co. Haan" 75.00
Plate
    7-1/2" d, Timor, multicolored Oriental dec, luster trim, mkd 40.00
    8" d, Canton, blue and white, luster trim 40.00
    9" d, polychrome floral dec, mkd "Maastricht" 35.00
    9-7/8" d, design spatter, red flowers, green leaves, blue border, mkd "Maastricht" 75.00
Platter, 15-1/4" d, farm scene, farm house and windmills in background, blue and white, mkd "Maastricht, Royal Sphinx" 150.00
Vegetable Dish, 8-1/4" sq, polychrome floral dec, wear and stains, mkd "Maastricht" 95.00

MAJOLICA

History: Majolica, an opaque, tin-glazed pottery, has been produced in many countries for centuries. It was named after the Spanish Island of Majorca, where figuline (a potter's clay) is found. Today, however, the term "majolica" denotes a type of pottery, which was made during the last half of the 19th century in Europe and America.

Saucer, ribbed, raised garlands at top, mkd "Society Ceramique Potrehe," 5-3/4" d, $10.

Majolica frequently depicts elements of nature: leaves, flowers, birds, and fish. Designs were painted on the soft clay body using vitreous colors and fired under a clear lead glaze to impart the rich color and brilliance characteristic of majolica.

Victorian decorative art philosophy dictated that the primary function of design was to attract the eye; usefulness was secondary. Majolica was a welcome and colorful change from the familiar blue and white wares, creamwares, and white ironstone of the day.

Marks: Wedgwood, George Jones, Holdcraft, and Minton were a few of the English majolica manufacturers who marked their wares. Most of their pieces can be identified through the English Registry mark and/or the potterdesigner's mark. Sarreguemines in France and Villeroy and Boch in Baden, Germany, produced majolica that compared favorably with the finer English majolica. Most Continental pieces had an incised number on the base.

Although 600-plus American potteries produced majolica between 1850 and 1900, only a handful chose to identify their wares. Among these manufacturers were George Morely, Edwin Bennett, the Chesapeake Pottery Company, the New Milford-Wannoppee Pottery Company, and the firm of Griffen, Smith, and Hill. The others hoped their unmarked pieces would be taken for English examples.

References: Susan and Al Bagdade, *Warman's American Pottery and Porcelain*, Wallace-Homestead, 1994; ——, *Warman's English & Continental Pottery & Porcelain, 2nd ed.*, Wallace-Homestead, 1991; Victoria Bergesen, *Majolica: British, Continental, and American Wares, 1851-1915*, Barrie & Jenkins, 1989; Leslie Bockol, *Victorian Majolica*, Schiffer Publishing, 1996; Helen Cunningham, *Majolica Figures*, Schiffer Publishing, 1997; Nicholas M. Dawes, *Majolica, Crown*, 1990; Marilyn G. Karmason and Joan B. Stacke, *Majolica, A Complete History and Illustrated Survey*, Abrams, 1989; Mariann Katz-Marks, *Collector's Encyclopedia of Majolica*, Collector Books, 1992, 1996 value update; Marshall P. Katz and Robert Lehr, *Palissy Ware: Nineteenth Century French Ceramics from Avisseau to Renoleau*, Athlone Press, 1996; Price Guide to Majolica, L-W Book Sales, 1997; Mike Schneider, *Majolica*, Schiffer Publishing, 1990, 1995 value update; Jeffrey B. Snyder and Leslie J. Bockol, *Majolica: European and American Wares*, Schiffer Publishing, 1994.

Periodical: Majolica Market, 2720 N 45 Rd, Manton, MI 49663.

Collectors' Club: Majolica International Society, 1275 First Ave., Ste. 103, New York, NY 10021.

Reproduction Alert: Majolica-style pieces are a favorite of today's interior decorators. Many exact copies of period pieces are being manufactured. In addition, fantasy pieces incorporating late Victorian-era design motifs have entered the market and confused many novice collectors.

Modern majolica reproductions differ from period pieces in these ways: (1) modern reproductions tend to be lighter in weight than their Victorian ancestors; (2) the glaze on newer pieces may not be as rich or deeply colored as on period pieces; (3) new pieces usually have a

SPECIAL AUCTIONS

Michael G. Strawser
200 N Main, P. O. Box 332
Wolcottville, IN 46795
(219) 854-2859

plain white bottom, period pieces almost always have colored or mottled bases; (4) a bisque finish either inside or on the bottom generally means the piece is new; and (5) if the design prevents the piece from being functional—e.g., a lip of a pitcher that does not allow proper pouring—it is a new piece made primarily for decorative purposes.

Some reproductions bear old marks. Period marks found on modern pieces include (a) "Etruscan Majolica" (the mark of Griffen, Smith and Hill) and (b) a British registry mark.

Advisor: Mary D. Harris.

Note: Prices listed below are for pieces with good color and in mint condition. For less-than-perfect pieces, decrease value proportionally according to the degree of damage or restoration.

Basket, 6" h, Etruscan, basketweave body, twisted twig handle, twig rim and base, pink int., Griffin, Smith and Hill monogram imp mark 440.00
Bowl, 8" d, Shell and Seaweed, Griffin, Smith and Hill monogram, "Etruscan Majolica" circle imp mark, imperfections 140.00
Bread Tray, Oak Leaf, minor edge chips 125.00
Butter Dish
　4" h, Shell and Seaweed, Griffin, Smith and Hill monogram, "Etruscan Majolica" circle imp mark, flakes on rim of bowl and lid 275.00
　8" d, butterfly topped lid, blue and yellow checkerboard design, circular ribbed body with brown glaze, Griffin, Smith and Hill monogram imp mark, minor chips under plate 220.00
Butter Pat, 3" d
　Begonia Leaf, pr, minor damage 70.00

Syrup, Sunflower, mottled blue ground, yellow and brown flower, green leaves, twig handle, pewter top, mkd "Etruscan Majolica," 8" h, $195.

　Geranium Leaf, pr, some damage 110.00
　Pansy 70.00
　Shell and Seaweed, pr, chips on underside 125.00
Cake Stand, 9-1/2" d, 5-3/8" h, Ivy, Griffin, Smith and Hill monogram imp mark, minor crazing 200.00
Cheese Keeper, 11" d, 6" h, Lily, Griffin, Smith and Hill monogram, "Etruscan Majolica" circle imp mark 2,310.00
Cigar Holder, match holder and striker, 7" h boy standing next to tree 125.00
Coffeepot, 6" h, Shell and Seaweed, Griffin, Smith and Hill monogram, "Etruscan Majolica" circle imp mark, small chip on lid rim, minor roughness to spout 550.00
Compote
　8" d, 6" h, Shell and Seaweed, Griffin, Smith and Hill monogram, "Etruscan Majolica" circle imp mark 385.00
　9" d, 7" h, Maple Leaf, Griffin, Smith and Hill monogram imp mark, minor imperfections 320.00
　10" d, 4" h, Classical Series, monotone green, classical center panel design, twisting left and vine border, Griffin, Smith and Hill monogram imp mark, hairline, chips 100.00
Cream Pitcher, 3" h
　Albino Coral, Griffin, Smith and Hill monogram, "Etruscan Majolica" circle imp mark 70.00
　Shell and Seaweed, Griffin, Smith and Hill monogram, "Etruscan Majolica" circle imp mark, flakes on rim 185.00
Cup and Saucer
　Bamboo, Etruscan, slight rim repair to cup 220.00
　Shell and Seaweed, 3" d cup, 5" d saucer 110.00
Cuspidor, 6" h, Shell and Seaweed, Griffin, Smith and Hill monogram, "Etruscan Majolica" circle imp mark 275.00
Dish, 6" l, Begonia Leaf, green, yellow butterfly perched in center, Griffin, Smith and Hill monogram imp mark, repair to tip 250.00
Jardiniere, 16" h, 13" d, three winged ladies around base, goat's feet, three medallions with birds, turquoise, brown, gray, green, and yellow, turquoise int., Minton, wear, restoration 925.00
Jug, 7" h, Baseball and Soccer Player, full color, pink glazed int., Griffin, Smith and Hill monogram, "Etruscan Majolica" circle imp mark, chip on rim 1,870.00
Oyster Plate, 9-1/4" d, Dolphin, Wedgwood 1,550.00
Pitcher
　5" h, Rustic, Griffin, Smith and Hill monogram, "Etruscan Majolica" circle imp mark, imperfections 125.00
　5" h, Wild Rose, butterfly lip, Griffin, Smith and Hill monogram imp mark, minor imperfections 135.00
　6" h, Fern, Griffin, Smith and Hill monogram, "Etruscan Majolica" circle imp mark, imperfections 180.00
　7-1/2" h, barrel, vine and floral design, lavender int., George Jones, restoration 150.00
Plate
　7-1/2" d, molded fruits and leaves, Sarreguemines 60.00
　8" d, Cauliflower, imperfections 135.00
　8-1/2" d, Shell and Fishnet, turquoise 250.00
　9-1/4" d, Strawberry and Apple, yellow border, Etruscan, hairline 115.00
　10" d, Blackberry, basketweave 75.00
Platter, 12" l, Geranium, Griffin, Smith and Hill monogram imp mark, chip on underside of rim 200.00
Punch Bowl, 12" d, 7" h, ftd, Bird and Fan, white ground, turquoise and multicolored birds, white, gray, and yellow fans, turquoise int., Wedgwood, minor professional hairline repair 990.00
Sardine Box, cov, detached underplate, 9" d
　Lily, swan finial, yellow background, white lilies, green leaves, brown rope border, pink int., Griffin, Smith and Hill monogram, "Etruscan Majolica" circle imp mark, chip on edge of lid, repair to swan neck 690.00
　Pointed Leaves, Etruscan, Griffin, Smith and Hill monogram imp mark, chips on box and lid 425.00
Sauce Dish, 8" l, Daisy, Etruscan, Griffin, Smith and Hill monogram imp mark, minor imperfections 275.00

Syrup Pitcher

   6" h, Coral, Griffin, Smith and Hill monogram, "Etruscan Majolica" circle imp mark, repair to handle..165.00

   8" h, Albino Sunflower, Griffin, Smith and Hill monogram, "Etruscan Majolica" circle imp mark, wear at base.............................200.00

Tea Set, Cauliflower, Etruscan, minor damage...........................675.00

Vase, 23" h, large cornstalk, corn on top, black boy figure in front of stalk, pink and lavender native garb, holding jugs and cup... 1,950.00

MAPS

History: Maps provide one of the best ways to study the growth of a country or region. From the 16th to the early 20th century, maps were both informative and decorative. Engravers provided ornamental detailing, such as ornate calligraphy and scrolling, especially on bird's-eye views and city maps. Many maps were hand colored to enhance their beauty.

Maps generally were published as plates in books. Many of the maps available today are simply single sheets from cut-apart books.

In the last quarter of the 19th century, representatives from firms in Philadelphia, Chicago, and elsewhere traveled the United States preparing county atlases, often with a sheet for each township and a sheet for each major city or town.

References: *Antique Map Price Record & Handbook for 1996*, available from Spoon River Press (2319C W. Rohmann, Peoria, IL 61604), 1996; Melville C. Branch, *An Atlas of Rare City Maps: Comparative Urban Design, 1830-1842*, Princeton Architectural Press, 1997; Carl Morland and David Bannister, *Antique Maps*, Phaidon Press, 1993; K. A. Sheets, *American Maps 1795–1895*, available from Spoon River Press (2319C W. Rohmann, Peoria, IL 61604), 1995.

Periodical: *Antique Map & Print Quarterly*, P. O. Box 254, Simsbury, CT 06070.

Collectors' Clubs: Association of Map Memorabilia Collectors, 8 Amherst Rd, Pelham, MA 01002; Chicago Map Society, 60 W Walton St, Chicago, IL 60610.

Museum: Hermon Dunlap Smith Center for the History of Cartography, Newberry Library, Chicago, IL.

Notes: Although mass produced, county atlases are eagerly sought by collectors. Individual sheets sell for $25 to $75. The atlases themselves can usually be purchased in the $200 to $400 range. Individual sheets should be viewed solely as decorative and not as investment material.

A Compleat Map of the Holy Land...Part 1st and IId, Samuel Dunn, pair engraved double page, hand colored in outline, wide margins, minor soiling, scattered browning in margins, each 355 x 505 mm 460.00

A Map Showing the Disputed Boundary of Missouri and Iowa, George A. Leakin, Washington, c1836, lithographed folding map, prepared for the Commissioner of the US, wide margins, 510 x 780 mm150.00

SPECIAL AUCTIONS

Swann Galleries, Inc.
104 E 25th St
New York, NY 10010
(212) 254-4710

Americae, Homann Heirs, engraved double page of the Americas, hand colored, wide margins, one soft vertical crease through portion of image, 465 x 530 mm...980.00

A New & Accurate Map of Asia, Thomas Bowen, London, 1777, engraved folding map, hand colored in outline, wide margins, small pin hole in ocean area, 325 x 425 mm 400.00

A New and General Map of the Southern Dominions Belonging to the United States of America, Laurie & Whittle, London, 1794, engraved double page, hand colored, ample margins, scattered minor foxing, small restored hole, 525 x 665 mm 1,265.00

A New Map of the Land of Canaan, Edward Wells, London, c1708, engraved, wide margins, 370 x 490 mm 230.00

A New Map of North America, John Cary, London, 1806, engraved double page, hand colored, wide margins, 525 x 600 mm.......230.00

A New Map Shewing the Travels of the Patriarchs, Edward Wells, London, c1708, engraved, wide margins, some wrinkling, 375 x 500 mm...200.00

Carolina, Herman Moll, London, 1740s, engraved, wide margins, chips at edges, few tears, matted, 210 x 285 mm 175.00

Carte Particuliere de l'Amerique Septentrionale, ou sont compris le Destriot de Davids, le Destroit de Hudson, Amsterdam, 1700, engraved two sheet joined, hand colored in outline, wide margins, scattered browning, one short tear on image repaired, 595 x 830 mm.........375.00

Chinese Plan of the City of Peking, T. B. Jervis, London, 1843, lithographed 16 section folding map, hand colored, folds into orig 4to orig case, covers loose, map tender along folds..930 x 1130 mm1,035.00

Hind, Hindoostan, or India, William Faden, London, 1800, engraved double page, hand colored, wide margins, 715 x 545 mm.......520.00

Lagoon Heights, Martha's Vineyard, MA, J. H. Bufford's Lithographers, 480 Washington St, Boston, 1873, litho on paper, 36-1/8" w, 27-1/8" h...1,035.00

Le Canada, Pieter Mortier, Amsterdam, 1700, engraved double page, hand colored in outline, wide margins, minor mildewing to side margins, 570 x 790 mm..575.00

Lutetiae Parisiorum, Mattaeus Seutter, Augsburg, c1730, double page city map of Paris and environs, hand colored, bottom margin trimmed close, 505 x 580 mm 1,495.00

Map of City of New York, G. Hayward, New York, 1842, lithographed folding map, partially hand colored, few small tears along right edge, 365 x 460 mm 150.00

Map of the City of New York with Fire & Watch Districts, G. Hayward, New York, 1841, lithographed folding map, district lines hand colored, minor and short separations along folds, cloth backed, 330 x 440 mm 100.00

Map of Ground in the Town of Harlem belonging to the Heirs of Peter Benson, Edward Doughty, City Surveyor, New York, 1877, manuscript map, property owned between Third and Fifth Avenues and 109th to 117th Streets, cloth-mounted, slight separation and minor loss along vertical fold, 490 x 380 mm 150.00

Map of Minnesota along the Chippewa River, Minnesota, c1850, manuscript map, showing land parcels, some identified as to ownership, on pc of cotton cloth, some dampstaining and smudging, 390 x 340 mm 175.00

Nouvelle Carte de la Hongrie, Henry Abraham Chatelain, Amsterdam, c1710, engraved double page, hand colored in outline, wide margins, 480 x 625 mm 230.00

Nouvelle Plan de Saint Petersbourg, A. R. Fremin, Paris, 1814, engraved double page city map, hand color, paper back, slightly soiled all over, 520 x 650 mm...635.00

Ocean Atlantique ou Mer du Nord, Amsterdam, 1700, shows Americas from Labrador to Brazil, engraved, hand colored in outline, wide margins, small area of mildew in lower margins, 475 x 600 mm....920.00

Palestine, Sidney Hall, London, c1840, engraved double page, hand colored in outline, wide margins, lightly toned all over, 530 x 445 mm 100.00

Plat of the Seven Ranges of Townships being Part of the Territory of the United States N. W. of the River Ohio, Thomas Hutchins, US, 1785, engraved folding map, hand colored in outline, scattered minor soiling, foxing, and offsetting, top margin trimmed close, 625 x 345 mm 435.00

Province de New York, John Montresor, Chez le Rouge, Paris, 1777, engraved 4 sheet map, hand colored in outline, inconsistent margins, tears and some discoloration along creases, vertical sheets joined, horizontal sheets unjoined, 1460 x 930 mm 1,955.00

Smith's New Map of London and Enrivons, London, 1856, engraved 44 folding map, hand colored in outline, linen backed, folded into orig 12mo cloth case with hinge and clasp, 705 x 1095 mm 1,160.00

South Africa, A. and C. Black, Edinburgh, 1840, engraved double page, hand colored, wide margins, 440 x 590 mm 50.00

The Grand Panorama of London, Charles Evans, London, c1844, wood engraved folding view showing London from the Thames, folds into orig sq 12mo cloth case, text missing, 160 x 3800 mm 980.00

The United States of America, Laurie & Whittle, London, 1794, engraved double page, hand colored, wide margins, minor loss to border rule, small chip in bottom margin extending into image, 475 x 520 mm 460.00

Virginia et Nova Francia, Petrus Bertius, Amsterdam, c1616, engraved single sheet, wide margins, French text on verso, slight dampstaining on upper corners, 100 x 140 mm 175.00

Western States, 1865, hand colored, from book Across the Continent by Samuel Bowles 325.00

West India Islands, John Thomson, Edinburgh, 1817, engraved double page, showing Guadaloupe, Antigua, and Mariegalante, hand colored in outline, scattered minor foxing, 540 x 650 mm 175.00

MARBLEHEAD POTTERY

History: This hand-thrown pottery was first made in 1905 as part of a therapeutic program introduced by Dr. J. Hall for the patients confined to a sanitarium located in Marblehead, Massachusetts. In 1916 production was removed from the hospital to another site. The factory continued under the directorship of Arthur E. Baggs until it closed in 1936.

Most pieces found today are glazed with a smooth, porous, even finish in a single color. The most desirable pieces have a conventional design in one or more subordinate colors.

Reference: David Rago, *American Art Pottery*, Knickerbocker Press, 1997.

Bookends, pr, 5-1/2" h, 5-1/2" w, emb with ship, green and orange glaze, blue ground, ship stamp, some running of glaze, flecks, restoration to one 800.00

Bowl
5" d, 2-3/8" h, squatty form, closed-in rim, matte dark cobalt blue glaze, imp mark, c1904-36 .... 375.00
4-1/8" h, tapered spherical form, dark teal blue glaze, imp mark on base 200.00

Vase, incised, dark brown panthers walking in front of lighter brown windows, light green ground, imp ship mark, "HT" for Hannah Tutt, 7" h, 5-1/4" d, $17,000. Photo courtesy of David Rago Auctions, Inc.

8" d, 3-3/4" h, flaring, emb lotus pattern, dark blue matte glaze ext. light blue semi-matte int., stamped ship mark, stilt pull chips 325.00

Chamberstick, 8-1/2" h, 5" d, rounded handle, smooth dark green matte glaze, imp ship mark 500.00

Tile, 6" sq, deep brown border of long dashes, green ground, solid dark brown edge band, matte glaze, imp mark, minor nicks 700.00

Vase
2-3/4" h, narrow mouth, flared bulbous form, teal blue matte glaze, black underglaze near rim, c1910 .... 250.00
3-1/4" h, 5" d, squatty bulbous, dark green semi-matte glaze, imp mark 450.00
3-5/8" h, short flared rim, squat bulbous body, repeating stylized trees, black trunks, blue leaves, gray ground, imp Marblehead cipher, initialed by Hannah Tutt, c1905 .... 2,415.00
4" h, 3-1/4" h, straight sided, imp stylized red flowers, green leaves, dark blue ground, ship mark and "M" 1,800.00
4-3/4" h, swollen cylindrical, dec at rim with repeating raised flower and leaf motifs in faint blue, red, and tan, speckled blue matte ground, imp mark on base, inscribed "HT" (Hannah Tutt) on foot 1,610.00
5" h, 3-3/4' d, ovoid, emb repeated pattern of stylized brown and blue fruit and leaves, speckled gray ground, imp ship and "HT," Hannah Tutt 1,300.00
5-1/2" h, 5" d, flaring, dark blue matte glaze, stamped ship mark, paper label 475.00
6-1/4" h, 3-3/4" d, bulbous, incised pattern of stylized brown trees, speckled green ground, imp ship mark and "MT," 1" hairline to rim 3,250.00
6-1/2" h, 5-1/2" d, bulbous, incised dark brown stylized blossoms, lighter brown ground, imp ship mark 8,500.00
7" h, 4" d, ovoid, olive green stylized trees, dark blue ground, stamped ship mark 3,250.00
7" h, 5-1/4" d, bulbous, incised dark brown panthers walking in front of lighter brown windows, light green ground, imp ship mark and "HT," Hannah Tuff, stilt pulls tobase 17,000.00
7-3/4" h, tapered oviform, flared rim, dark blue matte glaze, imp Marblehead cipher, early 20th C 800.00
8" h, ovoid, smooth speckled matte green glaze, stamped "MP" ship mark, remnant of paper label 1,000.00
8-1/2" h, corseted, incised ribs, checkered top and base bands, 3 shades of green matte glaze, imp ship mark, "A/B/T," Arthur Baggs 33,000.00
9" h, 4" d, cylindrical, lavender-gray matte glaze, imp ship mark 800.00

Vessel, 3" h, 4-1/4" d, squat, ribbed body, smooth green and charcoal matte glaze, incised winged "M" mark 400.00

MARY GREGORY TYPE GLASS

History: The use of enameled decoration on glass, an inexpensive way to imitate cameo glass, developed in Bohemia in the late 19th century. The Boston and Sandwich Glass Co. copied this process in the late 1880s.

Mary Gregory (1856–1908) was employed for two years at the Boston and Sandwich Glass factory when the enameled decorated glass was being manufactured. Some collectors argue that Gregory was inspired to paint her white enamel figures on glass by the work of Kate Greenaway and a desire to imitate pate-sur-pate. However, evidence for these assertions is very weak. Further, it has never been proven that Mary Gregory even decorated glass as part of her job at Sandwich. The result is that "Mary Gregory type" is a better term to describe this glass.

Reference: R. and D. Truitt, *Mary Gregory Glassware*, published by authors, 1992.

Museum: Sandwich Glass Museum, Sandwich, MA.

BOX Reproduction Alert: Collectors should recognize that most examples of Mary Gregory type glass seen today are either European or modern reproductions.

Barber Bottle, 7-1/8" h, deep sapphire blue, white enameled youngster playing tennis, cylindrical bulbous form, long neck, tooled mouth, pontil scar 150.00

Box, cov
   3-3/4" l, 2-1/4" d, 3" h, oval, boy with bunch of flowers in hand, jet black ground, metal fittings 285.00
   6-1/2" d, 6-1/2" h, round, ebony color, white enameled young boy offering nosegay to young girl sitting on bench beneath overhanging tree, white enamel garland around perimeter, gold colored metal fittings and scrolled legs 1,085.00

Cruet, 8-1/2" h, sapphire blue, sq dimpled sides, white enameled two girls facing each other, blue handle, orig stopper 495.00

Dresser Set, pr 10-1/2" h perfume bottles, 7" cov dresser jar, deep cobalt blue, enameled young children and angels, sprays of flowers, crown tops 895.00

Jewel Box, 3" x 3-1/2", cranberry, hinged lid 420.00

Lamp, 24-1/2" h, 6" d, facing pair, young boys in tree holding banner, white enameled flowers, red jeweled flowers, black amethyst, gold trim, frosted, ruffled shades with emb flowers, pr 1,800.00

Milk Pitcher, 6" h, cranberry ground, white enameled girl, clear applied handle 50.00

Miniature, pitcher, 1-3/4" h, cranberry ground, white enameled little girl blowing bubbles, clear glass handle with gold highlights 200.00

Mug, 4-1/2" h, amber, ribbed, white enameled girl praying 65.00

Paperweight, 2-1/2" w, 4" l, deep black ground, white enameled young boy and girl in garden setting 295.00

Patch Box, emerald green 295.00

Pitcher, 7-1/2" x 9-1/2", medium green, white enameled boy with bird and trees, girl with bowl and brush dec, pr 275.00

Plate, 6-1/4" d, cobalt blue, white enameled girl with butterfly net 125.00

Salt Shaker, 5" h, blue, paneled, white enameled girl in garden, brass top 190.00

Tumbler, 1-3/4" d, 2-1/2" h, cranberry, white enameled boy on one, girl on other, facing pr 100.00

Vase
   2-1/2" h, 1-1/2" w, cobalt blue ground, white enameled figure of young man standing among foliage, gold trim 325.00
   4" h, cranberry ground, white enameled boy and wagon 95.00

4-1/2" h, cranberry ground, 3 ftd, white enameled girl and boy 110.00

5-1/2" h, cranberry, white enameled girl 100.00

6-3/4" h, 3" d, pale amber, young girl in forest scene, reverse with spray of flowers and leaves, neck and shoulder with dec band 225.00

7" h, 2-1/2" w, bud, amber, white spatter background, young boy and girl among foliage, facing pr 550.00

8" h, ring, sapphire blue, young boy dec 195.00

8-1/4" h, 3-1/2" d, amber, ruffled top, white enameled young girl 185.00

10-1/2" h, 5" w, cranberry, white enamel of young girl holding a flower, paneled int. 295.00

MATCH HOLDERS

History: The friction match achieved popularity after 1850. The early matches were packaged and sold in sliding cardboard boxes. To facilitate storage and to eliminate the clumsiness of using the box, match holders were developed.

The first match holders were cast iron or tin, the latter often displaying advertisements. A patent for a wall-hanging match holder was issued in 1849. By 1880 match holders also were being made from glass and china. Match holders began to lose their popularity in the late 1930s with the advent of gas and electric heat and ranges.

Reference: Denis B. Alsford, *Match Holders, 100 Years of Ingenuity*, Schiffer Publishing, 1994.

Advertising
   Dutch Boy Paints, litho tin, emb, diecut, 6-1/2" h 275.00
   Ellwood Steel Fences, litho tin, red, white, and blue, 5" h 85.00
   New Process Gas Range, hanging, tin, gray stove, red ground 65.00
   Old Judson, J. C. Stevens, litho tin, 4-3/4" h 95.00
   Sharples Separator Co., tin, mother and daughter, farm scene ... 85.00

Bisque, 4" h, 3-5/8" d, natural colored rooster with beige basket, two compartments, round base with pink band 135.00

Brass, 3" h, bear chained to post, cast, orig gilt trim 225.00

Bronze, 3" h, shoe, mouse in toe 125.00

Cast Iron, figural,
   Bird 45.00
   High Button Shoe, 5-1/2" h, black paint, c1890 .... 50.00

Tumbler, pale blue, young boy holding floral branch, gold bands, ftd, 5-3/4" h, $145.

Advertising, Ceresota Prize Bread Flour, young boy cutting bread, seated on stool, barrel for matches, 2-1/4" w, 5-1/2" h, $90.

Glass, 3" h, 3-1/4" d, shaded rose to pink overlay satin, ball-shape, glossy off-white lining, ground pontil 155.00

Majolica

    Bull dog, striker, large 440.00

    Dog, striker, Continental, rim chips and repair...................... 165.00

    Happy Hooligan with suitcase, striker, rim nick to hat 110.00

    Monk, striker, hairline in base 140.00

Papier-Mâché, 2-3/4" h, black lacquer, Oriental dec.................... 25.00

Porcelain, seated girl, feeding dog on table, sgd "Elbogen" 125.00

Sterling Silver, 1-3/4" x 2-1/2", hinged lid, diecut striking area, cigar cutter on one corner, lid inscription "H. R." and diamond, inside lid inscribed "Made for Tiffany & Co./Pat 12, 09/Sterling" 95.00

MATCH SAFES

History: Pocket match safes are small containers used to safely carry matches in one's pocket. They were first used in the 1850s. Match safes can be found in various sizes and shapes, and were made from numerous materials such as sterling, nickel-plated brass, good, brass, ivory, and vulcanite. Some of the most interesting and sought after ones are figurals in the shapes of people, animals and anything else imaginable. Match safes were also a very popular advertising means in the 1895-1910 period, and were used by both large and small businesses.

References: Denis Alsford, *Match Holders, 100 Years of Ingenuity*, Schiffer Publishing, 1994; W. Eugene Sanders, Jr., and Christine C. Sanders, *Pocket Matchsafes, Reflectins of Life & Art, 1840-1920*, Schiffer Publishing, 1997; Audrey G. Sullivan, *History of Match Safes in the United States*, published by author, 1978.

Collectors' Club: International Match Safe Association, P. O. Box 791, Malaga, NJ 08328-0791.

Advisor: George Sparacio

BOX Reproduction Alert: Reproduction, copycat, and fantasy sterling silver match safes include:

    Art Nouveau style nude with veil, rectangular case with C-scroll edges

    Boot, figural

    Embracing wood nymphs

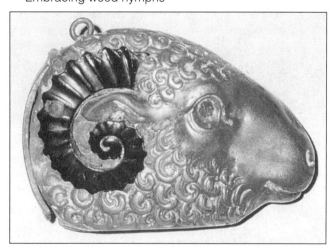

Ram's head, vulcanite horns, glass eyes, brass, 1-1/2" x 2-1/4", $625. Photo courtesy of George Sparacio.

Conquistador, figural, plated brass, 2-3/8" x 1-1/8", $495. Photo courtesy of George Sparacio.

Jack Daniels, 1970s fantasy item

Mermaid, with upper torso out of water, combing her hair

Owl and Moon

Many of these match safes are only marked "Sterling." Any match safe so marked requires careful inspection. Period American match safes generally are marked with the name of the manufacturer and/or a patent date. Period English match safes have the proper hallmarks. Beware of English reproduction match safes bearing the "DAB" marking.

Note: While not all match safes have a striking surface, this is one test, besides size, to distinguish a match safe from a calling card case.

Advance Thresher, multicolored graphics, celluloid wrapped, 2-3/4" x 1-1/2"... 250.00

Agatee, book shaped w/sterling silver trim, 1-5/8" x 1-1/4"......... 160.00

Artillery shell, figural, English hallmarks, sterling silver, 2-1/4" x 1-1/4"... 495.00

Art Nouveau, mother w/baby, by Unger, sterling silver, slant top, 2-5/8".. 295.00

Baby head in shirt, figural, brass, 2-7/8" x 1-1/2"...................... 245.00

Beaver, figural lid, Roden Bros., sterling silver, 2-1/2" x 1-1/2"... 325.00

Billiken, figural, brass, "Pat. Oct. 6, 08," 1-5/8" x 1-1/2"............. 265.00

Blatz Beer, plated brass, 2-1/2" x 1-1/2" 155.00

Butterfly Lady motif, Gorham, #B2297, sterling silver, 2-5/8" x 1-1/2"... 835.00

Bryant & May Wax, Vesta tin, 1893 Chicago World's Fair lithograph design, 1-3/4" x 6-1/4" 110.00

Columbian Expo, medallion on ear of corn, figural, plated brass, 2-1/2" x 1"... 325.00

Conquistador, figural, plated brass, 2-3/8" x 1-1/8".................... 495.00

Cow Brand logo, thermoplastic, slip top, 3" x 1-1/2" 140.00

Dog - Indian inserts, cigar cutter on bottom, plated brass ends, metal body, 2-7/8" x 1-1/2" 65.00

Dragon figural, holding opal, 4 sharp teeth, Japanese, brass, 2-3/4" x 1-7/8".. 550.00

Drunks in front of saloon, silver plated by Gorham, 2-3/8" x 1-3/8".. 35.00

Erotica, couple copulating, self winding, plated brass, 2-1/2" x 1-1/2".. 3,500.00

Filigree, floral motif, silver, 2-1/2" x 1-1/2"..................................150.00
Guide, book shaped, inside lady sitting on chamber pot, leather
     wrapped, French, 1-5/8" x 1-1/4"..425.00
Jack Knife, figural, Gorham Mfg. Co., simulated blades, sterling silver,
     2-1/4" x 7/8"...525.00
Lady in boat, stamped "Sterling", 2-1/2" x 1-3/4" 125.00
Love's Flight, celluloid wrapped, multicolored graphics, Whitehead &
     Hoag, 2-3/4" x 1-1/2" 200.00
Mythical figure, embossed on side, sterling silver, by Carter, 2-1/4 x
     1-1/4"...165.00
Oriental dragon, domed lid, quasi-figural, brass 2-1/2" x 1-1 /4" 300.00
Pickle, figural, brass with green patina, 2-1/2" x 3/4"..................395.00
Privy, figural, brass man in top hat, brass, 2" x 3/4" x
     1/2"..295.00
President Grant, portrait, figural, plated brass, 2-3/4" x 1-3/4" ...595.00
Ram's head, vulcanite horns & glass eyes, brass, 1-1/2" x 2 1/4" 625.00
Red Top Rye, slip-top, thermoplastic, 2-7/8" x 1-1/8" 85.00
Rebecca at the Well, sterling silver, 2-1/2" x 1-1/4" 250.00
Sorrento Ware, inlaid top, male figure, wood, sandpaper striker, 2-3/4"
     x 1-1/2"..130.00
Translucent enameling, sterling silver, 2-3/8" x 1-1/2" 625.00
Tooth w/boar surmounted, figural brass, 2-5/8" x 1" 140.00
Unger, Indian chief motif, sterling silver, 2-3/8" x 1 7/8".......... 1,350.00
Union Cigar Makers, cello wrapped, blue and black graphics, 2-1/2" x
     1-1/2"...155.00
Wolf's head, figural, glass eyes, plated brass, 1" x 2"................295.00

McCOY POTTERY

History: The J. W. McCoy Pottery Co. was established in Roseville, Ohio, in September 1899. The early McCoy company produced both stoneware and some art pottery lines, including Rosewood. In October 1911 three potteries merged creating the Brush-McCoy Pottery Co. This firm continued to produce the original McCoy lines and added several new art lines. Much of the early pottery is not marked.

In 1910, Nelson McCoy and his father, J. W. McCoy, founded the Nelson McCoy Sanitary Stoneware Co. In 1925 the McCoy family sold their interest in the Brush-McCoy Pottery Co. and started to expand and improve the Nelson McCoy Co. The new company produced stoneware, earthenware specialties, and artware.

Marks: Most of the pottery marked "McCoy" was made by the Nelson McCoy Co.

References: Susan and Al Bagdade, *Warman's American Pottery and Porcelain*, Wallace-Homestead, 1994; Bob Hanson, Craig Nissen and Margaret Hanson, *McCoy Pottery, Collector's Reference*, Collector Books, 1996, Book 2, 1999; ; Sharon and Bob Huxford, *Collector's Encyclopedia of Brush-McCoy Pottery*, Collector Books, 1996; ——, *Collectors Encyclopedia of McCoy Pottery*, Collector Books, 1980, 1997 value update; Martha and Steve Sanford, *Sanfords' Guide to Brush-McCoy Pottery*, Book 2, Adelmore Press (230 Harrison Ave., Campbell, CA 95008), 1996; --, *Sanfords' Guide to McCoy Pottery*, Adelmore Press, 1997; Jeffrey B. Snyder, *McCoy Pottery*, Schiffer Publishing, 1999.

Periodicals: NMXprss, 8935 Brecksville Road, Suite 406, Brecksville, OH 44141-2318, http://members.aol.com/nmxpress.

Reproduction Alert: Unfortunately, Nelson McCoy never registered his McCoy trademark, a fact discovered by Roger Jensen of Tennessee. As a result, Jensen began using the McCoy mark on a series of ceramic reproductions made in the early 1990s. While the marks on these recently made pieces copy the original, Jensen made objects which were never produced by the Nelson McCoy Co. The best known example is the Red Riding Hood cookie jar, which was originally designed by Hull and also made by Regal China.

The McCoy fakes are a perfect example of how a mark on a piece can be deceptive. A mark alone is not proof that a piece is period or old. Knowing the proper marks and what was and was not made in respect to forms, shapes, and decorative motifs is critical in authenticating a pattern.

Additional Listings: See *Warman's Americana & Collectibles* for more examples.

Basket, Rustic, pine cone dec, 1945...35.00
Bird Bath, 6"...38.00
Bowl
     Bird 35.00
     El Rancho Sombero, orig box...335.00
     Mt Pelee, lava type, charcoal irid, 1902................................350.00
Canister, Stonecraft, pink and blue bands, cov
     Large 45.00
     Medium...30.00
     Small..25.00
Cookie Jar
     Chairman of the Board 600.00
     Chef...125.00
     Mammy, yellow 450.00
     Teepee...250.00
Creamer and Sugar, Daisy, brown and green..............................25.00
Hurricane Lamp, Stonecraft, candle type....................................22.00
Iced Tea Server, El Rancho, orig box.......................................200.00
Jardiniere
     4" h, Blossomtime..35.00
     9" h, Rosewood, brown glaze, orange streaks 70.00
Lamp, cowboy boots, orig shade..150.00
Mixing Bowl, 12" d, Stonecraft, pink and blue bands..................55.00
Mug, Buccaneer..35.00
Planter
     Bird Dog with Pheasant, 8" x 13"..150.00
     Down By The Old Millstream..55.00
     Goat, gold trim, 11-3/4"...48.00

Cookie Jars, left: Jack-O-Lantern, repaired chip inside rim, darkened crazing, $375; right: World Globe, partial paint, small chip on lid, $200; Photo courtesy of Green Valley Auctions, Inc.

Spinning Wheel 48.00
Spreading Chestnut Tree.. 55.00
Spittoon, 4-1/2" d, pansies, mkd "Loy-Nel Art" 100.00
Tankard, corn, mkd "J. W. McCoy" 90.00
Teapot, cov, Stonecraft 40.00
Tea Set, 3 pcs, teapot, creamer, cov sugar
  English Ivory pattern, vine handles....................... 75.00
  Grecian, 7-1/2" h teapot.................................... 100.00
Vase
  8" h, double tulip 75.00
  8" h, pink 35.00
  9" h, white crackle, band of emb diamonds 45.00
  12" h, white 95.00
Wall Pocket
  Flower, rustic glaze, 1946................................... 35.00
  Lily 75.00
  Umbrella, yellow, 1955 .... 25.00

McKEE GLASS

History: The McKee Glass Co. was established in 1843 in Pittsburgh, Pennsylvania. In 1852 they opened a factory to produce pattern glass. In 1888 the factory was relocated to Jeannette, Pennsylvania, and began to produce many types of glass kitchenwares, including several patterns of Depression glass. The factory continued until 1951 when it was sold to the Thatcher Manufacturing Co.

McKee named its colors Chalaine Blue, Custard, Seville Yellow, and Skokie Green. McKee glass may also be found with painted patterns, e.g., dots and ships. A few items were decaled. Many of the canisters and shakers were lettered in black to show the purpose for which they were intended.

References: Gene Florence, *Kitchen Glassware of the Depression Years*, 7th ed., Collector Books, 1995, values updated 1999; ——, *Very Rare Glassware of the Depression Years*, 5th Series, Collector Books, 1997.

Additional Listings: See *Warman's Americana & Collectibles* for more examples.

Animal Dish, cov, dove, round base, beaded rim, vaseline,
  sgd 365.00
Berry Set, Hobnail with Fan pattern, blue, master berry and 8 sauce
  dishes 170.00
Bowl
  5" d, 4-1/2" h, Skokie Green 8.75
  6-1/2" d, Skokie Green 16.00
Butter Dish, cov, Wiltec pattern, Pre-Cut Ware, frosted 70.00
Candlesticks, pr, 9" h, Rock Crystal.........................165.00
Cereal Canister, cov, Skokie Green, 48 oz, round 35.00
Cheese and Cracker Set, Rock Crystal pattern, red..................170.00
Clock, tambour, vaseline 450.00
Coffee Canister, cov, Skokie Green, 24 oz, faded 30.00
Egg Beater Bowl, spout, Skokie Green......................32.00
Goblet, Rock Crystal, colorless 20.00
Lamp, nude, green 175.00
Measuring Cup, Skokie Green, nested set, 4 pc 125.00
Pitcher, 8" h, Wild Rose and Bowknot pattern, frosted, gilt dec....65.00
Punch Bowl Set, bowl, 12 mugs, Tom and Jerry, red scroll dec ...65.00
Reamer, pointed top, Skokie Green 45.00
Refrigerator Container, cov, 4" x 5", custard 45.00
Ring Box, cov, Seville Yellow 20.00
Salt and Pepper Shakers, pr, Skokie Green, 2-1/4", sq...............14.00
Server, center handle, Rock Crystal pattern, red.......140.00
Sugar Bowl, cov, Laurel pattern, French Ivory, tall.......................20.00
Sugar Canister, custard, round 115.00

Tea Canister, custard 130.00
Toothpick Holder, Aztec pattern 30.00
Tumbler, custard, ftd 15.00
Vase, 8-1/2" h, nude, Chalaine 175.00
Water Cooler, 21" h, spigot, vaseline, 2 pcs 325.00
Wine
  Plutec pattern, colorless 24.00
  Rock Crystal pattern, ruby 55.00
  Sunbeam pattern, colorless..................................35.00

MEDICAL AND PHARMACEUTICAL ITEMS

History: Modern medicine and medical instruments are well documented. Some instruments are virtually unchanged since their invention; others have changed drastically.

The concept of sterilization phased out decorative handles. Handles on early instruments, which were often carved, were made of materials such as mother-of-pearl, ebony, and ivory. Today's sleek instruments are not as desirable to collectors.

Pharmaceutical items include those things commonly found in a drugstore and used to store or prepare medications.

References: A. Walker Bingham, *Snake-Oil Syndrome: Patent Medicine Advertising*, Christopher Publishing House, 1994; Douglas Congdon-Martin, *Drugstore and Soda Fountain Antiques*, Schiffer Publishing, 1991; Patricia McDaniel, *Drugstore Collectibles*, Wallace-Homestead, 1994; J. William Rosenthal, *Spectacles and Other Vision Aids*, Norman Publishing (720 Market St., 3rd Fl., San Francisco, CA 94102), 1996; Keith Wilbur, *Antique Medical Instruments*: Revised Price Guide Schiffer Publishing, 1987, 1993 value update.

Periodical: *Scientific, Medical & Mechanical Antiques*, 11824 Taneytown Pike, Taneytown, MD 21787.

Collectors' Clubs: Maryland Microscopical Society, 8621 Polk St, McLean, VA 22102; Medical Collectors Association, 1685A Eastchester Rd, Bronx, NY 10461.

Museums: Dittrick Museum of Medical History, Cleveland, OH; International Museum of Surgical Science & Hall of Fame, Chicago, IL; National Museum of Health & Medicine, Walter Reed Medical Center, Washington, DC; National Museum of History and Technology, Smithsonian Institution, Washington, DC; Schmidt Apothecary Shop, New England Fire & History Museum, Brewster, MA; Waring Historical Library, Medical University of South Carolina, Charleston, SC.

Advertising Booklet, *Tales of the Jungle*, Alka-Seltzer, Dr. Miles Nervine adv, 29 pgs, giveaway by Theatre Pharmacy, LaPorte, Indiana,
  4-3/4" h...10.00
Amputation Saw, bow blade, ebony handle 125.00
Apothecary Chest
  6" x 11-3/4" x 21-1/4" l, poplar, gray repaint, 6 drawers, pulls
    replaced 495.00
  27" w, 12-1/2" d, 32" h, refinished pine and poplar, 24 drawers, wire
    nail construction, backboards replaced 550.00
Apothecary Jar, 13-1/4" h, colorless, blown, ground lid 140.00
Apothecary Shelf, hanging, 50" w, 6-1/4" d, 7-1/2" h, 24 drawers, gray
  repaint over worn softwood, pressed wood moldings, wire nail construction, edge damage, porcelain knobs 440.00

Book
Achilles, Rose, MD, *Carbonic Acid in Medicine*, Funk & Wagnalls, 1905, 1st ed., illus 18.00
Mould Guide For Trubyte New Hue Teeth, The Dentist's Supply Co. of NY, 1920s 125.00
The Physician Hand Book, 1879, leather bound 500.00
Box, 10-1/2" x 11" x 8-1/2", wood, black paint, stenciled "Dr. Greene's Nervura Nerve Tonic" 65.00
Capsule Filler, 8" x 16", Sharp and Dohme, chrome, orig wood box and instruction book, 1920-30 ....150.00
Catalog
Illinois Surgical Supply, Chicago, IL, 1940, 12 pgs, 3-3/4" x 7-1/4", Birth Control Means Freedom, Health & Happiness 20.00
Ritter Dental Mfg. Co, Rochester, NY, 1919, 112 pgs, 6" x 9", dental equipment 55.00
Display Case
Ashton & Parsons Homeopathic Medicines, cherry colored hardwood, curved glass front, reverse etched glass lettering and design on front glass panel, 33" h, 20" w, 13" d 1,200.00
Dr. Frost's Homeopathic Remedies Build Health, wood, stained, litho tin door panel, lists 38 aliment remedies, 19" h, ...450.00
Dr. M. A. Simmons Liver Medicine, wood, stained, imp letter in panels, 30-1/2" h 625.00
Dr. Morse's Indian Root Pills, 5 diecut cardboard pieces with Indian village, largest pc 27" x 41" 600.00
Dose Glass, clear, Royal Pepsi Stomach Bitters, 1900-10 ....40.00
Eyelid Retractor, ivory handle, mkd "Hills King St.," c1853 ....125.00
Forceps, dental, extracting, SP, handle design, F. Arnold 50.00
Jar, cov, glass, clear, label under glass
Dr. Kings New Light Pills 325.00
Dr. Mills Anti Pain Pills Cures Headaches 375.00
Magazine, *The Dental Cosmos*, S. S. White Dental Mfg., Philadelphia, PA, 1904, 164 pgs, 6-3/4" x 9-1/2" 50.00
Magazine Ad, 11" x 13-3/4", from Youth's Companion, April 23, 1925, Colgate's Ribbon Dental Cream, Coach Any Coakley 8.00
Manual, Johnson's First Aid Manual, ed. By Fred B. Kilmer, Johnson & Johnson, NJ, 1918, 8th ed., 8vo, 139 pgs 22.00
Mortar and Pestle, 9" h, ash burl, turned 130.00
Opthalmoscope, cased, Morton 120.00
Pill Making Device, 12" h, walnut and brass, star stamp on base, separate two handled device glides along top 220.00
Scale, chemist's, brass and steel, oak box with drawers, glazed to and sides, Becker's Sons, Rotterdam, c1920 ....225.00
Scalpel, ebony, c1860, 3 pc set 400.00
Sign
Dr. D. Jaynes Family Medicines, glass, emb silver and gold foil lettering, gold border, black background, framed, 11-1/2""h, 21-3/4" 195.00

Mortar and Pestle, burl, $250.

Dr. Pierce's Golden Medical Discovery, paper, Indians mixing roots, herbs, and bark for "Dr. Pierce's Golden medical Discovery for the Blood," matted and framed, 38" x 25" 700.00
Hill Liver, frosted glass, lady examining tongue in mirror, "Look At Your Tongue, If Coated You Need Hills Liver Tablets," framed, 9-1/2" x 11-3/4" 150.00
Stethoscope, monaural, metal 120.00
Medical Center Pharmacy Drugs, Perfumes, and Rubber Goods, reverse painted glass, gilt lettering, black background, 11-1/2" x 30-1/2" 250.00
Surgeon's Kit, pocket, scalpel, picks with horn or tortoise shell handles, probe, damage to case 150.00
Thermometer, 36-1/8" h, porcelain, Ex-Lax, black and white lettering, dark blue ground 125.00
Tin
Dr. Scholl's Foot Powder 30.00
Taylor's Blue Bird Talc sample size, multicolored, 2-1/8" x 1-1/4" 600.00

MEDICINE BOTTLES

History: The local apothecary and his book of formulas played a major role in early America. In 1796 the first patent for a medicine was issued by the U.S. Patent Office. At that time, anyone could apply for a medicinal patent; as long as the dosage was not poisonous, the patent was granted.

Patent medicines were advertised in newspapers and magazines and sold through the general store and at "medicine" shows. In 1907 the Pure Food and Drug Act, requiring an accurate description of contents on a medicine container's label, put an end to the patent medicine industry. Not all medicines were patented.

Most medicines were sold in distinctive bottles, often with the name of the medicine and location of manufacture in relief. Many early bottles were made in the glass-manufacturing area of southern New Jersey. Later, companies in western Pennsylvania and Ohio manufactured bottles.

References: Joseph K. Baldwin, *Collector's Guide to Patent and Proprietary Medicine Bottles of the Nineteenth Century*, Thomas Nelson, 1973; Ralph and Terry Kovel, *Kovels' Bottles Price List*, 11th ed., Three Rivers Press, 1998; John Odell, *Digger Odell's Official Antique Bottle and Glass Collector Magazine Price Guide Series*, vol. 5, published by author (1910 Shawhan Rd, Morrow, OH 45152), 1995.

Periodical: *Antique Bottle and Glass Collector*, P. O. Box 187, East Greenville, PA 18041.

Collectors' Club: Federation of Historical Bottle Collectors, Inc, 88 Sweetbriar Branch, Longwood, FL 32750.

American Expectorant, America, 1840-60, octagonal, greenish aquamarine, outward rolled mouth, pontil scar, 5-7/8" h 425.00
Arthurs Renovating Syrup, A. A., American, 1845-60, sq, narrow beveled corners, medium blue green, applied sloping collared mouth, iron pontil mark, 9" h 950.00
Atlas Medicine Co., Henderson, NC, 9-1/4" h, amber 35.00
Baker's Celery Kola, 10" h, amber 65.00
Blodgett's Persian Balm, 4-7/8" h, aqua, pontil 150.00
Booth & Sedgwick's London Cordial Gin, American, 1845-60, sq, beveled corners, deep blue green, applied sloping collared mouth with ring, iron pontil mark, 9-3/4" h 375.00
Brants Indian Balsam, America, 1840-60, octagonal, aquamarine, applied sloping collared mouth, pontil scar, 6-3/4" h 150.00
Celebrated Nectar/Stomach Bitters/And Nerve Tonic, sq, rounded corners, yellowish-green, fluted and swirled neck, 9-1/4" h 450.00

Maltine Manuf Co., NY, paper labels, $30.

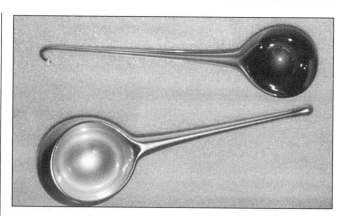

Ladles, gold colored int., maroon ext., hook at tip of handle, each, $175.

Thorn's Hop & Burdock Tonic, yellow, 6-3/8" h 40.00
Turner's Balsam, eight sided, aqua, 4-7/8" h 65.00
Vaughn's Vegetable Lithontriptic Mixture, aqua, 8" h 125.00
Web's Carthartic A No. 1 Tonic, amber, 9-1/2" h 60.00
Westlake's Vegetable Ointment, light cornflower blue, 2-7/8" h 75.00

MERCURY GLASS

History: Mercury glass is a light-bodied, double-walled glass that was "silvered" by applying a solution of silver nitrate to the inside of the object through a hole in its base.

F. Hale Thomas of London patented the method in 1849. In 1855 the New England Glass Co. filed a patent for the same type of process. Other American glassmakers soon followed. The glass reached the height of its popularity in the early 20th century.

Bowl, 4-3/4" d, gold, enameled floral dec 50.00
Cake Stand, 8" d, pedestal base, emb floral dec 80.00
Candlestick, 10-1/2" h 110.00
Cologne Bottle, 4-1/4" x 71/2", bulbous, flashed amber panel, cut neck, etched grapes and leaves, corked metal stopper, c1840 .... 160.00
Creamer, 6-1/2"h, etched ferns, applied clear handle, attributed to Sandwich 140.00
Curtain Tieback, 2-5/8" d, pewter fitting, starflower dec 65.00
Goblet, 5" d, gold, white lily of the valley dec 40.00
Pitcher, 5-1/2" x 9-3/4" h, bulbous, panel cut neck, engraved lacy florals and leaves, applied clear handle, c1840 .... 225.00
Salt, 3 x 3", price for pr 100.00
Sugar Bowl, cov, 4-1/4" x 6-1/4", low foot, enameled white foliage dec, knob finial 65.00
Vase, 9-3/4 h, cylindrical, raised circular foot, everted rim, bright enameled yellow, orange, and blue floral sprays and insects, pr 225.00
Wig Stand, 10-1/2" h, large sphere applied to baluster pedestal continuing to flaring round foot, 19th C 250.00

METTLACH

History: In 1809 Jean Francis Boch established a pottery at Mettlach in Germany's Moselle Valley. His father had started a pottery at Septfontaines in 1767. Nicholas Villeroy began his pottery career at Wallerfanger in 1789.

In 1841 these three factories merged. They pioneered underglaze printing on earthenware, using transfers from copper plates, and also were among the first companies to use coal-fired kilns. Other factories were developed at Dresden, Wadgassen, and Danischburg. Mettlach decora-

Compound Extract of Hops & Boneset, 4-3/8" h, aqua, pontil 65.00
Davis & Miller Druggist, Baltimore, attributed to Baltimore Glass Works, Baltimore, MD, 1845-60, cylindrical, brilliant sapphire blue, applied sq collared mouth, iron pontil, mark, 3" d, 7-1/2" h ... 1,800.00
Dr. Bowman's Indian Ointment, America, 1840-60, octagonal, aquamarine, applied sloping collared mouth, pontil scar, 6" h 275.00
Dr. Seymour's Balsam of Wild Cherry & Comfrey, America, 1840-60, octagonal, aquamarine, applied sloping collared mouth, pontil scar, 6-1/2" h 475.00
E. A. Buckhout's Dutch Liniment, Prepared At Mechanicsville, Saratoga Co NY, rect, beveled corners, figure of standing Dutchman, tooled mouth, pontil scar, 4-5/8" h 400.00
From The Laboratory of G. W. Merchant, Chemist, Lockport, N. Y., attributed to Lockport Glass Works, Lockport, NY, 1840-60, rect, chamfered corners, deep yellowish green, applied sloping collard mouth, tubular pontil scar, 5-1/2" h 500.00
Hunt's Liniment Prepared By G. E. Stanton, Sing Sing, N.Y., rect, wide beveled corners, bright yellow green, inward rolled mouth, pontil scar, 4-1/2" h 2,000.00
Iceland Balsam For Pulmonary Consumption, Iceland Balsam, America, 1830-50, rect, beveled corners, emb on 3 sides, yellow olive, short applied sloping collared mouth, pontil scar, 6-1/2" h, professionally cleaned, light emb lettering 5,500.00
I. Newport's Panacea Purifier Of The Blood Nerwich, VT, attributed to Stoddard Glasshouse, Stoddard, NH, 1846-60, cylindrical, indented emb panels, yellow olive, applied sloping collared mouth with ring, iron pontil ring, 7-3/8 h, shall chip on sloping collar 1,900.00
J. L. Leavitt, Boston, attributed to Stoddard Glasshouse, Stoddard, NH, 1846-60, cylindrical, yellow olive, applied sloping collard mouth with ring, iron pontil mark, 8-1/8" h 275.00
L. P. Dodge Rheumatic Liniment Newburg, America, 1840-60, rect, beveled corners, light golden amber, applied sloping collared mouth, pontil scar, 6" h, appears to have been cleaned 750.00
Smith's Green Mountain Renovator, attributed to Stoddard Glasshouse, Stoddard, NH, 1846-1850, rect, wide beveled corners, yellow olive amber, applied double collared mouth, iron pontil mark, 6-3/4" h 1,300.00
Swaim's Panacea Philada, America, 1840-60, cylindrical, indented panels, bright grayish green, applied sloping collared mouth with ring, pontil scar, 7-1/2" h, minor ext. wear 400.00

tions include relief and etched designs, prints under the glaze, and cameos.

Marks: The castle and Mercury emblems are the two chief marks although secondary marks are known. The base of each piece also displays a shape mark and usually a decorator's mark.

References: Susan and Al Bagdade, *Warman's English & Continental Pottery & Porcelain*, 3rd Edition, Krause Publications, 1998; Gary Kirsner, *Mettlach Book*, 3rd ed., Glentiques (P. O. Box 8807, Coral Springs, FL 33075), 1994.

Periodical: *Beer Stein Journal*, P. O. Box 8807, Coral Springs, FL 33075.

Collectors' Clubs: Stein Collectors International, 281 Shore Dr, Burr Ridge, IL 60521; Sun Steiners, P. O. Box 11782, Fort Lauderdale, FL 33339.

Additional Listings: Villeroy & Boch.

Note: Prices in this listing are for print-under-glaze pieces unless otherwise specified.

Coaster, 5" d, PUG
    #1032, dwarfs, small chip on edge, pr....................................328.00
    #1264, girl on swing and boy on bicycle, large chip on one,
        pr..260.00
Jardiniere, 5-1/2" h, 8-3/4 x 10", green ground, off-white cameo figures of Grecian men and women riding in carriage, sitting at table and drinking, base imp "#7000" and "#17" 425.00
Lazy Susan, #1570, PUG, 4 compartments, handle in center, bird design, 1" side hairline, 11" d 130.00
Plaque
    #1044-542, portrait of man, blue delft, 12" d 125.00
    .#1044-1067, water wheel on side of building, sgd "F. Reiss," PUG, gold wear on edge, 17" d 495.00
    #1044-5171, Dutch scene, blue delft, 12" d............................90.00
    #1108 enameled incised dec of castle, gilt rim, c1902, 17" d...230.00

#1168, Cavalier, threading and glaze, sgd "Warth," chip on rear hanging rim, 16-1/2" d...465.00
#2196, Stolzensels Castle on the Rhein, 17" d 1,100.00
#2621, man pouring, etched, 7-1/2" d 185.00
#2625, man singing, etched, small chip repair on edge, 7-1/2" d 115.00
#7072, Phanolith, woman, 8" x 6"..415.00
Punch Bowl, cov, stand, 14-1/2" h, dancing figures in relief, incised #2087, c1900 ....230.00
Stein
    #1078 (1528), The Gambler 150.00
    #1526, transfer and enameled, Student Society, Amico Pectus Hosti Frontem, dated 1902, roster on either side of crest, pewter lid, slight discoloration to int..465.00
    #2007, 1/2 liter, etched, black cat, inlaid lid..........................660.00
    #2018, 1/2 liter, character, pug dog, inlaid lid 1,100.00
    #2028, 1/2 liter, etched, men in Gasthaus, inlaid lid.............550.00
    #2057, 1/2 liter, etched, festive dancing scene, inlaid lid.......325.00
    #2091, pewter rim, lid missing..290.00
    #2093, 1/2 liter, etched and glazed, suit of cards, inlaid lid ...700.00
    #2100, 1/3 liter, etched, Germans meeting Romans, inlaid lid, H. Schlitt...495.00
    #2204, 1/2 liter etched and relief, Prussian eagle, inlaid lid ..780.00
    #2358, pewter top..250.00
    #2580, 1/2 liter, etched, Die Kannenburg, conical inlay lid, knight in castle 695.00
    #2811, 1/2 liter, etched, Art Nouveau design, inlaid lid, slight int. discoloration...750.00
    #2836, yellow, 3 reserves with white figures, pewter top.......350.00
    #2900, pewter top..330.00
    #2922, 1/2 liter, etched, men around campfire, inlaid lid, shallow factory flake on top...400.00
    #2950, 1/2 liter, cameo, Bavarian crest, pewter lid with relief crest 825.00
    #5001, 4.6 liter, faience type, coat of arms, pewter lid 850.00
Tile, 3-1/4" x 5-3/4", blue warrior...225.00
Tobacco Jar, #1231, 7" h, cattle, etched 350.00
Umbrella Stand, 24" h, stoneware, high relief figures and bands of masks..250.00
Vase, 10" h, #1808, stoneware, incised foliate dec, imp marks, pr 230.00

MILK GLASS

History: Opaque white glass attained its greatest popularity at the end of the 19th century. American glass manufacturers made opaque white tablewares as a substitute for costly European china and glass. Other opaque colors, e.g., blue and green, also were made. Production of milk glass novelties came in with the Edwardian era.

The surge of popularity in milk glass subsided after World War I. However, milk glass continues to be made in the 20th century. Some modern products are reissues and reproductions of earlier forms. This presents a significant problem for collectors, although it is partially obviated by patent dates or company markings on the originals and by the telltale signs of age.

Collectors favor milk glass from the pre–World War I era, especially animal-covered dishes. The most prolific manufacturers of these animal covers were Atterbury, Challinor-Taylor, Flaccus, and McKee.

References: E. McCamley Belknap, *Milk Glass*, Crown Publishers, 1949, out of print; Frank Chiarienza and James Slater, *The Milk Glass Book*, Schiffer, 1998; Regis F. and Mary F. Ferson, *Today's Prices for Yesterday's Milk Glass*,

Urn, detailed scene, female handle terminals, imp mark and "2209," 17-1/2" h, price for pair, one with repaired handle, $1,320. Photo courtesy of Garth's Auctions.

published by authors, 1985; ——, *Yesterday's Milk Glass Today*, published by authors, 1981; Everett Grist, *Covered Animal Dishes*, Collector Books, 1988, 1996 value update; Lorraine Kovar, *Westmoreland Glass*, 2 vols., Antique Publications, 1991; S. T. Millard, *Opaque Glass*, 4th ed., Wallace Homestead, 1975, out of print; Betty and Bill Newbound, *Collector's Encyclopedia of Milk Glass*, Collector Books, 1995, 1998 value update.

Collectors' Club: National Milk Glass Collectors Society, 46 Almond Dr, Hershey, PA 17033.

Museum: Houston Antique Museum, Chattanooga, TN.

Notes: There are many so-called "McKee" animal-covered dishes. Caution must be exercised in evaluating pieces because some authentic covers were not signed. Furthermore, many factories have made, and many still are making, split-rib bases with McKee-like animal covers or with different animal covers. The prices below are for authentic McKee pieces with either the cover or base signed.

Numbers in listings prefixed with a letter refer to books listed in the references, wherein the letter identifies the first letter of the author's name.

Animal Dish, cov
    Dog, setter, white base, sgd "Flaccus," repair to lid 150.00
    Fish, skiff base 90.00
    Hen, marbleized, head turned to left, lacy base, white and deep blue, Atterbury (F8) 165.00
Bowl
    8" d, 2-1/2" h, Wicket, Atterbury 70.00
    8-1/4" d, Daisy, allover leaves and flower design, open scalloped edge (F165) 85.00
Box, covered
    Coach 135.00
    Lion, English 95.00
Butter Dish, cov, 4-7/8" l, Roman Cross pattern, sq, ftd base curves outward toward top, cube shape finial (F240) 75.00
Calling Card Receiver, bird, wings extended over fanned tail, head resting on leaf, detailed feather pattern (F669) 150.00

Celery Vase, 6-5/8" h, Blackberry Pattern, scalloped rim, plain band above vertical surface, Hobbs Brockunier (F317) 110.00
Compote, Atlas, lacy edge, blue 185.00
Creamer and Sugar
    Blackberry 145.00
    Trumpet Vine, fire painted dec, sgd "SV" 130.00
Egg Cup, cov, 4-1/4" h, bird, round, fluted, Atterbury (F130) 135.00
Glove Box, Shell on Beach pattern 165.00
Goblet, Ivy in Snow 70.00
Jar, cov, eagle (Old Abe) 120.00
Lamp, 11" h, Goddess of Liberty, bust, 3 stepped hexagonal bases, clear and frosted font, brass screw connector, patent date, Atterbury (F329) 300.00
Match Holder, 5" l, Indian head, wall type 75.00
Mug, 3" h, Ivy in Snow 40.00
Pitcher, 7-1/2" h, owl, glass eyes 150.00
Plate
    6" d, 2 cats form upper edge, bracketed dog head, open work, swirling leaves, emb "He's all right" (B20d) 125.00
    7-1/2" d, Easter Sermon, preacher under tree, rabbits listening 85.00
    8" d, Wicket, Atterbury 42.00
    9" d, California Bears 125.00
Spooner, 5-1/8" h, monkey, scalloped top (F275) 125.00
Syrup, 6" h, Bellflower pattern, single vine, dated, Collins & Wright (F155C0) 245.00
Tumbler, Royal Oak, orig fired paint, green band 50.00
Water Set, C-Scroll pattern, tankard pitcher, six matching tumblers 225.00
Wine, Feather pattern 40.00

MILLEFIORI

History: Millefiori (thousand flowers) is an ornamental glass composed of bundles of colored glass rods fused together into canes. The canes were pulled to the desired length while still ductile, sliced, arranged in a pattern, and fused together again. The Egyptians developed this technique in the first century b.c. it was revived in the 1880s.

Reproduction Alert: Millefiori items, such as paperweights, cruets, and toothpicks, are being made by many modern companies.

Animal Dish, cov, boar's head, inset glass eyes, ribbed base, $1,200. Photo courtesy of Green Valley Auction, Inc.

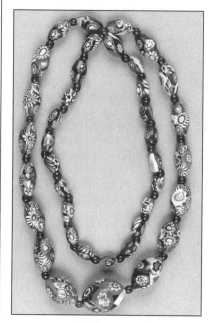

Beads, multicolored, green glass bead spacers, $125.

Bowl, 8" d, tricorn, scalloped, folded sides, amethyst and silver deposit 125.00
Creamer, 3" x 4-1/2", white and cobalt blue canes, yellow centers, satin finish 110.00
Cruet, bulbous, multicolored canes, applied camphor handle, matching stopper 120.00
Cup and Saucer, white and cobalt blue canes, yellow center, satin finish 90.00
Decanter, 12" h, deep black ground, all over multicolored flux and canes, including peachblow, and opal, enamel dec, Gundersen 1,450.00
Door Knob, 2-1/2" d, paperweight, center cane dated 1852, New England Glass Co. 395.00
Goblet, 7-1/2" h, multicolored canes, clear stem and base 150.00
Lamp, 14-1/2" h, 8-1/2" d dome shade, glass base, electric 795.00
Pitcher, 6-1/2" h, multicolored canes, applied candy cane handle 195.00
Rose Bowl, 6" d, crimped top, cased, white lining 145.00
Slipper, 5" l, camphor ruffle and heal 140.00
Sugar, cov, 4" x 4-1/2", white canes, yellow centers, satin finish 125.00
Vase
    4" d, multicolored canes, applied double handles 100.00
    5-1/2" h, purple bands, white oval lines, white bands with red flowers 165.00

MINIATURE LAMPS

History: Miniature oil and kerosene lamps, often called "night lamps," are diminutive replicas of larger lamps. Simple and utilitarian in design, miniature lamps found a place in the parlor (as "courting" lamps), hallway, children's rooms, and sickrooms.

Miniature lamps are found in many glass types, from amberina to satin glass. Miniature lamps measure 2-1/2 to 12 inches in height, with the principle parts being the base, collar, burner, chimney, and shade. In 1877 both L. J. Atwood and L. H. Olmsted patented burners for miniature lamps. Their burners made the lamps into a popular household accessory.

References: Marjorie Hulsebus, *Miniature Victorian Lamps*, Schiffer Publishing, 1996; Frank R. and Ruth E. Smith, *Miniature Lamps* (1981), Book II (1982) Schiffer Publishing; John F. Solverson, *Those Fascinating Little Lamps: Miniature Lamps and Their Values*, Antique Publications, 1988, includes prices for Smith numbers.

Collectors' Club: Night Light, 38619 Wakefield Ct, Northville, MI 48167.

Reproduction Alert: Study a lamp carefully to make certain all parts are original; married pieces are common. Reproductions abound.

Note: The numbers given below refer to the figure numbers found in the Smith books.

#5-1, rainbow, DQ, MOP, satin finish 565.00
#11-1, milk glass pedestal base and shade, colorless pressed font, Sandwich 265.00
#12-1, amber, emb, all orig 115.00
#23-I, time lamp, emb "Time & Light" 75.00
#29-I, nutmeg, white milk glass, brass band and handle 80.00
#50-I, log cabin, blue, handle 1,100.00
#51-I, amber, shoe, applied handle 1,00.00
#52-I, white milk glass, match holder 200.00
#59-I, colorless, emb "Vienna" 135.00
#68-I, finger lamp, blue with stars, emb "Wide Awake," 115.00

Smith, Figure VII, Santa Claus, milk glass, red and black dec, 9-1/2" h, $1,850.

#77-I, nickel, Beauty Night Lamp 55.00
#109-I, Beaded Heart, clear, emb 115.00
#110-I, Bull's Eye, clear, stem 45.00
#112-I, blue, emb "Daisy," nutmeg burner 75.00
#125-I, Christmas Tree, white milk glass, gold trim 125.00
#153-I, milk glass, pink and gold, emb 115.00
#171-I, Pond Lily, emb, inside painting 140.00
#204-II, blue, camphor shade 115.00
#211-I, Medallion, milk glass, emb 45.00
#212-I, pink milk glass with shells 245.00
#213-I, milk glass, emb, yellow, pink, and white 135.00
#230-I, Acanthus, milk glass, emb. yellow and white 125.00
#231-I, Drape pattern,, pink and white milk glass 75.00
#248-II, white milk glass, emb ribbed chimney shade, green, blue, and gold painted dec, hornet burner 135.00
#286-I, Cosmos, white 175.00
#309-I, Pan American Exposition, 1901, Buffalo, NY 2000
#317-I, white milk glass, painted brown, orange, and gray farm scene, nutmeg burner 185.00
#325-I, pink milk glass, angel dec 165.00
#327-II, swan, milk glass 400.00
#369-I, Beaded Swirl, end of day 300.00
#370-I, cranberry, Beaded Swirl 200.00
#389-I, satin, blue, melon ribbed base, pansy ball shade 195.00
#390-I, melon ribbed, cased, yellow 525.00
#400-I, green beaded 125.00
#459-II, satin, red shaded to pink, emb scrolled leaves and swirls 1,650.00
#474-I, Spanish Lace filigree 750.00
#497-I, owl, black, gray, orange eyes 1,100.00
#502-I, opalescent, amber, pink feet 3,000.00
#523-II, blue milk glass, medallion pattern 600.00
#548-II, colorless glass, swirled pattern, ruby and white spatter, nutmeg burner 1,750.00
#555-I, glossy satin glass, pink and butterscotch 1,550.00
#595-I, satin, MOP, DQ, shading from pink to apricot 2,000.00
#625-I, glow lamp, white milk glass, floral dec, burner 30.00

MINIATURE PAINTINGS

History: Prior to the advent of the photograph, miniature portraits and silhouettes were the principal way of preserving a person's image. Miniaturists were plentiful, and they often made more than one copy of a drawing. The extras were distributed to family and friends.

Miniaturists worked in watercolors and oil and on surfaces such as paper, vellum, porcelain, and ivory. The miniature paintings were often inserted into jewelry or mounted inside or on the lids of snuff boxes. The artists often supplemented commission work by painting popular figures of the times and copying important works of art.

After careful study miniature paintings have been divided into schools, and numerous artists are now being researched. Many fine examples may be found in today's antiques marketplace.

References: Daphne Foskett, *Miniatures: Dictionary and Guide*, Antique Collectors' Club, 1999; Dale T. Johnson, American Portrait Miniatures in the Manney Collection, The Metropolitan Museum of Art, 1990.

Museum: Colonial Williamsburg Foundation, Williamsburg, VA; Gibbes Museum of Art, Charleston, SC.

1-5/8" h, 3-7/8" l, on ivory, pair of oval portraits of gentleman and lady, burgundy dress, leatherized case with green velvet lining 1,320.00
2-5/8" h, on ivory, oval portrait of gentleman, blue eyes, minor wear and flaking, emb silver plated brass case 330.00
3" h, 4-3/4" w, on celluloid, pair of oval portraits of blond children, blue background, leatherized case with green velvet lining, early 20th C 125.00
3-1/8" h, on ivory, oval portrait of young woman, brown hair and eyes, white dress with red sash, leatherized case with dark burgundy velvet lining, edge uneven, colors worn 200.00
3-1/4" h, 2-3/4" w, on ivory, oval portrait of matron, lace bonnet, back mkd "Parcilaa Dean, Lynn, Mass," gilt insert, minor wear, incomplete leatherized case 474.00
3-3/4" h, 3" w, American School, early 19th C, watercolor on paper
  Young lady in green dress, elaborate jewelry, sgd "By Wm. S. Stevenson," toning, fading, staining to background 1,265.00
  Young man in black suit, unsigned, inlaid wood frame, toning, minor staining 1,035.00
3-7/8" h, 3-1/4" w, on ivory, oval portrait of young woman, blond hair, white dress, blue, white, and green background, incomplete frame 220.00
3-7/8" h, 3-1/4" w, on paper, woman in black dress, white bonnet, leatherized case 250.00
4" h, on paper, Robespierre, hair curls, blue jacket, ruffled shirt, sgd "Yerbout," French, late 19th C, gilt metal frame 250.00

4-1/8" h, 3-5/8" w, on ivory, oval portrait of young child, blond hair, blue yees, modern frame 385.00
4-1/4" h, on ivory, woman in large hat, elegant dress, indecipherable signature, oval gilt brass frame 200.00
4-3/8" h, 3-3/4" w, on ivory, oval portrait of young woman, blond hair, white dress, blue accessories, blue background, brass fame with backing sgd "Painted by Rd. Mills, Birmm, 1829", minor edge damage 385.00
4-1/2" h, 3-5/8" w, on ivory, oval portrait of gentleman, worn black lacquered frame with gilded fitting, revarnished, wear, some damage 275.00
5" h, 4-1/2" w, on ivory, oval portrait of woman, elaborate dark hair, brown eyes, black dress, blue shoulder scarf, worn black lacquered frame with gilded liner, minor wear 275.00
5" h, 5-3/4" w, on ivory, elegantly dressed lady, tortoiseshell and ivory veneered frame, sgd "Renoir", late 19th/early 20th C 250.00
5" h, 5-3/4" w, on ivory, woman with long brown curls, dressed in riding attire, dark background, French, Menardi, 19th C, wood frame 450.00
5-1/4" h, 4-1/2" w, on paper, oval portrait of matronly lady, bonnet, faded colors, black lacquered frame with gilded fittings 125.00
5-1/4" h, 4-3/4" w, on ivory, rect portrait of young man, black hair, leatherized case with burgundy velvet lining, wear and damage 55.00
5-1/2" h, 5" w, on ivory, oval portrait of woman, elaborate dark hair, hazel eyes, white dress, black lacquered frame with gilded fittings 275.00
5-3/8" h, on ivory, elegant lady in jeweled and feathered hat, low cut dress with lace collar, dec ormolu frame, French, sgd "Dark (?)" 350.00
5-5/8" h, 4-3/4" w, on ivory, oval portrait of woman, light brown hair, black dress, black lacquered frame with gilded fittings, chipped lens 200.00
6-3/4" h, 4-1/8" w, on ivory, lady, elegant dress, jewel and feather hairpiece, French school, rect gilt brass frame 400.00
7-1/8" h, 5-1/8" w, enamel, Renaissance-Revival style, maiden in yellow velvet dress, jeweled collar and headdress, long red hair draped over shoulders, sgd "T. Leroy," ormolu ribboned laurel wreath border frame, velvet backing, French 700.00
7-1/8" h, 5-1/8" w, on ivory, young woman, long hair, simple dress with brooch, French impressionist style, dec gilt bronze frame 700.00
7-1/4" h, 6-3/8" w, on ivory, rect portrait of young cleric, black coat, black lacquered frame with gilded fittings, wear, frame loose .. 200.00

MINIATURES

History: There are three sizes of miniatures: dollhouse scale (ranging from 1/2 to 1 inch), sample size, and child's size. Since most early material is in museums or is extremely expensive, the most common examples in the marketplace today are from the 20th century.

Many mediums were used for miniatures: silver, copper, tin, wood, glass, and ivory. Even books were printed in miniature. Price ranges are broad, influenced by scarcity and quality of workmanship.

The collecting of miniatures dates back to the 18th century. It remains one of the world's leading hobbies.

References: George M. Beylerian, *Chairmania*, Harry N. Abrams, 1994; Caroline Clifton-Mogg, *Dollhouse Sourcebook*, Abbeville Press, 1993; Nora Earnshaw, *Collecting Dolls' Houses and Miniatures*, Pincushion Press, 1993; Flora Gill Jacobs, *Dolls Houses in America*, Charles Scribner's Sons, 1974; ——, *History of Dolls Houses*, Charles Scribner's Sons; Constance Eileen King, *Dolls and Dolls Houses*, Hamlyn, 1989; Herbert F. Schiffer and Peter B. Schiffer, *Miniature Antique Furniture*, Schiffer Publishing, 1995; Margaret Towner, *Dollhouse Furniture*, Courage Books, Running Press, 1993.

Periodicals: *Doll Castle News*, P. O. Box 247, Washington, NJ 07882; *Miniature Collector*, Scott Publications, 30595

Portrait of Gentleman on ivory, $700.

Eight Mile Rd, Livonia, MI 48152; *Nutshell News*, 21027 Crossroads Circle, P. O. Box 1612, Waukesha, WI 53187.

Collectors' Clubs: International Guild Miniature Artisans, P. O. Box 71, Bridgeport, NY 18080; Miniature Industry Association of America Member News, 2270 Jacquelyn Dr, Madison, WI 53711; National Association of Miniature Enthusiasts, 2621 Anaheim, CA 92804-3883.

Museums: Colonial Williamsburg Foundation, Williamsburg, VA; Margaret Woodbury Strong Museum, Rochester, NY; Mildred Mahoney Jubilee Doll House Museum, Fort Erie, Canada; Museums at Stony Brook, Stony Brook, NY; Toy and Miniature Museum of Kansas City, Kansas City, MO; Toy Museum of Atlanta, Atlanta, GA; Washington Dolls' House and Toy Museum, Washington, DC.

Additional Listings: See Dollhouse Furnishings in *Warman's Americana & Collectibles* for more examples.

Doll House Furniture

Armoire, tin litho, purple and black..................................35.00
Bathroom, wood, painted white, Strombecker 40.00
Bedroom Suite
   French Provincial style, antique white, bed, dressing table, bench, pr night stands 195.00
   Victorian style, metal, veneer finish, bed, night stand, commode with faux marble tops, armoire and mirror, cradle, Biedermeier clock, metal washstand......................................675.00
Bench, wood, rush seat 25.00
Buffet Set, stenciled, 3 shelves, column supports, Biedermeier, 6" h 400.00
Chair
   Golden Oak, center splat, upholstered seat, German, c1875, pr .75.00
   Ormolu, ornate, 3" h, c1900, pr 75.00
Cradle, cast iron, painted green, 2" l...................................40.00
Desk, Chippendale style, slant front, drawers open.....................60.00
Dining Room, Edwardian style, dark red stain, extension table, chairs, marble top cupboard, grandfather clock, chandelier, candelabra, 5" h bisque shoulder head maid doll, table service for six, Gebruder Schneerass, Waltershausen, Thuringa, c1915 ....1,400.00
Hall Rack, walnut, carved fretwork, arched mirror back shelves, umbrella holder 450.00
Kitchen Set, litho tin, Modern Kitchen, all parts and pieces, animals, and related items, orig box, Louis Marx 250.00
Living Room Suite
   Empire style, sofa, fainting couch, 2 side chairs, upholstered tapestry, matching drapery 350.00
   Victorian style, settee, 2 parlor chairs, footstool, 2 plant stands, 2 gilt filigree tables, 3 panel screen, upholstered red velvet, Gone with the Wind style lamp 650.00
Piano, grand, wood, 8 keys, 5" h 35.00

Food, platters with fish, turkey, and ham, each 2" d, 2-3/4" l, center: cake plate with sliced cake, Viscoloid (celluloid), each $125. Photo courtesy of Julie P. Robinson.

Sewing Table, golden oak, drawer, c1880 ....100.00
Table, tilt-top, brass, 4-1/2" h 250.00
Tea Cart, Petite Princess 25.00
Vanity, Biedermeier 90.00

Doll House Accessories

Bird Cage, brass, bird, stand, 7" h 65.00
Candelabra, Petite Princess 25.00
Carpet Sweeper, gilt, Victorian...65.00
Christmas Tree, decorated 50.00
Clock, metal 35.00
Coffeepot, brass 25.00
Cup and Saucer, china, flower design, c1940............................10.00
Decanter, 2 matching tumblers, Venetian, c1920.........................35.00
Fireplace, tin, Britannia metal fretwork, draped mantel, carved grate...85.00
Plate, 4-1/4" d, redware, slip dec, America, 19th C, minor rim chips, glaze wear..805.00
Radio, Strombecker, c1930..35.00
Refrigerator, Petite Princess 75.00
Silhouettes, Tynietoy, c1930, pr 25.00
Telephone, wall, oak, speaker and bell, German, c1890 ....40.00
Towel Stand, golden oak, turned post....................................45.00
Umbrella Stand, brass, ormolu, sq, emb palm fronds.....................60.00
Urn, silver, handled, ornate 100.00

Child Size

Blanket Chest
   37" w, 13-3/4" d, 15-1/2" h, 6 board, molded lip top, dovetailed box, bracket feet, painted light blue, front yellow freehand dec, inscribed "J. J. H. 1820" in wreath flanked by tulips and meandering vines at ends above pinwheel Schoharie County, NY 2,645.00
   26-3/4" w, 11-1/2" d, 22" h, old dark green painted pine and poplar, molded hinged top, case with single drawer, cutout ends joined by valanced skirt, attributed to New England, c1800...........2,530.00
Bookcase, hp, scalloped cornice over 4 open shelves, base with 3 drawers, Peter Hunt dec 1,650.00
Chair
   Arm, Windsor, grain painted and parcel gilt, lowback, PA, first half 19th C, reserve scrolling concave crest continuing to downswept arms, six bulbous turned supports, plank seat, ring-turned tapering legs joined by stretchers, all over graining in brown and ochre, gilt highlights 850.00
   Side, 10-3/4" seat, 22" h, worn orig light green paint, black striping, gold stenciling, polychrome floral dec, pr..........................625.00
Chest of Drawers, Hepplewhite, serpentine, mahogany with inlay, cross banded top edge with stringing and banding, patera medallion on top, banding around base with fan in apron, banding around drawers, 5 dovetailed drawers, scrolled apron, French feet, top drawer as old pen and ink inscription "William Eaty, May 28, 1798," restored at Winterthur, 18-3/4" w, 24" h...............................30,800.00
Cook Stove, black and white enameled steel, nickel steel fittings, working gas range, mkd "Estate Fresh Air Oven," break in door frame, 15" l...2,420.00
Dresser, 23-1/4" h, cottage style, poplar, orig red paint, white striping, three drawers, high back mirror with shelves, wire nail construction, minor water damage to paint on feet.................................300.00
Rocker, Empire style, mahogany, vase shaped splat, rush seat, scrolled arms, 22" h..225.00
Table, drop leaf, Sheraton, walnut, pine secondary wood, leaves with decoratively cut corners, one dovetailed drawer, turned legs, old finish, minor edge damage, hinges replaced, age crack on top, 23-1/2" l, 12-1/4" w, 10-3/4" l leaves, 19" h.......................1,100.00
Tub, 5-5/8" d, 2-1/4" h, stave construction, metal bands, wire handles, orig blue paint, black bands 330.00

Doll Size

Bed, tester, mahogany, turned posts, arched tester frame, old finish, early 20th C, added plywood mattress support, repairs, 22-1/4" x 39-1/2" x 28-3/4" h 110.00

Blanket Chest, America, early 19th C
  Painted pine, six board, lift-off molded top, arched end boards, orig blue paint, 14" w, 5" d, 6-3/4" h, loss to leg, till missing ... 1,610.00
  Poplar, dovetailed case, molded edge lid, ogee feet, refinished, minor damage to feet and repair to lid, replaced hinges, 19" w, 9-1/4" d, 9-1/2" h 880.00
Chest of Drawers
  10" w, 8-1/4" h, poplar, old black paint, six board type construction, cutout feet, two nailed drawers 275.00
  13-1/2" w, 7-1/4" d, 13" h, Empire, mahogany and mahogany veneer, poplar secondary wood, 3 dovetailed drawers, S-curve pilasters, scrolled feet, some veneer damage 500.00
  25" h, 12" 2, 6-1/2" d, Tramp Art, swivel mirror with ornate crest over top with scalloped sides, 2 drawers over 3 long drawers on base with teardrop pulls, scalloped apron, late 19th/early 20th C, very minor losses 690.00
Cupboard, step back, wall-type, homemade
  Pine and poplar, gray paint, wire nail construction, 13-1/2" w, 8-1/4' d, 18-1/4" h 200.00
  Poplar, old red paint, white int. with shelves and pencil drawing, back inscribed "To Mary from Papa," 18-1/2" h 200.00
Stove, 18" w, cast iron, Jewel Range Jr., by Detroit Stove Works, Aesthetic Movement dec, six circular range lids, hot water reservoir, oven, grate, top and side warming ledges, one support detailed 525.00

MINTON CHINA

History: In 1793 Thomas Minton joined other men to form a partnership and build a small pottery at Stoke-on-Trent, Staffordshire, England. Production began in 1798 with blue-printed earthenware, mostly in the Willow pattern. In 1798 cream-colored earthenware and bone china were introduced.

A wide range of styles and wares was produced. Minton introduced porcelain figures in 1826, Parian wares in 1846, encaustic tiles in the late 1840s, and Majolica wares in 1850. Many famous designers and artists in the English pottery industry worked for Minton.

In 1883 the modern company was formed and called Mintons Limited. The "s" was dropped in 1968. Minton still produces bone-china tablewares and some ornamental pieces.

Marks: Many early pieces are unmarked or have a Sevres-type marking. The "ermine" mark was used in the early 19th century. Date codes can be found on tableware and majolica. The mark used between 1873 and 1911 was a small globe with a crown on top and the word "Minton."

References: Paul Atterbury and Maureen Batkin, *Dictionary of Minton*, Antique Collectors' Club, 1999; Susan and Al Bagdade, *Warman's English & Continental Pottery & Porcelain*, 3rd Edition, Krause Publications, 1998; Joan Jones, *Minton: The First Two Hundred Years of Design and Production*, Swan Hill, 1993.

Museum: Minton Museum, Staffordshire, England; Victoria & Albert Museum, London, England.

Bowl, 12" x 10", oval, Palissy style, minor base chip 3,080.00
Cabinet vase, 4" h, 3" d, squeezebag dec, red, olive, and white stylized poppies, mkd "Minton Ltd./7/A" 375.00
Center Bowl, 11" l, majolica, oval, pierced basketweave sides, putti on either end supporting foliage festoons, imp mark, c1868...... 2,875.00
Cup and Saucer, Aragon pattern, gilt scrolling band flanked by decorative borders 45.00
Dinner Service, Princess pattern, 160 pcs.................... 700.00
Ewer, 21-1/4" h, majolica, heron and fish, after model by J. Protat, imp mark, 1869 date code 2,400.00

Cup and Saucer, Tree Leaf pattern, sgd, 3-1/4" d cup, 4-7/8" d saucer, $40.

Figure, 10-1/2" h, putti, yellow basket and grape vine, 1867, professional repair at rim of basket 2,750.00
Floor Urn, 35" h, 18" d, majolica, Neoclassical, turquoise, massive foliage handles.. 12,650.00
Jardiniere, 7" h, molded wooden plants, white vines, lilac nt., majolica, matching stands, pr.. 475.00
Oyster Plate, majolica
  Cobalt blue 1,650.00
  Light green, 9" d 500.00
  Malachite, rim chips 1,210.00
  Mottled.. 935.00
  Pink, minor rim nick 1,100.00
  Turquoise.. 525.00
Oyster Server, 4 tier, majolica, green and brown, white wells, turquoise finial, rim damage to 6 wells, mechanical turning mechanism missing 3,575.00
Pitcher, 7" h, bulbous, loped shaped mouth, red flambé glaze, geometric gilt dec 200.00
Platter, 17" l, 14" w, blue and white transfer, "The Gem," imp maker's mark and date 420.00
Service Plate, 10-5/8" d, raised gold dec, wide light blue ground banded borders, 2 sets of 12, one with floral dec, other with urn and scrolled leaf dec, printed marks, mid 20th C 3,450.00
Soup Tureen, Cov, Stand, 14-1/4" l, oval, enamel dec black transfer printed Oriental garden landscape, imp marks, c1882............ 420.00
Sweetmeat Dish, 10" h, majolica, central shell form bowl flanked by standing putti, turquoise highlights, after model by Albert Carrier-Belleuse, some restoration...................................... 425.00
Tile, 5-3/4" sq, glazed pottery, mahogany frame, label indicates it was removed from U. S. Capitol in 1994 and that it was installed there in 1820 .... 100.00
Vase
  10" h, 5" d, bottle shape, 2 handles, squeezebag dec, teal, olive, gold, and white stylized plants, stamped "Minton Ltd./108," few minor nicks.. 1,000.00
  11-3/4" h, 5-1/2" d, cylindrical, 2 handles, squeezebag dec, red, olive, gold, and white stylized plants and swags, stamped "Minton Ltd./1" 950.00

MOCHA

History: Mocha decoration usually is found on utilitarian creamware and stoneware pieces and was produced through a simple chemical action. A color pigment of brown, blue, green, or black was made acidic by an infusion of tobacco or hops. When the acidic colorant was applied in blobs to an alkaline ground, it reacted by spreading in feathery designs resembling sea plants. This type of decoration usually was supplemented with bands of light-colored slip.

Types of decoration vary greatly, from those done in a combination of motifs, such as Cat's Eye and Earthworm, to a plain pink mug decorated with green ribbed bands. Most forms of mocha are hollow, e.g., mugs, jugs, bowls, and shakers.

English potters made the vast majority of the pieces. Collectors group the wares into three chronological periods: 1780–1820, 1820–1840, and 1840–1880.

Marks: Marked pieces are extremely rare.

References: Susan and Al Bagdade, *Warman's English & Continental Pottery & Porcelain*, 3rd Edition, Krause Publications, 1998.

Reproduction Alert.
Bowl
    5-5/8" d, 3" d, white dot dec in band, brown ground, cracks, chips, staining 195.00
    6-7/8" d, 3-1/2" h, brown seaweed dec, ochre ground, cracks, chips, staining 245.00
Chamber Pot
    8-1/2" d, tan band, blue and black stripes, blue, white, and black earthworm, wear, repair, handle replaced............................110.00
    8-3/4" d, two tone blue bands, black stripes, black and white earthworm, leaf handle, some wear and edge flakes 125.00
Creamer, 5-1/4" h, black and white checkered band on shoulder medium blue glaze 215.00
Cup, 2-7/8" h, imp border above brown and white earthworm design, blue ground, 19th C, imperfections 375.00
Jar, cov, 5" h, pale blue band, black stripes, white, black, and blue cat's eye and earthworm dec, repairs and hairline in lid...................500.00
Jug
    6-1/8" h, blue and white raise earthworm dec, two blue bands ..675.00
    8-1/2" h, 2 black and white checkered bands, blue glaze, foliate handle and spout 345.00
Measure, 5", 6", and 6-1/4" h, tankard, blue, black and tan seaweed dec, one with applied white label "Imperial Pint," other with resist label "Quart," minor stains, wear, and crazing, 3 pc set...........440.00
Mug
    3-1/4" d, 5" h, dark brown geometric design on cream ground, brown vertical geometric pattern on cream, dark brown and yellow alternating stripes, white handle with leaf impressed ends, cracks, handle repaired, chips 320.00
    3-3/8" d, 4-3/4" h, dark brown geometric pattern on cream ground, pumpkin, dark brown, and cream alternating stripes, white handle with leaf impressed ends, cracks, handle repaired 650.00
    3-3/8" d, 4-3/4" h, dark brown wavy dec on cream ground, bordered by ochre stripes, cream dot pattern on black stripe, blue impressed bands, cream handle with leaf impressed ends, minor glaze imperfections, minor chips 1,150.00
    4-1/4" d, 5-3/4" h, blue and brown earthworm pattern on olive ground, cream and ochre sunflower pattern on dark brown ground, light blue alternating stripes, white handle with leaf impressed ends, handle repaired, discoloration, cracks, minor chips 2,415.00
    4-3/8" d, 5-7/8" h, blue, brown, and cream earthworm pattern in vertical configuration on cream and white striped ground, green impressed band, dark brown alternating stripes, white handle with leaf impressed ends, handle and body repaired, cracks, chips....2,760.00
    5-1/8" h, yellow ware, molded and machined bands, leaf handle, brown, blue, and chocolate brown stripes, hairlines 715.00

6" d, 5-3/8" h, open chain pattern, pumpkin ground, upper and lower dark brown bands, white handle with leaf impressed ends, minor glaze imperfections, small hairline cracks 1,955.00
Mustard Pot, cov
    2-1/2" h, light blue, cinnamon, and dark brown earthworm pattern on blue ground, bordered by dark brown stripes, blue glazed collar, imp with laurel wreath leaves, top with applied finial, alternating impressed laurel wreath in blue with dark brown stripe on white ground, white handle with leaf impressed ends, minor chips, slight damage to lid...725.00
    2-3/4" h, light blue, white, and dark brown cat's eye on ochre ground, bordered by dark brown stripes, collar glazed in light blue, lid with finial and brown-ochre striping, white handle with leaf impressed ends, minor chips, slight damage to lid 650.00
Pepper Pot
    4" h, baluster form, dark brown seaweed dec on cinnamon ground, ochre dark brown and cream stripes, domed top, old chips, hairline crack...450.00
    4-3/8" h, ochre, dark brown and ginger tobacco leaf pattern on cream ground, plain domed top, old chips, staining, crazing 1,955.00
    4-3/8" h, white, cinnamon, and dark brown cat's eye on blue ground, dark brown, blue, and cinnamon stripes alternating on white ground, very minor chips 920.00
    4-1/2" h, baluster form, white, ochre and dark brown marbling on cream ground, dark brown stripes alternating on cream ground, dome top, old chips, hairline crack 515.00
    4-3/4" h, baluster form, white, brown, and cinnamon earthworm pattern on blue ground, green beading impressed band, blue dome top with dark brown stripe, foot with blue and brown stripes, foot repaired, old chips 820.00
    4-3/4" h, light blue, ochre, and cream cat's eye pattern on dark brown ground, cream and celadon alternating stripes, domed top with finial dec in blue with dark brown stripe, brown stripe on foot, minor chips, minor imperfections 1,100.00
Pitcher
    4" d, 5-1/4" h, blue, brown, and white earthworm pattern, brown ground, brown, blue, dark brown, and whit alternating stripes, white handle with leaf impressed ends, minor imperfections 1,380.00
    4" d, 6" h, white and brown zigzag earthworm pattern, green ground, white and brown cat's eye pattern on green ground, green impressed band, dark brown and white alternating stripes, white handle with leaf impressed handles, cracks...........1,380.00
    4" d, 6-1/4" h, blue, brown, and white earthworm pattern, brown ground, green imp bands, brown and white alternating stripes, white handle with leaf impressed ends, cracks, minor chips..........1,035.00
    4" d, 7-1/4" h, dark brown geometric pattern on cream ground separated by thin dark brown stripes, dark brown and blue alternating stripes, white handle with leaf impressed ends, cracks, spout, handle and bottom rim repairs 920.00
    4-1/4" d, 6-3/4" h, brown, cream, and ochre cat's eye pattern, blue ground, alternating with blue, cream, and dark brown cat's eye pat-

Pitcher, blue and white bands, stylized dec, $795.

tern on ochre ground, blue impressed band, dark brown and white alternating stripes, white handle with leaf impressed ends, cracks, minor chips, staining, minor glaze imperfections 1,495.00
4-3/8" d, 7-1/4" h, cream slip dec on dark brown ground, light blue, cream, and dark brown cat's eye pattern on ochre ground, green impressed leaf dec on raised shoulder, light blue and cream alternating stripes, white handle with leaf impressed ends, spout and neck repairs, crack on handle..3,795.00
5" d, 8" h, blue and brown earthworm pattern, celadon green and ochre ground, light green imp bands and alternating light blue stripes, white handle with leaf imp ends, spout and handle repaired, minor chips 2,530.00
8-1/8" h, white, brown and blue bands, dark brown stripes and cat's eyes, crow's foot hairline, minor crazing and wear 1,210.00
Salt, 3" d, 2-1/8" h, gray band, black stripes, white wavy lines, stains in foot, rim hairlines...330.00
Tea Canister, 4" h, blue, black, and white band on shoulder, white fluted band on bottom, medium blue glaze 125.00
Teapot, 5-7/8" h, oval shape, medium blue, fluted band on bottom, black and white checkered band on top, acorn finial 500.00
Waste Bowl
4-3/4" d, amber band, black seaweed dec separated into five segments by squiggly lines, green molded lip band, stains and hairlines 275.00
5-5/8" d, 2-7/8" h, orange-tan band, dark brown stripes, emb green band with blue, white, and dark brown earthworm, repairs.550.00

MONART GLASS

History: Monart glass is a heavy, simply shaped art glass in which colored enamels are suspended in the glass during the glassmaking process. This technique was originally developed by the Ysart family in Spain in 1923. John Moncrief, a Scottish glassmaker, discovered the glass while vacationing in Spain, recognized the beauty and potential market, and began production in his Perth glassworks in 1924.

The name "Monart" is derived from the surnames Moncrief and Ysart. Two types of Monart were manufactured: a commercial line which incorporated colored enamels and a touch of aventurine in crystal, and the art line in which the suspended enamels formed designs such as feathers or scrolls.

Marks: Monart glass, in most instances, is not marked. The factory used paper labels.

Basket, brown to light tan opal vertical striations, Cluthra type...600.00
Bowl
9" d, Aventurine, blue, mottled brown and goldstone, pebbled...165.00
11-1/2" d, mottled orange and green 195.00
Candlestick, two shades of green, goldstone, and mica flecks, paper label...120.00
Lamp Shade, 6-1/2" d, white opal..95.00
Vase
6-1/2" h, mottled shades of red and blue, white lining...........225.00
8-1/2" h, green rim shading to brown and clear body, green pedestal 95.00
9" h, bulbous ovoid, red ground, white and blue swirl dec, orig paper label 145.00

MONT JOYE GLASS

History: Mont Joye is a type of glass produced by Saint-Hilaire, Touvier, de Varreaux & Company at their glassworks in Pantin, France. Most pieces were lightly acid etched to give them a frosted appearance and were also decorated with enameled florals.

Note: Pieces listed below are frosted unless otherwise noted.

Chestnut Bowl, 8" d, colorless ftd and petal-form bowl, cameo etched and heavily enameled chestnuts on leafy branches, ochre, olive green, and rust, ice finished ground, gilt enameled foliate border, base with worn gold enamel "Mont Joye I. C." mark, c1910, wear to enamel........520.00
Pitcher, 10" h, amethyst, enameled flowers, aqua, blue, pink, and gold, sgd 350.00
Rose Bowl, 3-3/4" h, 4-1/4" d, pinched sides, acid etched, enameled purple violets, gold stems and dec..295.00
Vase
4" h, pink enameled poppy and gold leaves, frosted textured ground, mkd 275.00
5-1/2" h, swirled shape, green, enameled flowers, c1890, sgd "Mont Joye"..445.00
10" h, bulbous, narrow neck, clear to opalescent green, naturalistic thistle dec, gold highlights...375.00
18" h, green, enameled purple flowers, gold leaves, sgd......325.00
Violet Vase, 6" h, frosted etched surface, colorless glass, naturalistic enameled purple violet blossoms, gold highlights, base mkd "Dimier Geneve" 260.00

MOORCROFT

History: William Moorcroft was first employed as a potter by James Macintyre & Co., Ltd., of Burslem in 1897. He established the Moorcroft pottery in 1913.

The majority of the art pottery wares were hand thrown, resulting in a great variation among similarly styled pieces. Color and marks are keys to determining age.

Walker, William's son, continued the business upon his father's death and made wares in the same style.

References: Paul Atterbury, *Moorcroft: A Guide to Moorcroft Pottery 1897-1993, Rev. Ed.*, Richard Dennis and Hugh Edwards, 1990; Susan and Al Bagdade, *Warman's English & Continental Pottery & Porcelain*, 3rd Edition, Krause Publications, 1998; A. W. Coysh, *British Art Pottery, 1870-1940*, Charles E. Tuttle, 1976; Walter Moorcroft, *Walter Moorcroft Memories of Life and Living*, Richard Dennis Publications, distributed by Antique Collectors' Club, 1999; Frances Salmon, *Collecting Moorcroft*, Francis-Joseph Books, 1994.

Collectors' Club: Moorcroft Collectors' Club, Lipert International Inc., 2922 M. Street, NW, Washington, DC 20007.

Museums: Everson Museum of Art, Syracuse, NY; Moorcroft Museum, Stoke-on-Trent, England; Victoria & Albert Museum, London, England.

Marks: The company initially used an impressed mark, "Moorcroft, Burslem"; a signature mark, "W. Moorcroft" followed. Modern pieces are marked simply "Moorcroft" with export pieces also marked "Made in England."

Bowl, 9" d, 4" h, ftd, squeezebag dec, Waving Corn pattern, celadon ground, stamped "Moorcroft," sgd in ink, hairline from rim.......650.00
Cabinet Vase, 1-3/4" h, 2" d, stylized red roses, blue flowers, white ground, MacIntyre Burslem stamp mark, script "WM"..............850.00
Compote, 7-1/4" d, Lily motif, yellow and green ground 150.00
Ginger Jar, cov, 11-1/2" h, pomegranate dec............................525.00
Loving Cup, 4-1/4" h, tulip and cornflower dec, green, blue, and red, 3 handles, printed and painted signature, c1900 ....350.00
Marmalade Jar, cov, blue flowers, attached stand, sgd "MacIntyre" 175.00
Perfume Bottle, 2" h, 1-3/4" d, lavender and yellow pansies, cobalt blue ground, hallmarked silver cap 600.00

Vases, left: Poppy, bulbous, rolled lip, purple, rose, and green, cobalt blue ground, imp "W. Moorcroft/Potter to/ H.M. the Queen/Made in England," painted initials "W. M.," 11" h, $1,760; center: Orchid, bulbous tapering to flared neck, shades of blue, green, yellow and rose, pale blue-green ground, mkd "Moorcroft/Made in England," 4" h, $350; right: Pomegranate, bulbous body tapering to flared rim, rose, blue, green, brown, and purple, cobalt blue ground, mkd "Moorcroft/Made in England," sgd "W. Moorcroft," 9" h, $1,375. Photo courtesy of Alderfer Auction Co.

Pitcher, 5" h, 6" d, bulbous, yellow and pink irises, shaded blue to
  green ground, imp signature 350.00
Plate
  7-1/4" d, toadstool, blue ground, imp "Moorcroft Claremont" 620.00
  8-1/2" d, Natural War, green and blue glaze, pr 235.00
Potpourri Jar, 3-1/4" h, 3-1/2" d, heart shaped leaves, cinnabar glaze,
  ink script signature, chip to thread inside 400.00
Tea Set, 6-1/4" h coffeepot, teapot, creamer, open sugar, Pomegrante
  pattern, pewter mounts and lids, stamped "MOORCROFT," script
  sgd, "Liberty & Co." 2,500.00
Vase
  6-1/4" h, 3-1/2" d, bulbous, Ruby Lustre, cherry blossom design,
    imp script mark 900.00
  6-1/2" h, 3" d, Florian Ware, Poppy pattern, blue flowers, green
    leaves, white glaze, script sgd, McIntyre stamp............... 1,500.00
  6-3/4" h, 3" h, Florian Ware, tapering, squeezebag dec, blue jonquils,
    green leaves, blue ground, ink mark "W. Moorcroft/des" 1,800.00
  9" h, 3-3/4" d, Florian Ware, Violet pattern, yellow, blue, and cela-
    don, script sgd 1" hairline to rim.. 800.00
  12-3/4" h, Moonlit Blue, mounted as lamp............................. 900.00
  14-1/4" h, 6" d, Wisteria pattern, ruby flambé glaze, stamped
    "MOORCROFT/MADE IN ENGLAND" and script sgd 4,250.00

MORGANTOWN GLASS WORKS

History: The Morgantown Glass Works, Morgantown, West Virginia, was founded in 1899 and began production in 1901. Reorganized in 1903, it operated as the Economy Tumbler Company for 20 years until, in 1923, the word "Tumbler" was dropped from the corporate title. The firm was then known as The Economy Glass Company until reversion to its original name, Morgantown Glass Works, Inc., in 1929, the name it kept until its first closing in 1937. In 1939, the factory was reopened under the aegis of a guild of glassworkers and operated as the Morgantown Glassware Guild from that time until its final closing. Pur-

chased by Fostoria in 1965, the factory operated as a subsidiary of the Moundsville-based parent company until 1971 when Fostoria opted to terminate production of glass at the Morgantown facility. Today, collectors use the generic term, "Morgantown Glass," to include all periods of production from 1901 to 1971.

Morgantown was a 1920s leader in the manufacture of colorful wares for table and ornamental use in American homes. The company pioneered the processes of iridization on glass as well as gold and platinum encrustation of patterns. They enhanced Crystal offerings with contrasting handle and foot of India Black, Spanish Red (ruby), and Ritz Blue (cobalt blue), and other intense and pastel colors for which they are famous. They conceived the use of contrasting shades of fired enamel to add color to their etchings. They were the only American company to use a chromatic silk-screen printing process on glass, their two most famous and collectible designs being Queen Louise and Manchester Pheasant.

The company is also known for ornamental "open stems" produced during the late 1920s. Open stems separate to form an open design midway between the bowl and foot, e.g., an open square, a "Y", or two diamond-shaped designs. Many of these open stems were purchased and decorated by Dorothy C. Thorpe in her California studio, and her signed open stems command high prices from today's collectors. Morgantown also produced figural stems for commercial clients such as Koscherak Brothers and Marks & Rosenfeld. Chanticleer (rooster) and Mai Tai (Polynesian bis) cocktails are two of the most popular figurals collected today.

Morgantown is best known for the diversity of design in its stemware patterns as well as for their four patented optics: Festoon, Palm, Peacock, and Pineapple. These optics were used to embellish stems, jugs, bowls, liquor sets, guest sets, salvers, ivy and witch balls, vases, and smoking items.

Two well-known lines of Morgantown Glass are recognized by most glass collectors today: #758 Sunrise Medallion and #7643 Golf Ball Stem Line. When Economy introduced #758 in 1928, it was originally identified as "Nymph." By 1931, the Morgantown front office had renamed it Sunrise Medallion. Recent publications erred in labeling it "dancing girl." Upon careful study of the medallion, you can see the figure is poised on one tiptoe, musically saluting the dawn with her horn. The second well-known line, #7643 Golf Ball, was patented in 1928; production commenced immediately and continued until the company closed in 1971. More Golf Ball than any other Morgantown product is found on the market today.

References: Jerry Gallagher, *Handbook of Old Morgantown Glass*, vol. I, published by author (420 First Ave NW, Plainview, MN 55964), 1995; ——, Old Morgantown, Catalogue of Glassware, 1931, Morgantown Collectors of America Research Society, n.d.; Ellen Schroy, *Warman's Depression Glass*, Krause Publications, 1997; Jeffrey B. Snyder, *Morgantown Glass From Depression Glass Through the 1960s*, Schiffer Publishing, 1998; Hazel Marie Weatherman, *Colored Glassware of the Depression Era*, Book 2 published by author, 1974, available in reprint; ——, *1984 Supplement & Price Trends for Colored Glassware of the Depression Era*, Book 1, published by author, 1984.

Collectors' Clubs: Old Morgantown Glass Collectors' Guild, P. O. Box 894, Morgantown, WV 26507.

Bowl

#1 Berkshire, Crystal w/#90 Starlet Cutting, 8" d 60.00
#12-1/2 Woodsfield, Genova Line, 12-1/2" d 545.00
#14 Fairlee, Glacier decoration, 8" d.. 525.00
#19 Kelsha, Genova Line, 12" d 425.00
#26 Greer, Neubian Line, 10" d 750.00
#35-1/2 Elena, Old Amethyst, applied crystal rim, 8" d.............. 425.00
#67 Fantasia, Bristol Blue, 5-1/2" d... 75.00
#101 Heritage, Gypsy Fire, Matte Finish, 8" d 70.00
#103 Elyse, Steel Blue, 7" d 48.00
#1102 Crown, Moss Green, 9" d 45.00
#1933 El Mexicana, console, Seaweed, 10" d 385.00
#1933 El Mexicano Ice Tub, Ice or Seaweed, 6" d 210.00
#4355 Janice, Ritz Blue or Spanish Red, 13" d 445.00
#4355 Janice, Crystal, Glacier Decor w/Snow Flowers, 13" d.... 565.00
#7643 Truman, Spanish Red, crystal trim, rare, 10" d 4,500.00

Candleholders, pair

#37 Emperor, Stiegel Green or 14K Topaz, 8" h........................ 625.00
#80 Modern, Moss Green, 7-1/2" h.. 70.00
#81 Bravo, Peacock Blue, 4-1/2" h528.00
#82 Cosmopolitan, Moss Green, slant, 7" h................................ 75.00
#87 Hamilton, Evergreen, 5" h.. 75.00
#88 Classic, Nutmeg, 4-3/4" h 55.00
#105 Coronet, Ebony or Cobalt, slant, 8-3/4" h 120.00
#7620 Fontanne, Ebony filament, #781 Fontinelle etch........... 1,000.00
#7643 Golf Ball, Torch Candle, single, Ritz Blue, 6" h 280.00
#7662 Majesty, Randall Blue, 4" h 750.00
#7690 Monroe, Ritz Blue, 7" h, rare...................................... 1,200.00
#7951 Stafford, Crystal w/#25 gold band, 3-1/8" h 685.00
#9923 Colonial, Pineapple, 2-pc hurricane, 8-1/2" h................. 140.00

Candy Jar

#14 Edmond, Danube Line, #4 cover, rare, 8-1/2" h................. 625.00
#16 Rachel, Crystal, Pandora cutting, 6" h 385.00
#108 Bethann, Topreen Line, 5" h 595.00
#200, Mansfield, Burgundy matte, 12" h 195.00
#1212 Michael, Spanish Red, crystal finial, 5-1/2" h.............. 1,000.00
#7643-1 Alexandra, Randall Blue/Crystal Duo-Tone, 5" h 825.00
#9952 Palace, Ruby, 6-12" h 60.00

Champagne

#7577 Venus, Ritz Blue, Pillar Optic, 5-1/2 oz 55.00
#7606-1/2 Athena, Ebony filament, #777 Baden etch, 7 oz.......... 75.00
#7621 Ringer, Aquamarine, 6 oz.. 55.00
#7623 Pygon, D.C. Thorpe satin open stem, 6-1/2 oz.............. 165.00
#7640 Art Moderne, Ebony open stem, 5 oz............................. 85.00
#7643 Golf Ball, 5-1/2 oz , Spanish Red.................................. 50.00
#7678 Old English, 6-1/2 oz, Ritz Blue 52.00
#7860 Lawton, Azure, Festoon Optic, 5 oz................................ 50.00

Cocktail

Chanticleer, Pink Champagne bowl, 4 oz................................. 45.00
Mai Tai, Topaz stem, 4 oz 50.00
Old Crown, 6-1/4" h, 5-1/2 oz.. 85.00
#7577 Venus, Anna Rose, Palm Optic, 3 oz.............................. 38.00
#7577 Venus, Venetian Green, Palm Optic, 3 oz....................... 35.00
#7620 Fontanne, Ebony filament, #781 Fontinelle etch, 3-1/2 oz ... 135.00
#7643 Golf Ball, 3-1/2 oz, Ritz Blue 48.00
#7643 Golf Ball, 3-1/2 oz, Stiegel Green 45.00
#7654-1/2 Legacy, Spanish Red, 3 oz....................................... 45.00
#7654-1/2 Legacy, Manchester Pheasant silk screen, 3-1/2 oz . 185.00

Compote

#201 Inverness, Meadow Green, Peacock Optic, 4-1/2" d,
    7-1/2" h.. 155.00
#206 Colette, Burgundy, 7-1/2" h... 65.00

#7556 Toledo, high with cover, Crystal, Forever vutting, 4-1/2" d 315.00
#7654 Reverse Twist, Aquamarine, 6-1/2" d, 6-3/4" h 195.00

Cordial

#7565 Astrid, Anna Rose, #734 American Beauty etch, 3/4 oz.. 155.00
#7577 Venus, Anna Rose, #743 Bramble Rose etch, 1-1/2 oz... 165.00
#7643 Golf Ball, 1-1/2 oz, pastels.. 55.00
#7643 Golf Ball, 1-1/2 oz, Spanish Red.................................... 65.00
#7643 Golf Ball, 1-1/2 oz, Stiegel Green 60.00
#7617 Brilliant, Spanish Red, 1-1/2 oz.................................... 135.00
#7654 Lorna, Nantucket etch, 1-1/2 oz.................................... 105.00
#7668 Galaxy, Mayfair etch, 1-1/2 oz 87.50
#7673 Lexington, Ritz Blue filament, #790 Fairwin etch, 1-1/2 oz ... 165.00

Goblet

#300 Festival, Gloria Blue, 8 oz... 35.00
#7568 Horizon, #735 Richmond etch, 10 oz.............................. 48.00
#7577 Venus, Anna Rose, Palm Optic, 9 oz............................... 55.00
#7577 Venus, Crystal, #743 Bramble Rose etch, 9 oz.............. 80.00
#7604-1/2 Heirloom, 14-K Topaz, #751 Adonis etch, 9 oz....... 125.00
#7614 Hampton, Golden iris, Virginia etch, 9 oz...................... 65.00
#7617 Brilliant, Spanish Red, 10 oz.. 95.00
#7624 Paragon, Ebony open stem, 10 oz.................................. 200.00
#7630 Ballerina, Aquamarine/Azure, Yukon cutting, 10 oz........ 120.00
#7637 Courtney, D.C. Thorpe satin open stem, 9 oz................ 195.00
#7640 Art Moderne, Ritz Blue, crystal open stem, 9 oz............ 155.00
#7643 Golf Ball, 9 oz, Alabaster 150.00
#7643 Golf Ball, 9 oz, pastels 65.00
#7643 Golf Ball, 9 oz, Ritz Blue 65.00
#7643 Golf Ball, 9 oz, Spanish Red 60.00
#7643 Golf Ball, 9 oz, Stiegel Green 52.00
#7644-1/2 Vernon, Venetian Green, Pineapple Optic, 9 oz 55.00
#7659 Cynthia, #746 Sonoma etch, 10 oz................................ 68.00
#7664 Queen Anne, Manchester Pheasant silk screen, 10 oz... 275.00
#7678 Old English, 10 oz, Spanish Red 55.00
#7690 Monroe, Golden Iris, Amber, 9 oz.................................. 80.00

Guest Set

#23 Trudy, 6-3/8" h
    Alabaster 175.00
    Baby Blue 85.00
    Bristol Blue 125.00
    Opaque Yellow carafe, India Black tumbler.......................... 195.00
#24 Margaret, 5-7/8" h, Anna Rose, enamel decor 170.00

Jug

#6 Kaufmann, #510 Doric Star Sand Blast, 54 oz 275.00
#8 Orleans, #131 Brittany Cutting, 54 oz.................................. 385.00
#33 Martina, #518 Lily of the Valley Sand Blast dec, 46 oz,
    7-piece set.. 585.00
#36 Bolero, Pomona Two-Tone Line, 54 oz................................ 985.00
#37 Barry, Anna Rose handle and foot, Palm Optic, 48 oz........ 390.00
#303 Cyrano, #203 needle etch, 54 oz.................................... 385.00
#1933 LMX Del Rey, Randall Blue non-opaque, rare, 54 oz 675.00
#1962 Ockner, Crinkle Line, 64 oz, Amethyst........................... 145.00
#1962 Ockner, Crinkle Line, 64 oz, Pink Champagne, frosted ... 165.00
#7622-1/2 Ringling, 54 oz, Golden Iris.................................... 650.00
#7622-1/2 Ringling, 54 oz, Spanish Red 695.00

Plate, #1500

Alexandrite, #776 Nasreen etch, dessert, 7" d 135.00
Anna Rose, #734 American Beauty etch, dessert, 7" d 55.00
Crystal, Hollywood Platinum/Red band decor, torte, 14" d 395.00
Crystal, #810 Sear's Lace Bouquet etch, dessert, 7" d 25.00
Ritz Blue, Vernay decoration, dessert, 7-1/2" d 135.00
Stiegel Green, salad/luncheon, 8-1/2" d 55.00

Sherbet

#1962 Crinkle, 6 oz, Pink... 24.00
#3011 Montego, Gypsy Fired, 6-1/2" oz 38.00
#7620 Fontanne, #781 Fontinelle etch, 6 oz............................ 165.00

#7643 Golf Ball, 5-1/2 oz, pastels 40.00
#7643 Golf Ball, 5-1/2 oz, Ritz Blue 50.00
#7643 Golf Ball, 5-1/2 oz, Spanish Red.....................48.00
#7643 Golf Ball, 5-1/2 oz, Stiegel Green 45.00
#7646 Sophisticate, Picardy etch, 5-1/2 oz...............48.00
#7654-1/2 Legacy, Manchester Pheasant silk screen, 6-1/2 oz . 135.00
#7690 Monroe, Old Amethyst, 6 oz 85.00
#7780 The President's House, 6 oz 20.00

Tumbler

#1928 Ivy, Stiegel Green, ice tea, 15 oz 75.00
#1962 Crinkle, India Black, flat juice, 6 oz 85.00
#7622 Bracelet, Ritz Blue, ice tea, 14 oz 85.00
#7664 Queen Anne, Aquamarine/Azure, #758 Elizabeth etch,
    11 oz ....115.00 -
#7668 Galaxy, #778 Carlton etch, 9 oz 22.00
#9051 Zenith, Venetian Green, Peacock Optic, bar, 2 oz 45.00
#9074 Belton, Primrose, Vaseline, Pillar Optic, 9 oz..................125.00

Vase

#12 Viola, Rainbow Line, Spiral Optic, 8" d 120.00
#25 Olympic, #734 American Beauty etch, 12" h.......650.00
#26 Catherine 10" bud, Azure, #758 Sunrise Medallion etch 250.00
#35-1/2 Electra, Continental Line, Old Amethyst, 10"..............1,000.00
#53 Serenade 10" bud, Opaque Yellow 430.00
#53 Serenade 10" bud, Venetian Green, #756 Tinker Bell etch . 595.00
#67 Grecian, Ebony, Saracenic Art Line, 6" h..........1,200.00
#73 Radio, Ritz Blue, 6" 895.00
#90 Daisy, crystal, green and white wash, 9-1/2" w....450.00
#1933 Gaydos, LMX Seaweed, 6-1/2".......................785.00

Wine

#7565 Astrid, Anna Rose, #734 American Beauty etch, 3 oz 125.00
#7577 Venus, Anna Rose, #743 Bramble Rose etch, 3-1/2 oz... 145.00
#7643 Golf Ball, 3 oz, Alabaster 145.00
#7643 Golf Ball, 3 oz, Ritz Blue 75.00
#7643 Golf Ball, 3 oz, Stiegel Green............................65.00
#7640 Art Moderne, ebony stem, 3 oz 145.00
#7660-1/2 Empress, Spanish Red, 3 oz 85.00
#7668 Galaxy, #810 Sears' Lace Bouquet etch, 2-1/2 oz.............48.00
#7693 Warwick, Stiegel Green, 2-1/2 oz 55.00
#7721 Panama, Sharon decoration, 3 oz 225.00
#8446 Summer Cornucopia, Copen Blue bowl, 3 oz.................325.00

MORIAGE, JAPANESE

History: Moriage refers to applied clay (slip) relief decorations used on certain types of Japanese pottery and porcelain.

This decorating was done by one of three methods: 1) hand rolling, hand shaping, and hand application to the biscuit in one or more layers; the design and effect required determine thickness and shape, 2) tubing or slip trailing, which applied decoration from a tube, like decorating a cake, and 3) hakeme which involved reducing the slip to a liquid and decorating the object with a brush. Color was applied either before or after the process.

Bowl, 7" d, orange flowers and leaves, green wreath mark 150.00
Chocolate Pot, cov, 9" h, green ground, 4 floral medallions, heavy
    Moriage 245.00
Manicure Set, 3 tools, butter and cov trinket box, heavy dec 195.00
Planter, 3-3/4" h, 3-3/4" l, swan, figural, multicolored enameled dec..95.00
Powder Jar, 5" d, light green, raised turquoise beading, hp flowers...90.00
Tea Set, teapot, reamer, cov sugar, five cups and saucers, mauve
    ground, red roses, delicate white slipwork, unmarked 650.00
Vase
    9-1/4" h, pedestal base, green ground, white overall slipwork, floral
    medallions...265.00

Ewer, floral pattern, green, 10" h, $285.

12-1/2" h, tan ground, light green bands, blue and pink flowers, 3 panels of multicolored Bird-On-Limb dec, Japanese 265.00

MOSER GLASS

History: Ludwig Moser (1833–1916) founded his polishing and engraving workshop in 1857 in Karlsbad (Karlovy Vary), Czechoslovakia. He employed many famous glass designers, e.g., Johann Hoffmann, Josef Urban, and Rudolf Miller. In 1900 Moser and his sons, Rudolf and Gustav, incorporated Ludwig Moser & Söhne.

Moser art glass included clear pieces with inserted blobs of colored glass, cut colored glass with classical scenes, cameo glass, and intaglio cut items. Many inexpensive enameled pieces also were made.

In 1922 Leo and Richard Moser bought Meyr's Neffe, their biggest Bohemian art glass rival. Moser executed many pieces for the Wiener Werkstätte in the 1920s. The Moser glass factory continues to produce new items.

References: Gary Baldwin and Lee Carno, *Moser—Artistry in Glass*, Antique Publications, 1988; Mural K. Charon and John Mareska, *Ludvik Moser, King of Glass*, published by author, 1984.

Basket, 5-1/2" h, green malachite, molded cherubs dec, pr 800.00
Beverage Set, 10-1/4" h, frosted and polished smoky topaz decanter, 4
    cordials, molded nude women, 5 pc set...................................265.00
Center Bowl, 7-1/2" d, ribbed, green ground, etched border, gilded
    grapes on vine, acid-etched "Moser" within polished pontil, c1920,
    wear to gilding, rim flake 375.00
Cordial Set, 10-1/4" h decanter, six 2-1/2" h cordials, elongated neck
    on broad angular base of decanter, dichroic ice blue to pink glass
    entirely facet cut, matching faceted spire stopper, matching cordials
    with faceted flared cups, ball and disk base............................635.00
Cup and Saucer, 3" h, 5-3/8" d saucer, cobalt blue to white ext., swirl-
    ing raised gold tendrils and gold leaves, raised gold edges.....400.00
Cup, Paris, lime green, two applied acorns 350.00
Demitasse Cup and Saucer, amber shading to white, enameled gilt
    flowers 100.00

Box, cov, green ground, enameled floral motif, gilded leaf banding, ftd, script sgd "Moser," 4" d, 3" h, $145.

Cup and Saucer, mkd "Winterling/Bavaria/German/69" on cup, $17.50.

Ewer, 10-3/4" h, cranberry, gilt surface, applied acorns and clear jewels 2,000.00
Goblet, 8" h, cranberry, Rhine-style, enameled oak leaves, applied acorns, 4 pc set 1,800.00
Perfume, 4-3/4" h, pink-lavender Alexandrite, faceted panels, matching stopper, sgd in oval 275.00
Pitcher, 6-3/4" h, amberina, IVT, 4 yellow, red, blue, and green applied glass beaded bunches of grapes, pinched in sides, 3 dimensional bird beneath spout, allover enamel and gold leaves, vines, and tendrils 3,200.00
Portrait Vase, 8-1/2" h, woman, gold leaves, light wear 450.00
Rose Bowl, 5-1/2" d, 4-1/4" h, spherical, smoke colored body, heavily acid-etched stylized deer in garden setting, acid-etched "Moser" within polished pontil, c1920 .... 400.00
Urn, 15-3/4" h, cranberry, 2 gilt handles, studded with green, blue, clear, and red stones, highly enameled surface, multicolored and gilt Moorish dec 3,500.00
Vase
  7" h, paneled amber baluster body, wide gold medial band of women warriors, base inscribed "Made in Czechoslovakia-Moser Karlsbad" 550.00
  8" h, turquoise, flowers on panel 295.00
  9" h, cranberry, two gilt handles, medallion with hp roses, sgd 1,050.00
  10" h, heavy walled dark amethyst faceted body, etched and gilded medial scene of bear hunt, spear-armed men and dogs pursuing large bear 345.00
  15" h, 2-1/4" w, cylindrical, colorless ground, heavy enameled floral dec, pr 650.00
  23-1/2" h, cranberry ground, enameled leaf surface, applied acorns, three dimensional eagle and bird, sgd "Moser," stand 8,250.00

MOSS ROSE PATTERN CHINA

History: Several English potteries manufactured china with a Moss Rose pattern in the mid-1800s. Knowles, Taylor and Knowles, an American firm, began production of a Moss Rose pattern in the 1880s.

The moss rose was a common garden flower grown in England. When American consumers tired of English china with Oriental themes, they purchased the Moss Rose pattern as a substitute.

Butter Pat, sq, mkd "Meakin" 25.00
Coffee Mug and Saucer, mkd "Meakin" 42.00
Cup and Saucer, mkd "Haviland, Limoges" 25.00
Dessert Set, cake plate, eight 7-1/2" plates, cups and saucers, creamer and sugar, mkd "Fr. Haviland," price for 28 pc set 295.00
Gravy Boat, matching underplate, mkd "Green & Co., England" .. 30.00

Nappy, 4-1/2" d, mkd "Edwards" 15.00
Plate
  7-1/2" d, Haviland, Limoges 20.00
  8-1/2" d, mkd "KTK" 25.00
  9-1/2" d, mkd "Haviland" 20.00
Platter, 10" w, 14" l, rect, mkd "Meakin" 30.00
Salt and Pepper Shakers, pr, 5" h, sterling silver top and base, mkd "Rosenthal" 65.00
Sauce Dish, 4-1/2" d, mkd "Haviland" 20.00
Soup Plate, 9" d, mkd "Meakin" 20.00
Sugar, cov, mkd "Haviland, Limoges" 70.00
Tea Service, cov teapot, creamer, sugar, md "Meakin" 220.00
Teapot, 8-1/2" h, bulbous, gooseneck spout, basketweave trim, mid "T & V" 45.00
Tureen, cov, 12" l, gold trim 75.00

MOUNT WASHINGTON GLASS COMPANY

History: In 1837 Deming Jarves, founder of the Boston and Sandwich Glass Company, established for George D. Jarves, his son, the Mount Washington Glass Company in Boston, Massachusetts. In the following years the leadership and the name of the company changed several times as George Jarves formed different associations.

In the 1860s the company was owned and operated by Timothy Howe and William L. Libbey. In 1869 Libbey bought a new factory in New Bedford, Massachusetts. The Mount Washington Glass Company began operating again there under its original name. Henry Libbey became associated with the company early in 1871. He resigned in 1874 during the general depression, and the glassworks was closed. William Libbey had resigned in 1872 when he went to work for the New England Glass Company.

The Mount Washington Glass Company opened again in the fall of 1874 under the presidency of A. H. Seabury and the management of Frederick S. Shirley. In 1894 the glassworks became a part of the Pairpoint Manufacturing Company.

Throughout its history the Mount Washington Glass Company made different types of glass including pressed, blown, art, lava, Napoli, cameo, cut, Albertine, and Verona.

References: Edward and Sheila Malakoff, *Pairpoint Lamps*, Schiffer Publishing, 1990; John A. Shuman III, *Collector's*

Encyclopedia of American Art Glass, Collector Books, 1988, 1994 value update.

Collectors Club: Mount Washington Art Glass Society, P. O. Box 24094, Fort Worth, TX 76124.-1094.

Museum: The New Bedford Glass Museum, New Bedford, MA.

Additional Listings: Burmese; Crown Milano; Peachblow; Royal Flemish.

Advisor: Louis O. St. Aubin, Jr.

Beverage Set, satin, MOP
  Coralene, yellow sea weed dec, glossy finish, 9" h, bulbous water pitcher, three spout top, applied reeded shell handle, three matching 4" h tumblers, 2 blisters on pitcher, 3 pc set........750.00
  Herringbone, 9" h bulbous water pitcher, 7" w, applied frosted handle, deep rose to deep pink to pink, to off white, enameled and painted white wild roses, green, brown, and gold leaves, stems, branches, and thorns, 4 3-3/4" h tumblers, damage to tumbler, 5 pc set 1,750.00
Bon Bon Bowl, 2" h, 5-1/4" l, 4-1/2" w, Burmese, smooth satin finish, rectangular bowl, bulged-out optic ribbed sides with turned-in edges .285.00
Bowl, 4-1/2" d, 2-3/4" h, Rose amber, fuchsia, blue swirl bands, bell tone flint...295.00
Box, 4-1/2" h, 6-1/2" d, opalware, mint green ground, deep pink roses, small red cornflowers, gold trim, blown-out floral and ribbon design, #3212/20 .... 1,750.00
Collars and Cuffs Box, opalware, shaped as 2 collars with big bow in front, cov dec with orange and pink Oriental poppies, silver poppy-shaped finial with gold trim, base with poppies, white ground, gold trim, bright blue bow, white polka dots, buckle on back, sgd "Patent applied for April 10, 1894," #2390/128 .... 950.00
Cracker Jar, melon ribbing, squatty, white opal ground, cosmos and leaves dec, silver plate lid and handle 365.00
Cream Pitcher, 2-1/2" h, blue satin, "1893 World's Fair"............ 625.00
Flower Holder, 5-1/4" d, 3-1/2" h, mushroom shape, white ground, blue dot and oak leaf dec, ...425.00
Fruit Bowl, 10" d, 7-1/2" h, Napoli, solid dark green ground painted on clear glass, outside dec with pale pink and white pond lilies, green and pink leaves and blossoms, int. dec with gold highlight traceries, silver-plated base with pond lily design, 2 applied loop handles, 4 buds form feet, base sgd "Pairpoint Mfg. Co. B4704".......... 2,200.00
Humidor, 5-1/2" h, 4-1/2" d top, hinged silver-plated metalwork rim and edge, blown-out rococo scroll pattern, brilliant blue Delft windmills, ships, and landscape, Pairpoint 950.00
Jewel Box, 4-1/2" d top, 5-1/4" d base, 3-1/4" h, opalware, Monk drinking glass of red wine on lid, solid shaded green background on cover and base, fancy gold-washed, silver-plated rim and hinge, orig satin lining, artist sgd "Schindler"... 550.00

Biscuit Jar, yellow ground, orange and peach dec, lid mkd "Pairpoint 3932," base mkd "3932/222," 6" d, 4" h, $375.

Jug, 6" h, 4" w, satin, Polka Dot, deep peachblow pink, white air traps, DQ, unlined, applied frosted loop handle 475.00
Lamp, parlor, four dec glass oval insert panels, orig dec white opalware ball shade with deep red carnations, sgd "Pairpoint" base, c1890 .... 1,750.00
Lamp Shade, 4-1/4" h, 5" d across top, 2" d fitter, rose amber, ruffled, fuschia shading to deep blue, DQ... 575.00
Miniature Lamp, 17" h, 4-1/2" d shade, banquet style, milk glass, bright blue Delft dec of houses and trees, orig metal fittings, attributed to Frank Guba 795.00
Mustard Pot, orig silver-plated hardware
  3" h, hp barn swallow, brown-orange shaded ground 285.00
  4-1/2" h, ribbed, bright yellow and pink background, painted white and magenta wild roses.. 200.00
Perfume Bottle, 5-1/4" h, 3" d, opalware, dark green and brown glossy ground, red and yellow nasturtiums, green leaves, sprinkler top ..375.00
Pitcher, 6" h, 3" w, satin, DQ, MOP, large frosted camphor shell loop handle 325.00
Rose Bowl, 4" h, 5" d, satin, bright yellow, enameled red berries, pale orange leaves and branches, 8 large ribbed swirls.................. 145.00
Salt and Pepper Shakers, pr, 6 lobed body with cream colored ribs, hp enamel floral dec... 265.00
Sugar Shaker
  4-1/2" h, egg shape, pink and gold chrysanthemums on white to blue shaded ground 445.00
  4-1/2" h, egg shape, satin finish on upper half, allover green tint, vine laden with green leaves and naturalistic violet blossoms 385.00
  5-1/2" h, peachblow, satin finish with shiny base, delicate blossoms and leaves, SP top... 1,950.00
Tumbler, 4" h, satin, c1880
  Diamond Quilted, heavenly blue... 165.00
  Diamond Quilted, shaded yellow to white.............................. 165.00
  Herringbone, shaded blue.. 165.00
Vase
  3-1/2" h, amberina, applied rigaree necklace, 4 rows of optic thumbprints, last row enlonged and swirled..................... 575.00
  5" h, 4" w, melon ribbed, ruffled tricorn top, MOP satin, Alice Blue, white lining, applied frosted edge, 1880s.......................... 275.00
  5-3/4" h, 4-1/4" h, satin, heavenly blue shading to white, white lining, hobnails, 4 fold, folded in-top 675.00
  6" h, 3-1/4" w, bulbous stick, satin, flaring rim, apricot shading to white, DQ.. 375.00
  6-1/4" h, 5-1/2" w, satin, melon ribbed, MOP, Bridal White, muslin pattern, applied frosted edge, c1880 .... 425.00
  6-1/2" h, 3" w, satin, Raindrop, Bridal White, MOP, applied frosted edge, pr.. 550.00
  6-1/2" h, 6" w, satin, bulbous, DQ, deep rose shading to pink, two applied frosted "M" handles with thorns, cut edge, c1880 .. 750.00
  8" h, Ring, black ground, gold storks in flight, gold floral dec, spoke bottom, pr... 550.00
  8" h, satin, MOP, Raindrop, butterscotch, applied camphor edge.. 375.00
  8" h, 7" w, bulbous, satin, MOP, Alice Blue, Muslin pattern, applied frosted edge, 3 petal top 675.00
  8-1/4" h, 5" w, satin, amberina coloration, MOP DQ, deep gold diamonds, white lining, slightly ruffled top 1,250.00
  8-3/8" h, Napoli, int. dec of chickens in rain, gold ext. dec, some paint missing... 1,700.00
  9" h, 3-1/2" w at shoulder, MOP satin glass, deep gold, Raindrop pattern sheet lining, applied tightly crimped camphor edge, c1880285.00
  9" h, 5-1/2" w, pink opalware, Delft windmill with person in front, gold trim top and base, Pairpoint...................................... 725.00
  9-1/4" h, 4-1/4" w, satin, MOP, shaded rose, DQ, ruffled edges, white lining, c1880, pr.. 875.00
  10" h, Neapolitan Ware, yellow, purple, rust, and gold spider mums, green leaves, gold spider webbing on ext., sgd "Napoli", #880 .... 1,450.00
  11-1/4" h, gourd shape, 6" l flaring neck, satin, deep brown shading to gold, white lining, enameled seaweed design all over 550.00

11-7/8" h, bulbous stick, Colonial ware, glossy white, gold dec, all over vine and berry dec, two wreath and bow dec at top, sgd, #1010 .... 550.00

12-3/4" h, 5-1/2" w, Colonial ware, shaped like Persian water jug, loop handle on top, small spout, bulbous body, pedestal base, glossy white ground, pale pink and purple lilies, green leaves and stems, overlaid gold dec of leaves, stems, and daisies, sgd and #1022 .... 2,200.00

17-1/2" h, hp floral dec, white satin glass, swirl ribbed tall cylinder body 400.00

MULBERRY CHINA

History: Mulberry china was made primarily in the Staffordshire district of England between 1830 and 1860. The ware often has a flowing effect similar to Flow Blue. It is the color of crushed mulberries, a dark purple, sometimes with a gray tinge or bordering almost on black. The potteries that manufactured Flow Blue also made Mulberry china, and, in fact, frequently made some patterns in both types of wares. To date, there are no known reproductions.

References: Susan and Al Bagdade, *Warman's English & Continental Pottery & Porcelain,* 3rd Edition, Krause Publications, 1998; Ellen R. Hill, *Mulberry Ironstone,* published by author, 1993; Petra Williams, *Flow Blue China and Mulberry Ware,* revised ed., Fountain House East, 1993.

Advisor: Ellen G. King.

Balmoral, Beech & Hancoc
Butter Pat 40.00
Milk Pitcher, polychromed 350.00
Bochara, Edwards, pitcher to wash set 375.00
Bryonia, Utzschneider, bowl, 9" d, squared, open 255.00
Chusan, Holdcroft, tea cup and saucer 75.00
Corea, Clementson, vegetable tureen, cov 325.00
Corean, Podmore Walker
Creamer 175.00
Chamber Pot 375.00
Plate, 9" d 95.00
Platter, 14" 355.00
Punch/custard cup 60.00
Pitcher and Bowl Wash Set 1,050.00
Tea Cup and Saucer 90.00
Teapot, cov, coxcomb handle 575.00
Cyprus, Davenport
Soap Dish, lid, insert, bottom 850.00
Tea pot, cov 450.00
Delhi, M. T. & Co.
Plate, 9 1/2" d 65.00
Platter, 11" l 150.00
Flora, Walker

Bryonia, open bowl, 9", $255. Photo courtesy of Ellen G. King.

Marble, spittoon, $350. Photo courtesy of Ellen G. King.

Pitcher, to wash set 300.00
Plate, 8" d 55.00
Hong, Walker, teapot, cov, coxcomb handle 450.00
Jeddo, Adams
Cup Plate 65.00
Platter, 18" l 275.00
Under tray to sauce tureen 100.00
Wash Bowl, to wash set 295.00
Jeddo, Beech & Hancock, fruit compote, ftd, polychrome 175.00
Marble, maker unknown
Creamer 150.00
Plate, 9" d 60.00
Soap Dish, lid, insert, bottom 250.00
Spittoon 350.00
Teapot, cov 400.00
Medina, J. F. & Co.
Sauce/vegetable dish, 5" d 70.00
Teapot, cov, coxcomb handle 725.00
Percy, Morley, sauce tureen, top, ladle, bottom, tray 650.00
Rhone Scenery, Mayer, tea cup and saucer 65.00
Summer Flowers, Alcock, soup tureen, lid, bottom, undertray .. 325.00
Susa, Meigh, sugar bowl, cov 225.00
Vincennes, Alcock
Plate, 10 1/2" d 85.00
Platter, 15 1/2" l 250.00
Vegetable Tureen, cov 300.00
Vine Border, Bell, cake plate, handled 95.00
Washington Vase, Podmore Walker
Creamer 125.00
Plate
    8" d 60.00
    9" d 70.00
Relish, shell shape 180.00
Sugar, cov 275.00
Tea Cup and saucer 80.00
Teapot, cov 375.00
Vegetable Tureen, cov 375.00
Water Lily, L.P. & Co., pitcher and bowl wash set with shaving mug and hot water pitcher, polychromed 795.00
Wild Rose, maker unknown, pitcher to wash set 450.00
Wisteria, maker unknown
Cup Plate 60.00
Plate, 9" d 75.00
Zinnia, Bourne & Co., plate, 8" d 40.00

MUSICAL INSTRUMENTS

History: From the first beat of the prehistoric drum to the very latest in electronic music makers, musical instruments have been popular modes of communication and relaxation.

The most popular antique instruments are violins, flutes, oboes, and other instruments associated with the classical music period of 1650 to 1900. Many of the modern instruments, such as trumpets, guitars, and drums, have value on the "used" rather than antiques market.

The collecting of musical instruments is in its infancy. The field is growing very rapidly. Investors and speculators have played a role since the 1930s, especially in early string instruments.

References: Tony Bacon (ed.), *Classic Guitars of the '50s*, Miller Freeman Books (6600 Silacci Way, Gilroy, CA 95020), 1996; S. P. Fjestad (ed.), *Blue Book of Guitar Values*, 2nd ed., Blue Book Publications, 1994; Alan Greenwood, *Vintage Guitar Magazine Price Guide*, 6th ed., Vintage Guitar Books, 1998; George Gruhn and Walter Carter, *Acoustic Guitars and Other Fretted Instruments*, GPI Books, 1993; ——, *Electric Guitars and Basses*, Miller Freeman Books, GPI Books, 1994; ——, *Gruhn's Guide to Vintage Guitars*, GPI Books, 1991; Philip F. Gura and James F. Bollman, *America's Instrument: The Banjo in the 19th Century*, Univ of North Carolina Press, 1999; Mike Longworth, *C. F. Martin & Co.*, 4 Maples Press, 1994; Paul Trynka (ed.), *Electric Guitar*, Chronicle Books, 1993.

Periodicals: *Concertina & Squeezebox*, P. O. Box 6706, Ithaca, NY 14851; *Jerry's Musical Newsletter*, 4624 W Woodland Rd, Minneapolis, MN 55424; *Piano & Keyboard*, P. O. Box 767, San Anselmo, CA 94979; *Strings*, P. O. Box 767, San Anselmo, CA 94979; *Twentieth Century Guitar*, 135 Oser Ave, Hauppauge, NY 11788; *Vintage Guitar Classics*, P. O. Box 7301, Bismarck, ND 58507.

Collectors' Clubs: American Musical Instrument Society, RD 3, Box 205-B, Franklin, PA 16323; Automatic Musical Instrument Collectors Association, 919 Lantern Glow Trail, Dayton, OH 45431; Fretted Instrument Guild of America, 2344 S Oakley Ave, Chicago, IL 60608; Musical Box Society International, 887 Orange Ave E, St Paul, MN 55106; Reed Organ Society, Inc, P. O. Box 901, Deansboro, NY 13328.

Museums: C. F. Martin Guitar Museum, Nazareth, PA; International Piano Archives at Maryland, Neil Ratliff Music Library, College Park, MD; Miles Musical Museum, Eureka Springs, AR; Museum of the American Piano, New York, NY; Musical Museum, Deansboro, NY; Streitwieser Foundation Trumpet Museum, Pottstown, PA; University of Michigan, Stearns Collection of Musical Instruments, Ann Arbor, MI; Yale University Collection of Musical Instruments, New Haven, CT.

Musical Instruments

Accordion, 14-1/2" l, black lacquer, brass, silver, and abalone inlay, keys and decorative valve covers in carved mother of pearl, works, needs repair, some damage 95.00
Banjo
    Bacon Banjo Co., Style C, 17 fret neck, hard-shell
        case 185.00

Chamber Barrel Organ, Josephus Fuzelli, London, 1799, $5,925. Photo courtesy of Auction Team Breker.

Edgemere Banjo, 17 nickel plated hexagonal brackets, nickel, shell, wood lined, birch neck with faux mahogany finish, c1900 .... 300.00
Regina, 18 hook, 17 frets, peghead and fingerboard wood and metal trim, tone ring, metal resonator, 1920 patent date 125.00
Bassoon, 48-1/4" l, pearwood, 8 keys, brass mounts and keys, William Milhouse, branded "Milhouse/London" 525.00
Bugle, artillery, brass, c1900 .... 150.00
Caliola, Wurlitzer, wooden pipes, decorative front with name "Clancy O'Toole," drums, keyboard for manual play, also roll operation 14,500.00
Clarinet, 11-1/2" l, stained maple, brass mounts, 10 brass keys, stamped "F. Muss/Wien" 425.00
Cymbals, 10" d, leather handles, American, c1900 .... 90.00
Drum
    15" d, 12" h, snare, painted, labeled "Russell & Patee successors to Gilmore & Russell, 61 Court Street, Boston, Mass," ink inscription "sold 1849," imperfections 345.00
    16-1/2" d, worn orig varnish and transfer dec of eagle and shield, labeled "Carl Fischer, New York," replaced ropes and leather, old heads, two drum sticks 330.00
    17" d, 13-5/8" h, painted dec, reserve of musical instruments and "H. W. Maynard," labeled "William Sempf Manufacturer of Bass & Snare Drums 209 & 211 Grand Street, New York...," mid 19th C, minor losses 460.00
Flute, cocoa wood, silver trim, one key, German, late 19th C 85.00
Guitar, Super 400 C#SN, 1991, only 1 made 9,000.00
Harmonica, Classical, attributed to New England, 1830s, mahogany and mahogany veneer, rect hinged top with rounded corners banded in veneer, opens to int. with rounded open painted glass vessels identified by stenciled letters and musical notations, some case imperfections, 41" w, 23-1/4" d, 34" h 2,300.00
Harp, walnut, carved base, gilt traces, partially restored, restrung, Italian, c1620 .... 3,500.00
Melodian, D. B. Barlett Manufacturer, Concord, NH, rosewood and tiger maple, 5 octaves, ivory keys with centered articulated scale, grain painted fabric lined case with iron hardware, minor imperfections, 7" x 28-3/4" x 14" 865.00
Nicholodean, Cremona, style G, keyboard style, coin operated player piano, 29 flute pipes, 4 rolls, restored 12,000.00
Piano
    Grand, Classical, Wilkins & Newhall, Boylston St, Boston, early 19th C, mahogany, rosewood veneer piano case bordered by mahogany

crossbanding, supported on curule-form base, applied concentric ring bosses, tapered molded feet, 72" w, 31" d, 36" h 1,000.00

Upright, late Empire, Philadelphia, c1850, inlaid and ormolu mounted mahogany, molded cornice, rect case with drapery inset, flanked by turned columns, hinged lid, keys and inlay read "Loud & Brothers/Philadelphia," carved turned legs, casters, 52" w, 26" d, 76" h 3,000.00

Upright, Wurlitzer Style I, nickelodeon, carved oak case, red sharp key, reiterating feature on hammers, 10 rolls...................4,500.00

Pitch Pipe, 6" l, walnut, book form, paper label on int. "WN," America, 19th C, crack...200.00

Pump Reed Organ, 43" w, 22-3/4" d, 74" h, oak case, Eastlake detail, old worn finish, backboards incomplete, stop knob labels missing, not in working order...50.00

Saxophone
    Dupont, B-flat, baritone, highly polished brass 350.00
    Tourville & Co., tenor, silver 350.00

Trombone, Concertone, SP, gold plated bell, satin finish............300.00

Trumpet, Holton, B-flat, brass, nickel finish..........................550.00

Tuba, Dupont, E-flat, bass, nickel plated 475.00

Ukuele, The Serenader, B & G, NY, double binding around edge and hole, celluloid fingerboard and head 225.00

Violin
    American, labeled "Henry Richard Knopf New York Anno 1904, No. 139," 2 pc back of strong medium curl, ribs and scroll similar, top of medium grain, red color varnish, 14" l back, with case 2,530.00
    English, labeled "Antonius Stradivarius, Anno 1689," 1 pc back of irregular curl, ribs and scroll similar, top of fine to medium grain, gold-brown varnish, 13-7/8" l back, case and silver mounted bow stamped "F" 7,475.00
    English, labeled "William Tarr, Fecit No. 56, Manchester 1883," 1 pc back of strong narrow curl, ribs and scroll similar, medium grain top, gold-brown varnish, 14" l back...................................2,415.00
    German, labeled "Ernst Heinrich Roth Markneukirchen 1928, Reproduction of Antonius Stradivarius, Cremona 1718," stamped internally, 1 pc back of strong narrow curl, ribs and scroll similar, fine grained top, red-brown varnish, 14-1/6" l back 3,105.00
    Milan, labeled "Leandro Bisiach Da Milano Fece L'Anno 1924," 2 pc back of light irregular curl, ribs similar, scroll of broad curl, top of medium to wide grain, orange-brown varnish, 14-1/6" l back, with case 25,300.00
    Violincello, labeled "Degani Eugenio, Quatttordici Medagilie Di Metito, Fece Venezia Anno 1891, 2 pc back with strong medium curl, matching ribs and scroll, top with fine grain, orange color varnish, 29-1/16" back length, case and nickel mounted bow 59,700.00

Violincello Bow, silver mounted
    Nurnberger, Albet, octagonal stick stamped "Albert Nurnberger" at butt, ebony frog with pearl eye, silver and ebony adjuster with pearl eye, 78 grams 2,415.00
    Ouchard, Emile A., Paris, made in the style of J. B. Vuillaume, round stick stamped "Emile A> Ouchard" on both sides of the butt, ebony frog with missing pearl eye, silver and ebony adjuster, 80 grams 10,925.00
    Pfretzchner, Hermann Richard, round stick stamped "H. R. Pfretzchner" at the butt, later ebony frog with silver and pearl eye, silver adjuster, 86 grams 500.00
    Piernot, Marie Louis, round stick unstamped, ebony frog with parisian eye, plain silver adjuster, 76 grams 1,725.00

Zither, Columbia, 47 strings, c1900 ....275.00

Music Related

Advertising Sign, 19-1/2" x 27", Mason & Hamlin Grands & Upright Pianos, Boston, New York, Chicago, emb tin, shows grand piano, F. Tuchfarber Co. Mfg., framed 300.00

Book, Davey, History of English Music, London, 1895 ....20.00

Catalog
    Daniel F. Beatty, Washington, NJ, 1882, 32 pgs, 6-3/4" x 10", features organs...135.00
    Hamilton Piano Co., Chicago Heights, IL, c1910, 8" x 10-1/2" 45.00
    Kohler & Campbell, New York, NY, 1920, 5-1/2" x 8", pianos..32.00

McKinley Music Co, Chicago, IL, 1903, 50 pgs, 6-1/4" x 9-1/2", Catalog No. 22, music books....................................20.00

Guitar Case, canvas, brown, leather bound edges, strap, buckle, and handle, 1890 ....20.00

Music Stand, Classical, England, c1830, carved rosewood and rosewood veneer, leaf carved octagonal post, shaped platform base, 3 turned feet, old finish, 18" w, 48" h 1,955.00

MUSIC BOXES

History: Music boxes, invented in Switzerland around 1825, encompass a broad array of forms, from small boxes to huge circus calliopes.

A cylinder box consists of a comb with teeth, which vibrate when striking a pin in the cylinder. The music these boxes produce ranges from light tunes to opera and overtures.

The first disc music box was invented by Paul Lochmann of Leipzig, Germany, in 1886. It used an interchangeable steel disc with pierced holes bent to a point, which hit the star-wheel as the disc revolved, and thus produced the tune. Discs were easily stamped out of metal, allowing a single music box to play an endless variety of tunes. Disc boxes reached the height of their popularity from 1890 to 1910 when the phonograph replaced them.

Music boxes also were incorporated in many items, e.g., clocks, sewing and jewelry boxes, steins, plates, toys, perfume bottles, and furniture.

References: Gilbert Bahl, *Music Boxes*, Courage Books, Running Press, 1993; Arthur W. J. G. Ord-Hume, *Musical Box*, Schiffer Publishing, 1995.

Collectors' Clubs: Music Box Society of Great Britain, P. O. Box 299, Waterbeach, Cambridge CB4 4DJ England; Musical Box Society International, 1209 CR 78 West, LaBelle, FL 33935.

Museums: Bellms Cars and Music of Yesterday, Sarasota, FL; Lockwood Matthews Mansion Museum, Norwalk, CT; Miles Musical Museum, Eureka Springs, AR; The Musical Museum, Deansboro, NY; The Musical Wonder House Museum, Iscasset, ME.

Additional Listings: See *Warman's Americana & Collectibles* for more examples.

Adler, 14-3/4" disc, walnut inlaid case, crank wind, lithograph cov int. 1,950.00

Baker-Troll, 17" cylinder, walnut case, brass inlaid dec, 6 bells, 3 part comb, matching storage table 2,750.00

Birdcage, singing bird
    French, key wound, bird's head moves back and forth while chirping 1,800.00
    German...250.00

Bremond, Swiss reed cylinder, works only.............................3,250.00

Britannia, 9" disc, upright, walnut case, transfer and inlaid dec, double comb 1,250.00

Continental, 16-1/2" l, 6", 8 tune, cylinder, single comb, bird's eye maple case..345.00

Criterion
    Model 103, 14" disc 3,100.00
    Table, mahogany, carved, to hold Model 103 ....425.00

Cylinder
    17" x 3", ornate burled wood case, inlaid trim, excellent tone, cabinet need repair 1,500.00
    17" x 5-1/2" x 8", 6" cylinder, coin operated mechanism, mahogany inlaid case, 8 tunes 1,100.00

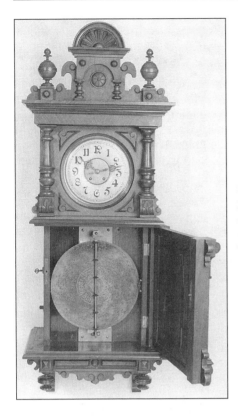

Symphonion No. 25B, c1900, $5,230. Photo courtesy of Auction Team Breker.

Ducommon Girod, 11-1/4" cylinder, walnut case, 3 control levers, six tune, c1840 .... 900.00

Edelweiss, 4-1/2" disc, table model, simple case, hand crank.... 300.00

Euphonia, 15-3/4" disc, mahogany case, metal corners, lithograph female on int. cov 1,200.00

Lochmann, Model 60, sold as is 2,325.00

Mills Vioano-Virtuoso, violin and piano combination, oak cabinet, orig DC motor, restored, converted from coin operated to automatic play 25,000.00

Paillard, NY, four 11" cylinders, full comb and bed, rosewood case with inlaid marquetry, base drawer stenciled "Paillard's Patent Feb 11th 1879, No. 48433," 41" w, 21" d, 16" h 5,500.00

Perfection, 10-1/2" zinc disc, table model, mahogany case 1,250.00

Regina

   Automatic Disc Changing, 15-1/2"

      Commercial Style 36, holds 12 discs, 5¢ coin operated, restored in early 1970s 11,500.00

      Mahogany case, bow front door, stained art glass panel, home model, temp regulator, 12 tune disc, 68" h 19,000.00

   Coin Operated Model, 27" automatic disc changing, walnut case, 12 discs, restored, replaced lower panel glass, mechanism cleaned and regulated 20,000.00

   Home Model, short bed plate, mahogany, serpentine case, double comb music box, 12 15-1/2" discs, 22" w, 13" h, 20" d, restored, mechanism cleaned and regulated 4,500.00

   Model 50, mahogany case, matching base cabinet 7,250.00

Snuff Box, early cylindrical musical snuff box, emb scene of Paris on lid, 4 x 1-1/2 x 2-1/2" 550.00

Subline-Harmonie, 15" cylinder, burl walnut on ebony and rosewood case, double comb, matching table with cabriole legs, c1870 .... 7,000.00

Swiss, cylindrical roll

   18" l, inlaid rosewood box.. 110.00

   25-1/2" l, case with marquetry bird and branch dec, orig works, 10 air cylinders, 5 bells, bell strikers, drum, Swiss, 19th C... 2,500.00

Symphonion, 10-1/2" l, 7-7/8" d, 6-7/8" h, oak case, side crank, lid opens to orig paper label, 6 interchangeable discs, works stamped and numbered 260134, German, working condition 750.00

NAILSEA-TYPE GLASS

History: Nailsea-type glass is characterized by swirls and loopings, usually white, on a clear or colored ground. One of the first areas where this glass was made was Nailsea, England, 1788-1873, hence the name. Several glass houses, including American factories, made this type of glass.

Bell, 11-3/4" h, rose loopings, white ground 95.00
Candlestick, 10" h, white loopings, colorless ground, folded socket rim, hollow blown socket drawn out to a double knop, bulb shaped stem, 2 additional knops, inverted cone shaped base, early 19th C.. 375.00
Fairy Lamp
    4-5/8" h, white loopings, powder blue, dome shaped shade, clear sgd "Clarke Criklite Trade Mark" candle cup........................ 275.00
    4-5/8" h, white loopings, ruby red ground, dome shaped shade, clear sgd "Clarke Criklite Trade Mark" candle cup, rim chip 215.00
    5-1/4" h, 6-1/4" d, opaque white loopings, frosted blue ground, colorless Clarke insert 695.00
    6-1/2" h, sweeping white loops, red ground, dome shaped shade, ruffled triangular base, colorless glass candle cup with ruffled edge, orig "Price's Royal Castle Night Light" candle........... 985.00
Flask
    7-1/4" h, broad oval form, white herringbone type loopings, ruby red ground, applied double collared mouth, pontil scar 400.00
    7-3/4" l, pink and white loopings, colorless ground................ 115.00
    8-3/4" h, pocket, teardrop form, profuse white loopings, teal green ground, sheared mouth, pontil scar 240.00
    9" l, white, red and blue loopings, colorless ground, short check at shoulder 90.00
Gemel Bottle, 8" h, flattened ovoid body, 2 necks, red, white, and blue loopings, colorless ground, white casing.................................. 400.00
Lamp, 11-1/2" h, pink and white loopings on colorless font and ruffled shade, applied colorless feet, berry prunt 2,500.00
Pitcher, 6-1/2" h, 4" d, white loopings, colorless ground, ftd, solid applied base, triple ribbed solid handle with curled end, flaring formed mouth, attributed t South Jersey, c1840-60 .... 1,200.00
Rolling Pin, 13-3/4" l, freeblown, rose and white loopings, colorless ground, ground mouth, smooth base, 1850-80 .... 220.00
Tumbler, white ground, blue loopings 120.00
Vase, 8" h, 5" d, cylindrical, flared mouth and base, colorless, white loopings, plain sheared rim, pontil, attributed to South Jersey. 195.00

Flask, colorless cased in white, red and blue loopings, 8-3/4" l, $200. Photo courtesy of Garth's Auctions.

Witch Ball
    4-3/8" d, pink and blue loopings, white ground...................... 450.00
    5-1/4" d, red loopings, colorless ground, opaque white casing, attributed to Pittsburgh.. 300.00

NANKING

History: Nanking is a type of Chinese porcelain made in Canton, China, from the early 1800s into the 20th century. It was made for export to America and England.

Four elements help distinguish Nanking from Canton, two similar types of ware. Nanking has a spear-and-post border, as opposed to the scalloped-line style of Canton. Second, in the water's edge or Willow pattern, Canton usually has no figures; Nanking includes a standing figure with open umbrella on the bridge. In addition, the blues tend to be darker on the Nanking ware. Finally, Nanking wares often are embellished with gold, Canton is not.

Green and orange variations of Nanking survive, although they are scarce.

Reproduction Alert: Copies of Nanking ware currently are being produced in China. They are of inferior quality and are decorated in a lighter rather than in the darker blues.

Bowl, 10" d, shaped, 19th C 880.00
Candlesticks, pr, 9-1/2" h 775.00
Cider Jug, 10" h, gilt highlights, 19th C, pr.................................. 825.00
Cup and Saucer, loop handle.. 65.00
Ewer, 11" h, small spout, blue and white, mid 19th C 300.00
Pitcher, cov, 9-1/2" h, blue and white, Liverpool shape.............. 550.00
Plate, 9-1/2" d, water's edge scene, c1780-1800 .... 85.00
Platter
    12-3/4" l, Chinese, 19th C, chips 415.00
    16" l, blue Fitzhugh border, minor chips and knife marks...... 575.00
Posset Pot, blue and white, intertwined handle, mismatched lid with gilded fruit finial 100.00
Rice Bowl, 19th C 100.00

Plate, water's edge scene, 1780-1800, 9-1/2" d, $85.

Salad Bowl, 10" h, 19th C 1,200.00
Soup Tureen, cov, 11-3/4" h, 19th C, imperfections 475.00
Teapot, 6-1/2" h, globular, diaper border above watery pagoda land-
    scape reserve 125.00
Tray, 9-3/4" l, 19th C 500.00
Tureen, cov, 13-1/2" l, 19th C 1,210.00

NAPKIN RINGS, FIGURAL

History: Gracious home dining during the Victorian era required a personal napkin ring for each household member. Figural napkin rings were first patented in 1869. During the remainder of the 19th century, most plating companies, including Cromwell, Eureka, Meriden, and Reed and Barton, manufactured figural rings, many copying and only slightly varying the designs of other companies.

Reference: Lillian Gottschalk and Sandra Whitson, *Figural Napkin Rings*, Collector Books, 1996.

Reproduction Alert: Quality reproductions do exist.

Additional Listings: See *Warman's Americana & Collectibles* for a listing of non-figural napkin rings.

Notes: Values are determined by the subject matter of the ring, the quality of the workmanship, and the condition.

Angel, seated on napkin rin, holding lead to crouching dog, collar with
    lock, rect, half circle ends, 3-1/2" h, James W. Tufts, c1876,
    Gottschalk #435 .... 350.00
Baby in cradle, James W. Tufts, Boston 300.00
Barrel, two cherubs holding dolls, Meriden Brittania Co. 150.00
Bird, wings spread over nest of eggs 175.00
Boy riding large dog, inscribed napkin ring, fancy rect ftd base, 3" h,
    James W. Tufts, c1876 .... 700.00
Boy with sitting-up dog, dressed in skirt and vest, plain rect base,
    Meridian Brittania, c1896, Gottschalk, #668 .... 350.00
Brownie, climbing up side of ring, Palmer Cox 185.00
Butterfly, perched on pair of fans 125.00
Cat, glass eyes, ring on back 270.00
Cherries, stems, leaf base, ball feet 120.00
Cherub, seated, back to napkin ring, draped attire, 4 ball feet support
    figure-8 base, Pairpoint, c1885, 4-1/4" h, Gottschalk, #431 ..... 700.00
Chicken, nesting beside ring 150.00

Child, crawling, ring on back 300.00
Dog, sitting next to barrel shaped ring, sgd "Tufts, #1531" 125.00
Dutch Boy, pulling on boots, resilvered 110.00
Frog, holding drumstick, pushing drum-like ring 300.00
Girl looking at bulldog sitting on ring, Kate Greenaway style, rect base
    with rounded ends, ball feet, 3-1/2" h, Wm Rogers, c1850 ..... 500.00
Goat, pulling wheeled flower cart 250.00
Horse, standing next to elaborate ring 250.00
Lily, oval napkin ring with engraved flowers, 1-1/2" h, Rogers and
    Brothers, c1870 .... 150.00
Owl, tufted center owl, 2 owlets perched on tree branch, fancy sq ftd
    base, 4" h, Simpson, Hall & Miller, c1870, Gottschalk #293 .... 700.00
Parrot, on wheels, Simpson, Hall, Miller & Co. 185.00
Rabbit, sitting alertly next to ring 175.00
Sailor leaning against an anchor, rope entwines anchor and ring, rect
    base, chamfered corners, 3-1/4" h, Simpson, Hall, Miller, c1870,
    Gottschalk, #674, silver worn 500.00
School Boy, wearing coat with tails, soft hat with tassel, carrying 2
    books under his arm, petting dog, rect base, 3-1/2" h, Wm Rogers,
    1850 .... 600.00
Sheep, resting on base near ring 195.00
Squirrel, eating nut, log pile base 185.00
Swan pulling wheeled napkin ring, Meriden Britannia, c1896,
    Gottschalk #282, shaft rings missing 500.00
Turtle, crawling, ornate ring on back 300.00
Twins on ladder, Greenaway type, rect tiered base, 3-1/2" h, Simpson,
    Hall, Miller, circa 1870, Gottschalk #529 .... 700.00
Vase, dark art glass vase with enameled flowers, supported by scrolls
    ending in rosettes, 6-7/8" h, Meriden Brittania, c1860, Gottschalk
    #305 .... 500.00

NASH GLASS

History: Nash glass is a type of art glass attributed to Arthur John Nash and his sons, Leslie H. and A. Douglas. Arthur John Nash, originally employed by Webb in Stourbridge, England, came to America and was employed in 1889 by Tiffany Furnaces at its Corona, Long Island, plant.

While managing the plant for Tiffany, Nash designed and produced iridescent glass. In 1928, A. Douglas Nash purchased the facilities of Tiffany Furnaces. The A. Douglas Nash Corporation remained in operation until 1931.

Bowl, 7-3/4" d, 2-1/2" h, Jewel pattern, gold phantom luster 285.00
Candlestick, 4" h, Chintz , ruby and gray, sgd 450.00
Compote, 7-1/2" d, 4-1/2" h, Chintz, transparent aquamarine, wide flat
    rim of red and gray-green controlled stripe dec, base inscribed "Nash
    RD89" 865.00

Sheep, rect base, Barbour, #13, $210.

Cologne Bottle, Chintz, wide pale green stripes, separatted by wide clear stripes with thin blue centers, clear stopper, mkd "Nash/ 1008/33," 5" h, $650.

Cordial, 5-1/2" h, Chintz, green and blue 95.00
Frame, 7-1/2" w, 9-1/8" h, Art Nouveau style silver overlay, flowing leaf and vine design, irid blue glass and bronze easel back, sgd on verse "Designed by L. H. Nash and made by him at Tiffany Furnaces, 1911, Corona, L.I., N.Y.," cracks to glass 1,840.00
Goblet, 6-3/4" h, feathered leaf motif, gilt dec, sgd.....................295.00
Plate, 8" d, Chintz, green and blue 195.00
Sherbet, bluish-gold texture, ftd, sgd, #417 ....275.00
Vase
    5-1/2" h, Chintz, brilliant red oval, controlled black, brown, gray striped dec, base inscribed "Nash" 865.00
    6" h, spherical, extended flared rim, Chintz, caramel int., cased to brown, yellow, and rust, zipper dec.....................................300.00
    9" h, Polka Dot, deep opaque red oval, molded with prominent sixteen ribs, dec by spaced white opal dots, base inscribed "Nash GD154" 1,100.00

NAUTICAL ITEMS

History: The seas have fascinated man since time began. The artifacts of sailors have been collected and treasured for years. Because of their environment, merchant and naval items, whether factory or handmade, must be of quality construction and long lasting. Many of these items are aesthetically appealing as well.

References: E. H. H. Archibald, *The Dictionary of Sea Painters of Europe and America*, Antique Collectors' Club, 1999; Donald F. Kuhlstrom, *Sunday Sailors: A Beginner's Guide to Pond Boats & Model Yachting Until the 1950s*, Turner Publications, 1998; J. Welles Henderson, Marine Art & Antiques, *Antique Collectors' Club*, 1999; David Joel, *Charles Brooking and the 18th Century British Marine Painters*, Antique Collectors' Club, 1999.

Periodicals: Nautical Brass, P.O. Box 3966, North Ft. Myers, FL 33918; Nautical Collector, P.O. Box 949, New London, CT 06320.

Collectors' Club: Nautical Research Guild, 62 Marlboro St., Newburyport, MA 01950.

Museums: Chesapeake Bay Maritime Museum, Saint Michaels, MD; Kittery Historical & Naval Museum, Kittery, ME; Lyons Maritime Museum, St Augustine, FL; Mariners' Museum, Newport News, VA; Maritime Museum of Monterey, Monterey, CA; Museum of Science and Industry, Chicago, IL; Mystic Seaport Museum, Mystic, CT; Peabody Museum of Salem, Salem, MA; Philadelphia Maritime Museum, Philadelphia, PA; San Francisco Maritime National Historical Park, San Francisco, CA; U.S. Naval Academy Museum, Naval Academy, MD.

Binnacle, 9" h, brass, compass, lamp 300.00
Book
    Arnott, D., ed., *Design and Construction of Steel Merchant Ships*, Society of Marine Archives, 1955, 1st ed 33.00
    Nansen, Fridtjof, *Farthest North Record of Voyage of Exploration of Ship Frame*, 1893-96 Polar Expedition, 2 volumes...............80.00
    Shay, Frank, *Iron Men and Wooden Ships*, Garden City, 1924, 8vo, orig boards, hand colored woodcuts, one of 200 copies 150.00
    The English Pilot, London, 1761, 3 volumes, folio.............1,380.00
Ephemera, accounts and correspondence ledger, from Boston Instrument Merchant Thomas Greenough, c1745-70, bills of laden, accounts, correspondence with agents in Philadelphia and London, cloth binder...9,200.00
Chart, 17" x 24", Boston Harbor, George W. Eldridge, 1876 ....195.00

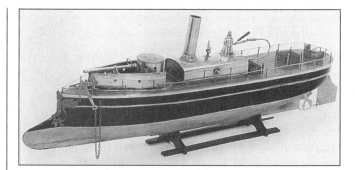

Model, steam boat, Radiguet, 40" l, $12,790. Photo courtesy of Auction Team Breker.

Chronometer, 6" sq, Hamilton Watch Co., cased........................550.00
Clock, 7" d, SS Kaponga, engine room bulkhead, brass 350.00
Diorama, 33" l, 5" d, 25" h, shadowbox, 3 masted schooner, last quarter 19th C 550.00
Foghorn, brass, hand crank..225.00
Inclinometer, 4-1/2" d, brass, cased, bubble type, Kelvin Bottomley & Baird Ltd...95.00
Lantern, 9-1/2" d, 13" h, copper, pressed glass lens, emb "Seahorse B. G. Trademark 35413 Anchor"...320.00
Lifeboat Compass, 8" sq, 7-1/4" h, boxed, 20th C 175.00
Medicine Chest, 50" l, 24" w, 27" h, *Halicone*, hinged top, compartment int., contains bottles, ceramic jars, other accessories...........1,450.00
Model
    29" l, *Albany*, steamboat, metal, wood stand.........................350.00
    35" l, cruising boat, mahogany, green and beige painted hull, stand 475.00
    35-1/4" l, 12" w, 23-1/2" h, bark, sailor's model, last half 19th C 600.00
Octant, Walker, Liverpool, ebony, brass fittings, ivory plates, orig case bears label "John Bliss & Co. 110 Wall Street," pencil inscription "John A. Ryder South Orrington Maine" 425.00
Painting
    13-1/2" x 16-3/4", ink and gouache on paper, Ship George Thomas West Master From Calcutta, Off Cap Ann Bound to Salem Mass, 1820, unsigned, titled beneath image, framed, stabilized tears, staining 1,725.00
    14" x 26", oil on canvas, sailing vessels off the coast, lighthouse in distance, sgd and dated "W. Plummer 1886" lower right, framed, repaired, retouched, craquelure.....................................1,035.00

Painting, oil on canvas, James Webb, (British artist, 1825-1895), framed, 44" x 29", $7,150. Photo courtesy of Jackson's Auctioneers & Appraisers.

21-1/4" x 31", oil on canvas, barque sailing off the coast, unsigned, English, 19th C, framer's label attached to stretcher, framed 2,875.00

21-1/4" x 36-1/4", oil on canvas, portrait of British two-masted schooner *Fanny*, unsigned, vessel identified on bow, framed, tear center left, scattered losses and punctures, surface grime 2,185.00

22" x 36", oil on canvas, portrait of American steamer *El Rio*, sgd, dated, and inscribed "A. Jacobsen 1893...705 Palisade Av. West Hoboken NJ" lower right, framed, scattered retouch, craquelure 12,650.00

22" x 36", oil on canvas, portrait of steamer *United States*, sgd, dated, and inscribed "A. Jacobsen 257 8 Av NY 1879" lower right, framed, slight damage to tacking edge, tears center left, surface grime, and craquelure.. 13,800.00

Porthole, 13-1/2" l, 9" h, Edwin Fox, rect, brass 110.00

Sea Chest, 30" w, 16-1/2" d, 15" h, *SS Mapourika*, splayed construction, carved crest, restored and refinished 700.00

Sextant, Spencer, Browning & Rust, London, brass, orig box bears label of "J. Sewell 61, South Castle Street, Liverpool," 19th C. 550.00

Ship's Bell, 8" d, *Alister Hardy*, brass, dated 1953...................... 145.00

Ship's Wheel
26" d, brass inlaid ring on each side, brass capped king spoke, John Hastie & Co., Greenock 350.00
42" d, brass 425.00

NAZI ITEMS

History: The National Socialist German Workers Party (NSDAP) was created on Feb. 24, 1920, by Anton Drexler and Adolf Hitler. Its 25-point nationalistic program was designed to revive the depressed German economy and revitalize the government.

In 1923, after the failed Beer Hall Putsch, Hitler was sentenced to a five-year term in Landsberg Prison. He spent only a year in prison, during which time he wrote the first volume of *Mein Kampf*.

In the late 1920s and early 1930s, the NSDAP developed from a regional party into a major national party. In the spring of 1933, Hitler became the Reich's chancellor. Shortly after the death of President von Hindenberg in 1934, Hitler combined the offices of president and chancellor into a single position, giving him full control over the German government as well as NSDAP. From that point until May 1945, the National Socialist German Worker's Party dominated all aspects of German life.

In the mid-1930s, Hitler initiated a widespread plan—ranging from re-arming to territorial acquisition—designed to unite the German-speaking peoples of Europe into a single nation. Germany's invasion of Poland in 1939 triggered the hostilities that led to the Second World War. The war in Europe ended on VE Day, May 7, 1945.

References: Bob Evans, *Third Reich Belt Buckles*, Schiffer Publishing, 1999; Gary Kirsner, *German Military Steins*, 1914 to 1945, 2nd ed., Glentiques Ltd., 1996; Ron Manion, *German Military Collectibles Price Guide*, Antique Trader Publications, 1995.

Periodicals: *Der Gauleiter*, P.O. Box 721288, Houston, TX 77272; *Military Collector Magazine*, P.O. Box 245, Lyon Station, PA 19536; *Military Collectors News*, P.O. Box 702073, Tulsa, OK 74170; *Military History*, 602 S. King St., Suite 300, Leesburg, VA 22075; *Military Trader*, P.O. Box 1050, Dubuque, IA 52004.

Iron Cross, first class, orig case, $50.

Autograph
Document, Adolf Hitler, 1 page 4to, Berlin, Oct 1, 1934, in German, sgd as Fuhrer and Reichs Chancellor, to celebrate school teacher's 14th year of service to German Reich, large emb spread wing eagle circled by wreath to left of signature .. 1,900.00

Note, Rudolf Hess, sgd with initials, on back of 4-1/8" x 2-1/4" calling card, Aug 13, 1933, asking management of National Gallery to assist with accommodation of Voltbehr war documents . 700.00

Photograph, Hans Baur, personal pilot and confidant of Hitler, glossy photo in Luftwaffe uniform, inscribed and sgd in German, 1969, folded horizontally 115.00

Banner, 7" x 38", double sided.. 35.00

Bayonet, police, dress, 13" blade, stag handle, attached police insignia, black leather scabbard, silvered fittings, orig black frog, guard marked "S. MG. 415," matching numbers 175.00

Belt, NSDAP, police officer's, light tan leather belt, clawed buckle 35.00

Cap Badge, RAD, silver finish, enameled, wreath 35.00

Car Pennant, 8-1/2" x 11-12", Teno, printed on both sides, white eagle on blue field, 2 tie strings 75.00

Cigarette Case, presentation, steel, painted, brass plate, emb heads of Mussolini and Hitler, "Vincere" above heads, eagle embracing wreath of swastikas, wreath with Italian emblem 175.00

Collar Tabs, NSDAP, Hauptgemeinschaftsleiter rank, 4 gold pips, gold eagle, double rows of gold ribbon, dark brown, white piping ... 100.00

Dagger, orange and yellow celluloid grip, SP fittings and scabbard, mkd "E & F Horstaer" 100.00

Emblem, 27" x 16" train engine, eagle with swastika.................. 250.00

Hat, police officer, black visor, bright eagle and wreath device, green-blue wool, silver cord, leather chin strap, pebbles side buttons 150.00

Holster, P-38, black leather, Nazi acceptance mark, pouch for extra clip 50.00

Magazine, NSDAP Der Schulungsbrief, 1940 .... 35.00

Medal, Eastern People's, 2nd Class, silver metal, ribbon 25.00

Membership Pin, swastika in circle, winged NSFK figure 15.00

Pennant, 54" l, 11" h, NSDAP, triangular, painted swastika, double sided 35.00

Photo Album, cigarette company premium, "Adolf Hitler-Bilder Aus Dem Leben Des Fuhrers Herausgegeben von Cigarette Bilder Dienst, Hamburg," 136 pgs with 100 tipped in glossy photocards recording Hitler's rise to power, 1936, 9-1/2" x 12-1/2" 235.00

Poster
12" x 20", Mein Kampf, portrait of Hitler, black and white........ 25.00
27" x 40, "Imperialists Cannot Stop The Winning Progress Of Our Five Year Plan!," Konstantin Elissev, snaggle-toothed top-hatted capitalist holds bomb throwing Nazi, Pope, French and Eastern

European Generals in his raised arm in front of booming factories of industry, red, black, and brown, expert restoration to left corners, 1930 .... 900.00
Shoulder Boards, police, Wactmeister Rank, black and silver cord, pink piping, removable style 12.00
Sword, dress, eagle and swastika, engraved brass handle, black wire wrapped plastic grip, black painted scabbard 120.00
Tinnie, Ten Years Of The Nazi Party In Weimer, silver, Standart .. 24.00

NETSUKES

History: The traditional Japanese kimono has no pockets. Daily necessities, such as money and tobacco supplies, were carried in leather pouches, or inros, which hung from a cord with a netsuke toggle. The word netsuke comes from "ne"—to root—and "tsuke"—to fasten.

Netsukes originated in the 14th century and initially were favored by the middle class. By the mid-18th century, all levels of Japanese society used them. Some of the most famous artists, e.g., Shuzan and Yamada Hojitsu, worked in the netsuke form.

Netsukes average from 1 to 2 inches in length and are made from wood, ivory, bone, ceramics, metal, horn, nutshells, etc. The subject matter is broad based, but always portrayed in a lighthearted, humorous manner. A netsuke must have smooth edges and balance in order to hang correctly on the sash.

Reference: Raymond Bushell, *Introduction to Netsuke*, Charles E. Tuttle Co., 1971; George Lazarnick, *The Signature Book of Netsuke, Inro and Ojime Artists in Photographs*, first edition 1976, 2 volume second edition 1981.

Periodicals: *Netsuke & Ivory Carving Newsletter*, 3203 Adams Way, Ambler, PA 19002; *Orientalia Journal*, P.O. Box 94, Flushing, NY 11363-0094, http://members.aol/com/Orientalia/index.html.

Collectors' Clubs: International Netsuke Society, P.O. Box 471686, San Francisco, CA 94147; Netsuke Kenkyukai Society, P.O. Box 31595, Oakland, CA 94604.

Reproduction Alert: Recent reproductions are on the market. Many are carved from African ivory.

Notes: Value depends on artist, region, material, and skill of craftsmanship. Western collectors favor katabori, pieces which represent an identifiable object.

Bone
    Bearded scholar with staff, 2" h, sgd 95.00
    Man with large fish, 2-1/8" h 75.00
    Young man holding fruit, 2-1/8" h, sgd 90.00
Horn
    Lotus leaf, stag horn, 19th C 100.00
    Shishi form, pressed, 19th C 50.00
Ivory
    Boy with fish, sgd, 19th C, 2" h 360.00
    Buddha, 19th C, 2-1/4" h 450.00
    Chick in egg, 2" l, ... 250.00
    Crouched figure, deep folds in clothing, 2 ivory figures with horned heads in sack over shoulder, carved by Seiji, 2" h 3,450.00
    Dragon, curled up, 19th C, 2-1/4" l 575.00
    Dutchman holding dog, carved by Maskazu 19th C, 3" h 375.00
    Entertainer being attacked by his monkey, carved by Masaka, early 19th C, 1-3/4" h 6,600.00

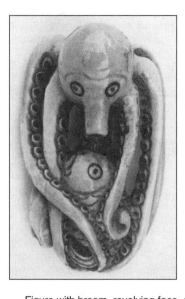

Carved ivory, 19th C, $95.

Figure with broom, revolving face, good and evil, 1-7/8" h 200.00
Fishmonger with revolving face, Chinese 75.00
Lady, carrying jar, folds of robe continue to left and then sweep top the right, baby boy in Chinese dress playing at her feet, inlaid horn hair knot on toddler, fingers of lady's left hand and flowers on her hair band, carved by Anraku, 4-1/4" h 11,550.00
Monkey on back of turtle, 1-7/8" h, sgd 60.00
Mouse, carved by Tomokasu, 1-3/4" l 350.00
Mythical elephant-like creature, 2" h, sgd 100.00
Pile of fish, stingray, octopus tentacles, and eel, carved by Kaigyokusai Masatsugu, 1-1/2"d 2,420.00
Plaque, elaborate city scene, carved by Kagetoshi 3,520.00
Samurai Warrior, 2-1/8" h, sgd 150.00
Shoki, holding oni in left hand, unsgd, 3-1/2" h 4,400.00
Skull, serpent entwined around toad, black onyx and MOP inlaid eyes, 2" h 425.00
Woman, flowing gown, cartouche surrounding signature, carved by Jutsuasi 1,870.00
Ivory and Boxwood, tortoise with small tortoise climbing over back, opens to reveal sleeping man with gourds and models of temples, carved by Ho Shu, Yoshihide, 19th C 12,650.00
Mother of Pearl, cat and kitten, 1-15/16" l 275.00
Porcelain
    Fruit and leaves, red, brown, and celadon, 19th C 60.00
    Hotei, mkd "Masakazu," 19th C 60.00
    Two puppies, 19th C 85.00
Wood
    Boy, seated, reading scroll, boxwood, carved by Masayuki, 19th C 200.00
    Geisha, seated, wearing flowing robe, holding tray, carved by Toshikazu, 19th C 245.00
    God, Jurojin stroking crane, silver with tarnished gray patina as helmet, neck guard, and sash and elbows, ivory face, hands, and crane's body, ebony feet, Jurojin, and crane, tortoiseshell sack on back, 2" h 3,850.00
    Karasu tengu, seated figure with beaked and fanged face, holding cucumber, carved by Jugyoko, 19th C 825.00
    Monkey, seated, clasping raised left knee, unsgd, first half 19th C 425.00
    Noblewoman, wretched beggar form, dying by roadside, carved by Ichihyo, first half 19th C 300.00
    Persimmon, stippled skin and leaves, unsgd, 19th C 295.00
    Rat, grooming 24,150.00
    Rice Mixer, boxwood, ivory inlaid eyes, teeth, and rice, carved by Tokoku, 19th C 5,750.00
    Scribe, sitting, holding writing slip and brush, carved by Shinsai, 19th C 275.00

Snail, crawling from shell, boxwood, 19th C 495.00
Woman, boxwood, nude, seated by basin, wringing towel, first half
  19th C 320.00

NEWCOMB POTTERY

History: The Sophie Newcomb Memorial College, an adjunct of Tulane University in New Orleans, LA, was originated as a school to train local women in the decorative arts. While metal working, painting, and embroidery were among the classes taught, the production of fine, hand-crafted art pottery remains their most popular and collectible pursuit.

Pottery was made by the Newcomb women for nearly 50 years, with earlier work being the rarest and the most valuable. This is characterized by shiny finishes and broad, flat-painted and modeled designs. More common, though still quite valuable, are their matte glaze pieces, often depicting bayou scenes and native flora. All bear the impressed NC mark.

References: Ralph and Terry Kovel, *Kovels' American Art Pottery*, Crown Publishers, 1993; Jessie Poesch, *Newcomb Pottery: An Enterprise for Southern Women*, Schiffer Publishing, 1984; David Rago, *American Art Pottery*, Knickerbocker Press, 1997.

Collectors' Club: American Art Pottery Association, P.O. Box 1226, Westport, MA 02790.

Museum: Newcomb College, Tulane University, New Orleans, LA.

Advisor: David Rago.

Cabinet Vase, 4-3/4" h, 2-3/4" d, painted amber and cobalt blue stylized dogs' heads, ivory ground, sgd "NC/SEW/JM/US/Q," Sabrina Wells, 1902 .... 3,500.00
Candlesticks, pr
  6-1/2" h, 3-1/2" d, carved white and yellow flowers, blue and green matte ground, carved "GM," Gertrude Maes, c1929, one bobeche reglued 900.00

Plaque, scene of live oak tree and Spanish moss by riverbank with cattails, by A. F. Simpson, 1915, orig frame, paper label, "AFS/HM7/263," 6" h, 9-1/4" w, $6,500. Photo courtesy of David Rago Auctions, Inc.

Teaset, high glazed, carved stylized floral design in gold, green, cobalt blue, and ivory, by Henrietta Bailey, 1907, stamped "NC/HB/JM/Q/BN99," 6" h x 8-1/2" w teapot, $14,000. Photo courtesy of David Rago Auctions, Inc.

7-1/4" h, 4-1/4" d, matte, pink spiderwort, blue ground, sgd "NC/JM/SI/NP82," paper label, Sadie Irvine, 1923 .... 1,700.00
Centerpiece Bowl and Flower Frog, 11-1/4" d, 4" h, matte, carved white and yellow flowers, blue ground, stamped "NC/AFS/JM/265," A. F. Simpson 1,600.00
Milk Pitcher
  4" h, 4" d, matte, stylized green leaves, dark blue ground, stamped "NC/AA/SI/UO1," Sadie Irvine and Aurelia Arbo, 1933, glaze nick to spout 1,200.00
  8" h, 5-1/2" d, carved ivory flowers, green leaves, cobalt blue band, ink mark "NC/YY38/M.T.RYAN/JM," Mazie Ryan, 1904, 2 small glazed-over firing lines 8,500.00
Mug, 4" h, 5" d, incised band of cobalt blue and green stylized flowers, denim blue ground, mkd "NC/EE43/JW/SEW," S. E. Wells, 1911 .... 1,500.00
Pitcher, 2-1/2" h, 3-1/4" d, carved yellow roses, blue-green glossy ground, "NC/HB/DD28," Henrietta Bailey, 1903 .... 1,600.00
Plate, 8-1/4" d, student china-painted porcelain, daisy border, yellow band, sgd "Mc/12-20-16" 100.00
Plaque, 6" h, 9-1/4" d, scene of live oak tree and Spanish moss, riverbank with cattails, orig frame, paper label, "AFS/HM7/263," A. F. Simpson, 1915 .... 6,500.00
Tea Set, high glaze, carved stylized gold,. Green, cobalt blue, and ivory floral design, 6" h teapot, stamped "NC/HB/JM?Q/BN99," Henrietta bailey, 1907 .... 14,000.00
Trivet, 6" d, carved wreath of stylized blue and green flowers, ivory ground, "NC/M/MWB/BH63," Mary Butler, 1906, short tight line to rim 1,400.00
Vase
  3" h, 5-1/2" d, squat, white blossoms, blue-green ground, "NC/JM/AFS/GR50," A. F. Simpson, 1914, small bruise at rim 850.00
  3-1/2" h, 5" d, squat, mate, white daffodils, green leaves, medium blue ground, "NC/271/KW46/S," Sadie Irvine, 1920 .... 1,500.00
  5-1/4" h, 4-1/2" d, bulbous, semi-matte raspberry glaze, periwinkle-blue int., stamped "NC" 400.00
  5-1/2" h, 3" d, ovoid, matte, live oak trees, Spanish moss, full moon, dark blue ground, "NC/SI/SI43," Sadie Irvine, 1930 .... 1,800.00
  5-1/2" h, 3" d, ovoid, white dogwood blossoms, blue-green ground, sgd "NC/JM/HA82/237/CL," Cynthia Littlejohn, 1914 ...... 1,600.00
  5-1/2" h, 3-1/4" d, carved white and yellow flowers, dark blue and blue-green ground, stamped "NC/AFS/JM/237/GP26/54/C," A. F. Simpson, 1914 .... 2,100.00
  7" h, 6-1/4" d, bulbous, butterflies and cotton blossoms, stamped "NC/100/SI/JM/PE71," Sadie Irvine, 1926 .... 8,000.00
  8-1/2" h, 3-1/4" d, classical shape, matte, carved wreath of pink bell shaped flowers, green leaves, dark blue ground, "NC/AFS/JM/92/QW25," A. F. Simpson, 1928 .... 3,250.00
  8-1/2" h, 3-1/4" d, corseted, carved tall white and yellow narcissus, green leaves, pale blue ground, sgd "NC/AFS/223/NT6," A. E. Simpson, 1924 .... 3,250.00
  8-1/2" h, 3-3/4" d, ovoid, tall oaks, Spanish moss, moonlit landscape, "NC/133/LE74/AFS," Anna Frances Simpson, 1920 .... 5,000.00

8-1/2" h, 4-3/4" d, tapering, matte, white gladiola blossoms, green leaves, medium blue ground, "NC/179/KH31/AFS," Anna Frances Simpson, 1919 .... 3,500.00

9" h, 3-1/2" d, landscape of live oak trees and Spanish moss, stamped "NC/SI/501/SI50," Sadie Irvine, 1930, minor glaze scaling to rim 4,500.00

9-1/2" h, 4-1/2" d, Español pattern, stamped "NC/229/SI/JM/PE95," Sadie Irvine, 1926 .... 6,500.00

11-1/4" h, 5" d, matte, carved moonlit landscape, barn surrounded by live oak trees, Spanish moss, sgd "NC/SI/JM/131/0041," Sadie Irvine, 1925, restored hole to base 3,750.00

12" h, 5-1/2" d, carved blue-green irises, light green leaves, blue ground, imp "NC," ink "SI," other illegible marks, Sadie Irvine, c1913, tight hairline from rim 3,000.00

Vessel

1-1/2" h, 4" d, squat, carved flowers, raspberry and blue matte glaze, stamped "NC/JM/SI/JK8," Sadie Irvine, 1918........ 1,000.00

2-1/2" h, 5-1/2" d, squat, carved ivory flowers, green leaves, cobalt blue band, green ground, ink mark "NC/FU99/AFS/JM," A. F. Simpson, 1913 .... 1,600.00

3" h, 5" d, squat, carved stylized flowers, purple overglaze, stamped "NC/AFS/JM/HE62/261/134," A. F. Simpson, 1915 .... 1,200.00

3-1/4" h, 6" d, squat, blue crocus, denim-blue ground, "NC/HB/HC75," Henrietta Bailey, 1916 .... 1,300.00

4-1/4" h, 5-1/4" d, spherical, white gladiola, green stems, blue ground, stamped "NC/JM/SI/75/PK97," Sadie Irvine, 1926 .... 2,400.00

5" h, 6" d, bulbous, matte, wild roses and leaves, denim blue ground, incised "NC/287/FM57/S.," Sadie Irvine, 1912, hairline to rim 1,200.00

5-1/2" h, 5" d, bulbous, carved, glossy, incised stylized cactus plants, large yellow blossoms, stamped "NC/MROSS/JM/X33," Marie Ross, 1903, small rim chip 12,000.00

5-1/4" h, 3" d, ovoid, matte, live oaks and Spanish moss, pale beige ground, "NC/AFS/NJ?JU82/291," A. F. Simpson, 1918, 2" hairline from rim 1,500.00

6-3/4" h, 8-1/2" d, squatty, carved live oak trees and Spanish moss, matte blue and green glaze, stamped "NC/HB/70JM/HR28/49," by Henrietta Bailey, 1915 .... 5,500.00

6-3/4" h, 8-3/4" d, bulbous, carved white and yellow narcissus, blue-green leaves, incised "NC/A.M./JM/GM10," attributed to Alma Mason, 1914, restored 2,400.00

Wall Pocket, 11" h, 4" w, conical, carved stylized cobalt blue and green trees, ivory band, high glaze, "NC/LN/JM/?y/59," Leona Nicholson, c1904 .... 8,500.00

NILOAK POTTERY, MISSION WARE

History: Niloak Pottery was made near Benton, Arkansas. Charles Dean Hyten experimented with native clay, trying to preserve its natural colors. By 1911, he perfected Mission Ware, a marbleized pottery in which the cream and brown colors predominate. The company name is the word "kaolin" spelled backwards.

After a devastating fire, the pottery was rebuilt and named Eagle Pottery. This factory included enough space to add a novelty pottery line in 1929. Mr. Hyten left the pottery in 1941, and in 1946 operations ceased.

Marks: The early pieces were marked "Niloak." Eagle Pottery products usually were marked "Hywood-Niloak" until 1934 when the "Hywood" was dropped from the mark.

References: Susan and Al Bagdade, *Warman's American Pottery and Porcelain*, Wallace-Homestead, 1994; David Edwin Gifford, *Collector's Encyclopedia of Niloak*, Collector Books, 1993.

Vase, wide flat rim, glazed int., 5-3/8" w, 3-1/8" h, $95.

Collectors' Club: Arkansas Pottery Collectors Society, P.O. Box 7617, Little Rock, AR 72217.

Additional Listings: See *Warman's Americana & Collectibles* for more examples, especially the novelty pieces.

Note: Prices listed below are for Mission Ware pieces.

Bowl, 4-1/2" d, marbleized swirls, blue, tan, and brown 65.00

Candlesticks, pr, 8" h, marbleized swirls, blue, cream, terra-cotta, and brown 250.00

Console Set, pr 8-1/2" h candlesticks, 10" d bowl, Mission ware, mkd 275.00

Humidor, 6-1/2" h, 6" d, bulbous, marbleized clay, stamped "Niloak," paper label 900.00

Pot, 2-3/4" x 3-3/4", marbleized swirls, red, brown, and chocolate, early 125.00

Toothpick Holder, marbleized swirls, tan and blue 100.00

Urn, 4-1/2" h, marbleized swirls, brown and blue 45.00

Vase

5-1/4" h, bulbous, stamped "Niloak" 265.00

8-1/4" h, tear shape, stamped "Niloak" 120.00

8-1/2" h, flaring, stamped "Niloak" 295.00

Wine Cooler, 4-1/4" h, low, stamped "Niloak" 125.00

NIPPON CHINA, 1891-1921

History: Nippon, Japanese hand-painted porcelain, was made for export between 1891 and 1921. In 1891, when the McKinley tariff act proclaimed that all items of foreign manufacture be stamped with their country of origin, Japan chose to use "Nippon." In 1921, the United States decided the word "Nippon" no longer was acceptable and required all Japanese wares to be marked "Japan," ending the Nippon era.

Marks: There are more than 220 recorded Nippon backstamps or marks; the three most popular are the wreath, maple leaf, and rising sun. Wares with variations of all three marks are being reproduced today. A knowledgeable collector can easily spot the reproductions by the mark variances.

The majority of the marks are found in three different colors: green, blue, or magenta. Colors indicate the quality of

REPRODUCTION ALERT

Distinguishing Old Marks from New

A common old mark consisted of a central wreath open at the top with the letter M in the center. "Hand Painted" flowed around the top of the wreath; "NIPPON" around the bottom. The modern fake mark reverses the wreath (it is open at the bottom) and places an hourglass form not an "M" in its middle.

An old leaf mark, approximately one-quarter inch wide, has "Hand" with "Painted" below to the left of the stem and "NIPPON" beneath. The newer mark has the identical lettering but the size is now one-half, rather than one-quarter, inch.

An old mark consisted of "Hand Painted" arched above a solid rising sun logo with "NIPPN" in a straight line beneath. The modern fake mark has the same lettering pattern but the central logo looks like a mound

the porcelain used: green for first-grade porcelain, blue for second-grade, and magenta for third-grade. Marks were applied by two methods: decal stickers under glaze and imprinting directly on the porcelain.

References: Joan Van Patten, *Collector's Encyclopedia of Nippon Porcelain*, 1st Series (1979, 1997 value update), 2nd Series (1982, 1997 value update), 3rd Series (1986, 1996 value update), 4th Series, (1997), Collector Books; 5th Series (1998); Kathy Wojciechowski, *Wonderful World of Nippon Porcelain*, Schiffer Publishing, 1992.

Collectors' Clubs: ARK-LA-TEX Nippon Club, 6800 Arapaho Rd, #1057, Dallas, TX 75248; Dixieland Nippon Club, P.O. Box 1712, Centerville, VA 22020; International Nippon Collectors Club, 1417 Steele St., Fort Myers, FL 33901; Lakes & Plains Nippon Collectors Society, P.O. Box 230, Peotone, IL 60468-0230; Long Island Nippon Collectors Club, 145 Andover Place, W. Hempstead, NY 11552; MD-PA Collectors' Club, 1016 Erwin Dr., Joppa, MD 21085; New England Nippon Collectors Club, 64 Burt Rd, Springfield, MA 01118; Sunshine State Nippon Collectors' Club, P.O. Box 425, Frostproof, FL 33843; Upstate New York Nippon Collectors' Club, 122 Laurel Ave., Herkimer, NY 13350.

Additional Listings: See Warman's Americana & Collectibles.

Basket, 10", pictorial lake scene 880.00
Bowl, ftd, matching ladle, hp flowers and scrolls 65.00
Bread Tray, Gaudy style, green and gold, pink asters 225.00
Butter dish, cov, floral hand, mkd "Hand Painted RC Nippon" 40.00

SPECIAL AUCTIONS

Jackson's Auctioneers & Appraisers
2229 Lincoln St.
Cedar Falls, IA 50613
(319) 277-2256
e-mail:jacksons@corenet.net

Calling Card Tray, 7-3/4" x 6", mythical dragon and bird, blue maple leaf mark 48.00
Candlesticks, pr, 10" h, Galle scene, moriage trees, maple leaf mark 400.00
Celery Tray, 15-1/4" l, flowered border, mark #84 .... 85.00
Charger, 12" d, rose tapestry 2,600.00
Chocolate Pot, 11" h, hp, pale pink, rose, violet, lavender, and yellow, gold beaded dec, turquoise jewels, blue maple leaf mark 90.00
Cigarette Box, cov, horse motif 470.00
Compote, 4-3/8" h, 8-1/2" d, Wedgwood and rose nosegay dec, wreath mark 200.00
Cracker Jar, melon ribbed body, bisque background, Indian in canoe shooting moose on river edge, ftd, wreath mark 425.00
Creamer, doll face 150.00
Demitasse Cup and Saucer, Woodland 110.00
Doll, 4-1/2" h, baby, bisque, broken foot 30.00
Egg Warmer, holds 4 eggs, stopper, sailboat scene, rising sun mark 115.00
Ferner, 6" w, floral dec, gold beading, 4 handles, green "M" in wreath mark 125.00
Hanging Basket, 4" 990.00
Humidor, cov, 5", elk dec 880.00
Hatpin Holder, 5" h, serpent in relief, mottled ground 175.00
Jam Jar, cov, matching underplate, deep cobalt blue, heavily raised gold cartouches, allover gold dec, pink and pale apricot flowers, 2 handles, blue leaf mark 145.00
Jug, 6-1/2" h, cylindrical, short slender neck, white flat shoulder, stylized dragons and jewels, orig stopper, green "M" in wreath mark 300.00
Liqueurs, stemmed, handpainted scene, set of 4 .... 150.00
Mug, Egyptian motif with warship 385.00
Napkin Ring, Egyptian scene 55.00
Nappy, 6-1/2" d, lake scene, forest in distance, moriage trim, gold beading 70.00
Pitcher, 7" h, slate gray ground, moriage sea gulls, leaf mark 250.00
Plaque, hanging
   7-3/4" d, Indian portrait, VP 124 .... 325.00
   9" d, quail, enameled leaves and berries, VP 1587 .... 325.00
   10" d, harbor scene, boats in full sail, shades of beige and brown, mkd "Hand Painted Nippon," and "M" in wreath mark 275.00

Plaque, monk, hand painted, 9-1/2" d, $660. Photo courtesy of Jackson's Auctioneers & Appraisers.

Plate
  8" d, handpainted, florals 20.00
  8-1/2" d, lake, house, and roses scene, cobalt blue and gold trim,
    leaf mark 185.00
  10" w, gold center, cobalt blue and gold trim, maple leaf mark ... 160.00
  12" d, rose tapestry 2,640.00
Potpourri, gold and white 50.00
Punch Bowl and Stand, 12-1/2" d, 6-1/2" h, bisque, bouquet of roses
  scene, wide rim dec with gold and jewels, wreath mark 350.00
Serving Tray, 11" d, gold and burgundy medallions inside gold fluted
  rim, multicolored roses and laves center, gold open pierced handles,
  Royal Kinran mark 225.00
Smoke Set, hoo bird 35.00
Stein, relief molded, dog heads, leash handle, green "M" in wreath
  mark 950.00
Sugar Shaker, 4-1/4" h, cobalt blue, floral maple leaf mark 150.00
Tankard, 11-1/2" h, oval body, ornate gold trim and base bands, gold
  handle, large blown out shaded green roses and foliage, pale green
  satin ground 250.00
Tea Set, teapot, creamer, and sugar, melon ribbed shape, gold handles and trim, gold overlay design, pink roses, leaf mark 265.00
Tea Strainer, pink roses 50.00
Urn
  8" h, floral dec, matching lid 935.00
  11" h, florals, dec scrolling, gold trim, small medallion depicting
    "Peace Bringing Abundance" 2,200.00
Vase
  5" h, tapestry, woodland scene, two small handles 690.00
  6" h, tapestry 990.00
  7" h
    Cartoon style ship 470.00
    Cobalt Blue, dec 470.00
  7-1/2" h, handles, bulbous, pedestal foot, cobalt blue, Madame
    Recamier portrait, three floral inserts, beaded 415.00
  8-1/2" h, scenic, gold, VP 216 .... 300.00
  9" h, two handles, moriage dec 155.00
  11" h, ovoid, double ribbon-shaped handles, cherry blossom motif,
    gilt accents, green "M" in wreath mark, pr 715.00
Wall Plaque
  9" l, heavy enamel rim, VP 3516 .... 300.00
  10" d, portrait 435.00
Whiskey Jug, 6-1/2" h, Egyptian motif, excessive wear 880.00

NODDERS

History: Nodders are figurines with heads and/or arms attached to the body with wires to enable movement. They are made in a variety of materials—bisque, celluloid, papier-mâché, porcelain, or wood.

Most nodders date from the late 19th century, with Germany being the principal source of supply. Among the American-made nodders, those of Disney and cartoon characters are most eagerly sought.

Reference: Hilma R. Irtz, *Figural Nodders*, Collector Books, 1996.; Tim Hunter, B*obbing Head Dolls*, 1960-2000, Krause Publications, 2000.

Collectors' Club: Bobbin' Head National Club, P.O. Box 9297, Lakeland, FL 32120.

Bisque
  Buttercup, German 180.00
  Chinese man, 4-1/2" h, seated, legs crossed, holding in hand, pink
    and beige dec, beading 170.00
  Colonial Woman, 7-1/2" h, bisque 190.00
  Indian Princess, 3-3/4"h, seated, holding fan, pale blue, gold
    trim 115.00
  Kayo, German 145.00

Baby in bath-tub, mkd "Patent/TT," 3-3/4" x 2-1/2" x 3-1/4", $30.

  Little Orphan Annie, German 115.00
  Monk, 5-3/4" h, standing, holding wine pitcher,
    German 150.00
  Oriental Couple, 8-3/4" h, pink robes, seated before keyboard and
    music book, gilt dec, Continental, 19th C 500.00
  Turkish Girl, 6" h, white beading 300.00
Ceramic
  Old Salt, 7" h sailor, white beard, blue shirt, brown pants, black
    boots 25.00
  Siamese Boy and Girl, 4-1/2" h, salt and pepper shakers, black,
    orange, and gold outfits, orig box mid "A Commodore Product,
    Japan" 20.00
Papier-Mâché
  Black Boy, clockwork, felt and cotton suit, 24" h, c1900 ..... 1,265.00
  Japanese Boy and Girl, 5-1/2" h, pr 50.00
  Mother Goose, red cape, black hat, white goose 3,960.00
  Rabbit, 8" h, sitting, light brown 90.00
Wood and Papier-Mâché
  Comical man, 6-3/8" h, top hat, worn orig polychrome 140.00
  Santa, clockwork, gray mittens, cardboard and wood 900.00

NORITAKE CHINA

History: Morimura Brothers founded Noritake China in 1904 in Nagoya, Japan. They made high-quality chinaware for export to the United States and also produced a line of china blanks for hand painting. In 1910, the company perfected a technique for the production of high-quality dinnerware and introduced streamlined production.

During the 1920s, the Larkin Company of Buffalo, New York, was a prime distributor of Noritake China. Larkin offered Azalea, Briarcliff, Linden, Modjeska, Savory, Sheridan, and Tree in the Meadow patterns as part of their premium line.

The factory was heavily damaged during World War II, and production was reduced. Between 1946 and 1948, the company sold its china under the "Rose China" mark, since the quality of production did not match the earlier Noritake China. Expansion in 1948 brought about the resumption of quality production and the use of the Noritake name once again.

Marks: There are close to 100 different marks for Noritake, the careful study of which can determine the date of production. Most pieces are marked "Noritake" with a wreath,

Dish, brown, gold, green, gray, figural nuts in center, 3 small legs, green mark, $90.

"M," "N," or "Nippon." The use of the letter N was registered in 1953.

References: Aimee Neff Alden, *Collector's Encyclopedia of Early Noritake*, Collector Books, 1995; Walter Ayars, *Larkin China*, Catalog Reprint, Echo Publishing, 1990; Joan Van Patten, *Collector's Encyclopedia of Noritake*, 1st Series (1984, 1997 value update), 2nd Series, (1994), Collector Books; David Spain, *Collecting Noritake, A to Z: Art Deco and More*, Schiffer, 1999,

Collectors' Club: Noritake Collectors' Society, 145 Andover Place, West Hempstead, NY 115532-1603.

Vase, fan shape, $135.

Additional Listings: See *Warman's Americana & Collectibles* for Azalea pattern prices.

Ashtray, Tree in the Meadow, 5-1/4" d, green mark 32.00
Berry Set, Tree in the Meadow, master bowl with pierced handles, 6
    sauce bowls 75.00
Bowl, figural, squirrel, Spain #8168 .... 65.00
Bread and Butter Plate, Margarita pattern, 6-1/2" d 9.00
Butter Tub, Pink Azalea, orig insert 65.00
Cake Plate, Tree in the Meadow, 7-1/2" sq 30.00
Cake Set, luster 70.00
Candlesticks, pr, luster, heavy gold 90.00
Celery Tray, windmill dec 40.00
Condiment Set, figural, ducks, 4 pcs 115.00
Creamer and Sugar
    Art Deco, pink Japanese lanterns, cobalt blue ground, basket type
        handle on sugar, wreath with "M" mark 50.00
    Tree in the Meadow, scalloped 85.00
Cruet, joined oil and vinegar, orig tops, Tree in the Meadow 75.00
Cup and Saucer, Florola, #83374 pattern 24.00
Demitasse Cup and Saucer, Tree in the Meadow 35.00
Demitasse Pot, Tree in the Meadow 95.00
Dinner Service, partial, Lazarre pattern, Oriental motif,
    89 pcs 200.00
Divided Dish, Tree in the Meadow 30.00
Fruit Bowl, Margarita pattern, 5-1/8" d 8.00
Gravy Boat, Tree in the Meadow 50.00
Hair Receiver, 3-1/4" h, 3-1/2" w, art Deco, geometric designs,, gold
    luster, wreath with "M" mark 50.00
Inkwell, owl, figural 125.00
Jam Jar, cov, basket style, handle, figural applied cherries on notched
    lid 55.00
Lemon Dish, Deco, tulip dec 35.00
Luncheon Plate, 7" sq, Azalea 75.00
Match Holder, underplate, camel scene, wreath with "M" mark 35.00
Napkin Ring, Art Deco man and woman, wreath with "M" mark,
    pr 60.00
Place Card Holder, figural, bluebird with butterfly, gold luster, white
    stripes, wreath with "M" mark, pr 35.00
Plate, 8-1/2" d, Tree in the Meadow 15.00
Platter, 11" l, Rosewin, #6584 .... 25.00
Salad Plate, Margarita pattern, 7-1/2" d 10.00
Salt, 3" l, swan, white, orange luster, pr 25.00
Salt and Pepper Shakers, pr, Tree in the Meadow, mkd "Made in
    Japan" 35.00
Soup Bowl, Florola 15.00
Spoon Holder, swans, blue background 50.00
Tea Set, Tree in the Meadow, 3 pcs 100.00
Tea Tile, Tree in the Meadow, 5" w, green mark 35.00
Vase, panoramic landscape, ducks, farm 75.00
Vegetable Bowl, cov, 9" d, round, Rosewin 35.00
Waffle Set, handled serving plate, sugar shaker, Art Deco flowers,
    wreath with "M" mark 50.00
Wall Pocket
    Butterfly, wreath with "M" mark 75.00
    Scenic 70.00

NORTH DAKOTA SCHOOL of MINES

History: The North Dakota School of Mines was established in 1890. Earle J. Babcock, a chemistry instructor, was impressed with the high purity level of North Dakota potter's clay. In 1898, Babcock received funds to develop his finds. He tried to interest commercial potteries in the North Dakota clay but had limited success.

In 1910, Babcock persuaded the school to establish a Ceramics Department. Margaret Cable, who studied under

Charles Binns and Frederick H. Rhead, was appointed head. She remained until her retirement in 1949.

Decorative emphasis was placed on native themes, e.g., flowers and animals. Art Nouveau, Art Deco, and fairly plain pieces were made.

Marks: The pottery is marked with a cobalt blue underglaze circle of the words "University of North Dakota/Grand Forks, N.D./Made at School of Mines/N.D. Clay." Some early pieces are marked only "U.N.D." or "U.N.D./Grand Forks, N.D." Most pieces are numbered (they can be dated from University records) and signed by both the instructor and student. Cable-signed pieces are the most desirable.

References: Darlene Hurst Dommel, *Collector's Encyclopedia of the Dakota Potteries*, Collector Books, 1996.

Collectors' Club: North Dakota Pottery Collectors Society, P.O. Box 14, Beach, ND 58621.

Bowl, 9" d, 4-1/4" h, carved heart-shaped leaves, matte green and white, glossy int., circular ink mark and "Schnell" 450.00
Figure, 4-1/2" h, 3-1/4" w, Bentonite cowboy, brick-red, black, and gold glaze, incised "JJ/13/UND," Julia Mattson, 1913 .... 650.00
Vase
    4-3/4" h, 6-1/4" d, sq tapering, repeating scenes of farmer and horse-drawn plough, green and brown matte glaze, circular ink mark, incised "The Plowman/Huck/119," F. Huckfield 1,200.00
    5" h, 4-1/2" d, bulbous, emb prairie roses, mottled green crystalline glaze, circular ink mark, incised "Steen-Huck-1100," Huckfield and Steen 1,200.00
    5-1/2" h, 6-1/2" d, ovoid, closed-in rim, carved lit lanterns, mustard yellow glaze, charcoal blue glossy ground, circular stamp mark, incised "R.L.H." 5,000.00
    6-3/4" h, 4-1/2" d, frieze of bronco riders, brown to green matte glaze, circular ink mark, incised "J.M./133," Julia Mattson 2,100.00
    7" h, 3-1/2" d, incised stylized turquoise blossoms, beige ground, stamped mark, illegible artist signature 1,300.00
    7-1/4" h, 5" d, bulbous, emb cowboy scene, matte chocolate brown glaze, circular ink stamp, sgd "Flora Huckfield," titled "N. D. Rodeo" 1,500.00
    8" h, 5-1/2' d, carved daffodils, mahogany matte glaze, circular ink mark, incised "McCosh '48" 1,100.00
    9" h, 5" d, carved mocha brown narcissus, dark brown ground, ink stamp, incised "E. Cunningham/12/6/50," E. Cunningham, 1950 .... 1,000.00
    10" h, 5-1/2" d, ovoid, carved sheaves of what, purple-brown matte glaze, ink stamped and incised "Huck 30/No. Dak. Wheat," F. Huckfield 1,300.00
Vessel
    3-1/2" h, 3-3/4" d, spherical, carved windows of silhouetted coyotes, cobalt blue and ivory, circular ink stamp and "JM/298," Julia Mattson, flat stilt pull nicks 1,200.00
    5-1/2" h, 6" d, spherical, Prairie Rose, carved coral stylized flowers, green leaves, sand ground, circular ink stamp and "M. Cable/131-A/Prairie Rose," Margaret Cable 900.00
    6" h, 7" d, spherical, Covered Wagon, carved frieze of wagons and oxen, sandy brown matte glaze, circular ink mark, incised "M. Cable" and title, by Margaret Cable 1,400.00

WALLACE NUTTING

History: Wallace Nutting (1861-1941) was America's most famous photographer of the early 20th century. A retired minister, Nutting took more than 50,000 pictures, keeping 10,000 of his best and destroying the rest. His popular and best-selling scenes included "Exterior Scenes" (apple blossoms, country lanes, orchards, calm streams, and rural American countrysides), "Interior Scenes" (usually featuring a colonial woman working near a hearth), and "Foreign Scenes" (typically thatch-roofed cottages). Those pictures which were least popular in his day have become the rarest and most-highly collectible today and are classified as "Miscellaneous Unusual Scenes." This category encompasses such things as animals, architecturals, children, florals, men, seascapes, and snow scenes.

Nutting sold literally millions of his hand-colored platinotype pictures between 1900 and his death in 1941. Starting first in Southbury, Connecticut, and later moving his business to Framingham, Massachusetts, the peak of Wallace Nutting's picture production was 1915 to 1925. During this period, Nutting employed nearly 200 people, including colorists, darkroom staff, salesmen, and assorted office personnel. Wallace Nutting pictures proved to be a huge commercial success and hardly an American household was without one by 1925.

While attempting to seek out the finest and best early-American furniture as props for his colonial Interior Scenes, Nutting became an expert in American antiques. He published nearly twenty books in his lifetime, including his ten-volume State Beautiful series and various other books on furniture, photography, clocks, and his autobiography. He also contributed many photographs which were published in magazines and books other than his own.

Nutting also became widely known for his reproduction furniture. His furniture shop produced literally hundreds of different furniture forms: clocks, stools, chairs, settles, settees, tables, stands, desks, mirrors, beds, chests of drawers, cabinet pieces, and treenware.

The overall synergy of the Wallace Nutting name, pictures, books, and furniture, has made anything "Wallace Nutting" quite collectible.

Marks: Wallace Nutting furniture is clearly marked with his distinctive paper label (which was glued directly onto the piece) or with a block or script signature brand (which was literally branded into his furniture).

Note: "Process Prints" are 1930s machine-produced reprints of twelve of Nutting's most popular pictures. These have minimal value and can be detected by using a magnifying glass.

References: Michael Ivankovich, *Alphabetical & Numerical Index to Wallace Nutting Pictures*, Diamond Press, 1988; ——, *Collector's Guide to Wallace Nutting Pictures*, Collector Books, 1997; ——, *Guide to Wallace Nutting Furniture*, Diamond Press, 1990; ——, *Wallace Nutting Expansible Catalog* (reprint of 1915 catalog), Diamond Press, 1987; *Wallace Nutting, Wallace Nutting: A Great American Idea* (reprint of 1922 catalog), Diamond Press, 1992; ——, *Wallace Nutting General Catalog* (reprint of 1930 catalog), Schiffer Publishing, 1977; ——, *Wallace Nutting's Windsors* (reprint of 1918 catalog), Diamond Press, 1992.

Collectors' Club: Wallace Nutting Collectors Club, P.O. Box 2458, Doylestown, PA 18901.

Museum: Wadsworth Athenaeum, Hartford, CT.

SPECIAL AUCTIONS

Michael Ivankovich Auction Co.
P.O. Box 2458
Doylestown, PA 18901
(215) 345-6094

Advisor: Michael Ivankovich.

Books

American Windsors	85.00
England Beautiful, 1st ed.	125.00
Furniture of the Pilgrim Century, 1st ed.	140.00
Furniture Treasury, Vol. I	125.00
Furniture Treasury, Vol. II	140.00
Furniture Treasury, Vol. III	115.00
Ireland Beautiful, 1st ed.	45.00
Pathways of the Puritans	85.00
Social Life In Old New England	75.00
State Beautiful Series	
Connecticut Beautiful, 1st ed.	75.00
Maine Beautiful, 1st ed.	45.00
Massachusetts Beautiful, 2nd ed.	45.00
New Hampshire Beautiful, 1st ed.	75.00
New York Beautiful, 1st ed.	85.00
Pennsylvania Beautiful, 1st ed.	48.00
Vermont Beautiful, 2nd ed.	40.00
Virginia Beautiful, 1st ed.	60.00
The Cruise of the 800	95.00
Catalog, Wallace Nutting's Original Studio	1,012.00

Furniture

Candle Stand, #17, Windsor	495.00
Chair	
#408, bent arm, Windsor	1,210.00
#412, comb back, arm, PA	1,045.00
#440, arm, writing, PA Windsor	2,805.00
#464, Carver, arm	965.00

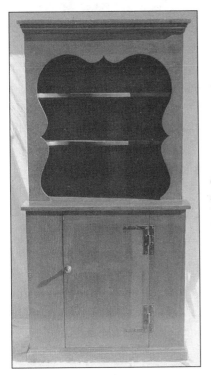

Cupboard, pine, scrolled, #923, $4,290. Photo courtesy of Michael Ivankovich.

Cupboard, #923, pine, scrolled	4,290.00
Table	
#619, crane bracket	685.00
#628b, Pembroke, mahogany	1,495.00
Pen and Pencil Tray, Nutting's personal item	195.00

Picture

A Fair Orchard Way, 11" x 14"	105.00
A Gettysburg Crossing, 14" x 17"	200.00
A Keene Road, 13" x 17"	165.00
A Lane In Sorrento	880.00
All the Comforts of Home, 13" x 15"	210.00
A Perkiomen October, 9" x 11"	250.00
Among the Ferns, 14" x 17"	165.00
An Elaborate Dinner, 14" x 17"	200.00
A Pennsylvania Stream	770.00
A Rug Pattern	690.00
Better than Mowing, 16" x 20"	490.00
Between the Games	800.00
Between the Spruces, 10" x 14"	200.00
Birch Hilltop, 15" x 22"	100.00
By the Fireside, 9" x 13"	100.00
California Hilltops, 11" x 14"	185.00
Christmas Welcome Home	1,100.00
Colonial Days, Nantucket	1,128.00
Dog-On-It, 7" x 11"	1,265.00
Elm Drapery, 15" x 22"	385.00
Fleur-de-lis and Spirea, 13" x 16"	685.00
Flume Falls, 12" x 15"	310.00
Four O' Clock, cows	1,295.00
Gloucester Cloister, 16" x 20"	1,100.00
Going for the Doctor, children	1,100.00
Grandmother's Hollyhocks, 9" x 11"	400.00
Helping Mother, 14" x 17"	410.00
Lockside Cottage	745.00
Parting at the Gate, 10" x 14"	550.00
Pennsylvania Arches, 14" x 17"	300.00
Priscilla's Cottage, 14" x 17"	360.00
Rapid Transit, stagecoach scene	1,540.00
Roses and Larkspur	1,210.00
Russet and Gold, 16" x 20"	315.00
Shadowy Orchard Curves, 11" x 14"	85.00
Stepping Stones to Bolton Abbey, 11" x 14"	330.00
The Coming Out of Rosa	300.00
The Delaware Canal Turn, PA	363.00
The Donjon Chenaceau, French Castle	660.00
The Meeting Place, horse and cows	2,420.00
The Old Homestead	880.00
To Meet The Rector	990.00
Tranquility Farm	880.00
Village Spires, 10" x 12"	125.00
Watching for Papa, 13" x 16"	420.00
Wilton Waters, 13" x 16"	155.00
Wrencote	565.00

Silhouettes

George and Martha Washington, 3" x 4"	90.00
Girl at Vanity Desk, 4" x 4"	90.00
Girl by Garden Urn, 4" x 4"	75.00
Girl by Spider Web, 5" x 4"	80.00
Scenes	45.00

WALLACE NUTTING-LIKE PHOTOGRAPHERS

History: Although Wallace Nutting was widely recognized as the country's leading producer of hand-colored photographs during the early 20th century, he was by no means the only photographer selling this style of picture. Throughout the country, literally hundreds of regional photographers were selling hand-colored photographs from their home regions or travels. The subject matter of these photographers was comparable to Nutting's, including Interior, Exterior, Foreign, and Miscellaneous Unusual scenes.

Several photographers operated large businesses, and, although not as large or well-known as Wallace Nutting, they sold a substantial volume of pictures which can still be readily found today. The vast majority of their work was photographed in their home regions and sold primarily to local residents or visiting tourists. It should come as little surprise that three of the major Wallace Nutting-like photographers—David Davidson, Fred Thompson, and the Sawyer Art Co.—each had ties to Wallace Nutting.

Hundreds of other smaller local and regional photographers attempted to market hand-colored pictures comparable to Wallace Nutting's during the period of 1900 to the 1930s. Although quite attractive, most were not as appealing to the general public as Wallace Nutting pictures. However, as the price of Wallace Nutting pictures has escalated, the work of these lesser-known Wallace Nutting-like photographers have become increasingly collectible.

A partial listing of some of these minor Wallace Nutting-like photographers includes: Babcock; J. C. Bicknell; Blair; Ralph Blood (Portland, Maine); Bragg; Brehmer; Brooks; Burrowes; Busch; Carlock; Pedro Cacciola; Croft; Currier; Depue Brothers; Derek; Dowly; Eddy; May Farini (hand-colored colonial lithographs); George Forest; Gandara; Gardner (Nantucket, Bermuda, Florida); Gibson; Gideon; Gunn; Bessie Pease Gutmann (hand-colored colonial lithographs); Edward Guy; Harris; C. Hazen; Knoffe; Haynes (Yellowstone Park); Margaret Hennesey; Hodges; Homer; Krabel; Kattleman; La Bushe; Lake; Lamson (Portland, Maine); M. Lightstrum; Machering; Rossiler Mackinae; Merrill; Meyers; William Moehring; Moran; Murrey; Lyman Nelson; J. Robinson Neville (New England); Patterson; Own Perry; Phelps; Phinney; Reynolds; F. Robbins; Royce; Frederick Scheetz (Philadelphia, Pennsylvania); Shelton, Standley (Colorado); Stott; Summers; Esther Svenson; Florence Thompson; Thomas Thompson; M. A. Trott; Sanford Tull; Underhill; Villar; Ward; Wilmot; Edith Wilson; and Wright.

References: Carol Begley Gray, *History of the Sawyer Pictures*, published by author, 1995 (available from Wallace Nutting Collector's Club, P.O. Box 2458, Doylestown, PA 18901); Michael Ivankovich, *Collector's Value Guide to Early Twentieth Century American Prints*, Collector Books, 1998; —, *Guide to Wallace-Nutting Like Photographers of the Early 20th Century*, Diamond Press, 1991.

Collectors' Club: Wallace Nutting Collector's Club, P.O. Box 2458, Doylestown, PA 18901.

Advisor: Michael Ivankovich.

Notes: The key determinants of value include the collectibility of the particular photographer, subject matter, condition, and size. Exterior Scenes are the most common.

Keep in mind that only the rarest pictures, in the best condition, will bring top prices. Discoloration and/or damage to the picture or matting can reduce value significantly.

David Davidson

Second to Nutting in overall production, Davidson worked primarily in the Rhode and Southern Massachusetts area. While a student at Brown University around 1900, Davidson learned the art of hand-colored photography from Wallace Nutting, who happened to be the Minister at Davidson's church. After Nutting moved to Southbury in 1905, Davidson graduated from Brown and started a successful photography business in Providence, Rhode Island, which he operated until his death in 1967.

A Puritan Lady	70.00
A Real D.A.R.	150.00
Berkshire Sunset	80.00
Christmas Day	160.00
Driving Home The Cows	120.00
Heart's Desire	30.00
Her House In Order	75.00
Neighbors	170.00
Old Ironsides	170.00
On A News Hunt	120.00
Plymouth Elm	20.00
Rosemary Club	40.00
Snowbound Brook	55.00
The Brook's Mirro	95.00
The Lamb's May Feast	130.00
The Seine Reel	190.00
The Silent Wave	35.00
Vanity	70.00

Sawyer

A father and son team, Charles H. Sawyer and Harold B. Sawyer, operated the very successful Sawyer Art Company from 1903 until the 1970s. Beginning in Maine, the Sawyer Art Company moved to Concord, New Hampshire, in 1920 to be closer to their primary market—New Hampshire's White Mountains. Charles H. Sawyer briefly worked for Nutting from 1902 to 1903 while living in southern Maine. Sawyer's production volume ranks third behind Wallace Nutting and David Davidson.

A February Morning	210.00
A New England Sugar Birth	300.00
At the Bend of the Road	35.00
Crystal Lake	65.00
Echo Lake, Franconia Notch	50.00
Indian Summer	35.00
Lake Morey	30.00
Lake Willoughby	50.00
Mt. Washington in October	55.00
Newfound Lake	73.00
Old Man of the Mountains	35.00
Original Dennison Plant	100.00
Silver Birches, Lake George	50.00
The Meadow Stream	80.00

Fred Thompson

Frederick H. Thompson and Frederick M. Thompson, another father and son team, operated the Thompson Art Company (TACO) from 1908 to 1923, working primarily in the Portland, Maine, area. We know that Thompson and Nutting had collaborated because Thompson widely marketed an interior scene he had taken in Nutting's Southbury home. The production volume of the Thompson Art Company ranks fourth behind Nutting, Davidson, and Sawyer.

Apple Tree Road	45.00

Blossom Dale	75.00
Brook in Winter	190.00
Calm of Fall	50.00
Fernbank	35.00
Fireside Fancy Work	140.00
High and Dry	45.00
Knitting for the Boys	160.00
Lombardy Poplar	100.00
Nature's Carpet	50.00
Neath the Blossoms	95.00
Peace River	30.00
Six Master	100.00
Sunset on the Suwanee	45.00
The Gossips	80.00
White Head	90.00

Minor Wallace Nutting-Like Photographers

Generally speaking, prices for works by minor Wallace Nutting-like photographers would break down as follows: smaller pictures (5" x 7" to 10" x 12"), $10-$75; medium pictures (11" x 14" to 14" x 17"), $50-$200; larger pictures (larger than 14" x 17"), $75-$200+.

Baker, Florian A., Rushing Waters	50.00
Farini, In Her Boudoir	30.00
Gibson, Mountain Road	20.00
Haynes, Untitled Waterfalls	20.00
Higgins, Charles A., A Colonial Stairway	65.00
Payne, George S., Weekly Letter	25.00
Watson, Edith, Pair of Bermuda	

OCCUPIED JAPAN

History: The Japanese economy was devastated when World War II ended. To secure necessary hard currency, the Japanese pottery industry produced thousands of figurines and other knickknacks for export. The variety of products is endless—ashtrays, dinnerware, lamps, planters, souvenir items, toys, vases, etc. Initially, the figurines attracted the largest number of collectors; today many collectors focus on other types of pieces.

Marks: From the beginning of the American occupation of Japan until April 28, 1952, objects made in that country were marked "Japan," "Made in Japan," "Occupied Japan," or "Made in Occupied Japan." Only pieces marked with the last two designations are of major interest to Occupied Japan collectors. The first two marks also were used during other time periods.

References: Florence Archambault, *Occupied Japan for Collectors,* Schiffer Publishing, 1992; Gene Florence, *Price Guide to Collector's Encyclopedia of Occupied Japan,* Collector Books, 1999 (updated prices for 5-book series *Collector's Encyclopedia of Occupied Japan);* Monica Lynn Clements and Patricia Rosser Clements, *Pocket Guide to Occupied Japan,* Schiffer Publishing, 1999; Carole Bess White, *Collector's Guide to Made in Japan Ceramics,* Book I (1996), Book II (1997), Collector Books.

Collectors' Club: The Occupied Japan Club, 29 Freeborn St., Newport, RI 02840.

Additional Listings: See *Warman's Americana & Collectibles* for more examples.

Ashtray
   2-1/4" w, bisque, heart shape, hp, floral sprays, white ground 17.50
   4-3/4" h, metal, spring-loaded head of young boy smoking cigar.50.00
Bowl, cov, Capo-di-Monte style, double handles, brightly colored enamel dec, winged cherubs in woodland scene, mkd "Occupied Japan" 20.00
Children's Play Dishes, play set, Blue Willow, 18 pc set 375.00
Cigarette Dispenser, mechanical, inlaid wood, spring-operated sliding drawer loads cigarettes into bird's beak 55.00
Clock, 10-1/2" h, bisque, double figure, colonial dancing couple, floral encrusted case 250.00
Cornucopia, 7" x 8", chariot, rearing horse and 2 cherubs, multicolored beading, gold trim, unglazed bisque 80.00
Creamer, bisque, figural cow 24.00
Doll Carriage, 2-1/4" h, celluloid, pink and blue, moveable hood, Acme 28.00
Figure, porcelain
   3" h, cherub, playing drum, pierced pedestal base 12.00
   4-1/2" h, 5-3/4" l, Chinese couple, woman playing stringed instrument, man smoking pipe 35.00
   6-1/2" h, boy standing by fence 24.00
Finger Bowl, 5-3/4" h, porcelain, winged cherub and raspberries. 30.00
Flower Frog, 6" h, figural, girl with bird on shoulder, pastel highlights, gold trim, bisque 45.00
Lamp, Colonial couple, gentleman with guitar, woman holding floral bouquet, floral emb base 25.00
Nut Dish, 6" d, metal, floral borders 12.00
Plate, 4-1/2" d, silvered metal, pierced scalloped fancy rim 12.00
Platter, 16" l, Courley pattern, heavy gold trim, mkd "Meito Norleans China" 30.00
Salt and Pepper Shakers, pr, coffeepots, cobalt blue glass, metal gray with red Bakelite handles, prig presentation box 25.00

Shelf Sitter, 4-3/4" h, bisque, Oriental girl, green 17.50
Tape Measure, 2-3/8" l, pig, stamped "Occupied Japan" 45.00
Tea Set, partial, blue luster, apple blossoms, 9" w x 5" h yellow teapot, 3-3/4"w sugar, and 7-6/8" d, plate, mkd "T" in red wreath 45.00
Toby Mug, 5-1/2" h, porcelain, blinking eyes 40.00
Toy, celluloid, monkey, playing banjo 165.00
Tray, 10-1/2" l, papier-mâché, rect, floral dec 45.00
Vase
   6" h, SP, Art Deco style, stylized blossoms, ftd 25.00
   10" h, bisque, figural, young lady and scrolled cornucopia 65.00
Wall Pocket, flying geese, set of 1 large and 3 smaller pockets, 4 pc set 25.00

OHR POTTERY

History: Ohr pottery was produced by George E. Ohr in Biloxi, Mississippi. There is a discrepancy as to when he actually established his pottery; some say 1878, but Ohr's autobiography indicates 1883. In 1884, Ohr exhibited 600 pieces of his work, suggesting that he had been a potter for some time.

Ohr's techniques included twisting, crushing, folding, denting, and crinkling thin-walled clay into odd, grotesque, and, sometimes, graceful forms. His later pieces were often left unglazed.

In 1906, Ohr closed the pottery and stored more than 6,000 pieces as a legacy to his family. He had hoped it would be purchased by the U.S. government, which never happened. The entire collection remained in storage until it was rediscovered in 1972.

Today Ohr is recognized as one of the leaders in the American art pottery movement. Some greedy individuals have taken the later unglazed pieces and covered them with poor-quality glazes in hopes of making them more valuable. These pieces do not have stilt marks on the bottom.

Marks: Much of Ohr's early work was signed with an impressed stamp including his name and location in block letters. His later work was often marked with the flowing script designation "G. E. Ohr."

References: Susan and Al Bagdade, *Warman's American Pottery and Porcelain,* Wallace-Homestead, 1994; Garth Clark, Robert Ellison, Jr., and Eugene Hecht, *Mad Potter of Biloxi: The Art & Life of George Ohr,* Abbeville Press, 1989; Ralph and Terry Kovel, *Kovels' American Art Pottery,* Crown Publishers, 1993; David Rago, *American Art Pottery,* Knickerbocker Press, 1997.

Cabinet Vase, 5" h, 2-1/4" d, bulbous, cupped rim, in-body twist, gunmetal glaze, stamped "G. E. OHR, Biloxi" 1,400.00
Chamberstick
   3" h, mottled greenish-brown glaze, solid pinched handle, imp "GEO E. OHR Biloxi, Miss" 460.00
   5" h, 3-3/4" d, bulbous, dimpled base, ribbed neck, glaze-drip feet, gunmetal glaze, incised "G. E. OHR" 1,500.00
Dish, 4-1/4" d, 1-1/2" h, crumpled
   Glossy orange glaze, stamped "GEO.E.OHR/BILOXI, MISS," minor rim nicks 1,600.00
   Green and gunmetal glaze, script sgd "Biloxi, Miss, 1897" 1,700.00
Figure, 3" h, touring cabin on slats, taupe-brown clay, mkd "GEO E. OHR Biloxi, Miss." Imperfections in making 525.00
Inkwell, 2" h, 6-1/2" w, 5-1/2" l, artist's palette shape, molded artist brushes, tools, green lustered glaze, stamped "G. E. OHR/Biloxi," old restoration to paint brush 3,750.00

Puzzle Mug, pink, mottled green glaze, mkd, 4-5/8" h, $850.

Mug
  3-1/2" h, 4-1/4" d, Joe Jefferson, deep in-body twist, blue, white, and pink sponged glaze, incised Jefferson's message "Here's to you and yours…," stamped "G. E. OHR, Biloxi, Miss/3-18-96" 6,500.00
  5" h, 5" d, ribbed top, applied snake, mottled gunmetal brown glaze, script sgd 3,250.00
Pitcher
  1-3/4" h, 4-3/4" d, leaf shape, gunmetal glaze, script sgd .. 1,300.00
  4" h, 5" d, pinched and cut-out handle, labial rim, gunmetal glaze, script sgd, restoration to rim 1,200.00
  4" h, 5-1/2" d, pinched and cut-out handle, mottled cobalt blue glaze, stamped "G. E. OHR/Biloxi, Miss," restoration to rim chip 1,800.00
  4-1/4" h, 2-1/2" d, ribbon handle, speckled moss green and indigo blue glossy glaze, imp "GEO E. OHR/BILOXI.MISS," restoration to lip 1,500.00
  8-3/4" h, 4" d, tapering, sponged umber and green bands, glossy clear glaze, stamped "GEO E. OHR.BILOXI, MISS" 5,000.00
Puzzle Mug
  3-1/2" h, mottled brown glaze, reticulated circular pattern near rim, stylized rabbit form handle, twist at base, imp "G. E. Ohr Biloxi Miss" 1,150.00
  3-1/2" h, 5-1/4" d, mottled gunmetal and green glaze, some tooling to body, stamped "G. E. OHR/Biloxi, Miss" 1,200.00
Vase
  2-1/2" h, circular, short neck, mottled brown glaze on red, thumbprint base, imp "GEO O OHR Biloxi Miss" 1,150.00
  4" h, 2-3/4" d, bulbous, folded rim, dark green glaze, stamped "G. E. OHR/Biloxi, Miss" 1,500.00
  4-1/2" h, 3" d, bulbous, triangular three lobed top, speckled olive-green glaze, stamped "G. E. OHR, Biloxi, Miss," minor nicks to top rim 2,200.00
  4-1/2" h, 4-1/2" d, bulbous, 2 rows of dimples, speckled green glaze imp "G. E. OHR/Biloxi, Miss" ....,1900.00
  4-3/4" h, cylindrical, crimped rim, thumbprint base, mottled black glaze, imp "G. E. Ohr Biloxi Miss" 1,380.00
  4-3/4" h, 2-1/2" d, bulbous, ruffled rim, sponged green, brown, and gunmetal glaze, rim fleck, stamped "G. E. OHR/Biloxi, Miss" 2,100.00
  5" h, 2-1/2" d, bottle shape, double-lobed opening, pear shaped body, green and gunmetal glaze, stamped "GEO O. OHR/BILOXI, MISS" 3,250.00
  5-1/2" h, 3" d, tear shape, cupped rim, vibrant green, brown, and ochre sponged glaze, stamped "GEO. E. OHR/BILOXI, MISS" 2,800.00
  5-1/2" h, 3-1/4" d, deep in-body twist, glossy raspberry glaze, stamped "G. E. OHR/Biloxi, Miss" 6,000.00

  7" h, 3-1/4" h, bottle shape, cupped ruffled rim, incised weeds, pink and green mottled glaze, stamped "G. E. OHR/Biloxi Miss" and "JHP" for assistant J. H. Portman, small rim flecks 4,000.00
  7" h, 4" d, bottle shape, cupped rim, deep in-body twist, brilliant green and gunmetal mottled glaze, script sgd, old restoration to in-making stilt pulls at base 2,700.00
  8" h, 4-1/2" d, bulbous, deep in-body twists, mirrored green, amber, and red mottled glaze, stamped "G. E. OHR/Biloxi, Miss"....5,500.00
  10" h, 5-1/2" d, deep full-height dimples, folded neck, green, pink, red, and gunmetal lustered glaze, stamped "G. E. OHR/Biloxi, Miss," restored 13,000.00
Vessel
  2-3/4" h, 3-3/4" d, squat, pink, purple, red, and green sponged glaze, stamped "G. E. OHR/Biloxi, Miss" and incised "Mobile Clay/5/9/99," touch-up to rim nick 1,700.00
  2-3/4" h, 4-1/2" d, dimpled sides, pinched opening, brown speckled glaze, stamped "G. E. OHR/Biloxi, Miss," restoration to one side 900.00
  3" h, 4-1/4" d, dimpled side, pinched, 3-sided opening, fine purple and green glaze, stamped "G. E. OHR/Biloxi, Miss" 5,000.00
  3" h, 4-1/2" d, dimples, pinched four lobed opening, mirrored black speckled glaze, stamped "G. E. OHR/Biloxi, Miss" 3,500.00
  3-1/2" h, 4" d, spherical, folded rim, mottled matte pink glaze, stamped "G. E. OHR/Biloxi, Miss./Mobile, Alabama clay" 2,400.00
  3-1/2" h, 4-1/4" d, dimpled sides, heart-shaped opening, brown and olive-green speckled glaze, stamped "G. E. OHR/Biloxi, Miss" 3,500.00
  4" h, 4-3/4" d, deep in-body twist, asymmetrical fanciful ribbon handles, green, raspberry, and gunmetal glaze, stamped "G. E. OHR/BILOXI" 7,000.00
  4-1/2" h, 4-1/4" d, deep in-body twist, closed-in rim, amber, gray, and pink mirrored and sponged glaze, stamped "G. E. OHR/BILOXI," kiln kiss to side..................................... 2,300.00
  4-1/2" h, 4-3/4" d, labial rim, pinched side, green and brown speckled mirrored glaze, stamped "G. E. OHR/Biloxi, Miss".....3,500.00
  5" h, 5-3/4" d, bisque, whimsical face, folded rim, script sgd, 2 small rim chips 6,500.00
  5" h, 7-1/2" d, bisque, asymmetrically pinched and folded, dendrite pattern, script mark, firing tear to body 5,000.00
  5-1/4" h, 5-1/4" d, spherical, pinched sides, ruffled top, pink volcanic glaze, green, black, and white sponged design, stamped "G. E. OHR/Biloxi, Miss" 5,000.00
  5-1/4" h, 5-1/2" d, pinched and dimpled body, red, green, blue, and gray mottled glaze, stamped "G. E. OHR/Biloxi, Miss," restoration to shoulder and parts of rim 1,300.00
  5-1/2" h, 4" d, asymmetrically folded and dimpled, script mark 1,200.00
  6-1/4" h, 5-3/4" d, ruffled rim, one large and deep in-body twist, mirrored brown mottled glaze, stamped "G. E. OHR/BILOXI," minute rim flecks 6,000.00
  6-1/2" h, 4-1/2" d, bulbous, pinched and folded top, red, green, blue, and amber mottled glaze, stamped "G. E. OHR/Biloxi, Miss" 4,750.00

OLD IVORY CHINA

History: Old Ivory derives its name from the background color of the china. It was made in Silesia, Germany, during the second half of the 19th century.

Marks: Marked pieces usually have a pattern number (pattern names are not common), a crown, and the word "Silesia."

References: Susan and Al Bagdade, *Warman's English & Continental Pottery & Porcelain,* 3rd Edition, Krause Publications, 1998; Alma Hillman, David Goldschmidt & Adam Szynkiewica, *Collector's Encyclopedia of Old Ivory China, The Mystery Explored,* Collector Books, 1997.

Periodical: *Old Ivory Newsletter,* P.O. Box 1004, Wilsonville, OR 97070.

Collectors' Club: Old Ivory Porcelain Society, Route 3, Box 188, Spring Valley, MN 55975.

Berry Bowl, individual
    #29, 3 pc set 65.00
    #40, 3 pc set 75.00
Biscuit Jar, cov, #15 ....350.00
Bowl
    6-1/2" d, #84 ....65.00
    9-1/4" d, #200 ....195.00
Cake Plate, #13, 10" d, open handles, roses around border, one in
    center 125.00
Celery Dish, 11-1/2" l, #15, mkd "Silesia & Ohme" 50.00
Chocolate Set, #84, chocolate pot, 6 cups and
    saucers 850.00
Chop Plate, #15, mkd "Silesia & Clarion" 120.00
Creamer, #32 ....50.00
Cup and Saucer, #84, mkd "Silesia" 35.00
Demitasse Pot, cov, #16 ....395.00
Hair Receiver 100.00
Mustard Pot, cov, #16 ....110.00
Oyster Bowl, #11 ....195.00
Place Setting, cup, saucer, and 8" plate, Eglantine pattern 85.00
Plate
    7-3/4" d, #16, 2 pc set 37.00
    8-1/4" d, #16, 3 pc set 44.00
    8-3/4" d, #84, 3 pc set 48.00
Sugar Bowl, cov, #75 ....60.00
Teapot, cov, #15 ....395.00
Toothpick Holder, #16 ....195.00
Waste Bowl, mkd "Silesia & Ohme" 225.00

OLD PARIS CHINA

History: Old Paris china is fine-quality porcelain made by various French factories located in and around Paris during the 18th and 19th centuries. Some pieces were marked, but most were not. In addition to its fine quality, this type of ware is characterized by beautiful decorations and gilding. Favored colors are dark maroon, deep cobalt blue, and a dark green.

Additional Listings: Continental China and Porcelain (General).

Basket, reticulated, gold and white dec, c1825........................1,400.00
Cake Stand, Honore style, green border, c1845..........................220.00
Dessert Service, partial, molded details, rose color striping, gilt border,
    pr 7-1/2" h corbels, 10 dessert plates, 6 ftd compotes of graduating
    height, shell form dish, cov ftd sugar urn, butter tub with attached
    underplate, 21 pcs...1,600.00
Dresser Bottles, pr, 7-1/4" h, squatty baluster, knopped elongated
    neck, neck with vertical gilt bands, base with roses and floral bou-
    quets, conforming stopper......................................400.00
Figure, 18-3/4" h, Napoleon, standing, one arm tucked behind back,
    other tucked into shirt, full military dress, gilt dec, low sq base,
    inscribed "Roussel-Bardell," late 19th C...................700.00
Luncheon Set, light blue ground banding, gilt and iron-red cartouche
    and monogram, 28 9-1/4" d plates, 18 8-1/4" d plates, 11 6-5/8" d
    plates, 12 sauce dishes, 11 soup plates, oval 12-1/2" l serving bowl,
    oval 17-1/2" l platter, 2 circular cov vegetable tureens, cov sauce
    tureen, cov oval 12-1/4" tureen with underplate, cov jam jar with
    attached dish, chips, gilt wear 1,610.00
Mantel Vase, bell-like flowered handles, blue ground, paneled enamel
    portraits of lowers, gilt trim, minor flower damage, pr...............350.00
Plate, 9-1/4" d, flower-basket center, gilt vine and borders, ochre
    ground, c1830, pr..250.00
Teapot
    8" h, ftd baluster, dec at mid section with wide gilt band of flowers
    flanked by decorative borders............................175.00

    8-1/2" h, tapering baluster form, gilt swag suspending foliage dec, con-
    forming gilt details on lid, molded rosebud finial, late 19th C...225.00
Tea Set, partial, 8" h sq teapot with canted corners, polychromed floral
    sprays, gilt borders, cov sugar, 8 teacups, 12 saucers, late 19th C, 22
    pcs...750.00
Urn, 17-3/4" h, figural and floral dec, green ground on body and plinth,
    two gilt scrolling foliate dec and handles, mounted as lamp 400.00
Vase
    9-3/8" h, portrait medallion on gilt dec ground, molded gilt floriform
    handles, pr 500.00
    9-1/2" h, fan shape, floral cartouche, cobalt blue ground, gilt foliate
    handles 200.00
    9-1/2" h, two handles, molded foliage, polychrome floral sprays and
    gilt highlights, pr..275.00
    20" h, molded openwork base, flower-form handles, conforming
    molded rim, gilt and polychromed borders centered by portrait
    medallions of male and female, orange-red ground, Louis-Phil-
    lippe, pr 950.00

OLD SLEEPY EYE

History: Sleepy Eye, a Sioux Indian chief who reportedly had a droopy eye, gave his name to Sleepy Eye, Minnesota, and one of its leading flour mills. In the early 1900s, Old Sleepy Eye Flour offered four Flemish-gray heavy stoneware premiums decorated in cobalt blue: a straight-sided butter crock, curved salt bowl, stein, and vase. The premiums were made by Weir Pottery Company, later to become Monmouth Pottery Company, and finally to emerge as the present-day Western Stoneware Company of Monmouth, Illinois.

Additional pottery and stoneware pieces also were issued. Forms included five sizes of pitchers (4, 5-1/2, 6-1/2, 8, and 9 inches), mugs, steins, sugar bowls, and tea tiles (hot plates). Most were cobalt blue on white, but other glaze hues, such as browns, golds, and greens, were used.

Old Sleepy Eye also issued many other items, including bakers' caps, lithographed barrel covers, beanies, fans, multicolored pillow tops, postcards, and trade cards. Regular production of Old Sleepy Eye stoneware ended in 1937.

In 1952, Western Stoneware Company made 22- and 40-ounce steins in chestnut brown glaze with a redesigned Indian's head. From 1961 to 1972, gift editions were made for the board of directors and others within the company. Beginning in 1973, Western Stoneware Company issued an annual limited edition stein for collectors.

Marks: The gift editions made in the 1960s and 1970s were dated and signed with a maple leaf mark. The annual limited edition steins are marked and dated.

References: Susan and Al Bagdade, *Warman's American Pottery and Porcelain,* Wallace-Homestead, 1994; Elinor Meugnoit, *Old Sleepy Eye,* published by author, 1979.

Collectors' Club: Old Sleepy Eye Collectors Club of America, P.O. Box 12, Monmouth, IL 61462.

Reproduction Alert: Blue-and-white pitchers, crazed, weighted, and often with a stamp or the word "Ironstone" are the most common reproductions. The stein and salt bowl also have been made. Many reproductions come from Taiwan.

A line of fantasy items, new items which never existed as Old Sleepy Eye originals, includes an advertising pocket mir-

Mug, Indian head on handle, 7-1/2" h, $375.

ror with miniature flour-barrel label, small glass plates, fruit jars, toothpick holders, glass and pottery miniature pitchers, and salt and pepper shakers. One mill item has been made: a sack marked as though it were old but of a size that could not possibly hold the amount of flour indicated.

Mill Items

Advertising Premium Cards, 5-1/2" x 9", full-color Indian lore illus, Old Sleepy Eye Indian character trademark, 10 pc set 875.00
Breadboard Scraper.. 625.00
Calendar, 1904.. 200.00
Cookbook, Sleepy Eye Milling Co., loaf of bread shape, portrait of chief 150.00
Label, 9-1/4" x 11-1/2" d, egg crate, Sleepy Eye Brand, A. J. Pietrus & Sons Co., Sleepy Eye, MN, red, blue, and yellow...................... 25.00
Letter Opener, bronze, Indian-head handle, mkd "Sleepy Eye Milling Co., Sleepy Eye, MN".. 750.00
Pinback Button, "Old Sleepy Eye for Me," bust portrait of chief.. 175.00
Teaspoon, silverplated 90.00

Pottery and Stoneware

Cigarette Box, 3" h, cobalt blue and white, mkd "W. S. Co. Monmouth, Ill," chips on lip 35.00
Creamer, 4" h, cobalt blue and white, stains............................. 140.00
Miniature Creamer, 2-1/4" h, cobalt blue and white 35.00
Mug, 4-3/8" h, cobalt blue and white, mkd "W. S. Co. Monmouth, Ill" 275.00
Pitcher, cobalt blue and white
 5-3/8" h, stains and crazing in base.. 165.00
 6-1/2" h, stains and hairlines 275.00
 7-7/8" h, interior stains.. 230.00
 8-7/8" h, repaired handle 165.00
Tile, cobalt blue and white.. 950.00

ONION MEISSEN

History: The blue onion or bulb pattern is of Chinese origin and depicts peaches and pomegranates, not onions. It was first made in the 18th century by Meissen, hence the name Onion Meissen.

Factories in Europe, Japan, and elsewhere copied the pattern. Many still have the pattern in production, including the Meissen factory in Germany.

Marks: Many pieces are marked with a company's logo; after 1891 the country of origin is indicated on imported pieces.

Reference: Robert E. Röntgen, *Book of Meissen,* revised ed., Schiffer Publishing, 1996.

Note: Prices given are for pieces produced between 1870 and 1930. Early Meissen examples bring a high premium.

Ashtray, 5" d, blue crossed swords mark 80.00
Bowl
 8-1/2" d, reticulated, blue crossed swords mark, 19th C 395.00
 10-1/2" w, sq, gilt border.. 265.00
Box, cov, 4-1/2" d, round, rose finial 80.00
Bread Plate, 6-1/2" d.. 75.00
Cake Stand, 13-1/2" d, 4-1/2" h 220.00
Candlesticks, pr, 7" h 90.00
Coffeepot, few chips 185.00
Compote, 11-1/2" l and 12-1/2" l, figural, reclining male and female figure, holding oval bowl, decorated overall in blue Onion pattern, Meissen, Germany, late 19th C, incised #2858, pr 2,875.00
Creamer and Sugar, gold edge, c1900 .... 175.00
Demitasse Cup and Saucer, c1890 .... 90.00
Dish, 12" d, circular, divided.. 175.00
Fruit Compote, 9" h, circular, openwork bowl, 5 oval floral medallions 375.00
Fruit Knives, 6 pc set... 75.00
Hot Plate, handles... 125.00
Ladle, wooden handle 115.00
Lamp, 22" h, oil, frosted glass globular form shade.................... 475.00
Plate, 10" d 100.00
Platter
 12-1/4" d 175.00
 13" l, 10" w, crossed swords mark.. 295.00
Pot de Creme... 65.00
Rolling Pin.. 175.00
Serving Dish, 9-1/4" w, 11" l, floral design on handle.................. 200.00
Soup Bowl, 9" d, molded and scrolled border, mkd "German," 11 pcs.. 175.00
Tray, 17" l, cartouche shape, gilt edge...................................... 425.00
Tureen, 13" h, fruit-form finial, lid repaired............................... 300.00
Vegetable Dish, cov, 10" w, sq... 290.00

OPALESCENT GLASS

History: Opalescent glass, a clear or colored glass with milky white decorations, looks fiery or opalescent when held to light. This effect was achieved by applying bone ash chemicals to designated areas while a piece was still hot and then refiring it at extremely high temperatures.

There are three basic categories of opalescent glass: (1) blown (or mold blown) patterns, e.g., Daisy & Fern and Spanish Lace; (2) novelties, pressed glass patterns made in limited quantity and often in unusual shapes such as corn or a trough; and (3) traditional pattern (pressed) glass forms.

Opalescent glass was produced in England in the 1870s. Northwood began the American production in 1897 at its Indiana, Pennsylvania, plant. Jefferson, National Glass, Hobbs, and Fenton soon followed.

References: Gary Baker et al., *Wheeling Glass 1829-1939,* Oglebay Institute, 1994, distributed by Antique Publications; Bill Banks, *Complete Price Guide for Opalescent Glass,* 2nd ed., published by author, 1996; Bill Edwards and Mike Carwile, *Standard Encyclopedia of Opalescent Glass,* 3rd ed., Collector Books, 1999; William Heacock,

Encyclopedia of Victorian Colored Pattern Glass, Book II, 2nd ed., Antique Publications, 1977; William Heacock and William Gamble, *Encyclopedia of Victorian Colored Pattern Glass,* Book 9, Antique Publications, 1987; William Heacock, James Measell, and Berry Wiggins, *Dugan/Diamond,* Antique Publications, 1993; ——, *Harry Northwood* (1990), Book 2 (1991) Antique Publications; Eric Reynolds, *The Glass of John Walsh,* Richard Dennis Publications, distributed by Antique Collectors' Club, 1999.

Blown

Barber Bottle
    Polka Dot, cranberry, old top 200.00
    Raised Swirl, cranberry 295.00
    Seaweed, cranberry 365.00
    Swirl, blue 225.00
Berry Bowl, master, Chrysanthemum Base Swirl, blue, satin 95.00
Biscuit Jar, cov, Spanish Lace, vaseline 275.00
Bride's Basket, Poinsettia, ruffled top 275.00
Butter Dish, cov, Hobbs Hobnail, vaseline 250.00
Celery Vase, Seaweed, cranberry 250.00
Creamer
    Coin Dot, cranberry 190.00
    Gonterman Swirl, blue, frosted 625.00
    Windows Swirl, cranberry 500.00
Cruet
    Chrysanthemum Base Swirl, white, satin 175.00
    Ribbed Opal Lattice, white 135.00
Finger Bowl, Hobbs Hobnail, cranberry 65.00
Lamp, oil
    Inverted Thumbprint, white, amber fan base 145.00
    Snowflake, cranberry 800.00
Mustard, cov, Reverse Swirl, vaseline 165.00
Pickle Castor, Daisy and Fern, blue, emb floral jar, DQ, resilvered frame 650.00
Pitcher
    Arabian Nights, white 450.00
    Fern, blue 450.00
    Hobbs Hobnail, cranberry 315.00
    Reverse Swirl, blue, satin, speckled 495.00
    Seaweed, blue 525.00

Miniature Lamp, Spanish Lace base, blue ground, Smith #40, 4" h, $225.

Spot Resist (Polka Dot) white, applied clear handle, closely ruffled top 245.00
    Windows, cranberry 695.00
Rose Bowl, Opal Swirl, white 40.00
Salt Shaker, orig top
    Consolidated Criss-Cross, cranberry 85.00
    Ribbed Opal Lattice, cranberry 95.00
Spooner, Reverse Swirl, cranberry 165.00
Sugar, cov, Reverse Swirl, cranberry 350.00
Sugar Shaker
    Coin Spot, cranberry 275.00
    Ribbed Opal Lattice, cranberry 325.00
Syrup, Coin Spot, cranberry 175.00
Tumbler
    Acanthus, blue 90.00
    Bubble Lattice, cranberry 135.00
    Christmas Snowflake, blue, ribbed 125.00
    Maze, swirling, green 95.00
    Reverse Swirl, cranberry 65.00
    Swirl, blue 95.00
Waste Bowl, Hobbs Hobnail, vaseline 75.00

Novelties

Back Bar Bottle, 12-1/4" h, robin's egg blue ground, opalescent stripes swirled to the right 100.00
Barber Bottle, 8" h, sq, diamond pattern molded form, light cranberry, white vertical stripes 275.00
Bowl
    Grape and Cherry, blue 85.00
    Ruffles and Rings, white 35.00
    Winter Cabbage, white 45.00
Bushel Basket, blue 75.00
Chalice, Maple Leaf, vaseline 45.00
Cruet, Stars and Stripes, cranberry 575.00
Epergne, 19" h, 10-1/2" d, clear to opalescent to cranberry edge, IVT bowl, resilvered base, lily vase holder 475.00
Jack-in-the-Pulpit, 7-1/2" h, 6" d, DQ base, opalescent shading to lighter to darker maroon, hobnail effect blossom 110.00
Vase, 16" h, 4-1/2" d, ruffled lily, pink vase, resilvered holder 295.00

Pressed

Berry Bowl, master
    Tokyo, green 60.00
    Wreath & Shell, blue 185.00
Berry Set, master, 6 sauces, Iris with Meander, vaseline 180.00
Butter Dish, cov
    Iris with Meander 395.00
    Water Lily and Cattails, blue 300.00
Card Receiver, Fluted Scrolls, white 40.00
Compote, Hearts & Flowers, Northwood, blue opale-scent 25.00
Cracker Jar, cov, Wreath and Shell, vaseline 750.00
Creamer
    Alaska, blue 85.00
    Inverted Fan and Feather, blue 125.00
    Swag with Brackets, green 90.00
Cruet, Fluted Scrolls, blue, clear stopper 295.00
Jelly Compote
    Intaglio, blue 30.00
    Iris with Meander, blue 42.00
Salt and Pepper Shakers, pr, Jewel and Flower, canary yellow, orig tops 250.00
Sauce
    Alaska, blue 55.00
    Wreath & Shell 45.00
Spooner
    Alaska, blue or white 85.00
    Jewel & Flower, blue, gold trim 85.00
Sugar, cov, Alaska, blue 225.00
Syrup, Coin Spot, blue, orig top, ring neck 145.00

Toothpick Holder, Ribbed Spiral, blue 90.00
Tumbler
    Alaska, blue 110.00
    Drapery, blue 90.00
    Jackson, green 50.00
    Jeweled Heart, blue 85.00
Vase, Northwood Diamond Point, blue 75.00
Water Pitcher, Jewel & Flower, white, gold trim 280.00

OPALINE GLASS

History: Opaline glass was a popular mid- to late 19th-century European glass. The glass has a certain amount of translucency and often is found decorated with enamel designs and trimmed in gold.

Biscuit Jar, cov, white ground, hp, florals and birds dec, brass lid and
    bail handle 165.00
Bouquet Holder, 7" h, blue opaline cornucopia shaped gilt dec flower
    holders issuing from bronze stag heads, Belgian black marble base,
    English, Victorian, early 19th C, pr 725.00
Box, cov, gilt metal, blue, Continental, early 20th C
    4-1/2" l, mint green 400.00
    5-3/8" l, rect, domed 250.00
    7-1/2" l, egg-shaped 295.00
Candelabra, Louis XV style, late 19th C
    18-1/2" h, gilt bronze and blue opaline, scrolled candle arms and
    base, two-light 175.00
    26-1/2" h, gilt metal and blue opaline, five-light 400.00
Chalice, white ground, Diamond Point pattern 35.00
Chandelier, 25" h, 16" d, French Empire style, ormolu mounted opaline
    glass bowl, acorn cast finial issuing 5 "S" scroll arms ending in opa-
    line glass candle cups, surmounted by opaline glass shaft with shell
    cast corona 1,500.00
Dresser Jar, 5-1/2" d, egg shape, blue ground, heavy gold dec . 200.00
Ewer, 13-1/4" h, white ground, Diamond Point pattern 135.00
Jardinieres, 5-1/4" h, gilt bronze and blue opaline, sq, Empire style,
    tasseled chains, paw feet, early 20th C, pr 1,610.00
Mantel Lusters, 12-3/4" h, blue, gilt dec, slender faceted prisms, Victo-
    rian, c1880, damage, pr 250.00
Oil Lamp, 24" h, dolphin-form stepped base, clear glass oil well,
    frosted glass shade, late 19th C, converted to electric, chips .. 460.00

Jack-In-The-Pulpit Vase, robin's egg blue body, applied amber feet, 5-1/2" h, $120.

Oil Lamp Base, 22" h, blue, baluster turned standard on circular foot,
    20th C, converted to electric, pr 635.00
Perfume Bottle, 3-1/8" d, 7-3/4" h, tapering cylinder, flat flared base
    white ,ring of white opaline around neck and matching teardrop stop-
    per, gold trim 115.00
Salt, boat shaped, blue dec, white enamel garland and scrolling ... 75.00
Sconces, pr, 14-1/2" h, 11" w, French Empire style, pointed oval black
    plate centering paterae supporting ormolu-mounted opaline glass
    flambeau with acorn cast finial, issuing pair of "S" scroll arms ending
    in opaline glass candle cups 1,900.00
Tazza, 5" h, opaline bowl, openwork base cast with acanthus and flow-
    ers, conforming ormolu mounts at rim, French, late 19th C 275.00
Vase, 13" h, enamel dec, ftd base with foliage bordered by stylized
    arabesques suspending beads, gilt wood base, French, late 19th C,
    mounted as lamps, pr 250.00

ORIENTALIA

History: Orientalia is a term applied to objects made in the Orient, an area which encompasses the Far East, Asia, China, and Japan. The diversity of cultures produced a variety of objects and styles.

References: Sandra Andacht, *Collector's Guide To Oriental Decorative Arts,* Antique Trader Books, 1997; —, *Collector's Value Guide to Japanese Woodblock Prints,* Antique Trader Books, 1999; Carl L. Crossman, *The Decorative Arts of the China Trade,* Antique Collectors' Club, 1999; Christopher Dresser, *Traditional Arts and Crafts of Japan,* Dover Publications, 1994; R. L. Hobson and A L. Hetherington, *Art of the Chinese Potter,* Dover Publications, 1983; Duncan Macintosh, *Chinese Blue and White Porcelain,* Antique Collectors Club, 1994; Gloria and Robert Mascarelli, *Warman's Oriental Antiques,* Wallace-Homestead, 1992; Nancy N. Schiffer, *Imari, Satsuma, and Other Japanese Export Ceramics,* Schiffer Publishing, 1997; Jana Volf, *Treasures of the Chinese Glass Work Shops,* Asiantiques, 1997.

Periodical: *Orientalia Journal,* P.O. Box 94, Flushing, NY 11363-0094, http://members.aol.com/Orientalia/index.html.

Collectors' Club: China Student's Club, 59 Standish Rd., Wellesley, MA 02181.

Museums: Art Institute of Chicago, Chicago, IL; Asian Art Museum of San Francisco, San Francisco, CA; George Walter Vincent Smith Art Museum, Springfield, MA; Morikami Museum & Japanese Gardens, Delray Beach, FL; Pacific Asia Museum, Pasadena, CA.

Additional Listings: Canton; Celadon; Cloisonné; Fitzhugh; Nanking; Netsukes; Rose Medallion; Japanese Prints; and other related categories.

Altar Coffer
    22" l, 16" d, 12" h, low, elm, rect top over single short drawer over
    single panel, flanked by shaped edges over shaped apron, block
    feet, Northern Chinese, mid 19th C 300.00
    58" l, 18-1/4" d, 31-1/2" d, cedar, rect top with short curved wings
    on either end, over three short drawers over two cupboard doors
    flanked by dragon with bat relief carvings, bracket feet, Chinese,
    19th C 550.00
Altar Stick, 20-1/2" h, cast bronze, Tibetan 250.00
Box, cov
    6-1/2" l, 7-1/2" h, four tier, lacquer, gilt cranes, sea and mountain
    landscape, Japanese 65.00
    16-1/2" l, 10-3/4" h, lacquered and painted, alternating figure in
    landscape and floral panels, metal lock, Chinese 125.00

Bowl, 6" d, 3" h, silver, chrysanthemum dec and shaped rim, pierced low foot, Canton, Sing Fat maker, early 20th C, 11 troy oz 345.00

Brush Washer, 5" l, carved green quartz, oval, relief carved vines, hardwood stand, Chinese 45.00

Candlestick, 10-1/4" h, bronze, figural, elegant lady, circular bronze base, Thai 150.00

Censor, 7-1/2" d, 5" h, bronze, flared sides, 3 elephant head feet, pierced rect form handles with scrolled corners, brown patination splashed all-over with irregular gilded areas, Chinese, 18th C 11,500.00

Cordial, 1-3/4" h, silver, applied chrysanthemum dec, Chinese, minor imperfections, 8 pc set 200.00

Dish, 8" d, Nabeshima, underglaze blue, iron red and green enamels, flowering branches, 3 mitsu tomoye, late 19th C, surface scratches 300.00

Dressing Box, 15" w, 11" d, 9-1/2" h, mother of pearl inlaid rosewood, fitted int. with mirror and drawers, ext. with scrolled foliage inlay, Chinese Export, late 19th C 850.00

Embroidered Picture, 80" x 41-1/2", Bird and Butterflies in Landscape with Bamboo and Peonies, silk, Chinese, 19th C 450.00

Figure

5-1/4" h, Buddha, seated in lotus position below serpent, bronze, Khmer 200.00

8" h, carved rose quartz, bird perched on tree trunk, hardwood stand, Chinese 190.00

10-3/4" h, Guanyin, holding basket, carved from rock crystal, separate rock crystal lotus-form base, Chinese, Qing dynasty ... 550.00

16-1/2" h, carved and painted wood, horse, standing, saddle and bridle, Chinese, 17th C 475.00

21" h, gilt bronze, Buddha, standing, hand raised, foliate dec tiered stand, Tibetan, 19th C 550.00

38" h, Foo Dog, green and mustard, two parts, glazed pottery, some chips, Chinese 250.00

Furniture

Altar Table, Chinese, late 19th C, carved rosewood, flush paneled molded rect top, scroll-carved frieze carved with thousand-gift motifs, rect section end supports of open panel form, 61-3/4" l, 16-1/2" w, 34-1/2" h 400.00

Armoire, Northern China, 18th C, red lacquer, rect top over front with pair of flush paneled doors, shelved int. with storage well, stile legs joined by pierced and carved frieze, 46-3/4" w, 18-3/4" d, 70-1/2" h 750.00

Chair, arm, Anglo-Chinese, c1900, carved and lacquered hardwood, arched cartouche shaped back centered by a quatrefoil panel painted with ho-ho bird, serpentine-fronted solid seat similarly painted, flanked by dragon-form arms, cabriole legs, carved throughout with dragons and scrolling clouds 120.00

Desk, Anglo-Chinese, partner's, rosewood, rect flush paneled top over frieze with 4 paneled drawers and 4 opposing drawers, each pedestal with further 2 drawers and 2 opposing drawers, beaded sq section legs joined by lattice work platform stretcher, 41-1/2" l, 28-1/4" d, 33" h 1,500.00

Low Table, Chinese, black lacquer, rect top, mother of pearl floral inlay, straight profusely carved legs, 22-1/4" w, 18" d, 22" h, pr 400.00

Low Table, Northern China, 19th C, bamboo and elmwood, rect molded top, inset lattice-work panel, lattice-work frieze on cluster legs, 51" l, 29-3/4" w, 18-1/2" h 600.00

Low Table, Northern China, 19th C, elmwood, rect molded flush paneled top, turned legs joined by pierced frame, 37-1/4" w, 37-1/4" d, 17-1/2" h 600.00

Music Table, Northern China, 19th C, black lacquered, rect flush paneled top, molded sq section legs with pad feet, pierced frieze continuing into brackets, 86" l, 18" d, 34" h 850.00

Official Armchair, Northern China, 19th C, painted elmwood, open rect back, yoke-form crest over bent splat, solid seat with molded sunken panel, out-curved arms, molded square section legs joined by box stretcher 625.00

Painting Table, Northern China, 19th C, bamboo, rect top over pierced frieze filled with geometric lattice-work panels, each end raised on four legs joined by box stretcher, 74-1/2" l, 20-3/4" w, 33" h 1,300.00

Painting Table, Northern China, 19th C, black lacquer, molded rect flush paneled top, molded sq section legs joined by pierced scroll frieze, tapered block feet, 71" l, 31-1/3" w, 34-1/2" h 850.00

Plant Stand, Chinese, late 19th C, 7-3/4" w, 7-3/4" d, 18-3/4" h, rosewood, rect molded flush paneled top, concave frieze centering foliate scrollwork, molded sq section legs joined by stepped box stretcher 95.00

Side Table, Chinese, painted, rect molded flush paneled top, front with arrangement of 3 frieze drawers over 4 molded panels, sq section legs, 51-3/4" l, 21-1/2" w, 35" h 375.00

Stool, Northern China, 19th C, elmwood, low, molded rect flush paneled top, molded sq section legs joined by arched frieze, molded box stretcher, 20-1/4" w, 17-1/2" d, 20-3/4" h 500.00

Writing Table, Anglo-Chinese, scarlet lacquer, molded rect top painted with figural landscape, front with central frieze drawer flanked on each side by 2 further drawers, kneehole flanked by scrolled brackets, sq section legs, floral sprays and scroll work dec, black highlights, 54-1/4" l, 24-1/2" w, 32" h 200.00

Loo Counter, 3-5/8" x 2-5/8", tabs inlaid with mother of pearl and semi-precious stone insects, center similarly inlaid with vase of flowers, ivory mounts, Chinese Export 200.00

Medicine Chest, Northern China, 19th C, elmwood, rect top with sunken panel, front with 16 drawers, each drawer front inscribed with Chinese characters, int. with compartments, stile legs with brackets, 36" w, 22" d, 43-1/4" h 800.00

Paste Box, cov, 3" d, Peking enamel, figural reserve, pink floral ground, Chinese 135.00

Pencil Box, 11-3/4" l, papier-mâché, int. with rust, silver, and gilt figures on blue ground, Japanese 75.00

Plaque, rect carved rosewood frame, center blue and white dec porcelain plaque, gilt bat and cloud dec on black ground, Chinese, 19th C . 650.00

Presentation Coffee Pot, 10-3/4" h, silver, pear-shaped, four scroll and shell feet, body chased and emb with leaves to lower portion and serpentine spout, reeded and leaf handle, ivory heat stops, lid with flower form finial, engraved with 1853 dated inscription, Khecheong maker, mid 19th C, 47 troy oz 3,150.00

Robe, silk, gilt thread and multicolored floral embroidery, blue ground, Chinese 250.00

Sake Pot, 4-1/4" h, iron, large spiked design shoulder, gently curving handle, Japanese, Edo Period, damage, later lid 150.00

Seal Box, 3" d, white biscuit, oval, 2 molded writhing dragons chasing pearl among sea and clouds, movable dragon's eyes and pearl, imp Qianlong seal mark on base, late 19th C 245.00

Shrine, 35" h, lacquer, pierced interior doors open to reveal elaborate interior, Japanese 475.00

Staff Handle, 4" l, rock crystal, lion head above carved floral motif, Mongol style, 19th C 475.00

Table Screen, 26" h, wood mounted brass, etched figural dec, Chinese, Qing dynasty 200.00

Tea Canister, 18" h, tin, painted and gilded, Chinese Export, mounted as lamp 750.00

Tea Service, silver, 6" h teapot, creamer, cov sugar, cov waste bowl, 6-1/2" h milk jug, stippled ground, applied dec of trees, chrysanthemums, and cranes, bamboo-style handles and lid finials, mkd "Zeewo" maker, early 20th C, 62 troy oz 1,840.00

Temple Fu Lions, 35-1/4" h, stone, one with paw raised on sphere, other with paw on dragon, Chinese, pr 4,500.00

Trunk, 34-31/2" w, 18-1/4" d, 16-1/4" h, camphorwood, brass bound, covered in painted leather, hinged rect lid, storage well, ext. painted with floral panels in shaded ivory on red ground, late 19th C .. 200.00

Tsuba, bronze, cast and pierced, Japanese, Meiji period

Dragon, gilt highlights 250.00

Mythological beast on rockery 400.00

Oni and figures in pavilion, gilt highlights 700.00

Umbrella Stand, 23-1/2" h, champleve enamel, Chinese 350.00

Urn, 9" h, 10-1/2" d, bronze, globular, stylized geometric banding, ridged ground, Chinese 250.00

Vase, earthenware, baluster, Imperial procession spirals around body, brocade panels at neck and foot, sgd in gold "yabu meizan," Japanese, c1890-1900, gilt wear, 5-7/8" h, $1,150. Photo courtesy of Freeman\Fine Arts.

Vase
  8-1/2" h, mixed metal, ovoid bronze vase, inlaid silver landscape dec 175.00
  9-3/4" h, bronze, cast, cranes dec, Japanese, Meiji period 175.00
  10" h, silver, cylindrical, engraved pagoda, trees, and mountains, Japanese, 22 oz, 4 dwt 450.00
  24-1/4" h, bronze, trumpet form, applied floral and leaf dec, Japanese, minor damage 250.00
Water Dropper, 4" d, melon glazed porcelain, flattened ovoid form, small rim, incised 4 character Chinese mark, 19th C 325.00
Writing Box, 16" w, 9-3/4" d, 20" h, mahogany, inlaid with MOP foliate spray, surrounded by border of birds and flowers, velvet writing surface and compartments, later stand, Chinese 475.00

ORIENTAL RUGS

History: Oriental rugs or carpets date back to 3,000 b.c.; but it was in the 16th century that they became prevalent. The rugs originated in the regions of Central Asia, Iran (Persia), Caucasus, and Anatolia. Early rugs can be classified into basic categories: Iranian, Caucasian, Turkoman, Turkish, and Chinese. Later India, Pakistan, and Iraq produced rugs in the Oriental style.

The pattern name is derived from the tribe which produced the rug, e.g., Iran is the source for Hamadan, Herez, Sarouk, and Tabriz.

References: J. R. Azizollahoff, *The Illustrated Buyer's Guide to Oriental Carpets,* Schiffer, 1998; Walter A. Hawley, *Oriental Rugs, Antique and Modern,* Dover Publications, 1970; Charles W. Jacobsen, *Check Points on How to Buy Oriental Rugs,* Charles E. Tuttle Co., 1981; Robert Pinner and Murray L. Eiland, Jr., *Between the Black Desert and the Red Turkmen Carpets from the Wiedersperg Collection,* Fine Arts Museum of San Francisco, distributed by Antique Collectors' Club, 1999; Pamela Thomas, *Oriental Rugs,* Smithmark, 1996.

Periodicals: HALI, P.O. Box 4312, Philadelphia, PA 19118; *Oriental Rug Review,* P.O. Box 709, Meredith, NH 03253, http://www.rugreview.com/orr.htm; *Orientalia Journal,* P.O. Box 94, Flushing, NY 11363-0094, http://members.aol/com/Orientalia/index.html; *Rug News,* 34 West 37th St., New York, NY 10018.

Reproduction Alert: Beware! There are repainted rugs on the market.

Notes: When evaluating an Oriental rug, age, design, color, weave, knots per square inch, and condition determine the final value. Silk rugs and prayer rugs bring higher prices than other types.

Afshar, South Persia, late 19th C, 4'8" x 3'6", 2 hooked diamonds and leaf motifs, red, royal blue, gold, and blue-green on midnight blue field, large ivory and midnight blue diagonal striped spandrels, red floral meander border, slight moth damage, minor end fraying 920.00
Akstafa, East Caucasus, third quarter 19th C, 8' x 3'9", 4 gabled sq medallions, 10 peacock motifs, red, royal blue, apricot, gold, aubergine, and blue-green on midnight blue field, ivory hooked sq border, small areas of wear, small rewoven areas, guard stripes and border partially missing from both ends 1,610.00
Bahktiari, West Persia, second quarter 20th C
  6'8" x 5'3", hexagonal lattice with flowering plants, navy blue, rd, black, ivory, rose, gold aubergine-brown, and dark blue-green, ivory palmette and vine border 2,300.00
  10'4" x 3', 3 notched medallions inset with cypress trees, surrounded by flowering plant motifs, red, royal blue, ivory, gold, aubergine-brown, light and dark blue green on midnight blue field, large gold spandrels, narrow red floral meander border, slight wear to center, border partially missing from one end, small hole, crude repairs 2,100.00
  13'4" x 10'8", serrated diamond lattice, flowering plants, boteh, and cypress trees, midnight, navy, and royal blue, red, rose, gold, red-brown, ivory, cream, and blue-green, abrashed navy blue rosette and diamond cartouche border, small areas of minorwear, small rewoven areas 6,325.00
Baluch, Northeast Persia
  Late 19th C, 3'6" x 2'7", 3 columns of flowering plants, navy and sky blue, light red, aubergine, camel field, multicolored compartmented "X" motif border, even center wear, small creases 1,265.00
  Late 19th/early 20th C, 5'2" x 3'2", column of 4 Turkoman-style octagonal turret guls, red, navy blue, ivory, brown, and aubergine, 2 navy blue and brown rosette borders, even center wear, brown corrosion 575.00
  Second half 19th C, 8'6" x 4'9", cruciform medallion surrounded by 4 large palmette motifs, 4 hooked triangles, rust, red, navy blue, ivory, and brown on midnight blue field, red hooked vine border, small areas of wear, brown corrosion 2,100.00
Bidjar, Northwest Persia, early 20th C
  5'3" x 4', dense overall Herati design, dark red, rose, royal blue, tan, and blue-green on midnight blue field, red palmette border, some moth damage 1,610.00
  13' x 10'4", Mina Khani floral lattice, royal and ice blue, red, black, gold, camel, and blue-green on ivory field, abrashed royal blue turtle border, slight moth damage 8,100.00
Chodor Mafrash, West Turkestan, second half 19th C, 4'5" x 1'7", staggered rows of Ertmann guls, midnight blue, red, ivory, and gold on dark aubergine field, diamond motif border of similar coloration, edges reduced into main border, stains 1,495.00
Ersari Chuval, West Turkestan, last quarter 19th C
  5' x 3'2", horizontal bands of geometric, floral, and border motifs, midnight and navy blue, apricot, gold, ivory, brown, and blue-green on rust-red field, flowering plant elem of similar coloration, even center wear, slight end fraying 1,035.00
  5'4" x 3'8", staggered rows of hexagons, apricot, ivory, midnight

and navy blue on rust field, hooked sq border, flowering plant
elem of similar coloration, even center wear, small repair .. 850.00
Ersari Torba, West Turkestan, last quarter 19th C, 3'10" x 1'5", staggered rows of diamonds, each surrounded by 4 rhomboids, red, rose,
gold, and ivory on variegated blue field, "C" motif border, slight moth
damage, small repairs 1,955.00
Fachralo Kazak, Southwest Caucacus, last quarter 19th C, 4'9" x 3'8",
large concentric gabled sq medallion, hooked motifs, ivory, royal
blue, gold, and blue-green, on red field, ivory floral meander border,
creases, slight end fraying 3,220.00
Fereghan-Sarouk, West Persia, last quarter 19th C, 6'6" x 4'2", large
lobed oval medallion and floral sprays, midnight, navy, and sky blue,
red, gold, rose, red-brown and blue-green on ivory field, red spandrels,
midnight blue rosette border, areas of minor wear, small tear .2,415.00
Gendje, South Central Persia, last quarter 19th C, 14'6" x 4'4", column
of ashik gul-in-squares flanked by chevron oriented diagonal stripes,
navy blue, sky blue, red, ivory, gold, light rust, aubergine, and blue-
green, multicolored ashik gul-in-diamond border, small areas of wear,
creases................... 3,795.00
Hamadan, Northwest Persia, second quarter 20th C, 17' x 12', overall
design of palmettes, rosettes, and blossoming vines, royal blue, sky
blue, dark red, rose, apricot, tan, ivory, and blue-green on abrashed
midnight blue field, red flowerhead and serrated leaf border .10,350.00
Heriz, Northwest Persia, early 20th C
    5' x 4', rosette medallion, palmette pendants, serrated leaves, red,
    rose, gold, red-brown, ivory, and abrashed blue-green on royal
    blue field, gold crab border, small areas of slight wear, slight end
    fraying 2,100.00
    7' x 4'10", indented hexagonal medallion surrounded by palmette
    motifs, midnight and sky blue, red, camel, ivory, and blue-green
    on dark rust-red field, ivory spandrels, midnight blue turtle border,
    small area of minor wear, slight end fraying.................... 3,220.00
Kashan, West Central Persia, second quarter 20th C
    6'8" x 4'3", large flowering tree with birds and animals, navy and
    sky blue, red, rose, tan, brown, olive and pale green on ivory field,
    red palmette border, slight wear to center 2,530.00
    7'8" x 5'2", circular medallion and dense blossoming vines,
    cochineal, royal blue, rose, camel, tan-gold, and light blue-green
    on midnight blue field, ivory spandrels, cochineal palmette and
    leafy vine border, new fringes added 4,715.00
Kazak, Southwest Caucacus, last quarter 19th C
    6' x 6'3", hooked diamond flanked by 2 notched medallions, red,
    ivory, gold, brown, and blue-green on abrashed sky blue field, ivory
    hook motif border, small areas of wear, small repairs.........2,645.00
    6'6" x 3'9", dated 1883, 3 stepped diamond medallions flanked by
    flowerheads, red, ivory, gold, rust, and dark blue-green on mid-
    night blue field, wide ivory "S" motif, serrated leaf border, small
    areas of wear, creases, selvage damage, small hole 2,760.00
Khamseh, Southwest Persia, early 20th C, 8'6" x 5'6", 3 stepped diamond medallions surrounded by small bird and geometric motifs, red,
ivory, navy blue, gold, and blue-green on midnight blue field, narrow
ivory floral meander border, slight even wear 1,840.00
Kuba, Northeast Caucasus, last quarter 19th C, 5'2" x 3'8", 3 Lesghi
stars, red, sky blue, ivory, gold, and blue-green on abrashed navy
blue field, navy blue hooked cross motif border, even wear to center,
black corrosion, slight end fraying........................ 2,415.00
Kurd, Northwest Persia, late 19th C
    8' x 5'9", rows of vases with flowers, red, sky blue, gold, ivory, dark
    gray, and blue-green on midnight blue field, wide abrashed red
    hooked octagon border, small areas of wear, small rewoven area,
    guard stripe partially missing from one end 1,380.00
    12'4" x 4'2", column of 6 hooked and serrated hexagonal medallions
    flanked by pairs of small medallions, red, medium blue, ivory, gold,
    and light olive on abrashed navy blue field, wide ivory crab border,
    even center wear, slight moth damage, small repairs........2,550.00
Mahal, West Persia, early 20th C
    12'6" x 8'10", overall floral sprays, red, rose, royal blue, apricot,
    gold, camel, ivory, and blue-green on abrashed midnight blue
    field, red flowerhead and vine border, small areas of wear, small
    tear, slight moth damage 1,380.00

Serapi, red, ivory, and blue geometric center medallion, red field, bold conforming corner pockets, stylized floral geometric ivory band borders, 15' x 11'4", stain, $21,280. Photo courtesy of Freeman\Fine Arts.

    14" x 10'9", overall Herati design, red, sky blue, rose, gold, ivory,
    olive, and blue-green on abrashed navy blue field, light blue-
    green flowerhead and vine border, small areas of wear, slight
    moth damage 3,220.00
Melas, Southwest Anatolia, second half 19th C, 5'4" x 3'9", 4 small diamond medallions, red, sky blue, ivory, gold, aubergine, light blue-
green on rust field, ivory diamond motif spandrels, gold star and
paired rosetted border, small re-piled areas, one end rewoven,
crease repair 2,300.00
Qashqai, Southwest Persia, late 19th C, 8' x 4'2", 3 diamond medallions surrounded by small floral, geometric, and bird motifs, ivory,
navy blue, red, gold, aubergine, and light blue-green on midnight
blue field, 3 narrow floral meander borders, slight even center wear,
small repairs........................ 4,890.00
Sarouk, West Persia, early 20th C, 6'8" x 4'3", vases of blossoms, floral
sprays, pendant flowering vines, midnight, slate, and sky blue, gold,
apricot, ivory, brown, green, and blue-green on rose field, midnight
blue palmette and serrated leaf border, slight edge wear........ 3,500.00
Seichour, Northeast Caucasus, second half 19th C, 3'10" x 3', 2 large
notched diamond medallions and small floral motifs, midnight and
sky blue, red, rose, gold, aubergine, and blue-green on ivory field,
red rosette border, sky blue and ivory "Georgian" outer border, even
wear, rewoven areas on ends and edges, other repairs 3,750.00
Senneh, Northwest Persia, last quarter 19th C, 3'2" x 3'2" saddle
cover, overall Herati design, red, rose, ivory, gold, and pale blue-
green on midnight blue field, red spandrels, gold floral meander border, outer guard stripe missing from both edges.................. 1,840.00
Shahsavan Soumak, Northwest Persia, last quarter 19th C, 2' x 1'10"
bag, single octagonal Memling gul surrounded by "S" motifs, red, sky
blue, ivory, gold, and blue-green on navy blue field, ivory pinwheel
border, small crude repairs.................... 1,265.00
Shirvan, East Caucasus, last quarter 19th C
    5'6" x 4', large keyhole type medallion inset with 8 octagons, red,
    abrashed sky blue, ivory, gold, red-brown, and dark blue-green on
    midnight blue field, ivory sq motif border, even wear, small areas
    of piling 1,955.00
    9'4", 3'10", column of 6 stepped hexagonal medallions flanked by
    14 squares, blue, red, ivory, gold, and blue-green on midnight
    blue field, reciprocal trefoil border of similar coloration, small
    areas of moth damage, crude repairs............................ 2,875.00
Sileh, Southweat Caucasus, last quarter 19th C, 6' x 5'4", rows of

squares each inset with four "S" motifs, red, sky blue, ivory, black, and blue-green on gold field, gold diamond-in-square border, 3 holes, slight moth damage 980.00

Sultanabad, West Persia, last quarter 19th C, 11'2" x 8'8", staggered circular rosette medallions, each surrounded by palmette motifs and leafy vines, midnight and slate blue, red, tan, rose, brown, and light blue-green on ivory field, blue-green turtle border, areas of wear, slight end fraying 3,450.00

Tabriz, Northwest Persia

Early 20th C, 5'4" x 3'8", silk, overall palmettes, cloud bands, and blossoming vines, blue, rose, ivory, and light green on red field, light green and metal thread spandrels and cross panel, cream palmette and paired leaf border 2,415.00

Late 19th C, 12'8" x 9'2", concentric hexagonal medallions, matching spandrels, overall Herati design, navy blue, rust, gold, and blue-green on ivory field, rust rosette and palmette border, even wear 9,775.00

Turkoman, West Turestan, late 19th/early 20th C, 7'4" x 7'4", trapping, diamond lattice design, various fabrics and techniques, dark red, black, gold aubergine, ivory, and green, fabric losses and replacement 350.00

Uzbek, Central Asia, l9th C, 6' x 4', horse cover, large rosette filled botch surrounded by long serrted leaves and floral groups, sky and ice blue, cochineal, rose, gold, ivory, apricot, and light blue-green on dark brown field, palmette border, embroidery losses 750.00

Yomud Chuval, West Turkestan

Early 20th C, 4' x 2'6", 16 chuval guls in navy blue, aubergine on dark rust-red field, ivory cross motif border, plain elem, slight moth damage 550.00

Last quarter 19th C, 4' x 2', 9 chuval guls, midnight blue, red, ivory, and blue-green on rust field, ivory syrga border, edges slightly reduced, re-overcast, elem missing 865.00

Yuruk, East Anatolia, late 19th C, 6' x 3'9", 4 hooked diamonds and rows of small stars, dark slate and sky blue, rust, apricot, ivory, gold, and blue-green on conchieal field, abrashed blue-green rosette and diamond border, re-piled and rewoven areas 1,265.00

OVERSHOT GLASS

History: Overshot glass was developed in the mid-1800s. To produce overshot glass, a gather of molten glass was rolled over the marver upon which had been placed crushed glass. The piece then was blown into the desired shape. The finished product appeared to be frosted or iced.

Early pieces were made mainly in clear glass. As the demand for colored glass increased, color was added to the base piece and occasionally to the crushed glass.

Pieces of overshot generally are attributed to the Boston and Sandwich Glass Co. although many other companies also made it as it grew in popularity.

Museum: Sandwich Glass Museum, Sandwich, MA.

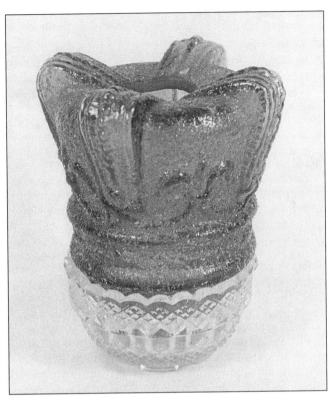

Fairy Lamp, crown shape, blue top, clear Clarke base, $150.

Basket, 7-1/4" h, 5" d, transparent green shading to colorless, ruffled swirled edge, sq thorn handle, melon-ribbed base with pineapple-like design, entire surface with overshot finish 285.00

Bowl, 6" d, 3-7/8" h, pale blue opaque, applied amber rigaree around top, applied green leaves, white, pink, and blue applied flowers 235.00

Celery Vase, 6" h, 3-1/2" d, scalloped top, cranberry ground 90.00

Cheese Dish, dome cov, 8" d, 7" h, cranberry ground, enameled crane and cattails, applied colorless faceted finial 425.00

Compote, 10" d, 10-1/4" h, cranberry ground, wide rounded bowl, scalloped crown gilt trimmed rim, compressed knop on cylindrical pedestal, wide flaring foot, late 19th C 300.00

Epergne, 9-1/2" d, 17" h, single lily, colorless ground, applied green snake coiled around lily and extending to pedestal base 220.00

Fairy Lamp, 4-1/4" h, 3" d, opalescent, figural, crown shape, colorless pressed "Clark" base 195.00

Pitcher

8-1/4" h, green ground, amber shell handle, Sandwich, c1875, brown age line near lip 225.00

9" h, tankard, cranberry ground, applied colorless reeded handle, hinged metal lid 195.00

Vase, 5-1/2" h, pink ground, applied random amber threading 225.00

PADEN CITY GLASS

History: Paden City Glass Manufacturing Co. was founded in 1916 in Paden City, West Virginia. David Fisher, formerly of the New Martinsville Glass Manufacturing Co., operated the company until his death in 1933, at which time his son, Samuel, became president. A management decision in 1949 to expand Paden City's production by acquiring American Glass Company, an automated manufacturer of bottles, ashtrays, and novelties, strained the company's finances, forcing them to close permanently in 1951.

Contrary to popular belief and previously incorrect printed references, The Paden City Glass Manufacturing Company had absolutely no connection with the Paden City Pottery Company, other than its identical locale.

Although Paden City glass is often lumped with mass-produced, machine-made wares into the Depression Glass category, Paden City's wares were, until 1948, all hand-made. The company's products are better classified as "Elegant Glass" of the era as it ranks in quality with the wares produced by contemporaries such as Fostoria, New Martinsville, and Morgantown.

Paden City kept a low profile, never advertising in consumer magazines of the day. It never marked its glass in any way because a large portion of its business consisted of sales to decorating companies, mounters, and fitters. The firm also supplied bars, restaurants, and soda fountains with glassware, as evidenced by the wide range of tumblers, ice cream dishes, and institutional products available in several Paden City patterns.

Paden City's decorating shop also etched, cut, hand painted, and applied silver overlay and gold encrustation. However, not every decoration found on Paden City shapes will necessarily have come from the factory. Cupid, Peacock and Rose, and several other etchings depicting birds are among the most sought after decorations. Pieces with these etchings are commanding higher and higher prices even though they were apparently made in greater quantities than some of the etchings that are less-known (but just as beautiful).

Paden City is noted for its colors: opal (opaque white), ebony, mulberry (amethyst), Cheriglo (delicate pink), yellow, dark green (forest), crystal, amber, primrose (reddish-amber), blue, rose, and great quantities of ruby (red). The firm also produced transparent green in numerous shades ranging from yellowish to a distinctive electric green that always alerts knowledgeable collectors to its Paden City origin.

Rising collector interest in Paden City glass has resulted in a sharp spike in prices on some items. Advanced collectors seek out examples with unusual and/or undocumented etchings. Colored pieces which sport an etching that is not usually found on that particular color are especially sought after, and are bringing strong prices. In contrast, prices for common items with Peacock and Rose etch remain static, and the prices for dinnerware in ruby Penny Line and pink or green Party Line have inched up only slightly, due to its greater availability.

References: Jerry Barnett, *Paden City, The Color Company*, privately printed, 1979, out-of-print; Lee Garmon and Dick Spencer, *Glass Animals of the Depression Era*, Collector Books, 1993; Naomi L. Over, *Ruby Glass of the 20th Century*, The Glass Press, 1990, 1993-94 value update, Book II, 1999; Hazel Marie Weatherman, *Colored Glassware of the Depression Era 2*, Glassbooks, 1974.

Advisor: Michael Krumme.

Color is crystal (clear) unless otherwise noted.

Bowl, nappy, #412 Crow's Foot Square
   5", ruby 35.00
   9-1/2" oval, ruby 45.00
Bowl, 2-handled serving:
   #215 Glades, Spring Orchard etch 50.00
   #221 Maya, light blue 57.50
Cake Salver, footed
   #300 Archaic, Gothic Garden etch, topaz 99.00
   #300 Archaic, Peacock and Rose etch, Cheriglo ... 95.00
   #300 Archaic, Lela Bird etch, green 125.00
   #411 Mrs. B., Ardith etch, yellow 145.00
Candy box, cov, flat
   #411 Mrs. B., Ardith etch, green 150.00
   #412 Crow's Foot Square, square shape, ebony w/crystal lid. 60.00
   #412 Crow's Foot Square, square shape, ruby ... 125.00
   #412-1/2 Crow's Foot Square, cloverleaf shape, cobalt ... 225.00
Candy dish, cov, footed, #555 w/beaded edge
   Crystal with floral cutting 85.00
   Ruby 67.00
Candleholders, pr
   #220 Largo, crystal, satin finish, silver deposit ... 30.00
   #412 Crow's Foot Square, 6-1/2" keyhole style, ruby ... 70.00
   #444 Vale three-light with cutting 40.00
Cocktail Shaker, orig strainer, rooster stopper ... 155.00
Compote, footed
   #444 w/ball stem, ruby $40.00
   #412 Crow's Foot Square, 6-1/2", ruby 70.00

Candy dish, #210 Regina, ftd, ebony, dots and floral vine wheel cutting, stepped dome lid, button finial, 6-5/8"h, $55.

#412 Crow's Foot Square, 6-1/2", Orchid etch, ruby 120.00
#412 Crow's Foot Square, 6-1/2", Orchid etch, yellow 40.00
#412 Crow's Foot Square, 6-1/2", opal, silver overlay 180.00
Console Bowl
    #220 Largo, three-footed, cupped up, light blue 70.00
    #411 Mrs. B., Gothic Garden etch, yellow 50.00
    #412 Crow's Foot Square, rolled edge, cobalt 60.00
Console Set, bowl and pr candleholders, #412 Crow's Foot Square,
    keyhole style candleholders, amber 62.00
Creamer and Sugar
    #191 Party Line, Cheriglo 24.00
    #412 Crow's Foot Square, ruby 45.00
    #412 Crow's Foot Square, Orchid etch, ruby 265.00
    #881 Gadroon, ruby 56.00
    #994 Popeye and Olive, rub 70.00
Cream Soup, #412 Crow's Foot Square, ruby 25.00
Cup and Saucer
    #220 Largo, ruby 22.50
    #411 Mrs. B., Ardith etch, topaz 15.00
    #412 Crow's Foot Square, ruby 17.50
Ice Bucket, metal bail, Cupid etch, pink, 225.00
Ice Tub, tab handles
    #191 Party Line, green 19.00
    #895 Lucy, Blue Willow etch 129.00
Mayonnaise, bowl and underplate:
    #215 Glades, Spring Orchard etch 33.00
    #300 Archaic, Nora Bird etch, Cheriglo 135.00
    #411 Mrs. B., Ardith etch, with ladle, yellow 48.00
    #555 beaded edge and "wing" handles, Gazebo etch 65.00
Plate, #412 Crow's Foot Square
    8-1/2", ruby 15.00
    11-1/2", ruby w/gold encrusted etch 90.00
Platter, oval, #412 Crow's Foot Square, ruby 45.00
Sugar Bowl, #411 Mrs. B., Gothic Garden etch, green 45.00
Sugar Pourer, #154 Rena, swirl pattern, metal top, Cheriglo 125.00
Syrup Pitcher, #180 with glass lid, floral cutting, green 69.00
Tray, center handle
    #220 Largo, ruby 95.00
    #412 Crow's Foot Square, Orchid etch, ruby 165.00
    #412 Crow's Foot Square, Delilah Bird etch, amber 95.00
    #412 Crow's Foot Square, opal, rare 350.00
    #701 Triumph, Delilah Bird etch 40.00
    #881 Gadroon, ruby 75.00
    #1504 swan shaped handle, Gazebo etch 85.00
    #1504 swan shaped handle, silver overlay 95.00
Tumblers and Stemware
    #191 Party Line footed soda, green 12.00
    #191 Party Line footed parfait, green 20.00
    #991 Penny Line flat ice tea, ruby 22.50
    #991 Penny Line wine, ruby 7.00
    #991 Penny Line footed goblet, mulberry 18.50
    #991 Penny Line low footed sherbet, mulberry 12.50
Vase
    #182 8" elliptical, Lela Bird etch, ebony 200.00
    #182 8" elliptical, Cupid etch, Cheriglo 650.00
    #182 8" elliptical, gold encrusted Peacock and Rose etch,
      ebony 335.00
    #184 10" bulbous-bottom, Lela Bird etch, ebony 150.00
    #184 10" bulbous-bottom, Utopia etch, ebony 195.00
    #184 10" bulbous-bottom, Peacock and Rose etch, Cheriglo 165.00
    #184 10" bulbous-bottom, Rose Bouquet etch, green 158.00
    #184 10" bulbous-bottom, Lady with Grapes etch, Cheriglo . 260.00
    #184 12" bulbous-bottom, Daisy etch, Cheriglo 167.00
    #184 12" bulbous-bottom, Eden Rose etch, ebony 142.00
    #210 Regina 6-1/2", Harvesters etch, ebony 145.00
    #210 Regina 6-1/2", Black Forest etch, green 150.00
    #412 10" Crow's Foot Square, flared, ruby 96.00
    #412 10" Crow's Foot Square, Gothic Garden etch, ruby 430.00
    Rectangular, 9" tall, 3" x 5" at top, Utopia etch 200.00

PAIRPOINT

History: The Pairpoint Manufacturing Co. was organized in 1880 as a silver-plating firm in New Bedford, Massachusetts. The company merged with Mount Washington Glass Co. in 1894 and became the Pairpoint Corporation. The new company produced specialty glass items often accented with metal frames.

Pairpoint Corp. was sold in 1938 and Robert Gunderson became manager. He operated it as the Gunderson Glass Works until his death in 1952. From 1952 until the plant closed in 1956, operations were maintained under the name Gunderson-Pairpoint. Robert Bryden reopened the glass manufacturing business in 1970, moving it back to the New Bedford area.

References: Edward and Sheila Malakoff, *Pairpoint Lamps*, Schiffer Publishing, 1990; John A. Shumann III, *Collector's Encyclopedia of American Art Glass*, Collector Books, 1988, 1996 value update.

Collectors' Clubs: Mount Washington Art Glass Society, P.O. Box 24094, Fort Worth, TX 76124.-1094; Pairpoint Cup Plate Collectors, P.O. Box 890052, East Weymouth, MA 02189.

Museum: Pairpoint Museum, Sagamore, MA.

China

Box, cov, 5" l, 3-1/2" w, 2-1/2" h, raised gold rococo scrolls, reverse on lid with 3 Palmer Cox Brownies playing cards, Pairpoint-Limoges logo, numbered 750.00
Chocolate Pot, 10" h, cream ground, white floral dec, gold trim and scrolls, sgd "Pairpoint Limoges 2500 114" 675.00
Gravy Boat and Underplate, fancy white china with scrolls, Dresden multicolored flowers, elaborate handle, Limoges, 2 pc 175.00
Plate, 7-3/8" d, hp harbor scene, artist sgd "L. Tripp," fuchsia tinted rim, gold highlights, back sgd "Pairpoint Limoges" 550.00
Vase
    7" h, 6-3/4" w, two handles, pink pond lily dec, soft beige ground, dark green trim on handles and ruffled top, sgd "P.M.C. 2004/261" 425.00
    9-1/2" h, 7" d base, hp chrysanthemum dec, gold highlights, putty colored body, sgd "Pairpoint Limoges 2008/262" 625.00
    14" h, portrait of little girl, framed by interlocking gold scrolls and stylized florals, fancy scrollwork of base, and rim, mahogany red ground, brushed gold highlights, reverse with well-worn gold dec 850.00

Glass

Candlesticks, pr, 9-1/2" h, Mt. Washington opalware glass, silver-plated overlay, deep pink painted ground, white peony dec, fancy Art Nouveau styled silver overlay base and socket, sgd "Pairpoint Mfg. Co." 1,250.00
Console Set, 3 pc set
    12" d bowl, matching 3" h candlesticks, Tavern glass, bouquet of red, white, and green flowers 575.00
    12" d, bowl, matching mushroom candlesticks, Flambo Ware, tomato red, applied black glass foot, c1915 .... 1,950.00
Compote, 10" h, 5-1/2" d, Fine Arts Line, Auroria, brilliant cut deep amber glass bowl, brass and onyx base with full figured cherub holding up bowl, mkd "C1413 Pairpoint" 475.00
Cracker Jar, cov
    6-1/2" h, 6" d, 16 panels, gold/beige ground, white and deep pink roses, green leaves, cov sgd "Pairpoint-3932," base sgd "3932/222," fancy metal work 595.00
    6-3/4" h, 7-1/2" w, Mt. Washington opalware, pistachios green top and bottom, 3-1/2" w band of deep pink and red roses, green leaves, gold trim, fancy silver-plated cov, handle, and bail, cov sgd "Pairpoint -3912," base sgd "3912-268" 725.00

Garniture, pr candlesticks and vase
- 10-3/4" h baluster shaped pr candlesticks, 10-7/8" h two handled vase, cobalt blue, overall cut and etched grape clusters and leafy vines, c1930...1,495.00
- 15-3/4" h pr candlesticks, 8-1/2" h vase, amethyst, cut and etched grape and vine pattern, c1930...1,955.00

Lamp, table
- 22" h, 17" d scenic reverse painted textured Exeter shade, pastoral scene of trees and grassy hillside, yellow, orange, blue, purple, green, and brown, shaded blue sky, yellow band about shoulder with repeating brown windmill motifs, three socket scrolling tripod base with bronze patina, imp "Pairpoint D3070" and logo on base, minor nick, wear to patina...2,100.00
- 27-1/2" h, 17" d Directorie scenic hexagonal heavy walled shade, reverse painted as six continuing panels, colorful landscaped ground with columnar waterfront building, irid background coloring, paneled borders above and below, "The Pairpoint Corp.n" on border, gilt metal, onyx, and cut glass candle lamp form base, imp "Pairpoint Mfg. Co. E30001"...2,645.00

Vase
- 5-1/2" h, 4-1/2" w, Tavern glass, bulbous, enameled floral dec of vase of flowers, base numbered...225.00
- 6" h, Tavern glass, bulbous, enameled sailing galleon on wavy sea, sgd "D. 1507," c1900-38 ....300.00
- 8-1/2" h, Tavern Glass, cylindrical, bubbled colorless ground, raised enameled dec of vase of flowers, obscured mark in polished pontil, c1920, slight wear to enamel 300.00
- 13" h, Adelaide pattern, tall trumpet form, cobalt blue cut to colorless, trapped bubble, colorless ball connector, disk shaped base, c1900-38, pr...2,530.00
- 15-1/4" h, Buckingham pattern, baluster, flared rim, colorless cut body, patinated metal and sq shaped onyx paw ftd base, imp "Pairpoint C1517," pr, abrasions to stone base 1,840.00

PAPER EPHEMERA

History: Maurice Rickards, author of *Collecting Paper Ephemera*, suggests that ephemera are the "minor transient documents of everyday life," material destined for the wastebasket but never quite making it. This definition is more fitting than traditional dictionary definitions that emphasize time, e.g., "lasting a very short time." A driver's license, which is used for a year or longer, is as much a piece of ephemera as is a ticket to a sporting event or music concert. The transient nature of the object is the key.

Collecting ephemera has a long and distinguished history. Among the English pioneers were John Seldon (1584-1654), Samuel Pepys (1633-1703), and John Bagford (1650-1716). Large American collections can be found at historical societies and libraries across the country, and museums, e.g., Wadsworth Athenaeum, Hartford, CT, and the Museum of the City of New York.

When used by collectors, "ephemera" usually means paper objects, e.g., billheads and letterheads, bookplates, documents, labels, stocks and bonds, tickets, and valentines. However, more and more ephemera collectors are recognizing the transient nature of some three-dimensional material, e.g., advertising tins and pinback buttons. Today's specialized paper shows include dealers selling other types of ephemera in both two- and three-dimensional form.

References: Warren R. Anderson, *Owning Western History*, Mountain Press Publishing, 1993; Patricia Fenn and Alfred P. Malpa, *Rewards of Merit*, Ephemera Society, 1994; John Henty, *The Collectable World of Mabel Lucie Attwell*, Richard Dennis Publications, distributed by Antique Collectors' Club, 1999; Gerard S. Petrone, *Cigar Box Labels: Portraits of Life, Mirrors of History*, Schiffer, 1998. Robert Reed, *Paper Collectibles*, Wallace-Homestead/Krause, 1995; Kenneth W. Rendell, *Forging History*, University of Oklahoma Press, 1994; Gene Utz, *Collecting Paper*, Books Americana, 1993.

Periodical: *Biblio*, 845 Willamette St., Eugene, OR 87401; *Paper & Advertising Collector*, P.O. Box 500, Mount Joy, PA 17552; *Paper Collectors' Marketplace*, P.O. Box 128, Scandinavia, WI 54977.

Collectors' Clubs: Calendar Collector Society, American Resources, 18222 Flower Hill Way #299, Gaithersburg, MD 20879; Cigar Label Collectors International, P.O. Box 66, Sharon Center, OH 44274; Citrus Label Society, 131 Miramonte Dr., Fullerton, CA 92365; Ephemera Society, 12 Fitzroy Sq, London W1P 5HQ England; Ephemera Society of America, Inc., P.O. Box 95, Cazenovia, NY 13035; Florida Citrus Label Collectors Association, P.O. Box 547636, Orlando, FL 32854; International Seal, Label & Cigar Band Society, 8915 E. Bellevue St., Tucson, AZ 85715; Society of Antique Label Collectors, P.O. Box 24811, Tampa, FL 33623; The Ephemera Society of Canada, 36 Macauley Dr., Thornhill, Ontario L3T 5S5 Canada; National Association of Paper & Advertising Collectors, P.O. Box 500, Mount Joy, PA 17552.

Additional Listings: See Advertising Trade Cards; Catalogs; Comic Books; Photographs; Sports Cards. Also see Calendars, Catalogs, Magazines, Newspapers, Photographs, Postcards, and Sheet Music in *Warman's Americana & Collectibles*.

Banners

Alaska, Eskimo child, totem pole, yellow and green, 1939, 3" x 7". 6.00
Montgomery, (AL), State Capitol, building, green and white lettering, 1939, 3-1/2" x 7-1/2" 5.00
Museum of Arts & Sciences, City of Culture Where Quality Predominates, Rochester, NY museum, blue, white lettering, 1929, 3-1/2" x 7-1/2"...5.00
Tucson San Xavier Mission Founded 1692, view of mission, blue and white, 1939, 3-1/2" x 7" 5.00

Billheads

Bethlehem Stove Depot, Bethlehem, PA, 1873, 8-1/2" x 14", Lehigh Valley RR Co. to R. W. Leibert, dealer in stoves, heaters, ranges, mantels, etc., placing order 12.00
Carson Hill Gold Mining Corp., 1934 ....6.00
F. C. Peterson, Gen. Blacksmithing, Dealer in Wagons and Buggies, bill for buggy repair, 1902...25.00
Fresno Agricultural Works, Manufactures and Importers of Farm Wagons, Agricultural Implements, Buggies, Carts, Raisin Machinery, etc., vignette of farm equipment and buggie, June 24, 1903, interesting content 15.00
Montgomery Door & Box Co., Buffalo, NY, 1903, 5-1/2" x 8-1/4", oval illus of factory buildings, smoke emerging from smoke stacks, statement of account...8.00
J. A. Norcross, Contractor/Builder, 1901, handwritten letter..........7.50
Newbury Company Building Materials, 1907, handwritten letter, 7" x 8-1/2" 10.00
Pocahontas Coal Co., Cincinnati, 1905, yellow and red invoice, 7" x 8-1/2"...10.00
Price Bros Groceries, El Paso, ...10.00
Southern Cultivator & The Dixie Farmer, Atlanta, GA, 1915, black and white vignette 8.00

Blotters

Badger Soap, You Want The Best, attached adv card, multi-colored 15.00
Kellogg's Corn Flakes, multicolored 10.00
None Such Mince Meat, factory illus, multicolored 8.00
Prudential Insurance Co., battleship, blue and white 8.00
Sundial Shoes, Bonnie Laddie, multicolored 10.00
Wayne Oakland Bank, Santa 12.00

Booklets

Henderson-Ames Co., Kalamazoo, MI, 6" x 9-1/2", c1929, metal badges, monograms, bag markers, etc., illus, folded in 3 folds . 10.00
200,000 for Breakfast with Tom Breneman, Tales by Tom, Corn by Corny, Bobbles by Bobbie, Cracks by Carl, introduction by Mrs. Bob Hope, 1943, Kellogg Co., 46 pgs, 5-1/2" x 7-1/4" 10.00

Bookmarks

Advertising
  Austin Young & Co., Biscuits, multicolored, 2" x 7" 5.00
  Bell Pianos, Art Nouveau woman, multicolored 12.00
  Eastman's Extract, silver gild, multicolored 10.00
  Palmer Violets Bloom Perfume, gold trim 15.00
  Youth's Companion, 1902, multicolored, 2-3/4" x 6" 8.00
Cross Stitch on Punched Paper
  Black Emancipation, black couple dancing, 1860s, 3-7/8" x 1-1/2" 40.00
  Ever Constant-Ever True, young girl with basket of flowers, 2-5/8" x 7" 10.00
  In God We Trust 10.00

Business Cards

Commercial Hotel, Grand Rapids, MI, $1.00 A day, printed, black and white 10.00
F. A. Howe, Jr, Contracting Freight Agent, MI, Central RR & Blue Line, Chicago, blue on white 12.00
Dexter Saloon, Nome, Wyatt Earp and C. E. Hoxsie, Proprietors, c1898-1900 .... 3,650.00
Keystone Tourist Camp, Miami, black and white photo on front, map on back, 1930s, 3-1/2" x 2" 7.00
Pfeiffer Brewing Co., Detroit, MI, printed, multicolored 7.50
Sheriff's Office, Los Angeles, CA, Hall of Justice with vignette of municipal buildings, Eugene W. Biscailuz, Sheriff, "Presented by George Contreras, Capt.," union label at bottom, 1940s 16.00
Silverthaw & Sons, Dealers in Diamonds & Watches, New Haven, CT, gold lettering, black ground, 1880s, printed 12.00

Calendars

1882, Canada First, The Great Literary-Political Journal, broadside type, 8" x 12" 65.00
1893, Benton Hall Dry Goods, Palmyra, NY, 2-1/2" 12.00
1894, Hoyt's, lady's, perfumed 12.00
1896, Singer Sewing Machines 40.00
1889, Pansies Bright, Taber Prang Art Co., 6 parts, pansy dec on each part 40.00
1900, Hood's, full pad, 2 girls 45.00
1901, Colgate, miniature, flower 20.00
1906, Hiawatha, multiple images of Indian scenes, monthly calendars placed throughout, metal band and grommet at top, metal band missing at bottom, 7-1/2" w, 36" h 125.00
1909, Bank of Waupun, emb lady 32.00
1914, Youth's Companion, marching scene, easel back 10.00
1916, Putnam Dyes 40.00
1922, Warren National Bank, Norman Rockwell illus 300.00
1923, Winona, F. A. Rettke, Indian Princess on cliff overlooking body of water, full pad, 6-1/2" w, 21-1/2" l 50.00
1929, Clothesline 65.00
1939, Rogers Statuary 20.00
1940, Columbian Rope 40.00

Checks, canceled

Arcata, CA, Arcata Branch of Bank of Italy, 1927 .... 7.00

C. J. Hoglund Lumber Co., vignette of lumper company, stove, barrel of nails, 1919 .... 15.00
Cloverdale, CA, Bank of Cloverdale, bank building illus, 1922 .... 8.00
Darlington, Indian Territory, Indian vignette, issued to Indian Bird Chief, sgd by Indian Agent 250.00
Farmers and Merchants Bank, Oakland, CA, ornate lettering, attached Spanish American War stamp on front, Dec 30, 1899 .... 8.00
Frank H,. Smith, Furniture Dealer & Undertaker, outdoor vignette of deer in woods, 1910 .... 10.00

Court Documents

Appointment of Estate Administrator, James Bell estate, killed by Billy the Kid 700.00
Citation, 1905, El Paso, Texas, charging Pat Garrett, with not paying promissory notes 400.00
Warrant, Montana Territory, 1884, paid for killing 14 bears, 14 mountain lions, 84 wolves, 115 coyotes 355.00

Decals

Alabama, The Cotton State, map motif, 1960s 6.00
Big Bear Lake, diecut brown bear, description of facilities on back, brown and yellow, 1930s, 2-3/4 .... 8.00

Flyers

A. B. T. Mfg. Co., Fayetteville, NC, 1930s, 9" x 12" folded as issued, 6 pgs, "The Watch Guard of Your Coin-Operated Machine, A. B. T. Mfg Co. Coin Chutes" 32.00
Electric, Gas & Steam Brokerage Co., Chicago, IL, 1920s, 5-3/4" x 8-1/2", lightning arresters, fuses, 11 illus 10.00
Hiram Wheaton & Sons, West Tisbury, MA, 1901, 5-1/2" x 8-1/2", orig company mailed envelope, dealers in soda water, wine, spirits, invoice for Pabst Beer, Faust & Cincinnati Beers 10.00
Puerto Rum, Party Kit, punch out tabs, recipes, 6 pgs, 1950, 10" x 8" 24.00
Standard Sanitary Mfg Co., Pittsburgh, PA, c1927, 6" x 13" sheet folded as issued, 8 pgs 10.00
Sunshine Court, N Palm Canyon Drive, Palm Springs, shows accommodations, black and white, 4 pgs, 1940, folded 6" x 9" 16.00
Tex Barber Shop, Oakland, CA, Specializing in Hair Cutting, No Fussing with Appointments…A Family Shop, Adults 50¢, children 35¢, pink paper, 1930s, 4-1/4" x 7" 7.00

Hotel Labels

Allis Hotel, Wichita, Kansas' Tallest Building, red, gray oval, 1930s, 3-3/4" 12.00
Arlington Hotel & Baths, Hot Springs, AR, 1930s, 4" x 3-1/2" 12.00
Condaldo-Vanderbilt Hotel, silhouette of building, night view from harbor, 1921, 5" x 6" 18.00
Daniel Boone Hotel, Charleston, hotel illus, red ground, 1930s, 4-3/4" 15.00
Hotel Winthrop, Gateway to Rainier Nat. Park, girl with toboggan, c1920, 3-1/2" x 5" 16.00
Mayflower Hotel, Washington, DC, gold ground, diecut scalloped edges, large ship in center, 1930s, 3-1/2" 15.00
McKinley Park Hotel, stamped diecut, multicolored, c1950, 4-1/2" x 4-1/2" 25.00
Ledger Account Book, Hamilton Carhartt Co., Detroit, MI, 64 pgs, 5" x 8", farm, stock, and crop accounts 15.00

Menus

Banquet To The Western Michigan Press, Reed City, 1883, fold-over, Robison Engraving Co., 1882, printed, black and white 15.00
El Mirador Hotel, Palm Springs, night scene of hotel, color photo litho, dinner menu on back, 1954, 8" x 10" 32.00
Francaise, Art Nouveau design, sgd "Mucha," dated 5 Janvier 1913, 5" x 9" 350.00
Johnson Line 15.00
Hotel Oakland, luncheon menu, 1929, honoring Japanese hotel men's delegation, front gold engraved hotel, tipped in real photo of Wild Ducks at Lakeside Park, 5" x 8" 20.00

Los Angeles Turf Club, insert for San Fransico Chronicle Harry B. Smith 6" Annual Santa Anita Handicap Tour Luncheon, March 1, 1941, engraving of Turf Club on front, 5 pgs, 7" x 10" 27.50
Royal Hawaiian Hotel, Hula Dancer cover by John Kelly, 1949, 10" x 14" 90.00
Metropolitan Hotel, 4 pgs, c1974 .... 35.00
SS City of Omaha, Christmas, 1940 .... 10.00
United States Hotel, Saratoga Springs, NY, 1892, 7" x 10" 15.00

Payroll Documents
Adams Express, routeman, 1918, 3-1/2" x 8" 8.00
Southern Express Co., wages for helper on L & N So. RY, Cot 16, 1918, Horace Green, Florence, AL, 3-1/2" x 8-1/2" 10.00

Programs
Invitation and Program for Carnival In Honor of George Washington, Request at Opera House, 1893, multicolored cover 12.00
Live Oak Union High School Graduation, 1926, lists grads, speakers, faculty, 4 pgs, 5" x 7-1/2" 9.00
Mardi Gras, New Orleans, 1949, 52 pgs, 9" x 12" 45.00
Richland Library Literary Society, Benefit Musical, opens, lists musical selections, poems to be read, black and white 5.00

Sheet Music
American Legion Song-Five Million Strong!, J. H. Benson, 1919 . 10.00
Birds Fly Over White Cliffs of Dover, Glenn Miller, 1941-42 .... 12.00
Break The News To Mother, 1897 .... 18.00
Full Moon & Empty Arms, Frank Sinatra, 1946 .... 10.00
In The Ghetto, Elvis, blue front 50.00
Kokomo, IN, Betty Grable, 1947 .... 8.00
Little Sweetheart of the Ozarks, Sandy Williams, 1937 .... 8.00
Moonlight & Shadows, Dorothy Lamour and Ray Milland, 1936 ... 10.00
Normandy Chimes, Powell, 1913 .... 10.00
Over the Rainbow, cast on cov 30.00
Red River Valley, Gene Autry, photo, 1935 .... 12.00
Song for Me, Bromo-Seltzer, c1890 .... 15.00
Those Ragtime Melodies, Hodgkins, 1912 .... 10.00
You Flew Over/Uncle Same Takes His Hat Off To You, 9-1/4" x 12-1/4", dedicated to Lindbergh 50.00
Tag, 4-1/2" x 9-1/2", heavy stock, Oshman & Sons, Inc., Cedar Rapids, IA, c1926, yellow, perforation, card sent to customer with red, green, and yellow tie-on tag for furs to be shipped to company, lists of guaranteed prices 10.00
Wallpaper Book, The Charles William Store, New York, NY, 126 pgs, 6-1/4" x 9-1/4", 1920, sample patterns, prices 45.00

PAPERWEIGHTS

History: Although paperweights had their origin in ancient Egypt, it was in the mid-19th century that this art form reached its zenith. The finest paperweights were produced between 1834 and 1855 in France by the Clichy, Baccarat, and Saint Louis factories. Other weights made in England, Italy, and Bohemia during this period rarely match the quality of the French weights.

In the early 1850s, the New England Glass Co. in Cambridge, Massachusetts, and the Boston and Sandwich Glass Co. in Sandwich, Massachusetts, became the first American factories to make paperweights.

Popularity peaked during the classic period (1845-1855) and faded toward the end of the 19th century. Paperweight production was rediscovered nearly a century later in the mid-1900s. Contemporary weights still are made by Baccarat, Saint Louis, Perthshire, and many studio craftsmen in the U.S. and Europe.

References: *Annual Bulletin of the Paperweight* Collectors Association, Inc., available from association (P.O. Box 1263,

Beltsville, MD 20704), 1996; Andrew H. Dohan, *The Dictionary of Paperweight Signature Canes: Identification and Dating*, Paperweight Press, 1997; Monika Flemming and Peter Pommerencke, *Paperweights of the World*, 2nd ed., Schiffer Publishing, 1998; Robert G. Hall, *Old English Paperweights*, Schiffer Publishing, 1998; John D. Hawley, *Glass Menagerie*, Paperweight Press, 1995; Sibylle Jargstorf, *Paperweights*, Schiffer Publishing, 1991; Paul Jokelson and Dena Tarshis, *Baccarat Paperweights and Related Glass*, Paperweight Press, 1990; Edith Mannoni, *Classic French Paperweights*, Paperweight Press, 1984; Bonnie Pruitt, *St. Clair Glass Collectors Guide*, published by author, 1992; Pat Reilly, *Paperweights*, Running Press, Courage Books, 1994; Lawrence H. Selman, *All About Paperweights*, Paperweight Press, 1992; ——, *Art of the Paperweight*, Paperweight Press, 1988; ——, *Art of the Paperweight*, Perthshire, Paperweight Press, 1983; ——, *Art of the Paperweight*, Saint Louis, Paperweight Press, 1981 (all of the Paperweight Press books are distributed by Charles E. Tuttle Co., 1996); Colin Terris, *The Charlton Standard Catalogue of Caithness Paperweights*, Charlton Press, 1999.

Collectors' Clubs: Caithness Collectors Club, 141 Lanza Ave., Building 12, Garfield, NJ 07026; International Paperweight Society, 761 Chestnut St., Santa Cruz, CA 95060; Paperweight Collectors Association Inc., P.O. Box 1059, Easthampton, MA 01027; Paperweight Collectors Association of Chicago, 535 Delkir Ct., Naperville, IL 60565; Paperweight Collectors Association of Texas, 1631 Aguarena Springs Dr., #408, San Marcos, TX 78666.

Museums: Bergstrom-Mahler Museum, Neenah, WI; Corning Museum of Glass, Corning, NY; Degenhart Paperweight & Glass Museum, Inc, Cambridge, OH; Museum of American Glass at Wheaton Village, Millville, NJ.

Antique
Baccarat
    Butterfly meadow scene 18,700.00
    Silhouette canes, lace ground 2,900.00
Clichy
    2-5/8" d, swirled, alternating purple and white pinwheels emanating from white, green, and pink pastry mold cane, minor bubbles 2,200.00
    2-3/4" d, mushroom, close concentric design, large central pink and green rose surrounded by pin, white, cobalt blue, and cadmium green complex millefiori, middle row of canes with 10 green and white roses alternating with pink pastry mold canes, pin and white stems 6,600.00
Degenhart, John, 3-3/16" x 2-1/4" x 2-1/4", window, red crystal cube with yellow and orange upright center lily, one to window, 4 side windows, bubble in center of flower's stamens 1,225.00
Gillinder, 3-1/16" d, orange turtle with moving appendages in hollow center, pale orange ground, molded dome 500.00
New England Glass Co.
    2-1/2" d, 2" h, nosegay, c1870, bouquet of 3 light blue and white millefiori cane flowers, 4 dark green leaves, white latticino ground, surrounded by 2 rows of blue, white, red, and yellow millefiori canes, rough pontil, light scratches 650.00
    2-3/4" d, crown, red, white, blue, and green twists interspersed with white latticino emanating from a central pink, white, and green complex floret/cog cane, minor bubbles in glass 2,400.00
Pinchbeck, 3-3/16" d, pastoral dancing scene, couple dancing before grouped of onlookers 650.00

Sandwich Glass Co.
2-1/2" d, 1-3/4" h, dahlia, c1870, red petaled flower, millefiori cane center, bright green leafy stem, highlighted by trapped bubble dec, white latticino ground 650.00
3" d, double poinsettia, red flower with double tier of petals, green and white Lutz rose, green stem and leaves, bubbles between petals, 3" d 1,200.00
St. Louis
3" d, 2-1/2" h, red and green ripening fruits, latticino base basket, central base cane 1,150.00
3-1/2" d, 2-1/2" h, Queen Victoria, c1840, sulfide portrait sgd "Victoria" in blue at base, few small inclusions 750.00
Val St. Lambert, 3-1/2" d, patterned millefiori, 4 red, white, blue, pistachio, and turquoise complex canes circlets spaced around central pink, turquoise and cadmium green canes circlet, canes set on stripes of lace encircled by spiraling red and blue torsade, minor blocking crease 950.00
Whitefriars, 3-5/8" d, close concentric millefiori, pink, blue, purple, green, white, and yellow cog canes, 1948 date cane, minor bubble in dome 900.00

Modern

Ayotte, Rick, 3-1/2" d, 2" h, Paradisa Butterfly, 1993, naturalistic butterfly, leaf green, yellow, and black, flying above white flowering branch, dark green leaves, "Ayotte Ed./50'93" inscribed near base 700.00
Baccarat
2-1/2" d, 1-3/4" h, pansy, yellow and purple pansy and bud, bright green leafy stem, flower centered by 6 pointed star motif cane, star cut base 550.00
2-3/4" d, 1-3/4" h, scrambled millefiori, pink, blue, green, and white millefiori twists, acid stamp on base 200.00
3-1/4" d, 2" h, 2 interwoven millefiori pink, green, blue, and white garlands, centered by ring of millefiori canes, latticino ground, faceted six and one, 2 annealing fissures 350.00
Banford, Bob, 3" d, 2-3/4" h, lily of the valley, white and yellow flowers, green striped leaves, wine red ground, "B" signature cane 500.00
Kaziun, Charles, 2-1/16" d, concentric millefiori, heart, turtle silhouette, shamrocks, 6 pointed stars, and floret canes encircled by purple and white torsade, turquoise ground flecked with goldstone, K signature cane 1,200.00
Monte Dunlavy, 4" d, 3-1/4" h, stylized lavender calla lilies issuing bubbles 75.00
Perthshire, Scotland
2-3/4" d, 2" h, millefiori and silhouette canes, lace ground, signature cane "P 1973" 275.00
3" d, 2" h, close packed millefiori carpet ground 225.00
3" d, 2" h, floral bouquet, blue, rose, lavender, gold, and green, hovering green dragonfly, crosshatched base, c1974 .... 400.00
Rosenfield, Ken
3-1/4" d, 2-1/2" h, desert scene, 2 mottled green flowering cacti plants, red and white flowers, sand ground, naturalistic rocks, signature cane, inscribed "Ken Rosenfield '93" 475.00
3-1/4" d, 2-3/4" h, blue and white morning glory blossoms and buds on entwined green vines, centered by ladybug, pink opaque ground, signature cane, inscribed "Ken Rosenfield '97" 450.00
Selkirk, 2-3/4" d, 2" h, clusters of purple grapes, bright green leaves on vine, "PH" (Peter Holmes) signature cane, base inscribed "Selkirk (illegible) Scotland 11/100 1982" 300.00
St. Louis
3" d, 2" h, gold inclusion of General Washington on his horse, surrounded by 13 blue and white star canes, one signature cane "SL 1976," blue ground, overlaid in red over white cut to colorless, five and one facets, orig box 200.00
3" d, 2-1/4" h, blue and coral clematis flower, millefiori cane center, one signature cane "M. 1975," light blue over white overlay cut to colorless, five and one facets, orig box 175.00
Stankard, Paul J.
2-1/2" d, Pineland pickerel-weed, yellow, brown, and green, spirit, bee, ant, and word canes on 4 orig plastic feet, inscribed "Paul J. Standard 1995 C-29" 2,300.00
3" d, bouquet, yellow meadow wreath, blue forget-me-nots, rd St. Anthony's fire, white bellflowers, and white chokeberry blossom and buds, 1977 .... 2,400.00
Tarisitano, Debbie
3-1/4" d, 2" h, pansy, open purple flower, stem and leaves, purple bud, one partially opened flower with white center, star cut base 600.00
3-1/4" d, 2-1/4" h, bouquet, 3 multi-petaled flowers, circular spray of leaves, pods, and berries, naturalistic blue, red, yellow, gold, and white, DT cane 865.00
3-1/2" d, 2-1/4" h, floral bouquet, intricate pink, yellow, and deep blue rose-like flowers, budded leafy green stems, signature cane beneath flower 750.00
Tarisitano, Delmo, 2-1/4" d, 2" h, strawberry, 2 white strawberry blossoms, 1 rd berry, green leaves, star cut base 635.00
Whittemore, Francis, 2-3/8" d, 2 green and brown acorns on branch with 3 brown and yellow oak leaves, translucent cobalt blue ground, circular top facet 5 oval punties on sides 300.00
Ysart, Paul, green fish, yellow eye, yellow and white jasper ground encircled by pink, green, and white complex cane garland, PY signature cane 550.00

PAPIER-MÂCHÉ

History: Papier-mâché is a mixture of wood pulp, glue, resin, and fine sand, which is subjected to great pressure and then dried. The finished product is tough, durable, and heat resistant. Various finishing treatments are used, such as enameling, japanning, lacquering, mother-of-pearl inlaying, and painting.

During the Victorian era, papier-mâché articles such as boxes, trays, and tables were in high fashion. Banks, candy containers, masks, toys, and other children's articles were also made of papier-mâché.

Box, cov, 3-3/8" x 2-1/8" x 7/8", rect, faux tortoiseshell finish, hinged lid, central cartouche, foliate borders, George IV 150.00
Candy Container, 5-3/8" l, egg shape, hen, chicks, and rooster standing on dirigible 200.00
Easter Egg, 18-3/4" l, 12-1/2" w, printed cotton covering with Quacky Doodles family, int. lined with gathered chartreuse crepe paper, early 20th C 750.00
Figure, 7" l, grasshopper, glass eyes, polychrome paint 250.00
Hen on Nest, 7" l, brown, beige, red, and green, glass bead eyes,

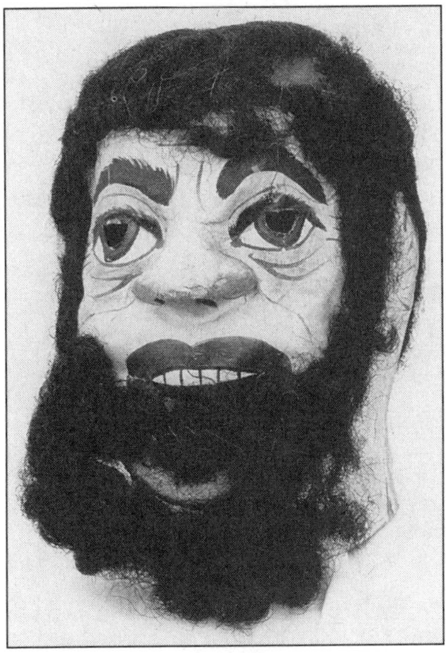

Mask, full face and beard, 13-1/2" h, $90.

labeled "Drake Process, Patented May 29, 1919 Copyright 1924 F. N. Burt Co. Ltd. Buffalo, N.Y.," some damage to base 165.00

Hobby Horse, 20" h, 21" l, black and cream horse, red saddle, leather ears, orig wheels, c1930 .... 195.00

Jack-O-Lantern, 5-1/2" h, startled expression............................ 225.00

Mask, 24" h, donkey head, brown and white, upright ears, shoulder cut-outs, polychrome paint 170.00

Nodder, 9-3/4" h, Easter Rabbit, oval cardboard base, orig polychrome paint 70.00

Parrot, 36" h, standing in metal ring, polychrome dec 435.00

Pip Squeak, 4-7/8" h, rooster, orig polychrome paint, bellows with loose leather, minor edge damage, faint squeak 50.00

Roly Poly, 4-1/8" h, clown, orig white and blue polychrome paint, green ribbon around neck 80.00

Sewing Box, 8-1/4" d, circular, mother-of-pearl bordered reserves with polychromed floral sprays on sides, hinged lid with inlaid border, central dec, fabric lined int., Victorian 275.00

Snuff Box, cov
  2-5/8" d, transfer dec of 2 men in farm yard, inscription 45.00
  3" l, rect, hinged lid with dec border, applied silver metal scrolls at corners, center conforming dec, Victorian, c1850.............. 300.00
  3-1/4" l, 2-3/8" w, painted man and 2 women in landscape, European... 300.00
  3-3/8" x 2" x 3/4", rect, faux tortoiseshell finish, hinged lid, applied metal border, central cartouche, George IV 425.00
  3-1/2" d, perpetual calendar transfer dec, brass fittings, French, minor chipping on inside rim 465.00

Tray, 22-1/4" x 28-1/2", Chippendale scalloped rim, orig black lacquer, nacre inlay, polychrome and gilt floral dec, wear, old touch-up, edge repair 450.00

Writing Box, 7" x 2-5/8" x 1-1/2", traveling type, rect, applied gilt brass corners, central tortoiseshell medallion with brass border, applied female portrait, int. fitted with 3 writing implements, ink pot, late Victorian 200.00

PARIAN WARE

History: Parian ware is a creamy white, translucent porcelain that resembles marble. It originated in England in 1842 and was first called "statuary porcelain." Minton and Copeland have been credited with its development; Wedgwood also made it. In America, parian ware objects were manufactured by Chistopher Fenton in Bennington, Vermont.

At first parian ware was used only for figures and figural groups. By the 1850s, it became so popular that a vast range of items was manufactured.

References: Paul Atterbury, ed., *The Parian Phenomenon*, Shepton Beauchamp, 1989; Susan and Al Bagdade, *Warman's English & Continental Pottery & Porcelain*, 3rd Edition, Krause Publications, 1998; G. A. Godden, *Victorian Porcelain*, Herbert Jenkins, 1961; Kathy Hughes, *Collector's Guide to Nineteenth-Century Jugs* (1985, Routledge & Kegan Paul), Vol. II (1991, Taylor Publishing).

Museum: Victoria & Albert Museum, London, England.

Bust
  10-3/4" h, Clytie, mounted on waisted circular socle, England, 19th C 200.00
  12-3/4" h, Shakespeare, raised circular base, Robinson and Leadbetter mark, c1875, minor chips 725.00
  16" h, maiden, garland in hair, black pedestal base 165.00

Creamer, 5" h, Tulip pattern, relief dec 95.00

Ewer, 10-1/2" h, blue and white, applied grapes dec, Bennington, c1850 .... 215.00

Figure
  10-1/2" h, two female figures clinging to rock above waves, cross to rear inscribed "Simply to Thy Cross I Cling," England, 19th C. 225.00

Pitcher, green and white, molded high-relief figures, 2 men drinking, seated man smoking, man and woman dancing, 9" h, $175.

  11-1/4" h, Jolly Cardinals, unmarked, England, 19th C 300.00
  12-3/4" h, four Apostles, standing with Biblical symbols, modeled by Eneret, Royal Copenhapen, 4 pc set 490.00
  22-1/2" h, fisherman, scantily clad male holding net, England, 19th C 1,150.00
  28" h, Egeria, partially clad nude figure, leaning on tree stump, artist sgd "J. H. Foley, R.A.," imp Copeland mark, c1870, footrim chips 750.00

Loving Cup, 8-1/2" h, relief figures of Bacchus and woman, grapes, and vines, Charles Meigh, c1840 .... 300.00

Pastile Burner, 8-1/2" sq, relief molded, bird and human figures, raised on turned column,s stepped sq base, pr 225.00

Pitcher, 8-3/8" h, hexagonal, paneled sides in relief with titled portraits in laurel wreaths of Shakespeare, Ossian, Milton, Homer, Dante, and Virgil, glaze int., gilt and iron red enameled acanthus leaves, painted mark, Union Porcelain Works, Greenport, NY, c1875, slight footrim chip.. 1,955.00

Vase, 10" h, applied white monkey type figures, grape clusters at shoulders, blue ground, c1850, pr........................... 275.00

PATE-DE-VERRE

History: The term "pate-de-verre" can be translated simply as "glass paste." It is manufactured by grinding lead glass into a powder or crystal form, making it into a paste by adding a 2% or 3% solution of sodium silicate, molding, firing, and carving. The Egyptians discovered the process as early as 1500 b.c.

In the late 19th century, the process was rediscovered by a group of French glassmakers. Almaric Walter, Henri Cros, Georges Despret, and the Daum brothers were leading manufacturers.

Contemporary sculptors are creating a second renaissance, led by the technical research of Jacques Daum.

Bookends, pr, 6-1/2" h, Buddha, yellow amber pressed molded design, seated in lotus position, inscribed "A Walter Nancy" 2,450.00

Bowl, 4" d, 8-3/4" h, Almeric Walter, designed by Jules Cayette, molded blue green glass, yellow center, green around border, three brown scarab beetles with long black antennas, inscribed "A. Walter Nancy," and also "J. Cayette," "Made in France" on base 4,600.00

Clock, stylized orange and black dec, G. Argy Rouseau, made for J. E. Caldwell & Co., metal back, 4-1/2" sq, $2,800.

Box, cov
    5-1/4" d, cylindrical, muted purple, central red flowers, amber and purple leaves on lid, repeating leaf border around box, G. Argy Rousseau, c1923 .... 4,320.00
    11-1/4" l, naturalistic modeled duck in muted blue shading to amber at head and breast, body forms top of box, colorless glass base, matching 4-1/2" l duckling, both frosted and polished to enhance design, both sgd "Daum Nancy" 575.00
Center Bowl, 10-3/8" d, 3-3/4" h, blue, purple, and green press molded design, 7 exotic long legged birds, central multi-pearl blossom, repeating design on ext., raised pedestal foot, sgd "G. Argy-Rousseau" 6,750.00
Clock, 4-1/2" sq, stars within pentagon and tapered sheaves motif, orange and black, molded sgd "G. Argy-Rousseau," clock by J. E. Caldwell 2,750.00
Dagger, 12" l, frosted blade, relief design, green horse head handle, script sgd "Nancy France" 1,200.00
Jewelry
    Earrings, pr, 2-3/4" l, teardrop form, molded violet and rose shaded tulip blossom, suspended from rose colored swirl molded circle .. 2,200.00
    Pendant, 1-1/4" d, molded amethyst portrait of Art Nouveau woman, flowing hair, gilt metal mount 400.00
Paperweight
    2-5/8" h, Papillion de Nuit, cube, internally streaked gray, deep forest green highlights, molded full relief moths, molded "G. Argy-Rousseau," c1923 .... 2,400.00
    4-1/2" d, yellow, stepped disk, centered by upright dark red and yellow flower among green leaves 500.00
Sculpture
    4-1/2" h, stylized dove, jade green, darker green base, initialed by designer Andre Houillon, mold imp "A Walter Nancy" 3,500.00
    9-5/8" l, crab in sea grasses, lemon yellow, chocolate brown, pale mauve, and sea green, sgd "A. Walter/Nancy" and "Berge/SC" 8,500.00
Tray, 6" x 8", apple green, figural green and yellow duck with orange beak at one end, sgd "Walter, Nancy" 950.00
Vase
    4" h, 4-1/2" h, molded inverted bell form, muted amber-tan, dec with band of raised maroon stylized flowers, dark green disk foot, imp "A. Walter Nancy" 1,495.00
    8-1/2" h, naturalistic form butterfly on leafy branch, mottled purple,

amber, and light blue, supporting slender colorless glass vase, base sgd "Daum Nancy" 400.00
Veilleuse, 8-1/2" h, Gabriel Argy-Rousseau, press molded oval lamp shade, frosted mottled gray glass, elaborate purple arches with three teardrop-shaped windows of yellow, center teal-green stylized blossoms on black swirling stems, imp "G. Arty-Rousseau" at lower edge, wrought iron frame, three ball feet centering internal lamp socket, conforming iron cover 6,900.00

PATE-SUR-PATE

History: Pate-sur-pate, paste-on-paste, is a 19th-century porcelain-decorating method featuring relief designs achieved by painting layers of thin pottery paste one on top of the other.

About 1880, Marc Solon and other Sevres artists, inspired by a Chinese celadon vase in the Ceramic Museum at Sevres, experimented with this process. Solon emigrated to England at the outbreak of the Franco-Prussian War and worked at Minton, where he perfected pate-sur-pate.

References: Paul Atterbury and Maureen Batkin, *Dictionary of Minton*, Antique Collectors Club, Ltd., 1996; Susan and Al Bagdade, *Warman's English & Continental Pottery & Porcelain*, 3rd Edition, Krause Publications, 1998; Bernard Bumpers, *Pate-Sur-Pate*, Barrie & Jenkins, 1992; G. .A. Godden, *Victorian Porcelains*, Herbert Jenkins, 1961.

Museums: National Collection of Fine Arts, Smithsonian Institution, Washington, DC; Victoria & Albert Museum, London, England.

Box, cov, 5-3/4" d, round, white female portrait, blue ground, Limoges, France, late 19th C................................. 690.00
Centerpiece, 16" l, elongated parian vessel, molded scroll handles and feet, pierced rim, 2 brown reserves, white pate-sur-pate amorini, gilding, dec attributed to Lawrence Birks, mkd "Minton," retailer's mark of Thomas Goode & Co., Ltd., London, c1889.......................... 1,400.00
Flask, 10-1/4" h, green ground, white slip, putti in moonlight, polychrome slip border, gold trim, artist sgd "Louis Solon," imp Minton mark, c1884, handle repaired, rim chip, gilt wear to top rim . 1,380.00
Lamp, 19" h, Neoclassical maiden and arabesque motif, pale green ground, circular gilt bronze base, late 19th C.......................... 425.00

Box, triangular, seated nude at stream bank, sgd "Gol" in design, F. M. Barbotine/Limoges/France, 5-1/2" x 5-1/2" x 2-1/4", $1,550.

Plaque

    5-1/4" x 11-1/4", Victoria Ware, Wedgwood, rust ground, gilt florets, applied white figure of Adam, imp mark, c1880, rim chip, framed 2,200.00

    7-5/8" d, one with maiden and cupid spinning web, other with maiden seated on bench with whip in one hand, sunflowers stalked with humanistic snail on other, artist sgd "Louis Solin," both mkd on back, framed, pr 2,500.00

    11" x 16", mottled blue-gray ground, colored slips of partially clad female holding lantern, putt figure lights torch, titled "La Nouvelle Psyche," unsgd, attributed to Louis Solon 27,600.00

    15" l, demi-lune shape, green ground, white slip, central figure of Venus holding mirror in each hand, tending off 2 groups of putti with their reflections, artist sgd Louis Solin, rosewood frame 9,200.00

    28-1/2" x 15-1/2", rect, depicting battle scene, warrior in classical dress stands poised to strike his foe, standing over body of fallen soldier, 2 other figures carrying slain soldier, sgd "Stahl," imp "Mettlach" on verso and numbered, carved and giltwood frame 2,300.00

Plate, 9-1/8" d, deep brown ground, gilt trim, white dec of nude child behind net supported by two small trees, artist monogram sgd "Henry Saunders," printed and imp Moore Brothers factory marks, c1885 .... 750.00

Portrait Medallion, 3-7/8" d, circular, blue ground, white slip side self-portrait profile, artist sgd "Louis Solon," dated 1892 .... 1,265.00

Vase

    6-1/2" h, cov, 2 handles, deep teal blue ground, gilt framed gray ground panel with white slip dec of reclining maiden, artist sgd Albione Birks, printed Minton factory marks, c1900, shallow restored chip on cov 1,840.00

    6-7/8" h, 2 handles, blue ground, white female subjects within oval mauve ground cartouches, German printed marks, 20th C, pr750.00

    7-1/4" h, 5-3/4" w, white flowers, green ground, gold serpent skin twisted handles, gold trim, pr 1,100.00

    7-1/2" h, 6" d, pate-sur-pate and modeled porcelain, maple leaves and white berries, enamel-like glossy glaze, cross hatched white bisque ground, mkd "U. C. 1913/MCL," for University City, 1913 ..... 3,750.00

    10" h, sq form handles with scrolled ends, stylized gilt foliate designs bordering pate sur pate cartouche of child with fruit basket on one side, enameled floral design on other side, KPM, Berlin, Germany, 19th C 5,175.00

    13-3/4" h, cov, dark brown ground, white slip of partially draped female figure holding flowering branch, shaped tripod base, gilt dec at rim, artist sgd Louis Solon, printed and imp marks, 1898, rim cover damage, minor gilt wear 2,300.00

    16-1/2" h, cov, deep green ground, circular panels dec in white slip, Psyche being carried heavenly by Mercury, maiden figures applied to shoulder, gilt trim, artist sgd Frederick Schenck, dated 1880, imp George Jones factory marks, cov damaged, hairlines to figures, light gilt wear 3,565.00

    37-1/2" h, blue ground, white clip depicting "Cupid's Tollgate," central frieze flanked by blue and green slip dec foliate designs, gold outlines, artist sgd Louis Solin, Minton factory marks, c1890.. 55,200.00

PATTERN GLASS

History: Pattern glass is clear or colored glass pressed into one of hundreds of patterns. Deming Jarves of the Boston and Sandwich Glass Co. invented one of the first successful pressing machines in 1828. By the 1860s, glass-pressing machinery had been improved, and mass production of good-quality matched tableware sets began. The idea of a matched glassware table service (including goblets, tumblers, creamers, sugars, compotes, cruets, etc.) quickly caught on in America. Many pattern glass table services had numerous accessory pieces such as banana stands, molasses cans, and water bottles.

Early pattern glass (flint) was made with a lead formula, giving many items a ringing sound when tapped. Lead became too valuable to be used in glass manufacturing during the Civil War; and in 1864 Hobbs, Brockunier & Co., West Virginia, developed a soda lime (non-flint) formula. Pattern glass also was produced in transparent colors, milk glass, opalescent glass, slag glass, and custard glass.

The hundreds of companies that produced pattern glass experienced periods of development, expansions, personnel problems, material and supply demands, fires, and mergers. In 1899, the National Glass Co. was formed as a combine of 19 glass companies in Pennsylvania, Ohio, Indiana, West Virginia, and Maryland. U.S. Glass, another consortium, was founded in 1891. These combines resulted from attempts to save small companies by pooling talents, resources, and patterns. Because of this pooling, the same pattern often can be attributed to several companies.

Sometimes various companies produced the same patterns at different times and used different names to reflect current fashion trends. U.S. Glass created the States series by using state names for various patterns, several of which were new issues while others were former patterns renamed.

References: Gary Baker et al., *Wheeling Glass 1829-1939*, Oglebay Institute, 1994, distributed by Antique Publications; George and Linda Breeze, *Mysteries of the Moon & Star*, published by authors, 1995; Bill Edwards and Mike Carwile, *Standard Encyclopedia of Pressed glass*, 1860-1930, Collector Books, 1998; William Heacock, *Encyclopedia of Victorian Colored Pattern Glass*: Book 1: *Toothpick Holders from A to Z*, 2nd ed. (1976, 1992 value update) Book 5: *U. S. Glass from A to Z* (1980), Book 7: *Ruby Stained Glass from A To Z* (1986), Book 8: *More Ruby Stained Glass* (1987), Antique Publications; ——, *Old Pattern Glass*, Antique Publications, 1981; ——, *1000 Toothpick Holders*, Antique Publications, 1977; ——, *Rare and Unlisted Toothpick Holders*, Antique Publications, 1984; Kyle Husfloen, *Collector's Guide to American Pressed Glass*, Wallace-Homestead, 1992; Bill Jenks and Jerry Luna, *Early American Pattern Glass—1850 to 1910*, Wallace-Homestead, 1990; Bill Jenks, Jerry Luna, and Darryl Reilly, *Identifying Pattern Glass Reproductions*, Wallace-Homestead, 1993; William J. Jenks and Darryl Reilly, *American Price Guide to Unitt's Canadian & American Goblets* Volumes I & II, Author! Author! Books (P.O. Box 1964, Kingston, PA 18704), 1996.

Minnie Watson Kamm, *Pattern Glass Pitchers*, Books 1 through 8, published by author, 1970, 4th printing; Ruth Webb Lee, *Early American Pressed Glass*, 36th ed., Lee Publications, 1966; ——, *Victorian Glass*, 13th ed., Lee Publications, 1944; Bessie M. Lindsey, *American Historical Glass*, Charles E. Tuttle, 1967; Robert Irwin Lucas, *Tarentum Pattern Glass*, privately printed, 1981; Mollie H. McCain, *Collector's Encyclopedia of Pattern Glass*, Collector Books, 1982, 1994 value update; George P. and Helen McKearin, *American Glass*, Crown Publishers, 1941; James Measell, *Greentown Glass*, Grand Rapids Public Museum Association, 1979, 1992-93 value update, distributed by Antique Publications; Alice Hulett Metz, *Early American Pattern Glass*, published by author, 1958 (reprinted by Collector Books, 1999, with revisions); ——, *Much More Early American Pattern Glass*, published by author, 1965; S. T. Millard, *Goblets I* (1938), Goblets II

(1940), privately printed, reprinted Wallace-Homestead, 1975; John B. Mordock and Walter L. Adams, *Pattern Glass Mugs*, Antique Publications, 1995.

Arthur G. Peterson, *Glass Salt Shakers*, Wallace-Homestead, 1970; Ellen T. Schroy, *Warman's Pattern Glass*, Wallace-Homestead, 1993; Jane Shadel Spillman, *American and European Pressed Glass in the Corning Museum of Glass,* Corning Museum of Glass, 1981; ——, *Knopf Collectors Guides to American Antiques*, Glass, Vol. 1 (1982), Vol. 2 (1983), Alfred A. Knopf; Doris and Peter Unitt, *American and Canadian Goblets*, Clock House, 1970, reprinted by The Love of Glass Publishing (Box 629, Arthur, Ontario, Canada NOG 1AO), 1996; ——, *Treasury of Canadian Glass*, 2nd ed., Clock House, 1969; Peter Unitt and Anne Worrall, Canadian Handbook, *Pressed Glass Tableware*, Clock House Productions, 1983; Kenneth Wilson, *American Glass 1760–1930*, 2 vols., Hudson Hills Press and The Toledo Museum of Art, 1994.

Periodical: *Glass Collector's Digest*, The Glass Press, P.O. Box 553, Marietta, OH 45750.

Collectors' Clubs: Early American Pattern Glass Society, P.O. Box 266, Colesburg, IA 52035; The National Early American Glass Club, P.O. Box 8489, Silver Spring, MD 20907.

Museums: Corning Museum of Glass, Corning, NY; Jones Museum of Glass and Ceramics, Sebago, ME; National Museum of Man, Ottawa, Ontario, Canada; Sandwich Glass Museum, Sandwich, MA; Schminck Memorial Museum, Lakeview, OR.

Reproduction Alert: Pattern glass has been widely reproduced.

Additional Listings: Bread Plates; Children's Toy Dishes; Cruets; Custard Glass; Milk Glass; Sugar Shakers; Toothpicks; and specific companies.

Advisors: John and Alice Ahlfeld.

Notes: Research in pattern glass is continuing. As always, we try to use correct pattern names, histories, and forms. Reflecting the most current thinking, the listing by pattern places colored, opalescent, and clear items together, avoiding duplication.

Items in the listing marked with an * are those for which reproductions are known to exist. Care should be exercised when purchasing such pieces.

Abbreviations:

ahapplied handle
GUTDODBGive Us This Day Our Daily Bread
hshigh standard
indindividual
lslow standard
osoriginal stopper

SPECIAL AUCTIONS

Mike Clum
P.O. Box 2
Rushville, OH 43150
(614) 536-9220

Green Valley Auctions, Inc.
Rt. 2, Box 434
Mt Crawford, VA 22841
(540) 434-4260

ACTRESS

Made by Adams & Company, Pittsburg, PA, c1880. All clear 20% less. Imperial Glass Co has reproduced some items, including an amethyst pickle dish, in clear and color.

Clear and Frosted

Bowl
　6," ftd..45.00
　7," ftd..50.00
　8," Miss Neilson................................85.00
　9-1/2," ftd...85.00
Bread Plate
　7" x 12," HMS Pinafore....................90.00
　9" x 13," Miss Neilson.....................72.00
Butter, cov..90.00
Cake Stand, 10".................................145.00
Candlesticks, pr.................................250.00
Celery Vase
　Actress Head.................................130.00
　HMS Pinafore, pedestal...............145.00
Cheese Dish, cov, The Lone
　Fisherman on cov, Two
　Dromios on base...........................250.00
Compote
　Cov, hs, 6" d..................................250.00
　Cov, hs, 12" d.................................300.00
　Open, hs, 10" d................................90.00
　Open, hs, 12" d..............................120.00
　Open, ls, 5" d...................................45.00
Creamer...75.00
Dresser Tray...60.00
Goblet, Kate Claxton (two portraits).....85.00
Marmalade Jar, cov..............................125.00
Mug, HMS Pinafore................................50.00
*Pickle Dish, Love's Request is Pickles.....45.00
Pickle Relish, different actresses
　4-1/2" x 7"...35.00
　5" x 8"..35.00
　5-1/2" x 9"...35.00
Pitcher
　Milk, 6-1/2," HMS Pinafore............295.00
　Water, 9," Romeo & Juliet..............250.00
Salt, master...70.00
Salt Shaker, orig pewter top.................42.50
Sauce
　Flat...15.00
　Footed..20.00
Spooner...60.00
Sugar, cov...100.00

ADONIS (Pleat and Tuck, Washboard)

Pattern made by McKee & Bros. of Pittsburgh, PA, in 1897

	Canary	Clear	Deep Blue
Bowl, 5," berry	15.00	10.00	20.00
Butter, cov	70.00	48.00	80.00
Cake Plate, 11"	25.00	20.00	32.00
Cake Stand, 10-1/2"	45.00	30.00	50.00
Celery Vase	35.00	25.00	40.00
Compote			
Cov, hs	65.00	40.00	75.00
Open, hs, 8"	45.00	30.00	50.00
Open, jelly, 4-1/2"	28.00	18.00	32.00
Creamer	28.00	22.50	32.00
Pitcher, water	55.00	35.00	60.00
Plate, 10"	25.00	18.00	32.00
Relish	10.00	15.00	20.00

	Canary	Clear	Deep Blue
Salt & Pepper, pr	40.00	35.00	45.00
Sauce, flat, 4"	10.00	8.00	12.00
Spooner	35.00	20.00	40.00
Sugar, cov	40.00	35.00	45.00
Syrup	150.00	50.00	150.00
Tumbler	20.00	16.00	20.00

ALMOND THUMBPRINT (Pointed Thumbprint, Finger Print)

An early flint glass pattern with variants in flint and non-flint. Pattern has been attributed to Bryce, Bakewell, and U.S. Glass Co. Sometimes found in milk glass.

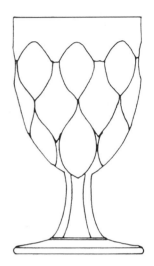

	Flint	Non-Flint
Bowl, 4-1/2" d, ftd	–	20.00
Butter, cov	80.00	40.00
Celery Vase	50.00	25.00
Champagne	60.00	35.00
Compote		
Cov, hs, 4-3/4," jelly	70.00	40.00
Cov, hs, 10"	110.00	45.00
Cov, ls, 4-3/4"	75.00	30.00
Cov, ls, 7"	70.00	25.00
Open, hs, 10-1/2"	70.00	–
Cordial	40.00	30.00
Creamer	60.00	40.00
Cruet, ftd, os	55.00	–
Decanter	70.00	–
Eggcup	45.00	25.00
Goblet	45.00	12.00
Punch Bowl	–	75.00
Salt		
Flat, large	25.00	15.00
Ftd, cov	45.00	25.00
Ftd, open	25.00	10.00
Spooner	20.00	15.00
Sugar, cov	65.00	40.00
Sweetmeat Jar, cov	75.00	50.00
Tumbler	60.00	20.00
Wine	28.00	12.00

APOLLO (Canadian Horseshoe, Shield Band)

Non-flint first made by Adams & Co., Pittsburgh, PA, c1890, and later by U.S. Glass Co. Frosted increases price 20%. Also found in ruby stained and engraved. Lamp found also in blue and yellowed, valued at $250.00

	Clear
Bowl	
4"	10.00
5"	10.00
6"	12.00
7"	15.00
8"	20.00
Butter, cov	40.00
Cake Stand	
8"	35.00
9"	40.00
10"	50.00
Celery Tray, rect	20.00
Celery Vase	35.00
Compote	
Cov, hs	65.00
Open, hs	35.00
Open, ls, 7"	25.00
Creamer	35.00
Cruet	60.00
Eggcup	30.00

	Clear
Goblet	35.00
Lamp, 10"	125.00
Pickle Dish	15.00
Pitcher, water	65.00
Plate, 9-1/2," sq.	25.00
Salt	20.00
Salt Shaker	25.00
Sauce	
Flat	10.00
Ftd, 5"	12.00
Spooner	30.00
Sugar, cov	45.00
Syrup	110.00
Tray, water	45.00
Tumbler	30.00
Wine	35.00

ARCHED GRAPE

Non-flint made by Boston and Sandwich Glass Co., Sandwich, MA, c1880.

	Non-flint
Butter, cov	45.00
Celery vase	35.00
Champagne	35.00
Compote, cov, hs	50.00
Creamer	40.00
Goblet	25.00
Pitcher, water, ah	60.00
Sauce, flat	8.00
Spooner	30.00
Sugar, cov	45.00
Wine	25.00

ARGUS

Flint thumbprint-type pattern made by Bakewell, Pears and Co., Pittsburgh, PA, in the early 1860s. Copiously reproduced, some by Fostoria Glass Co. with raised "H.F.M." trademark for henry Ford Museum, Dearborn, MI. Reproduction colors include clear, red, green and cobalt blue.

	Clear
Ale Glass	75.00
Bitters Bottle	60.00
Bowl, 5-1/2"	30.00
*Butter, cov	85.00
Celery vase	90.00
Champagne	65.00
Compote, open 8," scalloped	50.00
*Creamer, ah	115.00
Decanter, qt	95.00
Eggcup	30.00
*Goblet	60.00
Lamp, ftd	100.00
Mug, ah	65.00
Pitcher, water, ah	400.00
Salt, master, open	30.00
*Spooner	45.00
*Sugar, cov	65.00
*Tumbler, bar	65.00
Whiskey, ah	75.00
Wine	35.00

ART (Jacob's Tears, Job's Tears, Teardrop and Diamond Block)

Non-flint produced by Adams & Co., Pittsburgh, PA, in the 1880s. Reissued by U.S. Glass Co. in the early 1890s. A reproduced milk glass covered compote is known.

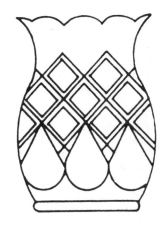

	Clear	Ruby Stained
Banana Stand	90.00	175.00
Biscuit Jar	135.00	175.00
Bowl		
6" d, 3-1/4" h, ftd	30.00	–
7," low, collar base	35.00	–
8," berry, one end pointed	50.00	85.00
Butter, cov	60.00	125.00
Cake Stand		
9"	55.00	–
10-1/4"	65.00	–
Celery Vase	40.00	100.00
*Compote		
Cov, hs, 7"	100.00	185.00
Open, hs, 9"	55.00	–
Open, hs, 9-1/5"	60.00	–
Open, hs, 10"	65.00	–
Creamer		
Hotel, large, round shape	45.00	90.00
Regular	55.00	100.00
Cruet, os	125.00	250.00
Goblet	60.00	–
Pitcher		
Milk	115.00	175.00
Water, 2-1/2 qt	100.00	–
Plate, 10"	40.00	–
Relish	20.00	65.00
Sauce		
Flat, round, 4"	15.00	–
Pointed end	18.50	–
Spooner	25.00	85.00
Sugar, cov	45.00	125.00
Tumbler	45.00	–
Vinegar Jug, 3 pt	75.00	–

ASHBURTON

A popular pattern produced by Boston and Sandwich Glass Co. and by McKee & Bros. Glass Co. from the 1850s to the late 1870s with many variations. Originally made in flint by New England Glass Co. and others and later in non-flint. Prices are for flint. Non-flint values 65% less. Also reported are an amber-handled whiskey mug, flint canary celery vase ($750.00), and a scarce emerald green wineglass ($200.00). Some items known in fiery opalescent.

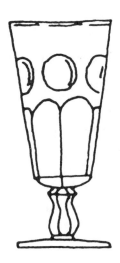

	Clear
Ale Glass, 5"	90.00
Bar Bottle	
Pint	55.00
Quart	75.00
Bitters Bottle	55.00
*Bowl, 6-1/2"	75.00
Carafe	175.00
Celery vase, scalloped top	100.00
Champagne , cut	85.00
*Claret, 5-1/4"	50.00
*Compote, open, ls, 7-1/2"	65.00
Cordial, 4-1/4" h	70.00
*Creamer, ah	210.00
Decanter, qt, cut and pressed, os	250.00
Eggcup	
Double	80.00
Single	30.00

	Clear
Flip Glass, handled	140.00
*Goblet	50.00
Honey Dish	15.00
*Jug, qt	90.00
Lamp	75.00
*Lemonade Glass	55.00
Mug, 7"	100.00
*Pitcher, water	450.00
Plate, 6-5/8"	75.00
Sauce	10.00
*Sugar, cov	90.00
Toddy Jar, cov	375.00
*Tumbler	
Bar	75.00
Water	75.00
Whiskey	60.00
Water Bottle, tumble up	95.00
Whiskey, ah	125.00
*Wine	
Cut	65.00
Pressed	40.00

ATLAS (Bullet, Cannon Ball, Crystal Ball)

Non-flint, occasionally ruby stained and etched, made by Adams & Co.; U.S. Glass Co. in 1891; and Bryce Bros., Mt. Pleasant, PA, in 1889.

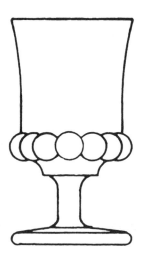

	Clear	Ruby Stained
Bowl, 9"	20.00	–
Butter, cov, regular	45.00	75.00
Cake Stand		
8"	35.00	–
9"	40.00	95.00
Celery Vase	28.00	
Champagne, 5-1/2" h	25.00	55.00
Compote		
Cov, hs, 8"	65.00	–
Cov, hs, 5," jelly	50.00	80.00
Open, ls, 7"	40.00	–
Cordial	35.00	–
Creamer		
Table, ah	30.00	55.00
Tankard	25.00	–
Goblet	35.00	65.00
Marmalade Jar	45.00	–
Molasses Can	65.00	–
Pitcher, water	65.00	–
Salt		
Master	20.00	–
Individual	15.00	–
Salt & Pepper, pr	20.00	–
Sauce		
Flat	10.00	–
Footed	15.00	25.00
Spooner	30.00	45.00
Sugar, cov	40.00	65.00
Syrup	65.00	–
Toothpick	20.00	50.00
Tray, water	75.00	–
Tumbler	28.00	–
Whiskey	20.00	45.00
Wine	25.00	–

AUSTRIAN (Finecut Medallion)

Made by Indiana Tumbler and Goblet Co., Greentown, IN, 1897. Experimental pieces were made in cobalt blue, Nile green, and opaque colors. Some pieces were made in Chocolate glass.

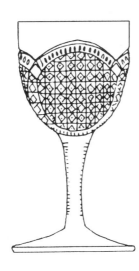

	Amber	Canary	Clear	Emerald Green
Bowl				
8," round	–	150.00	50.00	–
8-1/4," rect	–	150.00	50.00	–
Butter, cov	185.00	300.00	90.00	–
Children's table set	–	550.00	325.00	–
Compote, open, ls	–	150.00	75.00	–
Cordial	145.00	150.00	50.00	150.00
Creamer	120.00	125.00	40.00	120.00
Goblet	–	150.00	40.00	–
Mug, child's	–	–	45.00	–
Nappy, cov	–	135.00	55.00	–
Pitcher, water	–	350.00	100.00	–
Plate, 10"	–	–	40.00	–
Punch Cup	150.00	150.00	18.00	125.00
Rose Bowl	–	150.00	50.00	–
Sauce, 4-5/8" d	–	50.00	20.00	–
Spooner	–	100.00	40.00	–
Sugar, cov	–	175.00	45.00	–
Tumbler	175.00	85.00	25.00	–
Wine	175.00	150.00	30.00	150.00

BALTIMORE PEAR (Double Pear, Fig, Gipsy, Maryland Pear, Twin Pear)

Non-flint originally made by Adams & Company, Pittsburgh, PA, in 1874. Also made by U.S. Glass Company in the 1890s. Compotes were made in 18 different sizes. Given as premiums by different manufacturers and organizations. Heavily reproduced. Reproduced in clear, cobalt blue, and pink milk glass.

	Clear
Bowl	
6"	30.00
9"	35.00
Bread Plate, 12-1/2"	70.00
*Butter, cov	75.00
*Cake Stand, 9"	65.00
Celery vase	50.00
Compote	
Cov, hs, 7"	80.00
Cov, ls, 8-1/2"	45.00
Open, hs	30.00
Open, jelly	25.00
*Creamer	30.00
*Goblet	35.00
Pickle	20.00
*Pitcher	
Milk	80.00
Water	95.00
*Plate	
8-1/2"	30.00
10"	40.00
Relish	25.00
*Sauce	
Flat	10.00
Footed	15.00
Spooner	40.00
*Sugar, cov	50.00
Tray, 10-1/2"	35.00

BANDED PORTLAND (Virginia #1, Maiden's Blush)

States pattern, originally named Virginia, by Portland Glass Co., Portland, ME. Painted and fired green, yellow, blue, and possibly pink; ruby stained, and rose-flashed (which Lee notes is Maiden's Blush, referring to the color rather than the pattern, as Metz lists it). Double-flashed refers to color above and below the band, single-flashed refers to color above or below the band only.

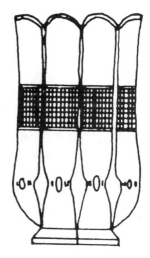

	Clear	Color-Flashed	Maiden's Blush Pink
Bowl			
4" d, open	10.00	–	20.00
6" d, cov	40.00	–	55.00
7-1/2" d, shallow	30.00	–	55.00
8"d, cov	50.00	–	75.00
Butter, cov	50.00	195.00	85.00
Cake Stand	55.00	–	90.00
Candlesticks, pr	80.00	–	125.00
Carafe	80.00	–	90.00
Celery Tray	25.00	–	40.00
Celery Vase	35.00	–	45.00
Cologne Bottle	50.00	125.00	85.00
Compote			
Cov, hs, 7"	75.00	–	125.00
Cov, hs, 8"	85.00	–	150.00
Cov, jelly, 6"	40.00	95.00	90.00
Creamer			
Individual, oval	25.00	55.00	40.00
Regular, 6 oz.	35.00	85.00	50.00
Cruet, os	60.00	175.00	300.00
Decanter, handled	50.00	–	100.00
Dresser Tray	50.00	–	65.00
Goblet	40.00	75.00	95.00
Lamp			
Flat	45.00	–	–
Tall	50.00	–	–
Nappy, sq	15.00	55.00	65.00
Olive	18.00	25.00	35.00
Pin Tray	16.00	–	25.00
Pitcher, tankard	75.00	115.00	240.00
Pomade Jar, cov	35.00	75.00	95.00
Punch Bowl, hs	110.00	–	300.00
Punch Cup	20.00	–	30.00
Relish			
6-1/2"	25.00	35.00	25.00
8-1/4"	20.00	40.00	45.00
Ring Holder	75.00	–	125.00
Salt & Pepper, pr	45.00	95.00	75.00
Sardine Box	55.00	–	90.00
Sauce, round, flat, 4 or 4-1/2"	10.00	–	25.00
Spooner	28.00	–	45.00
Sugar, cov	48.00	95.00	75.00
Sugar Shaker, orig top	45.00	–	85.00
Syrup	50.00	–	135.00
Toothpick	40.00	55.00	45.00
Tumbler	25.00	45.00	45.00
Vase			
6"	20.00	–	50.00
9"	35.00	–	65.00
Wine	35.00	–	85.00

BARBERRY (Berry, Olive, Pepper Berry)

Non-flint made by McKee & Bros. Glass Co. in the 1860s. The 6" plates are found in amber, canary, pale green, and pale blue; they are considered scarce. Pattern comes in "9-berry bunch" and "12-berry bunch" varieties.

	Clear
Bowl	
6," oval	20.00
7," oval	25.00
8," oval	25.00
8," round, flat	25.00
9," oval	30.00
Butter	
Cov	50.00
Cov, flange, pattern on edge	80.00
Cake Stand	90.00
Celery vase	55.00
Compote	
Cov, hs, 8," shell finial	85.00
Cov, ls, 8," shell finial	75.00
Open, hs, 8"	35.00
Creamer	30.00
Cup Plate	15.00
Eggcup	20.00
Goblet	25.00
Pickle	10.00
Pitcher, water, ah	100.00
Plate, 6"	20.00
Salt, master, ftd	25.00
Sauce	
Flat	10.00
Footed	15.00
Spooner, ftd	30.00
Sugar, cov	45.00
Syrup	150.00
Tumbler, ftd	25.00
Wine	30.00

BASKETWEAVE

Non-flint, c1880. Some covered pieces have a stippled cat's-head finial.

	Amber or Canary	Apple Green	Blue	Clear	Vaseline
Bowl	20.00	–	25.00	15.00	–
Bread Plate, 11"	35.00	–	35.00	10.00	–
Butter, cov	35.00	60.00	40.00	30.00	40.00
Compote, cov, 7"	–	–	–	40.00	–
Cordial	25.00	40.00	28.00	20.00	30.00
Creamer	30.00	50.00	35.00	28.00	36.00
Cup and Saucer	35.00	60.00	35.00	30.00	38.00
Dish, oval	12.00	20.00	15.00	10.00	16.00
Eggcup	20.00	30.00	25.00	15.00	25.00
*Goblet	28.00	50.00	35.00	20.00	35.00
Mug	25.00	40.00	25.00	15.00	30.00
Pickle	20.00	30.00	20.00	15.00	25.00
Pitcher					
Milk	95.00	95.00	95.00	95.00	95.00
*Water	75.00	75.00	75.00	45.00	80.00
Plate, 11," handled	25.00	35.00	25.00	20.00	30.00
Sauce	10.00	10.00	12.00	8.00	12.00
Spooner	30.00	36.00	30.00	20.00	30.00
Sugar, cov	35.00	60.00	35.00	30.00	40.00
Syrup	50.00	75.00	50.00	45.00	55.00
*Tray, water, scenic center	45.00	50.00	60.00	35.00	55.00
Tumbler, ftd	18.00	30.00	20.00	15.00	20.00
Waste Bowl	20.00	35.00	25.00	18.00	25.00
Wine	30.00	50.00	30.00	20.00	30.00

BEADED GRAPE (Beaded Grape and Vine, California, Grape and Vine)

Non-flint made by U.S. Glass Co., Pittsburgh, PA, c1890. Also attributed to Burlington Glass Works, Hamilton, Ontario, and Sydenham Glass Co., Wallaceburg, Ontario, Canada, c1910. Made in clear and emerald green, sometimes with gilt trim. Reproduced in clear, milk glass, and several colors by many, including Westmoreland Glass Co.

	Clear	Emerald Green
Bowl		
5-1/2," sq	17.50	20.00
7-1/2," sq	25.00	35.00
8," round	28.00	35.00
Bread Plate	25.00	45.00
Butter, cov	65.00	85.00
Cake Stand, 9"	65.00	85.00
Celery Tray	30.00	45.00
Celery Vase	40.00	60.00
*Compote		
Cov, hs, 7"	75.00	85.00
Cov, hs, 9"	100.00	110.00
Open, hs, 5," sq	55.00	75.00
Open, hs, 8"	55.00	70.00
Creamer	40.00	50.00
Cruet, os	65.00	125.00
*Goblet	35.00	50.00
Olive, handle	20.00	35.00
Pickle	20.00	30.00
Pitcher		
Milk	75.00	90.00
Water	85.00	120.00
*Plate, 8-1/4," sq	28.00	40.00
Salt & Pepper	45.00	65.00
Sauce, 4"	15.00	20.00
Spooner	35.00	45.00
Sugar, cov	45.00	55.00
Toothpick	40.00	65.00
*Tumbler	25.00	40.00
Vase, 6" h	25.00	40.00
*Wine	35.00	65.00

BEADED LOOP (Oregon # 1)

Non-flint made by U.S. Glass Co., Pittsburgh, PA, as Pattern Line No. 15,073. After the 1891 merger, reissued as one of the States series. Rare in emerald green. Reproduced in clear and color by Imperial.

	Clear
Berry set, master, 6 sauces	72.00
Bowl	
3-1/2"	10.00
6"	12.00
7"	15.00
Bread Plate	35.00
Butter, cov	
English	65.00
Flanged	50.00
Flat	40.00
Cake Stand	
8"	40.00
10"	55.00
Carafe, water	35.00
Celery Vase	30.00
Compote	
Cov, hs, 5," jelly	45.00
Cov, hs, 7"	60.00
Open, hs, 6"	30.00

	Clear
Open, hs, 8"	40.00
Creamer	
Flat	30.00
Footed	35.00
Cruet	50.00
*Goblet	35.00
Honey Dish	10.00
Mug	35.00
Pickle Dish, boat shape	15.00
Pitcher	
Milk	40.00
Water	60.00
Relish	15.00
Salt, master	20.00
Salt & Pepper Shakers, pr	40.00
Sauce	
Flat, 3-1/2" to 4"	5.00
Footed, 3-1/2"	10.00
Spooner	
Flat	24.00
Footed	26.00
*Sugar, cov	
Flat	25.00
Footed	30.00
Syrup	55.00
Toothpick	55.00
Tumbler	25.00
Wine	50.00

BIGLER

Flint made by Boston and Sandwich Glass Co., Sandwich, MA, and by other early factories. A scarce pattern in which goblets are most common and vary in height, shape and flare. Rare in color. The goblet has been reproduced as a commemorative item for Biglerville, PA.

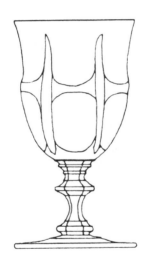

	Clear
Ale Glass	65.00
Bar Bottle, qt	95.00
Bowl, 10" d	40.00
Butter, cov	125.00
Celery Vase	100.00
Champagne	95.00
Compote, open, 7" d	40.00
Cordial	65.00
Creamer	75.00
Cup Plate	30.00
Eggcup, double	50.00
*Goblet	
Regular	48.00
Short Stem	50.00
Lamp, whale oil, monument base	155.00
Mug, ah	60.00
Plate, 6" d	30.00
Salt, master	20.00
Tumbler, water	65.00
Whiskey, handled	100.00
Wine	65.00

BIRD and STRAWBERRY (Bluebird, Flying Bird and Strawberry, Strawberry and Bird)

Non-flint, c1914. Made by Indiana Glass Co., Dunkirk, IN. Pieces occasionally highlighted by blue birds, pink strawberries, and green leaves, plus the addition of gliding.

	Clear	Colors
Bowl		
5"	25.00	45.00
9-1/2," ftd	50.00	85.00

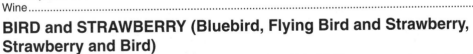

	Clear	Colors
10-1/2"	55.00	95.00
Butter, cov	100.00	175.00
Cake Stand	65.00	125.00
*Celery Vase	45.00	85.00
Compote		
*Cov, hs	125.00	200.00
Open, ls, ruffled	65.00	125.00
Jelly, cov, hs	150.00	225.00
Creamer	55.00	135.00
Cup	25.00	35.00
Goblet	600.00	1,000.00
Nappy	40.00	65.00
Pitcher, water	235.00	350.00
Plate, 12"	125.00	175.00
Punch Cup	25.00	35.00
Relish	20.00	45.00
Spooner	50.00	120.00
Sugar, cov	65.00	125.00
Tumbler	45.00	75.00
Wine	65.00	100.00

BLEEDING HEART

Non-flint originally made by King Son & Co., Pittsburgh, PA, c1875, and by U.S. Glass Co. c1898. Also found in milk glass. Goblets are found in six variations. Note: A goblet with a tin lid, containing a condiment (mustard, jelly, or baking powder) was made. It is of inferior quality compared to the original goblet.

	Clear
Bowl	
7-1/4," oval	30.00
8"	35.00
9-1/4," oval, cov	65.00
Butter, cov	75.00
Cake Stand	
9"	75.00
10"	90.00
11"	100.00
Compote	
Cov, hs, 8"	75.00
Cov, hs, 9"	95.00
Cov, ls, 7"	60.00
Cov, ls, 7-1/2"	60.00
Cov, ls, 8"	75.00
Open, ls, 8-1/2"	30.00
Creamer	
Applied Handle	60.00
Molded Handle	30.00
Dish, cov, 7"	55.00
Eggcup	45.00
Egg Rack, 3 eggs	350.00
Goblet, knob stem	35.00
Honey Dish	15.00
Mug, 3-1/4"	40.00
Pickle, 8-3/4" l, 5" w	30.00
Pitcher, water, ah	150.00
Plate	75.00
Platter, oval	65.00
Relish, oval, 5-1/2" x 3-5/8"	35.00
Salt, master, ftd	60.00
Salt, oval, flat	20.00
Sauce, flat	15.00
Spooner	25.00
Sugar, cov	60.00
Tumbler, ftd	80.00
Wine	150.00

BLOCK and FAN (Red Block and Fan, Romeo

Non-flint made by Richard and Hartley Glass Co., Tarentum, PA, in the late 1880s.
Continued by U.S. Glass Co. after 1891.

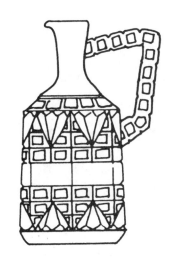

	Clear	Ruby Stained
Biscuit Jar, cov	65.00	150.00
Bowl, 4," flat	15.00	–
Butter, cov	50.00	85.00
Cake Stand		
9"	35.00	–
10"	42.00	–
Carafe	50.00	95.00
Celery Tray	30.00	
Celery Vase	35.00	75.00
Compote, open, hs, 8"	40.00	165.00
Condiment Set, salt, pepper and cruet on tray	75.00	–
Creamer		
Individual	–	35.00
Large	30.00	100.00
Regular	25.00	45.00
Small	35.00	75.00
Cruet, os	35.00	–
Dish, large, rect	25.00	–
Finger Bowl	55.00	–
Goblet	48.00	120.00
Ice Tub	45.00	50.00
Orange Bowl	50.00	–
Pickle Dish	20.00	–
Pitcher		
Milk	35.00	–
Water	48.00	125.00
Plate		
6"	15.00	–
10"	18.00	–
Relish, rect	25.00	–
Rose Bowl	25.00	–
Salt & Pepper	30.00	–
Sauce		
Flat, 5"	8.00	–
Ftd, 3-3/4"	12.00	25.00
Spooner	25.00	–
Sugar, cov	50.00	–
Sugar Shaker	40.00	–
Syrup	75.00	95.00
Tray, ice cream, rect	75.00	–
Tumbler	30.00	40.00
Waste Bowl	30.00	–
Wine	45.00	80.00

BOW TIE (American Bow Tie)

Non-flint made by Thompson Glass Co., Uniontown, PA, c1889.

	Clear
Bowl	
8"	35.00
10-1/4" d, 5" h	65.00
Butter, cov	65.00
Butter Pat	25.00
Cake Stand, large, 9" d	60.00
Compote, open	
hs, 5-1/2"	60.00
hs, 9-1/4"	65.00
ls, 6-1/2"	45.00
ls, 8"	55.00
Creamer	45.00

	Clear
Goblet	60.00
Honey, cov	55.00
Marmalade Jar	75.00
Orange Bowl, ftd, hs, 10"	110.00
Pitcher	
Milk	85.00
Water	75.00
Punch Bowl	100.00
Relish, rect	25.00
Salt	
Individual	20.00
Master	45.00
Salt Shaker	40.00
Sauce, flat	15.00
Spooner	35.00
Sugar	
Cov	55.00
Open	40.00
Tumbler	45.00

BRIDAL ROSETTE (Checkerboard)

Made by Westmoreland Glass Co. in the early 1900s. Add 150% for ruby-stained values. Reproduced since the 1950s in milk glass and, in recent years, with pink satin. The Cambridge Ribbon pattern, usually marked "Nearcut," is similar.

	Clear
Bowl, 9," shallow	20.00
Butter, cov	40.00
Celery Tray	20.00
Celery vase	30.00
Compote, open, ls, 8"	25.00
Creamer	25.00
Cruet, os	40.00
Cup	8.00
Goblet	28.00
Honey Dish, cov, sq, pedestal	45.00
Pitcher	
Milk	40.00
Water	35.00
Plate	
7"	15.00
10"	20.00
Punch Cup	5.00
Salt & Pepper	40.00
Sauce, flat	5.00
Spooner	20.00
Sugar, cov	35.00
Tumbler	
Iced tea	25.00
Water	20.00
Wine	15.00

BROKEN COLUMN (Bamboo Irish Column, Notched Rib, Rattan, Ribbed Fingerprint)

Made in Findlay, Ohio, c1888, by Columbia Glass Co.; and later by U.S. Glass Co. Notches may be ruby stained. A cobalt blue cup is known. The square covered compote has been reproduced, as have items for the Metropolitan Museum of Art and the Smithsonian Institution. Those for the Smithsonian are marked with a raised "S.I."

	Clear	Ruby Stained
Banana Stand	185.00	—
Basket, ah, 12" h, 15" l	125.00	—
Biscuit Jar	85.00	165.00
Bowl		
4" berry	15.00	20.00

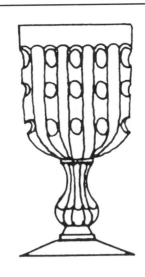

	Clear	Ruby Stained
*8"	35.00	–
9"	40.00	–
Bread Plate	60.00	125.00
Butter, cov	85.00	175.00
Cake Stand, 9" or 10"	75.00	225.00
Carafe, water	75.00	150.00
Celery Tray, oval	35.00	85.00
Celery Vase	50.00	135.00
Champagne	100.00	
Claret	75.00	–
Compote		
Cov, hs, 5-1/4" d, 10-1/4" h	90.00	200.00
Cov, hs, 10"	110.00	400.00
Open, hs, 8" d	75.00	200.00
*Creamer	42.50	125.00
Cruet, os	85.00	150.00
Decanter	85.00	–
Finger Bowl	30.00	–
*Goblet	55.00	100.00
Marmalade Jar	85.00	–
Pickle Castor, SP frame	225.00	450.00
*Pitcher, water	90.00	230.00
Plate		
4"	25.00	40.00
7-1/2"	40.00	95.00
Punch Cup	15.00	–
Relish	25.00	–
Salt Shaker	45.00	65.00
*Sauce, flat	10.00	20.00
*Spooner	35.00	85.00
*Sugar, cov	70.00	135.00
Sugar Shaker	85.00	200.00
Syrup	165.00	400.00
Toothpick	150.00	–
Tumbler	45.00	55.00
Vegetable, cov	90.00	–
*Wine	80.00	125.00

BUCKLE (Early Buckle)

Flint and non-flint pattern. The original maker is unknown. Shards have been found at the sites of the following glasshouses: Boston and Sandwich Glass Co., Sandwich, MA; Union Glass Co., Somerville, MA; and Burlington Glass Works, Hamilton, Ontario, Canada. Gillinder and Sons, Philadelphia, PA made the non-flint production, in the late 1870s.

	Flint	Non-Flint
Bowl		
8"	60.00	50.00
10"	65.00	50.00
Butter, cov	65.00	60.00
Cake Stand, 9-3/4"	–	30.00
Champagne	60.00	–
Compote		
Cov, hs, 6" d	95.00	40.00
Open, hs, 8-1/2"	40.00	35.00
Open, ls	40.00	35.00
Creamer, ah	120.00	40.00
Eggcup	35.00	25.00
Goblet	40.00	25.00
Pickle	40.00	15.00
Pitcher, water, ah	600.00	85.00
Salt		
flat, oval	30.00	15.00
footed	20.00	18.00
Sauce, flat	10.00	8.00
Spooner	35.00	27.50

	Flint	Non-Flint
Sugar, cov	75.00	55.00
Tumbler	55.00	30.00
Wine	75.00	35.00

BULL'S EYE

Flint made by the New England Glass Co. in the 1850s. Also found in colors and milk glass, which are worth more than double the price of clear.

	Clear
Bitters Bottle	80.00
Butter, cov	150.00
Carafe	45.00
Castor Bottle	35.00
Celery Vase	85.00
Champagne	95.00
Cologne Bottle	85.00
Cordial	75.00
Creamer, ah	125.00
Cruet, os	125.00
Decanter, qt, bar lip	120.00
Eggcup	
Cov	165.00
Open	48.00
*Goblet	65.00
Lamp	100.00
Mug, 3-1/2," ah	110.00
Pitcher, water	285.00
Relish, oval	25.00
Salt	
Individual	40.00
Master, ftd	100.00
Spill holder	85.00
Spooner	40.00
Sugar, cov	125.00
Sweetmeat, cov	125.00
Tumbler	85.00
Water Bottle, tumble up	125.00
Whiskey	70.00
Wine	50.00

BULL'S EYE and DAISY

Made by U.S. Glass Co. in 1909. Also made with amethyst, blue, green, and pink stain in eyes.

	Clear	Emerald Green	Ruby Stained
Bowl	15.00	20.00	30.00
Butter, cov	25.00	45.00	90.00
Celery Vase	20.00	25.00	40.00
Creamer	25.00	25.00	50.00
Decanter	—	110.00	—
Goblet	25.00	25.00	50.00
Pitcher, water	35.00	40.00	95.00
Salt Shaker	20.00	20.00	35.00
Sauce	7.50	10.00	20.00
Spooner	20.00	25.00	40.00
Sugar	22.00	30.00	45.00
Tumbler	15.00	20.00	35.00
Wine	20.00	25.00	40.00

BULL'S EYE with DIAMOND POINT

Flint made by New England Glass Co. c1869.

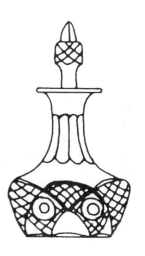

	Clear
Butter, cov	250.00
Celery Vase	150.00
Champagne	145.00
Cologne Bottle, os	90.00

	Clear
Creamer	200.00
Cruet, os	225.00
Decanter, qt, os	200.00
Eggcup	90.00
Goblet	135.00
Honey Dish, flat	25.00
Lamp, finger, ah	165.00
Pitcher, water, 10-1/4," tankard	650.00
Salt, master, cov	100.00
Sauce	20.00
Spill	75.00
Spooner	125.00
Sugar, cov	175.00
Syrup	175.00
Tumbler	145.00
Tumble-Up	165.00
Whiskey	150.00
Wine	135.00

BUTTERFLY and FAN (Bird in Ring, Fan, Grace, Japanese)

Non-flint made by George Duncan & Sons, Pittsburgh, PA, c1880 and by Richards and Hartley Glass Co., Pittsburgh, PA, c1888.

	Clear
Bowl	30.00
Bread Plate	50.00
Butter, cov	
Flat	100.00
Footed	75.00
Celery Vase	75.00
Compote	
Cov, hs, 8" d	95.00
Cov, hs, 7" d	95.00
Open, hs	30.00
Creamer, ftd	45.00
Goblet	65.00
Marmalade Jar	75.00
Pickle Jar, SP frame and cov	80.00
Pitcher, water	115.00
Sauce, ftd	15.00
Spooner	30.00
Sugar cov, ftd	50.00

CABBAGE ROSE

Non-flint made by Central Glass Co., Wheeling, WV, c1870. Reproduced in clear and colors by Mosser Glass Co., Cambridge, OH, during the early 1960s.

	Clear
Basket, handled, 12"	125.00
Bitters Bottle, 6-1/2" h	125.00
Bowl, oval	
7-1/2"	30.00
9-1/2"	40.00
Bowl, round	
6"	25.00
7-1/2," cov	65.00
Butter, cov	60.00
Cake Stand	
11"	40.00
12-1/2"	50.00
Celery Vase	48.00
Champagne	50.00
Compote	
Cov, hs, 8-1/2"	120.00
Cov, ls, 6"	95.00
Cov, ls, 7-1/2"	100.00

	Clear
Open, hs, 7-1/2"	75.00
Open, hs, 9-1/2"	100.00
Creamer, 5-1/2," ah	55.00
Eggcup	45.00
*Goblet	40.00
Mug	60.00
Pickle Dish	35.00
Pitcher	
Milk	150.00
Water	125.00
Relish, 8-1/2" l, 5" w, rose-filled horn of plenty center	35.00
Salt, master, ftd	25.00
*Sauce, 4"	10.00
Spooner	25.00
Sugar, cov	55.00
Tumbler	40.00
Wine	40.00

CABLE

Flint, c1860. Made by Boston and Sandwich Glass Co. to commemorate the laying of the Atlantic Cable. Also found with amber-stained panels and in opaque colors and other colors (rare).

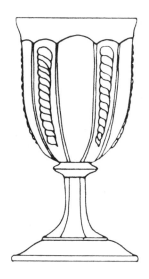

	Clear
Bowl	
8," ftd	45.00
9"	70.00
Butter, cov	100.00
Cake Stand, 9"	100.00
Celery Vase	70.00
Champagne	250.00
Compote, open	
hs, 5-1/2"	65.00
ls, 7"	50.00
ls, 9"	35.00
ls, 11"	75.00
Creamer	225.00
Decanter, qt, ground stopper	295.00
Eggcup	
Cov	225.00
Open	60.00
*Goblet	70.00
Honey Dish	15.00
Lamp, 8-3/4"	
Glass Base	135.00
Marble Base	100.00
Miniature Lamp	500.00
Pitcher, water, rare	650.00
Plate, 6"	75.00
Salt, individual, flat	35.00
Salt, master	
Cov	95.00
Ftd	45.00
Sauce, flat	15.00
Spooner	40.00
Sugar, cov	120.00
Syrup	225.00
Tumbler, ftd	200.00
Wine	175.00

CANADIAN

Non-flint possibly made by Burlington Glass Works, Hamilton, Ontario, Canada, c1870.

	Clear
Bowl, 7" d, 4-1/2" h, ftd	65.00
Bread Plate, 10"	45.00
Butter, cov	85.00

	Clear
Cake Stand, 9-1/4"	85.00
Celery Vase	65.00
Compote	
Cov, hs, 6"	90.00
Cov, hs, 7"	100.00
Cov, hs, 8"	110.00
Cov, ls, 6"	50.00
Cov, ls, 8"	75.00
Open, ls, 7"	35.00
Creamer	65.00
Goblet	45.00
Mug, small	45.00
Pitcher	
Milk	90.00
Water	125.00
Plate, 6," handles	30.00
Sauce	
Flat	15.00
Footed	20.00
Spooner	45.00
Sugar, cov	90.00
Wine	45.00

CANE (Cane, Insert, Hobnailed Diamond and Star)

Non-flint made by Gillinder and Sons Glass Co., Philadelphia, PA, and by McKee Bros. Glass Co., c1885. Goblets and toddy plates with inverted "buttons" are known.

	Amber	Apple Green	Blue	Clear	Vaseline
Butter, cov	45.00	60.00	75.00	40.00	60.00
Celery Vase	38.00	40.00	50.00	32.50	40.00
Compote, open, ls, 5-3/4"	28.00	30.00	35.00	25.00	35.00
Cordial	–	–	–	25.00	–
Creamer	35.00	40.00	50.00	25.00	30.00
Finger Bowl	20.00	30.00	35.00	15.00	30.00
Goblet	25.00	40.00	35.00	20.00	40.00
Honey Dish	–	–	–	15.00	–
Match Holder, kettle	20.00	–	35.00	30.00	35.00
Pickle	25.00	20.00	25.00	15.00	20.00
Pitcher					
Milk	60.00	55.00	65.00	40.00	55.00
Water	80.00	85.00	80.00	48.00	85.00
Plate, toddy, 4-1/2"	20.00	25.00	30.00	16.50	20.00
Relish	25.00	26.00	25.00	15.00	20.00
Salt & Pepper	60.00	50.00	80.00	30.00	70.00
Sauce, flat	–	10.00	–	7.00	–
Slipper	30.00	–	25.00	15.00	30.00
Spooner	42.00	35.00	30.00	20.00	30.00
Sugar, cov	45.00	45.00	45.00	25.00	45.00
Tray, water	35.00	40.00	50.00	30.00	45.00
Tumbler	24.00	30.00	35.00	20.00	25.00
Waste Bowl, 7-1/2"	32.50	30.00	35.00	20.00	30.00
Wine	35.00	40.00	35.00	20.00	35.00

CAROLINA (Inverness, Mayflower)

Made by Bryce Bros., Pittsburgh, PA, c1890 and later by U.S. Glass Co., as part of the States series, c1903. Ruby-stained pieces often were made as souvenirs. Some clear pieces found with gilt or purple stain.

	Clear	Ruby Stained
Bowl, berry	15.00	–
Butter, cov	35.00	–
Cake Stand	35.00	–
Compote		
Open, hs, 8"	38.50	–

	Clear	Ruby Stained
Open, hs, 9-1/2"	20.00	–
Open, jelly	10.00	–
Creamer	20.00	–
Goblet	25.00	45.00
Mug	20.00	35.00
Pitcher, milk	45.00	–
Plate, 7-1/2"	10.00	–
Relish	10.00	–
Salt Shaker	15.00	35.00
Sauce		
Flat	8.00	–
Footed	10.00	–
Spooner	20.00	–
Sugar, cov	25.00	–
Tumbler	10.00	–
Wine	20.00	35.00

CATHEDRAL (Orion, Waffle and Fine Cut)

Non-flint pattern made by Bryce Bros. Pittsburgh, PA, in the 1880s and by U.S. Glass Co. in 1891. Also found in ruby stained (add 50%).

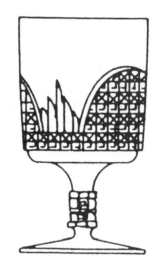

	Amber	Amethyst	Blue	Clear	Vaseline
Bowl, berry, 8"	40.00	60.00	50.00	45.00	45.00
Butter, cov	60.00	110.00	40.00	45.00	60.00
Cake Stand	50.00	75.00	65.00	40.00	65.00
Celery Vase	35.00	60.00	40.00	30.00	40.00
Compote					
Cov, hs, 8"	80.00	125.00	100.00	70.00	90.00
Open, hs, 9-1/2"	50.00	85.00	65.00	55.00	–
Open, ls, 7"	45.00	80.00	35.00	25.00	50.00
Open, jelly	–	–	–	25.00	–
Creamer					
Flat, sq	50.00	85.00	–	35.00	50.00
Tall	45.00	80.00	50.00	30.00	45.00
Cruet, os	125.00	–	–	65.00	–
Goblet	50.00	70.00	50.00	40.00	60.00
Lamp, 12-1/4" h	–	–	185.00	–	–
Pitcher, water	75.00	110.00	75.00	60.00	100.00
Relish, fish shape	40.00	50.00	50.00	–	45.00
Salt, boat shape	20.00	30.00	25.00	15.00	25.00
Sauce					
Flat	15.00	30.00	20.00	15.00	20.00
Footed	15.00	35.00	20.00	15.00	20.00
Spooner	40.00	65.00	50.00	35.00	45.00
Sugar, cov	70.00	100.00	60.00	50.00	60.00
Tumbler	40.00	40.00	35.00	25.00	40.00
Wine	40.00	60.00	55.00	30.00	50.00

COLORADO (Lacy Medallion)

Non-flint States pattern made by U.S. Glass Co. in 1898. Made in amethyst stained, ruby stained, and opaque white with enamel floral trim, all of which are scarce. Some pieces found with ornate silver frames or feet. Purists consider these two separate patterns, with the Lacy Medallion restricted to souvenir pieces. Reproductions have been made.

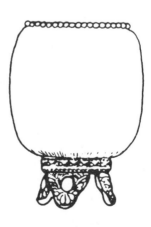

	Blue	Clear	Green
Banana Stand	65.00	35.00	50.00
Bowl			
6"	35.00	25.00	30.00
7-1/2," ftd	40.00	25.00	35.00
8-1/2," ftd	65.00	45.00	60.00
Butter, cov	175.00	60.00	100.00
Cake Stand	70.00	55.00	65.00
Celery Vase	65.00	35.00	75.00
Compote			
Open, ls, 5"	35.00	20.00	30.00

	Blue	Clear	Green
Open, ls, 6"	45.00	20.00	40.00
Open, ls, 9-1/4"	85.00	35.00	65.00
Creamer			
Individual	35.00	30.00	25.00
Regular	95.00	45.00	70.00
Mug	40.00	20.00	30.00
Nappy	40.00	20.00	35.00
Pitcher			
Milk	250.00	–	100.00
Water	375.00	95.00	175.00
Plate			
6"	50.00	15.00	45.00
8"	65.00	20.00	60.00
Punch Cup	30.00	18.00	25.00
Salt Shaker	65.00	30.00	40.00
Sauce, ruffled	30.00	15.00	25.00
Sherbert	50.00	25.00	45.00
Spooner	65.00	40.00	70.00
Sugar			
Cov, regular	75.00	60.00	70.00
Open, individual	35.00	24.00	30.00
*Toothpick	55.00	30.00	35.00
Tray, calling card	45.00	25.00	35.00
Tumbler	35.00	15.00	30.00
Vase, 12"	85.00	35.00	60.00
Violet Bowl	60.00	–	–
Wine	–	25.00	40.00

COMET

Flint, possibly made by Boston and Sandwich Glass Co. in the early 1850s.

	Clear
Butter, cov	200.00
Compote, open, ls	140.00
Creamer	175.00
Goblet	135.00
Mug	135.00
Pitcher, water	750.00
Spooner	95.00
Sugar, cov	175.00
Tumbler	110.00
Whiskey, w/handle	250.00

CONNECTICUT

Non-flint, one of the States patterns made by U.S. Glass Co. c1900. Found in plain and engraved. Two varieties of ruby-stained toothpicks ($90.00) have been identified.

	Clear
Biscuit jar	25.00
Bowl	
4"	10.00
8"	15.00
Butter, cov	35.00
Cake Stand	40.00
Celery Tray	20.00
Celery Vase	25.00
Compote	
Cov, hs	40.00
Open, hs, 7"	25.00
Creamer	28.00
Dish, 8," oblong	20.00
Lamp, enamel dec	85.00
Lemonade, handled	20.00
Pitcher, water	40.00
Relish	15.00

	Clear
Salt & Pepper	35.00
Spooner	25.00
Sugar, cov	35.00
Sugar Shaker	35.00
Toothpick	50.00
Tumbler, water	20.00
Wine	35.00

CRYSTAL WEDDING (Collins, Crystal Anniversary)

Non-flint made by Adams Glass Co., Pittsburgh, PA, c1890 and by U.S. Glass Co. in 1891. Also found in frosted, amber stained, and cobalt blue (rare). Heavily reproduced in clear, ruby stained, and milk with enamel.

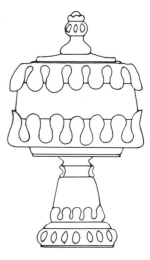

	Clear	Ruby Stained
Banana Stand	95.00	–
Bowl		
4-1/2," individual berry	15.00	–
7," sq, cov	75.00	85.00
8," sq, berry	50.00	85.00
8," sq, cov	60.00	95.00
Butter, cov	75.00	125.00
Cake Plate, sq	45.00	85.00
Cake Stand, 10"	65.00	–
Celery Vase	45.00	75.00
Compote		
*Cov, hs, 7" x 13"	100.00	110.00
Open, ls, 5," sq	50.00	55.00
Creamer	50.00	75.00
Cruet	125.00	200.00
*Goblet	55.00	85.00
Nappy, handle	25.00	–
Pickle	25.00	40.00
Pitcher		
Milk, round	110.00	125.00
Milk, sq	125.00	200.00
Water, round	110.00	210.00
Water, sq	165.00	225.00
Plate, 10"	25.00	40.00
Relish	20.00	40.00
Salt		
Individual	25.00	40.00
Master	35.00	65.00
Salt Shaker	65.00	75.00
Sauce	15.00	20.00
Spooner	30.00	60.00
Sugar, cov	70.00	85.00
Syrup	150.00	200.00
Tumbler	35.00	45.00
Vase		
Footed, twisted	25.00	–
Swung	25.00	–
Wine	45.00	70.00

DAISY and BUTTON

Non-flint made in the 1880s by several companies in many different forms. In continuous production since inception. Original manufacturers include: Bryce Brothers, Doyle & Co., Hobbs, Brockunier & Co., George Duncan & Sons, Boston & Sandwich Glass Co., Beatty & Sons, and U.S. Glass Co. Reproductions have existed since the early 1930s in original and new colors. Several companies, including L.G. Wright, Imperial Glass Co., Fenton Art Glass Co., and Degenhart Glass Co, too, have made reproductions. Also found in amberina, amber stain, and ruby stained.

	Amber	Apple Green	Blue	Clear	Vaseline
Bowl, triangular	40.00	45.00	45.00	25.00	65.00
Bread Plate, 13"	35.00	60.00	35.00	20.00	40.00

	Amber	Apple Green	Blue	Clear	Vaseline
*Butter, cov					
Round	70.00	90.00	70.00	65.00	95.00
Square	110.00	115.00	110.00	100.00	120.00
Butter Pat	30.00	40.00	35.00	25.00	35.00
*Canoe					
4"	12.00	24.00	15.00	10.00	24.00
8-1/2"	30.00	35.00	30.00	25.00	35.00
12"	60.00	35.00	28.00	20.00	40.00
14"	30.00	40.00	35.00	25.00	40.00
*Castor Set					
4 bottle, glass standard	90.00	85.00	95.00	65.00	75.00
5 bottle, metal standard	100.00	100.00	110.00	100.00	95.00
Celery Vase	48.00	55.00	40.00	30.00	55.00
*Compote					
Cov, hs, 6"	35.00	50.00	45.00	25.00	50.00
Open, hs, 8"	75.00	65.00	60.00	40.00	65.00
*Creamer	35.00	40.00	40.00	18.00	35.00
*Cruet, os	100.00	80.00	75.00	45.00	80.00
Eggcup	20.00	30.00	25.00	15.00	30.00
Finger Bowl	30.00	50.00	35.00	30.00	42.00
*Goblet	40.00	50.00	40.00	25.00	40.00
*Hat, 2-1/2"	30.00	35.00	40.00	20.00	40.00
Ice Cream Tray, 14" x 9" x 2"	75.00	50.00	55.00	35.00	55.00
Ice Tub	–	35.00	–	–	75.00
Inkwell	40.00	50.00	45.00	30.00	45.00
Parfait	25.00	35.00	30.00	20.00	35.00
Pickle Castor	125.00	90.00	150.00	75.00	150.00
*Pitcher, water					
Bulbous, reed handle	125.00	95.00	90.00	75.00	90.00
Tankard	62.00	65.00	62.00	60.00	65.00
*Plate					
5," leaf shape	20.00	24.00	12.00	12.00	25.00
6," round	10.00	22.00	15.00	6.50	24.00
7," square	25.00	35.00	25.00	15.00	35.00
Punch Bowl, stand	90.00	100.00	95.00	85.00	100.00
*Salt & Pepper	30.00	40.00	30.00	20.00	35.00
*Sauce, 4"	18.00	25.00	18.00	15.00	25.00
*Slipper					
5"	45.00	48.00	50.00	45.00	50.00
11-1/2"	40.00	50.00	30.00	35.00	50.00
*Spooner	40.00	40.00	45.00	35.00	45.00
*Sugar, cov	45.00	50.00	45.00	35.00	50.00
Syrup	45.00	50.00	45.00	30.00	45.00
*Toothpick					
Round	40.00	55.00	25.00	40.00	45.00
Urn	25.00	30.00	25.00	15.00	30.00
*Tray	65.00	65.00	60.00	35.00	60.00
Tumbler	18.00	30.00	35.00	15.00	25.00
Vase, wall pocket	125.00	–	–	–	–
*Wine	15.00	25.00	20.00	10.00	45.00

DAISY and BUTTON with CROSSBARS (Daisy and Thumbprint Crossbar, Daisy and Button with Crossbar and Thumbprint Band, Daisy with Crossbar, Mikado)

Non-flint made by Richards and Hartley, Tarentum, PA, c1885. Reissued by U.S. Glass Co. after 1891. Shards have been found at Burlington Glass Works, Hamilton, Ontario, Canada.

	Amber	Blue	Clear	Vaseline
Bowl				
6"	25.00	30.00	15.00	25.00
9"	30.00	40.00	25.00	30.00
Bread Plate	30.00	45.00	25.00	35.00

	Amber	Blue	Clear	Vaseline
Butter, cov				
Flat	55.00	55.00	45.00	55.00
Footed	–	75.00	25.00	60.00
Celery Vase	36.00	40.00	30.00	50.00
Compote				
Cov, hs, 8"	55.00	65.00	45.00	55.00
Open, hs, 8"	45.00	50.00	30.00	45.00
Open, ls, 7"	30.00	–	20.00	45.00
Creamer				
Individual	30.00	30.00	20.00	30.00
Regular	45.00	45.00	35.00	40.00
Cruet, os	75.00	85.00	35.00	100.00
Goblet	40.00	40.00	25.00	48.00
Mug, 3" h	15.00	18.00	12.50	20.00
Pitcher				
Milk	90.00	95.00	45.00	90.00
Water	145.00	110.00	65.00	125.00
Salt & Pepper	40.00	50.00	30.00	45.00
Sauce				
Flat	15.00	18.00	10.00	15.00
Footed	18.00	25.00	15.00	24.00
Spooner	35.00	35.00	25.00	35.00
Sugar, cov				
Individual	25.00	35.00	10.00	25.00
Regular	50.00	60.00	25.00	55.00
Syrup	125.00	125.00	65.00	125.00
Toothpick	40.00	40.00	28.00	35.00
Tumbler	20.00	25.00	18.00	25.00
Wine	30.00	35.00	25.00	30.00

DAKOTA (Baby Thumbprint, Thumbprint Band)

Non-flint made by Ripley and Co., Pittsburgh, PA, in the late 1880s and early 1890s. Later reissued by U.S. Glass Co. as one of the States patterns. Prices listed are for etched fern and berry pattern; also found with fern and no berry, and oak-leaf etching, and scarcer grape etching. Other etchings known include fish, swan, peacock, bird and insect, bird and flowers, ivy and berry, stag, spider and insect in web, buzzard on dead tree and crane catching fish. Sometimes ruby stained with or without souvenir markings; ftd. Sauce known in cobalt blue. There is a four-piece table set available in a "hotel" variant. Prices are about 20 percent higher than for the regular type.

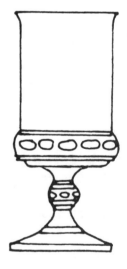

	Clear Etched	Clear Plain	Ruby Stained
Basket, 10" x 2"	205.00	175.00	300.00
Bottle, 5-1/2"	85.00	65.00	–
Bowl, berry	45.00	35.00	–
Butter, cov	65.00	40.00	125.00
Cake Cover, 8" d	300.00	200.00	–
Cake Stand, 10-1/2"	95.00	75.00	–
Celery Tray	40.00	25.00	–
Celery Vase	40.00	30.00	–
Compote			
Cov, hs, 5"	60.00	50.00	–
Cov, hs, 7"	70.00	55.00	–
Cov, hs, 10"	125.00	100.00	–
Open, ls, 6"	45.00	35.00	–
Open, ls, 8"	50.00	40.00	–
Open, ls, 10"	75.00	65.00	–
Condiment Tray	–	75.00	–
Creamer	55.00	30.00	–
Cruet	125.00	100.00	175.00
Goblet	35.00	25.00	75.00
Pitcher			
Milk	145.00	80.00	200.00
Water	125.00	75.00	190.00
Plate, 10"	85.00	75.00	–

	Clear Etched	Clear Plain	Ruby Stained
Salt Shaker	65.00	50.00	125.00
Sauce			
Flat, 4" d	20.00	15.00	30.00
Footed, 5" d	25.00	15.00	35.00
Spooner	30.00	25.00	65.00
Sugar, cov	65.00	55.00	85.00
Tankard	125.00	95.00	205.00
Tray			
Water, 13" d	100.00	75.00	—
Wine, 10" to 12"	125.00	90.00	—
Tumbler	35.00	30.00	55.00
Waste Bowl	65.00	50.00	75.00
Wine	30.00	20.00	55.00

DEER and PINE TREE (Deer and Doe)

Non-flint made by Belmont Glass Co. and McKee & Bros. Glass Co. c1886. Souvenir mugs with gilt found in clear and olive green. Also made in canary (vaseline). The goblet has been reproduced since 1938. L. G. Wright Glass Co. has reproduced the goblet in clear glass using new molds.

	Amber	Apple Green	Blue	Clear
Bread Plate	90.00	100.00	100.00	65.00
Butter, cov	165.00	165.00	165.00	95.00
Cake Stand	—	—	—	75.00
Celery Vase	—	—	—	75.00
Compote				
Cov, hs, 8," sq	—	—	—	100.00
Open, hs, 7"	—	—	—	45.00
Open, hs, 9"	—	—	—	55.00
Creamer	95.00	85.00	90.00	65.00
Finger Bowl	—	—	—	55.00
*Goblet	—	—	—	55.00
Marmalade Jar	—	—	—	90.00
Mug	40.00	45.00	50.00	40.00
Pickle	—	—	—	30.00
Pitcher				
Milk	—	—	—	90.00
Water	165.00	165.00	165.00	100.00
Platter, 8" x 13"	75.00	—	80.00	60.00
Sauce				
Flat	—	—	—	20.00
Footed	—	—	—	25.00
Spooner	—	—	—	65.00
Sugar, cov	—	—	—	85.00
Tray, water	100.00	—	90.00	60.00

DELAWARE (American Beauty, Four Petal Flower)

Non-flint made by U.S. Glass Co., Pittsburgh, PA, 1899-1909. Also made Diamond Glass Co., Montreal, Quebec, Canada, c1902. Also found in amethyst (scarce), clear with rose trim, custard, and milk glass. Prices are for pieces with perfect gold trim.

	Clear	Green with Gold	Rose with Gold
Banana Bowl	40.00	55.00	65.00
Bowl			
8"	30.00	40.00	50.00
9"	25.00	60.00	75.00
Bottle, os	80.00	150.00	185.00
Bride's Basket, SP frame	75.00	115.00	165.00
*Butter, cov	50.00	115.00	150.00
Claret Jug, tankard shape	110.00	195.00	200.00
Celery Vase, flat	75.00	90.00	95.00
*Creamer	45.00	65.00	70.00
Cruet, os	90.00	200.00	250.00
Finger Bowl	25.00	50.00	75.00

	Clear	Green with Gold	Rose with Gold
Lamp Shade, electric	85.00	–	100.00
Pin Tray	30.00	55.00	95.00
Pitcher, water	50.00	95.00	95.00
Pomade Box, jeweled	100.00	250.00	350.00
Puff Box, bulbous, jeweled	100.00	200.00	315.00
Punch Cup	18.00	30.00	35.00
Sauce, 5-1/2," boat	15.00	35.00	30.00
Spooner	45.00	50.00	55.00
*Sugar, cov	65.00	85.00	100.00
Toothpick	35.00	125.00	155.00
Tumbler	20.00	40.00	45.00
Vase			
6"	25.00	60.00	70.00
8"	25.00	70.00	75.00
9-1/2"	40.00	80.00	85.00

DIAMOND POINT (Diamond Point with Ribs, Pineapple, Sawtooth, Stepped Diamond Point)

Flint originally made by Boston and Sandwich Glass Co. c1850 and by the New England Glass Co., East Cambridge, MA, c1860. Many other companies manufactured this pattern throughout the 19th century. Rare in color.

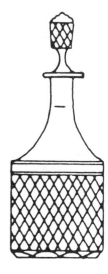

	Flint	Non-Flint
Ale Glass, 6-1/4" h	85.00	–
Bowl		
7," cov	60.00	20.00
8," cov	60.00	20.00
8," open	45.00	15.00
Butter, cov	95.00	50.00
Cake Stand, 14"	185.00	–
Candlesticks, pr	165.00	–
Castor Bottle	25.00	15.00
Celery Vase	75.00	30.00
Champagne	85.00	35.00
Claret	90.00	–
Compote		
Cov, hs, 8"	185.00	60.00
Open, hs, 10-1/2," flared	100.00	–
Open, hs, 11," scalloped rim	110.00	–
Open, ls, 7-1/2"	50.00	40.00
Cordial	165.00	–
Creamer, ah	115.00	–
Decanter, qt, os	200.00	–
Eggcup		
Cov	75.00	50.00
Open	40.00	20.00
Goblet	45.00	35.00
Honey Dish	15.00	–
Lemonade	55.00	–
Mustard, cov	25.00	–
Pitcher		
Pint	200.00	–
Quart	300.00	–
Plate		
6"	30.00	–
8"	50.00	–
Salt, master, cov	75.00	–
Sauce, flat	15.00	–
Spill Holder	45.00	–
Spooner	45.00	30.00
Sugar, cov	95.00	55.00
Syrup	170.00	–
Tumbler, bar	65.00	30.00
Whiskey, ah	85.00	–
Wine	75.00	30.00

EGG IN SAND (Bean, Stippled Oval)

Non-flint, c1885. Has been reported in colors, including blue and amber, but rare.

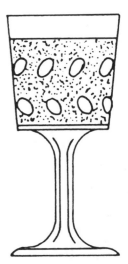

	Clear
Bread Plate, octagonal	25.00
Butter, cov	40.00
Compote, cov, jelly	45.00
Creamer	30.00
Dish, swan center	40.00
Goblet	30.00
Pitcher, water	45.00
Relish	15.00
Salt & Pepper	65.00
Sauce	10.00
Spooner, flat rim	30.00
Sugar, cov	35.00
Tray, water	40.00
Tumbler	30.00
Wine	35.00

EXCELSIOR

Flint attributed to several firms, including Boston and Sandwich Glass Co., Sandwich, MA; McKee Bros., Pittsburgh, PA; and Ihmsen & Co., Pittsburgh, PA, 1850s-60s. Quality and design vary. Prices are for high-quality flint. Very rare in color.

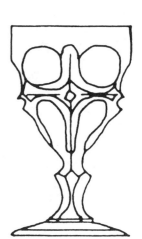

	Clear
Ale Glass	50.00
Bar Bottle	85.00
Bitters Bottle	95.00
Bowl, 10," open	125.00
Butter, cov	100.00
Candlestick, 9-1/2" h	125.00
Celery Vase, scalloped top	85.00
Champagne	60.00
Claret	45.00
Compote	
Cov, ls	125.00
Open, hs	85.00
Cordial	40.00
Creamer	85.00
Decanter	
Pint	85.00
Quart	85.00
Eggcup	
Double	45.00
Single	40.00
Goblet	50.00
Lamp, hand	95.00
Mug	30.00
Pickle Jar, cov	45.00
Pitcher, water	400.00
Salt, master	30.00
Spillholder	75.00
Spooner	60.00
Sugar, cov	110.00
Syrup	125.00
Tumbler, bar	50.00
Whiskey, Maltese Cross	65.00
Wine	45.00

EYEWINKER (Cannon Ball, Crystal Ball, Winking Eye)

Non-flint made in Findlay, Ohio, in 1889. Reportedly made by Dalzell, Gilmore and Leighton Glass Co., which was organized in 1883 in West Virginia and moved to Findlay in 1888. Made only in clear glass; reproduced in color by several companies, including L. G. Wright Co. A goblet and toothpick were not originally made in this pattern.

	Clear
Banana Stand, hs	135.00
Bowl	
6-1/2"	25.00
9," cov	75.00
*Butter, cov	70.00
Cake Stand, 8"	55.00
Celery Vase	45.00
*Compote	
Cov, hs, 6-1/2"	85.00
Cov, hs, 9-1/2"	150.00
Open, 7-1/4," fluted	65.00
Open, 4-1/2," jelly	45.00
Creamer	65.00
Cruet	65.00
*Honey Dish	40.00
Lamp, kerosene	125.00
Nappy, folded sides, 7-1/4"	30.00
*Pitcher, water	95.00
Plate	
7"	30.00
9," sq, upturned sides	65.00
10," upturned sides	85.00
Salt Shaker	35.00
Sauce	15.00
Spooner	35.00
*Sugar, cov	55.00
Syrup, pewter top	125.00
*Tumbler	45.00

FEATHER (Cambridge Feather, Feather and Quill, Fine Cut and Feather, Indiana Feather, Indiana Swirl, Prince's Feather, Swirl, Swirl and Feather)

Non-flint made by McKee & Bros. Glass Co., Pittsburgh, PA, 1896-1901; Beatty-Brady Glass Co., Dunkirk, IN, c1903; and Cambridge Glass Co., Cambridge, Ohio, c1902-03. Later the pattern was reissued with variations and quality differences. Also found in amber stain (rare).

	Clear	Emerald Green
Banana Boat, ftd	75.00	175.00
Bowl, oval		
7" x 9," ftd	35.00	–
8-1/2"	25.00	–
9-1/4"	20.00	75.00
Bowl, round		
6"	20.00	–
7"	25.00	75.00
8"	30.00	85.00
Butter, cov	55.00	150.00
Cake Plate	65.00	–
Cake Stand		
8"	45.00	175.00
9-1/2"	50.00	175.00
11"	70.00	175.00
Celery Vase 45.00	80.00	
Champagne	65.00	–
Compote		
Cov, hs, 8-1/2"	150.00	450.00
Cov, ls, 4-1/4," jelly	100.00	150.00
Cov, ls, 8-1/4"	150.00	–
Open, ls, 4"	20.00	–
Open, ls, 6"	25.00	–
Open, ls, 7"	35.00	–
Open, ls, 8"	40.00	–
Cordial	125.00	–
Creamer	40.00	85.00
Cruet, os	45.00	250.00

	Clear	Emerald Green
Dishes, nest of 3: 7," 8," and 9"	40.00	–
Goblet	55.00	150.00
Honey Dish	15.00	–
Marmalade Jar	125.00	–
Pickle Castor	145.00	–
Pitcher		
Milk	50.00	165.00
Water	75.00	250.00
Plate, 10"	50.00	75.00
Relish	20.00	–
Salt Shaker	35.00	70.00
Sauce	12.00	–
Spooner	25.00	60.00
Sugar, cov	50.00	85.00
Syrup	125.00	300.00
Toothpick	85.00	165.00
Tumbler	50.00	85.00
*Wine		
Scalloped border	40.00	–
Straight border	25.00	–

FINECUT (Flower in Square)

Non-flint made by Bryce Bros., Pittsburgh, PA, c1885, and by U.S. Glass Co. in 1891.

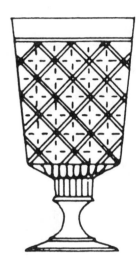

	Amber	Blue	Clear	Vaseline
Bowl, 8-1/4"	15.00	20.00	10.00	15.00
Bread Plate	50.00	60.00	25.00	50.00
Butter, cov	55.00	75.00	45.00	60.00
Cake Stand	–	–	35.00	–
Celery Tray	–	45.00	25.00	40.00
Celery Vase, SP holder	–	–	–	115.00
Creamer	60.00	40.00	35.00	75.00
Goblet	45.00	55.00	22.00	42.00
Pitcher, water	100.00	100.00	60.00	115.00
Plate				
7"	25.00	40.00	15.00	20.00
10"	30.00	50.00	21.00	45.00
Relish	15.00	25.00	10.00	20.00
Sauce, flat	14.00	15.00	10.00	14.00
Spooner	30.00	45.00	18.00	40.00
Sugar, cov	45.00	55.00	35.00	45.00
Tray, water	50.00	55.00	25.00	50.00
Tumbler	–	–	18.00	28.00
Wine	–	–	24.00	30.00

FLAMINGO HABITAT

Non-flint, maker unknown, c1870, etched pattern.

	Clear
Bowl, 10," oval	40.00
Butter, cov	65.00
Celery Vase	45.00
Champagne	45.00
Cheese Dish, blown	110.00
Compote	
Cov, 4-1/2"	75.00
Cov, 6-1/2"	95.00
Open, 5," jelly	35.00
Open, 6"	40.00
Creamer	40.00
Goblet	45.00
Sauce, ftd	15.00
Spooner	25.00
Sugar, cov	50.00
Tumbler	30.00
Wine	45.00

FLORIDA (Emerald Green Herringbone, Paneled Herringbone)

Non-flint made by U.S. Glass Co., in the 1890s. One of the States patterns. Goblet reproduced in green, amber, and other colors.

	Clear	Emerald Green
Berry Set	75.00	110.00
Bowl, 7-3/4"	10.00	15.00
Butter, cov	50.00	85.00
Cake Stand		
Large	60.00	75.00
Small	30.00	40.00
Celery Vase	30.00	35.00
Compote, open, hs, 6-1/2," sq	—	40.00
Creamer	30.00	45.00
Cruet, os	40.00	110.00
*Goblet, 5-3/4" h	25.00	40.00
Mustard Pot, attached under plate, cov	25.00	45.00
Nappy	15.00	25.00
Pitcher, water	50.00	75.00
Plate		
7-1/2"	12.00	18.00
9-1/4"	15.00	25.00
Relish		
6," sq	10.00	15.00
8-1/2," sq	15.00	20.00
Salt Shaker	25.00	50.00
Sauce	5.00	7.50
Spooner	20.00	35.00
Sugar, cov	35.00	50.00
Syrup	60.00	175.00
Tumbler	20.00	35.00
Wine	25.00	50.00

GALLOWAY (Mirror Plate, U.S. Mirror, Virginia, Woodrow)

Non-flint made by U.S. Glass Co., Pittsburgh, PA, c1904-19. Jefferson Glass Co., Toronto, Canada, produced it from 1900-25. Clear glass with and without gold trim; also known with rose satin and ruby stain. Vases known in emerald green. Toothpick reproduced in several colors.

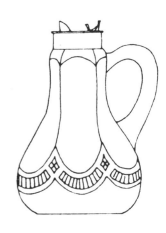

	Clear with Gold	Rose Stained
Basket, no gold	75.00	125.00
Bowl		
6-1/2," belled	20.00	35.00
8-1/2," oval	35.00	45.00
8-1/2," round	30.00	50.00
9," rect	30.00	45.00
11" d, round	45.00	65.00
Butter, cov	65.00	125.00
Cake Stand	70.00	95.00
Carafe, water	55.00	85.00
Celery Vase	35.00	75.00
Champagne	60.00	175.00
Compote		
Cov, hs, 6"	90.00	125.00
Open, hs, 5-1/2"	25.00	40.00
Open, hs, 10," scalloped	55.00	75.00
Creamer	30.00	50.00
Cruet	45.00	125.00
Eggcup	40.00	60.00
Finger Bowl	40.00	65.00
Goblet	75.00	95.00
Lemonade	35.00	45.00
Mug	40.00	50.00
Nappy, tricorn	25.00	50.00
Olive, 6"	20.00	30.00
Pickle Castor,		
sp holder and lid	75.00	200.00

	Clear with Gold	Rose Stained
Pitcher		
Milk	60.00	80.00
Tankard	75.00	125.00
Water, ice lip	65.00	175.00
Plate, 8," round	40.00	65.00
Punch Bowl	160.00	225.00
Punch Bowl Plate, 20"	80.00	125.00
Punch Cup	10.00	15.00
Relish	20.00	30.00
Rose Bowl	25.00	60.00
Salt, master	35.00	60.00
Salt & Pepper, pr	40.00	75.00
Sauce		
Flat, 4"	10.00	20.00
Footed, 4-1/2"	10.00	20.00
Sherbet	25.00	30.00
Spooner	30.00	80.00
Sugar, cov	55.00	85.00
Sugar Shaker	40.00	100.00
Syrup	65.00	135.00
*Toothpick	30.00	55.00
Tumbler	35.00	45.00
Vase, swung	30.00	—
Waste Bowl	40.00	65.00
Water Bottle	40.00	85.00
Wine	45.00	65.00

GARFIELD DRAPE (Canadian Drape)

Non-flint issued in 1881 by Adams & Co., Pittsburgh, PA, after the assassination of President Garfield.

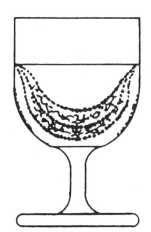

	Clear
Bread Plate	
Memorial, portrait of Garfield	65.00
"We Mourn Our Nation's Loss," portrait	75.00
Butter, cov	70.00
Cake Stand, 9-1/2"	70.00
Celery Vase	55.00
Compote	
Cov, hs, 8"	100.00
Cov, ls, 6"	85.00
Open, hs, 8-1/2"	40.00
Creamer	40.00
Goblet	40.00
Honey Dish	15.00
Pitcher	
Milk	70.00
Water, ah	75.00
Water, strap handle	100.00
Relish, oval	20.00
Sauce	
Flat	8.50
Footed	12.00
Spooner	35.00
Sugar, cov	60.00
Tumbler	35.00

GEORGIA (Peacock Feather)

Non-flint made by Richards and Hartley Glass Co., Tarentum, PA, and reissued by U.S. Glass Co. in 1902 as part of the States series. Rare in blue. (Chamber lamp, pedestal base, $275.00). No goblet known in pattern.

	Clear
Bonbon, ftd	25.00

	Clear
Bowl, 8"	30.00
Butter, cov	45.00
Cake Stand, 10"	50.00
Castor Set, 2 bottles	60.00
Celery Tray, 11-3/4"	35.00
Children's	
Cake Stand	35.00
Creamer	35.00
Compote	
Cov, hs, 5"	35.00
Cov, hs, 6"	40.00
Cov, hs, 7"	45.00
Cov, hs, 8"	50.00
Open, hs, 5"	20.00
Open, hs, 6"	25.00
Open, hs, 7"	30.00
Open, hs, 8"	35.00
Condiment Set, tray, oil cruet, salt & pepper	75.00
Creamer	35.00
Cruet, os	55.00
Decanter	70.00
Lamp	
Chamber, pedestal	85.00
Hand, oil, 7"	80.00
Mug	25.00
Nappy	25.00
Pitcher, water	70.00
Plate, 5-1/4"	15.00
Relish	15.00
Salt Shaker	40.00
Sauce	10.00
Spooner	35.00
Sugar, cov	45.00
Syrup, metal lid	65.00
Tumbler	35.00

HEART with THUMBPRINT (Bull's Eye in Heart, Columbia, Columbian, Heart and Thumbprint)

Non-flint made by Tarentum Glass Co. 1898-1906. Some clear and emerald green pieces have gold trim. Made experimentally in custard, blue custard, opaque Nile green, and cobalt.

	Clear	Emerald Green	Ruby Stain
Banana Boat	75.00	–	145.00
Barber Bottle	115.00	–	–
Bowl			
7" sq	35.00	100.00	95.00
9-1/2" sq	35.00	125.00	100.00
10" scalloped	45.00	100.00	90.00
Butter, cov	125.00	175.00	145.00
Cake Stand, 9"	150.00	–	195.00
Carafe, water	100.00	–	160.00
Card Tray	20.00	55.00	95.00
Celery Vase	65.00	–	110.00
Compote, open, hs			
7-1/2," scalloped	150.00	–	185.00
8-1/2"	100.00	–	200.00
Cordial, 3" h	140.00	175.00	175.00
Creamer			
Individual	30.00	45.00	50.00
Regular	60.00	110.00	175.00
Cruet	75.00	–	–
Finger Bowl	45.00	85.00	95.00
Goblet	65.00	125.00	130.00
Hair Receiver, lid	60.00	100.00	110.00

	Clear	Emerald Green	Ruby Stain
Ice Bucket	60.00	–	–
Lamp			
Finger	95.00	150.00	–
Oil, 8"	125.00	225.00	–
Mustard, SP cov	95.00	100.00	–
Nappy, triangular	30.00	60.00	–
Pitcher, water	200.00	–	–
Plate			
6"	25.00	45.00	50.00
10"	45.00	85.00	90.00
Powder Jar, SP cov	65.00	–	–
Punch Cup	20.00	35.00	40.00
Rose Bowl			
Large	60.00	–	110.00
Small	30.00	–	90.00
Salt & Pepper, pr	95.00	–	–
Sauce, 5"	20.00	35.00	40.00
Spooner	50.00	85.00	90.00
Sugar			
Individual	25.00	35.00	40.00
Table, cov	105.00	–	75.00
Tray, 8-1/4" l, 4-1/4" w	30.00	65.00	75.00
Tumbler	45.00	85.00	75.00
Vase			
6"	35.00	65.00	75.00
10"	65.00	100.00	110.00
Wine	55.00	150.00	165.00

HOLLY

Non-flint, possibly made by Boston and Sandwich Glass Co. in the late 1860s and early 1870s.

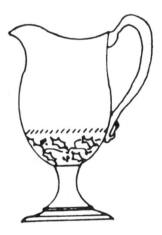

	Clear
Bowl, cov, 8" d	150.00
Butter, cov	150.00
Cake Stand, 11"	160.00
Celery Vase	90.00
Compote, cov, hs	165.00
Creamer, ah	125.00
Eggcup	95.00
Goblet	135.00
Pickle, oval	30.00
Pitcher, water, ah	225.00
Salt	
Flat, oval	65.00
Ftd	60.00
Sauce, flat	25.00
Spooner	60.00
Sugar, cov	135.00
Tumbler	95.00
Wine	165.00

HONEYCOMB

A popular pattern made in flint and non-flint glass by numerous firms, c1850-1900, resulting in many pattern variations. Found with copper-wheel engraving. Rare in color.

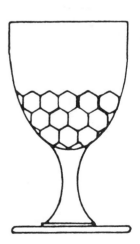

	Flint	Non-Flint
Ale Glass	50.00	25.00
Barber Bottle	45.00	25.00
Bowl, cov, 7-1/4" pat'd		
1869, acorn finial	100.00	45.00
Butter, cov	75.00	45.00
Cake Stand	55.00	35.00
Castor Bottle	25.00	18.00
Celery Vase	45.00	20.00
Champagne	50.00	25.00

	Flint	Non-Flint
Claret	35.00	35.00
Compote, cov, hs		
6-1/2" x 18-1/2" h	60.00	40.00
9-1/4" x 11-1/2" h	110.00	65.00
Compote, open, hs		
7" x 7" h	60.00	40.00
7-1/2," scalloped	40.00	25.00
8" x 6-1/4" h	65.00	40.00
Compote, open, ls		
6" d, Saucer Bowl	35.00	25.00
7-1/2," scalloped	40.00	25.00
Cordial, 3-1/2"	35.00	25.00
Creamer, ah	35.00	20.00
Decanter		
Pint, os	85.00	45.00
Quart, os	85.00	65.00
Eggcup	20.00	15.00
Finger Bowl	45.00	–
Goblet	25.00	15.00
Honey Dish, cov	15.00	25.00
Lamp		
All Glass	–	85.00
Marble base	–	90.00
Lemonade	40.00	20.00
Mug, half pint	25.00	15.00
Pitcher, water, ah	165.00	60.00
Plate, 6"	–	12.50
Pomade Jar, cov	50.00	20.00
Relish	30.00	20.00
Salt, master, cov, ftd	35.00	30.00
Salt Shaker, orig top	–	35.00
Sauce	12.00	7.50
Spillholder	35.00	20.00
Spooner	65.00	35.00
Sugar		
Frosted rosebud finial	–	50.00
Regular	75.00	45.00
Tumbler		
Bar	35.00	–
Flat	40.00	12.50
Footed	45.00	15.00
Vase		
7-1/2"	45.00	–
10-1/2"	75.00	–
Whiskey, handled	125.00	–
Wine	35.00	15.00

HORSESHOE (Good Luck, Prayer Rug)

Non-flint made by Adams & Co., Pittsburgh, PA, and others in late 1880s.

	Clear
Bowl, cov, oval	
7"	150.00
8"	195.00
Bread Plate, 14" x10"	
Double horseshoe handles	65.00
Single horseshoe handles	40.00
Butter, cov	95.00
Cake Plate	40.00
Cake Stand	
9"	70.00
10"	90.00
Celery Vase, knob stem	40.00
Cheese, cov, woman churning	275.00

	Clear
Compote	
Cov, hs, 7," horseshoe finial	95.00
Cov, hs, 8" x 12-1/4"	125.00
Cov, hs, 11"	135.00
Creamer, 6-1/2"	55.00
Doughnut Stand	75.00
Finger Bowl	80.00
Goblet	
Knob Stem	40.00
Plain Stem	38.00
Marmalade Jar, cov	110.00
Pitcher	
Milk	125.00
Water	100.00
Plate	
7"	45.00
10"	55.00
Relish	
5" x 7"	20.00
8," wheelbarrow, pewter wheels	75.00
Salt	
Individual, horseshoe shape	20.00
Master, horseshoe shape	100.00
Master, wheelbarrow, pewter wheels	75.00
Sauce	
Flat	10.00
Footed	15.00
Spooner	35.00
Sugar, cov	65.00
Vegetable Dish, oblong	35.00
Waste Bowl	45.00
Water Tray	125.00
Wine	150.00

ILLINOIS (Clarissa, Star of the East)

Non-flint. One of the States patterns made by U.S. Glass Co. c1897. Most forms are square. A few items are known in ruby stained, including a salt ($50.00) and a lidless straw holder with the stain on the inside ($95.00).

	Clear	Emerald Green
Basket, ah, 11-1/2"	100.00	–
Bowl		
5," round	20.00	–
6," sq	25.00	–
8," round	25.00	–
9," sq	35.00	–
*Butter, cov	60.00	–
Candlesticks, pr	95.00	–
Celery Tray, 11"	40.00	–
Cheese, cov	75.00	–
Compote, open		
hs, 5"	40.00	–
hs, 9"	60.00	–
Creamer		
Individual	30.00	–
Table	40.00	–
Cruet	65.00	–
Finger Bowl	25.00	–
Marmalade Jar	135.00	–
Olive	18.00	–
Pitcher, milk		
Round, SP rim	175.00	–
Square	65.00	–
Pitcher, water, square	65.00	–

	Clear	Emerald Green
Plate, 7," sq.	25.00	–
Relish		
7-1/2" x 4"	10.00	40.00
8-1/2" x 3"	18.00	–
Salt		
Individual	15.00	–
Master	25.00	–
Salt & Pepper, pr	40.00	–
Sauce	15.00	–
Spooner	35.00	–
Straw Holder, cov	275.00	400.00
Sugar		
Individual	30.00	–
Table, cov	55.00	–
Sugar Shaker	65.00	–
Syrup, pewter top	95.00	–
Tankard, SP rim	80.00	135.00
Toothpick		
Adv emb in base	45.00	–
Plain	30.00	–
Tray, 12" x 8," turned up sides	50.00	–
Tumbler	30.00	40.00
Vase, 6," sq	35.00	45.00
Vase, 9-1/2"	–	125.00

IOWA (Paneled Zipper)

Non-flint made by U.S. Glass Co. c1902. Part of the States pattern series. Available in clear glass with gold trim (add 20%) and ruby or cranberry stained. Also found in amber (goblet, $65.00), green, canary, and blue. Add 50% to 100% for color.

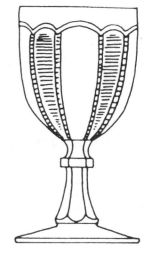

	Clear
Bowl, berry	15.00
Bread Plate, motto	80.00
Butter, cov	40.00
Cake Stand	35.00
Carafe	35.00
Compote, cov, 8"	40.00
Corn Liquor Jug, os	60.00
Creamer	30.00
Cruet, os	30.00
Cup	15.00
Decanter, 1-1/2 pts	40.00
Goblet	25.00
Lamp	125.00
Olive	15.00
Pitcher, water	50.00
Punch Cup	15.00
Salt Shaker, single	20.00
Sauce, 4-1/2"	6.50
Spooner	30.00
Sugar, cov	35.00
Toothpick	
Flat	20.00
Footed	50.00
Tumbler	25.00
Vase, 8" h	20.00
Wine	30.00

JACOB'S LADDER (Maltese)

Non-flint made by Bryce Bros., Pittsburgh, PA, in 1876 and by U.S. Glass Co. in 1891. A few pieces found in amber, yellow, blue, pale blue, and pale green. Bowls in variant of pattern found in flint, sometimes in metal holders.

	Clear
Bowl	
6" x 8-3/4"	15.00

	Clear
6-3/4" x 9-3/4"	20.00
7-1/2" x 10-3/4"	20.00
9," berry, ornate, SP holder, ftd (variant)	125.00
Butter, cov	75.00
Cake Stand	
8" or 9"	50.00
11" or 12"	60.00
Castor Bottle	18.00
Castor Set, 4 bottles	100.00
Celery Vase	45.00
Cologne Bottle,	
Maltese-cross stopper, ftd	85.00
Compote	
Cov, hs, 6"	80.00
Cov, hs, 7-1/2"	100.00
Cov, hs, 9-1/2"	135.00
Open, hs, 7-1/2"	35.00
Open, hs, 8-1/2," scalloped	30.00
Open, hs, 9-1/2," scalloped	38.00
Open, hs, 10"	40.00
Creamer	35.00
Cruet, os, ftd	85.00
Goblet	65.00
Honey Dish, 3-1/2"	10.00
Marmalade Jar	75.00
Mug	100.00
Pitcher, water, ah	175.00
Plate, 6-1/4"	20.00
Relish, 9-1/2" x 5-1/2"	15.00
Salt, master, ftd	20.00
Sauce	
Flat, 4" or 5"	8.00
Footed, 4"	12.00
Spooner	35.00
Sugar, cov	80.00
Syrup	
Knight's Head finial	125.00
Plain top	100.00
Tumbler, bar	100.00
Wine	30.00

JERSEY SWIRL (Swirl)

Non-flint made by Windsor Glass Co., Pittsburgh, PA, c1887. Heavily reproduced in color by L. G. Wright Co. The clear goblet is also reproduced.

	Amber	Blue	Canary	Clear
Bowl, 9-1/4"	55.00	55.00	45.00	35.00
Butter, cov	55.00	55.00	50.00	40.00
Cake Stand, 9"	75.00	70.00	45.00	30.00
*Celery Case	42.00	42.00	35.00	30.00
*Compote, hs, 8"	50.00	50.00	45.00	35.00
Creamer	45.00	45.00	40.00	30.00
Cruet, os	–	–	–	25.00
*Goblet				
Buttermilk	40.00	40.00	35.00	30.00
Water	40.00	40.00	35.00	30.00
Marmalade Jar	–	–	–	50.00
Pickle Castor, SP frame and lid	–	–	–	125.00
Pitcher, water	50.00	50.00	45.00	35.00
Plate, round				
6"	25.00	25.00	20.00	15.00
8"	30.00	30.00	25.00	20.00
10"	38.00	38.00	35.00	30.00
*Salt, ind	20.00	20.00	18.00	15.00

418

	Amber	Blue	Canary	Clear
Salt Shaker	30.00	30.00	25.00	20.00
Sauce, 4-1/2," flat	20.00	20.00	15.00	10.00
Spooner	30.00	30.00	25.00	20.00
Sugar, cov	40.00	40.00	35.00	30.00
Tumbler	30.00	30.00	25.00	20.00
*Wine	50.00	50.00	40.00	15.00

KANSAS (Jewel with Dewdrop)

Non-flint originally produced by Co-Operative Glass Co., Beaver Falls, PA. Later produced as part of the States pattern series by U.S. Glass Co. in 1901 and Jenkins Glass Co. c1915-25. Also known with jewels stained in pink or gold. Mugs (smaller and of inferior quality) have been reproduced in clear, vaseline, amber and blue).

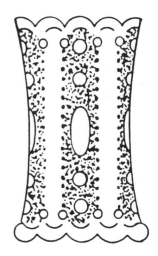

	Clear
Banana Stand	90.00
Bowl	
7," oval	35.00
8"	40.00
Bread Plate, ODB	45.00
Butter, cov	65.00
Cake Plate	45.00
Cake Stand	
7-5/8"	50.00
10"	85.00
Celery Vase	80.00
Compote	
Cov, hs, 6"	60.00
Cov, hs, 8"	85.00
Cov, ls, 5"	60.00
Open, hs, 6"	30.00
Open, hs, 8"	45.00
Creamer	40.00
*Goblet	55.00
*Mug	
Regular	45.00
Tall	25.00
*Pitcher	
Milk	80.00
Water	100.00
Relish, 8-1/2," oval	20.00
Salt Shaker	50.00
Sauce, flat, 4"	12.00
Sugar, cov	65.00
Syrup	125.00
Toothpick	65.00
Tumbler	45.00
Whiskey	25.00
Wine	50.00

KENTUCKY

Non-flint made by U.S. Glass Co. c1897 as part of the States pattern series. The goblet is found in ruby stained ($50). A footed, square sauce ($30) is known in cobalt blue with gold. A toothpick holder is also known in ruby stained ($150).

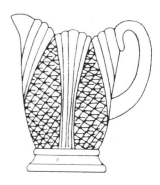

	Clear	Emerald Green
Bowl, 8" d	20.00	—
Butter, cov	50.00	—
Cake Stand, 9-1/2"	40.00	—
Creamer	25.00	—
Cruet, os	45.00	—
Cup	10.00	20.00
Goblet	30.00	50.00
Nappy	10.00	15.00
Olive, handle	25.00	—
Pitcher, water	55.00	—

	Clear	Emerald Green
Plate, 7," sq	15.00	–
Punch Cup	10.00	15.00
Salt Shaker, orig top	10.00	–
Sauce, ftd, sq	10.00	15.00
Spooner	35.00	–
Sugar, cov	30.00	–
Toothpick, sq	35.00	85.00
Tumbler	20.00	30.00
Wine	28.00	38.00

KING'S CROWN (Ruby Thumbprint, X.L.C.R.)

Non-flint made by Adams & Co., Pittsburgh, PA, in the 1890s and later. Known as Ruby Thumbprint when pieces are ruby stained. Made in clear and with the thumbprints stained amethyst, gold, green, and cranberry, and in clear with etching and gold trim. It became very popular after 1891 as ruby-stained souvenir ware. Approximately 87 pieces documented. Add 30% for engraved pieces. NOTE: Pattern has been copiously reproduced for the gift-trade market in milk glass, cobalt blue, and other colors. New pieces are easily distinguished: in the case of Ruby Thumbprint, the color is a very pale pinkish red.

	Clear	Ruby Stained
Banana Stand, ftd	85.00	195.00
*Bowl		
9-1/4" d, pointed	35.00	90.00
10" d, scalloped	45.00	95.00
Butter, cov, 7-1/2" d	50.00	135.00
*Cake Stand		
9" d	68.00	195.00
10" d	75.00	195.00
Castor Set, glass stand, four bottles	175.00	300.00
Celery Vase	40.00	60.00
*Champagne	25.00	35.00
*Claret	35.00	50.00
*Compote		
Cov, hs, 8"	65.00	245.00
Cov, ls, 12"	90.00	225.00
Open, hs, 8-1/4"	75.00	95.00
Open, ls, 5-1/4"	30.00	45.00
*Cordial	45.00	–
*Creamer, ah, 3-1/4" h		
Ind, tankard	25.00	35.00
Table, 4-7/8" h	50.00	65.00
*Cup and Saucer	55.00	70.00
Custard Cup	15.00	25.00
*Goblet	35.00	45.00
Honey Dish, cov, sq	100.00	175.00
*Lamp, oil, 10"	135.00	–
Mustard, cov, 4" h	35.00	75.00
Preserve, 10" l	35.00	50.00
*Pitcher		
Milk, tankard	75.00	125.00
Water, bulbous	95.00	225.00
Water, tankard	110.00	200.00
*Plate, 7"	20.00	45.00
*Punch Bowl, ftd	275.00	300.00
*Punch Cup	15.00	30.00
Salt		
Ind, rect	15.00	35.00
Master, sq	30.00	50.00
Salt Shaker, 3-1/8" h	30.00	45.00
*Sauce, 4"	15.00	20.00
Spooner, 4-1/4" h	45.00	50.00
*Sugar		
Ind, open, 2-3/4" h	25.00	45.00
Table, cov, 6-3/4" h	55.00	95.00

	Clear	Ruby Stained
Toothpick, 2-3/4" h	20.00	35.00
*Tumbler, 3-3/4" h	20.00	35.00
*Wine, 4-3/8" h	25.00	40.00

KOKOMO (Bar and Diamond, R and H Swirl Band)

Non-flint made by Richards and Hartley, Tarentum, PA, c1885. Reissued by U.S. Glass Co., c1891 and Kokomo Glass Co., Kokomo, IN, c1901. Found in ruby stained and etched. More than 50 different pieces manufactured.

	Clear	Ruby Stained
Bowl, 8-1/2" ftd	24.00	–
Bread Tray	30.00	45.00
Butter, cov	35.00	–
Cake Stand	45.00	165.00
Celery Vase	30.00	45.00
Compote		
Cov, hs, 7-1/2"	35.00	165.00
Open, hs, 6"	25.00	–
Open, hs, 8"	35.00	–
Open, ls, 7-1/2"	20.00	–
Condiment Set, oblong tray, shakers, cruet	80.00	195.00
Creamer, ah	35.00	50.00
Cruet	35.00	–
Decanter, 9-3/4," wine	65.00	165.00
Finger Bowl	25.00	35.00
Goblet	30.00	45.00
Lamp, hand, atypical, has no diamonds	50.00	100.00
Pitcher, tankard	55.00	100.00
Sauce, ftd, 5"	8.00	10.00
Spooner	25.00	45.00
Sugar, cov	45.00	65.00
Sugar Shaker	35.00	75.00
Syrup	45.00	135.00
Tray, water	35.00	90.00
Tumbler	25.00	35.00
Wine	25.00	35.00

LION (Frosted Lion)

Made by Gillinder and Sons, Philadelphia, PA, in 1876. Available in clear without frosting (20% less). Many reproductions.

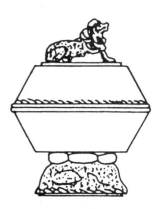

	Frosted
Bowl, oblong	
6-1/2" x 4-1/4"	55.00
8" x 5"	50.00
Bread Plate, 12"	90.00
*Butter, cov	
Lion's-head finial	90.00
Rampant finial	125.00
Cake Stand	85.00
*Celery Vase	85.00
Champagne	175.00
Cheese, cov, rampant	
lion's-head finial	400.00
Children's Table Set	500.00
*Compote	
Cov, hs, 7," rampant finial	150.00
*Cov, hs, 9," rampant finial, oval, collared base	150.00
Cov, 9," hs	185.00
Open, ls, 8"	75.00
Cordial	175.00
*Creamer	75.00
Cup and Saucer, child size	45.00
*Eggcup, 3-1/2" h	65.00

	Frosted
*Goblet	70.00
Marmalade Jar, rampant finial	90.00
Pitcher	
Milk	375.00
Water	300.00
Relish, lion handles	35.00
*Salt, master, rect lid	250.00
*Sauce, 4," ftd	25.00
*Spooner	75.00
*Sugar, cov	
Lion's-head finial	90.00
Rampant finial	110.00
Syrup, orig top	350.00
Wine	200.00

LOOP and DART

Clear and stippled flint and non-flint of the late 1860s and early 1870s. Made by Boston and Sandwich Glass Co., Sandwich, MA, and Richards and Hartley, Tarentum, PA. Flint adds 25%.

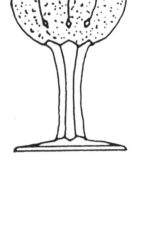

	Clear
Bowl, 9," oval	30.00
Butter, cov	45.00
Cake Stand, 10"	40.00
Celery Vase	35.00
Compote	
Cov, hs, 8"	85.00
Cov, ls, 8"	65.00
Creamer	35.00
Cruet, os	95.00
Eggcup	25.00
Goblet	25.00
Lamp, oil	85.00
Pitcher, water	75.00
Plate, 6"	35.00
Relish	20.00
Salt, master	50.00
Sauce	5.00
Spooner	25.00
Sugar, cov	50.00
Tumbler	
Footed	30.00
Water	25.00
Wine	35.00

LOUISIANA (Sharp Oval and Diamond, Granby)

Made by Bryce Bros., Pittsburgh, PA, in the 1870s. Reissued by U.S. Glass Co. c1898 as one of the States patterns. Available with gold and also comes frosted.

	Clear
Bowl, 9," berry	20.00
Butter, cov	75.00
Cake Stand	65.00
Celery Vase	30.00
Compote	
Cov, hs, 8"	75.00
Open, hs, 5," jelly	40.00
Creamer	30.00
Goblet	30.00
Match Holder	35.00
Mug, handled, gold top	25.00
Nappy, 4," cov	30.00
Pitcher, water	65.00
Relish	15.00
Spooner	30.00
Sugar, cov	45.00

	Clear
Tumbler	25.00
Wine	35.00

MAINE (Paneled Stippled Flower, Stippled Primrose)

Non-flint made by U.S. Glass Co., Pittsburgh, PA, c1899. Researchers dispute if goblet was made originally. Sometimes found with enamel trim or overall turquoise stain.

	Clear	Emerald Green
Bowl, 8"	30.00	40.00
Bread Plate, oval 10" x 7-1/4"	30.00	–
Butter, cov	48.00	–
Cake Stand	40.00	60.00
Compote		
Cov, jelly	50.00	75.00
Open, hs, 7"	20.00	45.00
Open, ls, 8"	38.00	55.00
Open, ls, 9"	30.00	65.00
Creamer	30.00	–
Cruet, os	80.00	–
Mug	35.00	–
Pitcher		
Milk	65.00	85.00
Water	50.00	125.00
Relish	15.00	–
Salt Shaker, single	30.00	–
Sauce	15.00	–
Sugar, cov	45.00	75.00
Syrup	75.00	225.00
Toothpick	125.00	–
Tumbler	30.00	45.00
Wine	50.00	75.00

MANHATTAN

Non-flint with gold made by U.S. Glass Co. c1902. A Depression glass pattern also has the "Manhattan" name. A table-sized creamer and covered sugar are known in true ruby stained, and a goblet is known in old marigold carnival glass. Heavily reproduced by Anchor Hocking Glass Co. and Tiffin Glass Co.

	Clear	Rose Stained
Biscuit jar, cov	60.00	100.00
Bowl		
6"	18.00	–
8-1/4," scalloped	20.00	–
*9-1/2"	20.00	–
10"	22.00	–
12-1/2"	25.00	–
Butter, cov	55.00	–
Cake Stand, 8"	45.00	55.00
Carafe, water	40.00	65.00
Celery Tray, 8"	20.00	–
Celery Vase	25.00	–
Cheese, cov, 8-3/8" d	–	115.00
Compote		
Cov, hs, 9-1/2"	60.00	–
Open, hs, 9-1/2"	45.00	–
Open, hs, 10-1/2"	50.00	–
*Creamer		
Individual	20.00	–
Table	30.00	60.00
Cruet		
Large	65.00	115.00
Small	50.00	–
*Goblet	25.00	–
Ice Bucket	–	65.00
Olive, Gainsborough	30.00	–

	Clear	Rose Stained
Pitcher, water, half gal		
Bulbous, ah	70.00	—
Tankard, ah	60.00	125.00
Plate		
5"	10.00	—
6"	10.00	30.00
8"	15.00	—
10-3/4"	20.00	—
Punch Bowl	125.00	—
Punch Cup	10.00	—
Relish, 6"	12.00	—
Salt Shaker, single	20.00	35.00
Sauce	14.00	20.00
*Spooner	20.00	—
Straw Holder, cov	95.00	150.00
*Sugar		
Individual, open	15.00	—
Table, cov	40.00	65.00
Syrup	48.00	200.00
*Toothpick	30.00	—
Tumbler		
Iced Tea	30.00	—
Water	20.00	—
Vase, 6"	18.00	—
Violet Bowl	20.00	—
Water Bottle	40.00	—
*Wine	15.00	—

MARYLAND (Inverted Loop and Fan, Loop and Diamond)

Made originally by Bryce Bros., Pittsburgh, PA. Continued by U.S. Glass Co. as one of its States patterns.

	Clear with Gold	Ruby Stained
Banana Dish	35.00	105.00
Bowl, berry	15.00	35.00
Bread Plate	25.00	—
Butter, cov	65.00	95.00
Cake Stand, 8"	40.00	—
Celery Tray	20.00	35.00
Celery Vase	30.00	65.00
Compote		
Cov, hs	65.00	100.00
Open, jelly	25.00	45.00
Creamer	25.00	55.00
Goblet	30.00	60.00
Olive, handled	15.00	—
Pitcher		
Milk	42.50	135.00
Water	50.00	100.00
Plate, 7," round	25.00	—
Relish, oval	15.00	55.00
Salt Shaker, single	30.00	—
Sauce, flat	10.00	15.00
Spooner	30.00	55.00
Sugar, cov	45.00	60.00
Toothpick	125.00	175.00
Tumbler	25.00	50.00
Wine	40.00	75.00

MASCOTTE (Dominion, Etched Fern and Waffle, Minor Block)

Non-flint made by Ripley and Co., Pittsburgh, PA, in the 1880s. Reissued by U.S. Glass Co. in 1891. The butter dish shown on Plate 77 of Ruth Webb Lee's Victorian Glass is said to go with this pattern. It has a horseshoe finial and was named for the famous "Maude S,"

"Queen of the Turf" trotting horse during the 1880s. Apothecary jar and pyramid jars made by Tiffin Glass Co. in the 1950s.

Bowl	Clear	Etched
Cov, 5"	–	35.00
Cov, 7"	–	45.00
Open 9"	35.00	40.00
Butter Pat	15.00	20.00
Butter, cov		
"Maude S"	100.00	110.00
Regular	50.00	65.00
Cake Basket, handle	80.00	95.00
Cake Stand	35.00	50.00
Celery Vase	35.00	40.00
Cheese, cov	70.00	80.00
Compote		
Cov, hs, 5"	35.00	40.00
Cov, hs, 7"	45.00	55.00
Cov, hs, 8"	60.00	75.00
Cov, hs, 9"	65.00	90.00
Open, hs, 6"	20.00	25.00
Open, hs, 8"	30.00	35.00
Open, ls, 8"	30.00	45.00
Creamer	30.00	45.00
Goblet	40.00	45.00
Pitcher, water	55.00	65.00
Plate, turned in sides	40.00	45.00
Pyramid Jar, 7" d, one fits into other and forms tall jar-type container with lid, three sizes with flat separators	50.00	55.00
Salt Dip	25.00	–
Salt Shaker, single	25.00	25.00
Sauce		
Flat	8.00	15.00
Footed	12.00	15.00
Spooner	30.00	35.00
Sugar, cov	40.00	45.00
Tray, water	40.00	55.00
Tumbler	20.00	35.00
Wine	25.00	30.00

MASSACHUSETTS (Arched Diamond Points, Cane Variant, Geneva #2, M2-131, Star and Diamonds)

Made in the 1880s, unknown maker, reissued in 1898 by U.S. Glass Co. as one of the States series. The vase ($45) and wine ($45) are known in emerald green. Some pieces reported in cobalt blue and marigold carnival glass. Reproduced in clear and colors, including cobalt blue.

	Clear
Bar Bottle, metal shot glass for cover	75.00
Basket, 4-1/2," ah	50.00
Bowl	
6," sq	17.50
9," sq	20.00
*Butter, cov	50.00
Celery Tray	30.00
Champagne	35.00
Cologne Bottle, os	37.50
Compote, open	35.00
Cordial	55.00
Creamer	28.00
Cruet, os	45.00
Goblet	45.00
Gravy Boat	30.00
Mug	20.00
Mustard Jar, cov	35.00

	Clear
Olive	8.50
Pitcher, water	65.00
Plate, 8"	32.00
Punch Cup	15.00
Relish, 8-1/2"	25.00
Rum Jug, various sizes	90.00
Salt Shaker, tall	25.00
Sauce, sq, 4"	15.00
Sherry	40.00
Spooner	20.00
Sugar, cov	40.00
Syrup	65.00
Toothpick	40.00
Tumbler	30.00
Vase, trumpet	
6-1/2" h	25.00
7" h	25.00
9" h	35.00
Whiskey	25.00
Wine	40.00

MICHIGAN (Loop and Pillar)

Non-flint made by U.S. Glass Co. c1902 as one of the States pattern series. The 10-1/4" bowl ($42) and punch cup ($12) are found with yellow or blue stain. Also found with painted carnations. Other colors include "Sunrise," gold and ruby stained.

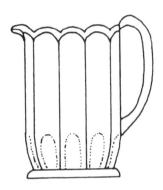

	Clear	Rose Stained
Bowl		
7-1/2"	15.00	30.00
9"	35.00	60.00
10-1/4"	35.00	62.00
Butter, cov		
Large	60.00	125.00
Small	65.00	—
Celery Vase	40.00	85.00
Compote		
Jelly, 4-1/2"	45.00	75.00
Open, hs, 9-1/4"	65.00	85.00
Creamer		
Ind, 6 oz., tankard	20.00	65.00
Table	30.00	70.00
Cruet, os	60.00	225.00
Crushed Fruit Bowl	75.00	—
Custard Cup	15.00	—
Finger Bowl	15.00	—
Goblet	45.00	65.00
Honey Dish	10.00	—
Lemonade Mug	24.00	40.00
Nappy, Gainsborough handle	35.00	—
Olive, two handles	10.00	25.00
Pickle	12.00	20.00
Pitcher		
8"	50.00	—
12," tankard	70.00	150.00
Plate, 5-1/2" d	15.00	—
Punch Bowl, 8"	50.00	—
Punch Cup	8.00	—
Relish	20.00	35.00
Salt Shaker, single, 3 types	20.00	30.00
Sauce	12.00	22.00
Sherbet cup, handles	15.00	20.00
Spooner	50.00	75.00
Sugar, cov	50.00	85.00
Syrup	95.00	175.00
*Toothpick	45.00	100.00

	Clear	Rose Stained
Tumbler	30.00	40.00
Vase		
Bud	35.00	40.00
Ftd, large	45.00	−
Wine	35.00	50.00

MINERVA (Roman Medallion)

Non-flint made by Boston and Sandwich Glass Co., Sandwich, MA, c1870, as well as other American companies. Shards have been found at Burlington Glass Works, Hamilton, Ontario, Canada.

	Clear
Bowl	
Footed	40.00
Rectangular	
7"	25.00
8" x 5"	30.00
Bread Plate	65.00
Butter, cov	75.00
Cake Stand	
9" x 6-1/2"	100.00
10-1/2"	120.00
13"	195.00
Champagne	285.00
Compote	
Cov, hs, 6"	135.00
Cov, hs, 8"	165.00
Cov, ls, 8"	165.00
Open, hs, 10-1/2," octagonal ftd	175.00
Creamer	45.00
Goblet	95.00
Marmalade Jar, cov	150.00
Pickle	25.00
Pitcher, Water	185.00
Plate	
8"	55.00
10," handled	60.00
Platter, oval, 13"	65.00
Sauce	
Flat	185.50
Footed, 4"	20.00
Spooner	40.00
Sugar, cov	65.00
Waste Bowl	50.00

MINNESOTA

Non-flint made by U.S. Glass Co. in the late 1890s as one of the States patterns.

	Clear	Ruby Stained
Banana Stand	65.00	−
Basket	65.00	−
Biscuit Jar, cov	55.00	150.00
Bonbon, 5"	15.00	
Butter, cov	50.00	
Carafe	35.00	−
Celery Tray, 13"	25.00	−
Compote		
Open, hs, 10," flared	60.00	−
Open, ls, 9," sq	55.00	−
Creamer		
Individual	20.00	−
Table	30.00	−
Cruet	35.00	−
Cup	18.00	
Goblet	35.00	75.00

	Clear	Ruby Stained
Hair Receiver	30.00	—
Juice Glass	20.00	—
Match Safe	25.00	—
Mug	25.00	—
Olive	15.00	25.00
Pitcher, tankard	85.00	200.00
Plate		
5," turned up edges	25.00	—
7-3/8" d	15.00	—
Pomade Jar, cov	35.00	—
Relish	20.00	—
Salt Shaker	25.00	—
Sauce, boat shape	10.00	25.00
Spooner	25.00	—
Sugar, cov	35.00	—
Syrup	65.00	—
Toothpick, 3 handles	30.00	150.00
Tray, 8" l	15.00	—
Tumbler	20.00	—
Wine	40.00	—

NEVADA

Non-flint made by U.S. Glass Co., Pittsburgh, PA, c1902 as a States pattern. Pieces are sometimes partly frosted and have enamel decoration. Add 20% for frosted.

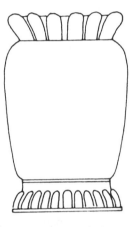

	Clear
Biscuit Jar	45.00
Bowl	
6" d, cov	35.00
7" d, open	20.00
8" d, cov	45.00
Butter, cov	70.00
Cake Stand, 10"	35.00
Celery Vase	25.00
Compote	
Cov, hs, 6"	40.00
Cov, hs, 7"	45.00
Cov, hs, 8"	55.00
Open, hs, 6"	20.00
Open, hs, 7"	30.00
Open, hs, 8"	35.00
Creamer	30.00
Cruet	35.00
Cup, custard	12.00
Finger Bowl	25.00
Jug	35.00
Pickle, oval	10.00
Pitcher	
Milk, tankard	45.00
Water, bulbous	50.00
Water, tankard	45.00
Salt	
Individual	15.00
Master	20.00
Salt Shaker, table	15.00
Sauce, 4" d	10.00
Spooner	35.00
Sugar, cov	35.00
Syrup, tin top	45.00
Toothpick	35.00
Tumbler	15.00

NEW HAMPSHIRE (Bent Buckle, Modiste)

Non-flint made by U.S. Glass Co., Pittsburgh, PA, c1903 in The States Pattern series.

	Clear with Gold	Rose Stained	Ruby Stained
Biscuit jar, cov	75.00	–	–
Bowl			
Flared, 5-1/2"	10.00	–	25.00
Flared, 8-1/2"	15.00	25.00	–
Round, 8-1/2"	18.00	30.00	–
Square, 8-1/2"	25.00	35.00	–
Butter, cov	45.00	70.00	–
Cake Stand, 8-1/4"	30.00	–	–
Carafe	60.00	–	–
Celery Vase	35.00	50.00	–
Compote			
Cov, hs, 5"	50.00	–	–
Cov, hs, 6"	60.00	–	–
Cov, hs, 7"	65.00	–	–
Open	40.00	55.00	–
Creamer			
Individual	20.00	30.00	–
Table	30.00	45.00	–
Cruet	55.00	135.00	–
Goblet	35.00	45.00	–
Mug, large	20.00	45.00	50.00
Pitcher, water			
Bulbous, ah	90.00	–	–
Straight Sides, molded handle	60.00	90.00	–
Relish	18.00	–	–
Salt & Pepper, pr	35.00	–	–
Sauce	10.00	–	–
Sugar			
Cov, table	45.00	60.00	–
Individual, open	20.00	25.00	–
Syrup	75.00	150.00	175.00
Toothpick	25.00	40.00	40.00
Vase	35.00	50.00	–
Wine	25.00	50.00	–

NEW JERSEY (Loops and Drops)

Non-flint made by U.S. Glass Co., Pittsburgh, PA, c1900-08 in States pattern series. Prices are for items with perfect gold. An emerald green 11" vase is known (value $75).

	Clear with Gold	Ruby Stained
Bowl		
8," flared	25.00	55.00
9," saucer	32.50	70.00
10," oval	30.00	85.00
Bread Plate	30.00	–
Butter, cov		
Flat	75.00	100.00
Footed	125.00	–
Cake Stand, 8"	65.00	–
Carafe	60.00	–
Celery Tray, rect	25.00	45.00
Compote		
Cov, hs, 5," jelly	45.00	65.00
Cov, hs, 8"	65.00	95.00
Open, hs, 6-3/4"	35.00	70.00
Open, hs, 8"	60.00	80.00
Open, hs, 10-1/2," shallow	65.00	–
Creamer	35.00	65.00
Cruet	50.00	–
Fruit bowl, hs, 12-1/2"	55.00	110.00
Goblet	40.00	70.00
Molasses Can	90.00	–

	Clear with Gold	Ruby Stained
Olive	15.00	—
Pickle, rect	15.00	—
Pitcher		
Milk, ah	75.00	185.00
Water		
Applied Handle	80.00	210.00
Pressured Handle	50.00	185.00
Plate, 8" d	30.00	50.00
Salt & Pepper, pr		
Hotel	50.00	120.00
Small	35.00	60.00
Sauce	10.00	35.00
Spooner	27.00	80.00
Sugar, cov	60.00	80.00
Sweetmeat, 8"	70.00	110.00
Syrup	90.00	—
Toothpick	55.00	225.00
Tumbler	30.00	60.00
Water Bottle	55.00	110.00
Wine	45.00	65.00

ONE HUNDRED ONE (Beaded 101)

Non-flint made by Bellaire Goblet Co., Findlay, Ohio, in the late 1880s.

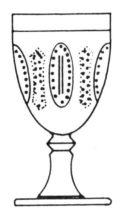

	Clear
Bread Plate, 101 border	
Farm implement center, 11"	75.00
Butter, cov	40.00
Cake Stand, 9"	65.00
Celery Vase	50.00
Compote	
Cov, hs, 7"	60.00
Cov, ls	60.00
Creamer	45.00
*Goblet	50.00
Lamp, hand, oil, 10"	80.00
Pickle	20.00
Pitcher, water, ah	125.00
Plate	
6"	20.00
8"	30.00
Relish	15.00
Sauce	
Flat	10.00
Footed	15.00
Spooner	25.00
Sugar, cov	45.00
Wine	60.00

PALMETTE (Hearts and Spades, Spades)

Non-flint, unknown maker, late 1870s. Shards have been found at Burlington Glass Works, Hamilton, Ontario, Canada. Syrup known in milk glass.

	Clear
Bottle, vinegar	80.00
Bowl, scalloped rim	
8"	25.00
9"	20.00
Butter Dish, cov	60.00
Cake Plate, tab handles	35.00
Cake Stand (two sizes)	100.00
Castor Set, 5 bottles, sp holder	125.00
Celery Vase	55.00
Champagne	75.00
Compote	
Cov, hs, 8-1/2"	75.00

	Clear
Cov, hs, 9-3/4"	85.00
Open, ls, 7"	30.00
Creamer, ah	65.00
Cup Plate	55.00
Eggcup	40.00
Goblet	35.00
Lamp, various sizes	95.00
Pickle, scoop shape	20.00
Pitcher, bulbous, ah	
Milk	135.00
Water	125.00
Relish (3 sauces)	18.00
Salt, master, ftd	22.00
Salt Shaker	55.00
Sauce, flat, 6"	10.00
Shaker, saloon, oversize	80.00
Spooner	35.00
Sugar, cov	55.00
Syrup, ah	125.00
Tumbler	
Bar	75.00
Water, ftd	40.00
Wine	110.00

PANELED FORGET-ME-NOT (Regal)

Non-flint, made by Bryce Bros., Pittsburgh, PA, c1880. Reissued by U.S. Glass Co. c1891. Shards have been found at Burlington Glass Works, Hamilton, Ontario, Canada. Made in clear, blue, and amber with limited production in amethyst, vaseline and green.

	Amber	Blue	Clear
Bread Plate	35.00	45.00	30.00
Butter, cov	50.00	60.00	45.00
Cake Stand, 10"	70.00	90.00	45.00
Celery Vase	45.00	70.00	36.00
Compote			
Cov, hs, 7"	90.00	110.00	65.00
Cov, hs, 8"	80.00	100.00	68.00
Open, hs, 8-1/2"	60.00	75.00	50.00
Open, hs, 10"	60.00	80.00	40.00
Creamer	45.00	60.00	35.00
Cruet, os	–	–	45.00
Goblet	50.00	65.00	32.00
Marmalade Jar, cov	80.00	100.00	60.00
Pickle, boat shape	25.00	35.00	15.00
Pitcher			
Milk	90.00	110.00	50.00
Water	90.00	110.00	75.00
Relish, scoop shape	55.00	55.00	65.00
Salt & Pepper, pr	–	–	65.00
Sauce, ftd	18.00	25.00	12.00
Spooner	40.00	50.00	25.00
Sugar, cov	60.00		40.00
Wine	55.00	65.00	60.00

PENNSYLVANIA (Balder)

Non-flint issued by U.S. Glass Co. in 1898. Also known in ruby stained. A ruffled jelly compote is documented in orange carnival.

	Clear with Gold	Emerald Green
Biscuit Jar, cov	75.00	125.00
Bowl		
4"	20.00	–
8," berry	25.00	35.00
8," sq	20.00	40.00
Butter, cov	60.00	85.00

	Clear with Gold	Emerald Green
Carafe	45.00	—
Celery Tray	30.00	—
Celery Vase	45.00	—
Champagne	25.00	—
Cheese Dish, cov	65.00	—
Compote, hs, jelly	50.00	—
Creamer	25.00	50.00
Cruet, os	45.00	—
Decanter, os	100.00	—
Goblet	24.00	—
Juice Tumbler	10.00	20.00
Molasses Can	75.00	—
Pitcher, water	60.00	—
Punch Bowl	175.00	—
Punch Cup	10.00	—
Salt Shaker	10.00	—
Sauce	7.50	—
*Spooner	24.00	35.00
Sugar, cov	40.00	55.00
Syrup	50.00	—
Tankard	110.00	—
Toothpick	35.00	90.00
Tumbler	28.00	40.00
Whiskey	20.00	35.00
Wine	15.00	40.00

PICKET (London, Picket Fence)

Non-flint made by the King, Son and Co., Pittsburgh, PA, c1890. Toothpick holders are known in apple green, vaseline, and purple slag.

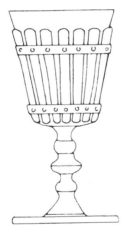

	Clear
Bowl, 9-1/2," sq	30.00
Bread Plate	70.00
Butter, cov	65.00
Celery Vase	40.00
Compote	
Cov, hs, 8"	135.00
Cov, ls, 8"	125.00
Open, hs, 7," sq	35.00
Open, hs, 10," sq	70.00
Open, ls, 7"	50.00
Creamer	50.00
Goblet	50.00
Pitcher, water	95.00
Salt	
Individual	10.00
Master	35.00
Sauce	
Flat	15.00
Footed	20.00
Spooner	30.00
Sugar, cov	50.00
Toothpick	35.00
Tray, water	65.00
Waste Bowl	40.00
Wine	85.00

QUEEN ANNE (Bearded Man)

Non-flint made by LaBelle Glass Co., Bridgeport. Ohio, c1879. Finials are Maltese cross. At least 28 pieces are documented. A table set and water pitcher are known in amber.

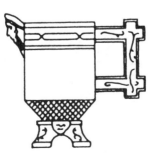

	Clear
Bowl, cov	
8," oval	45.00
9," oval	55.00

	Clear
Bread Plate	50.00
Butter, cov	65.00
Celery Vase	35.00
Compote, cov, ls, 9"	85.00
Creamer	45.00
Eggcup	45.00
Pitcher	
Milk	75.00
Water	85.00
Salt Shaker	40.00
Sauce	15.00
Spooner	40.00
Sugar, cov	55.00
Syrup	100.00

RED BLOCK (Late Block)

Non-flint with red stain made by Doyle and Co., Pittsburgh, PA. Later made by five companies, plus U.S. Glass Co. in 1892. Prices for clear 50% less.

	Ruby Stained
Banana Boat	75.00
Bowl, 8"	75.00
Butter, cov	110.00
Celery Vase, 6-1/2"	85.00
Cheese Dish, cov	125.00
Creamer	
Individual	45.00
Table	70.00
Decanter, 12," os, variant	175.00
*Goblet	35.00
Mug	50.00
Mustard, cov	55.00
Pitcher, water, 8" h	175.00
Relish Tray	25.00
Rose Bowl	75.00
Salt Dip, individual	50.00
Salt Shaker	75.00
Sauce, flat, 4-1/2"	20.00
Spooner	45.00
Sugar, cov	90.00
Tumbler	40.00
*Wine	40.00

REVERSE TORPEDO (Bull's Eye Band, Bull's Eye with Diamond Point #2, Pointed Bull's Eye)

Non-flint made by Dalzell, Gilmore and Leighton Glass Co., Findlay, Ohio, c1888-90. Also attributed to Canadian factories. Sometimes found with copper-wheel etching.

	Clear
Banana Stand, 9-3/4"	100.00
Basket	175.00
Biscuit Jar, cov	135.00
Bowl	
8-1/2," shallow	30.00
9," fruit, piecrust rim	70.00
10-1/2," piecrust rim	75.00
Butter, cov, 7-1/2," d	75.00
Cake Stand, hs	85.00
Celery Vase	55.00
Compote	
Cov, hs, 6"	80.00
Cov, hs, 7"	80.00
Cov, hs, 10"	125.00
Open, hs, 7"	65.00
Open, hs, 8-3/8" d	45.00

	Clear
Open, hs, 10-1/2 d, V-shaped bowl	165.00
Open, hs, jelly	50.00
Open, ls, 9-1/4," ruffled	85.00
Creamer	55.00
Doughnut Tray	90.00
Goblet	85.00
Honey Dish, sq, cov	145.00
Jam Jar, cov	85.00
Pitcher, tankard, 10-1/4"	160.00
Sauce, flat, 3-3/4"	10.00
Spooner	30.00
Sugar, cov	85.00
Syrup	165.00
Tumbler	30.00

ROMAN ROSETTE

Non-flint made by Bryce, Walker and Co., Pittsburgh, PA, c1890. Reissued by U.S. Glass Co. in 1892 and 1898. Also seen with English registry mark and known in amber stained.

	Clear	Ruby Stained
Bowl, 8-1/2"	15.00	50.00
Bread Plate	30.00	75.00
Butter, cov	50.00	125.00
Cake Stand, 9"	45.00	—
Celery Vase	30.00	95.00
Compote		
Cov, hs, 4-1/2," jelly	50.00	—
Cov, hs, 6"	65.00	—
Cordial	50.00	
Creamer	32.00	45.00
*Goblet	40.00	—
Mug	35.00	
Pitcher		
Milk	50.00	150.00
Water	65.00	140.00
Plate, 7-1/2"	35.00	65.00
Relish, oval, 9"	20.00	40.00
Salt & Pepper, glass tray	40.00	100.00
Sauce	15.00	20.00
Spooner	25.00	45.00
Sugar, cov	40.00	80.00
Syrup	85.00	125.00
Wine	45.00	65.00

ROSE-IN-SNOW (Rose)

Non-flint made by Bryce Bros., Pittsburgh, PA, in the square form c1880. Also made in the more common round form by Ohio Flint Glass Co. and after 1891 by U.S. Glass Co. Both styles reissued by Indiana Glass Co., Dunkirk, IN. Reproductions made by several companies, including Imperial Glass Co., as early as 1930 and continuing through the 1970s.

	Amber and Canary	Blue	Clear
Bowl, 8" sq	40.00	50.00	30.00
Butter, cov			
Round	65.00	125.00	45.00
Square	70.00	150.00	50.00
Cake Stand, 9"	125.00	175.00	90.00
Compote			
Cov, hs, 8"	125.00	175.00	80.00
Cov, ls, 7"	100.00	150.00	75.00
Open, ls, 5-3/4"	65.00	120.00	35.00
Creamer			
Round	60.00	100.00	45.00
Square	65.00	120.00	45.00
*Goblet	40.00	55.00	35.00

	Amber and Canary	Blue	Clear
Marmalade Jar, cov	70.00	125.00	60.00
*Mug, "In Fond Remembrance"	65.00	125.00	35.00
*Pickle Dish			
Double, 8-1/2" x 7"	85.00	110.00	100.00
Single, oval, handles at end	35.00	95.00	20.00
Pitcher, water, ah	175.00	200.00	125.00
Plate			
5"	40.00	40.00	35.00
6"	30.00	80.00	20.00
7"	30.00	80.00	20.00
*9"	30.00	85.00	20.00
Platter, oval	–	–	125.00
Sauce			
Flat	15.00	20.00	12.00
Footed	8.00	45.00	18.00
Spooner			
Round	30.00	80.00	25.00
Square	40.00	100.00	35.00
Sugar, cov			
Round	55.00	120.00	50.00
*Square	50.00	140.00	45.00
Sweetmeat, cov, 5-3/4" d	80.00	155.00	65.00
Toddy Jar, cov, under plate	150.00	155.00	125.00
Tumbler	60.00	100.00	50.00

SKILTON (Early Oregon)

Made by Richards and Hartley of Tarentum, PA, in 1888 and by U.S. Glass Co. after 1891. This is not one of the U.S. Glass States pattern series and should not be confused with Beaded Loop, which is Oregon #1, named by U.S. Glass Co. It is better as Skilton (named by Millard) to avoid confusion with Beaded Loop.

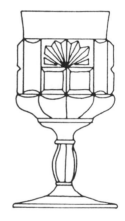

	Clear	Ruby Stained
Bowl		
5," round	15.00	–
7," rect	20.00	–
9," rect	30.00	–
Butter, cov	45.00	110.00
Cake Stand	35.00	–
Celery Vase	35.00	95.00
Compote		
Cov, hs, 8"	45.00	–
Open, ls, 8"	30.00	75.00
Creamer	30.00	55.00
Dish, oblong, sq	25.00	–
Goblet	35.00	50.00
Olive, handled	20.00	–
Pickle	15.00	–
Pitcher		
Milk	45.00	125.00
Water	50.00	125.00
Salt & Pepper, pr	45.00	–
Sauce, ftd	12.00	20.00
Spooner, flat	25.00	55.00
Sugar, cov	35.00	85.00
Tray, water	45.00	–
Tumbler	25.00	40.00
Wine	35.00	50.00

SPIREA BAND (Earl, Nailhead Variant, Spirea, Squared Do)

Non-flint made by Bryce, Higbee and Co., Pittsburgh, PA, c1885.

	Amber	Blue	Clear	Vaseline
Bowl, 8"	25.00	40.00	20.00	30.00
Butter, cov	50.00	55.00	35.00	45.00
Cake Stand, 11"	45.00	55.00	40.00	45.00

	Amber	Blue	Clear	Vaseline
Celery Vase	40.00	50.00	25.00	40.00
Compote, cov, hs, 7"	44.00	65.00	40.00	44.00
Cordial	38.00	42.00	20.00	38.00
Creamer	32.50	44.00	35.00	35.00
Goblet	30.00	35.00	25.00	35.00
Pitcher, water	65.00	80.00	35.00	60.00
Platter, 10-1/2"	32.00	42.00	20.00	32.00
Relish	30.00	35.00	18.00	30.00
Sauce				
Flat	10.00	12.00	5.00	10.00
Ftd	15.00	15.00	8.00	15.00
Spooner	30.00	35.00	20.00	35.00
Sugar, open	32.00	40.00	25.00	32.00
Tumbler	24.00	35.00	20.00	30.00
Wine	30.00	35.00	20.00	30.00

STATES, THE (Cane and Star Medallion)

Non-flint made by U.S. Glass Co., Pittsburgh, PA, in 1905. Also found in emerald green (add 50%). Prices given for clear with good gold trim.

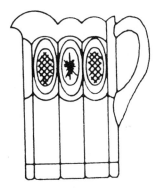

	Clear
Bowl	
7," round, 3 handles	25.00
9-1/4," round	30.00
Butter, cov	65.00
Celery Tray	20.00
Celery Vase	20.00
Cocktail	25.00
Compote	
Open, hs, 7"	30.00
Open, hs, 9"	40.00
Creamer	
Individual, oval	20.00
Regular, round	30.00
Goblet	35.00
Pickle Tray	15.00
Pitcher, water	45.00
Plate, 10"	25.00
Punch Bowl, 13" d	75.00
Punch Cup	10.00
Relish, diamond shape	35.00
Salt & Pepper	40.00
Sauce, flat, 4," tub shape	15.00
Spooner	25.00
Sugar	
Individual, open	15.00
Regular, cov	40.00
Syrup	65.00
Toothpick, flat,	
rectangular, curled lip	45.00
Tray, 7-1/4" l, 5-1/2" w	20.00
Tumbler	25.00
Wine	30.00

TENNESSEE (Jewel and Crescent, Jeweled Rosette)

Non-flint made by King, Son & Co., Pittsburgh, PA, and continued by U.S. Glass Co. in 1899 as part of the States series.

	Clear	Colored Jewels
Bowl		
Cov, 7"	40.00	–
Open, 8"	35.00	40.00
Bread Plate	40.00	75.00
Butter, cov	55.00	–

	Clear	Colored Jewels
Cake Stand		
8"	35.00	–
9-1/2"	38.00	–
10-1/2"	45.00	–
Celery Vase	35.00	–
Compote		
Cov, hs, 5"	40.00	55.00
Cov, hs, 7"	50.00	–
Open, hs, 6"	30.00	–
Open, hs, 8"	40.00	–
Open, hs, 10"	65.00	–
Open, ls, 7"	35.00	–
Creamer	30.00	–
Cruet	65.00	–
Goblet	40.00	–
Mug	40.00	–
Pitcher		
Milk	55.00	–
Water	65.00	–
Relish	20.00	–
Salt Shaker	30.00	–
Spooner	35.00	–
Sugar, cov	45.00	–
Syrup	90.00	–
Toothpick	75.00	85.00
Tumbler	35.00	–
Wine	65.00	85.00

TEXAS (Loop with Stippled Panels)

Non-flint made by U.S. Glass Co., Pittsburgh, PA, c1900, in the States pattern series. Occasionally pieces are found in ruby stained. Reproduced in solid colors, including cobalt blue, by Crystal Art Glass Co. and Boyd Glass Co., Cambridge, Ohio.

	Clear with Gold	Rose Stained
Bowl		
7"	20.00	40.00
9," scalloped	35.00	50.00
Butter, cov	75.00	125.00
Cake Stand, 9-1/2"	65.00	125.00
Celery Tray	30.00	50.00
Celery Vase	40.00	85.00
Compote		
Cov, hs, 6"	60.00	125.00
Cov, hs, 7"	70.00	150.00
Cov, hs, 8"	75.00	175.00
Open, hs, 5"	45.00	75.00
Creamer		
*Individual	20.00	45.00
Table	45.00	85.00
Cruet, os	75.00	165.00
Goblet	95.00	110.00
Horseradish, cov	50.00	–
Pickle, 8-1/2"	25.00	50.00
Pitcher, water	125.00	400.00
Plate, 9"	35.00	60.00
Salt Shaker	25.00	–
Sauce		
Flat	10.00	20.00
Footed	20.00	25.00
Spooner	35.00	80.00
Sugar		
*Individual, cov	45.00	–
Table, cov	75.00	125.00
Syrup	75.00	175.00
Toothpick	25.00	95.00

	Clear with Gold	Rose Stained
Tumbler	40.00	100.00
Vase		
6-1/2"	25.00	–
9"	35.00	–
*Wine	75.00	140.00

THOUSAND EYE

The original pattern was non-flint made by Adams & Co., Tarentum, PA, in 1875 and by Richards and Hartley in 1888 (pattern No. 103). It was made in two forms: Adams, with a three-knob stem finial, and Richards and Hartley, with a plain stem with a scalloped bottom. Several glass companies made variations of the original pattern and reproductions were made as late as 1981. Crystal Opalescent was produced by Richards and Hartley only in the original pattern. (Opalescent celery vase, $70; open compote, 8," $115; 6" creamer, $85; quarter-gallon water pitcher, $140; half-gallon water pitcher, $180; 4" footed sauce, $40; spooner, $60; and 5" covered sugar, $80). Covered compotes are rare and would command 40% more than open compotes. A 2" mug in blue is known.

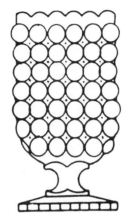

	Apple Green	Amber	Blue	Clear	Vaseline
ABC Plate, 6," clock center	60.00	70.00	60.00	50.00	60.00
Bowl, large, carriage shape	95.00	–	95.00	–	95.00
Butter, cov					
6-1/4"	75.00	85.00	80.00	50.00	100.00
7-1/2"	75.00	85.00	80.00	50.00	105.00
Cake Stand					
10"	60.00	90.00	60.00	35.00	95.00
11"	60.00	95.00	60.00	35.00	95.00
Celery, hat shape	60.00	75.00	70.00	40.00	60.00
Celery Vase, 7"	60.00	70.00	60.00	50.00	60.00
Christmas Light	35.00	50.00	40.00	30.00	45.00
Cologne Bottle	30.00	50.00	40.00	25.00	50.00
Compote, cov, ls, 8," sq	–	115.00	115.00	–	–
Compote, open					
6"	40.00	45.00	45.00	30.00	45.00
7"	50.00	60.00	50.00	40.00	50.00
8," round	45.00	60.00	50.00	40.00	60.00
8," sq, hs	45.00	60.00	60.00	45.00	60.00
9"	60.00	70.00	60.00	45.00	60.00
10"	60.00	75.00	70.00	50.00	70.00
Cordial	40.00	60.00	45.00	30.00	70.00
Creamer					
4"	40.00	45.00	45.00	30.00	45.00
6"	45.00	85.00	60.00	40.00	85.00
Creamer and Sugar Set	–	170.00	–	115.00	–
*Cruet, 6"	45.00	70.00	60.00	40.00	70.00
Eggcup	75.00	95.00	80.00	50.00	100.00
*Goblet	45.00	50.00	45.00	40.00	50.00
Honey Dish, cov, 6" x 7-1/4"	95.00	110.00	100.00	80.00	95.00
Inkwell, 2" sq	50.00	–	85.00	40.00	90.00
Jelly Glass	30.00	35.00	30.00	20.00	30.00
Lamp, kerosene					
hs, 12"	140.00	170.00	150.00	115.00	160.00
hs, 15"	145.00	180.00	150.00	130.00	170.00
ls, handled	130.00	130.00	130.00	105.00	140.00
Mug					
2-1/2"	30.00	35.00	30.00	25.00	40.00
3-1/2"	30.00	35.00	30.00	25.00	40.00
Nappy					
5"	40.00	–	45.00	35.00	50.00
6"	45.00	–	50.00	40.00	60.00
8"	50.00	–	60.00	50.00	70.00
Pickle	30.00	35.00	35.00	25.00	35.00
Pitcher					
Milk, cov, 7"	95.00	130.00	130.00	85.00	120.00

	Apple Green	Amber	Blue	Clear	Vaseline
Water, 1/4 gal	80.00	95.00	90.00	60.00	90.00
Water, 1/2 gal	90.00	110.00	95.00	75.00	95.00
Water, 1 gal	100.00	115.00	110.00	95.00	115.00
*Plate, sq, folded corners					
6"	30.00	35.00	35.00	30.00	35.00
8"	35.00	35.00	35.00	30.00	35.00
10"	40.00	60.00	45.00	30.00	40.00
Platter					
8" x 11," oblong	45.00	60.00	50.00	45.00	50.00
11," oval	85.00	90.00	60.00	45.00	85.00
Salt Shaker, pr					
Banded	70.00	80.00	75.00	70.00	75.00
Plain	60.00	70.00	60.00	45.00	70.00
Salt, ind	90.00	110.00	100.00	60.00	100.00
Salt, open, carriage shape	75.00	95.00	85.00	60.00	85.00
Salt					
Flat, 4"	15.00	25.00	20.00	10.00	20.00
Footed, 4"	20.00	25.00	20.00	15.00	25.00
Spooner	40.00	60.00	45.00	35.00	50.00
*String Holder	40.00	70.00	50.00	35.00	50.00
Sugar, cov, 5"	60.00	85.00	70.00	60.00	70.00
Syrup, pewter top	90.00	115.00	80.00	60.00	80.00
Toothpick					
Hat	45.00	70.00	80.00	40.00	60.00
Plain	40.00	60.00	60.00	30.00	45.00
Thimble	60.00	–	–	–	–
Tray, water					
12-1/2," round	75.00	90.00	85.00	60.00	85.00
14," oval	75.00	90.00	85.00	70.00	85.00
*Tumbler	35.00	75.00	40.00	30.00	35.00
Waste Bowl	–	–	–	75.00	–
*Wine	40.00	60.00	45.00	25.00	45.00

THREE-FACE

Non-flint made by George A. Duncan & Son, Pittsburgh, PA, c1878. Designed by John E. Miller, a designer with Duncan, who later became a member of the firm. It has been heavily reproduced by L. G. Wright Glass Co. and other companies as early as the 1930s. Imperial Glass Co. was commissioned by the Metropolitan Museum of Art, New York, to reproduce a series of Three-Face items, each marked with the "M.M.A." monogram.

	Clear
Biscuit Jar, cov	300.00
*Butter, cov	165.00
*Cake Stand	
9"	175.00
12-1/2"	225.00
Celery Vase	
Plain	110.00
Scalloped	110.00
*Champagne	
Hollow stem	250.00
Saucer type	150.00
*Claret	110.00
*Compote	
Cov, hs, 8"	175.00
Cov, hs, 9"	190.00
Cov, hs, 10"	225.00
Cov, ls, 6"	160.00
Open, hs, 9"	165.00
Open, ls, 6"	95.00
*Creamer	135.00
*Goblet	85.00
*Lamp. Oil	150.00
Marmalade Jar	275.00

	Clear
Pitcher, water	325.00
*Salt Dip	35.00
*Salt & Pepper	75.00
*Sauce, ftd	25.00
*Spooner	80.00
*Sugar, cov	125.00
*Wine	150.00

TORPEDO (Pigmy)

Non-flint made by Thompson Glass Co., Uniontown, PA, c1889. A black amethyst master salt ($150) is also known.

	Clear	Ruby Stained
Banana Stand	75.00	—
Bowl		
Cov, 7" d, 7-1/4" h	65.00	—
Open, 7"	18.00	—
Open, 9"	20.00	45.00
Butter, cov	85.00	—
Cake Stand, 10"	85.00	—
Celery Vase, scalloped top	40.00	—
Compote		
Cov, hs, 4," jelly	65.00	—
Cov, hs, 13-3/4"	165.00	—
Creamer	50.00	—
Cruet, os, ah	80.00	—
Cup and Saucer	60.00	—
Decanter, os, 8"	85.00	—
Finger Bowl	55.00	—
Goblet	45.00	85.00
Lamp		
3," handled	75.00	
8," plain base, pattern on bowl	85.00	
Marmalade Jar, cov	85.00	—
Pickle Castor, sp holder	125.00	
Pitcher		
Milk, 8-1/2"	75.00	150.00
Water, 10-1/2"	85.00	175.00
Punch Cup	25.00	—
Salt		
Individual	20.00	—
Master	35.00	—
Salt Shaker, single, two types	50.00	—
Sauce, 4-1/2," collared base	15.00	—
Spooner, scalloped top	45.00	—
Sugar, cov	65.00	—
Syrup	95.00	175.00
Tray, water		
10," round	85.00	—
11-3/4," clover shaped	75.00	—
Tumbler	45.00	60.00
Wine	90.00	—

TRUNCATED CUBE (Thompson's #77)

Non-flint made by Thompson Glass Co., Uniontown, PA, c1894. Also found with copper-wheel engraving.

	Clear	Ruby Stained
Bowl, 8"	—	40.00
Butter, cov	50.00	90.00
Celery Vase	40.00	55.00
Creamer		
Individual	20.00	30.00
Regular	35.00	65.00
Cruet, os, ph	35.00	90.00

	Clear	Ruby Stained
Decanter, os, 12" h	60.00	150.00
Goblet	30.00	50.00
Pitcher, ah		
Milk, 1 qt	50.00	100.00
Water, 1/2 gal	60.00	115.00
Salt Shaker, single	15.00	30.00
Sauce, 4"	30.00	50.00
Spooner	30.00	50.00
Sugar, cov		
Individual	20.00	35.00
Regular	30.00	65.00
Syrup	40.00	100.00
Toothpick	30.00	45.00
Tray, water	20.00	40.00
Tumbler	22.50	35.00
Wine	25.00	40.00

U.S. COIN

Non-flint frosted, clear, and gilded pattern made by U.S. Glass Co., Pittsburgh, PA, in 1892 for three or four months. The U.S. Treasury stopped production because real coins, dated as early as 1878, were used in the molds. The 1892 coin date is the most common. Lamps with coins on font and stem would be 50% more. Heavily reproduced for the gift-shop trade.

	Clear	Frosted
Ale Glass	250.00	350.00
*Bowl		
6"	170.00	220.00
9"	215.00	325.00
*Bread Plate	175.00	325.00
Butter, cov, dollars and halves	250.00	450.00
Cake Stand, 10"	225.00	400.00
Celery Tray	200.00	−
Celery Vase, quarters	135.00	350.00
Champagne	−	400.00
*Compote		
Cov, hs, 7"	300.00	500.00
Cov, hs, 8," quarters and dimes	−	550.00
Open, hs, 7," quarters and dimes	200.00	300.00
Open, hs, 7," quarters and halves	225.00	350.00
Open, 8-3/8" d, 6-1/2" h	−	240.00
*Creamer	350.00	600.00
Cruet, os	375.00	500.00
Epergne	−	1,000.00
Goblet	300.00	450.00
Goblet, dimes	200.00	295.00
Lamp		
Round font	275.00	450.00
Square font	300.00	−
Mug, handled	200.00	300.00
Pickle	200.00	−
Pitcher		
Milk	500.00	800.00
Water	400.00	800.00
Sauce, ftd, 4," quarters	100.00	185.00
*Spooner, quarters	225.00	325.00
*Sugar, cov	225.00	450.00
Syrup, dated pewter lid	−	650.00
*Toothpick	180.00	275.00
Tray, water, 10," round	450.00	550.00
*Tumbler	135.00	235.00
Waste Bowl	225.00	250.00
Wine	225.00	375.00

U.S. SHERATON (Greek Key)

Made by U.S. Glass Co., Pittsburgh, PA, in 1912. This pattern was made only in clear, but can be found trimmed with gold or platinum or with a green stain. Some pieces are marked with the intertwined U.S. Glass trademark.

	Clear
Bowl	
6," ftd, sq	15.00
8," flat	12.00
Bureau Tray	30.00
Butter, cov	35.00
Celery Tray	30.00
Compote	
Open, 4," jelly	12.00
Open, 6"	14.00
Creamer	
After dinner, tall, sq ft	12.00
Berry, bulbous, sq ft	15.00
Large	18.00
Cruet, os	25.00
Finger Bowl, under plate	24.00
Goblet	18.00
Iced Tea	20.00
Lamp, miniature	50.00
Marmalade Jar	35.00
Mug	15.00
Mustard Jar, cov	30.00
Pickle	10.00
Pin Tray	12.00
Pitcher, water, 1/2 gal	30.00
Squat, medium	30.00
Tankard	35.00
Plate, sq	
4-1/2"	8.00
9"	12.00
Pomade Jar	14.00
Puff Box	14.00
Punch Bowl, cov, 14"	90.00
Ring Tree	25.00
Salt Shaker	
Squat	12.00
Tall	15.00
Salt, individual	17.00
Sardine Box	35.00
Spooner	
Handled	25.00
Tray	12.00
Sugar, cov	
Individual	15.00
Regular	20.00
Sundae Dish	10.00
Syrup, glass lid	35.00
Toothpick	35.00
Tumbler	15.00

VERMONT (Honeycomb with Flower Rim, Inverted Thumbprint with Daisy Band)

Non-flint made by U.S. Glass Co., Pittsburgh, PA, 1899-1903. Also made in custard (usually decorated), chocolate, caramel, novelty slag, milk glass, and blue. Crystal Art Glass Co., Mosser Glass Co., and Degenhart Glass (which marks its colored line) have reproduced toothpick holders.

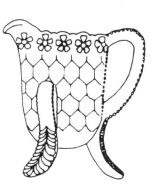

	Clear with Gold	**Green with Gold**
Basket, handle	30.00	45.00
Bowl, berry	25.00	45.00

	Clear with Gold	Green with Gold
Butter, cov	40.00	75.00
Card Tray	20.00	35.00
Celery Tray	30.00	35.00
Compote, hs		
Cov	55.00	125.00
Open	35.00	65.00
Creamer, 4-1/4"	30.00	55.00
Goblet	40.00	50.00
Pickle	20.00	30.00
Pitcher, water	50.00	125.00
Salt Shaker	20.00	35.00
Sauce	15.00	20.00
Spooner	25.00	75.00
Sugar, cov	35.00	80.00
*Toothpick	30.00	50.00
Tumbler	20.00	40.00
Vase	20.00	45.00

VIKING (Bearded Head, Bearded Prophet, Hobb's Centennial, Old Man of the Mountain)

Non-flint made by Hobbs, Brockunier, & Co., Wheeling, WV, in 1876 as its Centennial pattern. No tumbler or goblet originally made. Very rare in milk glass.

	Clear
Apothecary Jar, cov	60.00
Bowl	
Cov, 8," oval	55.00
Cov, 9," oval	65.00
Bread Plate	70.00
Butter, cov	75.00
Celery Vase	45.00
Compote	
Cov, hs, 9"	165.00
Cov, ls, 8," oval	95.00
Open, hs	60.00
Creamer, 2 types	50.00
Cup, ftd	35.00
Eggcup	40.00
Marmalade Jar	85.00
Mug, ah	50.00
Pickle	20.00
Pitcher, water	125.00
Relish	20.00
Salt, master	40.00
Sauce	15.00
Spooner	35.00
Sugar, cov	65.00

WAFFLE and THUMBPRINT (Bull's Eye and Waffle, Palace, Triple Bull's Eye)

Flint made by the New England Glass Co., East Cambridge, MA, c1868 and by Curling, Robertson & Co., Pittsburgh, PA, c1856. Shards have been found at the Boston and Sandwich Glass Co., Sandwich, MA.

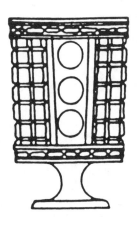

	Clear
Bottle, ftd	135.00
Bowl, 5" x 7"	30.00
Butter, cov	95.00
Celery Vase	105.00
Champagne	90.00
Claret	110.00
Compote, cov, hs	150.00
Cordial	100.00
Creamer	125.00

	Clear
Decanter, os	
Pint	165.00
Quart	195.00
Eggcup	45.00
Goblet, knob stem	65.00
Lamp	
9-1/2"	115.00
11," whale oil	175.00
Pitcher, water	500.00
Salt, master	45.00
Spooner	45.00
Sugar, cov	125.00
Sweetmeat, cov, hs, 6"	150.00
Tumbler	
Flip Glass	125.00
Water, ftd	75.00
Whiskey	75.00
Wine	70.00

WESTWARD HO! (Pioneer, Tippecanoe)

Non-flint, usually frosted, made by Gillinder and Sons, Philadelphia, PA, c1879. Molds made by Jacobus, who also made Classic. Has been reproduced since the 1930s by L. G. Wright Glass Co., Westmoreland Glass Co., and several others. This pattern was originally made in milk glass (rare) and clear with acid finish as part of the design. Reproductions can be found in several colors and in clear.

	Clear
Bowl, 5," ftd	125.00
Bread Plate	175.00
*Butter, cov	185.00
*Celery Vase	125.00
*Compote	
Cov, hs, 5"	225.00
Cov, hs, 8" d	455.00
Open, hs, 8"	125.00
*Creamer	115.00
*Goblet	120.00
Marmalade Jar, cov	200.00
Mug	
2"	225.00
3-1/2"	175.00
*Pitcher, water	350.00
*Sauce, ftd, 4-1/2"	35.00
*Spooner	95.00
*Sugar, cov	185.00
*Wine	200.00

WHEAT and BARLEY (Duquesne, Hops and Barley, Oats and Barley)

Non-flint made by Bryce Bros., Pittsburgh, PA, c1880. Later made by U.S. Glass Co., Pittsburgh, PA, after 1891.

	Amber	Blue	Clear	Vaseline
Bowl, 8," cov	35.00	40.00	25.00	55.00
Butter, cov	45.00	60.00	35.00	80.00
Cake Stand				
8"	30.00	45.00	20.00	60.00
10"	40.00	50.00	30.00	70.00
Compote				
Cov, hs, 7"	45.00	55.00	40.00	75.00
Cov, hs, 8"	50.00	55.00	45.00	75.00
Open, hs, jelly	32.50	40.00	30.00	55.00
*Creamer	30.00	40.00	28.00	55.00
*Goblet	40.00	55.00	25.00	75.00
Mug	30.00	40.00	20.00	55.00

	Amber	Blue	Clear	Vaseline
Pitcher				
Milk	70.00	85.00	40.00	110.00
Water	85.00	95.00	45.00	125.00
Plate				
7"	20.00	30.00	15.00	40.00
9," closed handles	25.00	35.00	20.00	45.00
Relish	20.00	30.00	15.00	40.00
Salt Shaker	25.00	30.00	20.00	40.00
Sauce				
Flat, handled	15.00	15.00	10.00	20.00
Footed	15.00	15.00	10.00	20.00
Spooner	30.00	40.00	24.00	55.00
Sugar, cov	40.00	50.00	35.00	65.00
Syrup	175.00	195.00	85.00	–
Tumbler	35.00	40.00	20.00	55.00

WILLOW OAK (Acorn, Acorn and Oak Leaf, Bryce's Wreath, Stippled Daisy, Thistle and Sunflower)

Non-flint made by Bryce Bros., Pittsburgh, PA, c1885 and by U.S. Glass Company in 1891.

	Amber	Blue	Canary	Clear
Bowl, 8"	45.00	40.00	50.00	20.00
Butter, cov	65.00	65.00	80.00	40.00
Cake Stand, 8-1/2"	55.00	65.00	70.00	45.00
Celery Vase	45.00	60.00	75.00	35.00
Compote				
Cov, hs, 7-1/2"	50.00	65.00	80.00	40.00
Open, 7"	30.00	40.00	48.00	25.00
Creamer	45.00	50.00	60.00	40.00
Goblet	40.00	50.00	60.00	30.00
Mug	35.00	45.00	54.00	30.00
Pitcher				
Milk	50.00	60.00	70.00	45.00
Water	55.00	60.00	75.00	50.00
Plate				
7"	35.00	45.00	50.00	25.00
9"	35.00	35.00	40.00	25.00
Salt Shaker	25.00	40.00	55.00	20.00
Sauce				
Flat, handled, sq	15.00	20.00	24.00	10.00
Footed, 4"	20.00	25.00	30.00	15.00
Spooner	35.00	40.00	48.00	30.00
Sugar, cov	68.50	70.00	75.00	40.00
Tray, water, 10-1/2"	35.00	50.00	60.00	30.00
Tumbler	35.00	40.00	45.00	30.00
Waste Bowl	35.00	40.00	40.00	30.00

WISCONSIN (Beaded Dewdrop)

Non-flint made by U.S. Glass Co. in Gas City, IN, in 1903. One of the States patterns. Toothpick reproduced in colors

	Clear
Banana Stand	75.00
Bowl	
6," oval, handled, cov	40.00
7," round	42.00
Butter, flat flange	75.00
***Cake Stand**	
8-1/2"	60.00
9-1/2"	70.00
Celery Tray	40.00
Celery Vase	60.00
Compote	
Cov, hs, 5"	60.00

	Clear
Cov, hs, 6"	65.00
Cov, hs, 7"	75.00
Cov, hs, 8"	90.00
Open, hs, 6"	35.00
Open, hs, 8"	50.00
Open, hs, 10"	75.00
Condiment Set, salt & pepper, mustard, horseradish, tray	110.00
*Creamer	60.00
Cruet, os	80.00
Cup and Saucer	50.00
*Goblet	75.00
Marmalade Jar, straight sides, glass lid	125.00
Mug	35.00
Pitcher	
Milk	75.00
Water	85.00
Plate, 6-3/4"	25.00
Punch Cup	12.00
Relish	25.00
Salt Shaker	30.00
Spooner	30.00
Sugar, cov	60.00
Sugar Shaker	90.00
Sweetmeat, 5," ftd, cov	40.00
Syrup	110.00
*Toothpick, kettle	55.00
Tumbler	45.00
Wine	75.00

X-RAY

Non-flint made by Riverside Glass Works, Wellsburgh, WV, 1896-98. Prices are for pieces with gold trim.

	Clear	Emerald Green
Bowl, berry, 8," beaded rim	25.00	45.00
Bread Plate	30.00	50.00
Butter, cov	40.00	75.00
Celery Vase	–	50.00
Compote		
Cov, hs	40.00	65.00
Jelly	–	40.00
Creamer		
Individual	20.00	50.00
Regular	35.00	65.00
Cruet Set, 4-leaf clover tray	125.00	350.00
Goblet	20.00	35.00
Pitcher, water	40.00	75.00
Salt Shaker	10.00	15.00
Sauce, flat, 4-1/2" d	8.00	10.00
Spooner	25.00	40.00
Sugar		
Individual, open	20.00	45.00
Regular, cov	35.00	65.00
Tumbler shape	–	75.00
Syrup	–	265.00
Toothpick	25.00	50.00
Tumbler	15.00	25.00

YALE (Crow-foot, Turkey Track)

Non-flint made by McKee & Bros. Co., Jeannette, PA, patented in 1887.

	Clear
Bowl, berry, 10-1/2"	20.00
Butter, cov	45.00

	Clear
Cake Stand	55.00
Celery Vase	40.00
Compote	
Cov, hs	50.00
Open, scalloped rim	25.00
Creamer	60.00
Goblet	45.00
Pitcher, water	65.00
Relish, oval	10.00
Salt Shaker	30.00
Sauce, flat	10.00
Spooner	45.00
Sugar, cov	35.00
Syrup	65.00
Tumbler	25.00

ZIPPER (Cobb)

Non-flint made by Richards & Hartley, Tarentum, PA, c1888.

	Clear
Bowl, 7" d	15.00
Butter, cov	45.00
Celery Vase	25.00
Cheese, cov	55.00
Compote, cov, ls, 8" d	40.00
Creamer	35.00
Cruet, os	45.00
Goblet	20.00
Marmalade Jar, cov	45.00
Pitcher, water, 1/2 gal	40.00
Relish, 10" l	15.00
Salt Dip	5.00
Sauce	
Flat	7.50
Footed	12.00
Spooner	30.00
Sugar, cov	45.00
Tumbler	20.00

PAUL REVERE POTTERY

History: Paul Revere Pottery, Boston, Massachusetts, was an outgrowth of a club known as The Saturday Evening Girls. The S.E.G. was composed of young female immigrants who met on Saturday nights to read and participate in craft projects, such as ceramics.

Regular pottery production began in 1908, and the name "Paul Revere" was adopted because the pottery was located near the Old North Church. In 1915, the firm moved to Brighton, Massachusetts. Known as the "Bowl Shop," the pottery grew steadily. In spite of popular acceptance and technical advancements, the pottery required continual subsidies. It finally closed in January 1942.

Items produced range from plain and decorated vases to tablewares to illustrated tiles. Many decorated wares were incised and glazed either in an Art Nouveau matte finish or an occasional high glaze.

Marks: In addition to an impressed mark, paper "Bowl Shop" labels were used prior to 1915. Pieces also can be found with a date and "P.R.P." or "S.E.G." painted on the base.

References: Susan and Al Bagdade, *Warman's American Pottery and Porcelain*, Wallace-Homestead, 1994; Paul Evans, *Art Pottery of the United States*, 2nd ed., Feingold & Lewis Publishing, 1987; Ralph and Terry Kovel, *Kovels' American Art Pottery*, Crown Publishers, 1993; David Rago, *American Art Pottery*, Knickerbocker Press, 1977.

Collectors' Club: American Art Pottery Association, P.O. Box 1226, Westport, MA 02790.

Bowl, cuerda seca
    5-1/4" d, 2" h, closed-in rim, stylized landscape of green trees, dark blue ground, ink mark "4-15 S.E.G./A.G." 850.00

Left: bowl, cuerda seca band of green grass against blue sky, moss green matte ground, mkd "S.E.G./4-15/S.G.," 3-1/4" h, 6-1/4" d, $2,700; center back: vessel, closed-in rim, cuerda seca band of stylized white flowers and green leaves, beige, celadon, and blue-gray ground, mkd "S.E.G. 339-12/11/S.G.," 4" h, 6" d, $3,750; center front: bowl, cuerda seca intricate and broad band of white orchids with green leaves, two-tone blue and beige ground, mkd "S.E.G./8/illegible initials," 2-3/4" h, 8-1/2" d, short, tight hairline, $2,000; right: cereal bowl, cuerda seca band of whimsical dancing rabbits in browns and ivory, paper label and ink mark, 2-1/4" h, 5-1/2" d, $2,100. Photo courtesy of David Rago Auctions, Inc.

    6-1/4" d, 3-1/4" h, band of green trees against blue sky, moss green matte ground, mkd "S.E.G./4-15/S.G.," crazing lines to rim..2,700.00
    8-1/4" d, stylized landscape, green, blue, and gray glazes, ink mark "SEG/y-20/bvc" 1,500.00
    8-1/2" d, 2-3/4" h, intricate broad band of white orchids, green leaves, two-tone blue and beige ground, "S. E. G./8/illegible initials," short title hairline 2,000.00
Cabinet Vase, 4-1/2" h, 2-1/4" d, cureda seca, brown and blue Greek key pattern, green ground, ink mark "S.E.G./E.G./4-1-?" 450.00
Cake Set, Tree pattern, black outline scene, blue sky, green trees, 10" d cake plate, six 8-1/2" d serving plates, each mkd "J.G., S.E.G.," three dated 7/15, three dated 1/4/15, one dated 3/15, price for 7 pc set 1,840.00
Cereal Bowl, cuerda seca
    5" d, 2-1/4" d, blue stylized trees, ivory sky, blue-green ground, paper label, incised "S.E.G./R.H./83-2-11" 1,000.00
    5-1/2" d, 2-1/4" d, band of whimsical dancing rabbits, browns and grays, paper label and ink mark 2,100.00
Cup and Saucer, 2" h, rim dec with dark blue outline, yellow floral border, cream ground, sgd on base "S. G. 91.7.12, 92.7.12, S.E.G.," 1912, some peppering old rim chip 575.00
Humidor, cov, 6-1/4" h, 5-3/4" d, spherical, blue matte glaze, pink int., minute int. rim nick, sgd in slip "P.R.P. 3/36" 400.00
Inkwell, 2-1/2" sq, 2" h, green and blue landscape of trees, ink mark and "Bowl Shop" paper label 850.00
Plate
    6-1/2" d, incised white mice, celadon and brown band, ink mark "Dorothy Hopkins/Her Plate," 1911 .... 1,300.00
    7-1/2" d
        Blue and green band, incised windmills, white center, 1911, ink S.E.G. mark 950.00
        Blue and white band, center medallion of blue scene, yellow sky and dock, initials "J.I.T.," mkd "S.E.G. F.L. 7/19" and "S.E.G., F.L. 8/15," price for pr 520.00
        Blue sky, green center, incised landscape of trees, 1912, ink S.E.G. mark 650.00
Ring Tray, 4" d, circular, blue-gray and green band of trees, blue-gray ground, mkd "S.E.G./J.G." 275.00
Teapot, 4-1/2" h, 9" d, brown and white wavy band of sailboats, yellow sky, 1918, restored 700.00
Tile, 3-3/4" sq, Washington Street, blue, white, green, and brown, mkd "H.S. S4 9/1/10," edge chips 420.00
Trivet
    4-1/4" d, medallion of house against setting sun, blue-gray ground, 1924, imp P.R.P. mark, 425.00
    5-1/2" d, medallion of goose standing on hill, dark blue ground, 1924, imp P.R.P. mark 550.00
    5-1/2" d, medallion of poplar trees in landscape, blue-green ground, 1925, imp P.R.P. mark 600.00
Vase
    5-1/4" h, 4-1/2" d, ovoid, abstracted landscape, green trees, frothy white sky, dark gray ground, sgd "3-22/S.E.G./E.G.," c1922 1,400.00
    7-1/8" h, bulbous, elongated neck, speckled dark blue glossy glaze, sgd "SEG 5. 25 M" on base, scratches 350.00
Vessel, 6" d, 4" h, closed-in rim, cuerda seca, band of stylized white flowers, green leaves, beige, celadon, and blue-gray ground, "S.E.G. 339-12-11/S.G." 3,750.00

PEACHBLOW

History: Peachblow, an art glass which derives its name from a fine Chinese glazed porcelain, resembles a peach or crushed strawberries in color. Three American glass manufacturers and two English firms produced peachblow glass in the late 1880s. A fourth American company resumed the process in the 1950s. The glass from each firm has its own identifying characteristics.

Hobbs, Brockunier & Co., Wheeling peachblow: Opalescent glass, plated or cased with a transparent amber glass; shading from yellow at the base to a deep red at top; glossy or satin finish.

Mt. Washington "Peach Blow": A homogeneous glass, shading from a pale gray-blue to a soft rose color; some pieces enhanced with glass appliqués, enameling, and gilding.

New England Glass Works, New England peachblow (advertised as Wild Rose, but called Peach Blow at the plant): Translucent, shading from rose to white; acid or glossy finish; some pieces enameled and gilded.

Thomas Webb & Sons and Stevens and Williams (English firms): Peachblow-style cased art glass, shading from yellow to red; some pieces with cameo-type relief designs.

Gunderson Glass Co.: Produced peachblow-type art glass to order during the 1950s; shades from an opaque faint tint of pink, which is almost white, to a deep rose.

Marks: Pieces made in England are marked "Peach Blow" or "Peach Bloom."

References: Gary E. Baker et al., *Wheeling Glass 1829-1939*, Oglebay Institute, 1994, distributed by Antique Publications; Neila and Tom Bredehoft, Hobbs, *Brockunier & Co. Glass*, Collector Books, 1997; James Measell, *New Martinsville Glass*, Antique Publications, 1994; John A. Shuman III, *Collector's Encyclopedia of American Glass*, Collector Books, 1988, 1994 value update; Kenneth Wilson, *American Glass 1760-1930*, 2 vols., Hudson Hills Press and The Toledo Museum of Art, 1994.

Gundersen

Cruet, 8" h, 3-1/2" w, matte finish, ribbed shell handle, matching stopper with good color 875.00
Cup and Saucer 275.00
Decanter
   10" h, 5" w, Pilgrim Canteen form, acid finish, deep raspberry to white, applied peachblow ribbed handle, deep raspberry stopper 950.00
   12" h, ovoiform, tapering to extended rim, raised dish base, tapered oval shaped stoppers, acid finished pink fading to white, pr 575.00
Goblet, 701/4" h, 4" d top, glossy finish, deep color, applied Burmese glass base 285.00
Jug, 4-1/2" h, 4" w, bulbous, applied loop handle, acid finish 450.00
Pitcher, 5-1/2" h, Hobnail, matte finish, white with hint of pink on int., orig label 550.00
Plate, 8" d, luncheon, deep raspberry to pale pink, matte finish. 375.00
Punch Cup, acid finish 275.00
Tumbler, 3-3/4" h, matte finish 275.00
Urn, 8-1/2" h, 4-1/2" w, two applied "M" handles, sq cut base, matte finish 550.00
Vase
   4" h, quatreform deep raspberry rim on angular body, applied reeded handles, c1940 .... 460.00
   4-1/4" h, 3" d, acid finish 225.00
   5" h, 6" w, ruffled top, pinched-in base 525.00
   9" h, 3-1/4" w, Tappan, acid finish........................... 425.00
Wine Glass, 5" h, glossy finish...................................... 175.00

Mount Washington

Bowl, 3" x 4", shading from deep rose to bluish-white, MOP satin int. 150.00
Pitcher, 6-7/8" h, bulbous, sq handle 3,750.00
Vase, 8-1/4" h, lily form, satin finish 1,850.00

New England

Celery Vase, 7" h, 4" w, sq top, deep raspberry with purple highlights shading to white 785.00

Cruet, shiny, intense Wild Rose color, pink-white handle, orig white ball stopper 1,250.00
Pitcher, 6-3/4" h, 7-1/2" w, 3-1/4" w at top, bulbous, sq top, applied frosted handle, ten rows of hobs, Sandwich 550.00
Spooner, sq top, acid finish.. 825.00
Tumbler
   3-3/4" h, shiny finish, deep color upper third, middle fading to creamy white bottom, thin walls 445.00
   3-3/4" h, velvety satin finish, deep raspberry red extends 2/3 down, faces to 1/2" pure white band 400.00
Vase
   3-1/4" h, 2-1/2" d, bulbous bottom, ring around neck, flaring top, matte finish 550.00
   5-1/2" h, satin finish, bulbous 485.00
   6-1/2" h, 3" w at top, lily, glossy finish, deep pink shading to white 650.00
   7" h, lily, crimson upper third, deep pink mid section, soft white color on lower third and wafer base................................... 945.00
   8-3/4" h, 4" w, bulbous stick, deep raspberry to white, matte finish 950.00
   10-1/2" h, 5" w at base, bulbous, tapering neck, cup top, deep color, orig glossy finish 1,250.00
   10-1/2" h, 5" w at base, bulbous gourd shape, deep raspberry with fuchsia highlights to white, coloring extends two-thirds way down, 4 dimpled sides 1,450.00
   15-1/2" h, 6" w at top, lily, deep raspberry pink to white 1,450.00

Webb

Cologne, 5" h, bulbous, raised gold floral branches, silver hallmarked dome top 900.00
Creamer, satin finish, coralene dec, rolled rim, flat base 650.00
Finger Bowl, 4-1/2" d, cased 195.00
Vase
   6" h, satin finish 375.00
   10-1/4" h, shiny, entrusted gold prunus blossom dec, rich gold shades to deep mahogany at top, pink to oyster white lower portion.. 875.00
   11-1/4" h, 6-1/2" d, pine needles, boughs, and trailing prunus blossoms, buds, and branches, two butterflies in flight, deep cherry red shading to pink-peach, creamy white lining, gold trim at top and base, dec by Jules Barbe 750.00

Wheeling

Cruet, 6-1/4" h, ball shaped, mahogany neck and spout, fuchsia shoulders, cream base, Hobbs, Brockunier................................. 1,950.00
Ewer, 6-3/4" h, 4" w, glossy finish, duck bill top, applied amber loop handle 3,500.00
Mustard, SP cov and handle.. 475.00

Vase, bulbous base, extended neck, 10" h, $995.

Pear, hollow blown

    4-3/4" w, 3" w base, matte finish, bright red and yellow, white lining, very tip of stem gone 900.00

    5-1/2" h, 3" w base, glossy finish, tip of stem gone 800.00

Pitcher, 5-1/4" h, quatreform raised rim on bulbous body, applied amber handle, int. bubbles, some staining................................ 375.00

Punch Cup, 2-1/2" h, Hobbs, Brockunier 535.00

Shaker, 5-1/2" h, cylindrical, tapering to neck, glossy finish, white opalk glass lining, metal screw top 320.00

Tumbler, shiny finish, deep colored upper third shades to creamy base 385.00

Vase

    9-1/4" h, ball shaped body, 5" slender neck, shape #11 .... 735.00

    13-3/4" h, elongated oval, tapered base and rim, acid finish, pin head size int. bubble 550.00

PEKING GLASS

History: Peking glass is a type of cameo glass of Chinese origin. Its production began in the 1700s and continued well into the 19th century. The background color of Peking glass may be a delicate shade of yellow, green, or white. One style of white background is so transparent that it often is referred to as the "snowflake" ground. The overlay colors include a rich garnet red, deep blue, and emerald green.

Bowl

    4-1/2" d, yellow, Chinese 275.00

    5-3/4" d, rounded form, ext. with cranes and lotus plants, green overlay, whit ground 90.00

    6-1/8" d, floral shaped rim, ext. with birds among lotus, lotus leaf form foot, red overly, white ground................................. 1,150.00

    7" d, raised lotus petals on ext., opaque blue with white int., 19th C 375.00

    7" d, rounded form, shaped rim, ext. with flowering lotus continuing to a lotus leaf-form foot rim, green overlay, white ground ... 575.00

Cup, 2-1/2" h, deep form, gently flaring rim, ring foot, continual band of overlapping dragons, cloud collar border, lappet border, red overlay, Snowflake.. 2,185.00

Dish, 11-3/4" l, flattened round form, bright yellow, 19th C 850.00

Jar, 5" h, wide ovoid sea green body, narrow short flared neck, Qianlong period, sgd... 4,400.00

Snuff Bottle, green, jade stopper, Chinese 65.00

Vase, Imperial Yellow, animals in garden setting motif, 7" h, $675.

Tray, 8-3/4" l, floral filled ground, oval shaped cartouche with maiden in garden 90.00

Vase

    7" h, high shouldered form, ducks swimming among tall lotus plants, green overlay, white ground, pr.............................. 500.00

    7-1/2" h, ovoid, elongated neck, red overlay, Snowflake pattern, body with 2 dragons and 2 phoenix, neck with dragon and phoenix, Qianlong period, pr..................................... 4,600.00

    8" h, high shoulder form, red overlay, white ground, female figures in garden, 18th C, pr... 1,840.00

    9-1/4" h, ovoid, opaque raised yellow flowers, translucent yellow ground, 19th C 525.00

PELOTON

History: Wilhelm Kralik of Bohemia patented Peloton art glass in 1880. Later it was also patented in America and England.

Peloton glass is found with both transparent and opaque grounds, although opaque is more common. Opaque colored glass filaments (strings) are applied by dipping or rolling the hot glass. Generally, the filaments (threads) are pink, blue, yellow, and white (rainbow colors) or a single color. Items also may have a satin finish and enamel decorations.

Biscuit Jar, 7" h, 6-1/2" d, powder blue body, white, yellow, blue, and vivid pink filaments, 48 molded-in vertical ribs, silverplated fittings, barn swallow emb on lid 785.00

Bowl, 6-1/2" d, 6" h, white ground, brown and yellow filaments, allover ribbed surface, 3 applied crystal thorn feet, 8 point star top 325.00

Finger Bowl, colorless, multicolored filaments 75.00

Pitcher, 6-1/2" h, sq blown clear body, applied colorless, pink, yellow, blue and white striped yellow filaments, applied colorless handle......... 250.00

Punch Cup, turquoise ground, multicolored filaments, enameled florals, set of six.. 325.00

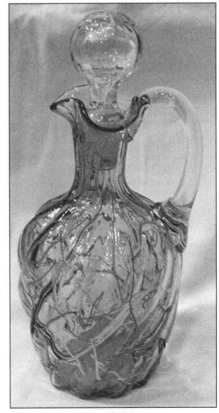

Cruet, light blue ground, multicolored filaments, applied colorless handle, colorless stopper, 7" h, $275.

Rose Bowl
    4" h, 4" w, ftd, 4 pulled edges, sq shape, applied crystal edge, 6 shell feet, glossy finish shaded blue ground, yellow, pink, white, blue, and red filaments 395.00
    6" h, 5-1/2" w, ftd, 8 point star shaped top, white lining, ribbed and swirled, brown shaded filaments 325.00
Toothpick Holder, 3" h, colorless, white filaments 145.00
Tumbler, 3-3/4" h, colorless ground, yellow, pink, red, light blue, and white filaments 125.00
Vase
    3-1/2" h, 3 x 3-7/8" d, orchid pink cased body, emb ribs, pink, blue, and yellow filaments, pinched together in center 195.00
    4" h, 4-3/4" d, bulbous base, folded over tricorn shape top, white ribbed cased body, pink, yellow, blue, and white applied filaments 290.00
    6" h, 5" w, ribbed, bright pink ground, yellow, blue, white, red, pink, and purple filaments, white lining, two applied ribbed handles 450.00
    6-3/4" h, 5-1/8" d, ovoid, emb ribs, flaring crimped rim, cased clear ground, royal blue filaments, white int. 225.00

PERFUME, COLOGNE, and SCENT BOTTLES

History: The second half of the 19th century was the golden age for decorative bottles made to hold scents. These bottles were made in a variety of shapes and sizes.

An atomizer is a perfume bottle with a spray mechanism. Cologne bottles usually are larger and have stoppers which also may be used as applicators. A perfume bottle has a stopper that often is elongated and designed to be an applicator.

Scent bottles are small bottles used to hold a scent or smelling salts. A vinaigrette is an ornamental box or bottle that has a perforated top and is used to hold aromatic vinegar or smelling salts. Fashionable women of the late 18th and 19th centuries carried them in purses or slipped them into gloves in case of a sudden fainting spell.

References: Joanne Dubbs Ball and Dorothy Hehl Torem, *Commercial Fragrance Bottles*, Schiffer Publishing, 1993; ––, *Fragrance Bottle Masterpieces*, Schiffer Publishing, 1996; Carla Bordignon, *Perfume Bottles*, Chronicle Books, 1995; Glinda Bowman, *Miniature Perfume Bottles*, Schiffer Publishing, 1994; ––, *More Miniature Perfume Bottles*, Schiffer Publishing, 1996; Jacquelyne Jones-North, *Commercial Perfume Bottles*, 3rd, Schiffer Publishing, 1996; –, *Perfume, Cologne and Scent Bottles*, 3rd ed., Schiffer Publishing, 1999; Jacquelyne Y. Jones-North, et. al., *Czechoslovakian Perfume Bottles and Boudoir Accessories*, Revised Ed., Antique Publications, 1999; Christie Mayer Lefkowith, *Art of Perfume*, Thames and Hudson, 1994; Monsen and Baer, *Beauty of Perfume*, published by authors (Box 529, Vienna, VA 22183), 1996; ––, *For The Love of Perfume*, published by authors, 1999; ––, *Legacies of Perfume*, published by authors, 1997; ––, *Memories of Perfume*, published by authors, 1998; Jeri Lyn Ringblum, *Collector's Handbook of Miniature Perfume Bottles*, Schiffer Publishing, 1996.

Periodical: *Perfume & Scent Bottle Quarterly*, P.O. Box 187, Galena, OH 43021.

Collectors' Clubs: International Perfume Bottle Association, 3314 Shamrock Rd, Tampa, FL 33629, http://www.perfumebottles.org; Mini-Scents, 7 Saint John's Rd, West Hollywood, CA 90069; Parfum Plus Collections, 1590 Louis-Carrier Ste 502, Montreal Quebec H4N 2Z1 Canada.

Atomizer
4-1/2" h, Moser, sapphire blue, gold florals, leaves, and swirls, melon ribbed body, orig gold top and bulb 275.00
6-1/4" h, Cambridge, stippled gold, opaque jade, orig silk lined box 140.00
8" h, Galle, cameo, lavender flowers and foliage, shaded yellow and frosted ground 1,250.00
8-1/2" h, DeVilbiss, bulbous, narrow neck, gold top rim, geometric designs, orange opalescent, blue-green spattered line dec, incomplete 995.00

Cologne
3-1/8" h, apple green, pressed base, cut stopper 150.00
4-1/2" h, vaseline, attributed to New England Glass Co., flint, orig stopper 225.00
5-7/8" h, Baccarat, colorless, panel cut, matching stopper 75.00
7" h, cut glass, cranberry cut to colorless, cane cut, matching stopper 250.00
7" h, 5" d, paperweight, double overlay, crimson red over white over colorless squatty bottle, five oval facet windows reveal concentric millefiore cane int., matching stopper 460.00
11" h, art glass, transparent green bottle, delicate floral design, colorless pedestal foot, faceted teardrop stopper 175.00

Perfume
2" h, 1-1/2" d, German, green glass, colored enamel coat of arms, fine enamel trim on body and matching green stopper 60.00
2-3/8" h, Venetian, globular body, Lion of Venice portrait cane on surface of opaque yellow and silver glass, crowned with ornate cap dec with flowers, no stopper 335.00
2-3/4" h, fluted and scroll designs, colorless, mkd "L'Heure Bleue," Guerlain fitted box 90.00
3-9/16" h, cherub sulphide surrounded by ornate faceting on all sides, gilded copper cap, glass stopper 365.00
3-11/16" h, Clichy, ext. dec with alternating blue and white swirled bands, stopper and base dec with 16K gold chased with delicate patterns, base mkd "D. J.," fitted leather carrying case 990.00
4-1/4" l, Cartier, broad ovoid body, deep blue-black ground, acid-etched geometric Art Deco designs, tapered cylindrical glass stopper, base inscribed "Cartier CA6 8430" 435.00

Silver Overlay, clear glass body, sterling silver vines and "Baraboo," orig stopper, both marked "862," $185.

4-3/8" h, Mary Gregory, cranberry, white enameled girl dec, colorless ball stopper...175.00

4-3/4" h, Schiaperlli Zut, colorless and froted, lower half of woman's torso, gold enamel stars, fringe, and ribbon, gilded stopper with green enamel "Zut"..325.00

5" h, Schuco bear, gold mohair, bead eyes, embroidered nose, wear 425.00

5-1/2" h, sunburst design, smokey, Volde Nuit, Guerlain fitted box 125.00

6-3/8" h, Baccarat, molded and frosted, acid stamped "Baccarat/France," mid-20th C 650.00

9" l, silver, elongated tapered conical form, end with single bead, below band of chased and emb flat leaves and flowers, central band of horizontal reeding, further band of flowers, rounded lid with flat leaves and flowers, Dominick & Haff, late 19th C, 5 troy oz 800.00

Scent

2-1/2" h, flattened oval body, marbled glass, silhouettes of Franchini, blue, green, brown, and white adventurtine, Murano, c1850 1,265.00

2-7/8" x 2-7/8" x 2-1/2", Botta-A-Parfum, ebonized wood, sq box silver mounted at mid section with floral swag border, cov by mother-of-pearl, centered miniature portrait on ivory of mother and child, sgd "Delacroix," int. fitted with cut glass scent bottle, French, late 18th/early 19th C 1,500.00

3" h, agate, flattened globe form, silver hinged rim and screw cap, mkd "Black, Starr, & Frost" 260.00

3-1/4" h, porcelain, figural, modeled as male and female, each holding dog, removable heads, Germany, 19th C, pr 435.00

3-3/4" h, ivory, figural, woman holding basket of flowers in one hand, fan in other, polychrome dec, Japan 90.00

3-3/4" h, satin, bridal white, Peacock Eye, MOP, orig glass stopper, push-on silverplated lid with monogram "C" 435.00

4" d, satin, bridal white, 24 white vertical stripes, 12 silk ribbons alternating with 12 muted satin ribbons, sterling silver flip top cap, collar stamped "CS, FS, STd, SILr," engraved name 400.00

4-1/8" h, Early American, blown, colorless, cranberry and white stripes, white and gold metallic twist..95.00

5-1/2" h, four triangular scenes encased in trelliswork banding, dec gilt metal foliate mounts, cut glass stoppers, French, early 20th C 115.00

6-7/8" h, rect box, shagreen covering, mounted at base with slightly stepped border rising to arabesques, conforming mounting at opening, int. fitted with 3 silver mounted scent bottles, George III, unmarked 1,300.00

Vinaigrette

7/8" l, SS, tooled purse shape, gilded int., John Turner, Birmingham hallmarks, 1792...250.00

1-1/4" l, SS, tooled purse shape, gilded int., S. Pemberton, Birmingham hallmarks, 1790...220.00

2-1/4" x 1", cranberry, rect, allover cutting, enameled tiny pink roses, green leaves, gold dec, hinged lid, stopper, finger chain 185.00

2-5/8" x 1-5/8", SS, Austrian, c1848, rect, lid chased with scene depicting house by river's edge, decorative borders, bottom chased with foliage, gilt washed int. 375.00

3-7/8" l, cut glass, cobalt blue, yellow flashing, SS overlay, emb SS cap 125.00

PETERS and REED POTTERY

History: J. D. Peters and Adam Reed founded their pottery company in South Zanesville, Ohio, in 1900. Common flowerpots, jardinieres, and cooking wares comprised the majority of their early output. Occasionally art pottery was attempted, but it was not until 1912 that their Moss Aztec line was introduced and widely accepted. Other art wares include Chromal, Landsun, Montene, Pereco, and Persian.

Vase, Moss Aztec, designed by Frank Ferrell, 7-7/8" h, $40.

Peters retired in 1921 and Reed changed the name of the firm to Zane Pottery Company.

Marks: Marked pieces of Peters and Reed Pottery are unknown.

Bowl, 10" d, Landsun, shades of blue...90.00
Candlesticks, pr, 10" h, mirror black glaze....................................35.00
Doorstop, cat, yellow..375.00
Ewer, 11" h ,orange and yellow raised grapes dec, brown ground50.00
Jardiniere, #249, Lions..65.00
Jug, bulbous, grape clusters and vine dec, standard glossy brown glaze, handle 75.00
Mug, blended glaze...30.00
Pitcher, 4" h, green and yellow raised fern leaves, gloss dark brown ground 65.00
Spittoon, Moss Aztec, stylized rose dec 90.00
Vase
  5" h, Zane Ware, underglaze rose dec.....................................45.00
  9-3/4" h, pine cones and needles, terra cotta with green wash 65.00
  12" h, Moss Aztec, relief grapes...75.00
  14" h, Chromal, scenic 195.00
Wall Pocket, 9" h, Egyptian...95.00

PEWTER

History: Pewter is a metal alloy consisting mostly of tin with small amounts of lead, copper, antimony, and bismuth added to make the shaping of products easier and to increase the hardness of the material. The metal can be cast, formed around a mold, spun, easily cut, and soldered to form a wide variety of utilitarian articles.

Pewter was known to the ancient Chinese, Egyptians, and Romans. England was the primary source of pewter for the American colonies for nearly 150 years until the American Revolution ended the embargo on raw tin, allowing the small American pewter industry to flourish until the Civil War.

References: Marilyn E. Dragowick (ed.), *Metalwares Price Guide*, Antique Trader Books, 1995; Donald M. Herr, *Pew-*

ter in Pennsylvania German Churches, Vol. XXIX, *The Pennsylvania German Society*, 1995; Henry J. Kauffman, *American Pewterer*, Astragal Press, 1994.

Collectors' Club: Pewter Collectors Club of America, 504 W. Lafayette St., West Chester, PA 19380-2210.

Museum: The Currier Gallery of Art, Manchester, NH.

Note: The listings concentrate on the American and English pewter forms most often encountered by the collector.

Baptismal Bowl, 9" d, Boardman, Hartford, CT, stamped "BX," mkd "Jacobs," 19th C 950.00
Basin
  6-5/8" d, 1-1/2" h, Blakeslee, Philadelphia, PA, partial eagle touch, wear and battering 175.00
  7-3/4" d, 1-7/8" h, Gershom Jones, Providence, RI, eagle touch, dents, wear, and scratches 375.00
  8" d, 2" h, Thomas Compton, English 220.00
Beaker, 5-1/8" h
  Thomas D. and Sherman Boardman, Hartford, CT, mkd "Laughlin," c1810-30 .... 650.00
  Timothy Boardman and Co., NY, mkd "Laughlin," c1825 .... 630.00
Bowl, 11-1/8" d, shallow, eagle touch mark, "B. Barns, Phila," (Blakslee Barns, Philadelphia), J#14, wear and scratches 360.00
Candlesticks, pr
  8-3/4" h, mkd "Jacobs," 1822-71 .... 950.00
  9-3/4" h, unmarked American, attributed to CT, with bobeches 275.00
  10" h, push-ups, one with repair to stem 300.00
Chamber Lamp, 4-3/4" h, lemon font, "R. Gleason" touch, (Roswell Gleason, Dorchester, MA), orig whale oil burner with one loose tube ...200.00
Charger
  12" d, London touch, wear 150.00
  13-1/8" d, George Lightner, Baltimore, eagle touch, some wear, minor edge damage 770.00
  13-1/2" d, Nathaniel Austin, MA, c1800 .... 750.00

Coffeepot, lighthouse shape, $600.

  14" d, David Melville, Newport, RI, 1804-10, dents 450.00
  15" d, John Townsend, London, smooth rim 250.00
Coffeepot, cov
  7" h, Israel Trask, Beverly, MA, lighthouse, bright cut engraving 350.00
  10-5/8" h, Freeman Porter, Westbrook, ME 470.00
  11" h, R. Dunham 275.00
  13" h, James Dixon, England 250.00
  13-1/2" h, Reed and Barton, mkd "Leonard Reed & Barton 3500" 250.00
Communion Chalice, 6-1/4" h, unmarked American, handles removed, pr 200.00
Creamer, 5-7/8" h, unmarked American, teapot shape 250.00
Deep Dish, 13-1/8" d, Stephen Barnes eagle touch, Middletown or Wallingford, CT, minor scratches and wear 415.00
Ewer, 8-1/8" h, hinged lid, European, dents and repairs 90.00
Flagon
  12-1/2" h, attributed to Israel Trask, Beverly, MA, 1807-56, minor dents 300.00
  14" h, Thomas D. and Sherman Boardman, Hartford, CT, mkd "Laughlin," 1810-30 .... 3,750.00
Inkstand, 3-1/2" h, 5-1/2" w, 9-1/2" l, unmarked, ftd 175.00
Lamp
  5-3/4" h plus brass and tin whale oil burner, Putnam touch, James Putnam, Madison, MA, some splits in rim of base 315.00
  7" h plus fluid burner, unmarked American, attributed to Meriden, reeded detail on base, ear handle, light pitting 110.00
  8-1/2" h plus burner, Yale and Curtis, NY 1 touch, matching fluid burner missing, snuffers and one brass tube loose 190.00
Measure
  2-3/8" to 8" h, assembled set, bellied, English, minor damage ...550.00
  5-3/4" h, John Warne, English, brass rim, battered, old repair, quart 100.00
Mug, quart
  4" h, Thomas Danforth Boardman, Hartford, CT, tankard, partial "T.D.B." touch, some battering, soldered repairs 500.00
  5-7/8" h, Samuel Hamlin, Hartford, Middletown, CT, and Providence RI, dent at base 625.00
Pitcher, 6" h, Freeman Porter, Westbrook, ME, 2 quart 225.00
Plate
  7-3/4" d, Thomas D. Boardman eagle touch, wear and scratches 275.00
  7-3/4" d, S. Kilbourne, Baltimore eagle touch, minor wear and dents 495.00
  7-7/8" d, Asbil Griswold, Meriden, CT, eagle touch some battering and knife scratches 160.00
  7-7/8" d, B. Barns, Philada and "B.B." eagle touch, wear and dents 200.00
  7-7/8" d, Joseph Danforth lion touch, minor wear 330.00
  8" d, crowned rose touch mark, "Jacob Whitmore," Middletown, CT, J#268, wear and scratches 220.00
  8" d, rampant lion touch, Edward Danford, Middletown and Hartford, CT, minor wear and scratches 220.00
  8-3/8" d, David Melville, Newport, RI, 1776-94, mkd on base, knife marks, minor pitting 520.00
Platter, 28-3/4" l, Townsend and Compton, London, pierced insert, mkd "Cotterell" 2,400.00
Porringer
  3-7/8" d, cast handle, mkd "TD & SB" touch (Thomas Danford Boardman, et al, Hartford) 220.00
  4-3/4" d, cast crown handle, mkd "I.G.," Boston area, pitting, pinpoint hole 140.00
  5-1/2" d, unmarked American, cast flowered handle 150.00
Soup Plate, 8-7/8" d, unmarked Continental, angel touch 75.00
Sugar Bowl, 6" h, Ashril Griswold, Meriden, CT, eagle touch 490.00
Syrup Pitcher, 4-1/2" h, hinged lid, unmarked, American 220.00
Tablespoon, rattail handle, heart on back of bowl, mkd "L. B.," (Luther Boardman, MA and CT). set of 6 .... 330.00
Tall Pot, 11" h, mkd "Simpson & Benham, NY," minor soldered repair 385.00

Tea Caddy, 3-3/4" h, B G S & Co, American, 1825-30, almond shape, bright cut designs, touch mark, wear, pitted 200.00

Teapot

　6-3/4" h, Roswell Gleason, Dorchester, MA, eagle touch 495.00

　6-3/4" h, Ashbil Griswold, Meriden, CT, eagle touch, some battering and repairs 200.00

　7" h, Eben Smith, Beverly, MA, 1813-56, minor pitting and scratches 375.00

　7-1/2" h, L. Boardman, Warranted touch, (Luther Boardman, South Reading, MA,) repairs, spout replaced 200.00

　7-5/8" h, Putnam touch (James H. Putnam, Walden, MA,) repairs 150.00

　7-3/4" h, Smith & Co touch, (Albany, NY,) some battering and damage 175.00

　8-1/8" h, A. Griswold eagle touch, (Ashbil Griswold, Meriden, CT,) some battering and repair, splits to bottom 200.00

　8-1/2" h, Continental, pear shaped, old soldered repair 160.00

Tobacco Box, 4-3/8" h, Thomas Stanford, cast eagle feet, engraved label with scroll work "Thomas Stanford, Gospel Hill, 1838," wear, final and one foot soldered 125.00

Tumbler, 2-3/4" h, Thomas Danforth Boardman, Hartford, CT, partial eagle touch 175.00

Warming Platter, 19" l, hot water type, tree and well, mkd "Dixon & Sons," English, repairs 250.00

PHOENIX GLASS

History: Phoenix Glass Company, Beaver, Pennsylvania, was established in 1880. Known primarily for commercial glassware, the firm also produced a molded, sculptured, cameo-type line from the 1930s until the 1950s.

References: Jack D. Wilson, *Phoenix & Consolidated Art Glass*, Antique Publications, 1989.

Collectors' Club: Phoenix & Consolidated Glass Collectors Club, P.O. Box 159, Burlington, VT 05402-0159.

Ashtray, Phlox, large, white, frosted 86.00

Bowl, Swallows purple wash 150.00

Cookie Jar, 9" h, Con-Cora, white milk glass, gilt dec 60.00

Creamer and Sugar, Catalonia, light green 45.00

Floor Vase, 18" h, Bushberry, light green 450.00

Lamp

　Ceiling, 15" sq, Flying Birds, heavy custard glass, metal mounts 1,500.00

　Table, 28" h, Lovebirds, green opalescent glass, brass fixtures 225.00

Pitcher, Wild Loganberry (Dewberry), irid marigold, milk glass body 700.00

Umbrella Stand, 18" h, Thistle, pearlized blue ground 450.00

Vase

　6" h, dragonflies and cattails, custard ground 110.00

　6-1/2" h, Line 700, blue crystal 350.00

　7" h, Bluebell, brown 125.00

　8-3/4" h, clear and frosted, grasshoppers and reeds dec 125.00

　10" h, Wild Geese, pearlized white birds, light green ground 195.00

　10-1/2" h, Zodiac, raised white figures, peach colored ground ... 700.00

　11" h, Wild Rose, blown out, pearlized dec, dark rose ground, orig label 275.00

　12" h, Dancing Girls, satin custard ground, blown out color enhanced figures, minor flake on inside rim 275.00

　14" h, Philodendron, blue, ormolu mounts 400.00

PHONOGRAPHS

History: Early phonographs were commonly called "talking machines." Thomas A. Edison invented the first suc-

cessful phonograph in 1877; other manufacturers followed with their variations.

References: Timothy C. Fabrizio and George F. Paul, *Antique Phonograph Gadgets*, Gizmos, and Gimmicks, Schiffer Publishing, 1999; —, *The Talking Machine: An Illustrated Compendium, 1877-1929*, Schiffer Publishing, 1997; Neil Maker, *Hand-Cranked Phonographs*, Promar Publishing, 1993; Arnold Schwartzman, *Phono-Graphics*, Chronicle Books, 1993; Eric L. Reiss, *The Compleat Talking Machine*, 3rd ed., Sanoran Publishing, 1998.

Periodicals: *Horn Speaker*, P.O. Box 1193, Mabank, TX 75147; *New Amberola Graphic*, 37 Caledonia St, St. Johnsbury, VT 05819.

Collectors' Clubs: Buckeye Radio & Phonograph Club, 4572 Mark Trail, Copley, OH 44321; California Antique Phonograph Society, P.O. Box 67, Duarte, CA 91010; Hudson Valley Antique Radio & Phonograph Society, P.O. Box 207, Campbell Hall, NY 10916; Michigan Antique Phonograph Society, Inc., 2609 Devonshire, Lansing, MI 48910; Vintage Radio & Phonograph Society, Inc., P.O. Box 165345, Irving, TX 75016.

Museums: Edison National Historic Site, West Orange, NJ; Johnson's Memorial, Dover, DE; Seven Acres Antique Village & Museum, Union, IL.

Advisor: Lewis S. Walters.

Phonolamp, Prairie du Chien, American, c1920, $2,900. Photo courtesy of Auction Team Breker.

Columbia
   BN, disc player 1,000.00
   BQ, cylinder player 1,200.00
   HG, cylinder player 2,400.00
Decca, Junior, portable, leather case & handle 150.00
Edison
   Amberola 30 .... 350.00
   Army - Navy, World War I 1,200.00
   Diamond Disc, VV-19, William & Mary 500.00
   Excelsior, coin op 2,500.00
   Fireside, original horn 900.00
   Gem, maroon, 2 - 4 minute reproducer 1,700.00
   Opera, moving mandrel, fixed reproducer 2,500.00
   Standard, Model A, oak case, metal horn 550.00
   Triumph, cygnet horn, mahogany case 2,500.00
   S-19 Diamond Disc, floor model, oak case 400.00
Graphone
   12.5 oak case, metal horn, retailer's mark, cylinder 450.00
   15.0 oak case with columns on corners, nickel plated platform,
      metal horn, stenciled cast iron parts 725.00
   Home Grand, oak case, nickel-plated works #6, spring motor 1,300.00
Harvard, trumpet style horn 300.00
Kalamazoo, Duplex -reproducer, original horns with decals, 1904
   patent date 3,300.00
Odeon Talking Machine Co., table model, crank wind, brass horn,
   straight tone arm 500.00
Silvertone (Sears), two reproducers 500.00
Sonora
   Gothic Deluxe, walnut case, triple spring, gold plated parts, auto-
      matic stop and storage 400.00
   Luzerne, Renaissance style case with storage 200.00
Talk-O-Phone, Brooke, table model, oak case rope decorations, steel
   horn 200.00
Victor
   Credenza, crank 1,100.00
   Monarch, table model, corner columns brass bell horn 1,500.00
   School House 2,500.00
   Victor I, mahogany case, corner columns bell horn 1,500.00
   Victor II, oak case, black bell horn 1,200.00
   Victor II, oak case, smooth oak horn 5,500.00
   Victor III, papier-mâché horn 1,400.00
   Victor V, oak case, corner columns, no horn 1,400.00

PHOTOGRAPHS

History: A vintage print is a positive image developed from the original negative by the photographer or under the photographer's supervision at the time the negative is made. A non-vintage print is a print made from an original negative at a later date. It is quite common for a photographer to make prints from the same negative over several decades. Changes between the original and subsequent prints usually can be identified. Limited-edition prints must be clearly labeled.

References: Diane VanSkiver Gagel, *Ohio Photographers, 1839-1900: A History and Directory*, Susan Herzig and Paul Hertzmann, William E. Dassonville, *California Photographer, 1879-1957*, Carl Mautz Publishing, 1999; Carl Mautz Publishing, 1998; Martin Gordon (ed.), *1999 Gordon's Photograph Price Annual International*, Gordon and Lawrence Art Reference, 1999; O. Henry Mace, *Collector's Guide to Early Photographs*, 2nd ed., Krause Publications, 1999; Susan Theran (ed.), *Leonard's Annual Price Index of Posters & Photographs*, Auction Index (30 Valentine Park, Newton, MA 02165), 1998; Craig A. Tuttle, *An Ounce of*

┌─────────────────────────────────┐
│   **SPECIAL AUCTIONS**   │
│   │
│   Swann Galleries, Inc.   │
│   104 E. 25th St.   │
│   New York, NY 10010   │
│   (212) 254-4710   │
└─────────────────────────────────┘

Preservation, A Guide to Care of Papers and Photographs, Rainbow Books, 1995.

Periodicals: *CameraShopper*, 313 N. Quaker Lane, P.O. Box 37029, W Hartford, CT 06137; *History of Photography*, 1900 Frost Rd, Suite 101, Tullytown, PA 19007; *On Paper*, 39 E. 78th St., #601, New York, NY 10021; *Photograph Collector*, Photographic Arts Center, 163 Amsterdam Ave. #201, New York, NY 10023.

Collectors' Clubs: American Photographic Historical Society, Inc., 1150 Avenue of the Americas, New York, NY 10036; Association of International Photography Art Dealers, 1609 Connecticut Ave. NW #200, Washington, DC 20009; Daguerrean Society, 625 Liberty Ave., Ste 1790, Pittsburgh, PA 15222; National Stereoscopic Association, P.O. Box 14801, Columbus, OH 43214; Photographic Historical Society, Inc., P.O. Box 39563, Rochester, NY 14604; Photographic Historical Society of Canada, P.O. Box 54620, Toronto, Ontario M5M 4N5 Canada; Photographic Historical Society of New England, P.O. Box 189, Boston, MA 02165; Western Photographic Collectors Association Inc., P.O. Box 4294, Whittier, CA 90607.

Museums: Center for Creative Photography, Tucson, AZ; International Center of Photography, New York, NY; International Museum of Photography at George Eastman House, Rochester, NY; International Photographic Historical Association, San Francisco, CA; National Portrait Gallery, Washington, DC.

Additional Listings: See *Warman's Americana & Collectibles* for more examples.

Album
   African-Americans, southern US, 42 albumen prints at various locales, featuring workers in cotton and orange fields, some posed on steps of prosperous looking house, street scenes, c1860 .... 1,265.00
   Maxime Du Camp, 14 Middle Eastern views, Middle and Upper Egypt, Thebes, ruins of palace of Karnak, Great Pyramid witih submerged Sphinx, Mosque of Ali Bey, Colossi or Gournah, Palace of Ramses, etc., salted paper prints, 6" x 8-1/4" or reverse, each with Du Camp's Gide et Baudry's and Blanquart-Evrard's printed credits, caption, and plate number on mount recto, oblong folio, lacks binding, partially disbound, American binder's blindstamp on front free endpaper, 1852 .... 4,850.00
   Francis Firth, Sinai and Palestine, 3 volumes, William Mackenzie, London, 1863, each illus with 37 mounted albumen prints, accompanying text leaves, 6-1/2" x 9" or reverse, several sgd in natavie, printed titled on mount recto, bound in gilt stamped morocco, some scuffs, light foxing to mounts 34,500.00
   Panoramic Views of the City of Sydney and Harbour, New South Wales, Charles Potter, Government Printer, Sydney, 1896, 11 fold-out multi-part panoramas of Sydney, 6-part panorama of grounds of the Sydney International Exposition, 8-part panorama of fairground with ladies show jumping trial in progress and agricultural exhibits, 3 part panorama of cricket match captioned "Stoddart's

Cabinet Card, outdoor scene, farm, horses, 6-3/8" x 4-1/4", $10.

team V combined. Australia First Test March 1895," 3-part panorama of the Zig-Zag Railway, albumen prints, various sizes, most titled in negative, oblong folio, gilt lettered morocco 25,300.00

Albumen Print
    4-1/2" x 3-1/2", Wild Bill Hickok, orig cabinet card mount, by George Rookwood, gilt credit and logo on back, c1874 10,350.00
    10" x 7-3/4", Julia Margaret Cameron, profile, photographer's ink signature, Colnaghi blindstamp on mount reverse, c1865........2,300.00
    12" x 10-1/4", Alfred Lord Tennyson, oval 9" x 7" print on orig mount with 8 miniature prints of literary and political notables, "Lord Tennyson" penciled in period hand on reverse, 1857 ....2,300.00
Ambrotype, cased, 3-1/4" x 3-3/4", officer holding sword, image has halo around liner, ornate thermoplastic case with edge hairlines sgd "Peck"..200.00
Carbon Print, 14" x 9-1/2", crane, Henry Dixon, credited and numbered in the negative, Dixon's blindstamp recto, 1870s..................1,265.00
Daguerreotype, cased
    Quarter-plate image, 2 young sisters, one standing, other seated in high chair, wearing identical striped dresses, delicate hand coloring on girls' cheeks, leather case, separated at hinge, mid 1850s...1,500.00
    Sixth plate image, young girl holding white rabbit on lap, full leather case, early mid 1850s..4,140.00
Orotone, 13-1/2" x 10-1/4", snow capped mountain by lake, by Norman Edson, sgd, orig Art Nouveau frame 1,200.00
Platinum Print on Tissue, 7-3/4" x 6", Myra Albert Wiggins, titled "Polishing Brass," 1903 ....1,495.00
Portfolio, Albert Arthur Allen, The Model Series No. 1, Allen Art Studios, Oakland, 1925, 15 classic photographs of seven girls, text pamphlet describing purpose of portfolio and a "Physical and Character Analysis" of each model, 6-1/2" x 9-1/2' silver prints, worn, loose as issued...8,050.00
Silver Print
    7" x 5-1/4", Ansel Adams, branches in snow, sgd in pencil on mount recto, hand editioned Portfolio III stamp on mount verso, 1959..1,380.00
    8" x 9", Eleanor, Harry Callahan, unsigned, framed, mounted....460.00
    8-1/2" x 7", Eugène Atget, Notre Dame, Voeu de Louis XIII, titled and numbered in pencil on verso, c1910 ....2,185.00
    9-1/2" x 7-1/2", Berenice Abbott, Trinity Church and Wall Street Towers, photographer's penciled signature and Maine handstamp on verso, 1934, printed 1950s 2,180.00
    11-1/2" x 9", Brassaï, backstage at Paris Opera, photographer's Paris handstamp on back, 1938 ....8,625.00
    12" x 15-1/4", Downtown Manhattan, 1936, sgd "Berenice Abbott" in pencil on the mat, identified on label from Alpha Gallery, Boston" on reverse, framed 865.00

    12-1/2" x 16", Dmitri Baltermants, Gorbachev and Reagan at Moscow Summit, photographer's handstamps, notation, and caption, in Cyrillic, on verso, mid 1980s 1,380.00
    13" x 10", Abraham Lincoln, sgd by Moses P. Rice, notations in pencil on back, typed letter authenticating print, sgd by Rice's grandson, 1863, printed 1891, framed............................1,840.00
    13" x 10-1/8", Berenice Abbott, Esso station, sgd in pencil on back, Maine handstamp, 1960s 1,100.00
    13-1/4" x 9-1/2", Margaret Bourke-White, US Supreme Court building, photographer's and 2 N.E.A. handstamps, penciled period caption on back, 1935..1,720.00
    14-3/4" x 19-1/4", Ansel Adams, Orchard, Portola Valley, CA, Adam's signature in pencil on mount verso, 1940, printed 1970s 2,760.00
    19" x 4", Exchange Place, Berenice Abbott photographer's stamps on reverse, inscribed "Series 1-13" in red pencil on reverse, mounted, framed...1,150.00
    19" x 15", San Francisco Bay Bridge Pier and Ferry Boat From the Air, sgd "Ansel Adams" in pencil on mount, titled in ink and identified with stamps on reverse of mount, 1954 negative, period print, mounted, unframed..4,315.00
Tintype
    2-3/8" x 2-7/8", sixth plate, soldier wearing kepi, holding telescope, cased 250.00
    3-1/8" x 3-1/2", sixth plate, enlisted man, wearing forage cap, open sack coat, checked shirt, cased..110.00
    3-1/8" x 3-5/8", sixth plate, seated sergeant, wearing striped pants, star on jacket, patriotic liner, minor spot on background.....250.00
    3-1/8" x 3-5/8", sixth plate, seated Union soldier, backdrop with colored flag, cased 220.00
    3-1/4" x 3-3/4", sixth plate, 3 standing Naval officers, scroll work thermoplastic case with leaves and star design, small edge chips 330.00
    4" x 4-7/8", quarter plate, infantry officer, identified as Lt. Jesse Horton, wearing gloves and epaulets, holding Hardee hat, paint dec case with pearl inlay, rust beneath liner..............................330.00
    4" x 4-7/8", quarter plate, standing cavalryman, holding saber, wearing forage cap, patriotic thermoplastic case with eagle and stand of flags, edge chips, labeled "Littlefield, Parsons & Co"..............420.00
Toned Silver Print, 34" x 26", Tom Baril, Sunflowers, sgd and dated in pencil on back, handstamp title, date, number, and edition "2/10," 1995 ....2,300.00

PICKARD CHINA

History: The Pickard China Company was founded by Wilder Pickard in Chicago, Illinois, in 1897. Originally the company imported European china blanks, principally from the Havilands at Limoges, which were then hand painted. The firm presently is located in Antioch, Illinois.

References: Susan and Al Bagdade, *Warman's American Pottery and Porcelain*, Wallace-Homestead, 1994; Alan B. Reed, *Collector's Encyclopedia of Pickard China with Additional Sections on Other Chicago China Studios*, Collector Books, 1996.

Collectors' Club: Pickard Collectors Club, 300 E. Grove St., Bloomington, IL 61701.

Bon Bon, basket-style, four sided, gold 45.00

SPECIAL AUCTIONS

Joy Luke Auctions
300 E. Grove St.
Bloomington, IL 61701
(309) 828-5533

Punch Bowl, red currants and leaves, maroon shading to yellow ground, artist sgd "Vokral," 1905-10 mark, 6" h, 13" d, $3,600. Photo courtesy of Joy Luke Auction Gallery.

Bowl, 9-3/4" d, landscape and bird design, gilded molded rim, sgd "E. Challinor" 300.00
Cake Plate, 10-1/2" d, open gold handles, Desert Garden pattern, black circles, multicolored fruit, shaded ground, gold trim........ 185.00
Chocolate Pot, cov, 9" h, conical, pink carnations, green leaves, gold arches, pink and white flowers, scrolling, gold handle, rim band and knob 300.00
Coffeepot, 7" h, mkd #5, c1905-10 .... 125.00
Creamer and Sugar, 4-1/4" h, Violets, c1898, artist sgd "H. Reury," Silesia blank, pr 325.00
Hatpin Holder, allover gold design of etched flowers, c1925 .... 50.00
Lemonade Set, tankard pitcher, 5 tumblers, bluebells and foliate, lemon-yellow ground 120.00
Perfume Bottle, yellow primroses, shaded ground, artist sgd and dated 1905, gold stopper, Limoges blank 200.00
Plate
  7-1/2" d, hp, currants, 1898 .... 75.00
  9-1/8" l, hp peaches, gilded and molded border, sgd "S. Heap" . 110.00
Platter, 12" d, hp, panted roses, gilded border, sgd "Seidel" 275.00
Punch Bowl, 12" d, orange grapes and plums design, artist sgd "F. Walton" 1,400.00
Tea Set, teapot, creamer, sugar, and cake plate, pink apple blossoms and green leaves, gilded trim, artist sgd 550.00

Vase, Walled Garden, gold rim and handles, sgd "E. Challinor," 1912-18 mark, 10-1/4" h, $1,800. Photo courtesy of Joy Luke Auction Gallery.

Tile, 6-3/4" d, Holland, Dutch Merchant Ship, GDA France Mark, c1905 .... 400.00
Urn, 11-1/2" h, allover gold, 3" band of grapes and strawberries, artist sgd, Belleek blank 500.00
Vase
  7" h, red poppies, maroon ground, wide gold irid band, narrow gilded rim and base band 250.00
  7-3/4" h, cylindrical, moonlight lake and pine forest scene, artist sgd "Challinor," Nippon blank 265.00
  9-1/2" h, 3-3/4" w, hp, 3 large dark orange poppies, gold, rust, an brown, sgd "Gasper" 365.00
  12" h, two handles, all over gilding, panel of lady with basket of flowers, sgd "F. Cimacty" 950.00

PICKLE CASTORS

History: A pickle castor is a table accessory used to serve pickles. It generally consists of a silver-plated frame fitted with a glass insert, matching silver-plated lid, and matching tongs. Pickle castors were very popular during the Victorian era. Inserts are found in pattern glass and colored art glass.

Amber, Cane pattern insert, silver frame 260.00
Amberina, melon ribbed IVT insert, SP lid, ftd frame, lid, tongs, c1875-95 .... 720.00
Bluebird, enameled, resilvered frame 725.00
Colorless, 11-3/4" h, acid etched insert, floral dec with bird medallion, octagonal SP frame, mkd "Meriden Co. 182" 200.00
Cranberry
  IVT insert, enameled blue and white florals, green leaves, shelf on frame dec with peacocks and other birds 325.00
  Paneled Spring insert, SP frame, c1875-95 .... 450.00
Double
  Colorless inserts, emb fans and flowers, matching cov, fancy tulip finials, Viking head ftd oval handled frame, sgd "Meriden" . 275.00
  Vaseline, pickle leaves and pieces, resilvered frame 800.00
Mt. Washington, 11" h, 6" d, decorated satin glass insert, blue enamel and painted yellow roses, green leaves, orange and yellow blossoms, silver-plated Rogers stand and tongs 875.00

Cranberry glass inserts, silver plated frames, left to right: white enameled flowers, 10" h; Hobnail, 11" h; Bulging Loop, 11" h; Inverted Thumbprint, 11" h, each $515. Photo courtesy of Alderfer Auction Co.

Opalescent
    Daisy & Fern, blue, emb DQ floral jar, resilvered frame 650.00
    Spanish Lace, vaseline, bulbous base, ornate frame............ 425.00
    Vertical white stripes, colorless ground, resilvered angel frame, elephant's head and trunk feet 725.00
Pink, shiny pink Florette pattern insert, white int., bowed out
    frame 325.00

PIGEON BLOOD GLASS

History: Pigeon blood refers to the deep orange-red-colored glassware produced around the turn of the century. Do not confuse it with the many other red glasswares of that period. Pigeon blood has a very definite orange glow.

Berry Bowl, 9" d, master, Torquay, SP rim 110.00
Bowl, 4-1/2" d, IVT 50.00
Butter Dish, cov, Venecia, enameled dec 350.00
Celery Vase, 6" h, Torquay, SP rim 225.00
Cracker Jar, cov, Quilted Phlox, Consolidated Glass Co, resilvered
    hardware 325.00
Creamer, Venecia, enameled dec.. 125.00
Decanter, 9-1/2" h, orig stopper 145.00
Hand Cooler, 5" l, cut panels, 2 compartments, SS fittings......... 145.00
Pickle Castor, Beaded Drape, Consolidated Glass Co, orig SP frame,
    cov, and tongs 425.00
Salt and Pepper Shakers, pr, Bulging Loops, orig top 150.00
Spooner, Torquay, SP rim.. 225.00
Syrup, Beaded Drape, Consolidated Glass Co., orig hinged lid . 250.00
Tumbler, 3-1/4" h, alternating panel and rib 85.00
Water Pitcher, Torquay pattern, metal rim and handle................. 450.00

PINK SLAG

History: True pink slag is found only in the molded Inverted Fan and Feather pattern. Quality pieces shade from pink at the top to white at the bottom.

Reproduction Alert: Recently, pieces of pink slag made from molds of the now-defunct Cambridge Glass Company have been found in the Inverted Strawberry and Inverted Thistle patterns. This is not considered true pink slag and

Tumbler, Inverted Fan and Feather, 4" h, $475.

brings only a fraction of the price of the Inverted Fan and Feather pieces.

Berry Bowl, 10" d 750.00
Butter Dish, cov, 70-5/8" d, 7" h cov, 2-1/4" h base with 4 molded feet,
    fiery opalescent coloring 1,485.00
Creamer... 465.00
Cruet, 6-1/2" h, orig stopper... 1,300.00
Jelly Compote, 5" h, 4-1/2" d, scalloped top 375.00
Marmalade Jar, cov... 875.00
Pitcher, water 975.00
Punch Cup, 2-1/2" h, ftd... 275.00
Salt Shaker 300.00
Sauce Dish, 4-1/4" d, 2-1/2" h, ball feet 225.00
Spooner 350.00
Sugar Bowl, cov 550.00
Toothpick Holder 825.00
Tumbler, 4-1/2" h.. 475.00
Water Set, 8" h water pitcher, four 4" h tumblers 5,000.00

PIPES

History: Pipe making can be traced as far back as 1575. Pipes were made of almost all types of natural and manmade materials, including amber, base metals, clay, cloisonné, glass, horn, ivory, jade, meerschaum, parian, porcelain, pottery, precious metals, precious stones, semiprecious stones, and assorted woods. Some of these materials retain smoke and some do not. Chronologically, the four most popular materials and their generally accepted introduction dates are: clay, c1575; wood, c1700; porcelain, c1710; and meerschaum, c1725.

Pipe styles reflect nationalities all around the world, wherever tobacco smoking is custom or habit. Pipes represent a broad range of themes and messages, e.g., figurals, important personages, commemoration of historical events, mythological characters, erotic and pornographic subjects, the bucolic, the bizarre, the grotesque, and the graceful.

Pipe collecting began in the mid-1880s; William Bragge, F.S.A., Birmingham, England, was an early collector. Although firmly established through the efforts of freelance writers, auction houses, and museums (but not the tobacco industry), the collecting of antique pipes is an amorphous, maligned, and misunderstood hobby. It is amorphous because there are no defined collecting bounds; maligned because it is perceived as an extension of pipe smoking, and now misunderstood because smoking has become socially unacceptable (even though many pipe collectors are avid non-smokers).

References: Ben Rapaport, *Collecting Antique Meerschaum Pipes: Miniature to Majestic Sculpture*, Schiffer Publishing, 1999; R. Fresco-Corbu, *European Pipes*, Lutterworth Press, 1982; Benjamin Rapaport, *Complete Guide to Collecting Antique Pipes*, Schiffer Publishing, 1979.

Periodicals: *Agricultural and Mechanical Gazette*, P.O. Box 930401, Wixom, MI 48939, http://www.digiscape.com/a&mgazette/BriarPipes.html; *Pipes & Tobaccos*, 3000 Highwoods Blvd, Suite 300, Raleigh, NC 27604-1029, http://www.pt-magazine.com.

Collectors' Clubs: Chicagoland Pipe Collectors Club, 540 South Westmore, Lombard, IL 60148-3028; International

Association of Pipe Smokers' Clubs, P.O. Box 930401, Wixom, MI 48393; New York Pipe Club, 440 East 81, Apt 1C, New York, NY 10028; North American Society of Pipe Collectors, P.O. Box 9642, Columbus, OH 43209-9642, http://www.naspc.org; Pipe Collectors Club of America, P.O. Box 5179, Woodbridge, VA 22194, http://www.pipesmoke.com; Pipe Club of London, 40 Crescent Drive, Petts Word, Orpington, Kent BR5 1BD; Society for Clay Pipe Research, 30 Ongrils Close, Pershore, Worcestshire WR10 1QE

Museums: Museum of Tobacco Art and History, Nashville, TN; National Tobacco-Textile Museum, Danville, VA; Pipe Smoker's Hall of Fame, Galveston, IN; U.S. Tobacco Museum, Greenwich, CT.

Carved Wood
   4" w, 8-1/2" to top of cover, Caucasian man's head, wearing tricorn hat, carved handlebar mustache, carved eyes, lips, and ears, carved fern designs under chin and back holder, orig painted dec, fitter for stem dark, possibly brass, early 19th C.................300.00
   5-1/2" l, 2-3/4" h bowl, head of black man wearing cap, hinged wood hat, glass eyes, exaggerated red lips, white teeth, orig case...225.00
   9-1/2" l, 4-1/2" h to top of bowl, front carved with coat of arms including leaping stag, carved eagle between bowl and stem connector, full carved fish at elbow, silver lid and stem connectors, wood, silver, and horn stem, horn mouthpiece, cracked bowl and back 175.00
   10-1/2" l, 4-1/2" h to top of bowl, front carved with draped female figure seated beside urn, relief carved plants nearby, carved eagle between bowl and stem connector, full carved fish at elbow, pierced engraved silver domed lid, carved wood stem, horn mouthpiece, intact chain 400.00
   11" l, 5" h bowl, peasant with removable stocking-type hat, mutton chop whiskers and handlebar mustache, red polychrome highlights on cap, ears, and lips, 19th C, some wear to paint ...300.00
   19" l, 4" to top of head, carved relief tavern scene with 7 men carved in high relief toasting with glasses up lifted, banner above script, silver molded lid, shaft carved wood, painted to resemble rosewood, late 18th/early 19th C, some small cracks on back of pipe bowl...400.00
   21" l, 5-1/2" to top of bowl, full standing hunter with dead stag, hounds, trees carved in deep relief, scroll carved beneath bowl, silver colored lid, wood stem, relief initials "FB" near back .225.00

Carved, folk art type, Civil War era, $1,300.

Ceremonial, Native American, Sioux, 19th C, 32-1/4" l, ashwood stem dec with fine quillwork, dyed horsehair and red silk ribbon, catlinite T-shaped pipe bowl 4,000.00
Figural Bowl
   2" l x 1-3/4" h, Nubian head, glass eyes, ivory colored teeth, highly detailed bowl, dark amber colored material, simple hollow reed stem, 19th C 300.00
   12-5/8" l, pottery, man's head coming out of shoe, fine cylindrical wood stem, horn mouthpiece, stamped "J. G." (Gambier) Paris, France, 19th C 350.00
Meerschaum
   4-1/2" h, 3" d bowl, intricately carved symbols of war, canons, armor, swords, center crown, elaborate scroll carving beneath bowl with grotesque face, 80% covered with high relief carving, silver top and stem mount, 18th C 300.00
   11" l, 4" h to top of lid, seated mustache figure holding ax, cottage on back, scroll carving beneath, brass lid hallmarked "H F N S," wood stem, horn mouthpiece, shades from light amber to dark amber, late 18th/early 19th C..100.00
   26-1/2" l, 4-1/2" bowl, carved bowl, Greek or Roman helmeted warrior head, detailed fully bearded face, helmet forms lid, mother-of-pearl shaft with engraved design and gold highlights, silver and painted ivory mounts, horn and amber stem, 19th C, small crack on helmet 650.00
Show Type
   Carved wood, 29" l, 9" to top of bowl, 4 section bowl, bottom, stem, and horn mouthpiece with gilt colored brass band at each attachment, relief designs on 2 of 3 bands, finely detailed brass cap with serpent closure, 19th C, some wear to gilt 400.00
   Glass, 26" l, 7-1/2" to top of bowl, white opaque Bristol glass, applied blood red top edge, some rough in-the-making texture 225.00
Display Case, 28" w, 39-1/2" h, single paned glass doored case, 8 velvet covered panels each displaying six different types of pipes, each paneled named "Packard Italian Briar, Seville National Walnut Briar" etc., includes 48 pipes, some with damage, cut stems 500.00

POCKET KNIVES

History: Alcas, Case, Colonial, Ka-Bar, Queen, and Schrade are the best of the modern pocket-knife manufacturers, with top positions enjoyed by Case and Ka-Bar. Knives by Remington and Winchester, firms no longer in production, are eagerly sought.

References: Jack Lewis and Roger Combs, *Gun Digest Book of Knives*, 5th edition, Krause Publications, 1999; Jerry and Elaine Heuring, *Collector's Guide to E. C. Simmons, Keen Kutter Cutlery Tools*, Collector Books, 1999; Jacob N. Jarrett, *Price Guide to Pocket Knives*, L-W Books, 1993, 1998 value update, Bernard Levine, *Levine's Guide to Knives and Their Values*, Krause Publications, 1997; ——, *Pocket Knives*, Apple Press, 1993; Jack Lewis and Roger Combs, *The Gun Digest Book of Knives*, 5th ed., Krause Publications, 1997; Jim Sargent, *American Premium Guide to Pocket Knives & Razors Identification and Value Guide*, 5th ed., Krause Publications, 1999; Ron Stewart and Roy Ritchie, *Cattaraugus Cutlery Co.*, Collector Books, 1999; ——, *Standard Knife Collector's Guide*, 3rd ed., Collector Books, 1993, 1995 value update; J. Bruce Voyles, *International Blade Collectors Association's Price Guide to Antique Knives*, Krause Publications, 1995; Ken Warner, *Knives 2000*, 20th edition, Krause Publications, 1999; Richard D. White, *Advertising Cutlery*, Schiffer Publishing, 1999.

Periodicals: *The Blade*, 700 E. State St., Iola, WI 54990; Knife World, P.O. Box 3395, Knoxville, TN 37927.

Collectors' Clubs: American Blade Collectors, P.O. Box 22007, Chattanooga, TN 37422; Canadian Knife Collectors Club, Route 1, Milton, Ontario L9T 2X5 Canada; National Knife Collectors Association, P.O. Box 21070, Chattanooga, TN 37421.

Museum: National Knife Collectors Museum, Chattanooga, TN.

Additional Listings: See *Warman's Americana & Collectibles* for more examples.

Notes: Form is a critical collecting element. The most desirable forms are folding hunters (one or two blades), trappers, peanuts, Barlows, elephant toes, canoes, Texas toothpicks, Coke bottles, gun stocks, and Daddy Barlows. The decorative aspect also heavily influences prices.

Banner Knife Co., folding, deer toe handle, 4" lock blade with corkscrew, wear, 9-1/2" l 30.00
Case
   3210-1/2, yellow composition, 3-1/8", 1920-40, Tested XX ... 150.00
   5205-1/2, stag, 3-3/4" l, 1920-40, Tested XX 550.00
   5265, stag, 5-1/4", saber ground, stamped "USA," 1965-70 . 100.00
   5391, stag, 4-1/2", 1920-40, Tested XX 2,000.00
   6205, green bone, 3-3/4", 1920-40, Tested XX 450.00
   6231LP, red bone, Shield, 3-3/4", Tested XX 225.00
   6250, green bone, 4-3/8", 1920-40, Tested XX 1,250.00
   6265, 5-1/4", flat blade, stamped "Tested XX," green bone, 1920-40 .... 300.00
   6276, green bone, 3-5/8", 1920-40, Tested XX 350.00
   6276-1/2, green bone, 3-5/8", sleeveboard, Tested XX 300.00
   6345-1/2Sh, bone, rare, 3-5/8", 1965-68, USA 400.00
   6347SHSP, Rogers bone, late, 3-7/8", 1940-64, stainless steel, all blades stamped, XX 350.00
   8271, genuine pearl, 3-1/4", long pull, stamped "XX," 1940-65 .. 450.00
   9251, imitation onyx, 5-1/4", 1920-40, Tested XX, knife-fork. 750.00
   9265, imitation pearl, 5-1/4", flat blade, stamped "Tested XX," 1920-40 .... 450.00
   12031LR, walnut, 3-3/4", 1965-69, electrician's, USA 30.00
   62005, spear, green bone, 3-3/8", 1920-40, Tested XX 550.00
   62009, red bone, 3-5/16", 1940-64, XX 65.00
   82103, genuine pearl, 2-7/8", 1920-40, Tested XX 200.00
   420657, white composition, 3-3/8", "Office Knife" mkd on handle, 1940-56 .... 100.00
   B151ISAB, imitation onyx, 1920-40, Tested XX 600.00
   PT10051L, SSP, pakkawood, brass bolstgers, 3-3/4" l 30.00
   Muskrat, red bone, 3-7/8", 1940-64, XX 350.00
Ka-Bar (Union Cut. Co., Olean, NY)
   6260KF 120.00
   24107 .... 1,100.00
   31187, 2 blades 185.00
   1161, light celluloid handle 125.00
   61187, Daddy Barlow 175.00
Keen Kutter (Simons Hardware, St. Louis, MO)
   K1881, Barlow 85.00
   K1920 .... 300.00

Ka-Bar, trapper, pearl handle, $45.

   6354, Scout 125.00
Queen Steel
   5, Senator, Winterbottom bone, 2-1/2" 20.00
   6, pearl handle, 2 blades with no tang stamp, 2-1/2", no etch. 45.00
   7, Rogers bone handle, 2 blades with tang stamp, Q, 2-1/2", bale, no etch 45.00
   12, simulated pearl handle, 1 blade, tang stamp, Q-Stainless, 4-1/8", no etch 65.00
   21, sleeveboard 40.00
   24, Slimline Trapper, Winterbottom bone, 4" 55.00
   29, jack, Winterbottom bone, 4-1/2" 75.00
   38, swell center jumbo, Big Q, Winterbottom bone, 5-1/4" 200.00
   61, Stockman, Winterbottom bone, 3-5/8" 50.00
Remington
   R73, 2 blade jack, brown bone, 3-1/8" 140.00
   R272, black 170.00
   R293, Field and Stream Bullet, bone, long pull 1,800.00
   R305, Pyremite, 3-3/4" 250.00
   R391, redwood, tear-drop jack, 3-3/8" 160.00
   R723, bone, large 1 blade, hawkbill, 4-1/2" 250.00
   R953, toothpick, bone 250.00
   R3273, Cattle, brown bone, equal end 275.00
   RC090, Barlow, 3-3/8", horn handle 125.00
Winchester
   1621, Budding, 4-3/4", ebony 150.00
   1920, Hunter, 5-3/8", bone, folding 1,000.00
   2337, Senator, 3-1/4", pearl 125.00
   2703, Barlow, 3-1/2", brown bone 160.00
   3944, Whittler, 3-1/4", bone 225.00

POISON BOTTLES

History: The design of poison bottles was meant to serve as a warning in order to prevent accidental intake or misuse of their poisonous contents. Their unique details were especially helpful in the dark. Poison bottles generally were made of colored glass, embossed with "Poison" or a skull and crossbones, and sometimes were coffin-shaped.

John H. B. Howell of Newton, New Jersey, designed the first safety closure in 1866. The idea did not become popular until the 1930s when bottle designs became simpler and the user had to read the label to identify the contents.

References: Ralph and Terry Kovel, *Kovels' Bottles Price List*, 10th ed., Crown Publishers, 1996; Carlo and Dorothy Sellari, *Standard Old Bottle Price Guide*, Collector Books, 1989.

Periodical: *Antique Bottle and Glass Collector*, P.O. Box 187, East Greenville, PA 18041.

Collectors' Club: Federation of Historical Bottle Collectors, Inc., 88 Sweetbriar Branch, Longwood, FL 32750.

Bowker's Pyrox Poison, colorless 30.00
Carbolic Acid, 3 oz, cobalt blue, hexagonal, flat back 48.00
Chloroform, 5-3/4" h, green, ribbed, label, 1900 .... 80.00
Coffin, 3-1/2" h, cobalt blue, emb, 1890 .... 100.00
Cylindrical, crosshatch dec, cobalt blue, flared mouth with stopper, smooth base, 6-1/4" h 250.00
Diamond Antiseptics, 10-3/4" h, triangular shape, golden amber, emb 385.00
Figural, skull, America, 1880-1900, cobalt blue, tooled mouth, smooth base
   2-7/8" h, small hole in nose area 475.00
   4-1/8" h 1,800.00
Imperial Fluid Co. Poison, 1 gallon, colorless 95.00
Lysol, 3-1/4" h, cylindrical, amber, emb "Not To Be Taken" 12.00
Melvin & Badger Apothecaries, Boston, Mass, irregular form, cobalt blue, tooled sq mouth, smooth base, 6-1/4" h 140.00

Aqua, embossed, blown, hobnail, diamond on front, rectangle on back, extended neck, imp "70," 3-5/16" h, $35.

Mercury Bichloride, 2-11/16" h, rect, amber.....................................18.00
Norwich Coffin, 3-3/8" h, amber, emb, tooled lip............................95.00
Owl Drug Co., 3-3/8" h, cobalt blue, owl sitting on mortar 70.00
Plumber Drug Co., 7-1/2" h, cobalt blue, lattice and diamond
   pattern 90.00
Poison, 3-1/2" h, hexagonal, ribbed, cobalt blue............................20.00
Tinct Iodine, 3" h, amber, skull and crossbones.............................45.00
USA Hospital Dept, Acetate Potassa, 6-1/2" h, cylindrical, aqua..65.00
Wilberts Javex, 9" h, amber, concave and ribbed...........................50.00

POLITICAL ITEMS

History: Since 1800, the American presidency has been a contest between two or more candidates. Initially, souvenirs were issued to celebrate victories. Items issued during a campaign to show support for a candidate were actively being distributed in the William Henry Harrison election of 1840.

There is a wide variety of campaign items—buttons, bandannas, tokens, pins, etc. The only limiting factor has been the promoter's imagination. The advent of television campaigning has reduced the quantity of individual items, and modern campaigns do not seem to have the variety of materials that were issued earlier.

References: Herbert Collins, *Threads of History*, Smithsonian Institution Press, 1979; Theodore L. Hake, *Encyclopedia of Political Buttons, United States, 1896-1972* (1974), Book II, 1920-1976 (1977), Book III, 1789-1916 (1978), revised prices for all three books (1998) Americana & Collectibles Press, (P.O. Box 1444, York, PA 17405); —, *Hake's Guide to Presidential Campaign Collectibles*, Wallace-Homestead, 1992; Edward Krohn (ed.), *National Political Convention Tickets and Other Convention Ephemera*, David G. Phillips Publishing (P.O. Box 611388, N. Miami, FL 33161), 1996; Keith Melder, *Hail to the Candidate*, Smithsonian Institution Press, 1992; James W. Milgram, *Presidential Campaign Illustrated Envelopes and Letter Paper 1840-1872*, David G. Phillips Publishing (P.O. Box 611388, N. Miami, FL 33161), 1996; Edmund B. Sullivan, *American Political Badges and Medalets, 1789-1892*, Quarterman Publications, 1981; —, *Collecting Political*
Americana, Christopher Publishing House, 1991; Mark Warda, *100 Years of Political Campaign Collectibles*, Sphinx Publishing (P.O. Box 25, Clearwater, FL 34617), 1996; —, Political Campaign Stamps, Krause Publications, 1998.

Periodicals: *Political Bandwagon*, P.O. Box 348, Leola, PA 17540; *Political Collector*, P.O. Box 5171, York, PA 17405.

Collectors' Clubs: American Political Items Collectors, P.O. Box 340339, San Antonio, TX 78234; Ford Political Items Collectors, 18222 Flower Hill Way #299, Gaithersburg, MD 20879; NIXCO, Nixon Collectors Organization, 975 Maunawili Cr, Kailua, HI 96734; Third Party & Hopefuls, 503 Kings Canyon Blvd., Galesburg, IL 61401.

Museums: National Museum of American History, Smithsonian Institution, Washington, DC; Western Reserve Historical Society, Cleveland, OH.

Reproduction Alert:

Campaign Buttons
The reproduction of campaign buttons is rampant. Many originated as promotional sets from companies such as American Oil, Art Fair/Art Forum, Crackerbarrel, Liberty Mint, Kimberly Clark, and United States Boraxo. Most reproductions began life properly marked on the curl, i.e., the turned-under surface edge.

Look for evidence of disturbance on the curl where someone might try to scratch out the modern mark. Most of the backs of these buttons were bare or had a paper label. Beware of any button with a painted back. Finally, pinback buttons were first made in 1896, and nearly all made between 1896 and 1916 were celluloid covered. Any lithographed tin button from the election of 1916 or earlier is very likely a reproduction or fantasy item.

Additional Listings: See *Warman's Americana & Collectibles* for more examples.

Advisor: Theodore L. Hake.

Autograph
   1-1/2" x 7" inscription on 6-1/2" x 9" photo of Charles Hughes, copyright Harris & Ewing, recently framed.........................150.00
   3-1/4" x 5-1/2" postcard, black and white, from "I'm For Dick Nixon How About You" folder, 1960 campaign, canceled Nov 4, Spokane, WA, postmark, addressed by Nixon in blue ink to Rose Mayes, leading Idaho Republican Party woman, regarding turn out at recent event, thanking for help, sgd "Richard," 2" l crease line 375.00
   8" x 10-1/2", letter sgd by Al Smith as governor to Mrs. Alton B. Parker, white paper, raised gold governor's seal..................70.00
Bandanna, 20" sq, silk, Harrison, red, white, and blue, inscription "Protection to American Labor and American Industries," some fading, small hole 75.00
Banner, 6" x 9", brown and white fabric banner, 4-1/4" x 5-1/4" browntone photo of FDR in center, facsimile signature in white, wooden

SPECIAL AUCTIONS

Hake's Americana & Collectibles
P.O. Box 1444, Dept. 344
York, PA 17405
(717) 848-1333

Magazine, *The Century Illustrated Monthly Magazine,* Lincoln Centennial Number, The Century Co., Union Square, NY, Vol. 77, No. 4, February 1909, printed black and yellow covers, color frontispiece miniature portrait, 134 pages, black and white photographs, color plates, 7" x 10", $25.

rod, with red painted barrel ends, blue fabric hanging cord and tassels 50.00
Bottle Opener, 3-1/4" x 3-1/4" cast iron figural donkey, unpainted, "FDR" on base 70.00
Button
   7/8" d, Grant, wearing uniform, multicolored portrait, gold ground, from Bastian Bros. 1910 set 20.00
   7/8" d, black and white, 1940, pre-Willkie, "Get From Behind The (Eight) Ball Be A Republican," curl reads "Acorn Badges Co., Chicago, IL" 50.00
   7/8" d, clock face, "16 to 1" Bryan, silver/dark blue, clock hands depicting slogan, 1896 .... 40.00
   1" d, Willkie, dark bluetone photo, dark blue ground, black ink imprint "Trapp Print Shop Topeka" 25.00
   1-1/4" d, brown and white button, FDR Inauguration, 3-D cello donkey hanger, "Dem" on pink and green blanket, red, white, and blue ribbons with "Roosevelt and Wallace Inauguration Jan 20, 1941" 60.00
   1-1/4" d, Teddy Roosevelt rebus, reddish pink rosebud at center accented by green stem and leaves, black lettering, cream ground, "For President (Rose) Velt," mint condition 350.00
   1-3/4" d, America Needs Dwight D. Eisenhower, litho, bluetone photo, reads "Draft Ike in 1956" 20.00
   1-3/4" d, For President Harry S. Truman, shades of gray 80.00
   4" d, If I Were 21 I'd Vote for Kennedy, tin litho, red and black letters, white background, AAA Novelty Co., Washington, DC 1960 ..... 10.00
Campaign Poster
   18" x 24", Kennedy for President, Leadership for the 60s, smiling black and white center photo, red background at top, blue background at base, plastic, numerous light handling creases, small tear at upper right edge 30.00
   22" x 28", Teddy Roosevelt for Vice President, striking 18" x 20" black and white engraved type portrait, bold caption "Theodore Roosevelt," Wm E. & Oscar Martial engraver's 1901 copyright, New York City 90.00
Carte de Visite, 2-3/8" x 3-7/8", emb frame, 3/4" h sepia real photo of Lincoln, captioned "Abraham Lincoln," adv for New Bedford, Mass, clothing store 150.00
Cartoon, litho print by John Childs, c1838-40, titled, bottom margin reads "New York, Published by J. Childs, Lithographer, 119 Fulton Street," and smaller type "Entered According to Act of Congress the Year 1838"
   12" x 15-1/2", Animal Magnetism, 3 men at right, watch as Andrew Jackson hypnotizes Van Buren, political satire text, light scattered aging, small holes 500.00

   13" x 15", Political Jugglers Losing Their Balance, Harrison, Kendall, Blair, Van Buren and Major Jack Dawning named at bottom edge, Harrison swings "Reform" club causing Amos Kendall and Francis Blair, supporting Van Buren, to fall backwards over hard cider barrel, log cabin in background, political satire text ... 500.00
   13-1/2" x 21", Whig Magnets Attracted by The Pole, man to right with "Whig Principles" flag "Uncompromising Hostility To The Re-Election of Martin Van Buren," Van Buren sits on throne like chair atop platform on pole, he says, "I'm Too Firmly Fixed in Popular Feeling To Be Shaken From My Seat," W. H. Harrison, Henry Clay, and Daniel Webster trying to ascend pole, additional political satire text, slight toning, some age spotting 500.00
Cuff Links Set, Goldwater 1984, 2" x 3-1/4" white glossy card, attached 3/4" white metal cufflinks with brass luster, image of elephant wearing black metal eyeglasses 35.00
Ferrotype
   1/2", Grant, wearing military uniform, blank reverse, narrow brass rim 120.00
   15/16", Lincoln and Hamlin, full name and date "1860"" on both sides, brass rim, near mint condition 700.00
Handkerchief
   12-3/4" sq, pink donkeys in white ovals, brown background, white edge trim, c1948 .... 20.00
   15" sq, black on white fabric, risque cartoon of happy Democratic donkey mounting battered and subdued Republican elephant, "Come November," c1940 .... 60.00
Inaugural Medal
   1-3/4" d, thick brass, FDR, name and portrait, "Fourth Inauguration 1945," reverse with early ship with many sails, inscribed "Thou Too Sail On O Ship Of State-Sail On O Union Strong and Great," only 3,500 issued 250.00
   2" d, bronze, Truman, 1949, 7,500 issued 140.00
Inauguration Clothing Button, George Washington, elaborate "GW" initials in center surrounded by "Long Live The President" which is surrounded by intertwined oval designs, each carrying one or two letters representing names of 13 orig states, orig finish, dark color brass 850.00
Jugate
   Dewey/Warren, black and white photos, red, white, and blue panels, blue names 35.00
   McKinley and Teddy Roosevelt, 1-1/4", black and white photos surrounded by gold beaded ovals and scrolling, dark blue ground 70.00
   Taft, Art Nouveau style, 1-1/4", black and white portrait on red, white, and blue 400.00
Knife, 1-1/2" l, silvered brass, knife blade and file blade, portrait of Wilson and slogan "Let Justice and Progress Go Hand in Hand," reverse "The White House," some tarnish on blades, 1916 .... 60.00
Lapel Stud
   Al Smith for President, enameled, threaded post back 30.00
   America First, 11/16", brass, red, white, and blue enameled brown eagle, gold accents, star designs, brass lettered inscription, c1916 .... 75.00
   McKinley, 7/8", real photo, "Victory Pennsylvania Will Head the Column in November/Victory" 20.00
   Roosevelt Business & Professional League, FDR, brass, dark blue enamel 10.00
   Taft, 1/2" d, name and tiny accents in gold, dark blue ground. 15.00
License Plate Attachment, 4-1/2" d diecut sunflower, Landon and Knox 50.00
Matches, 1-1/2" x 4-1/2", Kennedy for President/Johnson for Vice President, campaign type, black and white, red, white, and blue stars and stripes design, Universal Match Corp., St Louis, c1960, flattened, matches and staples removed, pr 24.00
Mechanical Pencil, 6" l, Friend of the People Harry S. Truman Foe of Privilege, "Compliments of the Mo. State Dem Com," red, white, and blue 50.00
Membership Certificate, 3" x 5-3/4", stiff paper, Progressive Party Contribution and Membership Certificate, black and white images of Teddy Roosevelt and Hiram Johnson on each side, green, red, and black, similar to $1 bill, reverse with images of green moose, quoted statements by Roosevelt and Johnson 30.00

Pinback Button, commemorates assassination of McKinley, black and white, black ribbon, orig paper insert, Whitehead & Hoag Co., Newark, NJ, 1896, 1-3/16" d, $24.

Paper Cup, 3-1/4" h, Coffee with Kennedy, bright red inscription on each side, unused 30.00
Pennant, 4" x 16", 4" l streamers, felt
    Hoover, green 30.00
    Smith, Al, red 30.00
Plate, 7" d, full color image, titled "Digging The Ditch At Panama," inscription above image at center "To Finish This Great Work We Need No Foreign Aid, For We Can Do It All Ourselves With Spirit And With Spade," Teddy Roosevelt like figure in background, wearing Spanish American war outfit with rifles, c1904 ....95.00
Pocket Mirror, 2" x 3", FDR, pale blue textured paper, black printing, FDR portrait, names of Vermilion County party leaders, "Retain The New Deal By Voting The Straight Democratic Ticket" 35.00
Postcard Folder, "I'm For Dick Nixon How About You," 3-1/4" x 5-1/2" black and white folder, 2 postcards, perforated seam in center, unused 18.00
Print
    9-1/2" x 13-1/2", Zachary Taylor The People Choice for 12th President, titled "The Presidents Of The United States," portraits of George Washington to Taylor, Currier, 12-1/4" x 16-1/4" varnished beveled wood frame 200.00
    12" x 14", black and white engraved 1864 image of Lincoln, orig thin cardboard mat with 2 gold accent oval lines, caption "Abraham Lincoln," dark wood oval frame, floral designs, gold accent inner border 250.00
    18" x 52", titled "The Inauguration of President Roosevelt March 4, 1905," published by Success Magazine of New York City, some heavy creasing 75.00
Ribbon
    1-3/4" x 6", red, white, and blue fabric, black and white celluloid piece with small McKinley facsimile signature at bottom, reads "Home Rule/Protection," stickpin 75.00
    1-3/4" x 7", parchment, black image, angel with trumpet laying wreath on head of Washington, inscription "Pro Patria/Washington Benevolent Society," c1824 ....100.00
    2" x 5" blue and white fabric ribbon, 2" long gold thread strands at bottom, Harrison Veterans, Lancaster, PA, 1888, ribbon reads "1840 Harrison Veterans, Harrison and Morton, Lancaster, PA, October 25, 1888" 80.00
    2" x 7-1/2", Fremont Republican 50th Anniversary, cello and brass

luster hanger, dark gold letters, blue fabric, "Semi-Centennial/Republican Party/1854-1904," center brass rim around sepia portrait 60.00
Sheet Music, 9" x 12", Nixon's The One, 4 pgs, red, white, blue, and purple cov, ©1968, words and music by Raymond J. Meurer Sr. and Jr. 4.00
Stereoscopic Card, 3-1/2" x 7", sepia colored, Roosevelt's Rough Riders Leaving Tampa, Florida, USA for Santiago," 1898 ....14.00
Stickpin
    Garfield, 1-1/4" h, emb eagle, flag, and ribbon border, inscribed "E. Pluribus Unum," raised center oval which holds crisp black and white ferrotype, vertical stickpin on reverse, bright silver luster 600.00
    Harrison, cardboard photo on brass shell, spring wing eagle at top, flag accents, brass 90.00
Tab, silver luster metal, silver inscription on dark green ground, "Cal 24/Coolidge," tab has been folded over, one of the first tabs ever used 50.00
Thermometer, 3-1/2" x 5-1/2", full color photo of FDR, ad for Martin's Ferry, OH, furniture store, metal frame holding glass over paper print, cardboard backing, 1934 ....45.00
Ticket, 3" x 10-1/2", red, white, and blue, FDR National Rally, bluetone photo of FDR, Washington, June 27, 1936, unused 20.00
Window Sign, 10" sq, This Is A Hoover Home, red, white, and blue, large 7" d black and white photo of Hoover 65.00

POMONA GLASS

History: Pomona glass, produced only by the New England Glass Works and named for the Roman goddess of fruit and trees, was patented in 1885 by Joseph Locke. It is a delicate lead, blown art glass which has a pale, soft beige ground and a top one-inch band of honey amber.

There are two distinct types of backgrounds. First ground, made only from late 1884 to June 1886, was produced by making fine cuttings through a wax coating followed by an acid bath. Second ground was made by rolling the piece in acid-resisting particles and acid etching. Second ground was made in Cambridge until 1888 and until the early 1900s in Toledo, where Libbey moved the firm after purchasing New England Glass works. Both methods produced a soft frosted appearance, but fine curlicue lines are more visible on first-ground pieces. Some pieces have designs which were etched and then stained with a color. The most familiar design is blue cornflowers.

Do not confuse Pomona with Midwestern Pomona, a pressed glass with a frosted body and amber band.

References: Joseph and Jane Locke, *Locke Art Glass*, Dover Publications, 1987; Kenneth Wilson, *American Glass 1760-1930*, 2 vols., Hudson Hills Press and The Toledo Museum of Art, 1994.

Bowl, 4-1/2" d, 3" h, first ground, rich deep amber staining 275.00
Butter Dish, cov, 4-1/2" h, 8" d underplate, first ground, gold stained acacia leaf dec, reeded curlicue handle 1,275.00
Celery Vase, 6-1/8" h, 4-1/2" d, first ground, acacia leaf dec......550.00
Champagne, 5" h, stemmed, second ground, amber staining....245.00
Creamer, second ground, Daisy and Butterfly, applied colorless handle, three applied colorless feet 275.00
Cruet, 7-1/4" h
    First ground, orig ball stopper...365.00
    Second ground, cornflower dec, ball stopper, petaled base with hint of amber irid stain 335.00
Finger Bowl, first ground...75.00
Goblet, 6" h, first ground, little amber stain remains 115.00
Lemonade Tumbler, second ground, pronounced blue cornflower dec 125.00

Pitcher, first grind, Cornflower pattern, light amber collar, 4-1/2" h, $500.

Pitcher, 5-1/2" h, first ground, applied unstained handle, sq mouth 235.00

Punch Cup

    Cornflower, first ground, blue staining 145.00

    Cornflower, second ground...110.00

    Inverted Thumbprint, first ground, amber staining...................85.00

Tankard Pitcher, 6-3/4" h, first ground, optic diamond quilted body, gold stain on clear glass handle and upper border 385.00

Tumbler

    3-3/4" h, 2-5/8" d, Cornflower, second ground, DQ glass, honey amber stain top and bottom, rich blue stained flowers........145.00

    3-3/4" h, second ground, irid amber butterfly and pansy dec, border of brilliant amber stain...235.00

    4" h, Cornflower, second ground, DQ, excellent staining 95.00

Vase

    3" h, 5-3/4" w, fan, second ground, optic baby thumbprint design on frosted portion, golden pedal form base 185.00

    6" h, first ground, rigaree around ruffled top and neck ring, etched waisted body, first ground, faded amber stain 215.00

    10" h, lily, frosted second ground, optic ribbed design, gold stain portion mouth with optic diamond quilted design, clear glass wafer base 385.00

PORTRAIT WARE

History: Plates, vases, and other articles with portraits on them were popular in the second half of the 19th century. Although male subjects, such as Napoleon or Louis XVI, were used, the ware usually depicts a beautiful, and often unidentified, woman.

A large number of English and Continental china manufacturers made portrait ware. Because most was hand painted, an artist's signature often is found.

Cabinet Plate, 9-1/2" d

    Female portrait, titled "Erblich," gilt foliate design on deep burgundy ground, German, early 20th C 1,955.00

    Mione & Amor, central figural scene, gilt foliate design on cobalt blue ground, Austria, Vienna, late 19th C 520.00

Bowl, woman watering flowers, green ground, gold raised border with flowers and foliage, Royal Coburg, 10" d, $2,310. Photo courtesy of Jackson's Auctioneers & Appraisers.

Nude female in landscape, gilt foliate design on deep burgundy border, freeform dec panel, Austria, Vienna, late 19th C . 1,890.00

Cup and Saucer

    3-1/2" h, cup with medallion of Louis XBVI, Madame de Lamballe and Marie Antoinette, blue celeste and jeweled ground, saucer with central crest, Sevres, 19th C, pr...............................2,200.00

    6-1/2" h cov cup, portrait reserve, floral spray, apple green ground, gilt highlights, Sevres style 250.00

Plaque

    3-1/4" h, General Hoche, green jacket, red collar, raised gilt border, cobalt ground, Hutschenreuther 150.00

    4-1/8" x 6", porcelain, rect, enameled female, artist sgd "Heubach Bros.," German, c1900 ....488.00

    6" d, bronze, Louis XIV, shown in right profile, inscribed "Bertinet Sculp cu privlegio," reverse dec with crowned interlaced L's with drapery and foliage, by Italian sculptor Bertinetti, 17th C 2,530.00

    16-1/2" d, circular, central portrait of Queen Elizabeth of England, scrolled gilt foliate on ruby red ground border, titled in German on reverse, Austria, Vienna, 19th C 2,300.00

Plate

    8" d, Daphnae, green ground, gilt foliate border, titled on verse, Richard Klem, Dresden, Germany marks, late 19th C........300.00

    9-3/8" d, Countess of Harrington, titled on reverse, central enamel portrait sgd "Wagner," raised gilt border, simulated jade medallions, Germany, late 19th/early 20th C................................500.00

    10" d, Napoleon, Louisiana Purchase souvenir, earthenware, blue and white, high glaze, fair buildings on rim, Victoria Art Company, NY 295.00

    10-1/8" d, enameled female portrait in center, gilt trimmed cobalt blue border, Austria, Vienna, 19th C 320.00

    12" d, youthful maiden, 3/4 profile, plumed hat, printed marks, elaborate carved giltwood frame, Continental, c1880 ....550.00

    14" d, Peter the Great and Catherine, portrait roundels border, Austrian, late 19th C 1,850.00

Vase

    3-1/8" h, 1-5/8" d, green ground, portrait of lady with wine glass, artist sgd "Sontagg," mkd "Royal Schwarzburg" 100.00

    7" h, portrait medallion of young girl, gilt surface dec, cranberry glass, mkd with crown and shield surrounded by oval........350.00

12" h, gilt ground, white porcelain body, sq enamel dec panels on each side, female taverner, other with topographical landscape with building, Paris, France, 19th C 345.00

14" h, baluster, portrait of elegant young woman by rose bushes, continuous landscape, printed factory Limoges marks, late 19th C 900.00

20-1/4" h, molded infants on scrolled foliate handles, body with matte blue ground, central circular cartouche with portrait of classical female, Paris, 19th C 600.00

POSTERS

History: Posters were a critical and extremely effective method of mass communication, especially in the period before 1920. Enormous quantities were produced, helped in part by the propaganda role posters played in World War I.

Print runs of two million were not unknown. Posters were not meant to be saved; they usually were destroyed once they had served their purpose. The paradox of high production and low survival is one of the fascinating aspects of poster history.

The posters of the late 19th and early 20th centuries represent the pinnacle of American lithography. The advertising posters of firms such as Strobridge or Courier are true classics. Philadelphia was one center for the poster industry.

Europeans pioneered posters with high artistic and aesthetic content, and poster art still plays a key role in Europe. Many major artists of the 20th century designed posters.

References: George Theofiles, *American Posters of World War I*, Dafram House Publishers; Susan Theran (ed.), *Leonard's Annual Price Index of Posters & Photographs*, Auction Index (30 Valentine Park, Newton, MA 02165), 1995; Jon R. Warren, *Collecting Hollywood*, 3rd ed., *American Collector's Exchange*, 1994; Bruce Lanier Wright, *Yesterday's Tomorrow*, Taylor Publishing, 1993.

Periodicals: *Biblio*, 845 Willamette St., Eugene, OR 87401; Collecting Hollywood, *American Collectors Exchange*, 2401 Broad St., Chattanooga, TN 37408; *Movie Poster Update*, American Collectors Exchange, 2401 Broad St., Chattanooga, TN 37408; *Plakat Journal*, Oskar-Winter Str. 3 D30160 Hannover, Germany.

Museum: Museé de la Publicité, 107 Rue de Rivoli, Paris, France.

Additional Listings: See *Warman's Americana & Collectibles* for more examples.

Advisor: George Theofiles.

Advertising

"Do It Electrically, Comfort, Convenience, Efficiency in the Home...Save Fuel, Food, Time, Money -By Wire," image of angel holding electric motor, period electrical appliances, full color, blue background, expert restoration to edges,c1915, 27" x 35".......600.00

SPECIAL AUCTIONS

Poster Auctions International
601 W. 26th St.
New York, NY 10001
(212) 787-4000

Biere Du Lion, Belgian beer poster, anonymous, full color litho, c1912, 23" w, 31" h, $350. Photo courtesy of George Theofiles.

Ferry's Seeds, full color image of pretty young lass amid towering hollyhocks, light fold lines, restoration to edges, thin tears, 1925, 21" x 28" 325.00

Fire! Fire! Fire!, "Chicago Lost But J. Dearman of Knoxville, Penna. Continues to Roll Up, Bundle Up, and Box Up As Many Goods As Ever!" red and black, some replacement to border, Oct.15th, 1871, 22" x 27" 225.00

Granite Iron Ware, paper, woman carrying milking pail, cow, "For Kitchen and Table Use," 12-1/2" x 28" 75.00

Lady Esther Face Cream, printed on board, beautiful young woman in oval vignette, "A Skin Food-An Astringent," c1920, 23" x 36" ..325.00

Kix Cereal, Lone Ranger 6-shooter ring, General Mills premium, "Only 15 cents plus Kix box top," c1948. 17" x 22" 225.00

Pabst Blue Ribbon - Now At Popular Prices, Aldridge, saloon scene, orig wood frame, litho image of turn of the century touring car crossing in front of huge 19th C locomotive, c1950, 40" x 23" 150.00

Popcorn Starch, packages and little girl, color litho, c1900, 10" x 13" 200.00

Richfield Gasoline, race driver in car, c1930, 39" x 53" 1,100.00

Royal Portable Typewriter, dark green detailed manual portable typewriter against leafed red and green ground, c1940, 24" x 36" .285.00

Shamrock Tobacco, canvas, seated man holding knife and tobacco, "Plug Smoking -10 cents a Cut," c1900, 17" x 23" 190.00

Vieux St. Jean, Robert Bon, placard for calvados-like drink of "Garnati Pur Vin," travel poster style, detailed bottle in front of ancient Swiss city, clock tower, c1920, 9-1/2" x 15" 95.00

Waterman's Ideal Fountain Pen, paper, Uncle Sam at Treaty of Portsmouth, early 1900s, 41-1/2 x 19-1/2" 950.00

Circus, Shows, and Acts

Barnum and Bailey Circus, Strobridge Litho, Co., "Jockey Races," 1908, 19" x 28" 900.00

Clyde Beatty-Cole Bros Combined Circus, The World's Largest Circus, "Clyde Beatty in Person," Roland butler, lion tamer, multicolored, 19" x 26" 90.00

Downey Bros Big 3 Ring Circus, "Leaps-Revival of that Astounding and Sensational exhibition," group of elephants, camels, and horses in line, aerial artist leaping overhead, audience background, c1925, 41" x 27" 125.00

Hollywood Peep Show, burlesque strip revue, c1950, 27" x 41" 150.00

Hot From Harlem, black burlesque show, color, Anon, c1947, 22" x 28" 250.00

Hoxie Bros Old Time Circus Land, One Mile West of Walt Disney

World, multicolored view of circus grounds and big top, 20" x 27" 65.00

Larry Breener's Fantasies of 1929, vaudeville and dance revue, Donaldson Litho, 14" x 22" 80.00

Ringling Bros Barnum & Bailey Liberty Bandwagon, color litho, ornate wagon with Merue Evans portrait, 1943, 30" x 19" 225.00

Tim McCoy's Wild West, circle of riders around red circle, on canvas, 1938, 54" x 41" 900.00

Magic

Buddha and Heartstone, Polish magician performing tricks, English and Polish text, c1914, 14" x 26" 100.00

Carter the Great-A Baffling Chinese Mystery- The Elongated Maiden, Otis Litho, "A pretty Chinese girl tied to a torture rack without seeming discomfort..," life-sized Chinese nobleman looking down on vignettes of complicated rack, stretched maiden, banshees, imps, devils, in color, c1920, 41" x 81" 650.00

Friedlander Stock Magic, Adolph Friedlander #6966, smiling devil holds card-like vignettes of magic acts in one hand, wand in other, yellow ground, c1919, 14" x 19" 150.00

Kar-Mi Swallows a Loaded gun Barrel, National, "Shoots a cracker from a man's head," Kar-Mi with gun in mouth blasts away at blindfolded assistant, crowd of turbaned Indians, 1914, 42" x 28" ..350.00

Movie

Action in Arabia, George Sanders and Virginia Bruce, 1944, 27" x 41" 75.00

African Queen, French release of classic Bogart and Hepburn film, color portraits of both above steamy jungle setting, c1960, 22" x 31" 150.00

Alias Boston Blackie, Columbia Pictures, Chester Morris, full color, 1942, 27" x 41" 100.00

Amazing Transparent Man, Miller Consolidated, D Kennedy, Marguerite Chapman, sci-fi silhouette against blue, 1959, 27" x 41" 125.00

Anatomy of a Murder, Columbia, Saul Bass design, 1959, 27" x 41" 125.00

Atlantic City, Republic, Constance Moore, Jerry Colonna in drag, by James Montgomery Flagg, 1941, 14" x 36" 200.00

Blondie in the Dough, Columbia Pictures, Penny Singleton, Chick Young's Blondie cartoon film, full color, 1947, 27" x 41" 95.00

Bad Boy, James Dunn and Louise Fazenda,, Fox, 1934, 27" x 41" 150.00

Buck Privates, Relart re-release, Bud Abbott, Lou Costello, the Andrews Sisters, full-color montage, 1953, 27" x 41" 95.00

Cheaters At Play, Thomas Meighan and Charlotte Greenwood, Fox, 1931, 27" x 41" 275.00

Double Danger, Preston Foster and Whitney Bourne, RKO, 1938, 27" x 41" 110.00

Dr. No, United Artist, Sean Connery, Ursula Andress, 1962, 27" x 41" 325.00

13 Rue Madeleine, Fox, James Cagney, Annabella, Cagney coming from behind looming door, printed in US for So American market. 1947, 27" x 41" 225.00

False Paradise, Hopalong Cassidy, United Artists, 1947, 27" x 41" 125.00

Farmer's Daughter, RKO, Loretta Young, Joseph Cotton, Ethel Barrymore, Cotton kneeling to pick up blond Young in maid's outfit, 1947, 27" x 41" 125.00

Flipper, MGM, Chuck Connors, 1963............................20.00

Goodbye Mr. Chips, Robert Donat and Greer Garson, MGM, 1939, 27" x 41" 450.00

I'll Be Seeing You, Ginger Rogers, Joseph Cotton, and Shirley Temple, United Artists 1945, 27" x 41" 150.00

Letter of Introduction, Universal, Charlie McCarthy, Edgar Bergen, Andrea Leeds, full-color dummy. 1938, 27" x 41" 300.00

Love Takes Flight, Bruce Cabot and Beatrice Roberts, Grand National, 1937, 22" x 28" 135.00

Mule Train, Columbia Pictures, Gene Autry, Champion, full-color portraits, 1950, 27" x 41" 150.00

New York, New York, United Artists, Robert Diniro, Liza Minnelli, 1977 .... 35.00

One-Eyed Jacks, Paramount, Marlon Brando, Karl Malden, full color, 1959, 27" x 41" 85.00

Pursuit Of The Graf Spee, John Gregson and Anthony Quayle, Rank, c1955, 22" x 28" 150.00

Raiders of the Lost Ark, Harrison Ford, Paramount, 1981........... 65.00

Smoldering Fires, Pauline Frederick and Laura La Plante, Universal, 1925, 14" x 22" 125.00

Political and Patriotic

America Lets Us Worship As We Wish - Attend The Church Of Your Choice, for American Legion sponsored "Americanism Appreciation Month," full color image of praying Uncle Sam, family at dinner table behind him, c1945,20" x 26" 225.00

Bridge of Peace, Venette Willard Shearer, anti-war poster from American Friends Service Committee, National Council to Prevent War, in color, children of all nations play beneath text of song of peace, c1936, 16" x 22" 125.00

Carry On With Franklin D. Roosevelt, portrait in gravure, black letters against white ground, framed, 1936, 9" x 11" 5.00

Confidence, large color portrait of Roosevelt over yacht at sea, "Election Day was our salvation/Franklin Roosevelt is the man/Our ship will reach her destination/Under his command...Bring this depression to an end...," c1933, 18" x 25" 250.00

United Nations Day, blue and white U.N. banner waves over airbrushed stylized brown and yellow globe, minor edge crumple, 1947, 22" x 23" 250.00

Theater

Black Dwarf, Beck & Pauli Litho, Milwaukee, detailed stag set with 9 strutting players, cat-like character, a knight, ladies, etc., folio fold, expert restoration to upper cream border, c1870, 28" x 21" 325.00

Bringing Up Father, McManus, "Jiggs, Maggie, Dinty Moore-George McManus's cartoon comedy with music," early newspaper cartoon characters against New York skyline, c1915, 41" x 81" 425.00

California Minstrels, J. H. Haverly, anonymous, broadsheet, company appearing at Hooley's Theater, Chicago, detailed wood engraving of minstrels and side men in center, advertises Billy Rice, Justine Robinson as a Phila drag act, red and black, c1880, 9" x 41" 550.00

Christmas Dollys - Paris Qui Marché, Choubrac, man and woman cabaret act imitating Victorian dolls, deep reds, blues, grays, and silver metallics, 1905, 36" x 52", evidence of folds, some expert restoration upper field 425.00

Claudine Clerice Fr, Collette Willy opera, full color, French, 1910, 26" x 35" 275.00

Dangers of a Great City, National show Print, Chicago, play by Oliver North, men fighting in an office, gleaming stock ticker, "Give me the papers or I'll...," c1900, 21" x 28" 150.00

Gondoliers, Gilbert & Sullivan, anonymous, pr of cavalier gentlemen in princely attire hold sword and crown, throne setting, bright multicolors, c1917, 20" x 30" 150.00

Irene Vanbrugh, Ernest Hamlin Baker, stage actress dressed in purple, grays, yellow, green, and orange hat, fur-collared coat, c1910, 20" x 28" 350.00

Key Largo, window card for play starring Paul Muni, portrait center, black and red motif, c1930, 14" x 22" 65.00

No No Nanette, Tony Gibbons, Theatre Mogador, Paris, European production of American musical, c1925, 15" x 22" 375.00

Transportation

Air France - North Africa, Villemot, stylized imagery of mosques and minarets, lave3nders, yellow, and blues against sky blue background, plane and Pegasus logo, c1950, 24" x 39" 225.00

Motorlobene-Fano, Alfred Olsen, Danish auto race, car raising cloud of dust, 1922, 24" x 35" 1,250.00

Royal Mail Atlantis, Padden, tourists in Royal mail motor launch approaching harbor village, mountains in background, c1923, 25" x 38" 675.00

SS France, Bob Peak, launching of French ocean liner, champagne and confection in front of huge, night-lit bow of ship, 1961, 30" x 46" 450.00

SS Michelangelo and SS Raffaello, Astor, detailed cutaway of Italian ocean liners, designed for use in travel office, printed on plasticized stock, metal frame, 1964, 54" x 22" 300.00
SS Rex, P Klodic, advertisement for Italian ocean liner, designed for use in travel office, framed, c1936, 40" x 29" 750.00

Travel

Alaskakans off to the Potlach, Northern Pacific Railway, seascape, Sidney Laurence, c1937, 30" x 40", restoration to left edge 375.00
Arizona - Fly TWA, Austin Briggs, full color western lass in 1950s style, c1955, 25" x 40" 300.00
Boston - New Haven Railroad, Nason, full color, stylized montage of Historic Boston by day and night, faint folio folds, c1938, 28" x 42" 275.00
Britain in Winter, Terence Cuneo, color rendering of horseman, hunters, and tourists outside rustic inn, 1948, 19" x 29" 125.00
Come to Ulster, Bernard Higham, beautiful lass points to grand mountainscape, c1933, 24" x 39", expert restoration to upper edge. 375.00
Hawaii - United Air Lines, Feher, stylized wahini, island behind her, full color, c1948, 25" x 40" 650.00
Palace Hotel Wengen, Klara Borter, hotel in foothills of Alps, 1928, 27" x 40" 800.00
Paris, Paul Colin, doves floating above stylized Eiffel tower and Arc de Triumph, 1946, 24" x 39" 600.00
Visitez La Tunisie, Yahia, multicolored Tunisian street scene, c1948, 25" x 39" 175.00

World War I

Call to Duty-Join the Army for Home and Country, Cammilli, recruiting image of Army bugler in front of unfurled banner, 1917, 30" x 40" 325.00
Clear the Way!, Howard Chandler Christy, Columbia points the way for Naval gun crew, c1918, 20" x 30" 250.00
Follow The Flag - Enlist in the Navy, James Daugherty, sailor plants flag on shore, 1917, 27" x 41" 450.00
Treat 'Em Rough - Jon The Tanks, A. Hutaf, window card, electric blue-black cat leaping over tanks in fiery battle, white border, c1917, 14" x 22" 900.00
You Wireless Fans - Help The Navy Get A Hun Submarine - A Thousand Radio Men Wanted, C. B. Falls, wireless operator reaching up to grab lightening bolt, starry night background, blue, green, red, and white, 1918, 27" x 44" 550.00
Which? Soldier Or Mechanic, L.H., "Enlist in the 57th Engineers (Inlaid Waterways) and Be Both... Camp Laurel, Maryland," 1918, 18" x 23" 200.00

POT LIDS

History: Pot lids are the lids from pots or small containers which originally held ointments, pomades, or soap. Although some collectors want both the pot and its lid, lids alone are more often collected. The lids frequently are decorated with multicolored underglaze transfers of rural and domestic scenes, portraits, florals, and landmarks.

The majority of the containers with lids were made between 1845 and 1920 by F. & R. Pratt, Fenton, Staffordshire, England. In 1920, F. & R. Pratt merged with Cauldon Ltd. Several lids were reissued by the firm using the original copper engraving plates. They were used for decoration and never served as actual lids. Reissues by Kirkhams Pottery, England, generally have two holes for hanging. Cauldon, Coalport, and Wedgwood were other firms making reissues.

Marks: Kirkhams Pottery reissues are often marked as such.

References: Susan and Al Bagdade, *Warman's English & Continental Pottery & Porcelain*, 3rd Edition, Krause Publi-

The Wolf and the Lamb, 4-1/8" d, $220.

cations, 1998; A. Ball, *Price Guide to Pot-Lids and Other Underglaze Multicolor Prints on Ware*, 2nd ed., Antique Collectors' Club, 1991 value update.

Note: Sizes given are for actual pot lids; size of any framing not included.

A False Move, c1850, 5" d 125.00
Arctic Expedition, T. J. & J. Mayer, multicolored, 3" d, rim chip .. 320.00
Bale's Mushroom Savoury, white glaze, brown and black transfer, 3-1/8" d, orig base 95.00
Begging Dog, c1860, 3" d 150.00
Bloater Paste, black label, white ironstone, 4-1/2" d, mkd "England" 45.00
Burgess's Genuine Anchovy Paste, white glaze, brown and black transfer, 3-1/4" d, shallow chips on reverse 50.00
Children Fishing, F. R. Pratt, 4" d 225.00
Children Sailing Boats, F. R. Pratt, 3" d 175.00
Cold Cream, white glaze, brown and black transfer, 2-1/2" d 40.00
Dr. Hassall's Hair Restorer, 1-3/4" d 250.00
Dublin Industrial Exhibition, multicolored, 3-3/4" d 65.00
Embarking For The East, Pratt, multicolored, 4-1/8" d, orig jar .. 125.00
Golden Eye Ointment, white glaze, brown and black transfer, 1-3/4" d 50.00
Hazard, Hazard & Co., Violet Cold Cream, 1150 Broadway New York, white glaze, brown transfer, 2-3/4" d 210.00
Jules Hauel, Saponaeceous Shaving Compound, 120 Chestnut St, Philadelphia, white glaze, red transfer, 4" d, minor staining, orig base 190.00
Hide and Seek, multicolored, 4" d, minor chips on reverse 75.00
Men and dogs boar hunting, 4" d 220.00
Morris's Imperial Eye Ointment 200.00
Mrs. Ellen Hale's Celebrated Heal All Ointment, black on white, 4" d 350.00
Pegwell Boy, c1850, 4" d 190.00
Persuasion, multicolored, 4-1/8" d 160.00
Queen Victoria on Balcony, T. J. & J. Mayer, large 275.00
Roussels's Premium Shaving Cream Philadelphia, white glaze, gray transfer, 3" d, minor age line in rim of lid, orig base 220.00
Tam O' Sahnger and Souter Johnny, 4" d, framed 275.00
The Rivals, multicolored, 4" d, minor chips on reverse 85.00

View of Windsor Castle, Pratt, 6-1/2" d.........................170.00
Walmer Castle, Kent, Tatnell & Son, 4-1/2" d 215.00
Windsor Ointment, Prepared Only By Hooks, bird on branch.....125.00

PRATT WARE

History: The earliest Pratt earthenware was made in the late 18th century by William Pratt, Lane Delph, Staffordshire, England. From 1810 to 1818, Felix and Robert Pratt, William's sons, ran their own firm, F. & R. Pratt, in Fenton in the Staffordshire district. Potters in Yorkshire, Liverpool, Sunderland, Tyneside, and Scotland copied the products.

The wares consisted of relief-molded jugs, commercial pots and tablewares with transfer decoration, commemorative pieces, and figures and figural groups of both people and animals.

Marks: Much of the early ware is unmarked. The mid-19th century wares bear several different marks in conjunction with the name Pratt, including "& Co."

References: Susan and Al Bagdade, *Warman's English & Continental Pottery & Porcelain*, 3rd Edition, Krause Publications, 1998; John and Griselda Lewis, *Pratt Ware 1780-1840*, Antique Collectors' Club, 1984.

Museums: City Museum & Art Gallery, Stoke-On-Trent, England; Fitzwilliam Museum, Cambridge, England; Potsdam Public Museum, Potsdam, NY; Royal Pavilion Art Gallert & Museum, Brighton, England; Royal Scottish Museum, Edinburgh, Scotland; Victoria & Albert Museum, London, England; William Rockhill Nelson Gallery of Art, Kansas City, MO.

Additional Listings: Pot Lids.

Creamer, 5-1/4" h, cow and milkmaid, yellow and black sponged cow, underglaze enamels, translucent green stepped rect base, horns chipped...450.00

Pitcher, Cottage, six sided, door and windows, orange rim, garland of berries and foliage, green grass base, green handle, 6" h, $350. Photo courtesy of Alderfer Auction Co.

Cup Plate, 3-1/8" d, Dalmatian, white, black spots 95.00
Figure
    5-1/2" h, Summer, pearlware, green, brown, and yellow ochre, chip on base 385.00
    9" h, Autumn, young woman, classical robes, holding armful of fruit, rockwork base, flaring rect plinth molded with leaf band, polychrome enamel trim, early 19th C 375.00
Jar, 7-3/4" h, molded oval panels of peacocks in landscapes, blue, brown, green, and ochre, lower section with vertical leaves, band of foliage on rim, c1790 ....620.00
Jug
    5-7/8" h, genre scenes in relief, "Sportive Innocence" on one side, "Mischievous Sport" on reverse 320.00
    7-3/4" h, large oval molded reserve, exotic barnyard fowl, still leaf-tip band at edge of reverse, molded rim band with flowering branches, base with long stiff leaves alternating with slender flowering branches, polychrome enamel highlights, c1800 ....1,4500.00
    8" h, molded leaves at neck and base, raised and polychrome painted hunting scene on colored ground, c1800 ....750.00
Miniature, 4-3/4" l, dish, center molded with spring of 2 ochre plums, green leaf, brown stem, feather molded rim, underglaze blue edging, small rim chip, c1800 ....350.00
Mug, 4" h, colorful tavern scene transfer 95.00
Mustard Jar, cov, dark blue hunt scene, tan ground 75.00
Pitcher
    6" h, cottage, six sided, cottage doors and windows, green grass base, berried garland, green handle, orange painted rim 350.00
    7-1/4" h, raised couple, mother, children, and trees dec, yellow, blue, brown, and green, 18th C 350.00
Plaque, 6-1/4" x 7-1/4", Louis XVI portrait, oval form, beaded border, polychrome enamels, c1793, rim nicks, glaze wear.................900.00
Plate, 9" d, Haddon Hall, classical figure border........................120.00
Pot Lid, 4" d, The New Blackfriars Bridge, c1860 ....95.00
Sauce Boat, 6-3/8" l, figural, dolphin, translucent green glaze over scales, brown eyes and fins, oval foot, yellow band border, chips, small hairlines in foot, c1790......................775.00
Tea Caddy, 6-1/4" h, rect, raised figural panels front and back, fluted and yellow trimmed lid, blue, yellow, orange, and green dec...350.00

PRINTS

History: Prints serve many purposes. They can be a reproduction of an artist's paintings, drawings, or designs, but often are an original art form. Finally, prints can be developed for mass appeal rather than primarily for aesthetic fulfillment. Much of the production of Currier & Ives fits this latter category. Currier & Ives concentrated on genre, urban, patriotic, and nostalgic scenes.

References: Jay Brown, *The Complete Guide To Limited Edition Art Prints*, Krause Publications, 1999; William P. Carl, *Currier's Price Guide to American and European Prints at Auction*, 3rd ed., Currier Publications, 1994; Clifford P. Catania, *Boudoir Art*, Schiffer Publishing, 1994; Karen Choppa, *Bessie Peace Gutmann*, Schiffer Publishing, 1998; Karen Choppa and Paul Humphrey, *Maud Humphrey*, Schiffer Publishing, 1993; Max Allen Collins and Drake Elvgren, *Elvgren: His Life & Art*, Collectors Press, 1998; Erwin Flacks, *Maxfield Parrish Identification & Price Guide*, 3rd ed., Collectors Press, 1998; Patricia L. Gibson, *R. Atkinson Fox & William M. Thompson Identification & Price Guide*, Collectors Press, 1994; Michael J. Goldberg, *Maxfield Parrish Vignettes*, Collectors Press, 1998; Martin Gordon (ed.), *Gordon's 1999 Print Price Annual*, Gordon and Lawrence Art Reference, 1999; *William R. Holland, Clifford P. Catania, and Nathan D. Isen, Louis Icart*, Schiffer

Publishing, 1994; William R. Holland and Douglas L. Congdon-Martin, *Collectible Maxfield Parrish*, Schiffer Publishing, 1993; Robert Kipp, *Currier's Price Guide to Currier & Ives Prints*, 3rd ed., Currier Publications, 1994; Stephanie Lane, *Maxfield Parrish*, L-W Book Sales, 1993; Coy Ludwig, *Maxfield Parrish*, Schiffer Publishing, 1973, 1993 reprint with value guide; *Maxfield Parrish*, Collectors Press, 1995; Ian Mackenzie, *British Prints*, Antique Collectors' Club; Rita C. Mortenson, *R. Atkinson Fox, His Life and Work*, Vol. 1 (1991, 1994 value update), Vol. 2 (1992), L-W Book Sales; N*orman I. Platnick, Coles Phillps*, published by author (50 Brentwood Rd., Bay Shore, NY 11706); Tina Skinner, *Harrison Fisher: Defining the American Beauty*, Schiffer Publishing, 1999; Kent Steine and Frederick B. Taraba, *J. C. Leyendecker Collection*, Collectors Press, 1996; Susan Theran and Katheryn Acerbo (eds.), *Leonard's Annual Price Index of Prints, Posters & Photographs*, Auction Index, published annually.

Periodicals: *Illustrator Collector's News*, P.O. Box 1958, Sequim, WA 98382; *Journal of the Print World*, 1008 Winona Rd, Meredith, NH 03253; *On Paper*, 39 E. 78th St., #601, New York, NY 10021; *Print Collector's Newsletter*, 119 East 79th St., New York, NY 10021.

Collectors' Clubs: American Antique Graphics Society, 5185 Windfall Rd, Medina, OH 44256; American Historical Print Collectors Society, P.O. Box 201, Fairfield, CT 06430; Gutmann Collector Club, P.O. Box 4743, Lancaster, PA 17604; Prang-Mark Society, P.O. Box 306, Watkins Glen, NY 14891.

Museums: American Museum of Natural History, New York, NY; Audubon Wildlife Sanctuary, Audubon, PA; John James Audubon State Park and Museum, Henderson, KY; Museum of the City of New York, NY; National Portrait Gallery, Washington, DC.

Reproduction Alert: The reproduction of Maxfield Parrish prints is a continuing process. New reproductions look new, i.e., their surfaces are shiny and the paper crisp and often pure white. The color on older prints develops a mellowing patina. The paper often develops a light brown to dark brown tone, especially if it is acid based or was placed against wooden boards in the back of a frame.

Size is one of the keys to spotting later reproductions. Learn the correct size for the earliest forms. Be alert to ear-lier examples that have been trimmed to fit into a frame. Check the dimensions before buying any print.

Carefully examine the edges within the print. Any fuzziness indicates a later copy. Also look at the print through a magnifying glass. If the colors separate into dots, this indicates a later version.

Apply the same principles described above for authenticating all prints, especially those attributed to Currier & Ives. Remember, many prints were copied soon after their period introduction. As a result, reproductions can have many of the same aging characteristics as period prints.

Additional Listings: See Wallace Nutting.

Note: Prints are beginning to attract a wide following. This is partially because prices have not matched the rapid rise in oil paintings and other forms of art.

Albright, Ivan Le Lorraine, *Fleeting Time, Thou Hast Left Me Old*, 1946, edition of 250, sgd "Ivan Le Lorraine Albright" in pencil lower right, titled in pencil lower left, litho on paper, 13-3/4" x 9-1/2", matted, unframed, deckled edges on 2 sides, subtle toning 1,265.00

Arms, John Taylor
  Early Morning, North River, second state, edition of 100, sgd and dated "John Taylor Arms, 1921" in pencil lower right, numbered "9/100" in pencil lower left, aquatint with etching on paper, 9-1/2" x 7-1/2" plate size, framed 1,495.00
  The Enchanted Doorway, Venezia, sgd and dated "John Taylor Arms - 1930" in pencil lower right, inscribed "Edition 100" in pencil lower left, sgd, dated and inscribed in plate lower right, etching on paper, 12-3/8" x 6-1/2" plate size, framed, light and mat toning 700.00

Audubon, John James, *Blue Jay*, Plate CII from *Birds of America*, c1830, "J. Whatman 1936" watermark, handcolored etching, engraving, and aquatint by R. Havell, 40-1/2" x 27-3/8" 750.00

Bacon, Peggy
  Dead Wood, sgd "Peggy Bacon" in pencil lower right, titled in pencil lower left, litho on wove paper, 13-1/8" x 9-3/8", unmatted, unframed...200.00
  The Chosen Few, sgd and dated "Peggy Bacon 1972" in pencil lower left, titled in pencil lower left, litho on Arches paper with watermark, 14" x 21-7/8", unmatted, unframed 200.00

Barnet, Will
  Reflection, 1971, edition of 225, published by Circle Gallery, Ltd., Chicago, sgd "William Barnet" lower right, numbered "Ed 40/225" in pencil lower right, titled in pencil lower left, color screenprint on paper, 22" x 14-1/4" image size, framed............................300.00
  Way to Sea, edition of 300, published by Styria Studios, NY, sgd and dated "©Will Barnet 1981" lower right, numbered "18/300" in pencil lower right, titled in pencil lower left, publisher's drystamps lower center, color screenprint with lithography on paper, 40" x 30" image size, unmatted, deckled edges, subtle handling marks 320.00

Bellows, George Wesley
  Dance in a Madhouse, 1917, edition of 69, sgd "Geo Bellows E.S.B." (by artist's wife) in pencil lower right, inscribed "No. 1" in pencil lower left, identified on paper label from H. V. Allison & Co., New York on reverse, litho on paper, 18-1/2" x 24-1/2" image size, framed...5,465.00
  Solitude, 1917, edition of 60, sgd "Geo. Bellows J.B.B." (by artist's daughter) in pencil lower right, inscribed "No. 29" in pencil lower left, litho on chine collé, 17" x 15-1/2", framed.................1,840.00

Benson, Frank Weston
  Ducks at Dawn, 1920, edition of 150, pencil signed in margin, etching and drypoint, 7-1/8" x 9"...150.00
  Morning, 1915, published state, edition of 35, sgd "Frank W. Benson" in pencil lower left, numbered "9/35" in pencil lower right, initialed and dated in the plate lower left, drypoint on paper, 7-3/4" x 9-3/4" plate size, framed...635.00
  Over Sunk Marsh, 1920, published edition of 150, sgd "Frank W.

SPECIAL AUCTIONS

Phillips Fine Art Auctions
406 E. 79th St.
New York, NY 10021
(212) 570-4830

Skinner Inc.
Bolton Gallery
357 Main St.
Bolton, MA 01740

Swann Galleries, Inc.
104 E. 25th St.
New York, NY 10010

Benson" in pencil lower left, drypoint on paper, 5-7/8" x 7-7/8"
plate size, framed 490.00

Benton, Thomas Hart, litho on paper

Edge of Town, 1938, edition of 250, distributed by Associated
American Artists, sgd "Benton" in pencil lower right and in the
matrix lower left, identified on AAA label affixed to backing, 8-7/8"
x 10-5/8", framed, mat burn, deckled edges 1,380.00

Jessie James, 1936, edition of 100, distributed by Associated American Artists, pencil signed in margin, 18-7/8" x 23-5/8" 4,250.00

Night Firing, 1943, edition of 250, distributed by Associated American Artists, sgd "Benton" in pencil lower right and in the matrix
lower left, 8-3/4" x 13-1/8" image size, framed 1,495.00

Old Man Reading, 1941, edition of 250, distributed by Associated
American Artists, sgd "Benton" in pencil and in the matrix lower
right, identified on AAA label affixed to backing, litho on paper,
10" x 12-1/8" image size, framed, deckled edges on 2 sides, subtle toning 1,100.00

The Farmer's Daughter, 1944, edition of 250, distributed by Associated American Artists, sgd "Benton" in pencil lower right, 9-3/4" x
13-1/4", framed, deckled edges on 2 sides 1,495.00

Berresford, Virginia, *Block of Houses*, sgd "Virginia Berresford" in pencil lower right, titled in pencil lower left, inscribed "12" in pencil lower
right, indistinctly identified within the matrix upper right, litho on
paper, 19" x 15-1/8" image size, unmatted 400.00

Bill, G. & F., *Bird's Eye View of Mt Vernon*, 1859, repaired, fold lines,
rebacked, 13-3/8" h, 16-1/2" w, gold gilt frame 220.00

Borein, Edward, *Bronco Busting*, sgd "Edward Borein" in pencil lower
right, remarque in pencil depicting horse and rider lower left, etching
on paper, 7-7/8" x 4-5/8" plate size, framed 1,955.00

Cady, Harrison, *The Ladies of the Sideshow*, sgd "Harrison Cady" in
pencil lower right, numbered "Imp/100" in pencil lower left, etching on
paper, 10" x 12-1/2" plate size, framed 400.00

Calder, Alexander

Circus, 1974-75, edition of 125, sgd "Calder" in pencil lower right,
numbered "23/125" in pencil lower left, identified on back, color
litho on paper, 26" x 38" sheet size, framed 1,380.00

Stabiles, edition of 125, edition of 125, sgd "Calder" in pencil lower
right, numbered "4/125" in pencil lower left, identified in information affixed to backing, color litho on paper, 25-1/2" x 19-1/2"
image/sheet size, framed 1,035.00

Chagall, Marc, *Le Cirque au Clown Jaune*, 1967, edition before letters
of 150, unsigned, color litho on paper, 27-7/8" x 22" sheet size,
unmatted, prevalent creasing 575.00

Chamberlain, Samuel, *Gateway in the Ghetto-Paris*, 1930, edition of
100, sgd "Samuel Chamberlain" in pencil lower right, numbered "87/
100" in pencil lower left, etching on laid paper, 7-5/8" x 5" plate size,
matted 230.00

Cook, Howard, *Rosanna*, 1939, edition of 250, sgd "Howard Cook" in
pencil lower right, litho on paper, 11-3/4" x 8-3/4" image size, matted,
unframed 345.00

Corinth, Lovis, *Springtime*, sgd "Lovis Corinth" in pencil lower right,
color litho on paper, 11" x 9-1/8" image size, framed 300.00

Currier and Ives

Majr. Genl. William T. Sherman, hand-colored litho, matted and
framed, 13-3/4" h, 10" w, Conningham 3932, minor damage ..220.00

The First Care, hand-colored litho, matted and framed, minor damage, 18" h, 13-1/2" w, Conningham #1962 .... 165.00

Trotting Cracks in the Snow, Louis Maurer, lithographer, identified
in inscriptions in matrix, hand-colored litho, 18-3/4" x 28-1/4",
framed, Conningham, 6170 .... 1,100.00

Currier, Nathaniel

American Farm Scenes, identified in inscriptions in matrix, hand
colored litho, 19-1/2" x 26" sheet size, framed 1,265.00

Catching a Trout, 1854, after Arthur Fitzwilliam Taft, identified in
inscriptions in the matrix, hand colored litho, 20-1/4" x 254-3/4"
sheet size, framed, repaired tears, foxing, toning, Conningham
845 .... 1,150.00

The Pursuit, identified in inscriptions in the matrix, hand colored
litho, 17-5/8" x 25-3/8", framed, bottom margin trimmed, toning,
few scattered fox marks 690.00

Currier & Ives, A Home in the Wilderness, $575.

Curry, John Steuart

Hounds and Coyote, 1931, edition of 25, sgd and dated "John
Steuart Curry 1931" in pencil lower right, titled and inscribed
"…25 prints" in pencil lower left, sgd and dated in matrix, litho on
paper with "France" watermark, 10-1/8" x 14" image size, matted,
unframed, deckled edges, subtle toning, annotations and copyright stamp on reverse 980.00

Summer Afternoon, 1939, edition of 250, published by Associated
American Artists, sgd "John Steuart Curry" in pencil lower right,
initialed in matrix lower left, litho on paper, 9-7/8" x 14", framed,
mat toning 750.00

Dine, Jim

A Nurse, edition of 30 plus proofs, published by Pyramid Arts Ltd.,
Tampa, numbered, sgd, and dated "11/30 Jim Dine 1976" in pencil lower left, drystamps, lower left, identified on fragmentary label
on reverse, soft ground etching with hand coloring on paper, 23-1/
2" x 19-3/4" plate size, framed 1,955.00

Olympic Robe, 1988, edition of 300 plus proofs, numbered, sgd,
and dated "CCLXXXIV/CCC Jim Dine '88" in pencil lower right,
drystamps lower left, color litho on paper, 35" x 27" sheet size,
unmatted 1,265.00

Dürer, Albrecht

The Angel with the Key to the Bottomless Pit, from Apocalipsis
Cum Figuris, 1498/1511, monogrammed and dated in the block
lower center, woodcut on laid paper with tower and crown watermark, 15-3/8" x 11", framed 1,380.00

The Holy Family with Joachim and Anne Under A Tree, monogrammed and dated in the block upper left, identified on label on
reverse, woodcut on paper with watermark of bull's head with initials "JZ," 9-1/4" x 6-1/4" image size, framed 4,900.00

Ehrgott & Forbriger, *Ohio White Sulpher Springs*, folio chromolithograph,
margins trimmed, 23-3/4" h, 38-7/8" w, matted and framed 425.00

Erni, Hans, *Nudes and Bulls*, edition of 20, sgd "Erni" in pencil lower
right, numbered "19/20" in pencil lower left, color etching with aquatint on paper, 11" x 18-1/2" image size, framed 550.00

Estes, Richard, *Ten Doors*, 1972, edition of 75 plus proofs, published
by Parasol Press Ltd., NY, sgd "Richard Estes" in pencil lower right,
numbered "26/75" in pencil lower left, color screenprint on paper, 14-
1/2" x 21-1/4" image size, framed 1,150.00

Frankenthaler, Helen, *The Red Sea*, edition of 58 plus proofs, published by Tyler Graphics, NY, lower right, numbered "13/58" in pencil
lower left, drystamp lower right, identified on label on reverse, color
litho on pink paper, 15-1/2" x 20-3/4" image size framed 2,300.00

Gardiner, Eliza Draper

At the Shoreline, Provincetown, edition of 40, sgd and dated "Liza
Gardiner '32" in pencil lower right, numbered "21/40" in pencil
lower left, color woodcut on gray paper, 9-1/4" x 11-5/8" image
size, matted 690.00

Passaconaway Number 3, edition of 40, sgd and numbered "Eliza D. Gardiner 22/40" in pencil lower left, color woodcut on cream paper, 9-7/8" x 7-1/2" image size, matted 1,725.00

Gearhart, Frances and May Gearhart, *Patty*, sgd "The Gearharts" in pencil lower right, titled in pencil lower left, color woodcut on tissue, 7-1/4" x 6" image size, matted....................... 400.00

Hassam, Frederick Childe, *The Red Cross Girl*, 1917, edition of 41, monogrammed in pencil lower right, monogrammed, dated, and inscribed "Heroland..." in plate upper left, etching on paid paper with cursive watermark "FJH," 6-7/8" x 5" plate size, shrink wrapped 750.00

Hyde, Helen
A Child of the People, 1901, sgd "Helen Hyde" in pencil lower right, monogrammed with HH chop within image upper right, numbered "113" in pencil lower left, copyrighted within block lower left, color woodcut on tissue paper, 10-7/8" x 3-7/8" image size, matted 300.00
In Kite Time, 1903, sgd "Helen Hyde" in pencil lower left, monogrammed in plate, circular chop within image lower right, numbered "54" in pencil lower right, color etching on tissue paper, 7-1/2" x 6", matted..350.00
Moonlight on the Viga Canal, 1912, monogrammed and sgd with clover chop within image lower left, copyrighted within block upper left, color woodcut on paper, 11-7/8" x 13-7/8" image size, framed....................400.00

Icart, Louis
L'Elan, 1928, sgd "Louis Icart" in pencil lower right, identified in copyright text upper left, windmill drystamp lower left, numbered "222" in pencil lower left, color etching and aquatint with additional coloring on paper, 20" x 15" plate size, framed 1,100.00
Moquerie, sgd "Louis Icart" in pencil lower right, identified in copyright text upper left and upper right, windmill drystamp lower left, color etching and aquatint wiith additional coloring on paper, 15-7/8" x 19" plate size, framed 920.00

Katz, Alex, *Ada with Flowers*, 1981, edition of 65, sgd and numbered "Alex Katz 56/65" in pencil lower left, printer's/publisher's drystamp lower right, identified from Obelisk Gallery, Boston, label on reverse, screenprint on paper, 48" x 36 image/sheet size, framed 2,070.00

Kellogg, *My Kitten*, girl and 2 cats on bench, handcolored litho, 9-7/8" h, 14" w, framed, minor stains and edge damage 200.00

Lindenmuth, Tod, *Fog Bound*, sgd "Tod Lindenmuth" in pencil lower right, titled in pencil lower left, color woodcut on paper, 14" x 11-1/8" image size, framed 800.00

Lum, Bertha Boynten, *Asia*, 1921, sgd, dated, and copyrighted and numbered "...Bertha Lum...131" at bottom of image, color woodcut on paper, 14-1/2" x 7-3/8", matted.................... 230.00

Markham, Kyra
Bleecker St. *Fire Hydrant*, 1942, edition of 25, sgd and dated "Kyra Markham '42" in pencil lower right, titled and numbered "...Ed. 25" in pencil lower left, litho on paper, Strathmore watermark, 8-1/2" x 10-1/2" image size, unmatted 1,265.00
Ohmpeer, 1944, edition of 25, sgd and dated "Kyra Markham '44" in pencil lower right, titled and numbered "...20/25" in pencil lower left, litho on paper, 13-1/4" x 10-1/8" image size, unmatted, deckled edge to 2 sides... 865.00

Marsh, Reginald
Irving Place Burlesk, 1930, final state, Whitney impression edition of 100, Whitney Museum drystamp lower right, annotated in lower margin, etching with engraving on paper, 9-3/4" x 11-7/8" plate size, unmatted, deckled lower edge, minor toning and soiling 460.00
Minsky's New Gotham Chorus, 1936, final state, Whitney impression edition of 100, initialed and dated in the plate lower right, Whitney Museum drystamps lower left, numbered "54/100" in pencil lower left, etching on paper, 8-7/8" x 11-7/8", unmatted..................... 660.00
Tenth Avenue at 27th St., 1931, sgd in pencil (posthumously) lower right and in the plate lower right, etching on paper, 7-7/8" x 10-7/8" plate size, framed... 635.00

Matisse, Henri, *La Robe D'Organdi*, 1922, edition of 50 plus proofs, sgd and numbered "Henri Matisse 41/50" in ink lower left, litho on paper, 16-3/4" x 10-7/8" image size, framed.................. 16,100.00

Parrish, Maxfield, *The Dinky Bird*, Schribner 265.00

Pennell, Joseph
New York Nocturne, sgd "J. Pennell imp" in pencil lower right, identified on fragmentary label from Frederick Kappel and Company, New York, affixed to reverse, mezzotint on paper, 13" x 9-7/8" plate size, framed, laid down between mats 1,725.00
Rouen From Bon Secours, 1907, sgd "J. Pennell imp" in pencil lower right, label from Doll and Richards, Boston, affixed to reverse, etching on paper, 7-3/4" x 12" plate size, framed . 230.00
The Eads Bridge, St. Louis, 1919, sgd "J. Pennell imp" in pencil lower right, identified on label on reverse, etching on paper, 9-3/4" x 11-3/4" plate size, framed, unobtrusive soiling and staining . 230.00

Ripley, Aiden :Lassell
Turkey Drive, sgd "A. Lassell Ripley" in pencil lower right, titled in pencil lower left, etching on paper, 8-7/8" x 11-3/4" plate size, framed.. 1,150.00
Wild Turkeys, sgd "A. Lassell Ripley" in pencil lower right, titled in pencil lower left, etching on paper, 11-1/4" x 9-1/2" plate size, framed.. 690.00

Rosenquist, James
Untitled, edition of 200, sgd "James Rosenquist" in pencil lower right, numbered "17/200" in pencil lower left, identified on label from Gimpel, New York, on reverse, color photo-lithograph on paper, 35" x 26-3/8" image size, framed 490.00
Waco Texas, edition of 225, sgd "James Rosenquist" in pencil lower right, numbered "40/225" in pencil lower left, color photo-lithograph on paper, 16-3/4" x 21-7/8" image/sheet size 260.00

Roth, Ernest David, *From Pier 5*, Coenties Slip, Manhattan, 1937, sgd "Ernest D. Roth K.K.H." in pencil lower right, sgd, dated, and titled in the plate lower left, etching on paper, 11-7/8" x 10-7/8" plate size, matted 230.00

Sarony & Co., NY, *Capitol of Ohio*, handcolored litho, minor stains, professional restoration, 16-3/8" h, 20-3/4" w, matted and framed 475.00

Senseney, George, *The Path Near The River*, 1917, sgd "Senseny" in pencil lower left, numbered "No. 29" in pencil lower left, dated and copyrighted below the plate, color aquatint on paper, 11-3/4" x 9-1/4" plate size 800.00

Soyer, Raphael
Immigrants, edition of 150, sgd "Raphael Soyer" in pencil lower right, numbered "62/150" in pencil lower left, litho on paper, 16" x 15-1/4" image size, framed.. 230.00
The Model, edition of 250, published by Associated American Artists, sgd "Raphael Soyer" in pencil lower right, titled in pencil lower left, identified on label from AAA on the reverse, litho on paper, 11-3/4" x 7-3/4", framed 525.00

Tobey, Mark, *Head*, edition of 150, sgd and dated "Tobey 1967" in pencil lower right, numbered "68/150" in pencil lower left, color litho on paper, 7-7/8" x 6" image size, framed 635.00

Toulouse-Lautrec, Henri, *Proces Arton, Deposition Ribot*, 1896, edition of 100, monogrammed and dated in the matrix, publisher's drystamp lower left, identified on label on reverse, litho on paper, 16-3/4" x 22-1/2", framed, subtle toning 2,100.00

Vicente, Esteban, *Chiva*, edition of 82, sgd "Esteban Vicente" in pencil lower right, titled in pencil lower center, numbered "33/82" in pencil lower left, color screenprint on paper, 29" x 37-1/2" imag size, framed ..300.00

Warhol, Andy, image from *Ladies and Gentleman*, 1975, edition of 125 plus proofs, printed by Alexander Heinrici, NY, published by Luciano Anselmnio, Milan, numbered and dated "101/125 Andy Warhol 75 @ A. W. E." in pencil on reverse, color screenprint on Arches paper, 35-3/8" x 26-1/4" image size, matted, pale foxing unobtrusive soiling, handling creases 700.00

Wengenroth, Stow
Railroad Cut, 1947, edition of 25, sgd "Stow Wengenroth" in pencil lower right, numbered "Ed/25" in pencil lower left, litho on paper, 9-3/4" x 15-1/4" image size, unmatted.............................. 635.00
Sunlit Dunes, 1951, edition of 60, sgd "Stow Wengenroth" in pencil lower right, numbered "Ed/60" in pencil lower left, litho on paper, 11-1/4" x 17-4/5", framed 375.00

Whitehead, Buell, *Three Brothers*, sgd and dated "Buell Whitehead 1946" in pencil lower right, titled in pencil lower left, color litho on paper, 13" x 17-3/8" image size, unmatted 175.00

Whistler, James Abbott McNeill

Drouet, sgd and dated "Whistler 1859" in the plate lower right, inscribed "Drouet Sculpteur" in the plate lower center, etching on paper, 8-7/8" x 5-7/8" plate size, framed 1,150.00

Thames Warehouses, sgd and dated "Whistler 1859" in the plate lower right, etching on paper, 3" x 8" plate size, framed .. 1,100.00

Wilson, John, *The Passing Scene*, sgd and dated "John Wilson 1945" in pencil lower right, titled in pencil lower left, litho on paper with watermark "LES BIBLIOPHILES," 11-1/4" x 14-3/4' image size, m atted 4,025.00

Wood, Grant

Fertility, 1939, distributed by Associated American Artists, sgd "Grant Wood" in pencil lower right, identified on label affixed to backing, litho on paper, 8-7/8" x 11-7/8" image size, framed 4,600.00

March, 1941, edition of 250, published by Associated American Artists, sgd "Grant Wood" in pencil lower right, identified on AAA label affixed to backing, litho on paper, 8-7/8" x 11-3/4" image size, framed 4,320.00

Zorn, Anders, *Ols Maria*, 1919, sgd "Zorn" in pencil lower right, sgd and dated in plate lower right, identified on label on reverse, etching on paper, 7-3/4" x 11-5/8" plate size, framed 800.00

PRINTS, JAPANESE

History: Buying Japanese woodblock prints requires attention to detail and abundant knowledge of the subject. The quality of the impression (good, moderate, or weak), the color, and condition are critical. Various states and strikes of the same print cause prices to fluctuate. Knowing the proper publisher and censor's seals is helpful in identifying an original print.

Most prints were copied and issued in popular versions. These represent the vast majority of the prints found in the marketplace today. These popular versions should be viewed solely as decorative since they have little monetary value.

A novice buyer should seek expert advice before buying. Talk with a specialized dealer, museum curator, or auction division head.

The following terms are used to describe sizes: chuban, 7-1/2" x 10" inches; hosoban, 6" x 12" inches; and oban, 10" x 15" inches. Tat-e is a vertical print; yoko-e a horizontal one.

Reference: Sandra Andacht, *Collector's Value Guide to Japanese Woodblock Prints*, Antique Trader Books, 1999.

Collectors' Club: Ukiyo-E Society of America, Inc., FDR Station, P.O. Box 665, New York, NY 10150.

Periodical: *Orientalia Journal*, P.O. Box 94, Flushing, NY 11363-0094, http://members.aol.com/Orientalia/index.html.

Museum: Honolulu Academy of Fine Arts, Honolulu, HI.

Note: The listings below include the large amount of detail necessary to determine value. Condition and impression are good unless indicated otherwise.

Album

Toyokuni III, Kuniyoshi, Hiroshige, mostly from series Ogura Imitations of the One Hundred Poets and Keniyshi Genji 2,645.00

Utamaro, Tokoyuni, Koyomine, Eizan, and Kuniyosu, 18 prints of women, trimmed, toned, some stains and wear 2,300.00

Chikanobu, framed triptych of women by lake, c1890, good impression, somewhat faded 125.00

Eishi, four courtesans in elaborate kimonos, 1790s, framed, good impression, somewhat faded 345.00

Eizan, Kikugawa, Bijin, color woodcut, Kakemono-e 350.00

Hiroshinge, people walking over bridge, fisherman below, 4-1/2" x 9-1/2", $250.

Harunobu, pillar print of woman carrying bucket, framed, very good impression, horizontal creases and tears................................. 345.00

Hasui, Kawase Bunjiro, woodblock

Chii Mountain Temple, 1940, oban tate 285.00

Mountainous landscape seen from inside room, matted and framed, 10" x 14"... 850.00

Rainy Night at Mekawa, 1932, oban tate............................... 300.00

Shinagawa, 1931, color woodcut, oban tate......................... 200.00

Zentsu Temple in Sanshu District, 1937, color woodcut, oban tate... 175.00

Hiroshige

Scene of small temple, from Edo Meisho series, framed, moderate impression and color, soiled 500.00

The Ferry on the Tenryn River near Mitsuke, from Upright Tokaido, Meiji printing, framed, good color....................................... 90.00

The Outer Bay at Choshi Beach in Simosa Province, from Sixty Odd Provinces series, good impression and color, some stains 230.00

Triptych of 3 women, each with umbrella in snowy landscape, c1850, framed.. 750.00

Hiroshige II, Mimeguiri Embankment and the Sumida River, from "Toto Meisho," 1862, good impression, fine color 350.00

Hiroshi Yoshida, evening street scene, sgd, Hiroshi seal, 14-1/2" x 19-1/2".. 270.00

Hokusai, In The Totomi Mountains, from Thirty-Six Views of Fuji, aizuri printing with blue outline, modern impression, wrinkled, torn, stains 1,610.00

Hui, Wang, attributed to, extensive landscape with figures, ink and color on silk, 52-1/2" x 22" 450.00
Junichiro Sekino, portrait of actor Kichiemon, "il ne etat," printed signature and seal lower right within the image, pencil sgd, 13/50 in lower margin, 22" x 18" 920.00
Kawamishi, the Water Lily Season, sgd and titled in pencil, dated, numbered, framed 425.00
Kunihisa, portrait of actor carrying bucket and broom over his shoulder, c1800 .... 425.00
Kunisada, courtesan and two kamuro, landscape in background, printed in blue, c1830, good impression and color 215.00
Kuniyoshi, Beauty with Small Dog, 13-7/8" x 9-5/8" 125.00
Okiie Hashimoto, Village in the Evening, sgd in pencil in margin, dated, Hashi seal, good impression, framed, 17 x 21-1/2" 250.00
Sekino, bridge in snow, sgd in image, seal, good impression, 18" x 12-1/2" 200.00
Shigenobu, surimono of courtesan in an interior, make-up table and mirror to left, fine impression and color 634.00
Toyokuni II, Kakemono-e portrait of monk peering under blanket on his head, bamboo flute in land, framed, very good impression, somewhat faded 230.00
Toyokuni III
Pentaptcyh of people in boat feeding goldfish, iris garden, framed, very good impression, missing leaf, somewhat faded 230.00
Two actors in roles, framed, very good impression and color, slight damage to bottom 115.00
Utamaro II, 3 women in an interior, c1811, good impression, faded, soiled 175.00
Yoshida, Hiroshi, color woodblock, matted and framed
Chionin Temple Gate, people climbing stairs in front of gate, flanked by blossoming apple trees, matted and sgd, printed calligraphy and chop marks, pencil titled and sgd, some foxing, 9-1/2" h, 14-3/4" w 600.00
Hirasaki castle, blooming apple trees in front of Japanese castle, matted and framed, printed calligraphy and chop marks, pencil titled and sgd, 14-3/4" h, 9-1/2" w 550.00
In A Temple Yard, figures by pond reflecting temple and cherry blossoms, printed cipher title and chop marks, pencil titled and sgd, 9-1/2" h, 14-3/4" w 450.00
Pagoda and trees reflected in pond, printed cipher title and chop marks, pencil titled and sgd, title partially obscured, 9-1/2" h, 14-3/4" w 700.00
Sarusawa Pond, 2 temples reflected in pond, matted and framed, mat obscuring side edges of print, printed chop mark, pencil titled and sgd, 9-1/2" h, 14-3/4" w 475.00
The Cherry Tree in Kawagae, figures by shrine under cherry tree, printed cipher title and chop marks, pencil titled and sgd, 9-1/2" h, 14-3/4" w 450.00

PURPLE SLAG (MARBLE GLASS)

History: Challinor, Taylor & Co., Tarantum, Pennsylvania, c1870s-1880s, was the largest producer of purple slag in the United States. Since the quality of pieces varies considerably, there is no doubt other American firms made it as well.

Purple slag also was made in England. English pieces are marked with British Registry marks. Other slag colors, such as blue, green, and orange, were used, but examples are rare.

Videotape: National Imperial Glass Collectors Society, *Glass of Yesteryears*, The Renaissance of Slag Glass by Imperial, RoCliff Communications, 1994.

Additional Listings: Greentown Glass (chocolate slag); Pink Slag.

Reproduction Alert: Purple slag has been heavily reproduced over the years and still is reproduced at present.

Animal Dish, covered, lion, lacy base 245.00
Ashtray, 6" sq, chocolate slag, Imperial IG mark 25.00
Bowl, 9" d, Rose, caramel slag, Imperial IG mark 45.00
Compote, cov, eagle finial 185.00
Compote, open, 4" h, 6" w, ruffled, hobnail, yellow, Kanawha 15.00
Creamer, Flwoer and Panel 85.00
Goblet, Flute 32.00
Match Holder, Daisy and Button 42.00
Nappy, 5" d, Floral, caramel slag, ring handle, Imperial IG mark .. 30.00
Plate, 10-1/2" d, closed lattice edge 60.00
Punch Cup, 3" h, light purple and white, open loop handle ending with small ball, Imperial 75.00
Spooner, Swan and Cattails, blue and brown swirl 90.00
Sugar, cov, Flute 175.00
Swan, 9-1/2" l, Imperial IG mark, orig sticker 125.00
Toothpick, Inverted Fan and Feather 65.00

PUZZLES

History: The jigsaw puzzle originated in the mid-18th century in Europe. John Spilsbury, a London map maker, was selling dissected-map jigsaw puzzles by the early 1760s. The first jigsaw puzzles in America were English and European imports aimed primarily at children.

Prior to the Civil War, several manufacturers, e.g., Samuel L. Hill, W. and S. B. Ives, and McLoughlin Brothers, included puzzles in their lines. However, it was the post-Civil War period that saw the jigsaw puzzle gain a strong foothold among the children of America.

In the late 1890s, puzzles designed specifically for adults first appeared. Both forms—adult and child—have existed side by side ever since. Adult puzzlers were responsible for two 20th-century puzzle crazes: 1908-1909 and 1932-1933.

Prior to the mid-1920s, the vast majority of jigsaw puzzles were cut out of wood for the adult market and composition material for the children's market. In the 1920s, the die-cut, cardboard jigsaw puzzle evolved and was the dominant medium in the 1930s.

Interest in jigsaw puzzles has cycled between peaks and valleys several times since 1933. Mini-revivals occurred during World War II and in the mid-1960s when Springbok entered the American market. Internet auction sites are impacting the pricing of puzzles, raising some (Pars, Pastimes, U-Nits, figure pieces) but holding the line or even reducing others (Straus, Victory, strip cut). As with all auctions, final prices tend to vary depending upon the time of yea and the activity of at least two interested bidders.

References: *Dexterity Games and Other Hand-Held Puzzles*, L-W Book Sales, 1995; Jack Matthews, *Toys Go to War*, Pictorial Histories Publishing, 1994; Chris McCann, Master Pieces, *The Art History of Jigsaw Puzzles*, The Collectors Press, 1998; Jerry Slocum and Jack Botermans, *Book of Ingenious & Diabolical Puzzles*, Time Books, 1994.

Collectors' Clubs: American Game Collectors Association., P.O. Box 44, Dresher, PA 19025.

Advisor: Bob Armstrong.

Note: Prices listed here are for puzzles which are complete or restored, and in good condition. Most puzzles found in attics do not meet these standards. If evaluating an old puzzle, a discount of 50% should be calculated for moderate damage (1-2 missing pieces, 3-4 broken knobs,) with greater discounts for major damage or missing original box.

Cardboard, Pre-1950

Lutz & Sheinkman, Snow Sleighing, artist Pruch, 14-1/2" x 18-1/2", 450 pcs, diecut, orig box, 1933, 13 figures 15.00
Milton Bradley/Big Ben, Along the Canal Bank, Flemish town, 26" x 20-1/4", 1,000 pcs, diecut, orig box 10.00
Tuco/Deluxe
    Signing the Constitution, artist Howard Chandler Christy, 19-1/4" x 15", 357 pcs, diecut, orig box 15.00
    When Seconds Count, fishing, 19-1/2" x 15-1/2", 357 pcs, diecut, crooked line stripe, orig box, 1940s 15.00
University Dist. Co./Jig Deluxe, Woman Peeling Apples, Goose Girl, 15-3/4" x 20-3/4", 500 pcs, diecut, sq knob stripe, interlocking, orig box, 1930s, 5 figures 25.00

Wood and/or Handcut, Pre-1930

Globe Puzzle Co., An Interesting Passage, Cardinal studying book with assistant, solid wood, 4-3/4" x 6-1/4", 50 pcs, orig box, push-fit, c1909, 1 pc replaced 20.00
Holabird Co./Silhouette, George Washington, c1909, plywood, 6" x 6-1/2", 26 pcs, push-fit, color line cutting, envelope, silhouette cut, reversible 35.00
Lowell, Abner/Lowlecrest, The Broken Doll, children and dog, plywood, 9" x 12-1/2", 206 pcs, angular, semi-interlocking, orig box, c1920 ...... 60.00
Parker Bros./Pastime, plywood
    Evening Mail, coaching, 17-3/4" x 11-1/2", 350 pcs, curve knob, color line cutting, semi-interlocking, 1930s, replaced box, 42 figures 140.00
    Spring Plowing, 6-3/4" x 13-3/4", 172 pcs, jagged, color line cutting,replaced box, 1910-20, 4 pcs replaced 65.00
    The Sisters, 11-3/4" x 17-1/4", 300 pcs, curl knob, push-fit, color line cutting, semi-interlocking, 1910s, replaced box, 30 figures 125.00
    The Village Festival, artist Sir Wilkie, 20" x 15", 400 pcs, curl knob, color line cutting, semi-interlocking, orig box, 53 figures, sawed by #14, 1 pc replaced 160.00
Pond, Mabel E., Patchwork Quilt, solid wood, 4-3/4' x 7-1/2", 74 pcs, push-fit, color line cutting, orig box, c1909 ...... 30.00
Ullman Mfg/Society, Christmas Eve, thick solid wood, 7-1/2" x 5-3/4", 75 pcs, orig box, c1909 ...... 30.00
Unknown Maker
    The Falconer, plywood, 6-1/4" x 9-1/2", 150 pcs, orig box, sq knob, push-fit, color line cutting, edge-interlocking, 1910-20, 2 pcs replaced 35.00
    Untitled, Christmas When American Was Young, solid wood, 14-1/4" x 8-3/4", 248 pcs, replaced box, push-fit, color line cutting,22 figures, artist J. L. G. Ferris, 1 pc replaced 100.00
    Untitled, old warship docking in port, plywood, 16-1/2" x 11", 197 pcs, push-fit, color line cutting, orig box, 5 figures 60.00
    Washington's Darkest Hour, Martha comforting George, artist J. L. G. Ferris, solid wood, 9-1/4" x 13", 211 pcs, replaced box, push-fit, color line cutting,c1909, 3 pcs replaced 80.00

Wood and/or Handcut, 1930s-40s, all plywood

Allen, John E., Mother's House by Brook, artist F. Tharlow, 13" x 9-3/4", 151 pcs, semi-color line cutting, interlocking, elongated cut, several figures, orig box, 1933 ...... 40.00
Bee-Cee/Busy Hour, Noonday Rest, 11-1/2" x 8-3/4", 200 pcs, interlocking, orig box, 8 figures, 2 pcs replaced 60.00
Bloomingdales, Floral Cottage, 12" x 9", 315 pcs, re knob, push-fit, color line cutting, semi-interlocking, orig box, 3 figures, 2 pcs replaced 100.00
Brenneman's Pharmacy, Ships at Sea, 21-1/2" x 13-3/4", 519 pcs, scroll, interlocking, orig box, 1 pc replaced, ex-lending library . 140.00
Davis, Calra/Interlochen, Colonial Sweetheart, 16" x 20", 494 pcs, interlocking, orig box, 1 pc replaced 110.00

Gleason, H. A./Cheerio, Eyes that Speak, dogs, 12-3/4" x 16", 330 pcs, color line cutting, interlocking, orig box, 10 figures. 3 pcs replaced 90.00
Hadley, Leon F., Palisades, artist F. Walker, 22" x 14", 782 pcs, interlocking, orig box, 1 pc replaced 160.00
Hammond, Leisure Hour, The Love Song, 6" x 8", 100 pcs, scroll, interlocking, orig box 25.00
Hayter/Victory/Super-Cut, The Conference, 18th C drawing room scene, 23-1/2" x 17-1/2", 800 pcs, round knob, color line cutting, interlocking, orig box, 60 figures, scalloped edges 300.00
Ken-Way Puzzle, Preparedness, bears, canoeing, artist Philip R. Goodwin, 14-1/2" x 10-3/4", 284 pcs, orig box, 1 pc replaced . 100.00
Madmar/Interlox
    First Tap of the Bell, artist J. L. G. Ferris, 12" x 9", 200 pcs, orig box, 4 pcs replaced 45.00
    Once in a Lovely Garden, artist Van Nortwick, 10" x 12-1/4", 250 pcs, orig box, 1 pc replaced 65.00
    The Squire's Story, 18th C drawing room, 18-1/2" x 15-1/2", 500 pcs, interlocking, orig box 120.00
    Valley of the Daffodils, 16-1/2" x 12", 400 pcs, scroll, interlocking, orig box 100.00
Madmar/Jig-Sawed, Stuart Painting Washington Portrait, 10" x 8", 158 pcs, orig box 35.00
Milton Bradley, Avenue of Trees, 15-3/4" x 11-3/4", 331 pcs, color line cutting, interlocking, orig box, 25 figures, sawed by #71, 1 pc replaced 100.00
Parker Bros./Pastime, Back from the Chase, artist Strachan, 22-1/4" x 15-3/4", 545 pcs, 1930-40, orig box, 64 figures, sawed by #756, 1 pc replaced 250.00
Par Co., High Noon, artist Ballendank, 18-1/2" x 13", 500 pcs, earlet, semi-color line cutting, interlocking, orig box, 2 seahorses, 1930-40 ...... 350.00
Parker Bros./Picture Puzzle Exchange, An Old English Cottage, 10" x 13-1/2", 255 pcs, curve knob, color line cutting ,interlocking, orig box, 30 figures 100.00
Parker, Frederick/Imperial, Unloading the Catch, artist Stuart Floyd, 18" x 10-3/4", 300 pcs, color line cutting, semi-interlocking, orig box, 31 figures, 2 pcs replaced 95.00
Robie, Douglas/Drocar, The Valley of Peace, 7-3/4" x 9-3/4", 168 pcs, push-fit, color line cutting, orig box, 1 pc replaced 40.00
S & H Novelty/Spare Time, The Last Load, winter farming sunset scene, 10" x 8", 150 pcs, sq knob, interlocking, orig box, 5 figures 40.00
Schwartz/Selected Pictures, Switzerland-Tis Paround onable to Envy the Swiss, 14-1/4" x 10-1/2", 200 pcs, interlocking, orig box, 11 figures 40.00
Straus, Joseph, Good Walk Everbody, 10" x 7", 150 pcs, knobby, interlocking, orig box, unusually tight cut, 1 pc replaced 25.00
Stoughton Studios/Tiz-A-Teeze, Ann Hathaway's Cottage, 11-3/4" x 10", 250 pcs, round and angular knob, interlocking, orig box, sawed by #4 ...... 60.00
Tri-Ply Wood Puzzle, Cozy Evening in Olden Days, 10" x 7", 137 pcs, sq knob, interlocking, orig box, 10 figures, sawed by #14 ...... 50.00
Tuck/Zag-Zaw
    A Rural Post Office, 19-3/4" x 15", 520 pcs, earlet, interlocking, orig box, 50 figures, 1 pc replaced 200.00
    The Colonel's Story, 15-1/2" x 11-3/4", 320 pcs, earlet, interlocking, orig box, 36 figures 115.00
Unknown Maker
    A Mariner in the Making, artist Hintermeister, 7" x 9-1/2", 197 pcs, replaced box, scalloped edges, loose cut 50.00
    Around the Bend in Shelburne, 10" x 7", 140 pcs, round knob edge, color line cutting, edge-link, orig box, push-fit color line cutting center, artist photo 30.00
    Don't Lose Him Dad, fishing, 15" x 12", 513 pcs, orig box, small pcs 100.00
    Hunting dog with bird , 14-3/4" x 12", 286 pcs, sq knob, color line cutting, orig box, 12 figures 100.00
    Nature's Wonderland, 6" x 8-3/4", 141 pcs, replaced box, loose cut 30.00
    Rounding the Cape, clipper ship, 10" x 12", 302 pcs, color line cutting, replaced box 90.00

Untitled, winter farm scene, 11-3/4" x 8-1/4", 266 pcs, semi-color line cutting, replaced box, 3 pcs replaced............................45.00

Venetian Canal, artist G. Boucart, 15-3/4" x 11-3/4", 450 pcs, color line cutting, interlocking, orig box...130.00

Wayside Inn, Sudbury, winter scene, artist N. Briganti, 14-1/4" x 10-1/2", 225 pcs, semi-interlocking, replaced box 50.00

Wenlock Christison Defying Court, artist F. C. Yomn, 10" x 7", 161 pcs, round knob, semi-color line cutting, orig box, trick edges, 1 pc replaced 40.00

Vandersloot, Carl/Vandee, Spring Unlocks Her Flowers, 12" x 16", 375 pcs, color line cutting, interlocking, orig box, 7 figures, 2 pcs replaced.. 120.00

Wood and/or Handcut, Post-1950, all plywood

Atlantic/Kingsbridge, Coaching Scene, artist L. Cow, 15-1/2" x 11-1/2", 360 pcs, round knob stripe, interlocking, orig box 45.00

Browning, James/U-Nit

The Boughs are Murmuring, 15-3/4" x 19-3/4", 500 pcs, earlet, interlocking, orig box, 50 figures, mahogany back..............175.00

The Water Carrier, 11-3/4" x 15-3/4", 300 pcs, random knob, jagged, interlocking, orig box, 42 figures, mahogany back, 2 pcs replaced 100.00

Glencraft, Strawberries, 13" x 8-1/2", 199 pcs, round knob strip, interlocking, orig box, 1 pc replaced...25.00

Hayter/Victory

Coronation of Queen Elizabeth, 9-3/4" x 7-1/2", 125 pcs, round knob stripe, interlocking, orig box 30.00

The Stirrup Cup, artist L. Carr Cox, 15-3/4" x 11-3/4", 350 pcs, round knob stripe, interlocking, orig box 50.00

Imbrie Mfg/Wastetime, A New England Landmark, winter scene, 8" x 10", 83 pcs, angular, semi-color line cutting, interlocking, orig box.........20.00

Straus, Joseph

Green Lake, 27-3/4" x 21-1/2", 1,000 pcs, round knob strip, orig box, 12 figures 120.00

Strike, Yellowstone fishing scene, 27-3/4" x 21-3/4", 1,000 pcs, round knob strip, interlocking, orig box, 11 figures..............140.00

The Land Beyond, 27-1/2" x 12-3/4", 1,000 pcs, round knob strip, orig box, 10 figures 130.00

Vera/Apollo, Fritillaries dans un vase de cuivre, flowers, artist Vincent Van Gogh, 9-1/2" x 10-3/4", 350 pcs, push-fit, color line cutting, edge-interlocking, orig box 100.00

QUEZAL

History: The Quezal Art Glass Decorating Company, named for the quetzal—a bird with brilliantly colored feathers—was organized in 1901 in Brooklyn, New York, by Martin Bach and Thomas Johnson, two disgruntled Tiffany workers. They soon hired Percy Britton and William Wiedebine, two more Tiffany employees.

The first products, which are unmarked, were exact Tiffany imitations. Quezal pieces differ from Tiffany pieces in that they are more defined and the decorations are more visible and brighter. No new techniques were developed by Quezal.

Johnson left in 1905. T. Conrad Vahlsing, Bach's son-in-law, joined the firm in 1918 but left with Paul Frank in 1920 to form Lustre Art Glass Company, which copied Quezal pieces. Martin Bach died in 1924 and by 1925 Quezal had ceased operations.

Marks: The "Quezal" trademark was first used in 1902 and was placed on the base of vases and bowls and on the rims of shades. The acid-etched or engraved letters vary in size and may be found in amber, black, or gold. A printed label which includes an illustration of a quetzal was used briefly in 1907.

Bowl, 9-1/2" d, gold calcite ground, stretch rim, pedestal foot, sgd "Quezal" 800.00
Cabinet Vase, 3" h, slight ribbing, bulbous base, flared neck, amber, strong allover gold irid, sgd "Quezal I 866" within polished pontil ..690.00
Candlesticks, pr, 7-3/4" h, irid blue, sgd 575.00
Chandelier, gilt metal
    14" h, 4 elaborated scroll arms, closed teardrop gold, green, and opal shades, inscribed "Quezal" at collet rim, very minor roughness at rim edge 2,000.00
    16" h, 3 shouldered flared opal shades, rib molded design, gold irid int., collet rim inscribed "Quezal," classic shaped socket, wheel with chain drop 450.00
Cologne Bottle, 7-1/2" h, irid gold ground, Art Deco design, sgd "Q" and "Melba" 250.00
Desk Lamp, 19" h, 10-1/2" d shade, heavy walled half-round opal glass

shade, lined with brilliant irid gold, ext. glossy surface with 5 broad pulled feather repeats, sgd "Quezal" on inside top rim, bronze three-arm spider mounting on black base with overlapping foliate devices, minor nicks to top rim 1,725.00
Lamp Shade, 5-1/4" h, 2-1/8" outside rim, bell form, gold irid, ribbed, green and white pulled feather design, inscribed "Quezal" on rim, price for pr 345.00
Toothpick Holder, 2-1/4" h, melon ribbed, pinched sides, irid blue, green, purple and gold, sgd 200.00
Vase
    4-5/8 h, double dec opal body, hooked and pulled gold feathers below green hooked elements, medial gold band, gold irid surface above and within flared rim, base inscribed "Quezal 490" . 2,070.00
    4-3/4 h, cased cylinder, five pointed gold irid feathers on opal white body, flared golden foot inscribed "Quezal" on base........... 575.00
    5" h, lily, pinched quatraform rim, slender transparent golden bud vase, five subtle green spiked feathers, large partial label covers pontil, "Art Quezal - rooklyn" 1,035.00
    7-3-4" h, 9-1/2" d, large flared bulbous ambergris body cased to opal, dec with green pulled and coiled feathers obscured by lavish overall gold irid, inscribed "Quezal C357" on base 5,175.00
    9" h, ovoid, green, raised gold irid neck, allover pulled gold luster leaves, brilliant irid, sgd "Quezal" within polished pontil .. 4,600.00
Whiskey Taster, 2-3/4" h, oval, gold irid, 4 pinched dimples, sgd "Quezal" on base.. 200.00

QUILTS

History: Quilts have been passed down as family heirlooms for many generations. Each one is unique. The same pattern may have hundreds of variations in both color and design.

The advent of the sewing machine increased, not decreased, the number of quilts which were made. Quilts are still being sewn today.

References: Cuesta Benberry, *Always There: The African-American Presence in American Quilts*, Kentucky Quilt Project, 1992; Kathryn Berenson, *Quilts of Provence*, Thames and Hudson, 1996; Mary Clare Clark, *Collectible Quilts*, Running Press, Courage Books, 1994; Anne Gilbert, *Instant Expert: Collecting Quilts*, Alliance Publishing, 1996; Liz Greenbacker and Kathleen Barach, *Quilts*, Avon Books, 1992; Carter Houck, *Quilt Encyclopedia Illustrated*, Harry N. Abrams and Museum of American Folk Art, 1991; Donald B. Kraybill, Patricia T. Herr, Jonathon Holstein, *A Quiet Spirit: Amish Quilts from the Collection of Cindy Tietze & Stuart Hodosh*, UCLA Fowler Museum of Cultural History (405 Hilgard Ave., Los Angeles, CA 90024); Elizabeth Kurella, *The Complete Guide To Vintage Textiles*, Krause Publications, 1999; Jeanette Lasansky et. al., *On the Cutting Edge*, Oral Traditions Project, 1994; Patsy and Myron Orlofsky, *Quilts in America*, Abbeville Press, 1992; Nancy and Donald Roan, *Lest I Shall be Forgotten*, Goschenhoppen Historians, Inc. (P.O. Box 476, Green Lane, PA 18054), 1993; Robert Shaw, *The Art Quilt*, Hugh Lauter Levin Associates, Inc., 1997; Shelly Zegart, *American Quilt Collections/Antique Quilt Masterpieces*, Nihon Vogue Ltd., 1996.

Periodicals: *Quilt Journal*, 635 W. Main St., Louisville, KY 40202; *Quilters Newsletter*, P.O. Box 4101, Golden, CO 80401; Vintage Quilt Newsletter, 1305 Morphy St., Great Bend, KS 67530.

Collectors' Clubs: American Quilt Study Group, 660 Mission St., Ste. 400, San Francisco, CA 94105; American

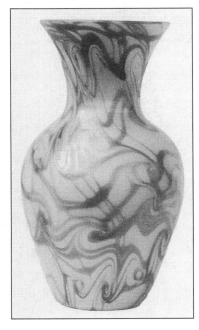

Vase, iridescent yellow with blue swirls, 7-1/4" h, $1,100. Photo courtesy of Garth's Auctions.

Quilter's Society, P.O. Box 3290, Paducah, KY 42001; National Quilting Assoc, Inc., P.O. Box 393, Ellicott City, MD 21043; Textile Group of Los Angeles, Inc., 894 S. Bronson Ave., Los Angeles CA 9005-3605.

Museums: Colonial Williamsburg Foundation, Colonial Williamsburg, VA; Doll & Quilts Barn, Rocky Ridge, MD; Museum of the American Quilter's Society, Paducah, KY; National Museum of American History, Washington, DC; New England Quilt Museum, Lowell, MA.

Notes: The key considerations for price are age, condition, aesthetic appeal, and design. Prices are now level, although the very finest examples continue to bring record prices.

Appliqué

Flower Basket
76-3/4" x 77", alternating squares of flower baskets with roses and looping geometric designs, surrounded by geometric and rose with leaf border, sky blue baskets, pink roses, dark green leaves, embroidered yellow flower centers, satin, heavily quilted ivory background, 20th C, some staining 700.00
79" x 66-1/2", baskets, birds, oak leaves, central floral medallion, red and white cotton, corner scroll and heart pendant devices, diamond pattern quilting, America, late 19th C, staining..... 400.00
87-1/2" x 89", sixteen baskets, with vining floral border, red, green, and goldenrod, some wear and stains 850.00
Floral Medallions, 82" x 90", pastel pink, green, and yellow, swag border, minor stains 415.00
Oak Leaf, 74" x 88", olive green printed fabric leaves, crimson printed fabric centers, stylized quarter moon border, PA, mid 19th C, minor stains 650.00
Pomegranate and Blossom, 80" sq, red, yellow, pink, and green patches, pierced and reverse appliquéd, white cotton ground, Arthur Schuman, Berne, Berks County, PA, late 19th C, top only 460.00
Rose of Sharon, 67-1/2" x 82-1/2", stylized floral medallions, pink calico, solid red and teal green calico, trapunto wreaths in center, edges frayed, greens faded 760.00
Stylized floral medallions, 74-1/2" x 76", nine medallions, vining border, red, pink, and green, minor wear 965.00
Tulip, 76" sq, ivory cotton squares, vivid red and gold tulips, green stems, each sq has 4 tulips radiating from center point, banded green border 900.00

Stars, red, green, and yellow, Berks County, PA, 19th C, $800.

Crazy, 72" x 74, pieced velvet, black, burgundy, purple, red, gold, gray, green, and brown solid and printed shaped patches, arranged in 16 squares, colorful velvet border, late 19th C 885.00

Pieced

Broken Star, 80" x 76", orange, yellow, green, red, brown, blue, and white printed calico patches, red and white calico Flying Geese border, PA, 19th C 460.00
Chinese Lanterns, 82" x 84", green, red, blue, yellow, and white printed calico and solid patches, blue and white ground, red border, diamond and rope quilting, PA, late 19th C, minor staining 1,495.00
Cobweb, 104" x 84", multicolored printed calico triangular patches, yellow, red, and green banded borders, inscribed "A Present from Grandmother, Mary Elizabeth Weider, to Charles Joel Weider, 1886," verso of Nine Patch pattern calico patches 750.00
Compass Star, 88" x 86", red, green, yellow, white, and pink calico patches, reverse triangle border, PA, 19th C 690.00
Courthouse Steps, 74" x 73", red, pink, brown, blue, green, and peach printed calico bars and patches, diagonal patch border, PA, late 19th C 920.00
Diamond and Chain, 85" x 85", blue, green, and pink calico with white, green, and calico machine sewn binding, white homespun back, Mennonite, stains 825.00
Diamond in Square Medallions, 70" x 96", teal green and goldenrod on white, pink calico ground, green calico border stripes, white homespun back, Mennonite 550.00
Embroidered, 102" x 110"blue and green florals on white squares, dark blue grid, pastel blue scalloped border, 20th C 425.00
Four Patch, 46-3/4" x 38", brown and gold calico on tan calico ground, mounted, America, early 20th C.. 345.00
Grandmother's Flower Garden Variant, 118" x 126", bright solid colors, prints, and white, 20th C 700.00
Log Cabin
68" x 90", multicolored, very worn, some moth damage, some tattered fabrics, ... 440.00
81" x 74", red, blue, green, orange, yellow, white, and burgundy printed calico and solid patches, yellow and green borders with diagonal line quilting, patches on verso, Mennonite, Bernville, Berks County, PA, 19th C, minor staining 460.00
81" x 81", red, yellow, blue, green, brown, pink, and white bars, broad red and black borders, rope quilting, verso with red, yellow and green calico horizontal bars, some staining................. 230.00
85" x 98", cotton, wool, and satin, brown, black, red, blue, purple, pink and white printed and solid bars, burgundy border, rope quilting, verso applied with patch with stamped signature "Annie N. Stephen," PA, late 19th C, wear 460.00
Flower Garden, red, white, and brown print, deep gray-green ground, red back, 83" x 86" 175.00
Lone Star, 76" x 79", pink, blue, lavender, and salmon, blue ground, quilted with horses, flowers, etc., Mennonite, minor stains 660.00
Monkey Wrench, 68" x 82", calico, yellow, gray on pink ground, gray border stripe, quilting binding, blue and white homespun back, Mennonite 470.00
Nine Patch, 80" x 72", red, blue, yellow, pink, and white printed calico patches, lightning dividers, white and red banded border, PA, 19th C.. 525.00
Philadelphia Pavements, 84" x 80", blue, red, orange, and white square printed and solid patches, orange and red banded borders with feather and floral fine quilting, PA, late 19th/early 20th C. 815.00
Pineapple Medallions, 76-1/2" x 94", pink calico and white 385.00
Pinwheels
68" x 70", blue and gold ground, minor stains 250.00
100" x 83", brick-red, yellow, blue, pink, brown, and white printed calico patches, 48 pinwheels within broad border printed in orange and red with leafy vines, diamond quilting, PA, 19th C 175.00
Rolling Stones, 82" x 84", pink, green, blue, and white patches, banded borders, Mennonite, PA, late 19th/early 20th C 425.00
Serrated Square, corresponding border, pink and green calico, shell and diamond quilting, 82" x 84".. 320.00
Small Star of Bethlehem, 87" x 84", red, blue, green, and yellow printed calico patches, 9 small stars within green calico borders, diamond quilting, PA, 19th C, some staining 345.00

Spider Web, 82" x 80", pink, red, blue, purple green, peach, and brown printed calico patches, wide purple calico border, diagonal line quilting, Mennonite, PA, late 19th C, some staining.........................825.00

Squares, 96" x 80-3/4", red, green, yellow, and white printed calico patches, 24 squares, broad brown, blue, green and white floral chintz border, minor staining, PA, 19th C..460.00

Star, 70" x 84" blue prints on white, machine sewn binding, stains and overall wear, early 20th C...495.00

Star of Bethlehem
    82" x 73-1/2", purple, green, red, blue, and pink calico, white ground, early 20th C, toning, minor staining, fabric wear....650.00
    85" sq, yellow, pink, purple, green, gray, and blue, white ground, pink and greed borders, c1940 ....715.00

Star Medallion, 70" x 82", multicolored prints, white on pink calico ground, green calico border stripe and binding, penciled quilting pattern visible, machine sewn binding, white homespun backing, Mennonite, minor age stains 500.00

Stars
    64" x 81", twelve stars in grid, red and white, minor wear, some fading to reds 315.00
    75" x 76", red, blue, pink, and yellow stars, colorful graphic design, some wear and facing, binding frayed in places.................275.00
    80" x 82", multicolored prints, red, and blue calico...............330.00
    90" x 86", 8-pointd star, saw tooth border, pink, yellow, and green bar back design, feather quilting...400.00

Stars and Squares, 87" x76", brown, red, blue and yellow printed calico, banded borders, Mennonite, PA, 19th C.............................635.00

Tulip, 80" sq, Le Moyne Star border, red, green, and orange, white cotton ground, machine pieced, hand quilted, minor staining, America, late 19th C...490.00

Tulips in Square, 94" x 91", red, green, and yellow printed calico patches, broad brown, red, green, and white coronation chintz and rosevine border, PA, 19th C 920.00

Unknown pattern, 88" x 86", 5 clusters of blossoms alternating with stylized flowerheads, red, yellow, and green patches, blue calico ground, red and yellow zigzag border, verso with red and blue calico bars, PA, 19th C 1,265.00

Windmill, 86" x 76", yellow, red, green, and blue printed calico patches, wide red calico with swag quilting, PA, late 19th C 690.00

Trapunto, white on white, feather wreaths alternating with wavy lines, wear and stains, 72" x 46"...495.00

QUIMPER

History: Quimper faience, dating back to the 17th century, is named for Quimper, a French town where numerous potteries were located. Several mergers resulted in the evolution of two major houses—the Jules Henriot and Hubaudière-Bousquet factories.

The peasant design first appeared in the 1860s, and many variations exist. Florals and geometrics, equally popular, also were produced in large quantities. During the 1920s, the Hubaudière-Bousquet factory introduced the Odetta line which utilized a stone body and Art Deco decorations.

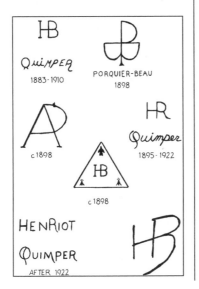

The two major houses merged in 1968, the products retaining the individual characteristics and marks of the originals. The concern suffered from labor problems in the 1980s and was purchased by an American group.

Marks: The "HR" and "HR Quimper" marks are found on Henriot pieces prior to 1922. The "Henriot Quimper" mark was used after 1922. The "HB" mark covers a long time span. Numbers or dots and dashes were added for inventory purposes and are found on later pieces. Most marks are in blue or black. Pieces ordered by department stores, such as Macy's and Carson Pirie Scott, carry the store mark along with the factory mark, making them less desirable to collectors. A comprehensive list of marks is found in Bondhus book.

References: Susan and Al Bagdade, *Warman's English & Continental Pottery & Porcelain*, 3rd Ed., Krause, 1998; Sandra V. Bondhus, *Quimper Pottery: A French Folk Art Faience*, printed by author, 1981, Revised Edition, 1995; Millicent Mali, *French Faience*, United Printing, 1986; Millicent Mali, *Quimper Faience*, Airon, Inc., 1979; Adela Meadows, *Quimper Pottery, A Guide to Origins, Styles, and Values*, Schiffer Publishing, 1998; Ann Marie O'Neill, *Quimper Pottery*, 2nd Edition, Schiffer Publishing, 1998; Marjatta Taburet, *La Faience de Quimper*, Editions Sous le Vent, 1979, (French text).

Museums: Musee des Faiences de Quimper, Quimper, France; Musee Departemental Breton, Quimper, France; Victoria and Albert Museum, French Ceramic Dept, London, England.

Bowl, male peasant, red, green, and blue florals, yellow inner band, 2 ext. blue bands, pierced for hanging, "Henriot Quimper France 85" mark, 6-1/4" d, $150. Photo courtesy of Susan and Al Bagdade.

Collectors' Club: USA Quimper Club, 2519 Kansas Avenue, Suite 108, Santa Monica, CA 90404.

Advisors: Susan and Al Bagdade.

Additional Terms:

A la touche border decor—single brush stroke to create floral

Breton Broderie decor—stylized blue and gold pattern inspired by a popular embroidery pattern often used on Breton costumes, dates from the Art-Deco era

Croisille—criss-cross pattern

Decor Riche border—acanthus leaves in two colors

Fleur de lys—the symbol of France

Ivoire Corbeille pattern—red dots circled in sponged blue with red touches forming half a floral blossom, all over a tan ground

Quintal—five-fingered vase

Biberon, 7" h, peasant man with floral sprays, blue striped overhead and side handles, "HenRiot Quimper France" mark side handle..........190.00
Biscuit Jar, cov, red, green, and blue floral sprays, blue dashes on handles, woven overhead handle, c1895......................................435.00
Bowl
    6-1/4" d, male peasant, blue pants, olive green shirt, red, green, and blue florals, yellow inner band, two exterior blue bands, pierced for hanging, "HenRiot Quimper France 85" mark... 150.00
    11"d, male peasant in center holding staff, orange-yellow flowers at sides, blue inner border, black wavy line with orange-yellow flowerheads on int., shaped wavy border with blue line on rim, "HB Quimper" on int. 425.00
Box, 5" l, horn shaped, male peasant with bagpipe, decor riche border, "Henriot Quimper" mark 565.00
Candlestick, 7-1/2" h, lighthouse shape, male peasant on one, female on other, orange and blue banding, "HenRiot Quimper, France" mark, pr 550.00
Chamberstick
    5-1/2" d, tri-lobed shaped base, female peasant with blue shirt, red apron, green shirt with 4 dots and florals, yellow top on candleholder, "HR Quimper" mark... 540.00

Cookie Plate, female peasant, blue, orange, red, and green florals, dark red inner chain border, orange and blue outlined rim, blue handles, yellow ground, "HenRiot Quimper France 110" mark, $200. Photo courtesy of Susan and Al Bagdade.

Cup and Saucer, orange, yellow, green, and blue bird, orange borders, "Henriot Quimper France" mark, $125. Photo courtesy of Susan and Al Bagdade.

    6-1/2" l, leaf shape base, female peasant, red, green, and blue floral stalks, stem with blue floret panels and blue crisscross design, orange border, "HenRiot Quimper France 75" mark 258.00
Charger, 12-5/8" d, "Breton Broderie" pattern, bust of female peasant in center wearing white coif, green dress, blue apron top, dark brown border with raised white enameled stylized dot flowerheads and dots, gold band of enameled leaf design, "HB Quimper A 64" mark, chip on reverse 500.00
Cheese Dish, cov, 8-1/4" d, male peasant on cov, bands of red and green florals with blue dot flowerheads, blue and orange outlined rims, green serpent handles, "HenRiot Quimper France" mark 425.00
Cider pitcher, 7-1/2" h, male peasant in blue pantaloons, orange shirt, walking stick, blue and yellow bands, "HenRiot Quimper" mark ... 345.00
Cigarette Holder, 3" h x 3-1/2" l, brown bust of camel on sides, dark red and blue arrowheads on border, blue shaped base, "HenRiot Quimper 82F" mark 575.00
Cookie Plate, 9" handle to handle, female peasant. dark blue dress, olive green top, dark red skirt, blue, orange, red, and green florals, dark red inner chain border, orange and blue outlined rim, blue handles, yellow ground, "HenRiot Quimper France 110" mark 200.00
Cup and Saucer
    Octagonal paneled shape, Modern Movement, bust of woman peasant on side panels, orange and blue geometrics and florals in others, "HB Quimper" mark.. 50.00
    Orange, yellow, green and blue bird, orange borders, "Henriot Quimper France" mark... 125.00
    Swirled and fluted body, peasant man and bluets on cup, blue sponged handle, bluet sprays on saucer, "HenRiot Quimper France" mark 60.00
Egg Cup, 2" h, figural swan, blue wing feathers, spotted breast and neck, orange accents, "HenRiot Quimper" mark 95.00
Egg Set, 12" l stand, walking male peasant with orange shirt, blue wavy-line and orange dots on overhead handle, 6 cups with blue trim, "HB Quimper" marks, cl895... 1,000.00
Figure, 4"h, Modern Movement, standing Breton man wearing blue

Jardiniere, female peasant on front, male pheasant on reverse, "HB Quimper France" mark, $650. Photo courtesy of Susan and Al Bagdade.

jacket, black pantaloons, yellow-brown cape, walking stick, "HenRiot Quimper France 140" mark 150.00
Fish Platter, 20-1/4" l, male peasant facing front, female facing back with head turned, scalloped border, pierced for hanging, "HR Quimper" mark 1,650.00
Gravy Boat, 4" h, 2 openings, overhhead handle, male peasant, florals, yellow ground, "HB Quimper France" mark................................. 70.00
Inkwell, 4-1/2" h, figural fleur de lys, alternating blue shade panels front and back, orange shades on sides 350.00
Jardiniere
    10-1/2" l, oval shape, male peasant with horn on front, crest on reverse, ribbed body, cornucopia feet, green border, scalloped top, "HenRiot Quimper" mark.. 980.00
    15-1/2" l, female peasant, red skirt, blue jacket, red, yellow green, and blue trim, male peasant on reverse, red jacket, blue pants, "HB Quimper France" mark.. 650.00
Melonnier, 13-1/4" handle to handle, dancing couple, "Breton Broderie" border, blue crest, green sponged handles with yellow shells, signed on front, "HenRiot Quimper" mark.. 780.00
Plaque, 18-1/4" h x 15" w, relief molded scene of peasant family kneeling before roadside cross, with "RUMENGOL" and "Pirhirined," Porquier Beau mark, chips 965.00
Plate
    6" d, geometric stylized star in center, red, green, and blue, c1920 .... 125.00
    6-1/2"d, female peasant. blue skirt, green shirt, rose apron, basket on head, 4 dots and florals, blue sponged piecrust edge, "Henriot Quimper" mark... 245.00
    8-1/2" d, dark blue, yellow, and white Deco style bust of female or male peasant, yellow "Breton Broderie" border, dark blue ground, "HB Quimper" mark, pr 350.00
    9 1/8"d, geometric, blue crisscross lattice panels, pink stylized 4 pointed stars, concentric blue, pink, and green border bands, "HB Quimper" mark, hairline 140.00

9-1/8" d, peasant woman seated on stump, blue, red and green floral sprays at sides, red and green single stroke dashes and blue dots on border, yellow and blue banded rim, "HB" mark..... 275.00
9-1/2" d, man with pipe, "Breton Broderie" border, "HB Quimper" mark.. 425.00
9-1/2" d, red, yellow, and blue extoic bird in center, red and green single stroke floral banded border, c1981 .... 400.00
Platter
    12" l, walking female peasant holding basket, blue, red, yellow and green vertical flowers, red and green floral band on border, indented rim, chip on reverse, unmarked 300.00
    14"l, oval, blue, yellow and red stylized flower heads in center, single stroke red and green floral banded border, indented rim, "HenRiot Quimper" on front, c1927 .... 325.00
Porringer
    3-1/2" d, yellow, red, and blue exotic bird, red half flowerhead, blue and yellow border bands, blue tab handles, "HR Quimper" mark on int. 125.00
    5-1/2" d, walking male peasant, red and green florals at side, yellow and blue banded border, blue tab handles, "HenRiot Quimper France" 75.00
Quintal
    3-1/2" h, "Ivoire Corbeille" pattern bust of peasant woman with tall coif in orange reserve, orange and blue banded tubes, "HenRiot Quimper 90" mark 75.00
    3-3/4" h, male peasant with horn, 4 dots and florals, blue edges, "Henriot Quimper" mark 225.00
Tray, 10-1/2" d, male peasant with bagpipe, female with jar on head, red, blue and orange crisscross border, open handles, "HenRiot Quimper France" mark 385.00
Trivet, 6" sq, standing female peasant holding flower bouquet, red, green, and blue floral garland on border, 4 small feet, "HenRiot Quimper France 128" mark 120.00
Vase
    4" h, 8-1/2" d, Modern Movement, relief of 3 dancing peasant women in yellow, pink, or blue aprons, black dresses, yellow-orange ground, orange wave margin, sgd "Sevellec," "HenRiot Quimper" mark.. 375.00
    8" h, shield shape, walking male peasant blowing horn on side, blue and orange wavy bands, orange curlicue handles with blue dashes, "HenRiot Quimper France" mark........................... 450.00
    12" h, ball shaped base, trumpet neck, peasant woman with jug on head, twin stylized sunflowers on reverse, flower sprays and scallop and dot designs on neck, "H.Q. HenRiot Quimper" mark, chips on base 220.00
Wall Pocket
    7-3/4" h, bagpipe shape, dancing peasant couple, pink and yellow ribbon, deco riche border, "HenRiot Quimper".................... 395.00
    8-1/2" h, figural bagpipe, frontal view of female peasant holding flower bouquet, molded blue ribbon at top, brown molded pipes, "HenRiot Quimper" on front 325.00
    8-1/4" h, walking female peasant, "St. Nazaire" below, red, blue, yellow, and green vertical florals.. 150.00

RADIOS

History: The radio was invented more than 100 years ago. Marconi was the first to assemble and employ the transmission and reception instruments that permitted the sending of electric messages without the use of direct connections. Between 1905 and the end of World War I, many technical advances affected the "wireless," including the invention of the vacuum tube by DeForest. Technology continued its progress, and radios filled the entertainment needs of the average family in the 1920s.

Changes in design, style, and technology brought the radio from the black boxes of the 1920s to the stylish furniture pieces and console models of the 1930s and 1940s, to midget models of the 1950s, and finally to the high-tech radios of the 1980s.

References: Robert Breed and Marty Bunis, *Collector's Guide to Novelty Radios, Book II,* Collector Books, 1998; Marty and Sue Bunis, *Collector's Guide to Antique Radios,* 4th ed., Collector Books, 1997; ——, *Collector's Guide to Transistor Radios,* Collector Books, 1994; Marty Bunis and Robert Breed, *Collector's Guide to Novelty Radios,* Collector Books, 1995; Philip Collins, *Radio Redux,* Chronicle Books, 1992; Harold Cones, and John Bryant, *Zenith Radio: The Early Years,* 1919-1935, Schiffer Publishing, 1997; Chuck Dachis, *Radios by Hallicrafters,* 3rd ed., Schiffer Publishing, 1999; Alan Douglas, *Radio Manufacturers of the 1920s,* Vol. 1 (1988), Vol. 2 (1989), Vol. 3 (1991), Vestal Press; Roger Handy, Maureen Erbe, and Aileen Farnan Antonier, *Made in Japan,* Chronicle Books, 1993; David and Betty Johnson, *Guide to Old Radios, Pointers, Pictures and Prices,* 2nd ed., Wallace Homestead/Krause, 1995; Mark Stein, *Machine Age to Jet Age, Radiomania's Guide to Tabletop Radios—1933-1959,* published by author (2109 Carterdale Rd., Baltimore, MD 21209); Eric Wrobbel, *Toy Crystal Radios,* published by author, 1997 (20802 Exhibit Court, Woodland Hills, CA).

Periodicals: *Antique Radio Classified,* P. O. Box 2, Carlisle, MA, 01741; *Horn Speaker,* P. O. Box 1193, Mabank, TX 75147; *Radio Age,* 636 Cambridge Road, Augusta, GA 30909; *Transistor Network,* RR1, Box 36, Bradford, NH 03221.

Collectors' Clubs: Antique Radio Club of America, 81 Steeplechase Rd, Devon, PA 19333; Antique Wireless Assoc, 59 Main St., Bloomfield, NY 14469; New England Antique Radio Club, RR1, Box 36, Bradford, NH 03221; Vintage Radio & Phonograph Society, Inc., P.O. Box 165345, Irving, TX 75016.

Museums: Antique Radio Museum, St. Louis, MO; Antique Wireless Museum, Bloomfield, NY; Caperton's Radio Museum, Louisville, KY; Muchow's Historical Radio Museum, Elgin, IL; Museum of Broadcast Communication, Chicago, IL; Museum of Wonderful Miracles, Minneapolis, MN; New England Wireless and Steam Museum, Inc., East Greenwich, RI; Voice of the Twenties, Orient, NY.

Additional Listings: See *Warman's Americana & Collectibles* for more examples.

Advisor: Lewis S. Walters.

Note: Prices of Catalin radios are dropping by about 10 to 15%. Collectors and dealers feel prices for these radios have reached their high side and are falling into a more realistic range.

Admiral
  Portable
    #33 .... 30.00
    #35 .... 30.00
    #37 .... 30.00
    #218, leatherette 40.00
    #909, All World 85.00
  Y-2127, Imperial 8, c1959 .... 45.00
Air King, tombstone, Art Deco 3,000.00
Arvin
  Hoppy with lariatenna 525.00
  Rhythm Baby #417 .... 275.00
  Table
    #444 .... 00.00
    #522A 65.00
  Tombstone, #617 Rhythm Maid 215.00
Atwater Kent
  Breadboard Style
    Model 9A 550.00
    Model 10, with tags 1,400.00
    Model 10C 930.00
  Cathedral, 80, c1931 .... 380.00
  Table
    #55 Keil 225.00
    #318, dome 115.00
  Tombstone, #854 .... 155.00
  Type R Horn 200.00
Bulova - clock radio
  #100 .... 40.00
  # 110 .... 25.00
  #120 .... 40.00
Colonial, "New World Radio" 1,000.00
Columbia. table radio, oak 125.00
Crosley
  ACE V 170.00
  Bandbox, #600, 1927 .... 80.00
  Dashboard 120.00
  Gemchest, #609 .... 425.00
  Litfella -1N cathedral 175.00
  Pup, no box 350.00
  Pup, with box 575.00
  Sheraton, cathedral 290.00
  Showbox, #706 .... 100.00

Fada, Art Deco case, Catalin, yellow, red trim, 1934, 10-1/2" l, 6" h, $600.

Super Buddy Boy..125.00
#4-28 battery operated 130.00
#10-135 ....45.00
Dumont, RA346, table, scroll work, 1938................110.00
Emerson
    AU-190 Catalin Tombstone............................1,500.00
    BT-245 ....1,200.00
    #274 Brown Bakelite..165.00
    #409 Mickey..1,400.00
    #411 Mickey..1,400.00
    #570 Memento...110.00
    #640 Portable 30.00
    #888 Vanguard 60.00
Fada
    #43..240.00
    #53X..200.00
    #60W 75.00
    #115, bullet shape 850.00
    #136..1,000.00
    #252..575.00
    #625, rounded end, slide rule dial 700.00
Federal
    #58DX..500.00
    #110..550.00
General Electric
    #81, c1934..200.00
    #400..30.00
    #410..30.00
    #411..30.00
    #414..30.00
    #515, clock radio 25.00
    #517, clock radio 25.00
    K-126..150.00
    Tombstone...250.00
Grebe
    CR-9..500.00
    CR-12..600.00
    MU-1..250.00
Halicrafters
    TW-600..100.00
    TW-200..125.00
Majestic
    Charlie McCarthy...1,000.00
    #92..125.00
    #381..225.00
Metrodyne Super 7, 1925.......................................265.00
Motorola
    #68X11Q Art Deco...75.00
    Jet Plane..55.00
    Jewel Box 80.00
    M logo 25.00
    Pixie...45.00
    Ranger, Portable...40.00
    Ranger #700...45.00
    Table, plastic..35.00
Olympic, radio w/phonograph 40.00
Paragon
    DA-2 table..475.00
    RD-5 table 600.00
Philco
    #17 - 20 - 38 cathedral 250.00
    #20, Cathedral...200.00
    #37 - 62 table 2tone..60.00
    #37 - 84 Cathedral 1937..................................175.00
    #40 - 180 console wood 150.00
    #46 - 132 table 20.00
    #49 - 501 Boomerang.......................................475.00
    #49 - 506 Transitone...35.00
    #52 - 544 Transitone...40.00
    #60, Cathedral...125.00

#551, 1928...145.00
T-7 126 transistor..65.00
T1000 clock radio 80.00
Radiobar, orig glasses and decanters..................1,500.00
Radio Corporation of America – RCA
    LaSiesta..550.00
    Radiola
        #18, with speaker..125.00
        #20..165.00
        #24..170.00
        #28 console..200.00
        #33..40.00
        #6X7 table, plastic...25.00
        8BT-7LE portable...35.00
        40X56 Worlds Fair 1,000.00
Silvertone - Sears
    #1, table..75.00
    #1582, cathedral, wood 225.00
    #1955, tombstone...135.00
    #9205, plastic transistor....................................45.00
    Clock Radio, plastic..15.00
Sony, transistor
    TFM-151, 1960...50.00
    TR-63, 1958...145.00
Sparton
    #506, Blue Bird, Art Deco...............................3,300.00
    "Blue Bird-REPRODUCTION".............................150.00
    #5218...95.00
Stewart-Warner, table, slant...................................175.00
Stromberg Carlson, # 636A console.........................125.00
Westinghouse -Model WR-602...................................50.00
Zenith
    #500, transistor, owl eye....................................75.00
    #500D, transistor..55.00
    #750L , transistor, leather case 40.00
    #6D2615 table w/boomerang dial........................95.00
    Trans-Oceanic 90.00
    Zephyr, multiband..95.00

RAILROAD ITEMS

History: Railroad collectors have existed for decades. The merger of the rail systems and the end of passenger service made many objects available to private collectors. The Pennsylvania Railroad sold its archives at public sale.

References: Stanley L. Baker, *Railroad Collectibles,* 4th ed., Collector Books, 1990, 1996 value update; Richard C. Barrett, *Illustrated Encyclopedia of Railroad Lighting,* Vol. 1, Railroad Research Publications, 1994; Barbara J. Conroy, *Restaurant China: Restaurant, Airline, Ship & Railroad Dinnerware,* Collector Books, Volume 1 (1998), Volume 2 (1999); Don Stewart, *Railroad Switch Keys & Padlocks,* 2nd ed., Key Collectors International, 1993; Joe Welsh, et. al., *The American Railroad,* MBI Publishing, 1999.

Periodicals: *Key, Lock and Lantern,* 3 Berkeley Heights Park, Bloomfield, NJ 07003; *Main Line Journal,* P.O. Box 121, Streamwood, IL 60107.

Collectors' Clubs: Chesapeake & Ohio Historical Society, Inc., P.O. Box 79, Clifton Forge, VA 24422; Illinois Central Railroad Historical Society, 14818 Clifton Park, Midlothian, IL 60445; Railroad Enthusiasts, 102 Dean Rd, Brookline, MA 02146; Railroadiana Collectors Assoc., 795 Aspen Drive, Buffalo Grove, IL 60089; Railway and Locomotive Historical Society, P.O. Box 1418, Westford, MA 01886;

Twentieth Century Railroad Club, 329 West 18th St., Ste 902, Chicago, IL 60616.

Museums: Baltimore and Ohio Railroad, Baltimore, MD; California State Railroad Museum, Sacramento, CA; Frisco Railroad Museum, Van Buren, AR; Museum of Transportation, Brookline, MA; National Railroad Museum, Green Bay, WI; New York Museum of Transportation, West Henrietta, NY; Old Depot Railroad Museum, Dassel, MN.

Additional Listings: See *Warman's Americana & Collectibles* for more examples.

Notes: Railroad enthusiasts have organized into regional and local clubs. Join one if you're interested in this collectible field; your local hobby store can probably point you to the right person. The best pieces pass between collectors and rarely enter the general market.

Baggage Tag, 1-1/2" x 2-1/2", SOO Line, celluloid, leather strap, "Tag Your Grip, Take a trip, the New Train" 20.00
Book
    Chicago Milwaukee St Paul & Pacific Railroad, *Chicago, Milwaukee, St. Paul & PacificRailroad Company Questions and Answers on Progressive Air Brake Promotional Examinations for Firemen,* effective date July 1, 1953, 119 pgs, 16 fold-out schematics 12.00
    Fagan, James, *Confessions of a Railroad Signalman,* Boston, 1908, 181 lbs 20.00
    Nock, O. S., *Railways in the Formative Years From 1851-1895,* MacMillian, 1973, 1st ed., 156 pgs, color illus by Clifford and Wendy Meadway, dg 8.50
    Ogburn, C., *Railroad The Great American Adventure,* National Geographic Society, 1977, 1st ed., 204 pgs 17.50
Builder's Plate, Schenectady Locomotive Works, 1899 .... 725.00
Button, uniform, 3/4" d, "Baggage Master," silvertone 8.00
Cabinet, American Railway Express, wood, countertop, front door stenciled "AM R.Y. EX. CO," several int. dividers missing, overall varnish loss, 33" x 25" x 11-1/2" 50.00

Ticket Case, oak, tin dividers, trim, from Connellsville railroad station, 16" l, 8-1/2" deep, 17-1/2" h, $200.

Calendar, 1938, Burlington Route, litho illus, steam and diesel trains in mountain landscape, vignette of covered wagons above, full pad, 18" x 27" 45.00
Cap Badge, 4-1/4" x 1-1/2" C&O RY, brakeman, emb black enameled lettering pebbled silvered ground, arched top, milled border 32.00
Catalog, The Mau-Sherwood Supply Co. for Mills, Mines, Railways, Hardware & Tools, ©1936 Cleve, OH, 448 pgs, fully ills 35.00
China
    Butter Pat, PA RR, backstamp 75.00
    Cereal Bowl, Union Pacific, Challenger pattern, no backstamp, Syracuse China 25.00
    Cup and Saucer, Chicago Burlington & Quincy, Chuck Wagon pattern, backstamp, Syracuse China 250.00
    Ice Cream Dish, B&O, Capitol pattern, ftd, no back stamp 50.00
    Plate, dinner, Wabash RR, Banner pattern, no backstamp, Syracuse China, 9-1/2" d 225.00
    Sauce Dish, Atchison Topeka & Santa Fe, Mimbreno pattern, backstamp "Made expressly for Santa Fe dining car service," Syracuse China, 5-1/2" d 80.00
Coach Seat, New Haven 8600 series, double 30.00
Engine Status Board, NY&NERR, used in Norwich, CT, engine shop, 60" sq 335.00
Glass, 3-1/2" d, 4-1/2" h, highball, weighted bottom, brown and white streamlined PA passenger train passing by landmarks of Philadelphia, New York City, Washington, DC, single PA Railroad keystone logo, 1930s 20.00
Grade Crossing Sign, wood, circular, black "RR" and white "X," white ground, worn 15.00
Lantern, Dietz
    11-1/2" h, Little Wizard, 4" ruby globe, emb "S & W B. D. N. O., NY, USA, DIETZ" 50.00
    14" h, Monarch, blue, 7" h ruby globe, orig Dietz sticker 50.00
    15" h, inspector's, Acme, orig globe, tin hood, silvered reflector at rear of wick, globe mkd "Dietz Fitzall, NY, USA, 4H Loc-Nob" 85.00
Map
    Map of the Canadian Pacific Railway, folding, colored, entire rail system from east to west, folded into orig cloth folder, Chicago, c1914, 425 x 825 mm 125.00
    Original Railroad Lines Map, Ohio with 100 Separate Lines Indicated and Titled, 1888, colored, 27" x 20-1/2" 135.00
    Railroad Lines Track Map of Alabama with 48 Separate Railroad Lines Titled and Indicated, 1888, orig colors, 20-1/2" x 14" 120.00
Membership Card, American Association Railroad Ticket Agents, 1931 .... 10.00
Napkin, 10-1/2" x 16-1/2", Milwaukee RR, cotton, printed magenta "Hiawatha" and Indian emblem, tan ground 20.00
Pass
    Reading Company, 1939, issued 10.00
    The Rocky Mountain Parks Transportation Co., 1930, issued 12.40
Patch
    2" d, G M & N, The Road of Service 4.50
    3-1/8" l, 2" h, S C L, L & N, Georgia Clinchfield West Point Route. 4.00
    3-3/8" l, 1-1/8" h, blue and white 4.00
Payroll Document, Southern Express, Florence, AL, Oct 31, 1918, for porter Horace Green, stamped "L & N So. RY," sgd by Green and witness, 3-1/2" x 8-1/2" 10.00
Photograph
    Group of 20, silver print photographs of steam locomotives used around the world, from early 1900s to 1940s, 10" x 15-1/2" and smaller, several numbered on negative, others with North British Locomotive Company handstamp and negative number, all with penciled dates and identifying captions on verso, 1904-40 ..2,000.00
    Group of 120 stereoview photographs titled "Pennsylvania Railroad Scenery," view of trains, machine shops, bridges, tracks, tunnels, stations, and scenery, along Delaware Water Gap, Watkin's Glen and waterfalls, gorges, and railroad towns from Philadelphia to Pittsburgh, by W. Purviance, arch topped, album prints, 6 stereo prs per page, mounted recto/verso, most titled and numbered in the negative, gilt bordered mounts with series title, photogra-

pher's credit and "Philadelphia" printed recto and verso, folio, linen, contemporary clamshell presentation box, c1875 .. 2,400.00
Playing Cards, 1" x 2-3/4" x 3-1/2", cardboard slipcase, complete deck, Southern Pacific Lines, back of each card with full color art of Southern Pacific Daylight streamliner passenger train passing thru scenic landscape, late 1930s 20.00
Pocket Watch
    American Waltham Watch Co., size 16, open face, gold filled case, damascened Vanguard movement, 23 jewels, wind indicator, adjusted for 6 positions 450.00
    Hamilton Watch Co., model 999, made for the Ball Watch Co., size 18, open face, gold filled case, 21 jewels, damascened plates, inscribed gold lettering, c1895 .... 300.00
Postcard, 8-3/4" x 5-1/2", mkd "Kodachrome Transparency by James W. Watson," c1974
    Milwaukee 419, Fairbanks-Morse H-16-44, Council Bluffs, Iowa ... 8.00
    Union Pacific #5010, North Platte, Nebraska, ... 8.00
Poster
    Eagle Nest Tunnel in the Bitter Root Mountains, Montana, "On the Route of the New Olympian, Chicago, Milwaukee, St. Paul and Pacific Railroad," tinted image of river gorge, c1927, 28" x 22" 250.00
    Fisherman Take Notice, Walt Kuhn, Union Pacific Railway, Sun Valley Lodge, Idaho, view of mountains, happy chef, list of fish to get in center, c1937, 23" x 29" 425.00
    Hoover Dam and Lake Mead, Union Pacific RR, c1947, 25" x 32" 350.00
    Kanawha River Near Montgomery, Adolph Hehn, C & O Railway, color litho, full color panorama of village and river, 1948, 28" x 23" 125.00
    Railroad Jack, comical farmyard scene, hobo riding homemade bicycle, dog, bites tire, matted and framed, 26" x 40" 275.00
    Red Man Tobacco, railroad conductor enjoying chew from pack held by engineer, 150s, 11" x 15-1/2" 80.00
Scale Model, NYC&HR, gondola freight car, 69" l, track 250.00
Silver Hollowware
    Coffeepot, Chicago & Northwestern RY, pine cone finial bottom mkd, "International, #05073," 1949, 14 oz 85.00
    Vase, 7-1/4" h, Great Northern RY, candlestick bud -type, mkd on side and bottom, International #05082, 1951 .... 175.00
Steam Whistle, 19" h, brass 250.00
Timetable
    1928, Louisville and Nashville Railroad 32.00
    1946, Charleston and Western Carolina 15.00
Water Bucket, metal, bail handle 25.00
Whistle Post, black "W," white ground, worn 25.00

RAZORS

History: Razors date back several thousand years. Early man used sharpened stones; the Egyptians, Greeks, and Romans had metal razors.

Razors made prior to 1800 generally were crudely stamped "Warranted" or "Cast Steel," with the maker's mark on the tang. Until 1870, razors were handmade and almost all razors for the American market were manufactured in Sheffield, England. Most blades were wedge shaped; many were etched with slogans or scenes. Handles were made of natural materials: horn, tortoiseshell, bone, ivory, stag, silver, or pearl.

After 1870, razors were machine made with hollow ground blades and synthetic handle materials. Razors of this period usually were manufactured in Germany (Solingen) or in American cutlery factories. Hundreds of molded-celluloid handle patterns were produced.

Cutlery firms produced boxed sets of two, four, and seven razors. Complete and undamaged sets are very desirable. The most-popular ones are the seven-day sets in which each razor is etched with a day of the week.

References: Ronald S. Barlow, *Vanishing American Barber Shop,* Windmill Publishing, 1993; Safety Razors: A Price Guide, L-W Book Sales, 1995; Jim Sargent, *American Premium Guide to Pocket Knives & Razors,* 5th ed., Krause Publications, 1999.

Periodical: Blade Magazine, P.O. Box 22007, Chattanooga, TN 37422.

Additional Listings: See *Warman's Americana & Collectibles* for more examples.

Notes: The fancier the handle or more intricately etched the blade, the higher the price. Rarest handle materials are pearl, stag, sterling silver, pressed horn, and carved ivory. Rarest blades are those with scenes etched across the entire front. Value is increased by the presence of certain manufacturers' names, e.g., H. Boker, Case, M. Price, Joseph Rogers, Simmons Hardware, Will & Finck, Winchester, and George Wostenholm.

American Blades

Case Bros., Little Valley, NY
    Hollow Point, arc etch, imitation ivory handles 150.00
    Hollow Point, candy-stripe handles 200.00
    Hollow Point, Tested XX, slick black handles, MOP inlaid tang.. 400.00
    Round Point, imitation ivory handles 100.00
Case, W. R. & Son Cutlery Co., Little Valley, NY
    Bulls Eye on markside, imitation ivory handles, silver endcaps, inlaid logo 285.00
    Square Point, mottled yellow celluloid handles 175.00
Cattaraugus Cutlery Co., Little Valley, NY, sq point, blue handles with white liners 35.00
Crandall Cutlery Co., Bradford, PA
    Square Point, blade etched "I. Must Kut," cream colored handles with beaded border 70.00
    Square Point, rear of tang stamped "Guilt Edge," smooth bone handles 85.00
Kane Cutlery Co., Kane, PA, hollow point, cream and rust twisted rope handles, c1884 .... 45.00
Kinfolks, Inc.
    Square Point, ivory bamboo handles 60.00
    Square Point, MOP inlaid tang, tortoise shell handles 125.00
    Square Point, red point, imitation ivory handles with silver endcaps 75.00
    Square Point, imitation ivory handles, Western Wedge 50.00
Platts Bros., Eldred, PA, square point, brown beaded border handles 85.00
Standard Knife Co., Little Valley, NY, arc mark, round point, yellow mottled handles with beaded borders, 1901-03 .... 150.00

J. R. Terry & Co., Worcester, MA, fully etched blade, tortoiseshell handle, $50.

Union Cutlery Co., Olean, NY, AJ Case Shoo-Fly, tiger-eye handle, c1912 .... 125.00

English Blades, Sheffield

George Wostenholme, etched adv on blade, emb ivory handle ... 40.00
Joseph Rodgers & Sons, wedge blade, stag handle with inlaid rect escutcheon plate 125.00
Wade & Butcher, hollow ground blade, name etched in ribbon, SS Art Nouveau handle, scrollwork, monogram 175.00

German Blades

Cosmos Mfg. Co., hollow ground blade, ivory handle, raised nude picking purple grapes, green leaves 125.00
F. A. Koch & Co., ivory handle, colored scene with deer, branches, and oak leaves 50.00
Imperial Razor, blade etched with US Battleship Oregon scene, dark blue celluloid handle 45.00
Wadsworth Razor Co., semi wedge blade, carved bone handle, c1870 .... 60.00

Sets of Razors

Crown & Sword, 7 day set, blades etched "The Crown & Sword Razor Extra Hollow Ground," black handles with raised "Crown and Sword," homemade wood case with felt lining, emb "RAZORS," plaque on top 85.00
G. W. Ruff's Peerless, 2, hollow ground blade, ivory handles, leather over wood case with "Gentlemen's Companion Containing 2 Razors Special Hollow Ground," red lining 70.00
Wilkinson Sword, 7 day, safety, 5" l, 2-1/2" d, 1-5/8" h orig box.. 125.00

RECORDS

History: With the advent of the more sophisticated recording materials, such as 33 1/3 RPM long playing records, 8-track tapes, cassettes, and compact discs, earlier phonograph records became collectors' items. Most have little value. The higher-priced items are rare (limited-production) recordings. Condition is critical.

References: Mark Allen Baker, *Goldmine Price Guide to Rock 'n' Roll Memorabilia,* Krause Publications, 1997; Mark Brown, Thomas Conner and John Wooley, *Forever Lounge,* Antique Trader Books, 1999; Les Docks, *American Premium Record Guide, 1900-1965,* 5th Edition, Kruase Publications, 1997; Goldmine Magazine, *Goldmine's 1997 Annual,* Krause Publications, 1996; ——, *Goldmine Roots of Rock Digest,* Krause Publications, 1999; Ron Lofman, *Goldmine's Celebrity Vocals,* Krause Publications, 1994; William M. Miller, *How to Buy & Sell Used Record Albums,* Loran Publishing, 1994; Tim Neely, *Goldmine Christmas Record Price Guide,* Krause Publications, 1997; ——, *Goldmine's Price Guide to Alternative Records,* Krause Publications, 1996; ——, *Goldmine's Price Guide to 45 RPM Records,* Krause Publications, 1996; ——, *Goldmine Record Album Price Guide,* Krause Publications, 1999; Tim Neely and Dave Thompson, *Goldmine British Invasion Record Price Guide,* Krause Publications, 1997; Jerry Osborne (comp.) *Rockin' Records, 1998 Ed.,* Antique Trader Books, 1997; Martin Popoff, *Goldmine Heavy Metal Record Price Guide,* Krause Publications, 2000; Charles Szabala, *Goldmine 45 RPM Picture Sleeve Price Guide,* Krause Publications, 1998; Neal Umphred, *Goldmine's Price Guide to Collectible Jazz Albums,* 1949-1969, 2nd ed., Krause Publications, 1994; ——, *Goldmine's Price Guide to Collectible Record Albums,* 5th ed., Krause Publi-

cations, 1996; ——, *Goldmine's Rock 'n' Roll 45 RPM Record Price Guide,* 3rd ed., Krause Publications, 1994.

Periodicals: Cadence, Cadence Building, Redwood, NY 13679; *DISCoveries Magazine,* P.O. Box 309, Fraser, MI 48026; *Goldmine,* 700 E. State St., Iola, WI 54990; *Jazz Beat Magazine,* 1206 Decatur St., New Orleans, LA 70116; *Joslin's Jazz Journal,* P.O. Box 213, Parsons, KS 67357; *New Amberola Graphic,* 37 Caledonia St., St. Johnsbury, VT 05819; *Record Collectors Monthly,* P.O. Box 75, Mendham, NJ 07945; *Record Finder,* P.O. Box 1047, Glen Allen, VA 23060.

Collectors' Clubs: Association for Recorded Sound Collections, P.O. Box 453, Annapolis, MD 21404; International Association of Jazz Record Collectors, P.O. Box 75155, Tampa, FL 33605.

Additional Listings: See *Warman's Americana & Collectibles* for more examples.

Note: Most records, especially popular recordings, have a value of less than $3 per disc. The records listed here are classic recordings of their type and are in demand by collectors.

After School Session, Chuck Berry, Chess, 1426 .... 50.00
Animal Tracks, The Animals, MGM E4305 .... 12.00
At Abbey Road, Helen Shapiro 17.50
Back in Black, AC/DC, Atlantic SD 16018 .... 10.00
Black Coffee, Peggy Lee, Decca 5482 .... 35.00
Blue Amberol, Edison, cylinder 10.00
Carneige Hall Jazz Concert, Benny Goodman, Columbia 160 ..... 45.00
Cuts Like A Knife, Bryan Adams, A & M SP 4919 .... 9.00
Don't Tell Me, Van Halen 10.00
Electric Barbella, Duran Duran, 15 track promo sampler 25.00
Electric Landlady, Jimi Hendrix, LP 30.00
Flick of the Switch, AC/DC, Atlantic 80 100-1 .... 12.00
For Those About to Rock, AC/DC, Atlantic SD 11111 .... 12.00
For You Sweet Love, Rick Nelson 15.00
Hiawatha, Laughing Water, Sodero's Band, Creole Belles and Soldiers in the Park march, New York Military Band, Edison Diamond Disc, 50514, 78 rpm 15.00
Highway to Hell, AC/DC, Atlantic SD 19244 .... 12.00
Hold That Tiger, Fabian, Chancellor 5003 .... 24.00
If I Can't Dream, Elvis 25.00
I'm With You, Pearl Bailey, Coral, 56078 .... 15.00
Introducing the Beatles, VeeJay LP 1062, cover split 60.00
It's a Mistake, Men at Work 12.00
Jailhouse Rock, Elvis 65.00
Jerome Kern Songs, Bing Crosby, Decca 5001 .... 24.00
Let There Be Rock, AC/DC 12.00
Marriage on the Rocks, Amboy Dukes, Polydor 24-4012 .... 10.00
Moody Blue, Elvis 25.00
Night has 1000 Eyes, Bobby Vee 18.00
Revelations, Santana 15.00
Rock and Rollin, Fats Domino, Imperial 9009 .... 65.00
Shades of Blue, Low Rawls, Family Reunion 12.00
Sheena is a Punk Rocker, Ramones, German 75.00
Spirits In It, In Love Again, Patti LaBelle 20.00
Tennessee Waltz, Patti Page, Mercury 25154 .... 17.50
The Byrds' Greatest Hits, Columbia CS 9516 .... 10.00
Tonight's The Night, Shirelles, Scepter 501 .... 35.00
Too Much Love Will Kill You, Queen 10.00
Too Much Monday, Buddy Holly, Crickets 18.00
Yesterday and Today, Beatles, Capitol T-2553 .... 42.00

REDWARE

History: The availability of clay, the same used to make bricks and roof tiles, accounted for the great production of red earthenware pottery in the American colonies. Red-ware pieces are mainly utilitarian—bowls, crocks, jugs, etc.

Lead-glazed redware retained its reddish color, but a variety of colored glazes were obtained by the addition of metals to the basic glaze. Streaks and mottled splotches in redware items resulted from impurities in the clay and/or uneven firing temperatures.

Slipware is the term used to describe redwares decorated by the application of slip, a semi-liquid paste made of clay. Slipwares were made in England, Germany, and elsewhere in Europe for decades before becoming popular in the Pennsylvania German region and other areas in colonial America.

References: Susan and Al Bagdade, *Warman's American Pottery and Porcelain,* Wallace-Homestead, 1994; William C. Ketchum, Jr., *American Pottery and Porcelain,* Avon Books, 1994.

Bank, 7-1/2" h, chest of drawers shape, yellow slip knobs and name "Albert Stewart," molded label "Savings Bank"..........195.00
Bottle, 5-3/4" h, pinched sides and tooling, green glaze, brown flecks, green striping, incised label, "Made by I. S. Stahl, 11-1-1939"...60.00
Bowl
    4" d brown streak dec, red glaze, double handle..................225.00
    6-1/2" d, white stripe dec, brown glaze....................................60.00
    12-1/2" d, 2-1/2" h, sgraffito, eagle, flowers, and "1827".......425.00
Charger, 13" d, molded bust of Washington, star ringed medallion, coggled rim, brown fleck glaze...475.00
Cooler, 18" h, ovoid, glaze flaking, mounted as lamp 75.00
Creamer
    4" h, brown dec, yellow glaze, stamped "John Bell" 2,900.00
    4-3/8" h, yellow slip design, green accents, ribbed strap handle 450.00
Cup, 3-3/4" h, flared lip, applied handle, clear glaze with mottled amber, minor wear and glaze flakes 90.00
Cuspidor, 8" x 4-1/4", tooled bands, brown and green running glaze, brown dashes, some wear and edge chips..............................265.00
Figure, 5-3/4" h, painted woman with child, chips......................145.00
Flask, 6-1/2" h, tooled lines and brown spotted glaze, old hairline to side, chip on lid 225.00
Food Mold, 7-7/8" l, oval, ear of corn, arched sides, crimped edge, four applied feet, clear glaze, sponging on rim, minor flakes 440.00
Jar, cov, 5-3/4" h, tooling, applied handles, dark glaze with black sponging, mismatched lid, minor wear and flakes....................110.00
Jar, open
    5-1/2" h, ovoid, imp "W. Smith, Womelsdorf," (PA), minor crazing, possible base hairline 95.00
    6-3/4" h, cream slip stripes, brown glaze, wavy lines, tooled lip 1,650.00

7-1/2" h, imp "John Bell, Waynesboro," int. glaze, hairline......90.00
    9" h, ovoid, ribbed strap handle, green tint glaze, wear, chips....220.00
Jug
    7" h, bulbous, applied handle, wheel thrown, dark brown slip 110.00
    9" h, ovoid, strap handle, clear glaze, black splotches, small chip on lip, glaze flakes 110.00
Loaf Pan, 16" l, very worn yellow slip dec, polka dot bird and foliage, coggled rim, wear, surface flaking, one corner damaged.........500.00
Milk Bowl
    8" d, rim spout 150.00
    9" d, white slip dec, greenish-amber glaze, surface chips.....250.00
Mold, 6" d, brown glaze, black dec 85.00
Mug, 5-1/4" h, butter print star design, strap handle, tooled lip, clear glaze with greenish highlights, minor glaze flakes and wear ...125.00
Pie Plate
    7-3/8" d, yellow slip wavy lines with green, chips and hairline....275.00
    7-1/2" d, yellow slip dec, minor edge chips 275.00
Pipkin, 8-1/4" h, manganese and colored slip dec, c1800 ....95.00
Pitcher
    7-1/2" h, wheel thrown, applied handle, coggled top edge and band at top of handle, slip colored with copper oxide (green) at top working down to iron oxide (rust) mottled with manganese (dark brown), attributed to Jacob Medinger, c1900-20 ....600.00
    8-7/8" h, brown Albany slip, New Geneva 55.00
Plate, 8-1/2" d, sgraffito floral design, white, green, and orange stripes, black German inscription on back, minor wear 660.00
Preserving Jar, cov, 10" h, green, orange spots, Galena............125.00
Turk's Head Mold
    8-1/4" d, swirled design, brown sponging, imp "John Bell Waynesboro," minor flakes...1,210.00
    8-3/4" d, fluted swirls, scalloped rim, clear glaze, brown sponging, hairline 75.00

RED WING POTTERY

History: The Red Wing pottery category includes several potteries from Red Wing, Minnesota. In 1868, David Hallem started Red Wing Stoneware Co., the first pottery with stoneware as its primary product. The Minnesota Stoneware Co. started in 1883. The North Star Stoneware Co. was in business from 1892 to 1896.

The Red Wing Stoneware Co. and the Minnesota Stoneware Co. merged in 1892. The new company, the Red Wing Union Stoneware Co., made stoneware until 1920 when it introduced a pottery line which it continued until the 1940s. In 1936, the name was changed to Red Wing Potteries, Inc. During the 1930s, this firm introduced several popular patterns of hand-painted dinnerware which were distributed through department stores, mail-order catalogs, and gift-stamp centers. Dinnerware production declined in the 1950s and was replaced with hotel and restaurant china in the early 1960s. The plant closed in 1967.

Marks: Red Wing Stoneware Co. was the first firm to mark pieces with a red wing stamped under the glaze. The North Star Stoneware Co. used a raised star and the words "Red Wing" as its mark.

References: Dan and Gail DePasquale and Larry Peterson, *Red Wing Collectibles,* Collector Books, 1985, 1997 value update; ——, *Red Wing Stoneware,* Collector Books, 1983, 1997 value update; B. L. Dollen, *Red Wing Art Pottery,* Collector Books, 1997; B. L. and R. L. Dollen, *Red Wing Art Pottery Book II,* Collector Books, 1998; Ray Reiss, *Red Wing Art Pottery Including Pottery Made for Rum Rill,* published by

Left: pitcher, brown, red, and green glaze, $390; center: bowl, brown and cream rings, $490; right: mug, brown dec, $440.

author (2144 N. Leavitt, Chicago, IL 60647), 1996; —, *Red Wing Dinnerware,* published by author, 1997.

Collectors' Clubs: Red Wing Collectors Society, Inc., P.O. Box 184, Galesburg, IL 61402; RumRill Society, P.O. Box 2161, Hudson, OH 44236.

Additional Listings: See *Warman's Americana & Collectibles* for more examples.

Basket, #1275 .... 45.00
Bean Pot, cov, stoneware, adv 85.00
Beater Jar, stoneware, half gallon, "Stanhope, Ia" adv 95.00
Bookends, pr, fan and scroll, green 20.00
Bowl
  8" d, 2-1/2" h, brown, 3 feet, mkd "Red Wing USA M 5010".... 20.00
  11-1/2" w, 3-1/2" h, dancing figures, mkd "Red Wing USA"..... 38.00
Bulb Planter, 9" d, low, chartreuse outside, drab olive green int., Rumrill 40.00
Butter Crock, 20#, large wing, tight hairline 550.00
Buttermilk Feeder, stoneware 75.00
Casserole, cov, 8" d, sponge band, chip on handle 165.00
Compote, 16" w, 10" h, orig deer flower frog, mkd "Red Wing 526".130.00
Cornucopia, 8-3/4" h, 4" w, 75th Red Wing anniversary sticker, mkd "USA M-1444" 40.00
Creamer and Sugar, #1376 .... 20.00
Crock, stoneware
  One Gallon, large wing 400.00
  Two Gallon, 4" wing 40.00
  Six Gallon, 4" wing 75.00
Dinnerware
  Casserole, cov, Bob White 70.00
  Casserole, cov, Pepe, 8-1/2" d 125.00
  Celery Tray, Merrileaf, 16" l, 3-1/4" w 20.00
  Coffee Pot, cov, Damask 45.00
  Creamer, Damask 25.00
  Creamer, Merrileaf, 4-3/4" h 10.00
  Cup and Saucer, Bob White 25.00
  Cup and Saucer, Damask 12.00
  Cup and Saucer, Magnolia, gray 16.00
  Dinner Plate, Damask 14.00
  Dinner Plate, Magnolia 14.00
  Dinner Plate, Town and Country 8.00
  Dish, divided, Capistrano, 13-1/2" l 20.00
  Gravy, cov, Merrileaf, 4-1/4" h, 9-1/4" l 25.00
  Platter, Magnolia, small 30.00
  Platter, Merrileaf, 9-1/4" x 13" 15.00

  Salad Plate, Bob White 25.00
  Salad Plate, Magnolia 10.00
  Salad Set, 8" bowl, 8 serving plates, Random Harvest 145.00
  Salt and Pepper Shakers, pr, Town and Country, dark green.. 65.00
  Soup Bowl, Magnolia 10.00
  Sugar Bowl, cov, Damask 25.00
  Vegetable, round, open, Damask 30.00
  Vinegar Bottle, Town and Country, blue 15.00
Ewer, 7" h, #184 .... 55.00
Figure
  Cowboy, rust 175.00
  Cowgirl, #B1414, white 175.00
  Giraffe, 1995 convention commemorative 90.00
Jug, five gallon, shoulder, large wing, "California White Wine" stencil 135.00
Mixing Bowl, 7" d, stoneware, "Cap," blue sponge dec, white ground 100.00
Pitcher, 9" h, stoneware, brown glazed grape dec, rick-rack border, waffle ground, "Red Wing North Star Stoneware" mark 90.00
Planter
  Bamboo, rectangular, 12" l, 3-1/2" w, 4" h, brown ext., butterscotch int., mkd "Red Wing USA #707" 28.00
  Deer, 7-1/4" x 7" x 2-3/4" deep, orig sticker, mkd "Red Wing #1120" 45.00
Teapot, cov, yellow rooster, gold trim 65.00
Vase
  6-1/2" h, bulbous, leaf design, molded ring handles, shiny jade green glaze, mkd "Red Wing Art Pottery" 80.00
  8-1/4" h, blue-gray, pedestal base, mkd "Red Wing, USA, 5021," c1957 .... 45.00
  10" h, lime green, #B2003 .... 42.00
  10" h, maroon mulberry dec, gray-cream ground, and yellow int., mkd "#1203 Red Wing USA," all over crazing 35.00
  10" h, 6-1/4" d, light green, mkd "Red Wing, USA M-1461" 80.00
  11-1/2" h, handles, #1376 .... 45.00
Wall Pocket, violins, turquoise, matched pr 175.00
Water Cooler
  Five gallon, small wing, no lid, small hairline 275.00
  Six gallon, small wing, no lid 385.00

RELIGIOUS ITEMS

History: Objects used in worship or as expression of man's belief in a superhuman power are collected by many people for many reasons.

This category includes icons since they are religious mementos, usually paintings with a brass encasement. Collecting icons dates from the earliest period of Christianity. Most antique icons in today's market were made in the late 19th century.

Reference: Penny Forstner and Lael Bower, *Collecting Religious Artifacts (Christian and Judaic),* Books Americana, 1995.

Collectors' Club: Foundation International for Restorers of Religious Medals, P.O. Box 2652, Worcester, MA 01608.

Museum: American Bible Society, New York, NY.

Reproduction Alert: Icons are frequently reproduced.

Additional Listings: Judaic, Russian Items.

Altar Cross, 10" x 6", polished brass, 2 pc construction, Russian 550.00
Altar Gospels, 12" x 14-3/4", silvered and gilded repousse and chased metal, front cover with repousse image of the Resurrection & Descent into Hades in center, corners with Old Testament Prophets, back cover with repousse and chased image of Crucifixion, corners

Cookie Jar, Jack Frost, orange pumpkin base, $500. Photo courtesy of Green Valley Auctions, Inc.

with the 4 Evangelists, matching clasps with double headed eagles, limited edition of the divine and holy Gospel in English 675.00
Altar Niche, 41" w, 22" d, 42" h, carved wood, fluted columns, fancy work, polychrome and gilding, 19th C 880.00
Altar Shrine, circumference 80", 41" h, Gothic style wood, ext. with applied cherub heads and 4 side mounted votive stands, int. rotates to reveal shine, when closed it exhibits a carved in relief Eucharistic Lamp beneath grapes and wheat, 19th C 935.00
Bible Cover, 10-1/2" x 7-1/2", vellum cover, front overlaid with massive gilded bronze and silvered plaque with champleve enamel, depicting crucifixion with the 4 Evangelists, back cover with gilded bronze Romanesque style angel and polished stone feet held in gilded and enamel frames, spine imp "Santa Biblia," matching bronze clasps..... 1,100.00
Candlesticks, pr
    15" h, Sabbath, brass, classical and floral design, Polish, minor wear, repair, dents 245.00
    28" h, bronze, Gothic style.. 935.00
Chair, Worshipful Masters, New Hampshire, 1850, painted black, gold highlights, back with pressed wood rosettes, carpet upholstery, 50-1/4" h.. 635.00
Chalice
    4-5/8" d, 4-1/2" h, English silver, Edward VII, London, 1902, W. Hutton & Sons, Ltd. Makers, Arts and Crafts style, shallow ovoid bowl engraved with circles and lappet pattern, rim engraved with Latin inscription in stylized block letters picked out with faux nail heads, trumpet foot chased and emb with band of leaves below lobing, 11 troy oz 350.00
    9" h, gold-washed silver, cup embellished with applied foliate design, engraved Latin inscription "This is the cup of my blood," paneled stem with fleur-de-lis engraving, central knop of thorn pattern, applied faceted purple stones, paneled flared foot with two panels tamped with wheat and grapes, one with applied cross, mkd "Sterling" on base, 19 troy oz 375.00
Crucifix, 15" h, carved ivory, figure, Continental 950.00
Doorstop, 6" h, 7-1/2" w, church door, painted cast iron, #9737 . 165.00
Figure
    11" h, carved limestone, Madonna and Child, French, 16th C.2,185.00
    28" h, carved and painted wood, trumpeting angel, attributed to northern Europe, 19th C, minor losses, repairs 2,185.00
    46" h, carved limewood, Madonna and Child, crowned Madonna, flowing hair and tunic, infant on left hip, attributed to Low countries, 16th C, losses, pieces off but present 2,645.00

Crucifix, carved ivory figure mounted to wooden cross, 10" h, $2,100. Photo courtesy of Jackson's Auctioneers & Appraisers.

Triptych, Russian, micro-mosaic, period of Tsar Nicholas I, removable center pendant of St. Nicholas, gilded silver frame with swivel mosaic of Eye of God, gilded silver sunburst, left and right wings both inset with removable pierced and carved bone crucifixes, left panel finely engraved with St. John Chrysostom, St. Gregory "Dvoeslova," Pope of Rhome, St. Basil the Great and St. Gregory the Theologian, right panel finely engraved with St. John, St. Philip, St. Peter, and St. Alexei, upper left and right wings engraved with continuous prayer, each section hallmarked St. Petersburg, central panel dated 1855, all with maker's mark "C. E.", 7-1/2" w open, 6-3/4" h, $19,600. Photo courtesy of Jackson's Auctioneers & Appraisers.

    54" h, Mary Magdalene, long black hair, painted naturalistically, flowing robes, painted, gilded, and carved wood and gesso, Continental, 19th C... 2,990.00
Gospel Cover, 13-1/4" x 15", gilded bronze and champleve enamel, one pc solid wood spine and back cover, hinged wood front with massive plaque, applied border dec, central gilded bronze and enamel Christ, corners with symbols of the 4 Evangelists, back cov with gilded bronze and enamel clover shaped medallions of an arch angel, matching bronze clasps.. 880.00
Icon, Greek
    19" x 15", The Mother of God of the Life Bearing Font, tempera on wood panel 1,25.00
Icon, Russian, tempera on wood panel, 19th C
    8-3/4" x 10-1/2", Baptism of Christ 1,155.00
    14" x 12", double sided processional, the Holy Village and Baptism of Christ, attributed to Palekh 3,025.00
    16" x 30", The Prophet Elijah with Life Scenes, gold leaf, Elijah in the desert in center, fiery ascension at top, surrounded by life scenes, overlaid with gilded metal riza 4,125.00
Mosaic, 24" x 36", The Lord Almighty, Venetian colored and gilded glass, attributed to Vatican workshop.................................... 3,300.00
Painting, Continental School, oil on canvas
    24" x 38", Abraham and Issac, indistinguishably sgd lower right, c1890 .... 420.00
    27" x 23", The Holy Family, nicely framed 330.00
    30" x 38", The Scared Heart of Mary, unsigned 770.00
Plaque, 8-1/2" x 5-3/4", painted porcelain, Ruth, retailed by Mermod & Jaccard of St. Louis, framed, German, c1900 .... 1,100.00

Processional Cross, 27" x 12", silvered and polished bronze, applied corpus, reverse with Mary Magdalene, receptacle base 715.00

Reliquary, 40" h, giltwood and composition, reliquary orb form dec with high relief grapes, wheat, and cherubim, central door for host, pedestal base, egg and dart detailing, acanthus trim, Continental, 19th C 1,725.00

Reliquary Cross, 10" x 15", tempera, gold leaf, porcelain on wood cross, reverse with old Slavonic inscription denoting that cross was blessed on Mt. Athos at the Russian Monastery of St. Panteleimon, relic inset on reverse is old square wood fragment, Russian, 19th C 1,650.00

Retablo, Mexican, painted on tin, late 19th C
  9-1/2" x 13-3/4", Our Lady of Sorrows...................................250.00
  9-3/4" x 13-1/2", Our Lady Refuge of Sinners, black flat iron frame..235.00

Santos, carved wood, polychrome and gesso, Spanish
  7-3/4 h, Infantata 375.00
  10" h, St. Mary in Glory, standing on cloudwork with seraphim ..115.00
  14" h, Crucified Christ..200.00
  15-1/4" h, Mary Magdeline..425.00
  16" h, Virgin Mary, jointed, glass eyes.......................................375.00
  16-1/2" h, Peasant Virgin..350.00

Sculpture
  10" h, 10" w, Christ with Crown of Thorns, bronze spelter, marble plinth 595.00
  10" h, 10" w, Mary Magdalene, bronze spelter, marble plinth 595.00
  27-1/2" x 24", Saint Elizabeth, carved wood and polychrome, German or Italian 1,650.00

Shrine, 35-1/2" h, Baroque, painted, gilded wood, and composition, Spanish, early 18th C, extensive worming, losses................1,955.00

Tabernacle, 26" h, 22" w, 8" x 8" door, cast bronze, form of cross, dec with sheaves of wheat, built-in exposition door....................... 110.00

REVERSE PAINTING on GLASS

History: The earliest examples of reverse painting on glass were produced in 13th-century Italy. By the 17th century the technique had spread to central and eastern Europe. It spread westward as the center of the glassmaking industry moved to Germany in the late 17th century.

The Alsace and Black Forest regions developed a unique portraiture style. The half and three-quarter portraits often were titled below the portrait. Women tend to have generic names while most males are likenesses of famous men.

The English used a mezzotint, rather than free-style, method to create their reverse paintings. Landscapes and allegorical figures were popular. The Chinese began working in the medium in the 17th century, eventually favoring marine and patriotic scenes.

Most American reverse painting was done by folk artists and is unsigned. Portraits, patriotic and mourning scenes, floral compositions, landscapes, and buildings are the favorite subjects. Known American artists include Benjamin Greenleaf, A. Cranfield, and Rowley Jacobs.

In the late 19th century commercially produced reverse paintings, often decorated with mother-of-pearl, became popular. Themes included the Statue of Liberty, the capitol in Washington, D.C., and various world's fairs and expositions.

Today craftsmen are reviving this art, using some vintage looking designs, but usually with brighter colors that their antique counterparts.

Portraits
  9-1/8" h, 6-1/2" w, Rosinia, polychrome, dark green ground, orig frame..450.00

Portrait, Jerome Napoleon, Baltimore, MD, framed, 12-3/4" x 15-3/4", $300.

  15" h, 11-5/8" w, Susan, blue dress, white collar, green ground, white border, minor wear, orig frame 550.00
  15-1/8" h, 11-7/8" w, Louise, green dress with white sleeves, gold scarf, brown ground, white border, minor wear, orig frame.550.00
  16" h, 11-1/2" w, Geisha, facing pr, geisha seated next to table, vase with flower, bamboo dec, mirrored ground, Chinese Export, 19th C, framed, losses...625.00
  21-1/2" h, 18" w, Abraham Lincoln, framed 425.00
  21-3/4" h, 19-3/4" w, George and Martha Washington, orig frames, minor edge wear 2,420.00

Scenes
  7" x 9", Perry's Lake Erie Victory, Sept 10, 1813, naval battle scene, multicolored 250.00
  10-1/2" h, 12-1/2" w, country house in winter, gold painted frame 75.00
  10-1/2" h, 12-1/2" w, *Ohio*, side wheeler steamship, poplar frame..175.00

Tray, 17-1/2" l, 19-1/4" w, colorful fruit, silver foil backing, black ground, old gilt frame...220.00

RIDGWAY

History: Throughout the 19th century, the Ridgway family, through a series of partnerships, held a position of importance in the ceramics industry in Shelton and Hanley, Staffordshire, England. The connection began with Job and George, two brothers, and Job's two sons, John and William. In 1830, John and William dissolved their partnership; John retained the Cauldon Place factory and William the Bell Works. By 1862, the porcelain division of Cauldon was carried on by Coalport China Ltd. William and his heirs continued at the Bell Works and the Church (Hanley) and Bedford (Shelton) works until the end of the 19th century.

Marks: Many early pieces are unmarked. Later marks include the initials of the many different partnerships.

References: Susan and Al Bagdade, *Warman's English & Continental Pottery & Porcelain,* 3rd Edition, Krause Publications, 1998; G. A. Godden, *Ridgway Porcelains,* Antique Collectors' Club, 1985.

Museums: Cincinnati Art Museum, Cincinnati, OH; Potsdam Puiblic Museum, Potsdam, NY.

Plate, Coaching Days & Coaching Ways, silver trim, 9" d, $70.

Additional Listings: Staffordshire, Historical; Staffordshire, Romantic.

Beverage Set, 9-1/2" h pitcher, six 4" h mugs, 12-1/2" d tray, Coaching Days, black coaching scenes, caramel ground, silver luster trim ..325.00

Bowl
  8-7/8" d, floral and foliage band, Imari palette, No. 21138.....300.00
  9-1/2" d, Coaching Days and Ways, "Henry VII and the Abbot," black and caramel brown 45.00

Cake Stand, 9-1/2' d, 2-1/4" h, Oriental floral design, butterflies, gilt trim, mkd "Ridgway, Old Derby," stains, gilt wear, chips, hairline, pr......150.00

Cup and Saucer, boy fishing on lake 30.00

Dessert Plate, 9" d, Harlequin patter, molded scalloped rim edge, gilt edge border of white beadwork with 4 clusters of gilt white blossoms, painted with assorted flowers and fruits, iron-red numbers, c1830, 19 pc set..2,750.00

Ice Pail, cov, 13" h, horizontal band of gilt edged orange feathery scrollwork reserved on pale yellow ground, above acanthus leaf molding, rope twist handles with trailing vine leaf terminals, cov with finials modeled as rhytons brimming with fruit, finial repaired, c1840, iron-red number...3,500.00

Mug, 4" h, Boating Days, New Haven and Eton, brown body, silver luster trim 45.00

Pitcher, 4-1/4" h, red transfers of family scenes on cream ground in roundels, reserved on cobalt blue ground, c1890, "Humphrey's Clock and William Ridgway" mark..225.00

Plate, 8-1/2" d, rose, rust, and purple Oriental-type florals with yellow centers, gray-green branches, raised, ribbed, scalloped edge, white ground, c1830, No. 2004... 65.00

Platter
  13" x 11", Asiatic Palaces, dark blue transfer, mkd "William Ridgway, Son & Co." 165.00
  18-1/2" x 15-1/2", Tyrolean, light blue transfer, molded well and tree, mkd "William Ridgway" 200.00

Teapot, cov, 6" h, 6" l, brown and white whooping cranes and foliage, emb leaves, dated 1877, mkd 125.00

Tray, 9-1/2" l, 7-1/2" w, Pickwick design, silver luster trim, scalloped rim, open handles.. 50.00

RING TREES

History: A ring tree is a small, generally saucer-shaped object made of glass, porcelain, metal, or wood with a center post in the shape of a hand, branches, or cylinder. It is a convenient object for holding finger rings.

Glass

Black, 3-7/8" d, 4" h, allover dec on saucer and post, lacy gold vines and green enamel leaves, light blue, white, orange, and cream flowers 95.00

Bristol, 3" h, 3-1/4" d, turquoise blue, lacy yellow leaves and large gold leaves dec 85.00

Cameo, 3-1/4" h, 4" d, acid cut, rd flowers, leaves, and stems, leaf ground, St. Louis 160.00

Clear, 3" h, 3-3/4" d, cut floral dec, black enameled bands 65.00

Cranberry, 3-1/4" d, 3-1/2" d, hp, multicolored flowers, gold leaves. 115.00

Moser, 4" h, 3-3/4" d, black amethyst, heavily enameled blue, white, orange, and yellow flowers, green leaves, all over lacy gold dec.. 115.00

Opalescent, 2-1/2" h, 3-1/2" d, vaseline, striped........................... 65.00

Waterford, crystal... 35.00

Porcelain

Austria, hp pink and green floral dec, gold trim, mkd "M. Z. Austria" . 70.00

Limoges, multicolored blossoms, white ground, mkd "T. & V. Limoges" 40.00

Minton, 3" h, pastel flowers, gold trim, mkd "Minton England" 45.00

Nippon, gold hand, rim dec... 35.00

Royal Worcester, 2-3/4" h, 4-1/2" l, oval dish, 3 pronged holder, hp pink and yellow flowers, beige ground, c1898 ....150.00

R. S. Germany, 2-3/4" h, 5-1/2" l, hp, pink flowers, green leaves, told tree, sgd "E. Wolff" 50.00

Wedgwood, 2-3/4" h, jasperware, center post, white cameos of classical ladies, floral border, blue ground, mkd 150.00

Zsolnay, 3-1/2" h, irid gold... 85.00

Silver

Tiffany & Co., angel shape...450.00

Wilcox, open hand, saucer base, engraved edge, sgd................. 60.00

Porcelain, center hand, rose floral motif, gilt trim, mkd with maple leaf and "Hand Painted," $55.

ROCKINGHAM and ROCKINGHAM BROWN-GLAZED WARES

History: Rockingham ware can be divided into two categories. The first consists of the fine china and porcelain pieces made between 1826 and 1842 by the Rockingham Company of Swinton, Yorkshire, England, and its predecessor firms: Swinton, Bingley, Don, Leeds, and Brameld. The Bramelds developed the cadogan, a lidless teapot. Between 1826 and 1842, a quality soft-paste product with a warm, silky feel was developed by the Bramelds. Elaborate specialty pieces were made. By 1830, the company employed 600 workers and listed 400 designs for dessert sets and 1,000 designs for tea and coffee services in their catalog. Unable to meet its payroll, the company closed in 1842.

The second category of Rockingham ware includes pieces produced in the famous Rockingham brown glaze that became an intense and vivid purple-brown when fired. It had a dark, tortoiseshell appearance. The glaze was copied by many English and American potteries. American manufacturers which used Rockingham glaze include D. & J. Henderson of Jersey City, New Jersey; United States Pottery in Bennington, Vermont; potteries in East Liverpool, Ohio; and several potteries in Indiana and Illinois.

References: Susan and Al Bagdade, *Warman's American Pottery and Porcelain,* Wallace-Homestead, 1994; Susan and Al Bagdade, *Warman's English & Continental Pottery & Porcelain,* 3rd Edition, Krause Publications, 1998; Mary Brewer, *Collector's Guide to Rockingham, Collector Books,* 1996.

Museum: Bennington Museum, Bennington, VT.

Additional Listings: Bennington and Bennington-Type Pottery.

Urn, campana form, ram's head handles, floral painted reserves, green ground, gilt dec, c1800-35, 12-5/8" h, gilt wear, one with repaired handle, price for pair, $1,150. Photo courtesy of Freeman\Fine Arts.

Bedpan, 15" l, Rockingham glaze, chip 40.00
Bottle, 6" h, figural, shoe, emb "Ann Reid 1859" 250.00
Bowl
    9-1/2" d, 3-1/4" h 65.00
    10-1/2" d, 4-3/4" h, molded ext. ribs, scalloped band 50.00
Casserole, cov, 12" l, 10-1/4" h, oval, fruit finial, applied handles 275.00
Creamer, figural
    5-7/8" h, Toby 215.00
    6-3/4" h, cow 19th C, minor chips 260.00
Dish, 11-1/2" l, octagonal, spotted Rockingham glaze 170.00
Figure, 10-1/2" h, seated dog, free standing front legs, molded base with deer and hounds design 440.00
Flask, 8" h, molded floral dec, band 45.00
Flower Pot, 10-1/4" h, emb acanthus leaves, matching saucer.... 45.00
Inkwell, 4-1/8" l, shoe shape 60.00
Loving Cup, 6-7/8" h, molded drinking scenes and dog fight, brown glaze, handles, chips on bottom edge 250.00
Mixing Bowl, 13" d, 6" h, Molded Gothic Arches, dark glaze, wear and scratches 140.00
Pie Plate, Rockingham glaze
    8-3/8" d 65.00
    10" d 80.00
Pitcher, Rockingham glaze
    4-3/8" l, squatty, C scroll handle 75.00
    6-3/8" h, molded Gothic Art design 65.00
    6-7/8" h, figural, seated dog, chip on base 185.00
    8" h, molded peacocks, rim chips 90.00
Plate
    9" d, painted center with exotic bird in landscape, raised C-scroll border with gilt and painting, puce griffin and green number marks..... 650.00
    9-1/4" d, painted vase of flowers overflowing onto marble table, medium blue ground, gilt line band, shark's tooth and S-scroll border, c1831-42 .... 875.00
Potpourri Vase, 4-3/8" h, waisted rect shape, painted front and reverse with river landscape between gilt formal borders, 4 paw feet, pierced cov with acorn knob, double handles, c1826, iron-red griffin mark 950.00
Scent Bottle, 6" h, onion shape, applied garden flowers, gilt line rims, c1831-40, printed puce griffin mark 465.00
Tray, 8-1/2" x 11", scalloped rim 100.00
Vase
    4-3/8" h, flared, painted view of Larington Yorkshire, figures and sheep, wide gilt border, dark blue ground, restored, c1826-30, iron-red griffin and painted title 420.00
    6-1/2" h, flared hexagon, painted sprays of colored garden flowers alternating with blue panels, gilt scrolls, c1831-42, puce griffin mark 800.00
Washboard, 24-1/4" h, 19th C, imperfections 350.00

ROCK 'N' ROLL

History: Rock music can be traced back to early rhythm and blues. It progressed until it reached its golden age in the 1950s and 1960s. Most of the memorabilia issued during that period focused on individual singers and groups. The largest quantity of collectible material is connected to Elvis Presley and The Beatles.

In the 1980s, two areas—clothing and guitars—associated with key rock 'n' roll personalities received special collector attention. Sotheby's and Christie's East regularly feature rock 'n' roll memorabilia as part of their collectibles sales. At the moment, the market is highly speculative and driven by nostalgia.

It is important to identify memorabilia issued during the lifetime of an artist or performing group as opposed to material issued after they died or disbanded. Objects of the latter type are identified as "fantasy" items and will never achieve the same degree of collectibility as period counterparts.

References: Jeff Augsburger, Marty Eck, and Rick Rann, *The Beatles Memorabilia Price Guide,* Antique Trader Books; Mark A. Baker, *Goldmine Price Guide to Rock N' Roll Memorabilia,* Krause Publications, 1997;Goldmine Magazine eds., *Goldmine Roots of Rock Digest,* Krause Publications, 1999; Marty Eck, *The Monkees Collectibles Price Guide,* Antique Trader Books, 1998; Joe Hilton and Greg Moore, *Rock-N-Roll Treasures,* Collector Books, 1999; Tom Neely and Dave Thompson, *Goldmine British Invasion Record Price Guide,* Krause Publications, 1997.

Periodicals: Beatlefan, P.O. Box 33515, Decatur, GA 30033; *Good Day Sunshine,* 397 Edgewood Ave., New Haven, CT 06511; *Instant Karma,* P.O. Box 256, Sault Ste. Marie, MI 49783.

Collectors' Clubs: Beatles Connection, P.O. Box 1066, Pinellas Park, FL 34665; Beatles Fan Club of Great Britain, Superstore Productions, 123 Marina St., Leonards on Sea, East Sussex, England TN 38 OBN; Elvis Forever TCB Fan Club, P.O. Box 1066, Pinellas Park, FL 34665; Graceland News Fan Club, P.O. Box 452, Rutherford, NJ 07070; Working Class Hero Club, 3311 Niagara St., Pittsburgh, PA 15213.

Reproduction Alert: Records, picture sleeves, and album jackets, especially for The Beatles, have been counterfeited. When compared to the original, sound may be inferior, as may be the printing on labels and picture jackets. Many pieces of memorabilia also have been reproduced, often with some change in size, color, and design.

Additional Listings: See The Beatles, Elvis Presley, and Rock 'n' Roll in *Warman's Americana & Collectibles* and *Warman's Flea Market Price Guide.*

Autograph
  Asher, Peter, sgd with black Sharpie on unlined white 5" x 3" card 17.50
  Berry, Chuck, sgd black and white photo, 10" x 8" 100.00
  Chapin, Harry, blue ink signature on white 5" x 3" card 100.00
  Clapton, Eric, sgd color photo, 8" x 10" 65.00
  Garrity, Freddie, sgd with blue Sharpie on unlined yellow 6" x 4" card 15.00
  Harry, Debbie, promo flat for French Kissin, sgd with blue Sharpie, 12" x 12" 40.00
  John, Elton, sgd 1989 WNEW 102.7 MCA Records, promo photo, 30th performance at Madison Sq Garden, 1989, 8" x 9" 55.00
  Jones, Booker T., sgd black and white photo, 8" x 10" 42.00
  Perkins, Carl, sgd color photo of Perkins, Eric Clapton, George Harrison, Ringo Starr, Dave Edmunds, Slim Jim Phantom, sgd by Perkins, 8" x 10" 75.00
  Richard, Little, black and white photo, inscribed "To you/With Love," 8" x 10" 70.00
  Young, Neil, sgd color photo, with guitar sitting in limo, 8" x 10" ...60.00
Backstage Pass, cloth
  Aerosmith, Pump Tour '89, afternoon 10.00
  Black Sabbath, working personnel 9.00
  Dylan/Petty, Temples in Flames 20.00
  Iron Maiden, World Slavery Tour, '84 .... 9.00
  Bon Jovi, NJ Guest 7.00
  KISS, 10th anniversary, after show, unused 7.00
  Cindi Lauper, Crew '86-87 .... 6.00
  Pink Floyd, Mixer '94 .... 9.00
  Rolling Stones, American Tour '81 .... 15.00
Book
  California Dreamin, Mamas and Papas 16.00

  Don't Be Denied, Neil Young 15.00
  Let Them All Talk, Elvis, Costello 12.00
Cigarette Lighter, Rod Stewart decal, chrome, c1975 .... 35.00
Concert Program
  Aerosmith, Nine Lives Tour, 1997 .... 10.00
  Clapton, Eric, Royal Albert Hall 10.00
  K. D. Lang, 1992 Ingenue Tour 6.50
  Paul Simon, Born at the Right Time Tour, 1991, over-sized 5.00
  The Who, Tommy, 1989, 18 pcs 6.00
Cover Artwork
  Rolling Stones, R'N'R Comics, orig full color artwork, 1989, 20" x 30", matted and framed, S. Jackson, pencil and ink cover drawing and 13" x 9" back cover H. Ras painting, set 250.00
  Frank Zappa, R'N'R Comics, 1994, 8-3/4" x 14-1/2", painting by Scott Jackson, used for front cover of "Via La Bizarre," issue #1 ...... 100.00
Counter Display, Rolling Stones, "Made In The Shade," 1976, 21" x 19", 3-D cardboard, bowed diecut, with four previous LP covers at left and "Rolling Stones & Tongue" logo on silver at top right .. 250.00
Crew Shirt
  Jimmy Buffet, white, American Tour '87, large parrot drawing 50.00
  Grateful Dead, white, "Local Crew 96" 30.00
  Metallica, black, "Metallic Lower Crew," drawing of blind justice over pocket area 30.00
  Pointer Sisters, gray, "Pointer Sisters Crew," silhouettes of sisters on sleeve 10.00
  Stryper, gray, "Staff, New Year's Eve, 86/87," photo of band .. 20.00
  Who, white, "Staff, Day on the Green," two Who as dog characters, 1989 .... 30.00
Divider Card, Yardbirds, LP bin type, Epic, 1988, 12" x 14" plastic, purple names and logos emb at top 200.00
Drumsticks
  Alice in Chains 25.00
  Black Crows, concerned used, logo 20.00
  Randy Castillo, Ozzy Osbourne 35.00
  Iron Maiden, 1985 .... 50.00
  Steve Riley, WASP 20.00
Flyer, concert
  Aerosmith, 1988. 8" x 6", 2 sided, Whitesnake Def Leppard on back 45.00
  Cramps, Horrible Halloween, Devonshire Fairgrounds, Northridge, CA, 1980s, 6" x 15" 40.00
  Led Zeppelin, Tarrant County Convention Center, Ft. Worth, TX, 8/22/70, 8-1/2" x 11-1/2" 60.00
  Motley Crue & Others, Glen Dale Civic Auditorium, Glen Dale, CA, 5/7/82, 8-1/2" x 11", two staple holes at top 35.00
Fun Kit, Beatles, 1964, oversized magazine, promoting Hard Day's Night 30.00
Label Sticker, Deep Purple, promo LP label made for Come Taste The Band 25.00
Lobby Card, Elvis, Blue Hawaii, 11" x 14", full color 40.00
Magazine
  Hit Parade Magazine, Jimi Hendrix and Fleetwood Mac, July 1969 .... 5.00
  SING Magazine, Marie McDonald on cov, June 1948 .... 4.50
Make-Up Kit, Kiss, MIB 10.00
Menu, Elvis Presley, Las Vegas Hilton Hotel, 8-1/2" x 11" 1000.00
Merchandising Kit, Queen, Night At The Opera, Elektra, 1985, 24" x 24" cardboard and tin paper poster with LP cover, two 15" x 24" 2 sided thin cardboard "Hanging Arrow" displays, two 9" x 10" oval posters with LP cover art 200.00
Pass, hospitality room, Rolling Stones, cloth, Lazar foil, Voodoo Lounge Tour, Oakland 45.00
Pennant, 29-1/2" l, We Love Lil Richard, felt, white, red design and border, orig 30" l wood stick 1950s 50.00
Plaque, Bon Jovi, Anytime, Anywhere, with unused tickets from Belgium, Italy, and Istanbul, gold CD, only 45 produced 250.00
Poster
  Alice Cooper, Warner Bros, black and white, heavy stock, 1970s 175.00

Appetite for Destruction, Guns N Roses, color, promo type 6.00
Kinks, Atlanta, GA, 1970, cardboard stock 180.00
Press Kit, photo, bio pages, etc.
    Captain and Tennille, 20 Years of Romance............................ 10.00
    Cheap Trick, One-On-One... 15.00
    Chicago, Night and Day.. 17.50
    Climax Blues Band, Shine-On 25.00
    Fleetwood Mac, The Dance, fold-out, 3D cutout of band 12.00
Print, Chuck Berry, by Red Grooms, color screenprint on paper, 1978, edition of 150, published by Marlborough Graphics, NY, sgd "Red Grooms" in pencil lower right, numbered "77/150" in pencil lower left, 24-1/2" x 18-1/2"... 345.00
Promotional Standee, Elvis Presley, "Aloha From Hawaii," RA, 1973, 34" x 56" 19.00
Radio Show
    Alice Cooper, King Biscuit Flower Hour, Michigan, 1978......... 18.00
    John Lennon, "What's It All About," 1982, 7", interview, for public service broadcast... 95.00
Record Award
    Beatles, "20 Greatest Hits," orig RIAA Gold strip plate award, gold wood frame 795.00
    Billy Joel, "Songs from the Attic," RIAA Platinum Strip plate, orig silver wood frame 450.00
    Eagles, "The Long Run," RIAA Platinum for 4 million sales .. 600.00
    Hootie & the Blowfish, "Fairweather Johnson," RIAA Gold LP ...600.00
    KISS, "Alive," Casablanca, in-house Platinum floater 595.00
    Midnight Oil, "Diesel & Dust," RIAA Gold award, with LP and cassette, old style round hologram.. 250.00
Scarf, Beatles, glossy fabric, half corner design, mkd "The Beatles/ Copyright by Ramat & Co., Ltd/London, ECI," 25" sq, c1964 ..160.00
Sheet Music, Love Me Tender, Elvis, deep pink cover.................. 50.00
Ticket
    Aerosmith, Pacific, 1989.. 5.00
    Bruce Springsteen, LA Sports, 1988 .... 5.00
    Elvis, 9/88... 75.00
    Ozzy Osbourne, sgd, last show, 10/92 .... 100.00
    Yardbirds/Doors, 1967... 50.00
    ZZ Top, sgd, 11/94... 50.00
Tour Book
    Michael Jackson, History World Tour, oversized 12.00

Tambourine, Monkees, colored disc, white ground, copyright 1967 Raybert Productions, Inc., trademark of Screen Gems, Inc., $42.

Jimmy Page and Robert Plant, World Tour, 1995................... 10.00
Rolling Stones, Bridges to Baylon, center fold-out 15.00
Sonny and Cher, 1972.. 100.00
Yes, Open Your Eyes, 1997.. 12.00
Yearbook, Dick Clark, 42 pgs, 1957, 8-1/2" x 11" 40.00

ROCKWELL, NORMAN

History: Norman Rockwell (Feb. 3, 1894-November 1978) was a famous American artist and illustrator. During the time he painted, from age 18 until his death, he created more than 2,000 works.

His first professional efforts were illustrations for a children's book; his next projects were done for *Boy's Life,* the Boy Scout magazine. His most famous works are those that appeared as cover illustrations on the *Saturday Evening Post.*

Norman Rockwell painted everyday people in everyday situations, mixing a little humor with sentiment. His paintings and illustrations are treasured because of this sensitive approach. Rockwell painted people he knew and places with which he was familiar. New England landscapes are found in many of his illustrations.

References: Denis C. Jackson, *Norman Rockwell Identification and Value Guide to: Magazines, Posters, Calendars,* Books, 2nd ed., published by author, 1985; Karal Ann Marling, *Norman Rockwell,* Harry N. Abrams, 1997; Mary Moline, *Norman Rockwell Collectibles,* 6th ed., Green Valley World, 1988.

Collectors' Club: Rockwell Society of America, 597 Saw Mill River Rd, Ardsley, NY 10502.

Museums: Museum of Norman Rockwell Art, Reedsburg, WI; Norman Rockwell Museum, Northbrook, IL; Norman Rockwell Museum, Philadelphia, PA; Norman Rockwell Museum, Stockbridge, MA.

Reproduction Alert: Because of the popularity of his works, the images have been reproduced on many objects. These new collectibles, which should not be confused with original artwork and illustrations, provide a wide range of collectibles and prices.

Additional Listings: See *Warman's Americana & Collectibles* for more examples.

Historic

Autograph, typed letter sgd, 1 page, 8vo, Stockbridge, April 24, 1973, answering questions relating to his work 450.00
Book
    A Rockwell Portrait, Donald Walton, 1978, book club edition, Sneed, Andrews, McMeel,, 285 pgs, black and white photos, dj 15.00
    My Adventures as an Illustrator, Rockwell, 1960 .... 25.00
    Norman Rockwell, Illustrator, Arthur A. Guptill, c1946, 3rd printing, Watson-Guptill, 208 pgs, Rockwell illus, orig box 25.00
Calendar, 1941, boy and dog illus, Hercules Powder Co. adv, 13" x 30-1/2".. 175.00
Magazine, cover illus
    Country Gentleman, Oct. 3, 1917.. 60.00
    Literary Digest, Aug. 17, 1918.. 40.00
Magazine Tear Sheet, Jell-O adv, *Country Gentleman,* 1922, matted 40.00
Poster
    Freedom of Speech, WWII, 1943 .... 60.00
    Maxwell House Coffee adv, 1932 .... 350.00

Modern

Coin, Ford Motor Co., 50th Anniversary 40.00
Figure
    Gorham Fine China, Four Seasons, Childhood, 1973, set of
       four 500.00
    Grossman Designs, Inc., Tom Sawyer, Series No. 1, 1976 ..... 95.00
Plate
    Scotty Gets His Tree, Christmas Series, Rockwell Society of Amer-
       ica, 1974 .... 175.00
    Triple Self Portrait, Gorham 75.00
Print
    Gilding the Eagle, Eleanor Ettinger, Inc., litho, 21" x 25-1/2" ... 3,500.00
    Music Hath Charms, Circle Fine Arts, sgd and numbered . 3,000.00
    People Praying, color offset litho, sgd in pencil lower right, num-
       bered, 28-1/4" x 22" 800.00

ROGERS & SIMILAR STATUARY

History: John Rogers, born in America in 1829, studied sculpture in Europe and produced his first plaster-of-paris statue, "The Checker Players," in 1859. It was followed by "The Slave Auction" in 1860.

His works were popular parlor pieces in the Victorian era. He produced at least 80 different statues, and the total number of groups made from the originals is estimated to be more than 100,000.

Casper Hennecke, one of Rogers's contemporaries, operated C. Hennecke & Company from 1881 until 1896 in Milwaukee, Wisconsin. His statuary often is confused with Rogers' work since both are very similar.

References: Paul and Meta Bieier, *John Rogers' Groups of Statuary,* published by author, 1971; Betty C. Haverly, *Hennecke's Florentine Statuary,* published by author, 1972; David H. Wallace, *John Rogers,* Wesleyan University, 1976.

Periodical: *Rogers Group,* 4932 Prince George Ave., Beltsville, MD 20705.

Museums: John Rogers Studio & Museum of the New Canaan Historical Soc, New Canaan CT; Lightner Museum, Saint Augustine, FL.

Notes: It is difficult to find a statue in undamaged condition and with original paint. Use the following conversions: 10% off for minor flaking; 10%, chips; 10 to 20%, piece or pieces broken and reglued; 20%, flaking; 50%, repainting.

Rogers

Checkers Up At The Farm 525.00
Coming To The Parson's 375.00
Council of War 1,300.00
Faust and Marguerite Leaving the Garden 1,300.00
Going For The Cows 450.00
Ha, I Like Not That 550.00
It Is So Nominated In The Bond 650.00
Parting Promise 400.00
Picket Guard 825.00
Rip Van Winkle at Home, damage 275.00
Speak for Yourself John 550.00
Taking The Oath 650.00
Union Refugee, broken gun 325.00
We Boys 475.00
Weighing The Baby, damage 575.00

Conquering Jealosy, $175.

Rogers Type

Can't You Talk 140.00
First Love, repainted 175.00
Holy Family 225.00
Romeo and Juliet 150.00

ROOKWOOD POTTERY

History: Mrs. Marie Longworth Nicholas Storer, Cincinnati, Ohio, founded Rookwood Pottery in 1880. The name of this outstanding American art pottery came from her family estate, "Rookwood," named for the rooks (crows) which inhabited the wooded grounds.

Though the Rookwood pottery filed for bankruptcy in 1941, it was soon reorganized under new management. Efforts at maintaining the pottery proved futile, and it was sold in 1956 and again in 1959. The pottery was moved to Starkville, Mississippi, in conjunction with the Herschede Clock Co. It finally ceased operating in 1967.

Rookwood wares changed with the times. The variety is endless, in part because of the creativity of the many talented artists responsible for great variations in glazes and designs.

Marks: There are five elements to the Rookwood marking system—the clay or body mark, the size mark, the decorator mark, the date mark, and the factory mark. The best way to date Rookwood art pottery is from factory marks.

From 1880 to 1882, the factory mark was the name "Rookwood" incised or painted on the base. Between 1881 and 1886, the firm name, address, and year appeared in an oval frame. Beginning in 1886, the impressed "RP" monogram appeared and a flame mark was added for each year until 1900. After 1900, a Roman numeral, indicating the last two digits of the year of production, was added at the bottom of the "RP" flame mark. This last mark

SPECIAL AUCTIONS

Cincinnati Art Galleries
635 Main St.
Cincinnati, OH 45202
(513) 381-2128

David Rago Auctions, Inc.
333 S. Main St.
Lambertville, NJ 08530
(609) 397-9374
web site: http://www.ragoarts.com

Treadway Gallery, Inc.
2029 Madison Rd
Cincinnati, OH 45208
(513) 321-6742

Vase, scenic vellum, painted birches by lake, E. D. Diers, 1920, flame mark/XX/ED/944A/V, restored drill hole at bottom, 18" h, 7-1/4" d, $5,000. Photo courtesy of David Rago Auctions, Inc.

is the one most often seen on Rookwood pieces in the antiques marketplace.

References: Anita J. Ellis, *Rookwood Pottery,* Schiffer Publishing, 1995; Herbert Peck, *Book of Rookwood Pottery,* Crown Publishers, 1968; ——, *Second Book of Rookwood Pottery,* published by author, 1985; David Rago, *American Art Pottery,* Knickerbocker Press, 1997.

Collectors' Club: American Art Pottery Association, P.O. Box 834, Westport, MA 02790-0697, http://www.amartpot.org.

Bookends, pr
  5-3/8" h, molded Jay bird figures, oak leaves, and acorns, creamy matte glaze, imp cipher 2829, 1929 .... 320.00
  6-1/2" h, molded open book, flowering branches and rooks, mottled mated green glaze, 1924 .... 1,150.00
Bowl
  5-1/2" d, 2-3/4" d, matte, garland of stylized green tulips, blue heart-shaped leaves, dark green ground, flame mark, "X/1109/WEH," William Hentschel, 1910 .... 900.00
  7-3/4" d, 3-1/2" h, hammered glaze, Limoges style underglaze pink blossoms dec, gold highlights, shaped #166, Laura A Fry . 775.00
Cabinet Vase, 4" h, 3" d
  Bulbous, carved matte, stylized fruit, dark green ground, flame mark, "V/969E/SEC," Sallie Coyne, 1905 .... 600.00
  Modeled matte, blue-green dragonflies, leathery rose ground, flame mark, "V/973/SEC," Salie Coyne, 1905 .... 1,100.00
Candlesticks, pr, 11-3/4" h, dolphins, twisted shaft and flaring bobeche, gunmetal glaze, flame mark, "XXI/2464," 1921 .... 650.00
Centerpiece Bowl, 13" d, 3" h, Jewel Porcelain, polychrome painted abstract bird on blossoming branch, flame mark, "XXIX/2574C/E. T. H.," E. T. Hurley, 1929 .... 1,300.00
Charger, 12-1/2" d, mauve and ochre galleon center, light blue splashed border, John Wareham, dated 1905 .... 1,450.00
Ewer
  5-1/2" h, 4-1/2" d, wild roses, blue ground, iris glaze, flame mark, "724D/W/ARV," A. R. Valentien, 1894 .... 2,000.00
  6" h, 4" d, silver overlay, standard glaze, painted hollyberries, shaded ground, flame mark, "40/W/SEC," Sallie E. Coyne, 1894 ..... 1,600.00
  9" h, 3-1/4" d, brown dragon, celadon ground, sea green glaze, flame mark, "379/MAD/G," Matt Daly, 1897 .... 4,250.00
Jardiniere, 7-1/4" h, 8-1/4" d, standard galze, blooming wild roses dec, double handled, shape #484D, Ameial Sprague, 1898 .... 900.00
Mug, 6" h, light standard glaze, blooming chrysanthemums dec, shape #501, William P. McDonald, 1889 .... 425.00
Plaque, scenic vellum
  5" h, 9-1/4" w, autumn landscape, orig frame, flame mark, "XVI/L.A.," Lenore Asbury, 1914 .... 3,750.00
  9-1/4" h, 5-1/4" w, The Willows, trees by river, orig gilded frame, flame mark, "XV/V," artist sgd on front, title penciled on reverse, orig gilded frame 4,750.00
  10" h, 7" w, snow scene, birches at dawn, orig frame, orig paper seal on back, sgd "SEC," Sallie Coyne, 1899 .... 4,250.00
Sketch, 10-1/2" x 15", orig study in watercolor and ink, flowering wisteria branch, green, purple, and black, Josephine Zettel, c1900, framed 500.00
Stein
  5-1/4" h, 4-3/4" d, Z-line, emb ears of corn, matte green glaze, flame mark, "11/332/Z/JDW," John D. Wareham, 1902, hairline to rim and handle 225.00
  6" h, 5" d, incised grave digger in cemetery, inscribed "To mingle with his native clay...," stamped "ROOKWOOD/1886," incised "Isaac Abbott/E.T.C.," Edward Cranch, 1886, 3" hairline from rim, hairline to handle 700.00
Tankard, 7-1/2" h, 4-1/2" d, carved matte, red tulips, green leaves, green ground, flame mark, "VII/1014D/V" and unknown artist's cipher, 1907 .... 500.00
Tile, 8" w, 10-1/4" l, rect, one with swallow in flight, shaded blue ground; other with 3 swallows perched on branch, shaded light green ground, imp marks, quarter moon ciphers, artist Albert Valentien initials, pr, crazing, chips 19,550.00
Umbrella Stand, 21" h, 17-1/2" d, cylindrical, caved matte, green and yellow wisteria, dark blue ground, flame mark, "XV/1753/CST," C. S. Todd, 1915, restored lines to body 1,800.00
Vase
  5" h, japonesque yellow blossoms, olive green glossy glaze ground, yellow glazed int., imp mark, 1343 and artist Sara Sax initials on base, 1923 .... 1,495.00
  5" h, 5-1/2" d, Jewel Porcelain, flaring, painted pink tulips, shaded gray ground, flame mark, "XLIII/6305/MHM," M. H. McDonald, 1943, orig factory certificate of authenticity, minor base nick 650.00
  5-1/4" h, bulbous, purple violets, shaded gray ground, iris glaze, uncrazed, flame mark, "II/914E/ED," E. D. Diers, 1902 ... 1,400.00
  5-1/2" h, 5-1/4" d, bulbous, vellum,cherry blossoms and blue flowers, shaded blue ground, flame mark, "XXV/2831/FR," Frederick Rothenbusch, 1925 .... 1,100.00
  5-1/2" h, 5-1/2" d, Jewel Porcelain, bulbous, painted yellow, pink, and blue crocus, blue-gray ground, flame mark, "XXV/2831," artist cipher K. Siryamadani, 1925 .... 1,800.00
  6" h, 3" d, fleshy pink poppy and green leaves, shaded pink ground, flame mark "IV/SX/30F," Sallie Sax, 1904 .... 1,100.00

Vases, left: Iris Glaze, Ed Diers, 1904, large pink and yellow roses, shaded pink to green ground, flame mark "IV/ 943C/ED," little crazing, 9-1/2" h, 5" d, $2,000; center: Jewel Porcelain, M. H. McDonald, 1940, landscape of blue and green trees, flame mark/XL/892B/MHM," uncrazed, 11" h, 5-1/2" d, $2,900; right: Iris Glaze, L. Asbury, 1905, white and gray poppies on shaded ivory to purple ground, seconded mark, flame mark/V/902C/L.A./X.," 9-1/2" h, 6-1/2" d, $2,000. Photo courtesy of David Rago Auctions, Inc.

6" h, 5-1/2" d, spherical, carved iris, white dogwood blossoms and branches, silver gray ground, flame mark, "531E/E.T.H.," E. T. Hurley, 1900 .... 4,250.00

7-1/4" h, 3" d, painted matte, orange rose, green leaves, purple ground, flame mark, "VII/950E, O.G.R.," Olga G. Reed, 1907 .... 2,600.00

7-1/4" h, 5" d, painted matte, red poppies, yellow ground, flame mark, "I/31BZ/ST," Sallie Toohey, 1901, restoration to hairline, another unrestored 1,300.00

7-3/8" h, tapered oviform, extended rim, soft brown and green leafy branches, red berry clusters, dark blue fading to cream glossy glaze, imp mark, "901D," artist Sara Sax cipher, c1902, crazing 1,495.00

8-1/4" h, 3" d, ovoid, Tiger Eye, Japanese landscape with flowers, bamboo, tall grasses, flame mark, "589E/R/H.E.W.," H. E. Wilcox, 1894 .... 1,100.00

8-1/4" h, 4" d, ovoid, scenic vellum, snowy scene, yellow sky, flame mark, "XII/917/CV/FR," Frederick Rothenbusch, 1912 .... 1,500.00

8-3/4" h, 4-3/4" d, corseted, Marine scenic vellum, fishing boats on ocean, flame mark "XXV/1358D," artist cipher for Carl Schmidt, 1925 .... 5,500.00

9" h, 4-1/4" d, painted vellum, blue trillum and green leaves, blue and green shaded ground, flame mark "XV/1356D/V/CS/X," Carl Schmidt, 1913, restoration to base, second mark for shaved bottom and glaze flaw 800.00

9" h, 5-1/4" d, Jewel Porcelain, bulbous, painted pink narcissus and green leaves, purple ground, uncrazed, flame mark, "XLIV/6869/ KS," K. Siryamadani, 1944 .... 2,400.00

9-1/8" h, tapered oviform, raised rim, large iris blossom dec, dark blue and olive green dark glaze, mustard yellow and brown ground, imp mark, "9 4 D O," artist Sallie E. Coyne cipher, inscribed "X" on base, 1903, crazing 550.00

9-1/4" h, 4" d, scenic vellum, tall pines in winter landscape, flame mark, "XVIISEC/1356D," Sallie Coyne, 1918 .... 2,800.00

9-1/2" h, wide shoulder tapering to base, extended neck with slightly flared rim, relief repeating stylized leaf and bud on stem pattern, dark blue-green matte glaze, imp cipher, 2379 on base, 1917, crazing, small nick on base 460.00

9-1/2" h, 3-3/4" d, iris buds and leaves, sea green ground, flame mark, "562/MAD/G.," Matthew Daly, 1897 .... 3,500.00

9-1/2" h, 4" d, scenic vellum, misty scene of trees by river, flame mark, "XII/V/2039D/ETH," E. T. Hurley, 1913 .... 1,600.00

9-1/2" h, 4" d, scenic vellum, tall pines in winter landscape, flame mark, "XVII/SEC/1660D," Sallie Coyne, 1917, restoration to drilled hole at base 2,500.00

9-1/2" h, 4-1/4" d, carved porcelian, Sung Plum, clusters of blue wisteria, green leaves, shaded celadon to burgundy ground, flame mark, "XXII/1120/" artist's cipher for K, Sirayamadani, c1917 .... 1,300.00

9-1/2" h, 6-1/2" d, Jewel Porcelain, bulbous, painted ivory dogwood blossoms, mottled taupe ground, flame mark, "XXVII/927D," artist cipher for Sara Sax, 1927, one small scaling to glaze flake at top rim, from firing 3,000.00

10" h, 4-3/4" d, bulbous, lavender, yellow, and purple iris, black to ivory ground, iris glaze, minimal crazing, flame mark, "VII/939B/ L.A.," Lenore Ashbury, 1907 .... 2,600.00

10-1/2" h, 5-3/4" d, wax matte, painted abstracted red flowers, green leaves, pink and blue butterfat ground, flame mark, "XXIX/ JH/614D," Janet Harris, 1929 .... 1,300.00

10-3/4" h, 4" d, lavender and purple iris, shaded gray ground, flame mark, "VII/907D/SEC," Sallie E. Coyne, 1907, 2 minute pock marks near rim 1,800.00

10-3/4" h, 6" d, scenic velum, misty landscape, blue, green, yellow, and purple, flame mark, "XXXIII/900B/L.A.," Lenore Asbury, 1923 .... 3,750.00

11" h, 6" d, Marine scenic vellum, bulbous, fishing boats on ocean, flame mark, "XXVI/827" and artist cipher for Carl Schmidt, 1926 .... 7,500.00

11-1/8" h, tapered oviform, flared rim, dark blue glazed applied blossom branches, glossy light blue shaded cream ground, imp "Rookwood 1885 197 D," artist Laura A. Fry cipher, 1885, crazing ... 920.00

11-1/4" h, 4" d, blue-gray iris, shaded gray to celadon ground, uncrazed, flame mark, "V/907D/SEC," Sallie E. Coyne, 1905 .... 2,600.00

14-1/4" h, 6" d, enameled vellum, stylized rd and blue flower clusters, green foliage, dark blue ground, flame mark, "XV/SX/261A/ V/X," Sara Sax, 1915, seconded mark for minor glaze scaling to rim 2,000.00

18" h, 7-1/4" d, scenic vellum, painted birches by lake, flame mark, "XX/ED/944A/V," E. D. Diers, 1920, restored drill hole at bottom .. 5,000.00

Vessel, 2-1/2" h, 3-3/4" h, carved matte squatty form, flowers, green to dark blue ground, flame mark and "VII/AP/536F," Albert Pons, 1908 .... 440.00

ROSE BOWLS

History: A rose bowl is a decorative open bowl with a crimped, scalloped or petal top which turns in at the top but does not then turn up or back out again. Rose bowls, which experienced their heyday in the late Victorian era, held fragrant rose petals or potpourri which served as an air freshener in the late Victorian period. Practically every glass manufacturer made rose bowls in virtually every glass type, pattern and style.

Reference: Johanna S. Billings, with Sean Billings, *Collectible Glass Rose Bowls,* Antique Trader Books, 1999.

Collector's Club: Rose Bowl Collectors, P.O. Box 244, Danielsville, PA 18038-0244, http://www.facets.net/~facets/ freeserve-edu/rosebowl.

Advisor: Johanna S. Billings

Reproduction Alert: Rose bowls have been widely reproduced. Be especially careful of Italian reproductions of Victorian art glass, particularly Burmese and Mother-of-Pearl, imported in the 1960s and 1970s.

Burmese, 2-1/4" h spherical, Thomas Webb, decorated with prunus blossoms, polished pontil, 8 softly rounded crimps 300.00

Carnival

> 3-3/4" x 5-1/2" Northwood Drapery, marigold, 6 crimps with opalescent edges, collar base, marked with an "N" in a circle on the bottom 325.00
> 5-1/2" x 4-1/2", Northwood Daisy & Plume, white, 2 minor flakes on underside of legs 310.00

Fenton, 5" h, spherical, white opalescent spiral pattern, swirling clockwise from bottom to top 55.00

Maize, 4-3/4" h x 7" w, dark blue overlay, white interior, squat shape, 8 crimps, made by L.G. Wright in the 1970s 85.00

Moser, 2-1/8" h, miniature, intaglio engraved, lily pattern, shaded green to clear, 6 crimps, polished pontil, unsigned 230.00

Mt. Washington, Crown Milano, 6" h, spherical, shaded tan top to lighter beige bottom, decorated with pink foxgloves and green foliage with a similar but smaller decoration on the back, 9 crimps, polished pontil, purple mark "616" 595.00

Murano, 6-1/2" h x 5-1/2" w, white opaque base with multi-colored inclusions, 8 crimps, rough pontil, has original red, silver and gold foil sticker identifying it as Venetian glass 55.00

Opaline, 3-1/2" h, pink blush top to white, matte finish, glossy base, rough pontil, Mezzotint decal of cherub above a light blue cloud, resting his chin on his right hand and looking off to the right, his other arm in front of him, 8 crimps, one with small glass inclusion 150.00

Opalescent, 4-1/2" h, spherical, green body, blue rim with band of opalescence just below the blue, enameled orange scrollwork, 8 crimps, polished pontil 100.00

Pattern Glass

> 2-1/4" h x 3" w, miniature, Robinson Glass Co. Puritan pattern, 24 tiny scallops along rim, top half plain 50.00
> 4" h x 5" w, Higbee's Thistle pattern, 6 little toes, scalloped top, some roughness along outer edges 60.00

Porcelain, 2" h, spherical, blue glaze over white base, white interior, oval scene captioned "Water St., Shullsburg, Vt." and outlined in gold, 6 crimps 40.00

Rubena, 2-3/8" spherical miniature, 6 crimps, polished pontil, slight ribbed design in glass 165.00

Satin

> 3-1/2" h, spherical, pink herringbone Mother-of-Pearl, white interior, rough pontil, 8 crimps 200.00
> 5" h, spherical, blue shaded to white with white interior, 8 crimps, ground pontil 50.00
> 6" h spherical, pink, with 8 indented swirls in the glass, ground pontil, decorated with a decal design of a man dressed in American

Pattern Glass, Puritan pattern, Robinson Glass Co., 24 scallops along rim, top half plain, 2-1/4" h, 3" w, $50. Photo courtesy of Johanna Billings.

Satin, pink herringbone Mother-of-Pearl, white int., rough pontil, 8 crimps, 3-1/2" h, $200. Photo courtesy of Johanna Billings.

> colonial garb, surrounded by scrollwork, all hilighted with gold enameling, probably Mt. Washington 250.00

Silver Overlay, 2-1/8" h miniature, spherical in sapphire blue with 6 crimps, silver overlayed in scroll design, signed in light script on polished pontil "Bailey Banks and Biddle, Philadelphia" 225.00

Stevens & Williams, satin, 4-3/4" h, spherical, brown shaded to rich yellow, 6 box pleated crimps, polished pontil 225.00

ROSE CANTON, ROSE MANDARIN, and ROSE MEDALLION

History: The pink rose color has given its name to three related groups of Chinese export porcelain: Rose Mandarin, Rose Medallion, and Rose Canton, and Rose Medallion.

Rose Mandarin, which was produced from the late 18th century to approximately 1840, derives its name from the Mandarin figure(s) found in garden scenes with women and children. The women often have gold decorations in their hair. Polychrome enamels and birds separate the scenes.

Rose Medallion, which originated in the early 19th century and was made through the early 20th century, has alternating panels of figures and birds and flowers. The elements are four in number, separated evenly around the center medallion. Peonies and foliage fill voids.

Rose Canton, which was introduced somewhat later than Rose Mandarin and was produced through the first half of the 19th century, is similar to Rose Medallion except the figural panels are replaced by flowers. People are present only if the medallion partitions are absent. Some patterns have been named, e.g., Butterfly and Cabbage and Rooster. Rose Canton actually is a catchall term for any pink enamel ware not fitting into the first two groups.

Periodical: *Orientalia Journal*, P.O. Box 94, Flushing, NY 11363-0094, http://members.aol.com/Orientalia/index.html.

Reproduction Alert: Rose Medallion is still made although the quality does not match the earlier examples.

Rose Medallion, left, lidded box, $975, center: covered vegetable, $685; right: cov sugar bowl, $475.

Rose Canton

Brush Pot, 4-1/2" h, scene with ladies, reticulated, gilt trim 275.00
Charger, 13" d, floral panels, 19th C 200.00
Garden Set, 18" h, barrel form 1,350.00
Plate, 9-3/4" d, 19th C, pr 550.00
Soup Tureen, cov, lozenge shape, figural scenes, gilt floral
  ground 315.00
Sugar, cov, handle 125.00

Rose Mandarin

Cup and Saucer, scenic panels, butterfly and floral
  border 165.00
Garden Seat, 18-1/2" h, barrel-form, court scene surrounding central
  body, upper and lower bands of butterflies and floral devices, chips at
  interior bottom edge, minor glaze wear 2,645.00
Pitcher, 5" h, scalloped rim, minor imperfections 320.00
Plate, 9-3/4" d, Qing dynasty 150.00
Platter, China, 19th C
  18-1/4" x 14-1/4", minor chip 1,610.00
  18-1/4" x 15-1/4", oval, minor imperfections 1,100.00
Serving Dish, 10-1/2" l, shaped, 19th C 120.00
Soup Tureen, cov, 14-1/2" l, 9" w, 10-1/2" h, minor glaze wear,
  19th C 3,450.00
Urn, cov, 16" h, baluster, foo dog finial on dome cover, minor glaze
  wear, 19th C 1,380.00
Vase
  17" h, baluster, scalloped flaring rim, foo dogs and kylins dec, minor
    glaze wear, 19th C 1,495.00
  17-1/2" h, panels and medallions of court scenes and figures sur-
    rounded by floral devices, rim and base cracks, pr 575.00

Rose Medallion

Bowl, 10-3/4" d 325.00
Bough Pot, cov, 8-3/4" h, squire form, cut corners, berries and squirrels
  in relief, 19th C 865.00
Bread and Butter Plate, 6-1/4" d, set of seven, minor glaze wear 290.00
Brush Holder, 4-3/4" h, cylindrical, 19th C 145.00
Candlesticks, pr, 7" h, minor glaze wear, 19th C 1,495.00
Charger, 19" d, minor glaze wear, 19th C 490.00
Compote, 14" d, 11" d, 3" h, low, diamond-shape, imperfections 750.00
Fruit Basket and Undertray, 10" l, 8-3/4" d, 14-1/4" h, reticulated, minor
  chips, 19th C 1,610.00
Garden Seat, 18" h, barrel form, paneled dec, alternating court scenes
  and floral devices, minor glaze wear 1,725.00
Jar, cov, 17-1/2" h, baluster, foo dog finial and masks, brass strapwork
  attached to cover and neck for locking purposes, imperfections 1,725.00
Luncheon Plate, 7-3/4" d, set of twelve, minor glaze wear 800.00
Mug, 6-1/4" h, woven strap handle, minor glaze wear, 19th C 425.00
Pitcher, 5" h, scalloped rim, minor imperfections 300.00
Punch Bowl, 16" d, minor glaze wear, 19th C 920.00
Salt, open, 4-1/2" l, 3-1/4" w, 1-1/2" h, minor imperfections, 19th C,
  pr 1,725.00

Sauce Tureen, cov, 9" h, monogram "A," minor glaze wear, pr 2,645.00
Shrimp Dish, 9-3/4" x 10-1/2", minor glaze wear 345.00
Teapot, dome cover, 8-1/2" h, restoration to spout, 19th C 320.00
Umbrella Stand, 24" h, Thousand Butterfly, cylindrical, ribbed, 3 rows
  of butterfly panels surrounded by Rose Medallion bands, minor
  imperfections 1,840.00
Vase
  10" h, baluster form, Kylin handles, pr 450.00
  25" h, gilt foo dogs and kylins, minor imperfections, 19th C, pr 2,990.00

ROSENTHAL

History: Rosenthal Porcelain Manufactory began operating at Selb, Bavaria, in 1880. Specialties were tablewares and figurines. The firm is still in operation.

Reference: Dieter Struss, *Rosenthal,* Schiffer Publishing, 1997.

Bowl, 10" d, multicolored, classical woman with paint brush and easel,
  cobalt blue rim, sgd 45.00
Box, cov, Studio Line, sgd "Peynet" 175.00
Cake Plate, 12" w, grape dec, scalloped ruffled edge, ruffled
  handles 75.00
Candlestick, 9-1/2" h, Art Deco woman holding candlestick 275.00
Chocolate Set, San Souci pattern, 6 cups and saucers, cov pot,
  creamer and sugar, mkd "Selb Bavaria," c1880, 15 pc set 425.00
Creamer and Sugar, pate-sur-pate type blue cherries dec 115.00
Cup and Saucer, 2" h cup, gilt band on colored ground, apple green,
  cinnamon, dark blue, and light blue, set of 4 .... 120.00
Demitasse Cup and Saucer, angular handle, gold clover, pale green
  ground, c1938 .... 45.00
Dinner Plate, 10" d, polychrome transfer dec, floral and gilt trim, center
  romantic scene, mkd "Rosenthal/Bavaria," crown and rose mark,
  also stamped "Patented USA/October 16th, 1923," 12 pc set . 525.00
Figure
  6" h, clown 225.00
  9" h, ram, mottled gray 200.00
  10-1/2" h, Fairy Queen, sgd "L. Friedrich-Granau" 325.00
  14" h, kneeling nude, sgd "Klimsch" 775.00
Plate
  8" d, Moss Rose pattern, 6 pc set 90.00
  10" d, girl and lamb dec, multicolored 40.00
Portrait Plate, 9-7/8" d, bust portrait of lady, pale yellow and white
  ground, faux green, turquoise, blue, and red hardstone jewels.. 350.00
Vase, hexagonal bulbous form, stepped flared base, burnt orange,
  cream colored egg shaped raised medallions on shoulder and flared
  rim, silver overlay of stylized floral and leaf motif 290.00

Vase, flying mallard dec, mkd "Germany, Rosental Kunt-stabeilung Selb Handgewalt R.K.," 4-5/8" h, $75.

ROSEVILLE POTTERY

History: In the late 1880s, a group of investors purchased the J. B. Owens Pottery in Roseville, Ohio, and made utilitarian stoneware items. In 1892, the firm was incorporated and joined by George F. Young who became general manager. Four generations of Youngs controlled Roseville until the early 1950s.

A series of acquisitions began: Midland Pottery of Roseville in 1898, Clark Stoneware Plant in Zanesville (formerly used by Peters and Reed), and Muskingum Stoneware (Mosaic Tile Company) in Zanesville. In 1898 the offices also moved from Roseville to Zanesville.

In 1900, Roseville introduced Rozane, an art pottery. Rozane became a trade name to cover a large series of lines. The art lines were made in limited amounts after 1919.

The success of Roseville depended on its commercial lines, first developed by John J. Herald and Frederick Rhead in the first decades of the 1900s. In 1918, Frank Ferrell became art director and developed over 80 lines of pottery. The economic depression of the 1930s brought more lines, including Pine Cone.

In the 1940s, a series of high-gloss glazes were tried in an attempt to revive certain lines. In 1952 Raymor dinnerware was produced. None of these changes brought economic success and in November 1954 Roseville was bought by the Mosaic Tile Company.

References: John and Nancy Bomm, *Roseville In All Its Splendor,* L-W Book Sales, 1998; Virginia Hillway Buxton, *Roseville Pottery for Love or Money,* updated ed., Tymbre Hill Publishing Co. (P.O. Box 615, Jonesborough, TN 37659), 1996; John W. Humphries, *Roseville Pottery by the Numbers,* published by author, 1999; Sharon and Bob Huxford, *Collectors Encyclopedia of Roseville Pottery,* 1st Series (1976, 1997 value update), 2nd Series (1980, 1997 value update), Collector Books; --, *The Roseville Pottery Price Guide,* Collector Books, 1997; James S. Jenkins, Jr., *Roseville Art Pottery, 1998-1/2 Price Guide, Volume II,* Clinical Pharmacology Consultants, 1998; Gloria Mollring, *1999 Roseville Price Guide, 5th ed.,* published by author (P. O. Box 22754, Sacramento, CA 95822); Randall B. Monsen, *Collectors' Compendium of Roseville Pottery,* Monsen and Baer (Box 529, Vienna, VA 22183), 1995, --, *Collectors' Compendium of Roseville Pottery, Volume II,* Monsen and Baer, 1997; David Rago, *American Art Pottery,* Knickerbocker Press, 1997.

Collectors' Clubs: American Art Pottery Association, P.O. Box 834, Westport, MA 02790-0697, http://www.amartpot.org; Roseville's of the Past Pottery Club, P.O. Box 656, Clarcona, FL 32710.

Additional Listings: See *Warman's Americana & Collectibles* for more examples.

Basket
Bushberry, 12", blue	400.00
Magnolia, tan, 384-8	150.00
Mayflower, brown	95.00
Ming Tree, green, 508-8	115.00
Pine Cone, brown, 408-6	250.00
White Rose, 8", green	195.00

Wincraft, blue, 609-12	185.00
Beer Mug, Futura, trial glaze	695.00
Bookends, pr, Bleeding Heart, green	175.00

Bowl
Dahlrose, 10" d, handle	185.00
Earlam, large, tan and blue	275.00
Imperial	115.00
Mostique, 8" d, rim chip	75.00
Pine Cone, small, green	105.00
Rosecraft, 6-1/2" d, yellow	40.00
Tourmaline, 6" d, turquoise	65.00
Vintage, 5" d, brown	110.00

Candlesticks, pr
Cremona, 1068-4, green	160.00
Gardenia, 4-1/2" h, gray	115.00
Magnolia, blue, 1157-4-1/2	150.00
Snowberry, blue, #1156-2-1/2	120.00

Console Bowl
Dahlrose, 6"	125.00
Foxglove, green, #410-10	210.00
Magnolia, tan, #450-10	175.00
White Rose, blue or rose, #391-10	195.00

Console Set, Apple Blossom, pink, #328-8 bowl, pr 2" h candleholders, #351	500.00
Cornucopia, Foxglove, rose, 163-6	130.00

Ewer
Clematis, blue, 17-10	185.00
Lowelsa, artist sgd	165.00
Magnolia, 15" h	700.00
Snowberry	155.00
Wincraft, chartreuse, 216-6	115.00
Floor Vase, Peony, 70-18	485.00
Flower Pot, Freesia, green, no saucer	100.00

Hanging Basket
Pine Cone, green	425.00
Snowberry, rose, 2 small ear chips	150.00
Zephyr Lily, green	225.00

Jardiniere
Artcraft, 6", green	275.00
Corinthian, 801-9, 9" x 12"	195.00
Donatello, 7-1/2"	135.00
Florentine, 6"	175.00
Futura, pink and lavender flowers, gray ground	
6" h, 9" d	400.00
8" h, 12" d, orig paper label	690.00
Peony, rose and green	100.00
Poppy, 4-1/2 x 7-1/2", rose, blemish on ear	125.00
Rozana, 7" d, cream, 1917	225.00

Vase, Laurel, yellow, orig triangular foil label, 1930s, 8" h, $225.

Vista, 10-1/4" h, 12" d, green, purple, and gray 550.00
Jardiniere and Pedestal
   Artcraft, 8" d, blue and green, restored small chip on top of
      pedestal 1,995.00
   Dahlrose, 10" 1,325.00
   Freescia, green, #669-8, 24 h 1,295.00
   Fuchsia, #645-10, tan, professionally repaired
      hairline 1,600.00
   Montique, blended 800.00
   Snowberry, 8" d, small nick on pedestal base 700.00
Lamp
   Orange and green 625.00
   Orian, orange, orig fittings 375.00
Plate, Juvenile, rolled edge
   Ducks, 8" d 150.00
   Puppy, 7-1/4" d 115.00
   Rabbits, 8" d 115.00
Rose Bowl, Baneda, pink, 235-6 ....535.00
Urn
   Camelian II, 5" h 165.00
   Earlam, green 185.00
Vase
   Blackberry, 5" h, #570-5 ....500.00
   Bushberry, blue, 35-8 ....185.00
   Columbine, blue, 24-10 ....125.00
   Cosmos, tan, 852-9 ....175.00
   Ferella, tan, 9" h 500.00
   Fuchsia, 8-1/2" h, #896-8 ....425.00
   Ixia, pink, 854-7 ....160.00
   Jonquil, 526-6-1/2 ....275.00
   Magnolia, 91-8, white on green, 2 handles 200.00
   Morning Glory, green, 7" h 500.00
   Mostique, gray, 154-10 ....225.00
   Peony, gold, 61-7 ....85.00
   Snowberry, green, IV-2 ....135.00
   Velmoss, #714-6, blue and brown 225.00
   Vista, 12" 600.00
   Wincraft, #247-7, green 185.00
   Wisteria, 7", blue...750.00
Wall Pocket
   Bushberry 350.00
   Cherry Blossom, brown 1,100.00
   Donatello, slight hairline near handle 255.00
   Florentine, large 300.00
   Foxglove, blue 425.00
   Iris..575.00
   La Rose 345.00
   Nude, brown 675.00
   Snowberry, pink 200.00
Window Box, green, 389-8...145.00

ROYAL BAYREUTH

History: In 1794, the Royal Bayreuth factory was founded in Tettau, Bavaria. Royal Bayreuth introduced its figural patterns in 1885. Designs of animals, people, fruits, and vegetables decorated a wide array of tablewares and inexpensive souvenir items.

Tapestry wares, in rose and other patterns, were made in the late 19th century. The surface of the piece feels and looks like woven cloth. Tapestry ware was made by covering the porcelain with a piece of fabric tightly stretched over the surface, decorating the fabric, glazing the piece, and firing.

Royal Bayreuth still manufactures dinnerware. It has not maintained production of earlier wares, particularly the figural items. Since thorough records are unavailable, it is difficult to verify the chronology of production.

Marks: The Royal Bayreuth crest used to mark the wares varied in design and color.

References: Susan and Al Bagdade, *Warman's English & Continental Pottery & Porcelain,* 3rd Edition, Krause Publications, 1998; Mary J. McCaslin, *Royal Bayreuth,* Antique Publications, 1994.

Collectors' Club: Royal Bayreuth Collectors Club, 926 Essex Circle, Kalamazoo, I 49008; Royal Bayreuth International Collectors' Society, P.O. Box 325, Orrville, OH 44667-0325.

Conch Shell
   Creamer and Sugar, 2-1/2" h, 3" d creamer, 2-1/4" h, 4" d sugar.....
      145.00
   Match Holder, hanging..225.00
   Mustard, orig spoon...85.00
Corinthian
   Chamberstick, 4-1/2" h, enameled Grecian figures, black ground ...
      60.00
   Creamer and Sugar, classical figures, black ground 85.00
   Pitcher, 12" h, red ground, pinched spout 225.00
   Vase, 8-1/2" h, conical, black, blue mark.........................225.00
Devil and Cards
   Ashtray 650.00
   Creamer, 3-3/4" h 195.00
   Mug, large...295.00
   Salt, master 325.00
Lobster
   Ashtray, claw 145.00
   Candy Dish 140.00
   Celery Tray, 12-1/2" l, figural, blue mark 245.00
   Pitcher, 7-3/4" h, figural, orange-red, green handle..............175.00
   Salt and Pepper Shakers, pr 150.00
Miscellaneous
   Ashtray, elk 225.00
   Bowl, 6" d, multicolored tavern scene 100.00
   Creamer
      Apple 195.00
      Bird of Paradise...225.00
      Bull, gray 225.00
      Cat, black and orange 200.00
      Clown, red 275.00
      Crow, brown bill...200.00
      Duck...200.00
      Eagle 300.00
      Frog, green 225.00
      Lamplighter, green 250.00
      Pear..295.00
      Robin..195.00

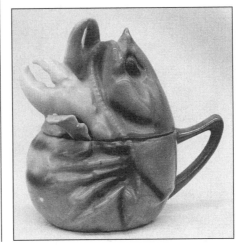

Lobster, covered mustard, orig leaf shaped spoon, $90.

Seal 695.00
   Water Buffalo, black and orange 225.00
Cup and Saucer, yellow and gold, purple and red flowers, green leaves, white ground, green mark 80.00
Hatpin Holder, courting couple, cutout base with gold dec, blue mark 400.00
Milk Pitcher
   Alligator 450.00
   Butterfly 1,200.00
   Owl 550.00
   Parakeet 495.00
Miniature, pitcher, portrait 95.00
Plate, 6-1/4" d, musicians 65.00
Ring Box, cov, pheasant scene, glossy finish 85.00
Salt and Pepper Shakers, pr, Elk 165.00
Toothpick Holder, Brittany Girl, 3 ftd, blue mark ...150.00
Vase, 3-1/2" h, peasant ladies and sheep scene, silver rim, 3 handles, blue mark 60.00
Wall Pocket, Strawberry 265.00
Nursery Rhyme
  Bell, Ring Around the Rosey, children dancing 295.00
  Planter, Jack and the Beanstalk, round, orig liner 225.00
  Plate
    Little Bo Peep, blue mark 90.00
    Little Jack Horner 125.00
    Little Miss Muffet 100.00
Snow Babies
  Bowl, 6" d 325.00
  Creamer, gold trim 110.00
  Jewelry Box, cov 275.00
  Milk Pitcher, corset shape 185.00
  Tea Tile, 6" sq, blue mark 100.00
Sunbonnet Babies
  Bell 425.00
  Cake Plate, 10-1/4" d, babies washing 400.00
  Celery Tray, open handle 275.00
  Cup and Saucer, babies fishing 225.00
  Dish, 8" d, babies ironing, ruffled edge, blue mark 175.00
  Fruit Bowl, 9-3/4" d, babies washing and hanging wash 125.00
  Hair Receiver 325.00
  Mustard Pot, cov, babies sweeping, blue mark 395.00
  Plate, babies ironing 100.00
Tomato
  Celery Tray 95.00
  Creamer and Sugar, blue mark 190.00
  Milk Pitcher 165.00
  Mustard, cov 125.00
  Salt and Pepper Shakers, pr 85.00

Rose Tapestry
Basket
  3-1/4" x 4-1/4", yellow roses, red rose border 375.00
  5" x 5", double pink roses, ruffled top 400.00
Bowl, 10-1/2" d, pink and yellow roses 675.00
Cache Pot, 2-3/4" h, 3-12/4" d, ruffled top, gold handles 200.00
Cereal Bowl, 6" d 185.00
Creamer
  3-1/2" h 225.00
  4" h 285.00
  4-1/2" h 350.00
Dresser Tray 395.00
Hairpin Box, pink and white 245.00
Jewelry Box, 5-1/2" w, 2" h, cov, shell shape 450.00
Nappy, handle 225.00
Nut Dish, 3-1/4" d, 1-3/4" h, 3 color roses, gold feet, green mark 175.00
Planter, 2-1/2" h, with liner 350.00
Plate, 4-1/2" d 195.00
Salt and Pepper Shakers, pr, pink roses 375.00
Stamp Box, cov, 2-1/2" sq, 2-1/2" h 265.00
Tray, 11" x 9" 350.00
Wall Plaque, 9-1/2" d, pierced for hanging 390.00

Tapestry, Miscellaneous
Bowl, 9-1/2" d, scenic, wheat, girl, and chickens 395.00
Box, 3-3/4" l, 2" w, courting couple, multicolored, blue mark 245.00
Charger, 13" d, scenic, boy and donkeys 300.00
Creamer, Desert scene, Arab riding horse 125.00
Dresser Tray, goose girl 495.00
Hatpin Holder, swimming swans and sunset, saucer base, blue mark 250.00
Match Holder, Arab scene 100.00
Tumbler, 4" h, barrel shape, castle in mountainous scene, blue mark 200.00

ROYAL BONN

History: In 1836, Franz Anton Mehlem founded a Rhineland factory that produced earthenware and porcelain, including household, decorative, technical, and sanitary items.

The firm reproduced Hochst figures between 1887 and 1903. These figures, in both porcelain and earthenware, were made from the original molds from the defunct Prince-Electoral Mayence Manufactory in Hochst. The fac-

Milk Pitcher, pastoral scene, blue mark, 5" h, $375.

Vase, bulbous, floral design, light yellow-green ground, burgundy neck, gilding at top, impressed and painted marks, 9" h, $200.

tory was purchased by Villeroy and Boch in 1921 and closed in 1931.

Marks: In 1890, the word "Royal" was added to the mark. All items made after 1890 include the "Royal Bonn" mark.

Cake Plate, 10-1/4" d, dark blue floral transfer 35.00
Cheese Dish, cov, multicolored floral dec, cream ground, gold trim.... 90.00
Cup and Saucer, relief luster bands, mkd 40.00
Ewer, 10-1/8" h, red and pink flowers, raised gold, fancy handle . 75.00
Jardiniere, 10-1/2" d, oval, scalloped rim, polychrome floral dec, raised gilding, shouldered by ornate scroll handles, base with satyr mask feet, ormolu mounts, late 19th C 475.00
Plate, 8-1/2" d, red and white roses, green leaves, earthtone ground, crazing, c1900 .... 20.00
Portrait Vase, 8-1/4" h, central female portrait, floral landscape, printed mark, c1900 .... 575.00
Tea Tile, 7" d, hp, pink, yellow, and purple pansies, white ground, green border, mkd "Bonn-Rhein" 35.00
Urn, cov, 13" h, hp, multicolored flowers, green, and yellow ground, 2 gold handles, artist sgd 120.00
Vase
  7" h, cylindrical, flared top and base, 3 vine shaped handles, hp polychrome floral dec, gilt accents, ivory ground, incised and printed mark "Royal Bonn, Germany" surrounding crest with "M1755" 220.00
  9-1/2" h, multicolored floral reserve, red ground, gold trim, two small handles on neck 225.00

ROYAL COPENHAGEN

History: Franz Mueller established a porcelain factory at Copenhagen in 1775. When bankruptcy threatened in 1779, the Danish king acquired ownership, appointing Mueller manager and selecting the name "Royal Copenhagen." The crown sold its interest in 1867; the company remains privately owned today.

Blue Fluted, Royal Copenhagen's most famous pattern, was created in 1780. It is of Chinese origin and comes in three styles: smooth edge, closed lace edge, and perforated lace edge (full lace). Many other factories copied it.

Flora Danica, named for a famous botanical work, was introduced in 1789 and remained exclusive to Royal Copenhagen. It is identified by its freehand illustrations of plants and its hand-cut edges and perforations.

Reference: Robert J. Heritage, *Royal Copenhagen Porcelain: Animals and Figurines,* Schiffer Publishing, 1997.

Marks: Royal Copenhagen porcelain is marked with three wavy lines (which signify ancient waterways) and a crown (added in 1889). Stoneware does not have the crown mark.

Additional Listings: Limited Edition Collector Plates.

Bowl, reticulated blue and white
  Round 125.00
  Shell shaped 150.00
Butter Pat, Symphony pattern, 6 pc set 35.00
Candlesticks, pr, 9" h, blue floral design, white ground, bisque lion heads, floral garlands 160.00
Cream Soup, #1812 .... 75.00
Cup and Saucer
  #1870 .... 75.00
  Plain Blue Lace, blue and white, ribbed cup 85.00
Dish, reticulated blue and white 175.00
Figure
  4" h, young girl, traditional dress, holding garland, No. 12418....250.00
  4" h, young girl, kneeling, flowers in lap, No. 21420 .... 265.00

Cup and Saucer, blue and white, mkd, $48.

4-1/2" x 4-1/2, wire haired fox terrier, #3165 .... 150.00
5" h, young girls wearing kerchiefs, holding garlands of flowers, one inscribed "yyland, #12421," other inscribed "amager, No. 12412," pr.. 525.00
5-3/4" h, young, native dress, kneeling and holding floral garland, No. 21413, No. 12414, pr 550.00
6" h, child in traditional dress, holding flowers, No. 12419 .... 225.00
6-3/4" h, girl knitting, No. 1314 .... 350.00
8-1/2" h, fawns on fluted columns, rabbit and lizard below, pr....375.00
9" h, two girls, native Scandinavian dress, plinth base, #12105, 20th C 375.00
12-1/2" h, gentleman in native Scandinavian dress, selling produce, No. 12103, 20th C 300.00
Fish Service, ten 10" d plates, different fish swimming among marine plants, molded and gilt border, light green highlights, gilt dentil edge, crown circular mark, 10 pc set 8,250.00
Inkwell, Blue Fluted pattern, matching tray 150.00
Pickle Tray, 9" l, Half Lace pattern, blue triple wave mark 70.00
Plate, 8" d, #1624 .... 50.00
Platter, 14-1/2" l, #1556 .... 140.00
Pot de Creme, cov, underplate, Flora Danica, violas dec 600.00
Salad Bowl, 9-7/8" d, Flora Danica, botanical specimen, molded gilt border, dentil edge, pink highlights, blue triple wave and green crown mark 825.00
Soup Tureen, cov, stand, 14-1/2" l, Flora Danica, oval, enamel painted botanical specimens, twin handles, finial, factory marks, botanical identification, 20th C.. 5,750.00
Tray, 10" l, Blue Fluted pattern... 65.00
Underplate for Cream Soup, #1626 .... 75.00
Vase
  6" h, coral and gray crackle glaze 42.00
  7" h, sage green and gray crackled glaze 150.00
Vegetable Bowl, #1622, sq 110.00

ROYAL CROWN DERBY

History: Derby Crown Porcelain Co., established in 1875 in Derby, England, had no connection with earlier Derby factories which operated in the late 18th and early 19th centuries. In 1890, the company was appointed "Manufacturers of Porcelain to Her Majesty" (Queen Victoria) and since that date has been known as "Royal Crown Derby."

Most of these porcelains, both tableware and figural, were hand decorated. A variety of printing processes were used for additional adornment. Today, Royal Crown Derby is a part of Royal Doulton Tableware, Ltd.

References: Susan and Al Bagdade, *Warman's English & Continental Pottery & Porcelain,* 3rd Edition, Krause Publications, 1998; John Twitchett, *Dictionary of Derby Porcelain 1748-1848*, Antique Collectors' Club; John Twitchett and Betty Bailey, *Royal Crown Derby,* Antique Collectors' Club, 1988.

Museums: Cincinnati Art Museum, Cincinnati, OH; Gardiner Museum of Ceramic Art, Toronto, Canada; Royal Crown Derby Museum, Osmaston Road, Derby; Derby Museums & Art Gallery, The Strand, Derby; Victoria & Albert Museum, London, England.

Marks: Derby porcelains from 1878 to 1890 carry only the standard crown printed mark. After 1891, the mark includes the "Royal Crown Derby" wording. In the 20th century, "Made in England" and "English Bone China" were added to the mark.

Cup and Saucer
    2" h cup, coral ground, gilt floral design and borders, floral dec inside cup rim, mkd "Bailey Banks & Biddle, Philadelphia". 115.00
    2" h, Japan pattern, alternating diamond and floral panel borders, stylized Oriental flowers, blue, iron-red, and gilt 90.00
    2" h cup, pale blue ground, turquoise star design, floral and butterfly gilt handle, mkd "Tiffany & Co." 100.00
    2" h, yellow ground, gilt paisley motif, red and blue enamel work 85.00
    5" d saucer, Imari pattern, 20th C 65.00
Dinner Service, partial, Rougement pattern, 47 pc set 450.00
Dish, 9" d, scattered rose sprays, floral border, late 19th C 160.00
Ewer
    7-1/2" h, cobalt blue, profuse gold gilt and floral dec, sgd 200.00
    12-1/2" h, mottled blue ground, raised gilt and iron-red dec bird and foliate design, pierced handle, shape #409, printed mark, c1888. 690.00
Jug, Imari palette, pink round, gold trim, c1885, pr 750.00
Mug, grapes and vines dec, blue and gold 175.00
Plate, 8-1/2" d, Imari palette, shaped rim, printed and imp marks, c1923, 12 pc set 375.00
Potpourri, 6" h, urn form, mounted masks, allover floral and gilt dec, pierced top with finial 85.00
Sauce Dish, Imari pattern, iron-red, cobalt blue and burnished gold, matching stand 1,200.00
Serving Dish, 11-3/8" l, Japan pattern, Imari palette, painted marks, c1865, slight staining to crazed glaze, gilt rim wear, pr 320.00

Plate, Pattern 2451, 7-1/8" d, $55.

Tea Service, Japan pattern, teapot, cov sugar, milk jug, thirteen cups, eleven saucers, ten 6" d plates, six 7" d plates, six 8" d plates, stylized oriental flowers within border of alternating diamond and floral panels, iron-red, cobalt blue, and gilt 1,250.00
Tea Set, Imari pattern, oval 9-1/4" h teapot, 3-1/4" creamer, 6" l cov sugar, c1883, rim repairs, gilt wear 260.00
Urn, 11-1/2" h, cobalt blue, red, and gold floral pattern, painted red crown mark 400.00
Vase
    7" h, dark red and gold, handles, c1884 .... 200.00
    7-3/4" h, mottled blue ground, iron-red enhanced gilt bird and foliate design, 1889, gilt wear 575.00

ROYAL DOULTON

History: Doulton pottery began in 1815 under the direction of John Doulton at the Doulton & Watts pottery in Lambeth, England. Early output was limited to salt-glazed industrial stoneware. After John Watts retired in 1854, the firm became Doulton and Company, and production was expanded to include hand-decorated stoneware such as figurines, vases, dinnerware, and flasks.

In 1878, John's son, Sir Henry Doulton, purchased Pinder Bourne & Co. in Burslem. The companies became Doulton & Co., Ltd. in 1882. Decorated porcelain was added to Doulton's earthenware production in 1884.

Most Doulton figurines were produced at the Burslem plants where they were made continuously from 1890 until 1978. After a short interruption, a new line of Doulton figurines was introduced in 1979.

Dickens ware, in earthenware and porcelain, was introduced in 1908. The pieces were decorated with characters from Dickens's novels. Most of the line was withdrawn in the 1940s, except for plates which continued to be made until 1974.

Character jugs, a 20th-century revival of early Toby models, were designed by Charles J. Noke for Doulton in the 1930s. Character jugs are limited to bust portraits, while Royal Doulton toby jugs are full figured. The character jugs come in four sizes and feature fictional characters from Dickens, Shakespeare and other English and American novelists, as well as historical heroes. Marks on both character and toby jugs must be carefully identified to determine dates and values.

Doulton's Rouge Flambé (Veined Sung) is a high-glazed, strong-colored ware noted primarily for the fine modeling and exquisite colorings, especially in the animal items. The process used to produce the vibrant colors is a Doulton secret.

Production of stoneware at Lambeth ceased in 1956; production of porcelain continues today at Burslem.

Marks: Beginning in 1872, the "Royal Doulton" mark was used on all types of wares produced by the company.

Beginning in 1913, an "HN" number was assigned to each new Doulton figurine design. The "HN" numbers, which referred originally to Harry Nixon, a Doulton artist, were chronological until 1940, after which blocks of numbers were assigned to each modeler. From 1928 until 1954, a small number was placed to the right of the crown mark; this number added to 1927 gives the year of manufacture.

References: Susan and Al Bagdade, *Warman's English &*

Continental Pottery & Porcelain, 3rd Edition, Krause Publications, 1998; Diana and John Callow and Marilyn and Peter Sweet, *Charlton Price Guide to Beswick Animals,* 2nd ed., Charlton Press, 1995; Jean Dale, *Charlton Standard Catalogue of Royal Doulton Animals,* 2nd ed., Charlton Press, 1998; ——, *Charlton Standard Catalogue of Royal Doulton Beswick Figurines,* 6th ed., Charlton Press, 1998; ——, *Charlton Standard Catalogue of Royal Doulton Beswick Jugs,* 5th ed., Charlton Press, 1999; ——, *Charlton Standard Catalogue of Royal Doulton Beswick Storybook Figurines,* 5th ed., Charlton Press, 1999; ——, *Charlton Standard Catalogue of Royal Doulton Figurines,* 4th ed., Charlton Press, 1994; ——, *Charlton Standard Catalogue of Royal Doulton Jugs,* Charlton Press, 1991; Jean Dale and Louise Irvine, *Charlton Standard Catalogue of Royal Doulton Bunnykins,* Charlton Press, 1999; Doug Pinchin, *Doulton Figure Collectors Handbook, 4th ed.,* Francis-Joseph Books, 1996.

Periodicals: *Collecting Doulton,* BBR Publishing, 2 Strattford Ave., Elsecar, Nr Barnsley, S. Yorkshire, S74 8AA, England; Doulton Divvy, P.O. Box 2434, Joliet, IL 60434.

Collectors' Clubs: Heartland Doulton Collectors, P.O. Box 2434, Joliet, IL 60434; Mid-America Doulton Collectors, P.O. Box 483, McHenry, IL 60050; Royal Doulton International Collectors Club, 700 Cottontail Lane, Somerset, NJ 08873; Royal Doulton International Collectors Club, 850 Progress Ave., Scarborough Ontario M1H 3C4 Canada.

Animal
  Alsatian, HN117 .... 175.00
  Bonzo Dog, model 883, blue glaze, brown and black detailing
    1-1/2" h, marked "Doulton," cracked 1,344.00
    2" h 1,312.00
  Bull Terrier, K14 .... 325.00
  Cocker Spaniel, HN1187 .... 160.00
  Dalmatian, HN114 .... 250.00
  English Bulldog, HN1074 .... 175.00
  English Setter, HN1050 .... 150.00
  French Poodle, HN2631 .... 150.00
  Salmon, 12" h, flambé, printed mark 435.00
  Scottish terrier, K18 .... 125.00
  Tiger, 14" l, flambé, printed mark 375.00
  Winnie the Pooh Set, Pooh, Kanga, Piglet, Eeyore, Owl, Rabbit, and Tigger, Beswick, boxed set 650.00
Bottle, 4-3/4" h, 4" d, gourd shape, Flambé, lustered gold, sang-de-boeuf and black flambé glaze, imp stamped "Royal Doulton Flambé / 9-23," spider lines to base 175.00
Bowl
  4" d, 2-1/4" h, Titanian, stork in flight, shaded blue and white ground, stamp mark, "134," artist sgd "H. Allen" 400.00
  9" d, 4" h, Dickens Ware, transfer dec, town scene and figures 160.00
  10" d, transfer dec, fox hunt scene, woman riding horse, green grape and dec leaf border, mkd "Geo Morland, Pinxt, 1784, England, Rd. No. 374874" 420.00
Cabinet Vase, 2-1/2" h, 2" d, swan, shaded green and blue ground, stamp mark, "1048/10-92/F.H." 400.00
Character jug, large
  Cardinal 150.00
  Poacher, D6781 .... 350.00
  Veteran Motorist 125.00
Character Jug, miniature
  Blacksmith 50.00
  Pickwick 65.00
Character Jug, small
  Pearly King 35.00

Character Jugs, left: Regency Beau, D6559, $800; center: Punch & Judy, D6590, $465; right: Mikado, D6501, $465. Photo courtesy of Andre Ammelounx Auctions.

  Pirate, no beard, 1967 .... 960.00
  Toby Philpots 85.00
Charger, 12-5/8" d, hp, allover incised leaf, berry, and vine border, central fruits and leaves, attributed to Frank Bragwyn, printed mark, c1930 .... 245.00
Child's Feeding Dish, Bunnykins in country store 135.00
Chocolate Set, 8" h chocolate pot, 6-1/2" hot water pot, creamer, sugar, eight cups and saucers, bone china, each dec with relief and enameled fox, crop-form handle and foot rim, 20th C 750.00
Clock Case, King's Ware, night watchman, c1905 .... 450.00
Figure
  Afternoon Tea, HN1747 .... 500.00
  Annabell, HN3273 .... 225.00
  Autumn Breeze, HN1934 .... 300.00
  Biddy Pennfarthing, HN1834 .... 175.00
  Fair Lady, HN2835, coral 175.00
  Flower of Love, HN3970 .... 160.00
  Forty Winks, HN1874 .... 325.00
  Hannah, HN3870, miniature 75.00
  Harlequin, HN2186 .... 250.00
  Lady MacBeth, Ellen Tracy, ivory glazed body, artist sgd "Noke," printed Burslem mark, 12-1/4" h, footrim chips 965.00
  Penelope, HN1901 .... 400.00
  Rose, HN1368 .... 75.00
  Schoolmarm, HN2223 .... 350.00
  Sweet Sixteen, HN2734 .... 250.00
  Thanksgiving, HN2446 .... 200.00
  Top o'the Hill, HN1830 .... 200.00
  The Foaming quart, HM2162 .... 250.00
  The Leisure Hour, HN2055 .... 400.00
  Victorian Lady, HN1208, 1926-38 .... 355.00
  Wigmaker of Williamsburg, HN2239 .... 300.00
  Yardley's Old English Lavender seller, c1925 .... 400.00
Fish Plate, 9" d, swimming fish centers, pale yellow ground, gold bands and rims, sgd "J. Hallmark," 10 pc set 700.00
Flask
  6-1/2" h, triangular, printed, Sydney Harbour, Dewars on reverse, c1914 .... 575.00
  7-1/2" h, King's Ware, Admiral Lord Nelson, Dewars on reverse, c1914 .... 550.00
Humidor, cov, 6" h, Chang Ware, squatty, molded ribs, brilliant shades of red, blue, yellow, and white, thick crackle finish, sgd in overglaze "Chang/Royal/Doulton" and "Noke" with monogram, c1925 . 1,975.00
Jar, cov, 2-3/4" h, 3-1/4" d, Noke Flambé, crimson-red glass, fully stamped 325.00
Jug, 10-1/2" h, Regency Coach, limited edition, printed marks, 20th C 930.00
Loving Cup
  9-3/4" h, Three Musketeers, limited edition, sgd "Noke, H. Fenton," orig certificate, 20th C 920.00
  10-1/4" d, King George V and Queen Mary, 25 year reign anniversary, c1935 .... 750.00
Mug
  4" h, gladiator, #D6553 .... 300.00

Plate, Gibson Girl, "They Take A Morning Run," copyright 1901 by Life Publishing Co., $145.

6-1/2" h, cardinal, A mark 100.00
8-1/4" h, St. John Falstaff 95.00
Pitcher
  8" h, Dickens Ware, Mr. Pickwick 100.00
  8-3/4" h, flow blue transfer, foliate ground, horseshoe framed panels of deer in landscape setting, printed mark, c1895 .... 245.00
  12-1/2" h, Coaching Days series, continuous scene, dark green rim 265.00
Plate
  8-1/2" sq, Dickens Ware, Mr. Micawber 85.00
  8-1/2" d, transfer ware, tall ships, unclear incised marking 40.00
  10-1/4" d, Roger Solem El-Cobler, No. D-6302 .... 45.00
Sauce Dish, Dickens Ware, Bill Skyes 40.00
Spirits Barrel, 7" l, King's Ware, double, silver trim rings and cov, oak stand, c1909 .... 1,200.00
Tankard, 9-1/2" h, hinged pewter lid, incised frieze of herons among reeds, blue slip enamel, imp mark, sgd, c1875 .... 1,600.00
Teacup and Saucer, cobalt blue, heavy gold dec 120.00
Tobacco Jar, 8" h, incised frieze of cattle, goats, and donkeys, imp mark, sgd, worn SP rim, handle and cover, dated 1880 .... 995.00
Toby, small
  Macauber 95.00
  Tony Weller 75.00
Tray, 9-1/2" d, Dickens Ware, Alfred Jingle 125.00
Umbrella Stand, 23-1/2" h, stoneware, enamel dec, applied floral medallions within diamond formed panels, framed by button motifs, imp mark, glaze crazing, c1910 .... 550.00
Vase
  5-1/4" h, 3" d, aventurine glaze, stamped "Royal Doulton/ England" 700.00
  6-3/4" h, Flambé, mottled red and yellow glazes, sgd "Harry Nixon," printed marks, c1930 .... 325.00
  7" h, 4-1/4" d, ovoid, Flambé, desert landscape silhouetted against crimson red ground, shallow scratch, stamped "Royal Doulton/ Flambé/Made in England" 225.00
  11" h, floriform, tapering base, pale yellow ground, pink accents, daisy and mixed flower designs, green crown mark, "England," "HB 3069" and "C 8549" 275.00

11-1/4" h, Sung Ware Flambé, mottled red and blue glazes, sgd "Noke" and "F. Allen," printed mark 420.00
11-3/4" h, cov, baluster, Athenic pattern, red glaze, acorn and leaf dec, silver mounted neck, sweeping scroll handle, foliate thumb piece, hinged lid,, ftd. Gorham Mfg. Co., Providence, c1905 .... 1,450.00
16-3/4" h, Hannah Barlow, central incised frieze of cows grazing, glazed stylized floral and foliate borders, sgd and imp marks, glaze flake to int. edge 635.00
24-1/2" h, 12" d, natural process dec, imp amber leaves and branches, blue-gray ground, spider-web hairline to base, dies-tamped mark 250.00

ROYAL DUX

History: Royal Dux porcelain was made in Dux, Bohemia (now the Czech Republic), by E. Eichler at the Duxer Porzellan-Manufaktur, established in 1860. Many items were exported to the United States. By the turn of the century, Royal Dux figurines, vases, and accessories, especially those featuring Art Nouveau designs, were captivating consumers.

Marks: A raised triangle with an acorn and the letter "E" plus "Dux, Bohemia" was used as a mark between 1900 and 1914.

Bowl, 17-1/2" l, modeled as female tending a fishing net, oval shell-form bowl, imp mark, early 20th C 490.00
Bust, 14" h, female portrait, raised leaves and berries on base, Czechoslovakia, early 20th C, unmarked, chips 290.00
Centerpiece
  16" h, central figure of Art Nouveau maiden holding open net with flask, flanked by shell-form bowls, naturalistically molded base 1,200.00
  18-1/2" h, molded high relief, branches and foliage, buff glaze, 4 maidens heads, large leaves forming bowl, mkd "Royal Dux Bohemia," large "E" in triangle, imp "833 13," restoration ... 750.00
Compote, figural
  14-1/2" l, modeled as female atop shell-form bowl, another figure within the wave modeled freeform base, imp mark, early 20th C 750.00
  20-1/4" h, leaf and floral molded bowl mounted to central free-form support, surrounded by three females, imp and printed marks, 20th C 635.00
Figure
  8-1/2" h, two dogs, naturalistically molded base 700.00
  9" x 8", dog sled team, 3 tethered dogs, pre-war "E" mark. 1,295.00

Vase, woman with outstretched arms, sea motif at base, mkd, 15-1/2" h, $125.

10" h, male, tricorn hat, long tail coat, cane, standing on stump, matte, pink triangle mark 350.00
14" l, retriever with duck in jaws, matte finish 400.00
14" x 8-1/2" x 15-1/2", lady, sedan chair, 2 courtiers, hound . 800.00
14-1/4" h, female with harp, incised scroll banding to raised base, imp mark, early 20th C...................................... 175.00
21" h, peasant couple, "E" mark, pr................................... 1,495.00
24" h, man and woman at water fountain, price for pr, some base chips 550.00
Jardiniere, 7-5/8" h, rect, large molded flower handles, centered by Art Nouveau maiden in flowing robes, top of body raised above rim... 850.00
Tazza, 19-1/2" h, figural, putti and classically draped woman supporting shell, price for pr, one with hairline in base 880.00
Vase, 19-1/4" h, bisque, Art Nouveau style female to one side of leaf and floral molded body, imp mark, early 20th C 290.00

ROYAL FLEMISH

History: Royal Flemish was produced by the Mount Washington Glass Co., New Bedford, Massachusetts. The process was patented by Albert Steffin in 1894.

Royal Flemish is a frosted transparent glass with heavy raised gold enamel lines. These lines form sections—often colored in russet tones—giving the appearance of stained glass windows with elaborate floral or coin medallions.

Collectors' Club: Mount Washington Art Glass Society, 60 President Ave, Providence, RI 02906.

Advisors: Clarence and Betty Maier.

Biscuit Jar, cov, 8" h, ovoid, large Roman coins on stained panels, divided by heavy gold lines, ornate SP cov, rim, and bail handle, orig paper label "Mt. W. G. Co. Royal Flemish".......................... 1,750.00
Ewer, 10-1/2" h, 9" w, 5" d, circular semi-transparent panel on front with youth thrusting spear into chest of winged creature, reverse panel shows mythical fish created with tail changed into stylized florals, raised gold dec, outlines, and scrolls, rust, purple and gold curlicues, twisted tope handle with brushed gold encircles neck, hp minute gold florals on neck, burnished gold stripes on rim spout and panels... 4,950.00
Vase
4" h, 4-1/2" d, mythical winged gargoyle, tail becoming part of stylized foliage that sweeps around the perimeter, gold embellishments, irregular-sized angular panels of subdued shades of brown, dark tan, lighter tan and frosted clear form background 985.00
6-1/2" h, 6" d, bold stylized scrolls of pastel violet, realistically tinted sprays of violets randomly strewn around frosted clear glass body, carefully drawn brilliant gold lines define violet nosegays and frame scrolls, daubed gold accents, two tiny handles, sgd with logo and "0583" 2,200.00
9-1/2" h, double bulbed body, allover training enameled roses, shades of pink and green, raised gold enamel outlines, stylized gilt trellis of blue spiral accents, red enamel mark on base, c1894, slight wear to gilt 3,335.00

ROYAL RUDOLSTADT

History: Johann Fredrich von Schwarzburg-Rudolstadt was the patron of a faience factory located in Rudolstadt, Thuringen, Germany, from 1720 to c1790.

In 1854, Ernst Bohne established a factory in Rudolstadt.

The "Royal Rudolstadt" designation originated with wares which Lewis Straus and Sons (later Nathan Straus and Sons) of New York imported from the New York and Rudolstadt Pottery between 1887 and 1918. The factory manufactured several of the Rose O'Neill (Kewpie) items.

Vase, ivory ground, orange and pink flowers, green and brown leaves, gold details, blue mark, #6320, 13-1/2" h, $165.

Marks: The first mark of the original pottery was a hayfork; later, crossed two-prong hayforks were used in imitation of the Meissen mark.

"EB" was the mark used by Ernst Bohne

A crown over a diamond enclosing the initials "RW" is the mark used by the New York and Rudolstadt Pottery.

Bottle, cov, 9-1/4" h, gourd shape, entrusted flowers, Ernest Bohne Sohne, late 19th/early 20th C, chips, pr 325.00
Bust, 15" h, classical figure, glazed to simulate marble.............. 165.00
Cake Plate, 12" d, pink, white roses, gold handles and trim......... 75.00
Creamer, Old Ivory style border gold trim, handpainted florals... 45.00
Ewer, 10" h, ivory, floral dec, gold handle and trim 125.00
Figure
7" and 7-1/2" h, woman in country dress with bundle of fire wood, male in country dress with sled, brightly polychromed, gilt dec base 700.00
7-1/2" h, maiden and 2 young girls with lamb, elegant dresses, applied flowers, polychrome details 300.00
Hatpin Holder lavender and roses 45.00
Nut Set, master bowl, 6 small bowls, white and green roses, fluted, ftd, "B" under crown mark.. 265.00
Plate, 8-1/2" d, pink, white, and yellow roses, gold molded piecrust rim 35.00
Teapot, cov, 5-1/2" h, hp, ivory, pink, lavender, and green floral dec.. 95.00
Urn, 10" h, mythological scene, Hector and Andro crowning maiden, cobalt blue ground, gold handles, artist sgd, stand.................. 145.00
Vase, 4" h, floral dec, elephant handles...................................... 90.00

ROYAL VIENNA

History: Production of hard-paste porcelain in Vienna began in 1720 with Claude Innocentius du Paquier, a runaway employee from the Meissen factory. In 1744, Empress Maria Theresa brought the factory under royal patronage; subsequently, the ware became known as Royal Vienna. The firm went through many administrative changes until it closed in 1864. The quality of its workmanship always was maintained.

Marks: Several other Austrian and German firms copied the Royal Vienna products, including the use of the "Bee-

Charger, three maidens and cupid attending central lady, elaborate cobalt blue ground, gold border, 16" d, $2,750. Photo courtesy of Jackson's Auctioneers & Appraisers.

hive" mark. Many of the pieces on today's market are from these firms.

Cabinet Vase
    3-1/2" h, children of four seasons, blue beehive mark 350.00
    7" h, oval reserve of Lemiramis, irid red and black ground, gold encrusted, Eolzner, late 19th C 775.00
Chocolate Pot, cov, 10" h, large reserve with artist dec a vase, woman looking on, cream ground, gilt handles and trim, Knoeller 350.00
Cup and Saucer, frieze figures and horses dec, cobalt blue border.145.00
Ferner, 7-3/4" w, 4" h, portrait of lady one side, portrait of different lady on other, burgundy, green , and gold, beaded, scalloped edges, ftd, mkd "Royal Vienna, Austria," artist sgd 425.00
Portrait Vase
    8" h, Art Nouveau young lady surrounded by rococo swirls and emb flowers, pale yellow, brown, and purple ground, two handles ..200.00
    10-1/4" h, maiden, green ground, gilt handles and trim, cov, c1900. 375.00
Stein, quarter liter, hp, copy of early Meissen Chinese scene, elaborate battle surmounted by gold border, 4 flowers painted in rear, similar scene of harbor of top of lid, floral design painted on underside of lid, eagle thumb lift, beehive mark 2,310.00
Urn, cov
    11-1/2" h, hp, elaborate scene of man, women, and cherub, cobalt blue ground, gold trim, beehive mark 1,200.00
    30" h, gilt intertwined serpent handles, gilt scroll dec and band, classical figures on cobalt blue ground, sq plinth painted with figural reserves on two sides, repaired, c1900 .... 4,000.00
Vase
    3-1/2" h, Meditation, artist sgd "Wagner," beehive mark 425.00
    11-1/4" h, bulbous, stick neck, scenes of gentleman and lady courting, landscape backgrounds, rococo gilding, mkd "Vienna" and beehive mark, c1885 .... 330.00

ROYAL WORCESTER

History: In 1751, the Worcester Porcelain Company, led by Dr. John Wall and William Davis, acquired the Bristol pottery of Benjamin Lund and moved it to Worcester. The first wares were painted blue under the glaze; soon thereafter decorating was accomplished by painting on the glaze in enamel colors. Among the most-famous 18th-century decorators were James Giles and Jefferys Hamet O'Neale. Transfer-print decoration was developed by the 1760s.

A series of partnerships took place after Davis's death in 1783: Flight (1783-1793); Flight & Barr (1793-1807); Barr, Flight & Barr (1807-1813); and Flight, Barr & Barr (1813-1840). In 1840, the factory was moved to Chamberlain & Co. in Diglis. Decorative wares were discontinued. In 1852, W. H. Kerr and R. W. Binns formed a new company and revived the production of ornamental wares.

In 1862, the firm became the Royal Worcester Porcelain Co. Among the key modelers of the late 19th century were James Hadley, his three sons, and George Owen, an expert with pierced clay pieces. Royal Worcester absorbed the Grainger factory in 1889 and the James Hadley factory in 1905. Modern designers include Dorothy Doughty and Doris Lindner.

References: Susan and Al Bagdade, *Warman's English & Continental Pottery & Porcelain,* 3rd Edition, Krause Publications, 1998; Anthony Cast and John Edwards, *Charlton Price Guide to Royal Worcester Figurines,* Charlton Press, 1997; G. A. Godden, *Victorian Porcelain,* Herbert Jenkins, 1961; Stanley W. Fisher, *Worcester Porcelain,* Ward Lock & Co., Ltd., 1968; David, John, and Henry Sandon, *Sandon Guide to Royal Worcester Figures,* Alderman Press, 1987; Henry Sandon, *Flight & Barr Worcester,* Antique Collectors' Club, 1992; Henry Sandon and John Sandon, *Dictionary of Worcester Porcelain,* vol. II, Antique Collectors' Club, 1995; ——, *Grainger's Worcester Porcelain,* Barrie & Jenkins, 1990; John Sandon, *The Dictionary of Worcester Porcelain,* vol. I, Antique Collectors' Club, 1993.

Museum: Charles William Dyson Perrins Museum, Worcester, England; Roberson Center for the Arts and Sciences, Binghamton, NY.

Basket, 8-1/2" d, flaring pierced sides mounted with floral heads, pine cone and floral cluster int., blue and white transfer dec, first period, mid 18th C 550.00

Vegetable Dish, covered, ram's head handles, green mark and registry mark, 8-3/4" x 5-1/2", $120.

Biscuit Jar, cov, 7-1/4" h, fluted body, raised spear head borders surrounding enamel floral design 550.00

Bowl, 10" d, scalloped border, shell molded boy, fruit and floral spray, blue and white transfer dec, first period, mid 18th C 320.00

Bud Vase, 3" h, bulbous, triangular handle, reticulated leaf design, ivory ground, hp polychrome floral dec, gilt accents, purple crown over circle mark, rect mkd "Rd. No. 43554," and "1139" 75.00

Butter Tub, cov, 4-1/4" d, 3-1/4" h, cylindrical, fully sculpted finial, painted floral sprays below geometric borders, first period, c1765 .... 450.00

Centerpiece, 6-1/4" h, oval, ftd, Royal Lily pattern, first period, c1800, repaired 125.00

Cup and Saucer, 5-3/8" d, cream colored ground, gilt highlighted enamel floral designs, c1900 .... 45.00

Demitasse Cup and Saucer, cobalt blue, gold crossbanding, pearl jewels, gold int., handle, and foot 275.00

Ewer, 10-1/2" h, classical form, elaborate scrolled handle, hp scene of swans in flight, light blue ground, peach and gilt accents, artist sgd "C. Baldwyn," green crown over circle mark, "Rd. No. 111573," c1900 .... 1,550.00

Figure
   5-1/4" h, politician, white glaze, late 19th C, staining, hat rim chip restored 290.00
   6-1/2" h, Welsh girl, shot enamel porcelain, sgd "Hadley," late 19th C 690.00
   7-3/4" h and 8-1/4" h, lady and gentleman, George III costumes, sgd "Hadley," pr. 1,100.00
   8-3/4" h, Cairo water carrier, 1895 .... 635.00

Fish Plates, 9-1/4" d, bone china, hp fish, gilt lattice and foliage border, sgd "Harry Ayrton," printed marks, c1930, 13 pc set 2,300.00

Fruit Cooler, 6-1/4" h, cylindrical, Royal Lily pattern, stylized floral reserve, stepped circular foot, first period, c1800 .... 225.00

Lizard Jug, 6" h, bulbous, relief lizard, molded basketweave body, late 19th C 460.00

Mustard Pot, 4" h, cylindrical, blue and white transfer, floral clusters, floral finial, first period, mid 18th C 325.00

Plate
   7" w, octagonal, landscape fan form reserves, cobalt blue ground, first period, 18th C, pr 350.00
   7-3/4" d, Blind Earl pattern, raised rose spray, polychrome floral sprays, scalloped border, first period, mid 18th C 1,100.00
   8" d, diaper pattern border surrounding floral spray, blue and white transfer dec, first period, mid 19th C 220.00
   9-1/4" d, bird center, blue enamel and gilt floral rim, c1886, set of 10 .... 300.00

Pitcher
   8" h, powder horn shape, twig-style handle, ivory ground, hp blue flowers, purple crown over circle mark, mkd "Rd. No. 37112" in rect above "1116," chip on spout 90.00
   8" h, squat vessel form, serpent handle, ivory ground, bird and fern design, moon and hummingbird on reverse, green crown mark, "Rd. 21627," also mkd "1048," sgd by artist 350.00
   8" h, squat vessel form, serpent handle, ivory ground, interlocking circles of various gilt dec, mkd "Patent Metallic" over green crown mark, illegible registry number, also mkd "1048," sgd by artist, minor damage on handle 145.00
   8-1/2" h, cylindrical, gilt leaf band around rim, cornucopia shaped handle, ivory ground, hp cherry blossom dec, gilt accents, purple crown atop circle mark, "Rd. No. 74149," and "1229" 135.00
   10" h, bulbous body, narrow neck, gilt bamboo styled handle, hp morning glory, cherry blossom, and dogwood dec.............. 150.00

Sauce Boat, 41/4" h, geometric band above foliate molded body, painted floral sprays, oval foot, first period, c1765, pr.............. 275.00

Sweetmeat, 6" l, leaf form, blue and white transfer Chinoisiere landscapes, first period, mid 18th C.. 325.00

Tea Bowl and Saucer, painted Chinoisiere vignette, blue border, first period, c1865 .... 185.00

Teapot, 9-1/2" h, narrow twist spout, C-scroll handle, acorn finial top, light blue and ivory ground, floral dec, purple crown mark, "Rd. No. 198833" and "1613" 450.00

Urn, cov, 11-1/2" h, pierced dome top, globular body, painted floral sprays, basketweave molded base, early 20th C 200.00

Vase, 9-1/2" h, urn shape, double handles, hp polychrome dec of flowers, gilt accents, ivory ground, green crown over circle mark, also mkd "Patent Metallic" in maroon 275.00

Waste Bowl, 5" d, 2-1/4" h, floral molded ext., floral spray int., lambrequin border, first period, c1765... 200.00

ROYCROFT

History: Elbert Hubbard founded the Roycrofters in East Aurora, New York, at the turn of the century. Considered a genius in his day, he was an author, lecturer, manufacturer, salesman, and philosopher.

Hubbard established a campus which included a printing plant where he published The Philistine, *The Fra,* and *The Roycrofter.* His most-famous book was *A Message to Garcia,* published in 1899. His "community" also included a furniture manufacturing plant, a metal shop, and a leather shop.

References: Kevin McConnell, *Roycroft Art Metal,* 2nd ed., Schiffer Publishing, 1994; The Roycrofters, *Roycroft Furniture Catalog, 1906,* Dover, 1994; Paul Royka, *Mission Furniture ,from the American Arts & Crafts Movement,* Schiffer Publishing, 1997; Marie Via and Marjorie B. Searl, *Head, Heart and Hand,* University of Rochester Press (34 Administration Bldg, University of Rochester, Rochester, NY 14627), 1994.

Collectors' Clubs: Foundation for the Study of Arts & Crafts Movement, Roycroft Campus, 31 S. Grove St., East Aurora, NY 14052; Roycrofters-at-Large Association, P.O. Box 417, East Aurora, NY 14052.

Museum: Elbert Hubbard Library-Museum, East Aurora, NY.

Additional Listings: Arts and Crafts Movement; Copper.

Ashtray, 9-1/2" d, hammered copper, table top, curled handle, normal cleaning to orig patina, orb and cross mark 900.00

Bench, Ali Baba, half ash log on keyed through tenon, oak trestle base, orig finish, carved orb and cross mark, some restoration to bark 6,500.00

Book
   A Message to Garcia, Elbert Hubbard, 1899, Levant binding, hand marbleized paper, sgd by Hubbard and Andrew Rowan 375.00
   Dreams, Olive Schreiner, copyright 1901, printed on Japan vellum, Levant binding, hand marbleized paper, suede lined slip case, sgd by Elbert Hubbard, numbered 61/100 .... 250.00
   Garnett and the Brindled Cow, Also Other Mothers, Alice Hubbard, 1913, Levant binding, hand marbleized paper, hand illuminated, sgd by Elbert Hubbard, numbered 888/1003 .... 100.00
   Life Lessons, Alice Hubbard, 1909, suede Levant binding, some loose pgs 50.00
   Ruskin and Turner, copyright 1895 G. P. Putnam, hand illuminated and illus, orig artwork, sgd by Elbert Hubbard, numbered 313/475, light wear to edges of binding 150.00
   The Book of Songs, Heinrich Heine, 1903, Levant binding, printed on Japan vellum, sgd by Elbert Hubbard, numbered 3/100 175.00
   The Book Worm, Browne, 1897, cloth bound 70.00
   The Deserted Village, Dr. Oliver Goldsmith, 1898, initialed and hand-illumined, sgd by Elbert Hubbard, numbered 9/470, light wear to edges, some foxing to pgs 150.00
   The Intellectual Life, O. G. Hammerton, 1899, initialed and hand-illumined, suede Levant binding, sgd by Elbert Hubbard, numbered 423/960 .... 100.00
   The Law of Love, W. M. Reedy, 1905, red suede binding, orig box 225.00

Chandelier, hammered copper, conical dome, orig hanging chains and ceiling plate, orig patina, few verdigris drips, unmarked, 8" h, 17-1/2" d fixture, $5,000. Photo courtesy of David Rago Auctions, Inc.

Bookcase, 34" l, 9-1/4" d, 65-1/2" h, overhanging top, chamfered back, 5 open shelves, bottom drawer with cast pulls, orig light finish, carved orb and cross mark 6,500.00
Bookends, pr
   4" h, 6-1/4" w, hammered copper, semi-circular, emb rivet dec, orig patina, orb and cross mark 300.00
   4-1/4" h, 4" w, brass washed hammered copper, pyramid, emb stylized floral dec, orig patina, orb and cross mark 200.00
   4-1/2" h, 5" w, brass washed hammered copper, sq, stylized dogwood dec, orb and cross mark........................... 300.00
   4-7/8" h, hammered copper, triangular, emb and etched sailing ship within circular rope twist border, dark patina, imp orb and cross mark, minor wear 290.00
   5" x 3-3/4", hammered copper, three-sided, garlands of roses, orig patina, orb and cross mark 300.00
Book Trough, 18" l, 5-3/4" d, 4-1/2" h, curved sides, hand-cut dovetailed construction, orig patina, carved orb and cross mark..... 900.00
Bowl, hammered copper, orb and cross mark
   3-3/4" d, 3" h, spherical, incised lotus design, new patina..... 350.00
   10-1/2" d, 3" h, squatty, closed-in rim, wear to orig patina..... 450.00
Bud Vase, 8" h, 3" sq, hammered copper, base emb with stylized dogwood blossom, orig glass liner, orig patina, orb and cross mark ...350.00
Calling Card Tray, 7" d, silver washed hammered copper, ftd, elaborate emb pattern, light wear to orig patina, design attributed to Walter Jennings, orb and cross mark....................... 375.00
Candle Sconce, pr, 9" l, 2-1/2" w, hammered copper, orb and cross mark
   Embossed arrowhead design on back plate......................... 500.00
   Flame covers, orig patina 400.00
Candlesticks, pr
   7-1/2" h, 3" sq, Princess, brash-washed hammered copper, double stem, faceted sq base, orb and cross mark....................... 475.00
   13" h, 5" d, hammered copper, twisted stems, large round base, orb and cross mark, remnants of brass wash 650.00
Candy Dish, cov, 5-1/2" d, 4-1/2" h, hammered copper, center emb with trefoil and starburst, orig patina 350.00
Chair
   Arm, 25" w, 22-1/2" d, 38" h, ladderback, 2 horizontal back slats, apron carved "Roycroft," inset tacked-on hard set, light cleaning to orig finish, new leather seat 2,600.00
   Desk, 17" w, 17" d, 43-1/2" h, mahogany, hourglass back slat with initial "H," tacked-on Japan leather seat, Mackmurdo feet, orig finish, carved orb and cross mark....................................... 1,400.00
   Dining, 17-1/4" w, 18" d, 40-1/4" h, side, hourglass back slats, orig tacked-on Japan leather seats, orig finish, unmarked, from estate of Wm Roth, Roycroft designer, set of six........................ 8,000.00
   Dining, 25-1/2" w, 16-1/2" d, 41" h, arm, Grove Park Inn, crest rail with carved {"GPI" over single broad vertical panel, orig tacked-on leather seat, orig finish, carved orb and cross mark 4,750.00

Side, 18" w, 18-1/2" d, 38-3/4" h, ladderback, 2 back slats, cloud-lift apron carved "Roycroft," inset tacked-on hard old, (non-orig) leather seat, overcoated finish.. 1,300.00
Chest of Drawers, 41" w, 24" d, 52" h to top, rect mirror, 2 small drawers over 4 graduated long drawers, hammered copper rect pulls, mint orig ebonized finish, carved orb and cross mark, mirror brackets missing, minor water damage to drawer face 7,500.00
Chiffoner, 41-5/8" w, 23-1/2" d, 58-1/2" h, mahogany, backsplash with shaped ends, rect top, 2 short drawers over 4 long drawers, hammered pulls, 4 shaped feet, branded mark centered on lower drawer, c1910 .... 1,840.00
Child's Chair, 6" w, 2" d, 4-1/2" h, mahogany, 4 vertical back slats, orb and cross mark.. 2,000.00
Cigar Box, 10" l, 5-1/2" w, 2-1/4" h, mgf by John Merriam & Co., Elbert Hubbard label on inside of lid.. 325.00
Clock, mantel, miniature, 6" w, 2" d, 4-1/2" h, tooled leather case, emb stylized flowers and leaves, orb and cross mark................... 7,300.00
Desk, 38-1/4" w, 19" d, 44" h, drop front, strap hardware, single drawer with large copper oval pulls, pull-out supports, Macmurdo feet, gallery int., orig finish, carved orb and cross mark, large chip to back of top 8,000.00
Desk Set, hammered copper, Indian motif, desk blotter, pen tray, letter holder, rolling blotter, perpetual calendar with orig cards, stamp box, letter opener, orig patina, orb and cross marks, 7 pc set 2,200.00
Dinner Bell, 3" h, 1-3/4" d, hammered copper, orig dark patina, orb and cross mark.. 450.00
Foot Stool, 17" l, 12" w, 14-1/2" h, inset green vinyl seat, refinished, carved orb and cross mark, new seat 900.00
Fruit Tray, 9-3/4" d, No. 805, circular, hammered copper, stylized rim dec, c1918, some pitting.. 520.00
Goodie Box, 23" l, 12-1/2" w, 9-1/2" h, mahogany, copper hinges and handles, orig finish, carved orb and cross mark, minor split to top... 1,100.00
Hall Mirror, 50" x 36", six hammered hooks, orig hanging chains and glass, fine orig finish, unmarked... 2,000.00
Hat Pin, hammered copper, unmarked, fine orig patina
   1-1/4" sq head, emb quatrefoil 375.00
   1-1/2" sq head, incised orb and cross mark 750.00
Humidor, 4-1/2" d, 5-1/2" h, hammered copper, lid emb with 4 pointed arrow, orig patina, orb and cross mark.................................... 1,100.00
Inkwell and Pen Tray, 15" l, 2-1/2" h, hammered copper, double leaded glass inkwells, orig patina, orb and cross mark........................ 600.00
Lamp
   Boudoir, 14-3/4" h, designed by Dard Hunter, leaded slag glass shade, band of stylized dogwood blossoms, yellow round, stem with 4

Clock, miniature mantel, tooled leather case, emb stylized flowers and leaves, orb and cross mark, 4-1/2" h, 6" l, 2" d, $7,300. Photo courtesy of David Rago Auctions, Inc.

curved flat bands, orig patina, small cracks in some panes, replaced copper cap, married to base, imp orb and cross mark 4,750.00

Desk, 14" h, 10" d, hammered copper and mica, 4 riveted acanthus leaf ribs over mica side panels, orb and cross mark, orig mica, new patina 2,600.00

Helmet, 14-1/4" h, No. 906, hammered copper, medium patina, c1919, minor dents and scratches 1,840.00

Library Table
  30" w, 22" d, 27-3/4" h, apron, lower shelf, Mackmurdo feet, skinned finish, carved orb and cross mark......................4,000.00
  59-1/2" l, 30" d, 30" h, single drawer, 2 oval copper pulls, flaring plank sides with Moorish cut-outs, carved orb and cross mark, new dark finish 3,250.00

Magazine Stand
  14" w, 12" d, 37-1/2" h, solid tapered sides, rounded top, 3 shelves, orig dark finish, carved orb and cross mark 8,500.00
  32-1/2" w, 15-1/2" d, 38-1/2" h, slatted sides and back, apron, 3 shelves, orig dark finish, carved orb and cross mark.......7,500.00

Motto Plank, carved ash, orb and cross mark
  42-1/4" l, 10" h, "Old Things are Best," orig hammered iron hanging chains, orig finish 6,500.00
  42-1/4" l, 10" h, "Self Reliance," orig hanging chains, refinished 3,250.00

Nut Bowl, hammered copper, closed-in rim
  6" d, 2-1/2" h, orig patina, orb and cross mark and "Roycroft" 550.00
  10-1/4" d, 2-3/4" h, 3 feet, new dark patina, orb and cross mark 400.00

Nut Set, 8" d, 4" h hammered copper bowl with center funnel holding 6 picks with brass tips and silver tines, and spoon, orb and cross mark, new patina 425.00

Picture Frame, tooled leather, orb and cross mark
  5-1/2" w, 8" h, emb Glasgow roses, standing missing from back, some stains to surface 1,300.00
  6-1/2" w, 9" h, emb daisy, light wear to corners 1,500.00

Poker Chip Rack, 6-1/2" d, 4-3/4" d, hammered copper, orig chips, orig dark patina, orb and cross mark...600.00

Rocker
  Open-arm, 26-1/2" w, 28" d, 35" h, 5 vertical back slats, replaced tacked-on leather seat, orig finish, carved orb and cross mark, torn seat cushion 1,200.00
  Sewing, 19" w, 21" d, 33" h, mahogany, 5 vertical back slats, replaced tacked-on leather seat, carved orb and cross mark 900.00

Saddle Purse, 3" x 3-1/4", tooled leather, emb day lily, orb and cross mark 700.00

Sideboard, 42" l, 20-1/4" d, 45" h, plate rack, single drawer with oval pulls, 2 cabinet doors with leaded glass fronts and round copper pulls, carved orb and cross mark, new dark finish 12,000.00

Table Mat, 17-1/2" d, tooled leather, emb trillium and Celtic rose design, orig condition, orb and cross mark 3,000.00

Tabouret
  15" sq, 20-1/2" h, sq overhanging top, four sided plank base, keyhole cut-outs, carved orb and cross mark, refinished 4,750.00
  15-1/2" sq, 21-1/2" h, sq overhanging top, orig brown tacked-on leather, apron carved "Roycroft,"" flaring legs, refinished 2,100.00

Tea Table, 36" d, 30" h, circular top, deep apron, cross stretchers, Mackmurdo feet, overcoated finish, carved orb and cross....4,250.00

Vase, hammered copper
  4" h, 3-3/4" d, flaring, ftd, orig patina, orb and cross mark 600.00
  5" h, 4-1/2" d, bulbous, closed-in rim, orig patina, rob and cross mark...475.00
  7" h, catalog #212, cylindrical, band of stylized diamond-shaped flowers on tall stems, with green triangles around rim, dark patina, imp mark on base 920.00
  9-1/4" h, 3-3/4" d, cylindrical, curled rim, emb bell-shaped flowers, verdigris patinated medallions, orig patina, unmarked.....1,000.00
  9-1/4" h, 4-1/2" h, cylindrical, brass-washed, curled rim, emb bell-shaped flowers, orb and cross mark, some wear to wash, few minor dents at rim 500.00
  10-1/2" h, 6" d, cylindrical, flaring riveted base, rich dark brown orig patina, orb and cross mark 4,750.00

12" h, 4-1/4" d, cylindrical, incised and emb diamond shaped pattern in band, unmarked, some pitting to orig patina, some discoloration 1,100.00

Writing Table, 48" l, 30" w, 30" h, mahogany, slatted sides, 2 drawers with hammered copper pulls, lower shelf mortised with keyed through-tenons, Mackmurdo feet, orig finish, carved orb and cross mark 5,000.00

RUBENA GLASS

History: Rubena crystal is a transparent blown glass which shades from clear to red. It also is found as the background for frosted and overshot glass. It was made in the late 1800s by several glass companies, including Northwood and Hobbs, Brockunier & Co. of Wheeling, West Virginia. Rubena was used for several patterns of pattern glass including Royal Ivy and Royal Oak.

Bowl, 4-1/2" d, Daisy and Scroll...65.00
Butter Dish, cov, Royal Oak, fluted 250.00
Compote, 14" h, 9" d, rubena overshot bowl, white metal bronze finished figural standard...170.00
Cracker Jar, cov
  Aurora, inverted rib, Northwood..325.00
  Cut fan and strawberry design, fancy sterling silver cov, 7" h, 6" w 1,150.00
Creamer and Sugar Bowl, cov, Royal Ivy 250.00
Decanter, 9" h, bulbous body, narrow neck, applied clear handle....170.00
Epergne, single-lily, tightly ruffled, overshot................................225.00
Finger Bowl, Royal Ivy 65.00
Pickle Castor, enameled daisy dec, ornate sgd frame with 2 handles, pickle fork in front 245.00
Salt Shaker, Coquette 150.00
Sauce Dish, Royal Ivy...35.00
Sugar Shaker, Royal Ivy 250.00
Toothpick Holder, Optic 150.00
Tumbler, Medallion Sprig 100.00
Tumble-Up, tumbler and carafe, Baccarat Swirl 175.00
Vase, 10" h, ruffled rim, hp enameled flowers, gold trim, Hobbs, Brockunier & Co. 175.00
Water Pitcher
  Opal Swirl, Northwood..275.00
  Royal Ivy, frosted 295.00

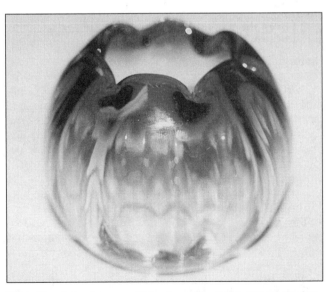

Rose Bowl, 6 crimps, polished pontil, slight ribbed design, 2-3/8", $165. Photo courtesy of Johanna Billings.

Vase, applied web dec, 2-1/4" d, 4" h, $245.

RUBENA VERDE GLASS

History: Rubena Verde, a transparent glass that shades from red in the upper section to yellow-green in the lower, was made by Hobbs, Brockunier & Co., Wheeling, West Virginia, in the late 1880s. It often is found in the Inverted Thumbprint (IVT) pattern, called "Polka Dot" by Hobbs.

Bowl, 9-1/2" d, Inverted Thumbprint , ruffled 175.00
Butter Dish, cov, Daisy and Button 250.00
Celery Vase, 6-1/4" h, Inverted Thumbprint 225.00
Creamer and Sugar Bowl, cov, Hobnail, bulbous, applied
  handle 550.00
Cruet, 7" h, Inverted Thumbprint pattern, tee pee shape, trefoil spout, 2/3
  flashed ruby top, intense vaseline color base, faceted stopper 550.00
Finger Bowl, Inverted Thumbprint 95.00
Jack In The Pulpit Vase, 8" h 250.00
Pickle Castor, Hobb's Hobnail, SP frame, cov, and tongs 500.00
Salt and Pepper Shakers, pr, Inverted Thumbprint 210.00
Syrup, 6-3/4" h, Inverted Thumbprint, orig hinged pewter cov 300.00
Tumbler, Inverted Thumbprint 125.00
Vase, 9-1/4" h, paneled body, enameled daises dec 85.00
Water Pitcher, Hobb's Hobnail 395.00

RUSSIAN ITEMS

History: During the late 19th and early 20th centuries, craftsmen skilled in lacquer, silver, and enamel wares worked in Russia. During the Czarist era (1880-1917), Fabergé, known for his exquisite enamel pieces, led a group of master craftsmen who were located primarily in Moscow. Fabergé also had an establishment in St. Petersburg and enjoyed the patronage of the Russian Imperial family and royalty and nobility throughout Europe.

Almost all enameling was done on silver. Pieces are signed by the artist and the government assayer.

The Russian Revolution in 1917 brought an abrupt end to the century of Russian craftsmanship. The modern Soviet government has exported some inferior enamel and lacquer work, usually lacking in artistic merit. Modern pieces are not collectible.

References: Vladimir Guliayev, *Fine Art of Russian Lacquered Miniatures,* Chronicle Books, 1993; P. Hare, *The Art & Artists of Russia,* Methuen & Co., 1965; L. Nikiforova,

SPECIAL AUCTIONS

Jackson's Auctioneers & Appraisers
2229 Lincoln St.
Cedar Falls, IA 50613
(319) 277-2256
email: jacksons@corenet.net

compiler, *Russian Porcelain in the Hermitage Collection,* Aurora Art Publications, 1973; Marvin Ross, *Russian Porcelains,* University of Oklahoma Press, 1968; A. Kenneth Snowman, *Fabergé,* Harry N. Abrams, 1993; John Traina, *The Faberge Case: From the Private Collection of John Traina,* Harry N. Abrams, 1998; Ian Wardropper, et. al., *Soviet Porcelain,* The Art Institute of Chicago, 1992.

Museums: Cleveland Museum of Art, Cleveland, OH; Forbes Magazine Collection, New York, NY; Hermitage, Leningrade, Russia; Hillwood, The Marjorie Merriweather Post Collection, Washington, DC; Russian Museum, Leningrad, Russia; Virginia Museum of Fine Arts, Lillian Thomas Pratt Collection, Richmond, VA; Walters Art Gallery, Baltimore, MD.

Enamels

Cigarette Case
  3" l, rect, rounded edges, silver gilt, guillouchè, translucent blue over diamond and wave ground, cover with cabochon thumbpiece, edges engraved with bands of laurels, St Petersburg, c1900, int. mkd "A. Tillander" 2,200.00
  3-1/2" l, 2-1/4" w, 84 standard, silver gilt, robin's egg blue enamel, feathered guillouchè ground, opaque white enamel borders, diamond chips on clasp, gilt in., Ivan Britzin, St. Petersburg, 1908-17, small losses and chips to enamel 1,200.00
Coffee Spoon, blue dot border in bowl, stylized polychrome enamel foliage, gilt stippled ground, twisted gilt stem, crown finial, G Tokmakov, c1890 .... 300.00
Egg, silver gilt and shaded enamel ware, 2 pc construction, cabochon stone, makers mark obliterated, 20th C, 3" h, ftd 700.00
  4" h, separate base 800.00
  Kovsh, 3" l, silver gilt, Art Nouveau style enameling, pointed prow, hooked handle, Maria Semenaova, Moscow, c1900 .... 1,900.00
  Letter Opener, 10-1/2" l, cylindrical handle, enameled translucent green guillouche ground, overlaid gilt trellis dec, horse head finial, red cabochon eyes, seed pearl border, agate blade 925.00
  Locket Compact, 1-3/4" w, silver guillochè, round, overall medium blue translucent enamel over sunburst ground, hinged lid

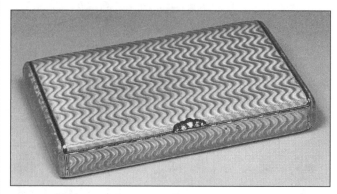

Cigarette Case, silver and guilloche enamel, Andre Gorlanov, 3-1/2" l, $5,600. Photo courtesy of Jackson's Auctioneers & Appraisers.

engraved around edge, St. Petersburg, 1908, Cyrillic makers mark "D. K." 400.00

Napkin Ring

1-3/4" x 1" x 1-1/2", enameled green, blue, pink, brown, white, light blue and maroon, Maria Semenova, Moscow, c1890 .... 700.00

2-1/4" l, oval, heavily enameled with scrolling foliage and skan edging, hallmarked Moscow, 1908-17, Cyrillic makers mark of Grigory Spitnev 225.00

Serving Spoon, 7" l, plique-a-jour enamel, round bowl, butterfly attached to long twisted handle with enameled orb finial, Moscow, 1888, makers mark of Pavel Ovchinnikov, Imperial Warrant. 1,400.00

Sugar Shifter

6" l, pierced bowl, band of colorful champleve enamel supported by long twisted stem, flat handle enameled on both sides, hallmarked Moscow, 1899-1908, 88 standard, Cyrillic makers mark of Khelbnikov 450.00

6-1/2" l, silver, back of bowl with colorful scrolling flowering foliage, front and back of handle with similar enamel dec, 11th Artel, Moscow, c1908 .... 1,100.00

Teaspoon, turquoise ground, filigree cloisons, white enamel dot border, red and white enamel flower in center of bowl, red flower on handle, gilt stern, V Akhimov, 1896 .... 300.00

Trinket Box, cov, oval, silver gilt, en plein enameling, slip on lid, Moscow, c1900 .... 2,200.00

Icon

7-1/2" w (open), 6-3/4" h, triptych, period of Tsar Nicholas I, central panel with ogee arch top containing removable micro-mosaic pectorial pendant of St. Nicholas, mosaic enclosed in gilded silver frame with acanthus leaves, velvet blacking and suspension loop, above hinged swivel mosaic is Eye of God set on gilded silver sunburst, left and right wings both inset with removable pierced and carved bone crucifixes, left engraved with St. John Chrysostom, St. Gregory "Dvoeslovia," Pope of Rome, St. Basil the Great and St. Gregory the Theologian, right panel finely engraved with St. John, St. Phillip, St. Peter and St. Alexei, upper right and left wings engraved with continuous prayer, each section hallmarked St. Petersburg, central panel dated 1855, all with makers mark "C. E." (attributed to Carl Ekqvist or Carl Ernst,) St. Petersburg 19,600.00

8-1/2" x 10-1/2", Three Hierachs, colorful and finely painted, St. Gregory the Theologian, St. Basil the Great, and St. John Chrysostom -

Icon, Archangel Michael, armor claid winged warrior, holding sword inscribed "At that time Michael, the great prince who protects your people will arise...," c1800, 42" h, 20-1/2" w, $12,100. Photo courtesy of Jackson's Auctioneers & Appraisers.

Golden Mouthed dressed as Bishops, Christ delivers blessing at to center, incised gold leaf, c1890 .... 1,120.00

9-1/2" x 11-1/2", Metrophan of Voronezhskiy and Miracle Worker, Monastic Bishop delivers blessing, holds crosior, Christ delivers blessing from top left, overlaid with silver repoussé and chased riza, applied halo, hallmarked St. Petersburg, Cyrillic makers mark "F. V." for Feodor Verhotsev, c1850 .... 1,680.00

11" x 8", Mother of God Helper in Birth, Mary, hair undone, hands together in prayer, Christ Child in mandoria of light below, gold leafed riza made with gesso stiffened cloth, scuttled, 19th C 1,235.00

11" x 9-1/4", Mary of Egypt, well painted, partially clothed ascetic with long stringy hair, background with scenes of her being discovered by Zosimus, etc., Christ delivers blessing from above, 19th C .. 1,960.00

11" x 12-1/4", Guardian Angel with Saints, center Guardian Angel above red clouds, left female Martyr St Nazoryeya, right female Martyr St Natalia, old Testament Trinity on upper border, 16th C revivalist style, c1900 .... 3,025.00

12" x 14", John the Forerunner with Life Scenes, winged John the Baptist in center, cradles diskos, delivers blessing, holds open scroll, top margin with God the Father, kovcheg intricately dec with scrolling foliate, title inscribed in abbreviated Slavonic near his gold leaf halo, attributed to Palekh or Mstera, 19th C 1,700.00

12" x 14" King of Kings, well painted Deisis variant, Christ enthroned and robed as bishop, John the Forerunner at left hand, Mary art right, Angels Michael and Gabriel behind holding seals bearing ICXC abbreviation, dec kovcheg and unique stippling within each halo, 19th C 3,475.00

12" x 14", Mother of God the Life-Giving Wellspring, Mary holding infant Christ seated in chalice-form fountain set in midst of pool, two angels standing on clouds, each hold disk with Cyrillic letters for Jesus Christ, c1800 .... 1,400.00

12-1/4" x 10-1/4", mid Pentecost, inscribed at top margin with title Prepolovenie, young Christ surrounded by learned men in the Temple, 16th C style, c1900 .... 1,680.00

12-1/4" x 10-1/2", Resurrection, Palekh, painted, Christ inside mondorla above empty tomb, two attending angels, background heavily incised, borders of faux enameling, titled at top, 1900 .... 3,100.00

12-1/4" x 10-1/2", The Nativity, Mary lying before cave in hill, newborn Christ lies in manger, 4 angels look on, 3 Magi approach with gifts, Joseph listening to shepherd, midwife Salome prepares to wash newborn, highly stylized Slavonic inscription, 16th C style, c1900.... 2,400.00

12-1/2" x 11", Korsun Mother of God, finely painted, mother and child in cheek to cheek embrace, overlaying veil and garments, intricate riza of seed pearls and paste stones, gilt repoussé and chased halo, 19th C 2,800.00

12-3/4" x 10-1/2", Mother of God of the Passion, Christ Child on her left arm, he folds her right hand, looks over his left shoulder at one of 2 flanking angels, angels bear instruments of the Passion, cross, spear, and sponge, gilt repoussé and chased metal riza with attached halo, borders with scrolling foliage and Bishop saints, 18th C 1,680.00

13" x 10-3/4", Smolensk Mother of God, painted in Usakov Armory School style, gown of Virgin and Christ Child in seed pearls, gemstones, and pastes, later repoussé and chased silver riza with haloes, dated 1779, hallmarked Nizhniy Nowgorod, borders of St Makary and Mary of Egypt, 18th C.. 6,200.00

14" x 12-1/2", St Nicholas, naturalistic rendering, delivering blessing, holds book of Gospels, overlaid with repoussé and chased 2 tone silver gilt riza, shaded enamel halo, corners and Gospel cover, title plaque with champleve enamel, custom fitted Karelian birch kiot, hallmarked Moscow, 1899-1908, Cyrillic makers mark of Ivan Aleskecvich Aleksev, c1900 .... 11,500.00

Metal

Brooch, 1-1/4" l, gold, large multi-faceted center garnet, surrounded by encrusted snake form with 51 diamonds, Faberge, Moscow, center mkd with workmaster Knut Oskar Phil O.P., 56 standard, 14 kt 4,480.00

Cigarette Case, 3-7/8" l, gold, Faberge, rect, rounded sides, hinged cov, embellished with oval of Tsar Nicholas II set in frame of diamonds and sapphires, crown finial, Cypher of Nicholas II set with diamond, two-tone gold laurels, workmaster Eduard Wilhemm

Schramm, St. Petersburg, c1900, mkd with initials of workmaster, 56 standard 3,920.00
Figure, 14-1/2" h, 12" l, bronze, equestrian group, officer and lady riding astride horse, dark brown patina, sgd, 20th C 865.00
Safe, 3" l, patinated, applied plaque with Russian characters 125.00
Samovar, 18" h, brass, bowl and tray 275.00

Porcelain

Butter Dish, 6" l, modeled as rams, 19th C, pr 400.00
Cabinet Plate, 9" d, cobalt blue, green, and red central rosette, gilt ground 275.00
Cup and Saucer
   3" h, gilt on white designs, F. Gardner, Moscow, early 20th C, set of six 395.00
   4-1/2" h, blue glazed, honoring coronation of Nicholas II, 1878, M. S. Kuznetsov 250.00
Demitasse Cup and Saucer, tall fluted cup, pink flowers, insects, green leaves, small circular handle, Lomonosov, c1940 .... 55.00
Dessert Plate, floral rim, magenta ground, Islamic script, printed mark, I. E. Kuznetsov, 19th C, set of six 265.00
Egg
   3" l, landscape and Christ Has Risen on front, reverse with swallows painted on pink ground, suspension loop 450.00
   4-1/2" l, floral and foliate polychrome dec, gilt high-lights 50.00
Plate
   6-1/4" d, central scene of women peasants in landscape, shaped flower filled panel rim, gilt highlights, Kustentzoff, price for pr .. 175.00
   9" d, bucolic scene, sepia, A. G. Popov, Moscow, 19th C, minor wear, chips, 10 pc set 690.00
Portrait Plate, 8" d, Empress Elizabeth, Safronov, early 19th C, hairline 315.00
Tankard, 8" h, figural, Turk's head, mkd "F. Gardner, Moscow," 19th C, restored 1,210.00
Tureen, cov, matching tray, Neoclassical roundel, cobalt blue banding, pink ground, gilt highlights, c1825 .... 1,250.00
Urn, 10-3/4" h, baluster, medallion handles, panel with Arab and maiden, polychrome dec, puce ground 425.00
Vase, 10" h, F. Gardner, Moscow, 19th C, campana form, painted scenes, pr 2,000.00

Silver

Altar/Reliquary Cross, 10-1/2" l, overall machine engraved, front with crucified Christ, hollow 2 pc construction, hallmarked Moscos, 1908-17, indistinguishable makers mark 675.00
Candlesticks, pr, 12" h, engraved and repousse stems and flower head socket, bell shaped base supported by base with grapes, resting on 3 feet, hallmarked Minsk, 1886, unknown maker 980.00

Chalice, 9-1/2" h, heavily engraved and repousse, dome shaped base, finely engraved with 4 Evangelists, bulbous stem supporting heavily engraved bowl depicting Christ, Virgin Mary, and John the Baptist, cross showing implements of crucifixion, rim engraved in Slavonic, hallmarked Moscow, 1892, indistinguishable makers mark, 14.5 oz 2,130.00
Cigarette Case, 3-7/8" x 2-1/2", .84 fine, c1890, rect, reeded ground, applied monogram, hinged match compartment, strike, and tinker cord, presentation inscription under hinged lid, 6.83 ozs 400.00
Cream Jug, 4-1/2" h, milk can shape, hallmarked St. Petersburg, 1841, Gracev Bros Plug lid, int. gilded 450.00
Crumber Tray, 11" l, early 20th C, blade shaped waisted rect form engraved with foliate scrolls and shells, applied geometric border, tapered cylindrical handle with domed cap and ring handle, monogrammed, 10 troy oz 200.00
Easter Egg, 2 pcs, 3" h, engraved in Cyrillic, "Christ Has Risen!," gilded int., hallmarked Moscow, 1899-1908, indistinguishable markers mark 675.00
Fruit Basket, 11-1/2" w, int. engraved with wreath of cherries, bail handle, hallmarked Moscow, 1889, Cyrillic makers mark 560.00
Icon Lampada, 19-1/2" l including chain, engraved foliage and crosses, three open fret work suspension arms, hallmarked Moscow, 1899-1908, Alexandr Fuld makers mark 675.00
Ladle, 16" l, 1862, handle with niello dec of bird above fruiting vine, applied female mask topped quatrefoil above bowl, ovoid floral repousse bowl gold washed to interior, exterior with incised banding and applied monogrammed shield, 13 troy oz 635.00
Letter Opener, 11-1/2" l, silver handle with Botgayrs on both sides, raised inscription, seaform semi-translucent stone blade carved to rounded point, Cyrillic makers mark "D. O." (attributed to Dimitry Orlov) ... 2,200.00
Salt, master, 3-1/2" w, Baroque style, hallmarked St. Petersburg 1841, Carl Magnus Stahle makers mark 150.00
Spoon, 8-3/8" l, 1886, ovoid bowl with central rect hand painted mineral enamel portrait of young woman in Russian dress, stylized enamel motifs, paneled stem picked out with enamel stringing, 4 troy oz 1,495.00
Tankard, cov, 7-7/8" h, 1894, "A.C." makers mark, tapered cylindrical body with bulbous lower section, stepped foot, engraved with central plain roundel flanked by geometric and foliate sprays with perching birds, geometric banding above and below, shaped ear handle, lid with thumb-piece and flattened urn finial, 14 troy oz 865.00
Tea Glass Holder, 4-1/4", Pan-Slavic style, Bogatyr in from of Kremlin gate, hallmarked Moscow, 1908-18, in Cyrillic "Moscow Platinum Factory" 400.00
Toasting Cup, 5-1/2" h, cylindrical body finely engraved with 2 winged cherubs blowing trumpets, flanking decorative panel with florals and scrolling foliage, dome shaped base with beading, hallmarked Moscow, 1891, Cyrillic makers mark for Pavel Mishukova 350.00

SABINO GLASS

History: Sabino glass, named for its creator Ernest Marius Sabino, originated in France in the 1920s and is an art glass which was produced in a wide range of decorative styles: frosted, clear, opalescent, and colored. Both blown and pressed moldings were used. Hand-sculpted wooden molds that were cast in iron were used and are still in use at the present time.

In 1960, the company introduced fiery opalescent Art Deco style pieces, including a line of one- to eight-inch high figurines. Gold was added to a batch of glass to obtain the fiery glow. These are the Sabino pieces most commonly found today.

Marks: Sabino is marked with the name in the mold, as an etched signature, or both.

Blotter, 6" l, rocker type, crossed American and French flags 275.00
Center Bowl, 10-1/4" d, 4-1/4" h, heavy walled, frosted, three high
  relief oyster shells, tripod feet, star, and pearls between, center mkd
  "Sabino France," int. wear 500.00
Charger, 11-3/4" d, opalescent, Art Deco molded spiral design, 3 nude
  women swimming, central molded mark "Sabino Paris" 550.00
Clock, 6-1/8" h, opalescent, arched case, overlapping geometric
  devices, molded festoons centered by circular chapter ring, molded
  "SABINO," c1925 .... 1,725.00
Figure
  Butterfly, opalescent, relief molded "Sabino" 25.00
  Fish, large 110.00
  Maiden, 7-3/4" h, opalescent, draped in contrapposto with raised
    right arm, etched "Sabino Paris" 885.00
  Pekinese, 1-1/4" h, begged, opalescent, relief molded
    "Sabino" 35.00
  Rabbit, 1" x 2" 75.00
  Turkey, 2-1/4" h, 21' l, molded signature "Sabino, France"...... 45.00
  Venus de Milo, large 75.00

Knife Rest, duck.. 25.00
Napkin Ring, birds, opalescent 45.00
Plaque, 12" l, 7-3/4" h, Dancing Nymphs, molded light lime green oval,
  frieze of figures in classical dress dancing among foliage, mold
  imperfections 230.00
Powder Box, small 45.00
Scent Bottle, Petalia.. 50.00
Vase, 9-7/8" h, opalescent, rounded rect form, Art Deco female nude each
  side, joining hands around vessel, etched "Sabino Paris" 1,870.00

SALOPIAN WARE

History: Salopian ware was made at Caughley Pot Works, Salop, Shropshire, England, in the 18th century by Thomas Turner. At one time the product was classified "Polychrome Transfer" because of the method of decoration, but the ware is better known by the more popular name "Salopian." Much of the output was sold through Turner's Salopian warehouse in London

Marks: Pieces are impressed or painted under the glaze with an "S" or the word "Salopian."

Bowl, 7-3/4" d, milkmaid milking cow in meadow scene, panels of men
  at work separated by florals, brown-black transfer with polychromed
  enamels.. 250.00
Creamer, 6" h, black transfer of maiden with urn, yellow and burnt
  orange accents, black and white frieze, black, white, orange, and yellow florals around rim border, c1790 .... 225.00
Cup and Saucer, Deer pattern, blue, black, yellow, and green transfer,
  chip on rim... 250.00
Plate, 7-1/4" d, white stag center, floral border, black transfer with polychrome enamels.. 115.00
Posset Pot, 4" h, brown transfer of large and small flowers highlighted
  by light blue, orange, yellow, and green................................... 350.00
Teabowl and Saucer, brown transfer of farm scene.................... 150.00
Tea Caddy, 4" h, black transfer of deer and cottage, pink and yellow
  accents... 275.00

Chicken, 6-1/2" w, 7-3/8" h, $420.

Plate, octagonal, Oriental pattern, 8-3/4" d, $185.

Teapot, 6-7/8" h, Castleford-type shape, Nelson's Victories at Nile, Copenhagen, and Trefalger in scalloped shell, flanked by two half serpents blowing trumpets, green-black transfer with red, yellow, flesh, green, and ochre accents, applied ochre border, swan finial, restored 650.00

Waste Bowl, classical cartouches in brown transfers with 3 maidens, cobalt blue, yellow, green, and ochre flowers, int. with brown transfer of florals 200.00

SALT and PEPPER SHAKERS

History: Collecting salt and pepper shakers, whether late 19th-century glass forms or the contemporary figural and souvenir types, is becoming more and more popular. The supply and variety is practically unlimited; the price for most sets is within the budget of cost-conscious collectors. In addition, their size offers an opportunity to display a large collection in a relatively small space.

Specialty collections can be by type, form, or maker. Great glass artisans, such as Joseph Locke and Nicholas Kopp, designed salt and pepper shakers in the normal course of their work.

References: Larry Carey and Sylvia Tompkins, *1003 Salt & Pepper Shakers*, Schiffer Publishing, 1997; —; *1004 Salt & Pepper Shakers*, Schiffer Publishing, 1998; Helene Guarnaccia, *Salt & Pepper Shakers, Vol. I* (1985, 1996 value update), Vol. II (1989, 1998 value update), Vol. III (1991, 1998 value update), Vol. IV (1993, 1999 value update), Collector Books; Mildred and Ralph Lechner, *World of Salt Shakers*, 2nd ed., Collector Books, 1992, 1996 value update; Arthur G. Peterson, *Glass Salt Shakers*, Wallace-Homestead, 1970, out of print; Irene Thornburg, *Collecting Salt and Pepper Shakers*, Schiffer, 1998.

Collectors' Clubs: Antique and Art Glass Salt Shaker Collectors Society, 2832 Rapidan Trail, Maitland, FL 32751-5013, http://www.cbantiques.com/ssc; Novelty Salt & Pepper Shakers Club, P.O. Box 3617, Lantana, FL 33465, http://members.aol.com/jlfuller1/jdf1.htm.

Museum: Judith Basin Museum, Stanford, MT.

Additional Listings: See *Warman's Americana & Collectibles* and *Warman's Flea Market* for more examples.

Notes: The colored sets, in both transparent and opaque glass, command the highest prices; crystal and white sets the lowest. Although some shakers, e.g., the tomato or fig, have a special patented top and need it to retain their value, it generally is not detrimental to replace the top of a shaker.

The figural and souvenir types are often looked down upon by collectors. Sentiment and whimsy are prime collecting motivations. The large variety and current low prices indicate a potential for long-term price growth.

Generally, older shakers are priced by the piece; figural and souvenir types by the set. Pricing methods are indicated in the listings. All shakers included below are assumed to have original tops unless otherwise noted. Reference numbers are from Arthur Goodwin Peterson's Glass Salt Shakers. Peterson made a beginning; there are hundreds, perhaps thousands, of patterns still to be cataloged.

Prices below are for individual shakers unless otherwise noted.

Art Glass (priced individually)
Burmese, 4" h, branches and leaves dec, metal top, Mt. Washington 85.00
Cobalt Blue, 4" h, deep color, sterling push-on lid with English hallmarks "E.E.," "HH" and a lion facing left, sterling collar mkd "E.E.," anchor, and lion facing left 285.00
Cranberry, Inverted Thumbprint, sphere 175.00
Fig, enameled pansy dec, satin, orig prong top, Mt. Washington 120.00
Scrollware, blue scrolling 170.00
Wave Crest, Erie Twist body, hp flowers, 2-1/2" h 185.00

Figural and Souvenir Types (priced by set)
Christmas, barrel shape
    Amber 80.00
    Amethyst 145.00
Ducks, 2-1/2" h, sitting, glass, clear bodies, blue heads, sgd "Czechoslovakia" 45.00
Egg shape
    Opaque white body, holly dec, 23 red raised enameled berries, Mt. Washington 185.00
    Pastel tint, pink enameled blossoms, lid loose 65.00
Strawberries, flashed amberina glass strawberry shaped shakers, white metal leaf caps, suspended from emb white metal fancy holder, 2-3/4" h strawberries, 5" h stand, sgd "Japan," c1921-41 .... 285.00

Opalescent Glass (priced individually)
Argonaut Shell, blue 65.00
Fluted Scrolls, vaseline 65.00
Jewel and Flower, blue, (164-J), replaced top 45.00
Seaweed, Hobbs, cranberry 60.00
Windows, Hobbs, blue, pewter top 50.00

Opaque Glass (priced individually)
Bulge Bottom, blue 20.00
Cathedral Panel, blue 20.00
Creased Bale, pink 20.00
Double, blue 20.00
Fanband, white 20.00
Fleur de Lis Scrolling, custard 25.00
Flower Blooming, white 20.00
Heart, blue 20.00

Christmas Salt, amber glass body, pewter top with agitator, $95.

Leaf Clover, blue	20.00
Little Shrimp, blue	25.00
Little Shrimp, white	20.00
Rib Pointed, blue	25.00
Spider Web, custard	20.00
Spider Web, pink	25.00
Swirl Wide Diagonal, white	20.00
Torch Wreath, white	20.00

Pattern Glass (priced individually)

Actress, pewter top	45.00
Beautiful Lady, colorless, 1905	25.00
Block and Fan, colorless, 1891	20.00
Crown Jewel, c1880, etched	35.00
Four Square, Billows	100.00
Franesware, Hobbs, Brockunier Co., c1880, hobnail, frosted, amber stained	45.00
Leaf Umbrella, old tops	350.00
Little Apple, ftd	110.00
Lobe, squatty	120.00
Medallion Sprig, 3-1/4" h, shaded cobalt blue to white, orig base, 33-S	75.00
Tulip	100.00
Twelve Panel, scrolled pink	130.00
Whirligig, colorless, tin top, (177-A)	20.00

SALT-GLAZED WARES

History: Salt-glazed wares have a distinctive pitted surface texture made by throwing salt into the hot kiln during the final firing process. The salt vapors produce sodium oxide and hydrochloric acid which react on the glaze.

Many Staffordshire potters produced large quantities of this type of ware during the 18th and 19th centuries. A relatively small amount was produced in the United States. Salt-glazed wares still are made today.

References: Susan and Al Bagdade, *Warman's English & Continental Pottery & Porcelain*, 3rd Edition, Krause Publications, 1998; Arnold R. Mountford, *The Illustrated Guide to Staffordshire Salt-Glazed Stoneware*, Barrie & Jenkins, 1971; Louis T. Stanley, *Collecting Staffordshire Pottery*, Doubleday & Co., 1963.

Museums: American Antiquarian Society, Worcester, MA; City Museum, Stoke-On-Trent, England; British Museum, London, England, Colonial Williamsburg Foundation, Williamsburg, VA; Fitzwilliam Museum, Cambridge, England; Museum of Art, Rhode Island School of Design, Providence, RI; Victoria & Albert Museum, London, England; William Rockhill Nelson Gallery of Art, Kansas City, MO.

Bowl, 11-1/2" l, oval, matching undertray, reticulated, edge wear and hairlines	1,320.00
Cache Pot, 7-1/2" d, taupe, applied classical dec, 1830	450.00
Cream Jug, 5-1/4" h, pear shape, raised rose branch band over drapery, lamb finial on lid	600.00
Creamer, pear shape, lyre handle, 18th C	
3" h, shield design, circular foot	550.00
3-1/4" h, raised leaf and putti dec, claw feet	750.00
Dish, 9" d, circular, scroll and latticino dec	325.00
Loving Cup, 4-1/4" h, white raised US seal, 2 gold initials on front, Britannia on verse, handles outlined in blue, Castleford	250.00
Plate, shaped reticulated rim	
8-1/4" d, emb border	600.00
9-3/4" d, emb diaper border	375.00
Platter, 16-3/4" d, molded diaper-work panels, scalloped rim, 18th C	250.00

Jug, raised Robert Burns commemorative design, beige ground, cream portrait, mask spout, hand handle, 8-1/2" h, $475.

Salt, helmet shape, latticino star and lion, bird and shell dec, claw feet, c18th C	880.00
Sauce Boat, 3-1/8" l, oval, relief molded diaper, ozier, and scrolling panels, loop handle	425.00
Tea Caddy, 4-1/4" h, pear shape, latticino dec, knob finial, 18th C	375.00
Teapot, cov, 7" h, ball shape, raised branch dec, bird finial on lid, 18th C	2,850.00
Tray, 7-3/4" l, oval, latticino dec, scalloped rim	350.00
Water Pitcher, 12-1/2" h, bulbous, incised fleck marks on body, hinged pewter lid	425.00

SALTS, OPEN

History: When salt was first mined, the supply was limited and expensive. The necessity for a receptacle in which to serve the salt resulted in the first open salt, a crude, hand-carved, wooden trencher.

As time passed, salt receptacles were refined in style and materials. In the 1500s, both master and individual salts existed. By the 1700s, firms such as Meissen, Waterford, and Wedgwood were making glass, china, and porcelain salts. Leading glass manufacturers in the 1800s included Libbey, Mount Washington, New England, Smith Bros., Vallerysthal, Wave Crest, and Webb. Many outstanding silversmiths in England, France, and Germany also produced this form.

Open salts were the only means of serving salt until the appearance of the shaker in the late 1800s. The ease of procuring salt from a shaker greatly reduced the use of and need for the open salts.

References: William Heacock and Patricia Johnson, *5,000 Open Salts*, Richardson Printing Corporation, 1982, 1986 value update; Allan B. and Helen B. Smith have authored and published ten books on open salts beginning with *One Thousand Individual Open Salts Illustrated* (1972) and ending with *1,334 Open Salts Illustrated: The Tenth Book* (1984). Daniel Snyder did the master salt sections in volumes 8 and 9. In 1987 Mimi Rudnick compiled a revised price list for the ten Smith Books; Kenneth Wilson, *American Glass 1760-1930*, 2 vols., Hudson Hills Press and The

Toledo Museum of Art, 1994.

Periodical: *Salty Comments*, 401 Nottingham Rd, Newark, DE 19711.

Collectors' Clubs: New England Society of Open Salt Collectors, P.O. Box 177, Sudbury, MA 01776; Open Salt Collectors of the Atlantic Region, 56 Northview Dr., Lancaster, PA 17601.

Note: The numbers in parenthesis refer to plate numbers in the Smiths' books.

Condiment Sets with Open Salts

German Silver, two castors, two salts, two salt spoons, Renaissance style with swan supports, c1900, mkd "800 fine" 800.00
Limoges, double salt and mustard, sgd "J. M. Limoges" (388) 80.00
Metal, coolie pulling rickshaw, salt, pepper, and mustard, blown glass liners, Oriental (461) 360.00
Quimper, double salt and mustard, white, blue, and green floral dec, sgd "Quimper" (388) 120.00

Early American Glass

2-3/8" h, 2-3/4" d, pressed vaseline, emb rib, SP ftd holder 55.00
2-5/8" l, colorless, variant, Neal MN3, chips 305.00
3" h, cobalt blue, paneled with diamond foot 125.00
3" h, colorless, blown, expanded diamond bowl, applied petal foot .145.00
3" l, colorless, lacy, eagle, Neal EE1, chips 200.00
3-1/8" l, cobalt blue, Neal CN 1a, 2 feet replaced, small chips ... 200.00
3-1/8" l, fiery opalescent, 3-1/8" l, Neal BS2, chips 275.00
3-1/4" l, fiery opalescent, eagles, Neal EE3b, chips 500.00
3-3/8" h, cobalt blue, facet cut, fan rim, sq foot, edges ground ... 125.00
3-5/8" l, sapphire blue, Neal BT 2, very minor flakes 1,075.00

Figurals

Basket, 3" h, 2-3/4" d, coral colored glass, SP basket frame, salt with cut polished facets 55.00
Boat, lacy, colorless, New England, Neal BT-9, slight rim roughness 160.00
Bucket, 2-1/2" d, 1-5/8" h, Bristol glass, turquoise, white, green, and brown enameled bird, butterfly and trees, SP rim and handle ... 75.00
Sea Horse, Belleek, brilliant turquoise, white base, supports shell salt, first black mark (458) 350.00

Individual

Colored Glass
    Cambridge, Decagon pattern, amber (468) 40.00
    Cameo, Galle, green pedestal, enamel dec, sgd (205) 295.00
    Moser, cobalt blue, pedestal, gold bands, applied flowers sgd (380) 70.00
    Purple Slag, 3" d, 1-1/4" h, emb shell pattern 50.00
Cut Glass, 2" d, 1-1/2" h, cut ruby ovals, allover dainty white enameled scrolls, clear ground, gold trim, scalloped top 60.00
German Silver, dolphin feet, 1890-1910 (353) 100.00
Mount Washington, blue Johnny Jump-ups, cream ground, raised gold dots on rim 135.00
Pattern Glass
    Crystal Wedding 25.00
    Fine Rib, flint.. 35.00
    Hawaiian Lei, (477) 35.00
    Pineapple and Fan 25.00
    Three Face 40.00
Royal Bayreuth, lobster claw (87) 80.00
Russian Enamel, 1-1/4" h, 1-3/4" d, colorless glass liner, gold finished metal, red and white scallop design, Russian hallmarks, c1940 ... 110.00
Sterling Silver, Georg Jensen, Denmark, porringer (238) 200.00

Intaglios

Niagara Falls, scene (368) 75.00
Tree, six intaglios, Venus and Cupid (423) 115.00

Master, Hobnail, sapphire blue, 3" sq, $12.

Masters

Coin Silver, made by Gorham for retailer Seth E. Brown, Boston, ftd, gold washed int., monogrammed, pair in fitted case, two coin silver spoons by Jones, Ball & Poor, pr, approx 4 troy oz 375.00
Colored Glass
    Cobalt blue, master, wafer base, 2-1/6" h, 2-1/16" d 150.00
    Cranberry, 3" d, 1-3/4" h, emb ribs, applied crystal ruffed rim, SP holder with emb lions heads 160.00
    Green, light, dark green ruffled top, open pontil (449) 90.00
        Raspberry, heavy, sq, Pairpoint (444) 75.00
        . Vaseline, 3" d, 2-1/4" h, applied crystal trim around middle, silverplated stand 125.00
Cut Glass, 2" d, 2" h, green cut to clear, SP holder 115.00
Pattern glass
    Bakewell Pears 30.00
    Barberry, pedestal 40.00
    Basketweave, sleigh (397) 100.00
    Diamond Point, cov 75.00
    Excelsior.. 30.00
    Snail, ruby stained... 75.00
    Sunflower, pedestal.. 40.00
    Viking 30.00
Pewter, pedestal, cobalt blue liner (349) 65.00
Sterling Silver, 1-3/4" h, Stieff Co., early 20th C, chased and emb allover floral pattern, applied floral rim, 3 scrolled shell feet, pr, 6 troy oz 260.00

SAMPLERS

History: Samplers served many purposes. For a young child, they were a practice exercise and permanent reminder of stitches and patterns. For a young woman, they were a means to demonstrate skills in a "gentle" art and a way to record family genealogy. For the mature woman, they were a useful occupation and method of creating gifts or remembrances, e.g., mourning pieces.

Schools for young ladies of the early 19th century prided themselves on the needlework skills they taught. The Westtown School in Chester County, Pennsylvania, and the Young Ladies Seminary in Bethlehem, Pennsylvania, were two institutions. These schools changed their teaching as styles changed. Berlin work was introduced by the mid-19th century.

Examples of samplers date back to the 1700s. The earliest ones were long and narrow, usually done only with the alphabet and numerals. Later examples were square. At the end of the 19th century, the shape tended to be rectangular.

The same motifs were used throughout the country. The name of the person who stitched the piece is a key factor in determining the region.

References: Ethel Stanwood Bolton and Eva Johnston Coe, *American Samplers*, Dover, 1987; Elizabeth Kurella, *The Complete Guide to Vintage Textiles*, Krause Publications, 1999; Glee Krueger, *Gallery of American Samplers*, Bonanza Books, 1984; Jack L. Lindsey, Worldly Goods, *The Arts of Early Pennsylvania, 1680-1758*, Pennsylvania Museum of Art, distributed by Antique Collectors' Club, 1999; Betty Ring, *American Needlework Treasures*, E. P. Dutton, 1987; Anne Sebba, Samplers, Thames and Hudson, 1979.

Museums: Cooper-Hewitt Museum, National Museum of Design, New York, NY; Smithsonian Institution, Washington, DC.

Note: Samplers are assumed to be on linen unless otherwise indicated.

1694, Mary Ogleed, silk on linen homespun, Adam and Eve with lion, unicorn, deer, birds, flowers, etc., alphabets, name, and date, three-dimensional apples and fig leaf on Eve, red, blue, green, brown, and white, very minor wear, framed, 11" w, 10-1/2" h 5,775.00

1788, Elisa Chapman, cotton homespun, silk stitches, inner floral wreath encircling verse, stylized streets, buildings, birds, and vining border, "Elisa Chapman 9 years old work'd May 1788," soft colors, gold painted frame, 18-1/2" x 14-1/2"....................................... 550.00

1796, Elizabeth Stone, linen ground, pink, green, and cream silk threads, rows of alphabets, zigzag border, trees, figures, "Elizabeth Stone was born in Danvers Janury (sic) 30th worked this in the 10th year of her age 1796," 7-1/2" w, 11-1/2" h.............................. 3,400.00

1806, Sarah Hodge, bands of alphabet letters separated by various stitches, 2 large flowering plants surrounding "Sarah Hodge/1806," top and bottom floral borders, 11-3/4 x 9-1/2", unframed...... 1,025.00

1815, E. Butler, silk on finely woven homespun, vining strawberry border, stylized flowers, bids, and houses, sgd "E. Butler, 1915," green, tan, black, and cream, war and holes, framed 300.00

1821, Mary Ward, Adam and Eve in the Garden of Eden, adorned with potted plants, dogs, peacocks, various birds, flowers, hearts, and bird house designs, embroidered cartouche in upper center that reads "Mary Ward/Jan' 12 1821," surrounded by geometric border, shades of green, brown, ivory, and blue, 9" x 12-1/2", framed, minor damage 1,800.00

1822, "W," initial and date enclosed in flowering wreath, alphabet panels surrounded by birds, trees, flowering vines, hearts, butterfly, floral devices, framed, losses to needlework, toning, fading, minor staining, 22" h, 17-1/4" w.. 865.00

1823, Catharine Foster, linen homespun, pink, olive, ivory, gray, green, and gold silk threads, flowering border, verse, birds, angels, flowers, and "Catharine Foster, Aged 12, 1823," some moth damage, orig molded black frame, 15-1/2" x 15".. 900.00

1824, Mary Hurd's Sampler Rochester Aged 15 Years February 9th 1824, five alphabet panels separated by rows of geometric devices, row of numbers, inspirational verse at lower left, bordered by ocean waves, toning minor staging, laid down on paper, 17-1/2" x 17" 1,100.00

1825, J. Melross, silk on linen homespun, alphabets, shepherdess, trees, green, red, white, and black, modern frame, 18" h, 19" w 880.00

1831, Mary Cockbill, Her work, Aged 12 Years, Quaker meeting house and figures, floral dec, framed, $1,100.

1827, Mary J. Keely, silk on linen homespun, alphabets, vining strawberry border, house, trees, hearts, initials and verse and "Mary J. Keely, born 1811, Aug 29, aged 16," faded brown, green, blue, black, and white, OH family provenance on back, framed, 19-1/4" h, 18-1/4" w 3,750.00

1831, Magdalen F. Parry, mixed floral borders surrounding designs of potted plants, birds, flowers, wreath, and text which reads "Extract/ Religions sacred lamp alone,/Unering pointe the way,/Where happiness forever shines,/ with unpoluted ray/Magdalen F. Parry/1831," 16" x 17", unframed... 2,450.00

1832, Susannah Funks, center floral arrangement in basket, flanked by other floral and bird designs, floral and ivy top and side borders, lower landscape of trees, stag, goose, other animals, "Susannah Funks Work done in the year of our lord 1832," 16-1/4" x 20-1/2" framed 2,450.00

1873, Jane A. Padbury, October 3rd 1873, Aged 13 Years, large brick building flanked by flowering trees, surrounded by animal, floral, and foliate devices, geometric border, fading and toning, 12-1/4" x 12-1/4" 980.00

Undated, American

Adam and Eve, upper panel of alphabet, unfinished center, lower panel of Adam and Eve beneath apple tree with entwined serpent, flowers, flowering vine border, unframed, minor fabric loss, minor staining, 16" x 13-1/2"... 345.00

Mary Elizabeth Beatty, Aged 8 Years, silk on linen homespun, green and pink vinine floral border, alphabets, verse, stylized floral groupings, wear and stains, faded colors, old gilded frame, 20-1/4" h, 20-1/4" w 450.00

Sara W. Cushing, Aged 10, alphabet panels above various pictorial symbols, central federal house flanked by flowering shrubs, trees, birds, black dog, surrounded by sawtooth border, toning, fading, minor staining, 13-1/2' x 17" 1,495.00

Elizabeth Donat, wool and bleached yarn, alphabets, birds, deer, olive green, red, and blue, worn and damage, some colors have bled, framed, 22" h, 14" w.. 110.00

Mary Fisher, 3 sets of alphabets, family initials, girl seated in garden with dog surrounded by flowers, rose and vine border, "Mary Fisher, Wrought in the 12th year of her life," 18" x 16-1/2", framed 550.00

Unnamed, silk on linen homespun, alphabets and stylized flowers, 2 people with bunch of grapes, initials, faded blue, yellow, green, and white, framed, 14-1/4" h, 25" w 550.00

SANDWICH GLASS

History: In 1818, Deming Jarves was listed in the Boston Directory as a glass factor. That same year he was appointed general manager of the newly formed New England Glass Company. In 1824, Jarves toured the glassmaking factories in Pittsburgh, left New England Glass Company, and founded a glass factory in Sandwich.

Originally called the Sandwich Manufacturing Company, it was incorporated in April 1826 as the Boston & Sandwich Glass Company. From 1826 to 1858, Jarves served as general manager. The Boston & Sandwich Glass Company produced a wide variety of wares in differing levels of quality. The factory used the free-blown, blown three mold, and pressed glass manufacturing techniques. Both clear and colored glass were used.

Competition in the American glass industry in the mid-1850s resulted in lower-quality products. Jarves left the Boston & Sandwich company in 1858, founded the Cape Cod Glass Company, and tried to duplicate the high quality of the earlier glass. Meanwhile, at the Boston & Sandwich Glass Company, emphasis was placed on mass production. The development of a lime glass (non-flint) led to lower costs for pressed glass. Some free-blown and blown-and-molded pieces, mostly in color, were made. Most of this Victorian-era glass was enameled, painted, or acid etched.

By the 1880s, the Boston & Sandwich Glass Company was operating at a loss. Labor difficulties finally resulted in the closing of the factory on Jan. 1, 1888.

References: Raymond E. Barlow and Joan E. Kaiser, *Glass Industry in Sandwich*, Vol. 1 (1993), Vol. 2 (1989), Vol. 3 (1987), and Vol. 4 (1983), distributed by Schiffer Publishing; ——, *Price Guide for the Glass Industry in Sandwich Vols. 1-4*, Schiffer Publishing, 1993; Ruth Webb Lee, *Sandwich Glass Handbook*, Charles E. Tuttle, 1966; ——, *Sandwich Glass*, Charles E. Tuttle, 1966; George S. and Helen McKearin, *American Glass*, Random House, 1979; Catherine M. V. Thuro, *Oil Lamps II*, Collector Books, 1994 value update; Kenneth Wilson, *American Glass 1760-1930*, 2 vols., Hudson Hills Press and The Toledo Museum of Art, 1994.

Museum: Sandwich Glass Museum, Sandwich, MA.

Additional Listings: Blown Three Mold; Cup Plates.

Basket, 5-1/2" h, 5-1/2" w, ruffled box pleated top, White Burmese, candy pink to yellow peachblow-type, applied frosted thorn handle 795.00
Bowl, 7-1/2" d, pressed, lacy, Tulip and Acanthus pattern 45.00
Butter Dish, cov, colorless, flint, Gothic pattern 195.00
Candlesticks, pr
    7" h, canary, pressed, loop base, Barlow #3047, very minor chips, gauffering marks 375.00
    7-1/2" h, hexagonal base, purple-blue petal socket, translucent white 575.00
    10-1/4" h, canary, dolphin, flint, one flake under petal, minor base roughness 850.00
Champagne, Sandwich Star 850.00
Compote, 10-1/2" w, 4-3/4" h, cranberry overlay, oval cuts, enameled birds and flowers on inner surface, c1890 .... 495.00
Creamer and Sugar, colorless, flint, Gothic pattern 125.00

Cup Plate, lacy
    Blue, ship 125.00
    Violet Blue, heart 325.00
Decanter, 6-3/4" h, cobalt blue, ribbed, tam o'shanter stopper 195.00
Goblet, colorless, flint, Gothic pattern, 12 pc set 650.00
Inkwell, 2-9/16", cylindrical domed form, colorless, pink and white stripes, sheared mouth, applied pewter collar and cap, smooth base 2,300.00
Lamp
    8-1/2" h, Waffle pattern, opaque blue and white, camphene burner, whale oil 950.00
    9-3/4" h, opaque white font, brass stem, marble base, gold dec 150.00
    11-3/4" h, colorless blown font, sq scrolled pressed base, lion head dec, paw feet, very minor chips and cracks 290.00
    12-1/2" h, pressed blue glass fonts, clambroth column and stepped base, minor base chips and cracks, pr 1,840.00
Paperweight, 3-1/2" w, 1-1/4" h, colorless and frosted, portraits of Queen Victoria and Prince Consort, 1851 .... 220.00
Pitcher, 10" h
    Amberina Verde, fluted top 325.00
    Electric Blue, enameled floral dec, fluted top, threaded handle 425.00
    Reverse Amberina, fluted top 400.00
Plate
    6" d, lacy, Shell pattern 165.00
    7" d, Rayed Peacock Eye 125.00
Pomade, cov, figural, bear, imp retailer's name
    3-3/4" h, clambroth, imp "F. B. Strouse, N.Y.," chips 525.00
    4-1/2" h, blue, base imp "X. Bazin, Philada," chips 300.00
Salt, 2" h, 3-1/8" d, blue, pressed, floral, Barlow 1460, minor chips, mold imperfections 690.00
Spooner, colorless, flint, Gothic pattern 85.00
Sugar, cov, translucent blue, Lacy Gothic pattern 1,300.00
Toy, lemonade cup, 1-5/8" h, canary, pressed, handle, tooled rim, pontil scar 140.00
Undertray, Heart, lacy, flint 400.00
Vase
    9-1/4" h, amethyst, Three Printie Block pattern, trumpet shape, gauffered rim, triple ring turned connector, pressed colorless base, hairlines to base 2,900.00
    10" h, dark amethyst, pressed, tulip, octagonal base, few chips to underside of base, pr 2,500.00
Whiskey Taster, cobalt blue, nine panels 185.00

SARREGUEMINES CHINA

History: Sarreguemines ware is a faience porcelain, i.e., tin-glazed earthenware. The factory which made it was established in Lorraine, France, in 1770, under the supervision of Utzschneider and Fabry. The factory was regarded as one of the three most prominent manufacturers of French faience. Most of the wares found today were made in the 19th century.

Marks: Later wares are impressed "Sarreguemines" and "Germany" as a result of changes in international boundaries.

Basket, 9" h, quilted, green, heavy leopard skin crystallization .. 250.00
Centerpiece, 14-3/4" h, 14-3/4" d, bowl with pierced ringlets to sides, supported by center stem flanked by sea nymphs either side, mounted atop circular base on 4 scrolled feet, polychrome dec, imp marks, chips, restorations, c1875 .... 900.00
Cup and Saucer, Orange, majolica, crack to one cup, nicks, set of 4 . 200.00
Dinnerware Service, white china, multicolored scenes, 6 luncheon plates, 6 bread and butter plates, 6 demitasse cups, 6 porringers, 2 platters, divided dish 150.00
Face Jug, majolica
    Danish woman, bonnet, minor nick 880.00

Vases, pr, fish eye pattern, green ground, mkd and numbered "1403DT C531" under foot, 11-1/2" h, $550.

Paul Kruger, repair	110.00
Smiling face, #3181, 5-1/2" h, minor rim nick	20.00
Suspicious Eyes, #3320	550.00
Upward Eyes, #3257, hairline	220.00

Garniture, Art Nouveau faience, 10-3/4" h pr of vases, shouldered trumpet form, shaped oval centerpiece bowl, each with wide gilt band of foliage within diamond borders centered by decorative medallion, verte ground 350.00

Humidor

Man with top hat, majolica	165.00
Pig, 6" h, #481, ear repair, no lid	220.00

Plate, 7-1/2" d, dec with music and characters from French children's songs, 12 pc set 375.00

Tankard, cov, 11" h, stoneware, continuous country scene of dancing and celebrating villagers, branch handle, pewter lid with porcelain medallion and painted polychrome coat of arms, dated 1869.. 325.00

Urn, 31-1/4" h, gilt metal mounted majolica, baluster form, cobalt blue glazed, mounted with the figure of a crowned lion holding sword, lion and mask handled sides, pierced foliate rim, raised on 4 scrolling foliate cast feet, imp "Majolica Sarreguemines," second half 19th C.....1,800.00

SARSAPARILLA BOTTLES

History: Sarsaparilla refers to the fragrant roots of a number of tropical American, spiny, woody vines of the lily family. An extract was obtained from these dried roots and used for medicinal purposes. The first containers, which date from the 1840s, were stoneware; glass bottles were used later.

Carbonated water often was added to sarsaparilla to make a soft drink or to make consuming it more pleasurable. For this reason, sarsaparilla and soda became synonymous even though they originally were two different concoctions.

References: Ralph and Terry Kovel, *Kovels' Bottles Price List*, 11th ed., Three Rivers Press 1998; Carlo and Dot Sellari, *Standard Old Bottle Price Guide*, Collector Books, 1989.

Stollo Co., Troy, NY, "The Temperance Beverage," paper label, 12 oz, $9.

Periodical: *Antique Bottle and Glass Collector*, P.O. Box 187, East Greenville, PA 18041.

Additional Listings: See *Warman's Americana & Collectibles* for a list of soda bottles.

Bristols Extract of Sarsaparilla, aqua, open pontil, 5-1/2" h	70.00
Bull's Extract of Sarsaparilla, beveled corners, 7" l	400.00
Carl's Sarsaparilla & Celery Compound, aqua, 7-3/8" h	70.00
Compound Extract of Sarsaparilla, amber, gallon	140.00
Dr. Ira Belding's, Honduras Sarsaparilla, colorless, 10-1/2" h	30.00
Dr. Townsend's Sarsaparilla, olive green, pontil	85.00
Foley's Sarsaparilla, light amber	40.00
Genuine Sands' Sarsaparilla, aquamarine, rect, beveled corners, applied double collared mouth, pontil scar	215.00
Guysott's Yellow Dock & Sarsaparilla	40.00
Lancaster Glassworks, barrel, golden amber	125.00
Old Dr. J. Townsend's Sarsaparilla, light bluish-green, sq, beveled corners, applied sloping collared mouth, iron pontil, 9-1/2" h	250.00
Radway's Sarsaparilla Resolvent	25.00
Skoda's Sarsaparilla, amber	25.00
Walker's, aqua	130.00
Warren Allen's Sarsaparilla Beer, tan, pottery	125.00

SATIN GLASS

History: Satin glass, produced in the late 19th century, is an opaque art glass with a velvety matte (satin) finish achieved through treatment with hydrofluoric acid. A large majority of the pieces were cased or had a white lining.

While working at the Phoenix Glass Company, Beaver, Pennsylvania, Joseph Webb perfected mother-of-pearl (MOP) satin glass in 1885. Similar to plain satin glass in respect to casing, MOP satin glass has a distinctive surface finish and an integral or indented design, the most well known being diamond quilted (DQ).

The most common colors are yellow, rose, or blue. Rainbow coloring is considered choice.

Tumbler, Raindrop pattern, Mother-of-Pearl, white ext. and lining, 3-3/4" h, $200.

Additional Listings: Cruets; Fairy Lamps; Miniature Lamps; Rose Bowls.

Reproduction Alert: Satin glass, in both the plain and mother-of-pearl varieties, has been widely reproduced.

Bowl, 6-1/2" d, 4-3/4" h, shaded blue, MOP, DQ, frosted thorny base feet extend to open crimped top.............................395.00
Bride's Basket, 15-1/2" h, deep rose, enamel swan and floral dec, heavy bronze holder with birds perched at top 450.00
Compote, 8" h, pink ruffled bowl, gilt edge, enameled floral dec, 3 ftd SP floral dec base 250.00
Creamer, 3-1/4" h, 3-1/4" d, globular, blue MOP, ruffled top, white lining, applied frosted handle 325.00
Cup and Saucer, 3" h, 5" d, Raindrop MOP, pink shading to white ..385.00
Epergne, 13-3/4" h, 10" d, pink and white, hobnail bowl, resilvered base and lily vase holder.........................395.00
Finger Bowl, 4-1/4" d, 2-3/4" h, pink, MOP, IVT, ruffled top.........165.00
Lamp, 17-1/8" h, 9" d, deep pink shading to lighter MOP, DG, ruffled, silverplated base emb designs of cupids, etc., white int. 895.00
Mustard Pot, 2-1/2" h, bright yellow, gold prunus dec, SP top, Webb 450.00
Salt Shaker, 3-1/4" h, rose shaded to white, MOP, DQ, tapered barrel, orig 2 pc lid..........................550.00
Scent Bottle, 7-1/2" h, 4-1/2" d, Peacock Eye, MOP, creamy yellow, hallmarked sterling crown like cap (with dent), collar with sterling chain..........................650.00
Sugar Shaker, 6-1/4" h, blue, Raindrop, MOP, SP top...............425.00
Tumbler, 3-1/2" h, Rainbow, DQ, enameled floral dec, pr..........375.00
Vase
    3" h, 4" d, deep yellow shading to lighter to white, DQ, MOP, white int. 145.00
    6-1/2" h, brown shaded to white, DQ, blue, white, and orange enameled forget-me-nots dec, MOP int. 825.00
    9-1/2" h, 5" w, blue shading to white, Coin Spot, lightly crimped rim pulled down to shoulder at 3 points, Mt. Washington 675.00

SATSUMA

History: Satsuma, named for a war lord who brought skilled Korean potters to Japan in the early 1600s, is a handcrafted Japanese faience (tin-glazed) pottery. It is finely crackled, has a cream, yellow-cream, or gray-cream color, and is decorated with raised enamels in floral, geometric, and figural motifs.

Figural satsuma was made specifically for export in the 19th century. Later satsuma, referred to as satsuma-style ware, is a Japanese porcelain also hand decorated in raised enamels. From 1912 to the present, satsuma-style ware has been mass-produced. Much of the ware on today's market is of this later period.

Reference: Nancy N. Schiffer, Imari, *Satsuma, and Other Japanese Export Ceramics*, Schiffer Publishing, 1997.

Periodical: *Orientalia Journal*, P.O. Box 94, Flushing, NY 11363-0094, http://members.aol.com/Orientalia/index.html.

Bowl, 5-1/2" d, cobalt blue ground, gilt dec, 19th C, worn gilt.....200.00
Box, cov, 3-1/2" d, round, lid dec with group of boys surrounded by floral border, base with band of fluttering butterflies above upright leaf border, int. base and lid with shaped cartouche of boys playing, surrounded by butterflies, sgd "Kinkozan," Meiji period 980.00
Cache Pot, 6-1/2" h, figural and landscape scene 120.00
Censor
    3-1/2" h, ovoid, 3 cabriole legs, 2 shaped handles rising from shoulder, lid with large shi shi seated on top, continual river landscape scene, patterned lappet border above, key fret border below, base sealed "Yabu Meizan," minor loss to one ear on shi shi 2,990.00
    10-1/4" h, tapering rect form, lobed base, 2 squared handles, pierced domed lid, allover dec or Arhats, Meiji period 635.00
Cup and Saucer, bird and floral motif, cobalt blue border, Kinkozan, Japanese.......................................115.00
Dish, 14" d, male and female figures gathered around a goddess, all in landscape, patterned border, Meiji period 115.00
Jar, cov, 8-1/2" h, cylindrical, paneled sides, bird and floral motif, phoenix on patterned border, sgd "Made in Kyoto, Japan," 19th C, discoloration 3,200.00
Koro, pierced lid
    2-3/4" h, ovoid, 3 short feet, continual scene of festival with men, women, and children playing games, eating, playing music, brocade shoulder border, 19th C 635.00
    3" h, hexagonal, 6 bracket feet, each side with flowers blooming behind garden fences, domed lid, sgd with Shimazu mon ...2,185.00

Incense Burner, courtesans on one side, Mandarins on obverse, c1875, 4" w, 3-3/4" h, $250.

Miniature
Jar, cov, 2-1/2" h, square form, small foot, each side with differing panel, musicians, Mt. Fuji, roosters, and women with children visiting a bird vendor, gilt floral designs on blue ground surrounding each panel and on lid, int. liner lid, 19th C, sgd "Kinkozan"............1,495.00
Teapot, 4" h, round form, panel of samuari and women with boys, blue ground, gilt floral and wave design, woven handle, base sgd "Kinkozan zo," Meiji period 635.00
Tea Cup and Saucer, 1-3/4" h cup,. 4-3/4" d saucer, colorful groups of flowerheads with scrolling gilt vines, minor gilt wear, sgd "Yabu Meizan" 900.00
Tea Set, 6-1/2" h teapot, creamer, sugar, 6 cups and saucers, 6 7-1/4" d plates, paneled designs of courtesans in courtyard settings, c1900 .... 290.00
Tray, 6-1/2" x 9-3/8", rect, scalloped corners, garden setting with women playing game, fan border, sgd "Ryozan," 19th C 1,400.00
Urn, 37-1/2" h, dragon handles, geishas in landscape 295.00
Vase
2-7/8" h, shouldered form, tall neck gradually flaring to rim, body dec with boys playing games, shoulder and neck with overlapping flowerhead designs, Yabu Meizan seal on base, Meiji period, pr ...2,300.00
4-1/2" h, slender ovoid, continual scene of fishermen in watery landscape, Mount Fuji in distance, floral lappet neck border, Yabu Meizan seal on base, Meiji period 2,100.00
6-1/4" h, high shouldered form, waisted neck, flared rim, two large panels, one with fisherman, other with immortals, background of shaped cartouches and butterflies, intricate brocade bands, 19th C, sgd "Seikozan" 1,495.00
6-1/4" h, ovoid, short waisted necks, flared rims, panels of figures in procession and in courtly pursuits on floral and patterned ground, one with rim damage, Meiji period, pr................................. 750.00
12" h, geometric banded borders, scene of artist decorating scrolls and birds, floral landscape, attached base, feet repairs, Japanese, late 19th C... 260.00
16" h, ovoid, short waisted neck, upturned rim, overlay design of monkeys chasing cabs, eating fruit, scrolling floral ground, black glazed neck, rim and root with sq scroll bands, unsgd, 19th C.......11,500.00

SCALES

History: Prior to 1900, the simple balance scale was commonly used for measuring weights. Since then, scales have become more sophisticated in design and more accurate. There are a wide variety of styles and types, including beam, platform, postal, and pharmaceutical.

Reference: Bill and Jan Berning, *Scales: A Collector's Guide*, Schiffer Publishing, 1999.

Collectors' Club: International Society of Antique Scale Collectors, 300 W. Adams St., Suite 821, Chicago, IL 60606.

Apothecary, 19-1/2" l, 15-3/4" h, walnut, fitted ivory dec.............250.00
Balance
14" l, cast iron, orig red paint with black and yellow trim, nickel plated brass pans, mkd "Henry Troemner, Phila. No. 5B, Baker's" 120.00
22" h, wrought iron, cast iron base, tin pans............................65.00
Candy
Dayton, metallic orange, brass pan......................................300.00
National Store Co., tin pan, c1910...95.00
Catalog, illus
Buffalo Scale Co., Buffalo, NY, 1882, 4 pgs 30.00
Chicago Scale Co., Chicago, IL, c1880, 24 pgs.....................80.00
E. & T. Fairbanks & Co., St. Johnsbury, VT, c1880, 34 pgs.....45.00
Computing, 15-1/4" h, 17-1/2" w, merchant's type, "Computing Scale Co., Dayton, Ohio" 225.00
Counter, blue, chrome with tan, mkd "Toledo" 175.00
Egg, Oaks Mfg. Co..20.00
Hand Held, wide side gauge, unusual cylinder, mkd "Chatilion, NY" 30.00

Fairbanks, 50% orig paint, 15-1/2" l, 8-3/4" h, $65.

Jeweler, brass pans, brass standard, 10 brass weights, green velvet lined box...160.00
Photographer, brass pans, brass weights, mkd "Made in Germany"...150.00
Platform
63" h, Peerless Junior, Peerless Weighing Machine Co., porcelainized steel, tiled platform, gold lettering 350.00
68" h, National Automatic Weighing Machine Co., cast iron, painted, relief patterns, porcelain sign and dial 995.00
Postal, 4-1/4" h, desk, SS, cased, monogram, mkd "Shreve & Co," c1900-22 ....250.00
Steelyard, wood, weighted bulbous end, turned shaft, 18th C....215.00
Store
Hanson Weightmaster, 6" x 14" x 10", cast iron, gold case with ground, black lettering and indicator......................................45.00
Howe, cast iron, red base, gold highlights, brass pan, 5 weights, patent June 18, 1887 ....75.00

SCHLEGELMILCH PORCELAINS

History: Erdmann Schlegelmilch founded his porcelain factory in Suhl in the Thuringia region in 1861. Reinhold, his brother, established a porcelain factory at Tillowitz in Upper Silesia in 1869. In the 1860s Prussia controlled Thuringia and Upper Silesia, both rich in the natural ingredients needed for porcelain.

By the late 19th century, an active export business was conducted with the United States and Canada due to a large supply of porcelain at reasonable costs achieved through industrialization and cheap labor.

The Suhl factory ceased production in 1920, unable to recover from the effects of World War I. The Tillowitz plant, located in an area of changing international boundaries, finally came under Polish socialist government control in 1956.

Marks: Both brothers marked their pieces with the "RSP" mark, a designation honoring Rudolph Schlegelmilch, their father. More than 30 mark variations have been discovered.

References: Susan and Al Bagdade, *Warman's English & Continental Pottery & Porcelain*, 3rd Edition, Krause Publications, 1998; R. H. Capers, *Capers' Notes on the Marks of Prussia*, Alphabet Printing (667 E. 6th St., El Paso, IL 61738), 1996; Mary Frank Gaston, *Collector's Encyclope-*

dia of R. S. Prussia and Other R. S. and E. S. Porcelain, 1st Series (1982, 1993 value update), 2nd Series (1986, 1994 value update), 3rd Series (1994), 4th Series (1997), Collector Books; Leland and Carol Marple, *R. S. Prussia: The Art Nouveau Years*, Schiffer, 1998; ----. *R. S. Prussia: The Early Years*, Schiffer Publishing, 1997.

Collectors' Club: International Association of R. S. Prussia Collectors Inc., 212 Wooded Falls Rd, Louisville, KY 40243.

Reproduction Alert: Many "fake" Schlegelmilch pieces are appearing on the market. These reproductions have new decal marks, transfers, or recently hand-painted animals on old, authentic R. S. Prussia pieces.

Dorothy Hammond, in her 1979 book Confusing Collectibles, illustrated an R. S. Prussia decal which was available from a china-decorating supply company for $14 a sheet. This was the first of several fake R. S. Prussia reproduction marks that have caused confusion among collectors. Acquaint yourself with some of the subtle distinctions between fake and authentic marks as described in the following.

The period mark consists of a wreath that is open at the top. A five-pointed star sits in the opening. An "R" and an "S" flank a wreath twig in the center. The word "Prussia" is located beneath. In the period mark, the leg of the letter "P" extends down past the letter "r." In the reproduction mark, it does not. In the period mark, the letter "I" is dotted. It is dotted in some fake marks but not in others.

The "R" and the "S" in the period mark are in a serif face and are uniform in width. One fake mark uses a lettering style that utilizes a thin/thick letter body. The period mark has a period after the word "Prussia." Some fake marks fail to include it. Several fake marks do not include the word "Prussia" at all.

The period mark has a fine center line within each leaf of the wreath. Several fake marks do not.

R.S. Germany

Biscuit Jar, cov, 6" h, loop handles, roses dec, satin finish, gold knob 95.00
Bonbon Dish, 7-3/4" l, 4-1/2" w, pink carnations, gold dec, silver-gray ground, looped inside handle 40.00
Bread Plate, iris variant edge mold, blue and white, gold outlined petals and rim, multicolored center flowers, steeple mark 115.00
Bride's Bowl, floral center, ornate ftd stand 95.00
Cake Plate, deep yellow, 2 parrots on hanging leaf vine, open handles, green mark 235.00

Cup and Saucer, purple and gilt flowers, white ground, $25.

Vases, cream and brown tone ground, white, and yellow floral dec, pr, 12" h, $150.

Celery Tray, 11" l, 5-3/4" w, lily dec, gold rim, open handles, blue label 120.00
Chocolate Pot, white rose florals, blue mark 95.00
Cup and Saucer, plain mold, swan, blue water, mountain and brown castle background, RM 225.00
Demitasse Cup and Saucer, 3" h, pink roses, gold stenciled dec, satin finish, blue mark 90.00
Dessert Plate, 6-1/2" d, yellow and cream roses, green and rich brown shaded ground, 6 pc set 135.00
Ewer, 7" h, 4 portrait panels of women in 19th C gowns, brown ground, heavy gilding, minor imperfections 475.00
Hatpin Holder, floral dec 95.00
Napkin Ring, green, pink roses, white snowballs 55.00
Nut Bow, 5-1/4" d, 2-3/4" h, cream, yellow, roses, green scalloped edge 65.00
Pitcher, 5-3/4" h, light blue, chrysanthemums, pink roses, gold trim 85.00
Plate, 9-3/4" d, white flowers, gold leaves, gilded edge, green ground, mkd "RS Germany" in dark green, script sgd "Reinhold Schlegelmilch/Tillowitz/Germany" in red 45.00
Powder Box, cov, green poppies, green mark 50.00
Punch Bowl, 17-1/4" d, 8" h, mahogany shading to pink, polychrome enameled flowers with gilt, imp fleur-de-lis mark with "J. S. Germany" 275.00
Sauce Dish, underplate, green, yellow roses, blue mark 45.00
Tea Tile, peach and tan, greenish white snowballs, RM over faint blue mark 165.00
Vase, 4" h, bottle shape, shaded green to cream, cottage scene, mkd 70.00

R. S. Poland

Berry Bowl, 4-1/2" sq, white and pale orange floral design, green leaves, small orange-gold border flowers, mkd 45.00
Creamer, soft green, chain of violets, applied fleur-de-lis feet, RM 110.00
Dresser Set, glossy, pink roses, pr 6-1/4" h candlesticks, 5" h hatpin holder, 13" x 9" tray, ... 425.00
Flower Holder, pheasants, brass frog insert 675.00
Vase
   8-1/2" h, 4-3/4" d, large white and tan roses, shaded brown and green ground 195.00

Relish, red floral center, iris in velvet on border, pink and lavender ground, 9-1/2" l, 4-1/2" w, $95.

10" h, cottage scene, woman with sheep in foreground, ornate handles, gold trim 650.00
12" h, 6-1/4" d, white poppies, cream shaded to brown ground, pr.. 750.00

R.S. Prussia

Bowl
10" d, Hidden Images, portrait of woman, hair in bun, additional molded florals, pastel green ground 240.00
10-1/2" d, carnation mold, white, peach shading, Tiffany carnations, pink roses dec, satin finish, RM 595.00
10-1/2" d, Iris mold, pink poppies and daisies, green ground, RM 300.00
Butter Dish, cov, porcelain insert, cream and gold shading, pink roses, raised enamel, RM 715.00
Cake Set, 9-1/2" d plate, six 7" d plates, carnation mold, pale greens, Tiffany carnations, pink and white rose dec, RM 995.00
Celery Tray
9" l, carnation mold, white, peach shading, Tiffany carnations, pink roses dec, RM 375.00
9" l, gold and lavender, roses, bar mark 350.00
Chocolate Set, cov chocolate pot, 6 cups and saucers, pink and red roses, gold luster, angular handles, RM 995.00
Creamer, floral 225.00
Demitasse Cup and Saucer, dainty flowers 100.00
Ferner, 7" d, mold 876, florals on purple and green ground, unsgd 165.00
Hair Receiver, green lilies of the valley, white ground, RM 95.00
Milk Pitcher, 5" h, Morning Glory mold, pink carnations dec 200.00
Mustard Pot, white, light blue and multicolored tiny roses 150.00
Plate, 11" d, Carnation mold, white, peach shading, Tiffany carnations, satin finish, slight wear to gilt 250.00
Relish Dish, 9" d, blown-out mold, lavender and pink gloss finish, pink and white roses, two handles, RM 95.00
Shaving Mug, with mirror (Gaston Book II, Plate 397) 450.00
Spoon Holder, 14" l, pink and white roses 200.00
Tankard, 11" h, Carnation mold, white, all-over pink poppies, Tiffany carnations, satin finish, RM 1,100.00
Toothpick Holder, green shadows, pink and white roses, jeweled, six feet, RM 250.00
Vase, 4-3/8" h, 2-5/8" d, Pheasant Scene, handle, Mold 918 ..... 500.00

R. S. Suhl

Coffee Set, 9" h, coffeepot, creamer, sugar, 6 cups and saucers, figural scenes dec, some mkd "Angelica Kauffmann" 1,750.00
Pin Tray, 4-1/2" d, round, Nightwatch 375.00
Plate
6-3/4" d, cherubs dec 90.00
8-1/2" d, windmill scene and water, green mark 125.00
Powder Dish, cov, Nightwatch, green shading 425.00
Vase, 8" h, 4 pheasants, green mark 275.00

R. S. Tillowitz

Bowl, 7-3/4" d, slanted sides, open handles, 4 leaf shaped feet, matte finish, pale green ground, roses and violets, gold flowered rim, mkd. 125.00
Creamer and Sugar, soft yellow and salmon roses 65.00
Plate, 6-1/2" d, mixed floral spray, gold beading, emb rim, brown wing mark 120.00
Relish Tray, 8" l, oval, hp, shaded green, white roses, green leaves, center handle, blue mark.. 45.00
Tea Set, stacking teapot, creamer, and sugar, yellow, rust, and blue flowers, gold trim, ivory ground, mkd "Royal Silesia," green mark in wreath 95.00
Vase
6" h, golden pheasants dec 265.00
10" h, pheasants, brown and yellow, 2 curved handles 125.00

SCHNEIDER GLASS

History: Brothers Ernest and Charles Schneider founded a glassworks at Epiney-sur-Seine, France, in 1913. Charles, the artistic designer, previously had worked for Daum and Gallé. Robert, son of Charles, assumed art direction in 1948. Schneider moved to Loris in 1962.

Although Schneider made tablewares, stained glass, and lighting fixtures, its best-known product is art glass, which exhibits simplicity of design and often has bubbles and streaking in larger pieces. Other styles include cameo-cut and hydrofluoric-acid-etched designs.

Marks: Schneider glass was signed with a variety of script and block signatures, "Le Verre Francais," or "Charder."

Bowl, 4-1/2" d, 2-1/2" h, mottled, slightly cupped........................ 195.00
Ewer, 10-3/4" h, elongated spout, mottled purples, pink, yellow, and orange splashes, applied purple handle, bulbed disk foot, acid stamp "France" on base, c1925 .... 450.00
Finger Bowl and Underplate, 4-1/2" d bowl, 7-1/4" d underplate, mottled red, burnt umber and clear, stamped mark 350.00
Tazza, 7-5/8" h, shallow white bowl rising to mottled amethyst and blue inverted rim, amethyst double bulbed stem, disk foot, sgd "Schneider," c1920 .... 865.00
Vase
7" h, bulbous, cylindrical neck, yellow and pink mottled ground, brown casing, 2 applied crimped orange handles, engraved "Schneider" and logo, slightly ground top 450.00
7-1/2" h, spherical, raised rim, colorless, etched band of stylized daisies with flashed green centers, inscribed "Charder Le Verre Francais," acid stamp "France Ovington" 900.00
13-3/4" h, baluster, smoky topaz, dec at shoulder with acid etched band of overlaid leaves, two applied floral cluster prunts, sgd "Schneider" near base, c1925 .... 980.00
14" h, tapering cylindrical, baluster neck, orange overlay, 5 clusters of pendant grapes, geometric pattern cut foot over yellow mottled ground, inset cane at base 650.00
14-3/4" h, teardrop shape, mottled cream and colorless overlaid in vitrified dark green and orange, acid-etched leaves descending from neck, c1925, base drilled.. 850.00

SCHOENHUT TOYS

History: Albert Schoenhut, son of a toy maker, was born in Germany in 1849. In 1866, he ventured to America where he worked as a toy-piano repairman for Wanamaker's in Philadelphia, Pennsylvania. Finding the glass sounding bars inadequate, he perfected a toy piano with metal sounding bars. His piano was an instant success, and the A. Schoenhut Company had its beginning.

From that point on, toys seemed to flow out of the factory. Each of his six sons entered the business, and it prospered until 1934, when misfortune forced the company into bankruptcy. In 1935, Otto and George Schoenhut contracted to produce the Pinn Family Dolls.

The Schoenhut Manufacturing Company was formed by two other Schoenhuts. Both companies operated under a partnership agreement that eventually led to O. Schoenhut, Inc., which continues today.

Some dates of interest:
1872—toy piano invented
1903—Humpty Dumpty Circus patented
1911-1924—wooden doll production
1928-1934—composition dolls made.

References: E. Ackerman and F. Keller, *Under the Big Top with Schoenhut's Humpty Dumpty Circus*, published by author (P.O. Box 217, Culver City, CA 90230), 1997; Carol Corson, *Schoenhut Dolls*, Hobby House Press, 1993; Elizabeth Stephan (ed.,) *O'Brien's Collecting Toys*, 9th ed., Krause Publications, 1999.

Collectors' Clubs: Schoenhut Collectors Club, 1003 W. Huron St., Ann Arbor, MI 48103; Schoenhut Toy Collectors, 1916 Cleveland St, Evanston, IL 60202.

Animal, wood, jointed
  4" h, 6-3/4" l hyena, glass eyes, leather ears, jointed at neck, shoulders, and hips, cord tail, orig paint flaking somewhat, left ear missing, unmarked..3,550.00
  5" h, 7-3/4" l, poodle, white, painted features, jointed at neck and hips, cord tail with looped cord at end, wear to nose and paint........145.00
  5-1/4" h, 8-1/2" l, cow, painted eyes, leather ears and horns, jointed at neck and hips, twine tail, small metal bell on old red ribbon, orig wood 2-1/2" x 2-1/4" x 3-1/4" wood manger 315.00
  6" h, donkey, narrow nose, glass eyes, leather ears, normal wear and aging, mane and tail missing, eyes cracked, unmarked...55,99
  8" h, gorilla, two-part head, composition-type face, painted features, leather ears, long arms with pink palms, some wear to paint, unmarked..3,400.00
  8" h, monkey, painted features, molded ears, cord tail, dressed in orig red felt costume and hat with gold trim, unmarked......375.00
  8-1/4" l, goat, black and white, painted eyes, leather horns and tail, leatherette ears, paint very good, minor chipping, ears damaged..175.00

Left: giraffe, painted eye, $495; center: polar bear, glass eye, $1,250; lion, painted eyes, $375.

8-3/4" l, dromedary camel, painted eyes, leather ears, woven cotton tail, minor chipping to orig paint, some wear 300.00
Character Figure
  Felix the Cat, 3-3/4" h, c1920, worn ears 175.00
  Felix the Cat, 8-1/2" h, label on foot, stringing loose, paint wear..215.00
  Maggie and Jiggs, 7" h Jiggs, 9" h Maggie, c1920, orig lunch bucket and rolling pin, minor flaking 750.00
Circus Box, Set No. 20/36, wooden sides, illus circus, animals, and people performing tricks on top, mkd "Schoenhut's Humpty-Dumpty Circus, Made in the U.S.A., The Toy Wonder, 10,001 New Tricks, Unbreakable," hinges slightly loose 350.00
Circus Character, 8" h, jointed wood
  Hobo, jointed shoulders and hips, orig red and white shirt, brown felt coat and hat, brown tweed pants, leatherette belt 200.00
  Negro Dude, painted features, leather ears, two part head with face molded as separate piece from head, orig red and white print shirt, white vest, black felt jacket, plaid pants, black felt hat, some crazing to face, unmarked 425.00
  Ringmaster and Lady Circus Rider, painted features, molded and painted hair, jointed, orig paint, ringmaster wearing orig white shirt and pants, yellow felt vest, red felt jacket, white top hat; lady circus rider with replaced gold body suit, orig skirt, some paint flaking, price for pair 165.00
Circus Set, reduced size, 4-1/2" h horse, 5-1/2" h giraffe, 4-1/2" h donkey, 4-1/2" h elephant, 6-1/2" h ringmaster, 6-1/2" h clown, 8-1/2" h ladders, 2-1/2" h barrel, 4-1/2" h chair, all with painted eyes, orig painted body, general wear and flaking.................................350.00
Circus Tent, 18" x 24" wood base, blue painted sides, bottom painted to resemble sand with red wood ring, wood support in back holds up canvas tent with red curtained door, wire supports have trapeze and metal rings on base, triangular flags of all nations on front with "Humpty-Dumpty Circus," mkd "Humpty Dumpty Circus, Reg. U. S. Pat. Off" on label on front and both sides of base, tent aged and discolored, normal wear 500.00
Doll
  14" h, 14/205 boy, wood socket head, brown intaglio eyes with molded eyelids, closed mouth and accent line between lips, carved and painted hair, wood body spring jointed at shoulders, elbows, hips, knees, and ankles, old knit outfit, mkd "Schoenhut Doll, Pat. Jan 17th, 1911, U.S.A." on label on back, normal wear 1,300.00
  14" h, girl, wood socket head, brown intaglio eyes, feathered brows, closed pouty mouth, auburn mohair wig, spring-jointed wood body with joints at shoulders, elbows, wrists, hips, knees, and ankles, antique white dress, mkd "Schoenhut Doll, Pat. Jan. 17th, '11, U.S.A. & Foreign Countries" incised on back, pale facial coloring, light crazing, overall light wear and aging 400.00
  15" h, baby, wood socket head, painted blue eyes, single stroke brows, accented nostrils, closed two-tone mouth, painted hair, bent-limb wood baby body with spring joints, old knit baby romper, mkd "H. E. Schoenhut, ©1913" round label on back of head, "Schoenhut Doll, Pat. Jan. 17th, 1911, U.S.A." on label on back, orig finish on head with slight touch-up, light overall wear, aging, and soil on body.....................................275.00
  15" h, baby, wood socket head, painted eyes, closed mouth, orig mohair wig, bent limb wooden baby body, new white baby romper, replaced socks and shoes, mkd "H. E. Schoenhut, ©1913" on round label on back of head, "Schoenhut Doll, Pat. Jan 17th, 1911, U.S.A." on oval label on back, brows worn off, small chip on lip, possibly factory repaint to body, crazed under right arm, left arm flaking 350.00
  15" h, boy, wood socket head, blue intaglio eyes, feathered brows, accented lips, closed pouty mouth, mohair wig, wood body spring jointed at shoulders, elbows, wrists, hips, knees, and ankles, copy of orig outfit, mkd "Schoenhut Doll, Pat. Jan 17'11 U.S.A. & Foreign Countries" incised on back, normal wear....................425.00
  16" h, boy, wood socket head, brown intaglio eyes, very faint brows, accented lips, closed pouty mouth, mohair wig, wood body spring jointed at shoulders, elbows, wrists, hips, knees, and ankles, copy of orig outfit, mkd "Schoenhut Doll, Pat. Jan 17'11

U.S.A. & Foreign Countries" incised on back, paint chips on face, sparse wig, orig body paint with wear and flaking...............350.00

Doll House

19" h, wood, white "stucco" covering, working front door, working door at 2nd story balcony, 2 windows on each end and 2 in front, removable red roof, back opens to four rooms with orig litho floor covering, plain yellow walls, mkd "Schoenhut Doll House. Made in U.S.A." on label on side of base, part of orig label missing, light wear 1,150.00

27-5/8" h, 25-1/2" w, 23-5/8" d, Daggle, No. 5/50, 1923, wood and fiberboard, 2 story, emb faux gray stone siding, emb faux green tile roof, off-white window and door trim, wooden front steps and chimney, 8 int. rooms plus attic, litho paper int., some wood, fiber, and paint damage 2,415.00

Roly Poly, papier-mâché head

9-7/8" h, red had, yellow, green, and light blue suit, separation in seam around middle 115.00

10" h, Buster Brown, painted blue eyes, single stroke brows, accent around eyes, closed mouth, molded and painted hair, one-piece papier-mâché body with arms molded to body, painted clothing, some paint flaking and wear 590.00

14" h, painted large eyes, feathered brows, open-closed smiling mouth with 6 painted teeth, molded and painted hair and yellow faux straw hat, papier-mâché round unjointed body, weight in base, molded and painted clothing, mkd "Schoenhut Rolly Dolly, Patented Dec 15, 1908, Other Patents Pending" on round label on base, some surface cracks on neck and edges of hat, light wear to finish.........................800.00

SCIENTIFIC INSTRUMENTS

History: Chemists, doctors, geologists, navigators, and surveyors used precision instruments as tools of their trade. Such objects were well designed and beautifully crafted. They are primarily made of brass; fancy hardwood cases also are common.

The 1990s have seen a keen interest in scientific instruments, both in the auction market and at antique shows. The number of collectors of this mechanical wonders is increasing as more and more interesting examples are being offered.

References: Florian Cajori, *History of the Logarithmic Slide Rule and Allied Instruments*, Astragal Press, 1994; Gloria Clifton, *Directory of British Scientific Instrument Makers 1550-1851*, P. Wilson Publishers, 1994; William H. Skerritt, *Catalog of the Charles E. Smart Collection: Antique Surveying Instruments*, published by author, (12 Locust Ave., Troy, NY 12180), 1996; Gerard L. E. Turner, *Scientific Instruments 1500-1900: An Introduction*, University of California Press, 1998.

SPECIAL AUCTIONS

Auction Team Köln
P.O. Box 50 11 19, D-50981 Koeln
Bonner St., 528-530, D-50968 Koeln
Köln Germany
0221/38 70 49

Skinner, Inc.
357 Main St.
Bolton MA 01740
(508) 779-6241

Tellurium, early mechanical planetarium, Orrery, 1880, $2,750. Photo courtesy of Auction Team Breker.

Periodicals: Tesseract, P.O. Box 151, Hastings-on-Hudson, NY 10706; Scientific, Medical & Mechanical Antiques, P.O. Box 412, Taneytown, MD 21787, http://americanartifacts.com/smma.

Collectors' Clubs: International Calculator Collectors Club, 14561 Livingston St., Tustin, CA 92680; Maryland Microscopical Society, 8261 Polk St., McLean VA, 22102; The Oughtred Society, 2160 Middlefield Rd, Palo Alto, CA 94301; Zeiss Historical Society, P.O. Box 631, Clifton, NJ 07012.

Museum: National Museum of American History, Smithsonian Institution, Washington, DC.

Alidade, cased, 11" l, W. & L. E. Gurley, Troy, NY, orig leather covered case, minor spots to lacquered finish.........................440.00

Anemometer, 6 register, 8 blade, 2-5/8" d, fan drives 2-1/4" d silvered dial, brass, mounting bracket, softwood case, c1875 ....345.00

Astronomical Theodolite, 15-1/2" h, 10-1/2" l telescope, 5-1/2" d, 2 vernier vertical circle, 6", 2 vernier 20" horiz. Circle, telescope and plate vials, microscope vernier readers, detachable alcohol lamp, detachable 4 screw leveling base, trough compass on telescope, orig dovetailed mahogany box with accessories, mkd "Stanley, Great Turnstile, Holborn, London, 7534," c1890, Heller & Brightly label mahogany ext. leg tripod.........................2,185.00

Astronomical Transit, 20" h, 8-1/2" w, 15-3/4" telescope with rt. Angle prism eyepiece with removable strider level, 7" d double frame, 2 vernier, vertical circle with indexing vial and circle control, 6" d, 2 vernier, 15", silver horizontal scale, plate vial with ivory scale, tribrach leveling base, bright brass finish, pine case, mkd "Blunt, New York," c1860 ....7,500.00

Circumferentor, 5-1/4" h, 9" d outside dia., 4-1/8" compass in center, attached to rotating sight vane/vernier arm, inset vial, silvered dial and outer ring, engraved with 8 point star, 2 outer fixed sight vanes, brass, mkd "Dollond London," c1825 ....1,955.00

Drawing Instruments, French, cased set, brass and steel instruments, wood scale, brass protractor, rosewood veneered case with warped lid.........................220.00

Globe, terrestrial

8" d, 9-1/2" h, Fitz's, mkd "Ginn & Heath," c1877, dec with revolving cast iron base, adjustable brass daylight/twilight boundary rings, brass moon, minor defects in Arctic Circle 3,220.00

18" d globe, 26" h, corrected to 1799, celestial corrected to 1800, each resting on turned fruitwood stand, George III, W. & J. H. Bardin, London, one missing compass, pr 11,500.00

Microscope, compound monocular

12" h, 8-1/4" l, 1-1/8" d tube with 1 obj, fine focus on arm, 3-1/2" d stage with condenser and diaphragm, double mirror on calibrated rotating arm, japanned and lacquered brass, case, extra obj., mkd "3373," c1885 .... 575.00

12" h, 8-1/2" l, 1-1/8" d, tube with 1 obj, fine focus on arm, rect stage, 5 hole diaphragm, double mirror on rotating arm, extra eyepiece, orig case, japanned and lacquered brass, sgd "Wm. H. Armstrong & Co., Indianapolis, Ind.," #11737, c1893 .... 635.00

13-1/4" h, 9" l, 1-1/2" d single nosepiece tube with 3-1/2" d. stage, condenser and double mirror revolve on arms centered on stage, against graduated vertical circular silvered dial, 4 obj. and 3 eyepieces, lacquered brass, case, mkd "14668, Pat. Oct 13, 1885" 1,840.00

15-1/2" h, 10-1/2" l, 1-1/4" d. tube with single nosepiece, fine focus on front of tube, 4-1/2" d stage, 2 sub-stage condenses, double mirror, detachable parabolic mirror, extra 8" l, 1-1/8" d draw tube, detachable stand condenser lens with "B" holder, prism eyepiece, 2 obj., 2 eyepieces, lacquered brass, orig case, mkd "Tolles Boston, 272," c1875 .... 2,275.00

Nonius Compass, 6 inch

15-1/8" x 6-7/8" x 7-1/8" h, 5-1/4" l detachable sight vanes, top designed to hold 7/8" d telescope, plate vials, silvered dial and edge engraved outer ring, unique 5' vernier moves the south sight vane by means of worn gear, mahogany case, mkd "J. Hanks," Troy, NY, c1825 .... 1,725.00

15-78" x 6-7/8" x 9-1/2" h, 7-1/4" l detachable sight vanes, 4-3/4" rad., 20°, 1' outside vernier ring, also edge graduated, staff adapter, lacquered brass, mkd "Phelps & Gurley, Troy, N.Y.," c1850 ..... 2,530.00

Octant, 10-7/8", Riggs & Bro., Philadelphia, ebony, ivory inlaid signature panel, scale with brass trim 550.00

Palmer's Computing Scale, 8-1/2" d computing wheel on 11-1/4" sq outer scale, instructions on reverse, 1 fixed and 1 rotating logarithmic scale, values and gauge points numbered and noted, red, yellow, gold, and black, mkd "Aaron Palmer, 1843 patent" 550.00

Pocket Compass

1-1/2 Inch, 2-1/4" x 2-1/4" mahogany case with hinged cov, 1-1/2" needle floats over engraved finely detailed mariner's star inside 2° increment quadrant outer ring, mkd "T. T. Rowe, Lockport, N.Y.," c1825 .... 230.00

2 Inch, 2-5/8" d, brass, worn silvered dial, full circle, 180° cliometer scale, mkd "Breiothaupt in Cassel," c1800 .... 565.00

Sextant, 3" d, brass, pocket, dial engraved "Stanley, Gt. Turnstile London," 19th C 460.00

Sketching Case, 10-1/2" l, 7" w, 4-1/2" x 6-1/8" plotting surface, 5" d graduated plotting scale, 2" l rotating trough compass, 2 paper rollers, varnished hardwood and lacquered brass, mkd "W. & L. E. Gurley, Troy, N.Y., patented Sept 28, 1897" 750.00

Solar Transit, 17" h, Burt Solar Attachment, hour circle on 6.45" engineer's transit, 11" telescope, 3" rad. vert. arc., 5" compass, telescope and plate vials, 4 screw leveling, brass construction, rubbed bronze finish, dovetailed mahogany case, label, and brass plummet, accessories, mkd "W. & L. E. Gurley, Troy, NY," c1890 .... 3,335.00

Surveyor's Compass

Davenport, Wm, Phila, 5" engraved face with tripod mount, plum bob, small magnifying glass, ivory scale, 14" l cherry case stenciled "A. C. Farrington" in gold and white 1,155.00

Patten, Richard, NY, 6" compass with engraved face, walnut case with litho label of eagle, ship, and signature, minor age cracks in lid, resoldered rim on brass cover, early tripod 990.00

Surveyors' and Engineers' Transit, 12" h, 11" telescope with vial, vert. arc., 6-1/4", 30" horiz. Circle with inlaid silver scales, plate vials, 4 screw leveling, green leather finish, orig dovetailed mahogany box with labels, mkd "Buff & Berger, Boston, #2149," c1890 .... 920.00

Surveyors' Vernier Transit Compass, 13-1/2" h, 11" telescope with vial, 3-1/2" d vert. circle, 5-3/4" compass, 4" rad. Declination vernier, 2 plate vials, cross sights, 4 screw detachable leveling base, staff adaptor, stiff leg tripod, brass plumb bob, orig case with labels, bronzed brass, mkd "W. & L. E. Gurley, Troy, NY," c1874 ..... 1,840.00

Telescope

5-7/8" l open, 1-3/4" d, brass mounts, shagreen, embossed scrolling foliage on leather draw, E. Nairne, London, first quarter 19th C 550.00

20-1/4" l, brass and leather, one draw, engraved "G. Young & Co. London Day & Night," England, 19th C, replaced leather ... 400.00

21" l, brass and mahogany, one draw, 19th C 320.00

Wye Level, 8-1/4" h, 4" w, 16-1/4" l, 1-3/8" d reversible telescope with 6-3/4" l, 4 screw leveling base, horiz. motion clamp and screw, eyepiece attachment, mkd "Kuebler & Seelhorst Makers Philada, 597, Oct 1, 1867 Patent" 500.00

SCRIMSHAW

History: Norman Flayderman defined scrimshaw as, "The art of carving or otherwise fashioning useful or decorative articles as practiced primarily by whalemen, sailors, or others associated with nautical pursuits." Many collectors expand this to include the work of Eskimos and French POWs from the War of 1812.

References: Stuard M. Frank, *Dictionary of Scrimshaw Artists*, Mystic Seaport Museum, 1991; Nina Hellman and Norman Brouwer, *Mariner's Fancy*, South Street Seaport Museum, Balsam Press, and the University of Washington Press, 1992; Martha Lawrence, *Scrimshaw*, Schiffer Publishing, 1993.

Museums: Cold Spring Whaling Harbor Museum, Cold Spring Harbor, NY; Kendall Whaling Museum, Sharon, MA; Mystic Seaport Museum, Mystic, CT; National Maritime Museum, San Francisco, CA; New Bedford Whaling Museum, New Bedford, MA; Old Dartmouth Historical Society, New Bedford, MA; Pacific Whaling Museum, Waimanalo, HI; Sag Harbor Whaling & Historical Museum, Sag Harbor, NY; San Francisco Maritime National Historical Park, San Francisco, CA; South Street Seaport Museum, New York, NY; Whaling Museum, Nantucket, MA.

Reproduction Alert: The biggest problem in the field is fakes, although there are some clues to spotting them. A very hot needle will penetrate the common plastics used in reproductions but not the authentic material. Ivory will not generate static electricity when rubbed, plastic will. Patina is not a good indicator; it has been faked by applying tea or tobacco juice, burying in raw rabbit hide, and in other ingenious ways. Usually the depth of cutting in an old design will not be consistent since the ship rocked and tools dulled; however, skilled forgers have even copied this characteristic.

Box, 2-1/4" d, 2" h, circular, engraved and stained, whaling scene, large whale surrounded by compass positions, late 19th C 225.00

Busk

11-7/8" l, whalebone, polychrome dec, memorial, foliate and geometric devices, 19th C, cracks 320.00

12-3/4" l, whalebone, polychrome dec, ship, foliate and geometric devices, 19th C, cracks, minor losses 195.00

13-7/8" l, wood, dec with eagle, shield, lovebirds, and ship under sail, heart and foliate devices, inscribed "GC & EW," dated 1840 ... 345.00

Cribbage Board

18" l, engraved and inked, pictorial, top with caribou, game board, sides with sled dog team and caribou in landscape, back with bears approaching walrus ice float, Inuit carved, early 20th C 750.00

19" l, engraved ivory, pictorial, tusk form, playing board flanks relief carved scene of pinniped head, pictorial style engraving, horse pulling sled, sea monster threatening hunter, canine in leg-hold trap, hunter getting close look at underside of caribou, attached pinniped form emerging from ice, sgd "A. LAMKA," loss to pegs and support 1,100.00

Whale's Tooth, engraved on one side, eagle clutching flag and banner, "Harrison and Tyler for President" over naval battle entitled "Constitution and Guerriere," 7-1/4" l, 3-7/8" w, $1,500.

Domino Box, 6-7/8" l, bone and wood, shoe form, pierced carved slide top with star and heart dec, domino playing pcs, Prisoner of War, 19th C, cracks, minor insect damage 520.00

Game Box, 5-3/4" x 6-1/2", bone, pierced carved box with geometric dec, 3 slide tops, compartmented int., backgammon and other playing pcs, traces of paint dec, Prisoner of War, 19th C, repair, warping to tops, very minor loses 690.00

Jagging Wheel, 7-1/4" l, dec with building flying American flag, berried vines, 19th C, very minor losses 520.00

Obelisk, 13-3/8" h, inlaid mahogany, inlaid with various exotic woods, abalone and ivory in geometric and star motifs, 19th C, minor losses, minute cracks 815.00

Paperweight, 3-1/8" l, carved block, inked caribou, salmon, and insect motifs, Intuit 325.00

Salt Horn, 5-1/2" l, engraved "John Snow March...1780 by S. H.," crosshatched borders enclosing reserve of ship, geometric, and foliate devices, insect damage 460.00

Seam Rubber, 4" l, whalebone, geometric designs on handle, traces of orig paint, 19th C 850.00

Snuff Box, 5" l, horn, architectural and marine motifs, dated "AD 1853" and "Willian Sandilands Plumber," English 950.00

Walrus Tusk
  12-1/2" l, polychrome engraving of whales, eagles, displays of arms, ships under sail, figure on horseback, 19th C, restoration, losses, pr 1,265.00
  17-3/4" h, reserves of animals, courting couples, ships under sail, memorials, sailors and armaments, later engraved brass presentation caps, "Presented by George M. Chase to Ike B. Dunlap Jan. 25th 1908," cracks, one restored, pr 2,530.00
  18-7/8" l, walrus, dec with two eagles, lady, Indian, and vulture, age cracks, 19th C 1,840.00

Watch Hutch, 11-7/8" h, bone, pierce carved floral and figural dec, brass backing, polychrome foliate highlights, Prisoner of War, 19th C, custom made case, minor cracks, losses, repairs 750.00

Whale's Tooth, 19th C
  4-3/8" l, dec with ship, woman resting on anchor holding flag, 2 potted plants, chips, minor cracks, 19th C 690.00
  5" h, courting couple on one side, Victorian building on other, geometric and foliate swag border, minor cracks 690.00
  5-1/4" h, young couple and two elegant ladies, cracks..........460.00

5-1/2" l, polychrome dec of fashionable lady on one side, other with child and hoop, geometric borders 690.00
5-3/4" h, young girl with jump rope on one side, other with young man, 20th C, cracks 260.00
6-1/4" h, dec with three-masted ship "Cyane" and memorial 2,300.00
6-1/2" h, four-masted shaping ship "Clipper Chip Great Republic Built E. Boston 1853" 550.00
6-5/8" h, historic landmarks, dec on both sides, very minor cracks and chips 865.00
6-7/8" h, various ships under sail and young lady, cracks 1,380.00
Whimsey, 5-3/4" h, carved bone, French soldier sharpening his sword on grinding wheel, Prisoner of War, 19th C, minor paint wear..........4,715.00

SEVRES

History: The principal patron of the French porcelain industry in early 18th-century France was Jeanne Antoinette Poisson, Marquise de Pompadour. She supported the Vincennes factory of Gilles and Robert Dubois and their successors in their attempt to make soft-paste porcelain in the 1740s. In 1753, she moved the porcelain operations to Sevres, near her home, Chateau de Bellevue.

The Sevres soft-paste formula used sand from Fontainebleau, salt, saltpeter, soda of alicante, powdered alabaster, clay, and soap. Many famous colors were developed, including a cobalt blue. The wonderful scenic designs on the ware were painted by such famous decorators as Watteau, La Tour, and Boucher. In the 18th century Sevres porcelain was the world's foremost diplomatic gift.

In 1769, kaolin was discovered in France, and a hard-paste formula was developed. The baroque gave way to rococo, a style favored by Jeanne du Barry, Louis XV's next mistress. Louis XVI took little interest in Sevres, and many factories began to turn out counterfeits. In 1876, the factory was moved to St. Cloud and was eventually nationalized.

References: Susan and Al Bagdade, *Warman's English & Continental Pottery & Porcelain*, 3rd Edition, Krause Publications, 1998; Carl Christian Dauterman, *Sevres Porcelain, Makers and Marks of the Eighteenth Century*, Metropolitan Museum of Art, 1986; Linda Humphries, *Sevres Porcelain from the Sevres Museum 1740 to the Present*, Hund Humphries, 1997; George Savage, *Seventeenth & Eighteenth Century French Porcelain*, Hamlyn Publishing Co., Ltd., 1969.

Museums: Art Institute of Chicago, Chicago, IL; British Museum, London, England; Frick Collection, New York, NY; Gardiner Museum of Ceramic Art Museum, Toronto, Canada; J. Paul Getty Museum, Los Angeles, CA; Metropolitan Museum of Art, New York, NY; Musee de Louvre, Paris, France, Musee National e Ceramique, Sevres, France; Victoria & Albert Museum, London, England; Wadsworth Atheneum, Harford, CT.

Marks: Louis XV allowed the firm to use the "double L" in its marks.

Reproduction Alert.

Box, cov
  5-3/4" l, cartouche with figure in landscape, cobalt blue ground, gilt foliate dec 200.00
  7" d, 6" h, circular, ormolu flame finial, dec with chateau in landscape, courting couple cartouches, gilt scrolling dec, cobalt blue

ground, two ormolu scrolling open handles, 3 ormolu scrolling feet, stamped "Chateau de Tuileries"..................................500.00

Bud Vase, 6" h, gilt ground, enamel Art Nouveau stylized leaf and flower design, printed mark 635.00

Bust, 13" h, Marie Antoinette, bisque bust, gilt highlights, cobalt blue ground, molded porcelain socle with central garland and monogram, 19th C...650.00

Cabinet Plate, 9-1/2" d, wide blue ground banding, gilt border with leafy vine, cartouche of cherubs flanking a Napoleonic "N," print marks, c1868, 3 pc set 488.00

Candelabra, pr, 30" h, porcelain urn, figure in landscape, fruit-filled cartouches, blue ground, candle nozzles and flowers, two handles cast with putti and floral dec, bronze mounts, worn gilt trim 5,250.00

Centerpiece, 20-1/4" h, 4 youths in procession, each supporting basket, mounted on freeform base, white biscuit, imp mark, early 20th C.320.00

Chocolate Cup, 3-3/4" h, wide dec entwined band of painted flowers, heavily gilt borders, molded acanthus capped handle with stylized eagle head, gilt highlights, first quarter 19th C, set of 3 ....250.00

Cup and Saucer, 3-1/8" h, cobalt blue ground, gilt framed oval cartouche on cup, enameled flowers 230.00

Figure, 18" h, bisque, Diana stands with attendants and dogs, ormolu base with cast rosette and circlet border, 4 acanthus feet, imp mark, second half 19th C 3,000.00

Ginger Jar, 12" h, blue flambé, ormolu mounts, pr...................2,000.00

Lap Desk, 11-1/4" x 8-1/8", rect porcelain plaque with central scene of cherubs at various artist pursuits cornered by floral reserves, gilt highlights, ormolu border, int. compartment for writing paper, late 19th C..950.00

Luncheon Plate, 9-3/4" d, central gilt six pointed star, border with hunt scenes, price for 6 pc set 325.00

Milk Jug, cov, 5" h, pear form, later neoclassical reserve dec, gilt highlights, c1870 ....185.00

Pin Box, cov, 6-1/2" l, oval, cartouche of romantic couple on cov, blue ground..275.00

Plate, 9" d, center reserve of pansies, trailing rose border, cobalt blue dec, rim, late 18th C 350.00

Platter, 13-1/4" l, oval, painted military camp scene reserve, scrolling gilt border, cobalt blue scalloped rim..625.00

Soup Plate, 9-1/2" d, scattered flower springs, 3 kidney shaped flower panes surrounded by apple green border with gilt tooled floral garlands, c1775, 6 pc set 1,400.00

Figures, white, unglazed, marble and gilt metal bases, c1758, 8" h, $3,200.

Tazza, 11-1/2" d, blue flambé, ormolu mounts 350.00

Urn, cov

6" h, figural and landscape cartouches, celeste blue ground, gilt dec, stamp of Chateau des Tuileries, pr 900.00

12" h, shouldered ovoid body, cobalt blue ground painted below mid section with scenes of courting couples and architectural views of river and landscape, top section with portraits of Louis XVI and Marie Antionette within raised gilt borders, circular foot, sq base with canted corners, cast female term handles, c1840, pr, restorations 1,700.00

17-1/2" h, ovoid body with scene of maiden and flowers holding garland within raised gilt borders, shouldered by rams masks holding loose rings, sq base with canted corners, cast with berried laurel, ormolu mounts, sgd "Domval(?)," late 19th C ...750.00

17-3/4" h, Art Nouveau style portrait medallion of woman, sgd "L. Heri," irid iris dec, gilt ground 2,000.00

Vase, 11" h, pink ground, oval cartouches with figural landscapes and ornaments, metal mount, pr 1,380.00

Wine Cooler, 10-1/4" h, Louis XVI style, circular tapering form, top section with gilded ram's heads over reeded band, base dec with ribboned garlands and entwined laurel, multicolored, white ground 2,300.00

SEWING ITEMS

History: As recently as 50 years ago, a wide variety of sewing items were found in almost every home in America. Women of every economic and social status were skilled in sewing and dressmaking.

Iron or brass sewing birds, one of the interesting convenience items which developed, were used to hold cloth (in the bird's beak) while sewing. They could be attached to a table or shelf with a screw-type fixture. Later models included a pincushion.

References: *Advertising & Figural Tape Measures*, L-W Book Sales, 1995; Elizabeth Arbittier et al., *Collecting Figural Tape Measures*, Schiffer Publishing, 1995; Carter Bays, *Encyclopedia of Early American Sewing Machines*, published by author, 1993; Ruth Miller Clark, *Carnival of Iridescent Luster Buttons*, 1986; Book II, 1992 (2100 Dawn Dr., Georgetown, TX 78628); Book III (Alan G. Perry, 7614 McKenry St., Houston, TX 77087-3834), 1997; Jane O. Dinkins, *Sketchbook of Little Carnival Glass Buttons*, (1100 Ridgeley Dr., Houston, TX 77055) 1996; Fink & Ditzler, *Buttons, The Collector's Guide To Selecting, Restoring and Enjoying New & Vintage Buttons*, 1993; Edith M. Fuoss and Nora O. Jones, *Black Glass Buttons*, 1945 (reprint by New Leaf Publishers); Edith M. Fuoss and Caroline Smith, *Black Glass Buttons, Return Engagement*, 1952; Elizabeth Hughes and Marion Lester, *The Big Book of Buttons*, 1981 (reprint by New Leaf Publishers); Lori Hughes, *A Century of American Sewing Patterns, 1860-1959*, C & B Press, 1998; Frieda Marion, *China Half-Figures Called Pincushion Dolls*, published by author, 1974, 1994 reprint; Bridget McConnel, *The Story of Antique Needlework Tools*, Schiffer Publishing, 1999; Wayne Muller, *Darn It!*, L-W Book Sales, 1995; Florence Zacharie Nicholls, *Button Handbook, with three supplements, 1943-1949*,(reprints by New Leaf Publishers); James W. Slaten, *Antique American Sewing Machines*, Singer Dealer Museum (3400 Park Blvd., Oakland, CA 94610), 1992; Glenda Thomas, *Toy and Miniature Sewing Machines* (1995), Book II (1997), Collector Books; Estelle Zalkin, *Zalkin's Handbook of Thimbles & Sewing*

Display Case, Boyce Needle Company, $350.

Implements, Warman Publishing Co., 1988, distributed by Krause Publications, http://www.krause.com.

Collectors' Clubs: Buckeye State Button Society, 251 Pfeiffer Ave., Akron, OH 44312-4137; Denton Button Club, 500 El Paseo, Denton, TX 76205-8502; International Sewing Machine Collectors Society, 551 Kelmore St., Moss Beach, CA 94038, http://ismacs.net; National Button Society, 2733 Juno Place, Apt. 4, Akron, OH 44313-4137; Pioneer Button Club, 102 Frederick St., Oshawa, Ontario L1G 2B3 Canada; The Button Club, P.O. Box 2274, Seal Beach, CA 90740; Thimble Collectors International, 2594 E Upper Hayden Lake Road, Hayden, ID 83835; Thimble Guild, P.O. Box 381807, Duncanville, TX 75138-1807; Toy Stitchers, 623 Santa Florita Ave, Millbrae, CA 94030.

Periodicals: *Button Bytes*, http://www.tias.com/articles/buttons; *That Darn Newsletter*, 461 Brown Briar Circle, Horsham, PA 19044; *Thimbletter*, 93 Walnut Hill Road, Newton Highlands, MA 02161-1836.

Museums: Antique Sewing Machine Museum, Oakland, CA; Button Bytes, http://www.tias.com/museum/clothing buttons.html; Fabric Hall, Historic Deerfield, Deerfield, MA; Frank Smith's Sewing Machine Museum, Arlington, TX, http://rampages.onramp.net/~arlprosv/museum.htm; Museum of American History, Smithsonian Institution, Washington, DC; Shelburne Museum, Shelburne, VT.

Advertising Thimble, Grants Hygienic Crackers, aluminum, enamel adv band, c1920 .... 20.00
Bodkins, whalebone and ivory, sealing wax inlaid scribe lines, 19th C, minor losses, 9 pc set 400.00
Book
  American Needlework 1776-1976, Leslie Tillett, forward by Rose Kennedy, NY Graphic Society, 1975 .... 15.00
  Book No. 8641, T. B. C. *Instructions & Designs for Tatting*, T. Buettner & Co., Chicago, IL, 1915, 32 pgs, 8" x 11" 25.00
  Ladies Complete Guide to Crochet, Fancy Knitting & Needlework By Mrs. Ann S. Stephens, NY, 1864, large fold-up patterns tipped in 115.00
Calendar
  1898, Betsy Ross sewing American flag 25.00
  1904, Singer Sewing Machine, diecut, Indian and animal skin 85.00
Catalog, Perry Mason Co., Boston, MA, c1929, Our Way, The New Companion Sewing Machine, 24 pgs 40.00

Epherma, letterhead, John B. Simpson, Darby, PA, 1910, sending sample of materials for regulation sailor suit, fabric swatches ... 17.50
Folder, 8-3/4" x 14-1/4", Wm. R. Moore Dry Goods Co., Memphis, TN, 3 pgs, c1937, heavy weight, "Guaranteed Fast Color No. 10 Batfast Suitings," 10 tipped-in blue Batfast Suiting swatches, 19 1-/4" x 2" colored swatches tipped in 28.00
Chatelaine, egg shape 80.00
Fan, Singer Ribbonaire, Bakelite 100.00
Instruction Manual
  Howe Sewing Machine, NY, 1872, 20 pgs, blue printed wraps 25.00
  Sears Roebuck Minnesota Model "A," early 1920s, illus, 32 pgs 30.00
Lady's Companion, 3-1/2" h, shagreen, oval, front with miniature on ivory of maiden at birdbath, within gold floral border, verse with mother and child in garden, lid with applied gold cartouches topped with birds and "D'amitier" and "Nesessaire," int. fitted with ivory needle case, mother-of-pearl handled pocket knife, scissors, spoon, ivory tablet, pencil, scent bottle, Louis XVI 1,300.00
Magazine
  Home Needlework Magazine, Florence Publishing Co, Florence, MA, 176 pgs, 1899, Vol. 1, No. 2, April 20.00
  Star Needlework Journal, American Thread Co., 1922, Vol. 7, No. 2, published quarterly 20.00
  The Ladies Standard Magazine, Standard Fashion Co., August, 1893 .... 20.00
Sewing Box
  5-3/4" l, figured mahogany veneer on pine, inlay, table clamp, dovetailed drawer, pincushion, wear and edge damage, thumb screw missing 220.00
  6-3/4" l, 5" w, 7" h, mahogany, lift off lid with pin cushion, single drawer, cathedral style 330.00
  11-1/8" l, 9-1/8" w, 6" h, Tunbridge, serpentine front, hinged lid and sides inlaid with florals, int. lid with inlay border surrounding pleated satin, center inlaid roundel, int. fitted with removable upper compartment, 4 inlaid flattened ball feet, England, late 19th C 260.00
Sewing Case, 4-1/8" l, 1-1/4" w, 7/8" h, ivory, rect, rounded corners, int. fitted with gilt-silver scissors and thimble, monogrammed, French, last quarter 19th C 325.00
Sewing Kit, 2-5/8" h, 1" d, vegetable ivory, carved, plain metal thimble 145.00
Sewing Stand, 12-5/8" h, pine, old red graining on yellow ground, shiny over varnish, four rotating tiers on turned spindle, wire pins for spools of thread, short cabriole legs and drawer in base, some damage to feet 36.00
Tape Measure
  Adv, round, multicolored litho of young girl with flowers, 1-1/2" d. 45.00

Pin Cushion, celluloid rabbit sitting with hands over two velour covered baskets, mkd "Germany," $135. Photo courtesy of Julie P. Robinson.

Egg, Chicago World's Fair, red 75.00
Pig, copper 65.00
Sentinel, pretty woman 45.00
Thimble
   Brass, fancy band design 15.00
   Cloisonné, China 12.00
   Meissen, hp, c1950 ....25.00
   Scrimshaw, whalebone 95.00
   Silver
      Cupid and garlands, Simons 95.00
      Cupid in high relief, c1900-40 ....120.00
      Engraved, 2 birds on branch 35.00
      Flowers, high relief 45.00
Thimble Holder
   3" h, fox with baton and open book leads a dog and cat in song, 2 thimble holders in front, oval base, mkd "Waters & Thorr New York" 350.00
   5-3/4" h, fisherman holding large rod, beautifully detailed large fish on ground, bucket by fish, post in front of fisherman, rect base, mkd "Miller Silver Co. Silver Plate" 350.00
Thread Cabinet
   Clarks, white lettering, 4 drawers, some damage to case 100.00
   Dexter Fine Yarn, oak, 4 drawers, 18-3/4" h, 18-5/8' w, 16" d..650.00
   Merrick's Spool Cotton, oak, cylindrical, curved glass, 18" d, 22" h...725.00
   Willimantic, 4 drawers, ornate Eastlake style case, 14-1/4" h.....550.00
Transfer Book, H. Heminway & Sons Silk, 1896, 24 artistic designs, 23 color plates with text on verso 40.00

SHAKER

History: The Shakers, so named because of a dance they used in worship, are one of the oldest communal organizations in the United States. This religious group was founded by Mother Ann Lee, who emigrated from England and established the first Shaker community near Albany, New York, in 1784. The Shakers reached their peak in 1850, when there were 6,000 members.

Shakers lived celibate and self-sufficient lives. Their philosophy stressed cleanliness, order, simplicity, and economy. Highly inventive and motivated, the Shakers created many utilitarian household forms and objects. Their furniture reflected a striving for quality and purity in design.

In the early 19th century, the Shakers produced many items for commercial purposes. Chairmaking and the packaged herb and seed business thrived. In every endeavor and enterprise, the members followed Mother Ann's advice: "Put your hands to work and give your heart to God."

References: Edward Deming Andrews and Faith Andrews, *Masterpieces of Shaker Furniture*, Dover Publications, 1999; Christian Becksvoort, T*he Shaker Legacy: Perspectives on an Enduring Furniture Style*, The Tauton Press, 1998; Michael Horsham, *Art of the Shakers*, Apple Press, 1989; John T. Kirk, *The Shaker World: Art, Life, Belief*, Harry N. Abrams, 1997; Charles R. Muller and Timothy D. Rieman, *The Shaker Chair*, Canal Press, 1984; June Sprigg and Jim Johnson, *Shaker Woodenware*, Berkshire House, 1991; June Sprigg and David Larkin, *Shaker Life, Work, and Art*, Stewart, Tabori & Chang, 1987; Timothy D. Rieman and Jean M. Burks, *Complete Book of Shaker Furniture*, Harry N. Abrams, 1993.

Collectors' Clubs: Shaker Heritage Society, 1848 Shaker Meeting House, Albany-Shaker Road, Albany, NY 12211, http://www.shakerworkshops.com/waterv.htm; Western Shaker Study Group, 1700 Pentbrooke Trail, Dayton, OH 45459; http://www.shakerwssg.org.

Periodical: Shaker Messenger, P.O. Box 1645 Holland, MI 49422; Shakers World, P.O. Box 1276, Manchester, CT 06045.

Museums: Canterbury Shaker Village, Canterbury, NH; Hancock Shaker Village, Pittsfield, MA; Shaker Historical Museum, Cleveland, OH; Shaker Museum and Library, Old Chatham, NY; Shaker Museum at South Union, South Union, KY; Shaker Village of Pleasant Hill, Harrodsburg, KY 40330.

Apothecary Cabinet, 66" x 14", stained wood, rect, front fitted with 12 small drawers, molded white glazed porcelain handles, identification labels, drawer sides inscribed with various content titles, New England, 19th C 450.00
Blanket Chest, 37" x 24-3/4", red painted wood, hinged rect top with molded edge, int. till, paneled front and sides raised on tapering cylindrical legs, lid int. inscribed in pencil "Bloomsburg, C. B. Hutton, Box 105, Orangeville," 19th C 1,200.00
Bonnet, dark brown palm and straw, black ribbons, 9" flounce, KY 395.00
Book, *How The Shakers Cook & The Noted Cooks of the Country, Feature The Chefs and Their Cooking Recipes*, A. J. White, New York, NY, 1889, 50 pgs, 3-3/8" x 6-1/8', bust of men illus, dusted, chips 15.00
Bottle, 9" h, aqua, emb "Shaker Pickles," base labeled "Portland, Maine, E.D.P. & Co." 90.00
Box, cov, bentwood
   5-3/8" l, oval, old natural finish, gray sawtooth borders, decoupage flowers, finger construction with copper tacks, 3 fingers on base, one on lid, age crack in lid 150.00
   9" l, oval, orig dark green paint, finger construction with copper tacks, two fingers on base, one on lid, minorwear...........1,265.00
Brush, 10-3/4" l, horsehair, turned wood handle.........................90.00
Candle Stand, 17-1/2" d, 24-1/2" h, New Lebanon, New York, c1820-50, cherry, circular top with bull-nose edge, circular disk support, turned, tapering post, tripod cabriole leg base, old red translucent varnish, top refinished, minor imperfections........................3,500.00
Carpet Beater, 41-1/2" l, bent willow, turned beech handle 85.00

Feather Duster, orig ribbon, turned maple, c1900, $175.

Chair
  28" h, 11" h seat, arm, child's, No. 1, Mt. Lebanon, NY, late 19th/
    early 20th C, maple, old finish, old tape seat 1,100.00
  41" h, 17-1/4" h seat, side, New England, early 19th C, orig red-
    brown painted surface, tops of front legs stamped "1," replaced
    tape seat, surface abrasions.. 4,315.00
Clothes Rack, 36-1/2" w, 72" h, red painted wood, 3 horizontal bars,
  top bar mounted on either side with 3 hooks, rect uprights continuing
  to form arched feet, New England,, late 19th C 2,750.00
Cobweb Broom, 94" l, Union Village, Oh, wear, incomplete
  stitching 145.00
Display Case, 8" x 10" x 10", pine, red stain, sliding lid, dovetailed, Mt.
  Lebanon 375.00
Dough Scraper, 4-1/2" l, wrought iron 40.00
Flax Wheel, 33-1/2" h, various hardwoods, old dark brown finish,
  stamped "SR. AL," (Deacon Samuel Ring of Alfred, Maine 1784-1848),
  two pieces of distaff replaced... 330.00
Grain Measure, 7-1/2" d, bentwood, stencil label "Shaker Society, Sab-
  bathday Lake, Me," minor edge damage 160.00
Hanger, 24" w, bentwood, chestnut.. 65.00
Publication, 9-1/2" x 13-1/2", bound copies of Shaker and Shakeress,
  Mt Lebanon, NY, 1873-1875, binding worn 250.00
Rocker
  No. 3, Mt. Lebanon, NY, 1875-80, shawl bar above shaped splats,
    one imp "3," another with image of decal used on production
    chairs, arms with tenon cap, red and green taped seat, rockers,
    orig dark surface, minor imperfections, 14" h, 33-1/2" h..... 460.00
  No. 7, Mt. Lebanon, NY, old dark finish, shawl bar, 4 slats, uphol-
    stered seat, top slat imp "7," 42" h 425.00
Scoop, 11-3/4", walnut 275.00
Sewing Box, 7-3/4" d, round, old varnish finish, lapped seams with
  copper tacks, swivel handle, worn white silk damask lining with pin-
  cushion, needle case and strawberry, ribbons missing 220.00
Sewing Desk, chestnut, pine, and maple, drawers, overhanging base,
  old refinish.. 11,500.00
Stand, 29-1/4" h, 19" x 19-3/8" top, South Union Kentucky, c1840, wal-
  nut, sq top overhangs base with one drawer, straight chamfered skirt,
  sq tapering chamfered legs, old refinishing, imperfections 690.00
Table, 34-3/4" x 35-1/2" x 28", maple, drop leaf, rect top, hinged rect
  leaves, single drawer, sq tapering legs, first half 19th C 6,500.00
Table Swift, 29-3/4" d extended, 25" h, maple, 19th C................ 230.00

SHAVING MUGS

History: Shaving mugs, which hold the soap, brush, and hot water used to prepare a beard for shaving, come in a variety of materials including tin, silver, glass, and pottery. One style, which has separate compartments for water and soap, is the scuttle, so called because of its coal-scuttle shape.

Personalized shaving mugs were made exclusively for use in barber shops in the United Sates. They began being produced shortly after the Civil War and continued to be made into the 1930s.

Unlike shaving mugs that were used at home, these mugs were personalized with the owner's name, usually in gilt. The mug was kept in a rack at the barber shop, and it was used only when the owner came in for a shave. This was done for hygienic purposes, to keep from spreading a type of eczema known as barber's itch.

The mugs were usually made on European porcelain blanks, that often contained the mark of "Germany," "France," or "Austria" on the bottom. In later years, a few were made on American-made semi-vitreous blanks. The artwork on mugs was done by decorators who worked for major barber supply houses. Occasionally, the mark of the barber supply house is also stamped on the bottom of the mug.

After a short time, the mugs became more decorative, including hand-painted floral decorations, as well as birds, butterflies, and a wide variety of nature scenes, etc. These are classified today as "decorative" mugs.

Another category, "fraternal mugs," soon developed. These included the emblem of an organization the owner belonged to, along with his name emblazoned in gold above or below the illustration.

"Occupational mugs" were also very popular. These are mugs which contained a painting of something that illustrated the owner's occupation, such as a butcher, a bartender, or a plumber. The illustration might be a man working at his job, or perhaps the tools of his trade, or a product which he made or sold.

Of all these mugs, occupationals are the most prized. Their worth is determined by several factors: rarity (some occupations are rarer than others), size of mug, and size of illustration (the bigger the better), quality of artwork, and condition. Although rare mugs with cracks or chips can still be valuable if the damage does not affect the artwork on the mug. Generally speaking, a mug showing a man at work at his job is usually valued higher than that same occupation illustrated with only the tools or finished product.

The invention of the safety razor by King C. Gillette, issued to three and one-half million servicemen during World War I, brought about changes in personal grooming—men began to shave on their own rather than visiting the barber shop to be shaved. As a result, the need for personalized shaving mugs declined.

References: Susan and Al Bagdade, *Warman's English & Continental Pottery & Porcelain*, 3rd Edition, Krause Publications, 1998; Ronald S. Barlow, *Vanishing American Barber Shop*, Windmill Publishing, 1993; Keith E. Estep, *Shaving Mug & Barber Bottle Book*, Schiffer Publishing, 1995.

Collectors' Club: National Shaving Mug Collectors Association, 320 S. Glenwood St., Allentown, PA 18104.

Museums: Atwater Kent History Museum, Philadelphia, PA; Barber Museum, Canal Winchester, OH; Lightner Museum, Saint Augustine, FL.

Advisor: Bill Boyd.

Note: Prices shown are for typical mugs which have no damage and show only moderate wear on the gilt name and decoration.

Fraternal

ARCIP, Retail Clerks Union, rd star, clasped hands,initials 195.00
B.L.E.E., Brotherhood of Locomotive Eng., "BLE" monogram...... 95.00
B.P.O.E., Elks, double emblem, Dr. title.................................... 300.00
F. of A., gilt deer's head, 2 crossed American flags, floral designs, gilt
  dec, fuchsia rim, mkd "Germany" 35.00
F.O.E., Fraternal Order of Eagles, eagle holding F.O.E. plaque.... 260.00
IB of PM, International Brotherhood of Paper Makers, paper making
  machine, clasped hands 275.00
I.O.M., International Order of Mechanics, ark ladder................. 270.00
Loyal Knights of America, eagle, flags, six-pointed star 275.00
Loyal Order of the Moose, gold circle with gray moose head, purple
  and green floral dec, gilt rim and base, mkd "Germany" 220.00
United Mine Workers, clasped hands emblem flanked by crossed picks
  and shovels, floral dec, rose garland around top, mkd "Germany" 125.00

Fraternal, Masonic emblems, name in gold, floral dec, $90.

Occupational

Barber, hp, pair of hair clippers, worn name 145.00
Bartender, hp, bartender pouring drink, mirrored back bar, 2 patrons
   drinking and smoking 450.00
Butcher, bull's head and butcher cutlery, G. M. Hardendorf,
   3-1/4" x 5" 350.00
Carpenter, hammer, saw, and plane, gilt dec, mkd "S. D. Show Barber
   Supply Co., Wichita, Kansas" 145.00
Chicken Farmer, rooster crowing 200.00
Cooper, man working on wooden barrel 375.00
Dentist, man wearing gray suit standing over man sitting in chair, den-
   tal office background, gilt sprig dec, mkd "OCKCI" 90.00
Engineer, red, gray, and yellow engine pulling gray and black tender,
   gilt sprig dec, mkd "Limoges France, The World Our Field, Koken St.
   Louis, Trademark" 175.00
Fabric Store, colorful hp shop int., owner waiting on well dressed
   woman, gold trim and name, 3-5/8" x 4-1/2" 700.00
General Store, pork, flour, and whiskey barrels, Limoges,
   4" x 4-3/4" 650.00
Hotel Clerk, clerk at desk, guest signing register 375.00
Ice Cream Parlor, metal dish of strawberry ice cream with spoon, worn
   gold trim 275.00
Locomotive and Coal Tender, F. M. Briggs, gold base band shows
   wear, 4" x 5" 105.00
Marksman, crossed rifles, target eagle wreath 200.00
Musical, banjo, owner's name 300.00
Painter, 2 men on scaffold painting house 375.00
Phonograph, outside horn photo 350.00
Photographer, ma with beard 250.00
Plasterer, hp, mortar board and 2 trowels, gilt springs, mkd "Teco Co.
   Semovit" 175.00
Shoemaker, hp, scene of shoemaker in shop, gilt foot and swags
   around name 195.00
Trainman, red plank caboose, gilt dec, mkd "H. & B. T RR" 185.00
Trolley Repair Wagon, horse drawn, scaffolding 1,250.00
Tugboat, boat in water, crew and captain 750.00
Writer, black desk inkwell with sander, pen, and brass
   handle 350.00

Other

Bicycle Racer, pink and yellow flowers, gilt banner with "Bicycle Rac-
   ers Madison Square Garden," trophy with inscription 550.00

Coronation of H M King Edward VII, 18th May 1937, British seal with
   monarch, flags on reverse, scuttle 40.00
Drape and flowers, purple drape, pot of flowers, gold name 85.00
Fish Shape, scuttle, green and brown 75.00
Horses in storm, white and black horses, copied from painting 100.00
Skull, white, gray, black, and cream, scuttle, mkd "Bavaria" 135.00

SHAWNEE POTTERY

History: The Shawnee Pottery Co. was founded in 1937 in Zanesville, Ohio. The company acquired a 650,000-square-foot plant that had previously housed the American Encaustic Tiling Company. Shawnee produced as many as 100,000 pieces of pottery a day until 1961, when the plant closed.

Shawnee limited its production to kitchenware, decorative art pottery, and dinnerware. Distribution was primarily through jobbers and chain stores.

Marks: Shawnee can be marked "Shawnee," "Shawnee U.S.A.," "USA #——," "Kenwood," or with character names, e.g., "Pat. Smiley" and "Pat. Winnie."

References: Jim and Bev Mangus, *Shawnee Pottery*, Collector Books, 1994, 1998 value update; Mark Supnick, *Collecting Shawnee Pottery*, L-W Book Sales, 1997; Duane and Janice Vanderbilt, *Collector's Guide to Shawnee Pottery*, Collector Books, 1992, 1998 value update.

Collectors' Club: Shawnee Pottery Collectors Club, P.O. Box 713, New Smyrna Beach, FL 32170.

Ashtray, Monte Carlo 38.00
Bank, Bulldog 50.00
Basket, 9" l, 5-1/2" h at handle, turquoise glaze, relief flowers and
   leaves, USA 688 .... 45.00
Batter Pitcher, Fern 65.00
Casserole, cov, Corn Queen, large 40.00
Cookie Jar/Bank, Winnie, 10-1/2" h, #61 mark and patent
   date 475.00
Cookie Jar, cov
   Dutch Girl, partial label 150.00
   Puss n' Boots 205.00
   Smiley
      Shamrocks dec 175.00
      Tulip dec 250.00

Cookie Jar, Smiley, $200. Photo courtesy of Green Valley Auctions, Inc.

Creamer
    Elephant 25.00
    Puss n' Boots, green and yellow 65.00
    Smiley Pig, clover bud 165.00
Figure
    Bear 45.00
    Gazelle 45.00
    Puppy 50.00
    Squirrel 30.00
    Rabbit 40.00
Fruit Bowl, Corn Queen 25.00
Mug, Corn King 35.00
Paperweight, Muggsy 65.00
Pitcher
    Bo Peep, blue bonnet, yellow dress 125.00
    Chanticleer 75.00
Planter
    Canopy Bed, #734 ....95.00
    Donkey with basket, #722 ....35.00
    Gazelle 25.00
    Horse with hat and cart 25.00
    Locomotive, black 65.00
    Mouse and Cheese, pink and yellow 25.00
    Rocking Horse, blue 32.00
    Wheelbarrow 20.00
Salt and Pepper Shakers, pr
    Chanticleer, large, orig label 45.00
    Dutch Boy and Girl, large 55.00
    Milk Cans 20.00
    Mugsey, small 65.00
    Puss n' Boots, small 30.00
    Smiley, small 30.00
    Watering Cans 27.50
Teapot
    Granny Ann, peach apron 115.00
    Horseshoe, blue 45.00
    Tom Tom, blue, red, and yellow 125.00
Utility Jar, Corn King 50.00
Wall Pocket
    Bird House 25.00
    Fern 35.00

SILHOUETTES

History: Silhouettes (shades) are shadow profiles produced by hollow cutting, mechanical tracing, or painting. They were popular in the 18th and 19th centuries.

The name came from Etienne de Silhouette, a French Minister of Finance, who cut "shades" as a pastime. In America, the Peale family was well known for the silhouettes they made.

Silhouette portraiture lost popularity with the introduction of the daguerreotype prior to the Civil War. In the 1920s and 1930s, a brief revival occurred when tourists to Atlantic City and Paris had their profiles cut as souvenirs.

Marks: An impressed stamp marked "PEALE" or "Peale Museum" identifies pieces made by the Peale family.

Museums: Essex Institute, Salem, MA; National Portrait Gallery, Washington, DC.

3-1/2" h, young woman, identified on bottom edge "Fanny Carmau 1811," hollow cut, re-cut to oval, stains, brass frame 100.00
3-1/2" h, 2-1/2" w, woman, hair up in bun, green dress with large ruffled sleeves, lace collar, gold pin, antique black molded frame 600.00
3-1/2" h, 2-1/2" w, woman, stamped brass frame attached to wood frame 95.00

Andrew Jackson, painted background, 10" h, 6-1/2" w, $200.

4" h, 4" w, gentleman, reverse painted glass with dec oval in gold surrounded by black, gold highlights, antique black molded frame, pencil inscription on back "Parker Emerson," some damage to reverse painting...90.00
4-3/4" h, 3-3/4" w, man and woman, oval portraits, Hat & Thomas Newell, mounted in lemon gold molded frame 150.00
5-1/8" h, 4-3/8" w, ink and watercolor on paper, young woman with blue dress, gilt highlights, mkd "H46," taped to paper line, 9-5/8" h, 8-1/8" w ogee bird's eye veneer frame with gilded liner 425.00
5-1/8" h, 4-1/2" w, boy wearing cap, ink, oval paper mat, framed.90.00
5-1/4" h, 4-1/2" w, man with pipe, hollow cut, gilded brass frame with minor damage 220.00
5-1/4" h, 7-3/8" w, two brothers, Issac and Rich Bucksput, together in later gilded frame 110.00
5-3/8" h, 6" w, military officer, ink and watercolor on paper, orange and gold uniform, mkd "F. Perring 1840" and "C. C. -1804," repainted black and gold frames, pr...3450.00
5-3/8" h, 8-1/4" w, man and wife, identified as Cal and Phoebe Holms, framed together in black lacquer frame, gilded liners, stains ...220.00
5-1/2" h, 4-5/8" w, two children, late 19th/early 20th C, modern gilt frames, pr 140.00
5-1/2" h, 4-3/4" w, hollow cut, bust, gentleman, traces of gilded detail, emb gilded paper and liner, black lacquered frame with gilded fittings, edge damage 175.00
5-5/8" h, 4-1/2" w, young man, penciled German inscription, modern gilt frame 115.00
5-3/4" h, 4-7/8" w, hollow cut, bust, lady with ornate hat, back mkd "Mrs. Norman" and "Mrs. Norman, Henley on Thames," black lacquered case with gilded fittings, wear and stain......................200.00
5-3/4" h, 5-1/4" w, young man with que, painted silhouette, gold repainted on old frame 55.00
6" h, 9" w, cut silhouettes of man and wife, ink wash details, ink stenciled mat with "We Are One" and blue hearts, dec frame with stenciled bronze powder designs on black, somestaining 3,630.00
6-1/4" h, 5" w, gentleman, hollow cut, old label "G. Saufer, Passe-Portouts, Philadelphia," framed, tears and repair......................90.00
6-3/8" h, 5-3/8" w, young man, old frame, stains and tears 100.00
6-3/8" h, 5-3/8" w, young woman, hollow cut, cut detail at collar, pencil inscription "Sarah Sage," stains 200.00

6-1/2" h, 10" w, man and woman, hollow cut, ink and watercolor details, framed together, sgd "Doyle," eglomise glass mat with 2 ovals, gilded frame 425.00

6-5/8" h, 5-1/2" w, man and wife, hollow cut, ink details, rosewood veneer frames, pr 580.00

6-3/4" h, 6" w, gentleman, black lacquer frame with gilded brass liner, minor stains 90.00

7-5/8" h, 9-1/2" w, boy and girl, full length, standing facing each other, hollow cut, gilt detail, bird's eye veneer ogee frame 725.00

8" h, 7" w, husband, wife, baby on knee, grandparents, 2 children, hollow cut, watercolor and pencil details, black cloth backing, paper professionally cleaned, orig bird's eye maple frames, turned dark wood buttons on corner blocks, 5 pc set 9,975.00

8-1/8" h, 5-1/8" w, hollow cut, full length, man in top hat, old molded pine frame 175.00

9-3/4" x 7", full length, young gentleman, Augt. Edouart, fecit Saratoga Springs, Aug 1844, sgd and dated lower left, cut and laid down on lithographed background, matted and framed, tears, minor stain, toning 520.00

16" x 14", hollow cut, portrait of young man, America, early 19th C, paper label on back with attribution to Ruth Henshaw Bascom, emb with dry stamp, staining, toning, creases 635.00

SILVER

History: The natural beauty of silver lends itself to the designs of artists and craftsmen. It has been mined and worked into an endless variety of useful and decorative items. Pure silver is too soft to be fashioned into strong, durable, and serviceable utensils. Therefore, a way was found to give silver the required degree of hardness by adding alloys of copper and nickel.

Silversmithing in America goes back to the early 17th century in Boston and New York and the early 18th century in Philadelphia. Boston artisans were influenced by the English styles, New Yorkers by the Dutch.

References: Louise Belden, *Marks of American Silversmiths in the Ineson-Bissell Collection*, University of Virginia Press, 1980; Frederick Bradbury, *Bradbury's Book of Hallmarks*, J. W. Northend, 1987; Bonita Campbell and Nan Curtis (curators), *Depression Silver*, California State University, 1995; Janet Drucker, *Georg Jensen: A Tradition of Splendid Silver*, Schiffer Publishing, 1997; Stephen G. C. Ensko, *American Silversmiths and Their Marks*, Dover Publications, 1983; Rachael Feild, *Macdonald Guide to Buying Antique Silver and Sheffield Plate*, Macdonald & Co., 1988; *Fine Victorian Gold-and Silverplate, Exquisite Designs from the 1882 Catalog of the Meriden-Brittania Co.*, Schiffer Publishing, 1997; Tere Hagan, *Silverplated Flatware*, 4th ed., Collector Books, 1990, 1998 value update; —, *Sterling Flatware*, L-W Book Sales, 1999; Stephen J. Helliwell, *Understanding Antique Silver Plate, Reference and Price Guide*, Antique Collectors' Club; William P. Hood Jr., *Tiffany Silver Flatware, 1845-1905, When Dining Was An Art*, Antique Collectors' Club, 1999; Kenneth Crisp Jones (ed.), *Silversmiths of Birmingham and Their Marks*, N.A.G. Press, 1981, distributed by Antique Collectors Club; Henry J. Kaufman, *Colonial Silversmith*, Astragal Press, 1995; Ralph and Terry Kovel, *Kovels' American Silver Marks*, Crown Publishers, 1989; Daniel Low and Co., *Gold and Silversmiths Catalogue*, 1901, reprinted by Bridgham Antiques, 1998; (Box 28204, San Diego, CA 92198); Everett L. Maffett, *Silver Banquet II*, Silver Press, 1990; Penny C. Morrill, *Silver Masters of Mexico*,

Schiffer Publishing, 1996; Richard Osterberg, *Silver Hollowware for Dining Elegance*, Schiffer Publishing, 1996; —, *Sterling Silver Flatware for Dining Elegance*, Schiffer Publishing, 1994; Ian Pickford, *Jackson's Silver and Gold Marks of England*, Scotland & Ireland, Antique Collectors' Club; – —, *Silver Flatware*, 1660-1980, Antique Collectors' Club; Dorothy T. Rainwater, *Encyclopedia of American Silver Manufacturers*, Revised 4th ed., Schiffer Publishing, 1998; Dorothy T. and H. Ivan Rainwater, *American Silverplate*, Schiffer Publishing, 1988; *Sterling Silver, Silverplate, and Souvenir Spoons*, revised ed., L-W Book Sales, 1987, 1994 value update; Charles Venable, *Silver in America 1840-1940*, Harry Abrams, 1994; Peter Waldron, *The Price Guide to Antique Silver*, Antique Collectors' Club; Joanna Wissinger, *Arts and Crafts Metalwork and Silver*, Chronicle Books, 1994; Seymour B. Wyler, *Book Of Old Silver*, Crown Publishers, 1937 (available in reprint).

Periodicals: *Silver & Gold Report*, P.O. Box 109665, West Palm Beach, FL 33410, http://www.wessinc.com; *Silver Magazine*, P.O. Box 9690, Rancho Santa Fe, CA 92067, http://www.silvermag.com; *Silver Update and Sterling Silver Hollowware Update*, P.O. Box 2157, Ellicott City, MD 21041-2157

Collectors' Clubs: International Association of Silver Art Collectors, P.O. Box 28415, Seattle, WA 98118-8415; New York Silver Society, 242 E. 7th St., #5, New York, NY 10009; Society of American Silversmiths, P.O. Box 704, Chepatchet, RI 02814, http://www.silversmithing.com.

Museums: Bayou Bend Collection, Houston, TX; Boston Museum of Fine Arts, Boston, MA; Colonial Williamsburg Foundation, Williamsburg, VA; Currier Gallery of Art, Manchester, NH; Yale University Art Gallery, New Haven, CT; Wadsworth Antheneum, Hartford, CT.

Additional Listings: See Silver Flatware in *Warman's Americana & Collectibles* for more examples.

American, 1790-1840

Mostly Coin

Coin silver is slightly less pure than sterling silver. Coin silver has 900 parts silver to 100 parts alloy. Sterling silver has 925 parts silver. American silversmiths followed the coin standards. Coin silver is also called Pure Coin, Dollar, Standard, or Premium.

Beaker, 3" h, 3" d, top and bottom molded rims, engraved, minor dents, Anthony Rasch, Philadelphia, 1807, 4 troy oz 490.00

Left: sugar bowl, fruit finial, $800; right: teapot, swan finial, $200.

Cake Server, 9-1/8" l, George C. Shreve, late 19th C, mark partially rubbed, shaped blade engraved with harbor scene within foliate cartouche, unfurling flag, engine-turned ground, fitted case, 3 troy oz 200.00

Creamer, 4-1/2" h, engraved wreath with ribbon and initials "C. G.," maker's mark, 4.7 troy oz..660.00

Creamer and Sugar, 7-3/4" h unmarked creamer, 9-1/2" h sugar with 2 handles and cover, repousse dec with vintage pattern, fine form finial and handles, engraved, minor dents, Allcock & Allen, New York City, c1820, 35 troy oz..980.00

Cream Jug, 4-3/4" h, oval form, applied rim, molded base and strap handle, engraved on bottom, minor dents, Joseph Foster, 1760-1839, 8 troy oz 490.00

Ewer
    7-5/8" h, Gorham, third quarter 19th C, chased and emb florals and foliage, plain central roundel with serpentine handle topped by flat leaf, low stem, stepped foot, 15 troy oz 435.00
    12" h, ftd, repousse vintage dec, vine form handle extending round shoulder and around base of both pieces, engraved, minor dents, William F. Ladd, New York City, 1828-45 ....1,200.00

Forks, 7-3/4" l, stem with applied medallion profile roundel of young woman, engraved details, 11 troy oz, 8 pc set 690.00

Jug, 7" h, J. B. Jones & Co. makers, 2nd quarter 19th C, inverted pear-shaped body, scroll handle and stepped neck, round stepped foot, name engraved under spout, 12 troy oz 700.00

Knives, 8-1/8" l, third quarter 19th C, medallion profile roundel to end of handle, engraved handle and blade, monogrammed on reverse, 14 troy oz, 9 pc set 920.00

Mug, 4" h, John L. Westervelt, Newburgh, NY maker, mid 19th C, cylindrical, fine beading to foot and rim, scroll handle, central cartouche engraved with name and dated 1863, engraved Greek key border, allover engine turned ground, 6 troy oz....................................200.00

Salt, 1-1/2" x 3-1/2", oval form, four hoofed feet, repousse floral and wreath dec at knees, gold wash bowls, minor dents, Ball, Black & Co., New York City, 1851-76, 7 troy oz, pr 290.00

Spoon, 9-1/4" l, Nicholas Geffroy maker, Newport, early 19th C, monogrammed, set of six, 11 troy oz 200.00

Sugar Bowl, cov, 8" h, Gorham, mid 19th C, squat baluster, stepped foot, wide band of engine-turning, one plain and one engraved cartouche, two serpentine handles, domed lid with flower form finial, 17 troy oz, minor dents...175.00

Tablespoon, 8" l, front tipt, back engraved, bowl with emb scallop shell below short drop handle, minor dents, wear, Samuel Edwards, Boston, 1705-62, 2 troy oz 635.00

Tea and Coffee Set, William B. Hever, New York City, 1776-1828, 11" h coffeepot, teapot, cov sugar, creamer, and waste bowl, graduated finial, rect gadrooned body, pedestal with 4 ball feet, die stamped band on shoulder with rural scenery, single narrow band of anthemion leaves on the finial, upper and lower rims, minor dents, 5 pcs, 110 troy oz 3,565.00

Harris and Schafer, Washington, DC, tea set, sterling, $6,000.

American, 1840-1920
Mostly Sterling

There are two possible sources for the origin of the word sterling. The first is that it is a corruption of the name Easterling. Easterlings were German silversmiths who came to England in the Middle Ages. The second is that it is named for the sterling (little star) used to mark much of the early English silver.

Sterling is 92.5 percent per silver. Copper comprises most of the remaining alloy. American manufacturers began to switch to the sterling standard about the time of the Civil War.

Basket, 9" d, 3" h, Whiting Mfg Co., late 19th C, reticulated, sides with scrolls and diapering, scroll rim, three scroll feet, fluted base, monogrammed, 11 troy oz 460.00

Bowl
    8" d, 2-1/2" h, Black, Starr & Frost, late 19th C, repousse, chased and emb with flowers and scrolling leaves, applied C-scroll rim, low base, monogrammed, gold washed int., 15 troy oz......350.00
    10-7/8" d, 4-1/2" h, International Silver, early 20th C, fluted bowl, vitruvian scroll band at top, domed base with low concave foot, 28 troy oz 600.00
    11-1/2" d, circular, broad border repousse with flowers and leaves on fine stippled ground, scroll and foliate border, mkd "S. Kirk & Son Sterling, #227," 1903-1925, 18 oz..............................650.00

Center Bowl, 14-1/2" d, Frank W Smith Silver Co., Inc., late 19th C, retailed by Bigelow, Kennard & Co., ovoid, engraved with quilted style pattern, edges reticulated with engraved leafy scrolls, edge with wide cast border of rocaille shells and C-scrolls, monogrammed center, 31 troy oz 1,840.00

Coffee Set, nesting, 7" h, Lebkuecher and Co., Newark, NY, 1896-1909, single serving, 3 part set, cov sugar, creamer, pot, 2 angled wood handles, cylindrical form, bulbous base, flared circular foot, imp maker's mark "Sterling, 02741 5 12 oz," 12 troy oz, repair to handle.........375.00

Compote, 8-3/4" d, 4-1/2" h, Bigelow, Kennard & Co., late 19th C, Etruscan-style, bowl with central roundel of classical man holding grapes, seated woman with baby, dog, beaded surround, engraved anthemion and flowerheads, short stem with single rib to center, trumpet foot, plain flattened loop handles, applied Greek key rim, 22 troy oz 700.00

Dish, cov, 5-1/2" h, Ball, Tompkins, & Black, New York, 1939, repousse, ovoid, shaped edge, four scroll and shell feet, domed lid with engraved mottoed crest and initials, ribbed mushroom finial, 19 troy oz 500.00

Dresser Set, Webster Co., late 19th C, hand mirror, hair brush, two nail brushes, nail buff, comb, nail file, shoe horn, glove stretcher, button hook, two glass jars with silver covers, all with foliage repousse against landscape ground, associated pair of German nail scissors, 22-1/2" w, 22-1/2" d, 30-1/2" h mahogany stand with top that opens to compartment with fitted int., sq section tapered legs joined by stretchers, 12 pc set...1,150.00

Flatware
    Alvin, Chateau Rose, 95 pcs, some serving pcs, 86 oz, 2 dwt 600.00
    Reed & Barton, Majestic, 100 pcs, some serving pcs, 82 troy oz..550.00
    Wanamaker, John, early 20th C, 56 pcs, some with monogram, some stainless steel blades, some serving pcs, 62 troy oz 345.00

Fruit Bowl, 12-1/2" d, Dominick & Haff, late 19th/early 20th C, retailed by Shreve, Crump & Low, fluted int., wide reticulated edge with realistically modeled chrysanthemums and daisies, 21 troy oz .. 1,150.00

Ice Cream Slice
    10" l, George W. Shiebler & Co., late 19th C, hammered finish, handle with Roman style male medallion on end, engraved bands of classical style designs, gold washed blade with further classical style engraving, medallion to lower right, central horizontal band to further of further small medallions, monogrammed on back of handle, 6 troy oz 4,025.00
    12-1/4" l, Dominick & Haff, late 19th C, Rococo pattern, retailed by Bigelow, Kennard & Co. monogrammed on back, 6 troy oz 320.00

Jar, cov, 3-1/8" d, 2" h, Whiting Mfg Co., late 19th C, lid with stamped band of scrolls and shells on edge, central commemorative style coin featuring Napoleon Francois Joseph in interior, underside engraved to Ruth Cleveland, dated 1893, 7 troy oz, descended in Grover Cleveland family 375.00

Kettle-On-Stand
   13" h, bombe repousse allover with flowers and leaves on fine stippled ground, hinged cover with similar dec, floral finial, fixed handle, circular base with conforming dec on 4 paw feet issuing from foliage, mkd "S. Kirk & So., #101," c1903-24, burner mkd "JI sterling silver," 56 oz 2,500.00
   15" h, Ball, Thompkins & Black, third quarter 19th C, bulbous baluster kettle with 2 horizontal bands of foliate heart-shaped motifs, scroll spout, hinged upright handle, domed lid with squatty ball finial, engraved with mottoed heraldic crest, scroll legs, 4 rocaille shell feet, 52 troy oz... 1,150.00

Mustard Pot, 4-1/2" d, S. Kirk & Son, Baltimore, mid 19th C, vegetal finial, glass liner, 7 troy oz 150.00

Pitcher
   8-1/4" h, Dominick & Haff, retailed by Bailey, Banks & Biddle, early 20th C, squat baluster form, stepped domed foot, stamped with wide band of flat leaves to lower section, scroll handle, scroll rim, monogrammed, 27 troy oz.. 635.00
   9" h, baluster shape, circular foot, scroll handle, inscribed and dated "1950," mkd "Cartier," and "Graff, Washborne, Dunn," 26 oz, 8 dwt 150.00
   10-3/4" h, Gorham, dated 1906, baluster form body cased and emb with Art Nouveau style flowers and leaves, handle terminating in flat leaves, shaped quatrefoil base, engraved presentation inscription, gold washed int., 45 troy oz 4,600.00

Platter, Dominick & Haff, oval, border repousse wiith flowers and leaves on fine matted ground, monogrammed, 16 oz.............. 475.00

Presentation Goblet, 8-1/2" h, Ball, Black & Co., New York, mid 19th C, baluster form cup with floral repousse, cartouche with chased and emb eagle with patriotic devices on one side, other with cartouche with chases, emb, and engraved gymnastic equipment on other, everted beaded rim, stem with flattened knop, beaded stepped foot, domed base with repousse foliate cartouches, engraved with inscription dated 1857, 11 troy oz... 690.00

Punch Bowl and Ladle, 14-3/4" d, 8-3/4" h, Gorham, bowl dated 1908, squat ovoid bowl, shaped edge, waterlilies dec, gold-washed int., domed foot, applied water lily dec, engraved with double monogram, names engraved on underside, 15" l ladle with fruiting berry vines, also monogrammed and dated, 92 troy oz.......................... 5,175.00

Punch Ladle, 9-1/2" l, terminal applied with scrolling foliage, monogrammed 100.00

Roast Platter, 20-5/8" l, 14-1/8" w, Gorham, early 20th C, Greek key border... 750.00

Salad Serving Set. spoon and fork
   9" l, Chambord pattern, Reed & Barton, monogrammed, 5 oz, 6 dwt 200.00
   11" l, Love Disarmed pattern, Reed & Barton, 14 oz, 2 dwt .. 650.00

Salt, open
   3-1/4" l, 1-3/4" h, Black, Starr & Frost, late 19th C, Classical Revival style, ovoid body, hoof feet terminating in lion's heads, red glass liner, 8 try oz, 4 pc set.. 430.00
   3-3/4" d, 1-1/2" h, Gorham, third quarter 19th C, bucket-shape, 3 bands of horizontal reeding, two reeded drop handles suspended from flowerhead roundels, small butterflies, frosted glass liner, pr, 6 troy oz 420.00

Salver, 7-1/4" x 7-1/8", Theodore B. Starr, late 19th C, sq, shaped edge reticulated with scrolls offset with small rocaille shells, pr, 14 troy oz 385.00

Tazza, 7-1/8" d, 2-1/2" h, Howard & Co., dated 1898, vessel with wide reticulated band and applied scroll rim, center monogram, applied scroll base, reticulated foot, pr, 19 troy oz............................... 700.00

Tea and Coffee Service, W. Gale & Son, New York, mid 19th C, 11-1/2" h coffeepot, teapot, creamer, cov sugar, open sugar, all with tapering cylindrical body, bands of beading and geometric pattern, open ovoid

handles with paterae to top with one male and one female profile medallions, spreading dome foot, 125 troy oz 5,175.00

Teapot, 9" h, Edward and David Kinsey makers, Cincinnati, mid 19th C, pear-shaped pot chased and emb overall with grapes and grape vines, reticulated cast scroll and shell base, crabstock handle and spout, domed lie with cast grape and leaf finial, 34 troy oz...... 920.00

Tea Service
   Ball, Black & Co., third quarter 19th C, tapered ovoid teapot, cov sugar, helmet-shaped open creamer, each with applied profile medallion and anthemion engraving, pendant handles, monogrammed, 36 troy ox.. 2,185.00
   Gorham, retailed by Bigelow, Kennard & Co., early 20th C, 5-1/4" l teapot, cov sugar, open creamer, ovoid with reeding, angular handle, reeded lids, monogrammed, 36 troy oz 575.00
   Shreve, Stanwood & Co., 1860, 16" h hot water urn on stand, creamer, cov sugar, open sugar, and 9" h teapot, ovoid, beaded detailing, lids with swan finials, domed stepped foot, urn with presentation inscription on side, burner and one sugar lid missing, 35 troy oz 2,185.00

Travel Clock, 3-5/8" l, 3-1/8" w, Wm Kerr & Co., late 1ith C, plain rect case with rounded corners, eight-day movement, oct goldtone engine-turned face, black Roman numerals, silver surround with engine turning, engraved scrolls and floral sprays, monogrammed cover 200.00

Tray, 22" l, 15-5/8" w, Frank M. Whiting & Co., early 20th C, oval, border engraved with classical revival band and floral swags, 60 troy oz 865.00

Vase
   11-1/4" h, I. N. Deitsch, early 20th C, reticulated tapered body, engraved flowers and leaves, trumpet foot, glass liner....... 690.00
   13-7/8" h, 6-3/4" d, Bailey, Banks, and Biddle, early 20th C, cylindrical body flaring outward at top, engraved husk swags and flowerheads, monogrammed roundel on one side, engraved inscription on other, slightly everted rim, domed base, 31 troy oz 635.00
   15-3/4" h, J. E. Caldwell & Co., late 19th/early 20th C, tapered baluster form with engraved laurel wreath on each side, one with monogram, everted rim with engraved band of lines and circles, trumpet foot with similarly engraved band, 34 troy oz 750.00

Vegetable Dish, cov, 11" l, Gorham, 1894, shaped oval, wide edge embellished with scrolls and rocaille shells, shallow lid with scroll edge and flat leaf handle, lid monogrammed, 25 troy oz 575.00

Arts & Crafts

Hand crafted silver from the Arts & Crafts period is one of the most sought after types of silver. Wonderful examples can be found, usu-

Alarm Clock, Liberty & Co., hammered, six enameled panels, early Bradley seven-jewel crystal faced clock, c1900, hallmarked, 6" h, 3-1/2" w, 2 small nicks to enamel, $3,750. Photo courtesy of David Rago Auctions, Inc.

ally with a hammered finish, and proudly displaying maker's marks, etc. Because much research has been done, individual makers in the various studios and shops are known to collectors.

Most pieces have impressed marks. Because the Arts & Crafts movement was international, guilds were located in the United States, Great Britain, Germany, and Austria, creating many forms.

Bowl

4-1/8" d, 2" h, Katherine Pratt, hammered finish, floriform, 5 petal like panels, scalloped rim, stepped circular base, engraved initials on one panel, date on base, imp "Pratt, Sterling" 200.00

7-1/8" d, 1-7/8" h, Kalo Shops, hammered finish, floriform, 5 petal like panels, rolled rim, imp "Hand Wrought At The Kalo Shops Chicago and New York, Sterling, 18" 400.00

8-1/4" d, 3-1/8" h, Arthur Stone, executed by Herbert A. Taylor, 1910-38, circular form, central tooled flower, dot, and engraved line border, circular stepped foot, makers mark "Stone, Sterling," and "T," 18 troy oz, scratches and spotting 1,150.00

8-7/8" d, 2" h, Kalo, Chicago, circular, 7 sided rolled rim, circular flared ftd base, hammered finish, imp "Sterling Kalo 57" 350.00

9-3/4" d, 1-3/4" h, Kalo Shop, Chicago, shallow circular 5 petaled form, inverted rim, inscribed presentation, base imp "Sterling Kalo M323" 425.00

Candy Dish, 5-1/2" d, 5-3/4" h, Kalo Shop, hammered finish, trumpet base, stamped "Kalo Shops/Park Ridge Ills/Serling" 900.00

Demitasse Spoon, Liberty, set of 6, orig leather case, spoons hallmarked, cast stamped "Liberty" 200.00

Ladle, 8-1/8" h, Kalo Shop, Chicago, hammered finish, notched handle, entwined raised "KP" monogram, imp "Sterling Kalo 8597" 260.00

Martini Pitcher, 9-1/2" h, 7" d, LeBolt, hammered finish, strainer spout, angular handle, die-stamped mark and "LeBolt/Hand Beaten/Sterling 801" 600.00

Martini Spoon, 13-1/2" h, Kalo Shop, Chicago, hammered finish, stamped "Sterling Kalo 243" 200.00

Plate, 9-3/4" d, Handicraft Shop, Boston, style of Mary Knight, circular, pinched and emb scrolling floral and leaf design around extended and rolled rim, imp Handicraft Shop mark, "Sterling, 1904" 435.00

Salt and Pepper Shakers, pr, Stone Associates, c1937, flattened baluster form, initials engraved on side, imp "Stone" with lower case "h" in shield, "Sterling" and "H" on base, 8 troy oz 460.00

Serving Spoon, 9" l, Th. Marthinsen, Norway, hammered finish bowl, squirrel and acorn motif handle, imp marks, "830S" 375.00

Tea Set, Arthur Stone, Gardner, MA, c1918, teapot, creamer, cov sugar, waste bowl, ivory finials and insulators, leaf detail on spout, bulbous body, initialed "H" for Arthur L. Hartwell, Master Craftsman, engraved with presentees initials and date, 44 troy oz 3,000.00

Continental

Generations have enjoyed silver created by Continental silversmiths. Expect to find well executed forms with interesting elements. Most Continental silver is well marked.

Austria-Hungary

Beaker, 3-1/4" h, late 19th C, base with thin beaded rim, engraved with diapering centered by flowerheads with central cartouche with coat of arms 175.00

Candlesticks, pr, 12-1/2" h, Rococo-style, late 19th C, paneled baluster stem and socket, scrolled weighted base, removable bobeche, lacquered 690.00

Continental

Asparagus Server, 11-1/4" l, late 19th C, reticulated handles topped by crowned lion's head, flowerheads and scrolls, standing figure, ending in cherub face above floral basket flanked by cherub herms over reticulation, blades reticulated with C-scrolls and engraved with flowers and further scrolls, monogrammed, 9 troy oz 230.00

Box, cov, 7-1/2" d, 2-3/4" h, late 19th/early 20th C, squatty ovoid, repousse foliate and scroll banding, hinged lid with floral roundel, 14 troy oz 345.00

Candelabra, 21-1/2" h, three-light, shaped sq lobed foot with scroll and floral rim rising to fluted stem applied with similar dec, 2

German, serving tray, shell form, scroll bead and leaf handles, textured rays, scalloped border, 15-3/4" l, 15" w, 74 oz, price for pair, $4,400. Photo courtesy of Freeman\Fine Arts.

scrolling foliate branches, central fixed sconce, detachable bobeches, convertible to candlestick, engraved with monogram below crown, weighted base 900.00

Condiment Jar, 4-3/4" h, late 19th/early 20th C, formed as sedan chair, stamped with scrolls and cartouches of dancing couples, hinged lid with quadripartite finial, cobalt blue glass liner, restorations, 5 troy oz 375.00

Creamer, 5-1/2" l, 4-1/4" h, figural, horned cow, fly hinged lid, 19th C 800.00

Danish

Sugar Tongs, Georg Jensen, Cactus pattern, early 20th C, 1 troy oz 115.00

Water Pitcher, 9-3/4" h, 20th C, tapered egg-shaped body, flared stem with beading to top, stepped foot, spout with curved reeding to underside, wooden handle with stylized floral terminal to top .. 750.00

Dutch

Bowl, 14-1/4" l, 3" h, 19th C, .833 fine, Dutch export mark, repousse, lobed, reserves with chased and emb country scenes, 2 pierced handles with putto to top, central flowers flanked by putto riding dolphins, 15 troy oz 460.00

Box, cov, 4-3/4" d, 3-1/8" h, late 19th C, .934 fine, sides chased and emb with classical style scrolls and husk swags, hinged lid with fluting, central engraved roundel with heraldic device and inscription, 10 troy oz 980.00

Coffeepot, 8" h, late 19th C, .833 fine, baluster form pot with allover scroll and foliage repousse, windmill vignette on one side, scroll cartouche topped by crown flanked by putto on other side, legs topped by crowned human masks, four ball and claw feet, turned wood handle set at right angle to ram-horned grotesque spout, flattened lid with vertical ribbing, rampant lion finial, 11 troy oz 800.00

Pitcher, 5-1/2" h, late 19th C, .833 line, baluster form, neck with band of fluting, repousse to lower section of foliage, birds and putti, domed foot with vertical ribbing, spout with putto, beaded serpentine handle, lid with vertical reeding, repousse and vegetal finial, base engraved "Esther Cleveland," 6 troy oz, descended in family of Grover Cleveland 260.00

French, .950 fine

Coffeepot, 8-1/2" h, Louis XVI, Bourdeaux, late 18th C, pear-shaped, scroll legs ending in plain cartouches, 3 hoof feet, turned wood handle in silver socket set at right angle to short fluted spout, domed hinged lid with scroll thumbpiece and flower finial, monogrammed, 22 troy oz 1,725.00

Coffeepot, 9-1/4" h, third quarter 19th C, pear-shaped, cast quadripartite scroll embellished serpentine spout and handle, heat stops, domed lid with flower form finial, 22 troy oz 460.00

Dish, cov, undertray, Paris, 1819-38, "C. P." maker's mark, cylindrical body with acanthus and flat leaf handles, rim with beading and flat leaf band, base with band of flat leaves, foot with band of laurel, lid with beaded edge, removable circular handle formed as cornucopia on leaf and flower base, fitted leather case, 30 troy oz 2,615.00

Fish Serving Platter, 27-3/4" l, 11-1/2" w, oval, reeded rim, monogrammed, 66 troy oz 1,265.00

Serving Dish, 11-3/4" l, 2-1/4" h, third quarter 19th C, oval, 2 shell handles, vertical reeded border, 17 troy oz........................... 490.00

Sweetmeat Dish, 5-1/2" l, 5" h, Odiot, Paris, maker, late 19th/20th C, shell form vessel drawn by sea creatures, reins held by two putti, flanking central standing putto poised as Neptune, holding trident-form fork, shaped rect base cast as water, 65 troy oz, pr......2,100.00

Tray, 17-3/8" l, 13" w oval, late 19th C, partially obscured maker's mark, beaded edge, engraved initial in center, 34 troy oz........575.00

Tureen, cov, 12-3/4" l, 10-1/2" h, third/fourth quarter 19th C, sprays of acorns and oak leaves to top, reeded rim, lid with flat leaf rim, stem with reeded shoulder, oval foot, flat leaf band, angular handles with flat leaf to bottom, stylized corn finial about flat leaf and lotus ground 1,840.00

Wine Taster, late 19th C, .950 fine, inset with crest to handle.....125.00

German, .800 fine

Basket, 14" l, shaped oval, paneled sides pierced with flowers, garlands, and scrolling foliage centering four vacant cartouches, center repousse with flowers, foliage, and 3 putti at play, 15 oz, 8 dwt 200.00

Beaker and Underplate, 2-1/2" h cup, 5-7/8" d underplate, cylindrical cup stamped with cartouches of courting couples, everted rim, gold-washed int., plates with foliage and scroll rim, well for cup, monogrammed, 14 troy oz, pr.. 375.00

Compote, 7-3/8" l, 6" h, late 19th C, four putto perm flanked by husk swags supporting ovoid reticulated body with winged putto, scrolls, swags, and foliate baskets, ovoid base with band of stamped scrolls and shells, monogrammed cartouche, clear glass liner, 34 troy oz, pr 1,850.00

Kettle-On-Stand, 16" h, compressed circular with lobed sides, four hoof feet, detachable cover with wooden finial, central swing partial wooden handle, multi-scroll stand with border, 48 oz, 8 dwt....325.00

Serving Dish, 12" d, 3-1/2" h, Wilhelm T. Binder, c1900, rounded trefoil shape, 3 handles, repousse leaf bud and line dec, scalloped, ribbed glass insert, imp "WTB, 800 fine"............... 1,150.00

Wedding Cup, 9" h, figural, beaded figure with chased and emb skirt, cup chased and emb with scrolls and grotesques, 15 troy oz1,955.00

Italian, punch bowl, 12-5/8" d, 10-1/2" h, late 19th/early 20th C, repousse, bowl with band of flat leaves to base below further continuous hunt scene of men attacking various animals, domed foot with band of flat leaves below continuous hunt scene, removable liner, 146 troy oz 4,025.00

Persian, box, cov, 7-1/4" x 7-1/4", 20th C, sq, hinged lid with slightly domed central plaque chased and emb with flowers and tropical birds, engraved foliate surround, sides with further foliate engraving, 26 troy oz 320.00

Wurtembergishe Metallwarenfabrik, candlesticks, pr, 7-1/2" h, plated, sq base applied with bow-tie garlands and foliage, rim with stylized leaves and beads rising to Corinthian column stems, detachable bobeches with beaded rims 375.00

English

From the 17th century to the mid-19th century, English silversmiths set the styles which inspired the rest of the world. The work from this period exhibits the highest degree of craftsmanship. English silver is actively collected in the American antiques marketplace.

Basket

6" d, 3-1/2" h, Victorian, London, 1884, J. R. Hennell maker, reticulated foliate pattern, circular banding, shaped edge with bead and flat leaf rim, four scroll and cylinder feet with husk swags, glass liner, 21 troy oz, pr 1,725.00

10" d, 7-3/4" h, London, 1911, maker's mark partially rubbed, applied scroll and floral rim, trumpet-form basket with similar reticulation, spreading base reticulated with scrolls, reticulated swing handle, 25 troy oz 1,610.00

17" l, 12-1/4" h, George II, London, 1751, Phillips Garden maker, body pierced in stylized scroll, shell, and cruciform pattern, rim with applied cast designs of bound fasces offset with shells on scrolls, busts of summer and autumn goddesses at either end, upright upright cast handle emerging from pierced anthemion above busts of putto flanked by sheaves of wheat, sides of handle formed as scroll below head with floral drapes, top of handle with flat leaves, central depiction of wind god in rocaille cartouche, 4 scroll feet topped by well modeled heads of Ceres, 92 oz 54,050.00

Berry Spoon, George III, marks partially obsured, later engraving, chasing and embossing, pr 200.00

Bowl, 5-1/4" d, 1-1/2" h, Edward VII, London, 1902, W. Comyns & Sons maker, shallow bowl emb with shield shaped panels, hand-hammered surface, low flower form foot, 7 troy oz 435.00

Candelabra, pr, 12-1/2" h, Victorian, London, 1875, maker attributed to Stephen Smith, Renaissance Revival-style, convertible, two foliage scroll and foliate candle arms each with flat leaf nozzle, foliate and acorn finial between arms, stem and foot with stamped foliage, masks, and herms, applied openwork scroll detailing to stem, round foot raised on three scroll feet, small engraved device on foot, 59 troy oz, pr ..4,600.00

Caudle Cup

4-3/4" h, London, 1894, makers mark "LG," also mkd "Lamber Coventry St.," cylindrical, lower body repousse with alternating leaves, 2 scroll handles, gilt int., 9 oz 250.00

6" h, 10-1/2" l, William III, Brittania Standard, London, 1704, Samuel Wastell maker, tapered cylindrical body with single applied molded band, cast ear-shaped handles, spreading domed foot, engraved on one side, heraldic device in rococo-style cartouche, 26 troy oz 2,990.00

Center Bowl, 17" l, 5-1/2" h, George III, London, 1811, Robert Garrard, lobed ovoid body, 2 short scroll and acanthus handles, gadroon and shell border offset with 2 scroll deetails to each side, 4 cast paw feet topped by group of scrolls, 51 troy oz 4,325.00

Chamberstick

4" l, 1-3/4" h, Victorian, London, 1888, W. Comyns maker, chased and emb with flowers and scrolls, removable bobeche, handle with monogrammed thumb-piece, 2 troy oz......................... 115.00

4-1/2" l, 4" h, Sheffield, 1824, "RG" maker's mark, molded foliate scroll and leaf base rim and socket, flying loop handle topped with flat leaf, removable scroll and shell edged bobeche, foliate chased and emb snuffer, all pcs fully marked, 10 troy oz ... 550.00

Charger, 11-3/4" d, George IV, London, 1826, Rebecca Emes and Edward Barnard, shaped edge, applied gadroon and shell border, engraved gartered heraldic device on rim, 29 troy oz 1,380.00

Coaster, 4-3/8" d, Edward VII, Birmingham, 1905, "W.H.H." maker's mark, round, inset to center with George III Irish ten pence bank tokens dated 1905, 4 troy oz, pr... 115.00

Coffeepot

11-1/2" l, 8-7/8" h, George III, London, 1806, Robert Hennell maker, partially reeded oblong body, fruitwood loop handle, oval trumpet foot, partially reeded lid, replaced finial, 35 troy oz............. 750.00

14-1/2" h, George III, London, 1767, William Grundy maker, baluster, spreading foot, scroll handle with ivory heat stops, serpentine spout with rocaille shell to base, flat leaf to spout, engraved monogram within foliate rococo-style cartouche, domed hinged lid with spiral reeded egg-shaped finial, 60 troy oz 5,750.00

Compote, 12-1/2" d, 7" h, Victorian, London, 1845, Benjamin Smith maker, bowl with shaped edge and vertical ribbing, everted rim with applied grapevine dec, tree-trunk form base with twining grapevine, 36 troy oz 1,150.00

Creamer, 2-7/8" h, William IV, London, 1831, Paul Storr, tapered cylindrical, short spout, scroll handle with shell terminal, applied stepped base, monogrammed, side mkd "Storr & Mortimer" 200.00

Creamer and Sugar, 4-1/2" h, George III, London, 1812, maker's mark rubbed, ovoid form, gadrooned rim, horizontal ribs to middle, reeding to lower portion of body, angular handles, 4 ball feet, 13 troy oz....... 320.00

Cup, 5-5/8" h, George III, London, 1800, Samuel Godbeheve, Edward Wigan and J. Bolt makers, baluster form, two handles, 4 drill holes in base, 11 troy oz.. 490.00

Demitasse Spoon, 5" l, George III, London, 1791, John Wren maker, bright cut engraved stem, fluted bowl, 3 troy oz, set of 6 .... 260.00

Dish Cross, 12" l, George III, London, 1772, "BD" maker's mark, (Burrage Davenport), pierced shell form feet and plate supports, burner with gadrooned rim, 15 troy oz 1,265.00

Egg Cup Frame, George III, London, 1800, Henry Nutting maker, reeded central handle, 4 ball feet, 6 associated Sheffield egg cups, 5 associated demitasse spoons, 18 troy oz 550.00

Entree Dish, cov, 12-1/8" l, 5-3/4" h, George IV, London, 1820, "BS" makers mark, lid modified with later band of foliate repousse and engraved with heraldic crest and monograms, base with gadroon and shell rim, removable leaf and shell handle, 67 troy oz 1,725.00

Epergne, 10-1/2" l, 11-3/4" h, George V, London, 1913, "GJ DF" maker's mark, central stem below navette-shaped reticulated basket with applied border, flanked by smaller removable baskets on scrolled arms, ovoid reticulated base with applied scroll and shell border, 4 scroll feet, 76 troy oz 6,325.00

Fish Server, 11-1/4" l, George III, London, 1770, attributed to John Neville, reticulated blade with scrolling foliage, stem end with shell, handle, engraved with gadrooned edge, central heraldic device, 4 troy oz 1,100.00

Goblet

6-1/2" h, George II, London, 1775, maker's mark partially obscured (attributed to Henry Greenway), beaded collar, tapered round funnel bowl, beaded trumpet foot, engraved coat of arms in roundel, 16 troy oz, pr... 1,955.00

7" h, George III, London, 1801, Daniel Pontifex maker, tapered ovoid bowl stamped with flat leaves to lower section, octagonal panel shaping above, plain wide rim, tapered stem with collar, ribbed trumpet foot, octagonal base, gilt washed int., 21 troy oz, pr... 1,150.00

Hot Water Kettle On Stand, 12" h, George III, London, 1807, John Emes maker, lid partially reeded with wood finial, pot with ovoid body partially reeded with gadrooned edging, on tapered circular foot, fluted tap, upright silver and wood handle, stand with gadrooned rim with burner and cover, flat leaf legs, four hairy paw feet with wooden ball supports, pot engraved with mottoed coat of arms, small heraldic device on pot lid, burner lid, and burner, 83 troy oz 2,100.00

Jug, 8" h, London, mid 18th C, mkd for Wm Shaw & Wm Preist makers, pear-shaped, stepped foot, serpentine scroll handle topped by flat leaf, short spout, engraved below spout with heraldic device, 26 troy oz 4,320.00

Jug, cov, 7-3/4" h, George III, London, 1769, "C. W." maker's mark, later Victorian adaptations, stamped bands flanking convex band at rim, ovoid body with twisted reeding and fluting to lower section, central cartouche flanked by C-scrolls, serpentine handle, domed foot, short spout, domed hinged lid with Victorian hallmarks, twisted reeding, fluting on urn finial, 18 troy oz 400.00

Mirror, 14-1/4" h, 10" d, Victorian, London, 1887, "JR SJ" makers, rect, curved top, reticulated with scrolls and flowers, mask center at base, grotesque beasts on either corner, beveled edge mirror, easel stand on back... 980.00

Muffineer

6-3/4" h, Brittania standard marks, London, 1894, Charles Stuart Harris maker, lid with three-tiered finial, cylindrical body with twisted banding, domed foot, 7 troy oz 290.00

8" h, Victorian, Birmingham, late 19th C, marks rubbed, lid with quatrefoil piercing, twisted ribbed finial, squat inverted baluster form, domed foot, one side engraved with heraldic device, 6 troy oz 400.00

8-1/2" h, Brittania standard marks, London, 1899, Charles Stuart Harris maker, tapered paneled lid with engraving, balusterpform finial, paneled baluster form, tiered foot, 14 troy oz 800.00

Presentation Cup, 9" h, George III, London, date letter parially rubbed, William Elliott maker, applied band of grapes and grape leaves below molded lip, cup reeded t lower section, stem with reeded collar, foliate carved serpentine handles, foot with flat leaf band, 43 troy oz ...1,610.00

Presentation Soup Tureen, cov, 17" l, 12-1/4" h, George IV, London, 1821, Rebecca Emes and Edward Barnard makers, ovoid body with

alt leaves, plain scroll and shell cartouche on one side, period presentation inscription on other side, foliate molded rim, handles topped by shells and terminating in lion's heads, four paw feet topped by flat leaves, cover with band of reeding, removable handled formed as two snakes twined with flat leaves, topped by fruit motif, 152 troy oz 8,625.00

Salt, open

1-3/4" h, George II, London, 1767, D & R Hennell makers, three shell-form legs with hoof feet, 3 troy oz 230.00

2-3/4" d, 2" h, George III, London, 1767, maker's mark rubbed, cased and emb with flowering vines, gadrooned rim, 3 scroll legs with shell feet topped by female masks, 8 troy oz, pr 260.00

Salver

5-5/8" l, George II, London, 1730, Gabriel Sleath maker, shaped molded border, four scroll feet, engraved center with heraldic device, 16 troy oz, pr 4,025.00

9-3/4" d, Edward VII, Sheffield, 1907, Harrison Bros. & Howson makers, round, molded border and gadroon and shell rim, raised on four scroll feet, center engraved with heraldic device, 15 troy oz ... 650.00

12-1/4" d, George III, London, 1762, attributed to Ebenezer Coker, shaped molded edge with reeded scroll and shell border, engraved center monogram within scroll and shell cartouche, 3 hairy ball and claw feet, each entwined with lion's tail, 30 troy oz 2,070.00

12-3/8" d, George II, London, 1783, John Tuite maker, shaped molded rim offset with shells, central engraved coat of arms in rococo cartouche, 4 scrolled leaf feet, 32 troy oz 2,185.00

16-1/4" d, George III, London, 1813, John Cotton & Thomas Head maker, beaded and ribbed border, four beaded and ribbed feet, center engraved with mottoed coat of arms, 64 troy oz... 3,750.00

17-1/4" d, London, 1946, Mappin & Webb makers, shaped edge with bead shell border, four scrolled feet, 60 troy oz 1,610.00

22-7/8" h, George II, London, 1750, Robert Abercomby maker, shaped edge, engraved with wide band of florals, fruits, shells, scrolls, and diapered cartouches, four paw feet topped by shells, engraved central Chinoiserie-style coat of arms, 156 troy oz 4,320.00

Sauce Boat, 7-3/8" l, 5" h, George III, London, 1763, no maker's mark, shaped edge, flying scroll handle, engraved initials on one side, 3 hoof feet topped by shells, 11 troy oz...................................... 550.00

Sauce Tureen, cov, 9-1/4" l, 5-1/2" h, George III, London, 1804, George Smith and Thomas Hayter makers, domed lid with urn finial, boat shaped body with ribbed rim, loop handles, pedestal foot, lid and body monogrammed, 33 troy oz, pr 2,760.00

Serving Spoon, 11-3/4" l, George III, William Eley and William Fearn, London, 1818, engraved crest, 3 oz, 6 dwt 175.00

Soup Tureen, cov, 14-1/2" l, 10-1/4" h, George III, London, 1819, William Elliott maker, gadrooned rim, acanthus handles, four paw feet terminating in shell and acanthus leaves, lid with two bands of gadrooning and ribbed removable handle, engraved coat of arms on body and lid, 136 troy oz.. 7,475.00

Standish, 11-3/8" l, 7-1/2" w, Edward VII, London, 1906, J. C. Vickery maker, rect, reeded border, two horizontal pen wells, two tapered inkwells with canted corners and hinged lids, central ovoid covered well, hinged lid fitted with eight-day clock, 4 ball and claw feet, some restoration needed, 32 troy oz 2,100.00

Sugar Bowl, 6" l, 5-3/8" h, Georgian, marks rubbed, beaded rim, ovoid body with ribbon-tied floral sprays and swags, roundels on each side, heraldic device, spiraled loop handles, trumpet foot with bands of bright cut engraving, 5 troy oz... 350.00

Sugar Tongs, Georgian, cast with shell, foliage, scrolls engraved with flowers, center vacant cartouche, 1 oz, 2 dwt 95.00

Sweetmeat Dish, 9-1/8" l, 5-5/8" w, 2-1/4" h, London, 1879, R & S Garrard maker, ovoid, flanked by male and female figure, auricular scroll and stylized shell handle, four periwinkle shell feet, 13 troy oz 1,495.00

Tablespoon, 8-3/4" l, George IV, London, 1826, William Eley, fiddle pattern, monogrammed, pr, 6 troy oz 200.00

Tankard, 7-3/4" h, George III, Newcastle, 1769, John Longlands I maker, tapered cylindrical form, plain body with engraved cartouche, serpentine handle with reticulated thumb-piece, gadrooned foot rim, slightly domed lid with gadrooned rim, engraved presentation inscription, lacquered, 26 troy oz.. 1,265.00

Tapersticks, pr, 4-1/4" h, George II, London, 1737, Jas. Gould maker, flattened knop, paneled step with ribbed shoulder, plain sconce, shaped stepped base, nozzles not present, 7 troy oz 1,035.00

Tazza, 7-3/4" d, 3-1/4" h, Edward VII, London, 1902, Charles Stuart Harris maker, body with gadrooned rim and stamped border of faces and Chinoiserie-style motifs, tapered stem, domed foot stamped with band of foliage dec, center monogrammed, 14 troy oz 385.00

Teapot
　5" h, William IV, London, 1837, Edward, Edward Jr., John and William Barnard, tapered ovoid, plain low foot, scroll ear handle, paneled serpentine spout, engraved to shoulder and edge of lid with diapered lozenges, scrolls, and flowerheads, flad lid with flattened ball finial, 15 troy oz 500.00
　5-3/4" h, Victorian, London, 1843, Edward, Edward Jr., John, and William Barnard, squat pear-shape, engraved upper portion with scrolls and cartouches, paneled serpentine spout, ear shaped handle, flush lid with melon finial, minor restoration, 22 troy oz 550.00
　6" h, 10-7/8" l, George III, London, 1798, Peter and Ann Bateman makers, paneled oval form, molded detailing, bands of bright-cut engraving to rim and base, serpentine spout and ear handle with ivory heat stops, domed lid with bright-cut engraving, urn shaped finial, 20 troy oz 865.00

Tea Set, assembled, 5-7/8" h teapot, George III, London, 1812, Crespin Fuller maker of teapot, maker's mark partially rubbed on all pieces, all with ovoid body and ball feet, angular handles and gadrooned rim on creamer and sugar, guilloche rim and ivory finial on teapot, 33 troy oz 920.00

Tea Service
　7-3/4" h teapot, George III, London, 1800, Peter, Ann, and William Bateman makers, ovoid teapot, helmet shaped cov creamer with angular handle, cov sugar with angular handles, all with partial vertical lobing, bands of bright cut engraving and engraved heraldic device, wooden pineapple finials, 33 troy oz 1,495.00
　9" h coffeepot, 16" h kettle on stand, George V, London, 1930, Crichton Bros. makers, coffee and teapots, kettle on stand, creamer, open sugar, cov sugar, all with ovoid body, arcaded and ribbed banding, teapot and coffeepot with wooden handles topped with silver flat leaves, lion's head roundels, reamer and sugar with curved handles terminating in lion's head roundels, 174 troy oz 2,990.00

Tea Urn, 15" h, London, 1778, maker's mark "I. R.," lid with tapered egg-shaped finial, beaded tape with ivory handle, beaded loop handles, four ball feet with stepped rect base and beaded edge, bright cut engraving throughout with husks, cartouches, and floral swags, 37 troy oz 2,100.00

Tray
　25" l, 16-1/4" w, George IV, London, 1822, "EB" makers mark, rect, gadrooned border, handles with shells and leaves, four paw feet flanked by floral roundels and stylized wings, engraved allover pattern of flowers and leaves, center with mottoed crest and later monogram, 120 troy oz.. 2,760.00
　25-1/2" l, 15-5/8" w, George III, London, 1817, "IM"makers mark, rect, gadrooned edge, handles terminating in stylized feathers, four gadrooned feet, engraved with wide band of florals, fruits, scrolls, and diapered cartouches, center with mottoed coat of arms, 104 troy oz, restoration 2,415.00
　28" l, 17-3/4" w, George III, London, 1802, Robert Garrand, oval, shaped edge, gadrooned border and handles, 108 troy oz ..3,220.00

Wine Coaster, 5-3/4" d, 2-3/4" h, Victorian, London, 1846, Joseph and John Angel makers, applied scroll and shell rim, reticulated sides, engraved to base with scrolls, shells, and central heraldic crest, pr 5,465.00

Irish

Fine examples of Irish silver are becoming popular with collectors.

Candlesticks, pr, George III/IV, Dublin, attributed to John Laughlin, Jr., larger gadrooned knob over gadrooned knob below partially vertically reeded stem with single horizontal beaded band, well with applied stylized wheat or grass fronds, domed gadrooned base, vertically

reeded sconce, removable nozzle with gadrooned rim, small heraldic crest engraved on foot and nozzle, 49 troy oz 7,475.00

Caudle Cup, cov, 7-1/4" h, Dublin, mid 18th C, mkd for John Hamilton, domed lid topped by ovoid finial, body with single molded band, crab-stock handles, lobed spreading foot, no date mark, 37 troy oz, pr 5,175.00

Cup, 4-7/8" h, mid 18th C, mkd for John Letabliere, tapered cylindrical body with leaf cut card work, band of foliate engraving, domed spreading foot, scroll handles topped with flat leaves, engraved on one side with cartouche, no date marks, 44 troy oz, pr......... 5,465.00

Salver, 6-1/2" l, George II/III, Dublin, William Townsend maker, shaped molded border, engraved center with heraldic crest in rococo cartouche, 3 pad feet with scroll legs, 8 troy oz 1,100.00

Snuffer Tray, George III, Dublin, 1798, William Doyle maker, octagonal boat shape, base with bright-cut engraved husk drops, heraldic crest within roundel flanked by leaves, sides reticulated with arcading, paterae, 4 troy oz 700.00

Scottish

Not to be outdone by their Irish and English neighbors, Scottish silversmiths also created fine objects.

Berry Spoon, Edinburgh, 1820, George Fenwick maker 75.00

Punch Ladle
　13-1/2" l, Edinburgh, 1789, maker's mark "CD," 6 troy oz..... 300.00
　14-1/2" l, Edinburgh, 1820, maker's mark "AH," ovoid bowl, twisted baleen handle, silver end cap 150.00

Sheffield, English

Sheffield Silver, or Old Sheffield Plate, has a fusion method of silver-plating that was used from the mid-18th century until the mid-1880s when the process of electroplating silver was introduced.

Sheffield plating was discovered in 1743 when Thomas Boulsover of Sheffield, England, accidentally fused silver and copper. The process consisted of sandwiching a heavy sheet of copper between two thin sheets of silver. The result was a plated sheet of silver which could be pressed or rolled to a desired thickness. All Sheffield articles are worked from these plated sheets.

Most of the silver-plated items found today marked "Sheffield" are not early Sheffield plate. They are later wares made in Sheffield, England.

Claret Jug, 11" h, cut glass body mounted at neck, hinged cover, baluster finial, multi-scroll foliate handle, c19435 .... 500.00

Soup Tureen, T. & J. Creswick, c1820, fluted bombé oval form, shell and acanthus scrolled feet, reeded bracket handles, domed lid, crested, 15-1/2" l, $1,600.

Domed Lid, 22" h, 11" l, engraved armorial whippet, oval handle, early 19th C..575.00

Plate, 9-3/4" d, circular, gadrooned rim, engraved Carlill crest, George III, price for pr 175.00

Platter and Meat Cover, 26" l oval tree platter, four ball feet, two wooden handles, gadrooned rim, armorials on both sides, dome cover with gadrooned rim, reeded handles, engraved armorials 2,750.00

Salver, 15-1/4" d, plated, shaped circular, three scroll and floral feet, chased field with scrolls and flowers centering monogrammed cartouche, shell and foliage rim 155.00

Serving Dish, 10-1/2" d, reservoir, handles.................................110.00

Vegetable Dish, cov, 13" l, plated, shaped rect, applied grapevine, scroll, and foliage handle, monogrammed 250.00

Wax Jack Bougie Box, 3-1/2" h, cylindrical, pierced dec, flat detachable top, reeded loop handle, snuffer attached by chain..........300.00

Wine Bottle Holder, 16" l, wooden base, vintage detail, ivory casters..275.00

Silver, Plated

Englishman G. R. and H. Elkington are given credit for being the first to use the electrolytic method of plating silver in 1838.

An electroplated-silver article is completely shaped and formed from a base metal and then coated with a thin layer of silver. In the late 19th century, the base metal was Britannia, an alloy of tin, copper, and antimony. Other bases are copper and brass. Today, the base is nickel silver.

In 1847, the electroplating process was introduced in America by Rogers Bros. of Hartford, Connecticut. By 1855 a number of firms were using the method to produce silver-plated items in large quantities.

The quality of the plating is important. Extensive polishing can cause the base metal to show through. The prices for plated-silver items are low, making them popular items with younger collectors.

Bun Warmer, 12-1/2" l, oval, cover chased with flowers and foliage, beaded rim, paw feet, liner and mazarine, 2 reeded handles ..275.00

Candelabra, pr, 12" h, Continental, 3-light, tapering stem issuing central urn-form candle-cup and two scrolling branches supporting wax pan and conforming candle-cup, oval foot with reeded border, vertical flutes 150.00

Candlesticks, pr, 14" h, English Regency-style, late 19th C, flat leaf socket, fluted standard, three monopodia supports offset with anthemion 550.00

Crumb Tray, mkd "P. S. Co. Sheffield NS 8435," $25.

Coffee Urn
    Continental, 19-1/2" h, vase form, body and lid fluted in sections, acanthus-capped handles, reeded spigot, sq pedestal base with ball feet 375.00
    Victorian, 16" h, baluster shape, repousse grapevines centering 2 vacant cartouches, 2 handles in form of branch applied with similar dec, circular base pierced with scrolls at internals on 4 scroll, foliate, and beaded supports, detachable cover, grapevine finial........125.00

Entree Dish, 11-1/2" l, oval, gadrooned rim, detachable foliage handles, monogrammed, American, pr..120.00

Epergne, 17-3/4" h, late 19th/early 20th C, lyre form standard supporting 2 scroll arms with round wirework baskets with cut glass liners, central navette shaped wirework basket with cut glass liner, oval wirework base, 4 fluted feet, rosing.......................................1,265.00

Fish Serving Set, 13-3/4" l knife, 10-1/2" l fork, English, late 19th C, carved reeded ivory handles, plated end caps emb with scrolls and birds, blades and tines engraved with leafy scrolls, fitted satin lined case..435.00

Hot Water Urn, Neoclassical style, 19th C, urn form body supported on 4 reeded monopodia topped by Adamesque urns with swags, quadripartite base with set in burner, 4 wooden ball feet, reeded spout with wooden tap carved as anthemion, 2 reeded loop handles with flat leaves on top and bottom, tapered lid with gadrooned shoulder below ovoid wood finial..690.00

Figure, 11-1/2" l, fighting roosters, naturalistically detailed, pr....120.00

Game Platter, 16" h, 26-1/2" l, English, late 19th C, well and three platter base with attached hot water pan, raised on four medallion-capped feet, associated domed cov with beaded bands and engraved wide border of entwined circlets, applied open handle surrounded by conforming engraved dec, body with engraved griffin.......................................700.00

Garniture, 6-1/4" h ftd compote with repousse floral and foliate bands, each side pc with conforming dec, Tiffany & Co. 350.00

Kettle On Stand, 15-1/2" h, circular, upper body engraved with scrolled foliage centering 2 cartouches engraved with armorials, leaf capped spout, flat hinged cover, nut finial, overhead fixed scroll and foliate handles, circular base with foliate apron, 4 scroll and foliate supports.............400.00

Tea Urn, 18-1/2" h, ovoid body engraved with flowers, diapers, reeded band at shoulder, two loop handles, sq base, detachable cover, baluster finial..400.00

Tray, 32" l, Victorian, oval, field engraved with floral and diaper medallions flanked by foliage with foliate garlands at intervals, beaded and geometrical design border and handles 350.00

Sheffield

English G. R. Elkington and H. Elkington are given credit for being the first to use the electrolytic method of plating silver in 1838.

Candlesticks, pr
    9" h, telescopic, circular base, gadrooned band rising to tapered cylindrical stem, vasiform scones, detachable bobeche with gadrooned rim, c1800 ....475.00
    24" h, ornate columns with composite capitals, pale blue blown glass hurricane shades with cut floral designs 425.00

Entree Dish
    11" x 8", shaped rect, gadrooned rim, detachable handle with gadroon dec..75.00
    14-1/2" l, shaped oval, grapevines applied at rim and cover, detachable branch form handle 100.00

Hot Water Urn, 22-3/4" h, early 19th C, Philip Ashberry & Sons makers, urn-form body with flat leaf engraving at base, wide central band of engraved anthemion, round domed base with beaded rim, trumpet foot with band of guillouche centered by flowerheads and accented with husks, angular handles terminating in flat leaves, anthemion handle on top, domed lid with flat leaf engraving and foliage baluster finial, inner sleeve 750.00

Sauceboat with Underplate, rim applied with grapevines 95.00

Soup Tureen, 16" l, 10-3/4" h, early 19th C, ovoid body with applied gadroon and shell border, two fluted handles with leaf terminals, four scroll and flat leaf feet, domed lid with reeded band, leaf-form finial, body and lid with let-in engraved heraldic device, fitted drop-in liner, restorations, rosing..1,725.00

Tankard, 5" h, Hy Wilkinson & Co makers, tapered cylindrical form, plain ear handle, gold washed int., fitted leather case, 10 troy oz 235.00

Tea and Coffee Service, baluster shaped coffeepot, 12-1/4" h kettle-on-stand, teapot, creamer, two handled open sugar, waste bowl, oval with canted corners, angular handles 425.00

SILVER DEPOSIT GLASS

History: Silver deposit glass was popular at the turn of the century. A simple electrical process was used to deposit a thin coating of silver on glass products. After the glass and a piece of silver were placed in a solution, an electric current was introduced which caused the silver to decompose, pass through the solution, and remain on those parts of the glass on which a pattern had been outlined.

Bowl, 10-1/2" d, cobalt blue ground, flowers and foliage, silver scalloped edge 85.00

Cologne Bottle, 3-3/8" h, clear ground, bulbous, floral and flowing leaf motif 165.00

Creamer, 2-3/4" h, clear ground, scrolling silver design................ 15.00

Decanter, 13-1/4" h, clear ground, Continental silver mounts, grape clusters, and leaves, dec, orig stopper...................... 90.00

Ice Tub, clear ground, floral and foliage dec, closed tab handles, matching sterling silver ice tongs 125.00

Perfume Bottle, 4-1/2" h, clear ground, vine and grape leaf dec .. 60.00

Sugar Shaker, clear ground, vine and grape leaf dec, SP top 65.00

SILVER OVERLAY

History: Silver overlay is silver applied directly to a finished glass or porcelain object. The overlay is cut and decorated, usually by engraving, prior to being molded around the object.

Glass usually is of high quality and is either crystal or colored. Lenox used silver overlay on some porcelain pieces. Most designs are from the Art Nouveau and Art Deco periods.

Reference: Lillian F. Potter, *Re-Introduction to Silver Overlay on Glass and Ceramics*, published by author, 1992.

Basket, 5-1/2" l, 6" h, deep cranberry body, allover floral and lattice design, sterling handle 600.00

Decanter, 11-1/2" h, molded, pinched oval bottle, surface bamboo dec overall, base disk imp "Yuan Shun/Sterling," faceted crystal hollow stopper 375.00

Flask, 5" h, clear bottle shaped body, scrolling hallmarked silver, hinged cov 275.00

Inkwell, 3-3/4" x 3", bright green ground, rose, scroll, and lattice overlay, matching cov, monogram..................... 650.00

Jug, 9" h, colorless glass, tapered baluster form, star-cut base, silver cased applied draw handle, overlay of twining grapes and grape vines, plain cartouche beneath spout, stylized cobweb overlay below, Alvin Mfg Co., late 19th/early 20th C.................. 1,380.00

Perfume Bottle

    4" h, bulbous, dark green glass, ornate silver overlay, floral and scroll dec, cased dec, monogrammed "CSE," pr 395.00

    4-1/4" h, squat baluster, colorless glass, large flowers and foliage overlay, central vacant cartouche 275.00

    5" h, baluster, elongated neck, colorless glass, scrolling foliage overlay, central monogrammed cartouche.................. 225.00

Tea Set, 8-3/4" h, Lenox porcelain body, Reed & Barton silver overlay, 3 pc set.. 325.00

Vase

    4" h, bronze, sterling floral and leaf overlay, Heintz, c1912, imp mark... 245.00

Whiskey Decanter, NYAC Travers Island Trophy, 1/24/14, 10-1/2" h, $145.

5-3/4" h, 3-3/4" d, bronze, overlaid sterling bird on branch, bronzed patina, stamped "HAMS" and "Patent," Heintz, shallow dent to shoulder 300.00

8" h, fan shape, floral silver overlay in geometric pattern, black opaque ground, mkd "Rockwell" and "no. 1371B" 260.00

8-1/4" h, colorless glass cylinder, flared to rim and foot, ruffled top edge, overlay of 2 large engraved roses, reticulated lozenge, Matthews Co., Newark, early 20th C 865.00

9-1/2" h, 3-1/2" d, bronze, cylindrical, overlaid sterling cyclamen, orig bronzed patina, stamped "HAMS" and "Patent," Heintz, shallow dent at rim an base...................... 400.00

12" h, 5" d, bronze, cylindrical, overlaid sterling daffodils, verdigris patina, stamped "HAMS" and "Patent," Heintz, minor restoration to patina behind flower...................... 1,000.00

SMITH BROS. GLASS

History: After establishing a decorating department at the Mount Washington Glass Works in 1871, Alfred and Harry Smith struck out on their own in 1875. Their New Bedford, Massachusetts, firm soon became known worldwide for its fine opalescent decorated wares, similar in style to those of Mount Washington.

Marks: Smith Bros. glass often is marked on the base with a red shield enclosing a rampant lion and the word "Trademark."

References: Kenneth Wilson, *American Glass 1760-1930*, 2 vols., Hudson Hills Press and The Toledo Museum of Art, 1994.

Reproduction Alert: Beware of examples marked "Smith Bros."

Biscuit Jar

    6-1/2" d, 9" h, realistic stalks of bearded wheat with raised gold highlights, cream body, melon ribbed body, metal fittings, lid sgd "S B 4402"..................................... 575.00

    7" d, 8-1/2" h, green and pastel brown tendrils of ivy wind around melon ribbed body, gold plated fittings, sgd "405" 885.00

Bowl

    6" d, 2-3/4" h, melon ribbed, two shades of gold prunus dec, beaded white rim 375.00

Salt and pepper shakers, hand painted herons, opaque white ground, 2 pc pewter top, 4-1/8" l, $90.

9" d, 4" h, melon ribbed, beige ground, pink Moss Rose dec, blue flowers, green leaves, white beaded rim 675.00

Bride's Bowl, 9-1/2" d, 3" h bowl, 16" h overall, opal glass bowl, painted ground, 2" band dec with cranes, fans, vases, and flowers, white and gray dec, fancy silver-plated holder sgd and numbered 2117 .... 1,450.00

Creamer and Sugar, 4" d, 3-3/4" h, shaded blue and beige ground, multicolored violet and leaves dec, fancy silverplated metalware.. 750.00

Humidor, 6-1/2" h, 4" d, cream ground, 8 blue pansies, melon-ribbed cov... 850.00

Juice Tumbler, blue, stork dec 50.00

Mustard Jar, cov, 2" h, ribbed, gold prunus dec, white ground ... 300.00

Plate, 7-3/4" d, Santa Maria, beige, brown, and pale orange ship ... 595.00

Rose Bowl

2-1/4" h, 3" d, cream ground, jeweled gold prunus dec, gold beaded top, sgd 285.00

4-1/4" h, 4" d, enameled pansy blossoms, row of raised dots on rim... 385.00

Sugar Shaker

5-3/4" h, pillar ribbed, white ground, pink wild rose and pale blue leaves, blue beaded top, orig cov fair 495.00

6" h, 2-1/2" d, cylindrical, vertical ribs, opaque white body, stylized dec of pink, blue, and gray summer blossoms, wispy stalks, pewter top... 575.00

Toothpick Holder

2" h, ribbed blank, purple and blue violets, beaded top.......... 285.00

2-1/4" h, barrel shape, opaque white body, swag of single petaled blossoms.. 265.00

2-1/4" h, pillar ribbed, white ground, pink wild rose and pale blue leaves, blue beaded top... 250.00

2-1/2" h Little Lobe, pale blue body, single petaled rose blossoms, raised blue dots on rim 245.00

Vase

5-1/4" h, 3-1/2" d, pinched-in, apricot ground, white wisteria dec, gold highlights, sgd 375.00

5-1/4" h, 4" d, triangular shape, pale yellow ground, white daisy-like flowers, sgd.. 425.00

5-1/2" h, petticoat shape, flared base, pink ground, multicolored foliage and herons, stamped mark on base, "Smith brothers- New Bedford, MA," pr 850.00

7" h, soft pink ground, inverted dec of white pond lily, blue-green and black leaves, brown stems, maroon trim, c1870, pr..... 375.00

7-1/4" h, 8" d, double canteen, pink rose sprays centered in 3 decorative reserves, lime-yellow ground, two restored enameled dots, small int. chip 325.00

8" h, conical shape, pink, white blossoms and hummingbird dec, script sgd, pr 225.00

8-1/2" h, double bulbed form, opal glass, repeating molded foliate panel at top, hp chrysanthemum blossoms and leaves, yellow, pink, brown, and green, cream ground, gold enamel highlights, wear to gilt, mold imperfection under neck 460.00

8-1/2" h, double bulbed form, repeating molded foliate and panel motifs at top, hp chrysanthemum blossoms and leaves, cream and green ground, stamped "Smith Brothers" trademark in red on base 1,150.00

10" h, 6" d, pillow, soft ground, purple wisteria, green, and gold leaves, slight roughage on base 925.00

10" h, 8" w, shaded rust, brown, yellow and gold ground, white apple blossoms, green leaves, and branches, painted beige int. 595.00

12-1/2" h, Verona, colorless ground, deep purple and white irises, gold trim, green leaves and stems, int. vertical ribs 550.00

SNOW BABIES

History: Snow babies, small bisque figurines spattered with ground porcelain that resembles snow, were made originally in Germany and marketed in the early 1900s. One theory about their origin is that German doll makers copied the designs from the traditional Christmas candies. While sales were modest at first, demand increased after the birth of Admiral Peary's daughter in Greenland in 1893 and her subsequent popularity as the "Snow Baby," so-named by the Eskimos.

Hertwig and Company, a German manufacturer of china doll heads and bisque figurines, was the first to make these small figures dressed in hooded snowsuits and posed in a variety of positions. They reached their greatest popularity between 1906 and 1910, when they were manufactured by a variety of German firms and imported by many American companies.

Reference: Mary Morrison, *Snow Babies, Santas, and Elves: Collecting Christmas Bisque Figures*, Schiffer Publishing, 1993.

Reproduction Alert: During the 1940s and as late as the 1970s, many inferior Japanese-made snow babies entered the market, some marked with an impressed "Japan," others with a paper label. Their crudely painted features, awkward poses, and coarser "snow" make them easy to distinguish from the original German examples. Since 1977, Dept. 56® has been marketing a line of products called The Original Snow Village.

Baby

In sleigh, sitting, both arms raised, reindeer in front.............. 150.00

Riding bear, red, white, and maroon, 2-7/8" h 150.00

Sitting, 2" 195.00

Sledding

Single baby pulled by huskies, 2-3/4" h 100.00

Three seated babies, bisque sled 165.00

Standing

Holding tennis racket, stamped "Germany".................... 115.00

Playing banjo, stamped "Germany"................................. 135.00

Waving 160.00

Bear

On four paws 100.00

Babies sledding, one pulling, one riding, 2-1/2" w, 1-1/2" h, $95.

Standing, 2-1/2" h 115.00
Elf, 1-1/2" h 70.00
Girl, seated on snowball, red skirt, arms raised 125.00
Ice Skaters, 2" h, boy and girl, pr 250.00
Sheep, 2" h 75.00
Snowman 65.00

SNUFF BOTTLES and BOXES

History: Tobacco usage spread from America to Europe to China during the 17th century. Europeans and Chinese preferred to grind the dried leaves into a powder and sniff it into their nostrils. The elegant Europeans carried their snuff in boxes and took a pinch with their finger tips. The Chinese upper class, because of their lengthy fingernails, found this inconvenient and devised a bottle with a fitted stopper and attached spoon. These utilitarian objects soon became objets d'art.

Snuff bottles and boxes were fashioned from precious and semi-precious stones, glass, porcelain and pottery, wood, metals, and ivory. Glass and transparent-stone bottles often were enhanced further with delicate hand paintings, some done on the interior of the bottle.

Collectors' Club: International Chinese Snuff Bottle Society, 2601 No Charles St, Baltimore, MD 21218.

Snuff Bottles

Agate, Chinese
Baluster, blue, carved and incised birds amid flowering branches, conforming stopper with floral finial, 3" h 175.00
Cameo, carved running horse 80.00
Carved, man rowing boat and pine trees 175.00
Ovoid, brown relief figure, honey ground, rose quartz stopper, 3" h 175.00
Amber, landscape and figures, caramel inclusions, conforming id, Chinese, late 19th C, 4" l 1,265.00
Celadon
Light jade, flattened ovoid short neck, 2-1/4" h 185.00
Mottled jade, gray and brown inclusions, dog mask and ring form handles, Qing dynasty, Chinese 400.00
Chrysoprase, flattened ovoid, light green, conforming stopper, 3" h 215.00

Cinnabar Lacquer, ovoid, continual scene of scholars and boys in a pavilion landscape, dark red, conforming stopper, 3-1/4" h 230.00
Cloisonné, auspicious symbols among clouds, yellow ground, lappet base border, ruyi head neck border, conforming stopper with chrysanthemum design, Qianlong 4 character mark 185.00
Coral, cylindrical, carved kylin, Chinese, 2-1/2" h 175.00
Enameled Glass, each side dec with deer beneath flowing trees, seal mark in red on base, 2-3/8" h 920.00
Famille Rose, porcelain, floral and scrolling foliate dec, blue ground, Qing dynasty, Chinese 80.00
Ivory, figural, 2 laughing, figures holding lily pad, base mkd with Qialong seal mark, Yongzheng seal mark, 3" h 1,840.00
Jade
Apple-green and celadon, silver mounted, Chinese 750.00
Black, flattened rect form, relief carved mountains, applied white jade figural grouping on one side, rose quartz stopper, wood base, 2-1/2" h 255.00
Green and brown, Buddha's hand form, relief flowering vine, conforming stopper, 3-1/2" h 175.00
Light green, disc form, enameled silver dec, conforming stopper, stand, 19th C, 2-3/4" h 230.00
White, flattened ovoid form, short cylindrical neck, raised double character mark on each side, 2-1/4" h 52.00
Lapis Lazuli, ovoid, relief carved, figures beneath tree, Chinese, 4" h 115.00
Malachite, carved, gourd, Chinese, 3" h 75.00
Opal, carved sage seated before gourd, Ch'ing Dynasty, 3" h ... 125.00
Overlay Glass, seven color, one side with floral designs in 2 archaic-form vases, reverse with immortal attending a crane and deer, bats flying above, each side with animal mask and ring handles, green, blue, mauve, coral, brown, and yellow, on white ground, 19th C 520.00
Peking Glass, Snowflake
Blue overlay, each side with prancing deer, head turned with a lingshi branch in mouth, 19th C, 2-1/2" h 490.00
Red overlay, flattened ovoid, one side with serpent and tortoise, other with frog sitting under lily pad, 2-1/4" h 1,265.00
Porcelain, Chinese
Blue and white
Floral dec, wood stand, Qianlong mark 450.00
Monkey dec, Qing dynasty 150.00
Red and white, dragon chasing flaming pearl of wisdom, Qing dynasty 200.00
White, molded fish, floral, foliate, and precious objects 275.00
Rose Quartz, flattened ovoid, relief carved leaves and vines, Chinese, 3" h 45.00
Stag Horn, flattened ovoid, one side with inset ivory panel with 2 laughing figures, reserve with inset panel with gold archaic script, 2-1/8" h 175.00

Peking Glass, pastel colored leaves, green jade top, 2-3/8" h, $220.

Turquoise, flattened body, high shoulder, relief carved auspicious symbol, agate stopper, wood stand, 2-3/8" h 165.00

Snuff Boxes

2-1/8" d, French
   Burl, gilded medallion under glass "Homage A Lafayette," tortoise shell lining, minor edge damage and repair 420.00
   Sterling silver, Paris, c1870, circular, sides with repousse borders of berried laurel, lid with circular band of garlands and scrolls, 1.68 troy oz 500.00
2-3/8" d, English, sterling silver, London, c1917-18, circular, floral border, central sunray motif, one hinge, 1.54 troy oz 315.00
2-3/4" l, Continental, early 19th C, silver mounted zebra shell, hinged lid chased with bird and dog among scrolls, central mounted hardstone 850.00
2-3/4" w, 2-1/4" d, 1" h, French, silver, 19th C, shaped oval, center oval portrait of gentleman flanked by military trophies within fueillage, hinged top, silver-gilt int. 325.00
2-7/8" l, French vermeil, jeweled, oval, sides repousse with scrolling foliage, lid with central basket of flowers, inlaid with seed pearls, sapphires, emeralds, and rubies within conforming repousse and jeweled border 450.00
2-7/8" x 2" x 5/8", French silver and niello, Paris, c1820, rect, sides and bottom with all over cross stitches, hinged lid depicting jousting match with castle and landscape in distance 300.00
3" d, French, sterling silver, c1880, circular, whole engine-turned, lid with border of berried leaves, 1.89 troy oz 275.00
3" l
   Continental, first half 19th C, mother-of-pearl, natural shell mounted at mid section with gilt metal 275.00
   Dutch, late 18th C, oval, silver mounted mother-of-pearl top and bottom, front engraved with basket of fruit and flowers over small cherub mask, scalloped border, stand-away hinge 425.00
3-1/8" l, Continental, .930 fine silver, oval, lid with repousse tavern scene, sides with scrolls, 2.3 troy oz 175.00
3-1/4" d, French
   Burl, relief carved scene of sea battle "Le Naufrage," machine tooled back 250.00
   Sterling silver, Keller, Paris, circular, beaded borders and central dec band on lid, central monogram, 4.43 troy oz 200.00
3-1/4" l, Continental, first half 19th C, mahogany and brass, rounded rect, brass caps at each end, hinged lid, small applied brass floral spray 175.00
3-1/2" d, papier-mâché, black litho, faded color, Reception of Genl. Lafayette at the City Hall New York, wear 525.00
3-3/4" x 1-1/8" x 7/8", Continental, silver, unidentified maker's marks, 18th C, later assayer's mark, rect, repousse border of scrolling foliage and flowers, lid with relief of putti jousting match, 2.65 troy oz 550.00
3-7/8" l, Continental silver and niello, c1880, unmarked, rect, rounded corners, allover matrix pattern 300.00
3-7/8" l, Continental silver inlaid ebonized wood, rounded rect, each end with reeded border, allover inlaid silver motif, lid with central elliptical scrolling vine and dec border, c1800 .... 650.00
4-3/4" x 1-5/8" x 7/8", Continental, .800 fine silver, early 19th C, rect, sides with repousse of foliate swags, lid with scene depicting baby baccante playing flute and lyre while others harvest grapes, 4.13 troy oz 450.00

SOAPSTONE

History: The mineral steatite, known as soapstone because of its greasy feel, has been used for carving figural groups and designs by the Chinese and others. Utilitarian pieces also were made. Soapstone pieces were very popular during the Victorian era.

Reference: *Soapstone,* L-W Book Sales, 1995.

Bookends, pr, 5" h, carved, block form, fu lion resting on top, Chinese 300.00

Candlesticks, pr, red tones, carved flowers and vases, 5-1/8" h, $85.

Candlesticks, pr, 5-1/8" h, red tones, flowers and foliage 85.00
Figure
   3-1/2" x 3-1/4", geisha, kneeling, Chinese, c1880 .... 125.00
   6-3/4" h, carved bird in flowering tree 50.00
   7" h, 7-1/2" w, seated Buddha 125.00
   8-1/2" h, carved loon, green, sgd "Pauloosie" 315.00
Hot Plate, 16" l, 8-1/2" w 75.00
Plaque, 9-1/2" h, birds, trees, flowers, and rocks 125.00
Sculpture, 10-1/4" h, 4-1/2" w, kneeling nude young woman, Canadian 95.00
Sealing Stamp, carved dec
   5" h, 1" d, curved scroll 95.00
   5-3/4" h, 2" d, fu dog on pediment, Oriental, c1900 .... 110.00
Toothpick Holder, 2 containers with carved birds, animals, and leaves 85.00

SOUVENIR and COMMEMORATIVE CHINA and GLASS

History: Souvenir, commemorative, and historical china and glass includes those items produced to celebrate special events, places, and people.

China plates made by Rowland and Marcellus and Wedgwood are particularly favored by collectors. Rowland and Marcellus, Staffordshire, England, made a series of blue-and-white historic plates with a wide rolled edge. Scenes from the Philadelphia Centennial in 1876 through the 1939 New York World's Fair are depicted. In 1910, Wedgwood collaborated with Jones, McDuffee and Stratton to produce a series of historic dessert-sized plates showing scenes of places throughout the United States.

Many localities issued plates, mugs, glasses, etc., for anniversary celebrations or to honor a local historical event. These items seem to have greater value when sold in the region in which they originated.

Commemorative glass includes several patterns of pressed glass which celebrate persons or events. Historical glass includes campaign and memorial items.

References: Pamel E. Apkarian-Russell, *A Collector's Guide to Salem Witchcraft & Souvenirs*, Schiffer Publishing, 1998; Monica Lynn Clements and Patricia Rosser Clements, *Popular Souvenir Plates*, Schiffer Publications, 1998; Bessie M. Lindsey, *American Historical Glass*, Charles E. Tuttle Company, 1967; David Weingarten and Margaret Majua, *Monumental Miniatures*, Antique Trader Books, 1998; Lawrence W. Williams, *Collector's Guide To Souvenir China*, Collector Books, 1997.

Periodicals: *Antique Souvenir Collectors News*, Box 562, Great Barrington, MA 01230; *Souvenir Building Collector*, 25 Falls Rd, Roxbury, CT 06783.

Collectors' Clubs: Souvenir Building Collectors Society, P.O. Box 70, Nellysford, VA 22958; Statue of Liberty Collectors' Club, 26601 Bernwood Rd, Cleveland, OH 44122.

Additional Listings: Cup Plates; Pressed Glass; Political Items; Staffordshire, Historical. Also see *Warman's Americana & Collectibles* for more examples.

Bell, 6-1/2" h, Elkhorn Fair, 1913, Button Arches pattern, ruby staining,
  clear paneled handle 75.00
Bottle, Columbus, oval, lay down, metal screw top.....................350.00
Bust, Gillinder
  Lincoln, frosted 325.00
  Napoleon, frosted and clear 295.00
  Shakespeare, frosted 150.00
Creamer
  New Academy, Truro, multicolored image on white medallion,
    cobalt blue ground, gold and white dec 30.00
  Wadsworth Atheneum, Hartford, CT, multicolored image on white
    medallion, lustered ground, 2" h, mkd "Wheelock China,
    Austria" 18.00
Cup, Entrance to Soldier's Home, Leavenworth, Kansas, multicolored,
  beaded dec, 2-1/2" h, mkd "Germany," slight wear to gold dec 18.00
Cup and Saucer
  Niagara Falls, cobalt blue ground, gold trim, 1-1/4" h x 1-3/4" d, 3-1/2" d
    saucer, scene of falls on saucer, mkd "Made in Japan," matching
    wooden display stand 20.00
  Souvenir of Edina, Missouri, white ground, rose dec, gold trim, 2-1/2" h
    x 3-3/4" w cup, 5-1/2" w cup, mkd "Japan" 20.00
  Souvenir of Rock City, Lookout Mountain, TN, 1-3/4" h x 1-3/4" w
    cup, 3-3/4" d saucer, mkd "Made in Japan" 12.00
  Washington and Lafayette, transfer print portraits on cup of George
    Washington and Lafayette, saucer with portrait entitled "Washing-
    ton His Country's Father," 1-3/4" h, creamware, England, early
    19th C 490.00
Demitasse Cup and Saucer
  My Old Kentucky Home, 2" h x 2" w cup, 4" d saucer, mkd "Hand-
    painted, Made in Japan, NICO" 15.00
  Souvenir of Chicago, Ill, Victorian man and woman on inside of
    cup, 2" h x 2-1/2" w cup, gold trim, mkd "Crest O Gold, Sabin,
    Warranted 22K"..17.50
Dish
  Beauvoir House, Jefferson Davis House, Biloxi, MS, 3-1/4" d, mkd
    "Made by Adams, England for the Jefferson Davis Shrine"..20.00
  DeShong Memorial Art Gallery, Lester, PA, yellow luster ground, 3-
    3/4" x 3-1/4", mkd "Made in Germany," wear to lettering and gold
    trim 12.00
Dish, cov, Remember the Maine, green opaque glass 135.00
Goblet
  G.A.R., 1887, 21st Encampment.......................................100.00
  Mother, Ruby Thumbprint pattern.....................................35.00
Mug
  Market Place and Town Hall, Preston, photos on front and back,
    pink luster ground, dated 1894, 3-1/2" h............................35.00

Plate, Admiral Dewey, green transfer, mkd "Semi-Vitreous/Canton China," 8-1/4" d, $20.

  Ross Castle, Killarney, Ireland, orange luster ground, dec handle,
    2-1/2" h, mkd "G. H. O., Austria"..................................25.00
Paperweight
  Moses in Bulrushes, frosted center 145.00
  Plymouth Rock, clear...95.00
  Ruth the Cleaner, frosted...125.00
  Washington, George, round, frosted center 295.00
Pitcher, 10-1/2" h, Trans-Atlantic Cable, ironstone, cable form
  inscribed "To God in the highest, on earth peace, good will towards
  men, Europe and America are united by telegraph," England, 19th C,
  cracks and chips to base..345.00
Plate
  Atlantic City, NJ, Rowland and Marcellus, 10-1/2" d.................50.00
  Florida, Saint Augustine, Vernon Kilns, mkd "Designed exclusively
    for J. Carver Harris" 20.00
  Hogg, James Stephen, first native born governor of Texas, brown
    print, Vernon Kilns, mkd "Designed for Daughters of the Republic
    of Texas" 25.00
  Idaho, state seal, Vernon Kilns.....................................20.00
  Marietta College 125th Anniversary, 1960, Wedgwood..........25.00
  Nebraska, University of Nebraska, Vernon Kilns....................30.00
  Oklahoma, Agricultural and Mechanical College, Vernon Kilns, mkd
    "Designed especially for Creech's Stillwater, Oklahoma" 32.00
  Oklahoma, Heart of the Great Southwest, state seal, Vernon
    Kilns 20.00
  President Nixon 15.00
  Sulphur Springs, Delaware, OH, light blue and black transfer, Stafford-
    shire, NY retailer's label, 10-1/2" d, chip on table ring.............200.00
  Texas, Southwest Methodist University, Dallas, Vernon Kilns, mkd
    "Made exclusively for Titche-Goettinger Co.".......................35.00
  University of Chicago 20.00
  Washington, Bellingham, green print, Vernon Kilns 50.00
Tile, 4" d, Detroit Women's League, multicolored irid glass........135.00
Tumbler, etched
  Lord's Prayer 15.00
  Niagara Falls, Prospect Point, gold rim 20.00
  Ten Commandments 15.00
  Whittier birthplace, waisted, tall.................................60.00

SOUVENIR and COMMEMORATIVE SPOONS

History: Souvenir and commemorative spoons have been issued for hundreds of years. Early American silversmiths engraved presentation spoons to honor historical personages or mark key events.

In 1881, Myron Kinsley patented a Niagara Falls spoon, and in 1884 Michael Gibney patented a new flatware design. M. W. Galt, Washington, D.C., issued commemorative spoons for George and Martha Washington in 1889. From these beginnings a collecting craze for souvenir and commemorative spoons developed in the late 19th and early 20th centuries.

References: Wayne Bednersch, *Collectible Souvenir Spoons: Identification and Values*, Collector Books, 1998; George B. James, *Souvenir Spoons* (1891), reprinted with 1996 price guide by Bill Boyd (7408 Englewood Lane, Raytown, MO 64133), 1996; Dorothy T. Rainwater and Donna H. Fegler, *American Spoons*, Schiffer Publishing, 1990; ——, *Spoons from around the World*, Schiffer Publishing, 1992; *Sterling Silver, Silverplate, and Souvenir Spoons with Prices*, revised ed., L-W Book Sales, 1987, 1994 value update.

Collectors' Clubs: American Spoon Collectors, 7408 Englewood Lane, Raytown, MO 64133; Dallas Souvenir Spoon Collectors Club, 9748 Broken Bow Road, Dallas, TX 75238; Northeastern Spoon Collectors Guild, 8200 Boulevard East, North Bergen, NJ 07047-6039; Southern California Souvenir Spoon Collectors Club, 3832 Denwood Ave., Los Alamitos, CA 90720; The Scoop Club, 84 Oak Ave., Shelton, CT 06484; Washington State Spoon Collectors, 1992 S. Elger Bay Road, Box 151, Stanwood, WA 98292.

Additional Listings: See *Warman's Americana & Collectibles* for more examples.

Adams, John, President, mkd "Rogers Silverplate," 6" l 10.00
Bingham Canyon, Utah, copper mine, mkd "Klephs Arts Copper Mine," copper, 5" l 12.00
Boulder, CO, name in bowl, Indian head handle.......................... 40.00
B. P. O. E. Elks #896, mkd "Reed & Barton Klitzner RI," silverplate, 4-1/2" l 15.00
Cawston Ostrich Farms, mkd "Sterling," 3-1/4" l.......................... 15.00
Denver, CO, sterling, gold washed bowl, acid etched pack mule, stem-end topped with winch with handle that turns, applied pick and shovel, stem entwined with rope, ending in bucket, opposed by modeled rock, 1 troy oz, late 19th C 85.00
Dodge City, KS, Boot Hill, mkd "Sterling," 4-1/4" l.......................... 17.50
Fort Dearborn, 1803-1857, mkd "Sterling, Hyman Berg," 6" l 20.00
Golden Gate Bridge, San Francisco, CA, mkd "Holland 90""and hallmark, 5" l 15.00
Gondola, mkd "Italy" on back of bowl... 35.00
Grand Army of the Republic, engraved bowl 70.00

New Orleans, LA, Canal Street, sterling silver, 5-3/8" l, $20.

King Cotton 45.00
Memorial Arch, Brooklyn, NY, round oak stove........................... 40.00
Palm Springs, Aerial Tramway, SP, John Brown, mkd "Antico" .. 100.00
Philadelphia, Independence Hall in bowl, SS 45.00
Portland, OR, SS 40.00
Prophet, veiled 135.00
Richmond, MO, SS 30.00
Rip Van Winkle.. 30.00
Rolex Bucherer, reclining lion in bowl, mkd "Bucherer of Switzerland," 4-1/4" l 12.00
Royal Canadian Mounted Police, "Victoria, British Columbia" in bowl, mkd "Made in Holland," 4-1/2" l... 30.00
Salem, MA, witch handle 45.00
San Antonia Hemisphere, World's Fair, 1968, applied emblem, chrome, 2-1/2" l 10.00
Seattle World's Fair, mkd "Sterling, 1961, Century 21 Exposition, Inc.," 6" l 42.00
SS Momus, Westfield Pattern, Meridan Britannia, 1903, back engraved "L. P. Co.," 6" l 10.00
St. Pauls, The Tower, Houses of Parliament, West Minister, each mkd "L. E. P. A1" on back, set of 4 in orig box 42.00
Thousand Islands, fish handle, engraved bowl, SS, Watson........ 45.00
Timberline Lodge, OR, mkd "Sterling," 5-1/2" l 32.00
Vista House, Columbia River, OR, detailed handle, mkd "Sterling" ... 32.00
Windmill, detailed curved handle, movable blades on figural windmill, hallmarked.. 38.00

SPANGLED GLASS

History: Spangled glass is a blown or blown-molded variegated art glass, similar to spatter glass, with the addition of flakes of mica or metallic aventurine. Many pieces are cased with a white or clear layer of glass. Spangled glass was developed in the late 19th century and still is being manufactured.

Originally, spangled glass was attributed only to the Vasa Murrhina Art Glass Company of Hartford, Connecticut, which distributed the glass for Dr. Flower of the Cape Cod Glassworks, Sandwich, Massachusetts. However, research has shown that many companies in Europe, England, and the United States made spangled glass, and attributing a piece to a specific source is very difficult.

Basket
7" h, 6" l, ruffled edge, white int., deep apricot with spangled gold, applied crystal loop handle, slight flake 225.00

Pitcher, white opalescent swirls with mica flakes, applied reeded handle, 6-3/4" h, $120.

9" h, lobed body, pink shading to white, mica flecks, applied clear handle 175.00
Beverage Set, bulbous pitcher, 6 matching tumblers, rubena, opalescent mottling, silver flecks, attributed to Sandwich, c1850-60 .. 250.00
Bride's Bowl, 10-3/8" d, multicolored, ruby, cranberry, and green, ivory-yellow ground, silver flecks 120.00
Candlesticks, pr, 8-1/8" h, pink and whit spatter, green aventurine flecks, cased white int. 115.00
Creamer, 3-1/4" d, 4-3/4" h, bulbous, molded swirled ribs, cylindrical neck, pinched spout, blue ground, swirled mica flecks, applied clear reeded handle 225.00
Cruet, Leaf Mold pattern, cranberry, mica flakes, white casing, Northwood 450.00
Ewer, 11" h, clear, cased pink, mica flecks, twisted applied handle 125.00
Pitcher, 7-1/2" h, bulbous, 4 sided top, apricot, gold mica flecks form diamond pattern, white casing, pontil 175.00
Rose Bowl, 3-3/8" d, 3-1/2" h, 8 crimp top, cased deep rose, heavy mica coral like dec, white int. 115.00
Salt Shaker, cranberry, cased white int., molded leaf design, Hobbs, c1890 .... 125.00
Sugar Shaker, cranberry, mica flakes, white casing, Northwood 115.00
Toothpick Holder, butterscotch, gold mica flecks, white lining 175.00
Tumbler, 3-3/4" h, pink, gold, and brown spatter, mica flecks, white lining 90.00
Vase, 4-3/4" h, 4" d, amethyst ground, collared scalloped top, goldstone flakes around body 145.00

SPATTER GLASS

History: Spatter glass is a variegated blown or blown-molded art glass. It originally was called "End-of-Day" glass, based on the assumption that it was made from batches of glass leftover at the end of the day. However, spatter glass was found to be a standard production item for many glass factories.

Spatter glass was developed at the end of the 19th century and is still being produced in the United States and Europe.

References: William Heacock, James Measell and Berry Wiggins, *Harry Northwood*, Antique Publications, 1990.

Flask, opaque white ground, blue spatter, 7-5/8" l, $150. Photo courtesy of Garth's Auctions.

Reproduction Alert: Many modern examples come from the area previously called Czechoslovakia.

Basket
6-1/2" h, 6-1/4" l, 5" w, rect, maroon, brown, yellow, blue, red, green spatter, white int. lining, clear thorn loop handle, tightly crimped edge with two rows of hobnails 250.00
7-1/2" h, 5" w, triangular form, bright pink and yellow spatter, white ground, clear twisted thorn handle, ruffled edge, c1890 ..... 225.00
7-1/2" h, 6" l, brown and jade green spatter, white ground, thorn handle, ruffled star shaped edge, c1890 .... 275.00
Bowl, 8-1/2" d, 4-1/4" h, Le Gras, Tigre, cranberry int., spattered cream opaque with goldstone, amber glass applied wishbone feet.... 220.00
Candlestick, 7-1/2" h, yellow, red, and white streaks, clear overlay, vertical swirled molding, smooth base, flanged socket 60.00
Cologne Bottle, 8-1/2" h, etched adv "Rich Secker Sweet Cologne, New York," applied clear handles 65.00
Creamer, 4-3/4" h, pink and white, applied clear handle, Northwood 50.00
Darning Egg, multicolored, attributed to Sandwich Glass 125.00
Ewer, cranberry spatter, applied clear handle 65.00
Finger Bowl and Underplate, 6" d, 3-1/4" d, tortoiseshell, ruffled 275.00
Jack-In-The-Pulpit, 5" h, 3-1/2" d, Vasa Murrhina, deep pink int., clear ruffled top 115.00
Rose Bowl, Leaf Mold, white mica spatter 185.00
Salt, 3" l, maroon and pink, white spatter, applied clear feet and handle 125.00
Sugar Shaker, Leaf Umbrella pattern, cranberry 495.00
Tumbler, 3-3/4"h, emb Swirl pattern, white, maroon, pink, yellow, and green, white int. 65.00
Vase
7" h, 4-1/2" d, golden yellow and white, enameled bird and flowers, applied clear handles, colored enamel dec 180.00
11" h, 6-1/2" d, sapphire blue ground, blue spatter, ruffled top with colorless edging, pr 450.00
Watch Holder, 3-3/4" x 4-1/4" dish, ruffled rim, blue spatter, 7" h ormolu metal watch holder 175.00

SPATTERWARE

History: Spatterware generally was made of common earthenware, although occasionally creamware was used. The earliest English examples were made about 1780. The peak period of production was from 1810 to 1840. Firms known to have made spatterware are Adams, Barlow, and Harvey and Cotton.

The amount of spatter decoration varies from piece to piece. Some objects simply have decorated borders. These often were decorated with a brush, requiring several hundred touches per square inch to achieve the spatter effect. Other pieces have the entire surface covered with spatter.

Marks: Marked pieces are rare.

References: Susan and Al Bagdade, *Warman's English & Continental Pottery & Porcelain*, 3rd Edition, Krause Publications, 1998; Kevin McConnell, *Spongeware and Spatterware*, Schiffer Publishing, 1990.

Museum: Henry Ford Museum, Dearborn, MI.

Reproduction Alert: Cybis spatter is an increasingly collectible ware in its own right. The pieces, made by the Polishman Boleslaw Cybis in the 1940s, have an Adams-type peafowl design. Many contemporary craftsmen also are reproducing spatterware.

Notes: Collectors today focus on the patterns—Cannon, Castle, Fort, Peafowl, Rainbow, Rose, Thistle, Schoolhouse, etc. The decoration on flatware is in the center of the piece; on hollow ware it occurs on both sides.

Aesthetics and the color of spatter are key to determining value. Blue and red are the most common colors; green, purple, and brown are in a middle group; black and yellow are scarce.

Like any soft paste, spatterware is easily broken or chipped. Prices in this listing are for pieces in very good to mint condition.

Creamer, 4-3/8" h, Rainbow, black and brown, wear and stains, tip of spout repaired 440.00
Cup and Saucer, handleless
    Four Petal Flower, red, blue, green, and black four petal flower, stains in cup, hairline and chip 300.00
    Hollyberry, red, green, and black, blue spatter, molded panels, very minor pinpoints 260.00
    Peafowl
        Blue spatter, red, blue, green, and black peafowl, chips on saucer 165.00
        Red spatter, blue, yellow, green, and black peafowl, mismatched, hairline in saucer 150.00
        Red spatter, red, blue, green, and black peafowl, imp "Adams," cup has edge wear, flaking repair on foot 110.00
    Rainbow, green and purple, rim repair 55.00
    Star, red, green, and yellow, blue spatter, minor damage, light overall stain 330.00
    Tulip, red and green, purple spatter 525.00
Dish, 6-3/4" l, oblong octagonal, Rose, red, green, and black rose dec, purple spatter, repair 165.00
Miniature
    Cup and Saucer, Rainbow, blue and purple, repair to saucer 315.00
    Jug, 3-1/4" h, blue and white sponge spatter 1,015.00
    Teapot, cov, 5-3/8" h, design spatter, red and white, minor stains 275.00
    Tea set, 4-1/4" h teapot, creamer, sugar, six cups and saucers, blue spatter, small chips, 9 pcs 650.00
Mug
    Blue, wear, stains, flakes on rim, 3-7/8" h 45.00
    Green stick spatter, red stripes, crow's foot 90.00
    Maroon and green, 2-3/4" h 250.00
Pitcher
    7" h, leaf handle, blue, minor wear, glaze flake on handle 150.00
    15-3/4" l, Peafowl, green, yellow, blue, and black peafowl, red spatter, stains, short hairlines, filled-in back rim chip 965.00
Plate
    6-1/4" d, Peafowl, red, yellow-ochre, green, and black, blue spatter, short hairline and stains 330.00
    7" d, Rainbow, red and blue, small edge damage 165.00
    7-1/4" d, Tulip, blue, red, green, and black, blue spatter, wear, stains, crazing, small rim chips 385.00
    8-1/4" d, Thistle, red and green, red spatter, red touched up on flower 140.00
    8-1/2" d
        Castle, brown, wear and crazing 275.00
        Peafowl, blue, green, yellow, and black, red spatter, light stains and minor edge chips 315.00
        Pomegranate, red, blue, green, and black, blue spatter, wear and rim chips 385.00
        Red, stains and crazing 75.00
        Rose, red, green, blue, and black rose, blue design spatter border 275.00
        Rose, red, green, blue, and black rose, green design spatter border, red stripes, ... 310.00
    8-5/8" d, Holly, red and green, minor stains 100.00
    8-7/8" d, Tulip, red, green, yellow, and black, blue spatter 385.00

Plate, Fort pattern, blue spatter, 9-1/2" d, $325.

    9" d, Tulip, red spatter border, red, green, and black, stains, small flakes, short hairline 250.00
    9-1/8" d, Peafowl, red, blue, green, yellow, and black, red spatter, light stains 630.00
    9-1/4" d, brown rabbit transfer, yellow stick spatter, gaudy red, blue, and green floral border 385.00
    9-3/8" d, gaudy floral dec, red, blue, and green, minor wear and scratches, minor glaze wear on edge 220.00
    10-1/8" d, black rabbit transfer rim, yellow and green stick spatter, gaudy red, blue, and green floral center, stains 385.00
Platter
    12-3/8" l, Columbine, green, purple, red, blue, and black, red border, stains 550.00
    13-5/8" l, Rainbow, blue and purple, oval bull's eye center, wear, stains, poorly executed edge repair 615.00
Saucer, Peafowl, red, blue, yellow-ochre, and black, red spatter 275.00
Soup Plate
    10-1/2" d, Columbine, green, purple, red, blue, and black flower, red spatter, stains 330.00
    10-3/4" d, gaudy stick spatter, red, blue, green, and yellow, floral design center, zigzag spatter border with stripes, mkd "Nimy, Made in Belgium," 3 pc set 185.00
Sugar, cov
    4-3/8" h, Rainbow, red and green, rim hairline 250.00
    4-1/2" h, Tulip, blue, red, green, and black, married lid, yellowed repairs 165.00
    4-5/8" h, Peafowl, blue, red, yellow-ochre, and black, stains, small chips on lid, rim repaired 135.00
    7-3/4" h, Peafowl, blue, green, red, and black, red spatter, paneled body, finial and rim poorly repaired 165.00
    8" h, Peafowl, red, dark yellow ochre, green, and black, blue spatter, octagonal body, mismatched lid repaired, small flakes on base 110.00
Teapot, cov
    6" h, Tree, green and black tree design, blue spatter, molded flower finial and handle, minor stains 330.00
    9-1/4" h, Hollyberry, red, green, and black, blue spatter, molded panels, minor chips, stains, heavily repaired lid 525.00
Waste Bowl, 5-3/8" d, Rainbow, red, blue, and green, hairlines, stains, and chips 150.00

SPONGEWARE

History: Spongeware is a specific type of decoration, not a type of pottery or glaze.

Spongeware decoration is found on many kinds of pottery bodies—ironstone, redware, stoneware, yellowware, etc. It was made in both England and the United States. Pieces were marked after 1815, and production extended into the 1880s.

Decoration is varied. On some pieces the sponging is minimal with the white underglaze dominant. Other pieces appear to be solidly sponged on both sides. Pieces made between 1840 and 1860 have circular or horizontally streaked sponging.

Blue and white are the most common colors, but browns, greens, ochres, and a greenish blue also were used. The greenish blue results from blue sponging with a pale yellow overglaze. A red overglaze produces a black or navy color. Blue and red were used on English creamware and American earthenware of the 1880s. Other spongeware colors include gray, grayish green, red, dark green on stark white, dark green on mellow yellow, and purple.

References: Susan and Al Bagdade, *Warman's American Pottery and Porcelain*, Wallace-Homestead, 1994; ——, *Warman's English & Continental Pottery & Porcelain*, 3rd Edition, Krause Publications, 1998; William C. Ketchum, Jr., *American Pottery and Porcelain*, Avon Books, 1994; Kevin McConnell, *Spongeware and Spatterware*, Schiffer Publishing, 1990.

Bowl, 7" d, fluted, brown and blue sponge, cream ground............ 60.00
Butter Crock
    4-5/8" d, 3" h, blue and white, back labeled "Village Farm Dairy," chips, hairlines, crazing 300.00

Pitcher, cobalt blue and tan, fluted top, 8" h, $220.

    9" d, 6" h, blue and white.. 300.00
Carpet Ball, 3-1/4" d
    Brown 85.00
    Green... 75.00
    Red and white plaid 90.00
Creamer, 3" h, green, blue and cream 100.00
Cup and Saucer, blue flower dec on cup 60.00
Dish, 6-1/2" x 8-1/2", blue and white, serpentine rim 200.00
Marble, 2" d, gray, blue sponge, late 19th C 220.00
Milk Pitcher, 7-1/2" h, black sponge, white ground 185.00
Miniature
    Bowl, cov, 3-1/4" d, blue and white sponge spatter, wooden handle and wire bail, hairline and chips... 475.00
    Pitcher, 3" h, cabin, teepee and bust of Harrison, two tone gray-white and blue dec... 300.00
    Sugar Bowl, 4-7/8" h, blue and white, paneled body, crazing, stains, mismatched lid 95.00
    Teapot, 4-1/8" h, blue and white dec, minor chips................. 850.00
Mush Cup and Saucer, blue and white, worn gilt trim, slight hairline in cup base... 85.00
Pitcher
    7-3/8" h, blue and white dec, minor chips on spout and rim 110.00
    8-1/4" h, blue and white dec, blue stripes............................. 225.00
    10" h, barrel shape, green, gold, and brown sponge............. 110.00
Plate, 9-1/2" d, red, green, and black central flower dec, red and green sponged border 190.00
Platter, 13-1/4" l, octagonal, central red and blue foliate chain, blue band border, cream ground, imp factory mark, Elsmore & Foster, Tunstall, 19th C 115.00
Sugar Bowl, cov, 4" h, floral reserve, brown sponge, English, 19th C... 95.00
Umbrella Stand, 21" h, American, 19th C 600.00
Wash Bowl, 14" d, 4-3/4" h, blue and white 150.00

SPORTS CARDS

History: Baseball cards were first printed in the late 19th century. By 1900, the most common cards, known as "T" cards, were those made by tobacco companies such as American Tobacco Co. The majority of the tobacco-related cards were produced between 1909 and 1915. During the 1920s, American Caramel, National Caramel, and York Caramel candy companies issued cards identified in lists as "E" cards.

During the 1930s, Goudey Gum Co. of Boston (from 1933 to 1941) and Gum Inc. (in 1939) were prime producers of baseball cards. Following World War II, Bowman Gum of Philadelphia (B.G.H.L.I.), the successor to Gum, Inc., lead the way. Topps, Inc. (T.C.G.) of Brooklyn, New York, followed. Topps bought Bowman in 1956 and enjoyed almost a monopoly in card production until 1981.

In 1981, Topps was challenged by Fleer of Philadelphia and Donruss of Memphis. All three companies annually produce sets numbering 600 cards or more.

Football cards have been printed since the 1890s. However, it was not until 1933 that the first bubble gum football card appeared in the Goudey Sport Kings set. In 1935 National Chickle of Cambridge, Massachusetts, produced the first full set of gum cards devoted exclusively to football.

Both Leaf Gum of Chicago and Bowman Gum of Philadelphia produced sets of football cards in 1948. Leaf discontinued production after their 1949 issue; Bowman continued until 1955.

Topps Chewing Gum entered the market in 1950 with its college-stars set. Topps became a fixture in the football card market with its 1955 All-American set. From 1956 thorough 1963, Topps printed card sets of National Football League players, combining them with the American Football League players in 1961.

Topps produced sets with only American Football League players from 1964 to 1967. The Philadelphia Gum Company made National Football League card sets during this period. Beginning in 1968 and continuing to the present, Topps has produced sets of National Football League cards, the name adopted after the merger of the two leagues.

References: *All Sports Alphabetical Price Guide*, Krause Publications, 1995; Mark Allen Baker, *All-Sport Autograph Guide*, Krause Publications, 1995; Tol Broome, *From Ruth to Ryan*, Krause Publications, 1994; *Charlton Standard Catalogue of Canadian Baseball & Football Cards*, 4th ed., The Charlton Press, 1995; *Charlton Standard Catalogue of Hockey Cards*, 7th ed., Charlton Press, 1995; Gene Florence, *Florence's Standard Baseball Card Price Guide*, 6th ed., Collector Books, 1995.

Jeff Kurowski and Tony Prudom, *Sports Collectors Digest Pre-War Baseball Card Price Guide*, Krause Publications, 1993; Mark Larson, *Complete Guide to Baseball Memorabilia*, 3rd ed., Krause Publications, 1996; —, *Complete Guide to Football, Basketball & Hockey Memorabilia*, Krause Publications, 1995; —, *Sports Collectors Digest Minor League Baseball Card Price Guide*, Krause Publications, 1993; Mark Larson (ed.), *Sports Card Explosion*, Krause Publications, 1993; Bob Lemke, ed., *2000 Standard Catalog of Baseball Cards*, 9th ed., Krause Publications, 1999; Bob Lemke and Sally Grace, *Sportscard Counterfeit Detector*, 3rd ed., Krause Publications, 1994; Michael McKeever, *Collecting Sports Cards*, Alliance Publishing, 1996; Alan Rosen, *True Mint*, Krause Publications, 1994; *Sports Collectors Digest, Baseball Card Price Guide*, 11th ed., Krause Publications, 1997; —, *Baseball's Top 500 Card Checklist & Price Guide*, Krause Publications, 1999; —, *Premium Insert Sports Cards*, Krause Publications, 1995; —, *Standard Catalog of Baseball Cards*, 7th ed., Krause Publications, 1997; —, *1998 Standard Catalog of Basketball Cards*, Krause Publications, 1997; —, *2000 Standard Catalog of Football Cards*, Krause Publications, 1999; —, *Standard Catalog of Football, Basketball, & Hockey Cards*, 2nd ed., Krause Publications, 1996, http://www.krause.com.

Periodicals: *Allan Kaye's Sports Cards News & Price Guides*, 10300 Watson Rd, St Louis, MO 63127; *Baseball Update*, Suite 284, 220 Sunrise Hwy, Rockville Centre, NY 11570; *Beckett Baseball Card Monthly*, 15850 Dallas Pkwy, Dallas, TX 75248; *Beckett Football Card Magazine*, 15850 Dallas Pkwy, Dallas, TX 75248; *Canadian Sportscard Collector*, P.O. Box 1299, Lewiston, NY 14092; *The Old Judge*, P.O. Box 137, Centerbeach, NY 11720; *Sport Card Economizer*, RFD 1 Box 350, Winthrop, ME 04364; *Sports Cards Magazine & Price Guide*, 700 E. State St., Iola, WI 54490; *Sports Card Trader*, P.O. Box 443, Mt. Morris, IL 61054; *Sports Collectors Digest*, 700 E. State St., Iola, WI 54990; *Tuff Stuff*, P.O. Box 1637, Glen Allen, VA 23060; *Your Season Ticket*, 106 Liberty Rd, Woodsboro, MD 21798.

Sports Cards Language

As in a dictionary, new terms and abbreviations are added to various antiques and collectibles categories. Here are some commonly used Sports Cards terms.

ACC—American Card Catalog, edited by Jefferson Burdick, Nostalgia Press, 1960. Lists alphabetical and numerical designations as it identifies card sets. They have devised a set of sub-abbreviations, such as F for food inserts. The one, tow, or three digit number which follows the letter prefix identifies the company and the series.

AS—All Star Card. A special card for players of the all star teams of the National League, American League, or Major League.

AU—Card with autograph.

Blank Back—refers to a card with no printing at all on the back.

Borders—white space, although sometimes colored, which surrounds the picture, used in establishing grading.

Brick—a wrapped group of cards, often of only one year.

Centering—the player should be centered on the card with even borders; an important grading factor.

Chipping—wearing away of a dark-colored border.

Combination Card—shows two or more players but not an entire team.

Common Card—ordinary player, lowest-valued card in a set.

CO—abbreviation for coach.

COR—corrected card.

CY—Cy Young award.

Ding—slight damage to the edge or corner of a card.

DP—double-quantity print run.

DR—draft choice.

ERR—error card. Card with a known mistake, misspelling, etc. When a variation card has been issued, the value of an error card goes down.

First Card—first card of a player in a national set, not necessarily a rookie card.

Foil—foil embossed stamp on card.

F/S—father and son on card.

Gloss—the amount of shine on a card, again a value determination.

Grade—condition that helps determine value.

Key Card—most important cards in a set.

Reverse Negative—common error in which picture negative is flipped so the picture comes out backward.

ROY—Rookie of the Year.

SP—single or short print, printed in lesser amounts than rest of series.

Team Card—card showing entire team.

Wrapper—paper wrapper surrounding wax packs.

YL—yellow letters, Topps, 1958.

Baseball

Allen & Ginter, N28, Cap Anson, 1887, PSA 5, framed 1,995.00
American Caramel, E90-1, 1909-11, Keeler, throwing, even corner
  wear 695.00
American Tobacco Cards
  0, Cobb, 1909, T-206, PSA Grade 5 .... 2,000.00
  0, Cobb, 1910, T-206, PSA Grade 5 .... 2,500.00
  0, Cobb, 1910, T-206, PSA Grade 5 .... 2,000.00
  0, Cobb, red, 1911, T-206, PSA Grade 3 .... 1,500.00

86, Jackson, 1915, M101-5 SN, PSA Grade 5 ....5,500.00
87, Jackson, 1916 M101-4 SN, PSA Grade 4 ....5,500.00

Bowman

1948
1, Eliot, PSA Grade 8 ....325.00
8, Rizzuto, PSA Grade 8 ....750.00
14, Reynolds, PSA Grade 7 ....100.00
24, Leonard, PSA Grade 8 ....75.00

1949
36, Reese, PSA Grade 7 ....2,750.00
50, Robinson, PSA Grade 8 ....2,000.00
84, Campanella, PSA Grade 8 ....1,500.00
131, Lather, PSA Grade 8 ....35.00
186, Kerr, PSA Grade 7 ....75.00
208, Trout, PSA Grade 8 ....175.00

1950
98, Williams, PSA Grade 5 ....500.00
157, Roe, PSA Grade 8 ....150.00
194, Cox, PSA Grade 8 ....125.00
215, Looat, PSA Grade 8 ....125.00

1951
1, Ford, PSA Grade 7 ....850.00
3, Roberts, PSA Grade 8 ....325.00
26, Rizzuto, PSA Grade 8 ....475.00
56, Branca, PSA Grade 7 ....125.00
152, Abrams, PSA 8 ....100.00
203, Law, PSA 8 ....100.00
253, Mantle, PSA 7 ....8,500.00
259, Dressen, PSA 8 ....200.00

1952
4, Roberts, PSA Grade 8 ....275.00
33, McDougald, PSA Grade 7 ....100.00
43, Feller, PSA Grade 8 ....500.00
101, Mantel, PSA Grade 7 ....2,500.00
217, Stengel, PSA Grade 8 ....425.00
232, Slaughter, PSA Grade 7 ....200.00

1953, color
6, Ginsburg, PSA Grade 7 ....50.00
9, Rizzuto, PSA Grade 7 ....275.00
18, Fox, PSA Grade 7 ....200.00
19, Dark, PSA Grade 8 ....125.00
32, Musial, PSA Grade 7 ....1,000.00
33, Reese, PSA Grade 6 ....675.00
46, Campanella, PSA Grade 7 ....525.00
59, Mantle, PSA Grade 4 ....1,250.00
68, Reynolds, PSA Grade 7 ....125.00
74, Mueller, PSA Grade 7 ....65.00

1954
19, Shantz 12.00
98, Kinder 17.00
171, Bernier 17.00
201, Thomson...10.00

Complete Set
1948, very good 1,100.00
1949, very good 4,250.00
1950, very good/excellent 1,750.00
1951, very good 3,000.00
1952, very good 2,000.00
1953, color, excellent/mint 5,750.00
1954, very good to excellent 5,750.00
1955, excellent/mint 3,500.00

Cracker Jack, 30, Ty Cobb, 1914, PSA 8, framed 24,950.00
Diamond Star, Ott, 50, 1935, PSA Grade 5 ....875.00

Fleer, complete sets
1959, near mint 1,750.00
1960, good to excellent 200.00
1961, excellent/mint 400.00
1963, good to excellent, mkd...............................750.00
1982, near mint..70.00
1984, near mint..100.00

1986, near mint...90.00

Goudey
75, Kamm, 1933, PSA Grade 7 ....125.00
87, O'Rouke, 1933, PSA Grade 5 ....75.00
91, Zachary, 1933, PSA Grade 6 ....100.00
92, Gehrig, 1933, PSA Grade 6 ....3,000.00
93, Welsh, 1933, PSA Grade 5 ....65.00
101, Coffman, 1933, PSA Grade 5 ....65.00
144, Ruth, 1933, PSA Grade 3 ....1,750.00
Sheet, uncut, 1933, printed backs, framed.......................6,995.00

Leaf
1, DiMaggio, PSA Grade 4 ....1,000.00
4, Musial, PSA Grade 6 ....750.00
76, Williams, PSA Grade 6 ....750.00

Playball
14, Williams, 1941, PSA Grade 5 ....1,750.00
27, DiMaggio, 1939, PSA Grade 7 ....2,500.00
27, DiMaggio, 1940, PSA Grade 7 ....2,500.00
71, DiMaggio, 1941, PSA Grade 5 ....2,000.00
92, Williams, 1939, PSA Grade 8 ....4,500.00
103, Berg, 1939, PSA Grade 3.............................300.00

Topps

1951
3, Ashburn, PSA Grade 8 ....325.00
20, Branca, PSA Grade 9 ....250.00
50, Mize, PSA Grade 8 ....250.00
52, Chapman, PSA Grade 8 ....175.00

1952
37, Snider, PSA Grade 7 ....425.00
44, Dempsey, PSA Grade 8 ....100.00
88, Feller, PSA Grade 7 ....325.00
124, Kennedy, PSA Grade 8 ....100.00
195, Minoso, PSA Grade 8 ....250.00
261, Mays, PSA Grade 5 ....1,750.00
311, Mantle, PSA Grade 5 ....11,000.00
312, Robinson, PSA Grade 6 ....1,250.00
313, Thompson, PSA Grade 7 ....425.00
314, Campanella, PSA Grade 8 ....5,000.00
333, Reese, PSA Grade 7 ....2,000.00
356, Atwell, PSA Grade 7 ....275.00
384, Crosetti, PSA Grade 6 ....375.00
392, Wilhelm, PSA Grade 7 ....900.00

1953
1, Robinson ,PSA Grade 7 ....750.00
4, Wade, PSA Grade 7 ....75.00

1954
11, Smith...15.00
22, Greengrass...24.00
65, Swift..24.00
94, Banks...250.00

Complete Sets
1951, blue...750.00
1952, good to very good/excellent..............................15,000.00
1953, good to very good/excellent...........................3,750.00
1954, good to very good..2,500.00
1955, very good to excellent....................................2,250.00
1956, good to very good..1,750.00
1957, very good to excellent....................................2,500.00
1958, good to very good..1,500.00
1959, good to very good/excellent...........................1,500.00
1960, excellent/mint...2,500.00

W. W. Gum
55, Gehrig, 1933, PSA Grade 4............................2,500.00
78, Ruth, 1935, PSA Grade 5...............................3,250.00
80, Ruth, 1933, PSA Grade 5...............................5,000.00

Basketball

Bowman

1948
2, Hamilton 18.00

3, Bishop	18.00
19, Ehliers	45.00
20, Vance	35.00
27, Norlander	18.00
31, Gilmur	35.00

Topps
1957

1, Cufton	90.00
2, Yardley	20.00
4, Braun	15.00
5, Sharman	60.00
12, Martin	50.00
19, Heinsohn	105.00
20, Thieben	25.00
21, Meineke	25.00
52, Spoelstra	25.00
58, Colin	15.00
77, Russel	675.00

1974-75

1, Jabbar	25.00
10, Maravich	18.00
39, Walton	50.00
200, Irving	40.00

Football

Bowman, 1950

80, Wildung	30.00
81, Rote	30.00

Fleer
1961

30, Unitas	18.00
197, Otto	25.00
204, Burford	4.00

1963

1, Garron	18.00
6, Long	95.00
36, Blanda	30.00
59, Powell	12.00
72, Alworth	175.00

Topps
1955, All Americans

4, Pinkert	5.00
12, Graham	75.00
22, Muller	12.00
65, Donchess	15.00

1959

44, Johnson	3.00
118, Cardinal team	6.00
126, Rams Pennant	4.00
161, Brown Team	6.00

1960

1, Unitas	27.00
4, Berry	10.00
23, Brown	120.00
31, Starr	23.00
60, Packer team	5.00
62, Ryan	7.00
1961, 166, Kemp	95.00
1964, 30, Kemp	110.00
1966, 96, Namath	60.00

Hockey

Topps

1966, 73, Beliveau	40.00
1966, 109, Howe	190.00
1971, 100, Orr	45.00
1973, 17, Dionne	10.00
1973, 88, Gilbert	5.00

SPORTS COLLECTIBLES

History: People have been saving sports-related equipment since the inception of sports. Some was passed down from generation to generation for reuse; the rest was stored in dark spaces in closets, attics, and basements.

In the 1980s, two key trends brought collectors' attention to sports collectibles. First, decorators began using old sports items, especially in restaurant decor. Second, card collectors began to discover the thrill of owning the "real" thing. By the beginning of the 1990s, all sport categories were collectible, with baseball items paramount and golf and football running close behind.

References: Mark Allen Baker, *Sports Collectors Digest Complete Guide to Boxing Collectibles*, Krause Publications, 1995; Don Bevans and Ron Menchine, *Baseball Team Collectibles*, Wallace-Homestead, 1994; David Bushing, *Guide to Spalding Bats 1908-1938*, published by author; —, *Sports Equipment Price Guide*, Krause Publications, 1995; Dave Bushing and Joe Phillips, *1996 Vintage Baseball Glove Pocket Price Guide*, No. 4, published by authors (217 Homewood, Libertyville, IL 60048), 1996; —, *Vintage Baseball Bat 1994 Pocket Price Guide*, published by authors, 1994; Bruce Chadwick and David M. Spindel authored a series of books on major-league teams published by Abbeville Press between 1992 and 1995; Duncan Chilcott, *Miller's Soccer Memorabilia*, Miller's Publications, 1994; Douglas Congdon-Martin and John Kashmanian, *Baseball Treasures*, Schiffer Publishing, 1993; *Ralf Coykendall Jr., Coykendall's Complete Guide to Sporting Collectibles*, Wallace-Homestead, 1996; Sarah Fabian-Baddiel, *Miller's Golf Memorabilia*, Millers Publications, 1994; Chuck Furjanic, *Antique Golf Collectibles, A Price and Reference Guide*, Krause Publications, 1997; John F. Hotchkiss, *500 Years of Golf Balls*, Antique Trader Books, 1997; Mark K. Larson, *Complete Guide to Baseball Memorabilia*, 3rd ed., Krause Publications, 1996; Mark Larson, Rick Hines and David Platta (eds.), *Mickey Mantle Memorabilia*, Krause Publications, 1993; Carl Luckey, *Old Fishing Lures and Tackle*, 5th ed., Krause Publications, 1999; J. L. Mashburn, *Sports Postcard Price Guide*, Colonial House, 1998; Kevin McGimpsey and David Neach, *Golf Memorabilia*, Philip Wilson Publishers, distributed by Antique Collectors' Club, 1999; Tim Mortenson, *2000 Standard Catalog of Sports Memorabilia*, Krause Publications, 1999; Dudley Murphy and Rick Edmisten, *Fishing Lure Collectibles*, 1995, 1997 value update, Collector Books; *1996 Vintage Baseball Glove Catalog Source Book*, The Glove Collector (14057 Rolling Hills Lane, Dallas, TX 75240), 1996; John M. and Morton W. Olman, *Golf Antiques & Other Treasures of the Game*, Market Street Press, 1993; Geroge Richey, *Made in Michigan Fishing Lures*, published by author (Rte. 1, Box 280, Honor, MI 49640), 1995; George Sanders, Helen Sanders, and Ralph Roberts, *Sanders Price Guide to Sports Autographs*, 1994 ed., Scott Publishing, 1993; Harold E. Smith, *Collector's Guide to Creek Chub Lures & Collectibles*, Collector Books, 1996; Mark Wilson (ed.), *Golf Club Identification and Price Guide III*, Ralph Maltby Enterprises, 1993.

Periodicals: *Baseball Hobby News*, 4540 Kearney Villa Rd, San Diego, CA 92123; *Beckett Focus on Future Stars*, 15850 Dallas Pkwy, Dallas, TX 75248; *Boxing Collectors News*, 3316 Luallen Drive, Carrollton, TX 75007; *Boxing Collectors Newsletter*, 59 Boston St., Revere, MA 02151; *Button Pusher*, P.O. Box 4, Coopersburg, PA 18036; *Diamond Angle*, P.O. Box 409, Kaunakakai, HI 97648; *Diamond Duds*, P.O. Box 10153, Silver Spring, MD 20904; *Fantasy Baseball*, 700 E State St, Iola, WI 54990; *Golfiana Magazine*, P.O. Box 688, Edwardsville, IL 62025; *Old Tyme Baseball News*, P.O. Box 833, Petroskey, MI 49770; *Sports Collectors Digest*, 700 E. State St., Iola, WI 54990; *Tuff Stuff*, P.O. Box 1637, Glen Allen, VA 23060; *US Golf Classics & Heritage Hickories*, 5407 Pennock Point Rd, Jupiter, FL 33458.

Collectors' Clubs: Antique Ice Skating Collectors Club, 70-104 Scott St., Meriden, CT 06450; Boxiana & Pugilistica Collectors International, P.O. Box 83135, Portland, OR 97203-0135; Collectors' League, 575 Hwy 73 N., West Berlin, NJ 08091-2440, http://www.gartlanusa.com; Eastern PA Sports Collectors Club, P.O. Box 3037, Maple Glen, PA 19002; Golf Club Collectors Association, 640 E. Liberty St., Girard, OH 44420; Golf Collectors Society, P.O. Box 241042, Cleveland, OH 44124, http://www.golfcollectors.com; International Hot Rod Association, 9-1/2 E. Main St., Norwalk, OH 44857, http://www.ihra.com; International Pin Collectors Club, 602 Chenango St., Binghamton, NY 13901-2029; Logo Golf Ball Collector's Association, 4552 Barclay Fairway, Lake Worth, FL 33467; Professional Skaters Association, International, 1821 2nd St. SW., Rochester, MN 55902; Society for American Baseball Research, 812 Huron Rd, E., #719, Cleveland, OH 44115; Sports Hall of Oblivion, P.O. Box 69025, Pleasant Ridge, MI 48069-0025; The (Baseball) Glove Collector, 14507 Rolling Hills Lane, Dallas, TX, 75240; Tennis Collectors Society, Guildhall Orchard, Mary Lane North, Great Bromley Colchester, Essex C07 7TUWorld Logo (Golf) Ball Association, P.O. Box 91989, Long Beach, CA 90809, http://www.hyperhead.com/wlba2.

Museums: Aiken Thoroughbred Racing Hall of Fame & Museum, Aiken, SC; International Boxing Hall of Fame, Canastota, NY; Kentucky Derby Museum, Louisville, KY; Metropolitan Museum of Art, The Jefferson Burdich Collection, New York, NY; Naismith Memorial Basketball Hall of Fame, Springfield, MA; National Baseball Hall of Fame & Museum, Inc., Cooperstown, NY; National Bowling Hall of Fame & Museum, St Louis, MO; New England Sports

SPECIAL AUCTIONS

Dixie Sporting Collectibles
1206 Rama Rd,
Charlotte, NC 28211
(704) 364-2900

Lang's
30 Hamlin Rd
Falmouth, ME 04105
(207) 797-2311

Box, Pointer Shot Gun Shells, $140.

Museum, Boston, MA; PGA/World Golf Hall of Fame, Pinehurst, NC; University of New Haven National Art Museum of Sport, W Haven, CT.

Baseball

Baseball, autographed, sgd by members of team
    American League All-Star Team, 1937, Foxx, Gehrig, DiMaggio 7,000.00
    Boston, 1964, Herman, Yastrzemski 250.00
    Los Angeles, 1983, Sax, Valenzuela, Welch, Stewart 150.00
    Milwaukee, 1979, Molitor, Young 200.00
    National League All-Star Team, 1955, Musial 600.00
    New York, 1960, Stengel, Kubek, Maris, Howard, Berra, Ford 700.00
    Oakland, 1981, Martin, Henderson........................ 200.00
Baseball Cap, autographed, game used
    Bench, Johnny, 1970s Cincinnati Reds 450.00
    Jackson, Bo, 1994 CA Angels 85.00
    Walker, Larry, 1995 Colorado Rockies 165.00
Baseball Glove
    Ashburn, Richie 45.00
    Berra, Yogi 100.00
    Reese, Pee Wee 65.00
Cabinet Card, John Clarkson, 1888, N173, Old Judge/Dogs Head.. 6,495.00
Jersey, game used
    1955, Ken Griffey.. 2,800.00
    1987, Reggie Jackson 700.00
    1988, Mark McQwire 1,500.00
Magazine, *Baseball*, December, 1926, cover with Ruby and Hornsby shaking hands during 1926 world Series 295.00
Pennant, felt
    Brooklyn Dodgers, Ebbert Field, blue, 1940s 190.00
    Cooperstown, blue, multicolored Braves style Indian head, 1940s 75.00
    Minnesota Twins A. L. Champs World Series, photo, 1965 .. 125.00
    New York Yankees, photo "M&M Boys Last Year Together!," 1966.. 90.00
Program
    All Star, Philadelphia, 1943.................................. 495.00

All Star, St. Louis, 1948 .... 325.00
New York Yankees, 1937 .... 195.00
New York Yankees, 1951 .... 195.00
Senators, 1955 .... 40.00
World Series, 1938, at New York, Yankees and Chicago
    Cubs 550.00
World Series, 1950, at Philadelphia 250.00
Roster Sheet, Pirates, 1927 .... 175.00

Basketball

Autograph, basketball
    Archibald, Nate 100.00
    Bing, Dave 100.00
    Bird, Larry 200.00
    Bradley, Bill 150.00
    DeBusschere, Dave 125.00
    O'Brien, Larry 125.00
    Thompson, John 100.00
Autograph, photograph, 8" x 10"
    Cooper, Charles 35.00
    Embry, Wayne 15.00
    McGuire, Dick 20.00
    Phillip, Andy 20.00
    Thurmond, Nate 20.00
Bumper Sticker, Kentucky Colonels, 4" x 15", ABA ball, team logo,
    name in blue and white, unused, 1974-75 .... 20.00
Magazine, *Sports Illustrated*, Feb, 1949, Ralph Beard, Kentucky
    cover 95.00
Pin, Chicago Americans Tournament Championship, brass,
    1935 .... 75.00
Program
    Basketball Hall of Fame Commemoration Day Program, orig
        invitation, 1961 .... 75.00
    NCAA Final Four Championship, Louisville, KY,
        1967 .... 175.00
    World Series of Basketball, 1951, Harlem Globetrotters and College
        All-Americans 55.00
Shoes, pr, game used, autographed
    Drexler, Clyde, Avais 225.00
    Newman, Johnny, Nike Air Flights 75.00
    Sikma, Jack, Converse 100.00
    Webber, Chris, Nikes 550.00
Souvenir Book, *Los Angeles Lakers*, with 2 records, Jerry West and
    Elgin Baylor on action cover 75.00
Ticket
    NBA Finals Boston Celtics at Los Angeles Lakers, 1963 .... 95.00
    San Antonio Spurs ABA Phantom Playoff, 1975, unused 15.00
    St. Louis Hawks at San Francisco Warriors, Dec 17, 1963 ..... 50.00
Yearbook
    1961-62, Boston Celtics 150.00
    1965-66, Boston Celtics 85.00
    1969-70, Milwaukee Bucks 40.00

Boxing

Autograph, photo, sgd
    Max Baer, 8 x 10" 180.00
    Mike Tyson 60.00
Badge, 4" d, Larry Holmes, black and white photo, red and black
    inscriptions, 1979 copyright Don King Productions 25.00
Boxing Gloves, 35 readable autographs 380.00
Cabinet Card, 4" x 6"
    Corbett, James F., dressed in suit 375.00
    Ryan, Paddy, full boxing post, dark brown border 395.00
    Sullivan, John L., dark brown border, "John L. Sullivan, Champion
        of the World" 495.00
Flipbook, 1-7/8 x 2-1/2", copyright 1897 by Cies & Co., 91 black and
    white pictures 60.00

Fishing

Book
    Koller, Larry, *The Treasure of Angling*, 1963, Ridge Press 15.00

Fishing Reel, George Snyder, Paris, KY, brass, c1820, $31,350. Photo courtesy of Langs.

Walton, Issac (1st) and Charles Cotton (2nd), *The Complete Angler:
    or Contemplative Man's Recreation: A Discourse on Rivers, Fish-
    Ponds, Fish & Fishing in 2 Parts*, supplementary and explanatory
    Sir John Hawkins 125.00
Catalog
    Evinrude Motors, Milwaukee, WI, 1961, 24 pgs, 8-1/4" x 11", Cat.
        Of Outboard Motors 32.00
    Shakespeare Co, Kalamazoo, MI, 1942, 86 pgs, 5-1/2" x
        8-1/2", Shakespeare's Wondereel Long Casts, No Backlash & No
        Thumbing, Angler Catalog 55.00
    The National Fisherman, 1951, 16 pgs, 8" x 10", Tackle 35.00
    Wallsten Tackle Co., Chicago, IL, 1940s, 20 pgs, 5-1/2" x
        8-1/4", Fishing Tips, Courtesy of Cisco Kid Lures 21.00
Sign, "The Flatfish, World's largest selling fishing plug," Helen Tackle
    Co., Detroit, metal framed glass, 8" x 16" 350.00
Tobacco Tin, Forest & Stream, pocket size, 4-1/4" x 3" x 7/8" 600.00

Football

Autograph, football
    Bell, Greg 65.00
    Bergey, Bill 70.00
    Ditka, Mike 125.00
    Flaherty, Ray 150.00
    Green, Roy 70.00
    Knox, Chuck 65.00
    Long, Howie 75.00
Autograph, helmet
    Aikman, Troy, Dallas Cowboys 265.00
    Dawson, Len, Kansas City Chiefs 250.00
    Elway, John, Denver Broncos 275.00
Autograph, photograph, 8" x 10"
    Bradshaw, Terry 40.00
    Brown, Jim 30.00
    Davidson, Ben 10.00
    Landry, Greg 12.00
    Moore, Herman 10.00
    Thomas, Thurman 25.00
Game, Tom Hamilton's Navy Football Game, 1940s 45.00
Pennant, felt, A.F.L.
    Boston Patriots, white on red, multicolored Patriot 75.00
    Buffalo Bills, white on blue, pink buffaloes 95.00
    Houston Oilers, white on light blue 75.00
Pinback Button, 1-1/4" d, Philadelphia Eagles, logo, football dangle,
    early 1950s 45.00
Playoff Guide, 1965 NFL, green Bay Packers vs. St. Louis
    Cardinals 40.00
Program
    Army vs. Duke, at the Polo Grounds, 1946 .... 40.00
    Army vs. Navy, Michie Stadium, 1952 .... 25.00
    Fordham vs. St. Mary's, at Polo Grounds, 1938 .... 40.00

Green Bay Packers, 1960 .... 30.00
Heisman Trophy, 1957, John David Crow 30.00
Pennsylvania vs. Cornell at Franklin Field.......................... 30.00
Rose Bowl, 1974, USC vs. Ohio State 40.00

Golf
Autograph, photo, sgd, Tiger Woods 60.00
Book
    George Fullerton Carnegie, *Golfiana: or Niceties Connected with the Game of Golf*, Edinburgh, 1833, 18 pgs of poetry ...21,850.00
    The Architectural Side of Golf, London, 1925.................... 14,950.00
Magazine, American Golfer, June, 1932................................. 10.00
Noisemaker, 2-3/4" d, 6-1/2" l, litho tin, full color image of male golfer, mkd "Germany" on handle, 1930s................................. 35.00
Print, Charles Crombie, *The Rules of Golf Illustrated*, 24 humorous lithographs of golfers in mediaeval clothes, London, 1905, ..1,265.00
Program, Fort Worth Open Golf Championship, Glen Garden Country Club, Ft Wort, TX, 1945.. 100.00

Hockey
Autograph
    Orr, Bobby, photograph, 8" x 10" 50.00
    Smith, Clint, photograph, 8" x 10"... 12.00
    Thompson, Tiny, puck.. 50.00
    Watson, Harry, puck... 55.00
    Worsley, Gump, sgd 1968-69 Topps card............................. 15.00
Hockey Stick, game used, autographed
    Beliveau, Jean, 1960s CCM, cracked 700.00
    Cashman, Wayne, Sher-wood, uncracked 175.00
    LeBlanc, J. B., Koho, cracked 50.00
Jersey, game used, Wayne Gretzky, Rangers, autographed 415.00
Magazine, Sport Revue, Quebec publication, Feb 1956, Bert Olmstead, Hall of Fame cov 15.00
Program, Boston Bruins, Sports News, 1937-382 .... 50.00
Stick, game used, autographed
    Bondra, Peter, Sherwood 90.00
    Lindros, Eric, Bauer Supreme 295.00

Hunting
Badge, Western Cartridge Co., plant type, emb metal, pin back, 1-3/4" x 1-3/8" 100.00
Book
    Batty, J., How to Hunt & Trap Buffalo, Elk, Moose, Deer, Antelope, 1878.. 65.00
    Dixon, William Scarth, Hunting in the Olden Days, 1912, Maynaud & Co. 40.00
    Ruark, R., Enough Gun: Ruark on Hunting Big Game, New American Library, 1966, dj.. 37.50
Box, Peters High Velocity, 2 pc cardboard shot gun shells, multicolored graphics, 25 16 gauge shells 250.00
Calendar Top, Winchester, paper, man atop rock ledge, hunting rams, artist sgd "Philip R. Goodwin," metal top rim, 20" x 14".......... 125.00
Sign
    Paul Jones Whiskey, game hunting scene, orig gold gilt frame, 43" x 57"... 750.00
    Remington UMC, diecut cardboard
        15" x 14", oversized shell next to box of ammunition 200.00
        15-1/2" x 9", Nitro Club Shells, English Setter atop pile of Remington Shotgun Shells 100.00
    L. C. Smith Guns, paper, two setters pointing to prey, 14" x 14-3/4" 1,200.00
    Winchester, diecut, cardboard, stand-up, Indian Chief with Winchester shotgun in one hand, additional barrels in other hand, 24" x 60"... 200.00
Tin, Kentucky Rifle Gunpowder.. 70.00
Watch Fob, Savage Revolver, figural, metal 110.00

STAFFORDSHIRE, HISTORICAL

History: The Staffordshire district of England is the center of the English pottery industry. There were 80 different potteries operating there in 1786, with the number increasing to 179 by 1802. The district includes Burslem, Cobridge, Etruria, Fenton, Foley, Hanley, Lane, Lane End, Longport, Shelton, Stoke, and Tunstall. Among the many famous potters were Adams, Davenport, Spode, Stevenson, Wedgwood, and Wood.

References: David and Linda Arman, *Historical Staffordshire* (1974), 1st Supplement (1977), published by authors, out of print; Susan and Al Bagdade, *Warman's English & Continental Pottery & Porcelain*, 3rd Edition, Krause Publications, 1998; A. W. Coysh and R. K. Henrywood, *Dictionary of Blue and White Printed Pottery* (1982), Vol. II (1989), Antique Collectors' Club; Mary J. Finegan, *Johnson Brothers Dinnerware*, published by author, 1993; N. Hudson Moore, *The Old China Book*, Charles E. Tuttle, Co., second printing, 1980; Jeffrey B. Snyder, *Historical Staffordshire American Patriots and Views*, Schiffer Publishing, 1995.

Museums: American Antiquarian Society, Worcester, MA; Cincinnati Art Museum, Cincinnati, OH; City Museum & Art Gallery, Stoke-on-Trent, England; Colonial Williamsburg Foundation, Williamsburg, VA; Elverson Museum of Art, Syracuse, NY; Henry Ford Museum, Dearborn, MI; Hershey Museum, Hershey, PA; Metropolitan Museum of Art, New York, NY; The National Museum of History & Technology, Washington, DC; The Henry Francis DuPont Winterthur Museum, Winterthur, DE; William Rockhill Nelson Gallery of Art, Kansas City, MO; Yale University Gallery of Fine Arts, New Haven, CT.

Notes: The view is the most critical element when establishing the value of historical Staffordshire; American collectors pay much less for non-American views. Dark blue pieces are favored; light views continue to remain underpriced. Among the forms, soup tureens have shown the largest price increases.

Prices listed below are for mint examples. Reduce prices by 20% for a hidden chip, a faint hairline, or an invisible professional repair; by 35% for knife marks through the glaze and a visible professional repair; by 50% for worn glaze and major repairs.

The numbers in parentheses refer to items in the Armans' books, which constitute the most detailed list of American historical views and their forms.

Adams
The Adams family has been associated with ceramics since the mid-17th century. In 1802, William Adams of Stoke-on-Trent produced American views. In 1819, a fourth William Adams, son of William of

SPECIAL AUCTIONS
The Armans Collector's Sales and Services
P.O. Box 4037
Middletown, RI 02842
(401) 849-5012

Plate, Don Quixote, knighthood ceremony, dark blue transfer, 10" d, $125.

Stoke, became a partner with his father and was later joined by his three brothers. The firm became William Adams & Sons. The father died in 1829 and William, the eldest son, became manager.

The company operated four potteries at Stoke and one at Tunstall. American views were produced at Tunstall in black, light blue, sepia, pink, and green in the 1830-40 period. William Adams died in 1865. All operations were moved to Tunstall. The firm continues today under the name of Wm. Adams & Sons, Ltd.

Bowl, 11" d, 2-1/2" h, English scenes with ruins, dark blue transfer, yellowed repair on back 165.00
Creamer, 5-3/8" d, English scene, imp "Adams," dark blue 175.00
Pitcher, 7-1/2" h, Seal of the United States, dark blue (443).... 1,200.00
Plate
    8-7/8" d, English scene, imp "Adams," dark blue, chip on table
      ring..250.00
    10-1/4" d, Mitchell & Freeman's China & Glass Warehouse,
      Chatham Street, Boston, imp "Adams," dark blue 715.00
Teapot, Log Cabin, medallions of Gen. Harrison on border, pink
    (458) 450.00

Clews

From sketchy historical accounts that are available, it appears that James Clews took over the closed plant of A. Stevenson in 1819. His brother Ralph entered the business later. The firm continued until about 1836, when James Clews came to America to enter the pottery business at Troy, Indiana. The venture was a failure because of the lack of skilled workmen and the proper type of clay. He returned to England but did not re-enter the pottery business.

Bowl, Landing of Lafayette, 9" d, ext. floral design, rim repair....410.00
Cup and Saucer, English scene with 2 men by river, dark blue transfer,
    imp mark, minor wear and pinpoint flakes................................. 110.00
Cup Plate, Landing of Lafayette at Castle Garden, dark blue..... 400.00
Plate
    7-7/8" d, Welcome Lafayette the Nations Guest and Our Country's
      Glory, molded rim with blue edge, imp "Clews," dark blue 1,155.00
    8-3/4" d, America and Independence, dark blue transfer, states bor-
      der, imp mark, wear, stains, crazing, minor scratches 275.00
    10" d, Landing of General Lafayette, imp "Clews," dark blue, very
      minor wear 350.00

    10-1/4" d, Landing of General Lafayette, imp "Clews," dark
      blue 360.00
    10-1/4" d, Peace, Plenty, dark blue transfer, imp mark, chip on table
      ring.. 495.00
    10-5/8" d, States series, America and Independence, fisherman
      with net, imp "Clews," dark blue, small rim flake................. 440.00
Platter, 17" d, Landing of Lafayette, imp "Clews," dark blue, scratches
    and wear 1,100.00
Soup Plate
    10-3/8" d, Winter View of Pittsfield, Mass, imp "Clews," dark
      blue 440.00
    10-1/2" d, Picturesque Views, Hudson, Hudson River, imp "Clews,"
      black transfer 165.00
    10-1/2" d, Picturesque Views, Pittsburgh, PA, imp "Clews," steam ships
      with "Home, Nile, Larch," black transfer, chips on table ring 330.00

J. & J. Jackson

Job and John Jackson began operations at the Churchyard Works, Burslem, about 1830. The works formerly were owned by the Wedgwood family. The firm produced transfer scenes in a variety of colors, such as black, light blue, pink, sepia, green, maroon, and mulberry. More than 40 different American views of Connecticut, Massachusetts, Pennsylvania, New York, and Ohio were issued. The firm is believed to have closed about 1844.

Deep Disk, American Beauty Series, Yale College (493) 125.00
Plate, 10-3/8" d, The President's House, Washington, purple
    transfer 275.00
Platter, American Beauty Series
    12" l, Iron Works at Saugerties (478)....................................275.00
    17-1/2" l, View of Newburgh, black transfer (463) 575.00
Soup Plate, 10" d, American Beauty Series, Hartford, CT, black transfer
    (476) 150.00

Thomas Mayer

In 1829, Thomas Mayer and his brothers, John and Joshua, purchased Stubbs's Dale Hall Works of Burslem. They continued to produce a superior grade of ceramics.

Cream Pitcher, 4" h, Lafayette at Franklin's Tomb, dark blue 550.00

Plate, American Scenery series, Fort Conanicut, RI, dark blue transfer, 7" d, $90.

Gravy Tureen, Arms of the American States, CT, dark blue (498) 3,800.00
Plate, 8-1/2" d, Arms of the American States, RI, dark blue (507) ...800.00
Platter
    8-1/4" l, Lafayette at Franklin's Tomb, dark blue....................525.00
    19" l, Arms of the American States, NJ, dark blue (503) 7,200.00
Sugar Bowl, cov, Lafayette at Franklin's Tomb, dark blue (510) .850.00

Mellor, Veneables & Co.

Little information is recorded on Mellor, Veneables & Co., except that they were listed as potters in Burslem in 1843. Their Scenic Views with the Arms of the States Border does include the arms for New Hampshire. This state is missing from the Mayer series.

Plate, 7-1/2" d, Tomb of Washington, Mt. Vernon, Arms of States
    border..125.00
Platter, 15" l, Scenic Views, Arms of States border, Albany, light blue
    (516)..265.00
Sugar Bowl, cov, Arms of States, PA, dark blue 350.00
Teapot, 9-1/2" h, Windsor pattern, dark blue...............................200.00

J. & W. Ridgway and William Ridgway & Co.

John and William Ridgway, sons of Job Ridgway and nephews of George Ridgway who owned Bell Bank Works and Cauldon Place Works, produced the popular Beauties of America series at the Cauldon plant. The partnership between the two brothers was dissolved in 1830. John remained at Cauldon.

William managed the Bell Bank Works until 1854. Two additional series were produced based upon the etchings of Bartlett's American Scenery. The first series had various borders including narrow lace. The second series is known as Catskill Moss.

Beauties of America is in dark blue. The other series are found in light transfer colors of blue, pink, brown, black, and green.

Plate
    6" d, Catskill Moss, Anthony's Nose (925)...............................85.00
    7" d, American Scenery, Valley of the Shenandoah from Jefferson's
    Rock, brown (289) 120.00
    10" h, Beauties of America, City Hall, NY, dark blue (260) 225.00
    10-1/4" h, Columbian Star, Harrison's Log Cabin, side view, green
    (277) 250.00
Platter, 19" l, Catskill Moss, Boston and Bunker's Hill, imp "William
    Ridgway Son & Co," medium blue, dated 1844, minor chips, knife
    marks, edge wear...525.00
Soup Plate, 9-7/8" d, Octagon Church Boston, imp "Ridgway," dark
    medium blue...330.00
Vegetable Dish, 1-" l, open, American Scenery, Peekskill Landing,
    Hudson River, purple (287) 195.00
Wash Bowl, American Scenery, Albany (279)..............................325.00

Rogers

John Rogers and his brother George established a pottery near Longport in 1782. After George's death in 1815, John's son Spencer became a partner, and the firm operated under the name of John Rogers & Sons. John died in 1916. His son continued the use of the name until he dissolved the pottery in 1842.

Cup and Saucer, Boston Harbor, dark blue (441) 650.00
Cup Plate, Boston Harbor, dark blue (441) 1,400.00
Plate, 9-5/8" d, The Canal at Buffalo, lace border, purple transfer, int.
    hairline...55.00
Platter, 16-5/8" l, Boston State House, medium dark blue (442) ...1,000.00
Waste Bowl, Boston Harbor, dark blue (441) 850.00

Stevenson

As early as the 17th century, the name Stevenson has been associated with the pottery industry. Andrew Stevenson of Cobridge introduced American scenes with the flower and scroll border. Ralph Stevenson, also of Cobridge, used a vine and leaf border on his dark blue historical views and a lace border on his series in light transfers. The initials R. S. & W. indicate Ralph Stevenson and Williams are associated with the acorn and leaf border. It has been reported

Plate, Fair Mount Near Philadelphia, dark blue transfer, 10-3/4" d, $225.

that Williams was Ralph's New York agent and the wares were produced by Ralph alone.

Cup and Saucer, , New Orleans, floral and scroll border..............95.00
Jug, 8-1/4" h, dark blue print...750.00
Plate
    6-1/2" d, Catholic Cathedral, NY, floral and scroll border, dark blue
    (395) 1,650.00
    6-7/8" d, Battery, NY, vine border (367) 800.00
    7-1/2" d, Columbia College, NY, acorn and oak leaves border, dark
    blue (350)..450.00
Soup Plate, 10" d, Erie Canal at Buffalo, lace border (386)..........95.00
Wash bowl, Riceborough, GA, lace border (388) 375.00

Stubbs

In 1790, Stubbs established a pottery works at Burslem, England. He operated it until 1829, when he retired and sold the pottery to the Mayer brothers. He probably produced his American views about 1825. Many of his scenes were from Boston, New York, New Jersey, and Philadelphia.

Pitcher, 6-1/2" h, Boston State House and New York City Hall, rose
    border, dark blue (335) 1,100.00
Plate
    6-1/2" d, City Hall, NY, spread eagle border, medium blue
    (323) 275.00
    10-1/4" d, Fairmount Near Philadelphia, imp "Stubbs," medium
    blue..220.00
Platter, 14-1/2" l, State House, Boston, spread eagle border, dark blue
    (331)...750.00
Salt Shaker, Hoboken in NJ, spread eagle border, dark blue
    (326)...700.00

Unknown Makers

Bowl, 11-1/8" d, 3-1/4" d, Franklin, scene of Ben flying kite, red trans-
    fer, minor wear 495.00
Pitcher
    6-7/8" h, America, Independence, mansion with winding drive, dark
    blue transfer, chips and hairline 660.00
    7-3/8" h, Seal of the United States with eagle, dark blue transfer,
    wear and stains...1,320.00

Pitcher, DeWitt Clinton Eulogy and Utica inscription, dark blue transfer, 6-1/2" h, $1,250.

Teabowl and Saucer, sea urchins and flowers, dark blue transfers, c1825, 3-3/4" bowl, 5-5/8" d saucer, $190.

Plate

7" d, Junction of the Sacandaga & Hudson River, black transfer, small rim glaze defect 95.00

7-3/4" d, Near Fishkill, small chip on table ring 100.00

8" d, View from Coenties-slip," scene of Great Fire, City New York, light blue transfer, wear, small edge flakes 385.00

8-1/2" d, Boston State House, dark blue transfer, unmarked, minor wear 200.00

8-3/4" d, Nahant Hotel near Boston, dark blue transfer, wear, chips on table ring 200.00

9" d, The Residence of the late Richard Jordon, New Jersey," brown, minor wear and stains 250.00

9-3/4" d, British Views, dark blue, minor wear and pinpoints. 215.00

9-3/4" d, City Hall, New York, dark blue transfer, minor wear 275.00

10-1/8" d, The Baltimore & Ohio Railroad, dark blue transfer, wear, stains 965.00

Platter, 16-5/8" l, Sandusky, dark blue, very minor scratches .. 8,525.00

Saucer, 5-7/8" d, scene of early railroad, engine and one car, floral border, dark blue 275.00

Soup Plate, 10-1/4" d, ---burgs, Yorkshire, medium blue 220.00

Teapot, 8-1/4" h, The Residence of the Late Richard Jordan, New Jersey, brown transfer, small chip, stain and repair to lid 715.00

Wood

Enoch Wood, sometimes referred to as the father of English pottery, began operating a pottery at Fountain Place, Burslem, in 1783. A cousin, Ralph Wood, was associated with him. In 1790, James Caldwell became a partner and the firm was known as Wood and Caldwell. In 1819 Wood and his sons took full control.

Enoch died in 1840. His sons continued under the name of Enoch Wood & Sons. The American views were first made in the mid-1820s and continued through the 1840s.

It is reported that the pottery produced more signed historical views than any other Staffordshire firm. Many of the views attributed to unknown makers probably came from the Woods.

Marks vary, although always include the name Wood. The establishment was sold to Messrs. Pinder, Bourne & Hope in 1846.

Creamer, 5-3/4" h, horse drawn sleigh, imp "Wood," dark blue, minor hairline in base 550.00

Cup and Saucer, handleless

Commodore MacDonnough's Victory, imp "Wood & Sons," dark blue, pinpoints on cup table ring 355.00

Ship with American flag, Chancellor Livingston, imp "Wood & Sons" 770.00

Plate

6-1/2" d, Catskill House, Hudson, imp "Wood & Sons," dark blue, white spot near center, pinpoint rim flake 495.00

7-5/8" d, The Capitol Washington, shell border, imp "Wood & Sons," dark blue 935.00

8-3/8" d, Chief Justice Marshall, Troy, imp "Wood & Sons," dark blue, small chip 600.00

8-5/8" d, The Landing of the Fathers at Plymouth, medium blue transfer, imp "Wood" 150.00

9-1/4" d, Commodore MacDonnough's Victory, imp "Wood," dark blue 385.00

9-1/4" d, The Baltimore & Ohio Railroad, (incline), imp "Enoch Wood," dark blue 770.00

10-1/8" d, Commodore MacDonnough's Victory, dark blue transfer, imp mark, wear, stains, crazing 385.00

10-1/4" d, Boston State House, imp "Wood & Sons," medium blue 165.00

10-1/4" d, The Baltimore & Ohio Railroad, (straight), imp "Wood," dark blue, minor scratches 825.00

10-3/8" d, Constitution and Guerriere, imp "Wood," dark blue minor scratches 1,760.00

Platter

16-5/8" l, London Views, St. George's Chapel, Regents Street, imp "Wood," dark blue, minor wear, scratches, pinpoint flakes . 660.00

18-1/2" l, Castle Garden Battery New York, dark blue transfer, imp mark, minor wear, shallow glaze flakes, stains 3,100.00

Toddy Plate

5-3/4" d, ship scene, shell border, scene not identified, imp "Wood," dark blue 330.00

6-1/2" d, dark blue transfer, Catskill House, Hudson, imp "Wood," minor wear and stains 525.00

STAFFORDSHIRE ITEMS

History: A wide variety of ornamental pottery items originated in England's Staffordshire district, beginning in the 17th century and still continuing today. The height of production took place from 1820 to 1890.

These naive pieces are considered folk art by many collectors. Most items were not made carefully; some even were made and decorated by children.

The types of objects are varied, e.g., animals, cottages, and figurines (chimney ornaments).

References: Susan and Al Bagdade, *Warman's English & Continental Pottery & Porcelain*, 3rd Edition, Krause Publications, 1998; Pat Halfpenny, *English Earthenware Figures*, Antique Collectors' Club, 1992; Adele Kenny, *Staffordshire Spaniels*, Schiffer Publishing, 1997; Griselda Lewis, *A Collector's History of English Pottery*, 5th ed., Antique Collectors' Club, 1999; Arnold R. Mountford, *The Illustrated Guide to Staffordshire Salt-Glazed Stoneware*, Barrie & Jenkins, 1971; Clive Mason Pope, *A-Z of Staffordshire Dogs*, Antique Collectors' Club, Ltd., 1996; P. D. Gordon Pugh, *Staffordshire Portrait Figures of the Victorian Era*, Antique Collectors' Club, 1987; Dennis G. Rice, *English Porcelain Animals of the 19th Century*, Antique Collectors' Club, 1989. Louis T. Stanley, *Collecting Staffordshire Pottery*, Doubleday & Co., 1963.

Museums: American Antiquarian Society, Worcester, MA; Brighton Museum, England; British Museum, London, England; City Museum and Art Gallery, Stoke-on-Trent, England; The Detroit Museum of Arts, Detroit, MI; Fitzwilliam Museum, Cambridge, England; Victoria & Albert Museum, London, England.

Reproduction Alert: Early Staffordshire figurines and hollowware forms were molded. Later examples were made using a slip-casting process. Slip casting leaves telltale signs that are easy to spot. Look in the interior. Hand molding created a smooth interior surface. Slip casting produces indentations that conform to the exterior design. Holes occur where handles meet the body of slip-cast pieces. There is not hole in a hand-molded piece.

A checkpoint on figurines is the firing or vent hole, which is a necessary feature on these forms. Early figurines had small holes; modern reproductions feature large holes often the size of a dime or quarter. Vent holes are found on the sides or hidden among the decoration in early Staffordshire figurines; most modern reproductions have them in the base.

These same tips can be used to spot modern reproductions of Flow Blue, Majolica, Old Sleepy Eye, Stoneware, Willow, and other ceramic pieces.

Note: The key to price is age and condition. As a general rule, the older the piece, the higher the price.

Bank, 5-1/4" h, cottage shape, repairs.........................195.00
Bowl, 14" x 8", rect, handles, all over cobalt floral dec, c1860....150.00
Cake Stand, blue and white transfer, Wild Rose pattern, crazing, 12" d, 2-1/2" h.........................400.00
Cheese Plate, cov, triangular, blue and white transfer, painted floral dec, ironstone.........................225.00
Child's Plate, 4-1/2" d, molded dressed goose, green, brown, and black enamel.........................55.00
Cup and Saucer, handleless, vase of flowers, birds, and shells, imp "Clews," some damage, pr.........................300.00
Figure
   3-1/4" h, rabbit, black and white, brown and green base, wear and enamel flaking.........................315.00
   4" h, dogs, seated, white, polychrome, orange pots in mouth, one with hairlines and chip to base, pr.........................400.00
   4-1/4" h, Spring, pearlware, brown and green glaze, small flakes, old repair.........................220.00
   4-1/2" h, Spring, canary, wear, small flakes.........................770.00
   4-5/8" h, Winter, canary, minor wear, small flakes.........................660.00
   5-1/2" h, 3-1/2" l, boy and girl under tree canopy, sheep and dog, oval base, 2 small nicks.........................90.00

Figures, Queen Victorian and Prince of Wales, 16" h, $880. Photo courtesy of Jackson's Auctioneers & Appraisers.

   6-1/2" h, 3-1/4" d, lad up in tree, bird in hand, nest nearby, girl seated below, oval base, repairs.........................65.00
   7" h, squirrel, sitting upright holding nut, naturalistic stump base, ear repaired.........................125.00
   7-3/4" h, King Charles Spaniel, pr.........................350.00
   13" h, King Charles Spaniel, pr.........................375.00
Hen on Nest, 10-1/2" l, polychrome, good color, minor edge wear and chips on inner flange of base.........................715.00
Jar, cov, 3-1/4" h, melon shape, alternating yellow and green stripes, cov with molded leaf, lead glaze, 18th C, hairline to cover, finial and rim chips.........................4,315.00
Mantel Ornament, 9" h, cottage, Potash Farm, hairlines.........................175.00
Pitcher, 4-7/8" h, mask, pink luster rim, glaze wear, hairline to spout.........................175.00
Plate, 10" d, feather edge, blue, emb rim design.........................55.00
Platter
   14-1/2" w, 19" l, blue and white transfer, sheep and cows in foreground, ruins in background, glaze imperfections.........................575.00
   16" l, 12" w, orchid ground, large colonial transfer scene, c1850.........................195.00
   19" l, Cambrian, Phillips, brown transfer.........................415.00
Sauce Boat, 7-7/8" l, fruit and flowers, molded feet and handle, dark blue, rim chips.........................330.00
Sauce Tureen, 7-1/2" l, blue transfer, pastoral scene, chips.......345.00
Teapot, 6-1/2" h, blue transfer, central dec of bird's nest with eggs.........................460.00
Waste Bowl, 5-5/8" d, Forget Me Not, red transfer, edge roughness.........................60.00

STAFFORDSHIRE, ROMANTIC

History: In the 1830s, two factors transformed the blue-and-white printed wares of the Staffordshire potters into what is now called "Romantic Staffordshire." Technical innovations expanded the range of transfer-printed colors to light blue, pink, purple, black, green, and brown. There was also a shift from historical to imaginary scenes with less printed detail and more white space, adding to the pastel effect.

Shapes from the 1830s are predominately rococo with rounded forms, scrolled handles, and floral finials. Over time, patterns and shapes became simpler and the earthenware bodies coarser. The late 1840s and 1850s saw angular gothic shapes and pieces with the weight and texture of ironstone.

The most dramatic post-1870 change was the impact of the craze for all things Japanese. Staffordshire designs adopted zigzag border elements and motifs such as bamboo, fans, and cranes. Brown printing dominated this style, sometimes with polychrome enamel highlights.

Marks: Wares are often marked with pattern or potter's names, but marking was inconsistent and many authentic, unmarked examples exist. The addition of "England" as a country of origin mark in 1891 helps to distinguish 20th-century wares made in the romantic style.

References: Susan and Al Bagdade, *Warman's English & Continental Pottery & Porcelain*, 3rd Edition, Krause Publications, 1998; Jeffrey B. Snyder, *Romantic Staffordshire Ceramics*, Schiffer Publishing, 1997; Petra Williams, *Staffordshire: Romantic Transfer Patterns* (1978), Staffordshire II (1986), *Staffordshire III* (1996), Fountain House East (P.O. Box 99298, Jeffersontown, KY 40269).

Museums: City Museum & Art Gallery, Stoke-on-Trent, England; Henry Ford Museum, Dearborn, MI.

Caledonia, Williams Adams, 1830s
Plate, 9-1/2" d, purple transfer, imp "Adams"...........................60.00
Platter, 17" l 500.00
Soup Plate, two color..175.00
Canova, Thomas Mayer, c1835; G. Phillips, c1840
Plate, 10-1/2" d...95.00
Pudding Bowl, two color 200.00
Vegetable, cov 325.00
Columbia, W. Adams & Sons, 1850
Creamer..115.00

Cup and Saucer...65.00
Cup Plate...65.00
Plate, 10" d..60.00
Relish...65.00
Dado, Ridgways, 1880s
Creamer, brown 75.00
Cup and Saucer, polychrome 80.00
Plate
7-1/2" d, brown 35.00
10-1/2" d, polychrome...70.00
Delzoni, plate, 8-3/4" d, brown transfer..60.00
India, plate, 9" d, red transfer scene, floral border.....................65.00
Japonica, creamer and sugar 275.00
Marmora, William Ridgway & Co., 1830s
Platter, 16-1/2" l...325.00
Sauce Tureen, matching tray 350.00
Soup Plate...100.00
Millenium, Ralph Stevenson & Son, 1830s, plate, 10-1/2" d 145.00
Palestine, William Adams, 1836
Creamer and Sugar..265.00
Cup and Saucer, two color 135.00
Cup Plate..75.00
Plate
5" d..45.00
7" d..60.00
9-1/2" d...65.00
Platter, 13" l..325.00
Vegetable, open, 12" l...200.00
Union, William Ridgway Son & Co., 1840s
Plate, 10-1/2" d...70.00
Platter, 15" l...165.00
Venus, Podmore, Walker & Co., 1850s, plate, 7-1/2" d 50.00

STAINED and/or LEADED GLASS PANELS

History: American architects in the second half of the 19th century and the early 20th century used stained- and leaded-glass panels as a chief decorative element. Skilled glass craftsmen assembled the designs, the best known being Louis C. Tiffany.

The panels are held together with soft lead cames or copper wraps. When purchasing a panel, protect your investment by checking the lead and making any necessary repairs.

Reference: Web Wilson, *Great Glass in American Architecture*, E. P. Dutton, New York, 1986.

Periodicals: *Glass Art Magazine*, P.O. Box 260377, Highlands Ranch, CO 80126; *Glass Patterns Quarterly*, P.O. Box 131, Westport, NY 40077; *Professional Stained Glass*, P.O. Box 69, Brewster, NY 10509; *Stained Glass*, 6 SW. 2nd St., #7, Lees Summit, MO 64063.

Collectors' Club: Stained Glass Association of America, P.O. Box 22462, Kansas City, MO 64113.

Museum: Corning Museum of Glass, Corning, NY.

Leaded

Firescreen, 48-1/2" w, 32" h, 3 panels, clear glass top half, hammered white glass lower half, central applied Art Nouveau floral design, green bull's eye highlights...2,750.00
Panel, 96" h, 20" w, rect, rippled, and opaque glass, turquoise, white, and avocado, clear glass ground, stylized flowering plant motif, c1910, 6 panels..6,000.00
Sketch for leaded glass window
Charcoal on paper, The Cruxification, 26" d, America, c1920....170.00

Platter, Spanish Convent, Adams, brown transfer, 9-1/8" x 11-1/8", $70.

Leaded window, Arts & Crafts, stylized landscape with redwood, oak, and mountains by river with bridge, polychrome slag glass, from 1901 house, mounted as door in oak frame, 80" h, 47" w, $7,000. Photo courtesy of David Rago Auctions, Inc.

Charcoal on paper, The Temptation, 26" d, America, c1920 . 150.00
Watercolor, garden scene, mother and child before Christ figure, sgd on mat "Louis Comfort Tiffany," 6-3/4" x 4-1/2" 1,725.00
Triptych, 34-3/4" h, 17-3/4" w, twining grapevines and grape clusters, green slag, textured purple and brown glass, amber border segments, textured colorless glass background, wood frame, cracks 1,380.00
Window
    23" h, 25-1/2" w, Prairie School, copper caming, textured clear and green glass, stylized floral pattern 1,000.00
    29-1/2" h, 18" w, attributed to Belcher Mosaic Glass Co., passion flower, pink ribbon, and rose bud against variegated amber ground, opalescent roundels, sea green and reddish umber frame of mosaic glass, unsigned 2,400.00
    36" h, 16-1/4" d, Prairie School, zinc caming, clear, white, green, and violet slag glass, stylized lilies and tulips, set of 5, few minor cracks in glass 4,250.00

Stained
Panel
    24" x 14", red, white, green, pink, and blue floral design, 2 layers of striated and fractured glass, green patinated bronze frame, stamped "Tiffany Studios New York" pr 2,400.00
    26" x 21", Richard the Lion-Hearted on horseback, 1883 ..... 675.00
Window
    32" x 24", Art Nouveau, yellow, blue, and orange geometric, oak frame, c1900 .... 275.00
    61-1/2" h, 61" l, over entry door type, blue and orange shield and geometric design, c1920 .... 490.00

STANGL POTTERY BIRDS

History: Stangl ceramic birds were produced from 1940 until the Stangl factory closed in 1978. The birds were produced at Stangl's Trenton plant and either decorated there or shipped to their Flemington, New Jersey, outlet for hand painting.

During World War II, the demand for these birds, and other types of Stangl pottery as well, was so great that 40 to 60 decorators could not keep up with the demand.

Orders were contracted out to be decorated by individuals in their own homes. These orders then were returned for firing and finishing. Colors used to decorate these birds varied according to the artist.

Marks: As many as ten different trademarks were used. Almost every bird is numbered; many are artist signed. However, the signatures are used only for dating purposes and add very little to the value of the birds.

References: Harvey Duke, *Stangl Pottery*, Wallace-Homestead, 1992; Robert C. Runge, Jr., *The Collector's Encyclopedia of Stangl Dinnerware*, 1998; Mike Schneider, *Stangl and Pennsbury Birds*, Schiffer Publishing, 1994.

Collectors' Clubs: American Art Pottery Association, P.O. Box 834, Westport, MA 02790-0697, http://www.amart-pot.org; Stangl/Fulper Collectors Club, P.O. Box 538, Flemington, NJ 08822.

Additional Listings: See *Warman's Americana & Collectibles* for more examples.

Advisor: Bob Perzel.

Note: Several birds were reissued between 1972 and 1977. These reissues are dated on the bottom and are worth approximately the same as older birds if well decorated.

3250, feeding Duck, natural colors 125.00
3250, standing Duck, Antique Gold 45.00
3273, Rooster, 5-3/4" h 850.00
3274, Penguin 475.00
3276, pair of Bluebirds 175.00
3285, 3286, Rooster and Hen shakers, pr 100.00
3400, Lovebird, old 100.00
3400, Lovebird, reused 60.00
3401, pair of revised brown Wrens 100.00
3401, pair of tan Wrens... 400.00
3404, pair of Lovebirds, original, kissing 350.00
3404, pair of revised Lovebirds, with bud 125.00
3406, Kingfisher 75.00
3408, small Bird of Paradise 125.00

Cockatoo, #3580, 8-7/8" h, $135.

3432, running Duck	700.00
3443, flying Duck, teal	300.00
3445, Rooster, yellow	200.00
3446, Hen, gray	275.00
3449, Parakeet	175.00
3454, Key West Quail/Dove, single wing up	300.00
3454, Key West Quail/Dove, both winds up	1,250.00
3459, Fishhawk/Osprey/Falcon	6,000.00
3491, Hen Pheasant	225.00
3518, pair of white-headed Pigeons	800.00
3581, group of Chickadees	180.00
3585, Rufus Hummingbird	75.00
3589, Indigo Bunting	90.00
3595, Bobolink	150.00
3625, Broadtail Hummingbird with blue flower	150.00
3634, Allca Hummingbird	75.00
3715, Blue Jay with peanut	700.00
3715, Blue Jay with peanut, black/blue Fulper glaze	1,400.00
3747, Canary with blue flower	200.00
3749, Western Tanager	350.00
3750, pair of Scarlet Tanagers	600.00
3751, Red Headed Woodpecker, pink glossy	475.00
3752, pair of Red Headed woodpeckers, red matte	525.00
3754, pair of white-winged Crossbills, pink glossy	400.00
3754, pair of white-winged Crossbills, red matte	450.00
3756, pair of Audubon Warblers	600.00
3757, Scissortail Flycatcher	800.00
3758, Magpie Jay	1,250.00
3925, Magnolia Warbler	2,500.00
3922, European Finch	900.00

STATUES

History: Beginning with primitive cultures, man created statues in the shape of people and animals. During the Middle Ages, most works were religious and symbolic in character and form. During the Renaissance, the human and secular forms were preferred.

During the 18th and 19th centuries, it was fashionable to have statues in the home. Many famous works were copied for use by the general public.

Reference: H. Nicholas B. Clark, *A Marble Quarry: The James H. Ricau Collection of Sculpture at the Chrysler Museum of Art*, Hudson Hills Press, 1997.

Note: Statuette or figurine denotes smaller statues, one-fourth life-size or less.

12" h, nude boy, seated on pillow incised with foliate designs, white marble, Continental, 19th C 635.00
12" x 24" x 16", Bear Hut with Cossacks, Eugene Alexandrovitch Lanceray, bronze, stamped in Cyrillic in base 2,100.00
14-1/2" h, The Eternal Woman, Ernst Hegenbarth, nude female, arms crossed over her chest, sits triumphantly atop her male victims, bronze, green brown patina, inscribed "ER Hegenbarth 1908," Wiener Gesell Schaft, Vienna foundry 1,200.00
28-3/4" h, La Nature Se Devoilant Devant La Science (Nature Revealing Herself Before Science), Louis Ernest Barrias, standing partially nude female emerging from under wraps, inscribed "E. Barrias," dated '20 Mars 1902, stamped "Susse Fres Edition" foundry seal, bronze and silvered bronze figure, gold, green, and silver patina 13,000.00
30" h, Master of the Hounds, Hippolyte Moreau, sgd in case, "Hippolyte Moreau, Lecourtier," dark brown patina 4,500.00
33" h, Madonna Nursing Child, carved stone, unknown 18th C German artist, some remaining polychrome paint 2,000.00
47-3/4" h, Stehender Torso, Herman Hubacher, sgd "Hubacher," dated "24," stamped foundry mark, "M. Pastori, cire perdue, Geneva," bronze lost wax process, greenish-black patina 3,750.00

Cupid and Psyche, Carrara marble, from Thurlow Lodge, Menlo Park, $176,500. Photo courtesy of Butterfield & Butterfield.

53" h, Young Neptune, marble, sgd, located, and dated "Pio fede, Sculp, Firenze, 1859," restorations 2,500.00
58" h, 45" l, Nude Woman, bronze, ballet pose, large green marble base, figure sgd "V. Salmones 88 B-20 PA" 3,300.00
63-1/2" h, Three Graces, marble, Continental, artist unknown, after the antique 2,500.00

STEIFF

History: Margarete Steiff, GmbH, established in Germany in 1880, is known for very fine-quality stuffed animals and dolls as well as other beautifully made collectible toys. It is still in business, and its products are highly respected.

The company's first products were wool-felt elephants made by Margaret Steiff. In a few years, the animal line was expanded to include a donkey, horse, pig, and camel.

By 1903, the company also was producing a jointed mohair teddy bear, whose production dramatically increased to more than 970,000 units in 1907. Margarete's nephews took over the company at this point.

Newly designed animals were added: Molly and Bully, the dogs, and Fluffy, the cat. Pull toys and kites also were produced, as well as larger animals on which children could ride or play.

Marks: The bear's-head label became the symbol for the firm in about 1907, and the famous "Button in the Ear" round, metal trademark was added.

References: Peter Consalvi, Sr., *2nd Collector Steiff Values*, Hobby House Press, 1996; Margaret and Gerry Grey, *Teddy Bears*, Running Press, Courage Books, 1994; Margaret Fox Mandel, *Teddy Bears and Steiff Animals*, 1st Series (1984, 1997 value update), 2nd Series (1987, 1996 value update), Collector Books; ——, *Teddy Bears*, Annalee

Left: Bear pull toy, gray mohair coat, glass eyes, leather collar, steel frame, cast iron wheels, wear, unmarked, 22" I, 14" h, $825; center: Dog pull toy, orange and white mohair coat, glass eyes, steel frame, cast iron wheels, one ear missing, ear button, voice box does not work, 15-1/2" I, 14" h, $280; right: Boxer, beige mohair coat, black trim, glass eyes, leather collar mkd "Steiff," head turns, minor wear, 16-1/2" I, 15-1/2" h, $175. Photo courtesy of Garth's Auctions.

Animals & Steiff Animals, 3rd Series, Collector Books, 1990, 1996 value update; Dee Hockenberry, *Big Bear Book*, Schiffer Publishing, 1996; Linda Mullins, *Teddy Bear & Friends Price Guide*, 4th ed., Hobby House Press, 1993.

Collectors' Clubs: Steiff Club USA, 31 E. 28th St., 9th Floor, New York, NY 10016, http://www.steiff-club.com; Steiff Collectors Club, 5001 Monroe St., Toledo, OH 43623, http://www.toystorenet.com.

Additional Listings: Teddy Bears. See also Stuffed Toys in *Warman's Americana & Collectibles* for more examples.

Notes: Become familiar with genuine Steiff products before purchasing an antique stuffed animal. Plush in old Steiff animals was mohair; trimmings usually were felt or velvet. Unscrupulous individuals have attached the familiar Steiff metal button to animals that are not Steiff.

Bear
   10" h, excelsior stuffed mohair plush, swivel head, black shoe-button eyes, black floss nose and mouth, back lump, jointed at shoulders and hips, elongated arms and oversized feet, beige felt pads with 4 floss claws, unmarked 650.00
   11" h, dark brown, cream muzzle and feet, fully jointed, glass eyes, excelsior stuffing, raised letter chrome ear buttons, 1950s, some fur and fiber loss 195.00
   11-1/4" h, ginger mohair, unjointed, black steel eyes, black embroidered nose and mouth, felt pads, underscored bottom, steel frame and spoked wheels, c1910, spotty fur and fiber loss 435.00
   11-1/2" h, blond mohair, fully jointed, black shoe button eyes, excelsior stuffing, c1905, re-embroidered nose, mouth, and claws, replaced pads, button missing 375.00
   13" h, cream mohair, fully jointed, black steel eyes, light brown embroidered nose, mouth, and claws, excelsior stuffing, felt pads, c1906, ear button, spotty fur and fiber loss...................... 1,035.00
   13" h, gold, fully jointed, black steel eyes, embroidered nose, mouth, and claws, tan felt pads, excelsior stuffing, c1906, slight fur loss, one leg restitched, slight moth damage on pads 2,185.00
   13-1/2" h, light tan mohair, fully jointed, glass eyes, brown embroidered nose, mouth, and claws, excelsior stuffing, felt pads, early 20th C, ear button, slight fur loss and matting, moth damage on pads 230.00
   17" h, Anniversary, light yellow mohair, fully jointed, glass eyes, black embroidered nose, mouth, and claws, felt pads, 1980s, ear button and tag, information sheet, orig box 375.00
   18" h, brown mohair, fully jointed, glass eyes, excelsior stuffing, tan

felt pads, black embroidered nose, mouth, and claws, early 1920s, underscored F button, spotty fur loss................... 2,100.00
   19" h, apricot mohair, fully jointed, black steel eyes, excelsior stuffing, embroidered brown nose, mouth, and claws, felt pads, c1906, underscored F button, moth damage on pads, some fur and fiber loss 3,795.00
   22" I, 14" h, pull toy, gray mohair coat, glass eyes, leather collar, steel frame, cast iron wheels, wear, unmarked................... 825.00
   23" h, cream mohair, fully jointed, black steel eyes, excelsior stuffing, light rust embroidered nose, mouth, and claws, c1906, blank button, slight moth damage, some fur loss on face 9,775.00
   31" I, 24" h, pull toy, brown mohair coat, glass eyes, ear button with ribbon, ring pull voice box, steel frame, sheet metal wheels with black rubber treads mkd "Steiff," added leather collar and rope pull 2,100.00
   65" h, brown mohair, jointed head and arms, glass eyes, cream face and feet, open mouth, black embroidered nose, excelsior stuffing, 1948, ear button and tag, right foot damaged 865.00
Beaver, 6" I, Nagy, mohair, chest tag, post WWII.......................... 95.00
Bison, 9-1/2" I, mohair, ear button, chest tag, post WWII 200.00
Boxer, 16-1/2" I, 15-1/2" h, beige mohair coat, black trim, glass eyes, leather collar mkd "Steiff," head turns, minor wear, straw stuffing. 165.00
Boxer Puppy, 4-1/4" h, paper label "Daly" 135.00
Cat
   7" h, beige velvet, black paint, faded red ribbon, pink hand warmer, ear button, wear, tail sewn back 550.00
   14" I, pull top, white mohair coat, gray stripes, glass eyes, worn pink ribbon with bell, pink felt ear linings, button, cast iron wheels.... 1,980.00
Cocker Spaniel, 5-3/4" h, sitting, glass eyes, ear button, chest tag, post WWII 125.00
Cocker Spaniel Puppy, 4-3/4" h, button 90.00
Dalmatian Puppy, 4-1/4" h, paper label "Sarras" 145.00
Dog, 15-1/2" I, 14" h, pull toy, orange and white mohair coat, glass eyes, steel frame, cast iron wheels, one ear missing, button in remaining ear, voice box does not work 280.00
Frog, 3-3/4" I, velveteen, glass eyes, green, sitting, button and chest tag 125.00
Goat, 6-1/2" h, ear button 150.00
Gussy, 6-1/2" I, white and black kitten, glass eyes, ear button, chest tag, post WWII 125.00
Kangaroo and Joey, 20-3/4" h mother, mohair, jointed head and arms, glass eyes, black embroidered nose and mouth, ear button and tag, 4" h velveteen baby with glass eyes, embroidered nose and mouth, ear button and tag missing 375.00
Koala, 7-1/2" h, glass eyes, ear button, chest tag, post WWII 135.00
Lion
   21" I, 18" h, pull toy, worn gold mohair coat, glass eyes, worn streaked mane incomplete, no tail, ring pull voice box, steel frame, sheet metal wheels with white rubber treads mkd "Steiff" 500.00
   26" I, recumbent, glass eyes, embroidered nose, mouth, and claws, post WWII, ears and button missing, spotty fur loss 55.00
Lizard, 12" I, Lizzy, velveteen, yellow and green, black steel eyes, chest tag 200.00
Llama, 10" h, glass eyes, ear button, chest tag, post WWII 125.00
Monkey, 5" h, Coco, glass eyes, ear button, chest tag, post WWII.. 125.00
Owl, 4-1/2" h, Wittie, glass eyes, ear button, chest tag, post WWII ... 95.00
Palomino Colt, 11" h, ear button, wear...................................... 330.00
Panda, 6" h, black and white mohair, fully jointed, glass eyes, excelsior stuffing, felt open mouth and pads, c1950, some fur loss, moth damage on pads, button and tag missing 260.00
Parakeet, 6-1/2" h, Hansi, bright lime green and yellow, airbrushed black details, plastic eyes, button tag, chest tag, plastic beak and feet.. 115.00
Penguin, 5-1/2" h, Peggy, glass eyes, ear button, chest tag, post WWII 95.00
Pig, 15" I, pull top, blonde mohair, button eyes, ear button, cast iron wheels, repairs, very worn mohair 330.00
Rabbit, 9-1/2" h, unmarked, wear 220.00
Soldier, 14" h, c1913, slight moth damage, hat and equipment missing 460.00

Sheep, 12-1/2" l, pull toy, woolly mohair coat, felt legs and face, button eyes, worn ribbon with bell, head turns, cast iron wheels, one ear incomplete, button missing..935.00
Squirrel, 6" h, unmarked 75.00
Tiger
    5-3/4" h, glass eyes, minor fading, not marked 50.00
    31" l, recumbent, unjointed, pink embroidered nose, black mouth and claws, ear button, post WWII, some damage 115.00
Turtle, 7" l, Slo, plastic shell, glass eyes, ear button, chest tag, post WWII.. 85.00
Walrus, 6-1/2" l, Paddy, plastic tusk, glass eyes, ear button, chest tag, post WWII.. 145.00

STEINS

History: Steins, mugs especially made to hold beer or ale, range in size from the smaller 3/10 and 1/4 liter to the larger 1, 1-1/2, 2, 3, 4, and 5 liters, and in rare cases to 8 liters. (A liter is 1.05 liquid quarts.)

    Master steins or pouring steins hold 3 to 5 liters and are called krugs. Most steins are fitted with a metal hinged lid with thumb lift. The earthenware character-type steins usually are German in origin.

References: Susan and Al Bagdade, *Warman's English & Continental Pottery & Porcelain*, 3rd Edition, Krause Publications, 1998; Gary Kirsner, *German Military Steins*, 2nd ed., Glentiques (P.O. Box 8807, Coral Springs, FL 33075), 1996; —, *Mettlach Book*, 3rd ed., 1994; Gary Kirsner and Jim Gruhl, *The Stein Book, A 400 Year History*, Glentiques, 1990.

Periodicals: *Regimental Quarterly*, P.O. Box 793, Frederick, MD 21705; *The Beer Stein Journal*, P.O. Box 8807, Coral Springs, FL 33075.

Collectors' Clubs: Stein Collectors International, P.O. Box 5005, Laurel, MD 20726-5005; Sun Steiners, P.O. Box 11782, Fort Lauderdale, FL 33339.

Museum: Milwaukee Art Center, Milwaukee, WI.

Character

Beethoven, half liter, porcelain, lire on side of body and on porcelain inlaid lid, E. Bohne & Sohn..570.00
Cat with Hangover, 1/2 liter, porcelain, inlaid lid, Schierholz, repaired chip on ribbon head bandage..330.00
Drunken Monkey, 1/2 liter, porcelain, inlaid lid, mkd "RPM"........220.00
Frederick III, in uniform, 1/2 liter, porcelain, porcelain lid, Schierholz, chips on lid repaired, int. color yellowing.............................. 1,735.00
Hunter Rabbit, 1/2 liter, inlaid lid, mkd "RPM" 295.00
Indian, 1/4 liter, porcelain, inlaid lid, E. Bohne & Sohn 440.00
L.A.W. high wheel bicycle, half liter, porcelain, lithophane of man falling onto woman, inlaid lid, Schierholz..440.00
Monk, 1/2 liter, pewter, pewter lid, heaving casting....................350.00
Monk, 1/3 liter, design by Frank Ringer, mkd "J. Reinemann, Munchen" on underside of base, inlaid lid, 5" h 580.00
Singing Pig, 1/2 liter, porcelain, Schierholz, inlaid lid................580.00
Skull, 1/3 liter, porcelain, large jaw, inlaid lid, E. Bohne & Sohn, pewter slightly bent 550.00

SPECIAL AUCTIONS

Andre Ammelounx
P.O. Box 136
Palantine, IL 60078
(708) 991-5927

Mettlach, #2065, 1-1/2 liter, etched, multicolored, jeweled base, sgd "Schlitt," $1,200.

Faience

Thuringen, 1 liter, 9-1/2" h, hp, floral design on front, purple trees on sides, pewter top rim and lid, pewter base ring, 18th C, tight hairline on side...1,155.00

Glass

9-1/2" h, 1 liter, blown, wedding type, hp floral design and verse, pewter lid with earlier date of 1779, pewter brass ring, c1850........ 925.00
15-1/4" h, 6-1/2" d, amber, encased in fancy French pewter frame, ram's heads around stein, hinged top lid 495.00

Ivory, hand carved, c1850-70

11-1/2" h, elaborate battle scene with approx. 100 figures, carving around entire body, silver top with figural knight finial, cherub bases and fruit in repousse o lid, figural handle of man in armor, silver base with touch marks, discoloration to ivory 6,700.00
13-1/2" h, elaborate hunting scene, 4 men on horseback, 15 dogs, ivory lid with various animals carved around border, 3-1/2" h finial of man blowing trumpet with dog, figural handle of bare breasted woman with crown, dog head thumblift, left arm and trumpet missing 11,550.00

Porcelain

Delft, 1/2 liter, elaborate scene of 2 people playing lawn tennis, porcelain inlaid lid of sail boat, mkd "Delft, Germany"....................1,390.00
Meissen, 1 liter, 7" h, hp, scene of 3 people in forest, floral design around sides, porcelain lid with berry finial and painted flowers, closed hinge, cross swords and "S" mark, c1820, strap repoured....................3,100.00
Schierholz, Musterchultz, Sad Radish, ... 295.00

Pottery

1/4 liter, transfer and enameled, color, Ulmer Splatz!, The Bird from the City of Ulm, pewter lid 115.00
1/2 liter, relief, tan, brown, and green, chicken with egg body design, relief pewter lid with bust of Bismarck, repaired tear in pewter, 2" hairline l body.. 130.00

Regimental, 1/2 liter, porcelain

2 Schwer. Reit. Regt. Erzh. Fz, Ferd u. Osterr-Este5 Esk Landshut 1899-02, named to Friederich Schmidt, 2 side scenes, lion thumblift, old tear on lid repaired, minor scruffs, 11-1/2" h...................... 675.00

11 Armee Corps, Mainz 1899, names to Res. Doring, 2 side scenes, plain thumblift, strap tear repaired, lines in lithophane, 10" h... 485.00

30 Field Artillery, Rastatt 1897-99, named to Freund Hilfstromp, 2 side scenes, roster, thumblift missing 375.00

50 Field Artillery, Karlsruhe 1899-01, named to Knonier Hillenbrand, 2 side scenes, roster, Griffin thumblift, minor pewter tear, 10-1/2" h. 550.00

61 Field Artillery, Dartmstadt 1910-12, named to Kanonier Boxheimer, 4 side sides, roster worn, lion thumblift 415.00

120 Infantry, Ulm 1899-01, named to Tambour Wurst, 2 side scenes, Wurttemberg thumblift, 10-1/2" h 520.00

123 Grenadier, Ulm 1908-10, named to Grenadier Schindler, 4 side scenes, roster, bird thumblift, open blister on int. base, finial missing 550.00

127 Infantry, Ulm 1910-12, named to Musketier Vollm, 4 side scenes, roster, bird thumblift, 11-1/2" h 475.00

Wood and Pewter, Daubenkrug

1/2 liter, 6-1/2" h, pewter scene of deer, vines and leaves on sides, pewter handle and lid, c1820, some separations to pewter 925.00

1/3 liter, 5-1/2" h, floral design on sides, oval with crown on front, pewter handle and lid, 18th C, splints in pewter and wood 1,270.00

STEUBEN GLASS

History: Frederick Carder, an Englishman, and Thomas G. Hawkes of Corning, New York, established the Steuben Glass Works in 1904. In 1918, the Corning Glass Company purchased the Steuben company. Carder remained with the firm and designed many of the pieces bearing the Steuben mark. Probably the most widely recognized wares are Aurene, Verre De Soie, and Rosaline, but many other types were produced.

The firm is still operating, producing glass of exceptional quality.

References: Thomas P. Dimitroff, Charles R. Hajdamach, Jane Shadel Spillman, and Robert f. Rockwell III, *Frederick Carder and Steuben Glass: American Classic*, Schiffer Publishing, 1998; Paul Gardner, *Glass of Frederick Carder*, Crown Publishers, 1971; Paul Perrot, Paul Gardner, and James S. Plaut, *Steuben*, Praeger Publishers, 1974; Kenneth Wilson, *American Glass 1760-1930*, 2 vols., Hudson Hills Press and The Toledo Museum of Art, 1994.

Museums: Corning Museum of Glass, Corning, NY; Rockwell Museum, Corning, NY.

Aurene, vase, Optic Rib, sgd "Steuben, Aurene, 6299," 5-3/4" h, $1,995.

Aurene

Bowl, 6" d, blue, irid surface 275.00

Candlesticks, pr, 10-1/8" h, catalog #686, amber, twist stems on applied disc foot, strong gold luster, sgd "Aurene 686," c1920 .... 1,100.00

Lamp Shade, 4-3/8" h, shape #2320, ribbed, bell shape, obscure silver fleur-de-lis paint stamp, pr 400.00

Perfume
4-1/4" h, tapered and paneled body, raised neck, floral molded stopper, strong blue irid with green and purple highlights, pontil sgd "Aurene 2758," c1920, light surface scratches 865.00
4-3/4" h, catalog #1455, melon ribbed, gold, ball top stopper with applied gold bead, base sgd "Aurene 1455" within polished pontil, c1910, stopper possible r
eplacement 635.00

Planter, 12" d, blue, inverted rim, three applied prunt feet, engraved "Aurene 2586" 775.00

Vase
4-3/4" h, catalog #209, green pulled loops, gold irid, inscribed "Aurene 209" 1,035.00
8" h, catalog #1124, gold, decumbent collar, trumpet form, strong irid, engraved "Aurene," numbered 550.00
8-1/2" h, catalog #2697, blue, flattened cone, raised pedestal foot, white vines and gold Aurene hearts, base engraved "Steuben Aurene 2697" 2,000.00

Celeste Blue

Candlesticks, brilliant blue, applied foliate form bobeche and cups, bulbed shafts, c1920-33, set of 4 .... 2,300.00

Center Bowl, 16-1/4" d, 4-1/4" h, catalog #112, swirled optic ribbed broad bowl, rolled rim, applied fluted foot, partially polished pontil, c1925 .... 400.00

Finger Bowl, Underplate, catalog #2889, 5" d flared bowl, 6-1/2" underplate, swirled ribbed design, c1925, set of 12, some chips 600.00

Iced Tea Goblet, 6-1/2" h, catalog #5192, blue, flared, light ribbon, c1918-32, set of 8 .... 400.00

Juice Glass, 4-1/2" h, catalog #5192, blue, flared, light ribbon, c1918-32, set of 8 .... 375.00

Luncheon Plate, 8-1/2" d, molded blue body, Kensington pattern variant, engraved border of leaves and dots, c1918-32, set of 12. 550.00

Cluthra

Lamp Base, 12-1/2" h, ovoid, creamy white cluthra acid-etched Art Deco flowers, acid-etched fleur-de-lis mark near base, orig gilded foliate bronze lamp fittings, c1925 .... 2,070.00

Vase, 6-1/4" h, catalog #2683, urn form, mottled royal blue and white, small trapped bubbles, polished pontil and acid fleur-de-lis, mkd "Steuben" 1,035.00

Wall Pocket, 15-1/2" w, 8" h, half round flared bowl, black and white cluthra, cut and mounted to foliate gilt metal framework, polished pontil, c1930, slight corrosion to metal 490.00

Crystal

Bud Vase, 6-3/4" h, elongated neck on swollen base, applied ball and scroll dec, base inscribed "Steuben," designed by Don Wier, 1947, Madigan catalog #7947, light staining 200.00

Goblet, 7-1/16" h, flared cylindrical vessel, knobbed stem, sq base, small "S" inscribed on base, designed by Arthur A. Houghton, Jr., 1938, Madigan catalog #7846, set of six, 2 with small chips ... 260.00

Vase
7-3/8" h, catalog #SP919, flared wing form, pedestal base, inscribed "Steuben" on base 330.00
10-1/2" h, catalog #7500, oviform, disk base, engraved grasses and stars, design by Walter Teague, acid stamp mark on pontil..... 575.00

Grotesque

Bowl, 11-1/2" l, 6-1/4" h, blue jade, Frederick Carder design, minor int. surface wear, fleur-de-lis mark 3,850.00

Vase, 9-1/4" h, amethyst, catalog #7090, pillar molded floriform body, ruffled rim shaded to colorless crystal at applied disk foot, acid script "Steuben" mark in polished pontil, c1930 .... 525.00

Ivory

Bowl, 9-1/2" d, 4-3/4" h, catalog #7337, inward curved shoulder, 4 double ribbed panels, bulbous body, unmarked 435.00

Jade

Candlesticks, pr, 10" h, No. 2956, jade candle cup and base, alabaster shaft, gold foil labels 550.00
Compote, 10" h, yellow, ftd 1,450.00
Lamp Base
    10-1/4" h, green jade bulbous base, long flared neck, rolled rim, applied spiral of alabaster glass ending with rosettes, silvered metal lamp fittings, c1925 .... 900.00
    12" h, catalog #7001, urn form, plum jade, intricately etched in Belgrade pattern, gilt-metal lamp fittings, c1925, chips to rim under mounting 2,415.00
    13" h flared double gourd shaped dark amethyst body cased to alabaster int., overlaid with amethyst, cameo etched in Chinese pattern, double etched with scrolling design, gilt metal fittings with 3 scroll arms, shallow chip under fixture 1,850.00
Parfait, 6" h, applied alabaster foot 350.00
Rose Bowl, 7" d, 7" h, spherical, smooth jade crystal 350.00
Vase, ovoid green body, flared neck, applied alabaster "M" handles, polished pontil, c1929 .... 1,100.00

Miscellaneous

Bowl, 6-1/2" h, Old Ivory, catalog #7307, pillar ftd, applied raised foot, c1930 .... 435.00
Candlesticks, pr, 11-3/4" h, catalog #2956, amber glass baluster shaped stems, wide disk foot, c1925 .... 690.00
Compote, 8" d, 2-1/4" h, circular, raised rim, pedestal base, rope-twist connector, clear, inscribed "Steuben" on base, mid 20th C 230.00
Exhibition Sculpture, 18" h, Salmon Run, designed by James Houston, engraved by George Thompson, number 14 in series of 20, orig red leather and velvet box 13,500.00
Lamp Base
    10-1/4" h, catalog #8023, urn form, swirled purple, blue, and red moss agate, gilt-metal lamp fittings, acanthus leaf dec, purple glass jewel at top, needs rewiring 2,415.00
    14" h, catalog #8006, bulbous, long flared neck, alabaster, etched Grape pattern, silvered metal lamp fittings, c1925 .... 1,150.00
Paperweight, Excalibur, designed by James Houston, 1963, catalog #1000, faceted hand polished solid crystal embedded with removable sterling silver sword, 18kt gold scabbard, base inscribed "Steuben" 1,955.00
Pitcher, 9" h, catalog #6665, Spanish Green, slightly ribbed oval, flared mouth, applied angled handle, raised disk foot, acid fleur-de-lis mark 460.00
Serving Plate, 14-1/4" d, 2" h, catalog #3579, Bristol Yellow, board convex and folded rim, slight optic ribbing, wear scratches 200.00
Vase, 12-1/2" h, 9-1/4" d, catalog #7389, Strawberry Mansion, flared bulb form, colorless, sq plinth base, two applied "M" handles, designed by Frederick Carder, 1934, nick at base 1,035.00

Rosaline

Bowl, 8" l, 7" w, 3-1/4" h, one end folded in, other pinched spout, inscribed "F. Carder Steuben 723" on edge of polished pontil . 350.00
Compote, 4" h, ruffled, alabaster stem and foot 275.00
Goblet, crystal foot 90.00
Perfume, 5-3/8" h, catalog #6412, teardrop shape, cloudy pink, applied alabaster glass foot, c1925, pr 435.00

Verre De Soie

Bonbon, 6" h, compote form, overall irid surface, swirled celeste blue finial, twisted stem 850.00
Perfume, 4-1/2" h, catalog #1455, ribbed body, celeste blue flame stopper, c1915 .... 400.00
Vase, 10" h, classic form, notched rim, all over floral motif 450.00

Wisteria, dichroic leaded glass, engraved Pillar pattern, reverse-engraved dots on base
Candlesticks, pr, 8-1/4" h, catalog #7093, fleur-de-lis stamp on polished pontil 1,035.00
Finger Bowl and Underplate, catalog #1679, 4-3/4" d three ftd bowl, 7-1/4" d tray, , fleur-de-lis mark, c1927, 3 bowls, 4 plates 750.00
Goblet, 9" h, catalog #7182, bell shaped, c1927, set of 4 .... 1,150.00

STEVENS and WILLIAMS

History: In 1824, Joseph Silvers and Joseph Stevens leased the Moor Lane Glass House at Briar Lea Hill (Brierley Hill), England, from the Honey-Borne family. In 1847, William Stevens and Samuel Cox Williams took over, giving the firm its present name. In 1870, the company moved to its Stourbridge plant. In the 1880s, the firm employed such renowned glass artisans as Frederick C. Carder, John Northwood, other Northwood family members, James Hill, and Joshua Hodgetts.

Stevens and Williams made cameo glass. Hodgetts developed a more commercial version using thinner-walled blanks, acid etching, and the engraving wheel. Hodgetts, an amateur botanist, was noted for his brilliant floral designs.

Other glass products and designs manufactured by Stevens and Williams include intaglio ware, Peach Bloom (a form of peachblow), moss agate, threaded ware, "jewell" ware, tapestry ware, and Silveria. Stevens and Williams made glass pieces covering the full range of late Victorian fashion.

After World War I, the firm concentrated on refining the production of lead crystal and achieving new glass colors. In 1932, Keith Murray came to Stevens and Williams as a designer. His work stressed the pure nature of the glass form. Murray stayed with Stevens and Williams until World War II and later followed a career in architecture.

Additional Listings: Cameo Glass.

Biscuit Jar, cov, 7-1/2" h, 5-1/2" d, cream opaque, large amber and green applied ruffled leaves, rich pink int., SP rim, lid, and handle 300.00

Rose Bowl, satin, brown shaded to rich yellow, 6 box pleated crimps, polished pontil, 4-3/4" h, $225. Photo courtesy of Johanna Billings.

Bowl, 6" d, 3" h, Matsu No Ke, creamy yellow satin, twisted knurled thorny frosted clear glass branch winds around perimeter, 36 florets, 3 feet, inscribed "Rd. 15353" 1,250.00

Calling Card Receiver, 10" l, applied amber handle, rolled edge, translucent opalescent ground, 3 applied berries, blossoms, and green leaves, 3 applied amber feet 750.00

Ewer, 8-1/2" h, 5" w, Pompeiian Swirl, deep rose shading to yellow, off white lining, frosted loop handle, all over gold enameled wild roses, ferns, and butterfly 1,500.00

Jardiniere, 6-1/2" d, 10" h, pink opalescent, cut back, 2 spatter flowers and sunflowers, 3 applied opalescent thorn feet, leaves, and stems, minor damage 350.00

Perfume, 4-3/4" h, spherical, heat reactive dark amber shaded to green satin, spiraled air-trap switch, hallmarked and chased silver cap, c1890 .... 635.00

Pitcher, 7" h, 4-1/2" d, mint green ext., robin's egg blue lining, 3 white and pink blossoms, amber leaves, twisting clear amber glass tendril which twists to form handle, end of handle ground smooth 385.00

Rose Bowl, Osiris, peacock eye mother-of-pearl 900.00

Vase
5-1/2" h, Pompeian Swirl, MOP, pink air trap, alternating blue air trap ribbons with satiny sheen, slight anomaly (possibly made-in-the-making) at rim 545.00
6-1/2" h, white cylinder cased to rose pink ext., acid etched floral spray, c1880 .... 325.00
7-1/8" h, gourd shape, spiraled air-trap swirls, bronze satin shaded to light blue cased to yellow int., polished pontil, c1885 ..... 350.00
10" h, pale rose pink cased to transparent green, wheel cut intaglio foliate panels, horizontal stepped flared rim 1,850.00
10-1/2" h, ovoid body, elongated and bulbed neck, deep red overlaid in white, cameo etched and engraved grosbeak on flowering branch with 2 butterflies, central stylized floral border, c1890, chip on base border 2,185.00

STICKLEYS

History: There were five Stickley brothers: Albert, Gustav, Leopold, George, and John George. Gustav often is credited with creating the Mission style, a variant of the Arts and Crafts style. Gustav headed Craftsman Furniture, a New York firm, much of whose actual production took place near Syracuse. A characteristic of Gustav's furniture is exposed tenon ends. Gustav published The Craftsman, a magazine espousing his antipathy to machines.

Originally Leopold and Gustav worked together. In 1902, Leopold and John George formed the L. and J. G. Stickley Furniture Company. This firm made Mission-style furniture and cherry and maple early-American style pieces.

George and Albert organized the Stickley Brothers Company, located in Grand Rapids, Michigan.

References: Donald A. Davidoff and Robert L. Zarrow, *Early L. & J. G. Stickley Furniture*, Dover Publications, 1992; *Furniture of the Arts & Crafts Period*, L-W Book Sales, 1992, 1995 value update; Thomas K. Maher, *The Kaufmann Collection: The Early Furniture of Gustav Stickley*, Treadway Gallery (2029 Madison Rd., Cincinnati, OH 45208), 1996; Paul Royka, *Mission Furniture, from the American Arts & Crafts Movement*, Schiffer Publishing, 1997.

Periodical: *Style 1900*, 333 Main St., Lambertville, NJ 08530.

Collectors' Club: Foundation for the Study of Arts & Crafts Movement, Roycroft Campus, 31 S. Grove St., East Aurora, NY 14052.

Museum: Craftsman Farms Foundation, Inc., Morris Plains, NJ.

Note: Gustav denotes Gustav Stickley and Craftsman Furniture; L & J G denotes L. and J. G. Stickley Furniture Company.

Bookcase
36-1/2" w, 12-1/8" d, 55-1/2" h, No. 643, L & J. G., gallery top, dual exposed tenons, 2 doors each with 8 panes of glass, hammered copper door pulls, labeled "The Work of L. & J. G. Stickley," c1912 .... 6,900.00
41-3/4" w, 12-3/4" d, 56" h, similar to No. 716, Gustav, gallery top, 2 doors each with 3 panes of glass, medium brown finish, large red decal, 1904-12 .... 9,200.00
43" w, 13" d, 56" h, gallery top, 2 doors each with 8 panes of glass, shaped pulls, Gustav circular device paper label, 1905-07 ..6,900.00
48" w, 14" d, 58-3/4" h, mahogany, rect top, pair sq leaded clear glass panels over 2 oak divided rect panels, arched lower apron, design by Harvey Ellis, red "Gustav Stickley" mark, c1904, some wear 21,850.00
60" w, 13" d, 56" h, No. 719, gallery top, 2 doors each with 12 panes of glass, shaped pulls, red Gustav decal, retailer's paper label "Walter F. Barnes, Broadway, New York," c1904..... 9,200.00

Card Table, 30" w, 18" d, 28-3/4" h, 2 side drawers with faceted wooden pulls, stretchers mortised through legs, keyed through-tenon center stretcher, orig finish, early red Gustav box decal, minor stains on top 20,000.00

Catalog, Craftsman Furniture Made by Gustav Stickley At The Craftsman Workshops, Eastwood, N.Y., dated Jan. 1909, paper bound 250.00

Cellarette, 20" w, 15" d, 29" h, single drawer and door, hammered copper pulls, arched apron, red Gustav mark, new finish........... 4,000.00

Chair
Arm, 38" h, 27-3/4" w, 20-1/2" d, No. 422, V-back over 6 vertical slats, spring cushion seat, L. & J. G. decal, c1912 .... 460.00
Dining, 17-1/2" w, 16" d, 41-1/4" h, tall back, spindled, fine orig hard leather seat, L & J G, Onondaga Shop 1,200.00
Side, 39-1/4" h, oak, No. 353, 3 vertical back slats, rush seat, arched apron, red Gustav decal, orig medium finish, scratches, roughness 460.00
Side, 40-1/4" h, oak, H-back, rush seat, No. 308, branded Gustav mark, c1912 .... 175.00

Chest of Drawers, 41" w, 21" d, 48" h, No. 906, oak, rect top over 2 short and 4 long drawers, hammered circular pulls, branded Gustav mark, c1912 .... 13,800.00

China Closet, 36" w, 15-1/4" d, 60" h, oak, Gustav, designed by Harvey Ellis, NY, c1904, rect overhanging top, arched single door with glass pane, arched rail below, shelved int. 8,625.00

Couch, 72-1/2" l, 28" d, 22" h, No. 295, slanted head rest, headboard and footboard with 4 horizontal slats centered by single wider slat, webbed support on slanted headboard, spring cushion seat, L. & J. G., Handcraft decal, c1910 .... 1,150.00

Desk
31-1/2" w, 9-3/4" d closed, 21-3/4" d open, 35" h, drop front, gallery top, 2 drawers, gate leg and 2 lower open shelves, medium finish, branded L & J. G. mark, stain, minor roughness 1,840.00
36" w, 24" d, 30" h, No. 650, rect top, single drawer, lower median shelf, paper Gustav label, worn rails, drill holes on top, roughness.... 920.00

Desk Set, hammered copper, blotter, letter holder, pen tray, rocking blotter, paper clip, inkwell with glass liner, stamp box, Gustav, most pcs stamped with joiner's compass, orig patina, 7 pc set 4,500.00

Dining Table, 54" l, 54" w, 30" h, No. 634, oval top, 4 heavy sq posts with large center post, cross stretchers with through tenons, 6 leaves, paper Gustav label, c1907-12 .... 11,500.00

Dresser with Mirror, 48" w, 22" d, 62" h, No. 905, oak, swivel mirror on rect top, 2 short drawers over 3 long drawers, large hammered brass ring pulls, branded Gustav mark, c1912 .... 9,775.00

Drugget Runner, 82" x 21", green and orange Coptic cross geometric pattern, oatmeal ground, Gustav, some wear to selvage 950.00

Foot Stool, 12" l, 12" w, 5" h, oak, dark brown orig leather, flared sq

feet, partial paper Gustav label, wear, older splintered wood, loss to one leg 490.00
Lamp, floor, 65" h, 26" d silk lined wicker shade, four-sided shaft with hammered copper rivets, long corbels, shoe feet, Gustav, unmarked, cleaned orig finish 7,000.00
Lamp Table, 40" d, 28-3/4" d, circular top, sq and arched apron, flaring plank legs, keyed through-tenons, arched cross-stretchers, early Gustav, unmarked, new finish, filled in hole on edge 4,250.00
Library Table
   40" w, 28" d, 29" h, No. 597, overhanging top, narrow lower shelf, mortised with keyed through tenons, orig dark finish, L. & J. G. Handcraft label, some wear to top 1,600.00
   42" w, 28" d, 29" h, single drawer, copper pulls, long corbels, "The Work of L. and J. G. Stickley" label, new finish 1,300.00
   42" w, 29-1/2" d, 30" h, No. 614, oak, rect top, 2 drawers, hammered copper pulls, lower median shelf with through tenons, branded Gustav mark, c1912 .... 2,100.00
   48" d, 30" h, No. 636, circular, orig tacked-on leather top, flaring plank legs, arched apron and cross-stretchers mortised with keyed through tenons, orig finish, large red Gustav box decal, c1902 .... 22,500.00
   65-1/2" l, 35-1/2" d, 30" h, 3 drawer, copper oval pulls, broad lower shelf, orig finish, early red Gustav box decal 5,000.00
Liquor Cabinet, 27-1/4" w, 16" d, 51" h, flush top, 2 door compartment with pull-out copper tray, single drawer, second 2 door cabinet, orig dark finish, unmarked, attributed to Stickley Bros 2,700.00
Magazine Stand, 19" w, 12" w, 45" h, chamfered back, arched backsplash and stretchers, 4 shelves, orig light finish, L & J G Handcraft dec 2,400.00
Mirror, table top, 22" w, 21-1/2" h, swivel, arched rect frame, angled shoe feet, branded Gustav mark, c1912 .... 690.00
Morris Chair, 37" d, 23-3/4" h, No. 2340, open bow-shaped arm, sgd with red Gustav decal in box, c1902-04, webbing missing.. 19,550.00
Music Cabinet, 20" w, 16" d, 46" h, No. 703, oak, gallery top, rect paneled door, branded Gustav mark, c1912 .... 7,475.00
Occasional Table, 30" d, 28-3/4" h, No. 644, round top, 4 cut-in leg posts, offset cross stretcher, base with through tenons, paper Gustav label, refinished, stains 2,070.00
Rocker
   28" w, 31-1/2" d, 38-1/2" h, No. 451, concave crest rail over 6 vertical slat, shaped flat arm with corbels over 6 vertical slat, branded "The Work of L. & J. G. Stickley," c1912, scratches on arm 1,380.00
   29" w, 30" d, 41" h, high backed, 5 vertical slats under each arm, corbels, loose seat cushion, branded Gustav mark, orig finish, arms recolored 1,800.00
Server
   40" l, 15" d, 37" h, backsplash, overhanging top, 2 shelves, new finish, L. & J. G. 2,100.00
   59-1/4" l, 24" d, 44-1/4" h, plate rack, chamfered back and sides, 3 drawers with heavy faceted wooden pulls, large red Gustav decal, new finish 14,000.00
Settle
   56" w, 22" d, 30" h, No. 205, back with 5 wide slats, even arm with one wide slat, spring cushion seat, side rails with through tenons, red Gustav decal, sgd "Stickley" 3,750.00
   76-3/4" l, 29-1/2" d, 31" h, cube, vertical slats, new blue leatherette cushions, very light overcoat over orig finish, Stickley Bros Quaint metal tag 2,300.00
Sewing Rocker, 19" w, 28" d, 40" h, mahogany, tall spindled back, sling seat, red Gustav decal, some alligatoring to orig finish 2,200.00
Shirtwaist Box, 32" w, 17" d, 16" h, oak, cedar lined, red, hammered copper lift handles, branded Gustav mark, c1912 .... 9,775.00
Side Chair, 37" h, three horizontal back slats, reupholstered slip seats, branded Gustav mark, c1912, set of 5 .... 2,185.00
Stand, 16" w, 16" d, 28-1/2" h, sq top, single drawer, circular wooden pull, lower median shaft, branded Gustav mark, c1912 .... 575.00
Tabouret
   15-3/4" d, 14" d, circular overhanging top, cloud-lift cross-stretchers, orig finished, branded "Ali Ik Kan," Gustav 1,000.00

17" h, No. 558, octagonal top, exposed leg joints, L. & J. G. red and yellow decal, c1912, nick, some roughness 400.00
20" h, No. 559, octagonal top, exposed leg joints, L. & J. G.refinished with faux stain 800.00
Tea Cart, 29" w, 17-1/4" d, 33" h, glass lined tray top, lower shelf, slat sides, branded Stickley Bros mark, new finish..................... 1,000.00
Tray, 11-1/4" w, 23-1/4" l, hammered copper, elongated oval, rolled rim, 2 riveted handles, orig patina, imp Gustav mark, c1912, scratches, spotting 575.00
Vanity, 36" l, 18" d, 54-1/4" h to top of mirror, overhanging top, 2 drawers with round wooden pulls, tapered legs, red Gustav mark, designed by Harvey Ellis, new dark finish, nick to pull 2,250.00

STIEGEL-TYPE GLASS

History: Baron Henry Stiegel founded America's first flint-glass factory at Manheim, Pennsylvania, in the 1760s. Although clear glass was the most common color made, amethyst, blue (cobalt), and fiery opalescent pieces also are found. Products included bottles, creamers, flasks, flips, perfumes, salts, tumblers, and whiskeys. Prosperity was short-lived; Stiegel's extravagant lifestyle forced the factory to close.

It is very difficult to identify a Stiegel-made item. As a result, the term "Stiegel-type" is used to identify glass made during the time period of Stiegel's firm and in the same shapes and colors as used by that company.

Enamel-decorated ware also is attributed to Stiegel. True Stiegel pieces are rare; an overwhelming majority is of European origin.

References: Frederick W. Hunter, *Stiegel Glass*, 1950, available in Dover reprint; Kenneth Wilson, *American Glass 1760-1930*, 2 vols., Hudson Hills Press and The Toledo Museum of Art, 1994.

Reproduction Alert: Beware of modern reproductions, especially in enamel wares.

Bottle, flattened globular, colorless, polychrome enameled lovebirds with heart, German inscription and "America" 1,595.00
Bottle, half post, colorless, pewter lip, minor enamel flaking
   5-1/8" h, polychrome enameled flowers and birds, stain 110.00
   5-3/8" h, polychrome enameled flowers and birds 360.00

Creamer, expanded diamond pattern, fiery opalescent, ftd, 3-1/2" h, $875.

5-3/8" h, polychrome enameled flowers, man with wine glass ...165.00

5-1/2" h, polychrome enameled flowers, bird in medallion, some residue, threads incomplete...250.00

5-3/4" h, polychrome enameled flowers, man with bell, threads on lip incomplete, broken blister on man's arm..........................55.00

5-7/8" h, polychrome enameled flowers, inscription, fox with birds in basket 300.00

6-3/4" h, polychrome enameled flowers, man with yoke, and buckets 175.00

Flip Glass, colorless, sheared rim, pontil scar, form similar to McKearin plate 22, #2

3-1/2" h, handle, engraved repeating swag motif around rim, lower body emb with graduated panels 210.00

6-1/4" h, engraved floral motif and sunflower 300.00

7" h, engraved basket and floral motif 350.00

7" h, engraved bird in heart dec within sunburst motif 400.00

7-7/8" h, engraved pair of birds perched on heart within sunburst motif 475.00

8" h, engraved large flower and floral motif 325.00

Flask

4-3/4" h, amethyst diamond and daisy 495.00

5" h, amethyst, globular, 20 molded ribs, minute rim chip ..1,380.00

Jar, cov, 10-1/2" h, colorless, engraved sunflower and floral motifs, repeating dot and vine dec on cov, applied finial, sheared rim, pontil scar, form similar to McKearin plate 35, #2 and 3 ....750.00

Miniature, flip glass, 3" h, colorless, engraved bird within sunburst motif, seared mouth, pontil scar 325.00

Tankard, handle, cylindrical, applied solid reeded handle, flared foot, sheared rim, pontil scar, form similar to McKearin plate 22, #4

5-1/2" h, milk glass, red, yellow, blue, and green enameled dec of house on mountain with floral motif, old meandering fissure around body of vessel...150.00

5-3/4" h, colorless, engraved with bird in elaborate sunburst motif 500.00

6-1/4" h, colorless, engraved elaborate bird and tulip dec.....475.00

Tumbler, 2-7/8" h, colorless, paneled, polychrome enameled flowers...220.00

STONEWARE

History: Made from dense kaolin and commonly salt-glazed, stonewares were hand-thrown and high-fired to produce a simple, bold, vitreous pottery. Stoneware crocks, jugs, and jars were made to store products and fill other utilitarian needs. These intended purposes dictated shape and design—solid, thick-walled forms with heavy rims, necks, and handles and with little or no embellishment. Any decorations were simple: brushed cobalt oxide, incised, slip trailed, stamped, or tooled.

Stoneware has been made for centuries. Early American settlers imported stoneware items at first. As English and European potters refined their earthenware, colonists began to produce their own wares. Two major North American traditions emerged based only on location or type of clay. North Jersey and parts of New York comprise the first area; the second was eastern Pennsylvania spreading westward and into Maryland, Virginia, and West Virginia. These two distinct geographical boundaries, style of decoration, and shape are discernible factors in classifying and dating early stoneware.

By the late 18th century, stoneware was manufactured in all sections of the country. This vigorous industry flourished during the 19th century until glass fruit jars appeared and the use of refrigeration became widespread. By 1910, commercial production of salt-glazed stoneware came to an end.

Butter Churn, N. A. White & Son, Utica, NY, large paddletail bird on flower, c1885, 18" h, $4,620. Photo courtesy of Vicki and Bruce Waasdrop.

References: Susan and Al Bagdade, *Warman's American Pottery and Porcelain*, Wallace-Homestead, 1994; Jim Martin and Bette Cooper, *Monmouth-Western Stoneware*, published by authors, 1983, 1993 value update; Don and Carol Raycraft, *Collector's Guide to Country Stoneware & Pottery*, 1st Series (1985, 1995 value update), 2nd Series (1990, 1996 value update), Collector Books; ——, *Stoneware*, Wallace-Homestead, 1995, ——, *Wallace-Homestead Price Guide to American Country Antiques*, 16th ed., Krause Publications, 1999; Terry G. Taylor and Terry and Kay Lowrance, *Collector's Encyclopedia of Salt Glaze Stoneware*, Collector Books, 1996.

Collectors' Clubs: American Stoneware Association, 208 Crescent Ct, Mars, PA 16066; Federation of Historical Bottle Collectors, Inc., 1485 Buck Hill Drive, Southampton, PA 18966.

Museum: Museum of Ceramics at East Liverpool, East Liverpool, OH.

Bank, 8-3/8" h, incised "Parnude Dennis," cobalt blue brushed foliate designs, stains, repair, bird finial rebuilt 880.00

Bottle

Cream Pot, John Burger, Rochester, NY, 3 gallon, large double-flower dec, glaze burn spots on side and back in-the-making, c1865, $880. Photo courtesy of Vicki and Bruce Waasdrop.

Cream Pot, N. Clark Jr., Athens, NY, 2 gallon, double brushed flower dec, very minor age-line at base, int. rim chip, c1850, 9-1/2" h, $210. Photo courtesy of Vicki and Bruce Waasdrop.

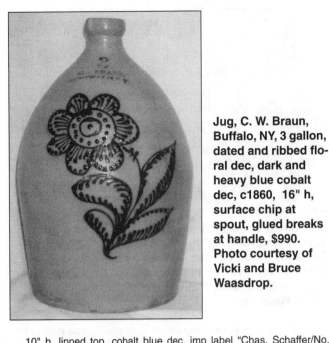

Jug, C. W. Braun, Buffalo, NY, 3 gallon, dated and ribbed floral dec, dark and heavy blue cobalt dec, c1860, 16" h, surface chip at spout, glued breaks at handle, $990. Photo courtesy of Vicki and Bruce Waasdrop.

6-1/2" h, imp label "P. Mansfield," blue bulbous lip, chips on base 90.00

9-5/8" h, imp label "F. Gleason, 1853," blue bulbous lip 200.00

Bowl, 13" d, 6-1/2" h, blue and white sponge spatter with ring, wear, rim chip 90.00

Butter Crock, 9-1/2" d, cobalt blue brushed dec, applied side handles 150.00

Churn, 19" h, ovoid, applied shoulder handles, cobalt blue brushed flower and "6," wood lid, handle with dasher, hairlines 200.00

Crock

6-1/2" h, 7-1/2" d, sealing lip, Albany slip int., cobalt blue brushed foliage scrolls, hairlines in base, small chips 400.00

7-1/2" h, applied handles, imp label "Whites Utica," cobalt blue quill work bird, hairline 275.00

9-1/2" h, applied handles, cobalt blue brushed flowers and "2" 165.00

12" h, applied handles, cobalt blue quill work flying polka dot bird with shield and medallion, "4" and flourish, damaged, stabilized cracks 470.00

13-1/2" h, applied handles, cobal blue brushed floral design, imp "6," chips 150.00

Figure, 4-3/4" h, rabbit, cobalt blue detail, chips, hairlines, broken ears 200.00

Flower Pot, 7-3/4" h, attached saucer base, red clay, cobalt blue brushed detail, chips and hairline 145.00

Ink Bottle, 6-5/8" h, New Geneva, broken and glued 330.00

Jar

3-3/4" h, imp label highlighted in blue "James Green & Co. Worcester Mass," chip on base 275.00

8" h, two handles, irregular ovoid shape, incised cobalt blue band around neck, firing crack, chips, glaze irregularities 290.00

8-1/2" h, ovoid, cobalt blue brushed flowers, stripes, polka dots and "Sug," domed lid, broken applied handles, chips 1,210.00

Crock, Macumber & Tannahill, Ithaca, NY, 3 gallon, double flower, c1875, 10" h, $495. Photo courtesy of Vicki and Bruce Waasdrop.

10" h, lipped top, cobalt blue dec, imp label "Chas. Schaffer/No. 215 Market St., Philadelphia" 290.00

10-1/2" h, cobalt blue slip flower, imp "1-1/2" 140.00

11-1/4" h, applied handles, cobalt blue slip flourish, date, and polka dots, damage and repair 410.00

11-1/2" h, applied shoulder handles, imp label "Pottery Works, Litt...2," bluish-gray brushed floral design, crow's foot and lip chip, mismatched lid 990.00

12" h, 8" d, two applied handles, 3 gallon, cobalt blue floral dec, chips to handle and rim 550.00

14" h, applied shoulder handles, cobalt blue slip bird on leaf, imp "4," minor lip chips 330.00

Jug

8-3/8" h, strap handle, incised label highlighted in cobalt blue, "Made by Charles Bless, March 26, 1877," (Whites, Utica potter) some in-making hairlines 440.00

8-1/2" h, ovoid, American, early 19th C, cobalt blue swirl and dot dec on shoulder and handle base, minor chips 400.00

9-1/2" h, face, America, late 19th C, shaped shoulder, single handle, applied facial features, cobalt glazed highlights to eyes, ears, hair, and handle, glaze imperfections, chips 750.00

10" h, strap handle, imp label "J. Fisher, Lyons, N.Y.," cobalt blue slip "C. Kamper's Sons, Mich. St. Buffalo, N.Y.," hairline in handle 110.00

11-1/4" h, ovoid, strap handle, imp label "I. M. Mead," cobalt blue "1" 200.00

12-1/2" h, strap handle, cobalt blue brushed "2" with blue at handle, small lip and handle chips 360.00

12-3/4" h, strap handle, imp label "Chollar Darby & Co., Cortland," cobalt blue brushed flower with blue at label 550.00

13-1/4" h, ovoid, strap handle, cobalt blue brushed floral designs, hairlines 635.00

13-1/2" h, strap handle, imp "2," cobalt blue slip floral design, pebbly finish 160.00

13-3/4" h, strap handle, imp label "Edmands & Co. 2," cobalt blue quill work design, feathery foliage, chips 250.00

15-1/2" h, ovoid, attributed to Jonathan Fenton, Boston, c1800, incised codfish dec, cobalt blue dec, glaze imperfections, chips at neck 1,495.00

15-1/2" h, strap handle, imp label "Co-Operative Pottery Co. Lyons N.Y.," cobalt blue quill work "Hammondsport, Vintage Co. Penn Yan, N.Y. 3," chips 165.00

17-1/4" h, ovoid, applied handle, imp label "N. B. Pearse ---3," cobalt blue brushed design, crazing and firing defects, chip on handle 245.00

Left: pitcher, unsigned, attributed to Edmands, 2 gallon, flower dec, c1870, 13" h, int. rim chip, $250; right: jug, Edmands & Co., 1 gallon, dotted bird on flowering branch, c1870, 12-1/2" h, professionally restored handle, repair to line in front, $250. Photo courtesy of Vicki and Bruce Waasdrop.

17-1/2" h, strap handle, imp label "Lyons Cooperative Pottery Co., Limited," with "5" and cobalt blue quillwork flourish 150.00

Marble

1-1/2" d, blue, light blue, and white on cream ground 95.00

1-5/8" d, blue and white 85.00

1-7/8" d, blue and white 165.00

Miniature

Churn, 2-7/8" h, applied shoulder handles, cobalt blue brushed floral dec, brown Albany slip int. 2,310.00

Churn, 6-1/4" h, applied handles and lid, chips and hairlines, filled in chip on base 1,210.00

Pitcher, 2-7/8" h, blue and white, molded Indian head medallion 110.00

Pitcher

10-1/2" h, dark brown Albany slip, incised lines, minor chips .. 55.00

13-1/4" h, strap handle imp "2," cobalt blue brushed floral dec 880.00

Planter, tree trunk, 12-3/8" h, brown glazed, vines in relief around trunk, imp "S. I. Pewtress & Co., New Haven, Conn," on base, chips 375.00

Preserving Jar

6-1/8" h, cobalt blue stenciled label "Manufactured for Green Dorsey, Pouhatan, Ohio," tin lid emb with emb eagle and "Pat. Apl'd For," chips 770.00

6-5/8" h, cobalt blue stenciled cherries and "Greensboro," broken and glued, emb strawberries on tin lid 220.00

6-7/8" h, cobalt blue brushed bands and tulip, emb lid with eagle and slot, chips on lip 635.00

7" h, cobalt blue stenciled apple and leaf, "Greensboro," hairlines, large lip chip, tin lid with emb vintage dec 750.00

8" h, cobalt blue stenciled "Peaches," emb tin lid with worn gold japannaing, shield and "Banner Jelly" 330.00

8-3/8" h, cobalt blue stenciled label "Hamilton & Jones" with pears, emb tin lid with shield and "Banner Jelly," small chips on inner lip 800.00

8-1/2" h, imp label "Frely & Bro. Strausburg, Va," brownish-gray salt glaze, small chips 75.00

8-3/4" h, cobalt blue stenciled label "Jacob Roemer, Dealer in Dry Goods, Groceries, etc. Clarington, Ohio," emb tin lid with shield and "Banner Jelly," minor hairline and chip 425.00

10" h, cobalt blue brushed flowers and stripes, base hairline 440.00

10" h, cobalt blue stenciled label "A. P. Donaghho, Parkersburg, W. VA" with eagle, hairlines 440.00

Salt, 2-1/2" d, 1-5/8" h, cobalt blue brushed dec, chips on foot, smaller chips on rim 880.00

Stove Leveler, 4-1/2" h, cobalt blue brushed designs, hairline and chips 440.00

Water Cooler, cov, cobalt blue bands, stenciled "3," orig spigot, minor chip on lid, 3 gallon 120.00

STRETCH GLASS

History: Stretch glass was produced by many glass manufacturers in the United States between 1915 through 1935. The most prominent makers were Cambridge, Fenton (which probably manufactured more stretch glass than any of the others), Imperial, Northwood, and Steuben. Stretch Glass is pressed or blown-molded glass, with little or no pattern, that is sprayed with a metallic salt mix while hot, creating a iridescent, onionskin-like effect, that may be velvety or shiny in luster. Look for mold marks. Imported pieces are blown and show a pontil mark.

References: Berry Wiggins, *Stretch Glass*, Antique Publications, 1972, 1987 value update.

Collectors' Club: Stretch Glass Society, P.O. Box 573, Hampshire, IL 60140.

Bowl, 10" d, Double Dolphin, #1602, Fenton, crimped edge, ice green, iridescence 215.00

Candlesticks, pr

8-3/4" h, #657, Northwood, vaseline 150.00

10" h, #349, Fenton, vaseline 95.00

Candy Jar, cov, #636, Northwood, vaseline, 1 pound size 85.00

Compote, Interior Paneled, ice green, sides pulled up on two sides 160.00

Console Bowl, 9-1/2" d, stretch, dark marigold, Imperial iron cross mark 90.00

Cornucopia Candlesticks, pr, Fenton, white 65.00

Creamer and Sugar, Rings pattern, tangerine 75.00

Hat, 4" h, purple, Imperial 60.00

Ice Cream Bowl, 8-1/2" d, Wide Panel, Imperial, deep 225.00

Nappy, 7" w, Fenton, vaseline 35.00

Plate, 8" d, Wide Panel, Imperial, red 85.00

Punch Bowl Base, Fenton, red 900.00

Sandwich Server, sq, green, center handle 35.00

Vase

4-3/4" h, Smooth Panels, Imperial, squatty, red to amberina 400.00

7-1/2" h, Smooth Panels, Imperial, red 220.00

10" h, Smooth Panels, Imperial, swung, red 350.00

11-1/2" h, #1531, Fenton, aquamarine, ruffled rim 235.00

STRING HOLDERS

History: The string holder developed as a useful tool to assist the merchant or manufacturer who needed tangle-free string or twine to tie packages. The early holders were made of cast iron, some patents dating to the 1860s.

When the string holder moved into the household, lighter and more attractive forms developed, many made of chalkware. The string holder remained a key kitchen element until the early 1950s.

Reference: Sharon Ray Jacobs, *Collector's Guide to Stringholders*, L-W Book Sales, 1996.

Reproduction Alert: As a result of the growing collector interest in string holders, some unscrupulous individuals are hollowing out the backs of 1950s figural-head wall plaques, drilling a hole through the mouth, and passing

Pairpoint, silver plated, repousse flame wreath around body, 3-3/4" d, 3-5/8" h, $80.

Porcelain, hand painted florals, 4-3/4" h, $60.

them off as string holders. A chef, Chinese man, Chinese woman, Indian, masked man, masked woman, and Siamese face are altered forms already found on the market. Figural wall lamps from the 1950s and '60s also are being altered. When the lamp hardware is removed, the base can be easily altered. Two forms that have been discovered are a pineapple face and an apple face, both lamp-base conversions.

Advertising
    Chase & Sanborn's Coffee, tin, 13-3/4" x 10-1/4" sign, 4" d wire basket string holder, hanging chain 825.00
    Dutch Boy Paints, diecut tin, Dutch Boy painting door frame, hanging bucket string holder, American Art Sign Co., 13-3/4" x 30" 2,000.00
    Es-Ki-Mo Rubbers, tin, cutout center holds string spool, hanging boot moves up and down on sign, 17" x 19-3/4" h 2,500.00
    Heinz, diecut tin, pickle, hanging, "57 Varieties," 17" x 14". 1,650.00
    Lowney's Cocoa, tin, cutout center holds string spool, cup and saucer hanger, 16" x 24" 3,000.00
    Mail Pouch Tobacco, metal, 2 pc, string held between 2 sections, hanging chains, hanging Mail Pouch tobacco tin, 15" x 31" h 2,000.00
Figural
    Ball of String, cast iron, figural, hinged, 6-1/2" x 5" h 100.00
    Black Boy, 8-1/2" h, cardboard head and arms, fabric body holds string, felt feet 50.00
    Black Man and Woman, chalkware, matched pair 275.00
    Boy, top hat and pipe, chalkware, 9" h 125.00
    Cat, ball of twine and bow, black cat, white face, green bow, chalkware, 6-1/2" h 100.00
    Chef, white, chalkware, 7-1/4" h 145.00
    Dutch Girl, chalkware, 7" h 100.00
    Mammy, holding flowers, chalkware, 6-1/2" h 185.00
    Pear, chalkware, 7-3/4" h 85.00
    Pineapple, face, chalkware, 7" h 165.00
    Strawberry, chalkware, 6-1/2" h 115.00

SUGAR SHAKERS

History: Sugar shakers, sugar castors, or muffineers all served the same purpose: to "sugar" muffins, scones, or toast. They are larger than salt and pepper shakers, were produced in a variety of materials, and were in vogue in the late Victorian era.

Reference: William Heacock, *Encyclopedia of Victorian*

Colored Pattern Glass, Book III, Antique Publications, 1976, 1991-92 value update.

China
Nippon, white, gold beading 60.00
R. S. Prussia, Schlegelmilch, 5" h, scalloped base, pearl finish, shaded roses, green leaves, red mark 250.00
Wedgwood, jasperware, white classical design, dark blue ground 50.00

Glass
Bristol, 6-1/4" h, tall tapering cylinder, pink, blue flowers and gree leaves dec 75.00
Cranberry, Parian Swirl 185.00
Crown Milano, melon shape, ribbed, dec, Mt. Washington two pc top 395.00
Custard, Paneled Teardrop 110.00
Cut Glass, Russian pattern alternating with clear panels, orig SS top 375.00
Depression Glass, Early American Sandwich pattern, Duncan & Miller, clear, orig top 95.00
Fig, 3-3/4" h, opaque cream ground, pale pink at creases, base, and rim, pale pink blossoms 1,950.00
Green Opaque, Parian Swirl, dec 110.00
Opalescent
    Beatty Rib, blue 250.00
    Bubble Lattice, blue, bulbous ring neck, orig top 225.00
    Coin Spot, blue, orig top 195.00
    Daisy and Fern, Parian Swirl mold, cranberry 385.00
    Leaf Umbrella, orig top, Northwood 295.00
    Ribbed Lattice, cranberry, orig top 135.00
    Spanish Lace, cranberry, orig top 150.00
Rubena, Royal Ivy, frosted, orig top 175.00
Satin, Leaf Mold, cased blue, orig top, Northwood 285.00
Smith Bros., Ribbed Pillar, dec 375.00
Spatter, Leaf Mold, vaseline, cranberry and white spatter, Northwood 465.00

SWANSEA

History: This superb pottery and porcelain was made at Swansea (Glamorganshire, Wales) as early as the 1760s, with production continuing until 1870.

Marks: Marks on Swansea vary. The earliest marks were "Swansea" impressed under glaze and "Dillwan" under glaze

Dish, Botanical series, c1805, 11-1/2" l, $325.

after 1805. "Cambrian Pottery" was stamped in red under glaze from 1803 to 1805. Many fine examples, including the botanical series in pearlware, are not marked but may have the name of the botanical species stamped underglaze.

References: Susan and Al Bagdade, *Warman's English & Continental Pottery & Porcelain*, 3rd Edition, Krause Publications, 1998; W. D. John, *Swansea Porcelain*, Ceramic Book Co., 1958.

Museums: Art Institute of Chicago, Chicago, IL; Glynn Vivian Art Gallery, Swansea.

Reproduction Alert: Swansea porcelain has been copied for many decades in Europe and England. Marks should be studied carefully.

Note: Fine examples of Swansea often may show imperfections such as firing cracks. These pieces are considered mint because they left the factory in this condition.

Bowl, 6-3/8" d, gilt cartouches with idyllic landscape scenes, gilt line borders, William Billingsley, c1815, red Swansea mark 750.00
Cup and Saucer, ribbed, gold fluted border and handle, white int., c1820 .... 175.00
Plate, wild rose and trailing blue flowers, elaborate gilt diaper and foliage well, molded flower wreath and C-scroll border, reserved with gilt green berried foliage, gilt line rim, William Pollard, red stencil mark, c1820 .... 990.00
Tureen, 6-5/8" h, multicolored floral sprays, gilt scrolling and borders, double handles, gilt triple ram's head finial, c1820................ 1,550.00
Vase, 6-3/4" h, floral band, gilt borders, flared base with painted flowers, applied bee handles, imp "Swansea" and triden mark, c1815-20, restored, pr.. 4,750.00

SWORDS

History: The first swords used in America came from Europe. The chief cities for sword manufacturing were Solingen in Germany, Klingenthal in France, and Hounslow and Shotley Bridge in England. Among the American importers of these foreign blades was Horstmann, whose name is found on many military weapons.

New England and Philadelphia were the early centers for American sword manufacturing. By the Franco-Prussian

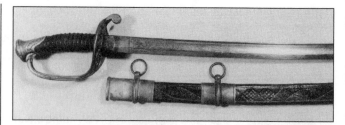

Ames 1850 infantry officer's, etched and engraved blade, "Chicopee, Mass" address, cast hilt with open work, leather scabbard with brass bands and drag, engraved "Lt. Geo. Trembley, 174th N.Y.S.I.," 36-1/4" l, $1,980. Photo courtesy of Garth's Auctions.

War, the Ames Manufacturing Company of Chicopee, Massachusetts, was exporting American swords to Europe.

Sword collectors concentrate on a variety of styles: commissioned vs. non-commissioned officers' swords, presentation swords, naval weapons, and swords from a specific military branch, such as cavalry or infantry. The type of sword helped identify a person's military rank and, depending on how he had it customized, his personality as well.

Following the invention of repeating firearms in the mid-19th century, the sword lost its functional importance as a combat weapon and became a military dress accessory.

References: *Swords and Hilt Weapons*, Barnes & Noble Books, 1993; Gerald Welond, *Collector's Guide to Swords, Daggers & Cutlasses*, Chartwell Books, 1991.

Museum: Fort Ticonderoga Museum, Ticonderoga, NY.

Note: Condition is key to determining value.

American
29-1/2" h, Model 1850 naval officer's, non-regulation, double fuller blade mkd "W./CLAUBERG/SOLINGEN" surrounding standing knight in armor, etching on one side of blade of eagle and fouled anchor, other side etched with fouled anchor "U.S.N." and "IRON/PROOF," plated brass guard with spread wing eagle over "US" cut to metal, iron scabbard with copper mounts 700.00
31" l, US War of 1812, officer's saber, curved blade mkd "PORTER" in dec on left side, "P" guard dec with ovals and globes, bone handle engraved with line and chevrons, simple brass throat carrying ring and drag on leather scabbard, 75% bright blue with scattered areas light to medium pitting, grip cracked full length......................... 550.00
32" l blade, cavalry officer's saber, c1870, slender curved highly polished black stuck maker's mark, sgd by retailer "The M. C. Liley & Co., Columbus, O," finely etched o matted panels both sides, owner's name "Capt. L. P. Hunt," "10th Cavalry U.S.A.," gilt brass hilt cast in relief, 3 bar guard, orig wire bound fish skin guard, orig nickel plated scabbard with presentation quality gilt brass mounts, orig sword knot and belt 2,100.00
32-1/4" l, Model 1872, unmarked thin straight blade, gilt hand guard with emblem representing building, overlay of "Constitution/Justice" in arcs, band of colored glass stones on crown pummel, scatted spots and pitting on blade and scabbard 350.00
33" l, 1842 pattern light artillery, moderately curved blade, 1-3/8" at ricasso, single wide fuller, left ricasso mkd with early Ames logo, and right "1862," surcharged "Conn," handle leather wrapped with braided brass wire, large oval plain pommel cap, single D-guard with ball quillion, plain nickel plated scabbard with 2 hangers.. 450.00
34" l, presentation grade, Tiffany US Model 1860 cavalry, "PDL" blade mkd "TIFFANT & Co.,/NEW YORK" on one side, "WAR-

RANTED TO CUT/WROUGHT IRON" on other, brass hilt with two branches of heavy leaf patterns, raysking grip with 3 wire wrap, plain iron scabbard, "US" etched on one side of blade, American eagle on other, dark patina on hilt, scattered spots of light pitting on blade, wire wrap loose at pommel 1,350.00

34-1/2" l, US Patent, Clauberg/Solingen, etched blade with "IRON PROOF" on top, leather covered grip with twisted brass wire wrap, much of etching worn off 800.00

34-3/4" l, US Model 1860, cavalry, double fuller blade mkd "Henry Boker/Solingen," patches of light surface rust o blade, most of leather covering on grip missing, iron scabbard 400.00

35" blade, light cavalry saber, Lansfield & Lamb, one wide and one unstopped narrow fullers, ricasso mkd with maker's name on wide side and "US/JCW/1864" on other, leather washer, 3-brnch brass handguard, plain pommel cap, leather wrapped handle with twisted wire, plain nickeled iron scabbard............................ 375.00

36-1/4" l, 1850 infantry officer, Ames, 30-1/4" l etched and engraved blade with "Chicopee, Mass" address, cast hilt wash with open work, leather scabbard with brass bands and drag, engraved "Lt. Geo. Trembley, 174th N.Y.S.I." 1,980.00

36-1/2" blade, heavy cavalry saber, S & K, spine mkd "FM 47" with proofmarks, 1-3/8" at ricasso, with one fuller and one unstopped narrow fuller, 3 branch handguard, leather wrapped with twisted brass wire and plain pommel cap, plain iron scabbard 350.00

40" very curved blade, heavy saber, 1806 Virginia Manufactory, 1-1/8" at ricasso with 2 unstopped fullers, one narrow, other more narrow, pierced flat iron knuckle guard with 8 holes of varying size plus a portapee slot, plain leather wrapped handle with single strand iron wire wrap, smooth iron backing, plain iron scabbard with small brazed tip, screwed on throat with fixed hangar button, dark even peppery brown patina 2,000.00

Austrian, 33" l, officer's, Damascus blade, single fuller on one side only, mkd "ECHT DAMAST/JOSEF/SZALLEY/WIEN" on right ricasso, "SOLINGER/EISENHAUER" on left, top of blade mkd "JOH. ZELINKA in WIEN," smooth gray patina, Hapburg double headed eagle guard, steel scabbard with light to medium pitting 150.00

French, 37" l, officer's, regulation, dated 1816, curved fullered dated Klingenthal blade etched on one side of the forte with fleur-de-lis above and below the inscription "Gardes du Corps Monsuier," martial trophies below, other side with radiant human mask, further trophies, Royal Arms of France between, brass hilt including semi-basket guard, orig grip and steel scabbard............................... 1,200.00

German, 42-1/2" l, processional, early 17th C, 2 handles, blade formed by 2 lugs ahead of leather cov ricasso, writhen and straight guillons with fish tail terminals, small inner and outer rings, wooden grip, spirally fluted pommel 2,750.00

Japanese

Katana, 27" cutting edge blade, Tachi style mountings, late Koto to Shinto period, Nakago displays one mekugi-ana, blade displays deep sori and Choki Hamon, unclear Hada, blade displays number of kizo and openings, 19th C mountings, Tsuka wrapped in green it-maki with matching pr of gold lacquered menunk of floral design 700.00

Waharyahi Samuari, suba, short 1,400.00

Polish, officer's, WWII period, cast brass dec hilt with Polish crest, single edged curved etched Solingen blade, mkd W. Kralka," brass mounted leather scabbard 150.00

Scottish or English, mid 18th C, unmarked 34" double edge blade with wear, staining, full basket hilt of iron with 2 small breaks in iron work and one or two razed repairs, handle twisted wire, large fluted octagonal pommel with peened rivet slightly loose............................ 850.00

TEA CADDIES

History: Tea once was a precious commodity and was stored in special boxes or caddies. These containers were made to accommodate different teas and included a special cup for blending.

Around 1700, silver caddies appeared in England. Other materials, such as Sheffield plate, tin, wood, china, and pottery, also were used. Some tea caddies are very ornate.

Chinese Export Porcelain, 3" x 3", sq, all roosters and floral dec ..350.00
Papier-Mâché, 9-1/4" l, 6-3/4" d, 6" h, Regency Chinoiserie-style, rect case with canted corners, ornately dec with figural reserves within flower blossoms bordered by wide bands of gilding, conforming hinged lid opening to int. fitted with two removable pewter tea canisters with dec chasing... 950.00
Quillwork, 8-3/8" l, 4-3/4" d, 5-1/4" h, hexagonal, inlaid mahogany frames, blue and gilt quillwork panels covered with glass, floral vintage and leaf designs with crown and "MC 1804," 2 int. lidded compartments, replaced foil lining, English................................. 2,750.00
Silver, 5" h, tapered ovoid form, chased and emb with reeding below foliate scrolls and cartouches, lid with beaded edge, rising to foliate finial, monogrammed, early 20th C, 6 troy oz 325.00
Wood
  6-3/8" l, 3-7/8" d, 3-1/8" h, bird's eye maple and burl veneer, rect, handed domed lid, applied handle, vacant int., Continental, late 19th C 150.00
  6-3/4" l, very worn geometric inlay, interior lid with ivory knob 275.00
  8-3/4" l, figured mahogany with inlay, ball feet, brass ring handles with dec escutcheons inlaid ivory key hole escutcheon, 2 int. compartments with inlaid lids, one with orig ivory knob, other with replaced wood knob, some veneer and inlay damage, English..............470.00
  9" l, 4-3/4" d, 4-3/4" h, Napoleon III, brass inlaid, ebonized wood, rect, canted corners, central brass inlaid vacant cartouche, brass borders, int. with 2 cov sections... 500.00
  10" l, Chippendale, cherry, mahogany cross banding, ogee feet, base and lid edge moldings, old finish, 3 int. compartments, orig brass escutcheon and bale with tooling, minor repairs....2,750.00
  12" l, Federal, mahogany veneer with edge inlay, almond shaped inlay key escutcheon, brass ring handles with lion escutcheons on ends, int. has mismatched mixing bowl and 2 inlaid mahogany lids with ivory knobs... 600.00
  12" l, 6-1/4" d, 7-3/8" h, Federal, rosewood veneer with inlay, brass ring handles with cornucopia escutcheons and batwing keyhole

Burl Walnut, line and ivory key inlay, chamfered corners, brass hinges, 2 compartments, 4-3/8" x 7-1/2" x 4-3/4", $575.

escutcheon, int. with 2 lidded compartments and clear cut glass mixing bowl 990.00
  12-1/2" l, 6" d, 7-1/2" h, George III, burl walnut, rect veneered case whit hinged stepped domed lid, well fitted int. with two conforming veneered compartments, each opening to lead lined interiors, center section for mixing bowl, associated glass bowl 650.00

TEA LEAF IRONSTONE CHINA

History: Tea Leaf ironstone flowed into America from England in great quantities from 1860 to 1910 and graced the tables of working-class America. It traveled to California and Texas in wagons and down the Mississippi River by boat to Kentucky and Missouri. It was too plain for the rich homes; its simplicity and durability appealed to wives forced to watch pennies. Tea Leaf found its way into the kitchen of Lincoln's Springfield home; sailors ate from it aboard the *Star of India*, now moored in San Diego and still displaying Tea Leaf.

Contrary to popular belief, Tea Leaf was not manufactured exclusively by English potters in Staffordshire. Although there were more than 35 English potters producing Tea Leaf, at least 26 American potters helped satisfy the demand.

Anthony Shaw (1850-1900) is credited with introducing Tea Leaf. The most prolific Tea Leaf makers were Anthony Shaw and Alfred Meakin (1875-present). Johnson Bros. (1883-present), Henry Burgess (1864-1892), Enoch Wedgwood, and Arthur J. Wilkinson (1897-present), all of whom shipped much of their ware to America.

Although most of the English Tea Leaf is copper luster, Powell and Bishop (1868-1878) and their successors, Bishop and Stonier (1891-1936), worked primarily in gold luster. Beautiful examples of gold luster were also made by H. Burgess; Mellor, Taylor & Co. (1880-1904) used it on children's tea sets. Other English potters also were known to use gold luster, including W. & E. Corn, Thomas Elsmore, and Thomas Hughes, companies which have been recently identified as makers of this type of ware.

J. & E. Mayer, Beaver Falls, Pennsylvania, founded by English potters who immigrated to America, produced a large amount of copper luster Tea Leaf. The majority of the American potters decorated with gold luster that had no brown underglaze beneath the copper luster.

East Liverpool, Ohio, potters such as Cartwright Bros. (1864-1924), East End Pottery (1894-1909) and Knowles, Taylor & Knowles (1870-1934) decorated only in gold luster. This also is true of Trenton, New Jersey, potters, such as Glasgow Pottery, American Crockery Co., and Fell & Thropp Co. Since no underglazing was used with the gold, much of it has been washed away.

By the 1900s, Tea Leaf's popularity had waned. The sturdy ironstone did not disappear; it was stored in barns and relegated to attics and basements. While the manufacture of Tea Leaf did experience a brief resurgence from the late 1950s through the 1970s, copper lustre Tea Leaf didn't recapture the hearts of the American consumer as it had a generation before.

Tea Leaf collectors recognize a number of "variant" decorative motifs as belonging to the Tea Leaf family: Teaberry,

Morning Glory, Coral, Cinquefoil, Rose, Pre-Tea Leaf, Tobacco Leaf, Pepper Leaf, Pinwheel, Pomegranate, and Thistle & Berry, as well as white ironstone decorated with copper lustre bands and floral and geometric motifs. Once considered the stepchildren of Tea leaf, these variants are now prized by collectors and generally bring strong prices.

Today's collectors eagerly seek out Tea Leaf and all of its variant motifs, and copper-lustre decorated white ironstone has once again become prized for its durability, beauty, simplicity, craft, and style.

References: Annise Doring Heaivilin, *Grandma's Tea Leaf Ironstone*, Wallace-Homestead, 1981, 1996 reprint distributed by L-W Book Sales; Jean Wetherbee, *White Ironstone, A Collector's Guide*, Tea Leaf Club International (324 Powderhorn Dr., Houghton Lake, MI 48629), 1996.

Collectors' Club: Tea Leaf Club International, 324 Powderhorn Dr., Houghton Lake, MI 48629.

Museums: Lincoln Home, Springfield, IL; Ox Barn Museum, Aurora, OR; Sherman Davidson House, Newark OH.

Advisor: Dale Abrams.

Notes: Tea Leaf values have increased steadily for the last decade, but there are some general rules of thumb for the knowledgeable collector. English Tea Leaf is still more collectible than American, except for rare pieces. The earlier the Tea Leaf production (1850s-1860s), the harder it is to find pieces and, therefore, the more expensive they are. Children's pieces are highly collectible, especially those with copper lustre decorative motifs. Hard-to-find Tea Leaf pieces include mustache cups, eggcups, covered syrup pitchers, ladles, oversized serving pieces, and pieces with significant embossing. Common pieces (plates, platters) of later production (1880-1900) need to be in excellent condition or should be priced accordingly as they are not that difficult to find.

Bone Dish
  Meakin
    Crescent shape 55.00
    Scalloped edge 65.00
  Shaw, fluted edge 60.00
Brush Vase
  Burgess, Pagoda 215.00
  Meakin, Fishhook 200.00
  Shaw
    Basketweave 425.00
    Plain round, drain hole 225.00
Butter Dish, 3pc, base, cover, liner
  Meakin, Fishhook 185.00
  Wedgwood, simple square 185.00
Butter Dish Liner, sq 25.00
Butter Pat, Meakin
  Square 15.00
  Round, Chelsea 25.00
Cake Plate
  Edwards, Peerless (Feather), sq, handles 185.00
  Meakin, Bamboo, 8-3/4" with handles 85.00
  Wilkinson, Senate shape, oval 150.00
Chamber Pot, Meakin
  Bamboo, 2 pc 265.00
  Scroll, 2 pc 285.00
Children's Dishes
  Mug, child's, Shaw 375.00

Creamer, Burgess, 5-1/2" h, $95.

Tea Set, Knowles, Taylor & Knowles, 4 cups and saucers, teapot, creamer and sugar 850.00
Tea Set, Mellor-Taylor, round bottom, gold luster, 6 cups and saucers, 6 plates, teapot, creamer, sugar, waste bowl 1,850.00
Coffeepot, cov
  Furnival, Gentle Square (Rooster) 325.00
  Meakin, Chelsea 300.00
  Shaw, Lily-of-the-Valley 475.00
Compote
  Mellor Taylor, sq, ridged 325.00
  Red Cliff, simple square, 1960s 150.00
  Shaw, plain, round 310.00
  Unmarked, unusually deep bowl, 8" d, 5" h 435.00
Creamer
  Edwards, Peerless (Feather) 285.00
  Meakin, Bamboo 185.00
  Red Cliff, Chinese shape, 1960s 80.00
  Shaw, Cable 250.00
Cup and Saucer
  Adams, Empress shape, 1950s 30.00
  Meakin 65.00
  Shaw, Lily-of-the-Valley 125.00
Egg Cup
  Meakin, Boston Egg Cup, 4" d, 1-3/4" h 395.00
  Unmarked, 3-1/2" h 325.00
Gravy Boat
  Johnson Bros, Acanthus, with stand 160.00
  Mayer, American 90.00
  Meakin, Bamboo 85.00
  Shaw, Basketweave, with stand 185.00
  Wedgwood, simple square 65.00
Mug
  Meakin, Scroll 195.00
  Shaw
    Chinese shape 115.00
    Lily-of-the-Valley 350.00
Mush Bowl, Meakin 85.00
Nappy
  Meakin, Fishhook, 4-1/4" sq 20.00
  Wedgwood, 4-1/4" sq, scalloped edge 24.00
Pitcher and Bowl Set
  Furnival, Cable 495.00

Meakin, Fishhook 285.00
Shaw, Cable 525.00
Pitcher/Jug
    Meakin
        Chelsea 375.00
        Fishhook...285.00
    Shaw
        Cable shape, 7" h...295.00
        Chinese shape, 7-1/2" 500.00
Plate
    Furnival, plain, round, 8-1/4"..................................12.00
    Johnson Bros., Acanthus, 9" d 22.00
    Meakin, plain, round, 6-3/4" d.................................10.00
    Shaw, plain, round, 10" d.......................................25.00
    Wedgwood, plain, round, 9-1/4" d 17.00
Platter
    Meakin
        Chelsea, 10" x 14", oval 65.00
        Plain, 9" x 13", rect...35.00
    Shaw, Lily-of-the-Valley, 13" 150.00
Punch Bowl, Shaw, Cable 525.00
Relish Dish, Shaw, Chinese shape 265.00
Sauce Tureen
    Furnival, Cable, 3 pc..185.00
    Meakin, Bamboo, 4 pc, including ladle 425.00
    Red Cliff, 4 pc, including ladle 175.00
Serving Bowl, open
    Grindley, round, scalloped edge 135.00
    Meakin, sq, scalloped edge, 6" sq 45.00
Soap Dish, cov
    Grindley, Bamboo, 3 pc, liner, rect........................225.00
    Shaw, Cable, 3 pc, liner, oval 300.00
Soup Bowl, Meakin, plain, round, 8-3/4" d...................25.00
Soup Plate, Meakin, plain, round, 10" d.......................50.00
Soup Tureen, Meakin, Bamboo, 4 pc with ladle........1,500.00
Sugar Bowl, cov
    Meakin
        Bamboo..95.00
        Fishhook...85.00
    Shaw
        Bullet 135.00
        Cable shape 145.00
Vanity Box, cov, Furnival, Cable, horizontal.................325.00
Vegetable, cov
    Meakin, Bamboo...165.00
    Shaw
        Basketweave 325.00
        Hanging Leaves 450.00
    Wilkinson, Maidenhair Fern 275.00
Waste Bowl
    Meakin, plain, round 110.00
    Shaw, Niagara Fan...120.00

TEAPOTS

History: The origins of the teapot have been traced to China in the late 16th century. Early Yixing teapots were no bigger than the tiny cups previously used for drinking tea. By the 17th century, tea had spread to civilized nations of the world. The first recorded advertisement for tea in London is dated 1658 and is called a "China drink...call Tcha, by other Nations Tay, alias Tee..." Although coffee houses were already established, they began to add tea to their selections.

While the Chinese had long been producing teapots and other tea items, the English were receiving these wares along with shipments of tea. By the early 1700s, British china and stoneware producers were manufacturing teapots. It was in 1706 that Thomas Twining bought his own coffee house and thwarted the competition of the many other such establishments by offering a variety of quality tea. Coffee houses were exclusively for males, thus women would wait outside, sending their footmen inside for purchases. For the majority of the 1700s, teapots were Oriental imports. British factories continued experimenting with the right combination of materials which would make a teapot durable enough to withstand the daily rigors of boiling water. Chinese Export Porcelain was an inspiration to the British and by the end of the 1700s, many companies found the necessary combinations of china clay and stone, fired at high temperature, which could withstand boiling water needed to brew precious pots of tea.

From the very first teapots, figural shapes have always been a favorite with tea drinkers. The Victorian era saw a change from more utilitarian teapots towards beautiful, floral, and Rococo designs, yet figural pots continued to be manufactured.

Early American manufacturers mimicked Oriental and British designs. While the new land demanded sturdy teapots in the unsettled land, potteries were established steadily in the Eastern states. Rockingham teapots were produced by many companies, deriving this term from British companies manufacturing a strong, shiny brown glaze on heavy pottery. The best known are from the Bennington, Vermont, potteries.

By the 1800s and the turn-of-the-century, many pottery companies were well established in the U. S., producing a lighter dinnerware and china including teapots. Figural teapots from this era are highly desired by collectors while others concentrate on collecting all known patterns produced by a company.

The last 20 years has seen a renewed interest in teapots and collectors desire not only older examples, but high-priced, specialty manufactured teapots such as those from the Lomonosov factory in Russia or individual artist creations commanding hundreds of dollars.

References: Edward Bramah, *Novelty Teapots*, Quiller Press, London, 1992; Tina M. Carter, *Teapots*, Running Press, 1995; —, *Collectible Teapots, Reference and Price Guide*, Antique Trader Books, 1999; Robin Emmerson, *British Teapots & Tea Drinking*, HMSO, London, 1992.

Periodicals: *Tea, A Magazine*, P.O. Box 348, Scotland, CT 06264; *Tea Talk*, P.O. Box 860, Sausalito, CA 94966; *Tea Time Gazette*, P.O. Box 40276, St. Paul, MN 55104.

Reproduction Alert: Teapots and other ware with blurry mark of shield and two animals, ironstone, celadon-colored body background, design made to look like flow blue, are new products, possibly from China. Yixing teapots have been reproduced or made in similar styles for centuries, study this type of teapot to help determine the old from the new.

Advisor: Tina M. Carter.

Automobile, figural, shaped like Austin, Carlton Ware, England.500.00
Belleek, sea urchin and coral, Echinus Tea Ware, Ireland, first black
    mark 850.00
Cadogan, brown Rockingham style pottery, no mark, possibly made in
    England, late 1800s 195.00
Blue Canton, reproduction of Chinese export porcelain, 1970s..150.00

Yixing, fixed bail handle, allover Chinese writing, padded storage box, imported by Midwest Importers, made in China, includes pamphlet explaining made in centuries old tradition, modern, $75. Photo courtesy of Tina Carter.

Clarice Cliff, teepee, 1946..850.00
Cloisonné, panel with butterflies and flowers, Chinese, late
    19th C 450.00
Copper, spun, E. W. Allen, 1940s 550.00
Flow Blue, Scinde pattern, Alcock, octagonal, 8 1/2" h 950.00
Graniteware, large teapot with pewter handle, lid and spout, Manning
    Bowman & Co. Manufacturers, called Perfection Granite Ironware,
    West Meriden, Connecticut 325.00
Lenox, Art Deco, applied sterling silver dec, c1930, 3 pc set 400.00

Porcelain, Sascha Brastoff, Surf Ballet, pink and white luster swirls, $250. Photo courtesy of Tina Carter.

Majolica, fish, multi-colored, Minton, no mark, late
    1800s 2000.00
Old Worcester, first period, Old Japan Star, 1765-70 ....5,250.00
Parian Ware, Brownfield, Mistletoe pattern......................450.00
Porcelain, pink and gray luster swirls, Surf Ballet, by California artist,
    Sascha Brastoff. mark includes artist name and chanticleer (rooster)
    used since 1953, especially large teapot 250.00
Rockingham Style, triple-spouted teapot, brown pottery, relief design,
    late 1800s, early 1900s...2,000.00
Sheffield, silver and ebony details, c1912......................1,500.00
Silver, repousse, S. Kirk & Sons, 6 pc set......................8,000.00
Wedgewood
    Earthenware, cabbage, lettuce, melon, various designs.......650.00
    Jasperware, unglazed porcelain with decoration in white relief, mod-
        ern set includes creamer and sugar, mark, Wedgwood, England,
        set...295.00
Yixing
    Bamboo handle, Chinese "chop mark" or signature, c1880 ..450.00
    Padded storage box, fixed handle, all over Chinese writing,
        imported by Midwest Importers, made in China, orig pamphlet
        explaining centuries old tradition, modern 75.00
Zurich porcelain, dragon spout, china series, rocco style, c1770..6,000.00

TEDDY BEARS

History: Originally thought of as "Teddy's Bears," in reference to President Theodore Roosevelt, these stuffed toys are believed to have originated in Germany. The first ones to be made in the United States were produced about 1902.

Most of the earliest teddy bears had humps on their backs, elongated muzzles, and jointed limbs. The fabric used was generally mohair; the eyes were either glass with pin backs or black shoe buttons. The stuffing was usually excelsior. Kapok (for softer bears) and wood-wool (for firmer bears) also were used as stuffing materials.

Quality older bears often have elongated limbs, sometimes with curved arms, oversized feet, and felt paws. Noses and mouths are black and embroidered onto the fabric.

The earliest teddy bears are believed to have been made by the original Ideal Toy Corporation in America and by a German company, Margarete Steiff, GmbH. Bears made in the early 1900s by other companies can be difficult to identify because they were all similar in appearance and most identifying tags or labels were lost during childhood play.

References: Shawn Brecka, *Big Book of Little Bears*, Krause Publications, 2000; Constance King, *The Century of the Teddy Bear*, Antique Collectors' Club, 1999; Margaret Fox Mandel, *Teddy Bears and Steiff Animals*, 1st Series (1984, 1997 value update), 2nd Series (1987, 1996 value update), Collector Books; ——, *Teddy Bears, Annalee Animals & Steiff Animals*, 3rd Series, Collector Books, 1990, 1996 value update; Carol J. Smith, *Identification & Price Guide to Winnie the Pooh Collectibles*, Hobby House Press, 1994; Ken Yenke, *Teddy Bear Treasury*, Identification & Values, Collector Books, 1999.

Periodicals: *Antique & Collectables*, P.O. Box 12589, El Cajon, CA 92022, http://www.collect.com/antiqueandcollectables; *Beans & Bears!* P.O. Box 3070, Richmond, VA 23228, http://www.beansmagazine.com; *National Doll & Teddy Bear Collector*, P.O. Box 4032, Portland, OR 97208; *Teddy Bear & Friends*, 741 Miller Drive, SE, Suite D2, Harrisburg, PA 20175; http://www.cowles.com/maglist.html;

Teddy Bear Review, 170 Fifth Ave., 12th Floor, New York, NY 10010; *Teddy Bear Times*, Avalon Court, *Star Road*, Partridge Green, West Sussex RH13 8RY, http://www.teddybeartimes.com.

Collectors' Clubs: Good Bears of the World, P.O. Box 13097, Toledo, OH 43613; My Favorite Bear: Collectors Club for Classic Winnie the Pooh, 468 W. Alpine #10, Upland, CA 91786; Steiff Club USA, 31 E. 28th St., 9th Floor, New York, NY 10016, http://www.steiff-club.com; Teddy Bear Boosters Club, 19750 SW Peavine Mountain Road, McMinnville, OR 97128.

Museum: Teddy Bear Museum of Naples, Naples, FL.

Additional Listings: See Steiff.

Notes: Teddy bears are rapidly increasing as collectibles and their prices are rising proportionately. As in other fields, desirability should depend upon appeal, quality, uniqueness, and condition. One modern bear already has been firmly accepted as a valuable collectible among its antique counterparts: the Steiff teddy put out in 1980 for the company's 100th anniversary. This is a reproduction of that company's first teddy and has a special box, signed certificate, and numbered ear tag; 11,000 of these were sold worldwide.

3-1/2" h, gold mohair, bead eyes, embroidered nose, perfume vial, Schuco 425.00

10" h, blond mohair, fully jointed, black steel eyes, excelsior stuffing, c1906, traces of fur, nose, mouth, and claws re-embroidered, replaced pads 175.00

10" h, ginger mohair, fully jointed, black steel eyes, black embroidered nose, mouth, and claws, felt pads, Steiff, blank ear button, spotty fur loss 1,150.00

10" h, light yellow short mohair pile, fully jointed, excelsior stuffing, black steel eyes, embroidered nose, mouth, and claws, felt pads, Ideal, c1905, spotty fur and fiber loss, pr 920.00

10-1/2" l, pull toy, brown wool, on all fours, glass eyes, leatherette muzzle, metal traces and wheels, early 20th C, some loss to wheels, fur loss 200.00

11" h, blond mohair, fully jointed, excelsior stuffing, black steel eyes, open composition mouth with full set of teeth, c1908, fiber wear around mouth and nose, some fur wear at seams 750.00

11-1/2" h, gold mohair, fully jointed, glass eyes, excelsior stuffing, Steiff, button missing, remnants of embroidered nose, mouth, and claws, spotty fur loss, extensive moth damage to pads 200.00

12" h, yellow mohair, fully jointed, glass eyes, embroidered nose and mouth, excelsior stuffing, felt pads, Schuco, early 1920s, moth damage, spotty fur loss 350.00

13" h, cream mohair, fully jointed, black steel eyes, embroidered nose, mouth, and claws, excelsior stuffing, felt pads, American, early 20th C, played-with, extensive fur loss, felt damaged 175.00

13" h, Peter, dark brown tipped beige mohair, fully jointed, molded composition head, googlie white and black eyes move in unison with tongue, full set of teeth, tan felt pads, Gebruder Sussenguth, 1925, orig carton with label, facsimile catalog and Peter papers, slight paint damage on nose, minor fur loss on back, some edge damage to box 1,725.00

13" h, yellow mohair, fully jointed, black steel eyes, embroidered black nose, mouth, and claws, excelsior stuffing, blue knitted sweater, English, early 20th C, spotty fur loss, pads replaced 260.00

15" h, curly cream mohair, fully jointed, glass eyes, shaved muzzle, yellow embroidered nose, mouth, and claws, "I Growl" chest tag, cream felt pads, Merrythought, 1930s, slight fur matting, muzzle soiled 635.00

15" h, Yes/No Bellhop, yellow mohair head, hands, and feet, glass eyes, red and black felt non-removable outfit, fully joined, excelsior stuffing,

cotton pads, embroidered nose, mouth, and claws, Schuco, c1923, minor fur loss, leather bag, hat tassel and strap missing 1,725.00

16" h, ginger mohair, fully jointed, excelsior stuffing, glass eyes, long arms, shaved muzzle, vertically stitched nose, felt pads, arrow ear button, Bing, c1907, very slight fur loss, head disk broken thru front of neck 2,300.00

16" h, light gold mohair, fully jointed, plastic eyes, Rexine pads, mouth opens and closes by squeezing knobs on back of head, Tara Toys, Ireland, early 1950s, cloth label sewn in foot seam, pads worn, fur loss around mechanism, replaced nose 175.00

16-1/2" h, ginger mohair, fully jointed, black steel eyes, black embroidered nose, mouth, and claws, beige felt pads, excelsior stuffing, American, c1919, patchy fur loss, felt damage 800.00

18" h, laughing Roosevelt bear, yellow mohair, fully jointed, glass eyes, embroidered nose and claws, 2 white glass teeth set in wooden jaw, pink felt pads, excelsior stuffing, Columbia Teddy Bear Manufacturers, NY, 1907, spotty fur loss around mouth, pads repaired . 1,265.00

18" h, yellow mohair, fully jointed, black steel eyes, excelsior and kapok stuffing, shaved muzzle, brown embroidered nose and mouth, felt pads, German, early 1920s, sold with frame photo of orig owner and bear, some fur and fiber loss, pads damaged 575.00

19" h, brown tipt gold mohair, fully jointed, glass eyes, shaved muzzle, black embroidered nose and mouth, excelsior stuffing, clipped mohair pads, Hermann, 1940s, fur slightly matted in spots 250.00

20-1/2" h, greenish-gold mohair, articulated body, glass eyes, ivory felt paw pads, worn coat 200.00

Back row, left to right: 26-1/2" h, gold mohair, articulated body, glass eyes, pink felt paw pads, some wear and repair, $550; 25" h, gold mohair, articulated body, glass eyes, ivory felt paw pads are worn, one replaced, wear, $525; 23" h, yellow mohair, articulated body, glass eyes, ivory felt paw pads, wear, ears loose, $200; 26" h, brown mohair, articulated body, glass eyes, ivory felt paw pads, $365; 26" l, light gold mohair, articulated body and glass eyes, ivory felt paw pads are very worn, one repaired, $250; front row, left to right: 20-1/2" h, greenish-gold mohair, articulated limps, glass eyes, ivory felt paw pads, worn coat, $200; 27" l, light gold mohair, articulated body, glass eyes, ivory felt paw pads are very worn, squeak voice box, $365; 22" h, gold mohair, articulated body, glass eyes, brown vinyl paw pads, labeled "Blue Ribbon Toys, Made in England," articulated mouth missing liner, $55. Photo courtesy of Garth's Auctions.

22" h, aqua rayon mohair, fully jointed, glass eyes, embroidered nose and mouth, excelsior stuffing, cotton pads, 1920s, some soiling, fading, and matting.. 115.00

22" h, gold mohair, articulated body, glass eyes, brown vinyl pad pads, labeled "Blue Ribbon Toys, Made in England," liner missing from articulated mouth...55.00

23" h, black long mohair, fully jointed, glass eyes, shaved muzzle, black embroidered nose, mouth, and claws, "I Growl" tag on chest, black felt pads, Merrythought, 1930s, slight fur loss 1,265.00

23" h, gold plush mohair, fully jointed, glass eyes, excelsior stuffing, Ideal, c1919, spotty fur loss, fiber loss on head, pad replaced, some possible restitching to nose and mouth 230.00

23" h, yellow mohair, articulated body, glass eyes, ivory felt paw pads, wear, ears loose 200.00

24" h, cream mohair, unjointed except arms, light bulb eyes, tan embroidered nose and mouth, excelsior stuffing, metal nose ring held electric cord and on/off button, brown felt pads, American-Made Stuffed Toy Co., NY, early 20th C, spotty fur loss, eyes not functioning 435.00

24" h, golden brown mohair, fully jointed, glass eyes, embroidered nose and mouth, kapok and excelsior stuffing, felt pads, wearing dress, bonnet, and glasses, 1920s, spotty fur loss and felt damage 350.00

25" h, gold mohair, articulated body, glass eyes, ivory felt paw pads are worn, one replaced, wear.. 525.00

25" h, yellow mohair, fully jointed, glass eyes, black embroidered nose, mouth, and claws, felt pads, excelsior stuffing, Ideal, 1920s, slight fur loss and matting 635.00

26" h, brown mohair, articulated body, glass eyes, ivory felt paw pads 360.00

26" h, light gold mohair, articulated body, glass eyes, very worn ivory felt paw pads, one paw repaired 250.00

26-1/2" h, gold mohair, articulated body, glass eyes, pink felt paw pads, some wear and repair 550.00

27" l, light gold mohair, articulated body, glass eyes, very worn ivory felt paw pads, squeak voice box 360.00

29" l, beige curly mohair, fully jointed, glass eyes, brown embroidered nose, mouth, and claws, excelsior stuffing, felt pads, Steiff, post WWII, ear button, some pad damage, wearing train engineer's outfit......575.00

32" l, curly mohair, fully jointed, glass eyes, shaved muzzle, open rose felt mouth, tan embroidered nose, cream felt pads, excelsior stuffing, Richard Cramer, Germany, 1930s, some spotty fur loss, moth damage to pads and mouth 1,955.00

TEPLITZ CHINA

History: Around 1900, there were 26 ceramic manufacturers located in Teplitz, a town in the Bohemian province of what was then known as Czechoslovakia. Other potteries were located in the nearby town of Turn. Wares from these factories were molded, cast, and hand decorated. Most are in the Art Nouveau and Art Deco styles.

Marks: The majority of pieces do not carry a specific manufacturer's mark; they are simply marked "Teplitz," "Turn-Teplitz," or "Turn."

Bust, 22-1/2" h, young woman, elaborate dress, fan, flowers, and hat with reticulated border, putto on shoulders, Ernest Wahliss, c1900, repaired 1,700.00

Candlestick, 13" h, applied flowers, gold trim 90.00

Ewer, 10-5/8" h, gilt trimmed ivory ground, enameled birds in paneled sides, c1900 .... 345.00

Figure

8" h, 8-1/2" l, two children, young boy in hat with pink ribbon, pushing young girl carrying umbrella and basket, soft beige ground, pink and blue highlights, sgd "Teplitz Bohemia," imp "4007".................. 450.00

21" h, gentlemen, 18th century style dress............................ 675.00

Pitcher, 12" h, cylindrical, bulbous base, leaf shaped handle, reticulated rim, ivory ground, iris and foliate dec, Ernst Wahliss Alexandra

Vase, base of handle sgd "G. Klint," mkd "Crown Oak Ware, Teplitz/Amphora BB 3903," 15" h, $385.

Porcelain Works, early 20th C, crown and shield mark on underside, hairline and crack at handle 110.00

Urn, 14" h, ovoid, two delicate handles, textured neck, handles, and base, ivory and pale green, gilding, hp floral center, mkd "Turn-Teplitz-Bohemia" in circle around vase mark, also mkd "RS + K Made in Austria" 295.00

Vase

11-1/2" h, stylized blue and green scene of sun through trees, lower band with ivory and blue insect and blue floral dec, gold accents, stamped "Turn-Teplitz-Bohemia/RS+K/Made in Austria" 490.00

12" h, lustered central panel with Art Nouveau style female portrait, c1900 .... 575.00

17" h, 12-1/2" d, tear shape, 2 handles, slip dec, yellow flowers, black stems, olive ground, stamped "Austria".................... 350.00

24" h, pierced foliate dec handles, floral dec, late 19th C 175.00

TERRA-COTTA WARE

History: Terra-cotta is ware made of hard, semi-fired ceramic. The color of the pottery ranges from a light orange-brown to a deep brownish red. It is usually unglazed, but some pieces are partially glazed and have incised, carved, or slip designs. Utilitarian objects, as well as statuettes and large architectural pieces, were made. Fine early Chinese terra-cotta pieces recently have sold for substantial prices.

Architectural Fragment, 38" l, lintel supports, from Solomon Blumenfield Flats, 1884, pr..550.00

Bust, 22" h, young woman, Chas Eugene Breton, 1916.............. 665.00

Figure

7-1/2" h, Aphrodite, dressed in tunic, open back, South Italian, third century B.C. 345.00

11" h, St. Joseph, wearing long loose robes, black hat, polychrome dec, Spanish, 19th C 600.00

18-1/4" l, nude reclining on natraulistic base, gazing to left, both hands on head, French, 20th C 650.00

18-3/4" l, reclining male figure with dog, inscribed "Claude Janin" 400.00

20" h, bulldog, Continental 1,850.00

**Wall Plaque, mkd "C. Conrad Charlottenstútte, Salzburg,"
8-1/2" h, $35.**

Planter
  10-1/4" h, garland and mask motif...100.00
  Rectangular, Italian...70.00
Plaque, 9-1/2" x 11-3/4", rect, woman weeping, Hebrew text below,
  reverse with imp "Menorah" mark, Bezalel, Jerusalem, c1914...3,450.00
Statue, 55" h, Minera, woman in draped toga, grape and cable head
  dress, holding wine cup...2,000.00
Tray, 9" x 7", hp, pilgrims resting, gilt dec, 1920 ....85.00
Urn, 29-1/2" h, molded putti and foliage dec, green glaze, waisted
  neck, two handles, circular base 395.00

TEXTILES

History: Textiles is the generic term for cloth or fabric items,
especially anything woven or knitted. Antique textiles that
have survived are usually those that were considered the
"best" by their original owners, since these were the objects
that were used and stored carefully by the housewife.

Textiles are collected for many reasons—to study fabrics, to understand the elegance of a historical period, for
decorative purposes, or to use as was originally intended.
The renewed interest in antique clothing has sparked a
revived interest in period textiles of all forms.

References: Dilys E. Blum, *The Fine Art of Textiles: The
Collection of the Philadelphia Museum of Art*, Philadelphia
Museum of Art, 1997; M. Dupont-Auberville, *Full-Color His-
toric Textile Designs*, Dover Publications, 1996; Loretta
Smith Fehling, *Terrific Tablecloths from the '40s and '50s*,
Schiffer, 1998; Frances Johnson, *Collecting Household
Linens*, Schiffer Publishing, 1997; Elizabeth Kurella, *The
Complete Guide To Vintage Textiles*, Krause Publications,
1999; Sheila Paine, *Embroidered Textiles: Traditional Pat-
terns from Five Continents, With a Worldwide Guide To
Identification*, Thames & Hudson, 1997; Mildred Cole Pel-
adeau, *Art Underfoot: The Story of Waldoboro Hooked*

Rugs, American Textile History Museum, 1999; Raffaella
Serena, *Embroideries and Patterns from 19th Century
Vienna*, Antique Collectors' Club Ltd., 1998; Jessie A. Tur-
bayne, *Hooked Rug Treasury*, Schiffer Publishing, 1997.

Periodicals: *HALI*, P.O. Box 4312, Philadelphia, PA 19118;
International Old Lacers Bulletin, P.O. Box 554, Flanders,
NJ 07836; Textile Museum Newsletter, *The Textile Museum*,
2320 S. St. NW, Washington, DC 20008.

Collectors' Clubs: American Needlepoint Guild, Inc., P.O.
Box 1027, Cordova, TN 38088-1027, http://www.needle-
point.org; Colonial Coverlet Guide of America, 5617 Black-
stone, La Grante, IL 60525-3420; Costume Society of
America, P.O. Box 73, Earleville, MD 21919, http://www.cos-
tumesocietyamerica.com; Stumpwork Society, 55 Ferncrest
Ave., Cranston, RI 02905-3510; International Old Lacers,
Inc., P.O. Box 554, Flanders, NJ 07836, Rug & Textile Society of Indiana, 8940 Sassafras Court, Indianapolis, IN
46260; Textile Group of Los Angeles, Inc., 894 S. Bronson
Ave., Los Angeles CA 9005-3605.

Museums: Cooper-Hewitt Museum, New York, NY; Currier
Gallery of Art, Manchester, NH; Ipswich Historical Society,
Ipswich, MA; Lace Museum, Mountain View, CA; Museum of
American Textile History, North Andover, MA; Museum of Art,
Rhode Island School of Design, Providence, RI; Philadelphia
College of Textiles & Science, Philadelphia, PA; Textile
Museum, Washington, DC; Valentine Museum, Richmond, VA.

Additional Listings: See Clothing; Lace and Linens;
Quilts; Samplers.

Banner, 36" x 60" l, Theodore Roosevelt and Hiram Johnson, Progressive Party, 1916, rust color printed on muslin, bullmoose flanked by
  portraits of Roosevelt and Johnson, minor staining 635.00
Bedspread, 104" x 91", 6 red linen and wool panels backed by 4 panels of brown printed cotton, wool batting, floral and diamond pattern
  quilting in center, running feather vine border, minor fabric loss and
  staining, America, mid 19th C 1,380.00

Close-up of corner block.

Coverlet, blue and white, Duchess County, NY, 1838, $990.

Coverlet, jacquard, one piece, double weave
 Central medallion with foliage border, bright red, purple, green, blue, and natural white, minor stains, wood damaged in few places, 72" x 78" 165.00
 Eagles with Liberty peacocks on fruited tree, floral border and corners, bust of General Washington, tomato red, navy blue, and natural white, minor wear and small holes, edge damage, 70" x 83" 3,100.00
 Regina Victoria, blue and white, center panel of queen with castle and crowns, lions in corners, floral border and diamond and flower border, dated 1870, 81" w, 101" l, minor staining 600.00
Coverlet, jacquard, one piece, single weave
 Alternating bands of sunbursts with heart centers and floral designs, rose border, olive green, red, and dark blue, "Mary Wismer, made by Samuel Gilbert, Trappe, Montgomery County, PA, 1848," 78" x 96" 1,035.00
 Central medallion with foliage borders, red, olive, gray-blue, and natural white, bottom edge labeled "M. by H. Stager, Mount Joy, Lancaster, Co., PA. Warranted Fast Colors No. 1," wear and stains, 78" x 83" 275.00
 Floral medallions and stars with double row floral border, four star corners with "J. B. 1857," magenta red, navy blue, olive tan, and natural white, moth damage and stains, 78" x 85" 385.00
Coverlet, jacquard, two piece, double weave
 Floral medallions, floral border with 4 houses and sailboat in each corner and "Year 1841," navy blue and white, attributed to Gilmour Brothers, IN, minor stains, wear, and some fringe loss, 74" x 91" 2,420.00
 Houses, man with plough, birds, plants, horse borders, corners labeled "The Farmer Fancy," navy blue and natural white, very worn with stains, 70" x 82" 6,930.00
 Oval medallion with flowers and birds, border divided into segments each having an eagle on branch, corners "C. M. 1835," tomato red, navy blue, natural white, minor wear, few small holes, 75" x 86" 4,180.00
 Peacocks in trees, turkeys, double floral border, navy blue and natural white, minor stains, 76" x 82" 1,980.00
Coverlet, jacquard, two piece, single weave
 Four rose medallions and floral border, buildings in corners and "Hol—Co. 1840," deep red, navy blue, olive gold, and natural white, patched repair, 68" x 86" 315.00
 Four rose medallions with stars, birds, and pots of flowers in border, corners labeled "S. F. Fancy Coverlet woven by G. Heilbronn, Lancaster, O, 1851," navy blue and natural white, 74" x 88" 660.00
 Geometric foliage design, buildings in borders, navy blue and natural white, wear, bottom end incomplete, 70" x 80" 330.00
 Stylized floral design, weeping willow borders, corners labeled "F. E. Hesse, Weaver, Logan, Ohio 1859," blue, red, olive gold, and

natural white, minor wear and fringe loss, unsewn, stains on edge, each panel 37-1/2" x 86" 2,420.00
 Vintage design, tulip border, corners labeled "Jacob Snyder, Stark Co., Ohio, 1850," navy blue, pink, olive yellow, and natural white, edge and overall wear, some missing fringe, 74" x 82" 495.00
Crochet Rag Rug, 27" x 56", elongated oval, "Ohio" in center, pink, gray, black, and white, wear and damage 220.00
Hooked Rug
 21" x 33-1/2", 3 white and gray cats playing with yarn, magenta ground with blue and white edge stripes, border with names "Skeeks, Shasta, and Minnie," mounted on stretcher, wear and minor damage 475.00
 29" x 24", half oval form, black cat and kitten, floral and leaf border, shades of black, brown, blue, red, and yellow, mounted, some wear and fading, America, late 19th or early 20th C 550.00
 38-3/4" x 29", sailing ship at sea motif, navy, red, blue, and rust, striated taupe and cream ground, navy border, minor fading, losses 175.00
 51-1/2" x 29-1/4", stylized floral sprays, shades of purple, red, blue, yellow, brown, and green, creamy yellow ground with black outlines, green and brown borders, wear, fading, America, early 20th C 115.00
 52" x 33", Noah's Ark, seated Noah with scroll, several pairs of animals, captioned "I Hope He Didn't Miss Any," shades of brown, green, purple-blue, and gray, mottled gray ground, minor wear, staining, America, 20th C 1,380.00
 54" x 30", Noah's Ark, Noah and wife, pears of animals disembarking from ark, captioned "Glad They Were To Be Ashore," shades of blue, brown, green, red, purple, yellow, and gray, multicolored ground, minor wear, staining, America, 20th C 1,380.00
Knitted Rug, 33" x 30", geometric squares of light and shadow, expanded diamond pattern, shades of brown, green, rose, and tan, framed, America, late 19th or early 20th C, minor losses 460.00
Needlepoint Panel, 27-5/8" w, 29" h, Giving Arms, Mary Anne Donnelly, all wool, multicolored yarn, good detail, orig eglomise glass and gilt frame, English, very minor damage 1,155.00
Needlework Family Record, Marlborough, MA, "wrought by Sarah Howe under the care of I. B., aged 13 years, Marlboro, Aug 3, 1819," 3 alphabet panels above family record, flanked by flowering vines, meandering floral border, fading, toning, silk thread loss to border, 18-1/2" x 16" 1,495.00
Needlework Panel, silk on linen homespun, painted features, oval scene of youth sowing seed, house and trees in background, old mellow shades of green, blue, black, brown, white, and yellow, matted, some damage to old gilt 12" h x 9-1/4" frame, 10-3/8" h, 7-3/4" w 600.00
Needlework Picture, England, 19th C
 14" x 14", Rebecca at the Well, solidly stitched crewel yarn and chenille, watercolor on silk ground, eglomise mat sgd "Ann Bentley," tear in sky, minor needlework losses, paint loss to mat 880.00

Hooked Rug, Little Bo Peep, red, pink, white, blue, and green, red borders, some fading, badly worn edges, $45.

16" x 18-3/4", Jesus as gardener meeting Mary Magdalene in garden following Resurrection, multicolored, solidly stitched in chenille and silk threads, handpainted silk features, cut and pasted to painted silk sky, oval picture pasted to linen backing, mounted to stretcher frame, eglomise mat, framed, toning, fading, repaint to mat 575.00

Penny Rug
   24-1/2" w, 35-1/2"l, black wool with chenille, red and pale green wool, olive velvet, black and yellow embroidery, worn scalloped edge, small holes and wear 200.00
   25" w, 37" l, hexagonal, repeating applied penny motif, scalloped border in shades of blue, red, black, brown, and olive wool, mounted, America, late 19th C 320.00
   28" x 46", appliquéd circles in various colors, predominately blue and black, red and green Ingrain carpet ground.................440.00
   42" x 50", hexagonal, appliquéd circles, multicolored, red felt centers, Ingrain carpet ground, pr 850.00
Rug, PA rag, wear and stains, 8'9" x 12'9" 150.00
Tablecloth, jacquard woven
   54" x 56", floral pattern, burgundy and natural white, knotted edge, light stains...250.00
   58" x 72", floral pattern, faded burgundy and natural white, very work, holes, and repair 55.00

THREADED GLASS

History: Threaded glass is glass decorated with applied threads of glass. Before the English invention of a glass-threading machine in 1876, threads were applied by hand. After this invention, threaded glass was produced in quantity by practically every major glass factory.

Threaded glass was revived by the art glass manufacturers such as Durand and Steuben, and it is still made today.

Biscuit Jar, cov, 7" h, vaseline glass, SP rim, lid, and handle 160.00
Bowl, 4-1/2" d, 2-1/4" h, raised rim, broad form, 8 trailing prunts over band of threading, gold irid ground, polished pontil base, sgd "L. C. T. o327" 575.00
Creamer, 4-3/4" h, clear, threaded neck and lip, applied ribbed handle, slight blue tint, Pittsburgh 175.00
Lamp Shade, 11-3/8" d rim, 13-3/8" d, 7" h, broad mushroom shape, amber mottled glass, internal random red-maroon threading, all over irid, Austrian 550.00
Pitcher
   6-3/4" h, aqua, threaded neck, applied handle......................425.00
   7" h, aqua, lily pad, threaded neck, applied tooled foot and handle...5,500.00
Rose Bowl, cranberry ground, cranberry threading, attributed to Mount Washington 100.00

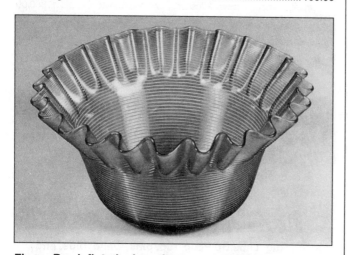

Finger Bowl, fluted edge, chartreuse, 5"d, $75.

Vase
   6-1/2" d, 12" h, wide ruffled form, green ground, ext. dec with green threading, int. with slight irid luster, polished pontil, attributed to Loetz, Austria, minor thread loss 450.00
   7" d, 7" h, shallow bowl, colorless ground, band of red threading, colorless shaft and round foot, base acid etched "Steuben," catalog #6886 c1925 ....325.00
   8" h, 5" d, gourd shape, light blue satin ground, allover applied colorless threading, MOP herringbone..............................450.00
   14-1/4" h, spiral ribbed form, extended neck, bulbous base, olive green, all over random threading in manner of Pallme-Konig, Bohemia, lightly irid surface, polished pontil, repair, crack . 500.00

TIFFANY

History: Louis Comfort Tiffany (1849-1934) established a glass house in 1878 primarily to make stained glass windows. In 1890, in order to utilize surplus materials at the plant, Tiffany began to design and produce "small glass" such as iridescent glass lamp shades, vases, stemware, and tableware in the Art Nouveau manner. Commercial production began in 1896.

Tiffany developed a unique type of colored iridescent glass called Favrile, which differs from other art glass in that it was a composition of colored glass worked together while hot. The essential characteristic is that the ornamentation is found within the glass; Favrile was never further decorated. Different effects were achieved by varying the amount and position of colors.

Louis Tiffany and the artists in his studio also are well known for their fine work in other areas—bronzes, pottery, jewelry, silver and enamels.

Marks: Most Tiffany wares are signed with the name "L. C. Tiffany" or the initials "L.C.T." Some pieces also are marked "Favrile" along with a number. A variety of other marks can be found, e.g., "Tiffany Studios" and "Louis C. Tiffany Furnaces."

References: Victor Arwas, Glass, *Art Nouveau and Art Deco*, Rizzoli International Publications, 1977; Alastair Duncan, *Louis Comfort Tiffany*, Harry N. Abrams, 1992; William P. Hood Jr., *Tiffany Silver Flatware, 1845-1905, When Dining Was An Art*, Antique Collectors' Club, 1999; Robert Koch, Louis C. Tiffany, *Rebel in Glass*, Crown Publishers, 1966; David Rago, *American Art Pottery*, Knickerbocker Press, 1997; John A. Shuman III, *Collector's Encyclopedia of American Art Glass*, Collector Books, 1988, 1996 value update.

Museums: Chrysler Museum, Norfolk, VA; Corning Glass Museum, Corning, NY; University of Connecticut, The William Benton Museum of Art, Storrs, CT.

Reproduction Alert: A large number of brass belt buckles and badges bearing Tiffany markings were imported into the United States and sold at flea markets and auctions in the late 1960s. The most common marking is "Tiffany Studios, New York." Now, more than 25 years later, many of these items are resurfacing and deceiving collectors and dealers.

A partial list of belt buckles includes the Wells Fargo guard dog, Wells Fargo & Company mining stage, Coca-Cola Bottling, Southern Comfort Whiskey, Currier and Ives express train, and U.S. Mail. Beware of examples that have been enhanced through color enameling.

An Indian police shield is among the fake Tiffany badges. The badge features an intertwined "U" and "S" at the top and a bow and arrow motif separating "INDIAN" and "POLICE."

Bronze

Ashtray, 4" d, 7/8" h, circular, two linear etched loop handles, imp "Tiffany Studios New York 1711," c1910, int. wear to patina 400.00

Bookends, set of 4, 4-5/8" w, 5-1/4" l, 6" h, Zodiac pattern, dark patina, imp "Tiffany Studios New York 1091" 690.00

Box, cov, 4-1/2" l, 3-1/2" w, 2" h, Zodiac pattern, imp "Tiffany Studios, New York 106" 920.00

Candlestick, 9-3/4" h, stylized plant form base, 3 legs supporting urn-form Favrile glass cup set with 7 green and gold iridized glass jewels, brown and green patina, base stamped "Tiffany Studios, New York, 7158" 1,610.00

Cigar Box, 6-1/2" l, 6" d, 2-1/2" h, rect hinged box, Zodiac pattern, multicolored enameling to each medallion, partial cedar liner, base stamped "Tiffany Studios New York 1655" 1,610.00

Cigarette Box, 6-1/4" l, 3-3/4" w, 2-1/8" h, etched finish, rect cedar lined hinged box, enameled blue and green dec, imp "Louis C. Tiffany Furnaces Inc., Favrile 130" 750.00

Compote, 6" d, 4-1/4" h, gilt, allover etched surface, imp "Louis C. Tiffany Furnaces Inc. Favrile 527" on base, minor discoloration..230.00

Desk Set, Zodiac pattern, #1009 and #10044 two-tiered letter holder, #1072 rocker blotter, pr #996 blotter corners, #414 stamp box, small tray, dark brownish-green patina, imp marks, 6 pcs 1,495.00

Frame, gilt, easel back
10-1/4" w, 12" h, cast Heraldic pattern, lower recessed finished in patinated brown, imp mark "Louis C. Tiffany Furnaces Inc. 61"..1,035.00
8" w, 10" h, etched, repeating freeform zigzag border in relief, recesses finished with patinated brown, imp Tiffany Furnaces mark, "Louis C. Tiffany Furnaces, Inc., Favrile 66" 750.00

Glove Box, 13-1/2" l, 4-1/2" d, 3-1/8" h, Grapevine pattern, striated green slag glass inserts, ball feet, imp "Tiffany Studios, New York" 980.00

Inkstand, 4" h, 7" l, No. 849, pierced bronze and blown opaque green glass, orig glass insert, stamped "Tiffany Studios/New York/25055," c1900 ....2,500.00

Letter Holder, two tier
5" h, Grape & Leaf, bronze and slag 700.00
6-1/8" h, Zodiac, imp "Tiffany Studios New York 1009," gilt wear 700.00

Letter Opener, 8-1/2" l, orig dark patina, scroll dec handle, imp "Tiffany Studios New York," c1910 ....115.00

Compote, encrusted jewels and gold doré finish, stamped "Louis C. Tiffany Furnaces, Inc., #504," Tiffany Art Glass Decorating Co. monogram, 7" d, 2-1/2" h, $495. Photo courtesy of James D. Julia, Inc.

Note Paper Holder, 4-1/8" w, 7-5/8" l, rect, geometric patterned border, enameled red, blue, and green inlay, imp "Louis C. Tiffany Furnaces, Inc. Favrile 610" on lower surface 260.00

Paperweight, 1-1/2" h, 2-1/4" l, sphinx, orig patina, some gilt, stamped "Tiffany Studios New York" 275.00

Thermometer, 8-3/4" h, Grapevine pattern, beaded border, green patina, green slag glass, easel stand, imp "Tiffany Studios New York" on reverse, minor corrosion 1,495.00

Tray
9-7/8" d, circular with extended rim and handles, etched, enameled blue, pink, and green floral cloisonné dec on handles, imp "Louis C. Tiffany Furnaces Inc., Favrile 512" under handle 460.00
14-3/4" d, circular, rolled rim, fire-polished random design, sgd with Tiffany Glass & Decorating monogram and "Tiffany Studios New York/8/9064" 995.00

Twine Holder, 3" h, Bookmark pattern, hexagonal form, hinged lid, reddish patina in lower recesses, imp "Tiffany Studios New York 905," minor spotting 1,035.00

Glass, all Favrile

Bowl
6-1/4" d, 2-3/4" h, ribbed, crimped edge, gold engraved leaf and vine border, mkd "L. C. Tiffany Favrile" 635.00
7" d, 2-3/4" h, shallow, ribbed ext., scalloped everted rim, irid blue, purple and green highlights, sgd "L. C. T., Favrile" 650.00
10-1/4" d, 4" h, flared, opalescent, leaf pattern, shaded turquoise blue at rim, sgd "L. C. Tiffany Inc. Favrile 5-1578" on applied colorless base 865.00

Bud Vase, 13" h, 3-1/4" d, gold body, enameled green and gold circular base, stamped "Louis C. Tiffany Furnaces Inc" 900.00

Carafe, 11" h, pinched ovoid body, elongated neck, topped with pinched and beaded stopper, ambergris, overall strong gold irid, polished pontil, base sgd "L. C. Tiffany Favrile 430," slight wear to rim 1,035.00

Compote
4" h, irid gold, 2 engraved butterflies, folded pedestal foot, inscribed "L. C. Tiffany Favrile 1149" 1,150.00
7" d, 6-1/2" h, shallow bowl with opalescent leaf pattern, pastel blue onion skin on top edge, colorless stem and disk foot with opalescent rim, base sgd "L. C. T. Favrile 1842" within polished pontil, shallow chip to underside of bowl 435.00
9" h, 3" h, cobalt blue bowl, strong blue irid, stretched irid on broad rim, base sgd "L. C. Tiffany Inc. Favrile X," very light wear to center 800.00

Finger Bowl and Underplate, 5-3/4" d bowl, 7" d underplate, 8-ruffled bowl, conforming underplate, fine gold stretched irid, both inscribed "L. C. T." 490.00

Flower Bowl, 12-1/2" d, circular, colorless body, brilliant gold irid vines and leaves, base inscribed "L. C. Tiffany Favrile 4034K" 980.00

Jack-In-The Pulpit, lustrous amber gold irid body, flared and ruffled rim with stretched irid to edge, pink optic ribbed throat tapering to slender stem supported by bulbous base, inscribed "L. C. T. Y5472," paper label on button pontil, c1905 ....14,950.00

Nut Dish, 4-1/8" d, 1-1/4" h, eight ribs and ruffled rim, irid gold, base inscribed "L. C. T." 375.00

Rose Bowl, 3-3/4" h, ten-ribbed form, ruffled rim, cobalt blue, overall blue irid luster, polished pontil sgd "L. C. Tiffany Favrile 1103-7725K," some scratches 865.00

Salt, 2-1/8" d, broad shouldered vessel, 8 pulled prunts, strong blue irid, base inscribed "L. C. T. FavrileX620" 800.00

Vase
4" h, broad ovoid, colorless body internally dec with white millefiori flowers among green trailing hearts and pale aubergine vines, base sgd "L. C. Tiffany Favrile V149," button pontil, c1904 ....3,450.00
4-1/4" h, floriform, bulbed body, ruffled broad blossom rim, stretched gold irid, disk foot, base inscribed "L. C. Tiffany Favrile 8651 D" 1,265.00
4-3/4" h, broad oval, emerald green body, 5 amber pulled and coiled leaves, gold irid descending from raised rim, inscribed "L. C. T. W6639" around prominent button pontil 2,415.00

4-3/4" h, ovoid, colorless body internally dec with pale mauve on cream morning glory blossoms, variegated green leaf vines, int. golden irid rising to cream at neck, base sgd "L. C. T. Y5626," c1905, base drilled, rust spotting to int. irid surface......... 3,450.00

4-3/4" h, ten ribbed form, wide pinched shoulders, raised ruffled rim, deep blue luster rising to lighter blue at top, polished pontil, sgd "L. C. Tiffany Favrile 1071-2666K," c1915, internal staining 1,035.00

5" h, flared amber Favrile glass oval body, 25 tiny white cane blossoms among emerald green leaf leaves, amber stems, overall irid luster, inscribed "LCT Tiffany Favrile 2889C" around button pontil ..2,415.00

5" h, ovoid, reactive ground of cream and cloudy blue at base shading to deep red, striated ochre, red, and light green trailing ivy leaves, base sgd "L. C. T. Y4812," c1905, button pontil ..6,900.00

5-1/2" h, floriform, bulbous body, cobalt blue ground, wide flaring and ruffled rim, stretch irid to rim, strong blue luster, short stem, applied disk foot, inscribed "L. C. Tiffany, Favrile 9041E" ... 980.00

6-1/4" h, slender elongated neck, bulbous cobalt blue body, silver shaded to purple irid, opal-green heart and vines, randomly trailing vines, inscribed "L. C. Tiffany Favrile 3811E"............. 2,185.00

7" h, waisted form, colorless glass, fine red craquelure to int. neck, cased with 5 intricate green, amber, and cream pulled feathers, base sgd "L. C. Tiffany Favrile 2306C" around button pontil..........4,600.00

7-1/4" h, ovoid, pale aqua ground, internally dec with yellow, red, and black millefiori flowers among dark green trailing heart leaves and vines, ochre swirls, base inscribed "L. C. Tiffany-Favrile 3527 P," partial paper label on button pontil, c1920 .... 6,900.00

9" h, swollen body tapering to bulbed stem, amber, dec with trailing vines and heart leaves, applied dark foot, sgd "L. C. Tiffany - Favrile 5603G," bubbles below surface 1,840.00

9" h, ten ribbed, bulbed, flared rim, applied ribbed base, strong blue irid, sgd "L. C. Tiffany Favrile 1524-3333 P" 2,415.00

9-1/2" h, pale transparent amber crystal stem, peach-opal petal blossom, applied irid folded foot, mkd "L. C. T. M1142," two folded blossom ribs.. 1,955.00

10-1/4" h, ten-ribbed gourd form, flared and ruffled rim above bulbed top, round disk foot, blue irid, inscribed "L. C. Tiffany Favrile 1089-68201" 1,495.00

13-1/2" h, cylindrical, amber gold irid glass, long green leaves, base mkd "L. C. T.," inserted into elaborate dark and gold dore bronze holder stamped "Tiffany Studios New York 717"..1,495.00

16" h, bud, slender cylinder of gold irid glass, 6 elongated green leaves rising from base, inscribed "L. C. T.," inserted into elaborate open scrolled bronze mount, stamped "Tiffany Studios New York 714".. 1,035.00

20-1/4" h, double bulbed form, elongated neck of ambergris grass, dec with blue irid pulled feathers rising to red and gold luster at top, base sgd "L. C. T. E550," paper label in polished pontil, c1895, rust colored blemish to irid on neck, inclusion on neck 2,760.00

Lamps

Boudoir, 15-1/2" h, dome shade, restored oviform base, irid gold glass dec with intricate intaglio carved green leaves, trailing budded vines, both sgd "L. C. Tiffany Favrile," shade also mkd "5594L"...... 9,775.00

Candle Lamp, 12-3/4" h, swirled gold irid candlestick base, with strong blue luster at base, white glass stem insert with five puled green leaves, ruffled gold to blue irid shade, both inscribed "L. C. T.," bases with paper labels, c1900, burst bubble in bobeche, needs rewiring 1,265.00

Floor, 55" h, 10" d spun bronze shade, reflective white int., swing socket, shaft with stylized leaf motif, scroll foot circular base, base stamped "Tiffany Studios New York 425," pr 7,475.00

Mantel Lamp, 8" h, slight octagonal form, cream colored glass rising to bulbed top, caramel and gold pulled petal design, fitted gilt bronze and wood base 1,150.00

Table

24" h, 14-1/2" d linen-fold shade, 12-sided Favrile fabric golden amber glass arranged in panel configuration, dark gold dore finish on leading and cap, matching gold dore 3-socket paneled lamp base, shade and base imp "Tiffany Studios New York," pr..................... 24,150.00

28" h, 18" d leaded geometric blue and green slag glass shade,

tree-shaped bronze base with 6 sockets, orig patina, shade stamped "Tiffany Studios/New York"............................. 21,000.00

28-1/2" h, 22-1/2" d leaded glass globe shade, mottled green geometric slag glass segments progressively arranged, stamped "Tiffany Studios" on rim, 4 socket bronze standard, domed, stepped, circular base, stamped "Tiffany Studios New York 532" on base 19,550.00

Silver

Bowl

5-3/4" d, 3" h, incised banding, everted rim, low domed foot, c1907-38, 11 troy oz 200.00

9-1/4" h, 3-5/8" h, stylized floral band flanked by vertical incised lines, low base, c1938-47, 28 troy oz 1,380.00

9-1/4" h, 4-1/4" h, ftd, shaped edge with applied flowerhead and fern rim, stylized pad and paw feet with scrolled legs topped by acanthus leaves, center monogram, 1891-1902, 24 troy oz................1,610.00

11-1/8" d, 5-3/8" h, tapered ovoid bowl, outward flaring rim, engraved date on base, low foot, c1907-38, 41 troy oz... 1,150.00

Brandy Saucepan, 10-1/4" l, 3-3/4" h, engraved on one side, inscription dated 1857, another inscription dated 1893, turned wood handle, 11 troy oz... 345.00

Cake Plate, edge with wide band of reticulating in arcade and fleur-delis pattern, reeded rim, low foot, center monogram, 1907-38, 17 troy oz 375.00

Candelabra, 12-1/4" h, 3-light, cornucopia shoulder and central sconce, flanked by reeded scroll candle arms and further cornucopia sconces, plain columnar stem, foliate cornucopia and shell edge, round floral repousse foot, removable beaded nozzles, sq base, 1902-07, 26 troy oz 1,150.00

Cigarette Case, 3-3/8" x 2-1/4", rect, rounded corners, gold-washed ovoid push button clasp, gold-washed interior, engraved on front with name and date, suspended from silver link chain, c1907-38, 4 troy oz..... 90.00

Cocktail Set, 6-3/8" h cocktail shaker, six 4-1/8" cordial glasses, tapered ovoid shaker with hammered surface, engraved initials and date in base, glasses with conical bowl, baluster stem, plaint foot, monogrammed, c1875-91, 26 troy oz 865.00

Dresser Set, 10 pcs, 3 brushes, comb, covered jar, receiving jar, hand mirror, shoe horn button hook, rect box, floral and scroll acid etched dec, gold-washed int. on jars and boxes, monogrammed, c1907-38, 23 troy oz 1,850.00

Flask, 5-1/4" l, c1860-70, glass body, silver ball stopper, plain cap, monogrammed 175.00

Flower Basket, flattened bell shape, flared sides, engraved husk drops and floral swags, reticulated to rim in guillouche pattern, overhead handle engraved with further husks, oval foot, 1907-38, pr, 26 troy oz 2,645.00

Ice Cream Spoon, 6" l, eggplant on vine on stippled ground, fluted gold washed bowl, late 19th/early 20th C, set of 8, 9 troy oz............ 2,300.00

Ladle, 10-1/2" l, Renaissance pattern, lobed ovoid bowl, handle monogrammed, 1902-07, 7 troy oz.. 920.00

Muffiner, 7-1/2" h, 1891-1902, urn form body with bat's wing fluting below applied stylized leaf banding, spiral reeded stem, sq base, screw-in domed lid with paneled ball finial,12 troy oz 635.00

Pie Server, 11-1/4" l, strawberry handle, gold-washed blade, early 20th C, 4 troy oz.. 920.00

Pitcher, 8-1/2" h, repousse, waisted baluster form, ear handle, short spout, chased and emb all over with flowers and leaves, 1891-1902, 32 troy oz 3,220.00

Serving Dish

11-1/8" l, 5-1/2" h , crenelated banding, lid with ovoid handle flanked by anthemion, c1854-70, 41 troy oz.................... 1,150.00

11-1/4" l, oval, divided into 2 wells, applied incised edge, 20th C, 22 oz 435.00

Side Plate, 8-1/4" d, 1875-91, silver gilt, stamped tear-drop pattern border, engraved center with fruit, elaborate engraved monogram on underside, set of 6, 77 troy oz... 14,375.00

Stuffing Spoon, 12-1/2" l, Chrysanthemum pattern, monogrammed, 8 troy oz 750.00

Tea and Coffee Service, 8-1/2" h coffeepot, teapot, cov sugar, and creamer, all with Classical Revival-style embossing, paneled baluster

coffeepot, angular handles, flattened urn finials, monogrammed, c1907-38, 69 troy oz 3,750.00
Tea Service, Aesthetic Movement, 1895-91, 4-1/2" h teapot, creamer, cov sugar, three-molded cylindrical form, engraved Chinoiserie-style flowers, birds, and insects, rim border of stamped band of lozenges and flowerheads, teapot with short spout, foliate angular handle and ball finial, three foliate angular handles on sugar, engraved with Chinese-style letter monogram, 19 troy oz.............................2,875.00
Travel Clock, 2-5/8" w, 3" l, rect, rounded corners, hand hammered surface, Arabic numerals, 20th C 490.00
Tray, 14-1/4" d, circular, hammered surface, raised edge, plain rim, mkd "Special Hand Work," 1907-38, 48 troy oz 2,185.00

TIFFIN GLASS

History: A. J. Beatty & Sons built a glass manufacturing plant in Tiffin, Ohio, in 1888. On Jan. 1, 1892, the firm joined the U. S. Glass Co. and was known as factory R. Fine-quality Depression-era items were made at this high-production factory.

From 1923 to 1936, Tiffin produced a line of black glassware called Black Satin. The company discontinued operation in 1980.

Marks: Beginning in 1916, wares were marked with a paper label.

References: Fred Bickenheuser, *Tiffin Glassmasters*, Book I (1979, 1994-95 value update), Book II (1981, 1994-95 value update), Book III (1985), Glassmasters Publications; Bob Page and Dale Fredericksen, *Tiffin Is Forever*, Page-Fredericksen, 1994; Jerry Gallagher and Leslie Piña, *Tiffin Glass*, Schiffer Publishing, 1996; Ed Goshe, Ruth Hemminger, and Leslie Piña, *Depression Era Stems & Tableware: Tiffin*, Schiffer Publishing, 1998.

Collectors' Club: Tiffin Glass Collectors Club, P.O. Box 554, Tiffin, OH 44883.

Bowl, Flanders, pink, 13" d, rolled edge.....................................345.00
Bud Vase, Fuchsia, crystal, 11" h..100.00
Celery, Flanders, pink 140.00
Champagne
  Cherokee Rose, crystal 20.00
  Flanders, pink 45.00
Cocktail
  Byzantine, crystal 18.00
  Byzantine, yellow 15.00
  Fuchsia, crystal 20.00
  June Night, crystal 20.00
Console Bowl, Fuchsia, crystal, flared, 12-5/8" d.......................135.00
Cordial
  Cordelia, crystal...10.00
  Flanders, pink 150.00
  Fuchsia, crystal 40.00
  Persian Pheasant, crystal...45.00
Cornucopia, Copen Blue, 8-1/4" 90.00
Creamer, Flanders, pink, flat..230.00
Cup and Saucer, Flanders, yellow 100.00
Decanter, Byzantine, crystal 600.00
Goblet
  Cerise, crystal..25.00
  Cherokee Rose, crystal 28.00
  Flanders, crystal 88.00
  Fuchsia, crystal 25.00
Iced Tea Tumbler, Flanders, pink, ftd...70.00
Juice Tumbler, ftd, Byzantine, crystal...18.00
Plate, Byzantine, yellow, 7-1/2" d...15.00

Sherbet
  Byzantine, crystal, low 12.00
  Cordelia, crystal, 3-3/4" h 8.00
Sherry
  June Night, crystal 30.00
  Shawl Dancer, crystal..55.00
Sugar
  Cerice, crystal..25.00
  La Fleure, yellow 40.00
Vase, Twilight, blue, 8-1/2" h...75.00
Wine
  Byzantine, crystal 18.00
  Flanders, pink 90.00
  Fuchsia, crystal..35.00

TILES

History: The use of decorated tiles peaked during the latter part of the 19th century. More than 100 companies in England alone were producing tiles by 1880. By 1890, companies had opened in Belgium, France, Australia, Germany, and the United States.

Tiles were not used only as fireplace adornments. Many were installed into furniture, such as washstands, hall stands, and folding screens. Since tiles were easily cleaned and, hence, hygienic, they were installed on the floors and walls of entry halls, hospitals, butcher shops, or any place where sanitation was a concern. Many public buildings and subways also employed tiles to add interest and beauty.

References: Susan and Al Bagdade, *Warman's American Pottery and Porcelain*, Wallace-Homestead, 1994; ——, *Warman's English & Continental Pottery & Porcelain*, 3rd Edition, Krause Publications, 1998; Norman Karlson, *American Art Tile, 1876-1941*, Rizzoli Publications, 1998; Ralph and Terry Kovel, *Kovels' American Art Pottery*, Crown Publishers, 1993; Richard and Hilary Myers, *William Morris Tiles*, Richard Dennis (distributed by Antique Collectors' Club), 1996; David Rago, *American Art Pottery*, Knickerbocker Press, 1997.

Periodical: *Flash Point*, P.O. Box 1850, Healdsburg, CA 95448, http://www.aimnet.com/~toolson/pages/tileorgs. thfinfo.htm.

Collectors' Clubs: Tiles & Architectural Ceramics Society, 36 Church St., Stony Stratford, Milton Kaynes MK11 1BD, UK, http://www.aimnet.com/~toolson/webtiles.htm

Museums: Boymans-van Beunigen Museum, Rotterdam, Holland; City Museum, Stoke-on-Trent, England; Iron Bridge Gorge Museum, Teford, England Lambert Van Meerten Museum, Delft, Holland; Mercer Museum & Tile Works, Doylestown, PA; Victoria & Albert Museum London, England.

Notes: Condition is an important factor in determining price. A cracked, badly scuffed and scratched, or heavily chipped tile has very little value. Slight chipping around the outer edges of a tile is, at times, considered acceptable by collectors, especially if these chips can be covered by a frame.

It is not uncommon for the highly glazed surface of some tiles to have become crazed. Crazing is not considered detrimental as long as it does not detract from the overall appearance of the tile.

Moravian, titled "Departure of Columbus," made in 1981 from orig mold, polychrome, framed, one of 3 made, 39-1/4" h, 45" w, $1,000. Photo courtesy of David Rago Auctions, Inc.

Art Pottery
   6" h, 12" w, landscape with birds and moose in foreground, dark green high gloss glaze 175.00
   6" h, 12" w, landscape with moose, dark green high gloss glaze 175.00
Arts & Crafts, 10" x 5-1/2", framed, scene of salt marsh landscape, blues, greens, and white, c1907 .... 2,100.00
Batchelder, 6" h, 18" l, beige bisque clay with blue engobe, stamped "Batchelder/Los Angeles"
   Bouquet of flowers and birds, slight abrasion to surface 375.00
   California desert landscape, abrasion to a few spots 850.00
   Peacocks, chips and abrasion, pr 1,000.00
California Art, 8" h, 12" l scene of California court yard with fountain, restored color and varnish, imp mark, mounted in Arts & Crafts frame 1,600.00
Cambridge Art Tile, Covington, KY, 6" x 18"
   Goddess and Cherub, amber, pr 250.00
   Night and Morning, pr 500.00
Claycraft
   7-1/2" h, 15-1/2" l, faience, Going West, molded Conestoga cov wagon, pastel glazes, stamped mark, mounted in contemporary Arts & Crafts frame 2,500.00
   13-1/4" h, 35" l, five tile faience panel, molded landscape of Mediterranean houses by sea, marks hidden by contemporary Arts & Crafts frame 2,400.00
Grueby, 6-1/4" sq, mottled matte green glaze, mustard yellow blossom, ftd copper frame, raised indecipherable mark on base 1,100.00
J. & J. G. Low, Chelsea, MA
   4-1/4" sq, putti carrying grapes, blue, pr 75.00
   6" d, circular, yellow, minor edge nicks and glaze wear........... 35.00
   6" sq, woman wearing hood, brown...................... 95.00
   6-1/8" x 4-1/2", rect, blue-green, woman, titled "Autumn"........ 90.00
KPM, 5-3/4" x 3-3/8", portrait of monk, titled "Hieronymous of Ferrara sends this image to the prophet to God," small nicks to corners ...245.00
Marblehead, 4-5/8" sq, ships, blue and white, pr 125.00
Minton China Works
   6" sq, Aesops Fables, Fox and Crow, black and white............ 75.00
   6" sq, Cows crossing stream, brown and cream 85.00
   6" x 12", wild roses, polychrome slip dec 50.00
   8" sq, Rob Roy, Waverly Tales, brown and cream.................. 95.00

Minton Hollins & Co.
   6" sq, urn and floral relief, green ground 45.00
   8" sq, Morning, blue and white 100.00
Mosaic Tile Co., Zanesville, OH
   6" sq, Fortune and the Boy, polychrome..................... 80.00
   8" sq, Delft windmill, blue and white, framed...................... 55.00
Pardee, C.
   4-1/4" sq, chick and griffin, blue-green matte 175.00
   6" sq, portrait of Grover Cleveland, gray-lavender 125.00
Providential Tile Works, Trenton, NJ, round, stove type, hold in center, flowered.......................... 20.00
Rookwood Faience, 8" h, emb pink, ochre, and green geometric floral pattern, Arts & Crafts frame, stamped "RP," chips to corners ..325.00
Sherwin & Cotton
   6" sq, dog head, brown, artist sgd 100.00
   6" x 12", Quiltmaker and Ledger, orange, pr 145.00
Trent, 6" sq, head of Michelangelo, sea green glaze, sgd by Isaac Broome, imp mark........................ 115.00
U. S. Encaustic Tile Works, Indianapolis, IN
   6" sq, wreath, flowered, emb, light green 20.00
   6" x 18", panel, Dawn, green, framed........................ 150.00
Wedgwood, England
   6" sq, Red Riding Hood, black and white 110.00
   6" sq, calendar, November, boy at seashore, peacock blue.... 95.00
   8" sq, Tally Ho, man riding horse, blue and white.................. 85.00

TINWARE

History: Beginning in the 1700s, many utilitarian household objects were made of tin. Because it is nontoxic, rust resistant, and fairly durable, tin can be used for storing food; and because it was cheap, tinware and tin-plated wares were in the price range of most people. It often was plated to iron to provide strength.

An early center of tinware manufacture in the United States was Berlin, Connecticut, but almost every small town and hamlet had its own tinsmith, tinner, or whitesmith. Tinsmiths used patterns to cut out the pieces, hammered and shaped them, and soldered the parts. If a piece was to be used with heat, a copper bottom was added because of the low melting point of tin. The industrial revolution brought about machine-made, mass-produced tinware pieces. The handmade era had ended by the late 19th century.

References: Dover Stamping Co, *1869 Illustrated Catalog*, Astragal Press, 1994 reprint; Marilyn E. Dragowick (ed.), *Metalwares Price Guide*, Antique Trader Books, 1995; John Player, *Origins and Craft of Antique Tin & Tole*, Norwood Publishing, 1995 (available from Christie & Christie Association, P.O. Box 392, Cookstown, Ontario, Canada L0L 1L0).

Museum: Cooper-Hewitt Museum, New York, NY.

Additional Listings: See Advertising; Kitchen Collectibles; Lanterns; Lamps and Lighting; and Tinware, Decorated.

Anniversary Top Hat, 6-1/2" h, band with bow 1,320.00
Book Box, 9-1/4" l, remnants of painted design.......................... 125.00
Candle Box, 14-1/2" h, cylindrical, hanging, some battering 220.00
Candle Lantern, 7-1/2" h, pyramidal top, glass in 4 sides, pierced star and ray air vents, mkd "Parker's Patent 1859, Proctor'sville, Vt," ring handle 365.00
Candle Mold
   5-1/43" h, 4 tube, half mold, ear handle, light rust................. 310.00
   10-1/2" h, 14-3/4" l, 48 tubes, ear handle, curved foot, minor separation of end seams in top gallery...................... 470.00
   11-1/4" h, 8 tubes, curved feet, ear handle............................ 315.00

Coffeepot, punched dec, $1,150.

Candle Sconce

9-1/2" d, round reflector with 3-D stamped cutouts in bright tin under glass, two socket candle arm soldered in place 1,815.00

10-1/2" d, round reflector backs with mirror mosaic, slight damage to one, pr 990.00

13-1/2" h, sunburst crest, star and two leaves, PA 1,265.00

14" h, raised vine and curved scalloped crest on back, slight rust 500.00

Candle Screen, 10" h, 10" w, girls with cats, painted in naturalistic colors, Victorian, 19th C, restorations, pr 1,610.00

Chafing Ball, 4" d, spherical 200.00

Cheese Sieve, 6" h, heart shape, resoldered hanging ring 360.00

Coffeepot

9-1/2" h, pewter knob on lid 250.00

11" h, replaced opalescent knob on lid 110.00

Colander, 4-1/2" d, heart shaped 235.00

Cookie Cutter, eagle, 4" wing span 50.00

Foot Warmer

7-1/2" x 9" x 5-3/4" h, punched heart and circles in tin panels, mortised wood frame with turned corner posts 200.00

8" x 9" x 5-3/4" h, punched panels in circle and heart design, mortised wood frame with traces of red paint, turned corner posts 215.00

Lamp

Grease, 1-5/8" h, colorful glaze 165.00

Petticoat, 4" h, orig whale oil burner, orig black paint 65.00

Skater's, 6-3/8" h, light teal-green globe 225.00

Lantern

7-5/8" h, mkd "Dietz Scout" 75.00

9-1/2" h, font with single spout burner, clear pressed paneled globe, ring handle 195.00

Match Box, 2-1/2" h, English post office dec, ivory socket 90.00

Muffin Pan, heart shaped wells 45.00

Roaster, 12" w, 9-1/4" h, hearth type 185.00

Sconce, 14" h, pr, candle, crimped circular crests 350.00

Teapot, 6-1/2" d, spout resoldered 150.00

TINWARE, DECORATED

History: The art of decorating sheet iron, tin, and tin-coated sheet iron dates back to the mid-18th century. The Welsh called the practice pontypool; the French, tôle peinte. In America, the center for tin-decorated ware in the late 1700s was Berlin, Connecticut.

Several styles of decorating techniques were used: painting, japanning, and stenciling. Designs were done by both professionals and itinerants. English and Oriental motifs strongly influenced both form and design.

A special type of decoration was the punch work on unpainted tin practiced by the Pennsylvania tinsmiths. Forms included coffeepots, spice boxes, and grease lamps.

Reference: Marilyn E. Dragowick (ed), *Metalwares Price Guide*, Antique Trader Books, 1995.

Box, cov

6-3/8" l, dark brown japanning, gold and orange stenciled floral dec, "Friendship," some wear and soldered repair at hinges 55.00

7" d, 6-1/2" h, cylindrical, orig dark brown japanning, red, white, yellow, green, and black floral dec, white band, hinged lid 750.00

Bread Tray, 12-1/2" x 8-1/4", red, green, and yellow floral dec, yellow swag border, red edge, black ground, minor paint loss 345.00

Canister, cylindrical

6-1/4" h, 6" h, red cherries, green leaves, white border, yellow stylized leaves and swag borders, lid centered with leaf dec, red japanned ground, minor scratches 400.00

8-1/2" d, 8-1/2" h, red cherries, green leaves, white border, red flowers, yellow stylized leaves, starburst at ring handle, black ground, minor paint loss 290.00

Coffeepot, cov, goose neck spout, dome top

9-1/2" h, red, green, yellow, and white floral dec, black ground, crusty surface with some touch-up, rust on int., some battering 825.00

10-1/2" h, red, green, brown, blue, and yellow floral dec, dark brown japanning, wear and old touch-up repaint, repairs ... 495.00

10-1/2" h, red and yellow flowers, stylized leaves, black ground, paint loss 490.00

10-1/2" h, yellow birds, red pomegranates, yellow stylized leaves, black ground, minor paint loss, lid unattached, repair to finial 1,100.00

Creamer, hinged lid, 4-1/4" h, dark brown japanning, yellow, green, red, and white floral dec, some wear 525.00

Document Box, dome top

4-1/4" l, worn dark brown japanning, white band, red and yellow dec, ring handle missing 55.00

5-1/2" x 8-1/2" x 4-1/2", red cherries, green leaves, white border, yellow stylized leaves and swags, nickel plated padlock, no key, broken hasp, minor paint loss 230.00

6-1/2" x 9-1/2" x 5-1/8", red, yellow, green fruit and foliage, yellow stylized leaf border, red japanned ground, minor scratches 5,470.00

8-3/4" l, dark brown japanning, yellow, red, green, and black floral dec, white band with painter's mark, minor wear, bottom seams loose 825.00

Tray, chamfered corners, yellow line, white bands with red flowers, green leaves, red corners with yellow lines, wear, 8-1/2" x 12", $125.

Hot Water Urn with Burner, 14" h, black ground, gilt dec, Chinoiserie scenes, three serpentine legs, 19th C 750.00
Milk Can, 8-1/2" h, black japanning, stenciled red and gold stylized floral design 200.00
Spice Box, 7-1/4" d, round, 7 int. containers, worn orig brown japanning, gold stenciled labels 175.00
Sugar Bowl, 3-1/2" h, worn orig red paint, brown and yellow comma type foliage, foot slightly battered 190.00
Tea Caddy, 8-1/4" l, dark ground, worn stenciled bronze powder dec, int. lift-out tray fits over two lidded compartments, orig emb brass handle, minor damage 220.00
Tray, 18" x 24-1/4", intricate stenciled scene of youth and maiden in garden, floral border, heavy over varnish 85.00
Urn, cov
   13-1/4" h, slender stem, ovoid foot, gilt florals, birds, and butterflies, 19th C, pr 1,725.00
   Two handles, acorn finials, dec with floral sprays and birds, scalloped floral and repeating gilt leaf borders, weighted base, French, 19th C, some paint loss, minor dents, pr 575.00

TOBACCO CUTTERS

History: Before pre-packaging, tobacco was delivered to merchants in bulk form. Tobacco cutters were used to cut the tobacco into desired sizes.

Brown's Mule, iron, counter top 70.00
Climax, 17" l 60.00
Cupples, Arrow & Superb 50.00
Drummond Tobacco C 75.00
JohnFinzer & Brothers, Louisville, KY 50.00
Griswold Tobacco Cutter, Erie, PA 70.00
Keen Kutter, E. C. Simmons 225.00
Lorillards Chew Climax Plus, brass, Penn Hardware Co., Reading, PA 100.00
Sprague Warner & Co. 75.00
Unmarked, graduated 6-1/4" to 7-1/2" w, 10-/12" l, cast iron cutter, wood base 45.00

TOBACCO JARS

History: A tobacco jar is a container for storing tobacco. Tobacco humidors were made of various materials and in many shapes, including figurals. The earliest jars date to the early 17th century; however, most examples seen in the antiques market today were made in the late 19th or early 20th centuries.

Reference: Joseph Horowitz, *Figural Humidors*, Mostly Victorian, published by author, 1997 (FTJ Publications, 3011 Fallstaff Rd, Baltimore, MD 21209).

Collectors' Club: Society of Tobacco Jar Collectors, 3011 Fallstaff Rd., Baltimore, MD 21209-2960.

Bear with beehive, 6-1/2" h, majolica, Continental 770.00
Black Boy, red hat with tassel, majolica, repainted, nicks 275.00
Bull Dog, porcelain, German 275.00
Creamware, 9" h, 6" d, plum colored transfers on side, one titled "Success to the British Fleet," striped orange, blue, and yellow molding, domed lid 900.00
Dog's Head, with pipe and green hat and collar, majolica 375.00
Dwarf in Sack, 8" h, terra cotta, multicolor dec, mkd "JM3478," chips, wear 255.00
Girl on side, pipe on lid, majolica, Continental 75.00
Indian, 5-1/2" h, black, majolica 330.00
Jasperware, raised white Indian chief on cov, Indian regalia on front, green ground 195.00

Pewter, Continental, 7" h, $225.

Mandarin, papier-mâché 95.00
Man with Pipe, large bow tie, with match holder and striker, rim chips, hairline 165.00
Man with Top Hat, majolica, Sarreguemines, hairline in base 165.00
Moose, porcelain, Austrian 200.00
Owl, 11" h, majolica, brown, yellow glass eyes 825.00
Rosewood, 12" l, 7-1/2" h, rect, four compressed bun feet, hinged lid, central compartment for mixing bowl flanked by two compartments for tobacco storage, removable lids, Continental, early 20th C 225.00
Toby Type, Shorter and Sons 55.00
Wave Crest, 5" sq, white opaque body, SP fittings 450.00
Winking Scotch Man, 6" h, porcelain, blue beret with plaid band and orange tuft, green collar 200.00

TOBY JUGS

History: Toby jugs are drinking vessels that usually depict a full-figured, robust, genial drinking man. They originated in England in the late 18th century. The term "Toby" probably is related to the character Uncle Toby from Tristram Shandy by Laurence Sterne.

References: Susan and Al Bagdade, *Warman's English & Continental Pottery & Porcelain*, 3rd Edition, Krause Publications, 1998; Vic Schuler, *Collecting British Toby Jugs*, 2nd ed., Kevin Francis Publishing Ltd., 1987.

Museums: American Toby Jug Museum, Evanston, IL; City Museum & Art Gallery, Stoke-on-Trent, England; Victoria & Albert Museum, London, England.

Additional Listings: Royal Doulton.

Reproduction Alert: During the last 100 years or more, tobies have been copiously reproduced by many potteries in the United States and England.

Bennington Type, 9-1/2" h, standing 175.00
Delft, 11-1/4" h, man seated on barrel, green hat, green and black sponged coat, blue and yellow pants, old cork stopper, c19th C .. 365.00
Luster Ware, 6-1/2" h, blue coat, spotted vest, 19th C 175.00
Majolica, 8-3/4" h, monk 165.00
Minton, 11-1/4" h, majolica, Quaker man and woman, polychrome dec, imp mark, pr 4,600.00
Portobello Pottery, 10" h, standing, spatter enamel dec, orig cov, c1840 .... 275.00

Staffordshire, Lord Nelson, multicolored, c1860, 11-1/2" h, $365.

Pratt
9-1/4" h, pearlware glaze, typical blue, brown, and ochre palette, hat inset, small chips 425.00
10-3/4" h, Hearty Good Fellow, blue jacket, yellow-green vest, blue and yellow striped pants, blue and ochre sponged base and handle, stopper missing, slight glaze wear, c1770-80 .... 1,500.00

Royal Doulton
6-1/2" h, stoneware, blue coat, double XX, Harry Simson..... 395.00
7" h, Baccachus, wreath of grapes and leaves on head, twisted vine handle 95.00

Staffordshire
9" h, pearlware, seated figure, sponged blue jacket, ochre buttons, ochre and lavender speckled vest and trousers, brown hair and hat, green glazed base, shallow flake inside hat rim, attributed to Ralph Wood, c1770-80 .... 1,950.00
9-1/4" h, Martha Gunn, translucent brown and ochre glazes, pearl body, brim repaired at hairline.. 1,265.00
9-1/4" h, Thin Man, full chair, green, blue and brown, holding pipe and foaming mug, attributed to Ralph Wood, c1765-75 .. 5,000.00
9-3/4" h, mottled and translucent glazes, cream colored body, small foot rim chips 460.00
10-1/2" h, King Charles Spaniel, enamel dec, restored hat, late 19th C 275.00
10-3/4" h, cat, enameled dec, holding letter, restored hat, late 19th C 300.00
11-3/4" h, Rodent's Sailor, black hat, green coat, white trousers with blue stripes, imp "65," on base, Ralph Wood, lid missing., c1765-75 .... 5,900.00

Whieldon, 9-1/2" h, pearlware, seated figure, yellow greatcoat, green vest, blue trousers, holding brow jug in left hand, raises foaming glass of ale towards mouth, lid missing, c1770-80 .... 1,600.00

Wilkinson
10" h, Marshall Joffre, modeled by Sir Francis Carruthers Gould, titled "75mm Ce que joffre," printed mark, c1918, hat brim restored.. 345.00
10-3/4" h, Field Marshall Haig, modeled by Sir Francis Carruthers Gould, titled "Push and Go," printed marks, c1917............. 460.00
11-3/4" h, Marshall Foch, modeled by Sir Francis Carruthers Gould, titled "Au Diable Le Kaiser," printed marks, c1918............. 345.00
11-3/4" h, Winston Churchill, multicolored, designed by Clarice Cliff, black printed marks, number and facsimile signature, c1940 ..825.00

Yorkshire-Type, 7-3/4" h, caryatid form handle, Pratt palette dec, sponged base and hat brim int. 750.00

TOOLS

History: Before the advent of the assembly line and mass production, practically everything required for living was handmade at home or by a local tradesman or craftsman. The cooper, the blacksmith, the cabinet maker, and the carpenter all had their special tools.

Early examples of these hand tools are collected for their workmanship, ingenuity, place of manufacture, or design. Modern-day craftsman often search out and use old hand tools in order to authentically recreate the manufacture of an object.

References: Ronald S. Barlow, *Antique Tool Collector's Guide to Value*, L-W Book Sales, 1999; Kenneth L. Cope, *American Machinist's Tools*, Astragal Press, 1993; Martin J. Donnelly, *Catalogue of Antique Tools*, published by author (31 Rumsey St., Bath, NY 14810), 1998; Garrett Hack, *The Handplane Book*, Taunton Press, 1997; Jerry and Elaine Heuring, *Collector's Guide to E. C. Simmons, Keen Kutter Cutlery Tools*, Collector Books, 1999; Herbert P. Kean and Emil S. Pollak, *Price Guide to Antique Tools*, Astragal Press, 1992; ——, *Collecting Antique Tools*, Astragal Press, 1990; Kathryn McNerney, *Antique Tools, Our American Heritage*, Collector Books, 1979, 1998 value update; Emil and Martyl Pollak, *Guide to American Wooden Planes and Their Makers*, 3rd ed., The Astragal Press, 1994; ——, *Prices Realized on Rare Imprinted American Wood Planes*, 1979–1992, Astragal Press, 1993; John Walter, *Antique & Collectible Stanley Tools, Guide to Identity & Value*, 2nd ed.., The Tool Merchant, 1996; C. H. Wendel, *Encyclopedia of American Farm Implements & Antiques*, Krause Publications, 1997; John M. Whelan, *The Wooden Plane*, Astragal Press, 1993; Jack Wood, *Early 20th Century Stanley Tools*, L-W Book Sales, 1996 value update; ——, *Town-Country Old Tools*, 6th ed., L-W Book Sales, 1997, 1999 value update.

Periodicals: *Fine Tool Journal*, 27 Fickett Rd, Pownal, ME 04069, http://www.FineToolJ.com; *Plumb Line*, 10023 St Clair's Retreat, Fort Wayne, IN 46825; *Stanley Tool Collector News*, 208 Front St., P.O. Box 227, Marietta, OH 45750, http://www.thetoolmerchant.com; *Tool Ads*, P.O. Box 33, Hamilton, MT 59840-0033.

Collectors' Clubs: American Barbed Wire Collectors Society, 1023 Baldwin Rd, Bakersfield, CA 93304-4203; Blow Torch Collectors Club, 3328 258th Ave. SE, Issaquah, WA 98027-9173, http://www.indy.net/~toper/BTCA; Collectors of Rare & Familiar Tools Society, 38 Colony Ct., Murray Hill, NJ 07974; Collectors of Rare & Familiar Tools Society of New Jersey, 38 Colony Street, New Providence, NJ 07974-2332, http://www.craftsofnj; Early American Industries Association, 167 Bakersville Rd, South Dartmouth, MA 02748-4198, http://www.eaiainfo.org; Early American Industries-West, 8476 West Way Dr., La Jolla, CA 92038; Long Island Antique Tool Collector's Association, 31 Wildwood Drive, Smithwotn, NY 11787-3452; Mid-West Tool Collectors Association, P.O. Box 8016, Berkley, CA 94707-8016; Missouri Valley Wrench Club, 613 N. Long St., Shel-

SPECIAL AUCTIONS

Auction Team Köln
Jane Herz
6731 Ashley Court
Sarasota, FL 34241
(941) 925-0385

Auction Team Köln
Postfach 501168 D 5000
Köln 50, W. Germany

Fine Tool Journal
27 Fickett Rd
Pownal, ME 04069

byville, IL 62565; New England Tool Collectors Association, 11-1/2 Concord Ave., Saint Johnsburgy, VT 05819; Ohio Tool Collectors Association, P.O. Box 261, London, OH 43140-0261; Pacific Northwest Tool Collectors, 5022 Erskine Ave., Seattle, WA 98136, http://www.tooltimer.com/PNTC.htm; Preserving Arts & Skills of the Trades, 2535 Grambling Way, Riverside, CA 9250y, http://www.tooltalk.org; Potomac Antique Tools & Industries Association, 6802 Newbitt Pl, McLean, VA 22101; Richmond Antique Tool Society, 2208 Lochwood Court, Richmond, VA 23233; Rocky Mountain Tool Collectors, 1435 S. Urban Way, Lakewood, CO 80028; Society of Workers in Early Arts & Trades, 606 Lake Lena Blvd., Auburndale, FL 33823; Southwest Tool Collectors Association, 712 S. Lincoln Lane Court, Mustang, OK 73069-4141, http://www/swtca.org; Three Rivers Tool Collectors, 310 Old Airport Road, Greensburg, PA 15601-5816; Tool Group of Canada, 7 Tottenham Rd, Ontario MC3 2J3 Canada; Western New York Antique Tool Collector's Association, 3162 Avon Road, Genesco, NY 14454, http://physics.sci.genesco.edu/WNYATCA/info.htm.

Museums: American Precision Museum Association, Windsor, VT; Barbed Wire Museum, La Crosse, KS; Living History Farms, Urbandale, IA; Mercer Museum, Doylestown, PA; National Agricultural Center & Hall of Fame, Bonner Springs, KS; Post Rock Museum, La Crosse, KS; Shelburne Museum, Shelburne, VT; Winchester Mystery House, San Jose, CA; World of Tools Museum, Waverly, TN.

Anvil, hand forged, 8" 60.00
Archimedian Drill, bit, c1915 .... 50.00
Awl, bone, 5" l 25.00
Bench Press, Sherman, solid brass, 12 lbs, 9-1/2" x 6" 65.00
Clamp, wood, jaws, 13-1/2" l, pr 115.00
Chisel, blade stamped "E. Connor," 22-1/2" l 45.00
Cooper's Howel, L. & I. J. White, Buffalo, NY, No. 20, beechwood,
    15" l 225.00
Drill
    Bow, ivory, brass, rosewood, Erlandsen type, 13" l 845.00
    Hand, Goodel and Pratt, brass ferrules 28.00
File, half round, 20" l 15.00
Hammer, claw type
    Iron, wood handle, c180 .... 35.00
    Winchester 55.00

Plane, round, molding, Ohio Tool Co., engraved carpenter's name, walnut, 9-1/2" l, $45.

Key Hole Saw, British, 15-1/2" l 30.00
Level, wood and brass
    Davis & Cook, patent "Dec, 1886" 45.00
    Goodell-Pratt, brass bound mahogany, orig decal,
        24" l 225.00
    Stanley, rosewood, patent 1896, 30" l 150.00
Mallet, burl, hickory handle, 34" l 200.00
Marking Gauge, Stanley, Williams' Patent, patented May 26, 1857,
    7" l 445.00
Mitre Box, laminated maple, birch, and oak, graduated quadrant,
    Stanley 45.00
Plane
    Keen Kutter, K110 .... 40.00
    Ohio Tool Co., walnut, inscribed with carpenter's name, 9-1/2" l .. 20.00
    Pond, W. H., New Haven, CT, carriage maker's molding planes,
        1840s, 7" l, 4 pc set 595.00
    Sandusky, 7/8" dado molding, No. 62, 9-1/2" l 115.00
    Stanley, #10-1/2 .... 120.00
    Varvill & Son, York, England, boxed bead molding planes, 9-1/2" l,
        10 pc set 595.00
    Winchester Repeating Arms Co. No. 3208, smoothing, metallic,
        mahogany handles, 9" l 185.00
Pruning Knife, hand forged iron blade, wood handle, c1800 .... 35.00
Router, Stanley, #71-1/2", patent date 1901 .... 40.00
Rule, Stanley, #32, two-fold, 12" l, caliper 120.00
Saw
    Band, mortised and pinned wood frame, orig red paint with blue
        and white striping, black and lade guides, laminated cherry and
        maple top, 76" 300.00
    Buck, wood, worn varnish finish, mkd "W. T. Banres," 30" 45.00
    Dovetail, Hague, Clegg & Barton, brass back, 9" l 95.00
    Turning, W. Johnson, Newark, NJ, Richardson blade,
        21" l 165.00
Screwdriver, flat wood handle, round sides, 9" blade 35.00
Scribe, curly maple adjustable fence and arm, 21" l 75.00
Shoot Board, Stanley, No. 51/52, orig decal, 14" l 1,295.00
Square, cherry, iron, brass bound blade, mkd "Set Tray" 50.00
Tire Gauge, Scharder, patent 1928 .... 40.00
Wagon Wrench 30.00
Wheel Measure, wrought iron, 14-1/2" l 45.00

TOOTHPICK HOLDERS

History: Toothpick holders, indispensable table accessories of the Victorian era, are small containers made specifically to hold toothpicks.

They were made in a wide range of materials: china (bisque and porcelain), glass (art, blown, cut, opalescent, pattern, etc.), and metals, especially silver plate. Makers include both American and European firms.

By applying a decal or transfer, a toothpick holder became a souvenir item; by changing the decal or transfer, the same blank could become a memento for any number of locations.

References: Neila and Tom Bredehoft and Jo and Bob Sanford, *Glass Toothpick Holders*, Collector Books, 1999; William Heacock, *Encyclopedia of Victorian Colored Pattern Glass*, Book I, 2nd ed., Antique Publications, 1976, 1992 value update; —, *1,000 Toothpick Holders*, Antique Publications, 1977; —, *Rare & Unlisted Toothpick Holders*, Antique Publications, 1984; National Toothpick Holders Collectors Society, *Toothpick Holders*, Antique Publications, 1992.

Collectors' Club: National Toothpick Holder Collectors, P.O. Box 417, Safety Harbor, FL 34695-0417, http://www.collectoronline.com/clubNTHCS.html.

Additional Listings: See *Warman's Americana & Collectibles* for more examples.

Bisque, skull, blue anchor shape mark 65.00
Burmese, 2-1/2" h, shiny, soft peach blush fading to buttery-yellow,
    eggshell-thin body 435.00
China
    Royal Bayreuth, elk 120.00
    Royal Doulton, Santa scene, green handles 75.00
    R. S. Germany, Schlegelmilch, MOP luster 40.00
Glass
    Amberina, DQ, sq top 350.00
    Cameo, Daum Nancy, winter scene, sgd 750.00
    Cranberry, coralene beaded flowers 285.00
    Cut, pedestal, chain of hobstars 145.00
    Milk
        Alligator, c1885 .... 70.00
        Florette, turquoise 110.00
        Parrot and Top Hat, c1895 .... 45.00
        Scroll, claw ftd, light pink and blue dec, c1900 .... 555.00
    Opalescent, Reverse Swirl, blue 85.00
Pattern Glass
    Arched Fleur-De-Lis 45.00
    Carnation, Northwood 75.00
    Daisy and Button, blue 75.00

Roller Skate, amber, high button shoe type, dated 1886, $45.

Delaware, rose stain, gold dec 175.00
Fandango, Heisey 55.00
Hartford, Fostoria 85.00
Florida, ruby amber 265.00
Kansas 45.00
Kentucky, green, gold trim 125.00
Michigan, clear, yellow stain 175.00
Spearpoint Band, ruby stained 195.00
Texas, gold trim 50.00
Truncated Cube, ruby stained 75.00
Vaseline, two children holding up barrel, on pedestal 35.00

TORTOISESHELL ITEMS

History: For many years, amber and mottled tortoiseshell has been used in the manufacture of small items such as boxes, combs, dresser sets, and trinkets.

Note: Anyone dealing in the sale of tortoiseshell objects should be familiar with the Endangered Species Act and Amendment in its entirety. As of November 1978, antique tortoiseshell objects can be legally imported and sold with some restrictions.

Also see *Celluloid* for imitation tortoiseshell items.

Box, cov, 9-3/8" l, 3-1/4" d, 1-5/8" h, rect, lid dec with raised gilt bird on
    perch, mother-of-pearl accents surrounded by foliate details, geo-
    metric Chinoiserie borders, Continental, late 19th C 700.00
Box, cov, with portrait
    2-3/8" d, circular, hand colored engraved portrait of bearded gentle-
      man, gold border, George IV 950.00
    3" x 2-1/4" x 5/8", tortoiseshell within silver borders, central pique
      inlaid dec monogram within border of arabesques, various ani-
      mals in corners, enameled scene of maiden reclining with child,
      attendant at side, face of satyr looking on from shadows, Louis
      XV, c1750, unmarked 1,550.00
Casket, 7" l, 2" h, shaped oval, tortoiseshell hinged lid, pique inlay of
    scrolling foliage suspending floral swag, silver case with floral and
    foliate feet, Birmingham, 1916 .... 750.00
Cigar Case
    5-1/2" l, rect, case inlaid with 3 color gold, reserve with vacant silver
      cartouche, hinged, pink silk lined int., fitted, expandable, Victo-
      rian, 19th C 450.00
    5-5/8" x 2-7/8", rect, silver inlaid crane and foliate stalks, brass bor-
      der with clasp, silk lined int., monogrammed, Continental, late
      19th C 550.00

Pin, tortoise shape, 1-1/2" l, $48.

Cigarette Case, 4-1/4" l, domed oval, applied central carved monogram, Continental, late 19th/early 20th C 325.00
Coin Purse, 2-3/4" l, tortoiseshell and metal framed purse, inlaid vacant gold cartouche, divided and expandable int., Victorian, 19th C 200.00
Diary
    3-3/4" x 2-5/8", silver inlaid floral bouquet and bird, silk lined int. fitted with pencil, monogrammed, French, late 19th C 400.00
    4-1/2" x 3-1/8", front inlaid with silver and gold fleur-de-lis suspending floral swag, gold clasp, silk lined int., French, late 19th C 425.00
Display Case, 21" w, 11-1/2" d, 19-1/2" h, veneer and ebonized, pieced gallery with finials over single door, conforming base, ebonized compressed bun feet, Dutch 1,080.00
Hair Comb
    5" l, carved band of openwork scrolling foliage, center cartouche 85.00
    6" l, diagonal openwork band of scrolling foliage, gold beaded top border 100.00
Lady's Suite, 4" x 2-7/8" carte-de-ball, ivory int.; miniature purse, leather int., both with rose gold fill monogram and hinges, orig leather case, emb monogram, Victorian 800.00
Longnette, 3-1/2" l closed, silver border with floral details, applied tortoiseshell over engine-turned ground, lever action, maker's mark rubbed, Continental, late 19th C 150.00
Miniature, mandolin, 5-1/4" l, tortoiseshell, ivory, and mother-of-pearl, Continental 175.00
Scent Box, 2-1/4" h, trapezoid, blond tortoiseshell veneer, divided int. compartments, late Regency, c1825, scent bottles missing 375.00
Snuff Box, cov
    2-1/2" d, circular, hinged lid inlaid with gold and silver bird within floral garland, Continental, l9th C 325.00
    2-5/8" d, circular, rose gold inlaid with foliate garland, center cartouche, Continental, late 19th C 250.00
    3" d, press dec with 2 men on bicycles on lid, geometric dec on bottom, European, cracks, chips, worm damage 275.00
    3-1/4" l, circular, stained ext. of geometric patterns, gilt mounted etching of man with wife and child, Victorian, second half 19th C ..425.00
    3-1/4" l, oval, blond tortoiseshell hinged lid, Continental, 19th C 250.00
    4" l, oval, blond tortoiseshell hinged lid, Continental, 19th C..275.00
Tea Caddy, 7-3/4" w, Regency, serpentine, MOP panels, ivory trim and escutcheon 1,500.00
Walking Stick, 34" l, handle with repousse and chased foliage, Continental, 19th C... 1,200.00

TOYS

History: The first cast iron toys began to appear in America shortly after the Civil War. Leading 19th-century manufacturers include Hubley, Dent, Kenton, and Schoenhut. In the first decades of the 20th century, Arcade, Buddy L, Marx, and Tootsie Toy joined these earlier firms. Wooden toys were made by George Brown and other manufacturers who did not sign or label their work.

Nuremberg, Germany, was the European center for the toy industry from the late 18th through the mid-20th centuries. Companies such as Lehman and Marklin produced high-quality toys.

References: Linda Baker, *Modern Toys, American Toys*, Collector Books, 1985, 1993 value update; Ronald S. Barlow (ed.,) *The Great American Antique Toy Bazaar, 1879-1945: 5,000 Old Engravings from Original Trade Catalogs*, Windmill Publishing, 1998; Robert E. Birkenes, *White Knob Wind Up Collectible Toys*, Schiffer Publishing, 1999; Larry Bloemker, Robert Genat, and Ed Weirick, *Pedal Cars*, MBI Publishing, 1999; Bill Bruegman, *Toys of the Sixties*, Cap'n Penny Productions, 1991; Dana Cain, *Collecting Monsters of Film and TV*, Krause Publications, 1997; Brad Cassity, *Fisher-Price Toys*, Collector Books, 1999; Jurgen and Marianne Cieslik, *Lehmann Toys*, New Cavendish Books, 1982; *Collector's Digest Price Guide to Pull Toys*, L-W Book Sales, 1996; Christopher Cook, *Collectible American Yo-Yos*, 1920s-1930s, Collector Books, 1997; Don Cranmer, *Collectors Encyclopedia, Toys—Banks*, L-W Books, 1986, 1993 value update; Greg Davis and Bill Morgan, *Collector's Guide to TV Toys and Memorabilia*, 2nd ed., Collector Books, 1999; Phillippe De LeSpinay, *Vintage Slot Cars*, MBI Publishing, 1999; Charles F. Donovan, Jr., Renwal, *World's Finest Toys*, published by author (11877 US Hwy 431, Ohatchee, AL 36271), 1994; Elmer Duellman, *Elmer's Price Guide to Toys*, Vol. 2, L-W Book Sales, 1996; James L. Dundas, *Gap Guns with Values*, Schiffer Publishing, 1996; ——, *Toys That Shoot and Other Neat Stuff*, Schiffer Publishing, 1998; Antoni Emchowicz and Paul Nunneley, *Future Toys*, New Cavendish, distributed by Antique Collectors' Club, 1999; Edward Force, *Corgi Toys*, Schiffer Publishing, 1984, 1997 value update; ——, *Dinky Toys*, Schiffer Publishing, 1988, 1992 value update; ——, *Lledo Toys*, Schiffer Publishing, 1996; ——, *Solido toys*, Schiffer Publishing, 1993; Tom Frey, *Toy Bop: Kid Classics of the 50's & 60's*, Fuzzy Dice Productions, 1994;

Christine Gentry and Sally Gibson-Downs, *Motorcycle Toys*, Collector Books, 1994; David C. Gould and Donna Crevar-Donaldson, *Occupied Japan Toys with Prices*, L-W Book Sales, 1993; Kurt Guile, Mike Willyard and Gary Konow, *Wyandotte Toys Are Good and Safe*, Wyandotte Toys Publishing, 1996; Ted Hake, *Hake's Price Guide To Character Toys*, Gemstone Publishing, 1998; Tom Heaton, *The Encyclopedia of Marx Action Figures*, Krause Publications, 1999; Morton Hirschberg, *Steam Toys*, Schiffer Publishing, 1996; Sharon and Bob Huxford (eds.,) *Schroeder's Collectible Toys*, 5th ed., Collector Books, 1999; Andrew Gurka, *Pedal Car Restoration and Price Guide*, Krause Publications, 1996; Dee Hockenberry, *Big Bear Book*, Schiffer Publishing, 1996; Don Hultzman, *Collector's Guide to Battery Toys*, Collector Books, 1998; Ken Hutchison & Greg Johnson, *Golden Age of Automotive Toys, 1925-1941*, Collector Books, 1996; Sharon and Bob Huxford, *Schroeder's Collectible Toys Price Guide: Antique to Modern*, 5th ed., Collector Books, 1999; Charles M. Jacobs, *Kenton Cast Iron Toys*, Schiffer Publishing, 1996; Alan Jaffe, *J. Chein and Co., A Collector's Guide to an American Toymaker*, Schiffer Publishing, 1997; Dana Johnson, *Matchbox Toys 1947-1996*, 3rd ed., Collector Books, 1999; Michele Karl, *Composition & Wood Dolls and Toys: A Collector's Reference Guide*, Antique Trader Books, 1998; Dale Kelley, *Die Cast Price Guide, Post-War: 1946-Present*, Antique Trader Books, 1997; Lisa Kerr, *American Tin-Litho Toys*, Collectors Press, 1995; ——, *Ohio Art: The World of Toys*, Schiffer Publishing, 1998; Sharon Korbeck and Elizabeth Stephan, *Toys & Prices, 2000*, 7th ed., Krause Publications, 1999.

Kathy and Don Lewis, *Talking Toys of the 20th Century*, Collector Books, 1999; Cynthia Boris Liljeblad, *TV Toys and the Shows that Inspired Them*, Krause Publications, 1996; Jerell Little, *Collector's Digest Price Guide to Cowboy Cap*

Guns and Guitars, L-W Book Sales, 1996; David Longest, *Antique & Collectible Toys 1870-1950*, Collector Books, 1994; ——, *Character Toys and Collectibles* (1984, 1992 value update), 2nd Series (1987), Collector Books; ——, *Toys*, Collector Books, 1990, 1994 value update; Charlie Mack, *Encyclopedia of Matchbox Toys, 1947-1996*, Schiffer Publishing, 1997; Bill Manzke, *The Encyclopedia of Corgi Toys*, Schiffer Publishing, 1997; Rex Miller, *The Investor's Guide to Vintage Character Collectibles*, Krause Publications, 1999; Richard O'Brien, *Collecting Toy Cars & Trucks*, 2nd ed., Krause Publications, 1997; ——, *Collecting American Made Toy Soldiers*, Krause Publications, 1997; ——, *Collecting Foreign-Made Toy Soldiers*, Krause Publications, 1997; Bob Parker, *Hot Wheels*, revised ed., Schiffer Publishing, 1996; ——, *Marx Toys*, Schiffer Publishing, 1996.

John Ramsay, *British Diecast Model Toys*, 6th ed., available from Tim Arthurs (Ralston Gallery, 109 Gover Ave., Norwalk, CT 06850), 1996; David E. Richter, *Collector's Guide to Tootsietoys*, 2nd ed., Collector Books, 1996; Vincent Santelmo, *The Complete Encyclopedia to G. I. Joe*, 2nd ed., Krause Publications, 1997; Martyn L. Schorr, *Guide to Mechanical Toy Collecting*, Performance Media, 1979; *Schroeder's Collectible Toys*, 3rd ed., Collector Books, 1996; Carole and Richard Smith, *Pails by Comparison*, published by author (P.O. Box 2068, Huntington, NY 11743), 1996; Elizabeth Stephan, ed., *O'Brien's Collecting Toys*, Ninth Ed., Krause Publications, 1999; Craig Strange, *Collector's Guide to Tinker Toys*, Collector Books, 1996; Carol Turpen, *Baby Boomer Toys and Collectibles*, 2nd ed., Schiffer Publishing, 1998; Gerald G. Walter, *Tin Dream Machines: German Tin Toy Cars and Motorcycles of the 1950s and 1960s*, New Cavendish, 1998; Stuart W. Wells, III, *Science Fiction Collectibles: Identification & Price Guide*, Krause Publications, 1999; Harry A. and Joyce A. Whitworth, *G-Men and FBI Toys and Collectibles*, Collector Books, 1998; Neil S. Wood, *Evolution of the Pedal Car*, Volume 5, L-W Book Sales, 1999.

Periodicals: *Antique Toy World*, P.O. Box 34509, Chicago, IL 60634; *Canadian Toy Mania*, P.O. Box 489, Rocanville, Saskatchewan SOA 3LO Canada; *Collectors Gazette*, Fleck Way, Thornsby, Stockton-On-Ters, Cleveland, T617 9J2, UK, http://www.icn.co.uk/cg.html; *Die Cast & Tin Toy Report*, 559 North Park Ave., Easton, CT 06612; *Master Collector*, 225 Cattle Barron Parc Drive, Fort Worth, TX 76108; *Model & Toy Collector Magazine*, 137 Casterton Ave., Akron, OH 44303; *Plane News*, P.O. Box 845, Greenwich, CT 06836; *Robot World & Price Guide*, P.O. Box 184, Lenox Hill Station, New York, NY 10021; *Toy Cannon News*, P.O. Box 2052-N, Norcross, GA 30071; *Toy Collector & Price Guide*, 700 E. State St., Iola, WI 54990; *Toy Collector Marketplace*, 1550 Territorial Rd, Benton Harbor, MI 49022; *Toy Gun Collectors of America Newsletter*, 312 Starling Way, Anaheim, CA 92807; *Toy Shop*, 700 East State St., Iola, WI 54990; *Toy Trader*, P.O. Box 1050, Dubuque, IA 52004; *Toybox Magazine*, 8393 E. Holly Rd, Holly, MI 48442; *U.S. Toy Collector Magazine*, P.O. Box 4244, Missoula, MT 59806; *Yo-Yo Times*, P.O. Box 1519, Herndon, VA 22070.

Collectors' Clubs: A. C. Gilbert Heritage Society, 1440 W. Rolley, Suite 252, New Haven, CT 06515; http://www.acghs.org; American Game Collectors Association, P.O. Box 44, Dresher, PA 19025; Antique Engine, Tractor & Toy Club, Inc., 5731 Paradise Rd, Slatington, PA 18080; Antique Toy Collectors of America, 13th Floor, Two Wall St., New York, NY 10005; Canadian Toy Collectors Society, 67 Alpine Ave., Hamilton, Ontario L9A1Z7, Canada; Capitol Miniature Auto Collectors Club, 10207 Greenacres Dr, Silver Spring, MD 20903; Diecast Exchange Club, P.O. Box 1066, Pineallas Park, FL 34665; Ertl Collectors Club, Highways 136 & 120, Dyersville, IA 52040; Farm Toy Collectors Club, P.O. Box 38, Boxholm, IA 50040; Ideal Toy Co. Collector's Club, P.O. Box 623, Lexington, MA 02173; Majorette Diecast Toy Collectors Association, 13447 NW Albany Ave., Bend, OR 97701; Miniature Piano Enthusiast Club, 633 Pennsylvania Ave., Hagerstown, MD 21740; San Francisco Bay Brooklin Club, P.O. Box 61018, Palo Alto, CA 94306; Schoenhut Collectors Club, 45 Louis Ave., West Seneca, NY 14224; Southern California Toy Collectors Club, Ste. 300, 1760 Termino, Long Beach, CA 90804.

Museums: American Museum of Automobile Miniatures, Andover, MA; Eugene Field House & Toy Museum, St. Louis, MO; Evanston Historical Society, Evanston, IL 60201; Forbes Magazine Collection, New York, NY; Hobby City Doll & Toy Museum, Anaheim, CA; Margaret Woodbury Strong Museum, Rochester, NY; Matchbox & Lesney Toy Museum, Durham, CT; Matchbox Road Museum, Newfield, NJ; Museum of the City of New York, New York, NY; Smithsonian Institution, Washington, DC; Spinning Top Exploratory Museum, Burlington, WI; Toy & Miniature Museum of Kansas City, Kansas City, MO; Toy Museum of Atlanta, Atlanta, GA; Washington Dolls' House & Toy Museum, Washington, DC; Western Reserve Historical Society, Cleveland, OH.

Additional Listings: Characters; Disneyana; Dolls; Schoenhut. Also see *Warman's Americana & Collectibles* and *Warman's Flea Market* for more examples.

Notes: Every toy is collectible; the key is condition. Good working order is important when considering mechanical toys. Examples in this listing are considered to be at least in good condition, if not better, unless otherwise specified.

Arcade, USA
 Fire Trailer Truck, red, blue fireman, detachable trailer, hose reel and ladder turntable, 16" l, ladders missing, paint loss....... 325.00
 Thresher, McCormick-Deering, gray and cream wheels, red lining, chromed chute and stacker, 12" l...................................... 320.00
 Tractor, cast iron, partial green and yellow paint, 3-1/2" l........ 70.00
 Trolley, Greyhound, New York World's Fair, blue and orange, nickel driver, decals, 3 cars with tinplate canopies, black tires, 16" l, some chipping and scratching 635.00
Arnold, USA, cycle, turquoise, no longer sparks........................ 650.00
Bing, Gebruder, Germany
 Open Tourer, 4 seater, litho tinplate, gray-green, black and yellow lining, red button seats, black wings, front steering, orange and gray wheels, twin lamps, windscreen frame, hand-brake operated clockwork motor, c1915, 12-1/2" l, chauffeur missing, lamps detached 2,400.00
 Union Ferry Boat, hand painted tin, clockwork, red hull, brown open deck, white deck housing, railing on side, window cut-outs on both sides, stack on roof, 12" l...................................... 1,200.00
Borgfeldt, George, NY, Pluto the Pup, articulated wood, orig maker's box, 6" l 920.00

SPECIAL AUCTIONS

Auction Team Breker
Jane Herz
6731 Ashley Court
Sarasota, FL 34241
(941) 925-0385

Auction Team Breker
Postfach 501168 D 5000
Köln 50, W. Germany

Bill Bertoia Auctions
1881 Spring Rd
Vineland, NJ 08360
(609) 692-1881

Jackson's Auctioneers & Appraisers
2229 Lincoln St.
Cedar Falls, IA 50613
(319) 277-2256
email: jacksons@corenet.net

James D. Julia, Inc.
P.O. Box 830
Fairfield, ME 04937
(207) 453-7125

Richard Opfer Auctioneering, Inc.
1919 Greenspring Dr.
Timonium, MD 21093
(410) 252-5035

Phillips Fine Art Auctions
406 E. 79th St.
New York, NY 10021
(212) 570-4830

Lloyd Ralston Toys
173 Post Rd
Fairfield, CT 06432
(203) 255-1233

Skinner Inc.
Bolton Gallery
357 Main St.
Bolton, MA 01740
(508) 779-6241

Stout Auctions
11 W. Third St.
Williamsport, IN 47993-1119
(765) 764-6901

Toy Scouts, Inc.
137 Casterton Ave.
Akron, OH 44303
(330) 836-0068
email: toyscout@salamander.net

Buddy L, USA
 Dump Truck, black, red chassis and wheels, open cab, front steering, decal under dashboard, hinged tailgate, 25" l, lacks chain to wheels, some scratches 1,150.00
 Electric Emergency Unit Wrecker, white pressed steel, rear hoist, 16-1/2" l, paint wear and staining....................... 215.00
 Outdoor Railroad, No. 1000 4-6-2 locomotive and tender, No. 1001 caboose, No. 1003 tank, No. 1004 stock, No. 1005 coal cars (one with orig decal), 121-1/2" l, repainted 1,840.00
 Shell Oil, 1938, Bud Krause restoration 3,850.00
 Steam Shovel, No. 220, black, red corrugated roof and base, cast wheels, boiler, decale and winch, 14" h, surface rust, paint crazing on roof... 115.00
 Telephone Maintenance Truck, No. 450, two-tone green, ladder, two poles, orig maker's box 350.00
 Wrecker, orig condition 3,950.00
Cast Iron, unknown American makers
 Dump Truck, green Mack style front, C-cab, red bed with spring lever, spoked nickel wheels, 7-3/4" l................................. 490.00
 Gasoline Truck, blue, Mack style front, C-cab, rubber tires, one tire missing. 7" l.. 200.00
 Milk Wagon, black cast iron horse, gilt harness, yellow wheels, blue steel wagon body, 6-3/4" l... 150.00
 Stake Truck, Ford Model A, red, 7" l................................... 200.00
Chein
 Barnacle Bill, tinplate, red hat, clockwork walking mechanism, 6-1/4" h.. 290.00
 Disneyland Ferris Wheel, clockwork motor, bell, six gondolas, litho Disney characters and fairgrounds scenes, 16-3/4" h, distortion and paint loss.. 350.00
 Easter Bunny, tinplate, pulling basket, multicolored, 10" l..... 145.00
 Hercules Ferris Wheel, clockwork motor, bell, six gondolas, litho children and fairground scenes, 16-1/2" l.......................... 325.00
Chromolithograph Paper on Wood, unknown maker
 Bagatelle Game, two clowns with cup hats, patent date "March 7, 1895," 15" l.. 290.00
 Battleship Texas, sides printed with anchor, guns, and gangway, deck with 2 wood cannons, funnel, mast, one flag pole, second one detached, red flag, attached manuscript Christmas tag, 14" l. 490.00
 Brownie Ten Pins, set of 10 different Palmer Cox Brownie figures, each with printed poem on reverse about their character, ©Palmer Cox 1892, two mallets and 3 balls, wood box... 1,150.00
 Noah's Ark, incised and applied dec, hinged roof, 4 carved humans, 40 animals, 19" l hull... 750.00
 Trinity Chimes, 8 chimes, cathedral scenes, upright case, 18" h... 150.00
Citroen, France
 Aviation Fuel Truck, pressed steel, clockwork, painted red, enclosed cab with opening driver's door, tanker body with filler cap and brass drain valve, electric headlights, rear decal "AVIA," 18" l.. 1,350.00
 5CV, open tourer, 2-seat, blue boat tail body, black wings and wheels, gray tires, front steering and clockwork motor, orig maker's box, 12" l... 2,070.00
 Fire Engine, painted tin, clockwork, red, open bench seats, removable hose reel, ladders mount on rear body, disc wheels, rubber tires, orig box, 18" l.. 2,900.00
 Race Car, pressed steel, clockwork, blue, molded seated figure with hand painted composition head, rubber tires, decal "Petite Rosalie," 12-1/4" l... 450.00
Converse, USA
 Heffield Farms Delivery Wagon, articulated horse, 21-1/2" l, considerable wear and paint loss.. 320.00
 Klondike Ice Co. Delivery Wagon, tinplate on wood, 2 litho horses, 17" l, paint poor.. 175.00
 Trolley, open sides, pressed steel, blue and mustard, stenciled dec, mkd "City Hall Park 175" on both ends, reversible benches, large clockwork motor, 16" l, paint poor, destination boards missing 260.00

Günthermann, Racing Teddy, mechanical, c1950, $2,050. Photo courtesy of Auction Team Breker.

Cragston
    Robot, 10-1/2" h, battery operated tinplate, silver-gray body, red arms and chest, domed clear-plastic head with visible mechanism, orig maker's box 1,725.00
    Shuttling Freight Train, locomotive, two wagons, accessories, orig box and wrapping 90.00
Dent, USA, dump truck, cast iron, green-gray, Mack-style front, C-cab, driver, red spoked wheels, spring-operated bed, swinging tailgate, 7" l, paint loss 320.00
Fisher-Price, USA, Mickey Mouse, No. 748, articulated paper on wood, pull-toy, xylophone, 9" l 350.00
French, unknown maker
    Clown, articulated, playing cymbals, papier-mâché head, blue and red costume, wood body, push-toy action, c1900, 8" h 460.00
    Soldier Pins, unopened set, 5 pins, knit-covered ball, c1900 ... 325.00
Gibbs, see-saw, yellow tower, handpainted boy and girl, 14-1/2" h .. 140.00
Girard/Woods
    Coupe, Pierce Arrow, pressed steel, pink and maroon, clockwork motor, battery operated lights, rubber tires and bell, 14" l, one headlight missing, scratches 1,200.00
    Man Pushing Wheelbarrow, red plaid jacket, yellow trousers, green cart with orange wheels, 5-3/4" l 150.00
Herolin, Germany, farm yard set, no. 744/2, pressed card, chromolithograph, house, family, animals, and trees, maker's box with label, early 20th C, 12-3/4" w, some damage to box 175.00
Hubley, Lancaster, PA
    Fire Wagon, painted cast iron, hook and ladder wagon, articulated triple team, two drivers, 4 ladders, red ground, yellow hitch and wheels, early 20th C, 31" l 1,650.00
    Indian motorcycle and side car, cast iron, cast aluminum handlebars, rubber tires, sprung steel noise-maker, some paint and decal loss, one tire damaged 865.00
Ives, Bridgeport, CT
    Cuzner Trotter, red tinplate carriage mkd "Pat'd March 7, 1871,"

Hubley, Firemen, 3 black and white horses, cast iron, repaired, $285.

Japanese Tin, Chrysler Imperial Le-Baron, 1962, tin, ATC-Asahi Toys, Japan, orig box, $20,455. Photo courtesy of Auction Team Breker.

    black spoked wheels, white horse with articulated legs, driver with striped trousers, black hat, brass clockwork motor, 11-1/2" l, some chipping 2,590.00
    Steamer, King, clockwork motor, black and red hull, brown superstructure with single funnel, 10-1/2" l, some wear 345.00
Japanese
    Haji, 8" l, car with boat trailer, friction powered, blue Ford convertible, red and cream Speedo motor boat with friction powered motor, red trailer, orig packing and maker's box 400.00
    San, tugboat, 12-1/2" l, battery operated tinplate, red, cream, yellow, and blue, smoking mechanism, orig maker's box 200.00
T.N.
    Dump Truck, 11" l, friction powered tinplate, red and cream, automatic side dump action, orig maker's box 150.00
    Great Swanee Paddle Wheeler, 10-1/4" l, friction powered tinplate, whistle mechanism, orig maker's box 175.00
    Space Patrol Car, 9-1/2" l, battery operated, litho, blue, cream, and silver, red astronaut, green laser, spinning antenna, orig maker's ox 1,265.00
Y.H./Daiwa, car with sailboat, 6-1/4" l, friction powered tinplate,

Kellermann, Socius, tin, clockwork, bike drives in wavy lines, pillion rider moves accordingly, c1938, $1,535. Photo courtesy of Auction Team Breker.

thunderbird style car, red body, black roof, red and cream sailboat with blue trailer..435.00

JEP Voisin, saloon car, No. 7392, tin, red body, black roof and wings, litho running boards, brass finished radiator, horn, battery operated spot light, front steering, clockwork motor, black disc wheels with gray tires, maker's and Paris retailer's labels, 14-1/2" l, one wing loose, one headlight front missing.....................................1,380.00

Kelmet Corp., New York, dump truck, sheet metal, orig black and red paint, mkd "White Big Boy, Kelmet Corp. New York, NY," minor wear, headlights missing, dump mechanism incomplete, 26" l..........990.00

Kenton, Kenton, OH
Bus, Nile Coach, cast iron 750.00
Elephant and Clown Chariot, remnants of silver paint and red blanket, yellow spoked wheels, detachable clown, 6-1/4" l, considerable paint wear and chips 130.00
Fire Pumper, cast iron, painted red, gold boiler top and lamps, driver, white tires, 10-1/4" l, some chipping 230.00
Hose Reel, cast iron, 3 white horses, white carriage and reel, driver, hose, and spoked wheels, 13-3/4" l, horses repainted, other paint poor...435.00
Overland Circus, cage wagon, red, yellow wheels, white horses, driver, and outrider, 14" l 425.00
Sulky and Driver, nickeled cast iron, red spoked wheels, 5" l 115.00

Keystone Mfg. Co., Boston, U. S. Mail Truck, Packard, black cab, green body, red chassis, 26" l, rear doors missing...................800.00

Kingsbury Toys, USA
Dump Truck 200.00
Streetcar, orange, black bumpers
No. 781, 9-1/4" l, scratching and chipping........................200.00
No. 784, clockwork motor, fixed turning and bell, 14" l, paint chipped 150.00

Lehmann, Germany
Autin, coil spring motor, wood grain litho cart, blue jacketed box, 3-3/4" l..290.00
Beetle, spring motor, crawling movement, flapping wings, maker's box, one leg detached, but present, early Adam trademark230.00
Na-Ob, red and yellow cart, blue eccentric wheels, gray donkey, mkd "Lehmann Ehe & Co.," 6" l, front wheel missing 145.00
Truck, tinplate, cream, red, and yellow, blue driver, fixed steering, clockwork motor, mkd "Lehmann Ehe & Co.," 6-3/4" l 435.00
Tut Tut Motor Car, white suited driver, horn, front steering, bellows, coil springs, paint loss, rust spotting, 6-1/2" l......................635.00
Walking Down Broadway, rack and pinion flywheel drive, litho couple, pug dog, orig lady's handbag, paint loss, 6-1/4" h 1,840.00

Linemar, Japan
Donald Duck, Huey, Louey, and Dewey Marching Soldiers, clockwork motor, rubber titles, 11-1/4" l, scratches 375.00

Fernand Martin, Paris, Le Petit Livreur, mechanical, 1911, $1,535. Photo courtesy of Auction Team Breker.

Gym Toy, Donald Duck, clockwork motor, celluloid figure, red bar, doing acrobatics, 4-1/2" h 245.00
Mickey Mouse with Xylophone, litho, clockwork motor, black, red, and yellow, foliate dec on xylophone, orig box lid, 7" h, chips, tears to lid 750.00
Popeye, rowboat, battery operated tinplate, orig controller and maker's box 9,200.00

Marklin, Goppingen, Germany, field cannon, 13" l, cast iron, olive finish, firing mechanism, adjustable barrel.............................115.00

Marx, Louis & Co., NY
Big Parade, moving soldiers, cannon, ambulance, clockwork motor, stationary buildings, 24" l, airplane missing, faded............200.00
Bulldozer/Tractor, gold body, rubber treads, plow and farmer driver, blue and red stake wagons, hitch, 2 discs, plow, corn planter, harvester 230.00
Bus, Royal Bus Line, orange, red, and green, driver, clockwork motor, 9-3/4" l...400.00
Charlie McCarthy Benzine Buggy, litho, black, cream, and red, clockwork motor, erratic action, 7" l, scratches and wear ...375.00
Dick Tracy Squad Car, battery operated motor and light, litho, green, characters in windows, 11-1/4" l, dent to roof, some scratches 175.00
G-Man Pursuit Car, pressed steel and tinplate, red and blue, armed agent, clockwork motor, 14-1/4" l, scratches 750.00
Honeymoon Express, clockwork motor, circular base...........100.00
Lumar Wrecker Service Truck, multicolored pressed steel, rear winch, 16" l, scratches and staining.................................200.00
Lumber Contractors Truck, steel, red and yellow, 20" l 115.00
Machinery Equipment Service Moving Truck, pressed steel, black, red, yellow, and silver, traversing crane, plastic motor, 2 wooden crates, maker's box, 22" l, truck rust and discoloration, box taped and water stained 175.00
Merrymakers Band, tinplate, one dancer missing 575.00
Popeye and Parrots, tinplate, clockwork motor, 8-1/4" h.......350.00
Railway Express Agency Delivery Truck, green, yellow details, silver roof, cream, red, and blue logos, operating tailgate, Wyandotte tires and accessories including dolly and miniature packages, 1950s, 20" l, few scratches and scuffs 375.00
U. S. Army Division Tank, No. 392, green, detailing, recoiling gun barrel, clockwork motor with start/stop action, 9-1/2" l..........60.00
Zippo the Climbing Monkey, multicolored litho tinplate, pull-string mechanism, 10" l 60.00

Metalcraft, Coca-Cola Delivery Truck, pressed steel, red and yellow, bottles, decals, 10-1/2" l, scratches....................................490.00

Paris Mfg. Co., South Paris, ME, Peerless No. 400 Wagon, pine body, stenciled and painted dec, handle, red disc wheels with solid rubber tires, 36" l wagon..175.00

Plank, Ernst, airship, shaded mustard colored superstructure and tubular fins, twin-bladed celluloid propeller, each emb with E. P. trademark, steel-blue colored gondola with Captain holding telescope, airman standing by engine, ventilator, rudder and tinplate forward propeller, cloth covered suspension wire and cast metal winding key, 11" l, excelsior filled maker's carton with chromolithograph label of Jules Verne style character riding rocket over German town, catalog no. label 962/1, torn triangular label with indistinct trademark, some damage and chipping..23,000.00

Pratt & Letchworth, hook and ladder truck, cast iron, horse drawn, one red and one white horse, black frame with red detailing, spoked wheels, seated front driver, seated rear steerer, 2 wood ladders and bell, 23" l..460.00

Schuco, trademark of Schreyer and Co., Germany
Acrobat Bear, yellow mohair, glass eyes, embroidered nose and mouth, turns somersaults when wound, orig key, 1950s, 5" h.575.00
Hopsta Dancing Monkey, red and yellow, baby mouse, clockwork motor, 4-1/2" h 175.00
Monkey Bellhops, Yes/No monkey with painted metal face, metal eyes, ginger mohair head and tail, red and black felt outfit and hands, Acrobatic monkey with painted metal face, metal eyes, ginger mohair head, red and black felt outfit and hands, winds by

rotating arms, oak Mission style settee, 1930s, 8-1/2" h, moth damage on both 435.00

Porsche Microracer, No. 1037, red, key missing 55.00

Teddy Bear on Roller Skates, wind-up, beige mohair head, glass eyes, embroidered nose and mouth, cloth and metal body and legs, cotton shirt, felt overalls, hands, and boots, rubber wheels, mkd "Schuco, U. S. Zone, Germany," clothes faded, key not orig 490.00

Teddy Bear on Scooter, friction auction, yellow mohair bear, black steel eyes, embroidered nose and mouth, black felt pants, blue litho scooter, 1920s, 5-3/4" h 1,035.00

Stevens & Brown, girl on velocipede, cast iron frame, brass clockwork motor, stencil dec red tinplate cover, red jacket and striped pantaloons, 11" l, steering rod missing 2,070.00

Strauss, Ferdinard, Corp., New York City

Flying Graf Zeppelin, aluminum, clockwork mechanism, maker's box, 16" l, some tabs broken 290.00

Jazzbo Jim, clockwork litho tinplate, banjo player, plaid jacket, cabin dec with caricatures, maker's box, hole in lid, 10-1/4" h 500.00

Red Cap Porter, bulldog popping out of trunk, lid missing, uniform faded 230.00

Sturditoy Construction Co., dump truck, pressed steel, rack lifting mechanism, 27" l, repainted, orig decals visible 635.00

Structo, hydraulic hook and ladder, pressed steel, red, 3" l 175.00

Technofix, cable car, clockwork motor, shaped tinplate base, litho Alpine scenes, maker's box, some tape on box, 18-1/2" w 130.00

Tinplate, unknown makers

Clown Violinist, stilt-legs, striped trousers, clockwork motor, 9" h, poor condition 60.00

Delivery Carriage, litho, black, red, yellow, and pink, flywheel drive, 4-1/4" l 150.00

Horse-Drawn Omnibus, attributed to Francis, Field and Francis, Philadelphia, 1850s, 2 white horses, black painted harnesses, wheel operated trotting, dark green roof with black fleur-de-lis and lining, emb gilt foliate surround, emb rear steps, door surround, driver's rear rest, emb window frames with painted curtains, rd front, rear upper section, lower half with handpainted polychrome floral and foliate dec, over blue-gray, ochre int. with ochre vis-a-vis bench seating along sides, wheels, 23" l, overall paint flaking, wheels detached, one window frame partially detached 48,300.00

Locomotive, attributed to Fallows, clockwork motor, cast wheels, high wings, cow catcher and bell, old repaint, 10" l 460.00

Locomotive, Victory, red boiler, bell, black and gilt stack, red and blue cab with green roof, silver stenciled windows, yellow chassis, spoked wheels, 4-3/4" l, one wheel damaged, scratches and paint loss 990.00

Porter and Trolley, clockwork motor in hinged trunk, blue uniform, red and orange electric-type trolley, 4-1/2" l 145.00

Steamer, 3 funnels, handpainted, red, cream, and gray hull, cream superstructure, 10" l 350.00

Two-Seater Tourer, litho, red, yellow, and cream, driver, fly-wheel drive, 3" l 400.00

Turner, Lincoln sedan, pressed steel, gray body, black roof and lines, green int., red wheels and rubber tires, 26-1/2" l, paint loss and surface rust 1,840.00

Unique Art, Newark, NJ

Hee Haw, litho tinplate milk cart, clockwork motor, milk cans, donkey, and hillbilly, 10" l 350.00

Jazzbo Jim, dancing figure, checkered jacket and trousers, log cabin dec with caricature figures, coil-spring motor, 9-1/2" h, some rust spotting and fading 260.00

Wilkins

Ladder Truck, pressed steel chassis, cast driver and operator, red spoked wheels, clockwork motor and ladder, 13-1/4" l, old repainting 230.00

Steam Pumper, cast iron, 2 black and one white horse, yellow frame, red wheels, nickeled boiler, 21" l 690.00

Wolverine Supply & Mfg. Co.

Car and Trailer, press-and-go motor, litho tin, blue and orange 1940s style four door sedan, four wheel blue, white, and orange trailer, some scratches, dent in auto roof, 27-1/2" l 200.00

Panama Pile Driver, gravity toy, falling ball-operated driver, patent date Dec 1905, 7 clay balls, 15-1/2" h, paint flaking 230.00

Zilotone, wind-up, figure plays tunes on xylophone, 3 interchangeable discs, repaired orig box lid, some paint chips 650.00

Wyandotte, USA

Airplane Carousel, multicolored tinplate, 4 planes, canopy and rack mechanism, 6-3/4" h 90.00

Ambulance, painted pressed steel, nickeled grill, operating rear door, minor scratches, 11" l 150.00

Car and Trailer, painted pressed steel, red, streamlined auto and travel trailer with operating rear door, replaced white rubber tires, paint worn, chips, and scratches, 25" l 215.00

Humphrey Mobile, litho tinplate, fixed steering, clockwork motor, rear door, moving hat and arm, 9" l, some scratching 350.00

Pan Am Clipper, painted pressed steel, red and white, brass engines, nickeled propellers, 9" l 275.00

TRAINS, TOY

History: Railroading has always been an important part of childhood, largely because of the romance associated with the railroad and the prominence of toy trains.

The first toy trains were cast iron and tin; wind-up motors added movement. The golden age of toy trains was 1920 to 1955, when electric-powered units and high-quality rolling stock were available and names such as Ives, American Flyer, and Lionel were household words. The advent of plastic in the late 1950s resulted in considerably lower quality.

Toy trains are designated by a model scale or gauge. The most popular are HO, N, O and standard. Narrow gauge was a response to the modern capacity to miniaturize. Its popularity has decreased in the last few years.

References: Paul V. Ambrose, *Greenberg's Guide to Lionel Trains*, 1945-1969, Vol. III, Greenberg Publishing, 1990; Paul V. Ambrose and Joseph P. Algozzini, *Greenberg's Guide to Lionel Trains 1945-1969*, Vol. IV, Uncatalogued Sets (1992), Vol. V, *Rare and Unusual* (1993), Greenberg Publishing; Susan and Al Bagdade, *Collector's Guide to American Toy Trains*, Wallace-Homestead, 1990; Tom Blaisdell and Ed Urmston, *Standard Guide to Athearn Model Trains*, Krause Publications, 1998; John O. Bradshaw, *Greenberg's Guide to Kusan Trains*, Greenberg Publishing, 1987; Pierce Carlson, *Collecting Toy Trains*, Pincushion Press, 1993; W. G. Claytor Jr., P. Doyle, and C. McKenney, *Greenberg's Guide to Early American Toy Trains*, Greenberg Publishing, 1993; Joe Deger, *Greenberg's Guide to American Flyer S Gauge*, Vol. I, 4th ed. (1991), Vol. II (1991), Vol. III (1992), Greenberg Publishing; Cindy Lee Floyd (comp.), *Greenberg's Marx Train Catalogues*, Greenberg Publishing, 1993; John Glaab, *Brown Book of Brass Locomotives*, 3rd ed., Chilton, 1993; John Grams, *Toy Train Collecting and Operating*, Kalmbach Publishing, 1999;

Bruce Greenberg, *Greenberg's Guide to Ives Trains*, Vol. I (1991), Vol. II (1992), Greenberg Publishing; —— (Christian F. Rohlfing, ed.), *Greenberg's Guide to Lionel Trains: 1901-1942*, Vol. 1 (1988), Vol. 2 (1988), Greenberg Publishing; ——, *Greenberg's Guide To Lionel Trains: 1945-1969*, Vol. 1, 8th ed. (1992), Vol. 2, 2nd ed. (1993), Greenberg Publishing; *Greenberg's Lionel Catalogues*, Vol. V, Greenberg Publishing, 1992; *Greenberg's Marx Train Catalogues, Greenberg Publishing, 1992; *Greenberg's Pocket Price Guide, American Flyer S Gauge*, , Kalmbach Publishing, 1998; *Greenberg's Pocket Price Guide, LGB*, 1969-1996, 3rd ed., Kalmbach Publishing, 1996; *Greenberg's Pocket Price Guide, Lionel Trains, 1901-1999*, Kalmbach Publishing, 1998; *Greenberg's Pocket Price Guide, Marx Trains*, 7th ed., Kalmbach Publishing, 1999; George Horan, *Greenberg's Guide to Lionel HO*, Vol. II, Greenberg Publishing, 1993; George Horan and Vincent Rosa, *Greenberg's Guide to Lionel HO*, Vol. I, 2nd ed., Greenberg Publishing, 1993; John Hubbard, *Story of Williams Electric Trains*, Greenberg Publishing, 1987; Steven H. Kimball, *Greenberg's Guide to American Flyer Prewar O Gauge*, Greenberg Publishing, 1987; Roland La Voie, *Greenberg's Guide to Lionel Trains*, 1970-1991, Vol. I (1991), Vol. II (1992), Greenberg Publishing.

Lionel Book Committee, *Lionel Trains: Standard of the World, 1900-1943*, Train Collectors Association, 1989; Dallas J. Mallerich III, *Greenberg's American Toy Trains: From 1900 with Current Values*, Greenberg Publishing, 1990; ——, *Greenberg's Guide to Athearn Trains*, Greenberg Publishing, 1987; Eric J. Matzke, *Greenberg's Guide to Marx Trains*, Vol. 1 (1989), Vol. II (1990), Greenberg Publishing; Robert P. Monaghan, *Greenberg's Guide to Marklin OO/HO*, Greenberg Publishing, 1989; John R. Ottley, *Greenberg's Guide to LGB Trains*, Greenberg Publishing, 1989; Peter H. Riddle, *America's Standard Gauge Electric Trains*, Antique Trader Books, 1998; Robert Schleicher, *Fun with Toy Trains*, Krause Publications, 1999; Alan R. Schuweiler, *Greenberg's Guide to American Flyer*, Wide Gauge, Greenberg Publishing, 1989; Gerry & Janet Souter, *The American Toy Train*, MBI Publishing, 1999; John D. Spanagel, *Greenberg's Guide to Varney Trains*, Greenberg Publishing, 1991; Elizabeth A. Stephan, *O'Brien's Collecting Toy Trains*, 5th ed., Krause Publications, 1999; Robert C. Whitacre, *Greenberg's Guide to Marx Trains Sets*, Vol. III, Greenberg Publishing, 1992.

Periodicals: *Classic Toy Trains*, 21027 Crossroads Circle, P.O. Box 1612, Waukesha, WI 53187, http://www2.classtrain.com; *Collectors Gazette*, Fleck Way, Thornsby, Stockton-On-Ters, Cleveland, T617 9J2, UK, http://www.icn.co.uk/cg.html; *LGB Telegram*, 1573 Landvater, Hummelstown, PA 17036; *Lionel Collector Series Marketmaker*, Trainmaster, P.O. Box 1499, Gainesville, FL 32602; *O Gauge Railroading*, P.O. Box 239, Nazareth, PA 18064.

Collectors' Clubs: A. C. Gilbert Heritage Society, 1440 W. Rolley, Suite 252, New Haven, CT 06515, http://www.acghs.org; American Flyer Collectors Club, P.O. Box 13269, Pittsburgh, PA 15234; Ives Train Society, P.O. Box 59, Thompson, OH 44086; LGB Model Railroad Club, 1854 Erin Drive, Altoona, PA 16602; Lionel Collectors Club of America, P.O. Box 479, LaSalle, IL 61301; Lionel Operating Train Society, 18 Eland Ct, Fairfield, OH 45014; Marklin Club-North America, P.O. Box 51559, New Berlin, WI 53151; Marklin Digital Special Interest Group, P.O. Box 51319, New Berlin, WI 53151; The National Model Railroad Association, 4121 Cromwell Road, Chattanooga, TN 37421; Toy Train Collectors Society, 109 Howedale Drive,

---

SPECIAL AUCTIONS

Bill Bertoia Auctions
1881 Spring Rd.
Vineland, NJ 08360
(609) 692-1881

Greenberg Auctions
7566 Main St.
Sykesville, MD 21784
(410) 795-7447

Joy Luke
The Gallery
300 E. Grove St.
Bloomington, IL 61701
(309) 828-5533

J. W. Auction Co.
54 Rochester Hill Rd
Rochester, NH 03867
(603) 332-0192

Lloyd Ralston Toys
173 Post Rd
Fairfield, CT 06432
(203) 255-1233

Stout Auctions
11 W. Third St.
Williamsport, IN 47993-1119
(765) 764-6901

Rochester, NY 14616-1534; The Toy Train Operating Society, Inc., Suite 308, 25 West Walnut St, Pasadena, CA 91103; Train Collector's Association, P.O. Box 248, Strasburg, PA 17579, http://www.traincollectors/org.

Museums: Delaware Train and Miniature Museum, Wilmington, DE; Toy Train Museum of the Train Collectors Association, Strasburg, PA.

Additional Listings: See *Warman's Americana & Collectibles* for more examples.

Notes: Condition of trains is critical when establishing price. Items in fair condition and below (scratched, chipped, dented, rusted or warped) generally have little value to a collector. Accurate restoration is accepted and may enhance the price by one or two grades. Prices listed below are for trains in very good to mint condition unless otherwise noted.

American Flyer

Boxcar, 33514, HO gauge, Silver Meteor, brown.........................45.00
Caboose
    935, S gauge, 1957, brown 60.00
    33515, HO gauge, C&O, lighted, yellow, center cupola 75.00
Crane Car, 944, S gauge, 1952-57, Industrial
    Brownhoist 30.00
Flat Car
    936, S gauge, 1953-54, Erie, depressed center, spool
    load 38.00
    24558, S gauge, 1959-60, Canadian Pacific, Christmas tree
    load 145.00

Gondola

    941, S gauge, 1953-57, Frisco 10.00

    33507, HO gauge, D&H, brown, canister load 60.00

Locomotive

    342, S gauge, steam, 1946, nickel plate, switcher, 0-8-0, tender mkd "Nickel Plate Road" 750.00

    345, S gauge, steam, 1954, Silver Bullet, Pacific, 4-6-2 .... 200.00

    426, HO gauge, B&O, blue and gray 150.00

Observation Car

    503, S gauge, 1952, silver finish 225.00

    24833, S gauge, 1957-58, silver, red stripe, "Washington" 50.00

Reefer, 24403, S gauge, 1958, Illinois Central, orange 15.00

Refrigerator Car, 123, HO gauge, orange 150.00

Tank Car

    500, HO gauge, Gulf, silver, single dome 15.00

    33500, HO gauge, Gulf, silver, single dome 25.00

Vista Dome, 502, S gauge, 1952, AFL, chrome finish 200.00

Ives

Baggage Car

    50, 1908-09, O gauge, 4 wheels, red litho frame, striped steps, white/silver body, sides mkd "Limited Vestibule Express, United States Mail Baggage Co." and "Express Service No. 50," 3 doors on both sides, one on each end, black roof with clerestory 150.00

    70, 1923-25, O gauge, 8 wheel, red litho body, simulates steel, tin roof with celestory stripe, sliding center door, mkd "The Ives Railway Lines, Express Baggage Service, 60, U. S. Mail" 30.00

Caboose, 67, 1918, O gauge, 8 wheels, red litho body, sliding door on each side, gray painted tin roof with red cupola, "The Ives Railway Lines" 45.00

Gravel Car, 63, 1913-14, O gauge, 8 wheels, gray litho, rounded truss rods, mkd "63" on sides 35.00

Livestock Car, 65, c1918, O gauge, 8 wheels, orange-yellow litho body, type D trucks, gray painted roof with catwalk, sides mkd "Livestock Transportation, Ives RR" 27.50

Locomotive

    11, 1910-13, O gauge, 0-4-0, black boiler and cab, litho plates beneath arched cab windows, cast iron wheels, L. V. E. No. 11 tender 165.00

    19, 1917-25, O gauge, 0-4-0, black cast iron boiler and cab, 2 arched windows and "IVES No. 19" beneath, cast-iron wheels, NYC & HR No. 17 tender 225.00

    25, 1906-07, O gauge, 4-4-2, black body, boiler tapers towards front, 4 separate boiler bands, 3 square windows on both sides of cab, gold frames and stripes, tin pony wheels, 4 wheel L.V.E. No. 25 tender 275.00

    3200, 1911, O gauge, 0-4-o, cast iron S-type electric center cab, green body, gold trim, cast iron six-spoke wheels, center door flanked by 2 windows, raised lettering "Ives" and "3200" below windows 250.00

    3236, 1928, Standard gauge, 0-4-0, electric box cab, tan tin body, stamped steel frame, diecast wheels, operating headlight, 3 windows per side, brass plates "The Ives Railway Lines" and "Motor 3236" 265.00

Parlor Car

    62, 1924-30, O gauge, 8 wheels, tin litho steel, red-brown, one pc roof with clerestory stripe,5 windows, 2 doors on each side, mkd "The Ives Railway Lines" above windows 75.00

    72, 1910-15, 1 gauge, 8 wheel, white tin body, litho to simulate wood, tin roof with clerestory stripe, 4 double windows, 3 small windows, door at each end, mkd "Twentieth Century Limited Express, No. 72, Chicago" 490.00

Passenger Car, 51, 1906-07, O gauge, 4 tin wheels, red litho spring detail on frame, vestibule at each end, litho body mkd Mohawk, Hiawatha or Iroquois, "Limited Vestibule Express," roof with clerestory strip 200.00

Tank Car, 66, 1921-35, O gauge, 8 wheels, gray painted body, black dome 25.00

Tender, 25, 1928-30, O gauge, diecast body, coal load, two 4-wheel trucks 150.00

Lionel, 390E steam engine and 390T tender, 1929-33, orig box, $990. Photo courtesy of Bider's Antiques, Inc.

Lionel

Baggage Car, 2602, O gauge, 1938, red body and roof 100.00

Boxcar

    00-44, OO gauge, 1939 .... 45.00

    HO-874, HO gauge, 1964, NYC 25.00

Caboose

    217, Standard gauge, 1926-40, orange and maroon 150.00

    2682, O27 gauge, 1938, red 12.00

    HO-841, HO gauge, 1961, NYC 10.00

Cattle Car, 213, Standard gauge, 1926-40, cream body, maroon roof 450.00

Hopper Car, 216, Standard gauge, 1926-40, silver, Sunoco decal 350.00

Gondola

    200, 2-7/8" gauge, motorized 1,000.00

    2452, O27 gauge, 1945, Pennsylvania 20.00

Locomotive

    38, Standard gauge, 1913-24, 0-4-0, electric, brown 200.00

    45, O gauge, 1960-62, US Marine Missile Launcher, olive shell, white missiles 225.00

    50, Standard gauge, 1924-0-4-0, electric gray 100.00

    209, 027 gauge, 1958, Alco AA, diesel, 2 units 450.00

    289E, O gauge, 1937, 2-4-2, steam, streamlined, black, 1689 tender 90.00

    HO-577, HO gauge, 1959, Alaska, diesel F-3, Dummy B 35.00

Observation Car

    322, Standard gauge, 1924 .... 95.00

    754, O gauge, 1934, streamliner 70.00

    2436, O27 gauge, 1954, Mooseheart 45.00

Pullman

    35, Standard gauge, c1915, orange 65.00

    420, Standard gauge, 1930, Blue Comet, light blue body, dark blue roof, mkd "Faye" 450.00

    607, O gauge, 1926 .... 45.00

    2533, O gauge, 1952, mkd "Silver Cloud" 85.00

Refrigerator Car, 214R, Standard gauge, 1929-40, ivory body, peacock roof 400.00

Set

    O gauge, No. 267W, electric Boston and Maine Flying Yankee streamliner, 616W locomotive with gunmetal nose, chrome rear, two 617 chrome coaches, 618 chrome observation with gunmetal tail, No. 65 whistle controller, instructions, papers, some accessories, each item in individual box 1,495.00

    O Gauge, No. 269E, electric freight trail, 261E 2-4-2 steam locomotive and 261T tender, 654 oil tank, 655 box car, 659 dump car, 657 caboose, all in individual boxes, instructions 980.00

    Standard Gauge, 402 electric 0-4-4-0 NY Central locomotive, 418 parlor car, 419 NY Central baggage/parlor car, incomplete station, 7 signals, gates, bumpers, transformer, track 550.00

Summer Trolley, 202, Standard gauge, 1910, motor car, mkd "202, Electric Rapid Transit" 1,200.00

Vista Dome, 2404, O27 gauge, 1964, Santa Fe, aluminum, blue lettering 50.00

TRAMP ART

History: Tramp art was an internationally practiced craft, brought to the United States by European immigrants. Its span of popularity was between the late 1860s to the 1940s.

Made with simple tools – usually a pocketknife, and from scrap woods—non-reusable cigar box wood and crate wood, this folk art form can be seen in small boxes to large pieces of furniture. Usually identifiable by the composition of thin layered pieces of wood with chip-carved edges assembled in built-up pyramids, circles, hearts, stars, etc. At times, pieces included velvet, porcelain buttons, brass tacks, glass knobs, shards of china, etc., that the craftsmen used to embellish his work. The pieces were predominantly stained or painted.

Collected as folk art, most of the work was attributed to anonymous makers. A premium is placed on the more whimsical artistic forms, pieces in original painted surfaces, or pieces verified to be from an identified maker.

Reference: Clifford A. Wallach and Michael Cornish, *Tramp Art, One Notch At A Time*, Wallach-Irons Publishing, (277 W. 10th St., NY NY 10014) 1998.

Advisor: Clifford Wallach

Bank, 6" h x 4" w x 4" d, secret access to coins 335.00
Bird Cage, 28" h x 22" w x 13-1/2" d, house with 2 compartments ..775.00
Box, ftd, 11-1/2" h x 15"w x 14"d, brass lions, date, and clasp for lock 265.00
Cabinet, 44" h x 22-1/2" w x 14" d, scratch built cabinet, embellished with pyramids, floral pattern on blue doors, crest and secret compartment 6,500.00
Chest of Drawers, 40" h x 29" w x 20" d, scratch built from crates with 4 drawers, 10 layers deep 2,400.00
Clock, mantel, 22" h x 14" w x 7" d, red stain with drawers at base .475.00

Box, pyramids made from alternating layers of yellow and orange, red paper lining, diecut of rabbit on lid, 7" x 8" x 5-1/4", $185.

Comb Case, 27" h x 17" w x 4"d, adorned with horseshoes, hearts, birds, 2 drawers and mirrors 700.00
Crucifix, 16" h x 7" w x 4-1/2" d, wooden pedestal base, wooden carved figure 185.00
Document Box, 14" h x 9-1/2" w x 9" d, diamond designs, sgd and date 375.00
Doll Furniture
    Chair, 10" h, 7" w, 12" d, dec with brass tacks 450.00
    Bureau, 14" h x 12" w x 9" d, drawers and mirror 650.00
Frame
    9" h, 6-3/4" w, photograph of maker, signed and dated "1906" ..275.00
    13" h x 12" w, horseshoe shape, light and dark wood 465.00
    14" x 12", hearts and diamonds, painted gold 255.00
    14" h x 24" w, double opening frame with oval opening for photos 325.00
    16" h x 18" w x 4-3/4" d. crown of thorns, multiple opening frame with minor losses, dark stain 495.00
    16" h, 22" w, block corner style, with painted hearts, pair of frames by same maker 225.00
    26" h x 24" w, velvet panels and sq corners 350.00
    48" h x 34" w, large, ornately carved, star decorated crown, 18 layers 2,200.00
Jewelry Box
    6" h x 11" w x 6" d, covered with hearts painted silver over gold, velvet lined 595.00
    6-3/4" h x 11-1/2" w x 7" d, hinged jewelry box with velvet top and sides 175.00
    8" h x 11" w x 7" d, hinged, pedestal, dark stain 175.00
    9" h x 11-1/2" w x 7" d, large, dated "1898," metal lion pulls . 300.00
    16" h x 14" w x 10"d , shallow drawers and carved finial on top. 395.00
Lamp
    24" h, 10" w, 10" d, table, double socket 550.00
    68" h, 17" w, 17" d, floor, heavy pedestal base, no shade.. 1,200.00
Match Safe, 9"h x 2" w x 2"d, strike surface, open holder for matches 75.00
Medicine Cabinet, 22" h x 18"w x 10" d, light and dark woods ... 675.00
Miniature
    Chair, 8" h x 6" w x 5-1/2" d, crown of thorns 245.00
    Chest of Drawers, 14" h x 5" w x 4" d, made of cigar boxes . 375.00
Music Box , 3" h x 7" w x 6" d, velvet sides 425.00
Night Stand, 37" h x 22" w x 14"d, dark stain, drawer on top and cabinet on bottom, no losses 1,600.00
Pedestal
    6 1-2" h x 10" w x 7" d, lift off lid, velvet lined 225.00
    14 1-2" h x 12" w x 8" d, multi-level, 6 drawers 675.00
    16" h x 7" w x 4-1/2" d, polychromed in green and black paint... 950.00
Pedestal Box
    8-1/4" h x 9" w x 6-1/2" d, double, bar connecting top pyramids, velvet lined, precise notching 325.00
    29-1/2" h x 16" w x 15" d, light and dark stained, made from fruit crates 1,850.00
Plant Stand, 22" h x 11" w x 11" d, painted gold, heavily layered 675.00
Pocket Watch Holder, 9" h x 6-1/2" w x 5-1/2" d, ftd 375.00
Radio Cabinet, 50" h x 33" w x 16" d, box type radio encased behind doors, ornate 3,600.00
Sewing Box
    8-1/2" h x 11-1/2" w x 8-1/2"d, velvet pin cushion on top....... 265.00
    9" h x 16-1/2" w x 8" d, painted red, white and blue sewing box, Uncle Sam cigar label under lid 1,600.00
Sewing Cabinet, 27" h x 16" w x 9"d, lift top and three drawers made from crate wood 1,400.00
Side by Side, bookcase/desk, 49" h x 29" w x 20" d, glass cabinet door with shelves on one side, other side is drop front desk......... 3,200.00
Vanity Mirror, 26" h, 14" d, 10" d, table top, heart on top and drawer 375.00
Wall Pocket
    7" h x 9" w x 4" d, open work and porcelain buttons............... 95.00
    8-1/2" h x 16" w x 4-3/4" d, shelf and diamonds for design ... 125.00

14" h x 11" w x 7"d, painted with hearts and stars, pr............ 700.00
20" h x 18" w x 5-1/2" d, carved leaves and acorns surrounding
mirror 1,400.00

TRANSPORTATION MEMORABILIA

History: Most of the income for the first airlines in the United States came from government mail-carrying subsidies. The first non-Post Office Department flight to carry mail was in 1926 between Detroit and Chicago. By 1930, there were 38 domestic and five international airlines operating in the United States. A typical passenger load was ten. After World War II, four-engine planes with a capacity of 100 or more passengers were introduced.

The jet age was launched in the 1950s. In 1955, Capitol Airlines used British-made turboprop airliners for domestic service. In 1958, National Airlines began domestic jet passenger service. The giant Boeing 747 went into operation in 1970 as part of the Pan American fleet. The Civil Aeronautics Board, which regulates the airline industry, ended control of routes in 1982 and fares in 1983.

Transoceanic travel falls into two distinct periods—the era of the great clipper ships and the era of the diesel-powered ocean liners. The golden age of the later craft took place between 1900 and 1940.

An ocean liner is a city unto itself. Many have their own printing rooms to produce a wealth of daily memorabilia. Companies such as Cunard, Holland-America, and others encouraged passengers to acquire souvenirs with the company logo and ship name.

Certain ships acquired a unique mystic. *The Queen Elizabeth*, *Queen Mary*, and *United States* became symbols of elegance and style. Today the cruise ship dominates the world of the ocean liner.

References: Carriages and Sleighs, Dover Publications, 1998; Barbara J. Conroy, *Restaurant China: Identification & Value Guide For Restaurant, Airline, Ship & Railroad Dinnerware*, Collector Books, Volume 1 (1998), Volume 2 (1999); Leila Dunbar, *Automobilia*, Schiffer Publishing, 1998; *Carriages and Sleighs: 228 Illustrations from the 1862 Lawrence, Bradley & Pardee Catalog*, Dover Publications, 1998; Lynn Johnson and Michael O'Leary, *En Route*, Chronicle Books, 1993; Karl D. Spence, *How to Identify and Price Ocean Liner Collectibles*, published by author, 1991; ———, *Oceanliner Collectibles*, published by author, 1992; Joshua Stoff, *Transatlantic Flight: A Picture History, 1873-1939*, Dover Publications, 2000; Rudolf H. Wackernagel, *Wittelsbach State and Ceremonial Carriages*, Volumes 1 and 2, Arnoldsche, distributed by Antique Collectors' Club, 1999; Richard R. Wallin, *Commercial Aviation Collectibles: An Illustrated Price Guide*, Wallace-Homestead, 1990; C. H. Wendel, E*ncyclopedia of American Farm Implements & Antiques*, Krause Publications, 1997.

Periodical: Airliners, P.O. Box 52-1238, Miami, FL 33152.

Collectors' Clubs: Aeronautic & Air Label Collectors Club, P.O. Box 1239, Elgin, IL 60121; Gay Airline Club, P.O. Box 69A04, West Hollywood, CA 90069; Bus History Association, 965 McEwan, Windsor Ontario N9B 2G1 Canada; Central Electric Railfans' Association, P.O. Box 503, Chicago, IL 60690; International Bus Collectors Club, 1518 "C" Trailee Drive, Charleston, SC 29407; National Association of Timetable Collectors, 125 American Inn Rd, Villa Ridge, MO 63089; Oceanic Navigation Research Society, P.O. Box 8005, Studio City, CA 91608-0005; Steamship Historical Society of America, Inc., Ste #4, 300 Ray Drive, Providence, RI 02906; Titanic Historical Society, P.O. Box 51053, Indian Orchard, MA 01151; Titanic International, P.O. Box 7007, Freehold, NJ 07728; Transport Ticket Society, 4 Gladridge Close, Earley, Reading Berks RG6 2DL England; World Airline Historical Society, 13739 Picarsa Dr., Jacksonville, FL 32225.

Museums: Howard Steamboat Museum, Jeffersonville, IN; Owls Head Transportation Museum, Owls Head, ME; South Street Seaport Museum, New York, NY, University of Baltimore, Steamship Historical Society Collection, Baltimore, MD.

Additional Listings: See Automobilia; Railroad Items. See also Aviation Collectibles, Ocean Liner Collectibles, and Railroad Items in *Warman's Americana & Collectibles*.

By Air

Advertising, fan, Air India 4.00
Baggage Label, 4-1/4" x 6", full color paper, *Graf Zeppelin*, German lettering for South Atlantic flight , c1929, unused 60.00
Counter Display Figure, 6-1/4" x 9" x 16" h, Air-India, painted composition, c1970 .... 185.00
Game, 13" x 14-1/2", United Air Lines Skyways, cardboard folder opens to 14-1/2" x 26" playing board, 1937 copyright, "Approved by United Air Lines," distributed by Levi & Gade, Chicago, Mainliner, 2 engine plane on cov 70.00
Paperweight, 2-1/2" d, dark luster lead, "Aero Club of America," raised image of eagle soaring beneath sun rays above world globe nestled in cloud banks, also inscribed "13th Annual Banquet Feb 19, 1919, Waldorf-Astoria" 20.00
Photo Card, 3-1/2" x 5-1/2", browntone, real photo, hovering over York Fairgrounds, airship suspends web and rudder, reverse with post card imprint and "AZO" marking at stamp, unused, 1900s 60.00
Ticket
2-1/2" x 3-1/2", black, white, and red, German zeppelin, c1930 .... 70.00
3-1/4" x 5-1/2", passenger, *Hindenburg*, US to Germany flight in connection with Transatlantic Airship Demonstration, 1936, inked name, unused 125.00

By Land

Blotter, 3" x 5-1/4", Firestone Bicycle tiers, black, white, orange and blue, unused, 1920s 20.00

Ink Blotter, "I got mine here," Firestone Bicycle Tires, Harvey R. Williams, Lancaster, PA, 3 boys, 1920s, 6" l, 3" w, $15.

Box Bed Wagon 575.00
Cap Badge, Pacific Greyhound Bus Line, chrome, blue and green cloisonné enameling, 2-1/2" x 2" 325.00
Conestoga Wagon Jack, 20" h plus adjustable arm, wrought iron and wood, initials and date "C. G." and "1758," very weathered wood...80.00
Milk and Ice Delivery Wagon, 1926, horse drawn, Cambridge City, IN 2,500.00
Horse and Pony Buggy, St Paris, OH, orig parasol and wicker seat 1,900.00
Luggage Tag, Canadian Pacific, stringed cardstock, red, white, and blue ship signs, c1930, 5" x 3" 15.00
Pin, 1" d, Schwinn Bicycles, dark maroon, world glove with "Ride the World Cycles" inscription on one side, other with "Arnold Schwinn & Co/Chicago," 1930s 35.00
Pinback Button, Tilton's Trolley Trip, multicolored, trolley excursion from CA, early 1900s 25.00
Poster, Cleveland Cycles, Indian riding bicycle looking back, 58" x 43" 525.00
Schedule and Timetable, New England Bus Transportation Co., 1955, 3" x 4-1/2" folded 12.00
Sign, National Trailways Bus Depot, porcelain, two-sided, multicolored, 18" x 22" 300.00
Stickpin, brass, bug pedaling bicycle, mkd "Compliments of United States Tire Co," 1920s 25.00
Stock Certificate, Brooklyn Rapid Transit Co., engraved, rear of street car vignette, c1910 .... 35.00
Wagon Wheel, wood 70.00

By Sea

Advertising Trade Card
  Lund's Pioneer Lion, 1860s Florida steam, red and black lettering 75.00
  National Line Steamships, S.S. The Queen, entire ship line and rates on reverse 150.00
Booklet, *St Lawrence Route to Europe*, Canadian Pacific, 1930, 16 pgs, 8" x 11" 25.00
Canoe, 201" l, painted wood, slatted timber construction, 2 caned suspended seats, ext. painted red and green, prow with American Indian profile, orig oar, maker's label "Old Town Canoe Co., Old Town, Maine, U.S.A." 2,700.00
Deck Plan, *S. S. Hamburg*, fold out, 1930 .... 35.00
Lighter, *R..M.S. Queen Elizabeth*, 1/2" x 1-3/4" x 2" h, chrome, metal disk official insignia on one side with red, blue, and copper enamel accents, 1950s 35.00
Manifest/Broadside, *Ship Dido*, hand colored, sgd by 28 crew members, 1822, 18" x 23" 450.00
Poster
  Allez En Corse, Ed. Collin, steamship, harbor village as seen through Corsican cave, c1950, 16" x 25" 200.00
  American Line - Red Star Line St. Louis and St. Paul, Orcutt Co. Litho, Chicago, SS St. Louis shown in black and green gravure, c1900, 37" x 20" 400.00
  Canada- Anchor Donaldson Line, *Odin Rosenvinge*, multicolor lithograph of steamer with Anchor Line logo at top, c1912, 25" x 40" 1,650.00
Sign
  Cunard Line, tin, *Aquitana* steam ship, old time paddle boat and sail boat sailing along side, artist sgd "A. F. Bishop," new frame with Cunard Line plaque, 33" x 43" 100.00
  Cunard Line, tin, ocean liner in New York Bay, Statue of Liberty in background, Berengaria, sgd on lower right corner "Bishop 1924," 43-1/2" x 34" 300.00
  Scandinavian-American, self framed tin, ocean liner in bay, *Frederick VIII*, 41" x 31" 1,200.00
Vase, 10-1/2" h, *Normandie*, silvered metal, trumpet form, sq base with beaded foot, Compagnie generale Translantique monogram, imp "E. Brandt" and "G. Bastard" 1,200.00

TRUNKS

History: Trunks are portable containers that clasp shut and are used for the storage or transportation of personal possessions. Normally "trunk" means the ribbed flat- or domed-top models of the second half of the 19th century.

References: Roseann Ettinger, Trunks, Traveling Bags and Satchels, Schiffer, 1998; Martin and Maryann Labuda, Price & Identification Guide to Antique Trunks, published by authors, 1980; Jacquelyn Peake, How to Recognize and Refinish Antiques for Pleasure and Profit, 3rd ed., Globe Pequot Press (P.O. Box 833, Old Saybrook, CT 06475), 1995.

Notes: Unrestored trunks sell for between $50 and $150. Refinished and relined, the price rises to $200 to $400, with decorators being a principal market.

Early trunks frequently were painted, stenciled, grained, or covered with wallpaper. These are collected for their folk-art qualities and, as such, demand high prices.

Chinese, brass bound camphor wood, 19th C, minor imperfections
  16" h, 36" w, 18" d, polychrome foliate dec on top, nailhead trim 1,035.00
  16-1/2" h, 36-1/4" w, 18-1/4" d, nailhead dec, monogrammed brass plaque 865.00
Dome Top
  11" h, 24" w, 13" d, paint dec, poplar, top with central floral device within yellow and green painted oval bordered by green, tan, and black, front initialed "PG" within foliate painted escutcheon rimmed by painted oval, light tan background, New England, early 19th C 1,035.00
  11-1/2" h, 28" w, 14" d, paint dec, black painted ground, central vined pinwheel bordered by meandering floral and arched vines, front with tassel and drape border, central MA, early 19th C 1,035.00
  19" l, fabric on wood, worn painted dec in ivory and green, red border designs and flowers, interior lined with green marbleized paper, worn 425.00
  28" w, 14" d, 12" h, grain painted, ext. covered with yellow and burnt sienna fanciful graining with green and yellow bordering

Hump back, metal, curved slats, c1890, $190.

simulating inlay, orig surface, some hardware missing, New
   England, early 19th C 260.00
33-1/4" w, 16-1/4" d, 18-3/4" h, black japanned brass mounts, gilt Chinoisiere dec of figures in garden landscape, side handles, late 18th/
   early 19th C, restoration 750.00
Flat Top
   14" x 8", Chinese, pigskin, red, painted Oriental maidens and land-
      scapes within quatrefoils, brass loop handles and lock, 19th C 125.00
   15-1/4" l, tooled leather on pine, iron straps, brass buttons and lock,
      lined with worn newspaper dated 1871, hinged replaced, some
      edge damage.. 385.00
   29-1/4" x 15-1/2" x 16-1/4", tin over wood, brass banded ends,
      wood rim, int. shelf missing................................. 100.00
Military, 21-3/4" w, 17" d, 12-1/2" h, brass bound camphor wood,
   hinged rect top, storage well, brass bail handles, English, second half
   19th C.. 200.00
Steamer
   21-3/4" h, 45" w, 21-1/2" d, Louis Vuitton, early 20th C, pigskin
      lining 2,100.00
   40-3/4" w, 22" d, 13" h, brass bound, Louis Vuitton, "LV" device, late
      19th/early 20th C 1,380.00

Tucker China

History: William Ellis Tucker (1800-1832) was the son of a
Philadelphia schoolmaster who had a small shop on Market Street, where he sold imported French china. William
helped in the shop and became interested in the manufacture of china.

In 1820, kaolin, a white clay which is the prime ingredi-
ent for translucence in porcelain, was discovered on a
farm in Chester County, Pennsylvania, and William ear-
nestly began producing his own products with the plentiful
supply of kaolin close at hand. The business prospered
but not without many trials and financial difficulties. He had
many partners, a fact reflected in the various marks found
on Tucker china including "William Ellis Tucker," "Tucker
and Hulme," and "Joseph Hemphill," as well as workmen's
incised initials which are sometimes found.

The business operated between 1825 and 1838, when
Thomas Tucker, William's brother, was forced by business
conditions to close the firm. There are very few pieces
available for collectors today, and almost all known pieces
are in collections or museums. But you can never tell!

Museum: Pennsylvania Historical Museum, Harrisburg, PA.

Coffee Cup and Saucer, large size, floral spray, green band dec, gilt
   edges and handle, from set made for Atherton family of Chester
   County, PA, monogram "A"..................................... 1,500.00
Creamer and Sugar, black transfer dec, landscape with house, c1830,

Water Pitcher, Walker type, gilt rim, mid band and base, 3 gilt fan reserves on molded neck and spout, loop handle with gilding, 2 painted spring flower reserves, c1830, 7-1/4" h, $2,240. Photo courtesy of Freeman\Fine Arts.

   sugar repaired 500.00
Fruit Dish, 11" l, oval, serpentine, gilt border, c1830............... 1,150.00
Miniature, tea service
   Hot water pot with lid, head spout (handle and rim repaired), teapot with
      bird's head spout, creamer, 4 straight sided cups with loop handles, 3
      saucers, classical form, Libeat pattern, white, gold trim 1,900.00
   Teapot with bird's head spout, creamer (handle repaired), open
      sugar bowl, 4 flaring rim tea cups with scroll handles (one cup
      with rim repair), 4 saucers, white, gold trim 1,800.00
Plate, 10" d, gold band and peach border, 3 gilt leaf dec, centered
   monogram "EMW," incised letter view on bottom..................... 625.00
Pitcher
   7-1/4" h, Walker type, gilt rim, mid band, and base, 3 gilt fan
      reserves to molded neck and spout, loop handle with gilding, 2
      spring flower reserves, c1830... 2,240.00
   8-1/4" h, modified Grecian form, gilt rim, mid band, and handle,
      wide summer flower mid band, conforming reserve at lip, c1830,
      star crack to bottom 400.00
   8-1/4" h, Walker type, gilded band on rim, mid band, and base,
      branch form handle, 2 summer flower reserves, c1830... 1,920.00
   9" h, white ground, grisaille scene dec, gilt highlights, minor gilt
      wear 980.00
   9-1/4" h, Grecian form, gilt edges, mid band and monogram "NMT"
      on both sides, c1830, minor wear to gilding 1,120.00
   9-3/8" h, Neoclassical form, strap handle, mid base, gilt detail,
      enameled bird on branch dec, minor gilt wear................ 6,720.00
Teapot, 9" h, pink and green floral dec, white ground, gold bands,
   restored 100.00
Tea Service, teapot, creamer, sugar, waste bowl, 10 7" plates, 7 cups,
   9 saucers, Forget-Me-Not pattern, white ground, gold band, wear,
   slight damage, 30 pc set 365.00

VAL ST.-LAMBERT

History: Val St.-Lambert, a 12th-century Cistercian abbey, was located during different historical periods in France, Netherlands, and Belgium (1930 to present). In 1822, Francois Kemlin and Auguste Lelievre, along with a group of financiers, bought the abbey and opened a glassworks. In 1846, Val St.-Lambert merged with the Socété Anonyme des Manufactures de Glaces, Verres à Vitre, Cristaux et Gobeletaries. The company bought many other glassworks.

Val St.-Lambert developed a reputation for technological progress in the glass industry. In 1879, Val St.-Lambert became an independent company employing 4,000 workers. The firm concentrated on the export market, making table glass, cut, engraved, etched, and molded pieces, and chandeliers. Some pieces were finished in other countries, e.g., silver mounts were added in the United States.

Val St.-Lambert executed many special commissions for the artists of the Art Nouveau and Art Deco periods. The tradition continues. The company also made cameo-etched vases, covered boxes, and bowls. The firm celebrated its 150th anniversary in 1975.

Bowl
   6-1/2" d, cov, cameo, deep cut purple florals, frosted ground, sgd "Val St Lambert" 750.00
   10" d, 4" h, red flashed overlay, sgd 350.00
Compote, 3-1/2" d, amberina, ruby rim, mottled glass bow, applied amber foot and handles 175.00
Decanter Set, cranberry cut to clear, ornate pattern, 5 wines with matching cutting, cobalt blue, cranberry, dark green, light green, and yellow 350.00
Dresser Box, colored 100.00
Finger Bowl, 4-1/2" d, crystal, half pentagon, cut edge, sgd 45.00
Pitcher, crystal, paneled, cut diamond design, sgd 95.00
Tumble-Up, decanter and matching tumbler, amber-crystal, mkd 95.00
Vase, 10" h, cranberry cut to clear, 3" acid cut band of Renaissance style chariots and people, Gothic arch panels, notched rim 300.00

VALENTINES

History: Early cards were handmade, often containing both handwritten verses and hand-drawn pictures. Many cards also were hand colored and contained cutwork.

Mass production of machine-made cards featuring chromolithography began after 1840. In 1847, Esther Howland of Worcester, Massachusetts, established a company to make valentines which were hand decorated with paper lace and other materials imported from England. They had a small "H" stamped in red in the top left corner. Howland's company eventually became the New England Valentine Company (N.E.V. Co.).

The company George C. Whitney and his brother founded after the Civil War dominated the market from the 1870s through the first decades of the 20th century. They bought out several competitors, one of which was the New England Valentine Company.

Lace paper was invented in 1834. The golden age of lacy cards took place between 1835 and 1860.

Embossed paper was used in England after 1800. Embossed lithographs and woodcuts developed between 1825 and 1840, and early examples were hand colored.

There was a big revival in the 1920s by large companies, like R. Tuck in England, who did lots of beautiful cards for its 75th Diamond Jubilee; 1925 saw changes in card production, especially for children with paper toys of all sorts, all very collectible now. Little girls were in short dresses, boys in short pants, which helps date that era of valentines. There was an endless variety of toy types of paper items, many companies created similar items and many stayed in production until World War II paper shortages stopped production both here and abroad.

References: Robert Brenner, *Valentine Treasury*, Schiffer Publishing, 1997; Dan & Pauline Campanelli, *Romantic Valentines*, L-W Book Sales, 1996; Roberta B. Etter, *Tokens of Love*, Abbeville Press, 1990; Katherine Kreider, *One Hundred Years of Valentines*, Schiffer, 1999; ——, *Valentines with Values*, Schiffer Publishing, 1996.

Collectors' Club: National Valentine Collectors Association, P.O. Box 1404, Santa Ana, CA 92702.

Advisor: Evalene Pulati.

Animated, large
   Felix, half tone, German 25.00
   Jumping Jack, Tuck, 1900 .... 65.00
Bank True Love note, England, 1865 .... 75.00
Bank of Love note, Nister, 1914 .... 38.00
Charm String
   Brundage, 3 pcs 45.00
   Four hearts, ribbon 45.00
Comic
   Sheet, 8" x 10", Park, London 25.00
   Sheet, 9" x 14", McLoughlin Co., USA, 1915 .... 20.00
   Woodcut, Strong, USA, 1845 .... 25.00
Diecut foldout
   Brundage, flat, cardboard 25.00
   Cherubs, 2 pcs 40.00
   Clapsaddle, 1911 .... 60.00
Documentary
   Passport, love, 1910 .... 45.00
   Wedding certificate, 1914 .... 45.00
Engraved
   5" x 7", American, verse 35.00
   8" x 10" sheet, English, emb, pg 65.00
   8" x 10" sheet, English, hand colored 45.00
Handmade
   Calligraphy, envelope, 1885 .... 135.00
   Cutwork, hearts, 6" x 6", 1855 .... 250.00
   Fraktur, cutwork, 1800 .... 950.00
   Pen and ink loveknot, 1820 .... 275.00
   Puzzle, purse, 14" x 14", 1855 .... 450.00
   Theorem, 9" x 14", c1885 .... 325.00
   Woven heart, hand, 1840 .... 55.00
Honeycomb
   American, kids, tunnel of love 48.00
   American, wide-eyed kids, 9" 40.00
   German, 1914, white and pink, 11" 75.00
   Simple, 1920, Beistle, 8" 18.00
Lace Paper
   American, B & J Cameo Style
      Large 75.00
      Small, 1865 .... 45.00
   American, layered, McLoughlin Co., c1880 .... 35.00
   Cobweb center, c1855 .... 250.00
   English, fancy
      3" x 5", 1865 .... 35.00
      5" x 7", 1855 .... 75.00
      8" x 10", 1840 .... 135.00

Hand Layered, scraps, 1855..65.00
Layered, in orig box
    1875, Howland 75.00
    1910, McLoughlin Co. 45.00
Orig box, c1890..55.00
Simple, small pc, 1875...22.50
Tiny mirror center, 4" x 6"..75.00
Whitney, 1875, 5" x 7"..35.00
Pulldown, German
    Airplane, 1914, 8" x 14"..175.00
    Auto, 1910, 8" x 11" x 4".......................................150.00
    Car and kids, 1920s...35.00
    Dollhouse, large, 1935..45.00
    Rowboat, small, honeycomb paper puff 65.00
    Seaplane, 1934, 8" x 9"..75.00
    Tall Ship, 8" x 16"...175.00
Silk Fringed
    Prang, double sided, 3" x 5" 24.00
    Triple layers, orig box 38.00
Standup Novelty
    Cupid, orig box 45.00
    Hands, heart, without orig box................................35.00
    Parchment
        Banjo, small, with ribbon 65.00
        Violin, large, boxed...125.00

VALLERYSTHAL GLASS

History: Vallerysthal (Lorraine), France, has been a glass-producing center for centuries. In 1872 two major factories, Vallerysthal glassworks and Portieux glassworks, merged and produced art glass until 1898. Later, pressed glass animal-covered dishes were introduced. The factory continues to operate today.

Animal Dish, cov
    Hen on nest, opaque aqua, sgd 75.00
    Rabbit, white, frosted..65.00
    Swan, blue opaque glass 100.00
Box, cov, 5" x 3", cameo, dark green, applied and cut dec,sgd 950.00
Butter Dish, cov, turtle, opaque white, snail finial.......................100.00
Candlesticks, pr, Baroque pattern, amber....................................75.00
Compote, 6-1/4" sq, blue opaque glass..75.00
Dish, cov, figural, lemon, opaque white, sgd...............................70.00
Mustard, cov, swirled ribs, scalloped blue opaque, matching cover with
    slot for spoon..35.00
Plate, 6" d, Thistle pattern, green...65.00
Salt, cov, hen on nest, white opal 65.00
Sugar, cov, 5" h, Strawberry pattern, opaque white, gold trim, sala-
    mander finial..85.00
Tumbler, 4" h, blue 40.00
Vase, 8" h, flared folded burgundy red rim, oval pale green body,
    matching red enamel berry bush on front, inscribed "Vallerysthal" on
    base 490.00

VAN BRIGGLE POTTERY

History: Artus Van Briggle, born in 1869, was a talented Ohio artist. He joined Rookwood in 1887 and studied in Paris under Rookwood's sponsorship from 1893 until 1896. In 1899, he moved to Colorado for his health and established his own pottery in Colorado Springs in 1901.

Van Briggle's work was heavily influenced by the Art Nouveau schools he had seen in France. He produced a great variety of matte-glazed wares in this style. Colors varied.

Artus died in 1904. Anne Van Briggle continued the pottery until 1912.

Marks: The "AA" mark, a date, and "Van Briggle" were incised on all pieces prior to 1907 and on some pieces into the 1920s. After 1920, "Colorado Springs, Colorado" or an abbreviation was added. Dated pieces are the most desirable.

References: Richard Sasicki and Josie Fania, *Collector's Encyclopedia of Van Briggle Art Pottery*, Collector Books, 1993, 1998 value update; David Rago, *American Art Pottery*, Knickerbocker Press, 1997.

Collectors' Club: American Art Pottery Association, 125 E. Rose Ave., St. Louis, MO 63119.

Museum: Pioneer Museum, Colorado Springs, CO.

Reproduction Alert: Van Briggle pottery still is made today. These modern pieces often are mistaken for older examples. Among the glazes used are Moonglo (off white), Turquoise Ming, Russet, and Midnight (black).

Cabinet Vase, 3" h, 3-1/4" d, No. 424, emb wreath of spade-shaped
    leaves, green and mauve matte glaze, incised "AA/Van Briggle/8/
    1906/424" 700.00

Left to right: Vase, tall, bulbous, emb stylized iris under semi-matte turquoise glaze, clay body showing through, mkd "AA/VanBriggle/Colo. Spgs/40," 1907-11, 10" h, 3-3/4" h, $1,000; vessel, spherical, emb mistletoe under sheer frothy dark green glaze, brown clay showing through, incised "AA/VAN BRIGGLE/Colo. Sp()," 4" h, 4-1/2" d, $700; vase, emb irises under sheer and frothy blue-gray glaze, red clay showing through, incised "AA/VAN BRIGGLE/19(?)/280," c1905, 13" h, 4" d, $3,500; vessel, squatty, emb pods under sheer frothy light blue glaze, brown clay showing through, incised "AA/VAN BRIGGLE/1905/288," 1905, 3" h, 6-1/2" d, $100.00; vase, bulbous, emb spade-shaped leaves under frothy green glaze, beige clay showing through, incised "AA/VAN BRIGGLE/19(?)/(?)85," c1905, 10" h, 5" d, $3,250; vase, emb flowers under matte light green glaze, incised "AA/VAN BRIGGLE/1903/219," 1903, 6-1/2" h, 4" d, hairline from rim, $850. Photo courtesy of David Rago Auctions, Inc.

Jug, 7" h, 5-3/4" d, Fire Water, scarabs and other Native American motifs, shaded blue to lavender matte glaze, orig matching stopper, incised "AA/Van Briggle/1902/III/12/A," 2 chips to stopper stem 2,600.00

Mug

4-1/4" h, 5-1/4" d, leathery apple green matte glaze, incised "AA Van Briggle/1906" 250.00

5" h, 5" d, emb eagle in flight, leathery matte green glaze, incised "AA/Van Briggle/1906/355" 400.00

Vase

4-1/4" h, 4-1/2" d, bulbous, emb sinewy poppy pods on stems, matte turquoise glaze, red clay showing through, incised "?O/AA/VAN BRIGGLE/COLO. SPRINGS/?52/190?," c1906 ......1,400.00

6" h, 3" d, bulbous, emb stylized tulips, semi-matte turquoise glaze, clay body showing through, mkd "AA/844/1915" 800.00

6-1/2" h, 4" d, emb flowers, matte light green glaze, incised "AA/VAN BRIGGLE?/1903/219," hairline from rim..................1,000.00

6-3/4" h, 3" d, cylindrical, emb daisies, frothy mustard glaze, incised "AA/VAN BRIGGLE/Colo. Spgs," 1907-11 ....1,600.00

7" h, 3-1/4" d, ovoid, curdled matte green glaze, incised "AA/Van Briggle," c1905 ....2,400.00

7" h, 4-1/2" d, bottle shape, emb stylized papyrus, semi-matte turquoise glaze, clay body showing through, mkd "AA/Van Briggle/Colo Spgs/734" 950.00

7-3/4" h, 4-1/2"d, emb stylized leaves, flowing matte green glaze, red clay showing through, incised "AA/VAN BRIGGLE/1905".....3,000.00

8" h, oviform body tapering to base, 4 large molded leaves of matte yellow-green glaze, incised mark "AA" in rect, "Van Briggle, 1902, III" 2,415.00

9-1/2" h, 3-3/4" d, corseted, emb stylized blossoms, frothy matte green glaze, incised "AA/Van Briggle/Colo Spgs/676," scaling to few high points, minor touchups to same 1,200.00

10" h, 3-3/4" d, bulbous, emb stylized irises, semi-matte turquoise glaze, clay body showing through, "AA/Van Briggle/Colo.Spgs/40," 1907-11 ....1,000.00

10" h, 5" d, bulbous, emb spade-shaped leaves, frothy green glaze, beige clay showing through, incised "AA/VAN BRIGGLE/19?/?85," c1905 ....3,250.00

11" h, 9-1/2" d, Lady of the Lily, nude leaning on large calla lily, fine matte light green glaze, incised "AA/VAN BRIGGLE/1902/III," firing line 37,500.00

11-1/4" h, 4-3/4" d, emb cornflowers, curdled raspberry red glaze, beige clay showing through, incised "AA/VAN BRIGGLE/COLO. SPGS/146," 1907-11, small flat kiln kiss to side 2,400.00

11-3/4" h, 4" d, cylindrical, No. 62, emb stylized peacock feather pattern, yellow and turquoise butterfat glaze, burgundy ground, incised "AA/VAN BRIGGLE/VX/1905," few minor burst glaze bubbles 1,800.00

13" h, 4" d, emb irises, sheer and frothy blue-gray glaze, red clay showing through, incised "AA/VAN BRIGGLE/19?/280," c1905 ....3,500.00

Vessel

3" h, 6-1/2" d, squat, emb pods, sheer frothy light bleu glaze, brown clay showing through, incised "AA/VAN BRIGGLE/1905/288"" 850.00

3-1/2" h, 4-1/4" d, squat, emb leaves, matte frothy brown glaze, incised "AA/VAN BRIGGLE/COLO. SPGS" 1,100.00

4" h, 4-1/2" d, spherical, emb mistletoe under sheer frothy dark green glaze, brown clay showing through, incised "AA/VAN BRIGGLE/Colo. Spg" 700.00

6" h, 4-1/2' d, bulbous, curdled blue matte glaze, incised "AA Van Briggle/1905/XV/349" 425.00

VENETIAN GLASS

History: Venetian glass has been made on the island of Murano, near Venice, since the 13th century. Most of the wares are thin walled. Many types of decoration have been used: embedded gold dust, lace work, and applied fruits or flowers.

Reference: Sheldon Barr, *Venetian Glass, Confections in Glass, 1855-1914*, Harry N. Abrams, Inc., 1998.

Plate, colorless, pastel enamel dec on rim, gold trim, 8" d, $40.

Periodical: *Verti: Italian Glass News*, P.O. Box 191, Fort Lee, NJ 07024.

Reproduction Alert: Venetian glass continues to be made today.

Bowl, 11" l, free form, cased, ice blue swirl with aventurine over white opaque and pulled clear handles 25.00

Center Bowl, 13" d, free form, amberina, elongated pulled edges, green partial Murano label 30.00

Chandelier, 48" d, 58" h, threaded and blown cranberry glass shaft, clear glass scrolled rods suspend faceted swags, 14 scrolled candle arms with molded drip pans 825.00

Cornucopia, 15-1/2" h, free form, emerald green shading............75.00

Epergne, 19-1/2" h, pale yellow, large central trumpet shaped vase surrounded by ten smaller vases, ruffled base, 20th C........1,150.00

Figure

11" h, swan, amber and green, elongated neck, ground and polished base, pr 50.00

12" h, bird, black sommerso, aventurine encased in clear and shaded amber, applied cobalt blue tail 35.00

13" h, dolphin, clear, shaded electric blue back, bullicante dec, free form base 90.00

Perfume Bottle, 5-5/8" h, pear form, twist-turned body, green, gold flecks 115.00

Pitcher, 3-1/2" h, green, gold trim 95.00

Vase

8" h, handkerchief shape, pale green and white pulled stripe, applied clear rope base, attributed to Barovier, 1930s 65.00

10" h, green ground, controlled bubbles, sgd "Barovier & Tosa" 500.00

10-1/2" h, floriform, pulled cobalt blue tips shading to ice blue 50.00

VERLYS GLASS

History: Originally made by Verlys France (1931-1960), this Lalique-influenced art glass was produced in America by The Holophane Co. from 1935 to 1951, and select pieces by the A. H. Heisey Co. from 1955 to 1957. Holophane acquired molds and glass formulas from Verlys France and began making the art glass in 1935 at its Newark, Ohio, facility. It later leased molds to the Heisey Co., and in 1966 finally sold all molds and rights to the Fenton Art Glass Co.

The art glass was made in crystal, topaz, amber, rose, opalescent, and Directorie Blue. Heisey added turquoise. Most pieces have etched (frosted) relief designs.

Marks: Verlys France marked the glass with mold impressed "Verlys France" and "A Verlys France." Holophane (also known as Verlys of America) marked pieces with the mold-impressed "Verlys" and a scratched-script "Verlys" signature. The A. H. Heisey Co. used only a paper label which reads "Verlys by Heisey."

Reference: Carole and Wayne McPeek, *Verlys of America Decorative Glass*, revised ed., published by authors, 1992.

Ashtray, 4-1/8" d, Rose, frosted amber, script sgd 175.00
Bookends, pr, 6-1/2" x 3-1/8" x 5-1/4", Girl and Deer, frosted, script
   sgd 675.00
Bowl
   8-1/4" w, 4-1/4" h, flowers, opalescent frosted, six sided, flowers
     and border panels, script sgd 465.00
   8-3/8" d, 2-7/8" h, thistle, frosted turquoise, by
     Heisey 400.00
   11-3/8" d, 2-1/4" h, birds, frosted dusty rose, mold
     sgd 450.00
Candlesticks, pr, 3-1/2" h, 2-3/8" h, Americana, three eagles, script
   sgd 575.00
Charger, 14" d, Orchid 120.00
Vase
   6-1/2" h, Gems, Directorie blue frosted, allover berry pattern,
     matching flower holder, mold sgd 600.00
   9" h, Alpine Thistle, fiery opalescent, script sgd 725.00
   9" h, Lovebirds, crystal, frosted birds, script sgd 145.00
   9-1/2" h, 5" d, Mandarine, frosted, Chinaman with umbrella, script
     sgd 550.00
   9-7/8" h, 6-1/4" d, Thistle, amber, high relief thistle, six clear arched
     panels, mold sgd 650.00
   11-1/2" h, Fleur de Chine, frosted, intaglio Chinese man, woman, tree,
     and bush, script sgd "Verlys," artist sgd "Carl Schmitz" 675.00

VILLEROY & BOCH

History: Pierre Joseph Boch established a pottery near Luxembourg, Germany, in 1767. Jean Francis, his son, introduced the first coal-fired kiln in Europe and perfected a water-power-driven potter's wheel. Pierre's grandson, Eugene Boch, managed a pottery at Mettlach; Nicholas Villeroy also had a pottery nearby.

In 1841, the three potteries merged into the firm of Villeroy & Boch. Early production included a hard-paste earthenware comparable to English ironstone. The factory continues to use this hard-paste formula for its modern tablewares.

References: Susan and Al Bagdade, *Warman's English &*

Punch Bowl, etched, multicolored, #2208, 15" h, $350.

Continental Pottery & Porcelain, 3rd Edition, Krause Publications, 1998; Gary Kirsner, Mettlach Book, 3rd ed., Glentiques (P.O. Box 8807, Coral Springs, FL 33075), 1994.

Additional Listings: Mettlach.

Beaker, quarter liter, couple at feast, multicolored, printed under
   glaze 115.00
Bowl, 8" d, 3-3/4" h, gaudy floral dec, blue, red, green, purple, and yel-
   low, mkd "Villeroy & Boch," minor wear and stains 50.00
Charger, 15-1/2" d, gentleman on horseback, sgd "Stocke" 600.00
Ewer, 17-3/4" h, central frieze of festive beer hall, band playing white
   couples dance and drink, neck and foot with formal panels between
   leaf molded borders, subdued tones, c1884, imp shape number, pro-
   duction number and date codes 900.00
Figure, 53" h, Venus, scantily clad seated figure, ribbon tied headdress, left arm raised across chest, resting on rock, inscribed "Villeroy & Boch," damage to foot and base 1,900.00
Mug, 4-1/2" h, Hires Root Beer, pottery 90.00
Plaque, 10-1/4" d, blue and white harbor scene, Mercury mark ... 90.00
Plate, 8" d, semi-porcelain, Napoleonic, black and white transfer battle
   scenes, alternating band of crowned "N's" within laurel wreath and
   cartouches, set of 6 .... 300.00
Platter, 17" l, elongated oval, black transfer, red, blue, green, and yel-
   low Gaudy Ironstone dec 55.00
Tray, 11-1/4" d, metal gallery with geometric cut-outs, ceramic base
   with border and stylized geometric pattern, white ground, soft gray
   high gloss glaze, blue accents, base mkd 200.00
Vase, 15" h, bulbous, cylindrical, deep cobalt blue glaze, splashes of
   drizzled white, 3 handled SP mount cast with leaves, berries, and
   blossoms, molded, pierced foot, vase imp "V" & "B," "S" monogram,
   numbered, c1900, pr 2,750.00

WARWICK

History: Warwick China Manufacturing Co., Wheeling, West Virginia, was incorporated in 1887 and remained in business until 1951. The company was one of the first manufacturers of vitreous glazed wares in the United States. Production was extensive and included tableware, garden ornaments, and decorative and utilitarian items.

Pieces were hand painted or decorated with decals. Collectors seek portrait items and fraternal pieces from groups such as the Elks, Eagles, and Knights of Pythias.

Some experimental, eggshell-type porcelain was made before 1887. A few examples are found in the antiques market.

Beer Pitcher, 7-5/8" h, decal bust of monk, shaded brown ground, gold trim, IOGA mark 90.00
Bowl, 8" d, 4" h, red poinsettia, shaded brown ground, IOGA mark 70.00
Chocolate Pot, cov, 7-1/2" h, cherries design 65.00
Cup and Saucer, Chateau pattern 10.00
Cuspidor, 6-1/2" h, floral dec, IOGA mark....................75.00
Dresser Tray, 10" l, 6" w, fluted, small blue and yellow flowers, pale blue and yellow ground, mkd "Warwick China" 35.00
Marmalade Jar, cov, pale yellow florals, brown ground, handles 115.00
Mug, monk reading paper, unsgd 40.00
Pitcher, 9-1/2" h, poppies, IOGA Mark 120.00
Plate
   8-1/4" d, swimming fish decal.................................50.00
   10" d, coach scene, yellow and gold bands...........95.00
Platter, 15" l, raised matte gold ribbed border design, scalloped trim, green helmet mark 45.00
Spirit Jug, 6" h, Dickens character with guitar, shaded brown ground 95.00
Spooner, platinum bands 60.00
Tray, 11-1/4" l, scattered bunches of pink and red roses, gold rim, open handles..25.00
Vase
   8-3/4" h, bud, rose design, helmet mark................125.00

9-1/2" h, bulbous oval base, narrow neck, flared rim with gold outline, 2 tapered loop handles, open red flower, green leaves, shaded brown ground, IOGA mark 155.00
10-1/2" h, red roses, blue-green ground................................95.00
Vegetable Bowl, cov, Chateau pattern 32.00

Pitcher, monk playing fiddle, brown tones, mkd "IOGA," 4-1/4" h, $85.

WATCHES, POCKET

History: Pocket watches can be found in many places—from flea markets to the specialized jewelry auctions. Condition of movement is the first priority; design and detailing of the case is second.

Descriptions of pocket watches may include the size (16/0 to 20), number of jewels in the movement, whether the face is open or closed (hunter), and the composition (gold, gold filled, or some other metal). The movement is the critical element since cases often were switched. However, an elaborate case, especially if gold, adds significantly to value.

Pocket watches designed to railroad specifications are desirable. They are between 16 and 18 in size, have a minimum of 17 jewels, adjust to at least five positions, and conform to many other specifications. All are open faced.

Study the field thoroughly before buying. There is a vast amount of literature, including books and newsletters from clubs and collectors.

References: T. P. Camerer Cuss, *Antique Watches,* Antique Collectors' Club, 1999; Roy Ehrhardt, *European Pocket Watches,* Book 2, Heart of America Press, 1993; Roy Ehrhardt and Joe Demsey, *Cartier Wrist & Pocket Watches,* Clocks, Heart of America Press, 1992; ——, *Patek Phillipe,* Heart of America Press, 1992; ——, *American Pocket Watch Serial Number Grade Book,* Heart of America Press, 1993; Alan Sherman, *Pocket Watches of the 19th and 20th Century,* Antique Collectors' Club, 1999; Cooksey Shugart and Richard E. Gilbert, *Complete Price Guide to Watches,* No. 19, Collector Books, 1999.

Periodicals: *The Premium Watch Watch,* 24 San Rafael Drive, Rochester, NY 14618; *Watch & Clock Review,* 2403 Champa St., Denver, CO 80205.

Collectors' Clubs: American Watchmakers Institute Chapter 102, 3 Washington Sq, Apt 3C, Larchmont, NY 10538; Early American Watch Club Chapter 149, P.O. Box 5499, Beverly Hills, CA 90210; National Association of Watch & Clock Collectors, 514 Poplar St., Columbia, PA 17512.

SPECIAL AUCTIONS

Phillips Fine Art Auctions
406 E. 79th St.
New York, NY 10021
(212) 570-4830

Skinner, Inc.
The Heritage on the Garden
63 Park Plaza
Boston, MA 02116
(617) 350-5400

Museums: American Clock & Watch Museum, Bristol, CT; Hoffman Clock Museum, Newark, NY; National Association of Watch and Clock Collectors Museum, Columbia, PA; The Time Museum, Rockford, IL.

Abbreviations:

gf	gold filled
j	jewels
S	size
yg	yellow gold

Bautte, Jq Fd. Geneve, 18K yg, white dial, Roman numerals, chased case with bi-color floral bouquet on one side, mixed meal and enamel dec on other, scalloped edges, enamel damage 260.00

Bijou Watch Co., lady's label, 14k yg, dec dial with ornate hands, subsidiary seconds hand and dial, diamond-set engraved crescent moon and star on case, 14k yg ribbon shaped watch pin, c1900 ...... 390.00

Bourquin, Ami, Locle, #30993, 18 kt yg, key wind, white porcelain dial, black Roman numerals, subsidiary seconds dial, engraved case with black and blue enamel, accented with rose-cut diamonds, fitted wooden box with inlaid dec 1,100.00

Boutte, #277389, 14k yg, 10 rubies, white dial, black Roman numerals, chased case with red and blue enamel star dec, Russian hallmarks, 29" l ropetwist chain, enamel loss 300.00

Champney, S. P., Worcester, MA, 18K yg, openface, gilt movement, #8063, key wind, white dial, Roman numerals, subsidiary seconds dial, hallmarks, orig key, c1850, dial cracked, nicks to crystal . 250.00

Elgin National Watch Co., openface, white porcelain dial, black Roman numerals, subsidiary seconds dial, 14K yg, inscribed dustcover dated 1889, hairline to dial 260.00

Frodsham, Henry, Liverpool, open face, 3/4 plate, case, and dustcover sgd "L & R. No. 2688," 18K yg engraved dial with Roman numerals, English hallmarks, scratches to dial 350.00

Hampden, hunting case, white porcelain dial, black Roman numerals, subsidiary seconds dial, engraved 14K yg case, scallop0ed edge, crystal loose 460.00

Jacot, Charles E., 18K yg hunter case, nickel jeweled movement, #9562, numbered on dust cov, case and movement, white porcelain dial, Roman numerals, subsidiary dial for seconds, monogrammed case, orig wood case with extra spring, 14k yg chain 750.00

Jurgensen, J. Alfred, Copenhagen, #784, 18K yd hunter case, highly jeweled movement, patent 1865, white porcelain dial, subsidiary dial for seconds, fancy hands, elaborate monogram 3,300.00

Kaston, Eye of Time, brooch, figural eye set with round and baguette diamonds, blue enamel clock for pupil, platinum mount, sgd "Dali" 5,290.00

Longines, lady's, hunting case, 17 jewel movement, 1370124, white enamel dial, Arabic numerals, subsidiary seconds dial, case set with 6 old mine-cut diamonds in crescent and star motif, verso monogrammed, 14K yg 150.00

Meylan, C. H., Brassus, no. 9105, lady's, hunting case, white porcelain dial, black Roman numerals, subsidiary seconds dial, 18K yg engine-turned case, engraved monogram, dustcover inscribed, dated 1898 .... 350.00

Moard, Remontoir Cylindre, 14k yg, engraved hunter case, white dial with Roman numerals, 56" l ropetwist chain, small slide, Russian hallmarks 375.00

Patek Philippe & Co., open face, triple-signed, 18 jewel movement, 8 adjustments, beige dial, black Arabic numerals, subsidiary seconds dial, 18K yg case 1,265.00

Pendant

Edwardian, octagonal shaped pendant, one side with classical female framed in rose-cut diamonds, other side with goldtone dial with black Arabic numerals, allover green and white enamel dec, some enamel loss 1,380.00

Eterna, 18K yg, rushed gold, rect form, black line indicators, hallmark, 23.10 dwt 230.00

Figural, insect, 18K yg, rose-cut diamond accents, blue enamel

Patek Philippe, Geneve, 18K gold, open face, minute repeating, split second chronograph, perpetual calendar, moon phases, register, and central alarm, c1920, $602,000.

hinged wings opening to reveal white dial, Roman numerals, flat 23-1/2" trace link chain 4,500.00

Swiss, gold filled, repeated, white dial, Arabic numerals, fancy hands, subsidiary seconds dial 300.00

Swiss, lady's, 10 jewel movement, cream colored dial, black Roman numerals and scroll hands, 18K yg gold case, muticolored enameled portrait of woman, rose-cut diamond accents, dents to dustcover, minor enamel loss 450.00

U. S. Watch Co,., Waltham, 14k yg, hunter, size 6, white dial, black Roman numerals, subsidiary seconds dial, engraved floral and scroll motifs on case 230.00

WATCHES, WRIST

History: The definition of a wristwatch is simply "a small watch that is attached to a bracelet or strap and is worn around the wrist." However, a watch on a bracelet is not necessarily a wristwatch. The key is the ability to read the time. A true wristwatch allows you to read the time at a glance, without making any other motions. Early watches on an arm bracelet had the axis of their dials, from 6 to 12, perpendicular to the band. Reading them required some extensive arm movements.

The first true wristwatch appeared about 1850. However, the key date is 1880 when the stylish, decorative wristwatch appeared and almost universal acceptance occurred. The technology to create the wristwatch existed in the early 19th century with Brequet's shock-absorbing "Parachute System" for automatic watches and Ardien Philipe's winding stem.

The wristwatch was a response to the needs of the entrepreneurial age with its emphasis on punctuality and planned free time. Sometime around 1930, the sales of wristwatches surpassed that of pocket watches. Swiss and German manufacturers were quickly joined by American makers.

The wristwatch has undergone many technical advances during the 20th century including self-winding (automatic), shock-resistance, and electric movements.

References: Hy Brown and Nancy Thomas, *Comic Character Timepieces,* Schiffer Publishing, 1992; Gisbert L. Brunner and Christian Pfeiffer-Belli, *Wristwatches, A Handbook and Price Guide,* Schiffer Publishing, 1997; James M. Dowling and Jeffrey P. Hess, *The Best of Time:* Rolex Wristwatches, *An Unauthorized History,* Schiffer Publishing, 1996; Roy Ehrhardt and Joe Demsey, *Cartier Wrist & Pocket Watches,* Clocks, Heart of America Press, 1992; ——, *Patek Phillipe,* Heart of America Press, 1992; ——, *Rolex Identification and Price Guide,* Heart of America Press, 1993; Sherry and Roy Ehrhardt and Joe Demesy, *Vintage American & European Wrist Watch Price Guide,* Book 6, Heart of America Press, 1993; Edward Faber and Stewart Unger, *American Wristwatches,* revised ed., Schiffer Publishing, 1997; Heinz Hampel, *Automatic Wristwatches from Switzerland,* Schiffer Publishing, 1997; Helmet Kahlert, Richard Mühe, Gisbert L. Brunner, *Wristwatches: History of a Century's Development,* Schiffer Publishing, 1999; Anton Kreuzer, *Omega Wristwatches,* Schiffer Publishing, 1996; Fritz von Osterhausen, *Movado History,* Schiffer Publishing, 1996; ——, *Wristwatch Chronometers,* Schiffer Publishign, 1997; Cooksey Shugart and Richard E. Gilbert, *Complete Price Guide to Watches,* No. 19, Collector Books, 1999.

Periodical: *International Wrist Watch,* 242 West Ave., Darien, CT 06820.

Collectors' Clubs: International Wrist Watch Collectors Chapter 146, 5901C. Westheimer, Houston, TX 77057; National Association of Watch & Clock Collectors, 514 Poplar St., Columbia, PA 17512; The Swatch Collectors Club, P.O. Box 7400, Melville, NY 11747.

Museums: American Clock & Watch Museum, Bristol, CT; Hoffman Clock Museum, Newark, NY; National Association of Watch and Clock Collectors Museum, Columbia, PA; The Time Museum, Rockford, IL.

Boucheron, gentleman's, dress tank, A250565, white gold, reeded bezel and dial, invisible clasp, black leather Boucheron strap, French hallmarks, orig leather pouch 2,150.00

Buccellati, Gianmaria, gentleman's, dress, 18K yg, fancy engrave dial, black tracery enamel, black leather strap, 18K yg clasp, Italian hallmarks 6,900.00

Bueche Girod, lady's, 18K yg, elongated oval goldtone dial, rect bezel with stylized hinge lucks, satin band, c1970 .... 980.00

Bucherer, lady's, 18K yg, Swiss movement, 17 jewel, designed as double-hinged engraved bangle, center covered watch, cream dial, applied goldtone Arabic and abstract indicators, Swiss hallmarks 165.00

Cartier, gentleman's, 18K hg, rect convex white dial, black Roman numerals, round gold bezel, black leather strap 1,380.00

Cartier, lady's

Art Deco, European watch and clock movement, back wind, slim tank style case encrusted with rose-cut diamonds, bezel set with 2 baguettes, cream colored dial with black Arabic numerals, rose-cut diamond shoulders, stamped "Made in France," French platinum marks, black leather cord strap, 18K gold deployant clasp 6,900.00

Santos, gold and stainless steel, round cream colored dial, black Roman numerals, gold bezel with new Cartier replacement bracelet in steel with gold accents, bracelet papers and Cartier box, back of case inscribed and dated 1987 .... 1,035.00

Tank, cream colored dial, black Roman numerals, 18K yg, aubergine lizard strap with Cartier deployant clasp, int. initialed, Carter suede pouch, cracks to dial, wear to strap 2,185.00

Chaumet, Paris, lady's, circular cream colored dial, black abstract indicators, Roman numeral 12, round 18K white gold bezel, quartz movement, back of case cov with protective film and date sticker mkd "04/96," French hallmarks, black lizard strap with 18K white gold Chamet clasp, orig box and papers 920.00

Chopard, Geneve, lady's, 18K yg, goldtone oval dial framed in carved coral with flanking pave-set diamond accents, gold mesh bracelet, buckle with "C" logo 1,725.00

Corum, man's, Admiral's Cup, stainless steel, round cream colored dial, nautical flag indicators, date function, gold, and stainless steel bracelet and case, water resistant, case initialed on reverse 1,035.00

Elgin, lady's, 14k yg, MOP dial, black abstract and Arabic numeral indicators, hinged freeform cover with diamonds and cultured pearl accent, tapering link bracelet with mesh edges, 33.80 dwt 500.00

Hamilton, Art Deco, platinum and diamond

Cushion shaped case with diamond bezel, foliate diamond shoulders and box-link diamond strap, (1.25 cts total), 17 jewel movement, 6-3/8" l 920.00

Sq cream colored dial, black Arabic numerals and abstract indicators, diamond set bezel and geometric shoulders set with 90 round and 20 baguette-cut diamonds (1.54 cts total), extra diamond set links, 6-1/4" l, replaced crystal, gold solder 865.00

Jaeger LeCoultre, lady's, oval gold dial, bezel set with 44 round diamonds, (0.44 cts), 18K yg cse, integral mesh band 750.00

Jurgensen, Jules, gentleman's, dress, 14k white gold, Swiss movement, silvertone brushed dial, abstract indicators, diamond-set bevel, black faux alligator strap 290.00

Le Coultre, gentleman's, Futurematic, goldtone dial, subsidiary seconds dial, power reserve indicator, 10k yg-filled mount, lizard strap, 1950s 435.00

Lehman, lady's, Retro, Uti movement, 18K yg, round goldtone dial with ruby indicators, one half framed in graduated calibre-cut channel-set rubies, snake like bracelet, French hallmarks, slight discoloration to dial 1,495.00

Lucien Piccard, lady's, Retro, 14k yg, MOP dial, Arabic numeral and abstract indicators, framed in channel0-set rubies, bracelet of circular links centered by gold discs framed in rubies, orig box 980.00

Nardin, Ulysse

Gentleman's, 14k yg, chronometer, goldtone dial, luminescent quarter sections, applied abstract and Arabic numeral indicators, subsidiary seconds dial, lugs with scroll accents, leather strap, discoloration and scratches to dial 290.00

Lady's, Retro, bi-color gold, stylized buckle motif, calibre-cut rubies and diamonds accent, snake link bracelet, slight discoloration to dial 2,185.00

Omega, gentleman's, 18K yg, round cream dial, goldtone Arabic numeral and abstract indicators

Heavy mesh bracelet, mild soil to dial, 44.80 dwt 460.00

Subsidiary seconds dial 225.00

Plaget, lady's, silvertone rect dial, black abstract indicators, cov with buckle design set with 17 round diamonds and 4 baguette diamonds (1.58 cts), integral textured 18K white gold band 2,530.00

Rolex Oyster

Lady's, Perpetual Datejust, gold and diamond, circular gold dial with diamond indicators, reeded bezel, President bracelet with central brushed finish, 18K yg, scratches to crystal 5,290.00

Man's, Perpetual Chronometer, stainless steel, tan dial, gold abstract indicators, steel Rolex bracelet, discoloration to dial, crystal chipped 750.00

Tiffany & Co.

Gentleman's, 18K yg, lapis lazuli color dial, stepped bezel, black crocodile strap 635.00

Lady's, Retro, round cream colored dial, gold Arabic numerals, International Watch Co. movement, 17 jewel movement, 2 adjustments, Cresaux case, 14kt yg snake bracelet, 6-1/2" l, reverse inscribed and dated 1942, some discoloration to dial 350.00

Ullman, M. & W, Art Deco, Swiss movement, 17 jewel, cartouche form, set with diamonds, accented with blue stones, cream dial, Arabic numerals, platinum mount, stainless steel band 200.00

Universal, Geneve, Uni-Compax, gentleman's, 18K yg, 2 dial chronograph, silver-tone dial, sweep seconds hand, black lizard strap ... 980.00

Uti, Paris, Spritzer and Furhmann, lady's, 18K yg, silvertone dial, applied goldtone indicators, leather strap with keyhole form closure, hallmarks, wear to strap 575.00

Vacheron & Constantin, Geneve
  Gentleman's, 18K yg, black dial, goldtone abstract and Arabic numeral indicators, subsidiary seconds dial, black leather strap.........1,725.00
  Lady's, round silvertone dial, black abstract indicators, textured 18K white gold bezel, integral mesh strap 1,035.00

WATERFORD

History: Waterford crystal is high-quality flint glass commonly decorated with cuttings. The original factory was established at Waterford, Ireland, in 1729. Glass made before 1830 is darker than the brilliantly clear glass of later production. The factory closed in 1852. One hundred years later it reopened and continues in production today.

Bowl
  6" d, allover diamond cutting 70.00
  8" d, DQ, thumbprint stem 125.00
  10" d, ftd, Benjamin Franklin Liberty Bowl, American Heritage collection 275.00
Cake Plate, 10" d, 5-1/4" h, sunburst center, geometric design....85.00
Cake Server, cut glass handle, orig box 80.00
Champagne Flute, 6" h, Coleen pattern, 12 pc set 450.00
Chandelier, 32-1/2" h, cut crystal, 12 alternating arms issuing candlecups hung with prismatic drops and swags of prismatic beads around cut crystal shaft surmounted by similarly hung crown 2,000.00
Compote, 5-1/2" h, allover diamond cutting above double wafer stem, pr 400.00
Creamer and Sugar, 4" h creamer, 3-3/4" d sugar, Tralee pattern 85.00
Decanter, 13-1/4" h, cut diamond and stylized fan pattern, matching stopper 200.00
Honey Jar, cov 70.00
Lamp, 23" h, 13" d umbrella shade, blunt diamond cutting, Pattern L-1122 ....450.00
Napkin Ring, 2" h, 12 pc set...225.00
Old Fashioned Tumbler, 3-1/2" h, Comeragh pattern, pr 70.00
Ring Dish, 5" d, colorless, cut glass, price for 3 pc set 110.00
Salt, master...85.00
Vase, 8" h, alternating diamond cut panels and horizontal notches
Wine
  5-1/2" h, Patrick, 8 pc set...220.00
  7-3/8" h, Coleen, 12 pc set 725.00

WAVE CREST

History: The C. F. Monroe Company of Meriden, Connecticut, produced the opal glassware known as Wave Crest from 1898 until World War I. The company bought the opaque, blown-molded glass blanks from the Pairpoint Manufacturing Co. of New Bedford, Massachusetts, and other glassmakers, including European factories. The Monroe company then decorated the blanks, usually with floral patterns. Trade names used were "Wave Crest Ware," "Kelva," and "Nakara."

References: Wilfred R. Cohen, *Wave Crest,* Collector Books, out-of-print; Elsa H. Grimmer, *Wave Crest Ware,* Wallace-Homestead, out-of-print; Carrol Lyle and Whitney Newland, *The C. F. Monroe Co. Catalogue No. 11, 1906-1907,* L & N Associates (P.O. Box 2013, Santa Barbara, CA 93120.)

Biscuit Jar, cov, unmarked
  5-1/2" d, 5-1/2" h, pink and white background, melon ribbed, hp flowers 250.00
  8" h, blue and white ground, swirled, cherry blossoms dec, lid with handle 150.00

Bowl, pink flowers, emb metal rim, 4-1/2" d, 1-1/2" h, $195.

  8" h, white ground, fern dec...200.00
Bonbon, 7" h, 6" w, Venetian scene, multicolored landscape, dec rim, satin lining missing 1,200.00
Box, cov
  3-3/4" d, 2-1/2" h, Cigar Band, ladies, royal personages, heraldic symbols, and bulldog dec, replaced closed lining............1,250.00
  4-1/4" d, bright blue ground, pink and white flowers, emb shell pattern, hinged..425.00
  4-1/4" d, 3-1/2" h, Bishop's Hat shape, brown-orange ground, pink flowers on lid, no lining, stamped "Nakara".........................340.00
  4-1/2" d, 3" h, round, blue and white ground, swirled, wild flowers on lid, unmarked 225.00
  5-1/2" d, 3-1/2" h, Bishop's Hat shape, gray-blue ground, pink and purple floral dec, orig lining, stamped "C.F.M. Co. Nakara" 425.00
  7-1/4" d, 3-3/4" h, Baroque Shell, raised pink-gold rococo shells, encircled by fancy pale turquoise Arabic design, natural opaque white ground, lace-like network of raised white enamel beads, satin lining missing, bright metal fittings 1,450.00
Cigar Humidor, 8-3/4" h, blue body, single-petaled pink rose, pink "Cigar" signature, pewter collar, bail, and lid, flame-shaped finial, sgd "Kelva"...685.00
Cracker Jar, cov
  10-1/2" h, 6" d, barrel shape, green-blue ground, yellow emb crests, hp yellow and brown wild roses, leaves, and stems, silver-plated cover and handle 675.00
  11-1/4" h, 5" w, square, four sides with blown-out dec, pink roses and buds, leaves, medium blue ground, emb metal hardware, sgd "Wave Crest" in pink banner 675.00
Dresser Box, cov
  3" h, round, opaque white satin, hp floral dec on lid, gilt-metal rim, Wave Crest trademark on base 320.00
  3" h, 5" l, ovoid box with hinged lid, four brass foliage and paw feet, pale pink ground, blue and white flowers with enamel accents........475.00
  3-1/4" h, square, light blue on white opal glass, hp floral dec, gilt-metal rim, Wave Crest trademark on base 300.00
  4" h, 7" d, round, hinged lid, brass closure band, swirled, cream colored ground, blue daisies, white enamel accents..............350.00
Ewer
  14-1/2" h, fishing scene, unmarked 110.00
  16" h, blue ground, melon ribbed, courting scene, unmarked, pr...250.00
Ferner, 7" d, 2-1/2" h, pale blue, swirled, yellow flowers, unmarked 150.00
Jewel Stand, 4" d, 3" h, green and white ground, scroll design, pink floral dec, unmarked 90.00
Mustard Jar, cov, spoon, green ground, floral dec, unmarked 140.00
Pickle Castor, 5-1/2" h, white ground, floral dec, fork holder on both sides of SP holder, unmarked 150.00
Pin Dish, open
  3-1/2" d, 1-1/2" h, pink and white, swirled, floral dec, unmarked ..35.00
  4-1/4" d, 2" h, pink and white, eggcrate mold, blue violets dec, mkd 80.00

5" d, 1-1/2" h, white, scrolls, pink floral dec, marked 80.00
Plate, 7" d, reticulated border, pond lily dec, shaded pale blue
ground 750.00
Salt and Pepper Shakers, pr
Shape No. 6, blue and white ground, fox and hound dec........ 75.00
Swirled, light yellow ground, floral dec, unmarked 75.00
Tulip, brown and white ground, birds and floral dec 60.00
Sugar Shaker, 3" h, 31/4" d, 8 Helmschmied Swirls, creamy pink
ground, hp Johnny Jump-Up sprigs, SP metal cov with emb blos-
soms and leaves 585.00
Syrup Pitcher, Helmschmied Swirl, ivory colored body, blue and white
floral dec, smoky-gray leafy branches, SP lid and collar.......... 485.00
Trinket Dish, 1-1/2" x 5", blue and red flowers 175.00
Vase, 10" h, pale pink accents on white, pink and orange chrysanthemums, enameled foliage, beaded white top............................. 600.00

WEATHER VANES

History: A weather vane indicates wind direction. The earliest
known examples were found on late 17th-century structures
in the Boston area. The vanes were handcrafted of wood,
copper, or tin. By the last half of the 19th century, weather
vanes adorned farms and houses throughout the nation.
Mass-produced vanes of cast iron, copper, and sheet metal
were sold through mail-order catalogs or at country stores.

The champion vane is the rooster—in fact, the name
weathercock is synonymous with weather vane—but the
styles and patterns are endless. Weathering can affect the
same vane differently; for this reason, patina is a critical
element in collectible vanes.

Whirligigs are a variation of the weather vane. Constructed of wood and metal, often by the unskilled, whirligigs
indicate the direction of the wind and its velocity. Watching
their unique movements also provides entertainment.

References: Robert Bishop and Patricia Coblentz, *Gallery
of American Weathervanes and Whirligigs,* E. P. Dutton,
1981; Ken Fitzgerald, *Weathervanes and Whirligigs,* Clarkson N. Potter, 1967; A. B. & W. T. Westervelt, *American
Antique Weathervanes* (1883 catalog reprint), Dover Publications, 1982.

Reproduction Alert: Reproductions of early models exist,
are being aged, and then sold as originals.

**Horse and Sulky, American, 19th C, metal, parcel gilt and
painted, full bodied running horse, minor repairs to horse,
48" l, 20" h, $4,500.**

Arrow, 54" l, 12" h, molded copper, mounting pole, small crease and
tear to feather end, America, late 19th C 490.00
Arrow Banner, 42" l, gilt zinc, America, 19th C, bullet hole, minor
dents 2,530.00
Black Hawk, 33" l, 18-1/2" h, molded copper, allover verdigris, traces of
gilt, minor imperfections, from MA... 6,555.00
Bull, copper, orig gilding, New England, late 19th C 6,500.00
Cow, 28" l, 15" h, narrow full bodied cow with horns, curved ears, long
broom type tail, tubular rod, newly painted with beige house paint
over orig gilt and green verdigris... 3,250.00
Eagle, 24" h, 29-1/2" w, A. L. Jewell & Co., copper, dark finish, some
green verdigris, cast head and feet, supporting rods on wings to body,
wood presentation base, bullet hole to inside of top of wing 3,500.00
Fire Engine, 48" l, 28" h, Cushing & White, Waltham, MA, 1875-85,
copper, two identical horses pulling 4 wheel fire engine cart with
driver and fireman on back, fire wagon with large seated man with
helmet, seat with lanterns on each side, two more lanterns on middle
section with large water tank, spigots, and wheels, man on back in
full cloak and fire helmet, tubular undercarriage supported by 4
shaped wrought iron metal rods, orig verdigris patina 200,000.00
Fish, 35-1/2" l, gilt copper, America, late 19th C, regilt, dents, seam
splints 1,380.00
Fox, 33" l, 7-1/2" h, solid iron, running in full stride, long bushy tail,
large mounting sleeve, some orig paint 6,000.00
Half Moon with Face, decorative wrought iron, 67" h, some
bending 5,550.00
Horse and Jockey, 32" l, 18" h, cast iron jockey mounted on copper
horse with iron head, full stride, detailed mane, tail, legs, and saddle,
copper shaft, dark copper finish with some green verdigris to iron
areas 3,750.00
Hunter, 25" l, 26-1/2" h, sheet iron, black painted silhouette of hunter
taking aim, from NH lodge... 1,265.00
Leaping Stag, 29-1/2" l, 69" h, molded copper, attributed to Harris &
Co., Boston, late 19th c, bush-gilt, cast iron stand with cardinals,
repair to antlers, minor seam imperfections 16,100.00
Lyre, 36" h, 59" l, copper and zinc, America, 19th C,
dents 4,890.00
Rooster, 28-1/2" h, 24" l, gilt over copper on iron stand, bullet
holes.. 770.00
Schooner, 29" h, 41" l, painted wood and zinc, Martha's Vineyard, MA,
early 20th C, minor cracks, losses, corrosion 1,150.00
Sulky and Driver, molded copper, attributed to J. W. Fiske, Boston, late
19th C, four wheeled sulky, mounted on wood base, allover brown
surface, 50" l, 19-1/2" h 17,250.00
Trotting Horse, 19" x 27", 49-1/2" h, molded copper, attributed to I. Harris and Sons, Boston, iron cardinals, round wooden base, allover verdigris, traces of gilt, holes.. 575.00
Whirligig
Locomotive, 10" h, 28-1/8" w, 10" d, painted and carved wood and
metal, mechanized engine and signal man, old weathered surface, minor imperfections, America, early 20th C 750.00
Man dancing and fiddle player, wood, tin, and wire, weathered,
repairs and replacements, 35" l 220.00

WEBB, THOMAS & SONS

History: Thomas Webb & Sons was established in 1837 in
Stourbridge, England. The company probably is best known
for its very beautiful English cameo glass. However, many
other types of colored art glass were produced, including
enameled, iridescent, heavily ornamented, and cased.

References: Charles R. Hajdamach, *British Glass,* 1800-
1914, Antique Collectors' Club, 1991.

Additional Listings: Burmese; Cameo; Peachblow.

Basket, 8" l, 6-1/2" h, vaseline opalescent shading to pink, petal edge,
twisted pink handle, DQ pattern, c1890 .... 265.00

Biscuit Jar, pink satin ground, gold banding, enameled Art Nouveau woman, floral dec, brass cover, cone finial, acid etched mark, 5-3/4" d, 7-1/2" h, $350.

Beverage Set, 11-3/4" h x 6" w pitcher, four 3-3/4" tumblers, pale cream ext., brilliant cranberry cased int., large cranberry loop handle, white, yellow, and magenta roses and leaves dec 875.00

Bowl
    4" d, 2-1/2" h, deep rounded sides, flat rim, ruby cut to green floral wreath and swag design, star cut base 235.00
    5-1/2" w, 5" h, Rainbow MOP satin, triangular, deep pink, yellow, blue, and white, applied thorn feet, raspberry prunt, sgd "Patent" .1,500.00
    5-3/4" d, 4-1/2" h, avocado green, sapphire blue stripes, mica flakes, crystal applied fancy drippings on sides, applied crystal rigaree around top edge, clear feet, clear berry pontil 235.00

Bride's Bowl, 6" h, MOP satin, herringbone pattern, green to white ext., chartreuse int., gold foliage dec 1,450.00

Cologne Bottle, 6" h, cameo, spherical, clear frosted body, overlaid white and red, carved blossoms, buds, leafy stems, and butterfly, linear pattern, hallmarked silver dec, molded and chased blossoms dec .3,200.00

Cream Pitcher
    3-1/4" h, sepia to pale tan ground, heavy gold burnished prunus blossoms, butterfly on back, gold rim and base, clear glass handle with brushed gold 385.00
    3-3/4" h, 2-1/2" d, bulbous, round mouth, brown satin, cream lining, applied frosted handle 210.00

Ewer, 9" h, 4" d, satin, deep green shading to off-white, gold enameled leaves and branches, 3 naturalistic applies, applied ivory handle, long spout, numbered base 425.00

Perfume Bottle, 4-1/4" h, undulating body, yellow overlaid in white, cut and carved as swimming dolphin, inscribed registry mark, "Rd. 18100," rim and cap missing 4,950.00

Punch Bowl, 2-3/4" h, 2-1/4" d, Alexandrite, barrel shape, blue shaded to rose to citron, citron applied handle, ground pontil, bell tone 500.00

Rose Bowl, 2-3/4" h, 3-1/2" d, deep rose, ground pontil, shiny signature "Patent" 385.00

Vase
    3-1/2" h, 5-1/2" w, pocket type, Flower and Acorn pattern, MOP satin, bridal white, gold flowers and leaves 650.00
    4" h, Burmese, shiny white, crimped top 685.00
    5" h, 6" w, 18" circumference, shaded blue, sky blue to pale white cream, applied crystal edge, enameled gold and yellow dec of flowers, leaves, and buds, full butterfly, entire surface acid-cut in basketweave design 425.00
    5-1/4" h, 3-1/2" d, opaque ivory, cut leaves and berries, brown staining, circular cameo mark on base "Simulated Ivory English Cameo Glass," hallmarked silver rim and frosted ball feet . 625.00

7" h, gourd-shaped body, butterscotch yellow shaded to turquoise blue, cased to opal white, outer layer etched and carved as five-petaled rose on front, ornamental grasses on back, linear borders above and below.. 1,955.00

7" h, 4" d, satin, robin's egg blue, leaves, berries, and vines dec, flowing gold and scroll design, white lining 450.00

7" h, 5" w, satin, basketweave mother of pearl, bulbous base shading from deep blue to pale blue, creamy lining 750.00

7-1/4" h, 4" w at shoulder, Rainbow MOP satin, pink, yellow, blue, and white, DQ, flaring top, broad shoulder, tapered body, glossy white int., sgd "Patent" 1,250.00

7-1/4" h, Japonesque, pale oval heat reactive body, white Burmese to pink at top, overall delicate oriental sepia scenes 345.00

7-1/2" h, 5-5/8" d, shaded orange overlay, off-white lining, gold flowers and fern-like leaves, gold butterfly on back, applied bronze-colored glass handles 255.00

8" h, 4" w, satin, pink and white stripes, fancy frilly top, bulbous base, unlined 425.00

10" h, 4" w, satin, pulled down edges, deep rose shading to pink, creamy lining, ruffled top, dome foot, pr............................... 550.00

10-1/2" h, gourd shape, satin, bright yellow shading to pale yellow, creamy white lining, bleed-through in pontil 285.00

10-1/2" h, 4" w, bulbous, gold floral prunus blossoms, leaves, branches, pine needles, and insect, satin ground shaded brown to gold, creamy white lining, Jules Barbe dec.................... 450.00

WEDGWOOD

History: In 1754, Josiah Wedgwood and Thomas Whieldon of Fenton Vivian, Staffordshire, England, became partners in a pottery enterprise. Their products included marbled, agate, tortoiseshell, green glaze, and Egyptian black wares. In 1759, Wedgwood opened his own pottery at the Ivy House works, Burslem. In 1764, he moved to the Brick House (Bell Works) at Burslem. The pottery concentrated on utilitarian pieces.

Between 1766 and 1769, Wedgwood built the famous works at Etruria. Among the most-renowned products of this plant were the Empress Catherina of Russia dinner service (1774) and the Portland Vase (1790s). The firm also made caneware, unglazed earthenwares (drabwares), piecrust wares, variegated and marbled wares, black basalt (developed in 1768), Queen's or creamware, and Jasperware (perfected in 1774).

Bone china was produced under the direction of Josiah Wedgwood II between 1812 and 1822 and revived in 1878. Moonlight luster was made from 1805 to 1815. Fairyland luster began in 1920. All luster production ended in 1932.

A museum was established at the Etruria pottery in 1906. When Wedgwood moved to its modern plant at Barlaston, North Staffordshire, the museum was expanded.

References: Susan and Al Bagdade, *Warman's English & Continental Pottery & Porcelain,* 3rd Edition, Krause Publications, 1998; Diana Edwards, *Black Basalt,* Antique Collectors Club, 1994; Robin Reilly, *The New Illustrated Dictionary of Wedgwood,* Antique Collectors' Club Ltd., 1995; —, *Wedgwood Jasper,* Thomas Hudson, 1994.

Periodical: *ARS Ceramica,* 5 Dogwood Court, Glen Head, NY 11545.

Collectors' Clubs: Wedgwood International Seminar, 22 DeSavry Crescent, Toronto, Ontario M4S 2I2 Canada; The Wedgwood Society, The Roman Villa, Rockbourne, Fording-

SPECIAL AUCTIONS

Skinner Inc.
Bolton Gallery
357 Main St.
Bolton, MA 01740
(508) 779-6241

bridge, Hants, SP6 3PG, England; The Wedgwood Society of Boston, 28 Birchwood Drive, Hampstead, NH 03841; The Wedgwood Society, of New York, 5 Dogwood Court, Glen Head, NY 11545; Wedgwood Society of Southern California, Inc., P.O. Box 4385, North Hollywood, CA 91617.

Museums: Art Institute of Chicago, Chicago, IL; Birmingham Museum of Art, Birmingham, AL; Brooklyn Museum, Brooklyn, NY; Cincinnati Museum of Art, Cincinnati, OH; City Museum & Art Gallery, Stoke-on-Trent, England; Cleveland Museum of Art, Cleveland, OH; Henry E. Huntington Library and Art Gallery, San Marino, CA; Jones Museum of Glass & Ceramics, East Baldwin, ME; Nassau County Museum System, Long Island, NY; Nelson-Atkins Museum of Art, Kansas City, MO; Potsdam Public Museum, Potsdam, NY; Rose Museum, Brandeis University, Waltham, MA; Victoria & Albert Museum, London, England; Wadsworth Atheneum, Hartford, CT; Wedgwood Museum, Barlaston, Stoke-on-Trent, England.

Basalt

Biscuit Jar, cov, 5-1/2" h, engine-turned body below band of children playing in relief, silver plated rim, handle, and cov, imp mark, late 19th C 520.00
Coffeepot, cov, 8-3/4" h, polychrome floral dec, imp mark, c1840 .... 700.00
Creamer, 4-3/4" h, Encaustic dec, iron red and white enameled scrolled vine and palmette banding, imp mark, early 19th C 635.00
Decanter, 10-1/4" h, banded key dec, silver rim, spout, and stopper, imp mark, late 19th C 690.00

Plaque, Erato, oval, framed, 6-3/4" h, $850.

Ewer, 7-3/4" h, feather molded rim, goat head terminals on each handle, applied foliage dec, imp mark, late 19th C, pr, each with handle restoration 1,380.00
Figure, mounted on titled circular base, imp mark, 19th C
  9" h, Cybele, standing with lion by her side, damaged 375.00
  10-1/8" h, Summer, scantily clad 635.00
Inkwell, 3-3/4" h, engine-turned body, cylindrical sander and inkwell, two handled urn form central handle on tray, imp marks, 19th C 900.00
Jardiniere, 8-7/8" h, classical relief of Muses below fruiting grapevine festoons, lion mask terminals, imp mark, early 20th C 375.00
Jug
  5-1/8" h, Dragon Kenlock Ware, enamel dec, rope twist handle, imp mark, c1900 .... 320.00
  6" h, pear form, beadwork and floral banding, inlaid white, imp mark, mid 19th C 375.00
  8-1/4" h, Egyptian, club form, iron red, black, and white dec, sphinx to either side of bird in flight, imp mark, c1854, footrim chip, surface wear 550.00
Lamp, oil, boat form receptacle molded with alternating acanthus leaves and bell flowers, berried leaf border, topped by seated classical female figure one reading book, other with ewer, fluted circular foot with knop molded with flowers within arches, sq base with canted corners, molded floral dec, imp "Wedgwood," pr 3,500.00
Model, designed by Ernest Light, imp mark, c1915
  2-1/2" h, bear 490.00
  7-1/2" h, egret, pierced rocky base, glass eyes, end of beak restored 200.00
Orange Bowl, 8-3/4" d, scroll work, floral festoons, basketweave dec, imp mark, late 19th C 1,200.00
Plaque
  6" h, 9-1/2" l, rect, Vulcan forming armor for Achilles, imp mark, 19th C, giltwood line oak frame with brass presentation plaque 1,265.00
  7-1/2" h, 10-3/4" l, oval, relief of Panther and Bacchanalian Boys, imp mark, late 18th/early 19th C 2,415.00
  8-3/4" h, 11-3/4' l, oval, Judgment of Hercules, imp mark, 19th C 1,035.00
Punch Pot, cov, 7-1/2" h, engine turned band below shoulder, imp mark, early 19th C, slight chips to shoulder 460.00
Teapot, cov, 8" l, oval, enameled palmette, leaf, and berry banding, sybil finial, imp mark, early 19th C, chip to cover 3,450.00
Vase
  5-3/4" h, applied classical and foliate relief, gilt and bronze dec, imp mark, c1880, cover missing 1,380.00
  7" h, Krater, upturned loop handles, imp mark, mid 19th C 700.00
  9-3/8" h, enameled floral dec, scrolled leaf molded handles imp mark, mid 19th C, rim and one handle restored 750.00
  9-5/8" h, trumpet, molded foliate dec, imp mark, early 20th C, pr 400.00
  11-1/2" h, trumped, molded foliate dec, imp mark, early 20th C, pr 550.00
Water Pitcher, 8-1/2" h, black, polychrome floral enameled dec, c1920, incised 750.00

Bone China

Clock Case, 8-3/4" h, "D" shape, paneled body, gilt dec cherubs centering foliage design, printed mark, late 19th C, top surface worn 1,035.00
Cup, 8-1/2" d, white body, cobalt blue framed panels, enamel painted flowers trimmed in gilt, 3 handles, artist sgd "J. Bond," printed mark, 20th C 750.00
Dresser Set, blue transfer print, scrolled foliate designs, 2-1/4" h low cov box, 4" h tall cov box, pr 5-3/8" h candlesticks, 2-1/2" h ring tray, 12-3/4" l oval tray with central cartouche of Bacchanalian Boys, printed marks, c1900, set 550.00
Vase, cov, 9-1/2" h, gilt figural finial, raised floral dec, printed marks, 20th C, chips to finial, gilt wear 350.00

Caneware

Bowl, cov, stand, 5" h, glazed, applied blue classical and foliate relief, imp mark, c1830, chip to footrim of bowl, saucer stained 375.00

Tobacco Jar, polychrome floral dec, lion door knocker type handles, 4-3/4" d, 5" h, $900.

Cream Jug, 2-1/2" h, molded bamboo leaves, enamel dec, imp lower case mark, 18th C 1,265.00

Custard Cup, 1-7/8" h, teardrop shape, blue enamel dice pattern, unmarked, late 18th/early 19th C, set of 4 .... 980.00

Game Pie Dish, cov, 7" l, oval, molded dead game hare finial, imp mark, c1871 .... 575.00

Garniture, 4-1/2" h, 3 bough pots, encaustic dec, blue, iron red, and white enamels, paneled sides with oval cartouches of cherubs and garden urns, imp upper and lower case marks, 18th C, missing covers, one with restored body 2,300.00

Inkwell

    8-1/8" l, rect, cut corners, applied blue foliate relief, 3 inserts, inkpot, sander, and cov, imp mark, c1830, damage or stains .. 230.00

    8-3/4" l, boat form, central loop handle, molded basketweave body, applied Rosso Antico foliate trim, pair of pots with covers, imp mark, late 19th C, slight damage and stains 2,645.00

Teapot, cov, 4-1/4" h, molded bamboo body, blue trim, imp lower case mark, 18th C, spout chipped 2,760.00

Carrara

Bowl, cov, stand, 4" h, molded sunflower body, imp mark, c1880, rim chip on bowl and stand 150.00

Figure

    13" h, England, modeled by Wm Beattie, imp title, date 1880 and mark, piece of wreath missing 400.00

    20-1/4" h, Venus Victrix, modeled from Venus de Milo, imp title and mark, c1880 .... 1,955.00

Drabware

Coffeepot, cov, 9-1/4" h, arabesque floral relief, stippled ground, spaniel finial, 19th C, spout chips 230.00

Potpourri, pierced cov, 2-3/8" h, applied blue classical and foliage relief, imp mark, mid 19th C 700.00

Sugar Bowl, cov, 1-7/8" h, applied blue floral banding, imp mark, 19th C 120.00

Teapot, cov, 2-3/4" h, applied blue floral banding, imp mark, 19th C 225.00

Vase, 3-3/4" h, enameled paneled flowers, imp mark, mid 19th C, covers missing, rim chips, pr 200.00

Earthenware

Jug

    6-1/4" h, ivory glaze, raised gilt floral dec, printed mark, c1885, wear to gilt rim 175.00

    14" h, cov, Islamic-style, gilt bronzed, enamel dec, imp mark, c1861, chip to spout 400.00

Pedestal, 35" h, enamel dec floral design, imp mark, c1862 ... 1,850.00

Vase, 7" h, flat sided, upturned loop handles, floral and butterfly dec, gilt trim, imp mark, late 19th C, one handle repaired 400.00

Jasperware

Barber Bottle, cov, three color dip, Bacchus heads on shoulder, white classical figures, fruiting grapevines and foliate designs in relief, imp mark

    8-3/8" h, lilac ground, green ground medallions, c1867, cov missing, shallow footrim chip 575.00

    9-3/4" h, white ground with green ground medallions, pale mauve frames, ram's heads and beadwork, late 19th C, heavily crazed, chips on cover rim 635.00

    10" h, dark blue ground with Bacchus heads on shoulder, lilac ground medallions, white classical figures of seasons, mid 19th C, two heads restored 750.00

Basket, 4-1/2" h, dark blue dip, basketweave molded loop handle, applied white openwork cells, imp mark, early 19th C, slight relief loss 435.00

Biscuit Jar, cov

    5-1/4" h, three color dip, central dark blue band bordered in light blue, applied white classical figures, silver plated rims, cov, and handle, imp mark, handle damaged 250.00

    5-1/2" h, light green dip, hp bird, bamboo branches, and berries, gilt trim, hinged pewter lid and rim, imp mark, mid 19th C 690.00

    6" h, three color dip, central dark blue band bordered by light blue, applied white classical figures in relief, silver plated rims, cov and handle, imp mark, late 19th C 350.00

    7-3/4" h, black dip, applied white classical and foliate relief, imp mark, c1876, matching stand 700.00

    8" h, light green dip, scrolled handles, applied white Dancing Houses figures, floral and foliate relief, imp factory mark and "McVitie and Price 1906," handle restored 635.00

Bottle, cov, 5-3/4" h, dark blue dip, applied white classical Muses and foliate relief, imp mark, c1864 .... 460.00

Bough Pot, 6-1/8" h, solid blue, sq, arched top, applied white classical subjects and foliate, paneled sides, imp mark, late 18th C, top rim, corner, and footrim chips, lid missing 260.00

Candle Holder, 2-3/4" h, dark blue dip, applied white classical and foliate relief, imp mark, mid 19th C 575.00

Candlesticks, pr

    6-7/8" h, dark blue dip, applied white classical and foliate relief, imp mark, mid 19th C 450.00

    8" h, black dip, applied white classical and foliate relief, imp mark, 19th C 865.00

Chandelier, 19-1/4" h, light blue dip, applied white classical and foliate relief to bowl and font, unmarked, late 19th C 1,100.00

Cheese Dish, cov, 4-3/4" h, dark blue dip, applied white classical and foliate relief, imp mark, mid 19th C 350.00

Clock, 14-3/4" h, light blue medallions, each with applied white relief, one with Three Graces, one with trophy emblem, floral painted enamel dial, child finial, mid 19th C, chips at key hole 3,800.00

Clock Case

    6" h, dark blue dip, rect, applied white classical and foliate relief, imp mark, c1900, shallow footrim chips 325.00

    6" h, three color, rect, white ground, mauve classical figures, green foliate relief, imp mark, c1900, footrim restored 575.00

    6-1/8" h, light green dip, rect, applied white classical and foliate relief, imp mark, c1900, footrim nicks 320.00

    6-3/4" h, dark blue dip, rect, stepped top, applied white classical and foliate relief, imp mark, c1900 .... 650.00

    7-7/8" h, light green dip, rounded top over pedestal base, applied white oak and acanthus leaves, imp mark, c1900 .... 400.00

    8" h, dark blue dip, rect, arched top, applied white classical and foliate relief, motto "Tempus Fugit" above relief of Father Time, imp mark, c1900 .... 800.00

    8-5/8" h, dark blue dip, rect, urn mounted to top, applied white classical and foliate relief, imp mark, c1900 .... 865.00

    9-3/4" h, solid light blue, sq form, fluted body, scrolled arched rim, domed top, applied white floral garlands terminating at ram's heads, palmettes, and gadroons, brass finial, imp mark, early 19th C, restoration to finial 1,955.00

12-1/4" h, light blue, applied white classical and foliate relief, imp mark, c1900, footrim chips 550.00

13-3/4" h, light green dip, tall case shape, applied white classical and foliate relief, dial frame dec with rhinestones, imp mark, c1900 .... 800.00

Coffee Cann and Saucer, 5-1/4" d saucer

Black dip, applied white trophies and classical medallions between fruiting festoons terminating at ram's heads, imp mark, mid 19th C 690.00

Solid light blue, engine-turned banding, imp mark, late 18th C, restored chips 260.00

Three color dip, Diceware, black ground, applied white foliage and yellow quatrefoils, imp mark, mid 19th C 2,530.00

Creamer

2-3/4" h, black dip, applied white fruit festoons between ram's head, classical and trophy designs, imp mark, mid 19th C . 750.00

4-1/2" h, blue, relief of Classical figures making offerings to gods 60.00

4-3/4" h, blue, two figures of muses within dec borders, applied metal hinged lid, 19th C 55.00

Cream Jug, 3-1/4" h, light green dip, hexagonal silver shape, applied white trophies and classical figures in relief, imp mark, early 19th C, handle repaired 200.00

Cup and Saucer, 5-1/2" d saucer, solid black, applied white classical and foliate relief, imp mark, 20th C 320.00

Half Buckle, 2-1/4" h, 3-5/8" w, dark blue dip, oval, faceted steel bead work on steel frame, jasper medallion with applied white classical relief and inlaid steel beads, imp mark, early 19th C, some bead loss, medallion repaired 490.00

Incense Burner

4-1/8" h, black dip, white dolphin form tripod base with foliage relief, imp mark, early 19th C, restoration to tails, cover missing . 200.00

5" h, light blue dip, applied whtie foliate relief, tripod dolphin base, imp mark, c1861, firing flaws at footrim, finial reglued 865.00

Jar, cov, 3-7/8" h, dark blue dip, applied white classical and foliate relief, imp mark, c1900, pr 300.00

Jardiniere

7" h, light blue dip, applied white floral band, imp mark, 19th C .. 300.00

8-3/8" d, black dip, applied white relief of Muses below fruiting grapevine terminating at lion's heads and rings, imp mark, mid 19th C 520.00

Jardiniere and Stand, 7-3/4" h, black dip, applied white Muses below fruiting grapevine festoons terminating at lion mask and rings, imp marks, mid 19th C 400.00

Jug

4-5/8" h, dark blue dip, commemorative, white relief portraits of Washington and Franklin within foliate framed cartouches, imp mark, early 20th C 275.00

6-1/8" h, three color dip, dark blue ground, applied yellow trellis, applied white foliate banding, hinged pewter lid, imp mark, mid 19th C, minor relief loss 635.00

6-1/8" h, three color dip, tapering sides, dark blue ground, yellow trellis, white foliate relief, hinged pewter lid, imp mark, 19th C 575.00

8" h, dark blue dip, Portland shape, applied white classical relief, hinged pewter lid, imp mark 525.00

8" h, dark blue dip, Portland shape, applied white classical relief, imp mark, mid 19th C, footrim chip 435.00

8-5/8" h, dark blue dip, lobe molded body, applied white classical figures, imp mark, mid 18th C, rim chips 920.00

9" h, dark blue dip, Portland shape, applied white classical relief, pewter rim and hinged cov, imp mark, mid 19th C 675.00

10-3/8" h, black dip, white classical relief, silver plated rim, cov, and handle, imp mark, late 19th C 350.00

Lamp, oil, 17-1/2" h, light blue dip, applied white classical and foliate relief, brass mounted collar, scrolled handles, circular base, imp mark, c1871 .... 920.00

Lantern, 11" h, light blue, cylindrical, paneled sides, 4 oval medallions, applied white Muses in relief, 19th C 635.00

Letter Box, 9-1/4" l, light blue oval medallion with applied white classi-

cal relief, brass frame, mounted to center of domed oak cover, applied brass rope work, late 19th C 2,100.00

Medallion

1" h, 2-3/8" w, three color dip, rect, cut corners, applied white classical relief, lilac ground with yellow trim, imp mark, 19th C, pr 635.00

1-1/4" h, 1-1/2" w, three color dip, octagonal, green trim, black center, white classical and foliate relief, imp mark, 19th C 230.00

1-1/2" h, 1-7/8" w, light green dip, oval, applied white classical relief of Sacrifice to Hymen and Marriage of Cupid and Psyche, imp mark, 19th C, pr 550.00

4-1/8" h, 2-1/4" w, yellow dip, oval, applied white classical female, imp mark, late 19th C 460.00

Milk Pitcher, dark blue dip, applied white scene of classical figures in relief 200.00

Pail, 6-1/8" h, dark blue dip, silver plated rim and handle, raised white banding, imp mark, mid 19th C 300.00

Patch Box, dark blue, oval, 3 inlaid oval medallions with applied white classical relief, ivory and cut steel mounts, early 19th C 800.00

Pawn, 2-1/2" h, white jasper, dark blue dip base, imp mark, late 18th C 325.00

Plaque, imp mark, framed

2-1/4" h, 6-1/2" l, light green dip, rect, applied white Seasons relief, ebonized and gilded frame, mark not visible, late 19th/early 20th C 350.00

3" h, 4" l, solid light blue, oval, applied white Muses in relief, late 19th C 490.00

3-3/4" h, 5-3/4" l, dark blue dip, oval, applied white relief, Bacchanalian Boys after design by Lady Diana Beauclerk, 19th C 750.00

4-1/8" d, black dip, circular form, applied white relief of the Seasons, mid 19th C, set of 4 .... 1,265.00

5" h, 8-1/4" l, black dip, black dip, rect, Dancing Hours, applied white classical figures, 19th C 400.00

5-1/4" h, 10-1/8" l, dark blue dip, rect, applied white classical subject, rim chips 1,380.00

5-3/4" h, 10" l, black dip, rect, Bacchus Entering the City, applied white classical relief 3,450.00

5-7/8" h, 17-7/8" l, black dip, rect, Dancing Hours, applied white classical figures, 20th C 1,265.00

6" h, 10" l, solid light blue, oval, applied white relief of Bacchus, 19th C 525.00

6" h, 18" l, black dip, rect, Dipping of Achilles, applied white classical relief, 19th C 1,955.00

6" h, 18" l, black dip, rect, Sacrifice to Peace, applied white classical relief, 19th C, some restoration 520.00

6" h, 18" l, solid black, rect, Blind Man's Bluff, applied white relief, c1900 .... 1,150.00

6-1/2" h, 9-3/4" l, dark blue dip, applied white relief, one with Marriage of Cupid and Pysche, other with Sacrifice to Hymen, 19th C, pr 2,530.00

7" h, 10" l, solid light blue, applied white Muse in relief, 20th C 375.00

26" h, 12" w, green ground, lilac medallions, applied white classical relief, imp mark, 19th C, repaired and restored surfaces, pr . 3,335.00

Plinth

3-5/8" h, light blue dip, sq, paneled sides, applied white classical and foliate relief, portraits of Mrs. Elizabeth Montagu and Jean-Jacques Rousseau, imp mark, 19th C 300.00

5" h, light green dip, paneled sides, applied white Seasons, bell flower, and foliate relief, imp mark, late 19th C 350.00

Potpourri, cov, 6-3/4" h, dark blue, applied white arabesque floral, foliate, and urn relief, pierced cover, imp mark, early 19th C 1,725.00

Potpourri Stand, 6" h, dark blue dip, applied white arabesque floral, foliate, and urn relief, imp mark, late 18th/early 19th C, covers missing, pr 750.00

Spill Vase

3-1/8" h, three color dip, green ground, applied white relief of ribbons, portrait heads on liliac ground medallions, imp mark, mid 19th C, firing lines on foot 700.00

4" h, black dip, applied white foliage, engine-turned striping, imp mark, mid 19th C, pr 1,150.00

Teapot, blue and white, Wesley, verse on front, damaged at spout, hairline crack, $60.

Teapot, cov, 4" h, three-color dip, white ground, green and lilac foliage, oval lilac ground medallions with white classical figures, imp mark, mid 19th C, slight chips to spout, handle restored 700.00

Tray, 6-3/8" h, 9-1/4" l, black dip, oval, applied white classical relief, imp mark, late 19th C 225.00

Trophy Vase, 14-3/4" h, dark blue dip, applied white classical figures and trophies in relief, foliate borders, handles, imp mark, c1900..........980.00

Urn, 11" h, blue, scene of Classical figures in relief, two handles, acanthus borders 275.00

Vase
  4" h, dark blue dip, Portland, applied whtie classical relief, imp mark, mid 19th C, pr 575.00
  6-1/8" h, dark blue dip, bottle shale, applied white classic and foliate relief, imp mark, mid 19th C, one base reattached, pr..460.00
  6-1/2" h, lilac dip, applied white classical and foliate relief, drum form plinth base with floral festoons and ram's heads, imp mark, c1864 ....400.00
  8" h, black dip, applied white Muses and foliate borders, imp mark, mid 19th C 865.00
  8-1/4" h, light blue dip, triangular, applied white classical and foliate relief, imp mark, mid19th C 575.00
  8-1/4" h, solid light blue, applied white Bacchus handles and foliate borders, imp mark, late 19th/early 20th C...........................435.00
  9-3/4" h, light green dip, 2 handles, undecorated body, c1900...690.00
  9-3/4" h, solid light blue, hp raised gilt floral dec, imp mark, 19th C 2,875.00
  9-7/8" h, dark blue dip, applied whtie classical, trophy, and foliate relief, imp mark, early 20th C...800.00
  10-1/4" h, dark blue dip, applied white classical and trophy relief, imp mark, late 19th C...750.00
  13" h, dark blue dip, tapered sides, applied white classical and foliate relief, imp mark, mid 19th C, cover missing, rim and footrim chips, hairline...635.00

Vase, cov
  6" h, black dip, applied white drapery swags and foliate borders relief, imp mark, mid 19th C, restoration to handles, pr . 1,3880.00
  6-3/4" h, solid white, Bacchus head handles, applied blue classical and foliate relief, imp mark, mid 19th C 635.00
  7" h, dark blue dip, trumpet form, applied white arabesque floral and foliate relief, imp mark, late 18th/early 19th C...........675.00
  8-1/4" h, light blue dip, applied white classical and foliate relief, two handles, pierced cov, imp mark, c1864...........................550.00
  8-3/4" h, three color dip, light blue ground, lilac medallions, white

relief of classical figures, trophies, foliate festoons, and borders, imp mark, c1900, married cover 865.00
  9-1/2" h, light blue dip, Apollo, applied white relief and Latin verse "CC Post Natum Conditorem Anno Viget Ars Etruriae Redintegrata," designed by John Goodwin to commemorate 200th anniversary of Josiah Wedgwood's birth, imp mark, mounted to ebonized wood base, c1930, slight rim nick, arm reglued, hairline to socle 635.00
  11-1/2" h, light green dip, applied white Muses and foliate borders, ormolu mounts, imp mark, cover restored 2,415.00
  11-3/4" h, solid black dip, applied white classical medallions between floral festoons terminating at ram's heads, imp mark, early 20th C, orig insert lid, married cover ....550.00.
  15" h, solid light blue, Dancing Hours, applied white foliate borders and Bacchus mask handles, imp mark, restored handles and socle 800.00
  16-1/2" h, light green dip, applied white oval medallions of Muses, floral festoons, palmette bands, stiff leaf borders, imp mark, mid 19th C 1,450.00
  18" h, solid light blue, applied white Muses and Apollo figures with assorted foliate border relief, upturned loop handles and urn finial, imp mark, early 19th C, restored handles, rim, and socle.....2,300.00

Wall Sconce, 22-1/4" h, green, 3 scrolled foliate arms, applied white classical relief to 2 oval and 2 circular medallions, no visible marks, c1860 ....3,750.00

Wine Cooler, 10-1/2" h, three color dip, Dice Ware, green ground, white swan handles, central band of relief depicting Roman Banquet, applied yellow quatrefoils, imp mark, 19th C, restoration to handle, lower body, and base 4,600.00

Majolica

Bird Feeder, 2-3/4" h, green glazed cylindrical form, pierced sides, imp mark, c1879 ....300.00

Biscuit Jar, cov, 6-1/2" h, marbleized enamel glazes, silver plated banding, handle, and cov, imp mark, c1878............................300.00

Cheese Dish, cov, 9-5/8" h, Bird and Fan, argenta ground, imp mark, slight stain to base, cov restored.................................375.00

Jug
  6-3/8" h, Bird and Fan, argenta ground, imp mark, c1878 .... 350.00
  7-1/2" h, Caterer, raised jeweling and banded motto relief, inscribed monogram under base for F. B. Rusel, imp mark, c1868 ... 375.00
  8-1/2" h, Caterer, raised jeweling and banded motto relief, imp mark, c1872, restored mouth chip 400.00
  10" h, tapering form, imp flower heads on drab body, silver plated rim and cov, imp mark, c1873..460.00
  10-3/4" h, tapered form, mottled brown, blue, and black glazes, silver plated banding, spout, hinged cover and handle, imp mark, c1880 ....460.00

Oyster Plate, 9" d, Sea Shells, basketweave body, set of 5, 2 yellow ground, 2 cobalt blue ground, 1 turquoise, imp mark, c1883 .....9,200.00

Plaque
  6" h, 12" l, rect, colored glaze, relief of Mercury and Zeus, spurious incised factory marks, mid or late 19th C, pr 400.00
  8" h, 12-5/8" l, rect, green glaze, Old Man, imp mark, c1860, rim chips 260.00

Salad Bowl
  7-3/4" d, relief foliate and floral festoons with ribbons, scrolled feet, silver plated rim, servers with shell molded handles, imp mark, c1870 ....400.00
  8-1/2" d, polychrome enamels, large oval panels of flowering branches, imp mark, one metal rim missing 360.00
  9-3/4" d, Bird and Fan, argenta ground, silver plated rim and foot, imp mark, c1880 ....230.00

Salt, open, 3-1/8" d, central cobalt blue banding framed in yellow beadwork, brown rim and foot, imp mark, c1867 ....110.00

Tile, 8" l, circular portrait of fox, oak leaf molded body, imp mark, c1875, framed 200.00

Pearlware

Foot Bath, 19-1/4" l, oval, blue transfer print of Tower of London scene, imp mark, early 19th C, hairlines to base.............................1,955.00

Plate, Water Nymph, blue on white, imp "Wedgwood Pearl," c1840-65, 9-1/2" d, $95.

Hand Basin, 12-3/8" d, gray marbleized dec, imp mark, c1878, glaze lines, wear to rim 230.00
Lazy Susan, 18-5/8" d, gilt and enamel dec, panels with insects and foliage, imp mark, c1863 .... 375.00
Tea Infuser, 13-1/4" h, gilt trim, polychrome dec transfer print foliate dec, scrolled handles, brass spigot, imp mark, Beanes Patent, c1863, inserts missing 320.00
Vase
   .5-1/8" h, slip dec, granular buff slip ground bordered in dark brown banded glaze, imp mark, early 19th C, covers missing, pr. 250.00
   8-1/2" h, porphyry dec, washed green glaze, applied white foliate relief, imp mark, late 18th C, cov missing, rim chip............ 350.00

Queen's Ware

Bouquetiere, brown and red slip dec, basketweave body, imp mark, late 18th C, cover missing, handle and rim chips restored....... 300.00
Dish
   13" l, oval shell shape, enamel dec cherubs, artist sgd "Emile Lesore," imp mark, c1860 .... 550.00
   13-1/4" l, oval boat form, bearded mask head handles, 2 circular cups, enamel dec fruiting grapevine dec, imp and printed marks, late 19th C 320.00
Plate
   8-7/8" d, shell shaped, enamel dec cherubs, artist sgd "Emile Lesore," imp mark, late 19th C 400.00
   9-1/4" d, enamel dec Aesop's Fable, titled on reverse "Don't put your nose in another's affairs," artist sgd "Emile Lessore," imp mark, c1863, enamel worn at rim 175.00
Vase, cov, 14-3/4" h, cream body, brown and blue flute and wreath banded borders, monogrammed "SL," imp mark, early 19th C, restored 525.00

Rosso Antico

Biggin, 5-3/4" h, molded arabesque floral dec, spaniel finial, imp mark, rim chip on insert strainer, c1840 .... 520.00
Font, 5-1/8" h, basalt, classical figure and foliate relief, imp mark, c1870 .... 230.00
Jardiniere, 6-1/2" h, basalt, banded relief of stylized motifs, engine-turned border, imp mark, early 19th C................................ 1,150.00

Jug, 5-3/4" h, basalt, pear shape, relief reeds and foliage, imp mark, early 19th C, star line in body.................................... 400.00
Lamp, oil, 4-7/8" h, enamel floral dec, imp mark, mid 19th C 520.00
Plate
   7" d, white stoneware, banded relief of hieroglyphs and stylized motifs, imp mark, early 19th C 690.00
   7-1/2" d, basalt, banded relief of hieroglyphs and stylized motifs, imp mark, early 19th C.. 400.00
Potpourri Jar, cov, insert, 14-3/4" h, allover enamel floral dec, pierced cover, imp mark, c1830, cov with rim chips......................... 3,335.00
Vase, 8-1/4" h, basalt, stylized Egyptian motifs, stiff leaves in relief, imp mark, early 19th C, cov missing, shallow chip under edge of plinth 490.00

Stoneware, white smear glaze

Crater Urn, pierced cover, 6-3/4" h, scrolled handles, applied blue fruiting grapevine and foliate dec, imp mark, c1830, insert cov missing ... 175.00
Hunt Jug, club form
   4-3/4" h, relief of Bacchanalian Boys, imp mark, c1840 .... 350.00
   5-7/8" h, applied blue fruiting grapevine banded border, imp mark, c1840, restored rim chip 230.00
Potpourri, cov, 3-1/2" h, applied green foliate dec, imp mark, c1830 550.00
Vase, 10-3/4" h, bearded male mask handles, applied blue lyre and wreath motifs, center foliate borders with acanthus leaves and palmettes, unmarked, c1830... 350.00

Terra Cotta

Bowl, cov, stand, 5-3/4" d, molded sunflower body, twig knop, imp marks, c1868, chips to cover, bowl rim, and footrim of stand .. 200.00

WELLER POTTERY

History: In 1872, Samuel A. Weller opened a small factory in Fultonham, near Zanesville, Ohio. There he produced utilitarian stoneware, such as milk pans and sewer tile. In 1882, he moved his facilities to Zanesville. Then in 1890, Weller built a new plant in the Putnam section of Zanesville along the tracks of the Cincinnati and Muskingum Railway. Additions followed in 1892 and 1894.

In 1894, Weller entered into an agreement with William A. Long to purchase the Lonhuda Faience Company, which had developed an art pottery line under the guidance of Laura A. Fry, formerly of Rookwood. Long left in 1895, but Weller continued to produce Lonhuda under the new name "Louwelsa." Replacing Long as art director was Charles Babcock Upjohn. He, along with Jacques Sicard, Frederick Hurten Rhead, and Gazo Fudji, developed Weller's art pottery lines.

At the end of World War I, many prestige lines were discontinued and Weller concentrated on commercial wares. Rudolph Lorber joined the staff and designed lines such as Roma, Forest, and Knifewood. In 1920, Weller purchased the plant of the Zanesville Art Pottery and claimed to produce more pottery than anyone else in the country.

Art pottery enjoyed a revival when the Hudson Line was introduced in the early 1920s. The 1930s saw Coppertone and Graystone Garden ware added. However, the Depression forced the closing of the Putnam plant and one on Marietta Street in Zanesville. After World War II inexpensive Japanese imports took over Weller's market. In 1947, Essex Wire Company of Detroit bought the controlling stock, but early in 1948 operations ceased.

References: Sharon and Bob Huxford, *Collectors Encyclopedia of Weller Pottery,* Collector Books, 1979, 1998 value update.

Collectors' Club: American Art Pottery Association, P.O. Box 834, Westport, MA 02790-0697, http://www.amartpot.org.

Museum: On-Line: http://www.weller.com.

Additional Listings: See *Warman's Americana & Collectibles* for more examples.

Basket, Florenzo, 5-1/2"	75.00
Bowl, Hudson dec	200.00
Candlesticks, pr, Glendale	165.00
Compote, Bonito, 4" h	65.00
Console Bowl, Sydonia, 17" x 6"	90.00
Cookie Jar, Mammy, bow on head, chip on back, 2 hairlines	1,100.00

Cornucopia
Lido, mauve	55.00
Wild Rose, peach and green	45.00
Ewer, Barcelona Ware, orig label	250.00
Flower Frog, Marvo, blue	55.00

Fountain Frog, 5-1/2" h, 6-1/2" w, Coppertone, bright green and brown glaze, hole in base and mouth for tube, mkd "12," glaze thinning at base 635.00
Jardiniere, Blue Ware	400.00

Mug, Dickensware, dolphin handle and band, sgraffito ducks 250.00
Pitcher, Louwelsa, 14" h, artist sgd, #750	600.00
Planter, Forest Tub, 4"	135.00

Umbrella Stand, 20-1/4" h, 10-3/4" d, Bedford Matt, emb stylized poppies, tulips, and daisies, dark green matte glaze, unmarked, bruise and sort firing line to rim, grinding, chips to base 750.00

Vase
Art Nouveau, 5"	160.00

Aurelian, 24-1/2" h, 13" d, oviform, flaring rim, four blossoming irises, high gloss glaze, sgd "L. J. Dibowski," base mkd "Weller, Aurelian No. 52," minor glaze nicks 1,955.00

Baldin, matte glaze, tan and green ground, red and yellow apples, c1917, 7-1/4" h 300.00
Eocean, sgd "Pillsbury"	725.00

Faience, Frederick Rhead
7-1/2" h, 6-1/2" d, oviform, white and green birds wearing hats on one foot, tobacco brown glaze, sgd "Rhead, Weller, Faience, V509" 1,840.00

9-1/2" h, 7" d, bulbous, incised standing rabbits playing trumpets, tobacco brown and yellow ground, high glaze, sgd "Rhead, Weller, Faience B489,7" 1,840.00

Forest, fan-shape, blue, tan, and green matte glaze, imp mark, c1920 ...... 200.00

Hudson
9-1/2" h, 4" d, white, blue, and green blooming iris, blue ground, sgd "Walch, Weller Pottery" 550.00

13" h, 4-1/4" d, tall cylinder, white floral blossoms, pink to blue ground, painted paper label, imp "Weller," sgd "Pillsbury" .. 690.00

Jap Birdimal, carved and painted by Frederick Rhead, row of stylized blue roses over white geese and trees, green ground, incised "Weller Faience/B-88," small wear glaze chips toward base 2,500.00
Lustre, 6" h, bud	40.00
Marbleized, 12" h	125.00

Sicard
4-1/2" h	550.00

5" h, 3" d, triangular form, foliate dec, irid glaze, sgd "Weller, Sicard" 490.00

7" h, 6" d, circular, foliate dec, rich irid glaze, imp "Weller" .. 2,415.00

8" h, 5" d, six rubbed sides tapering outward to base, green clover dec, irid glaze, mkd "27" 1,100.00

9" h, 4-1/4" d, cylinder, tapering outward to base, irid glaze, stylized peacock feathers, sgd "Weller, Sicard" 1,035.00
Solitone, 10" h, blue	160.00
Warwick, bud, 7" h	50.00

Woodcraft, 18" h, 7" d, owl and squirrel, green and brown tree trunk, imp "Weller" 750.00

Wall Pocket
Glendale, double bud, 203/15	425.00
Pearl, 8-1/2" l	150.00

WHALING

History: Whaling items are a specialized part of nautical collecting. Provenance is of prime importance since collectors want assurances that their pieces are from a whaling voyage. Since ship's equipment seldom carries the ship's identification, some individuals have falsely attributed a whaling provenance to general nautical items. Know the dealer, auction house, or collector from whom you buy.

Special tools, e.g., knives, harpoons, lances, and spades, do not overlap the general nautical line. Makers' marks and condition determine value for these items.

References: Nina Hellman and Norman Brouwer, *Mariner's Fancy,* South Street Seaport Museum, Balsam Press, and University of Washington Press, 1992; Martha Lawrence, *Scrimshaw,* Schiffer Publishing, 1993.

Museums: Cold Spring Harbor Whaling Museum, Cold Spring Harbor, NY; Kendall Whaling Museum, Sharon, MA; Mystic Seaport Museum, Mystic, CT; National Maritime Museum Library, San Francisco, CA; New Bedford Whaling Museum, New Bedford, MA; Pacific Whaling Museum, Waimanalo, HI; Sag Harbor Whaling & Historical Museum, Sag Harbor, NY; South Street Seaport Museum, New York, NY.

Additional Listings: Nautical Items; Scrimshaw.

Alphabet Game Set, whalebone and ivory, slide top box, 19th C, minor imperfections 195.00

Billet Head, 18-1/4" l, carved and painted wood, scrolling design, 19th C 920.00

Block, carved whalebone, 19th C, pr
2-1/2" l	575.00
3-1/4" l	1,095.00
Blubber Knife, 67" l, sheath, minor losses	550.00

Book
Andrews, Roy C., *Whale Hunting with Gun and Camera,* NY, 1925, 8vo, cloth 90.00

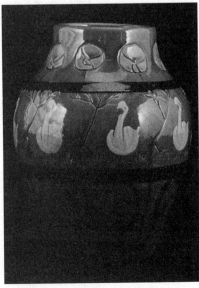

Vase, Jap Birdimal, carved and painted by Frederick Rhead, row of stylized blue roses over white geese and trees, green ground, incised "Weller Faience/B-88," small glaze chips toward base, 8-3/4" h, 6-1/2" d, $2,500. Photo courtesy of David Rago Auctions, Inc.

Stamp, whale ivory, tail entering ocean, mkd "_Marie 1837_," full whale stamp, 1-1/4" d, 1-3/4" h, $49.

Ashley, Clifford W., *The Yankee Whaler*, Boston, 1938, illus, gilt buckram, minor rubbing 125.00
Beale, Thomas, *The Natural History of the Sperm Whale*, London, 1838, 393 pgs, 3 plates, illus, 12 mo 690.00
Bennett, Frederick Debell, *Narrative of a Whaling Voyage round the Globe, from the Year 1833 to 1836*, London, 1840, folding map, 2 plates, 2 volumes, 8vo 1,620.00
Brown, John Ross, *Etchings of a Whaling Cruise, with Notes of a Sojourn on the Island of Zanzibar*, NY, 1846, plates and illus, 8vo 815.00
Stern, Edward, *Sketch of the Old New Bedford Whaling Bark "Stafford,"* Philadelphia, c1892, 30 pgs, 8vo, orig pictorial wrappers 420.00
Broadside
    255 x 175 mm, *Land of the West, Greenland Whale Fishery*, 12 stanza poem, London, second half 19th C 110.00
    490 x 580 mm, *List of Shipping Owned in the District of New Bedford, Jan 1, 1832, Employed in the Whale Fishery and Foreign Trade*, lists vessels, tonnage, managing owners, New Bedford, 1832 .... 575.00
Busk, 11-3/4" h, engraved whalebone, dec with sunburst, eagle and shield, fan, and other linear and geometric motifs, crack, 19th C ..435.00
Chart Square, 29-7/8", brass and wood, inscribed "MST," 19th C 200.00
Club, 11-7/8" l, whalebone, 19th C.. 950.00
Crimper, 9-1/4" l, whalebone, baleen and abalone inlay, 19th C, old repair to handle 980.00
Ditty Box, 5-7/8" l, whalebone, oval, single finger construction, 19th C.. 1,150.00
Doll bed, 10-3/8" h, 7-7/8" w, 10-5/8" d, whalebone, tall post, 19th C, very minor cracks 3,740.00
Domino Set, whalebone and baleen, sliding top box, 19th C, minor imperfections 190.00
Duster, 15-1/2" l, whalebone and carved wood, 19th C 415.00
Fid, 16" l, whalebone, 19th C, minor cracks.. 490.00
Figure, 16-3/8" l, carved baleen, whale, whalebone inlaid eye, 19th C, repair to tail 865.00
Game Board, 9-1/4" sq, whalebone and mahogany, 19th C, minor edge roughness 1,035.00
Harpoon
    39" l, double flue, inscribed "Alpha," 19th C, pitting, minor corrosion 290.00
    60" l, double-tined, cracks, loss to pole 285.00
    99-1/2" l, toggle, mounted on pole, 19th C 1,265.00
Horn Book, 3-7/8" l, whalebone, miniature.. 175.00
Ladle, 14" l, whalebone, coconut, and copper, 19th C................. 345.00
Lance, 103-1/2" l, minor corrosion 600.00

Lantern, 10-1/2" h, whalebone, pierced arched copper top, pierced base, ball feet, 19th C, replaced glass, minor loss............... 1,380.00
Marking Gauge, 9-1/8" l, whalebone, 19th C 1,035.00
Miniature, stool, 4-3/4" h, engraved whalebone, compass star and heart motif, top with lightly inscribed names, dates, and initials, baleen inlaid exotic wood, turned legs, 19th C, repair 1,150.00
Pan Bone, 2-1/4" x 3-1/4", double sided engravings of three-masted ships under sail, 19th C, crack, gouges 375.00
Parceling Tool, 5-7/8" l, whale ivory, crossbanded design, engraved "N. D. 1829," repair 175.00
Photographs, group of 8 silver prints, various sizes, taken aboard whaling ship *Thetis* during journey to Alaska, 3 images of Esquimaux aboard ship, another of crew, Captain Lovell Emory, several views from boat, each titled on back, c1885 .... 1,495.00
Pickwick, 3-3/4" h, whale ivory, green and red sealing wax inlaid scribe line dec, 19th C, minute chip to finial 1,495.00
Picture Frame, 6-1/4" h, 4" w, whalebone, pierce carved bird, star, and heart motif, 19th C, minute chip 4,600.00
Print, Sperm Whaling with its Varieties, John H. Bufford, 1870, identified within matrix, chromolithograph on paper, 18-3/4" x 34-1/2" sheet size, framed 1,725.00
Rattle and Whistle, 5-3/4" l, whalebone and whale ivory, 19th C, minor cracks.. 575.00
Rubber, whalebone, 19th C.. 425.00
Scribe, 8" l, whalebone, 19th C.. 1,150.00
Sewing Carrier, 6-7/8" h, 7" l, reticulated whalebone and pine, 19th C, repair, minor cracks.. 1,150.00
Ship Log Book, 13-1/2" h, 8-1/2" w, Bark *Mercury*, New Bedford, outlining trip to North Pacific, entries from Dec 1876 to May 1878, staining, toning 2,415.00
Spool Stand, 3 tiers, ftd, 19th C
    6-3/8" h, whale ivory and exotic wood, cup finial above 3 graduated circular tiers, 5 bun feet, 19th C, minor cracks 575.00
    7-1/8" h, whalebone, ivory, and wood, doughnut shaped ivory thimble holder above 3 graduated scalloped tiers, sealing wax inlaid scribe lines, tripod base, traces of blue pigment, missing 3 spool holders, very minor losses, minor cracks........................... 750.00
Swift, 19th C
    18-3/4" h, 18-3/4" d expanded, whale bone, expanding frame, dec with silk ribbon bows on circular wooden stand, heart-shaped mother-of-pearl inlay, fitted 22-1/2" h pine case 2,645.00
    22-5/8"l, whalebone and ivory, red and black sealing wax inlaid scribe lines, cup finial, barrel form clasp, cracks, minor losses 920.00
    23" l, whalebone, ivory, and wood, ball final, clamp carved with crosshatched diamond motif, minor losses, old repair........ 460.00
Try-Square, 9-3/8" l, whalebone, 19th C, very minor crack 290.00
Watch Hutch
    7-1/2" h, 5" w, 3-3/4" d, hanging, whalebone, arched crest pierce carved with star and crescent motifs, backed with painted cloth, 19th C, minor cracks, minute losses................................. 8,625.00
    9-1/8" h, whalebone and cherry, scrolled crest above ring turned posts, kidney shaped base, scribed bun feet, 19th C, minor cracks 690.00
    13-3/4" h, tall case clock form, baleen and ivory inlaid walnut, star and heart motif, 19th C, very minor losses 4,025.00
Whip, 24-1/4" l, whalebone handle, 19th C, losses to leather 175.00
Yardstick, 35-7/8" l, whalebone, 19th C 490.00

WHIELDON

History: Thomas Whieldon, a Staffordshire potter, established his shop in 1740. He is best known for his mottled ware, molded in the shapes of vegetables, fruits, and leaves. Josiah Spode and Josiah Wedgwood, in different capacities, had connections with Whieldon.

Whieldon ware is a generic term. His wares were never marked, and other potters made similar items. Whieldon ware is agate-tortoiseshell earthenware, in limited shades of green, brown, blue and yellow. Most pieces are utilitarian items, e.g., dinnerware and plates, but figurines and other decorative pieces also were made.

Coffeepot, cov, 7-1/2" h, molded spout and strap handle, brown tortoise shell glaze, blue and green, mismatched lid, old professional repair 475.00
Creamer, 4-1/4" h, Cauliflower, molded design, green and clear glaze, applied handle, old yellowed repair on spout, wear, stains, minor edge damage 385.00
Dish, 5-1/2" l, leaf shape, gray and brown mottling, splashes of green and yellow on white, three small feet, c1770 .... 425.00
Pitcher, 4-3/4" h 350.00
Plate
   9" d, shaped, late 18th C, hairlines, pr. 290.00
   9-1/4" d, majolica, rim nick. 165.00
   9-1/2" d, rim nick, hairline 140.00
   9-5/8" d, green, blue, and brown, black tortoiseshell glaze, emb rim 250.00
   9-3/4" d, mottled, rim nick 250.00
Platter, 10-3/8" l, blue and green, brown tortoiseshell glaze, emb rim 315.00
Sugar, cov, 4-3/8" d, 3-5/8" h, cauliflower, molded design, green and clear glaze, wear, stains, edge chips 3,245.00
Tea Caddy, 4-1/4" h, Cauliflower, molded design, green and clear glaze, lid missing, wear, light stains 550.00
Teapot, cov, 3-3/4" h, creamware body, Cauliflower, cream glazed florets, green glazed leaves, 18th C, restorations 475.00

WHIMSIES, GLASS

History: During lunch or after completing their regular work schedule, glassworkers occasionally spent time creating unusual glass objects known as whimsies, e.g. candy-striped canes, darners, hats, paperweights, pipes, and witch balls. Whimsies were taken home and given as gifts to family and friends.

Because of their uniqueness and infinite variety, whimsies can rarely be attributed to a specific glass house or glassworker. Whimsies were created wherever glass was made, from New Jersey to Ohio and westward. Some have suggested that style and color can be used to pinpoint region or factory, but no one has yet developed an identification key that is adequate.

Glass canes are among the most collectible types of whimsies. These range in length from very short (under one foot) to ten feet or more. They come in both hollow and solid form. Hollow canes can have a bulb-type handle or the rarer C- or L-shaped handle. Canes are found in many fascinating colors, with the candy striped being a regular favorite with collectors. Many canes are also filled with various colored powders, gold and white being the most common and silver being harder to find. Sometimes they were even used as candy containers.

References: Gary Baker et al., *Wheeling Glass 1829-1939,* Oglebay Institute, 1994, distributed by Antique Publications; Joyce E. Blake, *Glasshouse Whimsies,* published by author, 1984; Joyce E. Blake and Dale Murschell, *Glasshouse Whimsies: An Enhanced Reference,* published by authors, 1989; Wayne Muller, *Darn It,* published by author (P.O. Box 903, Pacific Palisades, CA 90272.)

Collectors' Club: Whimsey Club, 2 Hessler Court, Dansville, NY 14437.

Top: rolling pin, cobalt blue, worn gilded transfer design of ships, verse, and "Love & Live Happy," 27-1/2" l, $175; bottom: baton, clear blown, knob top, white, red, blue, and yellow swirls, 64" l, $200. Photo courtesy of Garth's Auctions.

Baton, blown glass
   9-3/4" l, green, twisted shank, applied knob 85.00
   41" l, opalescent blue, twisted ribs, rough end 85.00
   55-1/2" l, clear, blue and yellow spirals, stain, rough tip 150.00
   64" l, clear, swirls of white, red, blue, and yellow, knob top ... 200.00
Bellows Bottle, 16-1/2" h, ftd, colorless neck threading, colorless quilled rigaree on each corner, cranberry body, colorless applied standard and foot, pontil scar 125.00
Bird Fountain, 5-1/4" h, colorless, blown, cobalt blue finial 95.00
Buttonhook, 6-3/4" l, colorless, blown, applied flowers and other color dec 65.00
Cane, blown glass
   27-1/2" l, aqua, twisted detail, tip chipped 90.00
   30" l, amber, twisted detail, clear casing, ground end 65.00
   34" l, aqua, twisted detail, tip chipped 95.00
   38" l, aqua, twisted detail, knob handle, some damage 120.00
   42" l, clear, applied salmon and white, twisted handle and tip, tip chipped 145.00
Hat, blown three-mold
   2" h, cobalt blue, folded rim, McKearin GII-18 .... 600.00
   2-3/4" h, colorless, 15 ribs, applied cobalt blue rim 225.00
Rolling Pin
   12" l, ruby, white looping 385.00
   16-1/4" l, clear, cranberry and white looping 330.00
   27-1/2" h, cobalt blue, worn gilded transfer designs of ships, verse and "Love & Live Happy" 175.00
Walking Stick, blown glass
   35-3/4" l, pale aqua, silver painted int., bulbous end, tip chipped 95.00
   36" l, pale aqua, blue, yellow, red, and white stripes, bulbous end, tip chipped 90.00
   39" l, clear, twisted detail, knob handle, some damage 85.00
Witch Ball
   4-3/4" d, amber 95.00
   5-1/2" d, colorless, blown, white loopings 165.00

WHISKEY BOTTLES, EARLY

History: The earliest American whiskey bottles were generic in shape and were blown by pioneer glass makers in the 18th century. The Biningers (1820-1880s) were the first bottles specifically designed for whiskey. After the 1860s, distillers favored the cylindrical "fifth" design.

The first embossed brand-name bottle was the amber E. G. Booz Old Cabin Whiskey bottle which was issued in 1860. Many stories have been told about this classic bottle; unfortunately, most are not true. Research has proven that "booze" was a corruption of the words "bouse" and "boosy" from the 16th and 17th centuries. It was only a coincidence that the Philadelphia distributor also was named "Booz." This bottle has been reproduced extensively.

Prohibition (1920-1933) brought the legal whiskey industry to a standstill. Whiskey was marked "medicinal purposes only" and distributed by private distillers in unmarked or paper-labeled bottles.

The size and shape of whiskey bottles are standard. Colors are limited to amber, amethyst, clear, green, and cobalt blue (rare). Corks were the common closure in the early period, with the inside screw top being used between 1880 and 1910.

Bottles made prior to 1880 are the most desirable. When purchasing a bottle with a label, condition of that label is a critical factor. In the 1950s distillers began to issue collectors' special-edition bottles to help increase sales.

References: Ralph & Terry Kovel, *Kovels' Bottles Price List,* 11th ed., Three Rivers Press, 1998; John Odell, *Digger Odell's Official Antique Bottle and Glass Collector Magazine Price Guide Series,* Vol. 8, published by author (1910 Shawhan Rd, Morrow, OH 45152), 1995 Carlo and Dorothy Sellari, *Standard Old Bottle Price Guide,* Collector Books, 1989.

Periodicals: *Antique Bottle and Glass Collector,* P.O. Box 187, East Greenville, PA 18041; *Bottles & Extras,* P.O. Box 154, Happy Camp, CA 96039.

Museum: The Seagram Museum, Waterloo, Ontario, Canada.

Additional Listings: See *Warman's Americana & Collectibles* for a listing of Collectors' Special Edition Whiskey Bottles.

Argonaut, E. Martin & Co., amber, 11" h 35.00
Bininger's Regular, 19 Broad St., New York, 1840-50, clock shape, deep gold amber, applied double collared mouth, pontil scar, 5-7/8" h ..300.00
Bininger's Travelers Guide, A. M. Bininger & Co., No. 19 Broad St., NY, 1860-80, teardrop form, golden amber, applied double collared mouth, smooth base, 6-3/4" h 200.00
Black Cat, colorless, cut and polished fluted panels, orange enameled lettering, black and white enameled cat, tooled mouth with ring, ground pontil scar..275.00
Booz, E. G., Old Cabin Whiskey, qt, golden amber 300.00
Caspers Whiskey, Made by Honest North Carolina People, 1870-90, cylindrical, paneled shoulder, cobalt blue, tooled sloping collared mouth with ring, smooth base, 11-3/4" h 325.00
Chestnut Grove Whiskey, 1840-60, flattened chestnut form, applied handle, golden amber, applied mouth with ring, pontil scar, 9" h 110.00
Freeblown Jug, applied handle, America, 1840-60
  6-1/8" h, pear form, red amber, applied sloping collared mouth, pontil scar 220.00
  8" h, cylindrical corseted form, golden amber, applied double collared mouth, pontil scar 350.00
  8" h, flattened chestnut, golden amber, applied mouth with ring, pontil scar, 8" h 475.00
Griffith Hyatt & Co., Baltimore, 1840-80, globular, flattened label panels, applied handle, golden amber with olive tone, applied sq collared mouth, pontil scar, 7" h..375.00
H. Pharazyn/Phila/Right Secured, 1860-80, Indian Warrior form, brilliant light yellow amber, inward rolled mouth, smooth base, 12-1/2" h, incomplete mouth with roughness, some minor int. residue 800.00
Lancaster Glassworks, Lancaster, NY, 1860-80, barrel, puce amber, applied double collared mouth, smooth base, 9-5/8" h 180.00
Manhattan Club Pure Rye Whiskey, qt, amber 40.00
Old Continental Whiskey, yellow amber, 9-1/4" h 650.00
Richards, C. A., & Co., 99 Washington St, Boston, Mass, 1860-80, sq with beveled corners, yellow green, applied sloping collared mouth, smooth base, 9-1/2" h, 3/8" potstone 550.00
Ridgeway Straight Corn Whiskey, miniature, stoneware 50.00
Turner Brothers, barrel shape, yellow-amber, 9-7/8" h 120.00

Weeks Glass Works, Stoddard, NH, 1860-70, emb base, cylindrical, yellow amber with olive tone, applied sloping collared mouth with ring, smooth base, 11-1/2" h, retains cork and some int. residue..........200.00

WHITE-PATTERNED IRONSTONE

History: White-patterned ironstone is a heavy earthenware, first patented under the name "Patent Ironstone China" in 1813 by Charles Mason, Staffordshire, England. Other English potters soon began copying this opaque, feldspathic, white china.

All-white ironstone dishes first became available in the American market in the early 1840s. The first patterns had simple Gothic lines similar to the shapes used in transfer wares. Pattern shapes, such as New York, Union, and Atlantic, were designed to appeal to the American housewife. Motifs, such as wheat, corn, oats, and poppies, were embossed on the pieces as the American prairie influenced design. Eventually, more than 200 shapes and patterns, with variations on finials and handles, were made.

White-patterned ironstone is identified by shape names and pattern names. Many potters only identified the shape in their catalogs. Pattern names usually refer to the decorative motif.

References: Annise Doring Heaivilin, *Grandma's Tea Leaf Ironstone,* Updated Price Guide, L-W Book Sales, 1996; Dawn Stolzfus & Jeffrey B. Snyder, *White Ironstone, A Survey of its Many Forms, Undecorated, Flow Blue, Mulberry, Copper Lustre,* Schiffer Publishing, 1997; Jean Wetherbee, *White Ironstone,* Antique Trader Books, 1996.

Collectors' Clubs: Mason's Ironstone Collectors' Club, 2011 East Main St., Medford, OH 97504; White Ironstone China Association, RD #1, Box 23, Howes Cave, NY 12092.

Butter Dish, cov, Athens, Podmore Walker, c1857 ....85.00
Cake Plate, 9" d, Brocade, Mason, handled 140.00
Chamber Pot, cov, emb Fleur-De-Lis & Daisy o handle, 1883-1913, mkd "Johnson Bros." 135.00
Coffeepot, cov, Wheat and Blackberry, Clementson
Bros..120.00
Creamer
  Fig, Davenport..65.00

Left: covered vegetable dish, fig finial, center: wash pitcher and basin, Wheat and Clover pattern; right: coffeepot, Wheat and Clover pattern, $275.

Wheat in the Meadow, Powell & Bishop, 1870 .... 45.00

Cup and Saucer
   Acorn and Tiny Oak, Parkhurst...35.00
   Grape and Medallion, Challinor 40.00

Ewer, Scalloped Decagon, Wedgwood 150.00

Gravy Boat
   Bordered Fuchsia, Anthony Shaw 45.00
   Wheat & Blackberry, Meakin 35.00

Nappy, Prairie Flowers, Livesley & Powell..............................20.00

Pancake Server, octagonal, Botte, 1851...............................40.00

Pitcher
   Berlin Swirl, Mayer & Elliot 120.00
   Japan, Mason, c1915 ....275.00
   Syndenhaum, T. & R. Boote 195.00
   Wheat, W. E. Corn 85.00

Plate
   Ceres, Elsmore & Forster, 8-1/2" d.......................................15.00
   Corn, Davenport, 10-1/2" d..20.00
   Fluted Pearl, Wedgwood, 9-1/2" d..15.00
   Gothic, Adams, 9-1/2' d..20.00
   Prairie, Clemenston, Hanley, 6-5/8" d....................................12.00
   Wheat and Clover, Turner & Tomkinson..................................18.00

Platter
   Columbia, 20" x 15"..125.00
   Wheat, Meakin, 20-3/4" x 15-3/4"..75.00

Punch Bowl, Berry Cluster, J. Furnival...................................175.00

Relish
   Ceres, Elsmore & Forster, 1960 ....40.00
   Wheat, W. E. corn 30.00

Sauce Tureen, cov
   Columbia, underplate, Joseph Goodwin, 1855.....................115.00
   Prize Bloom, T.J. & J. Mayer, Dale Hall Pottery....................220.00
   Wheat & Blackberry, Clementson Bros. 175.00

Soap Dish, Bordered Hyacinth, cov, insert, W. Baker & Co., 1860s.150.00

Soup Plate, Fig, Davenport, 9-1/2" d 25.00

Sugar Bowl, cov
   Hyacinth, Wedgwood...45.00
   Fuchsia, Meakin 40.00

Teapot, cov, Ivy, Wm. Adams, 10" h...85.00

Toothbrush Holder
   Bell Flower, Burgess..50.00
   Cable and Ring, Cockson & Seddon 40.00

Wash Bowl and Pitcher, 12" h pitcher, 15" d, bowl, Alfred Meakin ...200.00

Vegetable, cov
   Blackberry..50.00
   Prairie Flowers, Livesley & Powell..85.00

WILLOW PATTERN CHINA

History: Josiah Spode developed the first "traditional" willow pattern in 1810. The components, all motifs taken from Chinese export china, are a willow tree, "apple" tree, two pagodas, fence, two birds, and three figures crossing a bridge. The legend, in its many versions, is an English invention based on this scenic design.

By 1830, there were more than 200 makers of willow pattern china in England. The pattern has remained in continuous production. Some of the English firms that still produce it are Burleigh, Johnson Bros. (Wedgwood Group), Royal Doulton (continuing production of the Booths' pattern), and Wedgwood.

By the end of the 19th century, production of this pattern spread to France, Germany, Holland, Ireland, Sweden, and the United States. Buffalo Pottery made the first willow pattern in the United States beginning in 1902. Many other companies followed, developing willow variants using rubber-stamp simplified patterns as well as overglaze decals. The largest American manufacturers of the traditional willow pattern were Royal China and Homer Laughlin, usually preferred because it is dated. Shenango pieces are the most desirable among restaurant-quality wares.

Japan began producing large quantities of willow pattern china in the early 20th century. Noritake began about 1902. Most Japanese pieces are porous earthenware with a dark blue pattern using the traditional willow design, usually with no inner border. Noritake did put the pattern on china bodies. Unusual forms include salt and pepper shakers, one-quarter pound butter dishes, and canisters. The most desirable Japanese willow is the fine quality NKT Co. ironstone with a copy of the old Booths pattern. Recent Japanese willow is a paler shade of blue on a porcelain body.

The most common dinnerware color is blue. However, pieces can also be found in black (with clear glaze or mustard-colored glaze by Royal Doulton), brown, green, mulberry, pink (red), and polychrome.

The popularity of the willow design has resulted in a large variety of willow-decorated products: candles, fabric, glass, graniteware, linens, needlepoint, plastic, tinware, stationery, watches, and wall coverings. All this material has collectible value.

Marks: Early pieces of Noritake have a Nippon "Royal Sometuke" mark. "Occupied Japan" may add a small percentage to the value of common table wares. Pieces marked "Maruta" or "Moriyama" are especially valued.

References: Leslie Bockol, *Willow Ware: Ceramics in the Chinese Tradition,* Schiffer Publishing, 1995; Robert Copeland, Spode's *Willow Pattern and Other Designs after the Chinese,* Studio Vista, 1980, 1990 reprint; Mary Frank Gaston, *Blue Willow,* 2nd ed., Collector Books, 1990, 1998 value update.

Periodicals: *American Willow Report,* P.O. Box 900, Oakridge, OR 97463; *The Willow Transfer Quarterly, Willow Word,* P.O. Box 13382, Arlington, TX 76094.

Collectors' Clubs: International Willow Collectors, P.O. Box 13382, Arlington, TX 76094-0382; Willow Society, 39 Medhurst Rd, Toronto Ontario M4B 1B2 Canada.

Reproduction Alert: The Scio Pottery, Scio, Ohio, currently manufactures a willow pattern set sold in variety stores. The pieces have no marks or backstamps, and the transfer is of poor quality. The plates are flatter in shape than those of other manufacturers.

Note: Although colors other than blue are hard to find, there is less demand; thus, prices may not necessarily be higher priced.

Berry Bowl, small
   Blue, Homer Laughlin Co 6.50
   Pink, mkd "Japan"...5.00

Bowl, 9" d, Mason...45.00

Cake Plate, tab handles, Royal China Co................................20.00

Charger, 13" d 35.00

Chop Plate, Royal China Co...20.00

Creamer and Sugar, Royal China Co. 20.00

Cup and Saucer
   Booths 30.00
   Buffalo Pottery 25.00

Child's Teapot, mkd "Made in Japan," $38.

Homer Laughlin	10.00
Japanese, decal inside cup, pink	25.00
Shenango	15.00
Gravy Boat, orig ladle, Royal China Co.	25.00
Pie Plate, 10" d	50.00

Plate, dinner

Allerton, 10" d	25.00
Buffalo Pottery, 9" d	20.00
Johnson Bros., 10" d	15.00
Royal China Co., 9" d	8.00
Platter, 12" l, Homer Laughlin	25.00
Soup Bowl, Royal China Co.	7.50
Sugar, cov, Allerton	65.00
Tea Cup and Saucer, scalloped, Allerton	45.00
Vegetable, Royal China Co., 9" d	20.00

WOODENWARE

History: Many utilitarian household objects and farm implements were made of wood. Although they were subjected to heavy use, these implements were made of the strongest woods and were well cared for by their owners.

References: Arene Burgess, *19th Century Wooden Boxes*, Schiffer Publishing, 1997; Jonathon Levi and Robert Young, *Treen for the Table,* John Campbell, *Fire & Light in the Home Pre 1820,* Antique Collectors' Club, 1999; George C. Neumann, *Early American Antique Country Furnishing,* L-W Book Sales, 1984, 1993 reprint.

Additional Listings: See *Warman's Americana & Collectibles* for more examples.

Note: This category serves as a catchall for wooden objects which do not fit into other categories.

Apple Box, 3-3/8" h, orig red and yellow paint	65.00
Bag Shorter, 16" h, poplar, orig varnish, black stenciled detail, rd trim, some damage and repair	550.00
Basket, 15" l, made from natural growth of burl, natural holes and cracks, four part handle	315.00

Bowl, burl

9" d,. 3-3/4" h, dark finish, rubbed down to mottled shine	330.00
12" x 14-1/2", 3-3/4" h, ash, scrubbed finish, edge and surface damage	825.00
13-1/2" d, 11-1/2" h, ash, old worn patina, protruding rim handles, minor rim damage	935.00

Food Masher, turned maple, early 20th C, $30.

Box

7-1/2" l, pine, old orange paint, brown, green, yellow, white, and blue rose mulling, domed lid, interior till	865.00
9" d, round, old blue paint, tape label "Rolled Oats," lapped seams, rusted steel tacks, minor edge damage	310.00
9" d, round, old blue paint, yellowed varnish, lapped seams with steel tacks	315.00
Bucket, 9-1/4" d, 12" h, staved and hooped construction, swing handle, attached by wooden pegs, painted red, wear, early 19th C	2,185.00

Tape Loom, walnut, cut-out decorative handle, $380.

Candle Box, 10-1/4" w, 4-1/2" d, 4-1/2" h, hanging, poplar, old worn bluish-green paint, scalloped crest, slant top lid with staple hinges, repaired splint in back board 200.00

Checkerboard

18-3/4" h, 26-3/4" w, pine, old red paint with black squares, applied gallery, edge damage 440.00

19" h, 27-1/2" w, poplar, old dark red and black paint with stars, applied gallery edge, wear 550.00

Churn, stave construction

22" h plus handle and dasher, old brown finish, wear and damage 150.00

24" h plus handle and dasher, worn old red paint, old repair to split lid 525.00

Compote, 12-1/2" d, 9" h, turned mahogany, old worn finish 275.00

Cup, 4-3/4" h, burl, decorative patches, some damage 200.00

Embroidery Stamp, 7-1/2" l, maple and copper, spread wing eagle with center shield, copper stripes set into wooden block, sgd "J. Preston Maker 193 Gorham St. Lowell, Mass," minor age splits........... 230.00

Figure

13" l, carved and painted, articulated Hessian soldier, wooden peg construction, black painted beard, arm and hand loss, age splits .. 175.00

13-1/4" h, articulated, pine, old patina, glass eyes 165.00

14-3/4" h, carved and painted, Indian maid, black hair, khaki colored costume with red trim, red necklace and beadband, black shoes, repairs to shoes, some loss to skirt fringe 980.00

26" l, 28" h, carved and painted, reindeer, pieced construction, stick legs 460.00

Game Board, paint dec

17-1/4" x 16-1/4", yellow and black, green ground, wear, America, late 19th C 2,185.00

20-1/2" x 21", pink, light blue, and orange on creamy white ground, outlined in black, cracks, minor paint wear, America, early 20th C 920.00

Game Box, 11-3/4" l, 9-1/2" w, 2-1/4" h, carved oak, rect, top profusely carved with flowers and leaves, conforming carved sides, hinged top, fitted int., mother-of-pearl chips, playing cards, small bun feet, Continental, late 19th C 250.00

Glove Box, 13" l, Turnbridge, marquetry inlaid, peasant dancers at beach, English 100.00

Humidor, 15-1/2" w, 9" d, 8-3/4" h, figured olive wood veneer on mahogany, metal lining, carved monogram in lid, edge and veneer damage, signs of added legs 225.00

Ladle, 6-1/2" l, treen, crooked handle, carving, chip in edge of bowl, patina 100.00

Lazy Susan, walnut, molded circular top, turned pedestal base, English, 19th C.. 1,150.00

Magazine Rack, hanging, oak, rose dec backing, c1890............. 75.00

Mask, winged cherub, carved, gessoed, and polychrome paint, gilt highlights, later giltwood 8-1/2" sq frames, pr 75.00

Mortar and Pestle, 12" d, 17" h, carved wood, tree trunk form, loss to base, age splits 275.00

Paddle

8-1/2" l, primitive, maple, burl bowl.. 165.00

9" l, ash, scrubbed finish, wear.. 375.00

Sugar Bucket, stave construction, lid

11-3/4" d, 11-1/2" h, old red paint, copper tacks, minor edge damage 500.00

12" d, 12" h, old blue repaint, branded "Ephram Murdock" 750.00

12" h, old light green paint.. 200.00

12" h, old refinishing, some damage 140.00

Tub, 10-3/4" d, 6" h, treen, poplar, worn orig red and yellow sponging, wear and deep age cracks in bottom 250.00

Wall Shelf

20" w, 9" d, 29" h, painted pine, ogee molded edge on shelf, extended backboard with box compartment, brown paint, wear, some wood loss, age cracks 400.00

28-1/2" w, 9-1/4" d, 30" h, grain painted, shaped sides joining 3 graduated shelves, 2 vertical back supports, old brown grain painted surface, New England, mid 19th C 1,035.00

Writing Box, 20" w, 10-1/4" d, 9" h, pine, old worn olive brown graining over red, dovetailed case and fitted int. with 4 pigeon holes and 2 drawers, orig brass bales, hinges and lock are replaced, age crack in lid, edge damage.. 275.00

WORLD'S FAIRS and EXPOSITIONS

History: The Great Exhibition of 1851 in London marked the beginning of the World's Fair and Exposition movement. The fairs generally featured exhibitions from nations around the world displaying the best of their industrial and scientific achievements.

Many important technological advances have been introduced at world's fairs, including the airplane, telephone, and electric lights. Ice cream cones, hot dogs, and iced tea were first sold by vendors at fairs. Art movements often were closely connected to fairs, with the Paris Exhibition of 1900 generally considered to have assembled the best of the works of the Art Nouveau artists.

References: *Crystal Palace Exhibition Illustrated Catalogue* (London, 1851), Dover Publications, n.d.; Robert L. Hendershott, *1904 St. Louis World's Fair Mementos and Memorabilia,* Kurt R. Krueger Publishing (160 N. Washington, Iola, WI 54945), 1994; Joyce Grant, *NY World's Fair Collectibles: 1964-1965,* Schiffer Publishing, 1999; Frederick and Mary Megson, *American Exposition Postcards,* The Postcard Lovers, 1992; Howard M. Rossen, *World's Fair Collectibles: Chicago,* 1933 and New York 1939, Schiffer Publishing, 1998.

Collectors' Clubs: 1904 World's Fair Society, 12934 Windy Hill Drive, St. Louis, MO 63128, http://www.inlink.com/~terryl; World's Fair Collectors' Society, Inc., P.O. Box 20806, Sarasota, FL 34276.

Museums: Buffalo & Erie County Historical Society, Buffalo, NY; California State University, Madden Library, Fresno, CA; 1893 Chicago World's Fair Columbian Exposition Museum, Columbus, WI; Museum of Science & Industry, Chicago, IL; Presidio Army Museum, San Francisco, CA; The Queens Museum, Flushing, NY.

Crystal Palace, 1851-53

Dollar, 1-3/4" d, seated Liberty and Crystal Palace 75.00

Pipe, white clay, 6" l, Crystal Palace on bowl............................. 100.00

Pot Lid, Pratt, 5" d.. 200.00

Print, Currier & Ives, Crystal Palace 400.00

Centennial, 1876

Bank, still, cast iron, Independence Hall, 9" h x 7" w 350.00

Glass Slipper, Gillinder

Clear... 35.00

Frosted 40.00

Medal, wooden, Main Building, 3" d.. 60.00

Scarf, 19 x 34", Memorial Hall, Art Gallery colorful 100.00

Columbian Exposition, 1893

Clock, shaped like sailing ship, cast iron, bronzed 225.00

Guide Book, Official 45.00

Pamphlet, illus.. 12.50

Plate, Wedgwood, dark blue and white, Administration Building in middle 45.00

Sheet Music, *World's Columbian Expo March*............................. 75.00

Watch Case Opener, Keystone Watch Case Co........................... 15.00

Trans-Mississippi, 1898, change purse, leather and MOP......... 45.00

Pan American, 1901
Cigar Case, hinged aluminum 2-1/2" x 5-1/2"...............................35.00
Frying Pan, pictures North and South America, 6" long..............75.00
Plate, frosted glass, 3 cats painted on dec, 7-1/2" d....................35.00

St. Louis, 1904
Medal, silvered brass, 2-3/4" d...60.00
Stamp holder, aluminum, 1-1/8" x 1-3/8" 35.00
Ticket...22.00
Tumbler 4" high, copper plated base, metal, Louisiana Purchase Monument, Cascades, Union Station and Liberal Arts Bldg 35.00
Alaska-Yukon, 1909, fob, 3 pc, State Building, Totem Pole, Fair Logo in Center, 4" l..75.00

Panama-Pacific, 1915
Pocket Watch, official, silver plated, 2" d 300.00
Post Card 5.00

Century of Progress, 1937
Playing Cards, full deck, views of the fair, all different, black and white 45.00

Poker Chip, red, white, or blue, 1-1/2" d 15.00
Ring , silver plated, blue and white, comet and star, adjustable ... 20.00
Tray, metal, 17" x 12", Ford Pavilion, brown 55.00

Great Lakes, 1936, pin back, Florida, with state flag on the face, 1-1/2" d...18.00

Texas Centennial, 1936, playing cards, colorful with Texas state flag on back, boxed 40.00

Golden Gate, 1939
Bookmark, typical view, 4" l 20.00
Match Book, orig matches, pictures Pacifica 10.00
Token, Sun Tower and Bridge, 1-1/8" d 15.00

New York, 1939
Candy Tin, miniature, Bagatele, very colorful, 4-1/4" x 6-1/2".......65.00
Cigarette Holder, Lenox, pink, yellow, blue, green, white, 2-1/2" h ..350.00
Pin, red enameled, from Russian Pavilion.................................150.00
Pipe, 5-1/2" l 125.00
Post Card, photo type 6.00

YARD-LONG PRINTS

History: In the early 1900s, many yard-long prints could be had for a few cents postage and a given number of wrappers or box tops. Others were premiums for renewing a subscription to a magazine or newspaper. A large number were advertising items created for a store or company and had calendars on the front or back. Many people believe that the only true yard-long print is 36 inches long and titled "A Yard of Kittens," etc. But lately collectors feel that any long and narrow print, horizontal or vertical, can be included in this category. It is a matter of personal opinion.

Values are listed for full-length prints in near-mint condition, nicely framed, and with original glass.

References: C. G. and J. M. Rhoden and W. D. and M. J. Keagy, *Those Wonderful Yard-Long Prints and More*, Book 1 (1989), Book 2 (1992), Book 3 (1995), published by authors (605 No. Main, Georgetown, IL 61846).

Reproduction Alert: Some prints are being reproduced. Know your dealer.

Advisors: Charles G. and Joan M. Rhoden, W. D. and M. J. Keagy.

Note: Numbers in parentheses below indicate the Rhoden and Keagy book number and page on which the item is illustrated, e.g. (3-52) refers to Book 3, page 52.

Animals

A Yard of Kittens, sgd Guy Bedford (BK 1-50) 450.00
Piggies in Clover, by The Art Interchange Co., New York, copyright 1904, (BK 3-25) 800.00
Yard of Chickens, sgd C. L. VanVredenburgh, by J. Onmann Lith. Co., N.Y., copyright 1905 (BK 2-19) 400.00
Yard of Puppies by Guy Bedford, Chicago (BK 2-26) 375.00

Calendar

1910 American Beauty Souvenir Clay, Robinson & Co., calendar and advertising at bottom, also advertising on back (BK 3-44) 550.00
1911 Pompeian Beauty by Forbes, calendar and advertising on back (BK 2-78) 450.00
1917 dark haired lady with left hand entwined in the pearls around her neck and pink roses at her waist, calendar on back (BK 2-90) 400.00
1918 Selz Good Shoes, copyright Selz, Schwab & Co., lady in black dress, long stem pink rose in right hand (BK 2-83) 500.00
1921 Fairbanks and Morse Quality 100% on logo at left, lady in sleeveless dark blue dress, light yellow shawl around arms, calendar and advertising at bottom (BK 3-49) 550.00
1924 John Clay & Company Live Stock Commission by Frank H. Desch, lady sitting on porch railing with hat in right hand and umbrella across lap, calendar at bottom, advertising on front and back (BK 3-52) ..550.00

Flowers and Fruits

A Shower of Pansies by Muller Lutchsinge & Co., N.Y., copyright 1895 (BK 2-41) 300.00
A Yard of Chrysanthemums by Maud Stumm (BK 2-33) 300.00
Carnations by Grace Barton Allen, basket of red carnations (BK 2-30) 250.00
Water Lilies by R. LeRoy, yellow bowl with white and yellow water lilies (BK 3-38) 350.00
Yard of Cherries and Flowers by LeRoy (BK 2-70) 300.00

Long Ladies

Alluring, Pompeian Art Panel, sgd Bradshaw Krandall, advertising on back (BK 2-99) 300.00

Liberty Girl, Pompeian Beauty, by Forbes, verse by Daniel M. Henderson, date 1919 and information on back (BK 1-28), $400. Photo courtesy of Joan Rhoden.

Barbara, 1912, sgd C. Allan Gilbert, by Brown and Bigelowe, St. Paul, USA and Sault Ste. Marie, Ont., lady in purple dress arranging yellow roses (BK 2-93) 450.00
Beatrice, by J. Baumgarth Co. Chicago, advertising "Belle of Drexel," Chicago's best 5 cent cigar, copyright 1911 (BK 3-41)............. 550.00
Indian Maiden in native attire, bowl of flowers in left hand, right hand at neck holding braids, river and trees in background (BK 3-89) . 450.00
Liberty Girl, Pompeian Beauty, by Forbes, verse by Daniel M. Henderson, date 1919 and information on back (BK 1-28)................. 400.00
Lovely lady in floppy hat, seated on bench with dog at side, sgd H. Dirch, "The Clay, Robinson & Co. Army of Employees" shown on back (BK 2-91) 400.00
The Stockman Bride, 1912 National Stockman & Farmer Magazine. bride in wedding dress, advertising on back (BK 1-12)............ 550.00

YELLOWWARE

History: Yellowware is a heavy earthenware which varies in color from a rich pumpkin to lighter shades, which are more tan than yellow. The weight and strength varies from piece to piece. Although plates, nappies, and custard cups are found, kitchen bowls and other cooking utensils are most prevalent.

The first American yellowware was produced at Bennington, Vermont. English yellowware has additional ingredients which make its body much harder. Derbyshire and Sharp's were foremost among the English manufacturers.

References: Susan and Al Bagdade, *Warman's American Pottery and Porcelain*, Wallace-Homestead, 1994; William C. Ketchum, Jr., *American Pottery and Porcelain*, Avon Books, 1994; Joan Leibowitz, Yellow Ware, Schiffer Publishing, 1985, 1993 value update; Lisa S. McAllister, *Collector's Guide to Yellow Ware*, Collector Books, 1996; Lisa S. McAllister and John L. Michael, *Collecting Yellow Ware*, Collector Books, 1993.

Bank, 3-5/8" h, house shape, molded detail highlighted in black, roof mkd "For My Dear Girl," firing crack at chimney 660.00
Canning Jar, 6-3/4" h, barrel shape 110.00
Creamer
    3-7/8" h, black stripes, white band, green seaweed dec, hairline at base of handle 165.00
    4-3/4" h, brown stripes, white band, blue seaweed dec, shallow flake on inside edge of table ring 440.00
Flask, 11" x 6", fish shape 1,000.00
Food Mold
    3-3/4" d, 1-1/4" h, miniature, Yellow Rock, Phila mark 185.00
    7-1/2" d, 2-3/4" h, turk's head 145.00

Game Dish, cov, 6-1/4" h, unglazed, cabbage leaf form, rabbit finial, chips 165.00
Measure, 5-3/4" h, 6-1/2"d, Spearpoint & Trellis 300.00
Miniature, iron, 3-3/4" l, brown sponging 425.00
Mug, 3" h, flared sides, white slip dec 150.00
Nappy, 10" d, Jeffords blue diamond mark 225.00
Pepper Pot, 4-1/2" h, blue seaweed dec, band dec 475.00
Pie Funnel, 2-1/2" h, unmarked 125.00
Pie Plate, 10" d, unmarked 90.00
Pitcher, 6-7/8" h, brown, green, and black sponging, wear, minor chips 175.00
Plate, 8" d, brown sponge dec, scalloped rims, English, rim chips, pr 440.00
Rolling Pin, wood handles, adv 125.00
Syllabub Cub, 3" h 125.00
Teapot, 6-1/4" h, applied ribbed and tooled handle, applied flowers on sides, brown sponging, chips, hairlines, lid missing 140.00
Wash Board, 12-3/4" x 25" h wooden frame, yellow ware insert with brown striping, gray weathered surface, wear and chips to pottery 200.00
Wash Bowl and Pitcher, 9-1/2" d bowl, 7-3/4" h pitcher, brown and blue sponged dec, brown stripe on pitcher 335.00

ZANE POTTERY

History: In 1921, Adam Reed and Harry McClelland bought the Peters and Reed Pottery in Zanesville, Ohio. The firm continued production of garden wares and introduced several new art lines: Sheen, Powder Blue, Crystalline, and Drip. The factory was sold in 1941 to Lawton Gonder.

Reference: Jeffrey, Sherrie, and Barry Hersone, *Peters and Reed and Zane Pottery Experience*, published by authors, 1990.

Additional Listings: Gonder; Peters and Reed.

Bowl
    5" d, brown and blue..45.00
    6-1/2" d, blue, mkd "Zanesware" 35.00
Figure, 10-1/8" h, cat, black, green eyes 500.00
Jardiniere, 34" h, green matte glaze, matching pedestal, artist sgd
    "Frank Ferreu" 375.00
Vase
    5" h, green, cobalt blue drip glaze 30.00
    7" h, flowing medium green over dark forest green ground.....85.00

ZANESVILLE POTTERY

History: Zanesville Art Pottery, one of several potteries located in Zanesville, Ohio, began production in 1900. At first, a line of utilitarian products was made; art pottery was introduced shortly thereafter. The major line was La Moro, which was hand painted and decorated under glaze. The firm was bought by S. A. Weller in 1920 and became known as Weller Plant No. 3.

Marks: The impressed block-print mark "La Moro" appears on the high-glazed and matte-glazed decorated ware.

References: Louise and Evan Purviance and Norris F. Schneider, *Zanesville Art Pottery in Color*, Mid-America Book Company, 1968; Evan and Louise Purviance, *Zanesville Art Tile in Color*, Wallace-Homestead, 1972, out-of-print.

Bowl, 6-1/2" d, fluted edge, mottled blue glaze.............45.00
Jardiniere
    7-1/8" h, 8-1/2" d, waisted cylindrical form, landscape scene, blue, green, and maroon matte glaze, c1908 ....175.00
    8-1/4" h, ruffled rim, cream to light amber peony blossoms, shaded brown ground..75.00
Plate, 4-1/2" d, applied floral dec 25.00
Vase
    8-3/4" h, cone shaped top, bulbous base, La Morro, mkd "2/802/4" 350.00
    10-1/4" h, light gray horse portrait, light olive green to blue-green ground, matte ext., glossy brown int., sgd "R. G. Turner" ...825.00

ZSOLNAY POTTERY

History: Vilmos Zsolnay (1828-1900) assumed control of his brother's factory in Pécs, Hungary, in the mid-19th century. In 1899, Miklos, Vilmos's son, became manager. The firm still produces ceramic ware.

The early wares are highly ornamental, glazed, and have a cream-colored ground. Eosin glaze, a deep rich play of colors reminiscent of Tiffany's iridescent wares, received a gold medal at the 1900 Paris exhibition. Zsolnay Art Nouveau pieces show great creativity.

Reference: Susan and Al Bagdade, *Warman's English & Continental Pottery & Porcelain*, Third Edition, Krause Publications, 1998; Federico Santi and John Gacher, *Zsolnay Ceramics: Collecting a Culture*, Schiffer Publishing, 1998.

Marks: Originally, no trademark was used; but in 1878 the company began to use a blue mark depicting the five towers of the cathedral at Pécs. The initials "TJM" represent the names of Miklos's three children.

Note: Zsolnay's recent series of iridescent glazed figurines, which initially were inexpensive, now are being sought by collectors and are steadily increasing in value.

Bowl, 6" d, reticulated Persian design, gold, burgundy, and blue . 95.00
Cache Pot, 13" d, young girls dance holding hands around stylized tree form, blue, pale silver, and pale lilac glazes.........................4,250.00
Chalice, 6" h, 4 flower stems as handles attached to upper body, flowers and berries in relief as terminals, green and blue Eosin glazes, red int., form #5668, c1899, millennium factory mark, ext. rim chip repaired 1,650.00
Compote, 11" d, ribbed, 4 caryatids molded as angels supports, blue-green irid glaze...1,100.00
Demitasse Cup and Saucer, slightly flared cup, floral and butterfly dec, broken loop handle, gold trim......................................50.00
Ewer, 17" h, polychrome, highly ornate, chipped scroll and base, craquelure, price for pr 150.00
Figure
    7-1/2" w, 4-1/2" h, polar bears, irid purple and green 225.00
    8-7/8" h, stylized tenor bass musician, black, red, yellow, and white glazes, green stamped mark 215.00
Garden Seat, 18-1/2" h, form #1105, c1882, wear to top surface, repairs to applied dec...1,850.00
Jardiniere, 16" l, ovoid, multicolored florals, protruding pierced roundels, cream ground, blue steep mark..................450.00
Jug, 10-1/2" h, yellow glaze, worn gilt highlights, form #109, c1882 500.00

Figure, irid green-gold, mkd "Made in Hungary, Zsolnay" and castle mark, 6-1/4" h, $125.

Pitcher, 71/2" h, form #5064, red/maroon metallic Eosin ground, cream and pale brown flower dec, c1898, millennium factory mark.... 750.00

Puzzle Jug, 6-1/2" h, pierced roundels, irid dec, cream ground, castle mark, imp "Zsolnay" 195.00

Vase

  3" h, circular, conforming rim relief, moth, irid green, gold, purple, and blue, deep red glossy ground, molded factory mark "6383," and "M" on base, c1901 .... 1,610.00

9-1/4" h, pink and gold Persian design................................. 425.00

10" h, 5" d, gourd shape, ruby red pomegranate, nacreous "Eocin" ground, die-stamped and wax resist mark with castle ...1,600.00

10-1/4" h, elongated oviform, extended neck and handle, brilliant orange-red, fiery purples and gold, floral and leaf motifs, sunset over tree lined landscape, raised round stamp trademark, imp 5572 M 23, c1900...1,610.00

UNCOVER THE HIDDEN VALUE IN YOUR COLLECTION

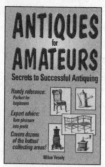

Antiques for Amateurs
Secrets to Successful Antiquing
by Milan Vesely
Satisfy your curiosity about the fascinating world of antiques with this helpful, informative beginner's guide. Novice antique enthusiasts will appreciate the easy-to-read-and-understand approach to a broad range of categories. Learn what antiques are, how to identify and collect them, and how to successfully buy them so that they grow in value.
Softcover • 6 x 9 • 192 pages
250 b&w photos
ANFA • $14.95

Warman's English & Continental Pottery & Porcelain
3rd Edition
by Susan and Al Bagdade
"The bible" for pottery and porcelain collectibles, the third edition is not only all new from cover to cover, it is also in a larger format for easier reading. The only price guide of its kind, it features 300 new photos; more than 200 categories; and more than 10,000 new price listings of today's hottest collectibles in the antiques market-place.
Softcover • 8-1/4 x 10-7/8 • 320 pages
300 b&w photos
ECPP3 • $27.95

Warman's Americana & Collectibles
9th Edition
Edited by Ellen T. Schroy
This proven bestseller gives you current prices and information on thousands of the most desired collectibles from the 1930s to today, including Barbie dolls, Coca Cola, Disney, sports memorabilia, toys and Western Americana. New categories include Beanie Babies, Haeger Potteries, Beswick, and Soakies. Collecting hints and expert advice help you collect with confidence.
Softcover • 8-1/4 x 10-7/8 • 408 pages
200+ b&w photos
WAMC9 • $19.95

Warman's Flea Market Price Guide
by Ellen T. Schroy and Don Johnson
Learn where to find flea markets and how to shop/sell successfully to get the best deals. In keeping with the Warman's tradition of quality, the value listings contain only the hottest collectibles and antiques. This book will be another best-selling reference that thousands of flea market lovers will use and treasure.
Softcover • 8-1/2 x 11 • 384 pages
650 b&w photos
WFM1 • $19.95

Warman's Glass
3rd Edition
by Ellen T. Schroy
Fully illustrated, this updated price guide covers more than 200 types of American and European glass and gives new prices for thousands of items. Glass types covered include Amberina, Carnival, Depression, Fire King, Lalique, Pattern, and Tiffany. From the finest art glass to utilitarian objects, you will discover everything you need to know about the colorful world of glass collecting.
Softcover • 8-1/4 x 10-7/8 • 384 pages
208 b&w photos
WGLA3 • $21.95

Warman's Jewelry
2nd Edition
by Christie Romero
Offers readers more listings and photos of the most popular and collectible jewelry from the 19th and 20th centuries. It also features the most current prices and gives collectors fascinating and valuable background information in each jewelry category including Victorian, Edwardian and Costume.
Softcover • 8-1/2 x 11 • 320 pages
600 b&w photos
WJEW2 • $22.95

Price Guide to Antique Clocks
by Robert and Harriet Swedberg
The time has arrived! Collectors and dealers were watching the clock for the release of this outstanding clock price and identification guide. Featured are hundreds of antique clocks with current values, along with valuable collecting tips and historical information that will aid both beginning and advanced clock collectors.
Softcover • 8-1/4 x 10-7/8 • 320 pages
600+ b&w photos
WCLOC • $27.95

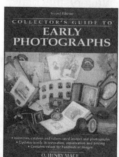

Collector's Guide to Early Photographs
2nd Edition
by O. Henry Mace
Covering every element of image collecting, this new edition gives updated prices for hundreds of 19th Century images and photographs. It also contains a wealth of new information including the latest improvements and trends in restoration, conservation, and pricing.
Softcover • 8-1/2 x 11 • 224 pages
226 b&w photos • 16 color photos
EPHO2 • $19.95

For a FREE catalog or to place a credit card order call
800-258-0929
Dept. ACBR
M-F, 7 am - 8 pm • Sat, 8 am - 2 pm, CST
Krause Publications, 700 E State St, Iola, WI 54990
www.krausebooks.com
Dealers call toll-free 888-457-2873 ext 880, M-F, 8 am - 5 pm

Shipping and Handling: $3.25 1st book; $2 ea. add'l. Call for UPS rates. Foreign orders $15 per shipment plus $5.95 per book.
Sales tax: CA 7.25%, IA 6%, IL 6.25%, PA 6%, TN 8.25%, VA 4.5%, WA 8.2%, WI 5.5%
Satisfaction Guarantee: If for any reason you are not completely satisfied with your purchase, simply return it within 14 days and receive a full refund, less shipping.